International Business

A Canadian Perspective

International Business

A Canadian Perspective

Terrance P. Power

ROYAL ROADS UNIVERSITY

THOMSON

NELSON

Australia   Canada   Mexico   Singapore   Spain   United Kingdom   United States

THOMSON

NELSON

International Business:
A Canadian Perspective

by Terrance P. Power

**Associate Vice President,
Editorial Director:**
Evelyn Veitch

Publisher:
Veronica Visentin

Marketing Manager:
Ann Byford

Developmental Editor:
Katherine Goodes, MY EDITOR

**Photo Researcher and Permissions
Coordinator:**
Mary Rose MacLachlan

**Senior Content Production
Manager:**
Tammy Scherer

Copy Editors:
Mariko Obokata and
Karen Rolfe

Proofreader:
Mariko Obokata

Indexer:
Dennis Mills

**Manufacturing
Coordinator:**
Joanne McNeil

Design Director:
Ken Phipps

Interior Design:
Jack Steiner

Cover Design:
Nelson Media Services

Cover Image:
© Stockbyte; *backcover, top right:*
Nicole Waring/Shutterstock

Compositor:
Integra

Printer:
Courier

Library and Archives Canada
Cataloguing in Publication

Power, Terrance P.
    International business :
a Canadian perspective / Terrance
P. Power.

Includes index.
ISBN-13: 978-0-17-625152-9
ISBN-10: 0-17-625152-9

    1. International trade—
Textbooks.   2. International
business enterprises—Textbooks.
3. International finance—
Textbooks.   4. Investments,
Foreign—Textbooks.
5. Globalization—Economic
aspects—Textbooks.
6. Globalization—Economic
aspects—Canada—Textbooks.
I. Title.

HD2755.5.I594 2007   658'.049
C2006-906942-5

Brief Contents

Contents

PART 7 EMERGING CURRENT BUSINESS ISSUES

www.power.nelson.com

Preface

Welcome to *International Business: A Canadian Perspective*. This text has been published to meet the specific needs of Canadian instructors and students. While there are a vast array of international business textbooks, written mostly by U.S. colleagues, those teaching international business studies in Canada note the information gaps and different perspectives found in these texts fail at times to address the realities faced by Canadian businesses in the global marketplace. *International Business: A Canadian Perspective* while recognizing that Canadian MNEs are at the forefront of international business, also provides significant focus on Canadian SMEs, which contribute 99 percent of our nation's GNP. This SME contribution is often overlooked in the current text offerings. During the past decade, globalization has made it possible for Canadian SMEs to make significant inroads into the international market. Services are now an appreciably larger portion of Canada's GNP, another fact often overlooked by current texts. The realities of these events and others are represented in this text.

International Business: A Canadian Perspective is suitable for graduate and undergraduate students. It provides a surface-level overview of international business supported by rote review questions, and is also designed as an outcome-based learning text for graduate learners and others wishing to drill down into the subject matter. Students are appropriately challenged by the many opportunities for critical thinking, reflective thought, and stimulating discussions that will lead to deep learning.

Be prepared to think differently! This text requires students to adopt a new mental model. *International Business: A Canadian Perspective* is not presented in the traditional academic journal format employed by other texts. In contrast, it is written as a fireside chat. Wordsworth, in response to criticism of his prose writing style, observed that if you wish to communicate with the common man you must use the common man's language. This sage advice is much in evidence in this text's content.

During the "chats," students are occasionally exposed to the author's Irish sense of humour and opinions as he deliberately "pokes the bear" to stimulate critical thinking. The reality of globalization and its many nuances means that there is seldom a right or wrong answer. Students are asked to question and test their hypotheses. The text assists them in exploring the truth.

Overview

Structure

This text has been crafted specifically for business leaders of SMEs interested in conducting international business from within or outside Canada. The discussions relate to international MNEs, but we have deliberately focused on the issues and challenges faced by small- and medium-sized businesses contemplating entering the global marketplace. There are few enterprises not touched by the shift toward integrated world economies; accordingly, decision makers must understand the difference between conducting a purely domestic enterprise and one that is international. Specifically, SMEs must recognize that countries are different, problems become more complex when offshore, impediments and constrictions to trade are prevalent, and foreign exchange markets and monetary systems all threaten the success of entry if not accommodated. All this takes place in an increasingly turbulent ecosystem.

Chapter 1 sets the stage and introduces the topic of globalization and its drivers. In a preliminary way, a number of global organizations are introduced; Canada's role and the importance of maintaining its position as an international trader is discussed; and the

There be dragons

merits of globalization are debated. Chapters 2, 3, and 4 focus on external factors: political, economic, societal, technological, cultural, and other attributes that must be understood and provided for by domestic enterprises when considering entering foreign markets. A failure to evaluate the impact of these attributes can destroy a firm. Chapter 5 introduces a number of regional formations and the current emerging issues they face. Chapter 6 reviews the essence of selected economic theories that support and explain free trade and globalization at the macro level. Globalization's shortcomings at the micro level, such as the growing gap between rich and poor, is also examined. In Chapter 7, foreign direct investment is examined along with its importance to the economic health of nations and the emerging troubling shifting FDI trends. Since the Bretton Woods Agreement in July 1944 and the U.S. decision to go off the gold standard in 1971, the world's foreign exchange markets and international monetary systems have become increasingly important to how enterprises conduct their business. These topics are examined in Chapters 8 and 9.

The text then transitions to an examination of SMEs' internal factors. Few international business textbooks break from their "silos" and examine strategic management and the role it plays in international studies; however, it is a must! Chapter 10 covers this, as well as a review of possible market entry strategies and modes of entry. Having selected the corporate strategy for the SME, the corresponding organizational design structure to support that strategy is put in place. Chapters 11 and 12 examine a number of organizational structures that can be considered by large and small organizations to support their chosen international strategy. Chapters 13 through 17 concentrate on different components of the firm's value chain that must be analyzed by business leaders when crafting SME strategies. These include the primary and secondary activities of marketing, purchasing, research and development, manufacture and supply chain management, human resource and labour management, global accounting issues, and then the text underscores the importance of ethics and corporate social responsibility throughout all aspects of the firm. These functional areas are viewed from the perspective of the units' decision maker, each charged with a responsibility to ensure that his or her functional area supports the corporate strategies and goals.

Features

Quotes

Chapters commence with five relevant and thoughtful quotes. These quotes provide a wonderful opportunity for reflective thinking and stimulating class dialogue following the reading of the chapter. Students will enjoy taking a position either for or against the author's observation.

CHAPTER 12

Export, Import, and Countertrade Practices

"The idea that Canada and China still have a special relationship has passed. We had a head start in the 1970s . . . but the rest of the world has caught up, and today, Canada has to compete for the attention of the Chinese government."[1]

—Yuen Pau Woo, chief economist of the Asia Pacific Foundation of Canada

"No nation was ever ruined by trade."[2]

—Benjamin Franklin

"Trade is the best cure for prejudice."[3]

—Baron de Montesquieu, (1689–1755), French lawyer and political philosopher

"My father's generation knew that they were playing by different rules from the West. When it came to trade, they pretended they didn't understand the rules. That's why they won."[4]

—Hideo Morita, executive at Sony Music Entertainment, Japan

"Americans should never underestimate the constant pressure on Canada which the mere presence of the United States has produced. We're different people from you and we're different people because of you."[5]

—Pierre Elliott Trudeau, Prime Minister of Canada, 1968–1979, 1980–1984

LEARNING OUTCOMES

- Understand why Canada must continue to be a world leader in exports.
- Evaluate the merits and reasons for exporting, importing, and countertrade practices.
- Understand the pitfalls for SMEs when crafting export strategy.
- Formulate opinions regarding Canada's need to diversify its international trade markets.

Learning Outcomes

Each chapter clearly sets out the learning outcomes to be achieved by students by the end of the chapter. The achievement of these outcomes is evidenced by critical thinking and the practical application of the chapter content to current global business issues.

Chapter Opening Vignettes

Chapters begin with a short exciting and relevant vignette to introduce a real-world issue. These vignettes have been specifically selected to encourage critical thinking as the chapter materials are read.

65

Canadian Atlantis Flight Training Devices Take Off

Courtesy of Atlantis Systems International, www.atlantissi.com

The terrorist attacks of September 2001 have had a profound effect on the airline industry, as well as national security throughout the world, especially in the United States and Canada. U.S. and Canadian regulatory authorities now require continuous aircrew training from the airlines and military because of the rapid technological advances in the aircrafts and the numerous industry standards that are emerging and evolving. A Canadian firm located in

tered under a number of quality management programs including ISO 9001:2000, AS 9100:2001, Boeing BQMS D6-82479, Rockwell Collins RC-9000, among others." In May 2002, Atlantis's Quality Management System, an ISO 9001 firm since 1995, was re-registered meeting the new ISO 9001:2000 standard. Atlantis is one of the first companies in the industry to achieve this distinction. These agile moves to meet the globally shifting

industry, and was awarded a prestigious Blue Ribbon Award for Innovation. Atlantis is succeeding because it is developing and introducing new standards and technology that meet or exceed the industry's demands.

With all of the products that Atlantis has developed over the years, it has done everything it can to protect its trademarks and patents. The company realizes that its trademark is an important asset to the organization and that it is how customers identify Atlantis products. Atlantis relies heavily on customer loyalty and aggressively pursues any unauthorized use of its trademark. Atlantis has operations worldwide in countries that are technologically advanced like Canada and the United States. It focuses on countries that have tax treaties and free trade agreements with Canada in order to increase sales and expand product lines. The company places great importance on risk management and therefore seeks stable governments with predictable political policies and the rule of law. This risk management policy has contributed to its success. Over the past few years, the company has become a major Canadian technology exporter. The government has recognized this and has

A Sun Tzu Moment

A unique feature to this text! This ancient strategist's thoughts have been given life by application to a Canadian conflict historical event. Students will enjoy these short historical insights as well as acquire a sense of Canadian culture and history. The relevance of Sun Tzu's thoughts of 2500 years ago and their application to Canadian business are remarkable.

During the past two decades, more than 1 million immigrants, primarily from Asia, have moved [t]here. Statistics show that in 2001, immigrants represented 26.1 percent of the 2005.[8] In December 2005, the United Nations Conference on Trade and Development reported that China remains the most attractive FDI destination in the world in 2005 for the tage and reflectively think about how we can best support and leverage our cultural diversity. It is an overlooked jewel that needs to be polished."[12]

A SUN TZU MOMENT. . .

Visual Arts Library, London/Alamy

"One whose upper and lower ranks have the same desires will be victorious."[13]

Some of the greatest human resource management (HRM) challenges Canada has faced were the transition of hundreds of thousands of men and women from peacetime jobs to wartime positions. At the commencement of the war with Germany in 1939, the RCAF had only 4,000 personnel and 195 mostly obsolete aircraft. By the end of the war, 131,000 pilots, navigators, and other air crew graduated from Canada's air training programs. Of this number some 70,000 were Canadians, and most of them served overseas. Eventually 47 RCAF squadrons served overseas, and a large number of RCAF personnel served in British units. Altogether, nearly a quarter of a million Canadians, including over 17,000 members of the Women's Division, served in the RCAF at home or abroad during World War II. Canada's air force had become the fourth largest among the Allied powers.[14]

The shifts experienced in military culture—hiring, staffing, controlling, and managing—were Herculean. Today globalization presents similar, significant, human resource challenges.

Evidence

Evidence sections provide practical and mostly Canadian current illustrations that support the position taken in the chapter's content. They are short insightful snippets that bring the real world into the chapter content. Visit www.power.nelson.com for additional chapter evidence sections.

International Strategic Thinking

International Strategic Thinking boxes stimulate students to reflect on the practical and applied implications of selected issues raised in the chapter.

performance of those assigned tasks to ensure the successful implementation of the selected strategy. Strategists must apply project management processes and tools to assist them. Visit www.power.nelson.com for The Five Signs of Failure: A Self-Test for CEOs.

INTERNATIONAL STRATEGIC THINKING

Strategies for Canadian SMEs Entering the Chinese Market

The following strategies are offered for consideration by Canadian SMEs considering entering the Chinese market:

· Recognize that infrastructure and technological capacity varies greatly between regions; a strategy for one area may not be possible, practical, or profitable elsewhere.
· If the SME's value lies in its knowledge, extra precautions should be taken to protect intellectual property.

· Long-term vision, patience, and presence are extremely important. Firms must be committed to either be stationed in or visit China regularly to develop relationships and seize opportunities as they arise.
· Prepare for the financial investment and time required to develop relationships and work through the bureaucracy. The costs of doing business in China can be high for small firms, including travelling, adapting to local market needs, and translation.
· Strategies for easing the transition and reducing the risk of failure in this new marketplace could include the following:

– Form strategic alliances with larger multinationals or Chinese companies to leverage market access and networks, and to more easily build credibility.

– Enter the Mainland Chinese market through Hong Kong. Hong Kong has the unique advantage of straddling East and West: its business, political, and legal environments have strong influences from Britain; however, it has ethnic and cultural ties to China.

Just Doing the Right Thing

Ethics and corporate social responsibility are increasingly considered by decision makers when crafting international business strategy. This section illustrates the importance of business decision makers "just doing the right thing" and the benefits that can flow to an organization by undertaking such action.

currency, nor a claim on the International Monetary Fund but rather an international reserve asset that exists only as accounting entries. SDRs' value are derived from a

JUST DOING THE RIGHT THING

Debt relief has become a significant vehicle of resource transfer to countries by the World Bank. However, many African countries' current debt ratios exceed the bank's sustainability level of 150 percent debt-to-exports ratio. Here is Canada's answer.

Canada Proposes 100 Per Cent Debt Relief for World's Poorest Countries

Minister of Finance Ralph Goodale today announced a debt relief proposal that will ease the burden of debt for the world's poorest countries by substantially increasing both the amount of relief available and the number of nations eligible for international debt relief assistance. He also called on other donor countries to support this Canadian initiative and provide similar debt relief for developing nations. "The Canadian proposal will provide low-income nations with the opportunity to invest in the future of their people, and

not the debt obligations of their past," said Minister Goodale. "A permanent debt relief solution may finally be within our reach." Under this initiative Canada will contribute approximately $172 million over the next five years to the International Development Association of the World Bank and the African Development Fund. This relief will be immediately open to the 15 countries that have completed the Heavily Indebted Poor Countries Initiative, a multilateral debt reduction strategy, as well as 4 other nations participating in the World Bank Poverty Reduction Support Credit program. A further 37 countries are potentially eligible for benefits. Strong governance and human rights considerations are built into this proposal, as is a link to the achievement of the Millennium Development Goals in 2015. This contribution represents 4 per cent of all debt payments to these institutions, or Canada's traditional share of global multilateral assistance. . . .

"Canada's proposal focuses on relieving the immediate burden of debt

by reducing debt-servicing obligations, and provides deeper relief than existing initiatives by effectively paying 100 per cent of debt-servicing payments coming due between now and 2015," said Minister Goodale. "Canada is also willing to explore various options to finance further debt relief through the IMF. However, if these options negatively affect the Fund's financial position or disrupt world gold markets, Canada calls upon donor countries to pay for 100 per cent debt-service relief on IMF claims directly."

Source: Department of Finance Canada, *Canada Proposes 100 Per Cent Debt Relief for World's Poorest Countries*, (February 2, 2005), retrieved August 21, 2006, from www.fin.gc.ca/news05/05-008e.html.

CRITICAL THINKING QUESTION
Are we doing enough as a developed nation? Given the corruption levels in some African nations, are we not just throwing good money after bad? Visit www.power.nelson.com to see the update on this initiative.

Practical Entrepreneurial Focus

Practical Entrepreneurial Focus boxes provide practical and applied real-world guidance for SME decision makers entering the international marketplace.

millenniums. In this text we will restrict our examination to the last 100 years or so. If a country backs any of its money with gold it is said to be using the gold standard. The United States and many other Western countries adhered to the gold standard during the early 1900s. Today, gold's role in the worldwide monetary system is negligible; however,

country backs its currency with gold and is prepared, under predetermined conditions, to exchange its currency for a fixed amount of gold.

PRACTICAL ENTREPRENEURIAL FOCUS

Canadian entrepreneurs envy the competitive advantages achieved by nations using the euro in the EU. Discussions emerge regularly as to whether Canada should dollarize (meaning adopting the U.S. dollar or the euro or some other global 'unit', as our currency). While admittedly there are many disadvantages for Canadian SMEs, there would seem to be strong support for the notion economically. Disadvantages include the loss of monetary fiscal policy; seigniorage; a perceived or actual loss of sovereignty, self-esteem, and national identity; and conveying the message to other nations that you cannot control your own affairs. (Seigniorage is discussed in Chapter 8, page 244.) Robert Mundell, a Canadian economist and a Nobel Laureate (1999) provided an interesting case in support of adopting a global currency.

"A few economists have recently recognized the merits of and need for a world currency. Whether that can be achieved or not in the near future will depend on politics as well as economics. But it is nevertheless a project that would restore a needed coherence to the international monetary system, give the International Monetary Fund a function that would help it to promote stability, and be a catalyst for international harmony. As Paul Volcker has put it, 'A global economy needs a global currency'. The benefits from a world currency would be enormous. Prices all over the world would be denominated in the same unit and would be kept equal in different parts of the world to the extent that the law of one price was allowed to work itself out. Apart from tariffs and controls, trade between countries would be as easy as it is between states of the United States. It would lead to an enormous increase in the gains from trade and real incomes of

all countries including the United States. Another dimension of the benefits from a world currency would be a great improvement in the monetary policies of perhaps two-thirds of the countries of the world. The benefits to each country from a stable currency that is also a universal currency would be enormous. If the whole world were dollarized, there would be a common inflation rate and similar interest rates, a considerable increase in trade, productivity and financial integration, all of which would produce a considerable increase in economic growth and well-being."[13]

CRITICAL THINKING QUESTION
From the perspective of Canadian business, do you agree with this Canadian-born (and educated at the University of British Columbia) Nobel Laureate's position? Should Canada take the first step and dollarize?

Supplements

Power Website (www.power.nelson.com)

The text-specific website contains, among other things:

- Over 40 current emerging issue papers written by former graduate students. These papers canvass an array of current emerging issues that are likely to affect Canadian business. The topics also serve as a jumping-off point for further research and investigation for students' major papers and class discussions, as well as materials to support advanced international business emerging-issues courses.
- A wealth of articles and information that "poke the bear," suited to create lively discussions in and out of class.
- The author's column in *Business Edge* magazine. Readers of this text are welcome to join his blog, Power's Strategic and International Studies Blog, at http://obelix.royalroads.ca/Powerblog. It contains ongoing dialogue about issues raised in this text, recent publications, and other background materials.
- Video clips connected to the video icons in the text.
- True/false and multiple-choice questions for students to hone their knowledge of the material.
- Internet exercises to further challenge students into debates.
- Web links to important global sites for international business.
- And much more!

Instructor's Resource CD

- **Instructor's Manual**: A valuable support tool for all instructors, the Instructor's Manual contains chapter-specific lecture plans, teaching suggestions, business projects, exercises, and suggested answers to Reflective Thinking Questions, Critical Thinking Questions, and Mini Cases, as well as other related International Business materials.
- **Computerized Test Bank**: The ExamView Computerized Testing Software contains all the questions in the printable Test Bank. This program is an easy-to-use test creation software compatible with Microsoft Windows. Instructors can add or edit questions, instructions, and answers, and can select questions by previewing them on the screen, selecting them randomly, or selecting them by number. Instructors can also create and administer quizzes online, whether over the Internet, a local area network (LAN), or a wide area network (WAN).
- **Test Bank**: The Test Bank consists of more than 160 questions per chapter. Included are multiple-choice, true/false, and essay-type questions to assess students' knowledge and critical thinking skills.
- **PowerPoint Slides**: These lecture presentation slides cover all the essential topics in each chapter.
- **CTV Videos on DVD**: Instructors can bring the real world into the classroom by using CTV video segments on a convenient DVD for *International Business: A Canadian Perspective*. This DVD contains a total of 30 video segments, providing current stories of interest to the international business world. Video icons in the text point to relevant video segments on the DVD.

Acknowledgments

Writing a text is a selfish activity. For the past three years, almost every weekend I have been able to pursue this passion. My three daughters, Victoria, Stephanie, and Jennifer; my son-in-law, Vince; and my grandchildren, Matthew "TJ" and Meaghan Anne McCluskey, have supported my quest with their patience and understanding of my frequent absences from family events.

I acknowledge and appreciated the research support of Monica Andrei and Maureen Cureton. My never-ending gratitude to my primary researcher and the wind beneath my wings, Tracy (Clemmy) Vickers, for her tireless efforts in making my deadlines hers.

Like all text authors, I am indebted to many of my colleagues who have written international business texts, and to those who have researched and published new thoughts in the discipline that I have drawn upon to advance the body of knowledge contained in this text. I am also intellectually indebted to my colleagues, and to students former and present. Many thanks to Katherine Goodes, Anthony Rezek, Karen Rolfe, Mariko Obokata, Joy Felsher, and Veronica Visentin, who have generously shared their encouragement, inspiration, and counsel over the years this book has been in development. For their collegial support in providing seasoned advice and suggestions for crafting this text, I thank the reviewers:

Sheng Deng, Brock University
Donald Prescott, Camosun College
Emile Hajjar, Dawson College
Linda Stockton, McMaster University
Nailin Bu, Queen's University
David Rutenberg, Queen's University
Dennis Ray, Royal Roads University
Algis Juzukonis, Seneca College
Rosalie Tung, Simon Fraser University
Elizabeth Croft, University of Northern British Columbia
Ronald Camp II, University of Regina
Andrew Shipilov, University of Toronto
Preet S. Aulakh, York University

I also applaud Steve Turnbull, British Columbia Institute of Technology, and Leslie Wilson, McMaster University, for their significant contributions to the text's Test Bank and Instructors Manual, respectively.

Finally, I would like to thank Royal Roads University for the research support, and specifically Mary Bernard and the recently appointed president of the University of Ontario Institute of Technology, Ron Bordessa, for their ongoing encouragement.

I dedicate this work to my wife of 32 years, Judith Anne. She is missed.

About the Author

Dr. Power is a professor of strategic and international studies at Royal Roads University, Victoria, Canada. He previously held appointments with the Faculty of Oxford—Brooks University, London; the University of Victoria; and Thompson Rivers University. Professor Power is a Wharton Fellow in the Wharton School of Business, University of Pennsylvania. He frequently undertakes consultation assignments with the public and private sectors and has been the keynote speaker at several national conferences. As a columnist, Dr. Power is a regular contributor to a number of business publications and is frequently identified as an authoritative media source. His next book, *Strategic Thinking Concepts* will be released in 2007. Dr. Power is an ex-Infantry officer who enjoys the works of Tom Clancy, espouses the teachings of Sun Tzu, and centres his universe on his grandson Matthew "TJ" and granddaughter Meaghan Anne McCluskey.

Author Note: With your feedback, together we will create *the* Canadian text for international business. I sincerely encourage you to visit www.power.nelson.com and post your thoughts and comments. You are also welcome to contact me directly at terry.power@royalroads.ca or visit Power's Strategic and International Studies Blog at http://obelix.royalroads.ca/Powerblog. Enjoy the read!

List of Videos

The Current Era of Globalization

Chapter 1 introduces the current era of globalization and the key drivers of this global phenomenon. As business leaders, we must understand the impacts of globalization on the marketing of goods and services, our environment, how we manage our global labour force, and how we accommodate the increasing pressure to change our culture. The tension between those advocating the merits of globalization and those wishing to "put the genie back in the bottle" is growing. The virtues of both positions of the great globalization debate are reviewed in this opening chapter; it is a debate that all political and business leaders must understand and participate in.

1

Globalization— The Quickening

"When you are describing a shape, or sound, or tint; don't state the matter plainly, but put it in a hint; and learn to look at all things, with a sort of mental squint."[1]

—Lewis Carroll

"Globalization is good and thank god it is also inevitable."[2]

—Amoroso, Kenya

"Globalization is a modern method of slaveholding and colonization of third world countries."[3]

—Mojtaba Ziaee, Tabriz, Iran

"Globalization has also been responsible for the rise of corporate social responsibility, i.e., multinational corporations, due to international pressure by NGOs, are spending money to promote peoples' living conditions and are concerned about the results of their operations, beyond economic success."[4]

—Luis Amorim, Brussels, Belgium

"Here in Africa people are wondering whether these violence-prone protesters are really interested in the plight of the underdeveloped countries. I think they are people venting their own frustrations. It's *not* the best way to get equity for the so-called 3rd World."[5]

—Tanya, Johannesburg, SA

LEARNING OUTCOMES

- Evaluate the current era of economic globalization.
- Examine and understand how the key drivers of globalization influence Canadian business.
- Assess the impacts of globalization on markets, goods and services, the environment, labour, and culture.
- Critically reflect on Canada's role in the new global economy.
- Explain why it is important for managers to have a global mindset.
- Analyze and form an opinion of the macro- and micro-level consequences of globalization.

Before beginning, read International Terminology at www.power.nelson.com. You will find the contents helpful. Additional terms will be defined as we proceed.

On China's Fast Track to Luxury

Massimiliano Lamagna/Shutterstock

The rapid growth of the Chinese economy is causing concern around the globe; other countries fear they will soon no longer be able to compete. It's a revolution based on a limitless supply of human resources. Watch out Japan and the United States: China already has the world's third biggest economy—and it just keeps growing.

In Beijing this summer (2004) the latest fashion statement is a Hummer H2. For the uninitiated a Hummer is an enormous gas-guzzling American 4×4. It's about the size of a small house. Just the thing for running around a congested city of 14 million people! "That has to be the stupidest car on the planet!" I commented to a Chinese friend on seeing yet another one blocking up a Beijing street. "I can't understand why anyone would want to buy one of those things." She laughed at me. "I thought you understood Chinese people!" she said. "They love cars like that. If you're rich in China, you want to show it off." And in Beijing there are plenty of new rich who like to show it off. I'm not

talking about rich compared to other Chinese. I'm talking rich compared to anywhere.

You can see it [in] the neighbourhood where I live on the outskirts of Beijing. Two years ago, it was surrounded by cornfields. Now huge new building sites for luxury housing complexes surround it. Places with names like Grand Hills, Riviera, or, my personal favourite, Yosemite Park. Here China's new rich can buy a fully packaged American lifestyle, five bedrooms, a real log fire, and of course an extra large garage for the 4×4. All yours for the bargain sum of $1 m, and there is no shortage of takers.

So where's all the money coming from? Well, much of it is far from clean. In my new area there are no doubt a fair number of corrupt officials, police officers and even the odd gangster. But an increasing number are from a class that 10 years ago hardly existed in China: private entrepreneurs. To see them in action you have to leave Beijing behind and head south, 1,500 miles south to the little city of Wenzhou on the coast of Zhejiang.

Wenzhou is crowded in between a wall of mountains and the wide expanse of the Pacific Ocean. Its physical isolation has forced its people to look outward across the sea. It's a city of traders and, interestingly, of churches. Christianity and capitalism have both found fertile souls among the people of Wenzhou. But as you drive from the airport into the city it's not the churches you notice, it's the factories. I'd been picked up by the driver of one of those factory owners. Snug inside the boss' V12 Mercedes Benz we sliced through the traffic at alarming speed, the driver's hand constantly on the horn.

We sped past factory after factory, their oversized gates proudly displaying names like Golden Dragon Footwear, or Bright China Leather. One even had a huge billboard showing Pierce Brosnan, better known as 007, purportedly wearing one of their suits. Here capitalism is raw and unregulated. The air is acrid. The rivers run black. It's not pretty, but it's thriving. Finally the large black car slipped through the gates of the East Wind cigarette lighter factory. On its steps stood a short man with a crew cut. He was the spitting image of China's late communist party chief Deng Xiaoping, the man who coined the phrase "to get rich is glorious." Mr. Feng has taken the words of his more famous doppelganger to heart. Starting with a small loan 15 years ago he now produces 100 m cigarette lighters a year. If you have a cigarette lighter in your pocket or your handbag the chances are it comes from Wenzhou, and there's a fair chance it comes from Mr. Feng's factory. Mr. Feng's formula for success is simple. Learn how to make something, and then make it cheaper than anyone else. The first part was easy; he bought samples of the best lighters from Japan, took them apart, and copied them. But it's cheap that Mr. Feng really excels at. He took a sleek red lighter from his pocket and gave it to me. "In Japan this costs about $25," he told me. "I can make it for $1!" Mr. Feng's secret is his work force. In a large hanger I found 600 of them sitting behind rows of desks assembling lighters. Most were young women. "They're better at the fiddly work," Mr. Feng told me. But men or women, they all have one thing in common; they are all migrants from China's countryside. And they'll all work for virtually nothing. Mr. Feng pays his workers about $90 a month. China today is like 18th century Manchester, only much, much bigger. There are now thousands of Mr. Fengs all over southern China, setting up factories and churning out goods. And there are 900 million poor farmers in China's countryside, all just waiting to up sticks [sic] and move to a factory.

The implications for the rest of the world are troubling. "Just think of it this way," one Chinese economist told me recently. "If all the industrial jobs in Europe and America moved to China tomorrow, we'd still have plenty of people left over!"

Source: Courtesy of the British Broadcasting Corporation, 2006 (http://news.bbc.co.uk/1/hi/programmes/from_our_own_correspondent/3939585.stm)

A SUN TZU MOMENT...

"Now to win battles and take your objectives, but to fail to exploit these achievements are an ominous, and may be described as a wasteful, delay."[6]

Visual Arts Library, London/Alamy

At Cambrai in France, Churchill as First Lord of the Admiralty recognized the potential of "land ships," the idea of Lieutenant-Colonel Earnest Swinton. The tracked fighting vehicles were kept a surprise (the element of surprise is one of the 10 principles of warfare) and were identified as "tanks." The word was out that the role of a "tank" was to carry water to the front. The mist hung over the Cambrai battlefield during the early hours of November 20, 1917, as 374 British tanks, for the first time in military history, shattered the stillness and set out to blow a hole in the Hindenburg line. The German soldiers viewing these emerging noisy beasts abandoned their posts. The tanks' mobility enabled the British forces to move on a six-mile front, five miles into German territory. This was unheard of; in World War I success was measured in yards! Unfortunately the British generals had not foreseen the degree of the tanks' success and the breakthrough could not be exploited. The Germans regrouped and the lines once again firmed up. Had the British been able to exploit the opportunity and continue with the initiative, the war and many lives would have been saved. During this monumental World War conflict, 619,636 served for Canada and over 66,000 gave their lives.[7]

Opening Thoughts—What Is Globalization?

We live in turbulent times with transformational changes in all sectors of the economy. What has happened to cause this quickening? How does the opening vignette make you feel? Do you feel threatened? Do you see an opportunity? Do you want to participate? Do you want to pull the covers over your head and go back to bed? Those are the feelings experienced by a great number of the world's 6.5 billion people. In 10 years, the population is expected to reach 7.5 billion. By 2010, it is estimated that there will be 23 "megacities" with populations of over 10 million each. Nineteen of these megacities will be in developing countries where over half of the population will be urbanized.[8] Turbulent times? You betcha! A Canadian was among the first to recognize the emerging interdependency of nations. In 1962, Marshall McLuhan observed in *Understanding Media* the role that communications would play and he coined the well-known phrases the "global village" and "the medium is the massage." (Note: *massage* is correct.) His global village theory posited the ability of electronic media to unify and retribalize the human race. We will see that McLuhan's insight into communications being one of the drivers of globalization was correct. We will also explore others.

This turbulence was also spawned in large part by Austrian Friedrich von Hayek's Nobel Prize–winning economic philosophy of free-market capitalism that advocated dispensing with trade and investment barriers. Among other honours, Hayek shared the 1974 Nobel Memorial Prize in Economics with Gunnar Myrdal, and in 1991 he received the US Presidential Medal of Freedom. Western developed nations increasingly embraced Hayek's thoughts as they rejected the long and widely held popular economic views of John Maynard Keynes. The earliest major adopter of Hayek's theory was British Prime Minister Margaret Thatcher in May 1979. "Thatcher's fresh new approach to governing was built on three pillars, trade union reform, deregulation and privatization. The Iron Lady created a truly competitive market economy for the first time in the 20th century, at a time when most continental nations embarked on exactly the opposite course."[9] Two years later, in January 1981, newly elected President Ronald Reagan of the United States followed Thatcher's lead and accepted to the views of Hayek. Building on Hayek's economic philosophy and the similar views of Nobel Prize–winning economist Milton Friedman, the seeds of a revitalized globalization took root.

Quickly, other Western developed nations adopted the economic theories of Hayek and Friedman. However, to many not-so-advanced nations, globalization seemed released by the opening of Pandora's "free trade" box. Like Pandora, once globalization had been released, there was no return to pre-Thatcher-trade-like relationships. As we will see, nations must continue down this expanding economic interdependence road or perish. We will also discover in this chapter that many in developing and underdeveloped nations increasingly view globalization as releasing "all the diseases, sorrows, vices, and crimes that afflict poor humanity"[10] while developed and other nations argue that the world is a better place because of globalization. By the end of this text, you will have formed your own opinion and will understand the reasons that support your position. Keep an open mind as we examine the issues.

The Cold War had political and economic rules of engagement. Each side knew the rules of the game. In foreign affairs, each was permitted to maintain its own territory and nurture its own national industry and spheres of interests. Words such as *détente*, *nonalignment*, and *perestroika* defined the dominant ideas of the system. Today globalization, with its overarching features of integration and interdependence, is built upon what can be increasingly described as a web. Countries and companies are connected to others, which gives rise to threats and opportunities. "Unlike the Cold War system where two people in charge were connected by a 'hotline,' today increasingly it seems that nobody is in charge. Businesses tend to be driving the globalization of international business."[11] Why? Survival! Corporations must search for opportunities to maximize shareholders' value and to ensure their survival by selling abroad. They must reduce their costs through exploiting location economies that can provide cheap key inputs for their products or services. Canadian businesses have little choice; if they don't join the global race, it won't be long before the firm's survival is in doubt. These views are also shared by Bradford De Long, a consultant who observed in a study undertaken for Industry Canada that "two global forces have dominated the development of the world economy for the past two decades, and promise to dominate the future economic development of the world for at least the next two decades. The first is the worldwide productivity slowdown that struck the industrial economies in the mid-1970s, and that ended the 'Great Keynesian Boom' of the first post–World War 2 generation. The second is the increasing integration of the world economy—what is often termed 'globalization.'"[12] (We will briefly discuss Bradford De Long's "global force of worldwide productivity" when we introduce Friedrich von Hayek's economic philosophy of free-market capitalism as initially adopted by British Prime Minister Margaret Thatcher in Chapters 6 and 7.)

It is important to remember that interdependent economic and political integration (globalization) took place long before 1980. The world has experienced globalization like this before. Consider the migration of people from Africa some 5,000 to 1,000,000 years ago; the invention of the wheel about 3,500 before the common era (B.C.E.); the establishment of well-travelled sea lanes in the Indian Ocean after 500 B.C.E.; the opening of the silk roads between China and what we now call Europe about 200 B.C.E.; the Phoenicians trading in the Mediterranean; the spread of epidemic diseases throughout the Eastern Hemisphere after 200 B.C.E.; the establishment of colonial linkages between the Eastern Hemisphere, the Western Hemisphere, and Oceania after 1492; and the founding of global trading companies after 1600, including Canada's oldest ongoing corporation, the Hudson's Bay Company (HBC), which was granted a Royal Charter in 1670. (HBC's chief interests for its first two centuries were the fur trade, exploration, and settlement in what was to become Canada in 1867).

Most recently, globalization established a presence between 1870 and the beginning of World War I. During this period, developed and developing countries had exponential economic growth. There was mobility of commodities, labour, and capital. There were advances in cheap transportation (e.g., shipping across the Atlantic); the telegram's underwater cables that linked the old and new worlds annihilated distance; and the automobile industry developed. Emigration from Europe to North America between 1880 and 1910 was 25 million people. (Today Canada's population is 32.4 million.) However, globalization was shattered during the four years of World War I. From 1914 to the last few decades of the 20th century, the line "firmed"; protectionism was the watchword. Be that as it may, never has there been such a profound and seemingly irreversible accelerated economic interdependence between developed and developing nations as we have witnessed during the past three decades. Thomas Friedman differentiated this modern version of globalization from the earlier ones when he remarked "Farther, faster, cheaper and deeper."[13] Few would argue. You'll note that I've not included underdeveloped nations in this observation; the reason will become clear later in the text. The other major driver, in addition to cheap transportation, was technological innovation. Technology driving convergence and interconnectivity in all business activities inexorably links us in a "web" whether we wish to be or not (more about this in a moment). We will also examine a number of other lesser but nevertheless significant drivers.

Globalization is often confused with globalism; however, the two are fundamentally different. **Globalism** is the ideology that advocates the liquidation of nations; it is the opposite of nationalism. Globalism describes the reality of being interconnected, while globalization is the speed at which these connections increase or decrease. **Globalization** is the increasing economic and political interdependence between nations in scope and intensity. It is not a fad or a passing trend, but rather a system that has quickly replaced the Cold War system after the fall of the Berlin Wall in 1989. Markets promote efficiency through competition and the division of labour—specialization that allows people and economies to focus on what they do best. "Global markets offer greater opportunity for people to tap into more and larger markets around the world . . . they can have access to more capital flows, technology, cheaper imports and larger export markets."[14] We will examine the underlying economic trade theory in Chapter 6.

As a result of this seismic shift, some countries are experiencing growing discomfort and tension as they move from economically autonomous, freestanding nation status toward a world without trade borders; a world that challenges their citizens, political beliefs, and economic philosophy, and brings into question the very core of the nation's culture and societal values. Indeed, the tsunamis that flow from these seismic shifts are increasingly evident. Daily newspapers report of the clash between the Islamic world and Western liberalized democracy, and growing tension between the developed and under-developed nations (the haves and have-nots). The world that McLuhan observed almost 50 years ago is a smaller place today, and many of its global citizens find the turbulence and change threatening. Do you? This fear of change gives rise to fundamentalist and neo-conservatives within counties. Through these ideological movements, people are trying to

Globalism is the ideology that advocates the liquidation of nations; it is the opposite of nationalism. Globalism describes the reality of being interconnected, while globalization is the speed at which these connections increase or decrease.

Globalization is the increasing economic and political interdependence between nations in scope and intensity. Globalism describes the reality of being interconnected, while globalization is the speed at which these connections increase or decrease. It is not a fad or a passing trend, but rather a system that has quickly replaced the Cold War system after the fall of the Berlin Wall in 1989.

protect their traditional views from the views of those they perceive to be "the barbarians at the gates." Fundamentalists are found not only in the Middle East but also in the right-wing spokespersons in the United States and in Canada. Quebec fundamentalists frequently express their concern about living in a sea of Anglophones. Many members of the Parti Québécois believe globalization is threatening traditional Francophone culture. Clearly a case can be made.

How extensive is this global transformation? Pause for a minute and look at the tag in the back of the shirt of the person next to you. I have asked students to do this many times in class and only on a few occasions have we found a Canadian-made garment. This is interesting because, as we will discuss in Chapter 17, most of you will express your desire not to support offshore textile sweatshops. However, when it comes to actually purchasing clothes, it seems price dictates what you will purchase. Therein lies the problem. International trade leads to lower costs and provides greater selection for the consumer; however, a great number of citizens in the global village are brutalized and left behind. What can we do to restore equity to the balance? It is a very emotional and ongoing debate. As global business practitioners and global citizens, you will have to formulate your own position on this issue.

In the headlong rush by business leaders to maximize shareholder value, they have left behind the supporting infrastructure to ensure stability of the global trade system. Global initiatives are underway. International accounting associations, international law, international banking, and other international institutions and initiatives are attempting to maintain their relevancy and to catch up with the exponential growth of international business. The globalization of supporting infrastructure initiatives will be discussed in Chapter 5, Chapter 8, Chapter 9, Chapter 14, and Chapter 16.

To illustrate the global dangers arising from growing independence without the appropriate infrastructures, consider the events of December 8, 1997, when the Thai government announced it was closing 56 of the country's top 58 financial houses. Global speculators began **selling short** the Thai baht (the Thai currency). The speculators, it turned out, were correct because the Thai economy was not as strong as most believed and the currency plummeted 30 percent. Overnight, Thailand's private banks declared bankruptcy. Many of the banks had borrowed heavily in U.S. dollars and in turn had loaned these funds to Thai investors and homeowners in return for mortgages and other debt instruments. Unfortunately, Thai borrowers were unable to make their payments, and the banks and investment houses collapsed. Owing to global economic interdependency, other nations' economies fell. A flight of currency, now possible because of global technology (electronic transfers), took place from all of the South East Asian emerging markets. This exodus drove down the value of the currencies of South Korea, Malaysia, and Indonesia. Investors scrambled to move their money to safer regions of the world, including Canada. This was the first global financial crisis in the new era of globalization. The Asian recession, subsequently termed the "Asian flu," had taken hold. In McLuhan's global village, flu in many forms is only a plane flight away! Asia's consumption of global commodities including those from Canada, particularly from British Columbia and Alberta, began to contract. Keep this example in mind as we discuss the current U.S. debt and deficit later in the text.

Selling short is an action taken by an investor to speculate on the pending decline of the future value of an asset with the expectation they will be able to profit from the subsequent decline in the value of the asset.

Another concern is that many see globalization as a threat to sovereignty. In trade terms, the growing economic interdependence is challenging national borders and changing attitudes toward policies designed to nurture national interests. The trend toward economic interdependence is not limited to industry. With recent trade agreements, such as the North America Free Trade Agreement (NAFTA) and the treaties that helped create the European Union (EU), countries' economic interests are becoming more closely intertwined. Trade barriers are being pulled down, and national policies are being challenged. This trend will have an increasing impact on both cultural and trade policies in the years ahead. We will expand this thought when we debate the merits of globalization, specifically as it impacts Canada. Alan Rugman states that globalization is a myth.[15] He argues that the majority of trade is regional within each of the "triad" regions of Europe, North America, and Asia. At the time of his book in 2001, intraregional exports were 62 percent for the EU, 56 percent for NAFTA, and 56 percent for Asia. Many see merit in Rugman's position. (For an overview of Rugman's argument, visit www.power .nelson.com.)

So, ready or not, globalization is here. We must be proactive in shaping the direction it takes. As decision makers, we have to think critically about how we can exploit its opportunities and how to mitigate possible problems. The Practical Entrepreneurial Focus boxes in each chapter provide some proactive steps Canadian small and medium-sized enterprises (SMEs) can undertake to shape their global environment. Like the British tanks, globalization has succeeded beyond the expectations of political leaders. The economic and political outcomes are outstripping traditional institutions' ability to keep pace with the advances and shifts caused by the growing interdependence between nations. Like the supply lines in a mobile battlefield, labour, finance, law, and banking, to name a few, are being stretched to the breaking point by the unforeseen success of globalization. New mental models about economic trade in the very broadest sense must be adopted. However, the real danger to the world is what happens if the momentum stalls. What if protectionism takes hold, and barriers to trade proliferate rather than shrink and much of what globalization's "tanks" have achieved is rolled back? Don't think it can happen? Read on.

Why Should I Study International Business?

I would be surprised if many of you did not ask "Why should I study international business?" and "What impact will globalization have on my life?" It is critical to understand emerging global issues because many of you will either be returning to the workplace or entering the workplace for the first time. You have the *duty* to constantly scan your global ecosystem for not only opportunities that you and your organization can exploit, but also threats that you must mitigate to prevent damage to your firm. Consider Nortel,[16] claiming to be a recognized leader in delivering communications capabilities that enhance the human experience, ignite and power global commerce, and secure and protect the world's most critical information. As an investor, it appeared to me that Nortel's management team failed to see emerging opportunities and threats and as a result Nortel's share value dropped from $124.50 in 2000 to only a few dollars in mid-2006. Nortel's management fell short of its duty. Don't let it happen to you. (Of course, there were additional issues regarding ethics and lack of corporate governance. These issues and the relationship between maximizing shareholder value and corporate social responsibility will be examined in Chapter 17.)

The second reason to study international business is that almost every firm today is global. Can you think of one firm that is not either directly or indirectly dependent for its welfare on goods or services from outside its region? I cannot. Indeed I would appreciate hearing from you at www.power.nelson.com if you believe you have found such a firm. You will be working in entities that are operating in diverse foreign environments and engaging in special types of transactions to include exporting, importing, and the conversion of currencies. Without deep learning and the ability to think independently and critically about international business and today's globalization challenges, you will be illiterate, contributing little to the well-being of your organization.

Economic Globalization

By definition, much of this text focuses on the business implications specific to small and medium-sized enterprises (SMEs) affected by globalization. Canada's multinational enterprises (MNEs) contribute over half of Canada's gross national income (GNI) so we will also examine them. We need to understand that the impact of globalization is far greater than merely the shift in ecosystem business variables. We will see that globalization not only is based on economics—the international integration of goods, technology, labour, and capital—but also has introduced profound changes, sometimes in a very turbulent fashion, to all aspects of the global human fabric.

Within this context, we will limit our examination to the drivers of globalization and the significant transformation it has brought about in both global markets and global products and services. There is one other aspect of globalization, the globalization of economies, which will not be covered in this text.

The Drivers of Globalization

Globalization has become a driving force for most nations and organizations whether they are public, private, or not-for-profit. C.A. Bartlett and S. Goshal suggest that the two primary forces driving globalization are widely recognized to be the reduction in trade and investment barriers, and technological innovation.[17] To these, practitioners tend to suggest additional drivers. While you may wish to include others, here are mine: the adoption of Hayek's and Friedman's economic theories; the fall of the Communist blocs in 1979 as China moved from a command economy toward a market system and the fall of the Berlin Wall in 1989; what I contend to also be a major driver—efficient inter-modal transportation infrastructure; and the growing access to the increasing mobility of labour.

These have all combined to dramatically accelerate the growing economic inter-dependence of nations and the industrialization of less developed countries. These drivers have contributed to the rapid, global shift to a free flow of goods, services, and capital. Globalization is significantly changing how we think about markets, and goods and services, and underscores the need for managers to adopt new mental models.

Declining Barriers

The genesis for declining trade and investment barriers can be found in the Bretton Woods agreement. As World War II concluded, initially 45 nations assembled at Bretton Woods, New Hampshire.[18] It was clear that the Allies would be victorious and that new trading institutions must be in place to ensure that at the cessation of hostilities, countries would not revert to the trading patterns and destructive economic theories of the 1930s. Accordingly, at Bretton Woods an agreement was reached to establish a number of global institutions to structure international trade and other aspects of international dependency. The International Monetary Fund (IMF) was among the first of the international organizations to be established. Its mission was to maintain order in the international monetary system and to be the lender of last resort to nations. A sister organization was also established—the World Bank (WB), which was charged with promoting economic development. Over the past 60 years the roles of these two global institutions have become somewhat blurred. Both institutions are criticized with respect to their relevancy. We will examine these institutions and others in Chapter 7, and will discuss the debate surrounding maintaining the status quo for these institutions.

Another major global institution was founded in 1947—the General Agreement on Tariffs and Trade (GATT), subsequently to become the World Trade Organization. GATT's prime purpose was to promote free trade through the reduction of tariff and nontariff barriers. In Chapter 6, we will explore the different types of trade barriers; however, "since 1947, average world tariff rates for manufactured goods have declined from approximately 40 percent to about 4 percent, largely as a result of agreements negotiated through GATT."[19] As a direct result, the volume of world trade and production has increased significantly, creating more prosperity and widening the gulf between rich and poor. The situation is becoming too dangerous to ignore. We must seek new ways to include the dispossessed and maintain stability in an interconnected world.

Advances in Technology

Technology innovation has enabled marketplace convergence on a number of fronts. Here are a few examples of technological advances that have significantly affected the growth of globalization.

THE WORLD WIDE WEB

The World Wide Web is a long way from the development of the first computer by German engineer Konrad Zuse in 1941. Most of us would claim a feeling of dependency on this several-decades-old technology. When was the last time the server went down? Did you feel there was little you could accomplish until it was back online? The introduction of Internet telephony, Internet addresses, and digital intellectual property are raising challenging issues for regulators in a global environment. The Web has led to connectivity and market convergence. Consider how customers now play a role in shaping the products and services SMEs provide. Today it is possible to visit a virtual automobile site where consumers can select options, tailoring an automobile to their specifications, and arrange payment and delivery of their vehicle online. Managers must think strategically about their industries' form and substance. As a substance, most would agree that banking is necessary, but are banks (form)? Automobiles as the substance are necessary, but are car dealerships (form) with acres of iron depreciating on their sales lots? The Web has democratized global customers. Can you think of an industry that must now consider form and substance as a result of the drivers of globalization?

INSTANT COMMUNICATION

The digital revolution has been here for more than a decade. It seems that technology has continued to abide by Intel co-founder Gordon Moore's 1965 law. Although only 11 words long—"the number of transistors on a chip doubles every twenty-four months"[20]—it has guided the high-tech industry. By continually shrinking the size of circuitry on silicon chips, the industry may eventually reach a point where individual elements would be no larger than a few atoms. Nanotechnology is emerging. The broad use of iPods, text messaging, camera phones; doctors making decisions based on handheld devices; and teachers using wireless technology all illustrate the exponential transformation communication has brought to industries. How many SMEs today rely upon "snail mail" to conduct their affairs? How many can afford to? Increasingly, reliance is placed on instant communications by e-mail, video conferencing, Voice-over-Internet Protocol (VoIP), faxes, electronic cash management, and electronic purchasing to name but a few new communication methods. Instant communication is transforming education. Again, it is a question of form and substance! Global conferences and classes can now be held in virtual classrooms supported by online white boards, video, pod casts, and discussion rooms. These technological advances have enhanced the efficiency of blended and distance-learning models over traditional educational institutions that continue to be grounded in bricks and mortar and "bums in the seats." Another example is medicine. Medicine is going global and leveraging the advances in technological communications. Telemedicine is very much part of Canada and other developed nations' health services program efficiencies.

COMPANY INTRANET AND EXTRANET

An **intranet** is a network based on an Internet protocol belonging to an organization. An intranet is used to share information among an organization's members, employees, and others with authorization. Intranet websites are similar to other websites, but a firewall blocks unauthorized access. Because they are much less expensive to build and manage than private networks based on proprietary protocols, secure intranets are now the fastest growing segment of the Internet.

Extranet refers to an intranet that is partially accessible to authorized outsiders. Whereas an intranet resides behind a firewall and is accessible only to people who are members of the same organization or are authorized, an extranet provides various levels of accessibility to outsiders. Outsiders will be issued a username and password. Your identity determines which "levels" of the extranet you can access. Extranets increasingly are becoming a tool for business partners to exchange information in real time.

Many large firms maintain an internal corporate **intranet** to communicate the firm's affairs privately within the organization. Employees telecommuting or working away from the office can access the gain entry to the firm's intranet to participate and retrieve data. Many firms, having recognized the importance and the efficiencies attained, are permitting suppliers and partners to have access to some portions of the company's intranet. By so doing, the net is then referred to as an **extranet**. We will see in Chapter 13 that extranets' electronic data interchange (EDI) systems can contribute to a firm's competitive advantage by permitting suppliers to have instant access to the company's inventory records and automatically triggering resupply as needed. Many large firms using EDI delight in saying, "The warehouse is on wheels and those wheels will be at the loading dock at 3:00 P.M." This ability to maintain a just-in-time (JIT) inventory represents important savings for SMEs with company extranets.

Adoption of Hayek's and Friedman's Economic Theories

Hayek shared the 1974 Bank of Sweden Prize in Economic Sciences in Memory of Alfred Nobel. Today, the thoughts of Adam Smith, Friedrich Hayek, and Milton Friedman are widely adopted as the economic grounding for globalization. In economic affairs, Adam Smith's *The Wealth of Nations* (1776) popularized the notion of the invisible hand. Smith observed that an individual who "intends only his own gain is, as it were, led by an invisible hand to promote . . . the public interest."[21] Friedman and Hayek argued that government discretionary fine-tuning of the economy, as advocated by their predecessor John Maynard Keynes (pronounced Canes), be abandoned and replaced with rules of **laissez-faire** policy—such as Freidman's famous "money supply growth" rule. These theories will be discussed in Chapter 3.

The Fall of the Communist Blocs

The shift from a command economy toward a market economy begun by China in 1978 and the fall of the Soviets' Berlin Wall in 1989 have allowed 2 billion new buyers and sellers to enter the global marketplace. Theoretically, Canadian firms now have access to 6.5 billion people in the global marketplace. This seismic event introduced significant turbulence into a reasonably stable, well-established, and predictable economic trading system. This turbulence presents great opportunities, as well as the potential to inflict great damage on businesses and industries. The global textile industry is one such example. Businesses in China, with significant competitive advantage because of location economies' primarily cheap labour and their new ability to avail themselves of the drivers of globalization, are sending shock waves through this industry.

Inter-modal Transportation Infrastructure

The expanding access to and lower costs of transportation have permitted firms to operate within global host countries and exploit their locations' economies. This makes more goods available at lower costs. For example, containerization has been instrumental in lowering costs over long distances. Ports such as Halifax can unload containers from Europe and use railways to have the containers to the head of the Great Lakes days before traditional shipping lanes could move the goods up the St. Lawrence River to Chicago. Today machines, containers, and a handful of dock workers complete the tasks of many in just a few hours. Similar cost savings were experienced in airfreight shipping owing to economies of scale and other transportation efficiencies.

Workers' Global Mobility

Changes in the world economy precipitated by globalization, free trade in services and unequal demand for some occupations have resulted in increased cross-national movement of workers and emphasized the need for easily transferable or international qualifications. Increasingly, some people are coming to understand the benefits of working abroad and are willing to do so. Pressure is building for policies to support the free movement of workers across borders and to facilitate the acquisition of skills for transnational employment. The demand for skilled workers is increasing exponentially and contributing to globalization and the harmonization of culture, language, and other attributes. But, as we will see, not without significant tension.

Globalization of Markets

The **globalization of markets** is the convergence of all countries' markets into one global marketplace. How we think about global markets has changed; some issues precipitated by the drivers of globalization will require critical thinking by business practitioners when considering operations outside the domestic market. Many Canadian SMEs and MNEs have specialized core competencies in proprietary products, designs, manufacturing processes, and technology. There is a global appetite for these goods and services, and

Laissez-faire is short for "*laissez faire, laissez aller, laissez passer,*" a French phrase meaning "let do, let go, let pass." The term was first used in France by the 18th-century enlightened thinkers as an injunction against government interference with trade. Today it is a synonym for strict free market economics, according to its own economic laws as stated by Adam Smith and others, and is generally understood to be a doctrine opposing economic interventionism by the state beyond what many believe to be the core roles of government—maintaining peace and preserving property rights.

The **globalization of markets** is the convergence or union of all countries' markets into one global marketplace.

through exporting or licensing, SMEs have found they can create strong competitive advantages within the global marketplace. For example, technology has certainly taken down barriers to cross-border prescription services. One example is Rx World—an SME that claims it can cut American prescription costs by up to 80 percent. Many Americans use Canadian pharmacies to obtain their medications at a lower cost, and the U.S. government has reluctantly permitted these drug imports for personal use. With growing opposition to the United States' new drug plan (in 2006), it would seem Rx World and others like this Canadian firm will do very well. The Internet has also made it easier for smaller airlines to compete with the large global carriers. By accessing the Internet, consumers compare multiple airlines' pricing and book their tickets without the assistance of an agent. This online competition and an informed consumer have made the industry's prices more competitive. Access to information by means of the Internet is a common theme supporting competitive advantage though most industries.

Global Acceptance and Preference

The ability to standardize the product or service so that it meets the needs of consumers in the global marketplace represents a significant cost savings to the business; the advantages of the economies of scale, learning curve, and experience curve can be exploited. (Chapter 6 contains detailed explanations of these curves.) The market for a product is driven toward globalization if that product has a high level of global acceptance and if patterns of consumer preferences are relatively similar across regions. Consumer preferences do not need to be homogenous; heterogeneity will not prevent globalization, as long as the heterogeneity is constant across regions. For example, the market for microchips is very globalized because consumers around the world use microchips in countless electronic products. The only preference that consumers express for a microchip is that it works according to specifications. In Canada, almost 40 percent of our exports are commodities, and therefore they can be marketed without much regard for the host consumers' tastes and preferences.

On the other hand, the automobile market is less globalized because consumers' preferences in automobiles vary greatly from country to country. Citizens of different countries prefer a number of different styles and modifications in their vehicles, from the size of the engine to the orientation of the steering wheel. There is no "world auto" because patterns of heterogeneity in consumer tastes and preferences differ across the regions of the world. Canadian SMEs can often improve efficiencies and productivity by establishing a critical mass resulting from entering additional international markets. In highly competitive, mature markets, a lower cost structure can improve SMEs' competitiveness internationally and domestically. However, there will be global consumers who want their consumer tastes and preferences attended to, including providing for their culturally embedded value systems; their distribution channels and business systems; and the recognition of their legal regulations. However, this tailoring comes at a cost.

Reduction in Trade Barriers

If Canadian businesses were restricted by global protectionist measures, they would be able to sell to only 32.4 million people. As a result of free trade, deregulation, regionalization, and other enabling initiatives, Canada now has access to over 6.5 billion people. This creates an abundance of marketing opportunities for Canadian SMEs and MNEs. (See the Canadian Global SME Market Success Story, p. 13.) For a market to move toward globalization, barriers to the flow of trade must be low enough to permit uniform pricing among markets worldwide. These barriers include both formal trade barriers, such as tariffs, and informal barriers, such as regulatory differences. In the market for automobiles, trade barriers exist that hinder it from achieving greater globalization. For example, strict government regulations concerning pollution may restrict the trade of autos in some countries. Auto companies themselves can also construct informal trade barriers by creating warranty structures that differ from one country to another. Impediments to trade are covered in Chapter 6.

Reduction in the Cost of Transporting Goods

Reduction in the cost of transporting goods from one country to another will lead to increasingly globalized markets. For example, consider the markets for Canada's oil and natural gas. A reduction in transportation costs has contributed to the globalization of the oil marketplace; however, natural gas continues to be expensive and difficult to transport over long distances because it explodes easily. The market for natural gas is therefore less globalized. When the cost of transporting a good is reduced, the price of that good tends to even out so that it costs the same in Bangkok as it does in Vancouver. Generally, the recent advances in shipping and freight technology have made transporting goods around the world more economical for many companies. Because these transportation costs are part of the price structure of the goods, companies that capitalize on lower transportation costs can pass the savings on to consumers in the form of lower prices. Unfortunately, the marketplace is not perfect, as we will see in subsequent chapters; at times, economic and political impediments, like taxes, impede the flow of these savings to the consumers. Lower transportation costs have also revealed new markets for products in locations that companies may have found prohibitively expensive to ship to in the past.

Expanded Low-Cost Communications

An effective worldwide communication network among buyers and sellers permits equal access to information, which leads to a reduction in search costs (global sourcing). The Internet makes it very efficient for buyers to source the lowest price or price–quality combination for a good. Informed customers pressure firms to offer the best value. For example, if you are responsible for purchasing raw materials for production, you want to ensure you get the best price for those raw materials. SMEs without access to communications networks, such as telephone, Internet, or the commodities market, might be limited to purchasing materials available within their local community. Although transportation costs might be lower if SMEs were to buy these raw materials from a supplier in their community, it is also possible that the supplier will realize that the SME has limited options and may, therefore, set a higher price. These expanded low-cost communications have levelled the playing field between MNEs and SMEs.

Diversification

SMEs with a diverse customer base achieved through expanding into new geographic regions can mitigate market cycles and economic downturns. Asian SMEs that had customer bases outside Asia at the time of the Asian economic "flu" understand the importance of this observation. Canadian SMEs and MNEs operating in different domestic and foreign regions can spread their business risk.

Canadian Global SME "Market" Success Story—Award-Winning Designs in China, ABCP Architecture and Urbanism, Saint-Hyacinthe, Quebec

"The largest school in Northeast China is on the verge of completion. It was designed by ABCP Architecture and Urbanism. The Shenyang Beida Jade Bird School is an 110,000 square-metre full-time boarding school that can accommodate 3,000 students at primary, secondary, pre-university and professional training levels and boasts a state-of-the-art sports facility. 'The scope of this project was huge. This type of construction is very rare in North America,' says Alain Bergeron, a partner at ABCP, a Quebec firm with several design awards under its belt in China—including a bronze for the 2008 Olympic Games Cultural and Sports Centre."

Source: Canada International Trade, *Award-Winning Designs in China: ABCP Architecture and Urbanism* (January 13, 2005), retrieved August 9, 2006, from www.dfait-maeci.gc.ca/tna-nac/stories112-en.asp.

The Beida Jade Bird School in Shenyang, designed by ABCP Architecture and Urbanism, is on the verge of completion.

Globalization of Goods and Services

Globalization requires us to see goods and services in a different light. Firms can decide which aspects of their business they are willing to decentralize and which aspects they want to remain centralized. In making this determination, globalization generally requires managers to undertake a value chain analysis. (Value chain analysis is discussed in Chapter 13.) A firm's value chain can be broken down into a series of connecting and interdependent activities. SMEs' management must isolate each activity and reflect on how they can reduce costs or add value to each activity to enhance the end product or service. Management can globalize goods and services by implementing efficiencies such as sourcing one or more inputs from anywhere in the world. This includes acquiring raw inputs, materials for assembly, and international services. Canadian call centres are a perfect example of the globalization of services. American firms seeking Canada's location economies and other attributes are increasingly moving part of their value chain (their call centre activities) to Canada. "McKinsey, a major global consulting firm, forecasts that worldwide jobs in the IT industry will grow from 6.7 million in 2004, to 10.6 million in 2008."[22] See the Canadian Global SME "Service" Success Story: Ringing in Profits, page 15.

The Business Benefits of Globalization of Goods and Services

- *Low-cost labour*—There have been transformational shifts in the supply of both skilled and unskilled labour. For instance, India has become a prime labour source of computer programmers and software developers, and China has captured 50 percent of the world's textile industry. Both illustrate the benefits of the globalization of services available to Canadian firms. Of course, Canadian workers and their unions, such as the textile workers from Montréal, view these results differently. We will examine these different perspectives later in the chapter.
- *Access to skilled labour expertise*—The Indian computer programmers and software developers are one example; another is animation services available in Ontario and British Columbia, used frequently by the U.S. film industry. Canada's technological know-how is highly prized.
- *Access to low-cost production or service inputs*—China is actively pursuing global access to resources to support its exponential manufacturing growth. In 2005, China provided $6 billion in funding to a very small, unknown Russian oil company to purchase Yukos Oil at a government foreclosure. The security China received from this small firm in return for the loan was its oil supply contracts. As a result, China has direct control over a significant portion of the Russian oil supply of 9.12 million barrels per day (bbl/day). We have seen similar resource takeover bids in Canada by Chinese firms wishing to ensure access to resources or to obtain commodities. "China National Petroleum Corporation (CNPC) has acquired oil concessions in Azerbaijan, Canada, Kazakhstan, Venezuela, Sudan, Indonesia, Iraq, and Iran. The Greater Nile Petroleum Operating Company (GNPOC), the Sudanese oil project in which CNPC owns a stake, began exports in August 1999, and CNPC's equity oil from the project is around 150,000 bbl/d. Sinopec also has begun purchasing overseas oil assets, with its most notable success being a contract for the development of Iran's Yadavaran oil field signed in November 2004. Yadavaran may eventually produce 300,000 barrels per day. Sinopec also acquired a 40 percent stake in Canada's Northern Lights oil sands project in May 2005, which is expected to produce around 100,000 bbl/d by 2010."[23] It is anticipated that China and the United States will also attempt to secure access to Canada's water.

Reflect for a moment on the issues these mergers and acquisitions present for Canadian government and business (see also Chapter 10). First, if Canada holds itself out as a free trader, can we allow our resources to be owned entirely by foreign countries? Second, the United States has long taken for granted that it would have access to Canada's oil, energy, water, and other commodities; the country has included them in its North American energy policy, oil policy, etc. What challenges will this American perspective present in the near future to Canadians? These are issues you may have to consider in your lifetime. We have reached the global commodities' "tipping point."[24] Standards of living will be directly affected by the ability to access commodities. From this time forward, these issues will not be far from the surface as nations formulate their national security and foreign policies and look toward commodity-rich countries like Canada. Visit www.power.nelson.com. On the website, the Note on Forecasting will explain basic economic terms, such as *trends, seasonality,* and *cyclical and random events.*

The past four decades have seen a broad structural shift toward services in the Canadian economy. Services have increased from just over half of Canada's gross domestic product (GDP) in 1961 to 69.7 percent in 2004. The percentage of workers employed in services is also on the rise: about three Canadians in four compared to just over half in 1961. Between 1992 and 2002, services created about 80 percent of new jobs. Cross-border export of services totalled just over $36.0 billion in 2004, representing about 57.3 percent of Canada's total services exports of $62.3 billion.[25] At this level, services exports amounted to 12.7 percent of total exports of goods and services. At the same time, Canada imported $73.5 billion in services, representing 16.8 percent of total imports of goods and services, with 56.9 percent coming from the United States. In addition to cross-border exports, many services are delivered through affiliates set up in foreign countries to sell services directly to foreign customers. In 2003, sales by foreign affiliates of Canadian services firms were $113 billion; almost twice the value of cross-border services exports.[26] The share of services exports relative to GDP rose steadily during the 1990s. Canada's services exports represented 5.2 percent of GDP in 2001, compared with 4.4 percent during 1993–96. Services imports have also expanded moderately from 5.8 percent in 1993–96 to 6.0 percent in 2001. The United States remains Canada's principal trading partner in services, accounting for 57.8 percent of Canada's total services exports in 2004 (compared with 81.8 percent of goods exports) and 56.9 percent of Canada's services imports. However, our services exports are less dependent on the U.S. market than is the case for our goods exports, and our fastest-growing export markets are elsewhere. For example, during 2004 services exports to Japan grew by over 33 percent; to other Organisation for Economic Co-operation and Development (OECD) countries by about 22 percent, to the EU by 8.9 percent; growth in services exports to the United States was only 1.1 percent.[27] International SME business managers must be aware of the significant transformation globalization has brought to markets, and products and services.

Video 1.1

Canadian Global SME "Service" Success Story

If you live in Seattle and you're on eBay and you call customer support because you're having trouble posting your collection of Beanie Babies, chances are you're talking to a Canadian. More specifically you're talking to one of 800 Canadians working in the eBay customer contact centre in Vancouver. American companies have long looked to Canada as a first-rate location to open a call centre, or to buy call centre services, for a number of compelling reasons: an exchange rate that allows U.S. companies to operate for substantially less, cultural affinity, access to an educated workforce and a state-of-the-art technological infrastructure. Each time a Canadian call centre sends an invoice to the American company that has contracted for these services, that is considered an export of services. "Exporting services works essentially the same way as exporting a traditional product in a box," says Todd Evans, EDC's Director of Economic Analysis and Forecasting. "The only difference is that we're basically billing for our knowledge." Diversifying Canada's export bundle by expanding into new industries is critical to Canada's future. "We anticipate that service exports will grow by 30 per cent over the next five years which will support more than one million jobs and $65 billion of GDP for Canada. The growth in call centre services is an important element in that growth."

Source: Excerpted from *Call Centres: Ringing in Profits* by Terri-Sue Buchanan, *ExportWise* (Winter 2005), www.edc.ca/english/publications_10819.htm.

Canada is a first-rate location for call centres.

INTERNATIONAL STRATEGIC THINKING

The rapid innovation of technology, the accelerating pace of global communications, and the other drivers present wonderful opportunities for SMEs but are accompanied by the constant threat of data overload; for decision makers, the more data available for analysis, the more complex and time-intensive the decision-making process can become. General Colin Powell, when asked how much information he required to make a decision during the first Gulf War, responded, 60 percent. In most cases, waiting until you have perfect information (100 percent) will be too long—the opportunity will have passed. SMEs have two advantages over MNCs: innovation and speed. SMEs must exploit both. International business adds to the decision-making complexity and the need for clarity and direction becomes increasingly important. Today, SMEs increasingly have access to statistics, research data, software packages, and competitive reports to assist in crafting their strategies. But the value of these tools and models is the reflective thinking—the critical thought—you apply to evaluating the data. A tool is not a substitute for the thinking process. You must identify key problems and constraints, and implement the strategy. You will find this is the most difficult part. Many SME managers fail, not because they have failed to craft a strategy, but because they have failed to implement it! It is about leadership, encouraging teamwork, and thinking strategically. Peter Drucker observed that it is increasingly important that managers should be first concerned with being effective and then with being efficient. Effectiveness is doing the right things; efficiency is doing things right.[28] Strategic thinking is determining the right thing to do.

It is important that we have a sense of history as we reflect on what the future holds for Canada in a globally interdependent world. It is our roots that support today's competitive advantage. Historical Canadian highlights can be found at www.power.nelson.com. They will assist in providing a context for discussions.

Globalization—Women Entrepreneur SMEs

Women in Canada have made great strides over the past 50 years, entering all aspects of work, from medicine and law, to firefighting and policing, to space exploration and diplomacy. Increasingly women undertake great managerial responsibilities in business, many as business owners. Women entrepreneurs owned, or partially owned, 45 percent of Canadian small and medium-size enterprises in 2000. In fact, Canadian women have been launching businesses at twice the rate of men in recent years. Women entrepreneurs are a vital and growing part of Canada's economy. However, women continue to be vastly underrepresented in export trade. Only 9 percent of export companies are owned by women at a time when Canadian exports have been growing exponentially over the last decade. There are many untapped opportunities for Canadian women in the global marketplace.[29]

Why Not Canada?

The role Canada plays in global business today is profound. Canada is a member of several economic organizations promoting world trade including the Group of Eight (G8), Asia-Pacific Economic Cooperation (APEC), and the Organization of American States (OAS; OEA in the other three official languages). Canada is a Dialog Partner in the Association of South East Asian Nations (ASEAN). The federal government has actively promoted trade trips abroad through "Team Canada," negotiating the North American Free Trade Agreement (NAFTA), an EU trade agreement, ongoing World Trade Organization (WTO) negotiations to reduce trade barriers, and promoting an Americas free trade agreement.

Canada is an exporting nation currently with trade surpluses. "As one of the most multicultural and cosmopolitan of states, a good global citizen in word and often in deed, with interests in every corner of the globe, Canada benefits from its close relationship with the United States and from an effective multilateral system of governance."[30] According to the World Economic Forum's *Global Competitiveness Report 2005–2006*, "Canada ranks fourteenth in competitiveness and the US ranks second, only to Finland."[31] To their benefit, international businesses can leverage the characteristics that make these countries competitive. Canada, for example, invests heavily in innovation, research, and development of globally marketed commercial goods.

"Canada has a vast reservoir of talents to create or strengthen the most diverse institutions in countries with the greatest need. That is what we are doing in Jordan, for example, where we are training Iraqi police officers. This kind of cooperation already exists among Francophone countries. The governments of Canada, Quebec and New Brunswick are working together to foster the development of the people and institutions of the less well-off countries of La Francophonie. But we can do so much more. For example, we can offer countries in need one of Canada's greatest assets: biculturalism. The coexistence in our country of common law and civil law affords us an influential role both in the Commonwealth and in La Francophonie, as well as in a number of Latin American countries."[32] Canada inspires confidence not only because it is a large industrialized nation, but also because it was neither a former colonial power nor a superpower. An example of Canada's nonthreatening role in international affairs was the very early recognition of Canada by the People's Republic of China (PRC).

It was not so long ago that China and Canada, home of Dr. Norman Bethune and Prime Minister Pierre Trudeau—leader of the first Western nation to provide diplomatic recognition and welcome the People's Republic of China into the community of nations in 1970—enjoyed a special relationship. Canada made this bold move two years before Henry Kissinger, the U.S. Secretary of State and then President Richard Nixon visited China following Canada's lead. It is unfortunate that Canada has allowed this competitive advantage with China to atrophy during the past two decades. Why not Canada? Canada is uniquely placed geographically, culturally, historically, politically, and societally to excel as a successful world trader.

China's Premier Chou En-lai appears alongside Margaret Trudeau and Prime Minister Pierre Trudeau while touring Buddhist statues during the Trudeaus' historic 1973 visit to China.

The Changing Picture of Foreign Direct Investments

Globalization has shifted the flow and stock of FDI from traditional recipients to new global venues. We will discuss in greater detail FDI turbulence and the resulting significant economic repercussions. For example, as a result of NAFTA, Canada and Mexico have attracted billions of dollars in FDI (see Figure 1.1). These investments create jobs and raise the standard of living for both Mexicans and Canadians—but at whose expense? In Chapter 7 we will explore this question and examine the importance of FDI to the well-being of nations.

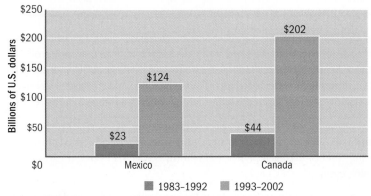

FIGURE 1.1

Change in Stock of Foreign Direct Investment (FDI) in Mexico and Canada, before and after NAFTA

Note: Stock of FDI measured as the total amount accumulated since 1979.

Source: Courtesy of International Monetary Fund (2003)

"Between 1983 and 1992, before NAFTA, the stock of FDI in Canada increased by $44 billion U.S. dollars [sic]. In the decade after NAFTA, between 1993 and 2002, the stock of FDI increased $202 billion, an increase of 354 percent over the decade before NAFTA. Inflows of FDI, along with bank loans and other types of foreign financing, have funded the construction of thousands of Mexican and Canadian factories that produce goods for export to the United States. Canada and Mexico have absorbed $326 billion in FDI from all sources since 1993."[33]

Globalization Leading to the New World Order

There is growing evidence that nations are moving toward the adoption of a new world order. Who will be the power brokers? Admitting China in 1979 and Russia in 1989 into the international community—followed by most of the rest of the communist world as they commence to adopt democratic institutions—has seriously disrupted the former world-order status quo. These new members of the global community want to play a part commensurate with their economic status and will transform the global leadership. At the end of the Cold War, the United States was alone at the centre of the world stage, but now we now find the global order moving toward an Orwellian world where a tri-polar global leadership (triad) is emerging. The triad comprises the United States, the European Union, and Japan/China. This triad is transforming global organizations and trade relationships.

Landov

Eisenhower included a warning in his farewell address to the nation, January 17, 1961.

New World Order—Eisenhower's Warning in His Farewell Address to the Nation, January 17, 1961

"This conjunction of an immense military establishment and a large arms industry is new in the American experience. The total influence—economic, political, even spiritual—is felt in every city, every Statehouse, every office of the Federal government. We recognize the imperative need for this development. Yet we must not fail to comprehend its grave implications. Our toil, resources and livelihood are all involved; so is the very structure of our society."[34]

Some observers see the United States shifting its foreign and domestic policy toward the right and, in an unabashed manner, taking control over the sovereignty, assets, and resources of regions deemed to be in the best interests of the United States. The framework for such a plan was written just before President George W. Bush came to office in 2000. It is called the "Project for the New American Century" (PNAC).[35] PNAC is a think-tank established in 1997 by Dick Cheney, Donald Rumsfeld, and Paul Wolfowitz, among others, which seeks to promote U.S. global leadership by increasing defence spending and adopting a "foreign policy that boldly and purposefully promotes American principles abroad."[36] Sound familiar?

Here are some quotes from the report that you might find interesting. Keep in mind that this plan was written in 1997.

"From an American perspective, the value of such bases [in Iraq] would endure even should Saddam pass from the scene. Over the long term, Iran may well prove as large a threat to U.S. interests in the Gulf as Iraq has. And even should U.S.–Iranian relations improve, retaining forward-based forces in the region would still be an essential element in U.S. security strategy given the longstanding American interests in the region."[37]

"The process of transformation (occupation of Iraq), even if it brings revolutionary change, is likely to be a long one, absent of some catastrophic and catalyzing event—like a new Pearl Harbour." [Was 9/11 such a catastrophic and catalyzing event?][38]

"We cannot allow North Korea, Iran, Iraq or similar states to undermine American leadership, intimidate American allies, or threaten the American homeland itself."[39]

JUST DOING THE RIGHT THING

Prime Minister Paul Martin stated: "while globalization has been of considerable benefit to us, it also poses a whole series of challenges that we cannot resolve without contemplating new approaches and taking new initiatives."[40] Is this call for ethics and global responsibility by the then prime minister a good or a bad thing? Every year, 14 million people die of diseases that could be avoided if they had access to affordable drugs. In the next 24 hours, 8,000 people will die of AIDS and 14,000 others will become infected with HIV, destroying families and devastating already fragile countries. Figures like these are mind boggling, and UN Secretary-General Kofi Annan has launched an urgent appeal to the international community. Canada was the first country to pass a law that will allow pharmaceutical manufacturers to produce low-cost drugs to combat HIV and AIDS in Africa. However, who speaks for the pharmaceutical firms? Is it fair to the investors and the firms who undertook the research and development in order to develop these drugs? With the prime minister's announcement, the Canadian government will prevent the enforcement of patents so that other pharmaceutical firms can manufacture generic drugs. What are the implications of just doing the right thing?

It is becoming increasingly clear that the United States sees itself as the world's most benevolent nation and that it should use its imperial power robustly to expand "freedom" across the globe. This perspective is troubling. With the world's second largest land mass, an abundance of resources including water and oil, and only 32.4 million inhabitants, what does this shift in global thinking by our neighbours to the south mean for Canada?

The Global Debate—The Rich Getting Richer and the Poor Getting Poorer

The world's increasing economic interdependence, driven by moving goods, services, money, technology, and raw materials swiftly across national borders, and accompanied by ideas and cultures circulating more freely, is a double-edged sword. Laws, economies, and social movements are forming at the international level; many politicians, academics, and journalists treat these trends as both inevitable and (on the whole) welcome. But for billions of the world's people, business-driven globalization means uprooting old ways of life and threatening livelihoods and cultures. The global social justice movement, itself a product of globalization, demands responsiveness to the individual's needs.

The consequences of globalization have incited a heated controversy among many people. Debated issues range from the inability of governments to control transnational firms to how to govern in the globalized world; others debate the relationship between international trade and economic development. Neoclassical economists, such as Hayek and Friedman, who advocate free market and trade liberalization policies, increasingly prevail. The economic evidence is compelling for supporters of globalization. Proponents of these theories contend that if opponents of free trade applied an open mind to these economic theories and the supporting evidence, much of the globalization debate would be put to rest. Supporters of globalization further argue that economic integration has many benefits, including better access to international markets, increased competition, cheaper goods and services, better mobility for workers, more efficient markets, more competitive industries, less government regulation, smaller bureaucracies, and lower taxes.[41] Opponents claim that globalization leads to lower wages and fewer employee benefits; higher unemployment; lower health and safety standards; lower environmental protection standards; weaker government; fewer social programs, such as health care and education; and less protection for developing industries and countries.[42] As you read the following sections and the materials in the balance of the text, formulate your own opinion on this issue. A strong argument can be made for either position.

Video 1.2

Is Globalization Working?

Increasingly, discord can be heard about the merits of globalization. The debate has been growing in intensity since the 1999 WTO meeting in Seattle and at every meeting thereafter, including the most recent in Hong Kong in December 2005, where a "quarter million people demonstrated."[43] We now take a brief look at the salient contentious issues.

Globalization Spreads Poverty

While he was finance minister, Paul Martin observed, "Globalization is not the source of the world's inequities. Nor, however, does globalization without development represent a panacea, automatically enriching the lives of those who fling their borders open to international trade and capital." Referring to the UN's Millennium + 5 Summit in 2005, Martin observed, "We have a duty . . . to all the world's people, especially the most vulnerable and, in particular, the children of the world, to whom the future belongs."[44]

How do we measure poverty? "Traditionally, poverty has been measured by the lack of a minimum income (or consumption level) necessary to meet basic needs. Measuring poverty on a global scale requires establishing a uniform poverty level across extremely divergent economies, which can result in only rough comparisons. The World Bank has defined the international poverty line as US$1 and $2 per day in 1993 Purchasing Power Parity (PPP), which adjusts for differences in the prices of goods and services between countries. The $1-per-day level is generally used for the least developed countries, primarily African; the $2-per-day level is used for middle-income economies, such as those of East Asia and Latin America. By this measure, in 2003 there were 1.2 billion of the developing world's 4.8 billion people living on $1 per day, while another 2.8 billion were living on less than $2 per day. In 2003, the richest 20 percent of the world's population received 85 percent of the total world income, while the poorest 20 percent received just 1.4 percent of the global income.[45]

"The $1- and $2-per-day measures offer a convenient albeit crude way to quantify global poverty. In the last several decades, poverty research has adopted a broader, multidimensional approach, taking into account a variety of social indicators in addition to income. The UN's Human Poverty Index, for example, factors in illiteracy, malnutrition among children, early death, poor health care, and poor access to safe water. Vulnerability to famine or flooding, lack of sanitation, exposure to disease, a diet poor in nutrients, and the absence of education are as much the signs of poverty as material deprivation. Providing the poor with basic social services and infrastructure would in many cases alleviate poverty to a greater extent than simply a rise in income level."[46] The world's poorest countries, as established by the United Nations in 2004, are Afghanistan, Angola, Bangladesh, Benin, Bhutan, Burkina Faso, Burundi, Cambodia, Cape Verde, Central African Republic, Chad, Comoros, Democratic Republic of Congo, Djibouti, Equatorial Guinea, Eritrea, Ethiopia, Gambia, Guinea, Guinea-Bissau, Haiti, Kiribati, Lao People's Democratic Republic, Lesotho, Liberia, Madagascar, Malawi, Maldives, Mali, Mauritania, Mozambique, Myanmar, Nepal, Niger, Rwanda, Samoa, São Tomé and Príncipe, Senegal, Sierra Leone, Solomon Islands, Somalia, Sudan, East Timor, Togo, Tuvalu, Uganda, Tanzania, Vanuatu, Yemen, and Zambia.

Sweatshops Are a Key Attribute of Location Economies

Many globalization opponents will readily find numerous stories of MNCs and SMEs using these sweatshops when seeking location economies to manufacture their products. A **sweatshop** is a place of employment in a host country that offends our cultural senses of laws governing minimum wage and overtime, child labour, industrial homework, occupational safety and health, workers' compensation, or industry registration. In most cases these sweatshops are operating within the laws of the host country. Sweatshops are usually found in labour-intensive, mass-production, and low-skilled industries, such as textiles, toys, and sporting products, and thus do not apply to highly skilled, labour-intensive industries, such as the IT, telecom, and telemarketing industries. "The apparel and textile industries are the largest industrial employer in the world. The apparel sector

A **sweatshop** is a place of employment in a host country that offends our cultural senses of laws governing minimum wage and overtime, child labour, industrial homework, occupational safety and health, workers' compensation, or industry registration.

FIGURE 1.2

Approximate Hourly Wage for
Apparel Workers around the World

Country	Approximate Hourly Wage Earned	Approximate Hourly Wage Required to Live
China	23 cents	87 cents
El Salvador	59 cents	$1.18
Haiti	30 cents	58 cents
Honduras	43 cents	79 cents
Nicaragua	23 cents	80 cents
Canada	$11.83[a]	$10.01

[a]Job Futures National Edition, *Machine Operators and Related Workers in Textile Processing (NOC 944)* (Service Canada, April 24, 2003), retrieved August 19, 2006, from http://jobfutures.ca/noc/944.shtml.

SOURCE: © NAPO-ONAP 2006

represents about half of global industry. Over 23.6 million workers are employed in the garment industry worldwide."[47] As it becomes the manufacturing capital of the world, China is frequently cited as the venue for an abundance of manufacturing sweatshops.

Proponents of cheap textiles will say, "Sure, they earn around 33 cents an hour, but isn't that a good wage in those countries?" See Figure 1.2 for the approximate hourly wages for apparel workers around the world.[48]

"In many cases, sweatshop workers employed by large multinational corporations are trapped in a system of modern day indentured servitude comparable to slavery and denied basic human freedoms like the right to join a union, attend religious services, quit or marry. Menial wages and reports of physical abuse are typical of a new economic world order in which the poor are getting poorer and the rich are growing richer. Workers in sweatshops have been forced to have abortions to keep their jobs, denied any bathroom breaks, sexually abused, and even killed for trying to organize protests. They typically work 12 and 16 hour days, with no overtime [pay]—and no choice."[49] Interestingly, sweatshops are not found only in developing countries. The apparel industry in Los Angeles depends almost exclusively on the labour of Latino and Asian immigrant workers. Despite low wages and few options for advancement, garment workers contribute greatly not only to the industry, but also to the Los Angeles economy as a whole. They reinvest in their local communities, spurring economic activity in the poorest parts of Los Angeles County.[50]

But what choices are available to Canada's SMEs? Can Canadian firms afford to not participate in location economies that are attractive because of very cheap labour? Consider: There is an increasing U.S. retail penetration in Canada. U.S. retailers bring not only their aggressive operating processes and technology, but also their own supplier bases, reducing further the "opportunities for Canadian apparel manufacturers in their home market."[51] For example, Wal-Mart is the world's largest retailer with $288 billion in 2005 sales, larger than the economies of 100 countries, including Israel and Ireland. With 1.6 million employees, it is the largest employer in the world. Wal-Mart aggressively continues its global expansion into host countries, including Canada; by using its own supplier base, largely overseas manufacturing, the company has a significant competitive advantage. (Wal-Mart Canada was named "Sweatshop Retailer of the Year" in 2000, 2001, 2003, 2004, and 2005. by the Maquila Solidarity Network.[52]) As retailers like Wal-Mart continue to merge or expand, their bargaining power increases, placing further pressure on Canadian manufacturers. These pressures come in the form of charge-backs, whereby retailers charge manufacturers for late deliveries or errors, markdowns, and provide estimated orders rather than firm orders. In order to compete, Canadian retailers are also sourcing their manufacturing activities overseas rather than using Canadian manufacturers.

Sweatshop workers are employed by some large multinational corporations.

Allowing more foreign competition in developing countries will assist workers to make their way out of poverty. History supports that sweatshop labour has helped poor economies leap to prosperity.[53] For example, China doubles its per capita GNI every 10 years whereas it took Britain 58 years to double its per capita GNI after its industrial revolution. Swedish economist Johan Norberg writes in his book, *In Defence of Global Capitalism*, that where it took Sweden 80 years to reach modernity, it has taken Taiwan and Hong Kong just 25 years. He predicts that "all of South and East Asia will be prosperous enough to ban child labour entirely by 2010."[54] These South and East Asian countries have **Export Processing Zones (EPZs)**, which are "industrial zones with special incentives to attract foreign investment."[55] "More than 30 million workers globally are employed in formal export processing zones, such as the maquiladora in Mexico and Central America."[56] These developing countries are competing with each other, for their own survival, to provide the lowest labour costs to attract MNCs. These companies are seeking greater profits in their efforts to market their products and remain competitive.

Proponents of globalization argue that SMEs and others seeking location economies by availing themselves of sweatshops increase jobs, raise wages, and increase employee benefits in developing countries. Mirek Kondracki, a former citizen of communist Poland at the time of the Cuban missile crisis and now a resident of America, observed, "Globalization is bad? OK. But there is one thing much worse than multinationals coming and exploiting the local labour force—multinationals NOT coming and NOT exploiting that force, which has to join the swelling ranks of the unemployed."[57] Moreover, many other researchers state that offshoring helps improve less developed countries' economies. Of course, offshoring and outsourcing provide us with cheaper products, which leads to more demand, higher productivity, and eventually the increase of wages in the less developed countries for those who accept a free trade economic policy. As a result, countries like China (pop. 1.3 billion, PPP $6,800 [2005 est.])[58] and India (pop. 1.09 billion [2006 est.], PPP $3,300 [2005 est.])[59] will become fully employed developed-world economies. Their wages will rise and labour will be paid according to its productivity. **Purchasing power parity (PPP)** is a method of measuring the relative purchasing power of different countries' currencies for the same "basket" of goods and services. PPP allows us to make more accurate comparisons of standards of living across countries.

The evidence to support this position is emerging. There has been a very discernable shift in competitive knowledge advantage toward less developed countries; India is fast becoming the software centre for the globe. "The economy has posted an excellent average growth rate of 6 percent since 1990, reducing poverty by about 10 percentage points. India is capitalizing on its large numbers of well-educated people skilled in the English language to become a major exporter of software services and software workers."[60] According to an annual Asia-Pacific salary survey by Hewitt Associates, the increase in Southeast Asian average wages will continue for the next several years due to high demand.[61] In India, wages rose 14 percent in the IT-enabled services industry. The Philippines, South Korea, and China also experienced increases in wages. However, when compared to American salaries, which rose by 3.3 to 3.5 percent, those wage increases are higher. In fact, America had the lowest growth reported by Hewitt—an indicator that Smith's invisible hand is at work in the IT-enabled services industry. Increasingly, neoclassical economists tend to view trade as mutually beneficial for developed and developing countries alike. Clearly our opening case, "On China's Fast Track to Luxury," supports this view.

We will see in subsequent chapters that trade liberalization is the best way for an economy to realize its comparative advantages[62] and to increase economic efficiency. Paul Krugman asserts that for 170 years the appreciation that international trade benefits a country has been one of the touchstones of professionalism in economics.[63] Trade provides imports of commodities, capital, know-how, and entrepreneurship at lower cost than developing entrepreneurship in-country because foreign educated nationals often are lured to host country firms that would have to spend significantly more money training location-indigenous management. Insofar as trade can be relied upon for growth, opening up to trade and exporting should accelerate development.[64] According

Export Processing Zones (EPZs) are formal industrial zones with special incentives to attract foreign investment.

The **purchasing power parity (PPP)** metric allows us to compare the purchase price for a fixed basket of goods in every country. The basket includes basic items that would be found in common use daily, such as apples, soap, toothpaste, and so on, thereby capturing the difference in the cost of living from country to country. PPP allows us to make more accurate comparisons of standards of living across countries.

to neoclassical economic theory, trade largely eliminates the handicaps of countries with limited natural resources or those in lower developmental stages. This is very much in evidence in 2005–06 as nations like China and India accelerate their consumption of global commodities. It is through trade that developmental opportunities will be more widely distributed throughout the world. Although the causal direction between open trade and growth is not clear[65] many empirical studies support the notion that free international trade promotes economic growth.[66]

Sebastian Edwards finds that there is a catch-up effect, in the sense that countries with a lower initial level of income per capita will tend to grow faster than other countries. Countries with more open trade policies have a greater ability to capture new technologies being developed in the rest of the world. In other words, trade liberalization makes the cost of imitating technological innovation lower than the cost of actual innovation by that country.[67] More than a century ago, Karl Marx foresaw the internationalization of capitalism. In *Manifesto of the Communist Party*, Marx and Engels argue that the need of a constantly expanding market for its products chases the bourgeoisie over the whole surface of the globe. It must nestle everywhere, settle everywhere, and establish connections everywhere. Through its exploitation of the world market, the bourgeoisie has given a cosmopolitan character to production and consumption in every country.[68] In 1917, Vladimir Lenin elaborated on this observation by defining imperialism, the highest (and therefore the last) stage of capitalism, as the colonial oppression and financial strangulation of the overwhelming majority of the world's people by a handful of advanced countries.[69] Today even those advocating against globalization recognize Lenin's view as flawed.

So there is a long way to go to close the gap between the rich and the poor but evidence can be produced to demonstrate that the number of poor, as defined by the UN, is decreasing. But is it decreasing quickly enough? What do you think? Visit www.power.nelson.com for a reading on this growing gap and the danger it presents in China.

Indigenous People Forgotten

Included in the number of poor are some of the world's indigenous people. They have special issues arising from globalization. "There are an estimated 350 million indigenous people spread over more than 70 countries. Many populations have been ravaged by new diseases, by changes in their habitat, by forced displacement from their land, by civil wars, and by the need to adapt to drastically different habits and lifestyles. Even the increased attention by **non-governmental organizations (NGOs)** to the plight of indigenous peoples can backfire when the agendas of large, powerful international organizations clash and often overwhelm smaller and weaker local groups."[70]

In Canada, Aboriginal people are an important group that federal and provincial governments continue to address. The Canadian government, for example, negotiated with the Tlicho ownership of a diamond-rich area in the Northwest Territories, equivalent in size to Switzerland, and negotiated another 75,000 square kilometres with the Labrador Inuit. The McKenzie pipeline debate arose from oil companies' plans to build a pipeline through Canada's Western Arctic to address the 1973 oil crisis. The proposed pipeline would carry oil and gas from the Prudhoe Bay field in Alaska south through the Mackenzie River Valley to the United States. But the land was also claimed by Dene and Inuit. In this case, the government and the Muskwa-Kechika successfully crafted an integrative landscape management initiative through a consensual agreement reached by all interest groups in a 63,000 square kilometre area of northeastern British Columbia.[71] Other challenges have not resulted in similarly amicable agreements. Nevertheless, there is evidence that the situation is improving not only in Canada but also globally.

At a gathering attended by various Latin American heads of state, Brazil President Luiz Inácio da Silva commented that his supporters, the workers of Brazil, had waited for decades to influence Brazilian politics. Alejandro Toledo, the first Peruvian president of indigenous descent, trumped da Silva's comments by observing that his own people had waited for 500 years! "The wait for indigenous people now seems to be over, not just in

A **non-governmental organization (NGO)** is an organization that is privately funded, generally by donations from the public, and is independent from the public sector and governments and their policies.

Peru, but all over the world. Their political empowerment has become a global trend."[72] Indigenous groups have gained political influence in Brazil, Colombia, and throughout Central America. The Confederation of Indigenous Nationalities of Ecuador is now a fundamental political force; so is Bolivia's Movement towards Socialism led by its new indigenous president, Evo Morales. Morales supports the Bolivian indigenous groups that depend on coca leaf production for their livelihoods.[73] His legitimizing the growth and harvesting of coca leaves is very troubling to the United States.

In Mexico, the rebellion in Chiapas, a poor and largely agricultural area brought its indigenous groups to the forefront of national politics in the last few years; the peasants had been struggling for land reform, health care, and educational institutions in their rural indigenous communities that had been ignored and discriminated against by the central government since the Mexican Constitution of 1917. In 2003, the peasants declared their autonomous government as being independent of Mexico in 30 municipalities.

Guatemala's Rigoberta Menchú, a Nobel Peace Prize winner, has become an international icon symbolizing the fight for indigenous groups' rights. Australia's Aborigines and New Zealand's Maori are regaining more and more control of their ancestral lands. The Maori increasingly elect government officials, and they are claiming rights to a significant area of New Zealand's oil reserves. This newly acquired political clout does not mean that the abject poverty, exclusion, and exploitation common among the world's indigenous populations are things of the past. Indigenous political influence is still quite recent and is often misused by politicians to advance their own interests; sadly, these abusive politicians are often indigenous themselves. But setting aside these caveats, the growth in political influence of indigenous groups over the past three decades has been enormous. Why? The short answer is globalization.

Environmentalists, human rights activists, antipoverty campaigners, and countless other NGOs are now able to recruit, raise funds, and operate internationally faster and farther than ever before. While technology has facilitated travel and communication among these latter-day Good Samaritans, the global spread of Western liberalized democracy has also produced other trends that highlight the plight of indigenous populations, thus enhancing their political weight. Decentralization of political power to state and local governments has enabled the election of indigenous representatives in areas where such populations are most numerous—for example, in Peru, Bolivia, and New Zealand. Global and local activism have transformed intolerance for human rights violations, ecological abuses, and discrimination of any kind into increasingly universal standards among governments, multilateral bodies, NGOs, and the international media.[74] Globalization has brought indigenous peoples powerful allies, a louder voice that can be heard internationally, and increased political influence at home. Constitutional changes in all these countries and regions have given indigenous peoples far more political advantages than ever before.

Disintegration of Sovereignty

Sovereignty is government free from external control. In a global economy, sovereignty is no longer what it was, and states no longer have the same power to protect, or to abuse, their citizens. Canada is no exception: it is but a shadow of its former self, with only a whisper for a voice. In the global marketplace, Canada is not as significant a player as it was 50 years ago. Indeed it is likely to become even less important as China, India, Brazil, Argentina, and Indonesia mature. Canada also faces a special challenge: it lives next door to the economic powerhouse—the United States.[75] See www.power.nelson.com for U.S. President Bush's definition of sovereignty.

The traditional view of international trade was that it always favoured the mother (developed) countries, which receive benefits from the colonies (underdeveloped). This view contends that inequality in the world system is not a temporary condition but a chronic one that allows some countries to maintain pre-eminence in a world economy by forcing others into positions of subservience. Can this be said of Canada? The question of national sovereignty is very much at the centre of the global debate in Canada. Our daily

Sovereignty is government free from external controls; in other words, a government that is the supreme authority within a territory.

economic interdependence on trade with the United States shapes our national security and economic policies; we are become increasingly less free from external control. This interdependence has been exacerbated by the events of September 11, 2001. The media is filled with stories: United States drug enforcement agencies having offices in Vancouver and Halifax; American airborne warning and control system (AWACS) surveillance aircraft routinely flying over Canada's southern border to monitoring government 400 miles north of the 49th parallel; the U.S. government proposes to erect towers along the Canadian–U.S. border; the U.S. government having increasing access to our databases and collaboration in data exchanges; the emergence of microchip information tracking devices; the passing of Canada's Anti-terrorism Act (containing similar provisions as the United States' Patriot Act); Canadian troops under U.S. command (e.g., the major Canadian Navy Operation Apollo in the Persian Gulf); and the missile defence shield program illustrate Canada's movement toward economic union with the United States. Strong words? We will revisit the validity of this statement in Chapter 5 where you will be encouraged to form your own position.

If Canadians understood the economic importance of trade with the United States, would they continue to protest?

ANTHONY BOLANTE/Reuters/Landov

The threat to sovereignty seems even stronger to those nations that have yet to adopt Western liberalized democracy. Globalization and support for America's foreign policy is prompting the adoption of this political and economic philosophy over all others. The actions of the United States, Britain, Australia, Canada, and others in the Middle East of recent date would seem to support this notion. Advocates for globalization will argue that it is necessary for us to accept some encroachment to our sovereignty by permitting external control because we will gain reciprocal advantage; it is necessary to jointly attack problems that one nation cannot do as effectively or efficiently alone; and nations are enabled to deal with issues and challenges outside their own territory.

The Environment

"The explosive growth of the global economy threatens the natural systems that sustain life on Earth. Despite some significant successes in reducing industrial pollution and increasing efficiency, globalization is devastating natural habitats, accelerating global warming, and increasing air and water pollution. At the same time, due to the increasingly global nature of trade and business, traditional national environmental protection techniques have become less effective."[76] With some justification, antiglobalization advocates point out that international businesses are "racing to the bottom." They argue that the decades of globalization have not delivered universal prosperity but rather have produced a race to the bottom as companies seek out the lowest possible global labour costs and the weakest environmental and worker safety standards.[77] The environmental standards adopted by international firms from developed countries tend to be lower in foreign countries. Indeed by definition, the lower standards and other lower cost inputs are what make the developing countries attractive as manufacturing venues. Without these very "advantages," the globalization movement by organizations would be less motivated to establish international operations.

Labour

"Globalization of production is creating a widening asymmetry in the world marketplace: on the one hand, there is an unprecedented volume of capital mobility and technology transfer across borders. On the other hand, labour mobility is subject to a myriad of restrictions, from visa requirements to occupational licensing. The freedom for monetary flows in capital markets does not exist for labour. While capital markets are being globalized, labour markets are 'blocked' and becoming increasingly dysfunctional."[78] Mexican immigrants in the United States and the Turkish workers in the EU illustrate significant labour market issues. Globalization of production results in the jobs, but not the workers migrating in regions. For example, a large number of IT jobs have migrated from the United States and Canada to India, but the workers remained in Canada and the United States. Canada maintains a number of barriers to prevent externally qualified skilled labour from gaining employment. Foreign-trained health care workers, such as doctors and nurses residing in Canada, are discouraged from entering the health care industry at a time when there are significant health care labour shortages.

Increasingly the developing countries are crying foul. Globalization has resulted in turbulence in the global labour market. Consider the United States, the economically strongest country. Advocates such as past presidential Democratic nominee (in 2004) John Kerry argue that since the North American Free Trade Agreement (NAFTA) was signed in 1993, the rise in the U.S. trade deficit with Canada and Mexico through 2002 has caused the displacement of production that supported 879,280 U.S. jobs. Most of those lost jobs were high-wage positions in manufacturing industries. American unions also are concerned about the loss of good-paying jobs to foreign firms. They observe that "The loss of these jobs is just the most visible tip of NAFTA's impact on the U.S. economy. In fact, NAFTA has also contributed to rising income inequality, suppressed real wages for production workers, weakened workers' collective bargaining powers and ability to organize unions, and reduced fringe benefits."[79] Clearly unions are experiencing difficulty in representing their workers in a global environment. We will examine labour and unions issues in Chapter 15.

Culture

"U.S. culture is now penetrating every continent through the dramatic growth of mass communications such as music, television, films and the Internet, as well as through the penetration of American corporations into foreign countries. From China to France and the Middle East, foreign leaders and activists alike have expressed fear that global cultures may become too Americanized, destroying unique cultural, economic, and religious traditions. Where does the public majority stand?"[80] Americans do not see this as an issue. The rest of the world does but to differing degrees. In October 1999, the Program in International Policy Attitudes (PIPA) asked, "How much of a threat, if at all, do you think American popular culture, such as music, television and films, is to the cultures of other countries in the world?" "Just 24 percent said American popular culture was a 'very serious' (7 percent) or 'serious' threat (17 percent) to other countries. By contrast, 33 percent considered it only a minor threat, and a plurality (41 percent) said it was not a threat at all."

The American public certainly does not view the spread of U.S. culture as a threat serious enough to provoke a lethal reaction. When Americans were asked about their feelings concerning the spread of American culture, the poll produced the results shown in Figure 1.3.

When you see or hear about McDonald's opening up in cities around the world, or when you hear about the popularity of U.S. TV shows in other countries, do you have mostly good feelings, mostly bad feelings, or mixed feelings?

Many would contend that this is a rather myopic view of cross-cultural issues held widely by Americans and demonstrates the cultural insensitivity that is contributing to those supporting antiglobalization. We will be examining the clash of global cultures in more detail in Chapter 2.

Globalization—Closing Thoughts

The weight of the evidence supports as a good thing an integrated and interdependent global economy. In the macro sense, it is good for all within the global village. The drivers of globalization increase trade, lower prices of goods and services, and make more products available for all. As a result, rising income permits consumers to purchase more, thereby creating jobs. In the subsequent chapters of this text there is much evidence to

FIGURE 1.3

Feelings about the Spread of American Culture

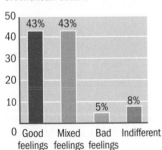

Source: © Program on International Policy Attitudes

PRACTICAL ENTREPRENEURIAL FOCUS

NuStride Corporation

If you have shopped for shoes or boots lately you are probably well aware that most of them are NOT made in Canada. In fact, the footwear industry—which used to employ thousands in Canada—has been one of the hardest hit by globalization. There is, though, a tiny flicker of hope. It brings together the unlikely combination of an Ottawa Jewish caterer who is famous in Hollywood, an Icelandic orthopedic genius, and some proud women shoemakers in Perth, Ontario. Together they're building the largest orthopedic shoe operation in the world, defying the forces of free trade, and further cementing the marriage of things Icelandic and Canadian.

The Canadian Orthopedic Shoe Company changed its name to NuStride Corporation. NuStride Corporation designs and manufactures custom orthopedic footwear for clients throughout North America. The company recently purchased and modernized the 230,000 square foot former Brown's Shoe Company facility, in Perth, Ontario, Canada where it is capable of producing more than 3,000 pairs of one-of-a-kind shoes each day. "We have made important new strides toward re-inventing the custom footwear industry," said Martin Horne, general manager. "Our goal is to become a leader in this field and the name NuStride captures perfectly the new energy we are bringing to the market place." NuStride is the exclusive Canadian licensee of the Bonus Ortho custom footwear fitting system developed in Iceland by Kolbienn Gislassen. The system is patented around the world and widely used throughout Europe. "One of the keys to NuStride's success is the Bonus Ortho fitting system," said Horne. "With this system NuStride's partners, practitioners offering orthopedic services, are able to fit many more clients in a normal work day. Other custom footwear makers require practitioners to create plaster casts, an antiquated and time consuming process," explained Horne. "With NuStride, the same practitioners can complete the entire measurement process in about 20 minutes and place a client's footwear order with a simple set of Bonus Ortho measurements submitted over the phone or via the Internet." Horne says the company has combined a high-capacity manufacturing operation, a highly skilled work force, and the mass customization made possible by the Bonus Ortho system to set new standards for quality, service, and price. "NuStride supplies precisely fitted custom footwear for about half of the current market price," said Horne, "and delivers that footwear right to the client's door in about a week."

SMEs are increasingly faced with stiff global competition. Do you think this Canadian company shows the way? Should SMEs specialize in value-added products and services, and abandon the traditional markets to the new location global economies countries? Consider the Montreal textile firms currently competing with China in a deregulated environment. Can they consider a similar strategy?

Source: From "The Shoemakers" in *The Sunday Edition*, CBC Radio One (Canada: 2005) © CBC 2006

support this position. Economic growth is an essential precondition to the alleviation of poverty, and globalization can be a tremendous force for good. Then finance minister Paul Martin said, "But in the end, Canada's argument has been that globalization is what we make of it. The choice is all of ours to make. Fundamentally, the answer lies in how we choose to govern ourselves as an international community. While there has been no disagreement on the ultimate goal—making globalization work and finding global solutions to both global and national challenges—there has been an ongoing debate about the best way of getting there."[81] The debate over how best to manage the international flow of labour, capital, ideas, goods, and services will continue. Canada's decision to trade is easy, but crafting the international trade rulebook with other nations is a challenge.

Management Implications

- International business requires all of the same elements of management that domestic business requires, with some additional challenges. These include complying with foreign laws and regulations; Canadian and foreign government trade barriers or interventions; different currencies, international monetary systems, and other financial forces; understanding economic and political systems; and understanding the cultural differences of doing business in a foreign land. Ultimately, a company confronting global issues must learn how to deal with a much more complex global business environment.

- There may be conflicts or confusion about foreign labour standards and expectations, and cultural or social differences that influence the way you interact with foreign business partners and associates, how you deal with bureaucrats, and how you market and distribute your products or services. Some factors may be within your control, while others are simply part of the risk of participating in the global business community.

- With more than 6.5 billion people on the planet, you can think *big*—opportunities for new markets in nearby or far corners of the earth. Yet with technological innovation, such as Internet communication and e-commerce, even the smallest firm can be a player in this global ballpark. Transnational business no longer belongs exclusively to transnational corporations.

- There are also threats. While Canadian firms seek offshore ventures, foreign companies are also making their presence felt in every sector of the Canadian economy. Can we compete with the high-skilled low-cost software developers and Internet-based services companies of India? Can we maintain market share when competing against cheap goods produced in China and Mexico? Does the quality of our goods stack up against German engineering and Japanese attention to detail in product quality?

- You have to determine how best to position your product or service in this global marketplace. Will you compete on price by finding offshore sourcing opportunities, or efficiencies associated with automation? Will you be an innovator, capitalizing on first-mover advantages in bringing new products or design improvements to foreign markets? Will you find ways to partner with foreign firms or use host-country agents to penetrate distant markets? The doors are open, and savvy business leaders are finding ways to carve their niche in the global marketplace. How will *you* capitalize on the big opportunities, and manage the increasing threats in this exciting era of globalization?

CHAPTER SUMMARY

- We live in turbulent times. Transformational changes in all sectors of the economy are evident from globalization. As a result of this seismic shift, countries experience growing discomfort and tension as they move from economically autonomous freestanding nations toward a world without trade borders and challenges to their political beliefs, economic philosophy, culture, and societal values. Indeed, the tsunamis that flow from these seismic shifts are increasingly evident; the clash between the Islamic world and the Western liberalized democracy, and growing tension between the developed and the underdeveloped nations (the haves and have-nots). The world that McLuhan observed almost 50 years ago is a smaller place today, and many of its global citizens find the change threatening.

- Globalization is the increasing economic and political integration of nations: greater international trade and greater movement of capital and labour among countries throughout the world. While trade between nations has taken place for hundreds if not thousands of years, this era of globalization began after World War II, and has escalated in recent decades. The end of the Cold War and the emergence of free market capitalism had significant roles in the growth and expansion of globalization. Nations are supporting this new era of globalization through their policies and regional trade agreements, but it is business that is leading globalization, generating the speed, volume, scope, and scale that is unprecedented throughout history.

- Global markets afford SMEs the opportunity to access new and larger markets. SMEs can access increased capital flows, technology, cheaper imports, and larger export markets. SMEs must think bigger than just domestic markets; they must think in terms of global markets.

- There are two key drivers of globalization: falling trade barriers and technological innovation. More and more, nations are removing trade barriers such as tariffs and duties, and eliminating policies that impede the free flow of products, labour, and capital. At the same time, technologies such as the Internet are enabling lower costs and faster international communications and global business transactions that were not possible in decades past. Technology is facilitating the convergence of all countries' markets into one global marketplace that brings both opportunities and challenges for Canadian businesses. There are a number of other significant drivers.

- Globalization of markets into one larger worldwide marketplace provides firms with opportunities to reduce marketing costs by standardizing products and services to gain economies of scale and greater efficiency. For Canadian firms, it also creates much larger opportunities beyond our borders, as free trade, deregulation, and regionalization support entry into larger foreign markets. Expansion into global markets also enables diversification, which provides protection against fluctuations in national or regional economies.

- In addition to influencing products, services, and markets, globalization influences labour, culture, and the environment. Business-driven globalization is affecting cultures by uprooting old ways of life, and generating heated controversy about whether the increasing competition and cheaper goods and services are the result of exploitation of low-cost labour in developing nations. Other concerns relate to the loss of sovereignty, as regional integration creates increasing political and economic integration, and threatens natural systems as the global expansion of industrial and business activities take their toll on the environment.

- Canada's role in globalization is increasing because we have what the world increasingly needs—commodities. Our export trade relies heavily on sales of timber, minerals, and energy including oil, natural gas, and electricity to the United States and other markets. Canada's historical roots support our competitive advantage in world markets resulting from sound economic management, free trade agreements with Mexico and the United States, and a strong trade relationship with China, an emerging dominant force in global markets. Canada is uniquely placed geographically, culturally, historically, politically, and societally to be a successful world trader.

REVIEW QUESTIONS

1. Why should we study international business?
2. How has globalization transformed the world's markets?
3. How has globalization transformed the marketing of goods and services?
4. What are the drivers of globalization?
5. Briefly discuss the issues most likely to emerge in a debate regarding the merits of globalization.

REFLECTIVE THINKING QUESTIONS

1. Having completed this chapter, reread the quotations on the first page, critically reflect on the validity of the authors' statements, and provide your opinion as to the validity of each. Evidence-based answers are preferred to rhetorical answers.
2. As business managers it is your duty to constantly scan your global ecosystem for both opportunities to exploit and threats that may affect your firm. What opportunities and threats do you see today when scanning the current international ecosystem?
3. Can you think of one firm that is not dependent on international relationships in some way for its well-being?
4. Select a Canadian SME and discuss the benefits of globalization (i.e., low-cost labour, access to skilled labour expertise, access to low-cost production or service inputs) and how they have affected that particular firm.
5. How important are Canada's commodities to Canadians' standard of living and our "petro" dollar? How would our standard of living be affected if China's economy stumbled?
6. Suppose an international organization had the power to shut down all sweatshops. How would international trade be affected? How would the Canadian economy and Canadian citizens be affected?
7. The United States has long taken for granted that it would have access to Canada's oil, energy, water, and other commodities, and has included them in its North American energy policy, oil policy, etc. What challenges will this American perspective present for Canada in the near future?
8. Do you think that globalization creates a threat to Canada's sovereignty? Support your position.

GLOBAL E-RESEARCH

Visit www.power.nelson.com for research suggestions, questions, and a number of background discussion papers on this topic.

MINI CASE

Free Trade Leaves World Food in Grip of Global Giants

Liem Bahneman/Shutterstock

Global food companies are aggravating poverty in developing countries by dominating markets.

Global food companies are aggravating poverty in developing countries by dominating markets, buying up seed firms and forcing down prices for staple goods including tea, coffee, milk, bananas, and wheat, according to a report to be launched today. As 50,000 people marched through Porto Alegre, in southern Brazil, to mark the opening of the annual World Social Forum on developing country issues, the report from ActionAid was set to highlight how power in the world food industry has become concentrated in a few hands. The report will say that 30 companies now account for a third of the world's processed food; five companies control 75 percent of the international grain trade; and six companies manage 75 percent of the global pesticide market. It finds that two companies dominate sales of half the world's bananas, three trade 85 percent of the world's tea, and one, Wal-Mart, now controls 40 percent of Mexico's retail food sector. It also found that Monsanto controls 91 percent of the global GM seed market.

Household names including Nestlé, Monsanto, Unilever, Tesco, Wal-Mart, Bayer and Cargill are all said to have expanded hugely in size, power, and influence in the past decade directly because of the trade liberalization policies being advanced by the United States, Britain, and other G8 countries whose leaders are meeting this week in Davos.

"A wave of mergers and business alliances has concentrated market power in very few hands," the report says. It accuses the companies of shutting local companies out of the market, driving down prices, setting international and domestic trade rules to suit themselves, imposing tough standards that poor farmers cannot meet, and charging consumers more. The report says that 85 percent of all the recent fines imposed on global cartels were paid by agrifood companies, with three of them forced to pay out $500 million (£266 million) to settle price-fixing lawsuits. "It is a dangerous situation when so few companies control so many lives," said John Samuel of ActionAid yesterday. The ActionAid report argues that many food behemoths are wealthier than the countries in which they do their business. Nestlé, it says, recorded profits greater than Ghana's GDP in 2002, Unilever profits were a third larger than the national

income of Mozambique, and Wal-Mart profits are bigger than the economies of both countries combined. The companies are also said to be taking advantage of the collapse in farm prices. Prices for coffee, cocoa, rice, palm oil, and sugar have fallen by more than 50 percent in the past 20 years.

The report feeds into growing calls at Porto Alegre for the regulation of multinational food companies. A coalition of the largest international environmental, trade, and human rights groups, including Greenpeace, Friends of the Earth, Amnesty, Via Campesina, and Focus on the Global South, yesterday said they would be working together to press for corporate accountability. Retailers such as Tesco, Ahold, Carrefour, and Metro are buying increasing volumes of fruit, vegetables, meat, and dairy products in developing countries, but their exacting food safety and environmental standards are driving small farmers out of business, says ActionAid. A spokeswoman for the Food and Drink Federation, which represents British food businesses, yesterday recognized that the industry's success "is closely linked to those at the beginning of the food supply chain." But she added: "Britain, the world's fourth largest food importing country, invests heavily and provides an enormous market for developing world farmers."

Excerpted from "Global Giants" by John Vidal (January 27, 2005), *The Guardian.*

MINI CASE QUESTIONS

1. Global food companies are aggravating poverty in developing countries by dominating markets. What happens to the SMEs in these host countries that have been making a meagre living on a small parcel of land when an MNC with its abundant resources decides to compete? It is happening even in developed countries like Canada. There is evidence that small prairie farm businesses have been outperformed by large international businesses that are able to achieve economies of scale and economies of scope as a result of globalization. Should we be concerned? Discuss.

2. Do governments or world organizations have a duty to monitor and control the wave of mergers and business alliances that is concentrating market power in the hands of a few? If you support the notion, how do you accommodate the economic trade theories of Hayek and Friedman? If so, by what authority? Consider Plato, Marx, Keynes, and other economic philosophers who support the notion of greater government involvement. Revisit your answer as you review Chapter 6. See if your position shifts as you come to understand the materials in the text. Be prepared to adopt new mental models!

3. Developed countries' exacting food safety and environmental standards are driving small farmers out of business. Is this a hidden barrier to free trade?

ENDNOTES

1 Lewis Carroll, *Phantasmagoria and Other Poems*, Classic Literature Library, retrieved October 16, 2006, from http://emotional-literacy-education.com/classic-books-online-c/fntsm10.htm.

2 BBC News, "Globalisation: Good or Bad?" *Talking Point* (July 25, 2001, 09:38 GMT UK).

3 Ibid.

4 Ibid.

5 Ibid.

6 Mark McNeilly, *Sun Tzu and the Art of Business: Six Strategic Principles for Managers* (New York: Oxford University Press, 1996).

7 Ibid.

8 Norman Foster, "Ecotecture to the Rescue," *The World in 2005* (London: The Economist, 2005).

9 Anatole Kaletsky, "End of the Golden Age," *The World in 2005* (London: The Economist, 2005).

10 H.A. Guerber, ed., *The Myths of Greece and Rome*, 1st ed. (London: G. Harrap & Co., 1907).

11 Thomas L. Friedman, *The Lexus and the Olive Tree*, 1st ed. (New York: Random Books, 2000).

12 Bradford De Long, "Canada in the 21st Century Series, No. 1: Global Trends: 1980–2015 and Beyond," retrieved August 19, 2006, from http://strategis.ic.gc.ca/epic/internet/ineas-aes.nsf/en/ra01741e.html.

13 Thomas L. Friedman, *The World Is Flat*, 1st ed. (New York: Farrar, Straus and Giroux, 2005).

14 International Monetary Fund, "Globalization: Threat or Opportunity?" (April 12, 2000), retrieved August 19, 2006, from www.imf.org/external/np/exr/ib/2000/041200.htm#II.

15 Alan Rugman, *The End of Globalization: Why Global Strategy Is a Myth and How to Profit from the Realities of Regional Markets* (New York: Random House, 2001).

16 See Nortel's webpage at www.nortel.com.

17 C.A. Bartlett and S. Goshal, *Managing across Borders: The Transnational Solution* (Cambridge, MA: Harvard Business School Press, 1989).

18 International Monetary Fund, *The IMF at a Glance* (September 2005), retrieved August 9, 2006, from www.imf.org/external/np/exr/facts/glance.htm.

19 C. Ford Runge, "Economic Stability Rides on Success of GATT Negotiations." *Feedstuffs*, Special Report, 64(20), 1992.

20 Gordon Moore, *Moore's Law*, retrieved August 9, 2006, www.intel.com/technology/mooreslaw/index.htm.

21 Adam Smith, *The Wealth of Nations* (New York: Modern Library, 1937).

22 Ben Edwards, "Learning to Love Outsourcing," *The World in 2005* (London: The Economist, 2005).

23 Lowell Feld, *China Country Analysis Brief*, retrieved August 9, 2006, from www.eia.doe.gov/emeu/cabs/China/Background.html.

24 Malcolm Gladwell, *The Tipping Point* (Boston: Little, Brown and Company, 2000).

25 Department of Foreign Affairs and International Trade, *Sixth Annual Report on Canada's State of Trade* (April 2005), retrieved August 9, 2006, from www.dfait-maeci.gc.ca/eet/trade/sot_2005/sot_2005-en.asp#the.

26 Statistics Canada, *The Daily: Foreign Affiliate Trade Statistics* (May 25, 2005), retrieved August 9, 2006, from www.statcan.ca/Daily/English/050525/d050525f.htm.

27 Department of Foreign Affairs and International Trade, *Sixth Annual Report on Canada's State of Trade* (DFAIT, Trade and Economics Division, April 2005), retrieved August 19, 2006, from www .dfait- maeci.gc.ca/eet/trade/sot_2005/sot_2005-en .asp#the.

28 *Brainy Quote* (2005), retrieved August 9, 2006, from www.brainyquote.com.

29 Foreign Affairs and International Trade Canada, *Why Trade Matters: Trade and the Canadian Economy* (FAITC, May 20, 2004) retrieved August 19, 2006, from www.dfait-maeci.gc.ca/tna-nac/stories96-en.asp.

30 Paul Heinbecker in *Canada among Nations*, eds. David Carment, Fen Osler Hampson, and Norman Hillmer (Montreal and Kingston: McGill-Queen's University Press, 2004).

31 Professor Klaus Schwab, *The Global Competitiveness Report 2005–2006* (September 28, 2005), retrieved August 9, 2006, from www.weforum.org/en/initiatives/gcp/Global %20Competitiveness%20Report/index.htm.

32 Prime Minister Paul Martin, "Speech by the Prime Minister" (paper presented at the CORIM, the CERIUM, the Institut d'études internationales de Montréal à l'UQAM, and the Montreal International organization, Montreal, PQ, May 10, 2004).

33 Robert E. Scott, "The High Price of 'Free Trade': NAFTA's Failure Has Cost the United States Jobs across the Nation," Economic Policy Institute, (November 17, 2003), retrieved August 19, 2006, from www.epinet.org/content.cfm/briefingpapers_bp147.

34 Paul Joseph Watson, *Eisenhower Warned America of New World Order* (Global Matrix Enterprises, 2003) retrieved August 9, 2006, from http://propagandamatrix.com/multimedia_old.html.

35 Thomas Donnelly, *Rebuilding America's Defenses: Strategy, Forces and Resources for a New Century,* (Washington: Project for the New American Century, September 2000), retrieved August 9, 2006, from www.newamericancentury.org/RebuildingAmericasDefenses.pdf.

36 Ibid.

37 Ibid.

38 Ibid.

39 Ibid.

40 Martin, "Speech by the Prime Minister."

41 Tom McFeat, *What Is Globalization* (2004), retrieved August 9, 2006, from www.cbc.ca/news/background/summitofamericas/globalization.html.

42 Ibid.

43 "Solidarity Action with Hong Kong WTO Defendants" (2006), retrieved August 9, 2006, from www.chinaworker.org/cgi-bin/index.cgi?action=viewnews&id=152.

44 Paul Martin, "Lessons from the Americas," *The World in 2005* (London: The Economist, 2005).

45 Information Please Database, "Measuring Global Poverty," (Boston: Pearson Education, 2005), retrieved August 19, 2006, from www.infoplease.com/ipa/A0908762.html.

46 Ibid.

47 Oxfam Canada, "What Is a Sweatshop: Just the Facts," *Oxfam Canada Campaigner*, Special Issue on Sweatshops, Fall 2000, retrieved October 16, 2006, from http://www .oxfam.ca/campaigns/downloads/OxCampFall2000.pdf.

[48] "How Do We Know that Hanes Are Really Made in Sweat Shops?" (2002), retrieved August 9, 2006, from www.she-net.com/nosweat/hanessweatshops.htm.

[49] Ibid.

[50] Timmy Lu and Karin Mak, *Crisis or Opportunity? The Future of Los Angeles' Garment Workers, the Apparel Industry and the Local Economy* (November 2004), retrieved August 9, 2006, from www.sweatshopwatch.org/media/pdf/garment_report_2004.pdf.

[51] Infomat, "Men's Apparel Industry in Canada," retrieved October 16, 2006, from http://www.infomat.com/research/infre0000200.html.

[52] Maquila Solidarity Network. 2000. A *Needle in a Haystack: Tracing Canadian Garment Connections to Mexico and Central America.* Retrieved August 19, 2006, from www.maquilasolidarity.org/resources/garment/haystack/1-canada.pdf.

[53] Roderick Benns, "Professor Says, 'Ethnocentric Perspective Impacts View of Sweatshops," *Axiom News*, July 6, 2004.

[54] Ibid.

[55] Oxfam Canada, "Don't Close Your Eyes to Sweatshop Abuses, Exploitation Is Never in Fashion."

[56] Garrett Brown, "Vulnerable Workers in the Global Economy," *Occupational Hazards*, 66(4), 2004.

[57] Mirek Kondracki, *Globalization: Good or Bad?* (July 25, 2001), retrieved August 9, 2006, from http://news.bbc.co.uk/1/hi/talking_point/1444930.stm.

[58] Central Intelligence Agency, *The World Fact Book: China* (2005), retrieved October 16, 2006, from https://www.cia.gov.cia/publications/factbook/geos/chi.html#Econ.

[59] Central Intelligence Agency, *The World Fact Book: India* (2005), retrieved October 16, 2006, from https://www.cia.gov.cia/publications/factbook/geos/in.html#Econ.

[60] Ibid.

[61] Hewitt, "Salaries Continue to Rise in Asia Pacific, Hewitt Annual Study Reports," retrieved October 22, 2006, from http://www.hewittassociates.com/Intl/AP/en-AU/AboutHewitt/Newsroom/PressReleases/2005/november-23-05.aspx.

[62] Anne O. Krueger, "Trade Policy and Economic Development: How We Learn," *American Economic Review,* 87(2), 1997.

[63] P.R. Krugman, "Is Free Trade Passé?" *Journal of Economic Perspectives* 1(2), 1987.

[64] Paul Martin, *Globalization, Terrorism and the World Economy* (November 16, 2001), retrieved August 9, 2006, from www.fin.gc.ca/news01/01-105e.html.

[65] Geoffrey Garrett, "The Causes of Globalization," *Comparative Political Studies,* 33(6–7), 2000.

[66] Sebastian Edwards, "Trade Orientation, Distortions and Growth in Developing Countries" *Journal of Development Economics*, 39(1), 1992.

[67] Ibid.

[68] Sangmoon Kim and Eui-Hang Shin, "A Longitudinal Analysis of Globalization and Regionalization in International Trade: A Social Network Approach," *Social Forces*, 81(2), 2002.

[69] Vladimir Lenin, *Imperialism: The Highest Stage of Capitalism* (New York: International Publishing Company, 1969).

[70] Moisés Naím, "An Indigenous World," *Foreign Policy* (November/December 2003).

[71] Muskwa-Kechika Advisory Board (2005), retrieved August 9, 2006, from www.muskwa-kechika.com.

[72] Naím, "An Indigenous World."

[73] Ibid.

[74] Ibid.

[75] President George W. Bush and Mark Trahant, *George Bush Stumbles over Sovereignty* (2004), retrieved August 19, 2006, from www.ifilm.com/player/?ifilmId=2646755&pg=default&skin=default&refsite=default&mediaSize=default&context=product&launchVal=1&data=.

[76] Pacific Institute, *Economic Globalization and the Environment* (2004), retrieved from www.pacinst.org/topics/globalization_and_environment.

[77] AFL-CIO American Federation of Labour—Congress of Industrial Organizations, "Global Economy" (2005), retrieved August 19, 2006, from http://stage.aflcio.org.

[78] Ozay Mehmet, Errol Mendes, and Robert Sinding, *Towards a Fair Global Market: Avoiding a New Slave Trade* (Ottawa: Human Rights Research Centre, 2004), retrieved August 9, 2006, from www.cdp-hrc.uottawa.ca/publicat/tfgmpub.html.

[79] Robert E. Scott, *The High Price of "Free" Trade: NAFTA's Failure Has Cost the United States Jobs across the Nation* (Economic Policy Institute, November 17, 2003), retrieved August 19, 2006, from www.epinet.org/content.cfm/briefingpapers_bp147.

[80] The Program on International Policy Attitudes (April 12, 2002), retrieved August 9, 2006, from www.americans-world.org/digest/global_issues/globalization/culture.cfm.

[81] Paul Martin, *Globalization, Terrorism and the World Economy* (November 16, 2001), retrieved August 9, 2006, from www.fin.gc.ca/news01/01-105e.html.

External—The International Business Ecosystem

2

Chapters 2, 3, and 4 are exciting and very relevant materials for business practitioners. In this part we examine how diverse global cultures, societies, political systems, economic systems, legal systems, and the presence or absence of technology can influence Canadian businesses. Since 9/11 it has become apparent that, when crafting our business plans, the traditional environmental industry scans are no longer sufficient. It is now essential we undertake broader analysis of the entire ecosystem within which the industry operates. We must think critically to understand fully the implications of an event far past its apparent surface-level impact on a specific industry. This was clear following 9/11; industries are linked, albeit to different degrees, and affected by events. The political and economic consequences of 9/11 are evident to most undertaking an environmental industry scan. But, as we will see within these chapters, the nexus to political, legal, and other ecosystem attributes must also be understood. Ecosystem means a living community of interacting organisms and their physical environment as opposed to the generally accepted term *environment*, which means the physical surroundings and industry conditions. I do this deliberately to remind you of the need to drill down in your analysis of the firm's ecosystem. We exist in a living interactive global village, and this text is about adopting new mental models.

Chapter 2 examines global cultures that are influenced by religious, societal, and other attributes, and then draws conclusions to include the necessity for businesses to develop cross-cultural sensitivity when crafting their host-country market-entry strategies. In Chapter 3 we examine the international political, economic, and legal attributes of a nation's ecosystems. In Chapter 4 we conclude our look at the international ecosystem by examining the presence or absence of technology as a driver of globalization. This is a fascinating section of the text, and I encourage you visit www.power.nelson.com for further discussions on these ecosystem attributes.

CHAPTER 2

International Business Environment: Culture and Society

"In this new world the most pervasive, important and dangerous conflict will not be between social classes, rich and poor, or other economically defined groups, but between people belonging to different cultural entities."[1]

—S. P. Huntington

"There is no conceivable human action which custom has not at one time justified and at another condemned."[2]

—Joseph Wood Krutch (1929)

"When in Rome, do as the Romans do."[3]

—St. Ambrose

"Living next to you is in some ways like sleeping with an elephant. No matter how friendly and even-tempered is the beast [USA], if I can call it that, one is affected by every twitch and grunt."[4]

—Pierre Elliott Trudeau, Prime Minister of Canada, 1968–1979, 1980–1984

"A culture may be conceived as a network of beliefs and purposes in which any string in the net pulls and is pulled by the others, thus perpetually changing the configuration of the whole."[5]

—Jacques Barzun, U.S. educator, author

LEARNING OUTCOMES

- Compare the specific cultural characteristics of selected nations.
- Evaluate the importance of developing cross-cultural literacy.
- Formulate opinions regarding the value of Canada's diversity as a strength or weakness in the global marketplace.
- Evaluate and apply Hofstede's model to selected countries you would consider as host countries.
- Evaluate the impact religious values have on culture and the conduct of business.
- Examine other selected attributes that influence culture, including politics, economics, value placed on lifestyle, language, societal forces, and changing demographics.
- Contrast the home and selected host countries' international verbal and nonverbal communication gaps.

Canadian Culture in a Global World

It may be Canada's greatest cultural coup in China since the days when students were required to memorize Mao Zedong's eulogy to revolutionary (Canadian) surgeon Norman Bethune. When classes begin at thousands of schools across China next month, as many as 15 million children will get a dose of Canada in their classrooms every day. Their textbooks will indoctrinate them with subtle but distinct references to Canadian holidays, Canadian weather, Canadian cities and Canadian variations of English words. As part of an upgrade in their English-language-teaching programs, Chinese elementary schools are switching to new textbooks, most written by Canadian authors who carefully planted their country's cultural references throughout the books. Two Canadian companies, Lingo Media Inc. of Toronto and Duval House Publishing of Edmonton, have played a key role in developing the textbooks that are replacing older British-based texts. After rapid growth in recent years, the two Canadian companies dominate as much as 75 per cent of the new teaching materials for students of English in China.

. . . With its booming economy and eagerness to join the global business culture, China has emerged as the world's biggest market for materials to teach English as a second language. Beijing has made it a mandatory subject for all students beginning in Grade 3, and more than 20 million elementary schoolchildren are believed to be studying English. China traditionally used British texts, but as Beijing develops much closer links across the Pacific Ocean to North American schools and businesses, educational authorities are giving preference to North American English. And because of its apprehension about a U.S. cultural invasion, Beijing sees the Canadian textbooks as less threatening. "Canadian English is becoming the standard in China," said Michael Kraft, president of Lingo Media. "Canadians have a great advantage in China. We wave the Canadian flag whenever we can. The Chinese officials much prefer to work with a Canadian company. They look at the Americans as cultural invaders, and they feel that learning American English would absorb China into U.S. culture."

Canadian culture and language is sprinkled liberally throughout the Lingo Media texts. Chinese students learn about Canadian Thanksgiving, the snow and autumn leaves in Canada, the Canadian flag, the urban landscape of Toronto and the Canadian love of ice hockey. Canadian spellings, such as "favourite" and "colour," are given preference over U.S. versions. In books for the older grades, the texts discuss the Inuit people and Canadian environmental values. Duval House takes a similar approach. In one of its textbooks for the Chinese market, there is a lengthy discussion of Canadian cities and their Chinatown areas. "The

Chinese people in Canada are very proud, and they work hard to keep their culture alive," says a Chinese character who visits Canada in one of the texts. "It's good that Canadians can tolerate other people."

After launching its China series in 2001, Lingo Media is using its partnership with China's top educational publisher to capture an estimated 60- to 65-per-cent share of the primary-school ESL market in China. "There was a demand for North American English because the Chinese tend to see British English as very colonial and inflexible," said Xia Bailing, a Chinese businessman who is a member of Lingo Media's board of directors. "The U.S. influence is a very sensitive issue for them. But Canadians never pose any economic or cultural threat to China, so they prefer Canadian English." Chinese government officials confirmed the preference. "In the past, we didn't know much about Canadian English education, but now many Chinese people are visiting Canada and there is much co-operation between the two countries," said Zhang Aizhen, director of the textbook review section of the Chinese Education Ministry. "We feel that Canadian experts have a good understanding of how to write textboooks that are suitable for Chinese students." It may be the biggest cultural influence that Canada has achieved in China. "If you plant something in the minds of young kids, it dominates them forever," Mr. Xia said.

Video 2.1

Lingo Media earned about $1-million last year in royalties on its Chinese textbook sales and has distributed more than 60 million books, plus other material. But it argues that it is motivated by more than just a desire for profits. "'Like most teachers, we care more about shaping the future than lining our wallets," an internal memo concludes. "The promotion of Canadian culture and language is an invaluable tool to help us achieve this goal." The Edmonton company, Duval House, estimates that 2.3 million Chinese students use its textbooks to learn English. Its texts were developed chiefly in Canada with Canadian editors, writers, illustrators and curriculum designers. The main characters in its texts are Chinese and Canadian children. "Our standard is Canadian English for vocabulary, grammar and pronunciation," said Glenn Rollans, a partner in Duval House. "We see Canadian English as effectively international English, drawing as it does on British, American and other influences."

Source: From "China's Schools Give Canadian English Top Marks" by Geoffrey York, *The Globe and Mail* (August 16, 2004). Reprinted with permission of the publisher.

A SUN TZU MOMENT . . .

"If one ignorant of military matters [military culture] is sent to participate in the administration of the army, then in every movement there will be disagreement and mutual frustration and the entire army will be hamstrung."[6] In World Wars I and II the allied junior officers were readily transferred from unit to unit. The German junior officers remained much longer in the lower ranks and also within the same units. The German officer corps also spent significantly more time training in the art of war. In over 60 quantitative studies[7] of World War II battles examining the combat effectiveness given the comparable equipment, the results indicated that German

soldiers were 2.5 times more combat effective than the Soviets, and 1.2 times more effective than the American, Canadian, and British soldiers. The difference was not because of a master race, but rather because of a higher degree of military professionalism and organizational learning. They were imbued with a strong military culture.

So what can we learn from this? We must not be myopic when viewing global, cultural, and societal differences. We cannot enter the global marketplace ignorant of the cross-cultural differences. Canadian businesses must develop a higher degree of cultural sensitivity and organizational learning. If we fail to develop cultural sensitivity and literacy, there will be disagreement, mutual frustration, and less success.

An **ecosystem** is a living community of interacting organisms and their physical environment.

Environment is the physical surroundings and conditions.

Opening Thoughts

In this chapter and the following two, we will examine some of the major attributes of our global **ecosystem** (**environment**) that domestic firms are likely to encounter as they enter a foreign marketplace. There are a great number of external, uncontrollable attributes that can impact and influence how firms conduct their international business. These attributes include the competitive, distributive, technological, labour, physical, financial, sociocultural, legal, socioeconomic, and economic distinctions of a nation. In order to succeed, firms must accommodate and understand the host country's unique features. We have selected the cultural, societal, political, economic, legal, and technological attributes for examination in this text. Although these are not the only characteristics you will encounter in a global marketplace, they tend to be the major influences. These attributes are also present in the domestic marketplace but, as we discussed in Chapter 1, they become far more complex in the nondomestic marketplace. It is also important to recognize that the weights of these attributes shift from time to time. Most would agree for example that, following 9/11, the political and economic attributes (e.g., significantly reduced air travel that affected the aero industry and also resulted in higher oil prices) became very important factors for analysis by SMEs conducting international business. It might help you to remember these attributes using the acronym "PEST-C" (political, economic, societal, technological, and, in the international setting, culture).

Generally the most obvious difference to the international business practitioner is the observable cultural differences between countries. The moment we get off the plane at a foreign airport we are aware of surface cultural differences. However, there are many deeper cultural differences below that we must also consider. It is imperative that Canadian managers develop **cross-cultural literacy**; we must create an understanding and an awareness of cultural differences between countries (and their citizens) and how these differences can affect the conduct and success of our business. The opening vignette dramatically illustrates that many nations view Canada's culture as nonthreatening. If it is true, then this education story raises the question and its challenges: does Canada do enough to exploit our nonthreatening cultural competitive advantage? What innovative exporting initiatives might SMEs consider in order to derive benefit from this view of Canadian culture?

> **Cross-cultural literacy** is an understanding and an awareness of cultural differences between countries (and their citizens) and how these differences can affect the conduct and success of our business.

What Is Culture?

Socrates declared, "I am not an Athenian or a Greek, but a citizen of the world." Culture slowly evolves; it cannot be forced. It is both a unifying and a divisive force. Canada has undergone and continues to undergo cultural transformation. Since confederation in 1867 our culture was largely based on British and French culture but it has increasingly morphed into a more cosmopolitan culture as Canada adjusts to accommodate the growing ethnic diversity of our nation's cultural mosaic. Cultural transformation sometimes causes tension among a nation's citizens. The lowering of the Red Ensign in 1965 and the adoption of the Maple Leaf flag caused great consternation among the Canadian veterans of World War I and II. The renaming of Dominion Day to Canada Day; the increasing use of the generic greeting, "Happy Holidays" during the statutory Christmas season (Christian); and no longer being permitted to sing *The Maple Leaf Forever* in school are all indicators of transformational change in Canada's culture. However, cultural changes are underway everywhere; culture is not static. As younger people in non-Western nations adopt and mimic what they see and hear on MuchMusic, wearing Levi jeans and drinking Coca-Cola, the cultural tension rises for those who seek to preserve the status quo. This very visual surface adoption of Western liberalized democracy can be very threatening particularly to those non-Western nations' citizens yearning to maintain their traditional culture.

So what is culture? You will find many definitions. One of the most widely adopted is that of Whitely and England who identified common threads in a hundred or so definitions. They define culture as "knowledge, beliefs, art, law, morals, customs, and other capabilities of one group distinguishing it from another."[8] I offer this definition: **culture** is an agreed-upon set of values, beliefs, and norms by a definable segment of people. **Values and beliefs** are abstract ideas relating to the concept of what is good and what is bad. **Norms** are generally specific social rules and guidelines that prescribe the acceptable behaviour of a member of a definable society. They can be morally or legally grounded and can be divided into folkways and mores. A breach of norms can have minor or major repercussions.

> **Culture** is an agreed-upon set of values, beliefs, and norms by a definable segment of people.
>
> **Values and beliefs** are abstract ideas relating to the concept of what is good and what is bad.
>
> **Norms** are generally specific social rules and guidelines that prescribe the acceptable behaviour of a member of a definable society.

Our values and beliefs are at the very core of our culture. To understand American values and beliefs, we can read the opening phrase of the United States Constitution that begins, "We the people . . ." This is indicative of the American bias toward individualistic values and is easy to recognize. These values are at the core of the American culture. Conversely, examining Canada's constitution (once known as the British North America Act of 1867, now, as part of our cultural change, referred to as the Constitution Act) we note language describing our values and beliefs in ". . . peace, order and good government." An examination of these two documents reveals the stark difference between Americans and Canadians. The United States' culture focuses strongly on the rights of the individual, while Canadians tend to place more value on the collective. Definable society beliefs about democracy; truth; justice; social obligation; individualism versus collectivism; roles of men, women, and children; and other beliefs are all deeply ingrained in nations' cultural values. When a society's values are threatened, strong emotive feelings are elicited. Can you think of a situation where you experienced strong feelings as a result of a shift or a failure to shift in Canada's culture?

Norms can be morally or legally grounded. They are the shared guidelines and rules for appropriate behaviour within a society. A breach of norms can have minor or major repercussions. Norms can be divided into folkways and mores. **Folkways** (minor repercussions) are grounded in acceptable social behaviour such as good table manners, dressing appropriately for dinner, standing when a lady enters the room. Yes, folkways shift! Transgressions seldom bring formal sanctions but those observing may well form a lower opinion of those who fail to observe the folkway social niceties. Attention to time, for example, is a folkway that is sometimes viewed differently in different countries. In Canada, when we call a meeting for 9:00 A.M., it is anticipated that all will be present at 9:00 A.M. or a few minutes before. In Jamaica, you may have ordered a taxi for 9:00 A.M. When it does not appear and you inquire of the dispatcher when you might expect the taxi, the response could be "Soon come, soon come"! You will find in an international context that hosts are often prepared to overlook breaches of folkways initially. **Mores** (major repercussions), on the other hand, are norms that have great impact on the functioning of society. They are the customs and conventions that are strongly held by a definable culture. Transgression of mores can bring sanctions. In Dubai (pop. 1.2 million; GNP $26,280), one of the seven emirates that make up the Federation of the United Arab Emirates (UAE), one of the strongly held mores is that women should dress modestly with their elbows and knees covered. The drinking of alcohol, while permitted at some upscale hotels, could bring quick retribution to Canadians consuming a little spirit in other locations. Indeed, in Dubai, this is one of many mores that have legal consequences. Figure 2.1 illustrates a macro view of culture.

Folkways are norms grounded in acceptable social behaviour such as good table manners, dressing appropriately for dinner, or standing when a lady enters the room. Transgressions seldom bring formal sanctions but those observing may well form a lower opinion of those who fail to observe the social niceties.

Mores (major repercussions) are norms that have great impact on the functioning of society. They are the customs and conventions that are strongly held by a definable culture. Transgression of mores can bring sanctions.

Characteristics of Culture

To understand the culture of the host nation, we will need to examine the country's specific characteristics concerning values, norms, folkways, and mores, including religious beliefs, values placed on life balance and lifestyle, political and economic philosophy, language, societal forces, changing global demographics, and negotiation considerations. In addition, there are a number of other unique characteristics that could also be examined including a country's attitudes toward foreigners, human rights, and other idiosyncratic factors that are not reviewed in these materials.

Religious Considerations

Religion is a system of shared beliefs and rituals concerned with the role of the sacred.[10]

Ethical values are grounded in religion and can be defined as the moral "ought to-do's" that sustain a civilized society.

The values and beliefs held sacred by religion shape cultures. The view of world religions toward toward work, savings, and material goods must be understood by business leaders intent on entering the international marketplace. **Religion** can be defined as a system of shared beliefs and rituals concerned with the role of the sacred.[9] Grounded in religion are ethical values. **Ethical values** can be defined as the moral "ought to-do's" founded in

FIGURE 2.1
A Macro View of Culture

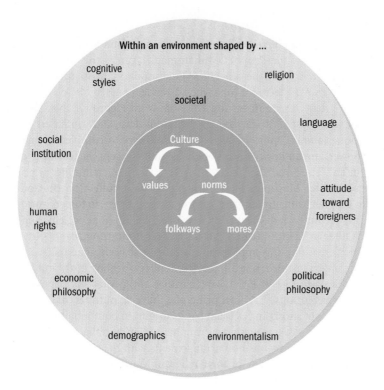

religion that sustain a civilized society. We will also see that the ethical use of the teachings of Confucianism, while not a religion, very much influences the values held by a great number of Chinese businesspeople.

The world's major religions are Christianity, Islam, Hinduism, Buddhism, Judaism, and Shintoism. In addition, we will examine Confucianism. Confucian views and beliefs in China affect business practices to the same extent that religion does in other countries.

Christianity and Business Implications

Christianity boasts some 300 denominations with the majority belonging to the Roman Catholic, Protestant, and Eastern Orthodox churches. Christianity is by far the largest of the world's religions and is adopted to some degree by about 30 percent (2,135,783,000)[11] of the globe's 6.5 billion people. Most Christians live in Europe and in the Americas. Increasingly, Christianity is developing a strong presence in Africa. Its fundamentals can be found in the teachings of Jesus of Nazareth over 2,000 years ago. Max Weber, a German sociologist, noted Christianity's impact on business; in 1904, he observed "business leaders and owners of capital, as well as the higher grades of skilled labour, and even more the higher technical and commercially trained personnel of modern enterprises, are overwhelmingly Protestant."[12] The focus on hard work, wealth creation (for the glory of God), frugality, and the accumulation of capital for investment was high on the list of Protestants' cultural values.[13] This tenet is known widely as the **Protestant work ethic.** Many believe it became the main driver of the development of capitalism and free enterprise, first in 19th-century Europe, and subsequently in the Americas. Roman Catholics, while supporting this tenet in part, are influenced by the teachings of the faith and as a result they "offer up" their work for the glory of God on earth in order to achieve gratification in the afterlife. Protestants grounded in the reformation place greater importance on the rights and obligations of the individual rather than the community. As a result you will note in Christian countries a raised awareness of the importance of individuals evident in their day-to-day business dealings.

Christianity boasts some 300 denominations with the majority belonging to the Roman Catholic, Protestant, and Eastern Orthodox churches. It is by far the largest of the world's religions and is adopted to some degree by about 30 percent of the world. Most Christians live in Europe and the Americas, with an increasingly strong presence in Africa. Its fundamentals can be found in the teachings of Jesus of Nazareth over 2,000 years ago.

The **Protestant work ethic** is a widely known tenet. Its focus on hard work, wealth creation (for the glory of God), frugality, and the accumulation of capital for investment was high on the list of cultural values of Protestants.[14]

Islam and Business Implications

Islam is the world's second
largest religion (1.3 billion)[17]
founded in 622 (the first year
of the Islamic calendar) by the
Prophet Muhammad and
followed by the majority in
more than 35 countries. Islam
is the youngest of the three
monotheistic world religions.
An adherent to Islam is a
Muslim, an Arab term for "one
who surrenders oneself to God."

Islam is the world's second largest religion (1.3 billion)[15] founded in 622 (the first year of the Islamic calendar) by the Prophet Muhammad. Islam is the youngest of the three monotheistic world religions (the others are Judaism and Christianity). An adherent to Islam is a Muslim, an Arab term for "one who surrenders oneself to God." Muslims are the majority in more than 35 countries. You will note from Figure 2.2 that Muslims can be found from the west coast of Africa, through the Middle East, and South East Asian nations, including Indonesia and China. Islam requires followers to completely surrender their uniqueness, power, and authority unconditionally and to accept the teachings of the Koran (also spelt Qur'an). The Koran, like the Christian Bible, sets out a number of principles that must be observed by Muslims. These principles are a collection of God's (Allah's) revelations to Prophet Muhammad. The paramount principle is to forego worldly ambition and seek Allah's favour by fulfilling the dictates of his will in hopes of entering paradise in the afterlife. Other teachings include respecting and honouring parents; respecting the rights of others; maintaining appropriate balance between generosity and frugality; avoiding killing unless justified; not committing adultery; dealing justly and equitably with others; being pure and just of heart; safeguarding and protecting orphans; and being humble and unpretentious.[16] These principles have a number of similarities with Christianity. This is not surprising as Islam has its origins in both Judaism and Christianity. The followers of Islam recognize Jesus as a prophet rather than the Son of God.

Canadian SMEs entering business arrangements with the followers of Islam will find that Muslims take a holistic view of their religion. Muslims cannot set their principles aside in "watertight compartments"; rather, they must observe these principles and be

FIGURE 2.2

Geographical Distribution of the
Religions of the World

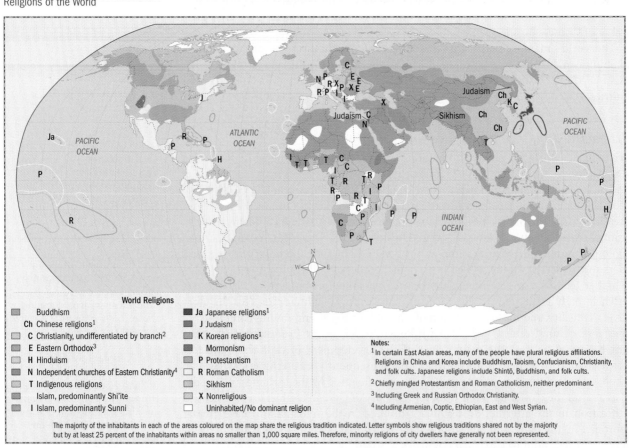

World Religions

▨	Buddhism	■ **Ja**	Japanese religions[1]
Ch	Chinese religions[1]	▨ **J**	Judaism
▢ **C**	Christianity, undifferentiated by branch[2]	▨ **K**	Korean religions[1]
▨ **E**	Eastern Orthodox[3]	▨	Mormonism
▢ **H**	Hinduism	▨ **P**	Protestantism
■ **N**	Independent churches of Eastern Christianity[4]	▢ **R**	Roman Catholic
▨ **T**	Indigenous religions	▨	Sikhism
▨	Islam, predominantly Shi'ite	▢ **X**	Nonreligious
▨ **I**	Islam, predominantly Sunni	▢	Uninhabited/No dominant religion

Notes:
[1] In certain East Asian areas, many of the people have plural religious affiliations. Religions in China and Korea include Buddhism, Taoism, Confucianism, Christianity, and folk cults. Japanese religions include Shintō, Buddhism, and folk cults.

[2] Chiefly mingled Protestantism and Roman Catholicism, neither predominant.

[3] Including Greek and Russian Orthodox Christianity.

[4] Including Armenian, Coptic, Ethiopian, East and West Syrian.

The majority of the inhabitants in each of the areas coloured on the map share the religious tradition indicated. Letter symbols show religious traditions shared not by the majority but by at least 25 percent of the inhabitants within areas no smaller than 1,000 square miles. Therefore, minority religions of city dwellers have generally not been represented.

constrained by them 24/7. The religion is not separate from the state as in most countries and it is at the very core of a nation's business practices and culture. Consider for example, Muslims' days for weekend prayer and holiday are Thursdays and Fridays according to the Christian calendar. Christians similarly are generally not available on Saturdays and Sundays. This results in a window of only three days per week in which to communicate and conduct international business. This can be further affected when adjusting to the difference between time zones. For example, between Vancouver, British Columbia, and Tehran, Iran, the difference is night and day—a time difference of 11.5 hours. Christian SME managers should also be aware that orthodox Muslims are required to pray five times a day. Be prepared for meeting stoppages to permit Muslim attendees an opportunity to fulfill their religious obligations.

Hinduism and Business Implications

Many see **Hinduism** as a way of life rather than a formal religion. It has no founder nor recognized central authority or spiritual leader. It is practised by more than 870 million[18] of India's population (1.1 billion). For Hindus, time is cyclical and as a result all members of society are in a process of birth, death, and reincarnation. The goal for a Hindu is to escape the cycle and reach eternal bliss (nirvana). Hindus' actions are shaped by the notion of moral retribution (karma). Karma motivates Hindus to behave properly in this life in order to achieve a higher spiritual status in the next life. Strict Hindus will not wilfully harm any living creature because of their belief that it may be an incarnated human soul. As a result, Hindus consider cows sacred animals and do not eat beef. For this reason, it is interesting to watch the market entry strategy of firms going into India. McDonalds' marketing literature for example provides, "We are committed to giving you wholesome, healthy, and delicious food. We ensure that the cooking area as well as cooking equipment for vegetarian products is visibly segregated from the non-veg sections. What's more—our crew members cooking vegetarian food items are identifiable by their green aprons."[19]

At the centre of the Hindu faith is the concept of the **caste system**. The caste system stratifies the entire society into four groups with each assigned a class of work. The religious word for caste is "varna." There are 3,000 castes and 25,000 sub-castes in India, each related to a specific occupation. These different castes fall under four basic varnas: Brahmins—priests; Kshatryas (politicians and landowners)—warriors; Vaishyas (merchants)—traders; and Shudras—labourers. Those not included in one of these basic four varnas are assigned to a fifth group referred to as the "outcasts—untouchables."

Caste not only dictates one's occupation, but also the dietary habits and the permitted interaction with members of other castes. Members of a high caste enjoy more wealth and opportunities while members of a low caste perform menial jobs. Outside the caste system are the outcasts/untouchables. "Untouchable jobs, such as toilet cleaning and garbage removal, require them to be in contact with bodily fluids. They are therefore considered polluted and not to be touched. The importance of purity in the body and food is found in early Sanskrit literature. Untouchables have separate entrances to homes and must drink from separate wells. They are considered to be in a permanent state of impurity. Gandhi named the untouchables 'Harijans' (Children of God). He tried to raise their status with symbolic gestures such as befriending and eating with Untouchables. Upward mobility is very rare in the caste system. Most people remain in one caste their entire life and marry within their caste."[21] Some might say Hindus in India do have social mobility. Hindus can move within the caste system but to do so must die and be reincarnated to achieve a higher or lower caste level. The Indian government has outlawed the caste system; however, there are daily examples of the tension that exists in the workplace because it continues to be imbedded in the culture. For recent business examples of tension in the Indian workplace visit www.power.nelson.com.

Hinduism is seen by many as a way of life rather than a formal religion. It has no founder nor recognized central authority or spiritual leader. It is practised by more than 870 million[20] of India's population (1.1 billion).

The **caste system** stratifies the entire society into four groups, called varnas, each with an assigned class of work. These are the Brahmins—priests; the Kshatryas (politicians and landowners)—warriors; the Vaishyas (merchants)—traders; and the Shudras—labourers. Those not included in one of these basic four varnas are assigned to a fifth group referred to as the "outcasts—untouchables."

Buddhism was founded by a Hindu Prince, Gautama, in India, 2,600 years ago. Buddhist teachings provided an alternative to Hinduism. There are currently approximately 378 million Buddhists[23] established mostly in Asian nations such as China, Korea, Tibet, Japan, Thailand, and Vietnam.

Judaism is one of the three monotheistic world religions and dates back to the 6th century B.C.E. Its religious and ethical beliefs are contained within a sacred text—the Hebrew Bible, particularly in the Torah (the five books of Moses) and the Talamud (the laws and commandments). Judaism's central authority is not vested in any person or group but rather in its writings and traditions. At the core of the religious belief is that the people of Israel are God's chosen people and every member of the faith strives to live within God's law.

Kosher describes food that meets the standards of Kashrut. Kashrut is the body of Jewish law dealing with what foods Jews can and cannot eat, and how those foods must be prepared and eaten. The word *kosher* can also be used, and often is used, to describe ritual objects that are made in accordance with Jewish law and are fit for ritual use. Contrary to popular misconception, rabbis or other religious officials do not "bless" food to make it kosher.

Shintoism, derived from the Chinese words *shin tao* ("the way of the Gods"), is the indigenous religion of Japan. Started about 500 B.C.E., arising from legends and without a founder or sacred text, over 4 million Japanese have accepted this native religion.

Buddhism and Business Implications

A Hindu Prince, Gautama, founded **Buddhism** in India 2,600 years ago. Buddhist teachings provided an alternative to Hinduism. There are currently approximately 378 million Buddhists[22] established mostly in Asian nations such as China, Korea, Tibet, Japan, Thailand, and Vietnam. Although founded in India, because Buddhist beliefs are contrary to Hinduism, Buddhism failed to take root in the subcontinent. Buddhists oppose the caste system and believe followers can attain enlightenment and achieve nirvana by abandoning the belief in the endless cycle of rebirth. The Buddhists' core belief is that, if people have no desire, they will not suffer. The Buddhist monks are active politically and influence the marketplace. One of the best known is the exiled honorary Canadian, His Holiness the 14th Dalai Lama; the political and cultural head of Tibet. Buddhists present a marketing challenge: it is hard to sell your goods and services to people who believe that if they have no desire, they will not suffer.

Judaism and Business Implications

Judaism was founded over 3,000 years ago and was the first of the world's monotheistic religions. "Judaism is an action-oriented system (a holistic lifestyle) rather than a spiritual one [adhered to only on "holy days"] and a community-oriented system rather than one that aims at the promotion of special individuals."[24] Statistically, the religion's numbers (15 million) understate their influence in international commerce. Similar to the Protestant work ethic, the approach of Judaism to wealth creation and, indeed, to the satisfaction of all human needs and wants is that "God created the world in such a way that these needs and wants were to be satisfied by human endeavour and provided the religious framework through the Torah [sacred text] whereby such endeavour would be moral and an expression of a religious way of life."[25] Orthodox Jews strictly adhere to important days in their religion. Be aware that from sundown Friday until sundown Saturday little work will take place. Jewish holidays will also influence the scheduling of business appointments. Like Hindus, the eating of pork is prohibited. In order to be **kosher**, among other things, meats are stored and served separately from dairy products. The preparation of foods according to Judaic dietary traditions (Rabbinic law) results in the foods being declared kosher.

Shintoism and Business Implications

Shintoism, derived from the Chinese words *shin tao* ("the way of the Gods"), is the practice of Japan's indigenous religion Shinto. Arising from legends and without a founder or sacred text, over 4 million Japanese have accepted this native religion. Shinto is an ancient Japanese religion that started about 500 B.C.E. (or earlier). Originally it was "an amorphous mix of nature worship, fertility cults, divination techniques, hero worship, and shamanism."[26] Up to the end of World War II, the followers of Shinto saw the Emperor of Japan as having divine status. As a term of peace, the Allied forces required that the Japanese Emperor relinquish this claim. Attendance at the Shinto shrines is not fixed as the religious days in the Christian and Islamic religions are rather, followers attend as they feel the need. Indeed, many homes contain a small Shinto shrine, thereby enabling the religion to be practised at home. At the heart of Shinto teachings is patriotism to the Japanese nation. It also requires followers to be sincere, observe ethical behaviour, value loyalty and respect toward others, and enjoy life. Underscoring these attributes is harmony and unity. The followers value trust and relationships. Family is seen as the main mechanism by which traditions are preserved. Adherence to the teachings of Shinto led Japan to an enviable economic position following World War II. These beliefs resulted in Japan having a loyal workforce with little union strife. Until the Asian crisis in 1997, there was little employee turnover as most of the workforce believed in the notion of a job for life with their organizations. However, with the economic downturn, this employment-for-life notion is, with increasing intensity, under attack as Japanese firms, anxious to restore their economic strength, adopt Western employment practices. It is difficult for a foreigner to embrace Shintoism. Unlike most other religions, there is no sacred text to assist those interested in learning about this religion. It is passed on from generation to generation by experiencing the rituals together as a group, similar to how Canada's First Nations transmit their culture, belief, values, and stories by word of mouth from generation to generation.

Confucianism and Business Implications

A politician and philosopher, K'ung-Fu-tzu (pronounced Confucius in English), founded **Confucianism** over 2,500 years ago. With over 225 million followers in China and partial acceptance by countries such as Japan, South Korea, and other nations with a large ethnic Chinese population, the teachings of Confucianism are growing as the economic stature of these countries develop. Interestingly, in 1949, Mao Zedong encouraged the downplaying of the importance of Confucianism as the official ethical system of China. However, H. Pierson French, professor of history and political science observed, "Confucianism by any other name is still Confucianism . . . You can't have traditions going on for 2,500 years without [them] sticking. We knock wood for luck; leave a house through the same door we entered. Those things still stay with people."[27] The teachings of Confucianism support the importance of obtaining personal salvation through taking the right actions in this world. These right actions are deeply embedded in the country's ethical codes that require high moral and ethical conduct and loyalty to others. Unlike other religions, such as Christianity and Islam, Confucianism spends little time thinking about the supernatural and supreme beings. Loyalty to one superior is highly prized. But not just loyalty up; loyalty down is equally expected. This reciprocal relationship (guanxi) is central to Confucianism. Confucian thinkers stress the importance of relationship building and establishing networks that are supported by reciprocal obligations. Confucianism teaches the importance of honesty. When individuals and companies cannot trust each other, then business relationships break down. Conversely, if you are able to create an atmosphere of total trust and loyalty in your workplace it will result in reducing the costs of doing business. Once accepted into the relationships, to break from the reciprocal understanding will cause the offending party a loss of "face" and will be subject to social sanctions from others in the network. "**Face** is a multi-faceted term, and its meaning is inextricably linked with culture and other terms such as honour and its opposite, humiliation. Saving face or *giving face* has different levels of importance, depending on the culture or society with which one is dealing. Perhaps the most familiar term to many is 'saving face,' which we understand simply to mean not being disrespectful to others in public, or taking preventive actions so that we will not appear to *lose face* in the eyes of others. Some will immediately associate the term 'face' with Sino-Japanese cultures, but it would be a mistake to think that those are the only cases where face issues are important. In the Cuban missile crisis, it was very important both sides not to lose face or credibility, and this need guided both sides' negotiating tactics."[28]

Other Religions and Business Implications

There are a number of other religions and near religions that you may encounter when entering a global market. They too will have to be understood and the impact they have on business practices accommodated. These include Jainism, a contemporary of Buddha; Sikhism an Indian military brotherhood; Taoism, founded by Lao-tzu a contemporary of Confucius; and Animism, a spirit worship that includes black magic generally found in African and certain Latin American countries. These other but not lesser religions and their potential impact on business are outlined at www.power.nelson.com.

Huntington's Eight Civilizations

In 1996, Samuel P. Huntington, a Harvard professor, published an insightful bestseller entitled *The Clash of Civilizations: Remaking of World Order*. At the core, his message was that the most important distinction between societies is culture. It is culture that defines who we are, and who we are not. Huntington prophesies a "clash of civilizations." No

Confucianism was founded over 2,500 years ago by a politician and philosopher, K'ung-Fu-tzu (pronounced Confucius in English). With over 225 million followers in China and partial acceptance by countries such as Japan, South Korea, and other nations with a large ethnic Chinese population, the teachings of Confucianism are growing as the economic stature of these countries develop. Loyalty to one superior is highly prized. But not just loyalty up; loyalty down is equally expected. This reciprocal relationship (guanxi) is central to Confucianism.

Face is a multi-faceted term, and its meaning is inextricably linked with culture and other terms such as honour and its opposite, humiliation. Saving face or *giving face* has different levels of importance, depending on the culture or society with which one is dealing. Perhaps the most familiar term to many is "*saving face*," which we understand simply to mean not being disrespectful to others in public, or taking preventive actions so that we will not appear to *lose face* in the eyes of others.

PRACTICAL ENTREPRENEURIAL FOCUS

International Consulting— Do Your Homework

"A Toronto telecommunications company targeted Southeast Asia as a promising new market for its services. The company successfully established a joint-venture partnership in Malaysia and had its sights set on Thailand's emerging market. A team of senior executives from the Toronto company traveled to Bangkok for a series of meetings with a potential joint-venture partner—a prominent, respected, and well-connected local company. The first day of meetings proceeded well and the Thai hosts invited the Canadians to a reception and dinner. During the reception the senior Canadian executive made an offhand remark about the Thai Royal family. His Thai counterpart smiled politely and soon excused himself from the conversation. Over the evening, the Canadian sensed something in the manner of his Thai host changed but could not understand why. This sense persisted over the next day of meetings,

AFP/Getty Images

The King of Thailand and the Royal Family

where the Thais seemed more reserved and formal. The Canadian team, baffled by this turn of events, returned home with little more than a vague commitment for future discussions. No discussions or agreement occurred and, over the ensuing months, the Canadian company found doors in Thailand closed, not only with the Thai company with whom they had hoped to form a partnership, but with other Thai firms they approached."[29]

This is a classic example of the consequence of not doing your homework. In Thailand, royalty is treated like deity. The Thais deeply

respect and revere their monarchy. I had the opportunity to travel to Thailand years ago and I specifically remember the tour guide admonishing us not to show any disrespect for the monarchy. Our Canadian culture, on the other hand, tolerates and encourages criticism of our government. The company's blunder caused that company a partnership opportunity, and the loss of other potential opportunities.

QUESTIONS

Are the Thai hosts being too sensitive and demonstrating a lack of tolerance of a remark made in a social setting by the Canadian firm's executive? Heated conversations are the norm in Canada as we discuss the latest antics of our political leaders. What is the problem? What action(s) might the Toronto firm's team of senior executives have undertaken to avoid this incident?

---

longer will there be dangerous conflicts between social classes, rich and poor, or other economically defined groups but rather conflicts will occur along "cultural fault lines." These thoughts were initially introduced in 1993 in *Foreign Affairs*.[30] Huntington predicted the most likely pending source of cultural conflict as being between the followers of Islam and Christianity. Yes, this was in 1993! Huntington's thesis responded to Johns Hopkins University professor and neo-conservative Francis Fukuyama, who previously postulated in his book *The End of History*[31] that the ultimate triumph of Western liberalized capitalism throughout the world is just about to arrive. Fukuyama states "this is the end point of mankind's ideological evolution and the universalization of Western liberalized democracy as the final form of human government."[32] For further insights into Dr. Fukuyama's belief that Western liberalized democracy will be the final form of human government and a short analysis of the document from a Canadian perspective, see www.power.nelson.com. Fukuyama was also one of the driving forces behind the "Project for the New American Century." It too can be found on the text site.

As we examine culture and the other environmental attributes that shape international business, we must consider these contradictory positions. We need to have a model in order to generalize about reality; to be able to understand causal relationships; to be able, with critical thinking, to anticipate and predict future developments; and to be able to discern what is important and what is not. Huntington was praised as a prophet who foresaw the 9/11 attacks. The term "clash of civilizations" has become a part of the political vernacular. The Muslims' global riots[33] of 2006, precipitated by a Danish cartoon, proved that there is merit in his observation. However, one caveat: we must be careful not to let Huntington's view become a self-fulfilling prophecy. The "War on Terror" is just that; it is not a war on Islam. What do you think? The lens you use to view the global environment will be influenced by which one of these perspectives resonates best with you.

Value Placed on Life Balance and Lifestyle

Cultures, as we have seen, can be differentiated by the importance the society or a group places on life balance and lifestyle. Death in India has significant religious meaning as a call centre owner quickly found out when part of its operations were effectively shut down for three days of mourning following a death in one worker's family. A Canadian human resource manager observed that Indian lunch periods must be extended, as that is the main meal period for the day, unlike Canadians who tend to favour short noon lunches for longer evening meals.[34] In considering life balance, the paid annual leave to which workers are entitled is a factor which obviously influences the annual duration of working time. In the EU, employees take 25.7 days off, in Japan 18 days and in Canada the average number of days off is 20 days. The cultural consideration of balance in life impacts directly on a nation's productivity. By examining the French hours of work we find about 1,589 hours per year vis-à-vis Canada's private sector workers at 1,775 hours per year.[35] It would seem that the French worker spends only 80 percent of the time producing goods and services compared to his Canadian counterparts. This reduction in work hours seems to have come at a cost. In the recent past (pre-2006) France's economy had outperformed Germany. However "Germany seems to be experiencing an economic revival under its Chancellor Angela Merkel that has recovered much of its lost competitiveness and is leading the pack, while France is lagging."[36] What conclusion can we draw about productivity and the value placed by these nations on maintaining a balance in life?

Political and Economic Philosophy

The prevailing economic and political systems dramatically impact the cultural practices that we will encounter as we move from country to country. We must keep in mind that these ecosystem attributes (PEST-C) are not to be viewed as independent "silos" but rather as multidimensional and nonlinear inputs. You will read more on political and economic philosophy and its impact on culture in Chapter 3.

Language

In many cases, language is a clear differentiator of culture. Language as a means of communication is both spoken and unspoken. In fact, there's much evidence to indicate that over 90 percent of our communication takes place without speaking. Accordingly, it is important in developing your cross-cultural literacy and an awareness of nonspoken communications in your host countries. In Canada, most of us use one word to communicate "snow." Other Canadians, the Inuit, have never developed a similar general descriptor for snow but rather use 24 differentiator descriptors for the various types of snow. Why? In the Inuit culture, the weather and snow are pervasive to all aspects of their life and therefore they need many discrete descriptions. Language shapes our culture and how we view our surroundings. Canada's culture is rich in that it has been shaped by two founding languages (English and French) and these in turn are increasingly being influenced by the growing diversity of languages introduced by new Canadians. Multiple languages within one nation are not unique to Canada. Belgium, Spain, Cyprus, and Switzerland all share two or more languages as part of their culture. See Figure 2.3, page 46, for the distribution of the world's major languages. Today the most common language, and the language of business, is English. Will it continue to be?

 Nonspoken language is communicated through gestures, facial expressions, eye contact, and the use of personal space. Want to test communicating using personal space? Next time you have an opportunity to use an elevator, enter the elevator and remain

FIGURE 2.3
Languages of the World

FIGURE 2.3
Languages of the World

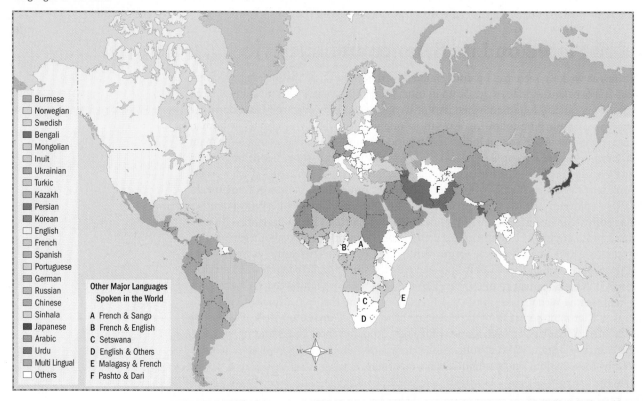

facing the back wall. You will be communicating a message, and all present will experience great discomfort with your action. Nonverbal communication is similarly as powerful when you fail to observe the prerequisite communication culture of a foreign country. The same level of discomfort experienced by those in the elevator will be felt by Iranians if you sit with the sole of your shoe visible to them. It is critical to your success that you understand all the ways you will be communicating within a host nation.

Societal Forces

It should be clear by now that the preceding cultural attributes, such as politics, economics, and religion, shape a society's social structure. A country's view of social groupings, social status, social mobility, and class system are influenced greatly by its political, economic, and religious beliefs.

Individual/Group

In Western cultures, particularly America and to a lesser extent Canada, the individual is seen as the basic unit of the social structure. In Islamic, Hindu, and Confucius nations, groups are seen as the basic units. It is common in all societies that their members cluster in collections ranging from a very few to a very large number. These social groupings contribute to our perception of who we are and are readily identifiable. The Hell's Angels, the Canadian Airborne Regiment (before it was disbanded), French Canadians, Newfoundlanders, and Western Canadians are examples of individuals who wish to be identified as part of a unique society.

After the individual, the basic group is the **nuclear** and **extended family**. Westerners will note strong bonds in the extended family found in Asia, the Middle East, Mexico, and Latin America. The propensity to hire extended family, regardless of qualifications, will be evident

A **nuclear** family typically includes parents and their children.

The **extended family** typically includes three or more generations, such as grandparents, aunts, uncles, and cousins, in addition to the nuclear family.

in these countries. In many nations, the distribution channels are built in large part on extended family. This can lead to a number of challenging human resources incidents. How do you fire or discipline a cousin? We will look at the role culture plays in influencing distribution channels in Chapter 14. We also examine the roles of individuals and groups from a political perspective in Chapter 3, commencing with Aristotle and Plato. We will come to see that individuals are very mobile and focused on their needs and wants while the group will be more focused on the values of the collective. There will be less movement between jobs and more loyalty to the organization when individuals feel part of the collective.

Social Status

Each country's social structure divides the population according to status, which is defined by the country's culture. Considerations in Canada are family heritage, income, and occupation. In Canada, we award status at the highest level to the Queen of Canada and her representatives (the governor general and the lieutenant-governors) followed by top government and business leaders. The middle level includes most university-trained professionals; while the bottom strata generally comprises blue-collar workers. This stratification is common within most Western developed nations. A different stratification will be found in other cultures. In China, for example, the value ingrained in society for lifelong learning places educators in the highest level of social status, while business leaders occupy the middle class.

Social Mobility

Different cultures have different levels of social mobility. **Social mobility** is the ease with which members of a society can move up or down the "ladder" of social status. The social mobility of countries can be placed on a continuum between the strict, legal caste system as found in India, which provides for no social mobility, to the other end of the continuum—a **class system** that permits social mobility. A class system is defined as social status determined by the family into which a person is born and subsequent socioeconomic achievements. A mobile class system provides the opportunity for individuals to significantly improve their placement within their society's social status. The United States generally is used to provide an example of the most mobile class system. Canada has a few glass ceilings that impede similar mobility. We will be looking closer at international glass ceilings in Chapter 15. It is important to be aware of the level of class-consciousness when doing business in foreign countries because you may encounter biases about dealing with individuals of "lower" rank.

Social mobility is the ease with which members of a society can move up or down the "ladder" of social status.

A **class system** is defined as social status determined by the family into which a person is born and subsequent socioeconomic achievements.

Changing Global Demographics

English political economist Thomas Malthus, in his famous work, *An Essay on the Principle of Population* (1798), postulated the theory that the world's population would grow unendingly without the natural constraints of war, famine, and disease. Malthus believed that the world would "starve itself" as it would be unable to maintain the food supply to meet the burgeoning global population. Fortunately, technology brought his theory into question just as recent Malthusian advocates were re-emerging in the 20th century. Global demographic trends are revealing new factors that will limit population growth and "suggest that by 2075 global population will have peaked and begun a substantial decline."[37]

Falling Birth Rates

Population predictions during the 20th century forecast explosive global population growth that would result in the Malthusian disaster. "During the 1990s, it was feared that global population would reach 12 billion. Today, new population studies indicate that the present global population of 6.5 billion will level off by 2050 at 9 billion, and that by

2075 it will have declined by 500 million."[38] A global fertility rate of 2.1 children is required to maintain populations at current levels. According to United Nations estimates, Asia, Latin America, and both Eastern and Western Europe have been experiencing declining birthrates for years, now approaching 1.85 children. The only exceptions seem to be the populations of the United States and France. The main reasons for the declining **fertility rate** phenomena seems to be the availability and increased use of contraception by women driven to achieve higher levels of education, enhanced opportunities for employment, and greater individual financial independence; the global trend toward urbanization that makes it harder to support more than one or two children; and certain governmental public policy initiatives that limit family size. (China and Iran have laws to limit the number of children permitted for each family.) China's one-child policy has drastically reduced the proportion of young people in its population. This public policy will have implications on the ability of companies to recruit enough staff. In China's case however, high population figures make the problem less serious. Other nations such as Australia, Estonia, Singapore, and Scandinavia, increasingly concerned about their falling populations, have devised incentives to encourage childbearing.[39]

> A country's **fertility rate** is the rate at which the population replaces itself.

The U.S. population is expected to expand from the present 300 million to 400 million over the next 50 years, with 80 percent of that growth coming from either immigrants or the descendants of immigrants. Conversely, Canada, even with an aggressive immigration policy, is projected to only maintain its current population of 31.4 million until 2050. Canada is experiencing a "baby bust" due to declining fertility rates, which will cause a number of significant impacts. At a time when commodities, such as energy and water, are experiencing growing global demand by developing nations, including China and the United States, Canada is an underpopulated, resource-rich country with the second largest land mass in the world. What emerging cultural and geopolitical issues can you see here? What can we do about them? Europe is in a similar state of decline. It is becoming depopulated faster than any time since the Black Death. The current estimates from the United Nations suggest that the European Union's population will decline by 7.5 million over the next 45 years. The economically active population (workers) will decline by 88 million. This will result in the Europeans' share of the world's population dropping from 6 percent to less than 4 percent,[40] resulting in worker shortages. The solution for many nations is increased immigration, but at what cost to existing culture?

Economic Implications

Population growth and sustainable consumption are necessary to fuel capitalism. This is the very core of globalization: increase living standards by reducing and removing trade barriers, thereby making more customers available to purchase more goods and services at lower prices. A significant reduction in population will have profound implications for both business and the economy. In general, as we have experienced in Canada, prosperity reduces birthrates, which constricts the workforce, and leads to an increase in the elderly population. In Canada, Germany, Japan, and many other developing countries, the declining workforces are becoming unable to maintain the necessary levels of productivity, or to support the countries' rapidly increasing elderly populations. Canada's social safety net, which includes health care and pensions, is increasingly showing the fissures precipitated by Canada's shifting age demographics. Indeed, many would argue that it is the social safety net that is at the core of Canadian culture. Economically and socially it is hard to predict what these complex demographic shifts will mean for either Canada's domestic economy or the global economy. It is clear that marketplace demand will realign along changing demographic lines. This suggests continually changing markets and shifting target audiences, presenting new challenges to both marketing and selling operations as they become more demographically targeted in their activities. Canadian SMEs operating in foreign countries will need to investigate the demographics and the projected shifts to determine whether they can recruit the right people for the right jobs. In countries such as Malaysia where the population pyramid is a triangle, i.e., the younger population is increasing in proportion, companies can worry less about whether they can recruit enough young workers for their manufacturing needs.

Much has been said in the media about Canada's **brain drain** and its impact. Brain drain is defined as emigration by the brightest and best of a nation's workplace talent to foreign countries. This phenomenon occurs for a number of reasons, including taxation levels, quality of life, and employment and research and development opportunities. Visit www.power.nelson.com for a reading on the topic. Is brain drain an issue we should be concerned about in Canada? Examine the Canadian health care industry and provide your reflective thoughts on this emerging issue and its likely impact on Canada's culture.

Brain drain is the emigration by the brightest and best of a nation's workplace talent to foreign countries.

The Cultural Globalization Index

Video 2.2

"Culture is the most visible manifestation of globalization, whether it is the appearance of new cultural forms (such as Disneyland Paris) or the transformation of traditional cultural expressions into something a bit different (such as Egyptian McDonald's restaurants serving their patrons the "McFalafel"). While there are ample data to track the cross-border movement of people (including the brain drain), merchandise, and money, it is extraordinarily difficult to measure the global spread of ideas and trends. However, it is possible to get a hint of a country's level of cultural integration by identifying **cultural proxies**—the conduits by which ideas, beliefs, and values are transmitted. One way to measure the globalization of culture is to chart the movement of popular media, which have more impact on our thinking than some of the other, more frequently cited symbols of cultural globalization (such as the proliferation of Starbucks coffee shops around the world)." The dissemination of movies would be an ideal indicator (proxy) of cultural globalization. Figure 2.4 shows "a ranking of the 20 most culturally globalized countries measuring each nation's exports and imports of books, periodicals, and newspapers. . . . The higher a country is on this ranking, the more likely an individual in that nation receives foreign cultural products."

"One clear pattern that emerges from this ranking index is that the globalization of culture may have a significant linguistic component. Three of the top five nations (Canada, Singapore, and Switzerland) have official bilingual legislation. English-language permeation also ties into a country's capacity to absorb international cultural products. Seven of the top 20 nations in this ranking index (Singapore, United Kingdom, Canada, Australia, Ireland, United States and Israel) are among the top ten English-speaking countries in the world. However, the bottom ten countries (Peru, Romania, Morocco, Thailand, Turkey, Philippines, Egypt, Indonesia, China, and Pakistan) are multilingual nations, and it would seem they are not guaranteed a high degree of cultural globalization. Indeed the Philippines and Pakistan, two countries where English is widespread, still rank near the bottom of the index. The biggest barrier to cultural globalization seems to be poverty, evident by these bottom 10 countries' per capita gross domestic product of under $8,000, and four of the ten having a literacy rate of less than 60 percent. In addition some countries, most notably China and Indonesia, have government regulations that restrict the import of foreign books, journals, and access to some Internet sites. Clearly poverty, illiteracy, and lack of social openness all are factors that contribute to a lack of cultural globalization."

Cultural proxies are the conduits by which ideas, beliefs, and values are transmitted. One way to measure the globalization of culture is to chart the movement of popular media (a proxy), which have more impact on our thinking than some of the other, more frequently cited symbols of cultural globalization such as the proliferation of Starbucks coffee shops around the world.

FIGURE 2.4
The 20 Most Culturally Globalized Countries

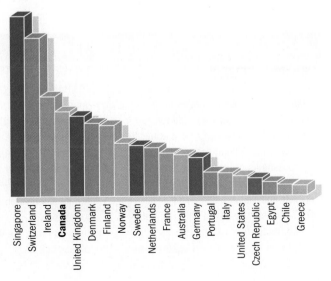

Source: From "Measuring Globalization" by Randolph Kluver and Wayne Fu, from *Foreign Policy* (March/April 2004). Reprinted with permission of the publisher.

Negotiation Considerations

Understanding the world's different cultures can make the difference between an SME's success and failure. Cultural understanding will be a necessity in order for you to communicate, act, negotiate, and make business decisions successfully. In a macro sense consider the cognitive styles, the negotiating strategies, and the value systems of people in the countries you intend to enter.

Cognitive Styles

You will need to understand the various cognitive styles and thought patterns adopted by different cultures. Some cultures are open-minded while others are close-minded. You may be surprised to learn that Canada tends to be a close-minded culture. Open-minded people are more apt to see all sides of an issue. They are prepared to listen and evaluate propositions before reaching a conclusion. Globally there are only a few cultures classified as open-minded. The transformation of Communist countries toward becoming democratic requires many former communist citizens to become open-minded. This demonstrates a willingness to adopt new mental models. **Mental models** are the decision-making frameworks that we apply when presented with a situation that requires us to make a decision. Neuroscience studies indicate that over 80 percent of the time we make our decisions within the context and framework of old mental models we have acquired over time. In this course, and in the operation of your business, you must adopt new mental models that examine all of the inputs before reaching your decision. Strategic critical thinking is in large part an art!

Mental models are the decision-making frameworks that are applied when presented with a situation that requires us to make a decision. Neuroscience studies indicate that over 80 percent of the time we make our decisions within the context and framework of mental models we have acquired over time.

Theocratic Cultures

Like Canadian culture, theocratic cultures are also close-minded. In Iran for example, God, through the Koran, informs members of this culture what values and beliefs are important. Anything that deviates from the teachings of the Koran is not acceptable. This closed-mindedness can be an impediment to business. For example, Islam prohibits the charging of interest on loans. With the cultural rigidity of a no-interest mental model, how does a Canadian firm undertake business with a Saudi Arabian firm (pop. 25.7 million, GDP $9,030) and convince them to pay interest on the balance of the money owing under the terms of a contract? Consider further: if during your meeting with a Saudi businessperson you raise your **ethnocentric view** regarding the need to charge interest, and he comments, "Canada is evil and should also become a theocracy," I would expect that you would have formulated your reply even before you heard more. Most of you would reply, "Never," without much thought. This illustrates the closed-minded cognitive

An **ethnocentric view** is holding a belief or demonstrating a behaviour that one's own ethnic group or culture is superior to others. At times the view is so extreme that the ethnic group will exhibit contempt or disregard other cultures.

JUST DOING THE RIGHT THING

Business Travellers, Beware

Here are some general rules for doing business in developing nations.

- You are the stranger—learn about the new environment, accept and adapt to aspects of the new culture, show respect for the people, the country and their customs.
- Conduct meaningful financial and character background checks—this usually requires expert agencies to

acquire specific information before you enter a deal. Don't rely just on your instincts, no matter how well they've served you in the past.

- Do a political and social risk assessment—a deal signed with a government about to be deposed in a coup is a deal worth reconsidering. Retain a reputable local lawyer to advise you on how to conduct business with the various levels of government.

- Implement a fraud prevention program—including effective controls, random/surprise audits, strong fraud policy, fraud education, an ethical work environment, annual employee declarations that they know/accept the company's policies.

Source: Paul McLaughlin, "Greasy Money," *CA Magazine.com* (2001), retrieved August 9, 2006, from www.camagazine.com/index.cfm/ci_id/6624/la_id/1.htm.

style of Canadians' reasoning. A truly open-minded person would consider the proposition. Following full consideration, it may well be that you would still reject the notion. But it is extremely important that you understand that you must adopt new mental models in an international business environment. This will be uncomfortable for many. Can you think of any of your old mental models that need testing?

Some cultures value abstract thinking of the nature required in this outcomes-based text where you are called upon to undertake reflective and critical thinking. Other cultures' education systems teach by rote and produce associative thinkers. One of the competitive advantages for Canadian SMEs is that Canadian managers tend to be abstract thinkers. I believe that this and the ability to innovate are the differentiators that can explain why Canada and the United States have done well economically over the past two centuries. Do you agree?

Negotiation Strategies

How do people decide if a business proposal is good? In essence they are asking, what is the truth? Different cultures establish the truth in different ways. They can be categorized as faith, fact, and feeling. Many small nations support culture-based decisions on a belief (faith) system, such as a religion or political ideology. For you to present facts such as a cost benefit analysis to such people who make decisions in this way is a waste of time. Their faith that will assist them in making business decisions independent of the facts and arguments you present. For example, they may believe that regardless of whether you can make a better quality product and offer it at a lower price, the right thing according to their beliefs is to have the product produced by local citizens. Islamic countries will generally be found in this category. Some cultures base their decisions on facts. Most Anglo-Saxon cultures fit in this category. For example, Canadian governments generally accept the low-cost bids. The third most common group is cultures where "feelings" make the decision. These cultures go by their gut instincts. They base their decisions on relationships. In some cases, it will take a long time to establish these relationships. However, once a relationship has been established, it is very strong and will not likely be replaced by new competitors. We will see later in this text that Asian cultures tend to rely heavily on feelings to make their decisions.

Value Systems

Every culture has a basis for determining good from evil, or right from wrong. There are three categories of value systems. You must be able to recognize these in your international business dealings. First, identify the locus of decision making; what is the core value—individualism or collectivism? The United States, and to a lesser extent Canada, are very individualistic nations while Asian countries such as China place great value on collective decision making. Understanding the focus of decision making will help you understand whether decision makers will consider only themselves or will abide by the consensus of the collective group. While this is presented as an either–or situation, the reality is that a cultural value system is seldom at either end of the continuum. You will be able to determine as you study the global cultures where along the continuum to place a nation's cultural value system. Second, we need to understand and to identify how different cultures cope with stress. Decision makers under stress will turn to interpersonal relationships, religion, technology, and the law for stress reduction. Once again, it is not an either–or proposition; rather, most use some combination of these four stress reducers. You will find it helpful to understand where your foreign business decision maker will turn for "comfort." Will it be an interpersonal relationship, such as seeking advice from his or her spouse, or will the individual be guided by religion, e.g., the Koran? Third, the issue of equality and inequality is an important characteristic of all cultural systems. Who controls the government, and who controls the business resources are frequently asked questions. The individualist in America relying on the sacred tenet found in her constitution that states "that all men are created equal" is quite different from what you will find underlining the class stratification in India. This issue of equality and inequality is not just between classes; it is also between genders. Most countries, including Canada, still maintain a glass ceiling for women in the workplace. It will be useful for you to understand the glass ceiling and how female business executives are regarded in a foreign country. "Half of all American university graduates are female and an equal number of men and women enter corporate training programs. But only 16% of corporate officers are women, only 11.7% of Fortune 500 company directors are female and only eight corporations have female CEOs. Fewer than 15% of law partners in the U.S. are female. In Canada, the situation is worse. Only a handful of CEOs are female and women hold only 9.8% of directorships. The public sector is better, but a glass ceiling exists everywhere."[41] Visit www.power.nelson.com for a paper on the topic of globalization and its impact on women in the workplace.

Cross-Cultural and Intercultural Negotiation Communication

We have noted that different cultures establish the truth in different ways (faith, fact, and feeling) when negotiating. In a more applied sense, let us examine selected countries' cross-cultural and intercultural communication. Understanding these critical elements is required for all international business people involved in negotiations. We briefly explain cross-cultural literacy required in several countries.

Canada

Canadians prefer to negotiate with facts rather than feelings. Although one must follow company policies, decision making can be classified as extremely high individualism. The negotiating style tends to be similar to U.S. practices; however, the pace may be slightly slower. When dealing with French Canadians, it is important that all material be written in French as well as English. Canadians expect a firm handshake, eye contact, and an open and friendly manner. They tend to be more reserved than U.S. citizens and appreciate acknowledgment of their Canadian identity. French Canadians will tend to be less reserved with their gestures, more expressive, and stand closer while talking than English-speaking Canadians. Canada is one of the most diverse, multi-ethnic nations in the world and, as a result, the etiquette of businesspeople may reflect the ethnic background of the individual. Gifts should be modest. When you visit a home, it is customary to bring a gift, such as flowers, candy, or alcohol. The best gifts are those that come from your home country and are generally given after the deal has been concluded.

Japan

Japan is home of lifetime employment, long work hours, extensive use of rules and government regulations, and dedicated single-minded companies. However, since the Asian "flu," the notion of lifetime employment is less prevalent. Punctuality is important because the Japanese believe it is rude to be late. The Japanese believe in collectivist values, with cooperation and harmony among all members of a group. This stands in stark contrast to the value Canadians and United States place on individualism and the emphasis on one's individual rights. Respect, sensitivity, and harmony are sometimes more important than the truth. Japanese will keep the peace with "little white lies" if necessary. It is a mistake to give the same gift to two or more Japanese of unequal rank. Red Christmas cards should be avoided, since funeral notices are customarily printed in this colour.

Australia

Arrange appointments one month in advance. Australians have a more casual attitude toward time. However, late arrival may result in the latecomer being perceived as a careless, unreliable person. Generally, gift giving is not part of the Australian business culture. Cynicism is an important part of the national character. A great deal of cynicism is directed at people who seem too wealthy or too powerful. Modesty, casualness, and an air of nonchalance are characteristic attitudes in Australian business culture. The work environment tends to be collaborative from top to bottom.

China

Being late for an appointment is a serious insult in Chinese business culture. Negative replies are considered impolite. Instead of saying "no," answer "maybe" or "I will think about it" and get into specifics later. When Chinese counterparts politely and enthusiastically say "no big problem" or "the problem is not serious," they usually mean "There are still problems." Causing embarrassment or loss of composure, even unintentionally, can be disastrous for business negotiations. The question, "Have you eaten?" is the equivalent to "How are you?" in North America. At present, official policy forbids giving gifts; this gesture is considered bribery, an illegal act. Never call anyone "Comrade" unless you are a communist also. Avoid wrapping in yellow paper with black writing, as it is related to death and bad luck.

United Kingdom

In the United Kingdom, appointments should be made at least a few days in advance, and, ideally, confirmed upon arrival in the country. Most British businesspeople will decline to meet a visitor when given relatively short notice. Cold calling is not appreciated. Giving gifts is not a normal part of British business culture. Indeed, British business colleagues are quite likely to feel embarrassed to receive any gift at all. The usual European caveats apply when giving flowers, i.e., no red roses, white lilies, or chrysanthemums (the last two are symbols of death).

United States

Americans' cultural norms reflect a more casual business style rather than one of intimacy. Business gifts are often presented after the deal is closed. In most situations, gifts are usually unwrapped immediately and shown to all assembled. Business people are direct and will not hesitate to disagree with you. This communication style often causes embarrassment to business travellers who are unaccustomed to dealing with Americans or direct communication in general.

Brazil

Brazil, initially colonized by Portugal, is the economic engine for South America. There is no official religion; however, 90 percent of the population has adopted Roman Catholicism. Brazilians place high value on home and family, and will not wish to discuss their private family affairs among casual acquaintances. They tend to be more analytical and abstract than other South Americans. They are prepared to look at individual cases rather than adopt a universal position. The concept of class and status are strong. Brazilian men expect women to be subservient. Be patient in negotiating, as several trips may be necessary to complete the bargaining process. Sometimes Brazilians find U.S. businesspeople's aggressive business attitudes offensive. Do not expect to get directly to the point. Like Canadians, be aware that Brazilians consider themselves "Americans" so do not use "in America" when referring to the United States. (Do you consider yourself American?) Brazilians communicate extremely close up and may keep in physical contact by touching arms, hands, or shoulders during the entire conversation. They are friendly and outgoing. Do not back away. The sign for "OK" (circle of the first finger and thumb) is considered vulgar. Conservative attire for women is very important in business. Avoid giving gifts of anything black or purple since these are colours of mourning.[42]

Canadian Culture in a Global World

"Our proximity to the United States (80% of Canadians live near the U.S. border) and the fact that we share a common language makes it very easy for English-speaking Canada to become an extension of the American market and for American cultural products to spill over the border. This is not the case in the Canadian French language market, which has the natural buffer of a different language. In fact, foreign competition dominates the Canadian cultural market. Foreign firms and products account for 45% of book sales in Canada; 81% of English-language consumer magazines on Canadian newsstands and over 63% of magazine circulation revenue; 79% (over $910 million) of the retail sales of tapes, CDs, concerts, merchandise and sheet music; 85% ($165 million) of the revenues from film distribution in Canada; and between 94 and 97% of screen time in Canadian theatres. The situation is most extreme in the film industry where the Hollywood studios have historically treated Canada as part of the U.S. market."[43] "The cultural sector is an important source of economic growth. Between 1989 and 1994, it grew by 9.9%, outstripping the growth in other key sectors such as transportation, agriculture and construction. Many of the jobs in the cultural industries are knowledge-based. They require creativity, critical thinking and the knowledge and skills to use advanced technology. People who are able to nurture this combination of creativity and high-tech skills are not only able to create the cultural products that add value to our lives; they are highly marketable in other fields. Cultural industries are a driving force in technological innovation. Compared to other sectors, more people working in cultural fields are successfully self-employed. The challenge for Canada is to develop, with other nations, open and transparent policies that acknowledge that cultural products are different from other goods and services, and allow us to maintain our national identity and cultural diversity in a rapidly changing world."[44]

Threats to Canada's Culture

In the past, Canada has faced a number of challenges to its cultural policies, primarily from America. When the United States–based *Sports Illustrated* began transmitting its publication electronically into Canada, the Canadian government responded by creating an 80 percent excise tax on the value of the advertising in **split-run magazines**. Producers of split-run publications cover the cost of production through sales and advertising in their own market. They compete for Canadian advertising dollars with Canadian-produced publications that need the advertising income to cover their production costs.

A **split-run magazine** is a Canadian edition of a magazine published originally in another country that has basically the same content as the original but replaces more than 5 percent of its original advertisements with ads targeted to Canadians.

As countries move to develop a freer trading world enabled by the exponential growth in technology (see Chapter 4), regulations may become stricter and the number of challenges to domestic cultural policies could increase. These challenges highlight a need for Canada to refine its cultural policies so it can continue to foster an environment where cultural expression and diversity thrive; we need to be open-minded. "Like Canada, many countries provide direct support to assist sustaining their cultural industries. For example: The European Union's MEDIA II program provides grants and loans to 'promote the development of [film] production projects . . . aimed at the European market'; the United Kingdom provides subsidies for a wide range of artistic activities through the Art Councils, which are funded by lotteries, while the British Film Institute provides direct grants for film production and exhibition; . . . [and] the United States directly supports everything from literature to drama through the National Endowment for the Arts. . . . Content requirements are a common cultural policy tool. France, Italy, Spain, Mexico and Australia have all established domestic content requirements that affect television, radio, film and pay-TV. . . . [For example,] France has ruled that 60% of its programming must be European and 40% French, and that all private and public radio stations must devote 40% of prime airtime to French songs. A number of countries have also set content requirements or screen quotas for the film industry. Cinemas in France must reserve five weeks per quarter for French feature films or four weeks per quarter for

Country	Maximum Foreign Investment/Ownership Allowed
Australia	15%
Canada	**33.3% of holding company 20% at licensing level**
United Kingdom	Ownership restricted to EU member states
United States	20% of conventional broadcasting

SOURCE: From Canada International Trade, *New Strategies for Culture and Trade—Canadian Culture in a Global World* (2003); available from http://www.dfait-maeci.gc.ca/tna-nac/canculture-en.asp. Copyright Public Works and Government Services Canada, 2006.

FIGURE 2.5

Comparison of Foreign Investment Restrictions on the Broadcasting Industry

theatres that include a French short during six weeks of the previous quarter; . . . [and] Mexico requires movie theatres to devote 10% of their screen time to domestic films (down from 30% in 1993)."[45] See Figure 2.5 for a comparison of foreign investment restrictions on the broadcasting industry.

Emerging Issues—Technology

New technologies are making the market for cultural products harder to regulate. Technology's impact on the ecosystem, including culture, is also addressed in Chapter 3. Past efforts to create a place for Canadian cultural products in the broadcast market succeeded because the government could control and regulate the relatively scarce number of bandwidths. Television broadcasters, cable companies, and pay and specialty TV services all had to be licensed to reach Canadian homes. With new convergence technologies, the number of channels will increase significantly, making the market more complex and fragmented, and more difficult to regulate. These new high-tech distribution networks may offer more highways into the Canadian market for foreign products, and government may find it more challenging to make a place for Canadian content on these new networks. Canada has attempted to constrict the cultural haemorrhaging by placing foreign investment restrictions on the broadcasting industry. Do you think this is a good or a bad thing?

A Canadian SMEs Cultural Success Story

50,000 Chinese Students in Speaking Competition about Canada—Maple Leaf Cup Considered the Gold Standard by Schools in Southwestern China

Southwest China, in partnership with the education departments of the provinces of Chongqing, Sichuan, Yunnan and Guizhow, held the first Southwest China Maple Leaf Cup public speaking competition finals at Sichuan International Studies University.

The theme was *Canada and China: Partners in Innovation,* and the competition included both English and French language entries. Each contestant's four-minute presentation was followed by a three-minute question and answer session between contestant and the judges. The judging panels for the English and French finals included members from the Canadian diplomatic corps in China, the Alberta Government Office in Beijing, the University of Windsor, Dalhousie University, the University of Alberta, Malaspina University-College, Alliance Française and the World Bank. Over 70 universities across the four provinces held competitions, leading to provincial finals and ultimately to the grand finale event in Chongqing. The finals attracted more than 1,600 students (in a theatre that seats 1,200), as well as over 100 local government officials, university administrators and professors who once studied in Canada. The competition benefited from corporate sponsorship by Penergy and IMAX.

Source: Department of Foreign Affairs and International Trade, 2005. Copyright Public Works and Government Services Canada.

50,000 Chinese students participate in a speaking competition about Canada.

Cultural Classification—Geert Hofstede's Model (A Useful "Tool")

"Culture is more often a source of conflict than of synergy. Cultural differences are a nuisance at best and often a disaster,"[46] observed Geert Hofstede, Emeritus Professor, Maastricht University.

The Hofstede model is a good tool to focus your analysis and to commence the critical thinking needed to form your foreign market-entry strategy. From 1967 to 1973, Hofstede conducted research and collected data from IBM Global employees. Over 100,000 employees in 64 different countries participated. Using this research he developed a cultural classification model to assist in differentiating cultures. Initially Hofstede examined cultures using four dimensions. A fifth dimension was subsequently added and has been applied to 23 of the countries he studied in his earlier research. This model has proven to be a valuable tool for SMEs to apply when considering market entry strategy. Hofstede's five cultural fundamental dimensions that have a high-level impact on human behaviour are power distance, individualism, masculinity, uncertainty avoidance, and long-term orientation.[47] See Figure 2.6 for countries positioned at each extreme of the five dimensions. Visit www.power.nelson.com for more discussion of Hofstede's valuable model and to identify where Canada places on the continuum of these five dimensions.

Power Distance Index (PDI)

The "Power Distance Index focuses on the degree of equality or inequality between people in the country's society. A High Power Distance ranking indicates that inequalities of power and wealth have been allowed to grow within the society. These societies are more likely to follow a caste system that does not allow significant upward mobility of its citizens. A Low Power Distance ranking indicates the society de-emphasizes the differences between citizens' power and wealth. In these societies equality and opportunity for everyone is stressed."[48]

Individualism (IDV)

"Individualism focuses on the degree the society reinforces individual or collective achievement and interpersonal relationships. A High Individualism ranking indicates that individuality and individual rights are paramount within the society. Individuals in these societies may tend to form a larger number of looser relationships. A Low Individualism ranking typifies societies of a more collectivist nature with close ties between individuals. These cultures reinforce extended families and collectives where everyone takes responsibility for fellow members of their group."[49]

Masculinity (MAS)

This dimension "focuses on the degree the society reinforces, or does not reinforce, the traditional masculine work role model of male achievement, control, and power. A High Masculinity ranking indicates the country experiences a high degree of gender

FIGURE 2.6

Hofstede's Data—The Five Cultural Dimension Extremes

Dimension	Position	Country	Score
Power Distance	Low	Belgium	11
	High	Malaysia	104
Uncertainty/Avoidance	Low	Singapore	8
	High	Greece	112
Masculinity/Femininity	Low	Sweden	5
	High	Japan	95
Individuality/Collective	Low	Guatemala	6
	High	USA	91
Long-Term Orientation	Low	Pakistan	0
	High	China	118

differentiation. In these cultures, males dominate a significant portion of the society and power structure, with females being controlled by male domination. A Low Masculinity ranking indicates the country has a low level of differentiation and discrimination between genders. In these cultures, females are treated equally to males in all aspects of the society."[50]

Uncertainty Avoidance Index (UAI)

The "Uncertainty Avoidance Index focuses on the level of tolerance for uncertainty and ambiguity within the society—i.e. unstructured situations. A High Uncertainty Avoidance ranking indicates the country has a low tolerance for uncertainty and ambiguity. This creates a rule-oriented society that institutes laws, rules, regulations, and controls in order to reduce the amount of uncertainty. A Low Uncertainty Avoidance ranking indicates the country has less concern about ambiguity and uncertainty and has more tolerance for a variety of opinions. This is reflected in a society that is less rule-oriented, more readily accepts change, and takes more and greater risks."[51]

Long-Term Orientation (LTO)

This dimension focuses on "the extent to which a society exhibits a pragmatic future-oriented perspective rather than a conventional historic or short-term point of view. Countries scoring high on this dimension are the Asian countries. These countries believe in many truths, have a long-term orientation, easily accept change and have thrift for investment."[52] A long-term orientation is thought to support a strong work ethic where long-term rewards are expected as a result of today's hard work. However, business may take longer to develop in this society, particularly for an outsider. "Cultures scoring low on this dimension believe in absolute truth, are conventional and traditional, have a short-term orientation and a concern for stability. Most Western countries score fairly low on this dimension."[53]

Criticism of Hofstede's Model

Critics of Hofstede's model point out, with some justification, that Hofstede generalizes about the entire national population in each country, yet his survey respondents were simply certain categories of employees in the subsidiaries of a single company (IBM). Critics ask what evidence he has that these respondents were nationally representative. Critics state that the 50,000 surveys conducted were an inaccurate measure of culture. They claim that one company can't provide information about entire national cultures; that the IBM data is old and obsolete; and that five dimensions can't tell the whole story. To which I respond yes, there is merit in these criticisms, but as Churchill stated, "It has been said that democracy is the worst form of government except all the others that have been tried."[54] So until a better model comes along . . . this one has value!

An Alternative to Hofstede's Model

Other researchers have put forward models for cultural classification that also have considerable merit. One well-known model is that of Trompenaars and Hampden-Turner. Their model classified cultures along a mix of behavioural and value patterns. They focused their research on the cultural dimensions of business executives unlike Hofstede's international IBM workers. Trompenaars and Hampden-Turner identify seven value orientations. Some are almost identical to Hofstede's dimensions while others offer a different perspective: universalism versus particularism; communitarianism versus individualism; neutral versus emotional; diffuse versus specific cultures; achievement versus ascription; Human-Time relationship; and Human-Nature relationship.[55] Of these seven value dimensions, the communitarianism/individualism value orientation closely replicates Hofstede's dimension of individualism and, to a lesser extent, power distance. Their achievement/ascription value orientation, describing how status is accorded, appears to be linked to Hofstede's power distance index, if one accepts that status is accorded by nature rather than achievement, and that this reflects a greater willingness to accept power distances. Trompenaars and Hampden-Turner universalism/particularism value orientation, describing a preference for rules rather than trusting relationships, seems to reflect Hofstede's uncertainty avoidance dimension and, to some extent, the collectivist/individualist dimension.[56] Their model does not have a single category to align with Hofstede's power distance index but, rather, includes elements of power distance in each category. Trompenaars and Hampden-Turner's classification diffuse/specific value orientation describes the range of involvement. Trompenaars and Hampden-Turner's other dimensions seem to focus more on the effects of underlying value dimensions. For example, their neutral/emotional dimension examines the extent to which feelings are openly expressed.

Hofstede's and Trompenaars and Hampden-Turner's methodologies both derive their data from questionnaires distributed among professionals—Hofstede among employees of IBM, and Trompenaars and Hampden-Turner among a large number of executives from different organizations. "Hofstede's work is based on a questionnaire originally designed to evaluate work values, and, not surprisingly, it is mostly focused towards that end. Trompenaars & Hampden-Turner's questionnaires on the other side asked respondents for preferred behaviour in a number of both work and leisure situations. What both studies have in common is that in both questionnaires the focus is on the ultimate goal state, and that the underlying values are derived from a series of questions about more outer layers of the 'culture onion.'"[57]

Cultural Classification of Likely Host Countries for Canadian Trade

Examine the bar graphs in Figures 2.7–2.12, produced by applying Hofstede's tool. What are the cultural implications for a Canadian firm entering the Argentine, German, Arab, Chinese, Brazilian, and Hong Kong marketplaces? Given these cultural insights, what would

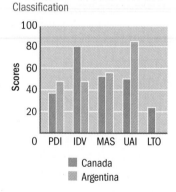

FIGURE 2.7
Canada versus Argentina, According to Hofstede's 5-D Model of Cultural Classification

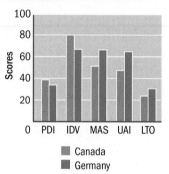

FIGURE 2.8
Canada versus Germany, According to Hofstede's 5-D Model of Cultural Classification

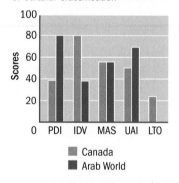

FIGURE 2.9
Canada versus the Arab World, According to Hofstede's 5-D Model of Cultural Classification

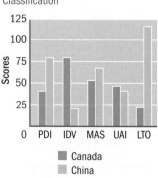

FIGURE 2.10
Canada versus China, According to Hofstede's 5-D Model of Cultural Classification

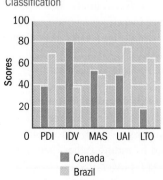

FIGURE 2.11
Canada versus Brazil, According to Hofstede's 5-D Model of Cultural Classification

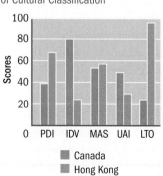

FIGURE 2.12
Canada versus Hong Kong, According to Hofstede's 5-D Model of Cultural Classification

you do differently? Can you identify the most likely areas of tension from Hofstede's models provided in Figure 2.6? Along which dimensions are the comparative national cultures aligned? Not aligned? (Note that it is clearly a weakness that Hofstede classifies the Arab world as a "collective," based largely on the role the Muslim faith plays in the lives of Arab people.)

Make a point of visiting www.geert-hofstede.com to explore the richness of Hofstede's model. The site also provides an abundance of cultural tips. For example, in China a quality writing pen is considered a favoured gift.

Management Implications

- Global managers must develop cultural awareness and sensitivity in order to operate successfully in an international environment. Business leaders understand that culture changes over time and management of that change is an important skill set they must possess. Managers crafting market entry strategies for their business must undertake research to identify the gaps between Canadian culture and the host country's culture. Then, having identified the gaps, they must undertake the cross-cultural training necessary to mitigate potential damage that these gaps could inflict on the firm's business if ignored.
- The international manager appreciates diversity and makes allowances for the cultural idiosyncratic factors when communicating with people of different cultural groups. The manager will avoid trying to impose his own cultural attitudes and

INTERNATIONAL STRATEGIC THINKING

It may be konnichiwa in Japan, Guten Tag in Germany and Merhaba in Turkey—saying hello is easy—but understanding cultural nuances for international business is far more challenging. Many people are familiar with business in the West, where there is little time for establishing relationships and getting straight down to business is not considered rude. But in other parts of the world, achieving mutual success with an overseas partner involves a lot more than a few quick meetings and a signature on the dotted line. "You could say that business is business in the West, and business is personal everywhere else," Neil Payne of Kwintessential, a culture specialist firm, told CNN. "In other parts of the world being mindful of other cultures can give you the upper hand and help you clinch that deal." For instance the consensual nature of Japanese society means that decision-making in a meeting can involve many members of a negotiating team. "It is important to build a relationship not only with the director or the manager or the head of the team but all those involved," explains Payne.

One way of recognizing how the hierarchy works in a Tokyo boardroom is that the head of the team may normally sit in the middle of the table, furthest away from the door. Payne suggests greeting the most senior person first—due to a respect for hierarchy—then greeting the rest of the team in descending order, in terms of rank.

In North Asia, handing out business cards with both hands in a respectful manner will also be noticed. For many in the West they are just bits of card, handed over as an after-thought, whereas in Asia they are tokens of value and esteem.

Speaking clearly and slowly, avoiding jargon and writing everything down can also help out in a meeting.

One common trait in Middle Eastern, Mediterranean, Asian and South American cultures is that many executives like to do business with people they know, trust and feel comfortable with. "It is important to understand what these people may like, so if they are into sport it may be worth going to a match or having

a round of golf," says Payne. "It is more about putting yourself in a context where both parties can be relaxed and both parties can get to know each other as people—not just as business people." It is best to remember that business will only continue once this relationship has been established. "(Many executives) will not enter into a relationship because they will not feel comfortable conducting business with someone that they do not feel 100 percent comfortable with," explains Payne.

A few words in the language of the country you are visiting as a sign of respect is always appreciated. And before you travel, contact your embassy to request briefing on business etiquette and cultural background. "If you are going to give one specific pointer to everyone, which is applicable across the world, that would be—always maintain a sense of professionalism," says Payne.

approaches on foreigners. He will demonstrate broad understanding and tolerance for different cultures' values and beliefs. Among the skills to be acquired is etiquette. In observing local customs and culture, cross-cultural leaders will avoid using the name of God in Islamic countries, they'll never call Muslims a Mohammedan; they will pronounce the national and individual names correctly; and they will adhere to the country's preferences for titles, dress, personal space distances, and other formalities.

CHAPTER SUMMARY

- It is imperative that Canadian SMEs develop cross-cultural literacy. We must develop an awareness and understanding of cultural differences between countries (and their citizens) and how they can affect the conduct and success of our business.
- Many nations view Canada's culture as non-threatening.
- Culture slowly evolves; it cannot be forced. It is both a unifying and a divisive force. Canada has undergone and continues to undergo cultural transformation. Our culture was largely based on British and French culture but it has become more cosmopolitan as it adapts to accommodate the growing diversity of our nation.
- Cultural transformation causes tension among a nation's citizens.
- Culture is a system of agreed-upon values, beliefs, and norms by a definable society. Values and beliefs are abstract ideas as to the concept of what is good and what is bad. Norms are generally concrete social rules and guidelines that prescribe the appropriate behaviour of a member of a definable society. Norms can be divided into folkways and mores.
- To understand the society and culture, we will need to examine a country's specific characteristics regarding its values, norms, folkways and mores; language; demographics; political and economic philosophy; social institutions; status symbols; cognitive styles; religious beliefs; attitudes toward foreigners; human rights; and environmentalism.
- Understanding the world's different cultures can make the difference between a SME's success and failure. Cultural understanding will be essential in order for you to communicate, act, negotiate, and make business decisions successfully. In a macro sense consider the cognitive styles, the negotiating strategies, and the value systems of people in the countries you intend to enter.
- Culture is more often a source of conflict than of synergy. Cultural differences are a nuisance at best and often a disaster.
- Geert Hofstede's four fundamental dimensions of culture with a high-level impact on human behaviour still serve today as basic criteria in most interdisciplinary, cross-cultural comparative research. The four basic dimensions are power distance, individualism, masculinity, and uncertainty avoidance. The more recently added fifth dimension is long-term orientation. With some justification, there are critics of the model.

REVIEW QUESTIONS

1. What is culture?
2. Outline the characteristics that influence a country's culture.
3. Describe briefly the six world religions and the beliefs most likely to be encountered by international business managers.
4. Briefly describe the business impact each of the six world religions, discussed in this chapter, is likely to have on how business will be conducted.
5. What point was Huntington trying to make in his book, *The Clash of Civilization and the Remaking of World Order*? Is there merit to his position?
6. Explain the different cognitive styles and thought patterns adopted by different cultures and provide an example of each.
7. What do we mean when we say she has an "ethnocentric view"?

REFLECTIVE THINKING QUESTIONS

1. Having completed this chapter, reread the quotations on the first page, critically reflect on the validity of the authors' statements, and provide your opinion as to the validity of each. Evidence-based answers are preferred to rhetorical answers.
2. Visit Hofstede's website (www.geert-hofstede.com/hofstede_canada.shtml) and prepare a report comparing Canada's cultural dimensions to a country of your choice.
3. The opening vignette and one of the chapter's videos describes what seems to be a competitive advantage for Canada, a perception that Canada's culture is less threatening than other developed nations. Do you agree? Support your opinion.
4. Are the various religious values outlined in this chapter less relevant today because of globalization?
5. How concerned should Canada be about retaining its culture while living in the shadow of the United States?

GLOBAL E-RESEARCH

Visit www.power.nelson.com for research suggestions, questions, and a number of background discussion papers on this topic.

MINI CASE

Recipe for Success

When Dinesh Paliwal, now head of global markets at the engineering company ABB, first arrived in Beijing in the mid-1990s to open one of its first offices there, he would spend several nights a week at banquets with local business executives, dining on Peking duck, drinking 20-proof alcohol and singing karaoke. "In those days, if you didn't drink with the Chinese and show them you wanted to understand their culture, you couldn't do business," said Paliwal, 48, an Indian-born American citizen. "It was only after karaoke that the negotiations really began."

Paliwal also runs the North American division of ABB, a Swedish-Swiss company that operates in more than 100 countries and is a leading maker of power-transmission and distribution equipment, like transformers and circuit breakers, and industrial robots. As global leaders gathered in Davos, Switzerland, to debate the emergence of India and China as economic powers, Paliwal, a straight-talking electrical engineer, said that much had changed since he lip-synched pop song lyrics more than 10 years ago. "Back then Chinese were hungry to learn what they needed to do to work for a Western company like ABB," he said Thursday. "But it was hard to break in. You were considered an acquaintance for two years before becoming a junior friend and then graduating to senior friend after four years."

Paliwal said Chinese employees were so embarrassed to be seen asking advice from a Westerner that they would drop by his office at 7 A.M. to question him on everything from Swedish engineering techniques to whether it was permitted to use the company credit card. He said many of the older engineers had a "Communist hangover" and told him they were embarrassed to be working for a profitable company. When he asked Chinese managers to do something, they routinely said "mayo," or "no" in Mandarin. Today, Paliwal said, the Chinese have shed any reluctance

about the profit motive and have adopted a can-do spirit because they are determined to match their manufacturing prowess with the engineering know-how that will help them become a more knowledge-based economy. But he said it was still essential for foreigners doing business in China to show respect. "You should never lose your cool or show anger during a negotiation with the Chinese," he said. "You must show you recognize this is a more than 1,000-year-old culture." Socializing, which may include karaoke, is also a must, he said. But despite China's superior infrastructure and logistics, Paliwal said ABB decided to base its global engineering center in Bangalore, India, rather than in China. Indians, he said, typically have more developed project management skills and speak good English, so they have an advantage in managing complex projects across the globe. "If a director from Norway calls the engineering center in India, they will get off the phone and feel confident that the job will be done," Paliwal said. "In China, because of the cultural differences, that is not always the case."

Meanwhile, while engineering wages are exploding in India and Indian companies are even outsourcing work to Chinese engineers, Indian engineers working on a multimillion-dollar project in the United States still typically cost $12 an hour, he said. Paliwal said his experience working in China helped prepare him for the task of turning around a chronically underperforming division. His biggest challenge, he said, was overcoming the legacy of Percy Barnevik, the former chief executive of ABB, who created a management structure so decentralized that divisions were undermining one another. He said he was horrified when he received a letter from the motorcycle maker Harley-Davidson, an ABB client, saying the company had received three different quotes for an ABB contract in the United States. Meanwhile, the company's U.S. division refused to outsource work to ABB's lower-cost Mexican division.

To overcome these divisions, Paliwal united operations in Mexico, Canada and the United States under one management structure, fired underperforming managers and reduced more than 54 North American units to a handful. The strategy appears to have worked.

MINI CASE QUESTIONS

1. "In those days, if you didn't drink with the Chinese and show them you wanted to understand their culture, you couldn't do business." What are the implications of this cultural folkway (socializing) for Canadian international business managers?

2. Culture can change over time. Can you find any evidence to support this observation in the article or from your other readings?

3. What do you think about a Canadian businessperson permitting her Chinese counterparts to save face? Can you think of a situation when you might not be so noble?

4. What cultural lesson have you learned from this short news article?

5. Would you have made the same market entry decision today e.g., choosing India over China for the ABB engineering centre?

6. Do you find any "aha" moments in the article? If so, what were they?

ENDNOTES

1 S. P. Huntington, *The Clash of Civilizations and the Remaking of World Order* (New York: Simon and Schuster, 1996).

2 *Human Action Quotes* (January 2004), retrieved August 9, 2006, from http://en.thinkexist.com/quotes/with/keyword/human_action.

3 David Wallechinsky and Irving Wallace, *Origin of Sayings*, retrieved August 9, 2006, from www.trivia-library.com/b/origins-of-sayings-when-in-rome-do-as-the-romans-do.htm.

4 James B. Simpson, *Simpson's Contemporary Quotations* (Boston: Houghton Mifflin, 1988).

5 Jacques Barzun, "The Culture We Deserve," in *The Bugbear of Relativism*, (Middletown, CT: Wesleyan University Press, 1989).

6 Mark McNeilly, *Sun Tzu and the Art of Business: Six Strategic Principles for Managers* (New York: Oxford University Press, 1996).

7 Ibid.

8 W. Whitely and G.W. England, "Managerial Values as a Reflection of Culture and the Process of Industrialization," *Academy of Management Journal* 20, no. 3 (1977).

9 N. Goodman, *An Introduction to Sociology* (New York: Harper Collins, 1991).

10 Ibid.

11 David B. Barrett and Todd M. Johnson, *Center for the Study of Global Christianity* (World Evangelization Research Center, 2005).

12 Max Weber, *The Protestant Ethic and the Spirit of Capitalism*, 1930 ed., (New York: Rutledge, 2000), p. 35.

13 Ibid.

14 Ibid.

15 Barrett and Johnson, *Center for the Study of Global Christianity.*

16 S.M. Abbasi, K.W. Hollman, and J.H. Murray, "Islamic Economics, Foundations, and Practices," *International Journal of Social Economics* 16, no. 5 (1990).

17 Barrett and Johnson, *Center for the Study of Global Christianity.*

18 Ibid.

19 McDonald's Corporation (India), *Welcome to McDonald's India* (2005), retrieved August 9, 2006, from www.mcdonaldsindia.com/home.html.

20 Barrett and Johnson, *Center for the Study of Global Christianity.*

21 Allison Elliott, *Caste and the God of Small Things* (Atlanta: Postcolonial Studies at Emory Pages, 1997), retrieved August 9, 2006, from www.english.emory.edu/Bahri/caste.html.

22 Barrett and Johnson, *Center for the Study of Global Christianity.*

23 Ibid.

24 Dr. Meir Tamari, *The Economics of Enough* (Business Ethics Center of Jerusalem), retrieved August 9, 2006, from www.besr.org/library/economicenough.html.

25 Dr. Meir Tamari, *Business Ethics D'var Torah: The Challenge of Wealth* (Business Ethics Center of Jerusalem), retrieved August 9, 2006, from www.besr.org/dvartorah/tamari/shelach.html.

26 Michael Scharding, *Green Book of Meditations Volume 4, The ill A.D. and the Odd Essay* (Washington DC, Drynemetum Press, September 1, 2002), retrieved August 16, 2006, from http://orgs.carleton.edu/Druids/ARDA2/ARDA2part6-4.pdf.

27 Bruce Kennedy, "Rulers of the Middle Kingdom: Have China's Communist Leaders Truly Broken with the Imperial Past?" (CNN Interactive, 2001), retrieved August 16, 2006, from http://edition.cnn.com/SPECIALS/1999/china.50/imperial.icon/rulers.

28 Sarah Rosenberg, *Face* (University of Colorado, 2004).

29 Shaben & Associates International Consulting, *Marco Polo: The Cross-Cultural Marketing Edge* (Industry Canada, 1999), retrieved August 9, 2006, from http://strategis.ic.gc.ca/epic/internet/insi-is.nsf/vwapj/macro-e.pdf/$FILE/macro-e.pdf.

30 Samuel P. Huntington, *The Clash of Civilizations?* (Summer 1993), retrieved August 9, 2006, from www.alamut.com/subj/economics/misc/clash.html

31 Francis Fukuyama, *The End of History and the Last Man* (New York: The Free Press, Simon and Schuster, 1992).

32 Ibid.

33 *Muhammad Cartoon Row Intensifies* (February 1, 2006), retrieved August 9, 2006, from http://news.bbc.co.uk/go/pr/fr/-/2/hi/europe/4670370.stm.

34 Canadian Marketing Association, "International

Outsourcing of Call Centre Operations: Lessons for Canadian Marketers" (2004), retrieved August 16, 2006, from www.the-cma.org/ council/downloads/ InternationalOutsourcingMarch2004.pdf.

[35] Roger Martin and James Milway, *Partnering for Investment in Canada's Prosperity* (June 29, 2004), retrieved August 9, 2006, from www.rotman.utoronto.ca/rogermartin/ PartneringforInvestment.pdf.

[36] "Gloom in France: The Unbearable Lightness of Being Overtaken" (February 2, 2006), retrieved August 9, 2006, from www.economist.com/displayStory.cfm?story_id=5471712.

[37] KLM Management Consultation, *Changing Global Demographics* (2003), retrieved August 9, 2006, from www.klminc.com/marketing/changing_global.html.

[38] Ibid.

[39] Ibid.

[40] Niall Ferguson, "Eurabia?" *New York Times Magazine* (April 4, 2004).

[41] Diane Francis, "We Haven't Come That Far after All," *National Post*, November 1, 2003.

[42] If you enjoyed these brief insights into selected cultures, read, "How to Do Business in Sixty Countries: Kiss, Bow or Shake Hands," Terri Morrison et. al., Adams Media Corporation (1994). See www.adamsmedia.com.

[43] Department of Foreign Affairs and International Trade, *New Strategies for Culture and Trade—Canadian Culture in a Global World* (1999).

[44] Ibid.

[45] Ibid.

[46] Geert Hofstede, *Cultural Dimensions* (1967–2003), retrieved October 22, 2006, from www.geert-hofstede.com.

[47] Ibid.

[48] Ibid.

[49] Ibid.

[50] Ibid.

[51] Ibid.

[52] Ibid.

[53] Ibid.

[54] *Brainy Quote* (2005), retrieved July 3, 2006, from www.brainyquote.com.

[55] Stephan Dahl, *An Overview of Intercultural Research— Trompenaars and Hampden-Turner* (Middlesex University Business School, 2004), retrieved August 9, 2006, from http://stephan.dahl.at/intercultural/Trompenaars.html.

[56] Ibid.

[57] Ibid.

The Business Environment of Nations: Political, Economic, and Legal Issues

"Render unto Caesar the things that are Caesar's and unto God the things that are God's."[1]

—Jesus to the Pharisees, making it clear that not all of life is under control of the state

"The first panacea for a mismanaged nation is inflation of the currency; the second is war. Both bring a temporary prosperity; both bring a permanent ruin. But both are the refuge of political and economic opportunists."[2]

—Ernest Hemingway, American writer

"Economic growth without social progress lets the great majority of people remain in poverty, while a privileged few reap the benefits of rising abundance."[3]

—John F. Kennedy, thirty-fifth president of the United States

"Some people regard private enterprise as a predatory tiger to be shot. Others look on it as a cow they can milk. Not enough people see it as a healthy horse, pulling a sturdy wagon."[4]

—Winston Churchill, British prime minister

"No nation was ever ruined by trade."[5]

—Benjamin Franklin, American scientist, publisher, diplomat

LEARNING OUTCOMES

- Understand selected political ideology terminology.
- Understand what attributes need to be considered in evaluating political risk.
- Evaluate the merits of the different political systems and some of the national political shifts taking place.
- Evaluate and formulate opinions about the appropriateness of different economic systems.
- Understand important economic indicators that must be considered when analyzing foreign markets.
- Evaluate different legal systems and understand how they can influence business.
- Examine the law relating to intellectual property globally.

Canadian Atlantis Flight Training Devices Take Off

Courtesy of Atlantis Systems International, www.atlantissi.com

Atlantis Systems Corporation, head-quartered in Brampton, Ontario, has earned international recognition through its ability to deliver fully-integrated, simulation-based training solutions to commercial and military customers in Australia, the Middle East, Europe, Asia, and North America. The company concentrates on customers whose operations include elements that must be controlled in a highly prescriptive way due to danger, regulations, or economics. The terrible events of September 2001 dealt a crushing blow to commercial aviation, and Atlantis suffered accordingly. By 2004, the company found itself on the verge bankruptcy in spite of an impressive record for engineering innovation.

The catalyst for change came in the form of a new management team with a new vision and the financial resources necessary to make the vision a reality. Recognizing the risks of maintaining a single market focus, Atlantis' management team quickly began to shift the firm's focus from the commercial sector to the military sector. Atlantis regained its footing during 2004 and since this time has increased its revenue by over

200 percent. The terrorist attacks had come at a time when there were increasing regulatory pressures across the aerospace industry. With globalization propelling agreements on international threats and regulations, Atlantis had already begun to evolve from building one-off training products to designing complete integrated training systems. At the human resource level, this meant a shift from a strong dependency on electrical and mechanical disciplines toward a greater dependency on simulation and systems engineering. This change in the workforce composite brought a new agility to the company and allowed Atlantis to address the larger training market.

The Integrated Maintenance Training System (IMTS), built to support customers of the Boeing F-18, was a $32 million proof statement that the company was on the right track. When the contract was delivered on time and on budget in late 2004, Atlantis became a trusted training systems provider for Boeing and their two major customers, the Royal Australian Air Force and the Canadian Forces.

An important factor in Atlantis' international success has been its

decision to qualify for and maintain international performance standards. Atlantis became an ISO 9001-registered company in 1995; it provided the company with access and credibility in international markets. Atlantis constantly evaluates its business processes against rigorous ISO and other industry standards as a means of improving the efficiency, economy, and profitability of its operations. When customers report high service levels, reduced defects, improved performance, or fewer environmental incidents, there is a direct relationship between their satisfaction and continued business.

Canada has a creative way of supporting exporters, based on the simple premise that the whole system will prosper if there can be increased confidence in the commercial viability and responsibility of all parties to an international business arrangement. One such support is the Canadian Commercial Corporation (CCC). It is dedicated to excellence in international contracting and procurement services in defence and developing markets. CCC guarantees the work undertaken by Canadian contractors will be delivered at the agreed-upon contract price. The strong relationship between Atlantis and CCC is another key to the company's success in the international arena.

During 2004, Atlantis adopted an underlying philosophy and strategy to provide a clear differentiator against the more traditional approaches to training. The shift was from training products, with an emphasis on tools and delivery, toward training systems, with a focus on how people learn. In other words, Atlantis believed that a truly integrated training system must focus on the management of knowledge—how it is acquired, maintained, and continually integrated into formal training in order to increase performance in the field.

Another undertaking of the company in 2004 precipitated by the US Sarbanes-Oxley Bill was its focus on corporate governance. Today Atlantis is fully compliant with United States and Canadian corporate governance regulations.

The workforce at Atlantis has doubled in three years, and the company has expanded its operations into the nuclear generation market. The first contracts, all in Ontario, were focused on determining the training needs of the market and looking for opportunities to apply the company's core competencies in simulation, knowledge management, and learning as the nuclear industry struggles to be ready for the large-scale attrition that it will face over the next few years.

By late 2006, Atlantis had become an important contributor to the positive side of Canada's international trade balance sheet, led by a strong management team. It is growing quickly, is profitable, and is expanding into new markets.

Courtesy of Atlantis Systems International, www.atlantissi.com.

A SUN TZU MOMENT . . .

Visual Arts Library, London/Alamy

"When the thunderclap comes, there is no time to cover the ears."

B.H. Liddell Hart describes the German strategy in France in 1940 as meeting with great success because of the Germans' speed and element of surprise. Similar to the success achieved by the United States in the first Gulf War when U.S. forces exploited the element of surprise, the Germans also attacked at unexpected points and with speed that had never been seen before on a battlefield. German airborne assaults used to secure bridges, and lightning attacks to secure the advantages of [their] armour, resulted in the British being driven back to the sea at Dunkirk in World War II.

In business, if you wait to hear the thunderclap it is often too late. Political, economic, and legal shifts within nations can take place with blitzkrieg speed. As a Canadian SME business leader, it is imperative that you scan your ecosystem for telltale signs of pending seismic shifts. Who foresaw the collapse of the Union of Soviet Socialist Republics? Is Vladimir Putin today indicating a return to some of Russia's former communist values? Will the euro rival the U.S. dollar as the world's reserve currency? Time spent in reconnaissance is never wasted.

Opening Thoughts

In Chapter 2 we commenced our examination of the attributes that influence a nation's business environment. We determined that culture shifts over time, meaning that globalization cultures are increasingly clashing, resulting in tensions, and further that culture is shaped by religion, education, language, and other influences. We also determined that in understanding a country's ecosystem, we should not view the attributes as watertight compartments but holistically in order to understand how each influences and is linked to the others. Keep this thought in mind as we examine countries' political, economic, and legal systems to understand how they will influence today's business environment.

Political Ideologies

Communism advocates social change that will result in a classless society and requires state ownership of all major factors of production.

Any discussion of political systems requires a cursory understanding of the political ideology terminology we will likely encounter:

Communism advocates social change that will result in a classless society. It requires state ownership of *all* major factors of production. Karl Marx (1818–1883), grounded to some extent in the thoughts of Plato (427–347 B.C.E.), conceived the notion of communism. The ideology was subsequently adopted by Lenin in Russia in 1917 after the Bolshevik revolution. Marx's ideology as amended by the thoughts of Chairman Mao Zedong was adopted in China at the end of the Long March in 1949.

Capitalism is grounded in the thoughts of Aristotle, Adam Smith, David Ricardo, John Stuart Mills, and others who supported the notion that all the major factors of production are to be privately owned rather than under the control of the state.

Capitalism is grounded in the thoughts of Aristotle, Adam Smith, David Ricardo, John Stuart Mills, and others who supported the notion that *all* the major factors of production are to be privately owned rather than under the control of the state. Capitalists believe that Smith's economic invisible hand will balance the marketplace so that only the appropriate quantity of goods and services will be provided and at the appropriate market price. PBS[6] makes available a free six-hour video called *Commanding Heights*. ("Commanding heights" is a phrase used by Valdimir Lenin in a speech to the Fourth Congress of the Communist International at St. Petersburg, Russia in 1922.) It is a wonderful historical documentary that traces the evolution of the struggle between the global communist states advocating the adoption of some form of Marxist ideology and those at the other end of the continuum advocating a free market of the nature advocated by Smith, Hayek, and others. It is a must-see for any serious international business learner. It will provide a solid context to derive the maximum benefit from this text.

Socialism ideology lies between the two polarized positions of communism and capitalism. Socialists support the notion that governments own or control the basic factors of production and that they should do so on a not-for-profit basis. The question becomes, of course, what industries are included in the basic factors of production? How this question is answered shifts the socialist country toward one pole or the other.

A **conservative ideology** in Canada generally means reducing governments' control or ownership of the basic factors of production and placing these factors in the hands of the private sector to operate at a profit. The father of modern conservatism was Edmund Burke. Within the notion of conservatism are left- and right-wing proponents. Right-wing proponents advocate greater and more aggressive reduction in government control or ownership; at the other end of the spectrum are left-wing proponents, who support a go-slow approach to conservative ideology. In other countries, conservatism means maintaining the status quo or returning to a previous state. In Russia and China, for example, those wishing to return to the previous command economies are referred to as *conservatives*.

Although this descriptor has evolved since its initial connotation, today **liberal ideology** means increasing governments' control or ownership of the basic factors of production on a not-for-profit basis. Liberals, like conservatives, have within their group left- and right-wing proponents. A left-wing Liberal would be seen as one who supports even greater government control or ownership of the basic factors of production rather than less. Right-wing proponents believe the opposite.

Libertarianism is grounded in the writings and beliefs of Lao-tzu, John Locke, Ayn Rand, F.A. Hayek, Milton Friedman, and many others. **Libertarians** advocate that individuals' liberty is to be preferred over the power of the state. "Politics may become a struggle between conservative paternalists, welfare state maternalists and libertarians who believe that adults should make their own decisions."[7]

Political Risk

In Chapter 2 we looked at culture and the importance of developing cultural literacy by SME business leaders intending to take their business international. One of the major risks businesses face is political risk. No matter how economically attractive the venture appears to be, firms can sustain serious financial damage if a host country inflicts financial penalties or some kind of unanticipated event that results in a loss of income-producing assets. Political risk assessments have become an expanding business during the past three decades. The term *political risk* is used to describe both anticipated and unanticipated risks. It is often impossible to forecast with certainty what governments will do in the future and which government actions will affect corporate profitability. Changes in economic variables, such as tax rates and output prices, will directly or partially influence some businesses while other businesses will be only indirectly affected by political actions. When a government that is philosophically inclined toward the free enterprise system is elected, one would anticipate encouraged optimism among investors leading to higher saving and investment rates, lower interest rates, and faster real income

Socialism is the notion that governments own or control the basic factors of production and that they should do so on a not-for-profit basis.

A **conservative ideology** in Canada generally means reducing governments' control or ownership of the basic factors of production and placing these factors in the hands of the private sector to operate at a profit. In other countries, conservatism means maintaining the status quo or returning to a previous state. In Russia and China for example, those wishing to return to the previous command economies are referred to as *conservatives*.

Liberal ideology today means increasing governments' control or ownership of the basic factors of production on a not-for-profit basis.

Libertarians advocate that individuals' liberty is to be preferred over the power of the state.

growth. However, the successful election of a socialist government might lead to a sharp escalation in inflationary expectations and deterioration in the value of the country's currency. When scanning a country's ecosystem, examples of political risks that you will attempt to identify include an analysis of the nation's political systems and ideologies, its political stability, the foreign investment climate, regulations regarding profit remittances and exchange controls, levels of taxation, the likelihood of expropriation, the political ruling party's attitudes toward foreign investors, the effectiveness of public administration, the constitutional guarantees, and the likelihood of labour strikes and unrest. In this chapter, we will focus our analysis of political risk by developing awareness and understanding of the different political systems and political ideologies and how they might affect business.

INTERNATIONAL STRATEGIC THINKING

Fidel Castro Has Banned the Dollar—Helped by America's Embargo

"Few things can irk Cuba's president, Fidel Castro, more than the fact that the greenback, the ultimate symbol of the global power of his archenemy, the United States, is also a mainstay of his own country's economy. And therefore few things can have satisfied him more than announcing this week, just days after a humiliating fall in which he fractured his knee and arm, that from November 8th, (2004) the dollar will no longer be legal for commercial transactions. Cubans will still be able to keep dollars and to swap them for 'convertible pesos'—equal in value, but thoroughly unconvertible anywhere outside Cuba—but they will pay a 10% commission.

"The dollar's introduction as legal tender in 1993, along with a slight loosening of restrictions on private enterprise, was an emergency measure to help the country earn hard currency after the Soviet Union, and its subsidies to Cuba, disappeared. But unlike many hopeful Cuba-watchers, Mr. Castro clearly never saw such measures as anything but temporary. The dollar's withdrawal is just the biggest and latest step in a series. American coins were taken out of circulation in October 2001, and last year state companies were forced to use only convertible pesos. The never-easy rules on private

entrepreneurship have been tightened bit by bit; a month ago there was a freeze on new licenses for many kinds of small business.

"The latest news sparked widespread dismay among ordinary Cubans, who are now rushing to bring dollars out from under the mattress and convert them before the November 8th deadline; but after that it may not make too much difference to them, or to tourists. The 10% commission will not apply to other currencies. Indeed Mr. Castro encouraged Cubans to ask their relatives abroad, who send home some $1 billion a year, to switch to other currencies for the transfers.

"Rather, the latest move seems designed both to restock the government's dollar reserves and to re-assert its authority over the financial system. Indeed, it makes a certain sense. It is not easy running monetary policy in a dual-currency system when the country that issues one of the currencies is doing its darnedest to prevent you from getting any. Under America's four-decade-old economic embargo, only the Treasury can allow the use of dollars in transactions with Cuba.

"But this also means that Mr. Castro has once again been able to use the embargo as a pretext for imposing new restrictions on his people. As part of what he calls America's 'imperialist economic warfare,' Mr. Castro cited the $100m fine that the Federal Reserve imposed on UBS, a Swiss bank, in May, for illegally transferring freshly printed

dollar notes to Cuba. According to some reports this had made it harder for Cuba to renew its stock of dollars in circulation. Hours before Mr. Castro's announcement, the Treasury had announced sanctions against Sercuba, a company with offices in Cuba and Europe that allows Americans to send money to Cuba via a website."[8]

This article provides an opportunity to reflect on a number of political, economic, and legal questions. Is the adopting of the euro by Cuba one more step toward a global weakening of the demand for the U.S. dollar? Does it signal a growing acceptance of the European Union as the trading partner of choice in Latin America? Is it a business opportunity for Canadian business practitioners? Will it signal U.S. debt holders—China, Taiwan, and Japan—to consider diversifying their foreign currency reserves to the euro, oil future contracts, and gold? And, if so, what will this mean for Canada's economy given our trade dependency (over 79 percent of Canada's exports go to the United States) on America's economic well-being? Is it legal for the United States to impose its law on other sovereign nations? There is much to critically reflect upon in this article. We will examine this issue and its possible business implications in subsequent chapters. Also visit the *www.power.nelson.com* website for further readings on this topic.

Adapted from "The Americas: Adios to the Greenback; Cuba's Currency," in *The Economist* (October 28, 2004).

Political Systems

Political systems make a difference. **Political systems** describe the structures, processes, and control mechanisms that support and sustain a nation's political ideologies. It is helpful to categorize different political systems into clusters. First we will differentiate the political systems by their political philosophy regarding the relationship between the collective and the individual. Second, we will differentiate the two systems by their political philosophy regarding the degree to which they are democratic or totalitarian regimes.

Political systems describe the structures, processes, and control mechanisms that support and sustain a nation's political ideologies. They can be differentiated along the political philosophies of collectivism versus individualism and democracy versus totalitarianism regimes.

Collectivism ⟵⟶ Individualism

On a continuum with collectivism and individualism at the extremes, we can cluster countries according to their political philosophy towards these two attributes.

COLLECTIVISM

In *The Republic*, Plato (427–347 B.C.E.) put forward the notion that an individuals' right should be subordinated to the interests of the collective (majority). He also advocated that property should be owned in common. As a political philosophy, Plato's thoughts have produced the golden thread used to stitch together today's collectivist ideology. Community needs taking precedent over the needs of the individual is the underpinning of communism and socialism.

INDIVIDUALISM

At the other end of the continuum we find individualism, grounded in the thoughts of another ancient Greek philosopher and a student of Plato's, Aristotle (384–322 B.C.E.). Aristotle opposed Plato's views and argued that individuals' rights and freedoms should take priority over the state's needs in all but a few situations. Further, he held that private property owned by the individual is to be preferred over state ownership for the economic well-being of the state. Supporters of individualism contend that an individual should have freedom over economic and political endeavours. Arguments against Aristotle's philosophy can be found in works like that of Garrett Hardin's *The Tragedy of the Commons*. Aristotle's thoughts can be traced through history to the political thinkers of today to include David Hume (1711–1776), Adam Smith (1723–1790), John Stuart Mills (1806–1873), Frederick August von Hayek (1899–1992), and Milton Friedman (1912–2006). Indeed F.A. Hayek said, "It seems to me that socialists today can preserve their position in academic economics merely by the pretence that the differences are entirely moral questions about which science cannot decide."[9] While Milton Friedman said, "A major source of objection to a free economy is precisely that it . . . gives people what they want instead of what a particular group thinks they ought to want. Underlying most arguments against the free market is a lack of belief in freedom itself."[10] Do you prefer Plato's collectivist or Aristotle's individualism view? Keep your bias in mind as you reflect on the issues encountered in this text as it is important to understand the lens you use.

Today, the thoughts of Adam Smith and F.A. Hayek are widely cited. "In economic affairs, Smith's *The Wealth of Nations* (1776) popularized the **"invisible hand"** notion that an individual who "intends only his own gain," is, as it were, "led by an invisible hand . . . [and] will promote . . . the public interest."[11] Adam Smith did not assert that this was invariably true, and perhaps neither did any of his followers. However, he contributed to a dominant tendency of thought that has interfered with positive action based on rational analysis ever since. This tendency is to assume that decisions reached individually will, in fact, be the best decisions for an entire society. "If this assumption is correct, it justifies the continuance of our present policy of laissez-faire in reproduction. If it is correct we can assume that men will control their individual fecundity so as to produce the optimum population. If the assumption is not correct, we need to re-examine our individual freedoms to see which ones are defensible."[12] What do you think?

John Stuart Mills reinforced Smith's assertion in his book *On Liberty* (1865) that, "the sole end for which mankind is warranted, individually or collectively, for interfering with the liberty of action of any of their number is self protection, . . . the only purpose for which

Adam Smith put forth that the **"invisible hand"** is the notion that an individual who "intends only his own gain," is, as it were, "led by an invisible hand . . . [and] will promote . . . the public interest."[13] Smith did not assert that this was invariably true, but he contributed to a dominant tendency of thought that assumes decisions reached individually will be the best decisions for an entire society.

power can be rightfully exercised over any member of the civilized community, against his will, is to prevent harm to others. His own good, either physical or moral, is not a sufficient warrant, . . . the only part of the conduct of anyone, for which he is amenable to society, is that which concerns others. In the part that merely concerns himself, his independence it is, of right, absolute. Over himself, his own body and mind, the individual is sovereign."[14] If you subscribe to this political theory you will no doubt experience discomfort with Canada's Anti-terrorism Act (see http://www.justice.gc.ca/en/anti_terr/faq.html). Advocates for freedom of the individual and private property opposed the ideas of Plato, Marx, and educator Garrett Hardin.

Democracy ←——→ *Totalitarianism*

On a continuum with democracy and totalitarianism at the extremes, we can similarly cluster countries according to political philosophy towards these two attributes.

DEMOCRACY

The ancient Greeks introduced a political system known as a democracy within their city-states. Initially, because of the small number of citizens, it was a **pure democracy** where all free male citizens participated freely and actively in the decision making required by the political process—the common people ruled. As the number of citizens grew, pure democracy where all participated was no longer a viable option. As a result, it morphed into a **representative democracy**. A representative democracy is a political system that permits citizens to delegate decision-making authority to representatives for an established period. At the expiry of the period, the representatives are accountable to the citizens (electorate) for their actions. Through voting processes, the existing representatives are affirmed for a further established period if it is the wish of the electorate; if not, new representatives are selected. The hallmarks of democracy include freedom of expression without fear of punishment; periodic elections that are transparent, open, and free from interference; protection of civil and property rights; protection of minorities; nonpolitical bureaucracies; a free press; and a free, transparent, and open judicial system. Examining a country's constitution can readily identify democratic hallmarks.

Canada's constitution can be used as a model of representative democracy. Prime Minister John G. Diefenbaker made the first attempt at limiting the federal government's power to violate basic Canadian human rights by enumerating rights and freedoms in the Canadian Bill of Rights Act (S.C. 1960, c.44). Up to that point, Canadians' rights and freedoms were grounded in a millennium of British constitutional guarantees contained initially in the Magna Carta Charter of 1215 followed by the English Bill of Rights and the common law precedents (*stare decisis*) over the years. Unfortunately, our basic rights had only statute status and were not incorporated or entrenched in Canada's constitution as set out in the Statute of Westminster of 1931 and the British North American Act of 1867. Prime Minister Pierre Elliott Trudeau and the United Kingdom passed The Constitution Act (1982). In the United Kingdom it was called The Canada Act. (1982 c.11). The purpose of this act was to repatriate the amending power and control of the Canadian Constitution to Canada. Trudeau was also concerned with the failure of Diefenbaker's Charter to entrench rights and freedoms in the constitution. So he seized the opportunity to remedy the situation. The Constitution Act includes the Charter of Rights and Freedoms (s.24, Part 1 of The Constitutional Act 1982). This law is the supreme law in Canada. Our Charter of Rights makes a good metric to determine what rights and freedoms should be considered in resolving whether or not a nation is a democracy.

The political environments of nations shift. Using these metrics (rights and freedoms), where would you place the United States in the light of the powers of the Patriot Act? Feeling smug? Recall that Canada passed similar legislation called the Anti-terrorism Act (Bill C-36). Has this legislation shifted both countries toward the totalitarian end of the continuum? Has our Charter protected our rights and freedoms? How many Canadians even knew the Anti-terrorism Bill was enacted on October 15, 2001? "The Act

A **pure democracy** is a political system where all citizens participate freely and actively in the decision making required by the political process.

A **representative democracy** is a political system that permits citizens to delegate decision-making authority to representatives for an established period. At the expiry of the period, the representatives are accountable to the citizens (electorate) for their actions. Through voting processes, the existing representatives are affirmed for a further established period if it is the wish of the electorate; if not, new representatives are selected.

gave law enforcement and national security agencies new investigative tools to gather knowledge about and prosecute terrorists and terrorist groups, as well as protect Canadians from terrorist acts, including: making it easier to use electronic surveillance against terrorist groups; creating new offences targeting unlawful disclosure of certain information of national interest; amending the Canada Evidence Act to guard certain information of national interest from disclosure during courtroom or other judicial proceedings; amending the National Defence Act to continue and clarify the mandate of the Communications Security Establishment (CSE) to collect foreign communications; within carefully defined limits, allowing the arrest, detention and imposition of conditions of release on suspected terrorists to prevent terrorist acts and save lives; requiring individuals who have information related to a terrorist group or offence to appear before a judge to provide that information; and extending the DNA warrant scheme and data bank to include terrorist crimes."[15] Does this sound like a democracy? Reflect on the warnings of Abraham Lincoln, "Don't interfere with anything in the Constitution. That must be maintained, for it is the only safeguard of our liberties."[16]

Man Arrested under Canada's Anti-Terrorism Law Denied Bail

A judge in Ottawa denied bail Friday afternoon for Mohammad Momin Khawaja, a Canadian accused of participating in a British bomb plot. Mohammad Momin Khawaja, 25, is the first person arrested under Canada's new Anti-terrorism Act. The Ottawa man is charged with participating in the activities of a terrorist group and facilitating a terrorist activity.

Khawaja's lawyer argued that his client doesn't pose a threat to the community, and is not a flight risk. The Crown, however, opposed his release. The court has imposed a publication ban on evidence heard in the proceedings. Khawaja's mother and three brothers were in court Friday, as they were Tuesday for the first day of his bail hearing. The RCMP has connected Khawaja with an alleged terrorist bomb plot in London, England. Five British men, all of Pakistani origin, have been charged with devising a bomb plot, and Khawaja is accused by British authorities of having a role in that plan.

Source: CBC News, *Man Arrested under Canada's Anti-Terrorism Law Denied Bail* (May 8, 2004). Copyright © CBC 2006.

CP PHOTO/Tom Hanson

Mohammad Momin Khawaja was arrested under Canada's Anti-terrorism Act.

Can democracy have universal application? Consider Formosa, now known as Taiwan. The political party founded by Sun Yat-sen and Sung Chiao-jen in 1912 and known as the Kuomintang (KMT), was driven from the Chinese mainland by the communists in 1949. The KMT withdrew to Formosa. Led by Chiang Kai-shek, and subsequently his sons and others, Taiwan has clearly demonstrated that 23 million Asians were able to establish a democratic system that is productive, healthy, wealthy, and extremely well educated. Taiwan has successfully established itself as the 17th largest economic nation in the world and holds the third largest foreign reserves. It has a **rule of law** and it encourages business at home and from foreign direct investment. Taiwan believes in free marketplace capitalism, observes human rights, and protects the environment. Recall that Asians typically (Chapter 2) place high value on the collective and the community; however, this seems to be no barrier to democracy. Taiwan has become the poster child for all other Asian nations grounded in Confucian thoughts. Clearly, democracy is a strong, viable, political–economic alternative for the Far East. Do you think the Islamic nations can follow Taiwan's example?

Despite these accomplishments, only 22 countries formally recognize Taiwan as an independent state. It continues to be barred from the United Nations and most international bodies. The reasons are political and economic. It seems that nations fearful of retribution by China conduct their foreign policy to avoid rewarding and recognizing the success of this 23 million–person democracy. This is an example of realpolitik. The term *realism* comes from the German compound word *realpolitik*, from the words *real*—meaning *realistic, practical*, or *actual*—and *politik*—meaning *politics*. **Realpolitik** is crafting a nation's foreign policy based on a pragmatic political analysis rather than ideals or ethics.

Rule of law states that everyone is subject to the law; no one, no matter how important or powerful, is above the law.

The term *realism* comes from the German compound word *realpolitik*, from the words *real*— meaning *realistic, practical*, or *actual*—and *politik*—meaning *politics*. **Realpolitik** is crafting a nation's foreign policy based on a pragmatic political analysis rather than ideals or ethics.

Political and Economic Positions Can Shift Quickly

On Thursday April 15th 2004, the challengers won a crucial battle in their bid to overturn South Korea's conservative, elitist and business-driven political system. Although the country's voters have been able to choose their leaders freely since the late 1980s, many of them, especially younger ones, still consider their brand of democracy to be corrupt, outdated and unfair. Many of the discontented enjoy the comforts that decades of market-friendly policies and high growth have delivered. But they resent the economic and political dominance of giant family-controlled business conglomerates, known as **chaebol**; their feelings towards the United States, a crucial ally, range from ambivalent to hostile; and they would rather deal with North Korean threats by placating its prickly regime than by standing up to it. And now, they have convinced mainstream voters to let them run the country for the next four years.

Source: "Young, Liberal and in Command," from *The Economist* (April 16, 2004).

Chaebol is the economic and political dominance of giant family-controlled business conglomerates.

TOTALITARIANISM

Totalitarianism is a political system adopted by citizens who support a government in which one person or political party exercises absolute control over all aspects of human life. It is imposed authority.

Totalitarianism is found at the other end of the political spectrum. This political system is adopted by citizens who support a government in which one person or political party exercises absolute control over all aspects of human life. It is imposed authority. Political parties that oppose totalitarian political systems are banned by the ruling totalitarian party. They are generally never completely removed from the nation's political stage, but must operate below the surface. Constitutional and individual rights of the nature provided by a democratic system like Canada are nonexistent within a totalitarian state. Totalitarian regimes require centralized political power and "differ from older concepts of dictatorship or tyranny. Totalitarian regimes seek to establish complete political, social and cultural control, whereas dictatorships seek limited, typically political, control. Two types of totalitarianism can sometimes be distinguished: Nazism and Fascism that evolved from 'right-wing' extremism, and Communism, which evolved from 'left-wing' totalitarian extremism. Traditionally, different social classes support each. Right-wing totalitarian movements have generally drawn their popular support primarily from middle classes seeking to maintain the economic and social status quo. Left-wing totalitarianism has often developed from working class movements seeking, in theory, to eliminate, not preserve, class distinctions. Right-wing totalitarianism has typically supported and enforced the private ownership of industrial wealth. A distinguishing feature of Communism, by contrast, is the collective ownership of such capital."[17] Currently, totalitarian states can be classified into four forms.

COMMUNIST Communist ideology is guided by the thoughts of Karl Marx (1818–1883), and Engels (1820–1895) who published the work *Manifesto of the Communist Party* in 1849. A communist political system is based on a dictatorship or small oligarchy as the ruling authority. North Korea (pop. 22 million, GNI unknown) is one of the few remaining prominent examples.

Profile: Kim Jong-il

"I know I'm the object of criticism in the world, but if I am being talked about, I must be doing the right things"[18]—Chairman of North Korea, Kim Jong-il

"Outside North Korea, little was known about Kim Jong-il when he was thrust into the limelight on the death of his father [in 1994]. The short bespectacled younger Kim is still in charge—although he remains very much a mystery. He has rarely appeared or spoken in public, and until a secretive trip to Beijing at the beginning of June [2002] it is thought he had not traveled outside North Korea since the 1980s. Within North Korea it's a different story. Kim Jong-il is regularly hailed by the media as the 'peerless leader' and 'the great successor to the revolutionary cause.' On the intellectual front, he's credited with having extended Kim Il-sung's [father] personal philosophy of Juche, or self-reliance, which has been the guiding light for North Korea's development.

"... He was officially designated successor to his father in 1980. But he didn't hold any positions of real power until 1991, when he took control of the armed forces—despite his lack of military experience. Analysts believe he was given the position to counter potential resistance to his eventual succession (de facto dictator). After the death of Kim Il-sung in 1994, it was three years before he took over the leadership of the ruling Korean Workers' Party."[19] In 1999, South Korean intelligence services claimed that somewhere between 2.5 million and 3 million North Koreans succumbed to starvation over the four previous years. This puts him third behind China's Mao Zedong and Russia's Josef Stalin for most people starved to death. "South Korean accounts portray Kim as a vain and capricious playboy, with permed hair and lifts in his shoes, and a penchant for foreign liquor. They have also consistently reported rumours of young women being kidnapped in Japan and elsewhere to be his companions in a string of luxury villas."[20] It is reported that his net worth is US$4 billion dollars.

"There's a more sinister side too—for years Kim Jong-il has been suspected abroad of being the man behind the 1983 bomb attack in Rangoon that killed several members of the South Korean Cabinet, as well as the bombing of a South Korean airliner in 1987. Some analysts also believe the younger Kim was responsible for developing North Korea's suspected nuclear weapons programme. But the secrecy surrounding Kim Jong-il and the difficulty of getting accurate information about North Korea means that it's virtually impossible to assess the true extent of his influence."[21] Chairman Kim may well encourage the myth making surrounding him precisely in order to keep the Western world guessing. North Korea has little to bargain with, and ignorance breeds fear. President George W. Bush included North Korea as one of the members of the "axis of evil." The free world hopes that a **coup d'état** will take place when North Korean citizens finally reach the breaking point. Such a coup may usher in a revolution, but usually it does not.

Chairman Kim Jong-il is regularly hailed as the "peerless leader" and "the great successor to the revolutionary cause."

A **coup d'état** (literally a "blow against the state") is a seizure of political power by a small number of people. Such a coup may usher in a revolution, but usually it does not.

THEOCRATIC Guided by religious teachings, **theocratic** totalitarians establish political systems with a religious dictatorship or small religious oligarchy as the ruling authority. "In theory, there is no reason why a theocracy and a democratic form of government are incompatible—vox populi, vox dei ("the voice of the people is the voice of God")—but historically those nations regarded as theocracies have been ruled by a theologically-trained elite. This may be a council of clerics, or a charismatic leader who may claim a special call from God and gain office by force of arms. The office might later become hereditary. The primary effort of government in a theocracy is to implement and enforce divine laws."[22]

When asked for examples of theocracies you will likely think immediately of Iran and its hardliner President Mahmoud Ahmadinejad or the Taliban that ruled Afghanistan from 1996 until 2001 and once again appears to be showing signs of increasing influence in the political affairs of Afghanistan and you would be correct. But let me challenge your mental model. The State of the Vatican City is one of the smallest independent states in the world both in area and population, a landlocked enclave surrounded by the city of Rome in Italy. Does it meet the definition of a **theocracy**? The Vatican, home of the Pope, forms the territory of the Holy See, the central authority of the Roman Catholic Church. The Vatican is technically a rare case of a nonhereditary elective monarchy; the monarch, the Pope, being elected for life by those Cardinals under the age of 80. The Pope appoints Cardinals as vacancies come due. The term *Holy See* refers to the composite of the authority, jurisdiction, and sovereignty vested in the Pope and his advisers to direct the worldwide Roman Catholic Church. As the "central government" of the Roman Catholic Church, the Holy See has a legal personality that allows it to enter into treaties as the juridical equal of a state. The Pope delegates the internal administration of the Vatican City to the Pontifical Commission for the State of the Vatican City. The legal system is based on canon, or ecclesiastical, law; if canon law is not applicable, the laws of the city of Rome apply. As an independent state, the Vatican has the right to send and receive

Theocratic is derived from "two Greek words meaning 'rule by the deity,' and is the name given to political regimes that claim to represent the Divine on earth both directly and immediately."[23]

A **theocracy** is a system in which political power rests with the clergy.

diplomatic representatives, including foreign embassies. The Holy See is a permanent observer in the United Nations, and in July 2004, gained all the rights of full membership except voting. What do you think? Have I taken it too far? There is evidence to support the notion.[24]

Tribal ethnocentric-based political systems are established by a specific "tribe" and ruled by a dictator or small oligarchy from that tribe.

TRIBAL **Tribal** ethnocentric-based political systems are established by a specific "tribe" and ruled by a dictator or small oligarchy from that tribe. From 1979 to 2003, Iraq was under Ba'ath Party rule led by President Saddam Hussein. The unicameral (comprising only one legislative chamber) Iraqi parliament, the National Assembly or Majlis al-Watani, had 250 seats and its members were elected for four-year terms. As in presidential elections, no non-Ba'ath candidates were allowed to run. The Ba'ath party membership comprised only members of the Sunni Arab "tribe." The other two Iraqi ethnic cultures, the Kurds and Shia Arabs, while representing the majority of the Iraqi population, were not permitted to have a voice in government. Sunni Arabs rule and Shia Arabs acquiesce. Under Hussein 60 to 65 percent of the population was governed by 20 percent of the population. With the intervention of the United States and others, this situation seems to have changed. The noncertified final results released in December 2005 saw 128 of the new Iraqi parliament's 275 seats go to the United Iraqi Alliance, the country's dominant Shiite coalition. Two Sunni Arab blocs took a total of 55 seats, while 53 seats went to the Kurdish Coalition comprising parties led by President Jalal Talabani and Kurdish leader Massoud Barzani. The success of this democratic initiative is yet to be determined.

RIGHT WING A right-wing totalitarian political system provides a limited number of economic freedoms but severely constrains political freedom. This political system is most likely to be the result of a military coup. The military, in order to maintain power and consolidate authority, severely constricts political freedom and the establishment of opposition parties. However, right-wing totalitarian rulers recognize the importance of economic freedom to the well-being of the nation and therefore extend freedoms to permit the economic infrastructure to continue operating. "Totalitarian regimes mobilize and make use of mass political participation, and are often led by charismatic cult-type figures. Examples of such cult figures in modern history are Mao Zedong (China) and Josef Stalin (Soviet Union), who led left-wing regimes, and Adolf Hitler (Germany) and Benito Mussolini (Italy), who led right-wing regimes. Right-wing totalitarian regimes (particularly the Nazis) have arisen in relatively advanced societies, relying on the support of traditional economic elites to attain power. In contrast, left-wing totalitarian regimes have arisen in relatively undeveloped countries through the unleashing of revolutionary violence and terror. Such violence and terror are also the primary tools of right-wing totalitarian regimes to maintain compliance with authority."[25]

Economic Considerations

An expert in international strategic planning observed that the effectiveness of strategic planning is strictly related to the capacity for environmental scanning. Most would agree. It is absolutely critical, as we will see in Chapter 10, that the firm's management must constantly scan and assess the environment within which it is operating. A failure to do this is just as negligent as a captain on an oil tanker failing to maintain a lookout and running the ship aground. A large number of business strategists suggest that economic environmental scanning should receive the most attention by corporate planners. They believe that economic variables will have the greatest influence on the corporate bottom line. While it is clearly an important variable, I'm unwilling to say it is number one. Today I believe technology is the most critical but the weights of the variables shift. The 9/11 attacks certainly brought economic and political considerations to the forefront.

Nevertheless, one can quickly list several dozen economic variables that need to be examined by SME business planners. Of course, this activity must be bound by the needs of the specific firm. For example, a natural resource firm will require different economic data from a distributor of consumer goods, which is more likely to be interested in income levels and household formation to include the head count per census period. Some of the attributes you might choose to look at may include real income, competitive and complementary products, barriers to trade, demographic factors, demand function, input–output analysis, and other statistics and data. A number of these items are covered in depth elsewhere in this text. In this chapter, we will develop an awareness and appreciation for the different economic systems we will encounter internationally.

Economic Systems: Command Economy ⟵— Mixed Economy —⟶ Market Economy

Economic systems determine the process surrounding and controlling the factors of production: land, capital, and labour. There are three broad classifications: command, mixed, and market economies, which can be placed on a continuum, with the command economy at one extreme and the market economy at the other. Between the two, are the nations with mixed economies. The key determining factor as to which system a nation will most likely adopt is found by examining its political ideology. Are the citizens democratic or totalitarian; are they collective in their views or individualist? Be aware that a country's position on the continuum can shift quickly. Business practitioners must scan the horizon for early warning signs of these movements as they can have significant impact on the firm's bottom line.

To illustrate, consider Canada's Prime Minister Trudeau who, in 1975, passed the Anti-Inflation Act "in response to a rapid acceleration in both wage and price inflation, which had pushed the Consumer Price Index inflation up to 10.7% in 1974 and 10.9% in 1975 [as compared to just 1.6% in January 2006]. It was the only time in Canada's history that such wage and price controls occurred during peacetime. The Bank of Canada warned that rising costs were undermining the country's ability to function efficiently and to compete internationally. The government responded to calls for action by introducing the Anti-Inflation Act. The Act was part of a larger federal government anti-inflation program that included limits on increases in government expenditures and tighter monetary and fiscal policies. The wage and price controls applied to the public sector and to private companies with 500 or more employees. Farmers, fishermen, and regulated industries were exempt from the price controls. Wage increases were capped at 10% in the first year of the anti-inflation program, 8% in the second year, and 6% in the third year. The Act was overseen by the Anti-Inflation Board. As well as monitoring the wage and price controls, the board investigated such things as gas prices, private-sector employee wages, insurance premiums, and even beef prices. The board's recommendations led to actions aimed at controlling inflation, such as rebates to consumers, wage rollbacks, and price reductions. Many groups were affected by the controls. Some 4.2 million working Canadians had their wage increases limited. Unions were severely restricted in their ability to bargain for higher pay. Wage and price controls were phased out in 1978, and then the Anti-Inflation Board was dissolved the following year."[26] The graph in Figure 3.1 provides evidence as to why Trudeau took such action.

Canada clearly shifted its position toward a command economy during this two-year period. With the phasing out of wage and price controls in 1978, Canada commenced moving along the continuum back toward the market economy pole. However, in 2003, the British Columbia Liberal Government adopted this same mental model, passing a law requiring zero wage increases for three years for the public service, and, in 2005, economic issues were such that once again Canada's political leaders were being put to the test. David Emerson, the federal industry minister in 2005, was on the hot seat. Minmetals, a Chinese state-owned corporation, considered a possible $7 billion takeover of Noranda Inc. A number of MPs—of all political stripes—called on Ottawa to block the deal, citing Minmetals's human rights record (U.S. Senate hearings in the late 1990s had heard allegations that Minmetals profited from forced labour in Chinese prisons). MPs wanted government intervention to prevent the sale. If successful, it would once again signal a shift

Economic systems determine the process surrounding and controlling the factors of production: land, capital, and labour. There are three broad classifications that can be placed on a continuum, with the command economy at one extreme, the market economy at the other, and the mixed economy somewhere between.

FIGURE 3.1

Canada's Trade Competitiveness
1970–1975

SOURCE: From "Hope for Canada?" by James
Grant, published in *Barron's National Business
and Financial Weekly* (November 1, 1979).
Copyright © 2006 Dow Jones & Company,
Inc. All Rights Reserved.

Grounded in the thoughts of Karl
Marx, a **command economy**, also
known as a centrally planned
economy, is one where the factors
of production are owned by the
government, and government
planning agencies specify the
production goals and the prices
for the country.

The **market economy**, located
at the opposite end of the
continuum, provides for all of
the factors of production to be
privately owned.

Laissez-faire is short for "*laissez
faire, laissez aller, laisser passer,*"
a French phrase meaning "let's
do, let go, let pass." The term
was first used in France by the
18th-century enlightened
thinkers as an injunction against
government interference with
trade. Today it is a synonym
for free market economics,
according to its own economic
laws as stated by Adam Smith
and others, and is generally
understood to be a doctrine
opposing economic
interventionism by the state
beyond what many believe to be
the core roles of government—
maintaining peace and
preserving property rights.

to the left in Canada's position along the continuum. However, to his
credit, Mr. Emerson stated he would follow the benchmarks set out in
the Investment Canada Act, which govern whether foreign takeovers are
of net benefit to Canadians—a very pragmatic approach to foreign
direct investments by Emerson, an economist. The factors considered
in undertaking a pragmatic approach to FDI include the effect on
economic activity; investment in productivity; competition within
the sector; and the contribution the deal will have in enhancing the
country's ability to compete globally. Interestingly, human rights are not
among the issues Mr. Emerson was required to review under this act.

Many nations have experimented either with both wage and price
controls or with just wage control. "America's most controversial
peacetime experiment with an incomes policy was during the period
1971–74, when inflation was fuelled by the costs of the Vietnam War, the
1973 oil embargo, and the later quadrupling in the world price of oil by the Organization
of the Petroleum Exporting Countries (OPEC). Wage and price controls during peacetime
have yielded minor gains at best in the United States; in postwar Western Europe, incomes
policies have been more frequently used. Britain, the Netherlands, Sweden, and Germany
have all implemented controls at various times and France has experimented with wage
and price controls many times since the 19th century."[27]

A **command economy**, also known as a centrally planned economy, is one where the
factors of production are owned by the government. Grounded in the thoughts of Karl
Marx, command economy governments' planning agencies specify the production goals
and the prices for the country. In many cases these goals form part of publicly announced
five-year plans. Chairman Mao Zedong implemented three successive five-year plans after
1949, attempting to grow the economic power of China. Each was a failure. There are no
examples of a pure command economy today; the closest would be North Korea,
discussed earlier in this chapter, pages 72–73. The theoretical concept of the economic
factors of production being used solely for the public good and all sharing equally is
attractive to many. In reality however, it has failed for many reasons. These reasons
include a failure to observe best business practices where failing economic unit(s) would
cease operation. China's factories continued to operate using state funds to subsidies
deficiencies. (In Chapter 6, pages 173–174, we examine the economic weakness of
providing subsidies and other supports to businesses.) Additionally, a command economy
fails to provide incentives to foster the growth of entrepreneurship and innovation.
Detractors have many examples to support their position: the Union of Soviet Socialist
Republic (1989), China (1979), North Korea, Cuba, and a number of Latin American
countries. Finally, those that cling to this model fail to meet the needs of the marketplace
as is evidenced by the thriving black markets operating in North Korea and Cuba.

The **market economy**, located at the opposite end of the continuum, provides for all
of the factors of production to be privately owned. The views of Adam Smith, David
Ricardo, and others we have and will talk about in Chapter 6, pages 161–165, prevail in
these economies. Smith's invisible hand in the marketplace guides what goods and
services will be provided. The market is based on economic demand and supply curves.
If there is a demand for a product, at a price that permits a profit, then the marketplace
will provide that product. On the other hand, if there is insufficient demand, the good or
service will cease to be offered. If the supply exceeds demand, the prices will fall and if
supply is less than what is demanded then the price will rise.

In a market economy, the concept of **laissez-faire** is accepted. Laissez-faire capitalism
is an economic doctrine that opposes governmental regulation of, or interference in,
commerce beyond the minimum necessary for a free-enterprise system to operate
according to its own economic laws as stated by Adam Smith. You will recall from our
discussions earlier that Adam Smith believes that a market economy will enable free choice,
encourage free enterprise and entrepreneurship, and allow prices be to supported only by
the market mechanism of demand and supply. No nations are pure market economies. The
United States, a mixed economy, might be the closest to this end of the continuum.

Between the two ends of the continuum represented by command and market economies, we will find the nations of the world classified as **mixed economies**. There is no end to the different combinations and permutations regarding the ownership of the factors of production in the world's mixed economies. Each nation has to be examined individually in order to find evidence to support where it is to be placed on the continuum. A nation's position on the continuum shifts as the economic and other variables in the ecosystem shift. Recall that Trudeau moved Canada toward a command economy because the economic realities dictated that such an action was prudent. Today, we have witnessed China moving from the command economy toward a market-based economy. Other countries are more entrenched in their position, such as North Korea, which officially shows little sign of shifting. However, North Korean farmers have developed an underground economy and are selling their small farm production out of the sight of the government. There also are market-based economies in South American nations like Brazil, Bolivia, Venezuela, and others that seem to be moving toward the command economy pole. Consider: in 2006, Ecuador used its military to seize some foreign oil concessions; Evo Morales, president of Bolivia announced plans to nationalize the country's natural gas resources; and Peru considered following faraway Mongolia's lead when the latter imposed a huge 68 percent windfall tax on foreign mining companies. Clearly, Canadian mining companies with interests in these countries are concerned with any shift in their economic ideology. It can be said with some degree of certainty that collectively, since the fall of the Bamboo Curtain (1979) and the Iron Curtain (1989), and the strengthening of Western liberalized democracy, a great number of nations have shifted along the continuum toward the market economy pole. See Figure 3.2 to compare the characteristics of the three market economies.

A **mixed economy** reflects some of the attributes of market and command economies. It is an economy whereby some production is done by the private sector and some by the state. The degree to which the private sector or the state control "commanding heights" determines where on the continuum the nation should be placed. The reality is all nations can be classified as mixed economies!

FIGURE 3.2

Characteristics of Command, Mixed, and Market Economies

Command (Socialism-Communism)	Mixed (between the Two Poles)	Market (Free Enterprise-Capitalism)
Controlled by strong, centralized government	Combination of market and command economic systems	Market consists of buyers and sellers
Generally focuses on industrial goods	Market forces control most consumer goods	Based upon supply and demand (Adam Smith)
Resources are tightly controlled by government	Government directs industry in needed areas (pragmatic decisions)	Usually focused on consumer goods
Economy can change direction very quickly (inviting mining companies then imposing, with little warning, significant windfall taxes)	Most of the global economies are clearly mixed and found between the two poles	Easy to adjust to changing consumer demands (Smith's invisible guiding hand at work)
Not designed to meet the wants of individuals (Aristotle) but rather collectivists (Plato)	Canada is mostly a market system but has elements of traditional and command systems; recall BC government's wage control	Freedom of choice for buyers
Lack of incentives		Little government control—individualism
Little variation in pay		Governments' main involvement in economy is to regulate and ensure "fair play"
Job security		Risk involved
Large bureaucracy		Large variety of goods available for buyers
Few new ideas or innovations		Things that ensure successful market economy are (1) competition; (2) resources (labour) are free to move around; (3) access to information, resulting in the ability to make informed choices
Very few nations can be found close to this end of this continuum (Cuba, North Korea)		Rule of law; constitution and rights and freedoms
Access to Internet monitored and controlled		Very few nations can be found close to this end of this continuum
No rule of law		Open access to Internet

Economic Dimensions

We now understand a number of the factors found in the different economic systems that we will encounter in international business. Those factors found in the command, mixed, and market economies will have to be accommodated when crafting a market entry strategy. In addition to the general understanding of these characteristics, through market research we can obtain a number of economic dimensions (metrics). To assist us in our planning, there are important economic indicators we must review, including gross national product (GNP) now referred to as gross national income (GNI), gross domestic product (GDP), purchasing power parity (PPP), Human Development Index (HDI), distribution of income (DI), private consumption expenditures (PCE), personal ownership of goods, private investment, union labour costs, foreign direct investment, exchange rates, inflation rates, and interest rates. It is critical that we undertake an analysis of these indicators, as it will enable us to determine with some degree of certainty the length and breadth of our selected foreign target market.

Gross domestic product (GDP) represents the total of the goods and services produced domestically within a 12-month period (normally the calendar year) to include income received from abroad. Since 1993, the World Bank adopted new terminology to refer to GNP as gross national income (GNI). **GNI** includes income received from other countries set off against similar payments made to other countries.

Throughout this text, when introducing nations we include the country's recent population and GDP (in U.S. dollars). The most common measures to assess the economic strength and health of a nation are GDP, GNI, PPP, HDI, DI, and PCE. Figure 3.3 shows the GNIs for Canada and a selected group of Canada's most likely trading partners, prepared by the World Bank. Study it for a moment. What conclusions can you draw when you consider the countries' populations and productivity?

Using another economic metric, Canada's US$714 billion GDP—equivalent to $23,000 per head—tell us about our selling strategy when compared to India's US$511 billion GDP (equivalent to $500 per head)? In part, the answer depends on the goods and services we propose to sell. If they are high-end, high-priced goods, then Canada may be the appropriate market. However if the goods and services are budget priced, then India might be the better venue. Most developed countries until recently did not consider developing and underdeveloped countries of significant importance to their global marketing strategies. Mistake! Consider Professor Vijay Mahajan's comments at a recent Wharton Fellows meeting in India. Mahajan explained that he had several eye-opening experiences when he returned to India. Eighty-six percent of the world's population lives in countries with an average GDP of less than $10,000 (the

Gross domestic product (GDP) represents the total of the goods and services produced domestically within a 12-month period (normally the calendar year) to include income received from abroad.

Gross national income (GNI) includes income received from other countries set off against similar payments made to other countries.

FIGURE 3.3
The World Bank Group, GNI Atlas Method—2005

Country	GNI in US$ (millions)
United States	$ 12,969,561
European Union (25)	$ 12,865,000
European Monetary Union	$ 9,912,405
Japan	$ 4,988,209
China	$ 2,263,825
Canada	$ 1,051,873
Mexico	$ 753,394
Brazil	$ 644,133
Russia	$ 639,080

The *World Bank Atlas* method converts data in the national currency to US dollars by averaging the exchange rate for that year and the two preceding years, and adjusting for differences in rates of inflation between the country and the United States. The resulting estimate of GNI/GDP in US dollars is divided by the midyear population to obtain the per capita GNI/GDP in current US dollars.[28]

Source: Adapted from World Bank Group, "WDI Data Query." © 2006 The World Bank Group. All Rights Reserved.

cutoff for developed countries). If we remove the two most populated nations, United States and Japan (total 330 million), the population of the (balance of the) developed world is a mere 6 percent of the global population (6.5 billion). Developing populations are growing rapidly while developed world populations are, by and large, shrinking. The developed world has to wake up and see this 86 percent opportunity. "You have no choice but to deal with the 86% world."[29] This is a powerful observation and clearly a new mental model for Canadian business.

Remember that all things change, including GDPs. The annual real GDP growth rates (India) for the Colonial period (1900–1950) was 1 percent, post-independence (1950–1980) was 3.5 percent; and reform period (1980–2003) a very desirable 6.0 percent. In contrast, the industrial revolution in the West took place at a rate of just 3 percent over a period of 100 years. Given current trends, India's per capita income will match that of the United States by 2066.[30] A caveat: be aware in your research that foreign statistics can be flawed. Canadian SMEs are cautioned to verify foreign economic metrics, as they may not have the same reliability as those produced by Statistics Canada. For example, India has an informal economy and experiences low tax filing. With a population in excess of one billion, only 15,000 Indians declared income of more than US$24,000 per year in 2004. So in determining the appropriate market entry strategy, can we rely solely on a country's GDP statistics to represent the purchasing power of our customers? No! We need also to consider other metrics. One such metric is purchasing power parity.

Simply comparing the gross product figures of the GNI, the GDP, or gross national product does not fairly reflect the cost of living in each country. These metrics can be misleading to business when determining whether or not there is a sufficient market in the host country for its goods or services. Accordingly, when determining a market entry strategy we should include a review of the **purchasing power parity** (**PPP**) index for the host countries we are considering. The PPP metric allows us to compare the purchase price for a fixed basket of goods in every country. The basket includes basic items found in common daily use, such as apples, soap, toothpaste, and so on, thereby capturing the difference in the cost of living from country to country. In reviewing the PPPs, we are able to obtain some understanding as to what a Canadian dollar, for example, can purchase in another country. It allows us to compare apples to apples. See Figure 3.4 for a ranking of countries by their PPP in **international dollars**. A review of this figure might lead you to conclude that the Indian market is far more attractive than we might have initially thought if our analysis considered only the GDP.

The **purchasing power parity** (**PPP**) metric allows us to compare the purchase price for a fixed basket of goods in every country. The basket includes basic items found in common daily use, such as apples, soap, toothpaste, and so on, thereby capturing the difference in the cost of living from country to country. PPP allows us to make more accurate comparisons of standards of living across countries.

The **international dollar** is a hypothetical unit of currency that has the same purchasing power that the U.S. dollar has in the United States at a given point in time. It is used to make comparisons both between countries and over time.

FIGURE 3.4

Purchasing Power Parity Index (PPP) Table (PPP GNI 2005)

Ranking	Economy	(International dollars)
3	United States	41,950
13	United Kingdom	32,690
16	**Canada**	**32,220**
19	Japan	31,410
23	France	30,540
25	Singapore	29,780
27	Germany	29,210
29	Italy	28,840
42	New Zealand	23,030
78	Russian Federation	10,640
81	Mexico	10,030
89	Brazil	8,230
107	China	6,600
144	India	3,460
191	Nigeria	1,040
202	Sierra Leone	780
208	Burundi	640

SOURCE: Adapted from "World Development Indicators Database" (World Bank Group, 2005).

FIGURE 3.5

The Big Mac Index

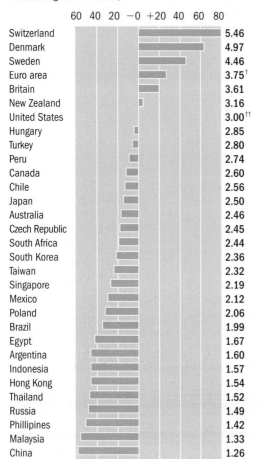

Local currency under (−)/over (+)
valuation against the dollar, %

		Big Mac price*, $
	60 40 20 −0 +20 40 60 80	
Switzerland		5.46
Denmark		4.97
Sweden		4.46
Euro area		3.75†
Britain		3.61
New Zealand		3.16
United States		3.00††
Hungary		2.85
Turkey		2.80
Peru		2.74
Canada		2.60
Chile		2.56
Japan		2.50
Australia		2.46
Czech Republic		2.45
South Africa		2.44
South Korea		2.36
Taiwan		2.32
Singapore		2.19
Mexico		2.12
Poland		2.06
Brazil		1.99
Egypt		1.67
Argentina		1.60
Indonesia		1.57
Hong Kong		1.54
Thailand		1.52
Russia		1.49
Phillipines		1.42
Malaysia		1.33
China		1.26

* At market exchange rate (December 13, 2004)
†Weighted average of member countries
††Average of four cities

SOURCE: "The Big Mac Index" from *The Economist* (December 16, 2004).

The Big Mac Index

Well-known British publication *The Economist* publishes in April and October of each year what can be described as a hybrid of the PPP metric. It is the Big Mac Index. McDonald's is a global multinational enterprise (MNE) that operates in so many different countries that *The Economist* suggests that there is value in preparing an index. The indexed "basket of goods" reflects the cost of McDonald's Big Mac in countries where McDonald's operates. *The Economist* makes the necessary adjustments for exchange rates and concludes whether not a country's currency is under- or overvalued.

"*The Economist*'s Big Mac index is based on the theory of purchasing-power parity (PPP), the idea that exchange rates should move to equalize the prices of a basket of goods and services across different countries. Our basket is the Big Mac. For example, the cheapest burger in the chart is in China, at $1.26, compared with an average American price of $3. This implies that the yuan is 58% undervalued relative to its Big Mac dollar-PPP. On the same basis, the euro is 25% overvalued, the yen 17% undervalued."[31] We can also conclude that the Canadian loonie was undervalued against the U.S. dollar as of December 2004. In hindsight, it seems that it was—CDN$1.29 to a US$1 (1 Jan 2004); then appreciating to CDN$1.14 Can to US$1 (1 February 2006).

The Economist also wondered how the globe looked when viewed through the bottom of a Coca-Cola bottle. The result of the study identified patterns. For one, there is a loose but clear positive relationship between Coke consumption and wealth. The study also noted a relationship between cola and the United Nations Human Development Index for surveyed countries' quality of life as measured by wealth, education, health, and literacy. Finally, the study noted that consumption rises with political freedom, as measured by Freedom House. (Established in New York in 1941, Freedom House is a nonprofit organization that monitors political rights and civil liberties around the world on a seven-point scale.)[32]

The Big Mac index is not an original concept. Historians have frequently used the cost of a loaf of bread to arrive at some sense of the cost of living in a specific period. Try it. Divide the cost of a loaf of bread today in Canada into the minimum wage. How many loaves can a worker buy? How does that compare with the minimum wage in the 1960s? Are we surging or falling behind? I think you will be surprised.

Amartya Sen,[33] a Nobel Prize–winning economist, underscores the importance of not completely evaluating countries by their wealth (GNI) or the PPP. Rather, he recommends that we analyze a nation's quality of life. The United Nations Human Development Index (HDI) meets this challenge and provides us with another metric for analysis when considering market entry strategies. The HDI augments the PPP that provided us with a sense of different countries' levels of economic development. The HDI measures how well a country's citizens' basic needs are being satisfied. Interestingly, Canada placed fourth in the world in 2002; the United States was 26th. Specifically, the HDI measures the longevity and overall health of its citizens, the levels and quality of education, and the standard of living. The index has three subclassifications—high human development, medium human development, and low human development. A review of Figure 3.6 will lead you to conclude that gross domestic product numbers are not necessarily a good indicator of the quality of life of a particular nation. Specifically, note that the United States with a very highly GDP per capita ranks significantly lower in life expectancy than Japan. Yes, you need money to put in place the necessary infrastructure such as schools and health care to improve the quality of life, but this outcome is not driven by money alone. Do you think individuals' personal values in Norway and Sweden contain a clue as to what other variables should be considered? Visit www.power.nelson.com for more on this.

FIGURE 3.6
Human Development Index

HDI Rank		Life Expectancy at Birth (years) 2002	Adult Literacy Rate (% Ages 15 and above) 2002	Combined Gross Enrolment, Ratio for Primary, Secondary and Tertiary Schools (%) 2001/02	GDP per Capita (PPP US$) 2002	Life Expectancy Index	Education Index	GDP Index	Human Development Index (HDI) Value 2002	GDP per Capita (PPP US$) Rank Minus HDI Rank
High Human Development										
1	Norway	78.9		98	36,600	0.9	0.99	0.99	0.956	1
2	Sweden	80		114	26,050	0.92	0.99	0.93	0.946	19
3	Australia	79.1		113	28,260	0.9	0.99	0.94	0.946	9
4	**Canada**	**79.3**		**95**	**29,480**	**0.9**	**0.98**	**0.95**	**0.943**	**5**
5	Netherlands	78.3		99	29,100	0.89	0.99	0.95	0.942	6
8	United States	77		92	35,750	0.87	0.97	0.98	0.939	-4
9	Japan	81.5		84	26,940	0.94	0.94	0.93	0.938	6
12	United Kingdom	78.1		113	26,150	0.88	0.99	0.93	0.936	8
53	Mexico	73.3	90.5	74	8,970	0.81	0.85	0.75	0.802	5
Medium Human Development										
57	Russia	66.7	99.6	88	8,230	0.69	0.95	0.74	0.795	3
88	Turkey	70.4	86.5	68	6,390	0.76	0.8	0.69	0.751	-12
94	China	70.9	90.9	68	4,580	0.76	0.83	0.64	0.745	5
127	India	63.7	61.3	55	2,670	0.64	0.59	0.55	0.595	-10
Low Human Development										
175	Burkina Faso	45.8	12.8	22	1,100	0.35	0.16	0.4	0.302	-20
176	Niger	46	17.1	19	800	0.35	0.18	0.35	0.292	-8
177	Sierra Leone	34.3	36	45	520	0.16	0.39	0.28	0.273	-1

SOURCE: Human Development Reports, *Human Development Index* (United Nations Development Programme, 2004).

The Human Development and Income Growth website provides a wonderful animated graphic display that demonstrates how, over time, changes in income (GDP per capita) affects changes in human development (health and literacy). Visit the site and watch the graphic demonstrating China, Sir Lanka, and Indonesia's economic growth following their investment in human development from 1975 to 2002. It is clear that high human development allows for fast economic growth but it is not automatic. The 1985 experience of Tajikistan is an example of a country with high human development and a declining economy. Following the animated graph of Botswana's growth from 1975 to 2002, the trend of increasing income is shown; there is severely declining human development despite significant growth in literacy. The sharp human development decline is the result of the reduced life expectancy caused by HIV/AIDS that has affected many African countries. For visual learners this is a great site! See the www.power .nelson.com website for the link.

Legal Systems

A cornerstone for a country's economic stability is the requirement to have a rule of law that is transparent and free from government interference. Nations without this attribute will not fully exploit the economic opportunities available to them. There is much

Law can be described as the body of rules that are enforced by nations' courts or by delegate government agencies such as provincial workers' compensation boards.

evidence that nations whose legal system rests in the hands of a political dictatorship or a powerful elite fail to encourage foreign direct investment into their nations.

Law can be described as the body of rules that are enforced by nations' courts or by delegated government agencies, such as provincial workers' compensation boards. In this portion of the text, we examine selected aspects of civil, common, theocratic, contract, and property law that will impact business. A careful examination and analysis of these aspects of the law will be critical to the success of any international business venture. Remember the words of Sun Tzu, "Those who do not use local guides are unable to obtain the advantages of the ground."[34] As a Canadian SME, you would be well advised the heed these wise words and engage the services of local guides (lawyers and others) to assist you through international legal systems. The other major body of law is criminal law. It varies significantly from nation to nation, as do the sanctions when the criminal law is breached. Criminal law will not be reviewed here but its impact must also be understood. The Evidence Box explains the case of an Indonesian criminal law sanction for writing graffiti. It demonstrates that you cannot assume the law you are familiar with in Canada will be the same in host countries. Regarding this specific offence, in Canada for the most part we turn a blind eye to graffiti in our downtown cores. Do you think such sanctions as applied by the Singapore criminal law would help rid Canadian downtowns of vandalism? There is a website[35] supporting such corporal action by legislators.

The Whipping Boy

"Should anyone much care whether an American boy living overseas gets six vicious thwacks on his backside? So much has been argued, rejoined and rehashed about the case of Michael Fay, an 18-year-old convicted of vandalism and sentenced to a caning in Singapore, that an otherwise sorry little episode has shaded into a certified International Incident, complete with intercessions by the US head of state. An affair that sometimes sounds—on editorial pages—equivalent to the abduction of Helen of Troy has outraged American libertarians even as it has animated a general debate about morality, East and West and the proper functioning of US law and order. The Trojan War this is not: the wooden horse is in America's citadel."[36]

"Which, to all appearances, is what Singapore wanted. The question of whether anyone should care about Michael Fay is idle though Singapore officials profess shock at the attention his case has drawn, they know Americans care deeply about the many sides of this issue. Does a teenager convicted of spraying cars with easily removable paint deserve half a dozen powerful strokes on the buttocks with a sopping-wet bamboo staff? At what point does swift, sure punishment become torture? By what moral authority can America, with its high rates of lawlessness and license, preach to a safe society about human rights? . . . The caning sentence has fascinated many Americans [; it] has concentrated minds wondrously on an already lively domestic debate over what constitutes a due balance between individual and majority rights. Too bad Michael Fay has become a fulcrum for this discussion. Not only does he seem destined to be pummelled and immobilized by an instrument of ordeal, but also the use of Singapore as a standard for judging any other society, let alone the cacophonous US, is fairly worthless.

". . . Even without its government's disciplinary measures, Singapore likely would be much the same as it is now. The major factor determining social peace and prosperity is culture—a sense of common identity, tradition, and values. Singapore is 76 percent ethnic Chinese, a people with one of the most self-disciplined cultures in the world. Prizing family, learning, and hard work, overseas Chinese have prospered wherever they have settled. . . . There is little crime [in Hong Kong and Singapore].

"Singaporeans have every right to be proud of their achievements. Does that justify Michael Fay's sentence? A letter writer to the *New York Times* advised that 'six of the best,' as he suffered at an English public (that is, private) school, might cure all that ails American youth. Comparing Fay's sentence to a headmaster's paddling is fatuous—but then, as John Updike once noted, old boys of Eton and Harrow can often 'mistake a sports car for a woman or a birch rod for a mother's kiss.' The pain from flaying with wet rattan, as it is done in Singapore, can knock a prisoner out cold."

Several large Asian countries, China among them, argue that the United States has no business criticizing Singapore's actions.

Adapted from James Walsh, "The Whipping Boy," *Time Magazine* (Singapore: Time, 1994). Copyright © 2006 Time Inc. All rights reserved.

Three Kinds of Civilian Legal Systems

In this section, we will look briefly at the three different kinds of civilian legal systems as differentiated from criminal law. They are common law, civilian law, and theocratic law. Undertaking business in an international environment will bring you into contact with one or more of these three legal systems. You cannot be a legal expert but you should develop an awareness and appreciation for the underpinnings of these three different types of law. You must understand how these legal traditions will shape and influence how you will do business in an international environment. Recall Canadian law finds the genesis for its constitutional law in the English Magna Carta Charter (1215) and the English Bill of Rights (1689). **Common law** developed from customs and traditions, and borrowed heavily on Roman civil law, canon or Church law, and law merchant. **Roman law** provides much of our property law today. **Canon law** contributes concepts to family and estate law. Law merchant provided legal concepts relating to commercial law and guilds (unions).

Common law grew incrementally over time to produce a body of law based on acts, regulations, and, most importantly, precedent. The process of following precedent of other courts is referred to as **stare decisis**. This means that courts generally follow previous rulings of cases based on similar facts within the same jurisdiction and from a court at a higher level. A lower court within the same jurisdiction must follow precedent established by a higher court. For example, in Canada if a case is being heard before a magistrate's court in Ontario, this court must follow previous rulings of a higher Ontario Court if that higher decision is based on similar facts. However, a magistrate's court in British Columbia may be guided by the Ontario higher court's decision but it is not bound to follow that decision (different jurisdictions). All courts are bound by the Supreme Court of Canada's rulings.

Business Implications

Most Anglo-Saxon countries have adopted common law as their legal system to adjudicate business matters. By definition, because of the vast array of combinations and permutations of factual situations, common law lawyers preparing contractual documents will go to great lengths to outline and describe every possible eventuality. Anglo-Saxon contracts tend to be long and give rise to litigation because of the difficulty to say with authority what each clause means in the event of a dispute. There can be some comfort taken in doing business in nations that have an Anglo-Saxon common-law system; South Africa, Australia, and the United States are examples.

Civil law is found at the other end of the continuum of civilian laws. This legal system is based on a "code." In Canada, for example, we have a code for criminal law (not civil law) called the Criminal Code of Canada. This code sets out in writing the criminal law with the elements of the crime and provides the sanctions if the act (code) is breached. It is relatively straightforward for the layperson to read the code and to understand the criminal law and its sanctions. In business matters, some countries have adopted civil law based on a written code to cover most eventualities. The 19th-century Napoleonic Code of France provides a good example. This code is the genesis for civil law in Quebec; it is a civil code of rules stated as broad principles. All other Canadian provinces and territories are governed by common law.

You will find that Cuba, Central and South America, most of Western Europe, and many nations in Asia and Africa have adopted the civil law tradition. From a practical

Common law developed from customs and traditions, and borrowed heavily on Roman civil law, canon or church law, and law merchant.

Roman law provides much of the property law we rely upon today.

Canon law contributes concepts to family and estate law. Law merchant provided legal concepts relating to commercial law and guilds (unions).

Stare decisis is the process of following the precedent of other courts. A lower court within the same jurisdiction must follow precedent established by a higher court and all courts are bound by the Supreme Court of Canada's rulings.

Civil law is found at the other end of the continuum of civilian laws. This legal system is based on a "code." Examples include the Criminal Code of Canada and Quebec's civil code, which is based on the 19th-century Napoleonic Code of France.

JUST DOING THE RIGHT THING

Product Safety

Increasingly, developed and developing countries are implementing safety standards for manufacturers' products. Breaches of safety standards and negligence give rise to product liability, and the resulting sanctions awarded by the courts are both civil and criminal. Civil remedies are generally qualified in dollar settlements. Criminal remedies can include fines but may also include incarceration for owners. Developed countries have well-established law for those injured by defective products. A major issue today is the costs incurred by developing countries in meeting safety standards and undertaking remedial action to ensure manufactured products will not cause injury to consumers.

QUESTION

How can developed countries compete with developing countries that pay little attention to product liability and safety issues? There have been a number of children's products, for example, introduced into the North American marketplace that have used lead-based paints in the manufacturing process.

Theocratic law is based on religious teachings. The most prominent theocratic laws are Islamic, Hindu, and Jewish law. While Hindu and Jewish law tend to be more cultural and spiritual forces now; Islamic law continues to be very much in evidence in Islamic countries today.

point of view, this means that you will experience less litigation in your business dealings because the contract clauses are codified, similar to the residential tenancy act in your province. This legislation sets out the law in a written code describing the rights and obligations of the leasing parties and the sanctions applicable if they are breached. Accordingly, in a private landlord–tenant relationship, there is generally little time spent crafting detailed leases as the contractual conditions are largely governed by the code.

Theocratic law is based on religious teachings. The most prominent theocratic laws are Islamic, Hindu, and Jewish law. When conducting business internationally, it will be important for you to develop a cultural sensitivity in your day-to-day dealings with countries that have adopted or at some point had these legal systems. You will most likely encounter Islamic theocratic law, as Hindu and Jewish law today is more a cultural and spiritual force. Islamic law, based on the Koran (also spelt Qur'an) and the writings of the Prophet Muhammad (Sunnah—the Prophet's words), continue to be very much in evidence in Islamic countries today. They must be observed if you are to be successful in Islamic countries.

Islamic banks will not charge interest on loans or pay interest on accounts; nor will Muslims invest in firms that market alcohol or tobacco. In Canada, Jewish law can determine legal disputes if both parties agree to be bound by the outcome. Using this as a precedent, Canadian Muslims have actively lobbied for the same recognition and wish to introduce Islamic theocratic law in Canada. Should Canadians be concerned that the use of Islamic theocratic law arbitration process is the beginning of a separate political identity for Muslims in Canada? How can Islamic theocratic law possibly align with the Charter of Rights and Freedoms in Canada?

Shariah Law

In 1991, Ontario was looking for ways to ease the burdens of a backlogged court system. So the province changed its Arbitration Act to allow "faith-based arbitration"—a system where Muslims, Jews, Catholics and members of other faiths could use the guiding principles of their religions to settle family disputes such as divorce, custody and inheritances outside the court system. It's voluntary—both parties (a husband and wife) have to agree to go through the process. But once they do, the decisions rendered by the tribunal are binding.

The Ontario government has been reviewing its Arbitration Act and on Dec. 20, 2004, it released a report conducted by former attorney general Marion Boyd. Among her 46 recommendations was that the Arbitration Act should continue to allow disputes to be arbitrated using religious law, if the safeguards currently prescribed and recommended by this review are observed. Earlier in the year, the Islamic Institute of Civil Justice said it wanted to set up its own faith-based arbitration panels under the Arbitration Act, based on Shariah law. The proposal ran into opposition from women's groups, legal organizations and the Muslim Canadian Congress, which all warned that the 1,400-year-old Shariah law does not view women as equal to men. In her report, Boyd noted that some "participants in the Review fear that the use of arbitration is the beginning of a process whose end goal is a separate political identity for Muslims in Canada, [however,] that has not been the experience of other groups who use arbitration."

What Is Shariah?

The word Shariah means "the path to a watering hole." It denotes an Islamic way of life—not just a system of criminal justice. It is a code of living that most Muslims adopt as part of their faith. Some countries formally institute it as the law of the land, enforced by the courts. However, the way Shariah law is applied from country to country can vary widely. How did it originate? According to Muslim scholars, the Prophet Muhammad laid down the laws. Some of the laws are said to be direct commands stated in the Qur'an; other laws were based on rulings Muhammad is said to have given to cases that occurred during his lifetime. These secondary laws are based on what's called the Sunnah—the Prophet's words, example, and way of life. One of the major concerns of people critical of Shariah law is that it is subject to interpretation and evolution. There is virtually no formal certification process to designate someone as being qualified to interpret Islamic law. As it stands today, almost anyone can make rulings as long as they have the appearance of piety and a group of followers.

Source: CBC News, "Shariah Law: FAQs," (2004). Copyright © CBC 2006.

VIDEO

Video 3.1

Property Rights

Property can be classified into two categories: **real property**, such as land and items considered fixed or attached to the land, and **personal property**, which includes ownership of all other things. Personal property includes intangible rights, such as a claim for a debt (called a **chose in action**—a right to sue). Bonds, shares, and negotiable instruments are examples of choses in action. **Intellectual property** is intangible personal property that includes copyright (provides the author control over the reproductions /use of her creative work); patents (a government-granted monopoly provided so that only the inventor can benefit/profit from the invention); trademarks (protects designs and symbols from use by unauthorized persons), industrial design (unique shapes or patterns); confidential information (private information that if disclosed would harm a business); and trade secrets (information that significantly contributes to a firm's competitive advantage).

Personal property also includes chattels (movable things), such as baggage, clothes, radios, animals, construction cranes, and boats. Be aware that in some cases chattels can cease to be personal property if attached to real property. Once attached, they become part of the real property. For example, a hot water heater in a home was clearly a chattel when purchased at the store, but becomes part of the real property—a fixture—when incorporated into the home heating system. Business owners must understand the varying property rights they are likely to encounter in host countries. Can they commence action against the state? Are the rights different between genders? Can they raise funds by pledging assets in the host country? Are there restrictions on foreign ownership? Can they buy land?

There are times when we experience an epiphany. One such moment for me came from reading Peruvian economist Hernando De Soto's bestseller, *The Mystery of Capital: Why Capitalism Triumphs in the West and Fails Everywhere Else.*[37] De Soto argues that the basic source of poverty and underdevelopment in nations such as Peru can be directly linked to the absence of a rule of law. In Peru and many other underdeveloped and developing countries, their citizens have, in many cases for generations, worked the same piece of land. Unlike Canada, where if a citizen exercises open use and exercises control over a piece of land for 60 years or more it is recognized by the Crown as a sufficient interest to represent ownership, Peru has no such law. As a result, although Peruvian farmers have been working the same tract of land or exercising the same ownership over waterfront property, because of the absence of law they are unable to raise capital through property

Real property are land and items considered fixed or attached to the land.

Personal property includes ownership of all things other than real property, including chattels; intangible rights, such as bonds, shares, and negotiable instruments; and intellectual property.

A **chose in action** means a right to sue and applies to intangible rights, such as a claim for debt. Bonds, shares, and negotiable instruments are examples of choses in action.

Intellectual property is intangible personal property that includes copyright, patents, trademarks, industrial design, confidential information, and trade secrets.

mortgages or in the case of goods, chattel mortgages, to invest in their businesses. De Soto contends that these people do not need external funding but rather a method to raise investment capital. We take this as a given in Canada as do many developing nations. This simple truth is the key to why Canada has done well economically and Peru has not. De Soto's book will stimulate creative thinking as to how underdeveloped and developing countries can alleviate poverty. Without the rule of law here is what can happen:

"Citing fresh evidence that a Moscow hotel was seized through fraudulent means, a Canadian businessman has asked Russia's top prosecutor to launch a civil case in a bid to regain control of the property. 'Our partners and myself have requested that the general prosecutor apply to the courts and have these properties returned,' Ken Rowe, chairman of Halifax-based IMP Group Ltd., told Canadian Press.[38]

"In a letter sent recently to Vladimir Ustinov, IMP alleges that ownership of the Aerostar Hotel was transferred to the Russian company Aviacity last August during bankruptcy proceedings that used a 'substantially undervalued' assessment of the building. The letter cites evidence gathered by Moscow's public prosecutor's office, which is conducting a criminal investigation into the seizure. Investigators discovered the 343-room Aerostar was valued at 267 million rubles ($11.93 million) by an unlicensed appraiser known as Business Problems LLC on July 1, 2002. An appraisal by an independent company put the building's value at more than 1.2 billion rubles.[39]

"'The buildings were given a value less than a third of their true price,' said Alexander Skoblo, IMP's lawyer in Moscow. 'We knew the buildings were undervalued, but the Ministry of Justice has confirmed this through their own evaluations.' Mr. Skoblo said the evidence is crucial because it shows the hotel was seized using false documentation. Under the Russian civil code, the entire transaction could be cancelled in short order, allowing IMP to go back into business, he said. Mr. Skoblo said a civil case could be resolved in a few months if Mr. Ustinov takes it to the civil courts. 'It's a more expeditious way of getting to the results,' the lawyer said, noting the criminal case could take years to complete. Mr. Rowe's battle for control of the hotel has been a lengthy one. Over the past decade, IMP had invested $45 million (US) in the Aerostar, one of the first international hotels to open in Russia following the collapse of the Soviet Union in the early 1990s.[40]

"Since Russian regulations prevented IMP and its partner, Russia's Aeroflot Airlines, from owning the hotel outright, they instead leased the property from the government through its Agency for Civil Air Transport. Last Aug. 17, IMP's executives were stunned when Aviacity produced documents saying they owned the building and then had IMP managers and 150 guests thrown out of the hotel. The Moscow prosecutor's office alleges that a fraudulent bankruptcy gave a small group of conspirators' control of the Aerostar and numerous other state assets."[41] The case remains unresolved in 2006!

Video 3.2

International Law

Sovereign nations craft and implement a law system, and have the moral and political authority to enforce their laws within their jurisdiction. But when issues arise in the normal course of business that fall outside the specific jurisdiction of a specific sovereign nation, then the question becomes, which rule of law should apply? This is the realm of international law. It is here that the business practitioner is at risk because of the lack of knowledge of the host countries' legal systems! With the success of globalization, increasingly we witness a rise in trade disputes between nations (public international law) and between individuals (private international law). In an attempt to resolve these disputes, a number of the world's nations have adjudicating institutions in place. One such initiative is the United Nations Convention on Contracts for the International Sale of Goods. This convention provides international rules governing commercial relationships between international buyers and sellers. Similarly, there is the United Nations Convention on the Carriage of Goods by Sea (The Hamburg Rules). This convention governs all contracts of shipping by sea between different states if certain conditions are met. Canada, as an exporter, frequently relies on conventions and acts of this nature. For arbitration, the

International Chamber of Commerce's International Arbitration Court in Paris has been most effective in settling disputes between buyers and sellers located in different countries. The World Trade Organization also provides adjudication services, as do most of the regional agreements such as NAFTA. (We will examine this dispute mechanism in greater detail in later chapters.) In the absence of better international institutions, business practitioners and nations are left with these conventions and their dispute resolution vehicles to resolve their differences. But what happens when one party, notwithstanding a signature to the international adjudication body, is unhappy and refuses to accept the determination? Read this article by former Canadian negotiator Gordon Ritchie.

"Who's Afraid of NAFTA's Bite? Not the US, Whose Dogged Attacks on Softwood Lumber Undermine Trade Agreements, Warns Former [Free Trade] Negotiator Gordon Ritchie."

"On the public stage, the Bush administration joins the chorus calling for improved Canada–US relations. Behind the scenes, it is threatening to launch an unprecedented attack that could leave the free-trade agreement in ruins. Its immediate target is the Canadian lumber industry. Stripped of legal technicalities, the underlying facts of the lumber situation are these: The US softwood industry, inefficient and undercapitalized, fears increased imports from Canada. Under the pretext that Canadian lumber enjoys an unfair advantage from provincial resource-management policies, the US industry has launched four trade actions since 1980."[42]

"In the first case, the action was dismissed as unwarranted by the US administration itself. In the second, before the free-trade agreement, the administration forced Canada to agree to impose border taxes on its own industry by its threat of unilateral action. By the third, Canada was able to use the protections of the free-trade deal to demonstrate that the US action was unfounded, and forced the administration to return the penalties illegally extracted from the Canadian industry. Rather than face the harassment of yet another trade case, Canada agreed to limit the volume of its exports to the United States (albeit to very high levels) for a promise of no further trade actions for five years. When that agreement was, unwisely, allowed to lapse, the US industry waited two whole days before launching yet another trade case, even more outlandish than its predecessors. That case is still, four years later, winding its way through NAFTA and World Trade Organization panels, which have consistently ordered the US authorities to clean up their act. So far, déjà vu all over again: The administration, acting as the agent of its protectionist industry, launches an unjustified trade action and imposes punitive duties; the Canadian industry and government are forced to spend millions to defend themselves; the free-trade panels declare the US actions improper and send them back to the authorities to correct."[43]

"A senior Commerce Department official has formally declared that when the administration finally loses its cases before the free-trade panels, after exhausting all reasonable (and some highly questionable) legal tricks, it will simply refuse to pay back the money illegally collected—now more than $4-billion Canadian—unless and until the Canadian government agrees to meet the demands of the US industry. This is indisputably in direct contravention of the NAFTA and amounts to nothing less than a unilateral abrogation of the central provisions of the free-trade agreement. Second, the administration is beginning to distribute these and other illegally collected duties to its own industries as a bounty, in direct defiance of the rulings of the WTO, leaving other countries no choice but to retaliate. Congress is blamed but experts say the Bush administration could have, but has not, used its discretion to interpret the offending legislation not to apply to Canada and Mexico. Third, in a highly cynical manoeuvre, the US Trade Representative has taken the unprecedented step of ordering the Commerce Department to amend the trade orders to overrule the NAFTA-panel decision (that found that imports from Canada had not been shown to injure, or threaten to injure, US producers). Finally, the US industry has pulled out all the stops in its campaign to evade the NAFTA tribunals. It is threatening to challenge the very constitutionality of the NAFTA panel process, enlisting the support, for a fee, of two former attorneys-general who, conveniently forgetting that the Justice Department certified to Congress that the system was perfectly constitutional, are prepared to argue that it is unthinkable that Americans would ever be subject to decisions in which foreign judges take part. If successful, this challenge could demolish the very provisions of NAFTA without which Canada (and Mexico) would never have ratified the agreement."[44]

From *Who's Afraid of NAFTA's Bite?* by Gordon Ritchie, *The Globe and Mail* (February 15, 2005). Reprinted with permission of the publisher.

Protection of Intellectual Property

In Western cultures, great value is placed in the products of intellectual activity. Developed nations advocate and support ownership rights over intellectual property through patents, copyrights, and trademarks. A **patent** is a grant to an inventor who has produced a new product. The grant provides for exclusive rights for a fixed period of time over the manufacture, use, or sale of the inventor's invention. **Copyrights** provide exclusive legal right to authors, composers, playwrights, recording artists, movie firms, and publishers for ownership of their work. **Trademarks** are the names and designs normally registered by producers of goods and services in order to differentiate their products.

A **patent** is a grant to an inventor who has produced a new product that provides for exclusive rights for a fixed period of time over the manufacture, use, or sale of the inventor's invention.

Copyrights provide exclusive legal right to authors, composers, playwrights, recording artists, movie firms, and publishers for ownership of their work.

Trademarks are the names and designs normally registered by producers of goods and services in order to differentiate their products.

Early Law—Intellectual Property

Extract from a Translation of the Venetian Decree of March 1474

There are in this city and its neighbourhood, attracted by its excellence and greatness, many men of diverse origins, having most subtle minds and able to devise and discover various ingenious artifices. And, if it should be provided that no one else might make or take to himself to increase his own honour the works and devices discovered by such men, those same men would exercise their ingenuity, and would discover and make things which would be of no little advantage to our state.

Therefore it is enacted by the authority of this body that whoever makes in this city any new and ingenious device, not previously made within our jurisdiction, is bound to register it at the office of the Provveditori di Comun as soon as it has been perfected, so that it will be possible to use and apply it. It will be prohibited to anyone else within any of our territories to make any other device in the form or likeness of that one without the author's consent or license, for the term of 10 years. But if anyone should act thus, the aforesaid author and inventor would be free to cite him before every office of this city, by which office the aforesaid infringer would be prepared to pay one hundred ducats and his artifice would be immediately destroyed. But our Government will be free, at its total pleasure, to take for its own use and needs any of the said devices or instruments on this condition, that others than the authors may not employ them.

Excerpted from "The English Patent as a Reward for Invention: The Importation of an Idea" by Jeremy Phillips, *Journal of Legal History*, 31, May 1982.

The ownership of ideas is an interesting concept. Asians (whose well-rooted culture goes back thousands of years), Canada's First Nations, the northern Inuit, and the Dene Nation, all with much older cultures than the West's, have difficulty understanding how Western cultures, established only for a few hundred years, can impose legal constraints on ideas. These older cultures initially put forward the position that surely the thoughts of man belong to all mankind. How can one man own an idea? Accordingly, with globalization's exponential growth in goods and services, Asian nations and others had difficulty accepting this Western view of ownership and tension became evident. Much has been written about the Chinese pirating of software, for example. Rightly or wrongly, most members of the world community are adopting the Western concept—ideas do not belong to all humankind. To enforce this notion, a number of legal steps have been taken

PRACTICAL ENTREPRENEURIAL FOCUS

38 Per Cent of Software Sold Last Year Pirated

More than a third of computer software sold in the world last year was counterfeit, with the highest rate of piracy in Latin America but the biggest losses to the industry in Europe, according to an industry-sponsored survey released Wednesday. The study, conducted by US-based market research firm IDC, found a global piracy rate of 36 per cent that cost the software industry $29 billion US ($38 billion CDN). The piracy rate was lowest—23 per cent—in North America, where losses were more than $7.2 billion ($9.5 billion). The losses were about the same, $7.5 billion ($9.9 billion), in the Asia-Pacific region, although the piracy rate there was more than double at 53 per cent, reflecting smaller sales.

In Latin America the piracy rate was 63 per cent, with losses of almost $1.3 billion ($1.7 billion), according to the survey. The Middle East and Africa had a piracy rate of 55 per cent with losses of nearly $900 million ($1,190 million). In the European Union, the rate was 37 per cent, costing software publishers more than 8 billion euros ($13.1 billion). The Business Software Alliance, the lobbying group that sponsored the survey, called on EU governments to quickly enact into national laws an EU directive, passed in March, to crack down on piracy. Under the bill, counterfeiters could face civil penalties, including seizure of property and bank accounts, if national courts find them guilty. Proposals for criminal sanctions were dropped from an earlier version.

The BSA also complained that less than half of the 25 EU countries have implemented a 2001 EU copyright directive, more than 18 months after the deadline. That attempt to harmonize protections across the continent tightened the definition of "private copy" and banned commercial use of copied material taken from the Internet. Beth Scott, a BSA vice-president, said a 10 per cent reduction in software piracy across Western and Eastern Europe could bring more than 250,000 new jobs and 19 billion euros ($31 billion) in tax revenues by 2006. "The costs reverberate up and down the supply and distribution chains," she said, adding that the addition of eight relatively poor but faster growing countries from Eastern Europe to the bloc this year made quick action even more necessary.

Source: "38 Per Cent of Software Sold Last Year Pirated" (Brussels, Belgium: Associated Press, 2004).

and international protocols established. See the Practical Entrepreneurial Focus box; improvements are being made.

Now, the Chinese regularly, with much media coverage, prosecute pirates. In 2003, 1 million pirated software discs, DVDs, and VCDs were destroyed by Beijing's police. According to the latest incomplete statistics, China deployed 67,908 personnel from the local copyrights administrations offices and reportedly suppressed some 3.6 million discs during September to November 2003.[45]

China reports that between 1995 and 2002, government officials smashed 197 million pieces of pirated products and China's courts heard 18,600 infringement cases.[46]

Management Implications

- With the success of globalization, more and more SME managers are interested in targeting foreign markets. Due diligence is essential to ensure business success in the international arena. This requires understanding of the political risks and the ability to make a dispassionate assessment of the political environment. During the last thirty years, political risk assessments have become an expanding business. Analysis must include an in-depth look at a country's political system and ideologies; political stability; foreign investment climate; profit remittances and exchange controls; taxation; expropriation; political party attitudes toward foreign investors; and labour conditions.
- Economic factors are as important. Managers have to perform a thorough economic analysis of real income; competitive and complementary products, barriers to trade, demographic factors, demand function, input–output analysis, and other statistics and data. Today, more than ever, managers need to develop an awareness and appreciation for the different economic systems they will encounter internationally. In order to determine the economic system of a country, they have to be able to identify the answers to questions such as, What goods and services are produced? How are goods and services produced? Who produces the goods and services? Who

consumes the goods and services produced? SME practitioners must understand the differences between market and command economies. Is there private ownership and free competition in the targeted market? Does the "invisible hand" of Adam Smith drive individual businesses to serve the best interests of society by providing the goods and services demanded by the people? Is the economy driven by state ownership and control, along with central planning and production? The correct identification of the economic system of the targeted country makes all the difference in the world. As history has proved, the pure command economy just does not work.

- In addition, business managers must understand the law. Canadian law finds the genesis for its constitutional law in the English Magna Carta Charter (1215) and the English Bill of Rights (1689). SMEs intending to internationalize have to be aware of the varying rights they are likely to encounter in host countries. Can they commence action against the state? Are the rights different between genders? Can they raise funds by pledging assets in the host country? Are there restrictions on foreign ownership? Can they buy land? It is critical that SMEs conduct an analysis of the political risk, economic indicators, and legal systems, so they can determine, with some degree of certainty, the business environment of their foreign target market.

CHAPTER SUMMARY

- Any discussion of political systems requires an understanding of the political ideology terminology to include communism, capitalism, socialism, conservative, liberal, and libertarianism.
- One of the major risks faced by businesses is political risk, both anticipated and unanticipated. Government actions cannot be forecast; thus, it is absolutely critical that the managers of SMEs constantly scan and assess the eco-system within which their firm is operating. Actions of governments may take the form of changes in economic variables such as tax rates and output prices. These actions may have the greatest influence on the corporate bottom line and they certainly affect corporate profitability.
- Political systems describe the structures, processes, and control mechanisms that support and sustain a nation's political ideologies. They are differentiated by their political philosophy regarding the relationship between the collective and the individual and by their political philosophy regarding the degree to which they are democratic or totalitarian.
- Economic systems determine the process surrounding, and the control over, the factors of production—land, capital, and labour. There are three broad classifications: command, mixed, and market economies. Command economies are characterized by (1) state ownership and control and (2) central planning of production. Market economies are defined by (1) private ownership and the freedom to buy and sell, (2) free competition, (3) prices set by the forces of supply and demand, (4) consumer sovereignty and (5) being profit-driven. Generally,

mixed economies will have areas that are public (most similar to a command economy) and areas that are private (closest in principle to the command economy). In reality, every economy of the world is some form of a mixed economy. Important economic indicators that we must consider when analyzing a targeted foreign market include gross national product, gross national income, gross domestic product, purchasing power parity, human development index, distribution of income, private consumption expenditures, personal ownership of goods, union labour costs, foreign direct investment, exchange rates, inflation rates and interest rates. Many of these metrics are covered in subsequent chapters.

- Legal systems within the host country require careful examination and analysis for an international business venture to be successful. Internationally, businesses are likely to encounter three different kinds of legal systems: common law, civil law, and theocratic law. Most legal systems distinguish between different types of property. In common law, property is divided into (1) real property, such as land and items considered fixed or attached to the land and (2) personal property, which includes ownership of all other things such as supporting ownership rights over intellectual property through (1) patents, (2) copyrights, and (3) trademarks. Trade disputes between nations (public international law) and between individuals (private international law) are resolved by adjudicating institutions sanctioned by some of the world's nations.

REVIEW QUESTIONS

1. Discuss the different dimensions of political systems and provide examples.
2. Discuss the four classifications of totalitarian states.
3. List a number of political risk variables you would examine in preparing your market-entry strategy.
4. Discuss the three kinds of economic systems. Is a mixed economy more desirable than the other economic systems? Why or why not? Use evidence to support your answer.

5. Reflecting on the advantages of a command economy, what impact would this economic system have on your SME?
6. Discuss the three kinds of civilian legal systems and, using examples, outline the possible business implications of each.

REFLECTIVE THINKING QUESTIONS

1. Having completed this chapter, reread the quotations on the first page, critically reflect on the validity of the authors' statements, and provide your opinion as to the validity of each. Evidence-based answers are preferred to rhetorical answers.
2. In economic affairs, Smith's *The Wealth of Nations* (1776) popularized the "invisible hand," the idea that an individual who "intends only his own gain, is, as it were, led by an invisible hand to promote . . . the public interest."[47] Do you believe we can rely upon business and the invisible guiding hand to act in our best interests?
3. A nation can employ a state-controlled strategy by implementing subsidies, price controls, wage controls, taxes, property rights, and other regulations or legislation. In times of inflation, would you as a SME owner support a government-controlled wage and inflation policy? Support your position.
4. Should Canadians be concerned that the use of the Islamic theocratic law arbitration process is the beginning of a separate political and legal identity for Muslims in Canada? Why or why not?

5. Recall the observation of Professor Vijay Mahajan from the Wharton School of Business, eighty-six percent of the world's population lives in countries with an average GDP of less than $10,000, the cutoff for developed countries. If we remove the two most populated nations, United States and Japan (total 330 million), the population of the balance of developed world is a mere 6 percent of the global population (6.5 billion). Developing populations are growing rapidly while developed world populations are, by and large, shrinking. The developed world has to wake up and see this 86 percent opportunity. "You have no choice but to deal with the 86% world."[48] This is a powerful observation and clearly a new mental model for Canadian business. Do you think this is a valid observation? What political, economic, and legal advantages does Canada have over some other developing countries?
6. In the light of former Canadian negotiator Gordon Ritchie's comments, should we continue our economic dependency with the United States or should we divest? Provide your reasoning.

GLOBAL E-RESEARCH

Visit www.power.nelson.com for research suggestions, questions, and a number of background discussion papers on this topic.

MINI CASE

Emerging Legal Threat

One of the most important threats to the well-being of Canadians and others in the virtual global community is the electronic collection, use, sharing, and storage of personal information by the public and private sectors. The convergence and seamless interface between the world's databases is a matter of grave concern to all citizens. The Orwellian danger to our individual privacy is not yet fully plumbed. The U.S. Patriot Act is but one example. Canada

and the United States have moved quickly to harmonize their national security systems; any impediment to this merger directly affects efficient border crossings in support of our trade and commerce. But this is a double-edged sword. The exchange of personal information also affects our national sovereignty and Canadian identity. We must be diligent to ensure efficient border crossings take place but that information is retained in "watertight compartments" and not used for other purposes. The pervasiveness of the "net" between organizations is the issue. The Canadian Federal Privacy Act allows for personal information to be transferred outside Canada, even without the consent of the individual the information pertains to.

"Beginning in stages since 2001, the Personal Information Protection and Electronic Documents Act (PIPEDA) has regulated the handling of personal information in the private sector across the country. Several provinces have enacted similar privacy standards. PIPEDA brings Canada law into line with privacy standards for personal information developed by the European Union, and means that our standards for the protection of personal information, when used by a commercial organization, are among the most stringent in the world. PIPEDA establishes a progressive framework, based on the highest international standards, against which to assess personal information management practices of the public and private sectors in Canada. It provides a framework for benchmarking best practices and encourages organizations that collect and process personal information to emulate those practices."[49]

It will require significantly more aggressive action by our governments to prevent the hemorrhaging of our rights to privacy in the coming decade. Visit www.power.nelson.com for further readings.

MINI CASE QUESTIONS

1. Do you believe this might be one of the most important political and legal issues you will face in the next 20 years? Explain.
2. Have you experienced organizations collecting data about you that they did not need to know? What action did you take? Do you feel the bargaining positions are equal, in that if you don't provide the information they refuse to give you service?
3. Are you concerned about Canadian citizens' data being provided to other nation's databanks? An example might be the requirement for American companies doing business in Canada to file reports under the U.S. Patriot Act.

ENDNOTES

1 King James Bible, Mark 12:17.
2 Brainy Quote (2005), retrieved August 9, 2006, from www.brainyquote.com.
3 John F. Kennedy, *Latin American Aid: H.R. 6518 Public Law 88206*, approved December 17, 1963, retrieved August 16, 2006, from www.jfklibrary.org/Historical+Resources/Archives/Reference+Desk/jfk_leg_record3.html.htm.
4 *Brainy Quote.*
5 US Embassy Lisbon, US Department of State, *The Benjamin Franklin Tercentenary: 1706–2006* (2006), retrieved August 9, 2006, from www.american-embassy.pt/BenFranklin.html.
6 William Cran, *Commanding Heights: The Battle for the World Economy* (Heights Productions, 2003), retrieved August 9, 2006, from www.pbs.org/wgbh/commandingheights/lo/index.html.
7 David Boaz, *Classic and Contemporary Writings from Lao-Tzu to Milton Friedman: The Libertarian Reader*, ed. David Boaz (New York: The Free Press, Simon and Schuster, 1998).
8 "The Americas: Adios to the Greenback; Cuba's Currency."
9 Brainy Quote.
10 Brainy Quote.
11 Adam Smith, *The Wealth of Nations* (New York: Modern Library, 1937).
12 Ibid.
13 Smith, *The Wealth of Nations.*
14 John Stuart Mill, *On Liberty* (London: Longman's, 1865).
15 Department of Justice, "Government of Canada Introduces Anti-Terrorism Act," (Canada Newsroom, 2001).
16 Brainy Quote.
17 Gary M. Grobman, *Nazi Fascism and the Modern Totalitarian State* (1990), retrieved August 9, 2006, from www.remember.org/guide/Facts.root.nazi.html.
18 Angie Knox, *Profile: Kimjong-il* (2000), retrieved August 9, 2006, from http://news.bbc.co.uk/1/hi/world/asia-pacific/783967.stm.
19 Ibid.
20 Ibid.
21 Ibid.
22 Paul J. Weber, "Theocracy," in *Encyclopedia of Politics and Religion*, ed. Robert Wuthnow (Washington, D.C.: CQ Press, 1998).
23 Ibid.
24 Weber, "Theocracy."
25 Grobman, *Nazi Fascism and the Modern Totalitarian State.*
26 Government of Canada, *1975-Anti-Inflation Act: Controlling Wages and Prices in Peacetime* (1975), retrieved August 9, 2006, from http://canadianeconomy.gc.ca/english/economy/1975economic.html.
27 Answers.com, *Incomes Policy* (Columbia University Press, 2006), retrieved August 9, 2006, from www.answers.com/topic/incomes-policy.
28 Columbia University, CIESIN, retrieved August 19, 2006, from www.ciesin.columbia.edu/IC/wbank/methods/mcgnp.html.
29 Robert E. Gunther, "Fellows India Master Class" (Wharton School of Business, July 2005).
30 Gurcharan Das, "Fellows India Master Class" (paper presented at the Fellows India Master Class, India, July 2005).
31 "Big Mac Index" *The Economist* (December 16, 2004), retrieved August 9, 2006, from www.economist.com/markets/bigmac/displayStory.cfm?story_id=3503641.
32 Ibid.
33 Amartya Sen, *Development as Freedom* (New York: Anchor Books, 1999).
34 Mark McNeilly, *Sun Tzu and the Art of Business: Six Strategic Principles for Managers* (New York: Oxford University Press, 1996).
35 Colin Farrell, *World Corporal Punishment Research* (April 1, 1994), retrieved August 9, 2006, from www.corpun.com/sgju9404.htm.

36 Ibid.

37 Hernando De Soto, *The Mystery of Capital: Why Capitalism Triumphs in the West and Fails Everywhere Else* (New York: Basic Books, 2000).

38 Ibid.

39 Ibid.

40 Ibid.

41 Ibid.

42 Gordon Ritchie, *Who's Afraid of NAFTA's Bite?* (February 15, 2005), retrieved August 9, 2006, from www.bclumbertrade .com/_images/GlobeMailOpEd.pdf.

43 Ibid.

44 Ibid.

45 "Million CDs Smashed in Campaign," *China Daily* (December 20, 2003).

46 Ibid.

47 Smith, *The Wealth of Nations*.

48 Gunther, "Fellows India Master Class."

49 Jennifer Stoddart, "Transferring Personal Information About Canadians across Borders—Implications of the USA Patriot Act," (Office of the Privacy Commissioner of Canada, 2004).

International Business Environment—Technology

"There is no New Economy. It's the same old economy with new technology."[1]

—Jack Welch, General Electric

"Airplanes are interesting toys but of no military value."[2]

—Marshall Ferdinand Foch, Professor of Strategy, Ecole Superieure de Guerre

"If it keeps up, man will atrophy all his limbs but the push-button finger."[3]

—Frank Lloyd Wright

"It has become appallingly obvious that our technology has exceeded our humanity."[4]

—Albert Einstein

"In a few hundred years, when the history of our time will be written from a long-term perspective, it is likely that the most important event historians will see is not technology, not the Internet, not e-commerce. It is an unprecedented change in the human condition. For the first time—literally—substantial and rapidly growing numbers of people have choices. For the first time, they will have to manage themselves. And society is totally unprepared for it."[5]

—Peter F. Drucker

LEARNING OUTCOMES

- Evaluate the impact of selected emerging technology on Canada's SMEs.
- Examine some of the leading technology advances transforming global commerce.
- Formulate an opinion as to Canada's global competitiveness in exploiting current technology.
- Evaluate the impact of convergence marketing driven by technology advances.
- Understand e-business customers' market segmentation.
- Examine technology infrastructure initiatives and assess if Canada could do more.
- Develop an awareness of taxation and personal privacy issues resulting for the exponential growth in technology.
- Judge Canada's environmental efforts to mitigate damage precipitated by selective emerging technologies.

Canadian Call Centres Are Calling

Photos.com

Americans applying for credit from the USA clothing giant Neiman-Marcus will be most likely speaking to a Canadian working as a service representative in an Albertan call centre. New low-cost telecom technology is creating a major new service industry in Canada. These white-collar jobs are migrating in large numbers from America to newly established Canadian centers. "The term 'call centre' is an umbrella descriptor for a wide range of services including travel reservations, technical support for customer service, customer contact centres, order entry, customer acquisition and retention capabilities, emergency response, online sales and market research, lead capture, account queries, direct response, customer support, comment lines, and multiple other solutions tailored to the needs of the US customers." Worldwide, call centres

are estimated to be a $50 billion industry, and growing 30 percent per annum. They are closely integrated with the growth of the $700 billion e-commerce industry. The fledgling health care call centres currently manage more than 100 million phone calls per year.

"A recent Economic Development Corporation publication forecast 800 new call centres would be established in Canada by 2008. This represents a significant increase from the current 450 centres operating today. Large American firms have established their call centre support north of the 49th parallel. They include Ford Credit, Dell Computer, Lehman Brothers, Neiman-Marcus, eBay, IBM, and AmeriCredit—a Texas-based consumer finance company in Ontario. This trend will continue. A Deloitte research survey of 100 of the world's largest financial services

companies indicates call centres operations, valued at $356 billion and representing about 2 million jobs, will move by 2008."

Why Canada? American companies, in order to be sustainable in an ever-increasing competitive global economy, must cut costs. They need suppliers who can deliver a similar level of service at a cheaper rate. As a supplier, Canada does this in spades. "Canadian call centres provide quality service at lower costs; however, the most significant advantages are the similar culture, common language, political and economic stability, lower employee turnover rates, lower payroll taxes, and a well-educated workforce. According to a 2004 KPMG study, *Competitive Alternative*, Canada's business costs are the lowest of the G-7 countries—from 5 to 20 percent lower than those offering similar services in the United States." *Site Selection Canada* reported that "in the 18 months ending September 30, 2003, more than 37,495 customer service representative positions were created and a further 118 customer contact centres were established across Canada, with about 98 percent coming from U.S.–based customers." In 2003, a typical U.S. firm, JP Morgan, opened a 1 million sq. ft. facility in Surrey, British Columbia. The press reported that the Surrey centre's opening signalled the end of 1,000 J.P. Morgan call centre positions in America.

"So are we creating fertile soil for this wonderful opportunity to take hold? No. We can do and must do much more to compete with the strength of our growing list of competitors—Mexico, India, Malaysia, and the Philippines. These countries have lower labour costs and are actively adjusting their economic climate to attract this expanding industry . . . [Do] we have the right financial and tax-incentive programs to attract companies to Canada? We did this for the movie industry with great success. Are we investing in the technology and infrastructure needed to support this industry? Our competitors are . . . . [The bottom line is that] in an era of rapid globalization jobs, like water, will flow where there is the least resistance and the greatest opportunity to 'pool' in the best global location."

Adapted from Terrance Power, "Call Centre Outsourcing Is an Opportunity," *The Business Edge*, March 31, 2005, and Teri-Sue Buchanan, "Call Centres: Ringing in Profits," *ExportWise* (Winter 2005).

A SUN TZU MOMENT. . .

Visual Arts Library, London/Alamy

"What is of the greatest importance in war is extraordinary speed; one cannot afford to neglect opportunity."[6]

It is not necessary to throw in the towel just because your global competitors have more and better technology. Speed and the correct application of the emerging technology you do have available can be a key success factor to allow your SME to exploit emerging global opportunities before the more technically advanced competition. Few know that in 1940 the French army, hiding behind the security of the Maginot Line, possessed better tanks and in greater numbers than the Germans. Yet the Germans won the battle. Why? Because unlike the French, who employed the tank by widely disbursing their armour in support of the foot soldier (and therefore proceeded only at the speed of the slowest foot soldier), the Germans exploited the new technology. The French found themselves no match for the German Blitzkrieg (lighting war). The German infantry were motorized, thereby enabling the new technology (tanks) to concentrate, outflank, and exploit their core competencies. Like water, they flowed quickly around the obstacles. In a global ecosystem, it is helpful to think of your business as water, and we will return to this notion frequently in the text. In this chapter you will be introduced to emerging technology. Think reflectively on the German experience and how you might be able to exploit the emerging technological advantages.

Opening Thoughts

In the proceeding chapters we briefly examined political, legal, economic, societal, and cultural attributes in a global ecosystem. Although there are a number of other attributes we could consider, the last one that we will look at in this text, and in my opinion the most important, is the transformational changes domestic and foreign businesses experience as a direct result of technological advances. As mentioned in Chapter 2, page 37, the acronym **PEST-C**—political (law), economic, societal, technological, and cultural—is helpful to remember these major attributes that must be thoroughly understood and analyzed in order to succeed in the international marketplace.

PEST-C is a common acronym for political (law), economic, societal, technological, and cultural (attributes that must be thoroughly understood and analyzed in order to succeed in the international marketplace).

The opening vignette illustrates how Canada's global call centre success was made possible by innovative low-cost technology. "Datamonitor estimates that the United States will lose about 3,000 call centres and some 133,000 agent positions by 2008, with a good portion of the contracts being outsourced to Canada." "The Canadian Customer Contact Centre Council Executive Director Elizabeth Thorn estimates that four out of every 100 employed Canadians work in this industry. Thorn believes call centers will be the workplace of the future, with projected growth of more than 7 per cent by 2008." This "will result in seven out of every 100 jobs in Canada by 2008"[7] being found in this industry.

Canada has been fast off the mark in harnessing many of the new technological breakthroughs during the past few decades. The call centre article demonstrates our ability to leverage our national advantages. Increasingly, developing countries are supporting their domestic firms by providing "fertile ground" to enable their fledging call centres to take root. Specifically, these countries provide favourable taxes, an educated labour force, and the latest technological infrastructure to support the industry. There are areas where Canada maintains the pole position (the most favoured position in horse racing—a good place to start from when the gate opens) such as in satellite technology and other communication initiatives. Canada has also been successful in carving out a niche in nanotechnology, and we are exploring medicine for the 21st century made possible by systems biology. (Systems biology seeks a holistic understanding of the complex interaction of DNA, RNA, protein, and cell elements and how these all function in a biological system integrated by computer. We will examine this technology and the business opportunities presented later in the chapter.) Many other nations also recognize the importance of technology to their economic well-being. The European Commission, for example, is promoting digital access to Europe's heritage. At least 6 million books, documents, and other cultural works will be available to anyone with a Web connection through the European Digital Library by 2011. Global competition in many aspects of the technology industry is intense and in some areas we are experiencing fierce competition from developing nations like India who daily encroach on our market share (see the Mini Case, Canada's SMEs Can Do Better, pages 118–119). In this chapter we explore some emerging technological advances that impact on SMEs in global commerce such as e-commerce's convergence marketing, cell phone and telecomm convergence, the exponential growth in the adoption of wide broadband, and selected environmental concerns arising from emerging technology success.

The danger for Canada, as a global middle-class income nation, was provided by Geoffrey Garrett who warned, "Both friends and foes of globalization overlook one of its critical effects: although it has served rich countries well and poor ones even better, globalization has left middle-income countries [Canada] struggling to find a niche in world markets. Because these countries cannot compete in either the knowledge or the low-wage economy, without help, they will fall by the wayside."[8] Canada has little choice but to maintain cutting-edge global technological prowess (a major part of a knowledge-based economy) or fall by the wayside as we are not a low-wage economy. Canadian SMEs must proactively seek these emerging opportunities, and adopt new emerging business technologies faster and smarter than the competition. Have you explored the possibility of VoIP, digital media, broadband, WiFi, WiMax, WiBro, IM, and 3G technologies? Indeed, how many SMEs have even heard the terms? Your global competitors have. Yes, we can leverage technology to enhance our national competitive advantage, we cannot ignore emerging business technologies—we must maintain currency.

The transformation is not just to be found in business technology. Technology permeates and is deeply embedded in our lives. For example, it has transformed the entertainment industry. Satellite television and radio give consumers more choices. Video game technology has come a long way from the 1980s' little yellow Pac-Man gobbling dots on a computer screen; today it is a $10 billion–a-year industry that produces realistic games that include escapes to fantasy worlds, sports, and even wars. The insatiable demand for bigger screens with more features to enable tailoring of programs or video games is met by technological improvements. Advancements continue to be made to our television and movie screens with plasma TV, HDTV, and IMAX; all reinforcing the family cocooning trend observed by Faith Popcorn in her bestseller, *The Popcorn Report.*[9] Popcorn's recent predictions include a number of emerging trends that are driven by technology. First, "*Big Mother*—Forget Big Brother, technology creates a new generation of super-observant moms. Consider her tools: classroom cams, RFID tags in backpacks, GPS chips in watches . . . or even embedded in kids' bodies. When children are never out of sight, a whole new mother–child emotional dynamic will result. A part of that: kids strike back. Call it the 'Mom Unplugged' syndrome. *Persona Propaganda*—Google has created the concept of the 'Public Resume'—a new kind of pervasive, email-able DigiTruth. Now that everybody can know everything about almost anyone, an industry will soon evolve to help you manage that public persona, creating the perfect online profile, optimizing your own Google search, giving us control over our digitized public identities. *Cocooning*— We are seeing clear evidence of our Cocooning and Anchoring Trends as of late as people are more and more feeling the need for security and safety in today's chaotic world, and are returning to the comforts of home. This migration back to the home is playing out in many areas, perhaps most notably in its impact on an activity like family dinner. *Identity Terrorism*—The most extreme from of 'Persona Propaganda', in which the Internet is used as a tool to malign a reputation, either of an individual or a corporation. This new kind of terrorism is bound to be an increasing problem in the years to come. *Profiling Paranoia*—As our personal choices become part of the digital ether (iPod playlists, TiVo configurations, Amazon choices) we will become increasingly worried about how this data can be used. The upside: Economical technology could match us to exciting content, information, even people. The downside: a new digital Gestapo could dictate all the content you see. *Porn as the Norm*—In a culture where, increasingly, anything is acceptable, pornography has become the sole source of titillation. Expect to see it emerge in more platforms, including on our cell phones. Wireless porn is projected to be one of the biggest mobile data applications. *The Idoling of America*—Pop-democratization, spearheaded by Zagat, made most visible with the vote-by-text-message phenomenon of *American Idol*, will soon spread throughout the culture to an unprecedented level. We foresee even personal decisions (should I have another child? should I marry this woman?) being put to vote by millions of Americans. *Mystic Messages*—Fundamentalism is booming. 49% of Americans call themselves 'Born Again,' and young people are very much a part of this explosion. We predict that major marketers will finally recognize this, and will develop products and services targeting this market. Jesus Barbie? Coca-Cola with religious messages on their cans?"[10] How can Canadian SMEs use the knowledge of these trends to shape their business?

Transformational changes can be seen in the explosive application of technology to study the genetic makeup of many organisms, advances in biotech, and DNA testing. These are not just for business applications. International security concerns, border initiatives, and the increasing incidence of identity theft and identity fraud have highlighted the need to strengthen the integrity of Canadian identity, immigration, citizenship, and travel documents. Biometric technology has emerged as a powerful and controversial tool that could potentially help address these public policy challenges. Transformational changes are also very much in evidence in the auto industry's use of alternative fuel for transportation, robotics in the manufacture of automobiles, fibre optics, smart bombs, lasers, and the Hubble telescope. In every field of endeavour, exponentially transformational changes are underway because of technology. The impact is incomprehensible, but we must do our best to bring critical thinking to emerging technology and its impact on business. We have shifted our marketing perspective from mass marketing developed by Henry Ford a century ago to a market segment of one. This transformational shift in marketing is possible because of technology.

The following McKinsey and Co. analysis cited in *BusinessWeek*[11] omits Canada as a major contender for cross-border IT services. Why do you think this is? Where would you place Canada on this matrix?

Remember, every business model decays. Never has the case been stronger for owners of Canadian SMEs to examine new technological advances and imagine how they could be exploited to provide a sustainable benefit to their firm. Internet technology has the potential to significantly shorten distribution channels in all industries. Reflect for a moment on the business or industry that you currently work in or hope to work in. What answer do you get to the "form and substance" question we discussed in Chapter 1, on page 10? Be a futurist. What innovative steps could you take to shorten the distribution channel? Or what new mental model could you introduce to the industry?

Technological advances drive a huge revolution where only the swift and innovative will be in a position to exploit technology and harness the power of the Web-dense global matrix of connections between people, ideas, and resources and survive. To borrow from Adolph Huxley, this is the "brave new world" of economic evolution—and the revolution will be permanent. Remember, SMEs don't fail because they failed to predict the impact of the PEST-C attributes; however, they will fail because they fail to imagine the unimaginable. "The future has already happened . . . it is just unequally distributed."[12] Imagine how this emerging technology will shape your business, but before you do, a closing caveat: "do not be a one-eyed prophet who sees only what new technology can do and are incapable of imagining what they will undo."[13] See the "Just Say No to e-Waste" box on page 114.

North and South Korea—Two Technological Solitudes

Canada's Hugh McLennan referenced the tension between Canada's English and French founding nations as "two solitudes" in his 1945 bestseller of the same name. The notion might also be used to described North and South Korea. Grounded in a common culture, and until recently the same history, one would expect to find very similar business environments in these two nations. Canada and the United States, for example, with the same British and European roots, illustrate the common business environment one might reasonably expect of two nations with similar history. However, the significantly different ecosystem attributes (PEST-C) have resulted in two very different nations. The very different political ideologies of North and South Korea have produced dramatically different business environments.

North and South Korea demonstrate the outcomes of nations willing and able to exploit technology and the outcome of nations that fall short. North Korea, a totalitarian regime led by its Chairman Kim Jong-il, is a country that presets all stations on televisions and radios to government frequencies prior to sale. As a result, North Korean citizens are not readily able to participate, in even the smallest way, in the democratization resulting from access to the World Wide Web. This Orwellian regime's dire economic results are well known. Chairman Kim Jong-il might consider Dakota tribal wisdom that suggests that if you find you are riding a dead horse, the best strategy is to dismount! In stark contrast is South Korea. With mobile phones in hand, South Koreans have become one of the most wired countries in the world. In 1960, South Korea had only one telephone for every 300 people (about one-tenth the world average at that time). By 2005, over 90 percent of South Korean households had a fixed-line phone, three times more than the global average. In addition, over three-quarters of the population, from young children to the elderly, carry mobile phones. South Korea has one of the highest Internet penetration rates in the world with more than 31 million of the 48.5 million people having daily access to the Web. Government fully supports technology and provides certification of the Internet speed available for every building, including residences, by posting the information on the outside of the buildings. In 2005, the South Korean government licensed the three main telecom firms (S.K. Telecom, KT, and Hanaro) to offer new high-speed wireless Internet service called WiBro. This new wireless Internet service allows mobile users to surf the Internet at very high speeds with enhanced reliability. South Korea's Ministry of Information and

Junko Kimura/Getty Images

Cell phones are used as debit cards in South Korea. Instead of handing over credit or debit cards that get swiped, users type their pass code on the phone keypad, point the device at a special receiver on a checkout counter and press a key. It's as simple as operating a TV remote.

SOURCE: Alberto Escarlate, *Cellphones Used as Debit Cards in South Korea* (October 12, 2003), retrieved August 9, 2006, from www.cacheop.com/archives/2003/10/cellphones_used.html.

Communication claims WiBro works even in a car travelling at 60 km/hr. The Ministry forecasts over 9 million people will subscribe to this new service within six years.

Consider these innovative outcomes as a result of South Korea's national strategy to support and exploit Internet. South Koreans will be able to watch high-quality video on their mobile phones, which will include built-in personal video recorders. They will be able to read radio frequency identification tags that will replace barcodes on goods, thereby obtaining further efficiencies and benefits that we will discuss in Chapter 14, pages 392–394. South Koreans will be able to check the expiry date of produce and then purchase the items using their mobile phones as debit cards. South Koreans currently have mobile handsets with the ability to send e-mail in the same way as a BlackBerry. However, they dislike the accompanying spam. As a result, e-mail is considered old-fashioned; increasingly, South Koreans send instant messaging (IM) text, requiring a more immediate response and providing certainty that the message had been delivered instantaneously. New Samsung mobile phones use voice recognition to convert speech to text, thereby enabling longer messages to be quickly crafted and ease of use for those of us blessed with large hands! Included in the mobile phones' new features will be the ability to instantaneously access menus in restaurants, pay electronically for the meal, and receive a receipt—all through a mobile phone. South Koreans' mobile phones are already configured for some basic e-commerce activities such as downloading music and making purchases in shops. In South Korea, it is forecast that in the very near future consumers will require only their mobile phone because it will have become a wallet—it will contain everything. (See the box—Will That Be Cash, Fingerprint, or Cell Phone?)

Will That Be Cash, Fingerprint, or Cell Phone?

"Imagine throwing away your wallet. No need to carry credit cards or cash. No need to haul around cards for the ATM, video store, gas station, or frequent-flier program. It would all be replaced by just your fingerprint. Or perhaps your cell phone. Or a round piece of plastic the size of a quarter. It would be the most fundamental change in personal finance since the introduction of the credit card in 1950. And it's not science fiction. Visa and MasterCard are aggressively testing devices and services that head in that direction. . . . 'We want to get people to think of payment apart from a piece of plastic card,' says Tolan Steele, vice president at Visa USA. John Gage, chief scientist for Sun [Microsystems] adds, 'Credit cards are just a physical variant of identity, so any way you can identify someone can be a way to pay for things.'

"Consumers in test markets around the world are already signing up to use some of these technologies. Within a year, the technologies that emerge as winners will be offered more widely. Within five years, they're expected to have a major effect on the way people use and think about money [form versus substance]. That will reverberate through society and business. A fingerprint system could let a mother and teenage daughter share a credit card account, but the system would know by the fingerprint which person is using it. That way, the daughter couldn't charge a case of beer, and the mom could set spending limits. When travelling, a cell phone–based system could let you store your itinerary; boarding passes, and identification inside your phone, changing the way passengers check in for flights and go through security. And one goal is to get people to use these new technologies for the kinds of small purchases that usually require cash. That has many implications, from helping lines at Starbucks move faster to helping tax collectors trace transactions.

The new ways of paying fall into three basic categories: radio frequency identification tags (RFID), gadgets, and biometrics." Visit www.power.nelson.com for a further discussion of these categories.

"Why bother with any of this? Credit cards have been good enough for more than 50 years. In fact, the new technologies promise benefits for every piece of the credit card puzzle. For issuers of credit cards, the new systems are expected to ultimately be far more secure, making it harder to steal information. That could save issuers billions of dollars a year that now are lost to fraud. For retailers, the new systems can speed up transactions.

Stores such as Gap or Starbucks would have more success issuing their own credit or stored value cards—consumers often don't sign up for such cards because they don't want more cards in their wallets. But if [an Old Navy clothing credit card] were virtual—through a fingertip or cell phone—an extra card would be just another item on an electronic menu. And consumers would likely get new ways to make purchases that are faster, easier to carry, more secure, and more flexible. Forces are lining up to push electronic wallets into the mainstream. 'The whole idea of money is about to be expanded,' Sun's Gage says."

Adapted from Kevin Maney, "Will That Be Cash, Fingerprint or Cell Phone?" *USA Today*, (November 16, 2003).

E-Commerce

Most agree with the South Koreans that the mobile phone with its expanding capabilities is the technological electronic tool of choice. The seamless integration of the mobile phone with every aspect of business is here. The day of the early adapter in accessing and using the World Wide Web has long passed. Today businesses recognize the need to participate in global **e-commerce**. E-commerce transactions are classified as business-to-business (B2B), business-to-customer (B2C) and customer-to-customer (C2C). Currently, the most successful of these classifications is the B2B market. **Business models** continue to be adjusted to reflect the reality of e-business convergence.

The business model specifies where the firm will be positioned in the distribution channel. Generally the **business paradigm**, reduced to its essence, is quite simple. A firm produces a good or service and sells it to customers with the expectation that the revenues from sales will exceed the cost of operation, resulting in a profit. Business models are a refinement of this basic paradigm. Internet commerce continues to spawn innovative business models, generally building on the old models. For example, one of the oldest forms of brokering, auctions, has been widely used. The Internet has popularized the auction model and broadened its applicability—the sale and purchase of goods and services. The online auction eBay comes to mind as a new mental model. New and interesting business model variations will continue to evolve. Some broad clarification of business models include brokerage, subscription, advertising, merchant, manufacturer (direct), affiliate, infomediary, community, and utility. Visit www.power.nelson.com for a discussion of these business models.

E-commerce, in many respects, has levelled the playing field between MNCs and SMEs. Using technology, Canadian SMEs have found a budget-priced way to compete with MNEs in presenting their goods and services to the global and domestic marketplaces. Figure 4.1 compares e-commerce activity by country, and Figure 4.2, on page 102, shows predicted B2C sales by world region.

Increasingly, a greater number of Canadians are using the Internet to shop. According to Statistics Canada, in September 2004, Canadian household spending on the Internet in 2003 grew 25 percent over 2002. Canadians spent $3 billion on everything from airplane tickets to goods on eBay. Stats Can estimates that 3.2 million Canadians bought something online in 2003, up from 2.4 million a year earlier.[14] Shopping in the global electronic cybermall is a reality.

E-commerce can be defined as the buying, selling, and distribution of goods and services over the Internet.

A **business model** is how a company sustains itself by generating revenue. It is a summary of how a company plans to serve its customers involving both strategy and implementation.

Reduced to its essence, the **business paradigm** is quite simple. A firm produces a good or service and sells it to customers with the expectation that the revenue from those sales will exceed the cost of operation, resulting in a profit.

Region	2000	2004
U.S.	46%	38%
Western Europe	20%	33%
Japan	21%	12%
Asia	5%	10%
Rest of World	7%	7%
Global total	$350.38 billion	$3.14 trillion

FIGURE 4.1
Where the e-Commerce Dollars Are, 2000–2004

NOTE: Amounts in US dollars.

SOURCE: "Where the E-Commerce Dollars Are, 2000–2004". Copyright © 2006 Verifone Inc. All rights are reserved.

FIGURE 4.2

Forrester Predictions for Global
Regional B2C Sales in 2004

World Region	Total ($Dollars)
United States	3.2 trillion
Asia-Pacific	1.6 trillion
Western Europe	1.5 trillion
Eastern Europe, MEA	68.8 million
Latin America	82 billion

NOTE: Amounts in US dollars.

SOURCE: *Marco Polo: The Cross-Cultural Marketing Edge* (prepared for Industry Canada, 1999). Courtesy of Shaben & Associates International Consulting.

While Canadians purchased $3 billion in goods and services in 2003, compared to $2.4 billion in 2002, it remains a small portion of the $688 billion in annual consumer spending. Three billion dollars represents about $956 per household. In addition, "a further 1.7 million households used the web to window-shop and/or conduct research prior to purchasing through conventional outlets."[15] See Figure 4.3 for Canadian online activities, from 2001 to 2003. Almost all automobile purchases today are made by consumers who first conduct their due diligence by researching the specifics of the automobile online first. This includes pricing comparison. No longer are auto dealerships able to conduct negotiations with the uninformed. Canadians are also increasingly purchasing goods online from both Canadian and foreign vendors. Stats Can reports that "newspapers, books, magazines, and other reading materials remained the most popular online purchases in 2003, bought by just under a third of e-commerce households. Travel ranked second on the shopping list: about 22 per cent arranged travel online. The percent of Canadian online shoppers who bought these most popular products or services in 2003: Books, magazines and newspapers 30%; Travel arrangements 22%; Clothing, jewellery and accessories 17%; Computer software 14%; Music (CDs, tapes, MP3) 11%; Consumer electronics 11%; Other entertainment, such as tickets 10%; Videos, DVDs 8%; Furniture and appliances 7%; Computer hardware 6%; Toys and games 6%; Sports equipment 6%; Health, beauty and vitamins 5%; and Hobbies 5%."[16] People aged 18 to 34 followed by those over age 55 make the most online purchases domestically. For every $10 spent by Canadian households on Internet purchases in 2003, $6.90 was spent within the country."[17] "Although more Canadians used their credit cards on the Internet to buy goods and services in 2003, three-quarters of them expressed concern about security. About one in five households—2.7 million—paid online for purchases, but 76 per cent of them said they worried about financial transactions on the web."[18] So does the law protect Canadians?

Canadians are protected by a number of acts and regulations in addition to those remedies available at common and civil law. First, "the Uniform Electronic Commerce Act (UECA) applies to all federally regulated industries. It served as a model for similar provincial legislation enacted everywhere in Canada except Nunavut and the Northwest Territories." The UECA confirms the validity of electronic documents, signatures and contracts. This means that contracts made online are just as binding as those paper contracts signed face to face. It requires sellers to disclose specific information to buyers. Under certain circumstances there are provisions in the Act for the reversal of credit card charges. The Act states that for online contracts, the "I agree" button is legally binding. Accordingly, once the buyer clicks "I agree," the contract is formed. Consumers must first

FIGURE 4.3

Percentage of Canadian Households
That Used Internet to Window-Shop
or Buy Goods and Services Online

	2001	2002	2003
Internet shopper (window-shopped or placed online orders)	33	37	40
Window-shopped only	14	14	14
Bought goods or services online	19	23	26
Paid online	15	19	22

SOURCE: "Electronic Commerce Households Spending in Canada and in Other Countries, by Region," Statistics Canada, February 18, 2005, www40.statcan.ca/l01/cst01/comm07a.htm. Copyright Public Works & Government Services Canada.

be allowed to review the terms of their contracts. If consumers make a mistake, they must be given an opportunity to prevent or correct the error. If this opportunity is not provided, then the contract is not binding.[19] Next time you make a purchase on eBay, note the opportunities that buyers are presented with to confirm the purchase or correct a mistake. They are well described! In addition to the provisions and protection provided by the UECA, the Personal Information Protection and Electronic Documents Act (PIPED) regulates the use of personal information collected in Internet transactions. PIPED has not gone as far as legislation in the United Kingdom that provides that financial information is never allowed to be merged with other personal information."[20] Unfortunately, there are no common international treaties concerning electronic contracts or transactions. This is a common thread through out this text; globalization is running ahead of the institutions, laws, and processes. Organizations such as the World Trade Organization are trying to craft and garner international support for universal law relating to electronic transactions. However, for now, disputes involving electronic transactions are governed by the rule-of-origin approach in common-law countries. For example, if an individual buys a book from an online business located in Britain, the laws where the business is headquartered prevail. This does not favour Canadian consumers, who must familiarize themselves with another country's laws and bring the application for a remedy within the foreign jurisdiction. This requirement adds significant costs to dispute resolution. However there is an exception you should be aware of: "If a person is located in Canada and the web server or computer is located outside Canada but uses Canadian Internet service providers, then the Canadian law applies. This landmark ruling is grounded in an Alberta Securities Commission (ASC) decision. The ASC asserted jurisdiction over the World Stock Exchange, an offshore online stock site that had contravened Alberta's securities laws. The Commission reasoned that although the website was outside the country, the effects were felt in Alberta."[21]

The law cannot keep up with the innovative illegal practices of those using the World Wide Web to scam us. "First online crooks went 'phishing,' and now they're getting into 'pharming' to reap their harvest of potential identity-theft victims. Pharming is a new scam that automatically directs computer users from a legitimate web site to a fraudulent copy of that site without any warning signs. The fraudulent site collects passwords, credit card numbers, or other private information for potential misuse and abuse. Security experts say such attacks are rare so far (April 2005) but could grow in the coming months in much the same way phishing scams have exploded."[22] The courts are increasingly aware of the damage crooks and unsolicited bulk e-mail distribution can cause. In April 2005, "a Virginia judge sentenced a spammer to nine years in prison . . . in the United States' first felony prosecution for sending junk e-mail. A jury had recommended the nine-year prison term after convicting Jeremy Jaynes of pumping out at least 10 million e-mails a day with the help of 16 high-speed lines, the kind of Internet capacity a 1,000-employee company would need."[23] Jaynes has appealed.

Another area of concern is the law relating to Internet intellectual property rights (IPR). In Chapter 3, pages 88–89, we noted that, increasingly, a firm's ownership of copyright, patents, trademarks, industrial design, confidential information, and trade secrets is challenged as a direct result of global technology. As science and technology rapidly develop worldwide, and the pace of economic globalization accelerates, the status of the intellectual property system in economic and social life has reached an historic high. The protection of IPR has drawn wide attention from international and local communities. For example, Canadian cable companies and others are concerned about the growing use of their signals without payment—an infringement of copyright law. We can copy music, television programs, movies, newspaper articles, and books effortlessly using technology. Canada funds IPR training programs to strengthen enforcement and patent examination, recognizing that a vibrant IPR regime is critical to the promotion of a creative, technologically advanced economy.

In a global world, who owns the Internet? Who sets the policies? Who controls the domain names and IP addresses? In 1998, Internet Corporation for Assigned Names and Numbers (ICANN, pronounced "I can") was established. It is a California-based nonprofit corporation created to oversee a number of Internet-related tasks previously performed directly on behalf of the U.S. Government by other organizations. Among other things, the Internet Non-Profit Corporation manages the assignment of domain names and IP addresses. "Some of ICANN's critics would like to see it internationalize itself, meaning that it would be reconstituted as some kind of public sector entity under international law and would cancel its contractual links to the U.S. Government and the U.S. Department of Commerce, which are historical in origin. Currently, there are 15 voting members of the ICANN Board of Directors, from six continents, and it has only two U.S. Directors. Proponents like Canada want the United States to maintain the authority it holds via the contract between ICANN and Commerce. This authority stems from the historical role of the United States in creating the Internet."[24] As you can imagine, the United States leadership is being questioned in favour of an international governing body.

The National Business Environment in Technology

Canada has undertaken a number of national business initiatives to nurture the technology industry. They include the establishment of technology parks, assistance programs for science and technology research, the Canadian Space Agency, Canadian Technology Network, and Federal Partners in Technology Transfer program. A **technology park** can be defined as "a property-based development that has a high-quality physical environment in a park-like setting; is located adjacent to or at a reasonable distance from a research institute or university; and emphasizes activities promoting growth of research, technology and knowledge-based enterprise."[25] Briefly, a technology park is not only a renter of space but also takes care of tenants' business needs. "The concept itself arose in the US in the 1950s, though there are schools of thought that believe the timeline begins with the founding of Hewlett-Packard in 1939 by a bunch of Stanford University graduates in Palo Alto. In India, this is a more recent phenomenon, coinciding with the boom in the IT services sector in the early 1990s. Things have changed recently, though—with bandwidth no longer an issue, other key factors are coming into play."[26] It is a global phenomenon. In India the "Northern states are waking up to the IT wave that has swept across states down southern and western India, there are a lot of initiatives underway promoting the setting up of integrated tech parks."[27] In Taiwan the science parks are part of a network of industrial parks set up over the years to provide a supportive environment for the manufacturing industry. They cater primarily to export-based companies. Government incentives are usually available for potential tenants: favourable loan conditions, tax breaks, reduced charges on utilities, favourable rentals, pre-existing factory and waste management facilities, etc. . . . The government has encouraged life science companies to locate in the island's science parks that have been designed especially to attract high-technology industries.[28] For a complete list of Canadian technology parks by province and some of the specific services they offer; links to federal and provincial financial and funding assistance programs; venture capital opportunities; and tax credit incentive programs for the science and technology community (S&T), visit www.power.nelson.com. There are also links to information products and other tools and resources.

The Canadian Space Agency (CSA) was established in March 1989 and is a member of the Industry Portfolio, a group of 12 federal departments and agencies that promote the government's goal of building a knowledge-based economy in all regions of Canada and advance the government's jobs and growth agenda. The mandate of the CSA is to promote the peaceful use and development of space, to advance the knowledge of space through science, and to ensure that space science and technology provide social and economic benefits for Canadians. Visit www.power.nelson.com for information on RADARSAT, to locate the current position of the International Space Station, or to read about the Canadian Astronaut Program. These programs drive advances in technology and enter into contracts with Canadian high-tech firms. IMP Corporation in Halifax and MacDonald, Dettwiler & Associates (MDA) of Vancouver

A **technology park** is a property-based development that has a high-quality physical environment in a park-like setting; is located adjacent to or at a reasonable distance from a research institute or university; and emphasizes activities promoting growth of research, technology, and knowledge-based enterprise.

are two such companies. MDA was under contract to the Canadian Space Agency as the prime contractor for The RADARSAT-2 project in 2003.

The Canadian Technology Network (CTN) links federal and provincial/territorial government laboratories and agencies, universities, community colleges, industry associations, technology centres, and economic development agencies. Collectively these organizations provide Canadian businesses with access to expertise, advice, and information about how to meet technology and related businesses challenges. Visit www.power .nelson.com for a list of specialized advisers from across Canada who provide free guidance to Canadian businesses. The Council of Science and Technology Advisors (CSTA) was established in 1998 in response to the government's science and technology strategy, *Science and Technology for the New Century*. The CSTA comprises representatives from academia, industry, and not-for-profit organizations. These representatives collaborate to provide strategic advice to the Government of Canada on the management of its internal science and technology. Visit www.power.nelson.com for more specifics on CSTA.

Finally, the Federal Partners in Technology Transfer (FPTT) initiative aims to establish common approaches, practices, and policies to effectively transfer research and technologies from government laboratories to the private sector. See www.power.nelson.com for information on training programs, a list of federal laboratories, success stories, resources, business opportunities, news and events, and information on the benefits of FPTT, as well as information on how to join.

Here are some interesting highlights related to Canada's efforts to support technology in the national business environment:

- Canada has a strong scientific research base with an international reputation in fields such as genomics, proteomics, bioinformatics, immuno-therapies, protein engineering, and new drug delivery systems.[29]
- Canada has the fastest rate of growth among the G-7 nations in the number of workers devoted to R&D, in external patent applications, and in business expenditures on R&D.[30]
- Nearly half of Canada's biotech employment is in skill-intensive positions requiring scientific research and technical expertise.[31]
- From 1999 to 2001, the number of existing and pending patents for Canadian biotech firms increased from 26 to 39 percent.[32]
- Investment in R&D by Canadian biotech firms totalled $1.3 billion in 2001—an increase of more than 60 percent over R&D expenditures in 1999.[33]
- Canada boasts a health sciences research community of over 30,000 investigators in 16 Canadian universities. They are affiliated with a network of more than 100 teaching hospitals, research institutes, and universities.[34]
- Canada has the world's best-educated workforce.[35]
- Canada has over 1,000 types of grants, as well as small business loans, R&D programs, export development, and medical research. SMEs must lever these support programs to their advantage these programs can make a significant contribution to the firm's bottom line.[36]

Worldwide Internet Users Top 1 Billion in 2005

An examination of Figure 4.4, on page 106, reveals the top 15 countries in broadband usage. The gap—the "digital divide"—is of increasing concern as it contributes directly to the disparity between the have and have-not countries. As well, note that South Korea is ranked 4th globally, whereas North Korea, which is not ranked, has a command economy that stifles entrepreneurship and innovation, as discussed in Chapter 3, page 76. In 2000, the entire continent of Africa had only 1.5 million Internet users. The digital divide between the underdeveloped world and the rest continues to grow. The worldwide number of Internet users topped 1 billion in mid-2005. There is little Internet user growth in the developed countries, but in the next five years many Internet users will be supplementing PC Internet usage with smartphone and mobile device Internet usage. (smartphone is a generic name for voice-centric mobile phones with information capability. Smartphones combine the functions of a cellular phone and handheld computer in a single device.) Internet usage is

FIGURE 4.4

Top 15 Countries in Broadband
Subscribers

Year-end 2005		
Broadband Subscribers (millions)		*Share %*
1. USA	46.9	21.6
2. China	35.9	16.5
3. Japan	26.4	12.2
4. South Korea	13.1	6.04
5. France	9.6	4.42
6. Germany	9.5	4.40
7. UK	8.9	4.35
8. Canada	**6.7**	**4.09**
9. Italy	6.6	3.05
10. Spain	4.6	2.12
11. Netherlands	4.4	2.00
12. Taiwan	4.3	1.97
13. Brazil	3.0	1.39
14. Australia	2.6	1.21
15. Belgium	2.1	0.97
Top 15 Countries	184.6	86.31
Worldwide Total	217.2	100

NOTE: Totals amended by author.

SOURCE: "Worldwide Broadband Subscribers Will Top 215m in 2005," *Computer Industry Almanac* (November 14, 2005). Copyright Computer Industry Almanac, Inc.

growing strongly in China, which surpassed Japan for second place in 2003. The growth of Internet users will continue in the developing countries for another decade.

It is anticipated that "Internet user growth will come from populous countries such as China, India, Brazil, Russia and Indonesia. . . . New Internet users will come from cell phone and smartphone Internet usage in developing countries."[37] Canada continues to maintain the lowest costs of any nation for Internet access (see Figure 4.5).[38] What difference will this adoption of this new technology by populated developing nations have on your business ventures? Will English continue to be the language of business? Consider Figure 4.6.

FIGURE 4.5

Access Prices and Internet Hosts

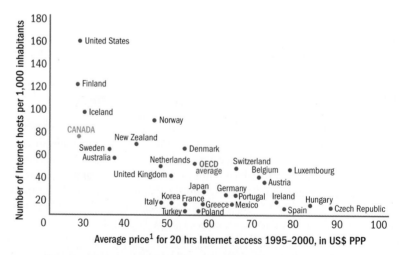

[1]Internet access costs include VAT and cover both peak and off-peak

NOTE: Data on hosts for Luxembourg is from mid-1999. Internet access costs include VAT.

SOURCE: OECD (www.oecd.org/dsti/sti/it/cm) and Telcordia Technologies (www.netsizer.com).

FIGURE 4.6
Top Ten Languages Used on the Web

(Number of Internet Users by Language)

Top Ten Languages in the Internet	Internet Users, by Language	Language as % of all Internet Users	World Population 2006 Estimate for Language	Internet Penetration by Language	Internet Growth for Language (2000–2005)
English	311,241,881	30.6%	1,125,664,397	27.6%	126.9%
Chinese	132,301,513	13.0%	1,340,767,863	9.9%	309.6%
Japanese	86,300,000	8.5%	128,389,000	67.2%	83.3%
Spanish	63,971,898	6.3%	392,053,192	16.3%	163.8%
German	56,853,162	5.6%	95,982,043	59.2%	106.0%
French	40,974,005	4.0%	381,193,149	10.7%	235.9%
Korean	33,900,000	3.3%	73,945,860	45.8%	78.0%
Portuguese	32,372,000	3.2%	230,846,275	14.0%	327.3%
Italian	28,870,000	2.8%	59,115,261	48.8%	118.7%
Russian	23,700,000	2.3%	143,682,757	16.5%	664.5%
TOP TEN LANGUAGES	810,484,459	79.6%	3,971,639,798	20.4%	150.5%
Rest of World Languages	207,572,930	20.4%	2,528,057,262	8.2%	453.9%
WORLD TOTAL	1,018,057,389	100.0%	6,499,697,060	15.7%	182.0%

SOURCE: "Internet Users by Language," *Internet World Stats* (December 31, 2005), retrieved August 9, 2006, from www.internetworldstats.com/stats7.htm.

Young Canadians Less Active Online Than Adults

Video 4.1

Canadian teens spend almost one-third (27.8 percent) less time online than their adult counterparts, with their Internet behaviour largely confined to social activities, according to a survey conducted by Ipsos-Reid Corporation. The online survey polled 1,226 teenagers between the ages of 12 and 17 in Canada, asking them to respond to a number of questions regarding their online behaviour. The survey found that the average teen spends approximately 13 hours online per week, compared to the 18 hours the average adult spends online. The report also found that Canadian teens use the Internet primarily for its social capabilities. Based on a list of 18 online activities, sending and receiving e-mail (73 percent do so a few times per week) and using instant messaging (70 percent) led all other categories by a large margin among respondents. Approximately 28 percent play games online versus friends, while 23 percent play games online against strangers.

Apart from those social online activities, Canadian teens appear to engage in other online activities far less than adults. Only 17 percent of teenagers reported having ever purchased something online, versus 50 percent of the adult online population. Other activities that more than half of adults engage in online also attract less teen interest. Few teens (9 percent) comparison-shop online; click online advertising (6 percent); or bank online (2 percent). Some of this lack of interest may simply be due to a lack of credit cards or bank accounts. The social nature of most teenage use of the Internet raises some concerns about safety. About 14 percent of teens reported that they had been asked at least once to meet in person with someone they originally met online. That number increases to 20 percent among respondents between ages 15 and 17.

Source: Rob McGann, *Young Canadians Less Active Online Than Adults* (December 7, 2004) retrieved August 9, 2006, from www.clickz.com/stats/sectors/demographics/article.php/3443981.

Demographics—Technology Types

The Retail Council of Canada has classified Canada's demographics into five types. The results are shown in Figure 4.7 on page 107. The technology types by gender are shown in Figure 4.8 on page 107. People considered technology-free comprise one-quarter of the

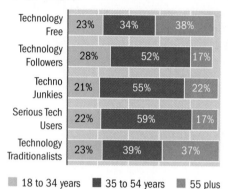

FIGURE 4.7

Technology Profile of Canadians, by Age Category

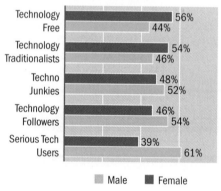

- ☐ 18 to 34 years ■ 35 to 54 years ▨ 55 plus

SOURCE: Retail Council of Canada and Industry Canada, *Glossary of Technology Types* (Industry Canada, 2005).

FIGURE 4.8

Gender Demographics of Canadians, by Technology Type

Technology Free — 56% / 44%
Technology Traditionalists — 54% / 46%
Techno Junkies — 48% / 52%
Technology Followers — 46% / 54%
Serious Tech Users — 39% / 61%

- ☐ Male ■ Female

SOURCE: Retail Council of Canada and Industry Canada, *Glossary of Technology Types* (Industry Canada, 2005).

Internet connectivity can be defined as the existence, availability, and affordability of the communication infrastructure.

population. These Canadians lag in technology adoption and typically have just the very basics in traditional technologies, such as telephone and cable. Technology-free consumers tend to be older and have lower household incomes; a solid proportion of this segment live in Quebec. Technology traditionalists comprise nearly one-quarter of the population and are similar to technology-free consumers in that they adopt just the very basics in available technologies—such as telephone and cable. Technology traditionalists however, tend to make greater use of these traditional technologies, including greater use of long distance calling and larger cable packages. The average consumer in this segment is older, with an average age of 49, and lives in a smaller household. Nearly 20 percent of Canadian consumers are technology followers. While they typically do not have the gamut of available technologies, they go beyond the telephone and cable services, and, adopt emerging technologies after they have been proven in the marketplace. Compared to the national average, technology followers are more likely to operate a home-based business. This segment also tends to be highly educated, with 43 percent having completed a university or college education, and 12 percent having completed a postgraduate education. Just less than one quarter of Canadians are techno junkies. They are driven to have the latest technologies, and adopt technologies as they emerge, including local, long distance, multiple phone lines, wireless, smart-touch services, Internet, satellite, and digital TV. These consumers tend to be located mainly in Ontario, are well educated, and have an average age of 45. Techno junkies live in large households, typically have annual household incomes of at least $40,000, and are more likely to have children 13 to 19 years old compared to the average Canadian household. Serious tech users make up the smallest percentage of Canadian consumers, comprising 11 percent of the population. Nearly half (47 percent) of these consumers are located in Ontario. Serious tech users are likely to adopt a broad range of technologies including local, long distance, multiple phone lines, wireless, Internet, satellite, and digital TV. They are also the heaviest users of technology and differ from techno junkies because tech users acquire the technology for a need. Not surprisingly, serious tech users tend to be male and affluent, with 36 percent earning over $80,000 annually, compared to 17 percent nationally.[39] See Figure 4.9 for an overview of Canadian online activities.

Compared to other nations, how prepared is Canada to exploit e-commerce? Canada, according to the *Economist* e-Readiness Survey, places 11th in the world (see Figure 4.10). The *Economist* measures a number of factors in order to arrive at this rating. It includes **Internet connectivity**, cost, online security, and privacy protection. It is clear Canada must do more to build supporting technological e-commerce infrastructure in order not to fall behind our global competitors.

FIGURE 4.9

Activities Online—Canadians with Internet Access

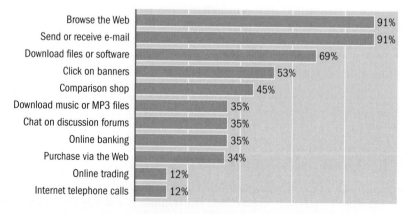

Browse the Web — 91%
Send or receive e-mail — 91%
Download files or software — 69%
Click on banners — 53%
Comparison shop — 45%
Download music or MP3 files — 35%
Chat on discussion forums — 35%
Online banking — 35%
Purchase via the Web — 34%
Online trading — 12%
Internet telephone calls — 12%

SOURCE: Retail Council of Canada and Industry Canada, *Glossary of Technology Types* (Industry Canada, 2005).

2004 E-readiness Ranking (of 64)	2003 Ranking	Country	2004 E-readiness Score (of 10)[a]	2003 Score
1	2	Denmark	8.28	8.45
2	3 (tie)	UK	8.27	8.43
3	1	Sweden	8.25	8.67
4	7	Norway	8.11	8.28
5	6	Finland	8.08	8.38
6	3 (tie)	US	8.04	8.43
7	12	Singapore	8.02	8.18
8	3 (tie)	Netherlands	8.00	8.43
9	10 (tie)	Hong Kong	7.97	8.20
10	8	Switzerland	7.96	8.26
11	**10 (tie)**	**Canada**	**7.92**	**8.20**
12	9	Australia	7.88	8.25
13	13	Germany	7.83	8.15
14	16	South Korea	7.73	7.80
15	14	Austria	7.68	8.09

FIGURE 4.10

Economist Intelligence Unit E-readiness Rankings, 2004

SOURCE: Economist Intelligence Unit and IBM Institute for Business Value, *The 2004 E-Readiness Rankings* (The Economist Group, 2004).

Nanotechnology

What is nanotechnology? The Greek prefix *nano* means one-billionth. In **nanotechnology**, this one-billionth relates to measurement. One nanometre equals one-billionth of a metre, where 75,000 nanometres measure the thickness of a human hair, and 1,000,000 nanometres match the width of a dime. Nanotechnology aims to create new materials from nano-sized resources. "Such atomic resources allow specific magnetic, thermal, and strength properties to be designed into any product. This enhances product strength, durability, and effectiveness since developers hold unprecedented flexibility when manufacturing one atom at a time. This process will lead to everything from cures of molecular diseases to a revolution in computing power."[40]

The traditional leaders in the game of technological development, the United States, Canada, and Western Europe, are for the first time being challenged by Japan, South Korea, and China. No one will be able to do research in all nanotechnology areas, and so all countries, including Canada, must find productive niches. "Canada has the people, the expertise, the international goodwill and respect, and the resources to take the global lead to establish the scientific foundation to understand and control the interactions of nano-materials in the environment and living organisms. This could be one of several areas in which this country could lead in the area of nanotechnology."[41] "Edmonton's biotech community is part of the larger nanotechnology cluster that's been developing for the past 20 years, thanks to the University of Alberta's strength in nanotech, engineering, medicine and computer science. Nanotechnology, a relatively new area of research, is the science of engineering devices at the molecular level. Applications of nanotechnology range from automotive sensors and land mine detectors to therapeutics and pharmaceuticals, where so-called nanorobots could be programmed to seek and destroy cancer cells. In 2001, the $120-million National Institute for Nanotechnology was established at the University of Alberta to further cement Edmonton's reputation as the place for nanotech research."[42] Nanotechnology will lead to everything from cures of molecular diseases to a revolution in computing power. The market is estimated to be 1.3 trillion euros by 2015.

Like other past disruptive technologies, such as electricity, the automobile, and the personal computer, nanotechnology has the potential to eliminate entire industries. During the Milken Institute Global Conference in April 2005, F. Mark Modzelewski, co-founder and managing director of Lux Research Inc., observed that nanotechnology will revolutionize virtually every industry, as well as impact everything from the way we live to how long we live. Think of it as the new industrial revolution. Modzelewski said

Nanotechnology aims to create new materials from nano-sized resources. The Greek prefix *nano* means one-billionth, which in nanotechnology relates to measurement. One nanometre equals one-billionth of a metre, where 75,000 nanometres measure the thickness of a human hair, and 1,000,000 nanometres is the width of a dime.

nanotechnology, just by enabling manufacturers to both put things together without waste and control the entire manufacturing process, is already very promising. Any Canadian SME that feels "blindsided" by this technology is simply not paying attention.

Quantum Computing Applications

Another transformational technology is quantum computing. Quantum computing adopts quantum physics concepts that enable exploitation of certain quantum physics properties of atoms or nuclei that transforms them to become quantum bits, or qubits, in the computer's processor and memory. Qubits can undertake computer calculation functions many times faster that conventional computer hardware. "The area of quantum computing applications has the potential to surpass the Internet and Industrial revolutions combined, in its impact on humanity. The world 25 years from now could very well be unrecognizable due to quantum computing. This is relevant as humanity is just entering 'another' world order versus a 'new' world order."[43]

"Currently, quantum computers and quantum information technology remain in the pioneering stage. . . . The knowledge needed to thrust quantum computers to their rightful position as the fastest computational machines in existence. Error correction has made promising progress to date, nearing a point now where we may have the tools required to build a computer robust enough to adequately withstand the effects of decoherence. Decoherence is the general term for the consequences of irreversible quantum entanglement. Generically, it describes a disturbance (change of state) *of the environment by the system.* Quantum hardware, on the other hand, remains an emerging field, but the work done thus far suggests that it will only be a matter time before we have devices large enough to test [quantum] . . . algorithms. Thereby, quantum computers will emerge as the superior computational devices at the very least, and perhaps one day, make today's modern computer obsolete. Quantum computation has its origins in highly specialized fields of theoretical physics, but its future undoubtedly lies in the profound effect it will have on the lives of all mankind."[44]

Systems Biology—Transforming Medicine

In the next few years, medicine will look different than it does today. Instead of following the traditional protocol of visiting your doctor's office and providing a blood sample for the physician to send to a lab for a dozen or so tests, you will be able to use a handheld nanotechnology device to take a thousand measurements from a single drop of blood. These measurements will be communicated, using your cell phone, to the laboratory server for analysis. You will receive the results within a few days attached to an e-mail that might say something like, "You are OK; complete the test again in six months." This will be routine in the era of systems biology.

Driven by the Human Genome Project (1990–2003), systems biology is now possible. **Systems biology** is the study of biological systems as a whole. Rather than analyzing individual components of systems such as genes and proteins, systems biology analyzes the entire system, and the various types of biological information (DNA and its genes and proteins) to reveal how biological systems work. Biological systems analysts are moving quickly to understand the role of DNA and its genes, the source code of life. Each of the 30,000 human genes encodes a specific protein. By seamlessly interfacing science and technology, we are now able to identify the probability of an individual developing a disease and, having done so, suggest the appropriate treatment to prevent its occurrence. For example, if you have a single copy of a mutant breast cancer gene, you have a 70 percent chance of developing breast cancer by the time you are 60 years old. But if you take preventive drugs commencing at 35, the chance of developing breast cancer drops to 5 percent. If men have a combination of certain defective genes, they have a 40 percent chance of getting prostate gland cancer by the age of 50 and an 80 percent chance of developing cardiovascular disease by 65. By undergoing a preventive regime, a similarly favourable outcome can be expected. Every six months, a person will be able to use a nanotechnology tool to take a thousand different

Systems biology is the study of biological systems as a whole rather than a collection of the individual components. It is a holistic approach to analyzing the entire system including all types of biological information (DNA and its genes and proteins) to reveal how biological systems work.

measurements to serve as a window into his own health status. This is a 21st-century science that will enable us to predict which diseases we might develop. It will result in extending the average lifespan by 20 years. See www.systemsbiology.org for more information on this emerging medical technology and its implications for Canadian demographics and business.

Convergence Marketing

We live in an age of marketing convergence—where traditional methods and new technology come together to enhance business effectiveness. Consumers, armed with more information, are consequently more demanding; they want to participate in the process of purchasing goods and services. A business that relies on the traditional **4Ps of marketing** (product, price, place, promotion), will have difficulty surviving in an increasingly competitive marketplace. A great deal of a firm's resources and energies are consumed in critically thinking about the 4Ps; however, in order to maintain a competitive advantage with the advent of Web-based digital technology, firms today must bring fresh new thinking. Businesses must combine traditional push/pull marketing models by harnessing the power of technology; use technology to understand their customers like never before; identify the needs and wants of their customers and cater to them in order to increase value; integrate traditional promotion with their IT technology; and develop a seamless distribution channel that incorporates technology. Convergence marketing adds value to your bottom line.

The traditional **4Ps of marketing** are product, price, place, and promotion.

Today, most customers will use the Internet to research their purchase options, and demand a change in service and product based on their research. By adapting convergence marketing, you can respond quickly to accommodate these new demands. Implementing an interactive approach to connect your business with your customer so that you can mutually exchange information before the sale will result in a new relationship with your customer. This relationship will become a critical part of your customer relationship management strategy.

Some examples might be helpful. Have you considered offering your product components in new individual-targeted combinations? Consider a furniture company that allows customers to purchase products after selecting the design, colour, and fabric separately. This personalization permits the customer to purchase exactly the product he wants. Your business can offer this service through your website by permitting customers to make selections and visually construct their desired furniture product before purchase. Today a number of large, Web-based catalogue companies, using the power of technology, let consumers try on clothes using a computer-generated model that closely resembles their own body shape.

Always be aware that the Internet enables the consumer to readily compare prices contacting a supplier. If you are operating in an industry where comparison-shopping is likely, it is important to provide your product information to potential customers online. Be aware of competitors' pricing and differentiate your product in some way that sets you apart while specifically addressing the needs of your target market. Ensure that your online pricing is consistent with your offline prices. A further caveat is the importance of the online site to be cross-culturally sensitive and internationally friendly.

Digital technology will continue to transform the traditional models of advertising and promotion that limited the consumer to viewing or reading promotional materials, calling or writing for information, or visiting the store. Technology is now emerging where it is possible for all these functions to be integrated in an immediate and ongoing dialogue between buyers and sellers. The new technology will enable us, while viewing our favourite television program, to take the cursor provided by the remote control and click on various products appearing in the picture on the TV screen. Do you like the clothes the actors are wearing? Pull down promotional information for review or purchase.

However, the exponential growth in convergence marketing technology results in the innovative and new quickly becoming outdated. The standard static banner that was splashed across web pages during the dot-com revolution is no longer considered an innovative promotional tool. We need to seek new mental models.

You will find that in the digital age the customer expects increased speed and convenience. She must be able to call, click, or visit your business, and quickly receive her goods or services. Increasingly in the international marketplace this is becoming a 24/7 activity. For digital products and services, it is fairly straightforward because the product can be downloaded and built entirely online. But physical products are more complex. The digital component is still present, but how do you get the product or service to your customer? To do this you must develop a seamless, integrated, just-in-time network. Amazon's supply chain management relationship with FedEx provides a good model for benchmarking. Reflective thinking about the strategic concept, convergence marketing, must be undertaken by business practitioners . . . because your competitor has done so!

Taxation Is a Growing Issue

Taxation is becoming a greater problem because of e-business. How does the government collect taxes on downloadable products? How does the government collect taxes on products you purchase in Canada on Canada's eBay site? "E-commerce gets more of the headlines, probably because it's recognized as such an important new feature of the global economy. It does beg fundamental questions about the way our taxation systems work—whether it's taxation of company profits or taxation of private consumption. The technology that makes e-commerce what it is puts more of a spotlight on the possible challenges to effective taxation—just how do you tax a cyber-business, or all those sales over the Net? E-commerce makes international trade in particular so much easier, and so the debate about taxation moves up the international level, too."[45] Canada's governments also engage e-commerce technologies to improve taxpayer service by offering electronic filing, electronic transfer of payments, and Internet access to tax-related information.

The potential speed, untraceability, and anonymity of electronic transactions may create tax avoidance and tax evasion. Consider Amazon.com; it started in 1995 and currently has customers in over 160 countries. E-commerce makes it easier for Amazon and others to complete transactions in an intangible manner; that is, without the need to physically provide the "good" to the customer, such as electronic transfer of digitalized books, or film developed and delivered electronically to the consumer. Taxation is not the only issue of concern; other issues are created by the Internet's borderless and intangible nature. The governing of online gambling and the distribution of materials harmful to minors are at the forefront of governments' concerns. In addition, consumer advocacy associations and others, with much justification, raise the need for enhanced consumer privacy laws.

Those arguing against e-commerce taxation put forward the notion that taxation is already at a sufficient level and further taxation by government is unsupportable; further, they argue that the additional charges incurred through shipping and handling costs added to the purchase price level the playing field with the local business market; and finally, because of the fledgling nature of this emerging business, it would be wrong to hinder its growth. What do you think?

A Global Technological Success Story

Like water—or like the motorized German infantry enabled by the new tank technology to concentrate, outflank, and exploit its core competencies— Canadian businesses must utilize technology to quickly flow around the obstacles and exploit opportunities. Read this success story and reflect on how you might apply emerging technology.

Planit Measuring

Forget about the old tape-measure method: A Mississauga, Ontario–based company called Planit Measuring has an updated version of the old measuring tape: a tablet PC equipped with a laser and computer-aided design software, which founder Mike Laurie calls the "measuring Board." It allows the company to come up with accurate floor plans and virtual tours. Planit was just recognized by the National Research Council as a Canadian Innovation Leader.

Source: Excerpted from Mathew Ingram, "Planit Measuring," *The Globe and Mail* (December 2, 2005).

INTERNATIONAL STRATEGIC THINKING

E-Commerce Best Practices: Ten Rules of the Road

Lauren Freedman president of E-Tailing Group provides these e-commerce "rules of the road"—key concepts that will help online merchants of all sizes navigate the challenges of Internet commerce.

"(1) The best technology doesn't make the sale. 'If someone has live chat but they have crummy products or bad prices, it's not going to make shoppers purchase.' . . . (2) The customer has more control than ever before. 'The consumer is incredibly demanding now,' Freedman said. 'They expect that anything's possible—they hit the submit button and expect that the FedEx guy is at the door. . . . Now, the Internet enables shoppers to be far more informed than the typical $7 an hour sales clerk—the uninformed sales associate is at the mercy of the educated e-shopper. . . . (3) Cross-channel selling is a killer app—if done right. Clearly, merchants who combine a bricks-and-mortar outlet with an e-commerce operation are positioned to move ahead of their competitors. Yet these two venues need to be fully integrated to truly romance customers. 'The customer demands a consistent experience from that merchant.' . . .

(4) Smart merchandising leverages the old rules. While the Internet introduces a blizzard of new techniques into merchandising, many of the timeless rules still apply. . . . 'The old rules still work because "what's hot" and "what's new" is still what shopping is all about.'" (5) The Web is the ultimate efficiency model for consumers. E-tailers need to make sure their e-business is set to compete for shoppers who are used to a highly efficient experience. (6) Be aware of e-commerce's limitations (and don't forget the catalogue). "There's still a huge role for touch and feel," Freedman notes. "The [bricks-and-mortar] store is not going to go away, contrary to what a lot of early venture capitalists tried to pretend would be the case." For those sites that don't have a bricks-and-mortar outlet, Freedman notes that catalogues allow touch, which can lend legitimacy to the business. The old-fashioned print catalogue, once thought to be on the verge of extinction, has proven to be an unbeatable sales driver in the online era. . . .

(7) Convenience and time saving often beat price—but the customer will pay only so much more. "People initially thought that price would be the only driver, but that's not true," Freedman said. Many online merchants make a tidy profit by tacking on a few bucks to a product that's delivered fast and hassle-free. We will be examining how marketers create value in the mind of the consumer in the section on value creation in Chapter 10, particularly in Figure 10.1, on page 282. (8) Personalization is in its infancy—but keep your eye on it. Early e-commerce futurists predicted that the Web would offer a one-to-one experience, yet we're still waiting for this. . . .

"When we surveyed merchants recently, they said, 'We are rudimentary when it comes to personalization,'" Freedman said. Some merchants are pushing the envelope—note Amazon's quasi-functional capability to offer items based on past visits—but they're the exception rather than the rule. So far, personalization has been lower on the radar screen. . . .

(9) "On-site search is the crux of most online activity and improving this function is clearly one of the hot topics in e-commerce today."

Canadian SMEs establishing an e-tailing component to their business would do well to remember these nine tenets.

Adapted from James Maguire, *E-Commerce Best Practices: Ten Rules of the Road* (January 11, 2005), from www.ecommerceguide.com.

Technology and the Environment— An Emerging Issue

"According to a recent GMIPoll [Global Market Insite Poll] survey of 20,000 consumers worldwide, the latest models of mobile phones are the most coveted in 20 of the world's top economies, including [Canada], the U.S., U.K., China, Russia, and India. When consumers were asked what technology they most frequently upgraded, 63 per cent cited mobile phones. . . . GMIPoll [notes that this finding highlights] how new consumer technology products are adding to a growing environmental problem of disposal of old technology being disposed. The firm notes that by 2005, 100 million mobiles will be thrown out annually in Europe alone. In the U.S., nearly 130 million cell phones, totaling about 65,000 tons of waste, will be thrown away every year . . . . Toxins associated with this waste include heavy metals and poisons such as arsenic, lead, and mercury."[46]

How did you dispose of your old computer? Would you be surprised to learn it may have made its way to a developing country for disposal? Read the "Just Doing the Right Thing" box.

Alberta has undertaken a similar initiative to address this emerging environmental issue by accepting computer donations and recycling in Edmonton. "The toxic time

JUST DOING THE RIGHT THING

Just Say No to e-Waste

Joe Fox / Alamy

Just say no to e-waste

"Most consumers are unaware of the toxic materials in the products they rely on for word processing, data management, and access to the Internet, as well as for electronic games. More than 1,000 materials, many of which are highly toxic, such as chlorinated and brominated substances, toxic gases, toxic metals, biologically active materials, acids, plastics and plastic additives are used in the production of computer hardware."[47]

According to Environment Canada seventy-one thousand tonnes of electronic products (TVs, computers, printers, cell phones, etc.) were discarded by Canadians in 2005. "They pose a serious risk to human health and the environment if inappropriately disposed of, land filled, or incinerated." Because managing e-waste is an expensive and dangerous process, "recyclers have turned to sheltered workshops for the developmentally disabled or prison labour rather than market labour."[48] Canada participated in the development of the Basel Convention on the Transboundary Movement of Hazardous Waste for Final Disposal and

was one of the original signatories on March 22, 1989.[49] "It was clear, however, that this was not enough to stop the transport of waste, which countries claimed was being exported for recycling purposes."[50]

In April 2000, China banned the import of certain electronic wastes including cathode ray tubes, copiers, telephones, and computers. On August 15, 2002, the government extended the list to more explicitly include such electronic wastes as printers circuit boards, keyboards and mice (data entry devices), printers, fax machines, etc. Here in North America, technology disposal is a major problem. Municipal incineration is the largest source of dioxins into the U.S. and Canadian environments and among the largest sources of heavy metal contamination of the atmosphere.

Are Canadians doing the right thing? Consider. Design: "A lot of the international attention on e-waste focuses on legislation when the answer could be in product design," explained Dr. Mitchell Eggers, Chief Pollster and COO of GMI. "There is an opportunity for marketers to tap into 'Generation Eco', the young green early adopters that are tech savvy and planet conscious. Marketers should explore designing responsible products that will retail at a premium."[51] Recycle: "Recycling programs, such as the Australian Mobile Telecommunications Association's pioneering partnership with Planet Ark, are role model examples of

excellent 'problem solution' marketing at work."[52] Organizations and individuals can now conveniently drop off their old computers at a participating location for donation or recycling. Consumers: Consumers should take environmental impact into account when upgrading new technology. In Canada only about 10 percent make this a consideration. "However, in other parts of the world, namely India and China, 20 and 26 percent respectively said environmental reasons could prohibit them from upgrading according to the GMIPoll."[53] Regulation: The British Columbia government is preparing an 'Extended Producer Responsibility' regulation for e-waste. The regulation is expected to become law by the spring of 2006,[54] ensuring brand owners will take full responsibility for their products' collection and management within an environmentally sound recycling program. This regulated responsibility puts the incentive squarely on manufacturers to design products that can be easily recycled. B.C.'s e-waste regulation is expected to follow the framework for other established product stewardship programs in B.C.: government-regulated, but producer-managed and –funded. The B.C. initiative was based on the European Union's regulations from five years earlier, requiring the reducing of e-waste from electronic products by making producers responsible for taking back their products. EU legislation requires producers to assume responsibility for their products at the end of their useful life (post-consumer stage). This is known as extended producer responsibility. Unfortunately, this concept has not taken hold in North America: "A pilot program that collected electronic scrap in San Jose, CA, estimated that it was 10 times cheaper to ship CRT monitors to China than it was to recycle them in the U.S."[55]

bomb of obsolete computers is being tackled by a new program—Electronic Recycling Association (E.R.A.), a non-profit organization. . . . . Managing director Bojan Paduh, a young entrepreneur from Calgary said: 'E-waste is the fastest-growing type of waste thrown out by corporations. A new PC is now obsolete in two years and millions of them end up on landfill waste sites each year. Every computer contains about four pounds of lead and small quantities of deadly cadmium and mercury. Other hazardous materials used in computers include hexavalent chromium, PVC plastic. All of these contribute to the poisonous cocktail of heavy metals found on landfills."[56]

Another major environmental problem created by technology—yet for many Canadians out of sight is out of mind—is space junk! The purity of space was broken on October 4, 1957, when the former Soviet Union launched Sputnik I, the first satellite to orbit the Earth. Sputnik was simple by today's standards, an aluminium sphere about the size of a basketball, weighing 183 pounds, with long antennae pointing to one side. It stayed in orbit for six months before falling back to Earth. That launch marked the beginning of the space age and of the space race between the United States and the U.S.S.R.[57] In January 1958, the United States followed with the launch of Explorer 1.[58] There are now approximately 700 operating satellites in near-Earth orbit, and this number is expected to grow to as many as 3,000 by 2020.

Also orbiting the Earth in this zone, 1,200 miles from the surface, are some 2,200 tons of orbital debris or space junk.[59] This includes spent rocket boosters, lens caps from cameras, parts of exploding separation bolts, even flecks of paint from the space shuttle. Spent or inoperative satellites are also considered space junk. The amount of orbital debris is growing every year, and the satellites launched each year add to the total. Obsolete satellites can explode or break up, and debris can strike other debris, generating thousands of smaller particles. Smaller particles cannot be tracked, however, and they often pose the greatest risk to spacecraft because they can't be seen and are travelling at very high speeds (about 7.5 km/second or 17,000 miles per hour!) At collision, the impact velocity is doubled or 34,000 miles per hour. Even a 1/4-inch nut at that speed can cause a lot of damage.[60] So far, more than 9,000 objects larger than about 4 inches have been catalogued. If the smaller but still lethal objects were included, the count could exceed 100,000.[61] "This debris silently zooms around the globe at speeds of up to 25,000 miles per hour with altitudes ranging from hundreds to thousands of miles."[62]

Another environmental issue driven by technology is global warming. Exponential growth fuelled by dirty energy has precipitated global warming to where it has reached the "tipping point,"[63] where change happens that may be irreversible. During the 1960s, many scientists identified emerging environmental issues leading to climate change and the potential for these to have serious impact if not addressed. Unfortunately, in the past 40 years, most nations have chosen to ignore the increasing cries for environmental sanity. Nevertheless, higher temperatures will result in stronger storms as evidenced by the increasing intensity and destructive power of recent hurricanes. Similarly, in 2004, Japan recorded its highest number of typhoons. There is mounting evidence of the economic losses generated by weather and flood catastrophes precipitated by changes in weather patterns. Without change, carbon dioxide levels in the atmosphere will quadruple and the associated 60 to 65 percent loss of soil moisture is expected to cause devastating erosion worldwide.

Of particular interest to Canada is the decreased number of frost days resulting in the development of vectors for infectious diseases. The transmission of diseases like malaria, West Nile virus, and avian flu, associated with climate changes, are now appearing in Canada. Global warming is of crisis proportion in Canada's north, and glaciers worldwide are disappearing at an alarming rate. Some glaciers in Latin America, Switzerland, China, Australia, South America, the Austrian Alps, Alaska, and northern Canada have nearly fully melted. By 2020, it is predicted that there will be no more snowfall on Mount Kilimanjaro. Greenland may disappear by the end of this century, which would result in a rise in sea level of 6 metres or 19.7 feet.[64] A rise of this magnitude would flood many coastal cities.

Currently the United States contributes more carbon emissions than the combined emissions of South America, Central America, China, the Middle East, and Indonesia, as reported by former Vice President Al Gore at the Milliken Institute Conference in 2005.

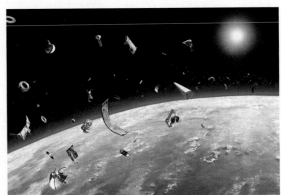

A few of the objects being tracked by USSPACECOM radar, including large pieces of orbital debris.

PRACTICAL ENTREPRENEURIAL FOCUS

What's All the Buzz about E-Biz?

Although an increasing number of Canadian businesses are using the Internet, many SMEs have not moved beyond basic services, such as e-mail and occasional web searches, to more sophisticated e-commerce applications that enable them to buy and sell over the Internet. Clearly e-commerce can boost productivity, cut costs, and expand sales internationally. Research indicates that Internet business is likely to account for a 40 percent increase in Canada productivity growth over the next 10 years. A study by the Canadian Federation of Independent Business concluded that Internet use will increasingly drive SMEs to do business outside Canada; every Canadian small business must explore and expand its cyberspace presence. "The range of e-business options is almost as vast as the medium: identifying new markets, promoting goods or services, creating a business website or increasing traffic to an existing site, ordering, buying and selling goods and services online, complementing customer relationships, and much more.

What are some of the factors to consider in crafting a business Internet strategy? First, identify what you want to accomplish. Do you want to lower costs of sales staff by providing information to clients electronically, or perhaps reach new markets by making your goods and services available for purchase online? Remember the "form versus substance" comments earlier. Your objectives should be specific, measurable, attainable, realistic, and time-dated (see Chapter 10). "Consider putting one aspect of your business online, and then build in ways to evaluate the desired result, whether it is generating more customer calls or lowering the cost of tracking your inventory." Second, companies that are already proficient in conducting business using e-mail and doing market research on the Internet are often ready to consider setting up a business website. A well-designed website should provide a clear image of the company; its history; its people, products, or services; and its location. Third, consider the firm's technological capabilities, including the condition of your computer hardware and the skills of your staff. Finally, consider your financial resources. There are various levels of fixed and variable costs associated with selecting an Internet service provider; registering a domain name; and designing, maintaining, and hosting your website.

Industry Canada offers an online technology diagnostic tool in its "Steps to Competitiveness" section at www.strategis.gc.ca.

For SMEs that seek to build business relationships with foreign firms or reach a wider consumer market, e-commerce simplifies access to company information and can increase the speed at which purchase orders or other transactions are completed. To ship internationally, you will have to understand international regulatory, financial, and logistical issues. For example, shipping outside Canada involves customs agents, duties, tariffs, and shipping fees. It also means you'll have to manage international payments, non-payment risk, and exchange-rate risk. (This text will introduce you to many of these concepts.) One of the best ways to familiarize yourself with your e-business options is to go online and visit competitors' sites. A little Internet searching will net big results in terms of information on everything from effective intelligence gathering to creating a website and making money through e-commerce.

Adapted from Suzanne Morris, "What's All the Buzz about E-Biz?" (Small Business Services, Export Development Canada, 2004).

Video 4.2

(Gore subsequently produced *An Inconvenient Truth*, a movie that included many of the conference materials.) Gore pointed out that the United States has lower emission standards than Japan, the EU, Australia, and Canada, and that it must do better. As Canadians and citizens of McLuhan's global village, we have a duty to protect our planet and ensure that it is passed to our children and grandchildren in better condition than we found it. We must learn to live off the "interest" of our ecosystem and not deplete its capital.

Management Implications

- SMEs must maintain awareness about the newest emerging technologies and their possible business applications. Applications are limited only by your imagination, so new mental models will be required. By understanding and applying the latest technology, you can increase your venture's efficiency. Be aware of the latest gadgets and consider which you should acquire to create a competitive edge and increase your bottom line.
- It is important to know about governments and their laws and regulations affecting e-commerce.

- You must also be aware of the international competitors in developing countries adopting new technology and "leap-frogging" over the current technology. They will make formidable competitors.
- Most importantly, you must recognize the new power of consumers. Adopting convergence marketing helps to accommodate these increasingly demanding customers. Customer relationship building is a key success factor for most businesses, and these relationships can be enhanced by the interactive nature of technology.
- The application of new technology to the organization's value chain can generate significant savings and increase efficiency thereby enabling the firm's flexibility and international reach.
- Technology, while providing great benefits, also presents many challenges. Challenges to our personal privacy and to our environment may well be the greatest threats in the next decade.

CHAPTER SUMMARY

- In this chapter we discussed the transformational changes that both domestic and foreign businesses experience as a direct result of technological developments.
- During the past few decades, while it continues to maintain a lead position in satellite technology and other communication initiatives, Canada has failed to exploit many of the new technological innovations. Governments of developing countries are specifically creating a favourable environment to encourage the establishment of call centres. Developing countries' favourable taxes, trained labour forces, and updated technological infrastructure are supporting their domestic firms.
- Canadian SMEs must use emerging business technologies faster and smarter than their competition. If they do not, their global competitors will.
- We have changed our marketing perspective from mass marketing, developed a century ago by Henry Ford, to "a market segment of one." This transformational shift was possible because of technology. Critical thinking is essential when considering emerging technology and its impact on how we do business. Every industry is experiencing transformational changes, and Canadian SMEs must examine new technological advances and exploit them.
- E-commerce enabled the SME to reach a broader segment of customers and levels the playing field between multinationals and SMEs. Using e-commerce technology, Canadian SMEs have found an economical way to conduct their business in both the global and domestic marketplaces.
- Today, more than ever, consumers have the resources and the power to become educated about global product and service offerings. As a consequence, customers are more demanding and sophisticated. Competitive Canadian businesses must understand how the traditional marketing models will be changed by technology.
- Increasingly, taxation of downloadable products is becoming an issue. While Canada is still reviewing the aspect of collecting taxes on products purchased in Canada from businesses such as Canada's eBay site, other jurisdictions are moving quickly to prevent the hemorrhaging of their taxation revenues. The European Union requires non–EU providers to register in one of the EU–15 nations and to pay taxes in that country for downloadable products. Once collected, the taxes are passed along to the country where the buyer is resident.

REVIEW QUESTIONS

1. How important is new technology to sustainable national competitive advantage for South Korea?
2. Research the definitions of VoIP, digital media, broadband, WiFi, WiMax, WiBro, IM, and 3G technologies?
3. What is e-commerce?
4. What impact does e-commerce have on a SME's distribution channels?
5. Classify your "technology type" and discuss the implications. Are you happy with this classification? If not, what can you do to change it?
6. What is nanotechnology? What are the implications of this new technology? Discuss.
7. What is convergence marketing? Explain how you could adopt this new marketing mental model to market a good or service of your choosing.

8. The "Global Technological Success Story" on p. 112 provided an example of a real firm exploiting technology. Identify three technical breakthroughs that Planit Measurements leveraged. Would this firm have been successful even if it had not adopted the new technology?

REFLECTIVE THINKING QUESTIONS

1. Having completed this chapter, reread the quotations on the first page, critically reflect on the validity of the authors' statements, and provide your opinion as to the validity of each. Evidence-based answers are preferred to rhetorical answers.

2. The article "*Will that Be Cash, Fingerprint, or Cell phone?*" on pages 100–101 provided an illustration of technological advances presenting threats that must be mitigated. Can you think of other examples of new technology that might be seen as a threat to privacy and the Canadian way of life?

3. In order to be sustainable in an ever-increasingly competitive global economy, American companies need Canadian suppliers and others who can deliver a similar level of goods and services at cheaper rates. As a service supplier, Canadian call centres provide quality service at lower costs to U.S. firms. Is this good for the Canadian economy? Is it bad for the United States? Change the countries. What happens if Canada outsources its service suppliers to developing countries in order to exploit location economies? Would your answer still be the same? How would such an action reflect on our economy? Does Canada have the right financial and tax incentive programs to compete with the strength of our growing list of competitors—Mexico, India, Malaysia, and the Philippines?

4. Do you think that Canadian SMEs demonstrate sufficient interest in utilizing some of the most advanced technology (i.e., VoIP, digital media, broadband, WiFi, WiMax, WiBro, IM, and 3G technology) when compared to developing countries such as South Korea?

5. What effect will the growth of e-commerce in developing nations have on Canadian SMEs?

6. Do you believe English will continue to be the language of business on the Web? If not, how will change affect Canadian SMEs?

7. In your opinion, how prepared is Canada to exploit e-commerce and compete with global, technologically-savvy competition?

8. How is e-commerce technology affecting governments' traditional taxation methods?

GLOBAL E-RESEARCH

Visit www.power.nelson.com for research suggestions, questions, and a number of background discussion papers on this topic.

MINI CASE

Canada's SMEs Can Do Better

In its Global Competitiveness Report, The World Economic Forum reviewed 102 economies of 2003–04 and produced the networked readiness index (NRI). The NRI measures the degree of preparation required for Canada and other countries to participate in and benefit from technology and telecom developments.

The Index placed Canada after the United States, Singapore, Finland, Sweden and Denmark. We must do better. . . . It is well recognized that one of the most powerful drivers of globalization is technology. SMEs must exploit the "power" of information and communication technologies (ICT) for their economic well-being. . . . Yes, there has been an unexpected confluence of variables beyond the control of Canada's small and medium-sized enterprises (SMEs) including the War on Terror, resulting in constricted border crossing; increasingly volatile foreign exchange dealings; and growing American protectionism. These and other variables contribute to our decreasing productivity. Size and reputation are not enough. During the 1980s, 46 percent of the top Fortune 500 companies ceased to exist. The golden age of marketing that claimed homogenous markets, predictable consumer behaviour, and mass marketing as key success factors is long gone; today the market is highly fragmented and complex. Increasingly SMEs are faced with a complex world where change is endemic. . . .

What can Canadian SMEs do to close the national competitive gap with our American cousins? First, consider the words of the former General Electric CEO, Jack Welsh who admonished, "Look at the world the way it is, not the way you think it should be." According to Industry Canada, SMEs represent 99.7% of Canada's one million employer businesses. Collectively SMEs are Canada's economic engine. Accordingly, if Canada is to improve our national competitiveness in ICT SMEs must propel this change.

Canada's U.S. exports, although fallen from a recent high of 85 percent 18 months ago (December 2004), are now

79 percent of our goods and services. SMEs can build value and take charge of their own destiny. They must adopt a new mental model that is driven by long-term growth rather than short-term bottom-line considerations. Although there are variables beyond the SMEs' entrepreneurial control, the remaining variables are controllable. SMEs will have to undertake proactive geographic expansion for growth rather than maintains their market share only in local markets. However, this will mean a significant shift from the current dependency on the U.S. market to emerging markets. Did you know that the exponential increase in the standard of living in China, for example, will increase China's eligible consumers tenfold by 2015? By 2020, China's GNP is estimated to be equal to America's. India, the "chained tiger," has been freed from its regulatory chains and bureaucracy and is now stalking the other Asian tigers' global markets. India's GNP will also exceed that of America shortly after China reaches the milestone.

If Canadian SMEs do not exploit this emerging opportunism, their global competitors will. SMEs must embrace the new emerging technologies faster and smarter than the competition.

Second, SMEs need to utilize the tools of e-business. By exploiting global network-enabled connections, accessing global markets easily, matching buyers and sellers across national boundaries, and saving transaction costs through efficient distribution tools, SMEs can play in the "sandbox" with larger multinational organizations. Third, SMEs need to understand the global village in order to engage it. It is a duty of SMEs' management to constantly scan the ecosystem and identify, at the earliest possibility, exploitable emerging opportunities and threats that have to be mitigated. Fourth, lobby government. Governments at all levels have a role in creating national competitiveness. Government can do this through in a number of ways:

- Enhancing advanced factor endowments such as infrastructure, education, research, transportation, science, and information technology. Unfortunately, the February 2005 federal budget did little to improve this situation.
- By creating an environment where consumers and society demand stringent standards. The Japanese lead the world in camera technology because Japanese consumers and government demand the best; they will not settle for a Kodak box camera.
- Deregulate industry, abolish monopolies, and eliminate interprovincial trade barriers. It is estimated that Canada wastes over $11 billion in national competitiveness because of interprovincial trade barriers? This when global barriers are falling.
- Adopt strong anti-trust policies. Mergers, collusion, controlling barriers to entry, and fixing prices all stifle innovation.
- Finally, encourage and enhance sustained investment through a tax rate for long-term capital gains to support new investment in corporate equity.

More than ever, we must intensify our efforts to enable individuals, businesses, and governments to benefit more fully from the use and application of technology and telecom advances.[65]

MINI CASE QUESTIONS

Have organizations asked you for data about yourself that they did not need to know? What action did you take? Do you feel the bargaining positions were equal? If you didn't provide the information, would they have refused to service you?

ENDNOTES

1 William A. McEachern, *The Teaching Economist*, 19 (Fall 2000), retrieved August 9, 2006, from www.thomsonedu.com/ economics/mceachern/teachingeconomist/wam19 .html#odds.

2 *Brainy Quote* (2005), retrieved August 9, 2006, from www .brainyquote.com.

3 Ibid.

4 *Albert Einstein Quotes* (2006), retrieved August 9, 2006, from http://en.thinkexist.com/quotation/it_has_become_ appallingly_obvious_that_our/220716.html.

5 Peter F. Drucker, *Managing Oneself* (Leader to Leader Institute, 1999), retrieved August 9, 2006, from www.pfdf.org/ conferences/drucker99.html.

6 Mark McNeilly, *Sun Tzu and the Art of Business: Six Strategic Principles for Managers* (New York: Oxford University Press, 1996).

7 Teri-Sue Buchanan, "Call Centres: Ringing in Profits," *ExportWise*, (Winter 2005), retrieved August 18, 2006, from www.edc.ca/english/publications_10819.htm.

8 Geoffrey Garrett, "Globalization's Missing Middle," *Foreign Affairs* (November/December 2004).

9 Faith Popcorn, *The Popcorn Report: Faith Popcorn on the Future of Your Company, Your World, Your Life*, 2nd ed. (New York: Harper Business, 1992).

10 Faith Popcorn, *Faith Popcorn's Predictions for 2004* (December 22, 2003), retrieved August 9, 2006, from www.azreporter.com/ news/features/2004/faithpopcorn.shtml.

11 "India Infotech," *BusinessWeek* (2001), retrieved August 9, 2006, from www.businessweek.com/adsections/indian/ infotech/2001/outlook.html.

12 Gary Hamel, *Leading the Revolution* (Watertown, MA: Harvard Business School Press, 2002).

13 Neil Postman, *Technopoly: The Surrender of Culture to Technology*, 1st ed. (Toronto: Random House Canada, 1993).

14 Statistics Canada, "*Electronic Commerce Households Spending in Canada and in Other Countries, by Region*," *(Canada)* (Statistics Canada, February 18, 2005), retrieved August 17, 2006, from www40.statcan.ca/l01/cst01/comm07a.htm.

15 Ibid.

16 Statistics Canada, "*Electronic Commerce Households Spending in Canada and in Other Countries, by Region.*"

17 Ibid.

18 "E-Commerce," CBC (September 23, 2004), retrieved August 9, 2006, from www.cbc.ca/news/background/internet/ecommerce.html.

19 Ibid.

20 Ibid.

21 Ibid.

22 Dan Lee, "Caught in the Web," *Wisconsin State Journal* (April 10, 2005), retrieved August 18, 2006, from www.madison.com/archives/read.php?ref=/wsj/2005/04/10/0504110128.php.

23 Terrance Power, "Canadian Firms Must Close Competitive Gap," *Business Edge*, 2, 6, retrieved August 9, 2006, from www.businessedge.ca/article.cfm/newsID/8817.cfm.

24 "ICANN," *Wikipedia*, (April 2, 2006), retrieved April 2, 2006, from http://en.wikipedia.org/w/index.php?title=ICANN&oldid=46597906.

25 "North India's Tech Park Dilemma: Can It Ever Play Catch-Up?" *Dataquest* (2003), retrieved August 9, 2006, from www.dqindia.com/content/top_stories/203052901.asp.

26 Ibid.

27 Ibid.

28 Morris Consulting-Incorporated, "Taiwan's Biotech-Focused Science Parks," *East Biotech* (2006), retrieved August 9, 2006, from www.biotecheast.com/index.php?module=htmlpages&func=display&pid=5.

29 *Why Canada Is Your Best Investment* (ICBS, 2004), retrieved August 9, 2006, from www.icbs.ca/foreign_%20investment_%20in_canada.shtml.

30 Ibid.

31 Ibid.

32 Ibid.

33 Ibid.

34 Ibid.

35 Ibid.

36 Ibid.

37 Egil Juliussen, "Worldwide Internet Users Top 1 Billion in 2005," *Computer Industry Almanac* (January 4, 2006), retrieved August 9, 2006, from www.c-i-a.com/pr0106.htm.

38 Raymond Chrétien, *Canada–U.S. Relations @ 2000: A Success Story* (October 27, 1999), retrieved August 9, 2006, from www.dfait-maeci.gc.ca/can-am/washington/ambassador/991027-en.asp.

39 Retail Council of Canada and Industry Canada, *Glossary of Technology Types* (Industry Canada, 2005), retrieved 2005, from www.retailinteractive.ca.

40 "Nanotechnology: Downsizing the Future," *Canadian Shareowner Magazine*, November/December 2004.

41 Jillian M. Buriak, "Beyond Hype and Fear," *National Post*, September 13, 2004.

42 Laura Bogomolny et al, "Biotech Nation," *Canadian Business*, September 27–October 10, 2004.

43 Jacob West, *The Quantum Computer: Future Outlook* (April 28, 2000), retrieved August 9, 2006, from www.cs.caltech.edu/~westside/quantum-intro.html.

44 Ibid.

45 Simon Woodside, *E-Commerce and Taxation: A Virtual Reality* (OECD, 2001), retrieved August 9, 2006, from www.oecdobserver.org/news/fullstory.php/aid/416/E-commerce_and_taxation:_a_virtual_reality.html.

46 *Cell Phones Most Frequently Upgraded Technology* (Marketnews.ca, 21 March 2005), retrieved 18 August 2006, from http://marketnews.ca/news_archive_detail.asp?nid=665.

47 *Just Say No to E-Waste: Background Document on Hazards and Waste from Computers* (Silicon Valley Toxics Coalition, 04/07/2006), retrieved 18 August 2006, from www.svtc.org/cleancc/pubs/sayno.htm.

48 Recycling Council of British Columbia, *Fact Sheet—Electronic Product Stewardship: A Made in BC Solution* (Recycling Council of British Columbia, 2001), retrieved 9 April 2005, from www.rcbc.bc.ca/about/Publications/factsheet/RCBC_E-Waste_Fact_sheet.pdf.

49 Environment Canada, "Basel Convention on the Control of Transboundary Movements of Hazardous Wastes and Their Disposal," (Ottawa: Environment Canada, 2003), retrieved October 20, 2006, from http://www.ec.gc.ca/TMB/eng/tmbbasel_e.htm.

50 United Nations Environment Programme, *Basel Convention on the Control of Transboundary Movements of Hazardous Wastes and Their Disposal* (October 8, 2005) (Secretariat of the Basel Convention, 2005, available from http://www.basel.int/text/con-e-rev.pdf.

51 *Just Say No to E-Waste: Background Document on Hazards and Waste from Computers.*

52 "Cell Phones Most Frequently Upgraded Technology" (Marketnews.ca, March 21, 2005), retrieved August 18, 2006, from http://marketnews.ca/news_archive_detail.asp?nid=665.

53 Ibid.

54 Ibid.

55 Michael Vanderpol, *Managing Risks Posed by E-Waste: A Canadian Approach* (May 17, 2005), retrieved August 9, 2006, from http://www.iaer.org/summit/presentation2005/Vanderpool.ppt.

56 Bojan Paduh, *Computer Donations and Recycling in Edmonton, Alberta, Canada* (March 22, 2005), retrieved August 9, 2006, from http://www.emediawire.com/releases/2005/3/emw220747.htm.

57 Steve Garber, *Sputnik and the Dawn of the Space Age* (February 21, 2003), retrieved August 9, 2006, from http://www.hq.nasa.gov/office/pao/History/sputnik/index.html.

58 Propulsion Laboratory Jet, *Past Missions—Explorer 1–5* (n.d), retrieved August 9, 2006, from www.jpl.nasa.gov/missions/past/explorer.html.

59 Peter N. Spotts, "Lots in Space" *The Christian Science Monitor* (October 9, 2003), retrieved August 9, 2006, from www.csmonitor.com/2003/1009/p11s02-stss.htm.

60 *Man-Made Junk and Natural Particles,* (NASA Johnson Space Centre, February 22, 2006), retrieved August 18, 2006, from http://hitf.jsc.nasa.gov/hitfpub/problem/environment.html.

61 Spotts, "Lots in Space."

62 "Space Junk," retrieved August 9, 2006, from www.bbc.co.uk/science/space/solarsystem/earth/spacejunk.shtml.

63 Malcolm Gladwell, *The Tipping Point* (Little, Brown and Company, 2000).

64 Stefan Lovgren, "Warming to Cause Catastrophic Rise in Sea Level?," National Geographic News, (April 26, 2004), retrieved 19 August 2006, from http://news.nationalgeographic.com/news/2004/04/0420_040420_earthday.html.

65 Adapted from Power, *Canadian Firms Must Close Competitive Gap.*

External—The Clustering of Nations and Global Institutions

The journey continues. In Part 1 we examined the revitalization of globalization and its drivers over the past three decades. In Part 2 we recognized the importance of undertaking an analysis of the PEST-C factors present in our external international business ecosystem. In Part 3 we shift from the external ecosystem considerations to an examination of selected global institutions, and economic and financial theories and concepts that influence international trade. First we examine the growing clustering of nations.

In this Part we will present an argument in support of globalization and selected global institutions that, when combined with economic trade theory (see Chapter 6) will convince most that at least at the macro level globalization works! However, on closer examination, globalization's shortcomings at the micro level significantly mar this brave new world. Opponents of these institutions and globalization also have cogent arguments that must be understood. This text will not provide you with the "correct position" on these significant and important issues, but will raise compelling arguments needed to defend your position. In Chapter 7 the importance of foreign exchange markets, international monetary systems, and the global capital markets supporting international trade are presented. An understanding of these financial institutions, theories, and concepts are essential for Canadian SMEs. I know you will find the materials fascinating and relevant to your understanding of daily business activities and some of the underlying drivers of international news.

Regionalization and Global Institutions

"Commerce with all nations, alliance with none, should be our motto."[1]

—Thomas Jefferson

"The developing coherence of Asian regional thinking is reflected in a disposition to consider problems and loyalties in regional terms, and to evolve regional approaches to development needs and to the evolution of a new world order."[2]

—Richard Nixon

"Good business leaders create a vision, articulate the vision, passionately own the vision, and relentlessly drive it to completion."[3]

—Thomas Hardy

"Small opportunities are often the beginning of great enterprises."[4]

—Demosthenes

"My contacts during my journeys through Asia and Europe have confirmed my view that the Union of African States will make for rapid economic advance on this continent. Its political advantages will be enormous, as the continent will be completely liberated, and a source of constant temptation to the Imperialist will be removed ... To hasten this change Africans must band themselves together into a Union."[5]

—Dr. M.I. Okpara, Premier of Nigeria's Eastern Region, (1961)

LEARNING OUTCOMES

- Understand the reasons for, and evaluate the merits of, regionalization.
- Examine the three major global regional trade blocs (the triad) and other regional groupings formulating opinions about their economic sustainability.
- Develop an awareness of emerging issues related to each of the major regional groupings.
- Compare the degrees of economic regional integration and formulate an opinion as to where Canada and other nations currently stand.
- Understand the implications of regional economic integration for Canadian SMEs.
- Evaluate the merits of the economic and political arguments supporting regionalization.
- Formulate opinions about the impact on nations from supranational bodies—the World Bank, the World Trade Organization (formally the General Agreement on Tariffs and Trade), and the International Monetary Fund—in regulating world trade.
- Consider the effectiveness of selected regional dispute resolution bodies.

Countdown to the 2005 Summit of the Americas in Argentina

JIM YOUNG/Reuters/Landov

In November 2005, the 34 democratically elected heads of state and government from the Americas will gather in Mar del Plata, Argentina for the Fourth Summit of the Americas. The central Summit theme proposed by Argentina is: 'Creating Jobs to Combat Poverty and Strengthen Democratic Governance.' Member states and civil society organizations are now submitting their comments on the proposed theme to Argentina, who will then release an updated document in early 2005 that will form the framework for

the eventual Declaration and Plan of Action for the Fourth Summit. On June 3, 2003, Canada officially handed over chairmanship of the Summit of the Americas process to Argentina after hosting the Third Summit in Québec City in 2001, where Canada strongly reaffirmed its identity as a nation of the Americas and as a busy crossroads for our hemispheric friends and neighbours.

What is the Summit of the Americas? The Summits of the Americas are periodic meetings that

bring together the thirty-four democratically elected Heads of State and Government of the Americas to discuss and seek solutions on diverse hemispheric issues. In addition to the Heads of State, the heads of the institution members of the Joint Summit Working Group participate as observers as well as other special guests including representatives from civil society, the private sector, academia and the media.

What is the main goal of the Summits of the Americas process? To analyze and discuss the challenges that the American continents faces in order to seek shared solutions and improve the quality of life of the citizens of the Americas. Why does Canada participate in the Summits of the Americas? Canada considers the Summit of the Americas process to be very important as a vehicle through which Canada can promote its hemispheric agenda, including issues such as commitment to democratic principles, promotion of human rights and human security, reduction of both poverty and inequality, and economic integration via a region-wide free trade agreement.

Source: Department of Foreign Affairs and International Trade, *Canada and the Americas— Closer Than Ever* (Government of Canada, 2004). Copyright Public Works and Government Services Canada.

A SUN TZU MOMENT. . .

Visual Arts Library, London/Alamy

"I reward my prospective allies with valuables and silks and bind them with solemn covenants. I abide firmly by the treaties and then my allies will certainly aid me."[6]

During World War II there was alignment of the interests of the Soviets and the Western Allies. Collectively they had a common purpose—to defeat Nazi Germany. They entered into

an alliance, albeit with a sense of discomfort and lack of trust. Nonetheless, these issues paled in magnitude against their paramount goal of defeating Hitler.

British politicians have been masters and deft strategists in implementing alliances to support their national best interest. During the 1800s it was in England's national best interest to ensure that no dominant continental power emerged. Accordingly, in 1820 it supported Greece's efforts to gain independence from the Ottoman Empire. Two decades later

Britain joined with the Ottoman Empire when Russia threatened Britain's interest. Only a few years later in the 1840s, Britain shifted its support to Russia in an effort to put down a rebellion in Hungary. Yet when Prussia defeated Austria (a former British ally) in 1866 in what was known as the Seven Week War, Britain took no action. It seems the British political leaders found Austria to be of little value to the national interest of Britain at that time. In the 1900s when Prussia, leading a united Germany as one of the most powerful European countries, emerged on the continent, Britain quickly allied herself with France and Russia to block Prussia's continental hegemony.

Today's regionalization initiatives are driven by the same underlying concerns for a nation's well-being. These interests are more than just trade. We will examine the "valuables and silks" that bind nations in regional groupings in this chapter. We will see that, while trade may be cited as the surface raison d'être for the alliances, lurking not far below is the extension of the regionally dominated nation's foreign and national security polices.

Zbigniew Brzezinski, former U.S. National Security Advisor to Jimmy Carter, wrote a wonderful book on the topic entitled *The Grand Chessboard: American Primacy and its Geostrategic Imperatives.*[7] Brzezinski boldly outlines why the world's nations are important to America's national interest and the actions required by U.S. leadership to influence them to support American initiatives. Visit www.power.nelson.com for a brief overview of this book and other suggested bestsellers that will interest those with a passion for international studies.

Opening Thoughts

One of the outcomes of globalization is the emergence of two or more countries entering into economically favourable trade agreements. In Chapter 1 we reviewed this growing economic interdependence, which is transforming global trade. Free trade economic theories, which promote economic interdependence, are outlined in Chapter 6. There we will see a strong argument for larger markets, and nations producing what they do best. The resultant efficiencies decrease unit costs and increase trade volumes—resulting in a comparative advantage for nations that exploit these new economic trade theories. Free and open trade, and investment, help participating economies grow, create jobs, and provide greater opportunities for further expansion of international trade and investment. In contrast, we will see that adopting protectionist practices (mercantilism) keeps prices high and fosters inefficiencies in certain industries.

Regionalization for our purposes refers to the clustering of trading nations.

Regionalism is the regional integration of nations by entering trade agreements. It can be traced back to early trading times when geographic proximity was an important factor in nurturing favourable trade arrangements. Often these trade agreements expand over time to other interdependencies between the trade "partners."

One major purpose of **regional trading blocs** is to reduce, and ultimately remove, all tariff and non-tariff barriers that impede the free flow of goods and services between participating members.

Clusters of nations (**regionalization**) have taken place, such as the North American Free Trade Agreement (NAFTA) and the Mercado Comun del Sur (Mercosur). The existence of **regionalism**, the regional integration of nations entering trade agreements, can be traced back to early trading times, when geographic proximity was an important factor nurturing favourable trade arrangements. "National economies are steadily becoming more integrated as cross-border flows of trade, investment, and financial capital increase. Consumers are buying more foreign goods, a growing number of firms now operate across national borders, and investors are committing more funds in distant places of the globe."[8] South Korea and Chile are among the more striking examples of countries that pursued strategies of trade liberalization. Accompanied by the appropriate macroeconomic policies, they have experienced dramatically accelerated growth as a result. In this chapter, we will examine a number of post–World War II nation clusters, driven by economic and other imperatives to form regional trading blocs both large and small. We will see that the composition of these clusters of trade blocs continues to take on new forms. One stated purpose of **regional trading blocs** is to reduce, and ultimately remove, all tariff and non-tariff barriers that impede the free flow of goods and services between the participating members. However, there are other rationales, sometimes unspoken or unintended, for supporting a free trade alliance between partnering nations. These secondary reasons occasionally require tradeoffs. For example, in some cases a country expresses the desire to promote democratic values, foster national security, prevent the loss of sovereignty, acquire secure commodity sourcing, or prevent non-member nations gaining easy access to the economic trade area. As you read about the different regional clusters, think critically about the underlying rationale for each agreement. See how many of these underlying reasons you can find. To assist your critical thinking, reflect on the Sun Tzu Moment on pages 123–124.

By the end of 2006, there were approximately 300 regional trade agreements. These initiatives are in addition to those implemented at a macro level by the World Trade Organization (WTO) and its 149 members. In this chapter we will examine the WTO and its efforts to encourage global free trade by reducing trade barriers, implementing rulings and directives, and providing dispute resolution processes. We also examine other important global institutions that support trade. International business practitioners entering a host marketplace would do well to understand and leverage the trade agreements in place.

Currently, the most successful regional trade region in terms of membership is the European Union (EU) established on January 1, 1993. On May 1, 2004, an additional 10 countries joined the regional grouping. With 25 member countries, the EU's population is 462 million with a GNI equal to the United States (2005). In addition, nations such as Turkey, with 69 million citizens, are eager to become members. Another regional free trade area we will examine is the North American Free Trade Agreement (NAFTA). NAFTA has proven to be an economic success for Mexico, the United States, and Canada, as the economic statistics will attest. However, some of you may be inclined to ask, at what cost to sovereignty?

A third region we will look at is the Mercosur Trade Agreement (1991) between Brazil, Paraguay, Argentina, and Uruguay as well as the region's recent addition, Venezuela. Mercosur is an attempt to replicate the U.S.–Canada Free Trade Agreement (FTA) of 1988, which took effect in 1989. The FTA was the precursor to the NAFTA initiative. It has long been the vision of some members of NAFTA, and several South American countries, to form a Free Trade Area of the Americas (FTAA). Economically, the FTAA would be the largest regional free trade grouping in the world. Membership would include most countries in the north and south of the Western Hemisphere. Cuba would be excluded if the United States prevails as gatekeeper for the FTAA, deciding who would and would not be members. Unfortunately, since 9/11 there have been setbacks, and some South American nations such as Brazil have grown tired of waiting for the United States to push ahead; they are now pursuing alternative free trade relationships with the EU, China, and some African countries. In 1996 this was further encouraged by populist President Hugo Chavez of Venezuela.

The fourth region we will examine is the Asia-Pacific Economic Cooperation (APEC) forum, established in 1994. It consists of 21 Pacific Ring countries including Mexico, the United States, Canada, Japan, and China. APEC is exploring a Pan-Pacific free trade area, building upon the principles of the Uruguay Round of the General Agreement of Tariffs and Trade (GATT, established in 1947, was the genesis for the WTO). (Completed in 1994, the Uruguay round was the eighth such meeting.)

We will also examine the formation of a customs union called the ASEAN Free Trade Area (AFTA), established in 1991. The ASEAN region is still under construction and forming new clusters.

After reading this chapter, you may conclude that, rather than globalization, we may be witnessing the emergence of three super, very economically integrated, regional trading blocs. (Read the Mini Case on page 153.) If so, ". . . it is not yet certain whether regionalization contradicts or complements globalization. How can we understand these complex and seemingly contradictory phenomena? Whereas globalization and regionalization may reflect the conflict between national, regional, and global interests, whether the two are contradictory or complementary is not yet certain."[9] Within these regional formations there are successes and failures as well as other emerging small and, unfortunately, weaker regional trade initiatives. As you read about these national clusters, think critically about the implications for Canadian SMEs in the global marketplace. But first, we need to establish a metric to measure the degree of economic integration.

FIGURE 5.1
Degrees of Economic Integration

FIGURE 5.1
Degrees of Economic Integration

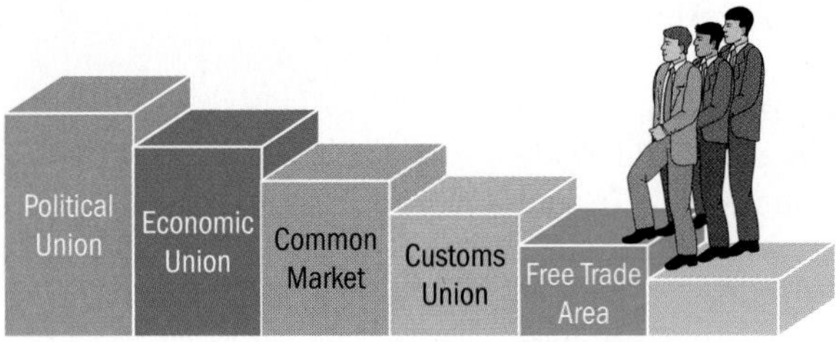

Political union is found at one extreme of a continuum or at the top of the stairs. There is political union when the regional groups centralize their political apparatus to coordinate all governance aspects generally associated with those found in a nation's state.

Degrees of Economic Regional Integration—A Metric

The degrees of economic regional integration can be seen as a continuum or stairs leading to full political union. At one extreme or the top of the stairs is a **political union**, where the regional groups centralize their political apparatus to coordinate all governance aspects that we generally associate with those found in a nation's state. Depending on the degree of economic integration, countries may participate concurrently in various trade groupings. The degrees can be thought of as a series of stairs shown in Figure 5.1. The hierarchy moving from low economic integration to high is free trade, customs unions, common markets, economic union, and, finally, political union. The closest free trade region to this end of the continuum or the top stair is the European Economic Union, which shows emerging signs of possible political union, the last step toward complete regional integration. The EU has adopted a common parliament, bill of rights, and rule of law, and 12 nations with as many different languages have accepted a common currency. Yet, most naysayers believe political union is not possible for the EU. Are there precedents? Proudly, yes. They need look no further than North America for successful models. The union of four British colonies in 1867, as well as, south of Canada's 49th parallel, the union of 13 English-speaking colonies in 1776, both validate that the current obstacles faced by the EU are surmountable if there is the will. Review the attributes of the degree of economic regional integration shown in Figure 5.2.

Regionalism Is Not Just about Trade

Concern over U.S. Militarism Brings China and India Closer

Chinese Premier Wen Jiabao's recent tour of South Asia on April 5–12 [2005] marked a further step in a still tentative rapprochement between China and India. . . . Indian Prime Minister Manmohan Singh summed up New Delhi's enthusiasm for the visit when he welcomed Wen, declaring, "India and China together reshape the world order". . . . At the conclusion, the two prime ministers issued a 21-point joint statement listing 12 agreements, protocols and memoranda of understanding between their countries. . . . On the economic front, the joint statement announced that trade between the two countries would be increased to $US20 billion by 2008—up from $13 billion in 2004. The two leaders agreed to establish joint economic groups, mechanisms for trade and investment promotion, closer financial relations, improved IT cooperation and the enhancement of direct shipping and aviation links. Over the past decade, India and China have experienced high rates of economic growth as foreign capital has flooded in to take advantage of their huge reserves

FIGURE 5.2
Attributes of the Degree of Economic Regional Integration

Forms of International Economic Integration

Stage (steps) of Integration	Abolition of Tariffs and Quotas among Members	Common Tariff and Quota System	Abolition of Restrictions on Factor Movements	Harmonization and Unification of Economic Policies and Institutions
Free trade area	Yes	No	No	No
Customs union	Yes	Yes	No	No
Common Market	Yes	Yes	Yes	No
Economic union	Yes	Yes	Yes	Yes
Political union	Yes	Yes	Yes	Yes

Adapted from Franklin R. Root, *International Trade and Investment,* Cincinnati, Ohio: South-Western Publishing Company, 1992.

of cheap labour. Whereas China has become "the workshop of the world," India has transformed into the "office of the world," with foreign investors exploiting its supply of cheap, educated, English-speaking technicians, computer programmers and office workers. The Indian and Chinese ruling elites both have ambitions to play a more prominent international role, making them rivals, not only for markets and resources, but also for influence in the Asian region. India and China, for instance, are each seeking to expand economic and political relations with the Association of South East Asian Nations (ASEAN) countries. China has longstanding relations with the military junta in Burma [Myanmar], which borders India and where New Delhi is trying to expand its presence. . . . Mentions of "multilateralism" and the UN's importance for global peace are oblique, but obvious are references to Washington's unilateral and illegal invasion of Iraq. The central factor pushing the two countries together is mutual concern over the consequences of unbridled US militarism. For China, the attempt to mend its fences with India is part of efforts to break out of what it fears is American encirclement. In the wake of the September 11 attacks on the US, the Bush administration occupied Afghanistan, established US military bases for the first time in Central Asia and sought to rebuild a military presence in South East Asia. . . .

China's relations with Pakistan and Bangladesh are also aimed at preventing any US encirclement. Beijing is building a deepwater port at Gwadar in Pakistan, strategically located near the Persian Gulf. The facility will be equipped with surveillance gear to monitor the surrounding ocean and will be open for use by Chinese vessels, including naval ships. Beijing's involvement in the construction will help extend its naval reach to protect China's vital oil supplies from the Middle East. . . . During Vajpayee's visit, China raised the prospect of a triangular relationship between Russia, China and India. . . . Beijing and New Delhi could, "through their combined leadership, impart a needed balance to global affairs." It went on to declare that a relationship with China was vital "at a time of unprecedented flux in international relations, rudely shaken by the American doctrine of pre-emption and war on Iraq."

. . . Following Wen's trip to India, US State Department spokesman Richard Boucher dismissed as "pure speculation" comments that India–China relations would harm America. Behind the scenes, however, it is not difficult to imagine that the White House is far from happy that its plans to use India against China have suffered something of a setback.

Source: K. Ratnayake, *Concern over U.S. Militarism Brings China and India Closer* (World Socialist website, February 5, 2005). Copyright 1998–2006 World Socialist website. All rights reserved.

Critical Thinking

There is much in this article that needs reflective thought. Should Western powers be concerned about an Axis growing between Russia, China, and India? Is this a new regional economic grouping? What tensions will be present as the United States and this Axis vie for oil pipelines and control over other Middle East commodities? Has U.S. foreign policy promoted this outcome as suggested by the article's author? If so, can it be reversed? On the surface, trade is clearly a driving force, but other significant considerations are not far below. What are the implications for Canadian business?

Visit www.power.nelson.com for a report on the growing strength of the Shanghai Cooperation Organization (SCO). Its members include six countries: China, Russia, Kazakhstan, Kyrgyzstan, Tajikistan, and Uzbekistan. Collectively the member states cover an area of over 30 million square kilometres, or about three-fifths of Eurasia, with a population of 1.455 billion people. Is there another Bamboo or Iron Curtain emerging?

Trading Blocs

Increasingly, the world is segregating into three major regional clusters or trading blocs. These supranational, regional blocs have been referred to as the **Triad**. The world's most powerful economies—the United States, the European Union, and, in combination, China and India—have each sought to forge links with neighbouring countries to enhance their trade access and influence over global rivals (see Regionalism Is Not Just about Trade,

The **Triad** refers to the world's three major global regional clusters or trading blocs. These supranational, regional blocs are also the world's most powerful economies: the United States, the European Union, and, in combination, China and India.

Road Blocks or Building Blocks
(Percentage of Total World Trade
[2004])

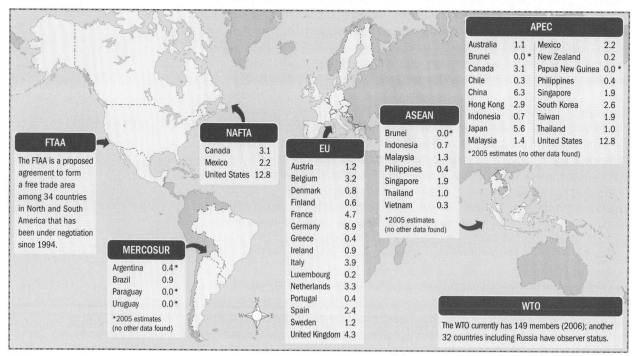

APEC			
Australia	1.1	Mexico	2.2
Brunei	0.0 *	New Zealand	0.2
Canada	3.1	Papua New Guinea	0.0 *
Chile	0.3	Philippines	0.4
China	6.3	Singapore	1.9
Hong Kong	2.9	South Korea	2.6
Indonesia	0.7	Taiwan	1.9
Japan	5.6	Thailand	1.0
Malaysia	1.4	United States	12.8

*2005 estimates (no other data found)

FTAA

The FTAA is a proposed agreement to form a free trade area among 34 countries in North and South America that has been under negotiation since 1994.

NAFTA

Canada	3.1
Mexico	2.2
United States	12.8

EU

Austria	1.2
Belgium	3.2
Denmark	0.8
Finland	0.6
France	4.7
Germany	8.9
Greece	0.4
Ireland	0.9
Italy	3.9
Luxembourg	0.2
Netherlands	3.3
Portugal	0.4
Spain	2.4
Sweden	1.2
United Kingdom	4.3

ASEAN

Brunei	0.0*
Indonesia	0.7
Malaysia	1.3
Philippines	0.4
Singapore	1.9
Thailand	1.0
Vietnam	0.3

*2005 estimates
(no other data found)

MERCOSUR

Argentina	0.4 *
Brazil	0.9
Paraguay	0.0*
Uruguay	0.0*

*2005 estimates
(no other data found)

WTO

The WTO currently has 149 members (2006); another 32 countries including Russia have observer status.

SOURCE: Author generated with data from "International Financial Statistics," International Monetary Fund. Retrieved May 2, 2006, from www.imfstatistics.org/imf/logon.aspx; and Ingolf Vogeler, *Road Blocks or Building Blocks? Percentage of Total World Trade, 1996.* (University of Wisconsin-Eau Claire, 1996), retrieved August 11, 2006, from www.uwec.edu/geography/lvogeler/w111/trade.gif.

pages 126–127). Other major trading countries, like the fast-growing exporters on the Pacific Rim and the big agricultural exporting nations, have also sought to create looser trade groupings to foster their interests. The formation of free trade zones and regional trade blocs is one of the major challenges facing the world trading system. See Figure 5.3 for a depiction of the world's major trading areas and their contributions to total world trade. Will their formation lead to increased protectionism, or will they promote trade liberalization and ultimately support a world trade bloc, with a new world order? If it is protectionism, there will be disastrous economic outcomes.[10] Visit www.power.nelson .com for a comprehensive overview of the countries by trade grouping.

Regional—Intra-trade Grouping

During the past 30 years, we have seen a substantial increase in the number of regional and subregional trade agreements. While this trend has helped many areas to intensify their mutual trade and allowed various countries to profit from expanding exports, it has not systematically resulted in increased **intra-trade** within all of the trade groupings that have been created. (Intra-trade is international trade among countries that belong to the same group whether it is a regional group or a trade grouping.) A caveat: "Regional trading arrangements can serve protectionist purposes, not least because of rules of origin (ROOs). ROOs can lead to trade diversion if they oblige partners to buy higher-priced intermediate goods from a partner rather than on the lower-priced world markets. They can even export protection from one partner to another. And all FTAs provide special interest groups with another opportunity to lobby against competition from imports. To the extent that regional trade agreements are inward-looking, and give lower priority to trade and economic engagement with the rest of the world, global trade will increase real incomes by less than it otherwise might."[11]

Intra-trade is international trade among countries that belong to the same group (for example, a regional or trade grouping).

Since 1980, intra-regional trade has grown in all regions except Central and Eastern Europe. The biggest absolute rise in intra-trade has occurred in the Asian region. After declining during the 1970s and 1980s, intra-trade in Africa has almost tripled during the past 20 years. While this statistic reads well, in 2001, it unfortunately still represented only 12 percent of total exports from that continent. For internal trade within trade groupings, the picture is more subdued. Despite the significant rise in intra-trade for the Asian region, trade within the region's trade groups did not keep pace, indicating that economic integration was broad-based. The past decade saw the emergence of sub-regional trading blocs in Latin America. This yielded mainly positive, although in some groups, modest results for the countries involved, increasing their exports to other members of the trade blocs. In Africa, numerous subregional trade agreements were signed, but none of the groups managed to surpass the 13 percent threshold of exports directed to other members within the trade bloc. For Central and Eastern European states, the prospect of their accession to the European Union boosted their trade with members of that group. A similar effect occurred with the North American Free Trade Agreement (NAFTA). Commercial exchange between Canada, Mexico, and the United States increased significantly before NAFTA came into force in January 1994.

The European Union

The EU (25) has become a powerful global trading bloc with a GDP now equal to the United States, as both have a 2005 estimated GDP of $12.3 trillion. The EU exports US$813 billion and imports US$801 billion in goods and services.[12] The long-term economic success of the EU is a product of the removal of internal trade barriers with the resulting growth of intra-European trade and of trade liberalization with the rest of the world. The EU's trade framework, by locking in the principle of tariff reduction, acted as a disincentive to protectionist lobbying. See Figure 5.4 for the distribution of exports among EU countries.

The Maastricht Treaty came into force on November 1, 1993, and provided the road map for the creation of the EU. The vision of the EU was to unite the member states in areas of public policy, including health, defence, and the European Monetary Union (EMU), which focused on economic policy and currency. By early 1995, the EU comprised 12 member countries: Belgium, Germany, Spain, France, Ireland, Italy, Luxembourg, the Netherlands, Great Britain, Greece, Portugal, and Denmark. Austria, Finland, and Sweden would join a few years later, in 1995. Three of the fifteen EU countries, Denmark, Sweden, and Great Britain, did not fix their currency's individual exchange rates on December 31, 1998, and thus did not join the EMU. The criteria for membership in the European Union can be found in three documents. First, the Copenhagen criteria, which comprise three basic membership criteria laid down at the Copenhagen Summit in June 1993.

FIGURE 5.4

EU (25)—Export of Goods and Services (Percentage of GDP (2004)

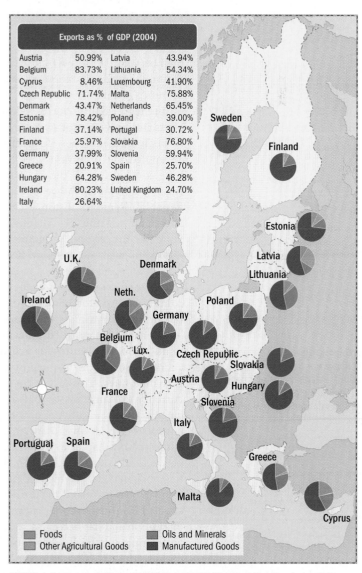

Exports as % of GDP (2004)			
Austria	50.99%	Latvia	43.94%
Belgium	83.73%	Lithuania	54.34%
Cyprus	8.46%	Luxembourg	41.90%
Czech Republic	71.74%	Malta	75.88%
Denmark	43.47%	Netherlands	65.45%
Estonia	78.42%	Poland	39.00%
Finland	37.14%	Portugal	30.72%
France	25.97%	Slovakia	76.80%
Germany	37.99%	Slovenia	59.94%
Greece	20.91%	Spain	25.70%
Hungary	64.28%	Sweden	46.28%
Ireland	80.23%	United Kingdom	24.70%
Italy	26.64%		

Foods
Other Agricultural Goods
Oils and Minerals
Manufactured Goods

SOURCE: Author generated with data from "Exports (% GDP): World Bank, World Development Indicators 2006," World Development Indicators database. Retrieved May 2, 2006 from http://devdata.worldbank.org/data-query; and International and Regional Studies Center for Global International and Regional Studies, *Regional Trade Blocs* (University of California, July 27, 2005), retrieved August 11, 2006, from http://ucatlas.ucsc .edu/trade/subtheme_trade_blocs.php.

These are the existence of stable institutions guaranteeing democracy, the rule of law, human rights, and respect for and protection of minorities; the existence of a functioning market economy as well as the capacity to cope with competitive pressure and market forces within the Union; and the ability to take on the obligations of membership, including adherence to the aims of political, economic, and monetary union.

The second criterion is a Framework for Negotiations entered into between the candidate nation and the EU on a case–by-case basis. The third criterion is the Maastricht Treaty, which provided five criteria: The applicant country could not have an inflation rate greater than 1.5 percent more than the average of the three countries with the lowest inflation rates; The applicant country must not have a prime interest rate more than 2.0 percent higher than the average of the three countries with the lowest inflation rates; The applicant country's currency could not have deviated from the euro by more than 15 percent during the preceding two years; The applicant country could not have a fiscal deficit of more than 3 percent of GDP; and the applicant country could not have a government debt to GDP ratio greater than 60 percent. Interestingly, some current members like France and Germany now have difficulty meeting these criteria while demanding that new applicants like Turkey get over the "bar"!

The creation of the euro as a single currency on January 1, 2002, for 12 EU members has led to ever-closer economic links. A growing number of other non-EU nations have adopted the euro as their currency, including Andorra, the Canary Islands, French Guyana, Guadeloupe, Kosovo, Madeira, Martinique, Mayotte, Monaco, Montenegro, Saint-Pierre-et-Miquelon, San Marino, and Vatican City.[13] Several countries and territories have linked their currencies to the euro (dollarization) through different types of agreements. (See www.power.nelson.com for a paper on the advantages and disadvantages of dollarization.) Some of these dollarization agreements were concluded with the EU, while others are unilateral. The unilateral ones include Bosnia, Botswana, Bulgaria, Cape Verde, Comoros Islands, Croatia, Cyprus, Czech Republic, Denmark, Estonia, FYR Macedonia, Herzegovina, Hungary, Israel, Jordan, Latvia, Libya, Lithuania, Malta, Morocco, Romania, Russia, Serbia, Seychelles, Slovakia, Slovenia, Tunisia and Vanuatu.[14] Napoleon's comment in 1807, "I want the whole of Europe to have one currency. It will make trading much easier"[15] has proved accurate. First, it removed the confusion caused by differing exchange rates. A common rate with a common currency ensures that consumers throughout Europe are now able to easily compare prices for goods and services. It also facilitates long-term planning for businesses operating within, and to a lesser degree outside, the EU, as they will no longer have to plan for currency fluctuations with the Euro-using countries. Second, it limits the opportunities for **arbitrage**, which is the artificial trade of goods between countries solely for the purpose of exploiting any price differential caused by shifting exchange rates. Third, it reduces the non-value-added currency exchange fees and currency exchange losses that occur when goods are purchased in one country with currency from another. Companies do not have to incur costs to provide hedging contracts based on potential currency fluctuations. (Hedging instruments are addressed in Chapter 8, pages 232–235). Fourth, it facilitates the movement of people between EU countries. And, finally, the euro increases the EU's competitive advantage in global markets. Having one currency backed by 12 nations and tied in part to a gold standard has increased the attractiveness of the EU to foreign investors. The euro has enabled EU firms to conduct their business with minimal administrative and economic disruption and has become a strong and valued currency on the international markets. Unfortunately, the EU has found it difficult to shed its protectionist past, in part because the EU is based on the idea of self-sufficiency in agriculture, which limits agricultural imports from other non–EU countries. We will examine the euro and its role as an international currency in Chapter 9.

Arbitrage (goods) is the artificial trade of goods between countries solely for the purpose of exploiting any price differential caused by shifting exchange rates.

FIGURE 5.5
European Union—Future Members

SOURCE: *Europe—Map of Member States of the European Union* (nationsonline.org, February 9, 2006).

European Union—Future Members

The EU will have 27 member states when further enlargement takes place in 2007, with the addition of Bulgaria and Romania. The next block of candidate countries well underway in their negotiations for admission include Croatia, Republic of Macedonia, and Turkey. Potential candidate countries and those demonstrating interest are Albania, Bosnia, Herzegovina, Montenegro, and Serbia and a further 15 states and a number of free trade associations; clearly an idea whose time has come. Figure 5.5 shows current and future EU members and countries with European Free Trade Association (EFTA) status. The most significant is application of an allied and NATO member, Turkey. Its acceptance or rejection will have significant consequences (see below). It is anticipated that this decision will take place in or before 2014. Visit www.power.nelson.com for a paper on the topic. Here are a few considerations.

Turkey Entering the European Union

EU officials continue to negotiate with Turkey concerning its application to join the union. Many in Europe and Turkey believe that Turkish membership in the EU is not a good idea: "There are many pitfalls that will have to be avoided. Even if the negotiations are successfully completed, France and Austria have said they will hold referendums on whether to ratify Turkey's accession treaty."[16] There are several arguments against Turkey joining the EU, specifically from countries within the EU. The main arguments include: ". . . that Turkey is not culturally 'European.' Another is that it will cause a wave of Turkish immigrants [pop. 69 million]. A third is that widening the EU to include Turkey will prevent further deepening of political and economic union. A fourth is that Turkey is too big, and will therefore exercise too much power within the EU. A fifth is that it is too poor [$2700 GDP/person] and will cost the rest of the EU too much."[17] Sixth, overall these EU countries opposing Turkey's membership are doubtful that the Union can handle such economic, social, and cultural differences. A further obstacle is Turkey's refusal to recognize Cyprus, a member of the union. "A declaration issued by EU member states in September 2005 says that Turkey must . . . normalize relations with all EU member states. The declaration indicates that the accession talks will proceed slowly if this does not happen soon. It also says that Turkey must fully implement its customs union with all EU states. At the moment Turkey is refusing to allow Cypriot ships and aircraft into its ports and airports."[18] This would potentially affect all EU members' relations and, at that point, Turkey's involvement would have to be reviewed. Finally, the current negotiations for entry are open-ended and the outcome can't be guaranteed.

An argument supporting Turkey's involvement ". . . is that its young and increasingly well-educated population can help the EU cope with its ageing population."[19] Another argument "is that it will help forge a bond between the West [Christian] and the Muslim world."[20] Unfortunately, not all of the directing minds of the EU support this position: "The former president of the European Commission, Jacques Delors, once said that the EU was a 'Christian Club.'"[21] This statement was alluding to the fact that new Muslim entrants would not be welcome in a Christian-dominated union. For Turkey, a particular attraction to becoming a member is that the country would be able to move forward with modernization. For example, Turkey's citizens would be able to gain the opportunity to work anywhere in the EU without a visa—a fact that has not gone unnoticed by France.

A caveat: rejection of this large Muslim's nation's application for the reasons that Delores suggests will have significant ramifications in the Muslim world. Indeed, I believe that rejection of membership might well provide the catalyst for the creation of a Muslim free trade region "crescent" running from Europe to India and China.

European Union—Background and Structure

"The European Union (EU) is not a federation like the United States. Nor is it simply an organization for co-operation between governments, like the United Nations. It is, in fact, unique."[22] The EU has its roots in the 1950s. The 25 member countries that comprise the EU, while remaining independent sovereign nations, as an economic union have moved toward abolishing or establishing common tariffs and quotas; removing restrictions on the movement of labour, capital, and equipment; and harmonizing and unifying economic policies and institutions among the member nations. As a result, EU members have delegated some of their "sovereign" decision-making powers to shared institutions. The three main EU decision-making bodies are the European Parliament, the European Union Council, and the European Commission.

The European Parliament (EP) has members elected by the citizens of the EU to represent their interests. The current parliament was elected in June 2004 and has 732 members representing all of 25 member countries. The current president of the EP, elected in 2004, is Josep Borrell Fontelles. The EP has three main purposes: (1) jointly with the EU Council, it passes European laws; (2) the EP exercises democratic supervision over other EU institutions, in particular the EU Commission; and (3) the EP shares authority over budgets and spending with the EU Council.

The European Union Council is the EU's main decision-making body. The Council has a president and a secretary-general. "The Presidency is held by the Member States in turn for a period of six months. The Council unanimously determines the order of rotation."[23] In the first half of 2006, Austrian Foreign Minister Ursula Plassnik will hold the Presidency. "Austria will be followed by Finland on 1 July 2006, then Germany and Portugal. Slovenia will take over the Presidency in the first half of 2008 as the first of the new Member States which joined the EU on 1 May 2004."[24]

The Council represents all member states and has ministerial representation from each. The working languages are English, French, and German. Within the council there are nine different sub-bodies including General Affairs and External Relations; Economic and Financial Affairs; Justice and Home Affairs; Employment, Social Policy, Health and Consumer Affairs; Competitiveness; Transport, Telecommunications and Energy; Agriculture and Fisheries; Environment; Education, and Youth and Culture. The Council has six main responsibilities including passing laws with the EP, coordinating economic policies, negotiating and concluding international agreements with other organizations, approving budgets and spending with the EP, developing the EU's common foreign and security policy, and coordinating the cooperation between the EU national courts and police forces.

The European Commission (EC) is a body independent of any of the member national governments. Its president is Jose Barroso. The EC represents the member states and has an appointed member from each. Its main focus is to uphold the interests of the EU as a whole. Part of its role is to implement the decisions for the EP and Council. The EC's responsibilities include proposing legislation for EP and Council consideration, managing and implementing EU policies and the approving budget, enforcing EU law, and representing the EU on the international stage. Visit www.power.nelson.com for an article on the European Union and its future.

A Few of the EU's Emerging Issues

The EU faces several significant issues in the years ahead:

- *National sovereignty.* Many believe the ruling elite is pushing to further concentrate and centralize power. In the EU, critics increasingly question whether "free trade" is destroying national sovereignties and imposing what they perceive as a tyrannical oligarchy in Brussels. The EU has become a supranational regional bloc (one of the triad) in the new world order.
- *Movement of labour.* Britain, Ireland, and Sweden were the only "old" EU-15 members to have maintained unrestricted access to their labour markets from the beginning of the Union's expansion. EU member states are to announce to the European Commission by the end of April (2006) whether they will extend the restrictions by another three years. Austria and Belgium are expected to continue to impose restrictions, in spite of the EU and independent experts' assurances that there is no reason to do so. In 2006, Germany had restricted labour movement until 2009 or possibly 2011.
- *Constitution.* The stunning fact that France and Holland rejected the European Union (EU) constitution in 2005 is a significant issue to many naysayers. Brussels has commenced damage control and is passing as many of the constitution's contents as possible under the existing legal framework. It is estimated that about 85 percent of the constitution can, with some creative interpretation, be implemented this way. There are several clauses that will require a formal treaty amendment (for example, the need to formalize the position of a European president to replace the existing system of member nations taking turns chairing EU meetings and to reform the current voting system). It is contemplated that these will be addressed at a miniature inter-governmental conference, probably in 2007. Recall that all 25 governments have accepted the constitution in principal so there could be little debate. The former president of France, Valery Giscard d'Estaing pronounced, "The rejection of the constitution was a mistake that will have to be corrected."[25] Visit www.power.nelson.com to review several papers on the European Union and the euro.

The North American Free Trade Agreement

Implementation of the North American Free Trade Agreement (NAFTA) began on January 1, 1994, and will be complete in 2008. This agreement removes most barriers to trade and investment among the United States, Canada, and Mexico. Under NAFTA, all non-tariff

NAFTA Exports of Goods and Services (Percentage of GDP 2005)

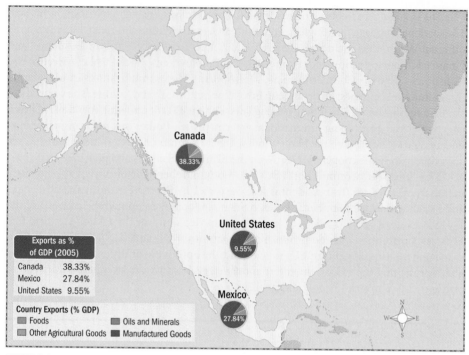

SOURCE: Author generated with data from "Exports (% GDP): World Bank, World Development Indicators 2006," World Development Indicators database. Retrieved May 2, 2006, from http://devdata.worldbank.org/data-query; and International and Regional Studies Center for Global International and Regional Studies, *Regional Trade Blocs* (University of California, July 27, 2005), retrieved August 11, 2006, from http://ucatlas.ucsc.edu/trade/subtheme_trade_blocs.php.

barriers to agricultural trade between the United States and Mexico were eliminated. In addition, many tariffs were eliminated immediately, with others being phased out over 5 to 15 years. All agricultural provisions will be implemented by the year 2008. For import-sensitive industries, long transition periods and special safeguards allowed for an orderly adjustment to free trade with Mexico. The agricultural provisions of the U.S.–Canada Free Trade Agreement (CFTA), in effect since 1989, were incorporated into NAFTA. Under these provisions, all tariffs affecting agricultural trade between the United States and Canada, with a few exceptions for items covered by tariff-rate quotas (TRQs), were removed before January 1, 1998. NAFTA exports $1,017 billion and imports $1,277 billion[26] in goods and services. See Figure 5.6 for a breakdown of NAFTA exports of goods and services.

Principles in Understanding NAFTA

NAFTA is the world's largest free trade area, with a total 2004 GDP of US$14.4 trillion, significantly larger than that of the European Union.[27] The NAFTA agreement includes **rules of origin**, where each country retains its external tariffs with non-member countries. Rules of origin provide the basis for customs officials to make determinations about which goods are entitled to preferential tariff treatment under NAFTA. This ensures that NAFTA's benefits are not extended to goods originally exported from non-NAFTA countries and that have undergone only minimal processing in North America.

What Are NAFTA's Positive Effects on Canada?

"By strengthening the rules and procedures governing trade and investment on this continent (within Canada, the United States, and Mexico), the NAFTA has allowed trade and investment flows in North America to skyrocket."[29] "From 1993 to 2005, trade among the NAFTA nations climbed 173 percent, from $297 billion to $810 billion. Each day the NAFTA countries conduct nearly $2.2 billion in trilateral trade."[30] In the period 1993 to 2002, "Canada's exports to its NAFTA partners increased by 87 percent in value. Exports to the United States grew from US$113.6 billion to US$213.9 billion, while exports to Mexico reached US$1.6 billion. US exports to Canada and Mexico grew from US$147.7 billion

Rules of origin are the "laws, regulations and administrative procedures that determine the origin of a good. Rules of origin may be designed to determine the eligibility of a good for preferential access under the terms of a free trade agreement, or they may be designed to determine a good's country of origin for various [other] purposes. . . . These rules can vary from country to country and from purpose to purpose."[28]

(US$51.1 billion to Mexico and US$96.5 billion to Canada) to US$260.2 billion (US$107.2 [billion] and US$152.9 billion, respectively). Mexican exports to the US grew by an outstanding 234 percent, reaching US$136.1 billion. Exports to Canada also grew substantially from US$2.9 [billion] to US$8.8 billion, an increase of almost 203 percent. The NAFTA has allowed both Canada and Mexico to increase their exports to the United States, but not at the expense of each other's share in the US merchandise import market. That's because substantial new trade has been generated throughout North America."[31] Canada provides the United States a market for 23 percent of its exports, and Mexico has increased from 6.8 percent in 1993 to a 13.6 percent share of U.S. exports in 1994. "U.S. manufacturing wages increased dramatically, with real hourly compensation up by 14.4% in the 10 years since NAFTA, more than double the 6.5% increase in the 10 years preceding NAFTA."[32]

Since the establishment of NAFTA, "the importance of trade with the US has increased for every Canadian province and nearly every industry. Canada now exports more manufacturing production to the US than it consumes domestically."[33] The U.S. economy has become heavily dependent on trade and investment linkages with Canada as the most important destination for exports from 39 U.S. states. In fact, Canada is the number one supplier of energy, including oil to the U.S.[34] Many of Canada's largest corporations suggest that liberalized trade provides advantages for both businesses and consumers because manufacturers in the NAFTA region benefit from a greater supply of inputs at lower prices. These organizations suggest that the result has been a rise in productivity, strengthening the competitiveness of these manufacturers in global markets. For consumers, NAFTA has provided more choices at competitive prices. Lower tariffs means that consumers pay less for products and have a greater selection of goods and services, which increases their standard of living.[35]

The NAFTA partners have recognized the importance of protecting the environment. Through the North American Agreement and Environmental Cooperation (NAAEC), they are promoting the effective enforcement of environmental laws in all three countries. Trilateral programs have been developed to facilitate the sharing of information, data, and best practices, to promote transparency and public participation, and to foster enhanced technical expertise and environmental policies among the three countries. In 2003, a strategic plan was developed for North American Cooperation in the Conservation of Biodiversity. This plan calls for protection of the shared environment and identification of potential opportunities for biodiversity conservation that arises from NAFTA–related trade.

What Are the Negative Effects on Canada?

Since the initiation of NAFTA, opponents, including labour, environmental, consumer, and religious groups, have argued that the agreement promotes the exploitation of low-paid labour, undermines domestic policy making, and threatens health and environmental standards. In addition, Canada's concerns also include a loss of sovereignty, primary dependence on a single market, and losses of natural resources and human capital. The 1989 U.S.–Canada Free Trade Agreement (FTA) and the 1994 NAFTA touched off a dramatic increase in Canada's trade and economic integration with the United States. By 2002, "over 40 percent of Canada–US trade [was] intra-firm, which points to the very high degree of integration between the two economies."[36] Today, Canada is even more dependent on its trade relationship with the United States, which has caused challenges in the Canadian softwood lumber and the beef industries. In 2005, Canada's six major import and export countries included those shown in Figure 5.7, page 136.

When NAFTA was originally debated, the majority of Canadian citizens did not realize that this trade agreement included a large number of non-trade policies to which every signatory country was required to adjust its domestic laws. "NAFTA sets limits on domestic meat and produce safety and inspection, environmental protections, service sector regulation, investment and development policy and banned buy-American and other procurement preferences. [In addition], NAFTA established

Canada's Imports and Exports in 2005

Country	Export %	Import %
United States	83.898	56.504
Japan	2.102	3.883
China	1.623	7.749
United Kingdom	1.893	2.737
Mexico	0.748	3.832
Germany	0.741	2.696

Note: Canada's exports to the United States are now reported at just over 79%.

SOURCE: Author generated with data from "Merchandise Trade by Country," Department of Foreign Affairs and International Trade database. Retrieved August 25, 2006, from www.dfait-maeci.gc.ca/eet/merchandise-trade-en.asp.

a number of closed-door committees empowered to set new standards outside the regulatory process which requires openness and public participation."[37] It has been suggested by a number of NAFTA opponents that the agreement attacks normal government activity, undermines control of domestic policy making, and creates a loss of sovereignty to Canada.

NAFTA includes a "proportional sharing" provision that grants other NAFTA countries rights in perpetuity to share natural resources. Accordingly, if Canada were to suffer a natural gas shortage, for example, it could not cease or substantially cut back exports to the United States. It could not give priority to domestic needs but would have to reduce domestic use and exports to other nations in order that the United States could maintain its share of the smaller remaining natural gas supplies. (Canada is required by NAFTA to continue exporting oil and gas to the United States, even if Canada experiences shortages.) Under "proportionality," Canada can cut exports to the United States to address shortages, but only if we cut in the same proportion to Canadians. Giant water corporations are ravenously eyeing Canada's massive freshwater supply. If any Canadian province agrees to sell bulk water to an international country, then all Canadian water could automatically be considered a traded good and not a natural resource over which Canada has sovereign control.[38] See www.power.nelson.com to review a discussion paper on this important emerging topic.

Lastly, NAFTA includes not only the trade of goods and services but also the movement of labour. Canada has seen a significant movement of Canadian trained professionals to the United States to take advantage of increased employment opportunities and salaries. As Canada subsidizes the education of students, this is a significant loss in intellectual capital, particularly in areas where Canada is in short supply of labour like doctors, nurses, and, increasingly, university professors. A further emerging issue is the General Agreement of Trades and Services (GATS). See www.power.nelson.com to review discussion papers on the brain drain, the General Agreement of Trades and Services, and NAFTA.

What Are the Impacts on International Business?

"The NAFTA has boosted competitiveness at the global level. The agreement has been instrumental in making North America one of the most active trading regions in the world."[39] The NAFTA countries account for 15 percent[40] of global exports. This is down from 19 percent in 2000 because of China's rapid growth in global exports.[41] "NAFTA fosters an environment of confidence and stability required to make long-term investments and partnering commitments. With a strong, certain and transparent framework for investment, North America has attracted foreign direct investment (FDI). In 2000, FDI in the three countries reached US$299.2 billion, more than double the US$136.9 billion figure registered in 1993. NAFTA has also stimulated increased investment from countries outside NAFTA. North America now accounts for 23.9 percent of global inward FDI and 25 percent of global outward FDI."[42] During 2004–05, increasing competition for FDI has been noted from China, Vietnam, and the East Asian tigers (Hong Kong, Taiwan, Singapore, and South Korea). You will read more about the shift in global FDI in Chapter 7. However, many opponents argue that NAFTA has had broad negative social impacts and increased inequality. In Mexico, NAFTA has been blamed for wage declines and forcing workers to move to big cities due to underemployment and unemployment. It has been suggested that the minimum wage in Mexico has declined by 20 percent; approximately 25 percent of Mexico's 40 million workers earn $4 a day.[43] For example, a manufacturing business moved from Cambridge, Ontario, to Juárez on the Mexican border. In Cambridge the workers were paid $8 per hour to produce brassieres that are sold for $20. This business generates economic activity within Cambridge in the form of workers living in homes locally, paying taxes, and generating local municipal taxes. When the manufacturing business moved to Juárez, Mexico, the wages for workers was reduced to $2 a day. This had a substantial impact on all the workers involved; Mexican workers are being paid inequitably and Canadian workers lose jobs.[44]

Today, many individuals chose to support or oppose NAFTA based on whether they are reaping the benefits or experiencing the negative consequences of free trade under NAFTA. The concerns of the opposition, although present, have been less substantial that those of interest groups who are more powerful and organized. Similarly, the Free Trade Area of the America's dream to eliminate or reduce trade barriers among all nations in the American continents is experiencing even greater push-back! In early 2006, the 34 potential members of FTAA met with the expectation that greater economic integration might be possible. However the program unravelled largely because of the growing tensions between the United States and some South American countries like Mercosur member Venezuela, and Bolivia. These setbacks are exacerbated by calls by American political leadership for more U.S. protectionism. Canadian SMEs must monitor these events and consider reducing their trade dependency on the United States though diversification.

Myth: NAFTA Hasn't Helped the United States; It Has Just Led to a Big Increase in U.S. Agricultural Imports

REALITY: While this is the perception in some quarters, the empirical evidence is quite the contrary. NAFTA's export benefits have been overwhelmingly positive for U.S. producers (see Figure 5.8) while the increase in imports that critics attribute to NAFTA are grossly overstated.

NAFTA's Emerging Issue

Manifest destiny. In 2005, the US Council on Foreign Relations, in *Building a North American Community*,[45] outlined a five-year plan to establish a North American Economic and Security Community with a common outer security perimeter by 2010. Described in the document is common economic space for all people in the region, a space in which to

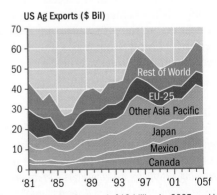

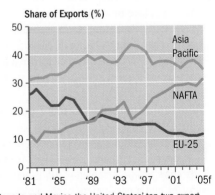

FIGURE 5.8

Canada and Mexico Account for Much of the Overall Growth in U.S. Agricultural Exports

Exports are expected to reach $19 billion by 2005, making Canada and Mexico the United States' top two export markets worldwide.

SOURCE: Foreign Agricultural Service, *Myths Regarding the Impact of NAFTA on U.S. Agricultural Trade* (May 2005) (United States Department of Agriculture, 2005), retrieved August 13, 2006, from www.fas.usda.gov/itp/Policy/NAFTA/NAFTA%20Myths.pdf.

trade, and a space where capital and people move freely. This plan contemplates that the three nations now become a customs union. The degrees of political and economic regional integration are discussed later in this chapter. This will require a harmonized visa and entry-screening process and full collaboration of Canada, the United States, and Mexico in sharing data about the exit and entry of foreign nationals. The document also calls for the establishment of a permanent tribunal for the North American Economic and Security Community to provide dispute resolution of issues. If this plan is implemented it will require an integrated continental transportation and infrastructure system (open skies and open roads) and the adoption of, among other things, national identification cards. The plan was silent as to the role of the 34 members of the Central America Free Trade Agreement (CAFTA). However, the inclusion of CAFTA would be consistent with the recently revitalized American vision of a north and south hemisphere trading bloc following the EU model of expanded membership. Consequently, it seems that Canada's ability to act with sovereignty, without being subject to the legal control of another country or international organization, will increasingly be an emerging issue for us to debate.

TRANSFORMATION TO ONE NORTH AMERICAN MARKET

Jim Miller, Senior VP, Corporate Affairs, Honda Canada observed, "There are no longer two separate Canadian and US marketplaces on this continent. It has become one North American market, and Canada is an ideal base from which to serve it."[46] Have we gone too far down the road to diversity with our portfolio of trading partners?

Free Trade Area of the Americas

The notion to unite the economies of the Americas into a single free trade area began at the Summit of the Americas, in December 1994. The heads of state and government of the 34 democracies in the region agreed to construct a Free Trade Area of the Americas (FTAA), in which barriers to trade and investment will be progressively eliminated. They agreed to complete negotiations toward this agreement by 2005. The FTAA negotiations were formally launched in April 1998 at the Second Summit of the Americas in Santiago, Chile.

"The Third Summit of the Americas was held in Quebec City, Canada on April 20–22, 2001. . . . Deadlines were fixed for the conclusion and implementation of the FTAA Agreement. Negotiations were to be concluded no later than January 2005; entry into force will be sought as soon as possible thereafter, no later than December 2005."[47] President Bush stated that the issue would be fast-tracked by the U.S. Government; however, following the events of 9/11, the sense of urgency provided by the United States dissipated, with disastrous results.

The final phase of FTAA negotiations was co-chaired by Brazil and the United States. Once again, the leaders "reaffirmed their commitment to the successful conclusion of the FTAA negotiations by January 2005, with the ultimate goal of achieving an area of free trade and regional integration."[48] The ministers of trade met with little success. The last summit took place in Argentina, in November 2005. It failed as Mercosur member states, led by Brazil's President Lula,[49] blocked ratification of the FTAA. However, with increasing trade interest being displayed in the region by China, South Africa, and the EU, U.S. Secretary of State Condoleezza Rice has been attempting to restart the FTAA talks. To date she has experienced little success, for the reasons we discussed earlier.

Venezuela Increases Cuba Ties with Show

Political allies Cuba and Venezuela began weaving their economies together more tightly Wednesday as scores of business people from the South American nation opened a trade show on the communist-run island. The opening of offices for Venezuela's state oil company and a government bank were among other major events planned for this week's trade and business meetings between the two left-leaning developing nations—a growing alliance that has increasingly alarmed Washington. Members of the administration of US President George W. Bush have expressed concerns that Venezuela has become increasingly authoritarian and that it is reinforcing its links to communist Cuba. Venezuelan populist President Hugo Chavez, elected in open, democratic elections 6 times considers himself an ally and personal friend of Cuban President Fidel Castro.... The new moves are aimed at cementing Cuba and Venezuela in a new 'Bolivarian Alternative for the Americas'— a trade pact they announced in December in opposition to the US–supported Free Trade Area of the Americas, or FTAA. The name refers to South American independence hero Simon Bolivar, frequently invoked by the Chavez government. 'While the FTAA retreats with its annexationist formulas, the (Bolivarian Alternative) advances, said Venezuelan Commerce Minister Barbara Castillo, using a term employed by FTAA opponents who say the United States wants to use the pact to 'annex' Latin America. Meanwhile, Venezuela's government-controlled Banco Industrial de Venezuela and the state oil company Petroleos Venezolanos were opening offices in Havana on Thursday—moves that could help the growing bilateral trade. Under Chavez, Venezuela, in 2000, began selling 53,000 barrels of crude a day to oil-import-dependent Cuba under preferential terms, allowing the island to cope with tough economic times that began with the Soviet Union's collapse more than a decade ago. In turn, communist Cuba has sent 13,000 Cuban doctors to work in Venezuelan state-run clinics located in poor neighbourhoods. The new office of Banco Industrial de Venezuela will help facilitate trade payments and has Cuban approval to offer everything from small business loans to letters of credit. Cuba, meanwhile, has plans to open in Venezuela a bank branch of its own, as well as a chain of 14 government-run stores that will sell goods at subsidized prices. Venezuela and China are also expanding trading relationships as China's global influence grows.

Source: *Venezuela Increases Cuba Ties with Show* (Forbes.com, April 27, 2005). © 2006 Forbes.com LLC™. All Rights Reserved.

Critical Thinking Questions

During the Milken Institute Global Conference in 2005, Brazilian Minister of Development, Industry, and Foreign Trade Luiz Fernando Furlan observed that Brazil and other South American countries are not waiting for the FTAA to come together. Brazil's trade with China has increased fourfold since 2000, and expectations are that it will double by 2008. Brazil's growth of GNI remains at approximately 5 percent. The minister forecasts that Brazil would be the world's fifth largest economy by 2050. Can NAFTA, through procrastination, afford to miss this opportunity?

FTAA's Emerging Issues

Decline in the attractiveness of Western liberalized democracy. Why is the vision waning? Internally, as the region increasingly embraced democracy at the end of the Cold War, Washington's market-oriented Western liberalized democracy began to take hold. Liberalization policies that cut social spending and privatized national industries in order to pay down national debts were implemented mostly in response to IMF loan conditions. But these initiatives have largely failed to deliver the goods. In their wake, a number of governments are bankrupt and beholden to the IMF and other foreign lenders. For Latin America's angry impoverished masses, already-threadbare social safety nets increasingly show strain—with far-reaching political ramifications. The shift has presented opportunities for proponents of new social and political movements in the region to begin marshalling their forces as many nations lurch to the left politically. In 2005, Bolivian "voters overwhelmingly elected former coca-grower Evo Morales, founder of Bolivia's 'Movement Toward Socialism' party, and a populist who fancies himself a 'nightmare' for the Bush administration. Then, in January [2006], Chilean voters chose socialist candidate Michele Bachelet, a torture victim of the Pinochet regime, as the nation's first woman president. Leftists [populists] also rule in Venezuela, Uruguay, Brazil and Argentina, and are leading in election campaigns in Peru and Mexico, the region's electoral grand prize. Even recycled Sandinista leader Daniel Ortega—'a hoodlum,' according to Roger Noriega, formerly the US's top Latin America official—appears poised for a comeback when

Nicaraguan voters go to the polls in November [2006]."[50] Has Che Guevara's[51] vision of pan-Latin cooperation already begun to materialize? Consider, "Venezuela, Brazil and Argentina recently announced a $20 billion plan to build a transnational gas pipeline through the Amazon. Chile has opened dialogue with landlocked Bolivia, easing a long-simmering feud over seaport access. Cuba . . . still employs doctor diplomacy, sending physicians all over the region, only now it receives billions of dollars worth of Venezuelan oil in return."[52] Externally, nations in the regions are proactively seeking new trade agreements with the EU, Africa, China, and others. The significance to Canada must be understood. The importance of Chile, Brazil, and other nations as Canada's trading partners is rising as we try to diversify our global customers. If FTAA is to fail, then we must have an exit plan. There are signs that the Bush administration now recognizes the political shift to the left and is growing increasingly concerned with the developments.

DR-CAFTA

Dominican Republic joined the five members of Central America Free Trade Agreement (DR-CAFTA), Costa Rica, El Salvador, Guatemala, Honduras, and Nicaragua, to create the second-largest free trade zone in Latin America for U.S. exports.[53] Negotiations with the five Central American countries began in January 2003. Eighty percent of DR-CAFTA imports already entered the United States duty-free; the remaining tariffs are to phased out over 10 years.[54]

"In 2003, the US exported $15 billion of goods to the Dominican Republic and Central American countries. Combined total of goods traded between the US and the original five CAFTA countries was $23.6 billion in 2003. The addition of the Dominican Republic represents an additional $8.7 billion in annual two-way trade, for a combined total trade relationship of approximately $32 billion."[55]

The United States and the DR-CAFTA countries have entered into an Environmental Cooperation Agreement that will promote environmental cooperation as a complement to the trade liberalization efforts.[56]

Will these six countries lead the way for other hemispheric nations and regions to join this new free trade region? Does this initiative help or hinder Canada's trade relationships? How much of this initiative was in response to the populist movements in South America and the growing interest in the region by other nations like China? See www.power.nelson.com to review a discussion paper on DR-CAFTA.

DR-CAFTA's Emerging Issues

Alliance partners are not in equal bargaining positions. "The US Trade Representative [USTR] has been insisting that the six countries involved in the agreement go beyond the original provisions, especially in the areas of intellectual property rights and sanitary regulations. In particular, US–based pharmaceutical companies have demanded legal changes in the Central American countries that would prevent generic drug companies from manufacturing low-cost medicines. The government of Guatemala has been particularly adamant in opposing such measures, and Guatemala's vice president has gone as far as to threaten to pull the country out of DR-CAFTA if the USTR does not let up."[57]

In addition, the Bush administration is demanding plant and animal health reforms before implementation, pushing Central American countries to eliminate domestic health regulations for U.S. meat exports. The costs for Central Americans to meet this demand will be very high. As a result, there is growing resistance; for example, El Salvador is reviving the anti-CAFTA movement, which is growing in strength.

Nevertheless, Peru, Panama, Colombia, and Ecuador are considering the possibilities of membership in DR-CAFTA.

Asia-Pacific Economic Cooperation Forum

The Asia-Pacific Economic Cooperation forum (APEC) is a loose grouping of the countries bordering the Pacific Ocean who have pledged to facilitate free trade. The Asian crisis hurt the economies of fast-growing newly industrialized countries like South Korea and Indonesia and seriously set back progress on free trade initiatives in the region.[58] APEC was established in 1989 to further enhance economic growth and prosperity for the region and to strengthen the Asia-Pacific community. APEC has worked to reduce tariffs and other trade barriers across the Asia-Pacific region, creating efficient domestic economies and dramatically increasing exports. The forum is the premier association for facilitating economic growth, cooperation, trade, and investment in the Asia-Pacific region. APEC is the only inter-governmental grouping in the world that operates on non-binding commitments, open dialogue, and equal respect for the views of all participants. Unlike the WTO or other multilateral trade bodies, APEC has no treaty obligations that must be observed by its membership. Decisions made within APEC are reached by consensus, and commitments are undertaken on a voluntary basis. "APEC has 21 members—referred to as 'Member Economies'—which account for approximately 40% of the world's population [2.6 billion people], approximately 56% of world GDP [US$ 19.254 billion] and about 48% of world trade. It ... represents the most economically dynamic region in the world having generated nearly 70% of global economic growth in its first 10 years. APEC's 21 Member Economies are Australia; Brunei Darussalam; Canada; Chile; People's Republic of China; Hong Kong, China; Indonesia; Japan; Republic of Korea; Malaysia; Mexico; New Zealand; Papua New Guinea; Peru; The Republic of the Philippines; The Russian Federation; Singapore; Chinese Taipei; Thailand; United States of America; [and] Viet Nam. . . . APEC also works to create an environment for the safe and efficient movement of goods, services, and people across borders in the region through policy alignment and economic and technical cooperation."[59]

APEC issues are of particular interest to Canada, as one of the largest gateways to Asia. For example, the specific threats posed by infectious diseases such as Severe Acute Respiratory Syndrome (SARS), avian flu, pandemic influenza, tuberculosis, malaria, and polio in the Asia-Pacific region and the requirement to strengthen the research into and production of relevant vaccines are of interest to Canada.[60] The very real possibility of pandemics is of great concern to Canada. See www.power.nelson.com to review a discussion paper on pandemics.

As a founding member of APEC, Canada has been involved in the organization since its creation in 1989. It has promoted trade liberalization and facilitation initiatives within the APEC forum specifically in the fields of customs, standards, and regulatory measures. Canada also believes that APEC has an important contribution to make on security issues and supports concrete initiatives in areas like "ship and port security, aircraft and airport security, cyber-security and anti-money laundering, [which] have helped secure the economic growth and prosperity of our region by reducing our vulnerability to terrorism."[61]

APEC's Emerging Issues

CANADIAN INFLUENCE

Canada needs to promote Canadian trade policy interests and our regional trade policy objectives, and to make the Asia-Pacific region more accessible to Canadian businesses through trade facilitation, transparency, and anti-corruption measures.

SECURITY—PANDEMICS

With increasing imports, Canada has to enhance security of both goods and people in the Asia-Pacific region by expanding adherence to counterterrorism agreements, capacity building, enhancing health security, and collaborating in crafting infectious-disease strategies. A SARS or similar outbreak can have serious business implications for the Canadian economy.

INFRASTRUCTURE NEEDS

Canada's SMEs in the Asia-Pacific region must be supported with trade policy measures that encourage our APEC partners to strengthen their legal infrastructure and narrow the digital divide.

The Association of Southeast Asian Nations (ASEAN)

The Association of Southeast Asian Nations (ASEAN) is a consensus-based inter-governmental organization for regional cooperation. Founded in 1967 by Indonesia, Malaysia, the Philippines, Singapore, and Thailand, and later joined by Brunei (1984), Vietnam (1995), Burma and Laos (1997), and Cambodia (1999), ASEAN is the region's major vehicle for dialogue on political, economic, security, social, and other key transnational issues. The ASEAN region has a population of about 500 million, a total area of 4.5 million square kilometres, a combined gross domestic product of US$737 billion, and a total trade of US$720 billion. "ASEAN total exports increased . . . to US$551.19 billion in 2004. ASEAN total imports likewise increased by 26.77% from US$388.79 billion in 2003 to US$492.86 billion in 2004."[62] Foreign direct investment (FDI), rebounded in 2004; "ASEAN FDI flow for 2004 reached US$25.1 billion, a 22% year-on-year increase."[63] The ASEAN economies' "real GDP expanded by 6.1% in 2004. Despite the current uncertainty in oil prices and rising interest rates, ASEAN's economic growth is likely to be sustained at around 5.5% in 2005."[64]

The region is now encouraging external membership. It began establishing special consultative relationships called dialogue partnerships with other selected countries in 1976. "Canada became a dialogue partner in 1977. Other dialogue partners are Australia, the People's Republic of China, the European Union, India, Japan, the Republic of Korea, New Zealand, Russia, and the United States of America."[65]

Canada has very significant interests in the Southeast Asian region and is strongly committed to a long-term partnership with ASEAN, as evidenced by its important political and trade ties with the region, strong people-to-people links, longstanding development cooperation, and ongoing support and promotion of peace and security in the area. The ASEAN economic region promotes a free flow of goods, services, investments, and capital, as well as equitable economic development and reduced poverty and socioeconomic disparities.[66] Interestingly, through political dialogue and collaboration, no tension has escalated into armed confrontation among ASEAN members since its establishment more than three decades ago.

The 10 members of the ASEAN region have opened a forum referred to as "ASEAN Plus Three" (China, Japan, and the Republic of Korea). This grouping is taking on increasing importance in the region and becoming the main vehicle for the realization of the East Asian community in the future because of the significant economic weight and growing political influence of the world stage these three nations bring to the region. The region is also moving to strengthen its relations with Russia. This is evidenced by the ASEAN–Russian Federation Joint Declaration on Progressive and Comprehensive Partnership and the Comprehensive Program of Action for 2005–2015, intended to strengthen ASEAN–Russia relations. A similar partnering "Plan of Action" with the President of the Republic of Korea was implemented in 2005.

ASEAN's Emerging Issues

CHINA'S INFLUENCE

While not a full member of the ASEAN, the hoped-for denuclearization of the Korean Peninsula and support of the efforts made by the "six-party talks"[67] to find a peaceful and comprehensive solution to the North Korean nuclear issue are dependent on China. China has called on all concerned parties to exert utmost efforts to move toward a peaceful resolution of the nuclear issue on the Korean Peninsula. However, the chance of a peaceful resolution was marred by North Korea's missile launch in July 2006 and nuclear testing later that year.

TERRORISM

Terrorist attacks in the region continue. The region's diversity of race, religion, nationality, and ethnic groupings will continue to be an issue.

PANDEMIC

The outbreak of avian influenza and the rise in oil prices have direct negative impacts on regional economic development and public health.

Mercosur

The Mercosur region was created in 1991 by Argentina, Brazil, Paraguay, and Uruguay, and the agreement was amended and updated in 1994. It created a common market/customs union between the participating countries. Canada had signed a Trade and Investment Co-operation Arrangement in 1998 with the largest South American trading bloc. Amid uncertainty surrounding the success of a FTAA hemispheric free trade zone, Canada inched forward in 2005 on a separate, but complementary, free trade arrangement.

In 2003, several important events contributed to Mercosur's strengthening. The newly elected presidents of Argentina and Brazil have put Mercosur at the top of the political agenda and a Dispute Settlement Court has been created to strengthen Mercosur institutionalization. See Figure 5.9 for a breakdown of Mercosur exports of goods and services.

Mercosur is expanding its influence. In 2004, it accepted Mexico and Venezuela as associate members, a status already enjoyed by Chile, Bolivia, and Peru. Mercosur and Mexico are continuing free trade talks, with a view toward the latter's eventual full admission to the South American trade bloc. In 2006, Venezuela became a full member of the Mercosur. Mercosur has also entered trade agreements with India, South Africa, and Egypt.

EU–Mercosur Relations, 1991–2005

The European Union has always supported a strengthening of regional integration in Mercosur. Notwithstanding the current cyclical downturn on both sides of the Atlantic, the EU continues to work toward a stronger relationship with Mercosur.

Mercosur as a whole is a "global trader": its internal regional customers and its suppliers account for less than one-quarter of its exports.

Mercosur's ambition to become a real common market is seen as an extremely positive element toward the creation of an association between it and the EU. The European Commission has encouraged Mercosur from the very beginning. In 1992, less than a year after its creation, the European Commission signed an Inter-institutional Agreement with Mercosur to provide technical and institutional support. The EU's primary reason for cooperating is to reinforce the process of regional integration of Mercosur, which in turn supplements the various cooperation relationships that the EU has with the individual members of Mercosur on a bilateral basis. "Mercosur's ratio of trade [imports + exports] to GDP is 25.1%. In the year 2003 imports and exports amounted to 62.3 and 93.6 billion euro respectively, representing 1.2% and 2% of the world flows."[68] The EU is Mercosur's largest trading partner for both imports and exports. "From 1993 to 2003, EU imports from Mercosur grew by 5.6% on average per year, and EU exports by 3.6%. In 2003, trade with Mercosur represented 2.8% of total EU imports and 1.8% of total EU exports. The EU is Mercosur's first trade partner with 22.9% of Mercosur total trade. At the end of 2003, 0.30% of the stock of EU inward FDI came from Mercosur, while 3.51% of the stock of EU outward FDI went to Mercosur."[69]

There is now movement toward a EU–Mercosur Regional Association Agreement. One main objective of the Mercosur Agreement was the preparation of negotiations for an Interregional Association Agreement between the EU and Mercosur, including a liberalization of trade in goods and services; free trade in conformity with WTO rules; as

FIGURE 5.9

MERCOSUR Exports of Goods and Services (Percentage of GDP, 2004)

Exports as % of GDP (2004)	
Argentina	25.28%
*Bolivia	30.70%
Brazil	18.02%
*Chile	36.26%
*Colombia	20.84%
*Ecuador	26.51%
Paraguay	35.99%
*Peru	20.90%
Uruagay	29.65%
**Venezuela	36.23%

* Bolivia, Chile, Columbia, Ecuador and Peru have associate member status.

** On 9 December 2005, Venezuela was accepted as a new member, to be officialized in late 2006.

Country Exports (% GDP)

▨ Foods　　▨ Oils and Minerals
▨ Other Agricultural Goods　　▨ Manufactured Goods

* Bolivia, Chile, Colombia, Ecuador, and Peru have associate member status.

** On December 9, 2005, Venezuela was accepted as a new member, and ratified in 2006.

SOURCE: Author generated with data from "Exports (% GDP): World Bank World Development Indicators 2006," World Development Indicators database. Retrieved from http://devdata.worldbank.org/data-query; and International and Regional Studies Center for Global International and Regional Studies, *Regional Trade Blocs* (University of California, July 27, 2005), retrieved August 11, 2006, from http://ucatlas.ucsc.edu/trade/subtheme_trade_blocs.php.

Trade within Mercosur

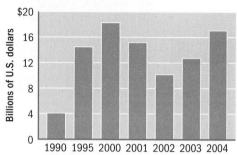

NOTE: Statistics include only MERCOSUR [4] = Argentina, Brazil, Paraguay, and Uruguay.

Source: Stephen Handelman, "Special Report: Summit of the Americas" (*Time*, April 19, 2001). Copyright © 2006 Time Inc. All rights reserved.

FIGURE 5.11
Mercosur [4]'s Geographic
Distribution of Exports and Imports

SOURCE: *Mercosur Outlook* (Ministry of Foreign Affairs, International Trade and Worship, International Economic Relations Secretariat, Argentine Republic, July 2002). Copyright Secretaria Comercio y Relaciones Economicas Internacional.

well as an enhanced form of cooperation and a strengthened political dialogue. In 2005, the Mercosur–EU Business Forum called for the revitalization of the EU–Mercosur negotiations. If successful, it will create one of the largest free trade areas in the world, involving almost 700 million people. It would be the first ever region-to-region free trade area.

Increasingly nations and trading blocs such as the South African Customs Union (SACU) are entering into preferential trade agreements with Mercosur. The Mercosur agreement with South America is small; about 1,000 products have been included in a special trade arrangement. . . . In 2005 the Mercosur commenced formal trade negotiations with China and India.[70]

Mercosur's Emerging Issues

FREE TRADE ALLIANCE WITH EU

"EU–Mercosur trade represents as much as EU trade with the rest of Latin America taken together. The EU is the 1st trading partner of Mercosur, representing [24%] of total Mercosur trade, and its first source of investment. Mercosur ranks 9th among EU trading partners, accounting for 2.3% of total EU trade."[71] See Figure 5.11 for the geographic distribution of Mercosur's exports and imports. The EU–Mercosur negotiations for an Association Agreement currently are moving toward conclusion (2005) and establishing a comprehensive political and economic partnership between the two regional trading blocs. If successful, the FTAA takes on diminished importance.

DIFFICULT TO BUILD CONSENSUS

Simon de Bolivar observed with exasperation that trying to promote Latin American unity was like "ploughing the sea." This observation continues to have merit.

Commonwealth of Independent States (CIS)

The Commonwealth of Independent States (CIS) was created in December 1991 in response to the breakup of the Soviet Union. Its purpose was to allow a "civilized divorce" between the Soviet republics. CIS is a confederation, or alliance, consisting of 11 former Soviet republics: Armenia, Azerbaijan, Belarus, Georgia, Kazakhstan, Kyrgyzstan, Moldova, Russia, Tajikistan, Ukraine, and Uzbekistan. Turkmenistan discontinued permanent membership as of August 26, 2005, and is now an associate member. Turkmenistan downgraded its status because of the doubt of the potential and continued worth of the CIS. For example, between 2003 and 2005, leaders of three CIS member states were overthrown in a series of "colour revolutions": Eduard Shevardnadze in Georgia, Leonid Kuchma in Ukraine, and Askar Akayev in Kyrgyzstan. The new governments of Ukraine and Georgia have adopted pro-Western stance, and Moldova seems to be quietly drifting toward the West. Many observers see the CIS as a tool that allows Russia to keep its influence over the post-Soviet states.

Since its formation, the CIS member-states have concluded a number of matters relating to integration and cooperation around economics, defence, and foreign policy. CIS participants interact on the basis of sovereign equality. In 1993, CIS states agreed to "the creation of an Economic Union to form common economic space grounded on free movement of goods, services, labour force, capital; to elaborate coordinated monetary, tax, price, customs, external economic policy; to bring together methods of regulating economic activity and create favourable conditions for the development of direct

INTERNATIONAL STRATEGIC THINKING

This chapter and others raise the question, how do we administer and manage this rapidly changing world? Do global challenges and issues require global government? Traditionally, using our old mental models, we think of economic units in terms of sovereign states. Is this mental model sustainable? What would replace it, if anything? The European Union may be showing us the way. It is changing the nature of sovereignty for 25 sovereign units. Without adopting this new mental model, how can we collectively address global environmental, human rights, and poverty challenges? It is doubtful that 193 sovereign governments will be effective. What do you think?

production relations."[72] In order to facilitate further deepening of integration in economic and humanitarian areas, additional agreements were signed in 1995. In February 1999, the Republic of Tajikistan was recognized as participant of the customs union.[73]

The Russian economy has recovered significantly in recent years, registering budgetary surpluses for five consecutive years. Russia has built up its foreign-currency reserves of US$180 billion (2004) and has made its debt repayments ahead of schedule. The Russian economy has begun integrating into the world economy, "According the Russian Academy of Sciences, in 1999–2005 Russia's GDP increased by nearly 57%, with average annual growth rates constituting 6.6%. The preliminary figure of Russia's GDP growth in 2005 cited by the Federal State Statistics Service [Rosstat] was 6.4%. . . . In 2005, the value of Russian exports exceeded $240 billion and that of imports $120 billion, registering a 35% and 29% increase respectively. Energy resources, ferrous and non-ferrous metals, fertilizers, and timber continued to dominate Russian exports. The investment climate in Russia is gradually improving; "Russia rose to the sixth place in the FDI Confidence Index 2005, after China, the United States, Britain, India and Poland (in March 2005, it was given eleventh place in the FDI Index)."[74] Inflation is an issue; it was 11.7 percent in 2004 to 10.9 percent in 2005.[75] Don't be mislead by these numbers, Russia today is not a superpower, and is nobody's enemy. It has significant internal problems such as the decline in population and the governance in its North Caucasus regions. These are profound and do not lend themselves to easy solutions. However, Russia is increasingly shifting its foreign policy activities to counter America's global initiatives and to enable it once again to play a role near the centre of the world stage. It will do this through regional alliances.

CIS's Emerging Issues

RISING TENSION WITH U.S. NATIONAL FOREIGN POLICY INITIATIVES

Is a U.S.–Russian partnership still feasible with the spectre of an unprecedented and provocative military encirclement by the United States in Asia and the Middle East? What will be the reaction of the CIS?

THE RUSSIAN PRESIDENT'S GROWING DOMINANCE OVER CIS

The move toward centralization of power in the Kremlin with a presidency that is strong, without countervailing institutions, can subvert democracy. Will the equal members of CIS accept this strong hand by the president and the Kremlin?

National Regions

We have looked at, and will continue to look at globalization and regionalization but as we leave this chapter, we should also be aware that there are emerging much smaller but nevertheless significant national and regional trading units that should be examined. They will increasingly affect Canadian SMEs and Canada's national sovereignty. In Canada, Cascadia is a good example. "Cascadia is a region controlled by the Pacific Northwest Economic Region (PNER), which has been created by compacts between five northwestern states—Oregon, Washington, Montana, Idaho and Alaska—and two Canadian provinces—British Columbia and Alberta. Cascadia is promoted as the 'two-nation vacation'; its 'main street' is the I-5 corridor from Eugene, Oregon, to Vancouver, BC; and Cascadia reports its own GNP. Former Washington State Senator, [Alan] Bluechel, president of the PNER, said, 'It's our version of the European Economic Region.' PNER has politically erased the national borders in Cascadia; in a publication advertising Cascadia, US Senator Mark Hatfield said, 'National regions are emerging as key environmental and economic units throughout the world.' They certainly are. Another example is Border Region 21, which has also erased national borders, in this case between Mexico and four southwestern states—California, Texas, New Mexico, and Arizona,"[76] as a result of NAFTA.

As this section on regionalization draws to a close, I would like you to think about Patrick Henry, who stated, "We are apt to shut our eyes against a painful truth . . . For my part, I am willing to know the whole truth; to know the worst; and to provide for it."[77] Review Figure 5.1 on page 126, and consider, what level (step) is Canada currently occupying and in which direction is Canada moving?

Multilateral Trade Liberalization

"Multilateral trade liberalization remains the best way to achieve a more open world economy where trade can flourish and expand and help fuel global economic growth. If regional trading arrangements erode support for the multilateral framework, it would be counterproductive. There is a danger that the emergence of regional trading blocs would be accompanied by increasing trade frictions and even rising trade barriers between competing blocs, or that countries' production is mostly destined for regional partners at high cost relative to world prices."[78]

The poster child for multilateral trade liberalization is Chile. Its government introduced strong fiscal and other reforms in the mid-1970s and, since the late 1980s, Chile has experienced strong, crisis-free growth. It withstood the economic downturn of 2001–02 more successfully than many of its Latin American neighbours. Trade liberalization was an integral part of these reforms. Tariffs in Chile have been progressively lowered over the years, to the current level of 6 percent, uniform across all commodities. Chile is one of the most open economies in the region and has one of the most diversified export structures. It serves as a model for those who would follow.

Will free trade agreements be subject to increased protectionist measures against non-members of the free trade cluster? No. International businesses' global strategies have resulted primarily in regional systems of production facilities. The gains from manufacturing and trading among these more widely dispersed facilities tends to offset the costs of managing such a complex organizational design. Therefore, it seems fair to conclude that multinationals' trade will remain mostly within the region of production, and would be little affected by the emergence of powerful trading blocs. The strategies of most Canadian multinationals and others would be threatened only if regional blocs restricted foreign investment. This seems unlikely, given the history of regional trade groups, and that restrictions on new investment would probably harm host competitors more than Canadian multinationals firms entering their market.

Global Institutions

As we discussed earlier, and will again in Chapter 9, page 258, the 1944 Bretton Woods agreement was driven by the need to establish rules for economic global trading relationships for most of the developed nations following World War II. We have briefly introduced several institutions formed to support this historic agreement. The primary organizations are the World Bank, the International Monetary Fund (IMF), and the General Agreement of Tariffs and Trade (GATT). GATT's mandate was subsequently enhanced at the Uruguay Round from 1986 to 1994 with the creation of the World Trade Organization (WTO). Originally created to provide stability in a global postwar economy where exchange rates were fixed, though adjustable, the IMF and the World Bank were born with outstanding survival instincts that have kept them going after exchange rates were floated in the early 1970s. Today these three institutions wield tremendous power and influence, especially in the developing world, resulting in an increasing number of critics accusing these institutions of lacking democratic decision-making processes, transparency, and accountability.

The World Bank

The World Bank, based in Washington, DC, is a multilateral institution that lends money to governments and government agencies for development projects. For more than 30 years, the bank has imposed stringent conditions, known as "Structural Adjustment Programs," on recipient countries, forcing them to adopt reforms such as deregulation of capital markets, privatization of state companies, and downsizing of public programs for social welfare. Privatization of water supplies, fees for public schools and hospitals, and privatization of public pensions are among the most controversial bank reforms. A shift in control of the Commanding Heights! Many critics express their dissatisfaction with this "cookie-cutter" approach to individual nations' varied economic difficulties.

The bank comprises two unique development institutions: the International Bank for Reconstruction and Development (IBRD) and the International Development Association (IDA). Each of the bank's institutions is owned by between 140 and 184 member countries. Governments can choose which ones they choose to join. Each institution plays a different but supportive role in global poverty reduction and the improvement of living standards. The IBRD focuses on middle-income and creditworthy poor countries, while the IDA focuses on the poorest countries in the world. The bank provides low-interest loans, interest-free credit, and grants to developing countries for education, health, infrastructure, communications, and many other purposes. However, while the Bank insists that "fighting poverty" is its first priority, many critics believe instead that it is responsible for increasing poverty. "Despite the Bank's noble mission, many detractors see their work as harmful. Labour unions protest that the IFC's [International Finance Corporation—an arm of the bank] encouragement of private business to go abroad reduces needed jobs in industrial countries."[79] The IFC is tasked with promoting growth in developing countries. "Human rights workers feel the private sector investment does not help the local people but enslaves them in factory and assembly line jobs. As the IDA grants a poor country money to build a dam that will provide electricity, environment activists complain that river wildlife will die as a result. The competing interests of worldwide organization groups can make project implementation difficult. The IMF has not avoided criticism. Many feel the IMF wastes money to prop up under-achieving economies. Often, money loaned to support currencies is diverted to support political parties. At times these political parties are corrupt but retaining the political party in power is often deem[ed] to be in the best interest of the institution's 'directing minds.' At times the terms and conditions of the loans are breached as no measures are taken to restructure a failing economy and the loans are never repaid. Yet all member governments continue to support the IMF and the World Bank as evidence[d] by their continued contributions. Although public scrutiny has forced the IMF and the Bank to reassess some of their policies, neither appears in danger of dissolving under this minor public pressure."[80] Many also criticize its cozy relationship with Wall Street and the United States Treasury Department. In 2005, Paul Wolfowitz, **neo-conservative** and former undersecretary of Defense, was appointed president of the World Bank. Wolfowitz was a co-author of *Rebuilding America's Defenses: Strategy, Forces and Resources of a New Century*. Visit www.power.nelson.com to access this article.

The International Monetary Fund

The IMF is a multilateral lending institution, also based in Washington, that maintains a loose relationship with the United Nations (UN). The IMF is an organization of 184 countries mandated is to foster global monetary cooperation, secure financial stability, facilitate international trade, promote high employment and sustainable economic growth, and reduce poverty. It provides loans to help stabilize faltering economies. It too has come under increasing criticism for its harsh neoliberal policies and

Neo-conservative, or neocon, refers to the political movement, ideology, and public policy goals of "new conservatives" in the United States. Proponents are mainly characterized by critics as having relatively interventionist and hawkish views on foreign policy of the nature conducted in Afghanistan and Iraq by the Bush administration. Neocons as conservatives generally lack of support for restricting the size of government and they tolerate more social spending, compared to other American conservatives such as traditional or paleoconservatives.

invasive loan conditions. Increasingly the IMF's operations have been the centre of growing controversy. Points of contention include:

A **moral hazard** is a situation in which someone will purposely engage in risky behaviour, knowing that any costs incurred will be compensated by the insurer (lender).

- *Moral hazard.* IMF bailouts encourage investors to assume additional risk in the expectation that losses will be absorbed by the IMF and ultimately the taxpayers of affected countries. Borrowers believe they will not be required to repay the loan.
- *Exposure of taxpayer funds.* Members' funds are used directly and indirectly in subsidized bailouts that promote perverse incentives leading to a more vulnerable financial system.
- *Inappropriate conditions.* The IMF sometimes imposes counterproductive policies that undermine economic performance as loan conditions. Recall the Asian Flu financial market meltdown materials earlier in the text.
- *Transparency.* The IMF is a closed and secretive organization that operates in a manner inconsistent with openness. We will examine other aspects of the IMF in Chapter 9, as it relates to international monetary systems and capital markets.

Video 5.1

The World Trade Organization

The WTO, formerly GATT, influences a wide range of global policy issues, including trade in goods, investment, patents, environmental regulations and many other issues. Since 1944, the world's merchandise trade expanded significantly, creating more prosperity and widening the gulf between rich and poor. The situation became of increasing concern, and new ways of using the WTO treaties to maintain stability in an interconnected world had to be found.

In 1994 the members of GATT established a new world organization with the powers to continue promoting free trade by reducing tariffs and non-tariff barriers on international trade and, very importantly, to enforce rules of international trade. The WTO has three main goals (see www.wto.org): to assist in the free flow of trade, to negotiate further opening of the global market, and to settle trade disputes between WTO members. All GATT trade agreements arranged since 1947 were ratified and assumed by the WTO. As of 2006, there are 149 members and a further 32 countries with "observer" status. These 149 members account for 97 percent of world trade. The last and ninth round of WTO negotiations was launched in 2001 and concluded in 2005. The WTO Doha, Qatar, round focused on lowering trade barriers and specifically assisting underdeveloped

JUST DOING THE RIGHT THING

Doha Round—Lift Millions out of Poverty

"World Trade Organization (WTO) Chief Pascal Lamy warned member states on Tuesday it would be a huge mistake to miss an April 2006 deadline for accords vital to an eventual global trade treaty. Although the 149-nation trade body has sometimes ducked major decisions rather than risk failure, Lamy said the end-April target for a sweeping pact on agricultural and industrial subsidies and tariffs must be hit. 'I believe we would be making a huge collective mistake if we thought we could postpone (a deal) by the end of April,' he told the Trade Negotiating Committee, the steering

body for the WTO's Doha round of free trade negotiations. The difficulties of striking a deal have led to speculation in Geneva that the WTO could let the April date slip."

The agreement for cuts to rich-nation farm subsidies and lower tariffs on farm and manufacturing goods was a key to unlocking other areas of the Doha round. The goal of the round was to boost the global economy and lift millions out of poverty, Lamy said. "While stressing the end-April date was 'do-able,' he warned leading WTO members against waiting until the last moment before announcing they were ready for a deal. . . . Lamy said the EU had to make further concessions on

opening up its highly protected farm market to imports, the United States had to agree to more farm subsidy cuts, and Brazil would have to accept deeper cuts in industrial tariffs. 'The question is not whether, but when,' he said."

Adapted from Richard Waddington, *WTO Chief Lamy Warns against Missing April Deadline* (The World Bank, March 29, 2006). © 2006 The World Bank Group. All Rights Reserved.

REFLECTIVE THINKING QUESTION

Do Canada and other developed members of the WTO really desire to "lift millions out of poverty"? Visit www.power.nelson.com to review a discussion paper on the WTO and its relationship to poverty in Africa.

nations in the area of agricultural products and textiles. It was intended that these new trade rules would be fairer for developing countries and level the playing field in order to permit them to share in the wealth of globalization. Unfortunately the July 2006 talks in Geneva failed to reach an agreement about reducing farming subsidies and lowering import taxes. A successful outcome of the Doha round has become increasingly unlikely, because the broad trade authority granted to President Bush expires in 2007. This was seen as critical to the WTO by a number of observers; "A delay in the conclusion of the Doha round of free-trade talks could derail Asian growth . . . Asia's future would also depend on how well China and India integrate with the rest of the regional and world economy."[81]

Intellectual Property (TRIPS)

The WTO is currently the only internationally recognized organization established to represent its member countries with respect to, among many trade issues, guidance on the international sale and use of intellectual property. (We discussed intellectual property in Chapter 4.) The WTO agreement, Trade-Related Aspects of Intellectual Property Rights (**TRIPS**) is an attempt to set global rules for trade and investment in ideas and creativity. The rules state how copyrights, patents, trademarks, geographical names used to identify products, industrial designs, integrated circuit layout designs, and undisclosed information such as trade secrets should be protected when trade is involved. Visit www.power. nelson.com for links to WTO streaming video clips on IP rights and clarification. These WTO videos outline the purpose of the TRIPS agreement and some of its challenges.

> The WTO adopted an intellectual property agreement commonly referred to as **TRIPS** (trade-related aspects of intellectual property rights). It is an attempt to set global rules for trade and investment in ideas and creativity.

Trade Disputes

In addition to the WTO's global free trade agreements between 149 different countries (China was admitted into the world body in 2005), there are a growing number of multilateral and bilateral trade agreements that also promote free trade among the signatories. Indeed, the WTO promotes a number of multilateral agreements. Many, as we have seen, are found in the growth of the regional clusters we have reviewed in this chapter. The WTO trade agreements are, for all purposes, legal contracts between members (countries), and these contracts contain sanctions if the contract is breached. The sanctions, designed to encourage compliance, include financial and trade damage awards. In most cases the sanctions work; however, we will see that in some cases countries can continue contravening the agreements and chose to pay the fine. Disputes brought before the WTO between countries can be settled between the parties or decided by dispute resolution panels, which have the authority to issue findings of WTO law. Parties that have been injured in such cases are entitled to impose sanctions that are sufficient to restrict imports from the offending country by an amount equal to the trade losses suffered by the injured party. While the findings of WTO panels are not legally binding on any country, the resulting penalties, imposed by the WTO ruling on the offending country, are often large enough to force countries to change their laws to conform to the WTO's demands. The WTO now covers not only trade in goods (the only area permitted under GATT), but also services and intellectual property. The scope for unilateral action has been considerably narrowed. Here are a few recent WTO trade disputes.

Canada imposed a 15 percent surtax on some U.S. products in retaliation for lingering trade dispute. The retaliatory surtax was seen by many to be a very weak response as it amounted to only $11.6 million. The announcement of the surtax on cigarettes, oysters, and live swine from the United States came just as the EU took a similar measure.[82] The EU also imposed similar duties of up to 15 percent "on such US imports as paper, textiles, machinery, and farm produce. The 25-member EU said it took the action 'in light of the continuing failure of the United States to bring its legislation in conformity with its international obligations.' "[83] "Both Canada and the EU have long asked Washington to repeal the Byrd amendment. The Byrd amendment allows American companies to keep the proceeds that Washington collects in antidumping disputes. . . . In November [2004], the WTO gave Canada and the other co-complainants the authority to retaliate. The other

PRACTICAL ENTREPRENEURIAL FOCUS

Trade and investment have always been at the core of Canada's economic development. Here are 10 initiatives that Canada's political and business leaders can undertake to promote more global trade and investment. A detailed discussion of each of these initiatives can be found at www.power.nelson.com.

1. Keep the lights on. Canada must enhance its open-door policy on trade and investment, and let the world know.
2. Keep it simple—cut red tape. There is nothing more harmful to Canadian SMEs than a complicated bureaucracy.
3. Create confidence. Creating confidence in Canada's ability to meet international investors' expectations is vital.
4. Develop fertile ground for FDI. Canada must ensure our capital markets are friendly, easily accessible, and well governed.
5. Foster a knowledge-based economy. Exploit emerging opportunities as Canada shifts to a strong knowledge-based nation.
6. Be transparent and predictable. A major determinant in FDI investors' preference is predictability. Canada's business processes must be transparent and above all predictable.
7. Don't put too many eggs in one basket. Canada's trade strategy must provide for greater diversity in our trading partners.
8. Encourage collaboration between business, academia, and industry. Another very important step toward securing more trade and investment is the need for greater dialogue between the public, private, and academic sectors.
9. Maintain technological "currency." Canada's governments must access intellectual capital and intelligence to be an early adopter of global business trends. Technological advancements and infrastructure are at the core of attracting FDI.
10. Undertake strategic thinking. In recent years, Canada has experienced strong economic activity due in part to the world's insatiable need to consume our commodities. This does not take strategic thinking! We just fill orders. Increasingly, the world seems unwilling to undertake FDI in Canada. Consider why. How Canada can remain a major destination for FDI?

As a business leader you can make a difference by influencing your member of Parliament.

countries involved include Mexico, Japan, India and Brazil."[84] Another "sensitive case is the long-running dispute between the United States and Europe over the banana trade, which the World Trade Organization settled over the heads of the Caribbean and Latin American countries most directly affected. Regional banana-producing nations argue that a change in the EU banana policy giving concessions to countries covered by the [Lomé Convention] would shatter their fragile economies."[85] The Convention affects a group of 79 countries made up of several EU nations, primarily former British, Dutch, and French colonies in Africa, the Caribbean, and the Pacific. Unfortunately after decades of dispute resolution process, the banana war continued in 2006. Similarly, the European Union was found to be subsidizing sugar production so the WTO made a ruling in favour of Australia.

Management Implications

- While the world is still coming to grips with the implications of globalization, tectonic shifts continue to affect the globe's economic and geopolitical future. In this chapter, we have read of the unfolding realignment of forces. Having examined some of these emerging shifts, a compelling case can be made that regionalization will replace globalization.
- The world is evolving into three huge economic and political regional unions (the triad), which will take shape by 2020. There is evidence that the EU will expand eastward as well as to the south, right to Southern Africa; that the Asian bloc, initially led by Japan and soon it is anticipated by China, will encompass a united Korea, ASEAN, Australia, and New Zealand, and create a vast free trade area by approximately 2015; that the United States and Latin American nations may not revive the FTAA, as South American nations will active seek other trading partners including the EU, South Africa, and the Asia bloc; and South Asia will have its own free trade area, which will eventually ally with the emerging new and stronger Latin American region.

- Like the EU, these other members of the triad may extract membership in return for free trade, as nations participate in monetary unions, cross-border infrastructure investments, regional development agencies, and conflict resolution mechanisms. However, Canada must be aware of the costs—the loss of sovereignty and foreign ownership of our commodities. There is evidence that freer trade promotes democratic values and human rights. The new alignments will present wonderful opportunities for Canadian business.

- Canada's political leaders must be proactive in playing a role in these evolving new regional trading blocs and secure a trading position. However, we must understand that the "pipe" runs both ways. Without a "valve" regulating the flow of trade, certain Canadian SMEs, as we saw with the Montreal textile industry, will face fierce competition. We must be ready to compete in a world with few barriers and impediments to trade.

- A clear understanding of the current regional free trade agreements will be critical to opening doors to international trade opportunities. Equally critical will be the awareness of newly emerging regional alignments and the appropriate repositioning Canada must undertake to exploit the new trading opportunities.

- One of Canada's competitive advantages is our ethnic diversity. Managers must remember to play to this strength as we seek new trading partners in the triad. Remember to visit www.power.nelson.com for an extensive outline of the many regional groupings.

- Canadian SMEs must think critically about the implications for their businesses in the global marketplace. How does the SME benefit from Canada's participation in the largest regional free trade grouping in the world? How does knowledge concerning these free trade groupings help Canadian SMEs? How does the creation of regional organizations, such as the APEC or ASEAN, affect Canadian business? How do single economic systems, such as CARICOM Single Market and Economy (CSME), designed to facilitate the pooling of the region's financial, human and natural resources, affect the Canadian economy?

- Trade liberalization is not a panacea, and it cannot replace broader economic reform. Rather, it is a key element of any strategy aimed at achieving sustained rapid growth. Other policy reforms are needed to ensure sustained growth; and these reforms will, in turn, increase the returns from trade liberalization. Sustained growth needs a sound macroeconomic framework: prudent fiscal and monetary policy aimed at reducing inflation and delivering price stability.

- Experience has taught us that flexible exchange rate regimes also have an important part to play in maintaining economic stability and thus paving the way for more rapid growth. Institutional reforms are also important if the proper incentives are to be in place to encourage enterprise. Property rights, the rule of law, and commercial codes are all vital ingredients of a well-functioning market economy. So are labour market reforms that lead to greater labour market flexibility.

- Infrastructure improvements must accompany trade liberalization to realize potential benefits. Low-cost transportation and communications are essential for productivity increases, and especially for trade. Improvements in administrative services and functions can also make an important contribution to trade growth. Reducing delays in ports, customs clearance, and red tape can contribute to overall economic growth as well as facilitate trade.

- Canadian managers must advocate for these improvements both at home and among our trading partners if we are to sustain our current standards of living.

CHAPTER SUMMARY

- During the last few decades, nations have accepted the need for regionalization—a need for two or more countries to enter into favourable regional trade agreements. Regionalism is not a new phenomenon; it started in the early trading times, when geographic proximity was identified as a significant factor that sustained positive trade arrangements. Today, with the unprecedented rapid pace of globalization and international trade growth, regionalism faces a new phase of development with the creation of new regional trading blocs and improvement of the existing ones. Their stated purpose is to reduce and ultimately remove all tariff and non-tariff barriers that obstruct the free flow of goods and services between the participating members. This is highly valued by the countries from each of the continents of the world. But, in almost all cases, other outcomes are also sought. We need to look beneath the surface for the reasons driving these clusters.

- There are three major global regional trading blocs. These supranational regional blocs have been referred to as the triad. The world's most powerful economies, the United States, the European Union, and Asia (China and India), have each sought to forge links with their neighbouring countries to enhance their trade access and influence over global rivals and mitigate other nations' influence in the region. Other major trading countries have also sought to create looser trade groupings to foster their interests. The regional blocs, including the triad, are continually transforming and adjusting, each with its own set of emerging issues that business leaders must be monitoring. As nations cluster, one can notice a shift in global economic power and influence.

- Currently, in addition to the agreements initiated at the macro level by the World Trade Organization (WTO) and its 149 members, the total number of regional trade agreements is estimated at 300. The regional free trade areas examined in this chapter included the North American Free Trade Agreement, the European Union, Mercosur, the Free Trade Area of the Americas, the ASEAN Free Trade Area, the United States–Dominican Republic–Central America Free Trade Agreement, the South Asian Association for Regional Cooperation, and the Commonwealth of Independent States. Other important regional agreements and a number of lesser economic "clusters" are reviewed at www.power.nelson.com.

- Regional trading arrangements can serve protectionist purposes, not least because of rules of origin (ROOs).

ROOs can lead to trade diversion if they oblige partners to buy higher-priced intermediate goods from a partner rather than on the lower-priced world markets.

- The degree of economic regional integration can be seen as a continuum or steps. At one extreme, or the top of the stairs, we find political union, where the regional groups centralize their political apparatus to coordinate all governance aspects that we generally associate with those found in a nation's state. Depending on the degree of economic integration, countries may participate concurrently in various trade groupings. Economic integration among countries ranges from strict trade integration to economic policy harmonization. The lowest degree of economic integration corresponds to a preferential trade arrangement—free trade agreements, customs unions, common markets, economic union. The highest degree of integration corresponds to a single free market—a political and economic union. The closest to political and economic union, the top step, is the European Economic Union.

- The Bretton Woods Agreement of 1944 was driven by the need to establish the rules for economic global trading relationships for most of the developed nations following World War II. The primary organizations are the World Bank, the International Monetary Fund (IMF), and the General Agreement of Tariffs and Trade (GATT), whose mandate was subsequently encased at the Uruguay Round during 1986 to 1994 by the creation of the World Trade Organization (WTO). Originally created to provide stability in a global postwar economy where exchange rates were fixed, though adjustable, the IMF and the World Bank were born with outstanding survival instincts that have kept them going long after exchange rates were floated in the early 1970s. Today these three institutions wield tremendous power and influence, especially in the developing world. An increasing number of critics accuse these institutions of lacking democratic decision-making processes, transparency, and accountability.

REVIEW QUESTIONS

1. What are the purposes of regional trading blocs?
2. Discuss the five levels of regional integration.
3. Briefly outline five regional trading blocs to include their membership, GNI, population, recent initiatives and future trends.
4. Outline the advantages and disadvantages of Canada as a member of NAFTA.
5. Briefly outline the function and some of the issues surrounding the global institutions put in place as a result of the Bretton Woods Agreement of 1944.

REFLECTIVE THINKING QUESTIONS

1. Having completed this chapter, reread the quotations on the first page, critically reflect on the validity of the authors' statements, and provide your opinion as to the validity of each. Evidence-based answers are preferred to rhetorical answers.

2. In the article "Concern over U.S. Militarism Brings China and India Closer," pages 126–127, the question was raised of the prospect of a emerging triangular regional relationship between Russia, China, and India. Indian Prime Minister Manmohan Singh declared, "India and China together reshape the world order." Should Canada be fearful of this new regional possibility?

3. Over the past 30 years, we have seen a substantial increase in the number of regional and sub-regional trade agreements signed worldwide. In your opinion, will the trade blocs affected by 9/11 lead to increased protectionism, or will they promote trade liberalization?

4. Would the FTAA be beneficial to Canadian SMEs?

5. Has NAFTA been a good thing for Canada?

6. Should Canada and Mexico seek greater economic union with the United States similar to the integration achieved by the EU to include dollarization by adopting the EURO?

7. Have the global institutions outlived their usefulness?

GLOBAL E-RESEARCH

Visit www.power.nelson.com for research suggestions, questions, and a number of background discussion papers on this topic.

MINI CASE

India for Pan-Asian Trade Agreement: ASEAN Seeks Ties with China, Korea and Japan.

India on Friday expressed its desire for eventually expanding the proposed comprehensive economic cooperation agreement (CECA) with ASEAN to a pan-Asian pact covering six more countries including Japan, China, Korea, Australia and New Zealand, aiming at a common economic community in East Asia. Finance minister P. Chidambaram said at a meeting with Asian leaders and the Asian Development Bank president H. Kuroda here at the World Economic Forum that India had already signed [a] framework agreement for free trade with ASEAN last year. But the minister outlined the need for a comprehensive economic treaty that takes care of investment and other financial matters. After the South Asian Free Trade Area ratification and the CECA with Singapore, India would sign a CECA with ASEAN soon. A senior official from an ASEAN country, however, cited the association's discord with India on the formulation of the Rules of Origin (which is meant to avoid occurrence of trade deflection under the guise of the proposed pact) as a stumbling block. The official also highlighted the substantial headway that has already been made by ASEAN towards formation of a trade bloc comprising ASEAN, China, Japan and Korea. ASEAN and China have already finalised the framework for a free trade pact, which is slated to be fully operational in 2010.

A similar agreement with Korea is in the works, too. A bloc that comprises ASEAN and the three Asian countries (China, Japan and Korea) would cover 86% of East Asian Trade. Among ASEAN countries, 99% of trade is already tariff-free. To a query on whether India could sign a[n] FTA with China, Chidambaram said, "it is not inconceivable. Trade with China is growing very fast. Some time in future there could be a FTA with China," he said. He also said there was a need to develop an Asian bond market where Asian nations could invest a significant portion of their burgeoning forex [foreign exchange] reserves. There was also a need to set up an Asian monetary fund, he said. "We will engage in dialogue (for all these initiatives)," he added.

Source: Economy Bureau, *India for Pan-Asian Trade Agreement: ASEAN Seeks Ties with China, Korea, and Japan* (Financial Express, January 28, 2006), retrieved August 24, 2006, from www.financialexpress.com/ fe_full_story.php? content_id=115880.

MINI CASE QUESTIONS

1. Should Canada be concerned that, "ASEAN and China have already finalized the framework for a free trade pact, which is slated to be fully operational in 2010"?

2. As this Asian trading bloc takes form, what initiatives, if any, should our political and business leaders undertake?

3. What could be the impact of Finance Minister P. Chidambaram's comment regarding the need for both an Asian bond market where Asian nations could invest a significant portion of their burgeoning forex reserves and an Asian monetary fund? We will cover some of these issues in subsequent chapters, but for discussion purposes here, consider whether Asia is moving toward monetary union. What would it mean to Canada as a recipient of FDI and our capital markets?

4. Do you see merit in establishing an Asian monetary fund?

ENDNOTES

1 Thomas L. Friedman, *The World Is Flat*, 1st ed. (New York: Farrar, Straus and Giroux, 2005).

2 Richard Nixon, "Asia After Viet Nam," *Foreign Affairs*, Vol 46, Iss. 1, October 1967.

3 *Brainy Quote* (2005), retrieved August 11, 2006, from www.brainyquote.com.

4 Ibid.

5 Dr. M.I. Okpara, *Notable Remarks on African Unification* (African Unification Front, 1961), retrieved August 11, 2006, from www.africanfront.com/quotes.php.

6 Mark McNeilly, *Sun Tzu and the Art of Business: Six Strategic Principles for Managers* (New York: Oxford University Press, 1996).

7 Zbigniew Brzezinski, *The Grand Chessboard: American Primacy and Its Geostrategic Imperatives*, 1st ed. (New York: Basic Books, 1997).

8 Sangmoon Kim, "A Longitudinal Analysis of Globalization and Regionalization in International Trade: A Social Network Approach," *Social Forces* 81, no. 2 (December, 2002).

9 Ibid.

10 *The World Trade Blocs* (BBC News, 1999) retrieved August 11, 2006, from http://news.bbc.co.uk/hi/english/static/special_report/1999/11/99/seattle_trade_talks/default.stm.

11 Anne O. Krueger, *Trade Policy and the Strategy for Global Insertion* (IMF External Relations Department, April 19, 2005), retrieved August 11, 2006, from www.imf.org/external/np/speeches/2005/041905.htm.

12 *The World Trade Blocs*.

13 Directorate General for Economic and Financial Affairs, *The Use of the Euro in the World* (European Commission), retrieved August 11, 2006, from http://europa.eu.int/comm/economy_finance/euro/world/ euro_world_main_en.htm.

14 Ibid.

15 Gwynne Dyer, "The Euro's Future" (January 1, 2003), retrieved August 11, 2006, from www.gwynnedyer.net/backup/articles/Gwynne%20Dyer%20article_%20%20Euro%20Anniversary.txt.

16 *Q&A: Turkey's EU Entry Talks* (BBC News, October 4, 2005), retrieved August 11, 2006, from http://news.bbc.co.uk/1/hi/world/europe/4107919.stm.

17 Ibid.

18 Ibid.

19 Ibid.

20 Ibid.

21 Ibid.

22 EUROPA, *Overviews of the European Union Activities: External Trade* (2004); retrieved August 24, 2006, from http://europa.eu/pol/comm/overview_en.htm.

23 EU-AT, *Presidency of the Council 2006* (Austria 2006—Presidency of the European Union, 2006), retrieved August 11, 2006, from www.eu2006.at/en/The_Council_Presidency/What_is_the_Presidency/index.html.

24 Ibid.

25 Daniel Hannan, "*So, You Thought the European Constitution Was Dead, Did You?*" (Telegraph Group, March 20, 2006), retrieved August 11, 2006, from www.telegraph.co.uk/opinion/main.jhtml?xml=/opinion/2006/03/20/do2001.xml&sSheet=/opinion/2006/03/20/ixop.html.

26 BBC News, "The World Trade Blocs," (BBC News, 2004), retrieved August 11, 2006, from http://news.bbc.co.uk/hi/english/static/special_report/1999/11/99/seattle_trade_talks/default.stm.

27 Foreign Affairs and International Trade Canada, *NAFTA: A Decade of Strengthening a Dynamic Relationship* (DFAIT, 2004), retrieved August 11, 2006, from www.dfait-maeci.gc.ca/nafta-alena/nafta10-en.pdf.

28 Foreign Affairs and International Trade Canada, *Chapter Eight—Glossary of Terms* (Government of Canada, April 4, 2004), retrieved August 11, 2006, www.dfait-maeci.gc.ca/tna-nac/2004/9_04-en.asp.

29 Foreign Affairs and International Trade Canada, *NAFTA: A Decade of Strengthening a Dynamic Relationship*.

30 Office of the United States Trade Representative, *NAFTA: A Strong Record of Success* (Executive Office of the President of the United States, March 2006), retrieved August 11, 2006, available from www.ustr.gov/assets/Document_Library/ Fact_Sheets/2006/asset_upload_file242_9156.pdf?ht=.

31 Foreign Affairs and International Trade Canada, *NAFTA: A Decade of Strengthening a Dynamic Relationship*.

32 Office of the United States Trade Representative, *NAFTA at 10: A Success Story* (12/01/2003) (Office, of the United States Trade Representative, December 1, 2003), retrieved August 11, 2006, from www.ustr.gov/Document_Library/Fact_ Sheets/2003/NAFTA_at_10_A_Success_Story.html.

33 Yuen Pau Woo, *Preferential Trading Arrangements in the Asia Pacific: A Canadian Perspective* (Taiwan Institute of Economic Research, November 30, 2004), retrieved August 11, 2006, from http://72.14.203.104/search?q=cache:rY0uN_ 8sxY4J:www.asiapacific.ca/analysis/pubs/speeches/pref_trading_30nov04.pdf+Canada+now+exports+more+manufacturing+production+to+the+US+that+it+consumes+domestically&hl=en&gl=ca&ct=clnk&cd=1.

34 Foreign Affairs and International Trade Canada, *NAFTA: A Decade of Strengthening a Dynamic Relationship*.

35 Foreign Affairs and International Trade Canada, *NAFTA Has Proven Its Value* (2003), retrieved August 11, 2006, from www.dfait-maeci.gc.ca/tna-nac/stories74-en.asp.

36 Woo, *Preferential Trading Arrangements in the Asia Pacific: A Canadian Perspective*.

37 Public Citizen, *The Ten Year Track Record of the North American Free Trade Agreement: Undermining Sovereignty and Democracy* (Global Trade Watch, 2004), retrieved August 11, 2006, from www.citizen.org/publications/release.cfm?ID=7295.

38 Ibid.

39 Foreign Affairs and International Trade Canada, *NAFTA: A Decade of Strengthening a Dynamic Relationship*.

40 Adrienne Warren, *Travel Follows Growth West* (December 2005) (Scotia Economics, December 2005); available from www.scotiacapital.com/English/bns_econ/nafta.pdf.

41 Ibid.

42 Foreign Affairs and International Trade Canada, *NAFTA, A Decade of Strengthening a Dynamic Relationship*.

43 Public Citizen, *The Ten Year Track Record of the North American Free Trade Agreement: The Mexican Economy, Agriculture, and Environment* (Global Trade Watch, 2004), retrieved August 13, 2006, from www.citizen.org/documents/NAFTA_10_mexico.pdf.

44 Alianza Social Continental Hemispheric Social Alliance, "Lessons from NAFTA. The High Cost of Free Trade," (2004).

45 Ibid.

46 Canadian Council of Chief Executives and Consejo Mexicano de Asuntos Internacionales, *Building a North American Community* (Council on Foreign Relations, 2005), retrieved August 13, 2006, from www.cfr.org/content/publications/attachments/NorthAmerica_TF_final.pdf.

47 Invest in Canada, NAFTA Advantage: Canada Is America's Number One Trading Partner—by a Long Shot (Government of Canada, December 6, 2005), retrieved September 9, 2006, from www.investincanada.gc.ca/en/872/Reasons_ to_Invest .html.

48 Tripartite Committee FTAA, *Free Trade Area of the Americas—FTAA* (FTAA Secretariat, 2005), retrieved August 13, 2006, from www.ftaa-alca.org/View_e.asp.

49 Luiz Inacio Lula da Silva, president of Brazil.

50 Nick Miroff, "Che Rides Again (on a Mountain Bike)" *The Nation Institute*, March 25, 2006), retrieved August 13, 2006, from www.tomdispatch.com/index.mhtml?pid=71996.

51 Commonly known as Che Guevara or el Che, Ernesto Guevara de la Serna was an Argentine-born physician, Marxist revolutionary, politician, and Cuban guerrilla leader. He firmly believed that only through revolution could Latin America's poverty and economic inequality be remedied. He was involved in many social revolutions as well as serving under Castro in various important Cuban government posts.

52 Miroff, "Che Rides Again (on a Mountain Bike)".

53 Office of the United States Trade Representative, *Dominican Republic Joins Five Central American Countries in Historic FTA with U.S.* (Executive Office of the President of the United States, August 5, 2004), retrieved August 25, 2006, from www.ustr.gov/Document_Library/Press_Releases/2004/August/Dominican_Republic_Joins_Five_Central_American_Countries_in_Historic_FTA_with_UShtml.html.

54 Ibid.

55 Ibid.

56 Ibid.

57 Burke Stansbury, *More CAFTA Failures for the Bush Administration* (Stop CAFTA Coalition, February 1, 2006); retrieved August 25, 2006, from www.stopcafta.org/article .php?list=type&type=43.

58 BBC, "The World Trade Blocs."

59 Economic Cooperation Organization, *About APEC* (APEC Secretariat, 2005), retrieved August 13, 2006, from www.apec .org/apec/about_apec.html.

60 Economic Cooperation Organization, *Santiago Declaration* (APEC Secretariat, November 20–21, 2004), retrieved August 13, 2006, from www.apec.org/apec/leaders__declarations/2004.html.

61 Foreign Affairs and International Trade Canada, *Asia Pacific: Regional Organizations* (DFAIT, April 12, 2005), retrieved August 13, 2006, from www.dfait-maeci.gc.ca/asia/main/regional/regional-en.asp.

62 Association of Southeast Asian Nations, *Chairman's Statement of the 11th ASEAN Summit: One Vision, One Identity, One Community* () (ASEAN Secretariat, December 12, 2005 [cited 2006]), retrieved August 13, 2006, from www.aseansec.org/18039.htm.

63 Ibid.

64 Ibid.

65 Foreign Affairs and International Trade Canada, *Asia Pacific: Origins and Membership* (DFAIT, February 10, 2006), retrieved August 13, 2006, from www.dfait-maeci.gc.ca/asia/main/regional/asean-origins-en.asp.

66 Association of Southeast Asian Nations, *Overview: Association of Southeast Asian Nations* (ASEAN Website, 2005), retrieved August 13, 2006, from www.aseansec.org/64.htm.

67 "Six-party talks" is the name given to meetings of the People's Republic of China, North Korea, South Korea, Russia, Japan, and the United States, held in order to find a resolution of the crisis over the North Korean nuclear weapons program.

68 European Commission External Relations, "The EU's Relations with Mercosur," retrieved October 22, 2006, from http://europa.eu.int/comm/external_relations/mercosur/intro/.

69 Ibid.

70 SABC News, *SA Union Signs Trade Agreement with Mercosur* (South African Broadcasting Corporation, April 12, 2005), retrieved August 13, 2006, from www.sabcnews.com/economy/business/0,2172,101992,00.html.

71 Europa, *Bilaterial Trade Relations: Mercosur* (August 2005) (European Commission, August 2005), retrieved August 13, 2006, from http://europa.eu.int/comm/trade/issues/bilateral/regions/mercosur/index_en.htm.

72 (CIS) Interstate Statistical Committee of the Commonwealth of Independent States, *Database Statistics of the CIS* (Information and Publishing Department, Russian Federation, 2005), retrieved August 13, 2006, from www.cisstat.com/eng.

73 Ibid.

74 Nina Kulikova, *Russian Economy: Forecasts for 2006* (Focus Information Agency, 2005), retrieved August 13, 2006, from http://en.rian.ru/analysis/20060327/44852175.html.

75 Ibid.

76 Jackie Patru, "Regionalism: Sneaking America into World Government," Council on Domestic Relations, retrieved October 22, 2006, from http://www.sweetliberty.org/issues/regionalism/sneaking.htm.

77 Patrick Henry, "Speech to the Second Virginia Convention (1775), retrieved October 22, 2006, from http://www.ifcwtc.org/words6.html.

78 Krueger, *Trade Policy and the Strategy for Global Insertion.*

79 Anonymous, *The World Bank and the International Monetary Fund* (Pagewise, 2002), retrieved August 13, 2006, from http://tntn.essortment.com/worldbankinter_riaw.htm.

80 Ibid.

81 Wong Choon Mei, *Asia Pacific Biz Leaders Warn Delay in Doha Free Trade Pact May Derail Growth* (Channel NewsAsia, January, 24, 2006), retrieved August 13, 2006, from www.channelnewsasia.com/stories/singaporebusinessnews/view/189798/1/.html.

82 *USA Today*, "Canada to Put Trade Surtax on U.S. Goods" (3/31/2005) (USA TODAY, March 31, 2005), retrieved August 13, 2006, from www.usatoday.com/money/economy/ trade/2005-03-31-trade-usat_x.htm.

83 Ibid.

84 Ibid.

85 BBC News, "*Business: The Economy Caribbean Moves Towards Trade Bloc*" (BBC News, April 18, 1999), retrieved August 13, 2006, from http://news.bbc.co.uk/1/hi/business/the_economy/322306.stm.

Economic Theories Advocating International Business

"For small firms to meet the significant and growing challenges of globalization, they need governmental and institutional back-up. A three-pronged approach can help build and strengthen competitiveness: closer business–government partnership; effective networking of national agencies involved in the value chain; and optimal use of new technologies."[1]

—R. Badrinath. Director, ITC Executive Forum, International Trade Centre

"I have always argued for freer trade, not as an objective but rather (in the context of the poor nations such as India, from where I come) as an often powerful weapon in the arsenal of policies that we can deploy to fight poverty."[2]

—Jagdish Bhagwati, Columbia University professor and author of In Defence of Globalization

"The bottom line is that the so-called China threat rings hollow in an era of globalization. China is not stealing jobs from rich, developed countries. Employment is growing in China's export sector because multinational corporations are expanding their Chinese subsidiaries. And China's demand for foreign-made goods is supporting employment elsewhere in the world."[3]

—Stephen S. Roach, chief economist at Morgan Stanley

"As President, Governor Bush will be committed to tearing down trade barriers abroad and keeping markets open at home because he understands that trade is increasingly important to continued U.S. prosperity."[4]

—Election website for George W. Bush

"I know this much. When we buy manufactured goods abroad, we get the goods and the foreigner gets the money. When we buy the manufactured goods at home, we get both the goods and the money."[5]

—Abraham Lincoln, sixteenth President of the United States (1861–1865)

LEARNING OUTCOMES

- Evaluate selected international trade theories to include the New Trade Theory and Porter's National Competitive Advantage Theory.
- Examine Canada and other selected countries' recent free trade agreements.
- Formulate opinions regarding the benefits and patterns of international trade.
- Examine the instruments available to governments wishing to intervene in free trade.
- Evaluate the political and economic arguments to support governments' intervention in free trade.

Stop or Cut Aid to Bombardier, Executives Say "Poor-Management Issue"

© 2006 Air Canada

A majority of business leaders want the federal government to stop or reduce assistance to aerospace and transportation company Bombardier Inc., according to a poll conducted for the *Financial Post* by COMPAS Inc. The poll of chief executives and business leaders found 63 percent of respondents believe the government should cut subsidies to the Montreal-based company either because they think the company has displayed poor management and proved unsuccessful with the financial aid it has received to date (36%) or because Canada can no longer afford the subsidies (27%). "Governments have trouble picking winners, but the losers don't seem to have much trouble picking governments!" said one executive. Canadian Prime Minister Paul Martin pledged last week to "give the necessary support to Bombardier" to ensure its survival.

The world's third-largest aircraft manufacturer recorded a US $64.5-million loss last fiscal year on sales of US $15.5-billion and has suffered a loss of US $141-million for the first nine months of 2004 and witnessed the departure of CEO Paul Tellier earlier this month. Just one third of those polled (33 percent) believe government should continue to financially back Bombardier, because they believe the aerospace industry is unique and competitors such as Brazil's Embraer, Boeing of the U.S. and Europe's Airbus are all heavily subsidized. "Certainly there is a minority who say they should continue receiving [subsidies] but you have others who say it may be a unique industry, but they are not succeeding with the money, so there is a poor-management issue and, certainly, in light of the fast and unexpected firing

of Tellier, that was a signal," said COMPAS's Tamara Gottlieb. Asked what industries, if any, should receive government assistance, technology was the only sector to receive a majority of support for some form of subsidies. Business leaders opposed giving financial assistance to airlines and automotive industries by greater than four to one.

"The best government assistance for many industries and the airline industry in particular, is the reduction of government fees, charges and taxes," said one respondent. The poll found there were instances when companies should receive assistance, such as in exceptional situations like SARS, or BSE in the case of the cattle industry. A "Buy Canadian" policy, touted by SNC Lavalin president Jacques Lamarre in the November issue of *National Post Business* was only favoured by 45% of executives. A majority (53%) said the federal government should concentrate on cutting spending and buying products and services based on "the best product for the lowest price." "Generally, business leaders are very sophisticated; fairly knowledgeable. They appear to be particularly sophisticated on the issue of corporate welfare," said Ms. Gottlieb. "They don't support it. They would rather have less regulation, fewer taxes and government charges across the board than special assistance packages."

Source: "Stop or Cut Aid to Bombardier, Executives Say 'Poor-Management Issue'" by Paul Brent, *National Post*, December 20, 2004. Reprinted with permission of the publisher.

A SUN TZU MOMENT . . .

"It is according to the shape that I lay the plan for victory, but the multitude does not comprehend this. Although everyone can see the outward aspects, none understands the way in which I have created victory."[6]

THE COLD WAR BEGINS

By the conclusion of World War II the United Kingdom as a global superpower was in decline and the void was filled by two nations with very different political ideologies—the United States and the Soviet Union. The tension between the two nations had escalated throughout the war and, with the collapse of Nazi Germany relations, quickly became polarized. Pre-war governments were re-established or new democratic governments were created by the Western powers; while in the areas occupied by Soviet troops, including the territories of former Allies such as Poland, communist satellite states were created. Within a few years following World War II, Europe became divided along ideological lines and the Iron Curtain went up.[7] The Cold War had begun, and two blocs emerged: NATO and the Warsaw Pact.[8] In the decades that followed, two trading blocs grounded in sharply contrasted fundamental ideologies, emerged. At times, the underlying reasons for emerging trade blocs seem obtuse, yet at other times the reasons appear very transparent as to the long-term national interest to be served.

Opening Thoughts

The Evolution of International Trade

Economists have shifted their core understanding of trade theory since the 1500s. The early focus was on a nation's basic factor endowments. These attributes explained a country's competitive advantage over other countries. A nation's basic factor endowments consist of natural resources, location, climate, and demographics. Mexico's close proximity to the world's largest market is an example of a basic factor endowment. Early classical economists did not spend a great deal of effort in examining why nations were competitive. During the last half of the 20th century, however, this changed. Increasingly, the study of trade theory began examining countries' governments and even private industries' ability to influence the competitiveness of national firms.

Michael Porter observes, "National prosperity is created, not inherited. It does not grow out of the country's natural endowments, its labour pool, its interest rates, or its currencies' values, as classical economists insist. The nation's competitiveness depends on the capacity of its industry to innovate and upgrade. Companies gain advantage against the world's best competitors because of pressure and challenge. They benefit from having strong domestic rivals, aggressive home-based suppliers, and demanding local customers. In a world of increasing global competition, nations have become more, not less, important. As the basis of competition has shifted more and more to the creation and assimilation of knowledge, the role of the nation has grown. Competitive advantage is created and sustained through a highly localized process. Differences in national values, culture, economic structures, institutions, and histories all contribute to competitive success. There are striking differences in the patterns of competitiveness in each country; no nation can or will be competitive in every, or even most industries. Ultimately, nations succeed in particular industries because their home environment is most forward looking, dynamic, and challenging."[9]

Porter's research contributes to our understanding of trade theory. He asks why certain industries in a given country have a greater share of the world trade than other countries. Porter's diamond model, which describes his theory of national advantage, has been widely accepted within the academic community and is a central model in many international business courses. We will be examining Porter's model in this chapter (see Figure 6.8, page 168). However Porter's theory does have critics in both academia and industry, including Canadian critic Alan Rugman. Rugman and his colleague, Joe D'Cruz, argued that the appropriate model was the double diamond.[10] Rugman and D'Cruz introduce 10 strategic clusters with a flagship firm, such as RIM or Bombardier, dominating their respective clusters. Visit www.power.nelson.com for an overview of the Rugman and D'Cruz double-diamond model.

Benefits and Patterns of International Trade

Why is it important that we understand trade theory? In the Bombardier case, the Canadian government wrestles with what products to import and export, how much should be traded, and with whom. Globalization, the growing economic interdependence between nations, requires decision makers in business and government to make choices. In Canada, answers to questions such as, "What is the appropriate balance between trade with the United States?" have significant ramifications. In 2005, Canada exported approximately 79.7 percent of our goods and services to the United States; in return we purchase 67.7 percent of our imports from the United States; approximately 10 percent of our exports are to Asia and 6.7 percent to the European Union. NAFTA drives this economic interdependence.

Increasingly, today Canada's political leaders recognize the need to diversify our trading partners. Accordingly, when considering which nations should be our trading partners, it is helpful to understand the different economic trade theories. One option would be for Canada to be protectionist and isolationist; striving for total economic independence from all other countries. This economic philosophy, called **mercantilism**, flourished in Europe from about 1500 to the 1700s. However, it continues today in isolated pockets—consider North Korea's political and economic philosophy espoused by Kim Jong-il. At the other end of the continuum we find nations that tend to be dependent on their wealthier neighbours and willingly seek ways to expand this growing trade interdependency. Canada directly derives its high standard of living as a result of its trade dependency on the United States. The growing interdependence is striking: In Europe, many Eastern European developing nations share a similar relationship with Germany, the economic engine of the European Union. In South America, Brazil is the economic engine that attracts its neighbours' trade, while Japan, followed closely by China, are the Asian engines. Nations should have a diversified portfolio of trading partners rather than becoming too economically interdependent and having all their eggs in one basket. When disputes between trading nations emerge, the distorted bargaining position can be detrimental to the weaker. Canada and the United States' dispute over U.S. barriers on lumber and beef industries illustrates the realities of this threat. Second, the economic conditions of a major trading partner can change quickly. Argentina's meltdown in 2002 was caused in large part by its economic dependency on Brazil and maintaining a currency board. The economic collapse resulted in the default on billions of dollars in foreign loans and 25 percent unemployment. So, what is the appropriate balance between dependency and independency? We need to examine the leading economic trade theories in order to arrive at an evidence-based rather than a rhetorical position.

> Nations that adopt **mercantilism** strive for total economic independence from all other countries by embracing protectionist and isolationist policies. This trade theory supports the notion that it is in the nation's best interest to sell as much of its exports as possible while restricting the value of its imports from its trading partners.

International Trade Theories

We will examine three leading economic theories—mercantilism, absolute advantage, and comparative advantage—and how they attempt to explain the *raison d'être* for international trade. See Figure 6.1, page 160, for the evolution of these theories.

Mercantilism

Mercantilism is seen as a zero-sum game. This means if I win, you lose. This trade theory supports the notion that it is in the nation's best interest to sell as much of its exports as possible while restricting the value of its imports from its trading partners. The result is a **trade surplus**. That is, the value of the nation's exports exceeds the value of the nation's imports. The losing nation in this trade arrangement is said to have a **trade deficit**—a condition where the value of the trade imports exceeds the value of the nation's exports.

Mercantilist theory was succinctly defined by Thomas Mun in 1630, who stated "The ordinary means therefore to increase our wealth and [treasure is] by foreign trade, wherein we must ever observe this rule: to sell more to strangers yearly than we consume

> A **trade surplus** occurs when the value of the nation's exports exceeds the value of the nation's imports. This is the goal of mercantilism.

> A **trade deficit** is the condition where the value of the trade imports exceeds the value of the nation's exports.

FIGURE 6.1
The Evolution of International Trade Theories

The Theory of Absolute Advantage
Adam Smith
Each country should specialize in the production and export of that good which it produces most efficiently.

The Theory of Absolute Comparative Advantage
David Ricardo
Even if one country was most efficient in the production of two products, it must be relatively more efficient in the production of one good. It should then specialize in the production and export of that good in exchange for the importation of the other good.

The Theory of Factor Proportions
Eli Heckscher and Bertil Ohlin
A country that is relatively labour abundant (capital abundant) should specialize in the production and export of that product which is relatively labour intensive (capital intensive).

The Leontief Paradox
Wassily Leontief
The test of the factor proportions theory which resulted in the unexpected finding that the United States was actually exporting products that were relatively labour intensive, rather than the capital intensive products that a relatively capital abundant country should, according to the theory.

International Product Trade Cycle Theory
Raymond Vernon
The country that possesses comparative advantage in the production and export of an individual product changes over time as the technology of the product's manufacture matures.

The Competitive Advantage of Nations
Michael Porter
A nation's competitiveness depends on the capacity of its industry to innovate and upgrade. Companies gain competitive advantage because of pressure and challenge. Companies benefit from having strong domestic rivals, aggressive home-based suppliers, and demanding local customers. Competitive advantage is also established through geographic "clusters" or concentrations of companies in different parts of the same industry.

SOURCE: Adapted from M. Czinkota, I. Ronkainen, and M. Moffett, *International Business*, 7th ed., Thomson Southwestern, 2005.

of theirs in value."[11] Most European nations readily adopted this economic philosophy in about 1500. The chief proponents were Britain, France, Portugal, Spain, and the Netherlands—all colonizing nations. To support mercantilism, these European nations and others, through a variety of means, including force, established colonies. The intention was that the colony would import products from the "mother" country. These colonies would in turn export essential raw materials to support the growing industrialized firms of the European nations. The wealth of these European nations grew dramatically as a direct result of their adoption of mercantile theory. With wealth came the ability to purchase the structure to sustain and defend holdings. European nations created armies and built navies to protect their global "branch plants." The European nations' economic growth provided the political power that remained largely unchallenged until the end of World War I.

However, mercantilism is not sustainable! The damage to society as a result of mercantilist policies is well documented. Through higher taxes, taxpayers pay government subsidies on exports. The restrictions placed on imports directly increase the cost and limit the supply of foreign products, thereby hurting consumers. (For example, the British Navigation Act of 1663 required that any European goods imported by its North American colonies be shipped via Great Britain. The British government also prohibited colonial competition with British firms. These policies were implemented to ensure an adequate supply of low-cost materials for British firms. The failure of mercantile economic policy was a major contributor to the overthrow of British rule by the 13 American colonies.) Yet, notwithstanding the evidence, neo-mercantilists or protectionists continue to support this "I win, you lose" economic policy. The support for this economic theory is prevalent among unions, textile manufacturers, steel companies, and farmers. Neo-mercantilists are found not only in North America but also in Asia. Japan grudgingly agreed to allow the importation of foreign rice; however, imports may not exceed 10 percent of its current market. The Europeans continue to impose barriers on beef, bananas, and other agricultural products. It is fair to say that almost every developed country has adopted and continues to adopt some neo-mercantilist policies to protect key industries within its economy.

Despite the support it receives, the mercantile philosophy that any nation could grow its wealth only at the expense of its neighbour is seriously flawed. This flaw was first made apparent in the late 1700s when Scottish economist Adam Smith first put forward the trade theory of absolute advantage in his landmark book, *An Inquiry into the Nature and Causes of the Wealth of Nations* (1776)— a new mental model.

Theory of Absolute Advantage

Many see Adam Smith as the father of free-market economics. He attacked the mercantile economic theory, demonstrating that mercantilism would weaken a country by preventing individuals from trading freely and benefiting from voluntary exchange. Mercantilism encouraged countries to squander their scarce resources producing products that were not suitable to produce; promoted inefficiencies; and reduced the wealth of the country as a whole by favouring small, select, and special interest groups. In *The Wealth of Nations*, Smith argued that free trade would enlarge a country's wealth by enabling a country to expand the goods and services available through imports while permitting the nation to specialize in the production of goods and services for which it is best suited. Smith's **theory of absolute advantage** holds that a country should export only those goods and services for which it is more productive than other countries and should import only those goods and services from countries that are more productive than it is. The theory is demonstrated by the following example shown in Figure 6.2.[12]

To understand Smith's theory, let us consider the effects of trade between the Western United States (Washington State, Oregon) and Western Canada (British Columbia, Alberta). In this case, the products will be lumber and apples. The production of any good requires inputs (factors of production). The production inputs include land, labour, and capital. Let us assume that both the Western United States and Western Canada have the same amount of resources (inputs) to enable them to produce *either* lumber or apples; and let us assume further that only 200 units of resources are available to each region. Imagine Western Canada can produce, by using its 200 units of resources, either 20 tonnes of lumber or 10 tonnes of apples. By examining Figure 6.2, you will note that Western Canada also has the opportunity to produce anywhere along the **production possibility frontier (PPF)** C to C1. Western Canada can produce more lumber than apples because the factors of production (resources) are used more efficiently to produce lumber. We can calculate that it takes 10 units of resources for each tonne of lumber and 20 units of resources to produce each tonne of apples. Similarly, imagine that the Western United States can use its 200 units of resources to produce 5 tonnes of lumber *or* 20 tonnes of apples. It too has the option to produce anywhere along the production possibility frontier (PPF) US to US1. Similarly, we can calculate that it will require 40 units of resources to produce each tonne of lumber and 10 units of resources to grow each tonne of apples.

The **theory of absolute advantage** holds that a country should export only those goods and services for which it is more productive than other countries and should import only those goods and services from countries that are more productive than it is.

The **production possibility frontier (PPF)** is a curve or line depicting all maximum output possibilities of two or more goods given a set of inputs (resources, labour, capital, technology etc.). The PPF assumes that all inputs are used efficiently.

FIGURE 6.2

The Theory of Absolute Advantage

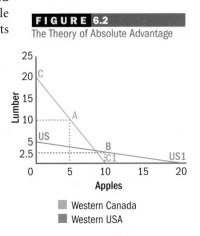

■ Western Canada
■ Western USA

In Figure 6.2 notice that Western Canada has an absolute advantage in the production of lumber while the Western United States has an absolute advantage in the production of apples. Both achieve a maximum return on their resources only if they *specialize* in what they do well! According to Smith, each nation should export only those goods and services for which it is more productive and should import from nations that are more productive in other goods and services. If these two "nations" in our example followed Smith's theory, and specialized in producing the goods in which they have an absolute advantage, the world would have 20 tonnes of apples from the Western United States and 20 tonnes of lumber from Western Canada. Recall either country can produce anywhere along the PPF. Suppose a country wishes to adopt protectionist, (mercantilist) trade policy measures and not trade with the other; it might choose to take its 200 units of resources and divide them equally between the production of lumber and apples.

If Western Canada followed this course of action, it would produce lumber and apples at point A on the PPF. By examining Figure 6.2, you will note that Western Canada will produce 10 tonnes of lumber and only 5 tonnes of apples. We will see in a moment that it has failed to achieve the maximum benefit (efficiencies) from its 200 units of resources. Similarly, by adopting a protectionist stance, the Western United States chooses to uses its resources at point B. The Western United States would be able to produce only 2.5 tonnes of lumber and 10 tonnes of apples. Once again reviewing Figure 6.2, we note that the protectionist trade model produced only 12.5 tonnes of lumber and 15 tonnes of apples for the world. I think you would agree that adopting a mercantilist policy results in a significant reduction in global availability of lumber and apples. Does Smith's theory of absolute advantage work when powerful trading nations like Canada, the United States, Germany, Japan, Brazil, and others deal with developing and underdeveloped nations that do not have the resources to provide an absolute advantage in any product or service? Can they still participate in globalization?

Theory of Competitive Advantage

The **theory of comparative advantage** was published by English economist David Ricardo who, building on Adam Smith's theory, proved that even though a nation was less efficient than other nations, it could still profit by exporting goods if it held an advantage in the production of the exported goods compared to the other nations.

English economist David Ricardo accepted Smith's theory of absolute advantage whereby market forces, not government, should determine the direction, volume, and composition of international trade. Ricardo raised the question, What happens if one country has Smith's absolute advantage in both lumber and apples? Should they still conduct international trade? The answer to the question came in 1817 when Ricardo published his **theory of comparative advantage**. Smith showed that a nation should export goods that it could produce with less labour (inputs) than other nations. Ricardo, building on Smith's theory, proved that even though a nation was less efficient than other nations, a nation could still profit by exporting goods if it held a *comparative advantage* in the production of the exported goods.

FIGURE 6.3

The Theory of Comparative Advantage

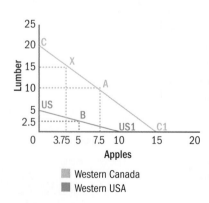

Western Canada

Western USA

Using the same example and looking at Figure 6.3, we now have a scenario where Western Canada produces and is more efficient in both lumber and apples. Western Canada can produce 20 tonnes of lumber or 15 tonnes of apples or any combination along the PPF (C to C1). Western United States, being less efficient, can produce either 5 tonnes of lumber or 10 tonnes of apples or any combination along the PPF (US to US1). The resources required by the nations to produce 1 tonne of apples and 1 tonne of lumber are shown in Figure 6.4. If Western Canada *adopted a protectionist* approach and used its 200 units of resources and applied them equally to the production of apples and lumber, Western Canada could produce 10 tonnes of lumber and 7.5 tonnes of apples (point A on the line PPF C-C1). Similarly, the Western United States could produce 2.5 tonnes of lumber and 5 tonnes of apples. If both countries adopt this trade policy, we note from Figure 6.5 that the total production and consumption of apples and lumber without trade yields a total of 12.5 tonnes of lumber and 12.5 tonnes of apples.

Resources Required to Produce 1 Tonne of Lumber and 1 Tonne of Apples		
	Lumber	Apples
Western Canada	10	20
Western USA	40	10

Production and Consumption without Trade (Mercantilism)		
	Lumber	Apples
Western Canada	10.0	0.0
Western USA	2.5	20.0
Total Production	12.5	20.0

Production with Specialization (Global Production)		
	Lumber	Apples
Western Canada	20.0	0.0
Western USA	0.0	20.0
Total Production	20.0	20.0

Adapted from Charles Hill, *International Business: Competing in the Global Marketplace*, 5th ed. (Boston: McGraw-Hill, 2005).

FIGURE 6.4

Smith's Absolute Advantage and Gains from Trade

Production and Consumption without Trade (Mercantilism)		
	Lumber	Apples
Western Canada	10	7.5
Western USA	2.5	5
Total Production	12.5	12.5

Production with Specialization (Global Production)		
	Lumber	Apples
Western Canada	15	3.75
Western USA	0	10
Total Production	15	13.75
Hence, the world is better off by:	2.5 tonnes	1.25 tonnes

Adapted from Charles Hill, *International Business: Competing in the Global Marketplace*, 5th ed. (Boston: McGraw-Hill, 2005).

FIGURE 6.5

Ricardo's Competitive Advantage and Gains from Trade

However, if the nations *adopt Ricardo's theory of comparative advantage*, can we demonstrate that they would be better off? Why should they trade if Canada is more efficient and has absolute advantage in both products? The answer is, because Canada, although having an absolute advantage in lumber and apples, has only a comparative advantage in lumber. Western Canada can produce 4 times the amount of lumber compared to the Western United States (20:5), but only 1.5 times as many apples (15:10). Western Canada is more efficient than the Western United States at growing trees when compared to apples. So following Ricardo's theory of specialization, what will be the level of production? In accordance with the theory, the two nations should enter into a trade agreement that provides for the Western United States to devote all of its 200 units of resources to the production of apples, thereby yielding 10 tonnes. Western Canada, adhering to the theory of comparative advantage, will under same trade agreement increase its lumber output by 5 tonnes. This shifts the production point upward along the PPF C-C1 from position A to position X (see Figure 6.3). Western Canada will produce 15 tons of lumber while its remaining units of resources (50 units) will produce apples (3.75 tons). So is the world better off as a result of this specialization? The answer once again is yes. The world now has 15 tons of apples and 13.75 tons of lumber, a significant increase in the global production of lumber and apples than if both regions adopted Mun's mercantilist trade theory.

PRACTICAL ENTREPRENEURIAL FOCUS

China can produce textiles with less labour cost than most other nations; it has an absolute advantage compared with other developing countries. Why shouldn't China be allowed to produce as much as it can and allow other developing countries to produce the products they are most efficient at producing?

A recent article reported that "while it's likely that China, with its seemingly limitless capacity for cheap skilled labour, will see a dramatic jump in market share, industry observers say they expect to see smaller countries specialize in an attempt to build a competitive advantage. What you're going to see is that competition will force manufacturers to focus on what they're competitive in. . . . Malaysia might focus on sweaters, while jeans production will be focused in Mexico and the Caribbean."[13] Yes, process streamlining will reduce costs for retailers, and increased competition should lead to additional savings. But it is not just about the unit cost. In a competitive environment, factories will be pressured to lower their prices. While in theory this transformation will benefit all retailers, it will be those with the most valuable contracts, like the box stores and high-end boutiques, that will benefit the most at the expense of smaller competitors. According to the Standard and Poor's report, the most likely to benefit will be those that can reduce their production cycle while maintaining or improving quality and value source.[14]

Do you agree with Standard and Poor's report that the only way for Canadian SMEs to compete in a highly competitive global industry is to reduce production cycles, improve quality, and seek out global value sourcing?

Heckscher-Ohlin Theory of Factor Endowments

Although Smith's and Ricardo's theories do much to explain trade theory, later economists also provide useful insights to assist in understanding why nations trade with one another. Economists Eli Heckscher and Bertil Ohlin shifted the focus of their study to the supply factors. Simply put, they contended that the cost of the resources (factors of production) has a direct relationship to supply and demand. If a country has a greater supply of a resource, then the cost of the resource will be lower. Accordingly, countries will trade in those abundant or oversupplied goods and services. This low cost of resources will result in an international competitive advantage for that industry or nation. The **Heckscher-Ohlin theory** states that when resources (factors of production both basic and advanced) are abundant in one nation, while at the same time scarce in other competing nations, the nation with the abundance will have an international competitive advantage in those specific resources and the goods or services that require those resources.

It is important to differentiate between absolute/comparative advantage and Heckscher-Ohlin theory. The first two theories focused on a country's production and the efficiencies achieved from specialization. The Heckscher-Ohlin theory is not grounded in production and productivity, but focused on the advantage of producing and exporting goods and services using factors of production that are most abundant and therefore cheaper compared to international competitors.

Heckscher-Ohlin theory provides for two classifications of factors of production. The first is labour; the second consists of land and capital equipment. China, as an example of the first classification, has an abundance of labour (1.3 billion people). According to Heckscher-Ohlin theory, China has a competitive advantage in producing goods that are labour-intensive. You only have to read the daily news to validate this observation. Canada, with the second-largest landmass in the world and a very small population of 31.2 million, illustrates the second classification of the Heckscher-Ohlin theory perfectly. Canada exports commodities to the world (currently representing over 50 percent of our exports). Many nations refer to us as the "breadbasket." To produce grains, a nation needs an abundance of land. Fortunately, Canada does have abundant land, which, according to the Heckscher-Ohlin theory, should result in Canada having a competitive advantage in the production of grain.

The **Heckscher-Ohlin theory** states that when resources (factors of production both basic and advanced) are abundant in one nation, while at the same time scarce in other competing nations, then the nation with the abundance will have an international competitive advantage in those specific resources and the goods or services that require those resources. This theory is focused on the advantage of producing and exporting goods and services using factors of production that are most abundant and therefore cheaper compared to international competitors.

The Leontief Paradox

A study by Wassily Leontief in the early 1950s suggested that the Heckscher-Ohlin theory might be flawed. Leontief undertook a significant study of the United States' trading patterns and applied the Heckscher-Ohlin theory. The United States, with an abundance of capital equipment, exports goods requiring capital-intensive production and imports goods requiring labour-intensive production. The trading pattern seems to align with the Heckscher-Ohlin theory. Yet Leontief's study concluded that, contrary to the Heckscher-Ohlin theory, it was the U.S. exports that required more labour-intensive production than those goods it imported! This paradox between the anticipated predicted outcome of the Heckscher-Ohlin theory and the actual trade flows is known as the Leontief paradox. This anomaly has since been supported by research studies of other nations. So our quest for a solid explanation as to why nations trade continues.

International Product Trade Life Cycle

During the mid-1960s, economist Raymond Vernon suggested international trade could be explained using his **international product-trade-life-cycle theory**. Those of you who have taken marketing courses will find the theory similar to the product-life-cycle model you have studied. Countries begin by exporting their product, and then at a later stage they undertake foreign direct investment and establish international facilities. Later, they enter the final stage and become an importer of the product. This cycle occurs because others will have entered the global market and captured market share by exploiting their own respective low-cost-factor endowments. Business is like water: it will seek out the location economies and use factors of production available in those venues to its best advantage. If a business does not follow this flow, its competitors will.

The Montréal textiles industry is world class. However, with NAFTA and WTO trade agreements, business flowed to the maquiladoras. The maquiladoras are tax- and duty-free factories initially created in 1965 to allow U.S. companies to assemble their products in Mexico. By 2004, companies from the United States and other countries had opened about 4,760 maquiladoras primarily along the northern border of Mexico. Mexico then became a world-class textile producer. Now some of the business has shifted from Mexico to less-developed countries like Malaysia and China, which have seen significant growth in their textile industries. Today China is recognized as a major world textile producer, while the Montréal textile industry market share continues to dissipate. "Chinese textile imports in Canada are up 40 percent in total since quotas were abolished. It has been reported that there is a fear of massive job losses among the 144,000 Canadian clothing industry workers, more than half of them in the French-speaking province of Quebec. Once the jewel of the Canadian textile industry, now on its last legs, Montréal had long benefited from the low Canadian dollar and low salaries to sell clothes to its southern neighbours, but neither factor will save it now as Mexican and Chinese goods flood the US market."[15] Between December 2003 and June 2004, factory closures or shift cuts forced 1,200 people in the sector out of work in Quebec, including 800 in Huntington, devastating the small town of 2,600 people south of Montréal.

The life cycle commences in stage 1 with the initial production of a new product by an innovative firm generally located in a developed nation like Canada. Figure 6.6, on page 166, graphically depicts the firm introducing its new product and growing its domestic market. The firm does well. For some reason, sooner or later, consumers outside the domestic market want the product. It may be that they became aware of the product by attending a trade show or though some other means. Now the firm enters stage 2 (mature product stage) and begins to export its surplus product internationally. Initially it draws from its surplus production capabilities. Later, because of the firm's international success, and the fear that competitors are aware of the initial firm's success and may

International product-trade-life-cycle theory is similar to the marketing product-life-cycle model. Countries begin by exporting their product; then they undertake foreign direct investment and establish international facilities. Later, they enter the final stage and become an importer of the product. This cycle will occur because others will have entered the global market and taken market share by exploiting their own respective low-cost-factor endowments.

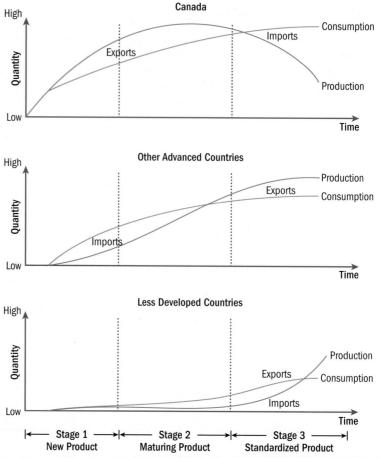

SOURCE: Adapted from Raymond Vernon, "International Investment and International Trade in the Product Cycle," *Quarterly Journal of Economics* (May 1966).

attempt to take away the firm's emerging international market, it now commits to international exports as part of its market-entry strategy.

Other advanced countries are initially importers of the new product in stage 1. However, before long, these countries commence production locally and enter their domestic market. As they do, they take export market share from the initial Canadian firm, and the firm's production levels drop although consumption levels continue to increase. The rising demand results in Canada importing some of the other advanced countries' products for the Canadian domestic market. Both the Canadian firm and the other advanced competitors have been exporting to less-developed nations during stages 1 and 2. Now, we enter stage 3 where the less-developed nations are able to access the factors of production and exploit their location economies so they commence production of the product. Generally, cheap labour needed to produce labour-intensive products is the primary success factor less-developed nations use to enter the global market; see stage 3 (standardized product). The Chinese textile manufacturing experience reversed the global textile trading relationship and follows Vernon's model closely. Today, China is able to sell domestically, to innovative international firms like those in Montréal's textile industry, and to other industrialized countries' markets. This evolution in international product life cycles results in a production downturn in the innovating countries as well as the other industrialized countries. At the micro level, people, including 800 in the Huntington textile industry, are hurt; but at the macro level there is a greater abundance of budget-priced textiles for global consumers. Look at the tag in the shirt you are wearing today—Canadian or Chinese?

New Trade Theory

Early in the 1970s, a variety of explanations emerged to assist in understanding international trade patterns. The economists advocating this new trade theory stressed the importance that luck, entrepreneurship, and innovation play in explaining why firms are successful in international trade. The **new trade theory** states three premises: First, firms can gain an advantage through specialization and by exploiting economies of scale; second, companies that are first into the marketplace will gain a number of advantages as well as the ability to put in place barriers to entry by competitors; third, on occasion, governments can play a very important role in assisting home companies to succeed internationally (see the Bombardier story, on page 157).

Most of us have firsthand experience regarding the advantages to be gained by specialization and exploiting economies of scale. Consider for a moment that you have to make one hamburger. Now consider that you have to make 10 hamburgers. Most would agree that there would be a savings in the production process. Preparing 10 burgers at one time, placing in buns, and wrapping them for delivery to the consumer will take less time than producing 10 hamburgers individually. The savings will be in labour, energy costs, and economies of scale in purchasing power by buying buns in packages of 10 rather than buying a single bun. These savings are derived from what are referred to as the learning curve, the experience curve, and the economies of scale curve (see Figure 6.7). You will note the cost (labour, cash, time) of each unit declines with the number of units produced.

The **first-mover advantage** premise states that companies that are first into the marketplace will gain a number of economic and strategic advantages over those that enter the market subsequently. First movers may also have the ability to put in place barriers to entry for their competitors. The strategic and economic advantages of being first to market can include establishing a brand name; identifying and partnering with the strongest alliances available in the host country; shaping and influencing government regulations and regulators regarding the industry; contracting to be provided with the best factors of production; and, by moving down the economy of scale curve, making their unit costs low enough to become a barrier to entry for competitors considering entering the marketplace. Indeed, a persuasive case can be made for governments to support their national firms establishing a presence in a host country. This argument is particularly strong if the particular industry can support only a few firms globally. Canadians have seen with pride the success of Research In Motion's (RIM) BlackBerry being first in the global marketplace. It has become the industry standard and has retained its significant market share in spite of major global competitors attempting to copy the product. RIM received two major federal government Technology Partnerships Canada grants—one in 1998 ($6 million) and the other in 2000 ($34 million). These federal supports contributed significantly to the early success of the company. Apple's very successful MP3-type player, the iPod, also illustrates the advantages of first-mover advantage.

Porter's Theory—Competitive Advantage of Nations

In the early 1990s, a group of scholars under the direction of Michael Porter studied 100 industries in 10 nations to understand how a nation achieved international success in a particular industry.[16] Why, for example, does Canada have a leading telecommunications industry, whereas Mexico is among the world leaders in textiles? In responding to this question, Porter and his team established four determinants that, when analyzed, shed light on the strength or weakness likely to explain a firms' national competitive advantage. This is widely referred to as Porter's diamond theory.

Porter's theory of competitive advantage of nations holds that four types of determinants affect the ability of domestic firms to utilize the nation's resources to gain international competitive advantage. The four specific country attributes are factor

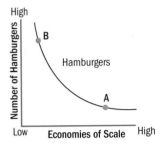

FIGURE 6.7
The Learning Curve, Experience Curve, and Economies of Scale Curve

The **new trade theory** states three premises: firms can gain an advantage through specialization and by exploiting economies of scale; companies that are first into the marketplace will gain a number of advantages as well as the ability to put in place barriers to entry by competitors; and, on occasion, governments can play a very important role in assisting home companies to succeed internationally.

Those first to enter the market attain **first-mover advantage** and gain a number of economic and strategic advantages over those that subsequently enter the market, which may include establishing a strong customer base, securing the best inputs and outputs, moving down the experience curve, and increasing switching costs.

Porter's theory of competitive advantage of nations holds that four kinds of determinants affect the ability of domestic firms to utilize the nation's resources to gain international competitive advantage. The four specific country attributes are factor endowments; demand conditions; related and supporting industries; and the firm's strategy, structure, and rivalry.

FIGURE 6.8
Porter's Determinants of National
Competitive Advantage

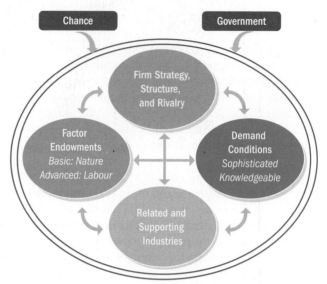

Source: Adapted from "The Competitive Advantage of Nations" by Michael D. Porter, *Harvard Business Review* March–April 1990.

The **basic factor conditions** are those found naturally and without enhancements within a nation, such as a large labour force, natural resources, surface features, and geography.

Advanced factor conditions are enhancements made to improve the competitive advantage of the nation's industry.

endowments; demand conditions; related and supporting industries; and the firm's strategy, structure, and rivalry. You'll note in Figure 6.8 that each determinant is interrelated with each of the others while chance and government influence them. Porter's theory suggests that it is the interaction of these determinants that governs a nation's competitive advantage. He differentiates factor conditions into basic and advanced. The **basic factor conditions** are those found naturally and without enhancements within a nation. They would include a large labour force, natural resources, surface features, and geography. **Advanced factor conditions** are enhancements made to improve the competitive advantage of the nation's industry. Examples would be educating the nation's work force (e.g., India); providing inter-modal transportation (e.g., Japan), upgrading infrastructure to facilitate the rapid movement of goods and services (e.g., the United States), and upgrading communications (e.g., Canada).

Are the customers of the domestic industry sophisticated? Demanding customers will force the industry to undertake research and development and to be on the leading edge in the production of goods and services. Imagine for a moment that you are a Japanese firm selling a Kodak box camera. The domestic manufacturer might readily find a market for the camera in Nigeria but would not be successful marketing it in Japan. Why? Because the Japanese are demanding in their expectations of camera equipment and the attributes they expect in the camera. Anything less than meeting those high expectations will not do well in the Japanese market. Accordingly, we can readily understand why Japan has a world-class camera industry.

Industries recognize the synergy that can be obtained by clustering related and supporting industries in close proximity to the main industry. The movie industry in Canada is clustered around Vancouver and Toronto. The movie industry's related and supporting industries, such as food services, video, editing, and grips, establish their presence in close proximity to these centres. The synergy is derived from the daily interaction and experience both industries share.

Finally, the stronger the domestic competition, the greater the need for strategic planning. Firms in a competitive environment constantly look for efficiencies that in turn will enhance their international competitiveness. "Structure follows strategy"—so strong domestic competition forces firms to adopt the most efficient and effective structure and organization, thereby enhancing their global competitive stature. We will explore this notion in more detail in Chapter 11, pages 311–324. Together, these four determinants operate within an ecosystem where chance and government can significantly affect the strategic fit of the diamond. A chance event, such as the tragedy of 9/11, can create destruction and reshape industries. Clearly the airline and tourism industries were affected by this horrific event. It is the task of political leaders and decision makers to exploit these opportunities or to mitigate the dangers that chance presents. By doing so, they can contribute to strengthening Porter's diamond. Similarly, government can directly affect its nation's competitive advantage through proactive or reactive initiatives or indeed by a failure to respond in any capacity. Within Canada, the wheat, milk, and egg marketing boards shape the nation's competitive advantage of these industries. Do you think they do this in a positive way?

Porter's theory of competitive advantage states that the degree of an industry's success will be a function of how successfully the factors are aligned (i.e., strategically fit) within Porter's diamond. There would be little competitive advantage for a nation to expend the resources to create advanced factor endowments (e.g., developing a skilled labour force and the infrastructure required for the telecommunications industry), if government establishes trade barriers constricting the necessary related and supporting telecommunication industries. Nations need national strategies to achieve national competitive advantage. Political leaders must ensure these four determinants are aligned and fully supportive of each other. It is like planting seeds: the ground must be fertile for the plants (industries) to thrive. By applying Porter's diamond we can better understand how the patterns, scale, and scope are linked among trading nations. It is this macro view that assists in understanding the global trade theory and enriches the theories of Adam Smith and David Ricardo.

Although Porter permits us to focus on the roles of capital and labour, technological change, patterns of innovation, and the nature of demand in shaping trade links among nations, there are exceptions to the diamond. Although governments can support a particular determinant, such as advanced factor endowment conditions to assist an industry (e.g., the automobile industry in Ontario is supported by governments providing an educated workforce, cheap energy, and tax incentives), the industry can still fail. It would seem that Ontario should have comparative advantage in the production of automobiles. Yet other resource constraints, such as the high Canadian dollar, or the import of budget-priced Chinese automobiles, may shift the balance within Porter's diamond such that Canada will no longer be able to compete in the global automobile market. It might be better for us to take our limited resources to enhance the factor endowment conditions that support call centres or the telecommunications industry. China's Geely Automobile Holdings said it planned to step up car exports in 2004 after testing overseas markets in late 2003, with an eye to selling 30 percent of its output abroad by 2010.[17] In 2005, Geely produced fewer than 200,000 cars, according to *Automotive News*, an industry trade magazine, and most of those were sold in China. However, to tap the ASEAN market, the assembly of Geely cars will start in Malaysia in October 2006. While the Geely cars are not ready for the North American market, Visionary Vehicles has partnered with Chery Automobile Co., another Chinese automaker to begin importing cars to the United States by the end of 2008. Geely also manufactures the Haoqing minicar, the cheapest on the Chinese market (US$3,867). What proactive actions do you think Canada's auto industry should take? Is the Ontario government throwing good money after bad in order to assist current automobile manufacturers?

Occasionally an individual company may succeed globally despite Porter's diamond model predicting a nation's competitive advantage is unlikely. E-business has afforded the opportunity for a number of firms to gain international competitive stature because of their ability to access and to focus on the external nations as their core market. Clear proof of this is seen by observing the phenomenal growth of Chinese firms since 1979 under Deng Xiaoping (in power from 1978 to 1997)[18] when China formally moved from a command economy toward a more market economy. Clearly, an examination of the national competitive advantage of China through the 1980s and 1990s would not lead one to the conclusion that individual industries could be so globally competitive.

Closing Thoughts on International Trade Theory

We started with the question, Why do nations trade? It is an important question to understand the direction, composition, and volume of trade that takes place within and between nations. It is important for Canada as an international trading nation to reflect upon the theories of Smith, Ricardo, Heckscher-Ohlin, Vernon, the economists who advocated the new trade theory, and, most recently, Porter's theory, in order to seek out the nuggets that might give Canada an edge over international competitors. You probably now recognize that we have not found a definitive economic trade theory to explain why nations trade. Therefore, we must content ourselves by taking the best from these economic trade theories and making them our own. Who knows, maybe one of you will answer the questions—why do nations trade, and how can they get the edge?

Does Free Trade Work?

There are advocates on each side of this question. While there are issues, it is anticipated that by the time you have completed this chapter, you will agree, on an academic level at least, that free trade works. However, on the micro level, there are many challenges that must be addressed. Consider, for example, Chile's experience. Chile has the strongest bond rating in South America and a reputation for strong financial institutions and sound economic policy. If there is any place in Latin America where the poor have thrived because of globalization, it is Chile. The country's success shows that poor nations can exploit globalization but only if they have governments that can make it happen. Chile reduced poverty by growing its economy 6.6 percent per year from 1985 to 2004. One of the few points economists can agree on is that economic growth is the most important thing a nation can do for its poor. However, the debate swirls around basics like whether poverty in the world is up or down in the last 15 years (the number of people who live on less than $1 a day is slightly down, but the number who live on less than $2 is slightly up). "Inequality has soared during the last 15 years, but economists cannot agree on whether globalization is mainly at fault or whether other forces, like the uneven spread of technology, are responsible. They can't agree on how to reduce inequality—growth tends not to change it. They can't agree on whether the poor who have not been helped are victims of globalization or have simply not yet enjoyed access to its benefits—in other words, whether the solution is more globalization or less. But economists agree on one thing: to help the poor, you'd better grow."[19]

Trade Restrictions

Business managers are aware of the importance of continually scanning the economic venues—both those where they currently operate and those in which they propose to operate. Government leaders, national press, and other spokespersons for the business community often telegraph the government's economic plans. At times, these plans provide for implementation or removal of trade restrictions. Business leaders must adopt proactive strategies to exploit the opportunities and to mitigate the damage of the anticipated changes indicated by these spokespersons. By understanding the underlying theories driving these changes, business decision makers will be able to use this trade knowledge to their advantage. Consider how the Marxist regime of Salvador Allende in Chile played a direct role in its economy. It is generally well known that the Allende government implemented high import duties in support of its protectionist stance, and enacted an excessive income tax on the private sector to fund its government's direct investment to include significant subsidies for the friends of government.

General Pinochet, upon taking power as a military dictator (1973–1990), appointed a conservative group of about 25 Chilean economists known as the Chicago Boys. "Most of the Chicago Boys received their basic economic education from the School of Economy in

Universidad Católica, and were later postgraduate exchange students at the University of Chicago"[20] and devotees of the free-market economic philosophies of Nobel Prize winner Milton Friedman. Friedman's economic philosophies supported Hayek, whose thoughts took centre stage in the 1980s and were adopted widely by Margaret Thatcher (former Prime Minister of Britain), Ronald Reagan (former President of the United States), and others, including Stephen Harper, Prime Minister of Canada, as we discussed in Chapter 1, on page 5. Those familiar with Hayek and Friedman's philosophies were not surprised when a free-market economic system and massive restructuring took place within Chile. The Chilean government reduced import duties from over 1,000 percent to a basic level of 10 percent. Pinochet removed almost all of the import barriers and enabled free trade with the world. This, of course, meant that Chilean businesses had to quickly become globally competitive or die. The removal of import duties permitted Chilean businesses to import state-of-the-art manufacturing equipment, thereby improving their productivity. So, then, can a case be made to interfere with the free trade theories of Smith, Ricardo, Hayek, and Friedman when we witness the success of countries like Chile? And if so, what "instruments" are available to political decision makers?

Instruments of Trade Policy

We can now make a persuasive case in support of free trade based on the classical theories of Smith, Ricardo, and Heckscher-Ohlin augmented by Raymond Vernon's product life cycle theory and the emerging new trade theory offered by Michael Porter. We have seen that pure **free trade** could exist when governments make no attempt to interfere with businesses buying or selling products or services directly or indirectly in the global marketplace. Understanding the academic arguments that support these trade theories, so why do our political leaders continue to interfere with free trade by providing subsidies, imposing tariffs, and applying other instruments to distort and impede free trade? It is to this question, the political reality of international trade, that we now turn.

> **Free trade** exists when governments make no attempt to interfere with businesses buying or selling products or services directly or indirectly in the global marketplace.

We noted in the opening vignette, on page 157, that Bombardier has been an ongoing recipient of federal government supports that enhance the firm's competitiveness in the aero industry.

A government can consider implementing six main instruments to interfere with free trade. These instruments are tariffs, subsidies, voluntary export restraints (VERs), local-content requirements, administrative policies, and anti-dumping duties.

Tariffs

A **tariff** is a tax levied on imports. In most countries, tariffs fall into two categories; Canada has three. A **specific tariff** is a fixed charge levied for each unit of an imported good. For example, a tax of 50¢ for each bushel of California tomatoes being imported into Canada would be a specific tariff. An **ad valorem tariff** is a percentage based on the value of the goods imported. For example, imported garlic bulbs from China are taxed at 10 percent of the garlic bulb's declared value. Canada is one of the few countries with a third classification, a **compound tariff**. This is a combination of both a specific and an ad valorem tax being levied. Tariffs on exports result in the product costing more in the importing country. This impediment to trade is reduced with the signing of free trade agreements. For example, Australian wine exports have increased dramatically in the last few years, yet the Asian market was not increasing at all. This changed when a Thailand–Australia Free Trade Agreement was signed in 2003. The ad valorem "tariff on Australian wine was reduced from 60 to 40 per cent and will be phased to zero by 2015. Australian exports of wine for the first ten months of the agreement's operation were up 8 per cent to $6.5 million."[21] Is there a lesson here for Canada's governments at all levels?

The Auto Pact, an agreement between the United States and Canada, was developed in 1965 and was said to be the key behind the success of the Canadian auto industry. In 2001, the WTO, after a complaint by Japan and the EU, ruled that the agreement was unfair because Canada was imposing tariffs on imported vehicles that were not made by

> A **tariff** is a tax levied on imports. In most countries, tariffs fall into two categories. Canada has three: specific, ad valorem, and compound.
>
> A **specific tariff** is a fixed charge levied for each unit of a good imported. For example, a tax of 50¢ for each bushel of California tomatoes being imported into Canada would be a specific tariff.
>
> An **ad valorem tariff** is a percentage based on the value of the goods imported. For example, imported garlic bulbs from China are taxed at 10 percent of the declared value of the garlic bulbs.
>
> A **compound tariff** is a combination of both a specific and an ad valorem tax being levied. Canada is one of the few countries with this tariff classification.

North America's three big car manufacturers. Chrysler, Ford, and General Motors were able to import cars to Canada duty-free, but car manufacturers like Honda and Toyota had to pay tariffs of 6.1 percent. The WTO ruled that this practice was discriminatory.[22] The United States, Europe, Japan and other countries have experienced ongoing disputes regarding tariffs on steel, oranges, and clothing. In March 2002, President Bush imposed tariffs of 8 to 30 percent on steel imports until 2005. However, many U.S. manufacturers need steel to make their products. The result was that the cost of these tariffs was passed along to the consumer and affected the global competitiveness of these steel users. This once again demonstrates how tariffs are a double-edged sword. During the first year of these tariffs, U.S. manufacturers paid $680 million more for steel than they had previously.[23] In another example, before 2001, China's government imposed a tariff of nearly 100 percent on imported cars. With China's accession into the WTO, the tariff was gradually reduced over five years to 25 percent in 2006. High tariffs discourage consumers from choosing imported cars, and allow domestic car sellers to charge unreasonably high prices. In addition, high tariffs also encourage foreign automobile manufacturers that are interested in the Chinese market to set up joint ventures with domestic manufacturers instead of exporting cars directly into China.

Japan imposes a 50 percent tariff on fresh beef imports to protect the domestic cattle industry. This greatly hurts beef sales from Australia, a major exporter to Japan. U.S. shrimp producers were delighted when their federal government imposed tariffs on Chinese and Vietnamese imports of shrimp into the country. Duties on imports of Chinese frozen and canned warm-water shrimp were subject to tariffs ranging from 27 to 112.8 percent while Vietnamese imports were subject to tariffs from 4.1 to 25.8 percent. The United States lobbied successfully to impose tariffs on the grounds that its investigation found unfair dumping practices being conducted by China and Vietnam that were hurting the U.S. shrimp industry.[24] Dumping is defined as selling goods in a host market below the cost of production.

In 2004, Canada announced measures aimed at improving the global competitiveness of the textiles and apparel industries. These measures include the elimination of tariffs on imported fibres and yarns, as well as the elimination of tariffs on imported fabrics used in the production of apparel. To minimize adverse effects on current domestic production, Canada retained tariffs on fibres, yarns, and fabrics where domestic suppliers can demonstrate production in Canada.[25] So when nations impose countervailing duties and anti-dumping tariffs, who wins and who loses? Tariffs raise the price of imported products and will generally protect domestic producers from foreign competition. In the lumber dispute, the American government collected over $5 billion (CDN) from Canadian lumber producers. The U.S. lumber producers argued that the stumpage fees paid by Canadian firms did not represent world prices and were in effect a hidden subsidy. (Governments can be very creative in this way.) The United States government gained from increased government revenues. U.S. lumber producers gained because they have protection from foreign Canadian lumber producers and therefore are able to charge higher prices in the U.S. homebuilding marketplace. Consumers lose. In this case, American homeowners paid significantly more for both imported and domestic building materials.

Whether or not a business case can be made to support a tariff must be determined on a case-by-case basis. Was the increased cost of housing less than the possible impact of losing forestry jobs in the American Northwest? Many economists say yes. "The U.S. consumer perspective could be very important. A study by the Cato Institute in the United States found that trade restrictions increased the price of lumber in the United States between 20 and 35 percent or US$50 to $80 per thousand board feet. This resulted in the cost of the average new home in the United States being between US$800 and $1,300, higher than it would be had free trade prevailed. According to the Bureau of the Census, every $1,000 increase in housing prices means that an additional 300,000 families are unable to purchase a home. Lumber-using workers outnumber lumber-producing workers by about 25 to 1 in the United States."[26] however, it seems the lumber-producing workers' lobby group's interests were stronger. While a deeper analysis is beyond the scope of this text, it is clear that tariffs are pro-producer and anti-consumer. Having examined

Adam Smith's demand–supply curves, you now understand what happens when the supply is artificially constrained by tariffs and the demand remains unchanged: the cost of the product rises.

A further consideration is that tariffs tend to promote the status quo in home industries. The American lumber industry has less reason to improve its efficiency when it is not forced to compete in a free trade global marketplace. The U.S. steel industry is yet another example of government intervention resulting in an industry becoming reliant on protectionist measures. During the 1990s, little money was spent upgrading and improving the efficiency of American steel mills while, during the same period, the Europeans made significant capital investments. As a result, the European firms were able to provide the global marketplace with cheaper steel products. In response, the U.S. government imposed an ad valorem tariff on steel of between 8 and 30 percent to protect its industry's hemorrhaging market share.

The removal of tariffs can also be disruptive to the status quo. Uruguay Round WTO members, for example, agreed to eliminate non-tariff barriers, such as quotas, VERs, and orderly marketing agreements, and bring textiles and agricultural products under the general trading rules for all products over a 10-year period. Consequently, the Multi-Fibre Agreement (MFA) established in the 1970s expired on December 31, 2004. It was a system of quotas and voluntary export restraints that were implemented to protect certain textile industries. The new trade rules don't provide for quotas. All countries, including Canada, knew what would happen in the global textile industry in 2004; the developed and developing countries had a 10-year adjustment period to prepare for the tariff removal as the December 31, 2004 deadline approached. Many firms failed to use this time to invest in new more productive machinery and innovative products, and now find themselves competing against the location economies of China. Even countries like Bangladesh that rely heavily on the textile industry have also been adversely affected because of competition from China.[27] What are the remedies available for nations that feel they have been unfairly treated in the global marketplace? This topic was discussed when we looked at the World Trade Organization and other global institutions' dispute resolution processes in Chapter 5, pages 149–150.

Subsidies

A **subsidy** is the gratuitous direct or indirect payment of monies by a government to a domestic firm. The Canadian government has provided subsidies to firms such as Bombardier and Research In Motion (RIM) in several forms. Subsidies can take the form of cash grants, low-interest loans, tax breaks, or the government acquiring an equity position in the firm. As a result of their financial advantage, firms have an increased competitive advantage in the marketplace.

Many in the United States, like the Institute of American Textile Manufacturers Institute, believe the reason for the economic distress currently experienced by the domestic industry has been the sustained depreciation of Asian currencies against the U.S. dollar. U.S. pundits argue that this is a hidden subsidy. "This decline in currency values, which has averaged 40% over the past five years, has allowed Asians to drop their export prices by as much as 25% which has caused an enormous surge in imports from Asia. The end result has been [between 2003 and 2005] the closure of [many Canadian and] over 150 textile plants in the United States and the loss of over 100,000 textile jobs. . . . While other currencies—notably the euro—have strengthened recently against the dollar, the Chinese yuan, the Korean won and the Taiwan dollar have remained dramatically undervalued."[28] These pundits contend that these major exporting countries manipulated their currencies to gain a competitive advantage over U.S. manufacturers. It is a serious issue: these three countries have built up over $1 trillion in foreign reserves over the past five years. China is adding to its cache of U.S. dollars at the rate of $7 billion per month. Viewed from an American perspective, the effect of these foreign reserve accumulations is to make U.S. dollars scarce vis-à-vis these Asian currencies, thereby driving down the value of Asian currency in relation to the dollar. However, we could argue that these

A **subsidy** is the gratuitous direct or indirect payment of monies by a government to a domestic firm.

actions are preventing a global economic collapse by acquiring U.S. Treasury bills. Either way, the end result has been record imports of manufactured goods at what some claim to be artificially depressed prices. "Chinese exports of all goods to the U.S. jumped 20% last year [2003] with China, at $102 billion, surpassing Japan as the single biggest slice of the U.S. trade deficit. China benefits by getting a 40% advantage (subsidy) on the goods it exports because of its undervalued currency."[29] We will examine this issue further in Chapter 8, pages 226 and 231.

Canada's Bombardier, in order to compete with its aero industry counterpart, Brazil's Embraer, continues to benefit from subsidies, tax breaks, loan assistance for global customers, and other trade advantages. These benefits, received by both Embraer and Bombardier, have been the subject of ongoing disputes before the WTO.[30]

In March 2003, Brazil, Australia, and Thailand brought forward a dispute to the WTO regarding subsidies that the EU provides to its sugar industry. They argued that only sugar manufactured from beets or cane harvested in the EU, not sugar imported into the EU, should benefit from a "guaranteed high intervention price" and that these subsidies create an unfair playing field and affect world markets. In addition, Brazil, Australia, and Thailand claimed that the EU provided an "export subsidy" to sugar produced above a certain quota.[31] As a result of adjudication in June 2004, the EU announced a reduction in its quotas, a major reduction of its subsidies to help poor countries in the sugar industry, a reduction in subsidized exports, and a reduction of guaranteed prices by 30 to 40 percent.[32] It seems the WTO dispute resolution process can work when the parties participate in good faith.

The BBC website contains an article that compares two dairy farmers, one in Africa and one in France. The African farmer, who has a herd of 14 dairy cows, gets no subsidies from his government and makes £11 per month. The French farmer has 98 hectares of land and 45 dairy cattle and makes £60,000 a year from the milk. This income includes an EU subsidy of 30 euro cents per litre. In all, about 75 percent of the French farmer's income comes from government subsidies. This example illustrates the advantage that farmers have when their government subsidizes the industry and how the subsidy unfairly disadvantages farmers in countries that cannot afford to do the same.[33] "Fisheries in Massachusetts have been awarded with cash grants. Global subsidies to international fisheries amount to around $10 [billion] to 15 billion annually. Environmental groups want this amount reduced because it further depletes the world's fish stocks; 25 percent of the world's fish stock is overexploited or depleted."[34] The U.S. government awarded commodity and disaster subsidies to farmers totalling $131 billion during the period 1995–2003. Recipients, for instance, were farmers affected by the hurricanes and tornadoes that destroyed crops in Florida.[35] Since 1978, the United States government has granted a multitude of tax incentives and subsidies to corn growers, which are largely the multinational oil companies, to promote the growth of a domestic ethanol industry.

So once again we have to ask, who benefits and who loses? Clearly, subsidies are taxpayers' money, so an argument can be made that the taxpayers lose. The domestic producers cushioned by the gratuitous payments have less of an incentive to become efficient. Subsidies can be seen as beneficial when viewed as an aid to a domestic firm in order to obtain a first-mover advantage in new markets, particularly when the new market will accommodate only one or two players within the industry. The subsidized firm will experience increased revenues that will in turn provide additional tax revenues to the government. While a detailed analysis is not within the scope of this text, a cost-benefit analysis could be done to pragmatically determine whether the specific subsidy contemplated is a good or bad thing.

Import Quotas and Voluntary Export Restraints

The international free trade pipeline flows in both directions. It seems that developed countries lost sight of this possibility during the initial days of globalization. Their products and services flowed freely and quickly as the developed counties eliminated the free trade constraints into developing countries. Today, the bidirectional nature of the pipeline's flow is very clear. China is now flooding the global markets using this same pipeline, raising growing concerns in the developed countries. In an attempt to shut off or constrict the influx of goods, nations will consider introducing import quotas and voluntary export restraints.

Import Quotas

An **import quota** is a government restriction on the quantity of a product that will be admitted into the host country. It is customary for the host government to implement import quotas by issuing import licences to specific groups or firms. Canada, for example, has implemented quotas on imports of ice cream and yogurt. The U.S. imposes import quotas on dairy products as well as an administrative import-licensing requirement that costs US $200.[36] Mexico imposes similar quotas on imported U.S. turkeys.[37]

It seems China will benefit the most from the elimination of the quota system. In view of the country's cheap and abundant labour, more efficient production, and better-integrated infrastructure, it is anticipated that China will gradually expand its share of the U.S. garment market to 50 percent from the current 16 percent. At the same time, China is expected to increase its share of the EU market from 20 percent to 29 percent according to recent estimates by the World Trade Organization.[38] If China dominates in polyester segments, other developing countries like Indonesia, India, and Pakistan might have a comparative advantage in the cotton categories and should still compete in the market through specializing in something that can be produced in a short period.[39] U.S. textile industry leaders, warning of U.S. losses of up to 600,000 jobs if pre-emptive action was not taken, petitioned their administration to block the anticipated flood of Chinese imports. The request is unusual because petitions normally seek to limit imports only after they have done damage to a domestic industry. American textile groups joined dozens of other industry groups from other countries in unsuccessfully appealing to the World Trade Organization to delay the elimination of the textile quotas.[40] While there are advantages and disadvantages in eliminating the quota, Clay Risen, assistant editor at *The New Republic* explains, "it will radically alter the industry—thousands of jobs will be lost, thousands more will be created, supply chains will be overhauled, and clothing retailers will come under pressure to reduce prices significantly."[41] So the removal of the textile quota is great for the thousands more who will have jobs, but what about for those who will lose their jobs? How can Canada compensate the Montréal textile workers and what employment alternatives are available for them? What about those people in the developing world who stand to lose their jobs? Will they have compensation or alternatives? We win as consumers; we have quality products at lower prices. Indeed at the macro level it is a good thing given "studies have predicted that the phase-out will benefit the world economy to the tune of up to $324 billion."[42]

Voluntary Export Restraints

On occasion, foreign countries, industries, or firms sense that an importing country is not pleased with the current trade arrangements for a particular product. To prevent the introduction of draconian measures to constrict imports by the host country, exporting countries sometimes implement a **voluntary export restraint (VER)**. A **VER** is a quota that has been self-imposed by the exporting country. On many occasions VERs are put in place at the request of the importing country's government. One of the best-known examples occurred in the early 1980s. During the 1960s and 1970s, Japanese car manufacturers were dramatically acquiring North American market share to the chagrin of the Big Three auto manufacturers. You may recall North American automobiles with their low gas mileage, steel bodies, large fins, and lack of attention to quality going head to head against the more efficient and economical Toyota and Honda vehicles from Japan. The Japanese recognized that President Ronald Reagan might, as a result of lobbyists' pressure, implement very severe import quotas on foreign automobiles. Fearing the worst, the Japanese government responded quickly to reduce American concerns and to

An **import quota** is a government restriction on the quantity of a product that will be admitted into the host country.

A **voluntary export restriction (VER)** is a quota that has been self-imposed by the exporting country. On many occasions, VERs are put in place at the request of the importing country's government.

permit the U.S. manufacturers time to preserve their remaining domestic market share. In fact, Chrysler would have gone bankrupt if it weren't for Japan's intervention.[43] A United States Federal Trade Commission study found that this VER cost American consumers about $1 billion a year between 1981 and 1985. These monies primarily made their way to the Japanese car producers in the form of higher prices resulting from the reduced supply of their sought-after autos in the U.S. market. The cash windfalls strengthened the Japanese firms and made them better able to compete in the global marketplace. This type of financial windfall continues today. Toyota is becoming every bit as dominant as Ford was with its Model-T in the 1910s and 1920s, and General Motors in the 1950s and 1960s with Chevrolet and Cadillac. "In a comprehensive report on the world auto industry published by Standard & Poor's, Efraim Levy says that U.S. automakers, despite restructuring efforts, new product introductions, and incentives will continue to lose market share in 2006."[44] Today NAFTA specifically provides that VERs are not permitted.[45]

So again we ask, who wins and who loses? Certainly in the face of protectionist measures, a VER is a worthwhile instrument to consider potentially making the best of a bad situation. Because the North American supply of their vehicles was artificially restricted, the Japanese automobile producers were therefore able to charge more for their cars; they won. North American auto industry producers also won; the Japanese VER gave them time to retool and commence crafting automobiles that could meet or exceed the Japanese standards. How well the U.S. industry used that time is a question for debate. What's not debatable is that the consumer was again the loser. By restricting the number of quality automobiles available, North American consumers were disadvantaged, paying a higher price for Japanese automobiles than could have been commanded in a free and unrestricted marketplace.

Recall our discussion concerning the textile industry and the end of the 40-year-old quota system, on page 175. As the deadline loomed, global pressure mounted against the Chinese textile export industry. In order to prevent Canada, the United States, and the European Union from imposing temporary limits on Chinese textile imports and to prevent claims of anti-dumping, on December 12, 2004, the Chinese government volunteered to increase its export tariffs on some textiles. Interestingly, under the World Trade Organization, VERs have been illegal since the 1980s. Nevertheless, the pragmatic view is that no WTO member would likely challenge China's VER and therefore the validity of China's action is a moot point. Occasionally, VERs may be used as a government tool to increase the price of a product to the benefit of both the host manufacturer and the foreign exporter. Governments consider using this tool when the combined production of both the host and exporting countries is insufficient to meet consumer demand.

Local-Content Requirements

Local-content requirements are implemented by nations by specifying that some portion of the product must be produced domestically.

Many nations will implement a **local-content requirement** by specifying that some portion of the product must be produced domestically. The requirement will be expressed as a percentage of the materials or as a percentage of the value of the product. Countries such as Canada employ this instrument to assist in the transformation of basic component supply firms into firms that also supply some added value before passing the product on to the consumer. Australian TV, like Canadian TV, has local-content requirements for broadcasting, advertising, and motion pictures. With the signing of the

INTERNATIONAL STRATEGIC THINKING

In crafting strategies for your business, you should be aware of a number of methods available to you to circumnavigate import quotas. One popular method is to review the trade agreements of third-party nations with the intention of benefiting from the special concessions that permits them quota-free entry into the marketplace you wish to enter. Once you've identified such a nation, then you establish facilities in that nation in order to acquire their status with respect to trade with your target country.

Free Trade Agreement between the United States and Australia, however, Australians have recently agreed not to impose local-content requirements on any new media forms that emerge in the future.[46] Canada's local-content requirements are generally justified as necessary for cultural preservation. The National Association of Broadcasters of Africa requires 30 percent of the programming to be local and would like to see it increased to 50 percent for radio stations.[47] The Pakistani government supports local industry by providing price preferences of up to 25 percent for domestic suppliers, especially in engineering-goods contracts. The government also allocates 10 percent of the annual purchasing budget of public-sector agencies to domestic purchases. The local-content requirement in Pakistan, called the Indigenization/Deletion Program goes against the WTO Agreement on Trade-Related Investment measures and is slated for elimination by the WTO.[48]

From 1963 to 1998, the Volvo assembly plant[49] in Dartmouth, Nova Scotia, implemented an innovative way to get around NAFTA's trade barriers. The plant "manufactured" Volvos, employing what is known as a Completely Knocked Down (CKD) process. These are basically kits or packs shipped from Sweden for assembly within NAFTA's borders. Some refer to them as "screwdriver" plants. By adopting this strategy of maintaining a certain ratio of total sales to Canadian production, Volvo could import one car duty-free for every car it assembled in Canada. Unfortunately for Dartmouth, Volvo argued, without success, that it met the local-content requirement. Volvo moved the assembly of cars to Mexico in 1999. The General Agreement on Tariffs and Trade (GATT) started phasing out tariffs in 1994, and as the tariff rate has declined so has the advantage of assembling in Canada. Similarly, the U.S. has established vehicle-part manufacturing plants in India. India maintains regulations that require auto manufacturers in India to sign memoranda of understanding (MOU) imposing local-content requirements. At least 10 percent local parts must be used in the manufacturing process.[50] McDonnell Douglas Corporation (MDC) has had full-fledged co-production operations in China since 1986, when it launched the MD-82 assembly operation that used 15 to 20 percent local airframe content. However, the Trunkliner deal MDC signed with China Aero Technology Import-Export (CATIE) in 1992 called for 65 percent local content initially, increasing to 80 percent by 2001.[51]

The Boeing Company has been successful in the Chinese market in part because the company agreed to transfer technology. Boeing's strategy has allowed Chinese firms a greater role in producing fuselage assemblies and parts in exchange for a continued share of its market. Boeing has promised to establish a headquarters in Beijing, build a spare parts service centre, ship two flight simulators to the Civil Aviation Administration and provide training for Chengdu Aircraft Maintenance & Engineering Company. Many companies have found that technology transfer is often the price of admission to China's vast markets. Having recognized that most of the world's major multinational firms would like to operate in China, the government in Beijing is able to demand access to up-to-date technologies with a high degree of success. Motorola, for example, has agreed to build a US$720 million silicon-wafer fabrication plant in northeastern China and train the local workforce for all the labour involved with the plant. "The decision was not entirely altruistic on Motorola's part. Wu Jichuan, Minister of Posts and Telecommunications said recently, 'Motorola has earned quite a lot of money in the mobile telephone market in China. It's high time for them to transfer some technology'. Paul M.F. Cheng, chairman of Inchcape Pacific Ltd., also addressed this issue with regard to other foreign firms, 'It's been said that while Chinese consumers may love Coke, Pepsi and Kentucky Fried Chicken— which is why the companies want to be there—that's not how they got there'. They got the business because the authorities they were dealing with wanted Coke's and Pepsi's water analysis purification technology and KFC's technology for food preparation and preservation."[52]

Once again, who wins and who loses? Similar to import quotas, local-content requirements protect local firms by restricting foreign competition. So domestic producers win, and the restriction on the supply of imported materials increases the costs to consumers.

Administrative Policy

Administrative trade policies are bureaucratic rules and regulations that are specifically designed to impede free trade.

There are also informal instruments available to government to restrict trade. Governments can implement **administrative trade policies**—bureaucratic rules and regulations that are specifically designed to impede free trade. While governments will openly proclaim that the nation is open for business, from time to time they will put administrative policies in place to make it difficult for other countries to enter their market. Many countries use customs and inspection processes to interfere with imports. For example, Japan had a practice of inspecting all tulip bulbs by slicing them open (and thus ruining them);[53] France used to require that all imported VCRs be processed through a remote, understaffed office, resulting in costly delays. For cosmetics imports,[54] Japan had a list of ingredients that were not allowed. Unfortunately, the list was not made public, so foreign cosmetics companies had to guess which ingredients were allowed when they submitted a product for approval. Middle East and North African (MENA) regional trade has been greatly hampered on both the import and export sides. Their customs clearance, certification of conformity with local standards, and trans-shipment regulations add almost 11 percent to the cost of trade in these regions, partly in the form of official fees and partly in the form of bribes.[55] In Central Asia, there have been excessive regulatory and licensing requirements, inspections by various enforcement agencies, and complex and arbitrary taxation. For example, an investor from Issyk Kul, located in northwestern Kyrgyzstan, wanted to start a water bottling plant. She was required to open a bank account; register with the local government and tax inspectorate; verify paperwork with the regulating government; obtain a "code of enterprise" from the statistics committee; obtain a certificate of registration based on this code; notarize all documents; and present a detailed business plan providing her financial forecast. The woman was to do all of this within a 30-day period. Needless to say, she was unable to establish the bottling plant.[56]

Video 6.1

In Malaysia there is no import duty on chicken parts but the imports are regulated through licensing and sanitary controls.[57] The Czech Republic requires selected imported goods including oil, natural gas, pyrotechnical products, sporting guns, and ammunition to go through a licensing process.[58] In Canada, we have many administrative bodies creating similar policies. Under the authority of Canadian Wheat Board Act, the Canadian Wheat Board[59] (CWB) is the sole exporter of prairie-grown wheat and barley, marketing Western grain to some 70 countries around the world, including the sale of wheat and barley for human consumption within Canada. The CWB's regulations govern permit books, producers' certificates, and licences; the designation, transportation, and pooling points of wheat and barley; as well as delivery contracts and payments.

On occasion the issue is not black and white. A number of countries have introduced laws that have the double effect of protecting the environment and restricting imports. A number of these rules have been challenged under the WTO's dispute settlement process. Typically, the WTO has ruled against such laws. See Just Doing the Right Thing: Tuna Dispute—Protecting Environment or Restricting Imports? on page 180.

Anti-dumping Policy

Dumping is defined as the selling of goods in a host market below the cost of production. This definition has been expanded by those affected who argue that dumping also takes place when goods are sold in the host market below the fair market value.

The final instrument we will examine is anti-dumping policies. **Dumping** is defined as selling goods in a host market below the cost of production. This definition has been expanded and argued by those impacted that say dumping can take place if goods are sold in the host market below the fair market value. In the lumber case, this was the claim made by U.S. lumber producers. They argued that Canadian lumber producers were selling lumber at lower than the world fair-market price. Firms dump their products in other nations' markets for a number of reasons: they may simply want to reduce surplus inventory outside their home market in order to recover some monies; or dumping may be part of a predatory strategy to make the product available much cheaper in the host country until the local producers are forced out of business, at which time the predator firm will increase its prices (indeed, sometimes the final price will exceed the original fair market price as the predator firm is now in a monopoly position). Anti-dumping policies generally also include bringing forward a dumping challenge if there is any material harm to the domestic industry.

On December 17, 2004, Australia announced that it was beginning an anti-dumping investigation against South Korea for its exports of paper products into Australia. Australian paper product manufacturers complained that Koreans were reducing prices on these paper exports, unfairly cutting into the Australian markets, negatively affecting profits. They claimed that the South Korean manufacturers were breaking world trade laws by offering their products at much cheaper rates than Australian manufacturers. The Korea Trade Investment Promotion Agency (KOTRA) was expected to decide the case in 2005.[60]

In 2000, the EU imposed a 34.8 percent anti-dumping duty on the export of malleable fittings from Brazil. Brazil opposed the EU's claims and after consultations were unsuccessful, Brazil asked a WTO panel to rule. In March 2003, the WTO ruled in favour of the EU and accepted only two of Brazil's 40 arguments. The WTO also determined that there was injury to the industry caused by Brazil's low export pricing. An interesting point that Brazil tried to argue was that the EU did not honour the fact that Brazil was an exporter from a developing country. (The WTO regularly provides special treatment to exports from developing countries). Nevertheless, the WTO ruled that this was not so and that the EU "appropriately explored constructive remedies."[61]

In the fibre optics industry, in July 2003, Chinese producers lodged a complaint against the U.S. fibre maker Corning, Inc., accusing it of selling fibre at extremely low prices.[62] In January 2005, while punitive tariffs ranging from 7 to 46 percent were initiated against other fibre optics makers, Corning was found to be dumping fibres at a margin of only 1.51 percent, and was exempted from the punitive tariffs. Chinese rubber producers initiated an anti-dumping complaint with regard to styrene butadiene rubber, used to make rubber products such as car tires.[63] Eighteen months later, in September 2003, China initiated anti-dumping duties of up to 38 percent against the Russian, South Korean, and Japanese styrene butadiene rubber producers.

So who wins and who loses this time? Once again, consumers lose; they are unable to purchase the cheaper foreign products. The inefficient, domestic firms win. They are protected and do not have to seek efficiencies in order to become competitive in the global marketplace. The governments that impose anti-dumping policies win; they get the money, just as we saw in the lumber dispute where the U.S. Government held back over $5 billion from Canada's lumber exporters.

Political and Economic Arguments to Support Government Intervention in Free Trade

Imagine for a moment that you are the prime minister of Canada and have just announced a loan guarantee for Bombardier. A news reporter approaches you and, being well read and familiar with trade theories, asks how you, as prime minister, can justify interfering with free trade. How would you reply? Generally, political leaders respond using one or some combination of the following generic political and economic arguments to support their decision. Most of these will be well known to you, as they appear regularly in local media in response to similar questions posed to our government officials. The range of political justifications will include protecting industries that are necessary for national security, protecting jobs, retaliating in response to some real or perceived unfair trade practice or unfair advantage by a foreign competitor, supporting the political foreign goals of the country, and providing protection and encouraging the enhancement of human rights in other exporting countries.

In the computer industry, **offshoring** involves giving jobs to foreigners in developing countries instead of keeping those jobs at home. The United States has documented that 830,000 service jobs will have shifted to low-cost economies by 2005.[64] "Widely cited figures predict that by 2015, roughly 3.3 million U.S. business-processing jobs will have

Offshoring involves giving jobs to foreigners in developing countries instead of keeping those jobs at home.

JUST DOING THE RIGHT THING

Tuna Dispute— Protecting Environment or Restricting Imports?

In recent years, the U.S. had a dispute with Mexico and other Pacific Latin American countries concerning trade in tuna. At issue are the yellow-fin tuna whose territory in the Pacific Ocean ranges from about Los Angeles down to Santiago, Chile. The territory extends from the continental coast to about 500 miles from the coast. For reasons that baffle scientists, yellow-fin tuna like to swim below schools of dolphins. This habit is very convenient for fishermen, since dolphins swim at the surface and therefore signal that there are tuna below. So fishermen surround areas with dolphins with nets up to a mile wide, to capture the tuna. Historically, many dolphins have been killed in this process—several hundred thousand per year in the 1970s.

Since then, new techniques have been developed to allow dolphins to escape. In addition, the U.S. government sought to protect dolphins by imposing a dolphin-kill quota on American fishermen. . . . (That is, American fishermen had to ensure that dolphin casualties did not exceed 8 percent of the number of captured tuna.) In addition, each boat had to have an independent observer to ensure that this quota was kept. Some of the American sellers of tuna (e.g., StarKist) then adopted a policy of accepting tuna only from boats that did not use "dolphin sets"—the method most likely to result in dolphin casualties.

However, these rules applied only to American fishermen. Dolphin populations were still threatened by Latin American fishermen, and fish from those countries could enter the U.S. at a much lower cost. So the U.S. banned tuna

Latin American countries agreed to impose quotas on their fishermen and to properly count the number of dolphin kills when fishing for tuna and other types of fish.

imports from the other countries that harvest yellow-fin tuna. The Latin American countries took the matter to the WTO, arguing that the United States cannot discriminate against tuna from those countries, because the product is identical to those captured by American fishermen.

The WTO ruled in favour of the Latin American countries. (This ruling is one example of why many environmental groups oppose freer trade and the WTO.) While the WTO rules do allow governments to restrict trade for justifiable environmental reasons, the WTO panel concluded that the U.S. measures were not justifiable. The panel found that the United States did not adequately explore other means of achieving its environmental objectives. For example, the United States could have attempted to negotiate an environmental treaty that commits these governments to keep dolphin casualties down to some level. In addition, the WTO panel rejected the U.S. argument that it had always been prepared to lift its ban on Mexican tuna if Mexico's dolphin kill was reduced to the actual levels of U.S. casualties. The WTO

panel considered this stipulation to be unreasonable, since it did not allow Mexico to know whether trade was open until after the U.S. actual casualties for a year were known.

As a result of the WTO's decision, the United States and the Latin American countries had to find a way to come to an agreement, with the proviso that what the United States had been doing was not allowed. The agreed-upon result was that the Latin American countries agreed to impose quotas on their fishermen, and to require that each boat had an international observer on board to report dolphin kills. However, some people worry that the quotas are not really kept. The observers are quite vulnerable to harm when they are out at sea, so some captains intimidate the observers into underreporting dolphin kills.

Source: Don Wagner, *Tuna Dispute* (University of British Columbia, 2002). 1996–98 by PACIFIC (Werner Antweiler).

moved abroad; as of July 2003, around 400,000 jobs already had. Other research suggests that the number of U.S. service jobs lost to offshoring will accelerate at a rate of 30 to 40 percent annually during the next five years.[65] It is a major political issue in the United States, and government leaders are calling for political intervention to stop the perceived hemorrhage.

U.S. politicians resort to political reasons to justify trade barriers to protect the steel industry and constrict what they claimed to be illegal and unfair imports of steel. They contend employment in this sector has dropped 60 percent since 1980.[66] Dissident economists say that although wealth is generated, it has gone to only a few Americans, while there have been tremendous numbers of jobs lost.[67] Outsourcing of U.S. jobs has become a major problem according to U.S. politicians. The U.S. candy cane manufacturers report that 90 percent of the world's candy canes are consumed in the U.S. yet manufacturers have sent production offshore for the past five years. Senator Joe Lieberman claims that America is "hemorrhaging manufacturing jobs." He wants a crackdown on piracy of intellectual property, elimination of a $2 billion loophole for offshore corporations, and the number of overseas U.S. trade law enforcers doubled. Lieberman claims that 3.1 million jobs have been lost during George W. Bush's term, 80 percent of which have been in the manufacturing sectors.[68]

For several years, trade between Israel and Egypt has been stalled because of differences in political ideologies. In particular, Egypt has not agreed with Israel's approach to the peace process with Palestine. In December 2004, the two countries entered into a trade agreement with the United States whereby all Egyptian goods made in partnership with Israeli firms had free access to American markets. This protocol established "qualified industrial zones" in Egypt, meaning that products produced in these zones have duty-free access to the United States, as long as 35 percent of their components are made within the Israeli–Egyptian partnership.[69] The qualified industrial zones that were established in Egypt will not only open up the U.S. market to the Egyptians, but also protect jobs in Egypt's textile industry. Because the Multi-Fibre Agreement of 2004 eliminated import quotas, countries like Egypt are unable to compete with China's production costs. Fearing they would be squeezed out of the market and sustain massive job losses, they signed the agreement with the United States and now cooperate with Israel. Hence Egypt is able to export to the United States duty free and save jobs.[70]

From time to time, nations will claim that it is necessary, for *national security* reasons, to intervene and protect certain domestic industries. Japan, the United States, the European Union, and Canada have all identified defence-related industries as needing protection. For the purpose of national security and to further its foreign policy, the United States has placed trade sanctions on a number of countries. For example, the U.S. rice industry has been hit hard by trade restrictions. Since 1962, the United States hasn't exported rice to Cuba because of trade sanctions and in 1990, Iraq, which was the largest importer of U.S. rice, placed sanctions on it.[71] Japan included national defence among the reasons to justify constricting the import of rice. "In a nation where rice once served as a currency, cultural and social feeling has long been used by Japan to protect its politically connected rice farmers from foreign invaders. Tariffs as high as 490 percent have discouraged exporters such as the United States and Australia from selling beyond the current tariff-free 770,000 tonnes a year. This has enabled Japan's inefficient rice industry to . . . continue charging consumers six times the average world price for their rice. It's not all about culture and tradition, however. Domestic political considerations also loom large as Japan comes under growing pressure to lower agricultural barriers. . . . Japan doles out seven times the cost of production in government support, with ¥3–4 billion [$CDN 30 million–40 million] in direct subsidies, according to Japan's Rice Data Bank."[72]

The fluidity of goods across the American and Canadian borders is a building block to both countries' economic well-being. However, terrorists could very easily exploit this. So with some justification, the United States and other countries use national security to constrict free trade. A typical shipping container is passed through 12 to 15 different locations and comes into contact with at least 25 different parties, generating 30 to 40 documents, and using 2 to 3 different transportation methods. A low-yield nuclear bomb at Los Angeles Port could kill as many as 500,000 to 1 million people, causing initial monetary losses of $100 million to $200 billion and a further indirect $1.2 trillion of incurred costs.[73] It is by far the largest port for Asian imports in America. The threat is real. Many will remember the strong opposition from the U.S. Congress, and the pressure exerted against a Dubai-owned company to forego its plans to take over operations at U.S. ports.[74]

Another political argument in support of government intervention is that it is *necessary to protect jobs and industries*. Most developed countries including Canada use this argument frequently. Recall it was the protection of jobs that also motivated Egypt to enter into a partnership with Israel and the United States in order to mitigate the damage of the Chinese multi-fibre threat. Again in 2002, the U.S. imposed the Farm Security and Rural Investment Act that was said to give $180 billion to protect U.S. farm industry jobs over the next 10 years. Critics argue that such subsidization will result in further U.S. production and lead to a worldwide drop in the prices of agricultural goods.[75]

With some regularity, *countries retaliate* against what they perceive as unfair trade practices by other governments. There have been a number of political leaders and media in Canada who have argued that Canada should retaliate against the U.S. trade policy that prevents Canadian beef and lumber from entering the American market. (In order to encourage the Americans to play by the rules of the game, these pundits suggest that Canada "turn off the tap" for water, oil, and natural gas and appoint a royal commission to study the circumstances surrounding the issues relating to export of these commodities. It would probably take five years for the Commission to reach a finding.) Genetically altered food has provided grounds for preventing free trade in beef and other food goods. Although the evidence is clear that genetically altered food is not a health risk, protecting consumers continues to be used as one political argument for preventing free trade in these foodstuffs (see below). In 1989, the European Union banned the import of beef treated with growth hormones because of what it felt were serious health concerns associated with this practice. The United States and Canada say that the use of growth hormones in cattle is safe and support their position with evidence from the World Health Organization, Health Canada, and the Food and Drug Administration (FDA). After the United States imposed the WTO retaliation tariff on European imports awarded as a result of this issue, the French retaliated against the Americans with a 100 percent tax on Coca-Cola.[76] However, while retaliation is a viable, sanctioned, trade practice, it is not always an option for smaller, poorer countries. An example of this is a banana dispute in which Ecuador won a case against the EU. The sanction gave Ecuador the authority to impose retaliatory sanctions to the value of US$201 million on European imports. However, Ecuador is reliant on EU goods; consequently, making EU goods more expensive for its citizens would do serious harm to the economy while not economically affecting the EU. Therefore, it was not workable for this small country to place the sanctioned retaliation measures on EU goods.[77] The United States has effectively used retaliation against Cuba. Canada's approach has been different. Through trade, we have attempted to influence the actions of the Cuban government.

Taking protectionist measures, U.S. politicians moved to stop burgeoning, low-cost Vietnamese catfish imports that were taking market share from catfish farmers in Mississippi, Alabama, Louisiana, and other Southern U.S. states. Southern politicians wrote a tiny paragraph into a Gargantuan Agricultural Appropriations Bill to say that these whiskered fish from Vietnam cannot be imported under the name "catfish." President Bush later signed the bill on the grounds Vietnam was exploiting cheap labour.[78] Undertaking a retaliatory measure in *support of the country's foreign political goals is risky*.

Video 6.2

Another political argument for restricting free trade is to *protect consumers*. Consider the growth hormones in cattle case above and the international trade in prescription drugs. A human rights organization, Doctors Without Borders, wants poor people in developing countries to have access to the medicines they so desperately need. Pharmaceutical companies, backed by the U.S. government, want to maintain their patent monopolies. However, these patents raise the price of drugs by several hundred percent.[79] It is a difficult question with convincing arguments on both sites. We looked at the issue of intellectual property in Chapter 3, on pages 88–89.

Finally, there is the political argument of *human rights*. The EU has stated that progress on human rights, terrorism, and nuclear production must be made before negotiations for a trade and co-operation agreement between the EU and Iran can begin. Human rights groups support the EU in its position.[80]

So What Is the Correct View of Free Trade?

It is clear on an academic level that strong arguments by classical trade theorists, such as Adam Smith, David Ricardo, and others, support unrestricted free trade. On the other hand, are we to adopt the pragmatic political and economic arguments that prevail when the free trade issues to be decided are close to home? Many argue that free trade enhances liberty, democracy, and the opportunity to displace anticompetitive policies that increase global poverty. Nevertheless, each day 29,000 children die of hunger, over 30,000 children die of preventable diseases, 2.8 billion people live on less than $2 a day, and worse still, 1.2 billion live on less than $1 per day.[81]

Jadish Bhagwati states in his book, *In Defence of Globalization*, that in order to examine the merits of free trade objectively, we must not accept the fallacy that "if one is for free trade, one must be for free trade direct investment, for free trade capital flows, for free emigration, for free love [and] for free everything else."[82] Free trade is necessary but not sufficient. Amartya Sen, Nobel laureate observed, "[Adam] Smith's intellectual arguments were partly aimed at countering the power and effectiveness of advocacy and the entrenched interests."[83] At the core of the debate is the question, Are the interests of the many to be preferred over the entrenched interests of the few? If you accept this as the preferred view, then it follows that nations require a system to protect private property; establish a rule of law that is transparent, open, and equitable, with access to a fair and effective judicial system; have the infrastructure in place to support a healthy and educated population; and to be governed by a transparent and responsible-to-the-citizens government; and practise free trade.

Does free trade in its purest sense actually exist? No, in 2003, the average Most-Favoured-Nation tariff rate in low-income countries was nearly 14.5 percent; it was close to 4 percent in industrial nations, and all countries have in place countless non-tariff barriers including quotas and administrative impediments such as slow border crossings to gain economic advantage for domestic firms.[84] Most free trade economists today, including Paul Krugman, support a pragmatic view where decisions are made on a case-by-case basis determined based on a cost-benefit analysis. However, adopting Krugman's view has inherent dangers. First, the pragmatic view evokes all that is bad in mercantilism and may well serve as a catalyst for retaliation by those foreign nations affected by the decision to intervene in free trade. The danger of retaliation, of course, leads to counter-retaliation that can escalate into a full-blown trade war. It may be utopian, but it would seem that the solution is not retaliation but rather to avail the services of the international adjudicating bodies that we discussed in Chapter 5, on pages 149–150. The major dispute resolution forums are found within the WTO and, in Canada's case, within NAFTA when issues involve Mexico or the United States. The second concern with adopting a pragmatic approach to free trade is that on occasion, whether real or perceived, governments intervene as a direct result of lobbyists and advocates. One does not have to look far within any nation to find evidence to support this concern. Krugman warns of the danger of special-interest groups shaping domestic politics for their own ends at a cost to the nation as a whole. We can look at the lumber dispute for validity of Krugman's observation. He concludes that in the United States, "to ask the Commerce Department to ignore special interest politics while formulating detailed policy for many industries is not realistic; to establish a blanket policy of free trade, with exceptions granted only under extreme pressure, may not be the optimal policy according to the theory but may be the best policy that the country is likely to get."[85] I believe that the same observation is equally true in Canada.

Management Implications

- What relevance do trade theories have for international business managers? Understanding theories behind trade may help you to identify some of the strengths and weaknesses of potentially competitive foreign firms. By identifying the factors or conditions that support a nation's dominance in one or more market sectors, these trade theories explain why specific countries export selected goods. Why does Canada have a strong export market in wheat, timber, oil, and natural gas? Because the factor conditions or comparative advantages in Canada are due to the abundance of these natural resources. Michael Porter's theory of national competitive advantage identifies additional considerations as to why nations are strong in certain market sectors. Why are Japan and Germany world leaders in automobile manufacturing? Why is India becoming powerful in the Internet, communications-related services, and software development sectors? By observing the conditions in the four categories identified in Porter's diamond, you may determine some of the risks and opportunities for entering a market and competing against the domestic rivals. Analysis of the factors driving the success of nations' domestic industries may also help you understand why they are also successful in these sectors internationally.

- Do we need to apply international trade theories to compete in global markets? No. While analysis of the macroeconomic conditions can be enlightening for firms, it is more important for governments to apply the trade theories to help identify which industry sectors need support, and the best policies or initiatives should be introduced to assist the domestic firms when entering foreign markets, and when competing against incoming foreign firms. You can influence government!

- Are policies and instruments of trade important considerations for international business managers today? Yes. Firms entering foreign markets must consider a host of forces and conditions when evaluating the risks and potentials with regards to export or foreign direct investment in offshore markets. Administrative delays due to bureaucracy can hamper delivery schedules and result in very dissatisfied customers. Tariffs can push up costs, making it difficult if not impossible to compete on price with domestically produced goods in a target overseas market. Similarly, competing against subsidized industries can create unequal playing fields.

- While independent businesses, especially SMEs, have little control over the existence or enforcement of the various instruments of trade, it is imperative that you are aware of these policies and restrictions, as they can make or break your foreign enterprise.

CHAPTER SUMMARY

- Theoretically, companies from different nations have greater or fewer advantages in trading different goods or services, depending on the cost and efficiencies they can achieve in production. There are several trade theories, beginning in the 1500s with mercantilism, which advocates a strong export market with restrictions on imports. It is still a popular approach to international trade in some countries such as Japan. Adam Smith introduced the theory of absolute advantage in the 1700s, which advocates free trade with nations specializing only in the export of those goods or services that they produce more efficiently than any other goods. Later, in the early 1800s, economist David Ricardo, with his theory of comparative advantage, suggested that if a nation is more efficient in production of certain goods in comparison to other nations, it should capitalize on all those export opportunities, irrespective of whether those goods can be produced with absolute advantage. In the 20th century, the Heckscher-Ohlin theory of factor endowments considered national advantages based on the supply (and cost) of labour, land, and capital.

- In the 1960s, international product trade life cycle theory (IPLC) posited that products follow a life cycle from new to maturing to standardized products, which begin as exports and are later manufactured in countries with lower-cost labour forces, at which time competitors enter the market and take over the export country's production. New trade theory provides explanations for international trade patterns, observing advantages through specialization and economies of scale. It also observes strategic and economic advantages for the firms that are first to enter new markets (first movers). The most recent international trade theory is Porter's theory of competitive advantage of nations, which posits that the ability of a nation's firms to compete internationally depends on domestic conditions. Porter identifies four determinants that affect a nation's firms competitive advantage. These are factor endowments, such as natural resources; demanding domestic markets; a strong presence of related and supporting industries; and effective firm strategy, structure, and domestic competition. According to Porter's theory, it is these factors that drive innovation and upgrades in domestic industries, which in turn influence the competitiveness of firms internationally.

- Free trade refers to the removal of barriers to trade among nations. Free trade may include bilateral agreements, such as between Canada and Chile, or multilateral agreements between more nations, such as NAFTA between Canada, Mexico, and the United States. Nations typically agree on removal or reduction of tariffs, quotas, and bureaucratic barriers that hamper the flow of goods between free trade partners, and other trade restrictions among the partners to the agreement.

- Trade policies and instruments of trade policy are imposed by governments and political leaders to intervene in international trade. Tariffs, which are taxes levied on imports or exports, are still common today. Tariffs include special tariffs, ad valorem tariffs, and compound tariffs. Most tariffs result in the importing country paying more for the product, which may discourage the export market. Subsidies are direct and indirect payments by governments to domestic firms. Import quotas and voluntary export restraints (VERs) impose limitations on the volume of goods being traded. Administration trade policies are bureaucratic rules and regulations that are specifically designed to impede free trade. Tariffs, subsidies, quotas, VERs, and administrative policies help protect domestic industries from international competition. Local-content requirements specify that a foreign firm operating in a host country must locally produce a percentage of the materials or of the finished-goods' value. This may also apply to media, such as magazines, television, and radio broadcasting content. The intent of a local-content policy is to support domestic businesses or, with regard to media, protect a nation's culture.

- There are a number of political and economic arguments to support government intervention in free trade.

REVIEW QUESTIONS

1. Explain mercantilism.
2. Briefly outline Smith's theory of absolute advantage.
3. Briefly outline Ricardo's theory of comparative advantage.
4. Describe briefly the Heckscher-Ohlin theory of factor endowments.
5. Describe briefly Raymond Vernon's international product life cycle theory.
6. Using Michael Porter's diamond model, explain his competitive advantage of nations theory.
7. Briefly describe the six main trade policy options available to governments to intervene in free trade.
8. Outline the political and economic arguments used to support governments' intervention in free trade.

REFLECTIVE THINKING QUESTIONS

1. Having completed this chapter, reread the quotations on the first page, critically reflect on the validity of the authors' statements, and provide your opinion as to the validity of each. Evidence-based answers are preferred to rhetorical answers. Specifically note the economic trade theories of Lincoln and Bush.
2. One driver of mercantilism was that the colony would import products from the "mother" country and export essential raw materials to support the growing industrialized firms of the European "mother" nation. Can you make a case to support the notion that Canada continues to perpetuate this aspect of mercantilism given its significant export of commodities with little or no added value?

3. The media reports, "China's Geely Automobile Holdings Ltd. said it plans to step-up car exports in 2004 after testing overseas markets in late 2003, with an eye to selling 30 percent of its output abroad by 2010."[86] Geely also manufactures the Haoqing minicar, the cheapest on the Chinese market at just US$3,867. What proactive steps do you think Canada's auto industry should take? Would the Ontario government be throwing good money after bad if it adopted one or more of the intervention instruments available?
4. Given the threat of Chinese imports, Canada intends to retain tariffs on fibres, yarns, and fabrics where domestic suppliers can demonstrate production in Canada.[87] Who wins and who loses when the Canadian

government retains tariffs on fibre, yarns, and fabrics? Substantiate your answer.

5. Can you think of examples of developing countries that grow their industries at the expense of developed countries? How does it affect SMEs? How does it influence the Canadian economy? How does it affect the global economy?

6. Neo-mercantilists are found in almost every developed country. Identify and discuss how the barriers imposed by these neo-mercantilists are affecting domestic business.

7. As the manager of a Canadian SME, you know that countries' governments and even private industries have the ability to influence the competitiveness of national firms. Identify a Canadian international SME and outline how it has been able to support this proposition.

8. According to the Heckscher-Ohlin theory, countries will trade in the goods and services in which they have abundance or an oversupply, providing an international

competitive advantage for that industry or nation. Leontief dismissed this theory in the early 1950s when he conducted a study showing that exports required more labour-intensive production than imports. What is your opinion of the Leontief paradox? Can you think of an example of Canada gaining competitive advantage by trading goods or services of which the country has abundance? Can you identify an industry that would be in this position compared to other industries?

9. Is Krugman too cynical when he concludes that in the United States, "to ask the Commerce Department to ignore special interest politics while formulating detailed policy for many industries is not realistic; to establish a blanket policy of free trade, with exceptions granted only under extreme pressure, may not be the optimal policy according to the theory but may be the best policy that the country is likely to get"?

GLOBAL E-RESEARCH

Visit www.power.nelson.com for research suggestions, questions, and a number of background discussion papers on this topic.

MINI CASE

BC Ferries' Board Approves $325 Million in Contracts

Following the completion of an extensive competitive bidding process, BC Ferries has selected Flensburger Schiffbau-Gesellschaft (FSG) of Germany to build three Super C-class vessels. The contracts, with a total value of (€206.4 million or approximately $325 million Canadian (based on [then] current exchange rates), were approved today by BC Ferries' Board of Directors. The Board also approved a total project budget of $542 million, which includes Canadian taxes, financing, and project management costs that would have been incurred regardless of where the vessels were built. It also includes a contingency for federal duty. On behalf of the Board of Directors, Board Chair Elizabeth J. Harrison issued the following statement, "We are extremely pleased with the excellent terms negotiated with Flensburger Shipyard. We believe the terms and conditions that BC Ferries achieved in these new contracts are second to none in the industry. In selecting the best overall bid, we have put our customers first and significantly enhanced our ability to keep fares as low as possible in the years ahead'. . . . 'These are design-build, fixed-price contracts that provide BC Ferries with substantial guarantees related to delivery dates, performance criteria, cost certainty and quality construction,' said David Hahn, BC Ferries' President and CEO. 'We have also been able to negotiate extremely favourable payment terms with 80 per cent of the contract price due only

upon completion of each vessel'. . . . 'Flensburger scored first overall on the criteria we and our independent consultants defined at the outset of this process,' said EVP, Business Development, Mike Corrigan, who was the company's lead negotiator. 'With respect to price, this contract is approximately 40 per cent or about $130 million less than the Canadian price we received during the early phase of the bidding process. In addition, the excellent Flensburger payment schedule saves BC Ferries another $30 million in interest payments. Even assuming the additional $81 million in duty, there is still an $80 million advantage with the chosen contractor,' he said. . . . FSG is one of the world's leading shipyards with state-of-the-art design and production facilities. FSG has extensive experience building large, complex vessels, having built 724 ships in total, including 17 passenger/vehicle ferries since 1999. Flensburger has not delivered a vessel late in over twenty years. FSG was short listed along with two other shipyards following a competitive bidding process. Three Canadian shipyards and 11 international shipyards were invited to bid in the process. Criteria for selection included the design and construction plan, recent experience building large ferries, customer satisfaction (references from other customers), delivery schedule, price and payment terms, financial stability and the ability to provide guarantees.

Source: British Columbia Ferry Services, "BC Ferries Board Approves $325 Million in Contracts," (media release, September 17, 2004), retrieved September 13, 2006, from www.bcferries.com/news/files/04-071-super_c_vessels.pdf.

MINI CASE QUESTION

1. Many see free trade as selling out Canadian jobs. Proponents of this view adopt the logic succinctly stated by Abraham Lincoln in his case against free trade: "I know this much. When we buy manufactured goods abroad, we get the goods and the foreigner gets the money. When we buy the manufactured goods at home, we get both the goods and the money." As a member of the BC Ferries' Board, announcing the successful bidder, Flensburger Schiffbau-Gesellschaft (FSG) how would you respond to this anti-free trade argument?

ENDNOTES

1. R. Badrinath, "Building Business Competitiveness" (paper presented at the International Trade Forum, Geneva, 2004).

2. Jagdish Bhagwati, *Coping with Anti-Globalization: In Defense of Globalization* (New York: Oxford University Press, 2004). Peter Coy, "Book Review," *BusinessWeek,* March 22, 2004.

3. Stephen S. Roach, "Why We Ought to Be Thanking the Chinese," *Fortune,* March 22, 2004.

4. *George W. Bush 2000 on the Issues: International Trade* (4President Corporation, 2000), retrieved August 11, 2006, from www.4president.org/issues/bush2000/bush2000trade.htm.

5. Thomas K. McGraw, ed., *Creating Modern Capitalism* (Cambridge, MA: Harvard University Press, 2000).

6. Mark McNeilly, *Sun Tzu and the Art of Business: Six Strategic Principles for Managers* (New York: Oxford University Press, 1996).

7. "Realpolitik," *Wikipedia*, retrieved August 11, 2006, from http://en.wikipedia.org/w/index.php?title=Realpolitik&oldid=44574128.

8. Ibid.

9. Michael D. Porter, "The Competitive Advantage of Nations," *Harvard Business Review* March–April (1990).

10. If you have an interest in learning more about the double diamond and the arguments supporting this revisionist model, review the article by Rugman and D'Cruz, "The 'Double Diamond' Model of International Competitiveness: The Canadian Experience," *Management International Review*, 33(2), 1993.

11. H.W. Spiegel, *The Growth of Economic Thought* (Durham, NC: Duke University Press, 1991).

12. This example has been adapted from Charles W.L. Hill, *International Business* (New York: McGraw-Hill Irwin, 2005).

13. Clay Risen, "Elimination of Global Textile Quotas Will Accelerate Retail Shake Out," *World Trade* (January 2005).

14. Ibid.

15. *Canada China Business Trends* (Canada China Business Council, August 2004), retrieved August 12, 2006, from www.ccbc.com.

16. Porter, "The Competitive Advantage of Nations."

17. Alison Leung and Ben Blanchard, *China's Geely to Step up Car Exports, Eyes US* (Reuters, June 24, 2004), available from www.planetark.com/dailynewsstory.cfm/newsid/25661/newsDate/24-Jun-2004/story.htm.

18. Roberto Ortiz de Zárate, *Leaders of China (People's Republic of China)* (2003), retrieved August 13, 2006, from www.terra.es/personal2/monolith/china.htm.

19. Tina Rosenberg, "The Free-Trade Fix," *The New York Times*, August 18, 2002.

20. "Chicago Boys," *Wikipedia*, retrieved August 13, 2006, from http://en.wikipedia.org/wiki/Chicago_Boys.

21. The Hon. Mark MP Vaile, *Australian Exporters Taking Advantage of Thailand-Australia Free Trade Agreement (TAFTA)* (Media release, Commonwealth of Australia, February 20, 2006), retrieved August 13, 2006, from www.trademinister.gov.au/releases/2006/mvt010_06.html.

22. CBC News, *Ottawa Unsettled as WHO Strikes Down Auto Pact* (Canadian Broadcasting Corporation, 1999), retrieved August 13, 2006, from www.cbc.ca/stories/1999/10/14/autopact991014.

23. Chris Nammour, "Newshour Extra with Jim Lehrer," in *Online Newshour* (United States: Public Broadcasting System, 2004).

24. Newschannel KATC 3 Acadiana's, "KATC 3 Acadiana's Newschannel: World Now," in *KATC 3 Acadiana's Newschannel: World Now* (United States: Associated Press, 2004).

25. Ralph Goodale, "Inquiry into the Availability of Certain Apparel Fabrics Produced in Canada," (Minister of Public Works and Government Services Canada, April 2006), retrieved August 26, 2006 from www.citt.gc.ca/refer/reports/mn2f001_e.asp.

26. Institute of Chartered Accountants of BC, "Softwood Lumber Dispute: Canada's Chances Better at the Next Stage?" *CA Public Policy Review,* no. 2001–07 (August 2001).

27. "Textile Sector to Struggle after Quota Termination," *Jakarta Post,* (December 28, 2004).

28. American Textile Manufacturers Institute, "Statement of American Textile Manufacturers Institute," (US House Committee on Ways and Means, 2004).

29. Ibid.

30. International Centre for Trade and Sustainable Development, "WTO Disputes Rise Again: Bananas, Patents & Aircraft," (*ICTSD Bridges Weekly Trade News Digest,* February 6, 2001), retrieved August 26, 2006, from www.ictsd.org/html/weekly/story3.06-02-01.htm.

31. WTO, *"European Communities—Export Subsidies on Sugar; Request for Consultations by Thailand"* (2003), retrieved August 13, 2006, from www.wto.org/english/tratop_e/cases_e/ds283_e.htm.

32. BBC, "Europe Plans Sugar Subsidy Cuts," (BBC News, June 24, 2004), retrieved August 26, 2006, from http://news.bbc.co.uk/go/pr/fr/-/2/hi/business/3837007.stm.

33. *Dairy Farmers North and South* (BBC News, September 8, 2003), retrieved August 13, 2006, from http://news.bbc.co.uk/1/hi/business/3198113.stm.

34. Jack Sackton, *Seafood.Com News Greenwire* (December 10, 2003), retrieved 2004, from www.seafood.com/Default.aspx?tabid=36.

[35] *Environmental Working Group* (December 9, 2004), retrieved 2004, from www.ewg.org/farm/findings.php.

[36] *The U.S Dairy Import Licensing Program. FAS Online* (December 12, 2004), retrieved 2004 from www.fas.usda.gov .itp/imports/dairy.html.

[37] FAS Office of Agricultural Affairs in Mexico, *FAS Office of Agricultural Affairs in Mexico. FAS Online* (December 11, 2004), retrieved 2004, from www.fas.usda.gov/info/ agexporter/1998/February%201998/us.html.

[38] Risen, "Elimination of Global Textile Quotas Will Accelerate Retail Shake Out."

[39] Jakarta, "Textile Sector to Struggle after Quota Termination."

[40] "Textiles" (*A&A Economic News Digest,* November 2004), retrieved August 26, 2006, from www.aacb.com/publications/ ed/view.asp?type=economic&newsletterID=96.

[41] Risen, "Elimination of Global Textile Quotas Will Accelerate Retail Shake Out."

[42] Ibid.

[43] Steven Suranovic, *US–Japan Automobile VERs* (August 16, 2003), retrieved August 13, 2006, from http://internationalecon .com/v1.0/ch10/10c071.html.

[44] Standard & Poor's, Market Share for U.S. Autos May Continue Slipping but Staying Power Stronger Than Recent Trends Suggest, Says S&P CreditWeek Special Report (New York, March 9, 2006), retrieved October 27, 2006, from http://www.theautochannel.com/news/2006/03/09/ 0002767.html.

[45] North American Free Trade Agreement (International Trade Canada, 2002).

[46] The Hon. Mark MP Vaile, *Free Trade Agreement with the United States* (February 8, 2004) (Commonwealth of Australia, 2004), retrieved August 13, 2006, from www.trademinister.gov.au/releases/2004/mvt008_04.html.

[47] National Association of Broadcasters of Africa, *Casa Reviews Local Content Requirements* (December 13, 2004), retrieved 2004, from www.nab.org.za.

[48] Don Wagner, *Lecture Notes: Trade Barriers and the WTO* (October 24) (University of British Columbia, October 24, 2000), retrieved August 13, 2006, from http://pacific .commerce.ubc.ca/wagner/lec13.PDF.

[49] "Volvo Assembly Plants," retrieved August 13, 2006, from www.volvoadventures.com/assemblyplants.html.

[50] Office of the United States Trade Representative, *U.S. Wins WTO Case on Indian Auto Restrictions* (December 21, 2001), retrieved 2004, from http://www.ustr.gov/Document_Library/ Press_Releases/2001/December/Section_Index.html.

[51] Ashley Moretz, *Countertrade Opportunities in the People's Republic of China* (2005); available from www.barternews .com/countertrade_republic_of_china.htm.

[52] Ibid.

[53] Christian Tyler, "West Remains Wary of Japanese Markets," *The Financial Times,* April 22, 1985.

[54] *The Survey on Actual Conditions Regarding Access to Japan Cosmetics* (Japan External Trade Organization, June 1997), retrieved August 26, 2006, from www.jetro.go.jp/en/stats/ survey/access/cosmetics.html.

[55] Sereen Juma, *Sector Brief: Trade, Investment and Development in MENA* (The World Bank Group, December 10, 2004), retrieved October 27, 2006, from http://lnweb18.worldbank .org/mna/mena.nsf/Attachments/Trade+Brief-ENG/ $File/TRADE-ENG-2004AM.pdf.

[56] Elaine Kurtenbach, *U.S. Commerce Secretary to Press China over Anti-Dumping Disputes* (Associated Press, June 22, 2004), retrieved August 26, 2006, from www.signonsandiego.com/ news/business/20040622-0605-china-us-trade.html.

[57] Robert B. Zoellick, "National Trade Estimate Report on Foreign Trade Barriers (Nte)," *Foreign Trade Barriers* (The Office of the United States Trade Representative (USTR), 2004).

[58] Fabiana Borges da Fonseca, *Exporting to Brazil? Try High-Value Products* (FindArticles, August 2002), retrieved August 13, 2006, from www.findarticles.com/p/articles/mi_m3723/ is_8_14/ai_93026200.

[59] The Canadian Wheat Board homepage is located at www.cwb.ca/en/index.jsp.

[60] "Australia Starts S. Korean Paper Import Antidumping Probe," *Asia Pulse,* (Seoul, South Korea, December 17, 2004)

[61] European Commission, *Making Globalisation Work for Everyone: The European Union and World Trade* (Office for Official Publications of the European Communities, 2003), retrieved August 13, 2006, from http://ec.europa.eu/trade/ icentre/publications/ww_730en.pdf.

[62] Li Weitao, "China Probes Dumping Accusations," *China Business Weekly* (July 8, 2003), retrieved August 26, 2006, from www.chinadaily.com.cn/en/doc/2003-07/08/content_ 244707.htm.

[63] "China Targets Foreign Raw Materials Dumpers" (*China Daily,* September 10, 2003), retrieved August 13, 2005, from www.chinadaily.com.cn/chinagate/doc/2003-09/ 10/content_263007.htm.

[64] Ed Frauenheim, *Study Supports Controversial Offshore Numbers* (CNET News.com, May 17, 2004), retrieved August 27, 2006, from http://news.zdnet.com/2100-3513_ 22-5213391.html.

[65] Vivek Agrawal and Diana Farrell, "Who Wins in Offshoring?" (*The McKinsey Quarterly,* October 2003) retrieved August 26, 2006, from http://news.com.com/2030-1014-5096283.html.

[66] Aaron Lukas, "Protection without Protectionism: The Challenges of Trade," in *Trade Policy Analysis,* no. 27 (CATO Institute, 2004).

[67] Mark Wiesbrot, *Protectionism Trumps Free Trade at the WTO* (CounterCurrents.org, September 10, 2003), retrieved December 12, 2004 from http://www.countercurrents.org/ glo-weisbrot100903.htm.

[68] Joe Lieberman, "Lieberman Vows to Save Manufacturing Jobs," *USA Today: Politics,* July 21, 2003

[69] BBC News, *Egypt and Israel Seal Trade Deal* (BBC News, December 14, 2004), retrieved August 16, 2006, from http://news.bbc.co.uk/1/hi/business/4095011.stm.

[70] Jeremy Howell, *Egyptian Cotton Makers Fight to Survive* (BBC News, December 7, 2004), retrieved August 16, 2006, from http://news.bbc.co.uk/1/hi/business/4073365.stm.

[71] Foreign Agricultural Service, *A Review of U.S. Trade Restrictions and Grain Exports* (United States Department of Agriculture, November 13, 2003), retrieved August 13, 2006, from www.fas.usda.gov/grain/circular/1997/97-09/feature/ trd_rstr.htm.

[72] "WTO on a Sticky Wicket against Japan's Rice Bowlers" (Reuters, September 12, 2003), retrieved August 27, 2006, from www.theage.com.au/articles/2003/09/11/1063268512176.html.

[73] Eric Marquardt, "Trade Protectionism in Developed Countries Exploits Vulnerable Economies in Developing

Countries" (*Power and Interest News Report*, July 18, 2003), retrieved August 26, 2006, from www.globalpolicy.org/socecon/ffd/2003/0718exploits.htm.

74 Jonathan Weisman and Bradley Graham, *Dubai Firm to Sell U.S. Port Operations* (*Washington Post*, March 10, 2006), retrieved August 16, 2006, from www.washingtonpost .com/wp-dyn/content/article/2006/03/09/ AR2006030901124.html.

75 Daniel W. Drezner, "The Outsourcing Bogeyman," *Foreign Affairs*, (May/June 2004).

76 Paul Rauber, "Raging Hormones: Europeans Protest Genetically Engineered, Hormone-treated Food" (Sierra Magazine, March 2000), retrieved August 16, 2006, available from www.findarticles.com/p/articles/mi_m1525/is_2_85/ai_62828677.

77 Reuters, "Africa Asks for Mass Retaliation in Trade Rows" (Reuters News Services, September 11, 2002), retrieved August 13, 2006, from www.globalpolicy.org/socecon/bwi-wto/2002/0911retaliation.htm.

78 George Hager, "Bush Plays Free Trade Game," US Today: Money (July 2, 2002).

79 "Access to Medicines at Risk across the Globe: What to Watch Out for in Free Trade Agreements with the United States" (MSF Campaign for Access to Essential Medicines, May 2004), retrieved September 13, 2006, from www.doctorswithoutborders.org/publications/reports/2004/ftaa_05-2004.pdf.

80 BBC News, "Iran Rebukes EU on Rights Abuses" (BBC News, June 21, 2004), retrieved August 16, 2006 from http://news.bbc.co.uk/1/hi/world/middle_east/3825337.stm.

81 United Nations Development Program, "The State and Progress of Human Development," in *Human Development Report* (New York: Oxford University Press, 2002).

82 Bhagwati, Coping with Anti-Globalization: In Defense of Globalization.

83 Amartya Sen, *Development as Freedom* (New York: Anchor Books, 1999).

84 World Bank, *Average MFN Applied Tariff Rates by Sector in Recent Years* (World Bank, November 21, 2004), retrieved August 13, 2006, from http://siteresources.worldbank.org/INTRANETTRADE/Resources/tar2000a.xls.

85 P.R. Krugman, " Is Free Trade Passe?" *Journal of Economic Perspectives* (Autumn 1987).

86 Leung and Blanchard, *China's Geely to Step up Car Exports, Eyes U.S.*

87 Goodale, "Inquiry into the Availability of Fabrics Produced in Canada."

Foreign Direct Investment

"The social object of skilled investment should be to defeat the dark forces of time and ignorance which envelope our future."[1]

—John Maynard Keynes (1883–1946), British economist

"States are now being forced to join an international beauty contest to compete for foreign investment."[2]

—Zwelinzima Vavi, General Secretary of Congress of South African Trade Union (COSATU)

". . . The establishment can't admit [that] it is human rights violations that make . . . countries attractive to business—so history has to be fudged, including denial of our support of regimes of terror and the practices that provide favourable climates of investment, and our destabilization of democracies that [don't] meet [the] standard of service to the transnational corporation."[3]

—Edward S. Herman, economist, author, and U.S. media and foreign policy critic

"The inherent vice of capitalism is the unequal sharing of blessings; the inherent vice of socialism is the equal sharing of miseries."[4]

—Winston Churchill (1874–1965), British Prime Minister

"Only after the last tree has been cut down, only after the last river has been poisoned, only after the last fish has been caught, only then will you find that money cannot be eaten."[5]

—Cree Indian Prophecy

LEARNING OUTCOMES

- Evaluate the role of foreign direct investment (FDI) in a nation's economic and security interest.
- Understand the benefits and costs of FDI to the host nation.
- Understand the benefits and costs of FDI to the recipient nation.
- Understand why firms undertake FDI.
- Evaluate the merits of economic and political instruments that can influence the flows of FDI.
- Evaluate the merits of protectionism as a remedy for unwanted FDI.
- Compare the FDI flows to developed and underdeveloped nations and understand the reasons for the wide gap between these two clusters of nations.
- Assess the degree of national economic globalization by reference to FDI.
- Evaluate the emerging shifts in Canada's current FDI economic climate.
- Identify the emerging shifts in global FDI and the likely impact on Canada.

China's a Cautious Oilsands Investor

© Jason Lee/Reuters/Corbis Canada

"China's strategy as it enters the Canadian oilsands business is playing out in a series of small steps rather than the big splash that was once predicted, industry observers said yesterday. Representatives from China's three major oil companies made trips to Calgary last year, prompting speculation deals as large as a takeover of Husky Energy Inc. were in the offing. But China's three recent forays suggest it's behaving more like a safe investor diversifying a portfolio and learning about the business. 'For China, you get security of supply through diversity of supply and in the end, that's really what these [deals] have been all about,' said Robert Ebel, director of the energy program at the Center for Strategic and International Studies in Washington. The latest plunge was when Sinopec Group invested $105-million with privately held, Calgary-based Synenco Energy Inc. in a deal that gives China's second-largest oil producer a 40% share, or about 40,000 barrels a day, worth of production from Synenco's proposed Northern Lights oilsands mine. The deal ensures, for the first time, a share of production. A pact in mid-April between PetroChina Co. Ltd. and pipeline company Enbridge Inc. aims to secure 200,000 barrels a day of future supply from various producers in northeastern Alberta to be moved west to the B.C. Coast. The oil would then be shipped by tanker to China. That same week, CNOOC Ltd. acquired a 17% interest in oilsands start-up MEG Energy Inc. . . . China's daily consumption of oil has grown at a faster rate than any other country over the past two years, rising from an average of 4.97-million barrels in 2002 to a projected 6.9-million barrels this year [2005]. But China still produces about half of what it consumes from its own fields, so its situation is not yet desperate and may be why it can move at a calculated pace into Canada."[6]

In 2004, as China's interest in the oilsands was growing, there were fears that the Chinese government-owned nationals would compete against the U.S. to secure reserves. In Canada many doubt there is any political motivation behind China's entry into the Alberta oilsands; however, there are an increasing number of voices expressing national security concerns. I am of the opinion that this concern is unfounded—it is about securing a reliable supply of energy. Canada is a preferred venue for FDI as it has little political risk and the dollar is stable. Furthermore, it is a good fit as the tar sands are about chemical engineering—an area of Chinese oil industry expertise.

A SUN TZU MOMENT...

Visual Arts Library, London/Alamy

"Win all without fighting."[7]

To win all without fighting, nations must first decide to which other nations they want to expand their sphere of influence. An examination of the conflicts during the 20th century presents excellent illustrations of both strategies for examination. World Wars I and II, and wars in Korea, Vietnam, Iraq, and Afghanistan illustrate the heavy cost of ill-conceived strategies employed by nation(s) attempting to expand their sphere of influence. Another model was the cessation of the Cold War brought about because of President Reagan's strategy to use investment to stop communism from dominating the world. Reagan won without fighting as Sun Tzu counselled. Nations with command economies like the Union of Soviet Socialist Republic were unable to "keep the financial pace" and collapsed as Western liberalized democracy prevailed.

Foreign direct investment is a very effective tool to win all without fighting. Developed countries frequently use FDI to bring recipient nations into alignment with their national policy interests. Consider Canada's economic interdependence with the United States; certainly it influences Canada's national policies. Zbigniew Brzezinski observes, "One must consider as part of the American system the global web of specialized organizations, especially the international 'financial' institutions. The International Monetary Fund (IMF) and the World Bank mandate was initially to represent 'global' interests and their constituency was construed as the world. In reality, however, these institutions are heavily American dominated and their origins traceable to [the] Bretton Woods Conference of 1944."[8]

We examined these global institutions in Chapter 5. Some suggest because they are of little geopolitical and strategic importance, North African nations fair poorly in obtaining their share of global FDI. There are, of course, other reasons that we will review in this text.

A Chinese proverb states, "The greatest conqueror is he who overcomes the enemy without a blow." Keep this proverb in mind as we look at FDI and the part it plays in supporting national interests and the global economy.

Opening Thoughts

The volume and growth of capital FDI flows are important parts in the globalization story. "In 2003, the total size of world international trade flows reached US$7.4 trillion while total world FDI stock reached US$8.2 trillion. Canada's foreign direct investment overseas is an important aspect of Canada's relations with the rest of the world. Canadian foreign direct investment abroad (CFDIA) more than tripled since the late 1980s to reach $399 billion by the end of 2003. By comparison, Canada's total exports of goods and services more than doubled (growing 174 percent) over the same period."[9] Given the growth and size of Canadian FDI and impact on international trade, it is important to understand the nature and patterns of CFDI.

Globalization is driven by improved technology, cheap transportation, deregulation, and other factors that have made McLuhan's global village even smaller. In *The World Is Flat*,[10] Thomas L. Friedman validates this observation in his thesis that the dimensions of trade know no borders. The liberalization of the freer movement of Lenin's factors of production, combined with the ability to communicate and control activities globally, have increasingly permitted more FDI and trade. These global ownership advantages and location economies are driving the exponential growth of FDI.

From the end of Mao Zedong's Long March in 1949 until 1979, China was a command economy behind a bamboo curtain that permitted little FDI and foreign trade. China's isolationist policies and dismal attempts at economic reform resulted in decades of failure. This did not come as a surprise to economists familiar with the new trade theory.

Remarkably, since 1979 and its rapid move toward a socialist market economy, China has become the largest recipient of FDI in the world. In 2003, China replaced the United States as the number one recipient of FDI. Unfortunately as China, India, and other nations increasingly attract FDI (see Figure 7.1), Canada's inward flows of FDI have been dropping because investment capital seeks these new, more advantageous investment locations. Since joining the WTO in November 2001, China has significantly integrated into the global marketplace. China is opening its markets and encouraging FDI outflows as well as inflows. The opening vignette illustrates one of China's FDI initiatives in Canada, undertaken to ensure an oil supply to meet its insatiable thirst for commodities. We must also recognize that India, as a result of the 1995 reforms, will also become a global commodities "Pac-man" that will increasingly compete for global commodities. This increase in demand is good for nations rich in commodities, like Canada, but troubling for those that must acquire these inputs. Open markets will result in disruption and competition in the global marketplace for scarce resources. Competition will be a source of increasing tension as nations concerned for their national security and their economies see their traditional input suppliers actively "courted" in the global marketplace. Many Canadians feel the United States has taken for granted Canada's water, energy, and other commodities as their secure source. While the opening vignette reveals otherwise in a global free market place; NAFTA does put some fetters on Canada's energy sales.

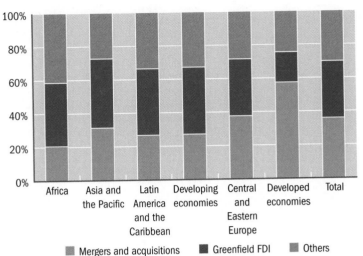

FIGURE 7.1
Preferred Modes of FDI and Internationalization of Business, 2004–2005

SOURCE: United Nations Conference on Trade and Development, *Research Note #3: Prospects for FDI Flows and TNC Strategies, 2004–2007* (United Nations, June 7, 2004). Copyright UNCTAD.

The various **types of FDI** include mergers and joint ventures, wholly owned subsidiaries, acquisitions, and greenfields. In this chapter we will consider these and answer a number of questions: Why would managers undertake these FDI modes of entry into foreign markets that are a greater risk than other modes such as licensing and export? Can a nation have too much FDI? How can a nation attract or discourage FDI? What are the advantages and disadvantages of FDI?

What Is Foreign Direct Investment?

It is important that we differentiate between **FDI** and **foreign portfolio investment (FPI)**. FPI can be defined as investments undertaken by individuals, firms, and governments that represent less than 10 percent equity interest in the target investment. The foreign content in your mutual funds or your registered retirement savings plans are considered FPI, not FDI. The distinction is whether or not the FDI can influence (control) the recipient entity. Arbitrarily, convention is that 10 percent ownership is deemed to be sufficient to influence the directing minds of the company. FDI is measured by referring to the flow and stock of FDI. The **flow of FDI** is the amount of FDI flowing in and out of a country over a fixed period (generally reported over a one-year period). An analogy would be the reporting of Canada's deficit or surplus for a particular fiscal year. The **FDI stock** is the accumulated total of all of a nation's FDI. An analogy would be Canada's debt, approximately $499.5 billion in 2006. There are further materials on these and other modes of entry in Chapter 10, pages 293–300. The current global FDI boom is driven by massive merger and acquisition (M&A) deals.[11]

Why Is FDI Important?

Canada comprises only 1.9 percent of the world economy and has only 0.5 percent of the world's population. Forecasts indicate that Canada is likely to grow at a slower pace economically than the world average in coming years (see Figure 7.2, page 194). Accordingly, Canada's government must play a role in helping businesses reap economic gains provided by increased trade.[12] To sustain our economic standard of living, we need capital to grow our businesses, and our domestic market is unable to provide all of the capital required. Accordingly, FDI is encouraged. However, there are both advantages and disadvantages of encouraging FDI that must be considered, as we will see in a moment. Government must help SMEs explore FDI opportunities and exploit the opportunities globalization presents.

Types of FDI include mergers and joint ventures (the combining of two or more firms into generally a new entity), subsidiaries acquisitions (the 100 percent takeover of another firm), and greenfields (establishing from the ground up a new operation in a foreign country).

Foreign direct investment can be defined as significant investment made by external individuals, firms, and governments (investors) in local facilities to produce or market goods or services. Significant investment will be deemed to have taken place whenever a 10 percent or greater equity interest in the target investment has been obtained by the external entity.

Foreign portfolio investment (FPI) can be defined as investments undertaken by individuals, firms, and governments that represent less than 10 percent equity interest in the target investment.

The **flow of FDI** is that amount of FDI flowing in and out of a country over a fixed period of time.

The **FDI stock** is the accumulated total of all of a nation's FDI.

FIGURE 7.2

IMF 2005 Economic Growth
Forecasts for Selected Countries

World Average	4.3%
Canada	**3.4%**
U.S.	3.5%
Germany	0.8%
France	1.5%
Italy	0%
Ireland	5%
Japan	2%
U.K.	1.9%
Australia	2.2%
China	9%
India	7.1%
Brazil	3.3%
Mexico	3%
Nigeria	3.9%
Kenya	4.7%
Zimbabwe	-7.1%
Morocco	1%

SOURCE: Author generated from World Economic Outlook Database (International Monetary Fund, September 2005), retrieved August 27, 2006, from www.imf.org/external/pubs/ft/weo/2005/02/data/index.htm.

Zwelinzima Vavi's quote at the beginning of this chapter, "States are now being forced to join an international beauty contest to compete for foreign investment"[13] reflects the reality and the importance of FDI to nations' economic well-being. During the first decade of the new millennium most would agree that the FDI stories of India and China have dominated the press. Is FDI a good or a bad thing? How do we decide? How do we encourage or impede FDI?

Host Country Benefits

Nations support and encourage FDI because of the benefits they receive. There are four FDI benefits to host countries: the resource transfer effect, the balance of payments effect, the employment effect, and the effect on competition and economic growth.

The Resource Transfer Effect

Most countries quickly recognize that, at one level, the advantages of incoming capital, technology, and management resources augment their own capital, technology, and management resources. For example, how can Canada finance the estimated $90 billion required to develop the Alberta oil sands? And if Canada did raise the capital internally, that would mean that $90 billion of investment capital would not be available for other capital projects in Canada. So on the surface, FDI for major projects is generally welcome. At times, a nation's credit rating is so poor it may not be able to raise sufficient capital to undertake major capital initiatives. How would Uzbekistan raise capital in the global financial market (see Chapter 9) to fund pipelines and other infrastructure necessary to move energy supplies to market? Often in situations like this, private-sector enterprise will have greater capacity to raise funds and at lower cost (interest) than governments.

Another resource transfer is that of technology resources. There are many recent examples of American firms, such as AOL-Time Warner, Yahoo, and Microsoft, transferring their technology and some components of their research and development as preconditions established by China to permit FDI in the Middle Kingdom. China adopts a pragmatic nationalist view toward FDI and maintains distortionary preferential policies. See the Mini Case on page 219. For example, China often insists that a number of foreign technology initiatives be 51 percent owned by Chinese firms. Over time, domestic technological skills will grow as a result of these Chinese initiatives. At some point, Chinese workers will develop technological breakthroughs that should flow back to developed companies that originally made the FDI. In 2002, Microsoft Corporation "signed its first shareholder agreement in China . . . to set up a software joint venture called Zhongguancun Software Co. Partnering with Beijing Centergate Technologies (Holding) Co., Ltd. (CENTEK) and Stone Group. The joint venture will develop business and government software applications and industry solutions for Chinese and overseas markets."[14] CENTEK, Stone, and Microsoft ownership is 51%, 30%, and 19% respectively.[15] Another example of strategic partnership in China's rapidly growing online communication market is the joint venture (JV) between Chinese firm TOM On Line (China's leading wireless Internet company) and VoIP Skype (the pioneering global Internet communications company providing free high-quality phone calls to anywhere in the world). The JV will make China one of Skype's top three markets.[16] Once again, notice the share distribution. "The joint venture holding structure will be 51% and 49% by TOM Online and Skype, respectively."[17] The technological advances will be transferred back to the two companies' other global initiatives.

Resource transfer also includes transferring financial management skills. Consider those acquired by developing countries to support JV FDI. Firms adopting geocentric human resource management practices hire the best global management to operate the JV in the host country (see Chapter 15, Figure 15.2 (page 420), and page 421). This benefits the host country by growing the country's advanced factor endowment of skilled human resources (recall Porter's diamond in Chapter 6, pages 167–168.) Other firms in the host country, recognizing the competitive advantage gained by employing highly skilled foreign personnel, make job offers to attract them away from the JV. This retains advanced management business skills in the host nation.

The Balance of Payments Effect

Much has been written recently about the United States' balance of payment (BoP) accounts. Many nations are concerned about this issue, particularly Canada because of our high economic interdependence with America. FDI affects a country's BoP. As a result, it is important to have a basic understanding of what contributes to a country's BoP and how it can be affected by FDI.

Balance of payment tracks both a nation's payments to and receipts from other nations. You will note in Figure 7.3, page 196, that **BoP** accounts are divided into two sections. The **current-account section** reflects credits and debts (exports and imports) of all transactions involving the export and import of goods and services, income receipts from abroad, and income payments for foreign assets inside the country. The first chart of accounts is "merchandised goods." Merchandised goods are tangible goods. Expenditures incurred from importing and exporting physical goods are recorded here either as credits (+) or debits (−). Services form the second chart of accounts in the current account section. Services include, for example, tourism and consulting services. This chart reflects the Canada's revenues and expenditures for services in 2004. These values are recorded as credits or debits. The third chart of account is investment income. It represents both the inflows or income receipts (+), and outflows or income payments (−) of global income from a Canadian perspective. Inflow of income earned on FDI abroad is recorded here as a credit. Canada's payment of interest and dividends to foreign holders of Canadian bonds and equities are recorded here as an outflow (debit) to all those countries and individuals providing FDI. A **current account surplus** exists when a nation exports more goods and services than it imports. This was the case in 2004 when Canada had a credit of $14.232 billion. A country is said to have a **current account deficit** when it imports more goods and services than it exports.

The second section contains the capital account. The **capital account** records the sale and purchase of Canadian assets. For example, in 1983, Hong Kong billionaire Li Ka-shing's company, Hutchison Whampoa Limited, purchased Canadian Husky Oil. This sale would be included as a credit in the capital account. This is because capital (the money used to purchase the shares) flows as FDI into Canada. However, when income payments or dividends flow out to Hutchison Whampoa Limited in Hong Kong, the annual value will be recorded in Canada's current account as a debit.

A country's balance of payment (**BoP**) account tracks both payments to and receipts from other nations.

The **current-account section** of the BoP account reflects credits and debits of all transactions involving the export (credit) and import (debit) of goods and services, income receipts from abroad, and income payments for foreign assets inside the country.

A **current account surplus** exists when a nation exports more goods and services than it imports.

A **current account deficit** exists when a country imports more goods and services than it exports.

Canada's **capital account** records the sale and purchase of Canadian assets. For example, when Husky Oil was sold to a Hong Kong company in 1983, the transaction was included as a credit on Canada's capital account. This is because the capital (the money used to make the purchase) flowed into Canada as FDI.

FIGURE 7.3
Canadian Balance of Payments
Accounts, 2004

Current Account	Credits	Debits
Exports of goods, services, and income	$529,335	
Merchandised Goods	429,134	
Services	61,816	
Income receipts on investments	38,385	
Imports of goods, services, and income		−$500,887
Merchandised Goods		−363,076
Services		−74,490
Income payments on investments		−63,321
Unilateral transfers		−14,216
Balance of current account	14,232	
Capital Account		
Canadian assets abroad		−955,436
Foreign assets in Canada	1,136,563	
Balance on capital account	189,087	
Statistical discrepancy		−6,272

SOURCE: *Canada's Balance of International Payments: Capital and Financial Accounts* (Statistics Canada, May 30, 2006). © Copyright Public Works & Government Services Canada, 2006.

The Employment Effect

FDI proponents claim additional jobs will be created because the FDI funds would not otherwise be available in the host country. However, this is a double-edged sword. Those who oppose the FDI initiative and adopt a "radical" view of FDI argue that many of the new jobs promised would, in fact, be jobs transferred to the new FDI facility from existing businesses already in the host country. There is some evidence that FDI has resulted in closures of existing smaller and less competitive domestic enterprises and a number of these firms' employees have found work with the new company. The argument that local jobs are lost is even stronger when the FDI takes the form of a merger or acquisition rather than a greenfield mode of entry (see Chapter 10, pages 299–300). Which view should be upheld is a question for the host country's governing bodies. They must undertake a cost-benefit analysis. Many adopt a pragmatic nationalist FDI solution.

The Effect on Competition and Economic Growth

An examination of Porter's diamond (see Chapter 6, pages 167–169) is instructional to understand how FDI will contribute to a nation's competitive position. Specifically, the inward investment will enhance competition and stimulate additional investment by those wishing to remain in the industry. Porter's country attributes—the advanced factor endowments (management skills, technology, and infrastructure); related and supporting industries; demand conditions; and the firm's strategy, structure, and rivalry—will all be affected positively by FDI. Second, arguments supporting the positive effect on competition and economic growth caused by FDI can be found in Adam Smith's economic theory. In a free marketplace without impediments, supply and demand will promote competition, thereby resulting in the lowest prices for goods and services and in the quantity that the market can support.

A number of economies have seen an improvement in their outward FDI performance over the past 15 years. The fact that a nation's FDI grew faster than its share of global GDP indicates that its businesses are building ownership advantages rapidly and/or are increasingly choosing to exploit their competitive advantages by establishing operations in foreign locations.

Host Country Costs

There are three costs to host countries as recipients of FDI. They have the potential to negatively affect on competition within the host country's industries; to adversely affect the balance of payments over time; and, for many within the host country, a perceived or actual loss of sovereignty and autonomy as foreign nations acquire ownership of the host country's entities and assets.

Negative Impact on Competition

Earlier we discussed the impact of the largest capitalized company in the world, Wal-Mart entering the Canadian retail market (see Chapter 1, page 21). With its distinctive and core competencies, Wal-Mart has globally demonstrated its business acumen. The company's access to capital, global sourcing, and state-of-the-art technology (such as RFID and EDI) present a great threat to indigenous competitors within Canada and other host nations. While developed countries are affected when multinational enterprises enter their marketplaces, the effects are not as devastating as they are to the **developing countries** and **undeveloped countries**. Consider, for example, small domestic sugarcane producers in the Dominican Republic, Guatemala, Fiji, and Malawi. Do they have the skill sets and resources to compete against developed countries' FDI in their marketplace? Do they have the resources to survive the market price swings? Are they able to access forward, future, and hedging instruments to protect themselves from currency turbulence in the marketplace (see Chapter 8, pages 230–231)? There is considerable evidence that the answer to these questions is "no."[18] Small indigenous firms soon close or sell their operations to the larger foreign firms.

Negative Impact on the Balance of Payments over Time

Earlier, on page 195, we discussed the positive impact of FDI on the host country's BoP. When Wal-Mart makes its initial capital expenditures to establish its facilities in Canada, the expenditures are recorded in the year the investment is made, thereby positively affecting the inflow of Canada's FDI. The adverse side of this, of course, is that over time, as these new facilities accrue profits, the profits are repatriated to Wal-Mart's home office. This represents an ongoing debit in Canada's BoP accounts. From time to time, governments become concerned about this type of outflow. This is particularly true when they, like the United States, are in a BoP–deficit position. Countries in this position sometimes consider implementing restrictions on FDI earnings that can be repatriated to the home country. Another potential adverse consideration can be found in manufacturing industries. Bombardier offered to establish aircraft manufacturing facilities in Ireland as part of its strategy to obtain incentives from the Irish government. However, the number of jobs and revenues may not meet the Irish government's anticipated inflow of FDI, as many of the parts would be outsourced from other venues including Montréal.

Perceived or Actual Loss of Sovereignty and Autonomy

At times, government leaders and citizens express their concerns when the perceived or actual loss of sovereignty and autonomy resulting from inflows of FDI is seen as excessive. Canada implemented the Foreign Direct Investment Review Act as the federal government's response to our national concern about loss of sovereignty and autonomy. National FDI concerns shift over time with economic circumstances. The German acquisitions of PEI real estate in 1982 precipitated the PEI government to pass the Prince Edward Island Lands Protection Act. The act provides, "A person who is not a resident person shall not have an aggregate land holding in excess of five acres or having a shore frontage in excess of one hundred and sixty-five feet unless he first receives permission to do so from the Lieutenant Governor in Council."[22] Similarly, all three prairie provinces restrict sales of farmland to foreign-owned corporations, but only Saskatchewan restricts Canadian corporations from purchasing more than 10 acres of farmland.[23] These and other initiatives were taken in response

Developing countries and less developed countries are used interchangeably in this text. The terms describe a country whose per capita income is low by world standards but does not meet the UN criteria for least developed nation status in at least two of the three categories. It does not necessarily connote that the country's income is rising.[19]

Undeveloped countries and least developed countries are used interchangeably in this text. The term describe countries with no more that 10 percent of their GNP resulting from manufacturing.[20] Since 1971, the United Nations has denominated Least Developed Countries (LDCs) a category of low-income states that are deemed structurally disadvantaged in their development process, and facing more than other countries the risk of failing to come out of poverty. The three measurement criteria are low income, weak human assets, and economic vulnerability.[21]

to the Japanese, German, and American acquisitions of Canadian farmland in the 1980s and early 1990s and were driven by Canadians' fear of the perceived loss of sovereignty and autonomy.

Why Do Organizations Undertake FDI?

All firms, large and small, from developed and developing countries alike, driven by the competitive pressures of a globalizing world economy, undertake FDI to invest abroad by establishing foreign affiliates (FDI). These affiliates contribute to the economic well-being of the investing organization. Organizations consider a variety of factors when deciding whether to undertake FDI. The major factors are political, the potential for market share growth, and the location economies that might be achieved. Visit www.power.nelson.com for a list of the world's top 100 nonfinancial multinationals (also referred to as transnational corporations) ranked by 2003 foreign assets.

Political Radical View ←→ Pragmatic Nationalism View ←→ Free Market View

> Those who accept the **free market view** adopt the position that nations must not interfere with FDI, but open up their country and permit the free flow of FDI.

The political factors (see Chapter 3, pages 67–74) have to be fully evaluated when considering FDI. Where along the continuum between the radical view of FDI and the free market view is the potential host country's current political and economic ideology? Those of you who have watched *Commanding Heights*[24] will understand the underlying political philosophies as to who should control the nation's major industries—the public or the private sector? Proponents of the **free market view** argue that nations must not interfere with FDI but open up their country and permit the free flow of FDI. Supporters of this view take comfort that Smith's invisible hand will guide the marketplace to the appropriate FDI balance between supply and demand. Since 9/11, many would contend there has been a perceivable shift away from this pole toward the left. Evidence to support this observation can be seen in America's response to the textile imports from China that resulted in the United States proposing a 27.5 percent tariff. The cry, "Made in America" is heard increasingly. This is at best pragmatic globalization, at worst mercantilism. Nations wishing to access U.S. markets are encouraged to create jobs within America. Similarly, Latin American nations, such as Bolivia, Venezuela, and others, are quickly shifting to the left and adopting a radical view, particularly relating to ownership of their energy industry.

> Supporters of the **radical view** of FDI, grounded in the thoughts of Plato and shaped by Karl Marx, hold an economic rationale for rejecting or nationalizing developed countries' FDI because they fear that FDI will spread Western liberalized democracy and imperialism that will suffocate and exploit lesser developed and underdeveloped nations that accept FDI.

The other end of the continuum, the **radical view** of FDI, is grounded in the thoughts of Plato and shaped by Karl Marx. The economic rationale for rejecting or nationalizing developed countries' FDI is that FDI will spread Western liberalized democracy and imperialism that will suffocate and exploit lesser developed and underdeveloped nations that accept FDI. The countries closest to this far-left end of the continuum are North Korea and Cuba. Between these two positions we find the pragmatic nationalism FDI view. Nations shift between the two pole positions (free market–radical FDI philosophies); a nation's current placement on the continuum depends on, among other things, its current political ideology and the economic realities present at that particular moment in time. The **pragmatic nationalism view** utilizes a cost-benefit analysis to determine whether to accept FDI. If the benefits outweigh the costs to the host country then FDI should be encouraged; if not, it should be rejected.

> The **pragmatic nationalism view** utilizes a cost-benefit analysis to determine whether to accept FDI. If the benefits outweigh the costs to the host country then FDI should be encouraged; if not, it should be rejected.

Governments wishing to encourage FDI should consider offering attractive incentives and aggressively marketing themselves as a host country open for business. If on the other hand, the costs outweigh the benefits, then it is permissible for the host country to impose restrictions of the inflow of FDI. For instance, in 1980, faced with a low Canadian dollar and attracting more FDI than many Canadians felt comfortable with, Prime Minister Pierre Trudeau launched socialist liberal initiatives to stem the inflow of FDI. Many Canadians supported these initiatives, and Canada dramatically shifted along the continuum toward the radical pole. The Trudeau government passed and implemented the Foreign Investment Review Act. This Act required all foreign organizations contemplating FDI in Canada involving a proposed transfer in excess of 50 percent of the target organization to submit a proposal for approval to the federal government. No merger or acquisition was permitted until this bureaucratic process—sometimes taking many months—had been completed. Needless to say, this FDI barrier retarded the growth of Canada's FDI inflow. Today, one can readily conclude that Canada's position along the FDI continuum has shifted back towards the free market pole. Governments at all levels in Canada today actively encourage FDI. For example, consider the very generous tax incentives provided by the federal, Ontario, and British Columbia governments to encourage American and other national film-making companies to produce their product in Canada.

Political impediments can include trade barriers and administrative regulations. A way around a country's protectionist measures is for firms to undertake FDI. In 1980, the Japanese government had to implement voluntary export restraints to curtail the success of Japanese automobile sales in the United States. There was a sense of "fortress America" emerging that weighed heavy in Toyota's decision to undertake FDI to build cars in America and to also implement a VER. Toyota was strongly encouraged by different levels of American government to build and invest in the United States, thereby creating jobs for U.S. autoworkers.

JUST DOING THE RIGHT THING

JOE GIZA / Reuters/ Landov

Americans protesting the sale of U.S. ports operations to Dubai Ports World.

President George W. Bush has said opposition in the US to a deal giving a Dubai-based company control of six US ports sends a bad signal to allies. Mr. Bush said the United Arab Emirates [UAE] was a "valued and strategic partner" in the US-led war on terrorism. Dubai Ports World has agreed to cede control of the ports to a "US entity" after an outcry from lawmakers worried the deal would harm national security. Meanwhile, US–UAE trade talks set for Monday have been postponed. Officials from both sides downplayed the delay and said it was unrelated to the ports row. Spokeswoman for the US Trade Representative's Office Neena Morjani said both sides were committed to the free trade talks but needed

"additional time to prepare for the second round of negotiations." The US and the UAE have been discussing a free trade deal since March 2005. Mr. Bush told a conference of the National Newspaper Association that the US needed allies like the UAE. "They are a key partner for our military in a critical region, and outside of our own country, Dubai services more of our military, military ships, than any country in the world," he said. Mr. Bush added: "In order to win the war on terror we have got to strengthen our friendships and relationships with moderate Arab countries in the Middle East." But the president admitted Congress was "still very much opposed" to the deal.

Dubai Ports World is taking over P&O, which currently runs the ports. Lawmakers have threatened to block the takeover on security grounds. They have called for a comprehensive review of ownership of key transport assets, despite the concession from Dubai Ports World. The company has not explicitly said it will sell the subsidiaries respon-

sible for US ports, although the White House has suggested that this will be the end result. Trade experts agreed with Mr. Bush that the Dubai Ports World saga would set a damaging precedent for other Middle Eastern firms planning to invest in the US. "It is just assuming that if a company is from the Middle East it is de facto disqualified from investing in the United States, and I think that is a terrible message to send," said Daniel Griswold, director of the Cato Institute's Centre for Trade Policy Studies.

It has now emerged that a second Dubai-owned firm is already providing shipping services in the US. The other company—Inchcape Shipping Services (ISS)— has been owned since January by the United Arab Emirates investment firm Istithmar. ISS, whose clients include the US Navy, has had extensive interests in the US for many years. It arranges pilots, tugs and dock workers for shipping companies and works with the US Customs to ensure the smooth arrival and departure of vessels at ports such as New York, New Jersey and San Francisco.

Source: BBC News, *Bush Warns over Port Row 'Signal'* (BBC News, March 10, 2006). Copyright British Broadcasting Corporation, 2006.

FDI to Grow Market Share

Potential for the firm to grow market share in the host country must be considered. In Chapter 6, pages 165–166, we discussed, as part of the underlying explanation for economic trade theory, economist Raymond Vernon's "international product trade life cycles." Vernon's theory also explained why firms undertake FDI. Companies export their product and subsequently make FDI in foreign countries as their product moves through its life cycle. Initially, the product is manufactured in the home country where domestic demand can be closely monitored, and research and development activities can be brought to bear quickly to enhance the product. As the domestic market matures, sales from exporting (demand) increase, resulting in offshore firms being presented with the opportunity to make FDI in production facilities in these foreign markets.

Having made the choice to become more active in the host market, a significant question becomes what is the appropriate mode of entry? In Chapter 10, pages 293–300, we explore the advantages and disadvantages of the available modes for FDI. FDI might be selected as one strategy in order to mitigate the risk (e.g., losing control) that licensing, franchising, or continuing to export might present. A firm's specific competitive strengths, such as innovation, brand names, managerial and organizational skills, access to information, financial or natural resources, and size and network advantages, present an opportunity for the firm to lever its core competencies and competitive advantages by making FDI in the host country, thereby enabling growth of its market share. Keep in mind that a firm's customers are also exploiting the benefits of globalization, e.g., location economies. Consequently, in order to preserve their market share, there are times when firms will have little choice but to "tag along" and follow their customers into new international locations. Firms cannot afford to allow their rivals to expand into new venues unchallenged if they want to maintain their global competitive position. This fact becomes increasingly more important as emphasis on supply chain management contributes to the success of international firms (see Chapter 14, pages 404–410).

Firms also undertake FDI to make them the dominant firm within the industry. Dominant MNE–sized firms like Wal-Mart are able to dictate terms to their suppliers and achieve the best price points for their merchandise. To support a firm's strategy to achieve the dominant position within the industry may require undertaking **vertical integration** (backward or forward). In order to control quality bauxite when little was available globally, Canada's Alcan purchased bauxite mines in Jamaica. The company did so to ensure a supply of inputs and to control the best source of quality bauxite for years, thereby preventing other global aluminium producers from accessing this quality source. Today, with energy looming as a major issue, a number of MNEs are entering the energy industry to ensure their supply and control over their cost. We will be discussing vertical and horizontal integration in Chapter 14, pages 407–408.

Vertical integration is the extension of a firm's activities into adjacent stages of production. It can mean taking control of the inputs (backward) or control over the outputs (forward). Firms undertake FDI in industries abroad that provide inputs into that firm's domestic industries, or provide FDI to foreign industries that sell and distribute the goods of the domestic firm.

Location Economies

Business, as Sun Tzu observes on page 310, is to be thought of as water; it will flow around obstacles to seek out the lowest locations (location economy, sometimes referred to as the eclectic theory) as well as to ensure a supply of inputs. It will do so without national loyalties in order to carry out its raison d'être mandate of survival and maximizing shareholders' value. The decreasing impediments to trade resulting from globalization enable organizations to seek out location economies (low-cost nations) and actively undertake FDI to enhance their **value chains**. A value chain is determined by viewing and identifying, as watertight compartments, all of the firm's functions, activities, and processes that contribute to the design, production, marketing, delivery, and after-sales servicing of a good or a service. It is a way of viewing the firm that can be used as a tool for analysis. Value chain analysis will be covered in Chapter 14, pages 404–410.

In order to compete globally, managers must exploit every opportunity to "wring out the pennies" from the firm's value chain by seeking the low-cost options and/or moving part of the value chain activities to locations that can provide either better quality or a more secure supply of "inputs" for their products. Managers also seek ways to add value in the mind of the consumer to the chain, thereby increasing the value of the product or service. Accordingly, there is little choice but for firms competing globally to exploit these nondomestic opportunities to enhance their value chains. FDI is one mode of entry to accomplish this. **Location economies**, which reflect primarily economic factors conducive to the production of different goods and services in home and host economies, such as relative market size, production or transport costs, skills, supply chains, infrastructure, and technology support, are to be fully considered. Firms must examine competing locations against the costs of production in order to determine where they will derive the best value for money. Is there access to cheap capital in the host country (e.g., Japan's interest rate was 0 percent in 2006), to skilled and abundant labour (e.g., IT in India), and to land with the supporting infrastructure necessary for the firm's particular needs (e.g., China— Beijing/Shanghai)? Firms are not static in the global economy and will actively consider emerging economies as possible alternative new sites for their operations. Business leaders must identify market imperfections created by strengths and weaknesses found in the attributes of Porter's diamond, such as factor endowments, trade barriers, and the wide range of other variables we discussed in Chapter 6, pages 167–169. Constant analysis of the industry's shifting global ecosystem to identify advantages might result in a firm's exploiting an emerging location economy in a host country. Business will use FDI to mitigate the damage or exploit the opportunities these market imperfections present from time to time.

Competitors who fail to exploit emerging global opportunities will soon see their market share taken by those prepared to undertake FDI or other modes of entry (see Chapter 10, pages 293–300) as being in the best interest of their firm. Managers must determine what mode is most suitable. There are a wide range of options, each with advantages and disadvantages that are accompanied by different degrees of risk that must be considered by the decision makers. For example, will the firm export, license, franchise, joint venture, or undertake FDI?

Instruments Available to Government to Encourage or Impede FDI Flows

Governments have a wide range of policy instruments to affect positively or negatively on inflows and outflows of FDI in order to meet national interests.

Restrict Incoming FDI

Host countries can implement ownership restrictions and performance demands to restrict incoming FDI. In Canada, the airline industry has been subject to government regulation that prevented more than 25 percent ownership by non-Canadians. Many point to this as one of the causes of Air Canada's economic woes. We noted earlier China's ownership restriction in the telecommunications industry. Governments can also constrict FDI by making performance demands of foreign countries wishing to establish facilities within their country. Performance demands relating to product content and whether it will be sourced locally; the percentage of local content; stipulations about the amount of output that must be exported; and requiring the transfer of research and development and other skill sets to the host country as preconditions to permitting the FDI are not uncommon.

A **value chain** is defined as viewing and identifying all of the firm's functions, activities, and processes as "watertight compartments" that contribute to the design, production, marketing, delivery, and after-sales servicing of a good or a service.

Location economies can be defined as those locations that offer the lowest cost factors of production—land, labour, and capital—in the broadest sense.

Encourage Inflows of FDI

In order to encourage the inflows of FDI, governments can offer financial incentives and infrastructure improvements. The financial incentives are evident in Canada's film industry. Governments waive taxes, and provide subsidies and possibly low-interest loans to encourage FDI. The danger, as we've seen in the film industry example, is that foreign firms play one government off another; British Columbia and Ontario found themselves competing for the same foreign film clients. Bombardier exploited this strategy when looking for financial incentives to assist with the cost of development of its new C-series plane. They encouraged the Irish, U.S., and Quebec governments to enter a bidding war. Infrastructure improvements are often used as a method for government to encourage FDI. Multimodal transportation that provides efficient movement of goods is always a favourite, as are technological incubator parks. Education support for the skill sets required by the FDI facilities was used with great effect by the Celtic Tiger[25] to attract FDI to the Emerald Isle. Canada is the most generous of all G-7 nations in the after-tax cost of R&D, providing over $1.5 billion per year in tax credits. This program has been very successful at enticing multinational chemical companies, for example, to move their R&D operations to Canada. Two of the largest chemical manufacturers, Rhodia Inc. and Nova Chemicals, moved their entire R&D operations to Mississauga, Ontario. They have built large industrial plants that employ hundreds of employees and create great economic spinoffs for the community.

Quebec Wins New Bombardier Plant: Radio Canada

Bombardier Aerospace has decided to build its new passenger jets in Quebec if Montreal-area employees agree to a new collective agreement, says Radio-Canada. Sources in Ottawa and at Bombardier confirm they have selected the city of Mirabel, north of Montreal, to build its much-anticipated C-Series jet, says the report. Toronto, Belfast and New Mexico have all lobbied to build the jet, which will seat 110–135 passengers.

. . . Radio-Canada says the federal government has agreed to $400 million in loans, while Quebec will add $350 million in tax incentives. CBC's French-language broadcaster also says the city of Mirabel will give the company a tax break the first year. But the deal hinges on whether 6,300 unionized employees agree to a new contract. Company and union representatives agreed to the contract in principle on Wednesday. The employees will vote on the deal on Sunday. Dave Chartrand, local president of the International Association of Aerospace Workers, says the workers know what they have to do. "The only thing we hope is that the people will listen to the entire presentation and make an educated vote. That's the most important thing," said Chartrand. Bombardier has said it is looking for $60 million per year in concessions from its Montreal workforce, otherwise, it says it will be cheaper to build the planes in Toronto. The union won't say if those concessions form part of the agreement. Bombardier, which could not be reached for comment, has said it will make the official announcement about where the C-Series jets will be built later this month.

Source: CBC News Online Staff, *Quebec Wins New Bombardier Plant: Radio Canada* (CBC News, March 3, 2005). Copyright © CBC 2006.

Restrict Outbound FDI

Home countries can restrict outbound FDI by imposing a higher tax rate on income earned abroad. On occasion, governments prohibit domestic firms from making investments in other countries; U.S. firms are subject to such prohibition in terms of investing in Cuba. In the Helms-Burton Act, the United States formally set out sanctions against Cuba, ". . . its provisions include the right to deny US visas to executives, majority shareholders and their families of companies that have invested in property that had belonged to US companies prior to the Communist revolution."[26] The act was used against the Canadian mining company Sherritt International. President Clinton amended the act to allow American companies and individuals to sue in U.S. courts foreign companies benefiting from confiscated American property in Cuba. Many countries were upset by this legislation, including major Cuban investors, Canada, Mexico, France, and Britain. They were not consulted about the contents of the legislation and that it effectively tries to control sovereign nations' foreign policies and their companies.[27] In 2004 the United States fined "Alpha Pharmaceutical Inc.; ICN Farmaceutica S.A. de C.V.; Laboratorios Grossman, S.A. based in Panama and Mexico DF—US$198,711.73 for importing and exporting goods to and from Cuba between 1998 and 2003. Trinity Industries of Mexico, S.A. de C.V., based in Mexico City, Mexico—US$55,000 for selling goods destined for Cuba and for financing their carriage in 2001. Chiron Corporation Ltd., in name of Chiron S.p.A. and Chiron Behring GmbH, located in Emerville, California, USA—$168,500 for the exportation of vaccines to Cuba between 1999–2002. And Daewoo Heavy Industries America Corp., with offices in Suwanee, Georgia, USA— $55,000, for the exportation of merchandise to Cuba in 1999."[28] The EU has fought the Helms-Burton law at the WTO; Canada and Mexico through NAFTA. Neither avenue has been successful to date. Most countries argue that engagement, rather than sanctions, is the best way to reform the Cuban government. The act certainly restricts outbound FDI.

Encourage Outbound FDI

The home country can encourage outbound FDI by offering insurance to cover the risk of investment abroad through insurance for security of the assets, receipts, and individuals. All countries can provide attractive loans to support investment abroad; these generally take the form of government-guaranteed loans. Governments can negotiate with foreign governments to gain special tax treaties and tax breaks on profits earned abroad. These tax treaties reduce the practice of double taxation. Governments can also bring moral suasion and political pressure on other nations to get them to relax their restrictions on inbound investments. Through the many programs and incentives offered by the Canadian government, Canadian businesses are being encouraged to expand globally. The strengthening of the Canadian dollar will stimulate outbound FDI. Stephen Poloz, a chief economist with Export Development Canada estimates "that each dollar of outbound FDI creates around two dollars of future Canadian exports."[29] See Chapter 12, pages 349–351, for Canadian government supports for outbound FDI. In addition, visit www.power.nelson.com for a comprehensive overview of Canadian federal and provincial tax measures, incentives, grants, credits, and other corporate tax advantages available to SMEs.

Overview of Global FDI

"Historically, the United States (US) has attracted the largest amount of annual FDI flows. However, during the 1990s, China began attracting increasingly larger amounts of FDI inflows.... As investment inflows into the US slumped markedly between 2001 and 2003, China supplanted the US as the top country for FDI inflows"[30] See Figure 7.6, on page 206, for the regional distribution of FDI inflows and outflows, 1992–2004. Although more recent statistics are not yet available, anecdotal evidence would support the notion that the gap continues to grow. What does this mean to the world and to Canadian business in particular?

We must bear in mind the nature and origin of some FDI flows and stocks, as these will sometimes influence the accuracy of the numbers. One problem is **round tripping**. This occurs when an investment is made abroad for tax reasons and ends up back in the home country. The ranking of countries by outward FDI performance index confirms these expectations (see Figure 7.7, on page 207). Relatively small economies (e.g., Denmark, Finland, the Netherlands, Sweden, and Switzerland) figure prominently at the top of the list. This suggests that these economies have highly competitive enterprises with ownership advantages that enable them to compete successfully in international markets, overcoming the disadvantages of operating in foreign locations. On the other hand, it also reflects the relatively small size of markets in their home economies, which

Round tripping occurs when an investment is made abroad for tax reasons and ends up back in the home country.

FIGURE 7.4

Foreign Direct Investment, Net Inflows (BoP, Current US$)

(Data shown in billions)					
Countries	1999	2000	2001	2002	2003
Canada	**25**	**66**	**28**	**21**	**6**
China	39	38	44	49	54
India	2	2	4	4	4
United States	289	321	167	72	40

SOURCE: Author generated from World Bank Group. *World Development Indicators Database*, (World Bank Group, 2002), retrieved August 27, 2006, from http://devdata.worldbank.org/data-query.

in turn drives them to expand abroad. Countries at the top of the index also include a number of developing economies from Southeast Asia (e.g., Malaysia). Firms from these relatively small, open economies are subject to the same competitive pressures of the globalizing world economy as their counterparts from developed countries, and are thus increasingly building their competitive strength by expanding through FDI. A number of developed countries with large home markets have an index value below 1.0 and rank relatively low on the list (e.g., the United States (29) and Japan (47)—both major outward investors in absolute terms but small in relation to the size of their economies. Given their size, one would expect considerably higher outward FDI. Yet, the index indicates a slight decrease relative to their size.[31]

"China increased its share of global FDI inflows into developing countries from 9.3% in 1990 to 27.7% in 2003 and its share of FDI into Asian developing countries from 14.4% to 49.9% over the same period. With the increase in these inflows, China's share of the

FIGURE 7.5

Matrix of Inward FDI Performance and Potential, 2001–2003

	High FDI performance	Low FDI performance
	Front-runners	*Below-potential*
High FDI Potential	Bahamas, Bahrain, Belgium and Luxembourg, Botswana, Brazil, Brunei Darussalam, Bulgaria, Chile, China, Costa Rica, Croatia, Cyprus, Czech Republic, Denmark, Dominican Republic, Estonia, Finland, France, Hong Kong (China), Hungary, Ireland, Israel, Kazakhstan, Latvia, Lithuania, Mexico, Netherlands, Panama, Portugal, Qatar, Singapore, Slovakia, Slovenia, Spain, Sweden, Switzerland, Trinidad and Tobago, Tunisia, and Vietnam	Argentina, Australia, Austria, Belarus, **Canada**, Germany, Greece, Iceland, Iran, Islamic Rep., Italy, Japan, Jordan, Kuwait, Lebanon, Libyan Arab Jamahiriya, Malaysia, Malta, New Zealand, Norway, Oman, Philippines, Republic of China, Thailand, Ukraine, United Arab Emirates, United Kingdom, and the United States
	Above-potential	*Under-performers*
Low FDI potential	Albania, Angola, Armenia, Azerbaijan, Bolivia, Colombia, Congo (Republic), Ecuador, Ethiopia, Gambia, Georgia, Guyana, Honduras, Jamaica, Mali, Mongolia, Morocco, Mozambique, Namibia, Nicaragua, Nigeria, Peru, Republic of Moldova, Romania, Sudan, Syrian Arab Republic, TFYR Macedonia, Togo, Uganda, United Republic of Tanzania and Zambia	Algeria, Bangladesh, Berlin, Burkina Faso, Cameroon, Congo (Democratic Republic), Cote d'Ivoire, Egypt, El Salvador, Gabon, Ghana, Guatemala, Guinea, Haiti, India, Indonesia, Kenya, Kyrgyzstan, Madagascar, Malawi, Myanmar, Nepal, Niger, Pakistan, Papua New Guinea, Paraguay, Rwanda, Senegal, Sierra Leone, South Africa, Sri Lanka, Suriname, Tajikistan, Turkey, Uruguay, Uzbekistan, Venezuela, Yemen, and Zimbabwe

SOURCE: United Nations Conference on Trade and Development, *Matrix of Inward FDI Performance and Potential, 2001–2003* (United Nations, September 29, 2005). Copyright UNCTAD, 2006.

global FDI stock thus advanced from 1.3% in 1990 to 6.1% in 2003. China's share now lags only those of the US (18.8%), the UK (8.2%) and Germany (6.6%)."[32] The opening vignette, on page 191, illustrates China's active inflows into Canada's oilsands.

Note the trend of Canada and the United States compared to China. Should Canada and the United States be concerned? See Figures 7.4 and 7.5. Are we doing enough to attract FDI?

What Is Happening?

Annual FDI outflows from developing countries have grown faster over the past 15 years than those from developed countries. See Figure 7.6 for a comprehensive distribution of FDI inflows and outflows for developed and developing economies. Negligible until the early 1990s, outward FDI from developing countries accounted for over one-tenth of total world stock and some 6 percent of total world flows in 2003 ($900 billion and $36 billion, respectively). FDI from developing countries to other developing countries seems to be growing faster than that from developing countries to developed countries.

Firms from some developing economies (such as Malaysia) already have an established track record as outward investors. Others—including India, Chile, Mexico, and South Africa—have become players relatively recently. Indeed, some recent developing economies have become large investors, by international standards. In 2003, for instance, Hong Kong, China, had a larger outward FDI stock than Sweden—even if round tripping and indirect FDI are taken into account. Its multinational corporations— along with those from Singapore, the Republic of Korea, Mexico, and, more recently, South Africa—figure prominently among the world's leading MNCs. This fact reflects the recognition that firms from developed and developing countries need global production assets to be competitive internationally. Their investments span all sectors and country groups and involve complex as well as simple industries.

If FDI outflows are viewed in relation to **gross fixed capital formation,** a number of recent developing economies (Singapore; Hong Kong, China; Taiwan Province of China; and Chile) rank higher than some developed countries (Germany, Japan, and the United States). (Gross fixed capital formation, as defined by the European System of Accounts (ESA), consists of "resident producers' acquisitions, less disposals, of fixed assets during a given period plus certain additions to the value of non-produced assets realised by the productive activity of producer or institutional units.")[33] Indeed, the United Nations Conference on Trade and Development (UNCTAD) is "predicting that the share of recent developing countries in outward FDI can be expected to rise as recent developing-country businesses become more competitive and their governments permit or even encourage outward FDI, thereby strengthening the 'emerging new geography of investment.'"[34]

Gross fixed capital formation, as defined by the European System of Accounts (ESA), consists of "resident producers' acquisitions, less disposals, of fixed assets during a given period plus certain additions to the value of non-produced assets realised by the productive activity of producer or institutional units."

Overview of Canada's Foreign Direct Investment

The success of the BlackBerry as a leading wireless platform is evidence that Canada offers a positive business environment for high-tech firms, with exceptional research and educational institutions and a very attractive quality of life.[35] As shown in Figure 7.8, on page 207, the United States is Canada's largest source of FDI. In 2003, the U.S. share of foreign direct investment in Canada was 63.9 percent. Canada and the United States have one of the world's largest direct investment partnerships, with the stock of investment between the two countries totalling CDN$393 billion in 2003. Increasingly, more FDI inflows go to knowledge-based industries in high-tech manufacturing, such as electronics, communications, and chemicals.

Since 1996, Canada's outbound FDI abroad has exceeded FDI into Canada. By investing in foreign countries abroad, Canadian companies expand their markets and strengthen their operations through the acquisition of new technologies, resources, and skills. According to Statistics Canada, outbound FDI from Canada contributed about $82.4 billion to the wealth of Canadians in 2002.[36] "Canadians are diversifying their foreign investments worldwide and especially in the US, Europe, and the Far East."[37]

FIGURE 7.6

Regional Distribution of FDI Inflows and Outflows, 1992–2004

Region/country	FDI inflows (Billions of dollars)							FDI outflows (Billions of dollars)						
	1992–1997 (Annual average)	1998	1999	2000	2001	2002	2003	1992–1997 (Annual average)	1998	1999	2000	2001	2002	2003
Developed countries	180.8	472.5	828.4	1 108.0	571.5	489.9	366.6	275.7	631.5	1 014.3	1 083.9	658.1	547.6	596.6
Western Europe	100.8	263.0	500.0	697.4	368.8	380.2	310.2	161.7	436.5	763.9	859.4	447.0	364.5	350.3
European Union	95.8	249.9	479.4	671.4	357.4	374.0	295.2	146.9	415.4	724.3	806.2	429.2	351.2	337.0
Other Western Europe	5.0	13.1	20.7	26.0	11.4	6.2	15.1	14.8	21.2	39.6	53.3	17.9	13.3	13.3
Japan	1.2	3.2	12.7	8.3	6.2	9.2	6.3	20.2	24.2	22.7	31.6	38.3	32.3	28.8
United States	60.3	174.4	283.4	314.0	159.5	62.9	29.8	77.6	131.0	209.4	142.6	124.9	115.3	151.9
Canada	**8.1**	**22.8**	**24.7**	**66.8**	**27.5**	**21.0**	**6.6**	**11.0**	**34.4**	**17.2**	**44.7**	**36.1**	**26.4**	**21.5**
Developing economies	118.6	194.1	231.9	252.5	219.7	157.6	172.0	51.4	53.4	75.5	98.9	59.9	44.0	35.6
Africa	5.9	9.1	11.6	8.7	19.6	11.8	15.0	2.2	2.0	2.6	1.3	-2.5	0.1	1.3
Latin America and the Caribbean	38.2	82.5	107.4	97.5	88.1	51.4	49.7	9.5	19.9	31.3	13.7	12.0	6.0	10.7
Asia and the Pacific	74.5	102.4	112.9	146.2	112.0	94.5	107.3	39.6	31.6	41.6	83.9	50.4	37.9	23.6
Asia	74.1	102.2	112.6	146.1	111.9	94.4	107.1	39.6	31.6	41.7	83.8	50.3	37.9	23.6
West Asia	2.9	7.1	1.0	1.5	6.1	3.6	4.1	0.5	-1.0	2.1	3.8	5.1	2.5	-0.7
Central Asia	1.6	3.0	2.5	1.9	3.5	4.5	6.1	–	0.2	0.4	–	0.1	0.8	0.8
South, East and South-East Asia	69.6	92.1	109.1	142.7	102.2	86.3	96.9	39.0	32.5	39.2	80.0	45.1	34.7	23.5
South Asia	2.5	3.5	3.1	3.1	4.0	4.5	6.1	0.1	0.1	0.1	0.5	1.4	1.2	0.9
The Pacific	0.4	0.2	0.3	0.1	0.1	0.1	0.2	0.1	-0.1	–	0.1	0.1	–	–
Central and Eastern Europe	11.5	24.3	26.5	27.5	26.4	31.2	21.0	1.2	2.5	2.5	4.0	3.5	4.9	7.0
World	310.9	690.9	1086.8	1 388.0	817.6	678.8	559.6	328.2	1 092.3	1 092.3	1 186.8	721.5	596.5	612.2

Adapted from United Nations Conference on Trade and Development, *World Investment Report 2004: The Shift Towards Services.* Copyright UNCTAD, 2006.

Rank	Economy	1988–90	1993–95	1999–2001	2001–03
1	Hong Kong, China	1.9	4.7	11.7	10.7
2	Switzerland	3.7	4.5	4.9	5.1
3	Singapore	2.6	3.7	3.9	4.5
4	Belgium and Luxembourg	2.4	2.9	3.6	4.0
5	Netherlands	4.5	4.1	4.3	3.8
6	United Kingdom	2.9	2.7	3.0	2.9
7	Panama	8.9	6.3	2.3	2.8
8	Sweden	2.5	2.9	2.7	2.8
9	Finland	0.9	1.2	2.0	2.1
10	Denmark	0.6	1.3	2.0	1.9
11	France	1.0	1.4	1.7	1.8
12	**Canada**	**1.8**	**1.9**	**1.8**	**1.7**
13	Spain	0.4	0.6	1.4	1.4
14	Ireland	3.4	2.3	1.9	1.4
15	Malaysia	0.7	1.1	1.3	1.4
16	Germany	1.1	1.0	1.3	1.4
29	United States	0.9	0.9	0.7	0.8
47	Japan	0.7	0.6	0.3	0.3

FIGURE 7.7
Outward FDI Performance Index of
the Top Economies, 1988–2003

Note: Economies are ranked in descending order of their performance index in 2001–2003. Figures were calculated based on outward stock.

SOURCE: United Nations Conference on Trade and Development, *World Investment Report 2005: Transnational Corporations and the Internationalization of R&D* (United Nations, 2005). Copyright UNCTAD, 2006.

"The cumulative stock of Canadian direct investment abroad (CDIA) rose 9.8 percent, or $39.3 billion, to $438.4 billion in 2004. Some $191.2 billion, or 43.6 percent of the total CDIA, is placed in the United States. Total foreign direct investment in Canada edged up 2.9 percent, to $367.9 billion last year [2004]. About two-thirds (or 65.1 percent) of the total is held by American investors. Since 1997, Canada has been a net exporter of FDI capital."[38]

FDI Trends from a Canadian Perspective

According to the Economist Intelligence Unit, which provides research and analysis for *The Economist,* Canada is the world's most attractive business environment, while the *World Competitiveness Yearbook 2004* rates the country the third most competitive globally. KPMG's *2004 Competitive Alternatives* study reports that Canada is the lowest-cost G-7 country in which to do business. KPMG claim Canada is holding a 9 percent cost advantage relative to the United States and that Canada is the most cost-competitive country in 9 of the 17 industry sectors studied, including biomedical research and development, clinical trials, and back office/call centres.[39]

The Patterns of Canada's FDI

Figure 7.9 summarizes the geography of CFDI across countries and covers two periods (averages over 1987–91 and 1999–2003). The United States remained the most favoured location for CFDI, accounting for 47.1 percent of CFDI in recent years, though its share

Country	%
United States	63.9
France	8.9
United Kingdom	7.6
Netherlands	4.3
Japan	2.7
Switzerland	2.1
Others	10.6

FIGURE 7.8
Geographic Distribution of Inward
FDI Stock in Canada

SOURCE: *Invest in Canada: Canada at a Glance,* (Government of Canada, June 26, 2006). Copyright Public Works and Government Services Canada, 2006.

FIGURE 7.9

Top 15 Destinations of Canadian
Direct Investment Abroad
(Outward Flow)

	Ave (1987–91)	Ave (1999–2003)	% of Total
United States	55,981	176,450	47.1
United Kingdom	11,205	36,307	9.7
Barbados	1,351	23,136	6.2
Ireland	1,173	11,763	3.1
Netherlands	1,188	10,316	2.8
Bermuda	1,769	9,823	2.6
Bahamas	1,872	7,738	2.1
Japan	890	7,023	1.9
Cayman Islands	143	6,827	1.8
Hungary	2	6,807	1.8
Brazil	1,521	6,557	1.7
Germany	800	5,917	1.6
Chile	230	5,704	1.5
France	1,456	5,634	1.5
Australia	2,091	5,131	1.4

SOURCE: Department of Foreign Affairs and International Trade, *Sixth Annual Report on Canada's State of Trade* (DFAIT, Trade and Economics Division, October 10, 2005). Copyright Public Works and Government Services Canada, 2006.

in total CFDI fell gradually from the 1987–91 high of 62 percent. The balance of CFDI is geographically dispersed across countries in Europe, the Caribbean, Latin America, and Asia. Almost 10 percent of CFDI between 1999 and 2003 went to the United Kingdom.[40]

"What determines the pattern of what countries outbound FDI reaches? Recent research examining the bilateral pattern of foreign direct investment has found that the main determinants of the location of Canada's outbound FDI are host country income levels, geographic proximity, and whether the two countries share a common language." As SME business decision makers you should note these attributes. These determinants have been used extensively in explaining trade flows. Two-thirds of the geographical pattern of trade can be explained by these few determinants. The United States, the U.K., and countries in non-US North America (mainly Bahamas, Barbados, and Bermuda), Japan in Asia, and Brazil and Chile in South and Central America were among the top destinations of Canadian direct investment abroad.[41] Adjusting for host country income levels, proximity, and language, a major portion of CFDI is headed toward offshore financial centres, the countries with low taxes, or those endowed with natural resources. From 1990–2003, Canadian investment in official financial centres increased from $11 billion to $88 billion, or more than a quarter of the total increase in CFDI. Barbados, Bermuda, the Cayman Islands, and the Bahamas are the top destinations among official financial centres that experienced the strong growth in the past decade. Why? See Chapter 16, pages 457–459. In Europe, Canadian investment is concentrated in the Netherlands and two low-tax countries (Ireland and Hungary), rather than in big continental European countries, such as Germany and France. "Canadian investment in Central and South America is showing significant improvement particularly in resource-rich Brazil and Chile. Canadian direct investment in these countries is larger than that in Mexico. In non-Japan Asia, Canadian direct investment focused on resource-rich Indonesia and two Asian financial centres, namely, Singapore and Hong Kong. Unfortunately, Canadian direct investment in the two Asian emerging markets of China and India remains relatively small. Average Canadian direct investment in China during the period of 1999–2003 was only $602 million, which was smaller than Canadian investment in countries such as Colombia and New Zealand. Canadian direct investment in India over the same period was $178 million, which was similar to Canadian investment in Panama. Given our diversity, we should and can do much more FDI in China and India. The 1980s was a lost decade for developing countries as the share of CFDI slipped back to 13-15 percent of total CFDI. Since 1989, however, the share of CFDI heading toward developing countries came back and surpassed the previous peak in the 1970s to reach 25.2 percent in 2000 from the low of 13.4 percent in 1989."[42]

(Millions of dollars)	Ave (1987–91)	Ave (1999–2003)	Growth (%)
Barbados	1,351	23,136	1,612.7
Bermuda	1,769	9,823	455.2
Bahamas	1,872	7,738	313.4
Cayman Islands	143	6,827	4,674.4
Hungary	2	6,807	340,240.0
Brazil	1,521	6,557	331.2
Chile	230	5,704	2,377.7
Argentina	128	4,924	3,746.7
Singapore	1,795	3,730	107.8
Indonesia	997	3,668	267.9
Mexico	218	3,293	1,413.2
Hong Kong	522	3,134	499.9
Peru	9	1,924	21,282.2
Thailand	33	918	2,724.0
South Korea	28	821	2,867.5

FIGURE 7.10

Top 15 Destinations of Canadian Direct Investments in Developing Countries, 1987–2003

SOURCE: Department of Foreign Affairs and International Trade, *Sixth Annual Report on Canada's State of Trade* (DFAIT, Trade and Economics Division, October 10, 2005). Copyright Public Works and Government Services Canada, 2006.

A surprising development in the recent pattern of CFDI is the dramatic rise of CFDI in Hungary. CFDI in that country increased from $2 million in 1987–91 to $6.8 billion in 1999–2003 (see Figure 7.10). CFDI in Peru, Cayman Islands, China, Argentina, Costa Rica, and Colombia also reported very strong growth. It is important to note that the rapid growth of CFDI in many developing countries occurred from a very small base. CFDI also grew rapidly in some advanced industrialized countries including Sweden and Luxembourg (see Figure 7.11).[43]

Canadian FDI Abroad, by Sector

With respect to the industrial distribution of CFDI, by far the largest share was concentrated in finance and insurance, followed by energy and metallic minerals, services, and machinery and transport equipment (see Figures 7.12 and 7.13, page 210).

(Millions of dollars)	Ave (1987–91)	Ave (1999–2003)	Growth (%)
Hungary	2	6,807	340,240.0
Peru	9	1,924	21,282.2
Sweden	11	1,268	11,225.0
Luxembourg	9	800	8,788.9
Cayman Islands	143	6,827	4,674.4
China	16	602	3,781.3
Argentina	128	4,924	3,746.7
Costa Rica	3	103	3,320.0
Colombia	25	794	3,050.0
South Korea	28	821	2,867.5
Thailand	33	918	2,724.0
Austria	26	645	2,380.8
Chile	230	5,704	2,377.7
Ecuador	9	212	2,253.3
Barbados	1,351	23,136	1,612.7
Mexico	218	3,293	1,413.2
Norway	32	423	1,228.9
British Virgin Islands	29	313	997.5
Panama	17	187	973.6
Ireland	1,173	11,763	903.1

FIGURE 7.11

Fastest Growing Canadian Direct Investment Destinations, 1987–2003

SOURCE: Department of Foreign Affairs and International Trade, *Sixth Annual Report on Canada's State of Trade* (DFAIT, Trade and Economics Division, October 10, 2005). Copyright Public Works and Government Services Canada, 2006.

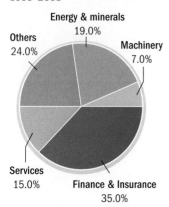

FIGURE 7.12

Canadian Direct Investment Abroad by Sector, Industrial Countries, 1999–2003

Energy & minerals 19.0%

Others 24.0%

Machinery 7.0%

Services 15.0%

Finance & Insurance 35.0%

SOURCE: Department of Foreign Affairs and International Trade, *Sixth Annual Report on Canada's State of Trade* (DFAIT, Trade and Economics Division, October 10, 2005). Copyright Public Works and Government Services Canada, 2006.

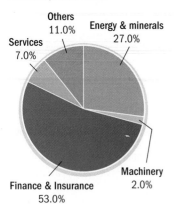

FIGURE 7.13

Canadian Direct Investment Abroad by Sector, Less Developed Countries, 1999–2003

Others 11.0%

Energy & minerals 27.0%

Services 7.0%

Machinery 2.0%

Finance & Insurance 53.0%

SOURCE: Department of Foreign Affairs and International Trade, *Sixth Annual Report on Canada's State of Trade* (DFAIT, Trade and Economics Division, October 10, 2005). Copyright Public Works and Government Services Canada, 2006.

Royal Bank of Canada Acquires Liberty Corp.'s Insurance Operations

Royal Bank of Canada has agreed to acquire Liberty Corp. units Liberty Life Insurance Co. and Liberty Insurance Services Corp., a third-party administrator, for $580 million in cash. The deal, for which regulatory and shareholder approval is pending, is expected to be completed by September 30. . . . Royal Bank, whose primary U.S. operations consist of banks and asset management companies, said it was buying the Liberty companies to gain a foothold in the U.S. insurance market and to cross-sell a wider range of financial products to all of its U.S. customers. "This is a strategic opportunity for us to really get into the business in the United States," Royal Bank Insurance CEO Jim Westlake said in a conference call with members of the media."

. . . Foreign financial services companies have become the natural buyers for U.S. insurance companies, said Nutmeg Securities analyst Ira Zuckerman. Not only do foreign insurers have excess cash on their hands, but also the opportunity for expansion is much greater in the United States than in their domestic markets, Zuckerman said. In most foreign countries the insurance market is dominated by a few large companies, while in the United States the industry remains highly fragmented, he said.

Source: *Royal Bank of Canada Acquires Liberty Corp.'s Insurance Operations* (SNL Financial, June 19, 2000). Copyright © 2006 SNL Financial.

Canada's Declining Share of Global Inward FDI

Canada's declining share of inward FDI in recent years has generated concern amongst many observers. The decline, as shown in Figure 7.14, is linked to Canada becoming a relatively less attractive global investment location.[44] Canada's inflows peaked as a share of economy in 1961 at 35.0 percent of GDP. Until 1989, FDI inflow fell sharply. In the early 1990s a welcome turnaround took place and the share rose from 19.5 percent in 1993 to 30.8 percent in 2001. With China, India, and others competing in the global FDI marketplace, Canada's share of FDI inflows in 2004 a decline to 28.4 percent. There are news reports in mid-2006 that this decline may be reversing.[45] There are conflicting views from others such as the Economist Intelligence Unit and KPMG studies that point out the *World Competitiveness Yearbook 2004* rated Canada the third-most competitive globally. The report notes Canada has a 9 percent cost advantage relative to the United States. Further Canada is the most cost-competitive country in 9 of the 17 industry sectors the report studied, including biomedical research and development, clinical trials, and back office/call centres and yet Canada still enjoys the lowest cost of living among G-7 countries.[46]

FDI stocks carry years of history from previous investment decisions like that of Trudeau's Foreign Investment Review Act, as well as exchange rate movements and other changes in market value. FDI flows are a more relevant and meaningful measure of a country's attractiveness as an investment destination. These trends are "likely a reflection of the rising importance of competing destinations for global FDI flows."[47] Would it be fair to say that Canada does not seem to have the will to undertake long-term planning to build and support Porter's determinants to grow the national competitive advantage we discussed in Chapter 6? Remember the words of Sun Tzu: business should be thought of as water; FDI will flow to where it is most attracted.

A Canadian FDI Success Story

A Calgary firm, Enbridge Inc., is North America's biggest oil pipeline network operator with 13,500 km of pipeline moving two-thirds of the oil from the Western Canadian sedimentary basin along with its operations in the United States and in the Arctic. It owns Canada's largest gas distribution company in Ontario, Quebec, New Brunswick, and New York and operates lines in Columbia and Spain. Its strategy in 2004 was to expand geographically along the energy value chain in North America. To contribute to this strategy it acquired the American company Shell Gas Transmission Line and renamed it Enbridge Gulf Offshore Ltd. The $613 million purchase will provide stakes in pipelines that carry about half of all deepwater gas production in the Gulf, and southern Louisiana and Mississippi. The Royal Dutch/Shell Group unit owned or had an interest in 11 transmission and gathering pipelines in five corridors with a landed capacity of about 4.7 billion cubic feet per day.

Laying pipe in trench: Alliance Pipeline construction, 1999–2000.

Selected Countries' FDI Overviews

The most significant recent changes in FDI have taken place in China. The Chinese have opened their markets to stimulate economic growth and meet the terms of admission to the WTO. Foreign investors quickly saw the huge opportunities to decrease manufacturing costs and access the very large and growing domestic markets of China and the rest of Asia. By 2003, "China recorded inward investment of $53 billion USD which was further enhanced by an additional $13 billion USD of investment in Hong Kong (Trends and Recent Developments in Foreign Direct Investment—2004). In comparison, the United States and Canada saw declines in FDI that only reached $39.9 [billion] and $6.6 billion USD respectively."[48] China's economic potential is widely recognized, witnessed by the recent investment made by Bank of America into one of China's leading financial institutions, the Construction Bank. The Bank of America paid US$3 billion in order to attain a 9 percent ownership of the company and an entry into the middle kingdom. It is estimated that FDI growth could surpass the US$100 billion mark within the next decade. India is also opening up its markets to foreign investors. The two primary benefits offered by China and India have previously been unavailable to the foreign investor: first, enormous new marketing opportunities for their products, and second, access to a quality, low-cost labour market. India, like China, is also benefiting from the recent shifts in FDI. Prior to the early 1990s India had virtually no FDI inflows and fairly consistent investments between US$2 billion and $4 billion per year.

FIGURE 7.14

Canada's Declining Share of Global Inward FDI

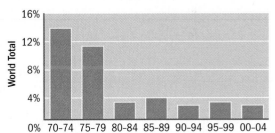

SOURCE: Department of Foreign Affairs and International Trade, *Sixth Annual Report on Canada's State of Trade* (DFAIT, Trade and Economics Division, October 10, 2005). Copyright Public Works and Government Services Canada, 2006.

The United States has received relatively stable FDI inflows and continues to be one of the greatest recipients of FDI. However, there are emerging causes for concern. "In 2000, the level of FDI in the U.S. was over $321 billion USD. Over the next few years that number continued to decline and by 2003 reached $39.9 billion USD. To a large degree, this decline can be attributed to such events as the terrorist attacks on 9/11, the corporate mismanagement with such companies as Enron, and a generally sluggish economy."[49]

Why Doesn't More FDI Flow to Africa?

Most international studies tend to overlook the nations of Africa. The growing gap between rich and poor, starvation, struggling national economies, and corruption are all part of the story. FDI could help. So why doesn't more FDI flow to Africa? For a number of reasons, including high taxes, lack of reforms, corruption, and bureaucracy. Significant impediments constrict the inflow of FDI to most African nations. "A report released by the World Bank [2005] . . . has placed Uganda among African countries that levy the highest business taxes in the world."[50] High taxes directly affect a nation's ability to create jobs. That in turn leads to high youth unemployment rates. "African countries levy the highest business taxes in the world: on average, 62 percent of gross profits is taxed away."[51] These high taxes create an incentive toward tax evasion, thereby driving many firms into the underground economy. The result is reduced revenue inflows to governments. In Mauritania, business taxes are so high that if firms evaded 20 percent of them, their company's gross profit would increase by as much as 60 percent. Unfortunately, African nations continue to obstruct SMEs with heavy legal burdens and piecemeal reforms, which complicate doing business, all of which discourage FDI. (See www.power.nelson.com for a discussion paper on the scope and impact of Canada's underground economy.)

Compare the African experience with the FDI climate of Eastern Europe, the fastest-reforming region in the world. Eastern Europe actively courts FDI by implementing far-reaching reforms, streamlining business regulations, and reducing taxes. "Doing more to improve regulation and help entrepreneurs is key to creating more jobs and more growth. It is also a key to fighting poverty. Women, who make up three quarters of the work force in some developing economies, will be big beneficiaries. So will young people looking for their first job," said Paul Wolfowitz, President of the World Bank Group.[52]

When we review and compare selected regulatory indicators related to business startup, payment of taxes, operation, trade, and closure by measuring the time and cost associated with various government requirements, it is clear that the failure to attract FDI by most African nations is a self-inflicted wound. There are other variables such as macroeconomic policy, quality of infrastructure, currency volatility, investor perceptions, and crime rates that must be addressed to make the ground fertile for FDI in Africa. "For example, an entrepreneur in Mozambique must complete 14 separate procedures taking 153 days to register a new business. In Sierra Leone, 164 percent of a company's gross profits are required to pay all business taxes."[53] In Burundi, it takes 55 signatures and 124 days to move imported goods from the country's ports to the factory gate. There have been some small steps forward; e.g., Ghana, Senegal, and Tanzania revamped their tax codes and eased tax burdens on businesses; Rwanda abolished mandatory preshipment inspections; and Cameroon established time limits to clear customs, thereby reducing delays. However, Madagascar increased the minimum capital requirement for starting a new business to US$5,350 (unfortunately this is still 25 times the average annual income); Chad increased notary fees, and transfer and registration taxes, resulting in the total cost of registering property increasing from 17 percent to 22 percent of the property value; in Ethiopia, exporters require 33 bureaucratic signatures to move goods to the port of exit. As you can see, for manufacturers in Africa, often the administrative burdens of trading can pose larger costs than government's tariffs and quotas. Administrative costs in Nigeria can account for as much as 18 percent of the value of exports! But some African nations are trying. Rwanda is among the biggest reformers of courts, customs procedures, and upgrading of credit registries. Mauritius and South Africa are among the countries with the most business-friendly environment. Unfortunately, for every three African countries that improved business regulations, another one made them more costly.[54]

"The top 30 economies in the world in terms of the . . . ease-of-doing-business index, in order, are New Zealand, Singapore, the United States, Canada, Norway, Australia, Hong Kong/China, Denmark, the United Kingdom, Japan, Ireland, Iceland, Finland, Sweden, Lithuania, Estonia, Switzerland, Belgium, Germany, Thailand, Malaysia, Puerto Rico, Mauritius, the Netherlands, Chile, Latvia, Korea, South Africa, Israel, and Spain. Other African countries with high ranks are Namibia (33), Botswana (40), Zambia (67), and Kenya (68). Nine of the 10 countries with the lowest rank on the ease-of-doing-business indicators are African: Democratic Republic of Congo, Burkina Faso, Central African Republic, Chad, Sudan, Niger, Togo, Congo Republic, and Mali."[55] If Africa is going to participate in the opportunities globalization presents, then it must address these and other issues.

FDI Global Forecast

Notwithstanding rising FDI from the developing world, developed countries continue to account for over 90 percent of total outward FDI. "Prospects for global foreign direct investment (FDI) are expected to be positive in both the short term (2004–2005) and the medium term (2006–2007). The extent and the speed of the FDI recovery, however, will vary by region and industry. Despite the FDI recovery, competition for FDI is expected to become fierce in the years to come. The stage for the expected FDI recovery is set by

INTERNATIONAL STRATEGIC THINKING

The Celtic Tiger was very successful in making Ireland fertile for FDI. Have a look. Once again, keep in mind Porter's diamond as you read about these initiatives.

Ten Reasons to Invest in Northern Ireland

1. *Fresh talent and skills in abundance*. Northern Ireland's highly educated and skilled English-speaking workforce provides a steady stream of fresh talent for knowledge-based companies. Northern Ireland has one of the youngest populations in Europe and educational achievements are high, with students consistently performing well above other UK regions at A-minus level. Northern Ireland employees have a strong work ethic and are highly loyal, best illustrated through their low levels of absenteeism and labour turnover rates that are amongst the lowest in Europe.

2. *Competitive operating costs*. Northern Ireland's operating costs are highly competitive and significantly lower than the rest of the UK and Europe. In software, for instance, junior level salaries are up to 29 percent lower than the rest of Europe, while the difference at senior levels can be even higher. The cost of a 3-minute phone call to mainland Europe is on average 48 percent cheaper than other EU tariffs. A wide variety of business facilities are available at highly competitive costs with prime office rents among the lowest in the world; as little as £12.50 per sq ft in the greater Belfast area compared to £31.05 per sq ft in Dublin and £23 per sq ft in Washington.

3. *Advanced telecommunications infrastructure*. The UK was the first EU country to deregulate and privatize its telecommunications sector and is one of the most cost-effective locations for telecoms services in Europe. The UK's vast support infrastructure ensures excellent service support to business. A resilient, digital network provides high-speed voice and data connections throughout the world. Northern Ireland is set to become the first UK region to provide 100% coverage of broadband services by the end of 2005.

4. *Sector/cluster strengths*. Knowledge-based sectors accounted for 83 percent of all FDI into Northern Ireland in 2003/04. Software, contact centres and financial services are experiencing the fastest growth. Major new arrivals in these sectors have included: Citigroup, LBM, Yell and Fighting Bull Technologies. Northern Ireland also boasts world-class companies in the Aerospace, Engineering and Health Technologies sectors.

5. *Excellent university/business linkages*. Northern Ireland's two internationally known universities have been key drivers in the development of the region's technology and knowledge industries. Queen's University, Belfast and the University of Ulster have globally recognized research centres across a range of disciplines, which are producing new ideas that change the world we work and live in. They each have a strong track record in commercialization of research and in spinning-off successful business ventures.

6. *Accessible to Europe*. As part of the European Union, companies in Northern Ireland can take advantage of tariff-free access to the world's largest consumer market of over 400 million people. With Northern Ireland's modern road infrastructure, busy seaports and air links, businesses can deliver to their customers on time, every time. Daily direct flights out of three airports in Northern Ireland connect to major European and US locations, and London is only an hour away by air. Northern Ireland is the only part of the UK that shares a land border with a Euro participant (the Republic of Ireland). As a result, the business community and the Banking and Financial Services sector in Northern Ireland regularly conduct business in Euro.

7. *Strong and dynamic economy*. Northern Ireland has unemployment levels currently at a 25-year low and strong growth in manufacturing output, well above the UK level. Northern Ireland's GDP had the largest increase between 1990 and 1999 of all the UK regions, growing 1% per annum faster than the UK during this period. It has grown to 3% in 2004 and is projected to grow another 0.5% to 3.5% in 2005. The Q1 estimates for manufacturing output show that there was an increase of 0.7% since the last quarter and an increase of 3.8% compared to the same period last year. Comparisons with the UK show that Northern Ireland's manufacturing output is more promising than the UK, which had a decrease of 0.4% during Q1 2004.

8. *Pro-business climate*. Northern Ireland has a strongly pro-business climate. The regional Government is committed to developing the knowledge-based economy and encouraging innovation and entrepreneurship. Regulation is kept to a minimum. As part of the UK, the region benefits from the strength of the UK economy and its low-inflation, low-interest rate climate. Companies have ready access to a broad range of funding options as well as a developing venture capital market.

9. *Generous financial assistance and support*. Northern Ireland offers a highly attractive and competitive package of financial incentives, recruitment and training, R&D and other development support tailored to each company's needs. Invest Northern Ireland works in an ongoing partnership with investors to ensure all the necessary support is given throughout the lifetime of a commercial venture to develop and expand your business and to improve your capability and international competitiveness.

10. *Our existing investors—success speaks for itself*. Northern Ireland has become increasingly successful in attracting foreign direct investment (FDI) in recent years. Invest Northern Ireland now has nearly 300

externally owned client companies and these employ almost 36,000 people in Northern Ireland. Key investors include leading multi-national companies such as Seagate Technology, Bombardier Aerospace, Caterpillar, Citigroup, Allstate, Liberty Mutual, HCL, BT, Halifax and Prudential. A testament to the success of these investments is the fact that nearly three-quarters of these companies have already re-invested in Northern Ireland or are gearing up to invest more.

Source: Invest Northern Ireland, *Ten Reasons to Invest.* Copyright Invest Northern Ireland, 2006.

CRITICAL THINKING QUESTIONS
Can Canada and other nations learn from the Celtic Tiger?
How do these 10 reasons align with and validate Michael Porter's competitive advantage of nations model discussed in Chapter 6, on pages 167–169?

the acceleration of global GDP growth, the relatively low levels of interest rates in major capital exporting economies, and the increase in domestic investment and industrial output. Corporate profits of MNCs are also rising, as are stock valuations. All groups surveyed by UNCTAD agreed that investment confidence is returning and that global FDI flows are likely to increase during the period 2004–2007. Services are expected to be the sector most attractive to FDI, particularly in tourism, telecommunications and IT. Prospects for manufacturing are also expected to be good, although varying by industry. Electronics, automobiles and machinery are expected to perform better. The primary sector is expected to see a moderate FDI recovery. Asia and Central and Eastern Europe are viewed as the most attractive regions for FDI, while relatively weaker FDI recovery is expected in Western Europe and Africa in 2004–2005, and in Latin America in 2006–2007. The top FDI recipients for 2004–2005 are likely to be China and India in Asia, South Africa and Egypt in Africa, Brazil and Mexico in Latin America and the Caribbean, Poland and Russia in Central and Eastern Europe, and the United States and the United Kingdom among the industrialized countries. The United States, the United Kingdom, France, Germany and Japan will continue to be the main sources of FDI, but newcomers such as China and South Africa will also be on the list of top FDI providers."[56]

"FDI in OECD countries jumped 27 percent to reach US$622 billion in 2005 [see Figure 7.15], up from US$491 billion in 2004 and US$465 billion in 2003, according to the latest estimates from the OECD. These are the highest inflows since 2001 and the near-term outlook for FDI remains strong, with OECD economies forecast to stay buoyant for the rest of 2006. The United Kingdom was the world's largest recipient of inward FDI in 2005, attracting US$165 billion of FDI from OECD countries. France was the world's most active outward investor in 2005, with aggregate flows totalling 116 billion. Outside the OECD area, China continues to hit new records. In 2005 its total

FIGURE 7.15
FDI into OECD Countries Jumps 27% in 2005

	Outflows				Inflows			
	2002	*2003*	*2004*	*2005*	*2002*	*2003*	*2004*	*2005*
Australia	8.0	15.5	17.5	-39.8	17.7	9.7	42.0	-36.8
Austria	5.8	7.1	7.4	9.4	0.4	7.2	3.7	8.9
Belgium	12.7	36.9	33.5	22.9	15.6	32.1	42.1	23.7
Luxembourg	125.6	99.9	81.7	52.4	115.2	90.3	77.3	43.7
Canada	**26.8**	**21.5**	**43.2**	**34.1**	**22.1**	**7.6**	**1.5**	**33.8**
Czech Republic	0.2	0.2	1.0	0.9	8.5	2.1	5.0	11.0
Denmark	5.7	1.1	-10.4	8.1	6.6	2.6	-10.7	5.0
Finland	7.6	-2.3	-1.1	2.7	7.9	3.3	3.5	4.6

FDI inflows reached US$72 billion—their highest level ever, and worldwide exceeded only by the United Kingdom and United States. Outward investment from China is also rising. Chinese official figures estimate the 2005 outflows at close to US$7 billion."[57]

"Mergers and acquisitions (M&A) are expected to resume their popularity in developed economies, while greenfield investments (see Chapter 10, pages 299–300) will be preferred in developing countries. The surge in offshoring worldwide indicates that lower-labour-cost countries will benefit most from FDI, in activities such as production, logistics and support and sales & marketing. Infrastructure and skill-dependent investments will also expand in certain countries. Policy competition for FDI is getting fierce. Most host countries are expected to intensify their efforts in investment targeting, in addition to offering more generous investment incentives and further liberalization."[58] Of course, this outlook can shift dramatically with a global geopolitical event such as a significant escalation in Middle East tensions and the subsequent interruption to global energy supply, higher inflation, and a contracting global economy. That's why we must scan our business ecosystem in order to identify emerging issues.

Are These FDI Trends a Concern for Canada?

These FDI trends present a number of concerns for Canadian businesses. First, Canadian businesses may not be able to remain competitive with goods that enter Canada at a much lower labour cost. Second, lower labour costs will cause some Canadian producers to invest overseas in order to remain competitive, increasing unemployment in Canada. There is also the concern that as investment increases in these countries' technological sectors, Canadians will progressively be faced with even greater domestic competition as skilled foreign labour immigrates to Canada in search of better economic opportunities. Decreasing FDI will also have repercussions for the Canadian economy. A decrease in FDI could lead to a devaluation of the Canadian dollar, which in turn may attract foreign investors wishing to exploit the weaker dollar. (Recall the Trudeau period.) However, the impact on local manufacturers requiring external inputs could be negative in that their cost of doing business would increase and further minimize their competitiveness in the marketplace. The investment trends in China and India look like they will continue. Therefore, the Canadian government needs to be proactive in promoting Canada if it is to retain investment dollars. It must also need seek new investors abroad.

What are the risks to Canada's FDI sustainability? "[There are] a number of risk factors, including oil price volatility, the rise of new protectionism impeding trade and outward FDI, regional conflicts and increased threats from terrorism. Also on the down side, some major developed and developing countries continue to struggle with structural impediments to economic growth and FDI flows."[59] Canadian political and business leaders must scan their environment to identify these risks at the earliest opportunity.

Corruption—A Risk to FDI

Increasingly, **corruption** is becoming a risk to Canadian FDI. In Chapter 17, we will examine what some pundits see as the weakening of Canadian values and the steps we are taking to correct this growing problem. In 2003, Canada occupied 12th position on the **Corruption Perceptions** Index of nations. Placement on this list indicates how a country is viewed in terms of corruption risk for global FDI. In 2005, Canada had fallen to 14th position. Yes, 14th position! As shown in Figure 7.16, page 216, Iceland is considered the least corrupt, followed by Finland, New Zealand, Denmark, and Singapore. Following Canada are Hong Kong, Germany, and the United States. The nations considered most corrupt are Haiti, Myanmar, Turkmenistan, Bangladesh, and—in last place—Chad. To learn more and scan numerous charts and graphs, visit www.power.nelson.com.

Corruption is a lack of integrity or honesty (especially susceptibility to bribery) or use of a position of trust for dishonest gain. For example, political corruption is the misuse of public office for private gain.

Corruption perception scores relate to the perceptions of the degree of corruption as seen by business people, academics, and risk analysts, and range between 0 (highly clean) and 10 (highly corrupt). This includes police corruption, business corruption, political corruption, etc.

FIGURE 7.16
Transparency International's 2005
Corruption Perceptions Index

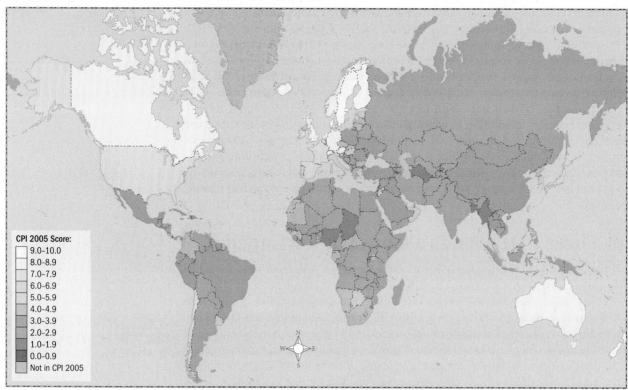

SOURCE: Dr. J. Graf Lambsdorff, *Corruption Perceptions Index 2005* (Transparency International, 2005). Copyright Transparency International, 2006.

Country Rank	Country	2005 CPI Score
1	Iceland	9.7
2	Finland	9.6
	New Zealand	9.6
4	Denmark	9.5
5	Singapore	9.4
11	Netherlands	8.6
	United Kingdom	8.6
13	Luxembourg	8.5
14	**Canada**	**8.4**
17	USA	7.6
19	Ireland	7.4
21	Chile	7.3
	Japan	7.3
32	Botswana	5.9
	Taiwan	5.9
40	Italy	5.0
	South Korea	5.0
59	Cuba	3.8
	Thailand	3.8

SOURCE: Dr. J. Graf Lambsdorff, *Corruption Perceptions Index 2005* (Transparency International, 2005). Copyright Transparency International, 2006.

PRACTICAL ENTREPRENEURIAL FOCUS

Canadian SMEs Relying on FDI Alone Is a Risky Path to Export Growth

Canadian SMEs relying on FDI alone are on a risky path to export growth. Yes, FDI is an essential component of any national export development strategy. However, business should attach a higher priority, and invest more resources, in stimulating and supporting business alliances with local host firms and organizations. Indeed, the outcomes from such alliances can be significantly increased by the right strategy, such as Sun Tzu's advice in the Art of War—when in foreign lands use local guides. Alliances between SMEs, MNEs, and nongovernmental organizations (NGOs) can improve your competitiveness in developing countries.

What are the alternatives? The first is to concentrate on FDI. Competition among countries for FDI continues to become more challenging for Canadian exporters due in part to the emerging success of the BRIC (Brazil, Russia, India, China) nations and others with their attractive benefits. It's a winner-takes-all game, in which there can be only one winner for a project. For FDI to succeed, Canadian SMEs need an established FDI track record, a natural competitive advantage as contemplated by Porter (and explained in his diamond theory), proximity to the target export market, or a key input to contribute. Further, the Canadian government must support and nurture a national export strategy that ensures and maintains a pro-investment environment, a competitive investment regime, a proactive promotion program, and an efficient investor-servicing capacity. However, at the end of the day, the decision to make FDI to increase Canadian business exports rests with the foreign investor over whom the Canadian SME has little direct influence.

Fortunately the situation is different when it comes to SMEs developing export capacity and value addition, if they promote "in-country" partnerships in the host countries rather than attempting only to attract FDI to stimulate their growth globally. Remember it's not a question of "one-upping" international competition but of fostering cooperation within the local business community, particularly within the host country's SME sector. In fact, focusing on in-country alliances to create incremental export capacity is largely a matter of working with SMEs, not multinationals, which primarily focus on FDI as part of their market-entry strategy. For SMEs, the scope for creativity, innovation, proactive strategic thinking, and flexibility is substantially wider and remains largely within the control of the Canadian SME. In short, I believe the chances of success are greater.

While the impact of a single in-country alliance on export capacity is likely to be considerably smaller than a venture involving FDI, the cumulative value of a number of local, export-oriented partnerships should not be underestimated. FDI generally concentrates incremental capacity and value addition in specific regions of a country, while an SME in-country alliance can be tailored to developmental considerations such as rural development, poverty alleviation, and geographic diversification of productive capacity. These are all issues that the firm's export strategy should address.

Here are three best-practice strategic thinking concepts for Canadian SMEs to consider when contemplating in-country alliances.

First, a trade support network should play the role of catalyst. This is even more important in developing countries where more often than not partnerships require an external agent or broker. Within the public sector generally you will find appropriate national trade support organizations. They are a good starting point to facilitate and assist in country alliances. Often, creative thinking will be needed. For example, you might consider forming a public sector–private sector partnership (P3s), in which government agencies partner with private-sector alliances.

In-country alliances need not be partnerships between the public and private sectors only—consider NGOs. Increasingly NGOs are becoming relevant in trade promotion and in developing alliances. This is particularly true in developing rural communities. NGOs can provide the technical glue that holds many export-oriented alliances together. They can play a large role in growing the SME's management competency necessary for export production. Consider NGOs such as universities and technical training centres as potential partners when forming an export alliance.

Finally, ensure that you broker partnerships between the big and the small. Often, partnering with local subsidiaries of multinationals, even informally, can enhance the international competitiveness of the SME's venture. There is evidence that these partnerships are viable in both developmental and commercial aspects of the enterprise. Consider the PRONAMAZON-Poverty and Environment in the Amazon (POEMA)-DaimlerChrysler alliance in Brazil. It is an excellent case example. Further information on these types of business relationship to include P3s can be found at www.power.nelson.com.

Management Implications

- Canadian business leaders have little choice but to undertake business opportunities globally in order to participate in the exponential growth in world trade. Firms can choose among a number of models, including FDI. Recently Canada has seen its share of the world's FDI fall due to the emergence of more attractive competing destinations. Today and in the near future the BRIC countries (Brazil, Russia, India, and China) offer attractive opportunities for Canadian MNEs' and to a lesser extent SMEs' outward FDI. Two of the major factors making the BRIC countries attractive are their low labour costs and emerging internal markets. Canada's business leaders must consider these new BRIC countries as FDI opportunities.

- Canadian governments of all levels must develop proactive strategies to promote Canada and its firms in order to retain our current stock of FDI as well as to encourage investors from abroad. The Celtic Tiger's initiatives to attract FDI are worth examination.

- The perception of external investors regarding the level of corruption in a nation is an important factor in attracting FDI. Canada has fallen to the 14th least-corrupt nation with which to do business. This must be improved.

SUMMARY

- FDI has expanded faster than the global GNP. In 2003, China supplanted the United States as the top country for FDI inflows. FDI contributed about $83 billion of wealth to Canada in 2002. Canada's shrinking share of FDI in recent years is generating concern. In 1961, inward FDI in Canada represented 35 percent of the country's GNP; by 2004, that figure had dropped to 28.4 percent. Depending on the economic and political climate, nations increase and decrease their interference in the free flow of FDI.

- Host countries benefit from FDI as a result of the resource transfer effect, the balance of payments effect, the employment effect, and the effect on competition and economic growth. However, there are costs to the host country as a result of FDI, which include any negative impact on competition, the gradually adverse effect of the nation's balance of payments as a result of flow out of the country (repatriated profits and/or dividends), and a perceived loss of sovereignty and autonomy.

- Firms undertake FDI because of the country's favourable political and economic ideology, in order to grow market share, and to exploit location economies.

- Governments have instruments available to encourage or impede the flow of FDI. To restrict incoming FDI, governments can implement ownership restrictions and make performance demands as a condition of permitting FDI in the country.

- To encourage inflows of FDI, governments can offer financial incentives and infrastructure improvements. The International Strategic Thinking box detailing the Celtic Tiger success, on pages 213–214, provides a good example of a government encouraging inflows of FDI.

- To restrict outbound FDI, home countries can impose a differential tax rate on income earned abroad. They may also put an outright prohibition on FDI in what is perceived as a hostile nation.

- A home country can encourage outbound FDI by offering insurance to cover the risk of investment abroad, such as the Economic Development Corporation (see Chapter 12, pages 349–351); negotiating special tax increases; and providing moral suasion and political pressure on other nations to get them to relax their restrictions on outbound investments.

- Corruption remains a risk to FDI. Canada has fallen to 14th position on the corruption perception index of nations. Canada is considered more corrupt than the United Kingdom, Austria, and Singapore.

- The distribution of FDI is inequitable. Underdeveloped nations, such as those in Africa, do not receive their share due to corruption and the lack of other attributes. As a result, this makes Africa an unattractive destination for FDI. There are some indications of small improvements in the inflow of Canadian and other FDI to the African continent.

REVIEW QUESTIONS

1. What is FDI?
2. What do we mean by the terms *flow* and *stock* of FDI?
3. Why do countries generally encourage FDI?
4. Discuss the benefits and costs of FDI, using Canada as the host nation.
5. Discuss the benefits and costs of FDI, using Canada as the recipient nation.
6. Governments have a wide range of policy instruments to affect positively or negatively on FDI flows in order to meet their national interests. Briefly describe those instruments using examples.
7. Why doesn't more FDI flow to Africa? Discuss.
8. Identify the emerging shifts in global FDI and the likely impact on Canada.

REFLECTIVE THINKING QUESTIONS

1. Having completed this chapter, reread the quotations on the first page, critically reflect on the validity of the authors' statements, and provide your opinion as to the validity of each. Evidence-based answers are preferred to rhetorical answers.
2. Reflect for a moment on the Chinese proverb, "The greatest conqueror is he who overcomes the enemy without a blow"[60] Do you think FDI plays a role in supporting a country's national interest in the global economy? Can you provide evidence to support your conclusion?
3. Can Canada and other nations learn from the Celtic Tiger? How do the "10 Top Reasons," on page 213, align with and validate Michael Porter's competitive advantage of nations model discussed in Chapter 6, on pages 167–169?
4. Do you have a growing concern about corruption in business dealings? If so, explain why it is a risk to Canada's FDI inflows. If not, explain why it should not be seen as a risk to Canada's inflows of FDI?

GLOBAL E-RESEARCH

Visit www.power.nelson.com for research suggestions, questions, and to view a number of background discussion papers on this topic.

MINI CASE

China Needs a New FDI Strategy to Retain Its Global Leadership

According to the *World Investment Report 2004: The Shift towards Services*, China topped the global FDI inflows with a realized total value of US$54 billion in 2003. China has ranked among the top five FDI recipients since 2001. This fact reflects China's attractiveness as a destination for global manufacturing bases. China has been proactive in its efforts to bring in foreign companies, large and small. However, in order to sustain its FDI advantage, China may have to rethink its FDI strategy.

Currently China's FDI strategy is attractive because of location economies and large internal markets. These factors, combined with an appetite for technology, acquiring management know-how, and expanding export markets as well as something unique to China—institutional barriers that prevent state-owned enterprises (SOEs) from operating on a market mechanism-based model—have proven extremely effective in attracting FDI. Indeed as an aside, large and small Canadian firms should consider establishing joint ventures with these SOEs to avail their firms of both preferential treatment and the economic freedom that the current strategy provides.

However, the strategy needs to be revisited. With the advent of China's WTO accession, it has accelerated the opening of industries that were previously closed to foreign investors. The removal of entry barriers has encouraged more FDI, especially in services. However, this success is being affected by the current performance requirements for some industries. As stated, business, like water, will flow from economies that impose stringent performance requirements or barriers.

Another reality of the current strategy relates to SOEs. To date many, if not the majority of China's best SOEs, are in industries that are accessible to foreign investors, have set up joint ventures with foreign companies. The SOEs that remain "unattached" are less attractive partnering targets. Accordingly, China's new FDI strategy must accommodate the entry of private domestic firms into alliances with international firms if it is to maintain its torrid pace of FDI growth. But foreign business will tend grow their own affiliates rather than look for Chinese domestic partners. This may be a mistake for Canadian SMEs as we have noted in this chapter.

More broadly, the new FDI strategy must make provision to steadily remove the distortions created by FDI and alleviate the reliance of its GDP growth on foreign-invested enterprises (FIEs). The new FDI strategy needs to complement this fact with an active domestic investment promotion strategy by "facilitating market entry for domestic non-SOEs and improving the competitive environment so that domestic entrepreneurship can grow faster. . . . China needs to learn from post–World War II Germany and avoid the experiences of Botswana. The former encouraged foreign investments but was not dominated by them—instead, it succeeded in strengthening its own innovation capacities. By contrast, foreign companies have to a large extent dominated the economy of Botswana, with daunting social and political consequences, even though FDI has contributed to the economic growth of the country."[61] China must have an open and fair competitive environment for all firms, domestic and foreign alike. It must move quickly to establish the rule of law that respects policy transparency, protects intellectual property rights, and upholds fair competition. China needs to expand and encourage Asian production integration. If Asian countries encourage a fierce competitive market place, few nations win. Competition is good according to the economic trade theory because it can compel countries to improve their investment climates. However, with apologies to Adam Smith, "too much competition, especially in granting preferential treatments to FIEs, may have distortional effects on the competing countries' domestic economies. As manufacturing constitutes two-thirds of FDI into Asia, it is dangerous for Asian countries to compete too heavily with each other on this front. To curb unhelpful intra-regional competition and experience the benefits of regional integration, China and other Asian countries should consider creating a division of labour among themselves."[62] Accordingly, China can maintain FDI inflow leadership in support of its economic growth only if it crafts a new FDI strategy that provides for upgrading its institutional environment, phasing out distorted preferential policies, and promoting greater integration with its neighbours.

Interestingly, if ASEAN plus China, India, and South Korea integrated as a single market, the entity would have the largest population and the third-largest GDP in the world. If Japan were included, these economies would form the world's largest free trade economic union with a market size bigger than the North American Free Trade Agreement and EU combined. Something to think about in the middle of the night!

MINI CASE QUESTIONS

1. The case states, "China needs to expand and encourage Asian production integration. If Asian countries encourage a fierce competitive market place, few nations win." This implies that expansion of China's FDI into Asia seems economically sound. Do you think the Japanese and Americans might hold a different view? If so why? If not, why not?

2. According to the case, "China needs to learn from post–World War II Germany and avoid the experiences of Botswana. The former encouraged foreign investments but was not dominated by them—instead, it succeeded in strengthening its own innovation capacities." Reflect for a moment on this observation and ask if Canada is dominated by FDI, or have we controlled it and thereby strengthened our own innovation capacities? Whatever your position, support it using economic and political examples (instruments) the Canadian government has employed to achieve those outcomes.

3. The case states, "Competition is good according to the economic trade theory because it can compel countries to improve their investment climates." Do you think China's investment climate has significantly improved because of this economic trade theory?

4. Interestingly, if ASEAN plus China, India, and South Korea integrated as a single market, the entity would have the largest population and the third-largest GDP in the world. If Japan were included, these economies would form the world's largest free trade economic union with a market size bigger than the North American Free Trade Agreement and EU combined. What do you think the impact would be on Canada? What proactive actions can Canadian business and governments leaders undertake to exploit this emerging issue?

ENDNOTES

1 *Brainy Quote* (BrainyMedia.com, 2005), retrieved August 15, 2006, from www.brainyquote.com.

2 Ibid.

3 Edward Herman, *The Real Terror Network: Terrorism in Fact and Propaganda* (South End Press, 1982), retrieved August 15, 2006, from www.thirdworldtraveler.com/Herman%20/ Quotes_RealTerror_EH.html.

4 *Brainy Quote.*

5 James Neill, *Wilderness Quotes* (October 17, 2005), retrieved August 16, 2006, from www.wilderdom.com/Quotes Wilderness.htm.

6 Jon Harding, "China's a Cautious Oilsands Investor," *National Post*, June 2, 2005.

7 Mark McNeilly, *Sun Tzu and the Art of Business: Six Strategic Principles for Managers* (New York: Oxford University Press, 1996).

8 Zbigniew Brzezinski, *The Grand Chessboard: American Primacy and Its Geostrategic Imperatives*, 1st ed. (New York: Basic Books, 1997), p. 27.

9 Department of Foreign Affairs and International Trade, *Sixth Annual Report on Canada's State of Trade* (DFAIT, Trade and Economics Division, October 10, 2005), retrieved August 27, 2006,

from www.dfait-maeci.gc.ca/eet/trade/sot_2005/sot_ 2005-en.asp#the.

10 Thomas L. Friedman, *The World Is Flat*, 1st ed. (New York: Farrar, Straus and Giroux, 2005).

11 United Nations Conference on Trade and Development, *Prospects for Foreign Direct Investment and the Strategies of Transnational Corporations, 2004–2007* (United Nations, 2002), retrieved August 16, 2006, from www.unctad .org/Templates/webflyer.asp?docid=5600&intItemID=2983 &lang=1.

12 Craig Alexander and Eric Lascelles, *Globalization: Peril or Panacea for Canadian Business? Canadian Business Goes Global for Growth* (June 14) (TD Group Financial Services Site, 2004); available from www.td.com/economics/special/ sb04_exec.pdf.

13 *Brainy Quote.*

14 *Microsoft Announces Its First Software Joint Venture in China* (Microsoft, 2002), retrieved August 16, 2006, available from www.microsoft.com/presspass/press/ 2002/jan02/ 01-16Chinapr.mspx.

15 Ibid.

16 Online TOM and Skype Limited, *Tom Online, Skype Announce Joint Venture in China*) (Skype, September 5, 2005), retrieved August 16, 2006, from www.skype.com/company/news/ 2005/skype_jointventure.html.

17 Ibid.

18 Belinda Coote, ed. *The Trade Trap*, Oxfam, UK and Ireland (Oxford, England: Alden Press, 1993).

19 *Statistical Profiles of the Least Developed Countries,* (United Nations Conference on Trade and Development, 2005), retrieved August 28, 2006, from www.unctad.org/en/ docs/ldcmisc20053_en.pdf.

20 Ibid.

21 *Statistical Profiles of the Least Developed Countries.*

22 Island Regulatory and Appeals Commission, *Lands Protection Act* (Prince Edward Island—The Island Regulatory and Appeals Commission, March 30, 2005), retrieved August 16, 2006, from http://consumerinformation.ca/app/oca/ccig/abstract.do?- language=eng&abstractNo=EB000026&text=&language=eng.

23 Craig Docksteader, *Farmers for Economic Freedom* (2001), retrieved August 16, 2006, from www.enterstageright.com/ archive/articles/1201/1201cfen.htm.

24 William Cran, *Commanding Heights: The Battle for the World Economy* (Heights Productions, 2003), retrieved August 16, 2006, from www.pbs.org/wgbh/commandingheights/ lo/index.html.

25 A term for the recently thriving Irish economy.

26 PBS Online News Hour, *Cuban Discord & Helms-Burton* (7/19/96) (MacNeil/Lehrer Productions, July 19, 1996), retrieved August 16, 2006, from www.pbs.org/newshour/ forum/july96/helms_burton_7-19.html.

27 Ibid.

28 Cuban Government, *Cuba Report to UN on Why USA's Blockade Must End* (New Zealand Independent News Media, 2005), retrieved August 16, 2006, from www.scoop.co.nz/ stories/WO0510/S00197.htm.

29 Stephen S. Poloz, *Foreign Investment Mutually Beneficial* (March 6, 2002) (Export Development Canada, March 6, 2002), retrieved 2006 from www.edc.ca/docs/ereports/ commentary/weekly_commentary_e_387.htm.

30 Department of Foreign Affairs and International Trade, *A Quarterly Review of Canada's Trade Performance: Second Quarter 2004* (DFAIT, November 9, 2004), retrieved August 16, 2006, from www.dfait-maeci.gc.ca/eet/trade/2-CTQR2004/ 2ctqr-2004-en.asp.

31 United Nations Conference on Trade and Development, *World Investment Report 2005: Transnational Corporations and the Internationalization of R&D* (United Nations, 2005), retrieved August 16, 2006, from www.unctad.org/en/docs/wir2005_ en.pdf.

32 Department of Foreign Affairs and International Trade, *A Quarterly Review of Canada's Trade Performance: Second Quarter 2004.*

33 *European System of Accounts—ESA 1995,* (Office for Official Publications of the European Communities, Luxembourg, 1996), retrieved August 28, 2006, from http://forum.europa .eu.int/irc/dsis/coded/info/data/coded/en/gl006867.htm.

34 United Nations Conference on Trade and Development, *UNCTAD Hails Increase in Developing Countries' Foreign Direct Investments* (Weekly) (UN Information Centre (UNIC), Issue No. 32, August 11, 2004), retrieved August 13, 2006, from www.un.org.pk/unic/newsletters/ NEWSLETTER040811.htm.

35 United Nations Conference on Trade and Development, *World Investment Report 2004: The Shift Towards Services*—Annex tables B.1 and B.2. (United Nations, 2004), retrieved August 16, 2006, from www.unctad.org/en/docs/wir2004overview_ en.pdf.

36 Industry Canada, *Business Support and Financing, SME Guide* (Industry Canada website, 2004), retrieved 2005, from http://strategis.ic.gc.ca/SSG/me00005e.html.

37 Patrick Luciani and Neil Seeman, *Foreign Investment Fear-Mongering* (The Fraser Institute, 2003), retrieved August 16, 2006, from www.fraserinstitute.ca/admin/books/chapterfiles/ Foreign%20Investment%20Fear-Mongering-luciani0603.pdf.

38 Department of Foreign Affairs and International Trade, *Sixth Annual Report on Canada's State of Trade* (DFAIT, Trade and Economics Division, April 2005), retrieved August 16, 2006, from www.dfait-maeci.gc.ca/eet/trade/sot_2005/sot_2005- en.asp#the.

39 "Foreign Direct Investment" (*Financial Times Business*, 2004), retrieved August 16, 2006, from www.fdimagazine.com/news/ printpage.php/aid/1007/Canada.html.

40 Department of Foreign Affairs and International Trade, *Sixth Annual Report on Canada's State of Trade.*

41 Ibid.

42 Ibid.

43 Ibid.

44 Jeff Sanford, "As Direct Foreign Investment Wanes, Canada's Search for New Deals Grows," *Canadian Business* (March 31, 2005).

45 Ibid.

46 "Foreign Direct Investment" (*Financial Times Business*, 2004), retrieved August 16, 2006, from www.fdimagazine.com/ news/printpage.php/aid/1007/Canada.html.

47 Ibid.

48 Department of Foreign Affairs and International Trade, "A Quarterly Review of Canada's Trade Performance: Second Quarter 2004," *Canadian Trade Review*, (November 2004), retrieved August 27, 2006, from www.dfait-maeci.gc .ca/eet/trade/2-CTQR2004/2ctqr-2004-en.asp.

49 Ibid.

[50] Gerald Rulekere, *Taxes Killing Businesses in Africa—Report* (The Monitor Publications, October 4–10, 2005), retrieved August 16, 2006, from www.monitor.co.ug/archives/a2005/oct/bizfin/1010/bf10042.php.

[51] International Finance Corporation, *Doing Business in 2006: African Nations Lag Behind in Efforts to Encourage Businesses through Regulatory Reforms* (World Bank Group, September 13, 2005), retrieved August 16, 2006, from www.doingbusiness.org/documents/DB2006_PR_AFR_English.pdf.

[52] Ibid.

[53] International Finance Corporation, *Doing Business in 2006: African Nations Lag Behind in Efforts to Encourage Businesses through Regulatory Reforms.*

[54] Gerald Rulekere, *Taxes Killing Businesses in Africa—Report.*

[55] Ibid.

[56] United Nations Conference on Trade and Development, *Prospects for Foreign Direct Investment and the Strategies of Transnational Corporations, 2004-2007.*

[57] Organisation for Economic Co-operation and Development. *FDI into OECD Countries Jumps 27% in 2005* (OECD, June 28, 2006), retrieved August 16, 2006, from www.oecd.org/document/39/0,2340,en_2649_201185_37011943_1_1_1_1,00.html.

[58] Ibid.

[59] Ibid.

[60] *Chinese Proverbs Quotes* (ThinkExist.com Quotations, 2006), retrieved August 16, 2006, from http://en.thinkexist.com/quotation/the_greatest_conqueror_is_he_who_overcomes_the/157323.html.

[61] Yong Zhang, *China Must Adjust Its FDI Policies If It Wants to Retain Its Global Lead in Inflows* (*Financial Times Business*, April 12, 2005), retrieved August 16, 2006, from www.fdimagazine.com/news/fullstory.php/aid/1211/Tips_for_the_top.html.

[62] Ibid.

External— Money, Money, Money

To conclude our examination of the external international business ecosystem for Canadian SMEs, we must examine global financial systems and their structures. The ebb and flow of world currencies and their relationship to each other can often make or break firms engaged in international business. Currency volatility enabled by global technology can be seen in media real-time reports. How do Canadian firms protect themselves from a Canadian dollar trading at 63¢ to the U.S. dollar and 18 months later trading at 87¢ to the U.S. dollar? The impact of currency turbulence can sometimes have a greater shock on the firm's bottom line than the cost of inputs. Business leaders must have a working knowledge of global foreign exchange markets or risk losing it all! It is to this subject that we now turn.

Global Foreign Exchange Markets

"No one would remember the Good Samaritan if he only had good intentions. He had money as well."[1]

—Margaret Thatcher, British Prime Minister (1979–90)

"It is a socialist idea that making profits is a vice; I consider the real vice is making losses."[2]

—Winston Churchill 1874–1965, British Prime Minister

"The chief value of money lies in the fact that one lives in a world in which it is overestimated."[3]

—H. L. Mencken, American writer

"A dollar picked up in the road is more satisfaction to us than the 99 that we had to work for, and the money won at Faro or in the stock market snuggles into our hearts in the same way."[4]

—Mark Twain

"This planet has—or rather had—a problem, which was this: most of the people living on it were unhappy for pretty much of the time. Many solutions were suggested for this problem, but most of these were largely concerned with the movements of small green pieces of paper, which is odd because on the whole it wasn't the small green pieces of paper that were unhappy."[5]

—Douglas Adams, English humorist and science fiction novelist

LEARNING OUTCOMES

- Examine the global foreign exchange (FX) market and the three functions it performs.
- Consider the merits of the Tobin Tax as a solution to reducing the amount of harmful speculation in the FX market.
- Formulate opinions about international currency risks.
- Examine a number of hedging instruments to include forward and future contracts, options, and swaps.
- Understand how to evaluate the four determinants of FX rates.
- Understand the implications of, and how to predict, FX rate changes.
- Evaluate the merits of governments' restrictions on the movement of exchange rates and currency convertibility.
- Form an opinion as to whether the U.S. dollar will continue to dominate global financial markets.

Interest-Rate Swap Deal Covers Electrification Project

STEVEN SHAVER/BLOOMBERG NEWS/Landov

For investors venturing into emerging markets, insurance against non-commercial risks cushions them against political events detrimental to their projects. MIGA [Multilateral Investment Guarantee Agency] went a step further recently by also offering insurance to a group of lenders to a Vietnam power plant to cover their interest rate hedging instrument. By covering a derivative, the agency is enabling project financiers to use instruments that are widely available in developed countries, but rarely in emerging markets. The deal represents an important first for MIGA in terms of product offerings. The debt financing is provided at a floating interest rate, which presents financial risks. To offset the need to either buy an interest rate cap (which could have been prohibitively expensive) or to put together a separate fund to cover severe interest rate increases, the enterprise chose instead to engage in a swap that allows it to pay a fixed interest rate. This is particularly important in the utilities sector where companies relying on a fixed revenue stream benefit from managing their exposure to interest rate fluctuations.

In this case, the interest-rate swap is associated with a non-shareholder loan—part of the project financing—issued by a bank syndicate composed of five lead arranging banks (the agent being Crédit Lyonnais). MIGA covers losses in the event that the swap is cancelled as a result of a political event. "What's innovative here is that for the first time, MIGA has offered coverage against non-payment of incurred swap losses by the utility to the swap provider due to covered political events," says Philippe Valahu, MIGA Regional Manager for Asia. . . . MIGA and the Asian Development Bank (ADB) are [providing coverage for the lenders' loan to the project]—the first project-specific collaboration between the two institutions. "The project is an environmentally friendly solution to the supply problem. It will feed the national power grid, as well as the industrial and residential areas in South Vietnam," says Kurumi Fukaya, ADB's project team leader. "This will make the areas served by the project attractive to investment, which can spur economic growth and help reduce poverty." . . . This represents one of the largest foreign direct investments ever made in Vietnam. In addition to the project loan, ADB is providing $32 million in political risk guarantee. MIGA is providing another $138 million in political risk guarantees. Of this, $15 million is for coverage of the interest rate hedging instrument. Another $38 million is covering Singapore based SembCorp Utilities Private Limited's Equity, and the balance covers principal and interest. Nippon Export and Investment Insurance is also covering political risk. For MIGA, the importance of the deal goes beyond the opportunities accessed by the new coverage products. It is also an indication to the marketplace of the benefits of joint projects involving a number of multilateral development banks, and signals more such programs in Asia going forward.

Source: World Bank Group, "Vietnam: Interest-Rate Swap Deal Covers Electrification Project" (Multilateral Investment Guarantee Agency, Jan-Mar, 2004).

A SUN TZU MOMENT...

"Display profits to entice them. Create disorder and take them."[6] Sun Tzu

THE GERMAN HYPERINFLATION, 1923

Prior to World War I Germany was a thriving, developed country, with a gold-backed currency, expanding industry, and world leadership in optics, chemicals, and machinery. The German mark, the British shilling, the French franc, and the Italian lira all had about equal value, and all were exchanged four or five to the dollar. By 1923, at the most fevered moment of the German hyperinflation, the exchange rate between the U.S. dollar and the mark was one trillion marks to one dollar. A wheelbarrow full of marks could not even buy a newspaper. "Most Germans were taken by surprise by the financial tornado. 'My father was a lawyer,' says Walter Levy, an internationally known German-born oil consultant in New York, 'and he had taken out an insurance policy in 1903, and every month he had made the payments faithfully. It was a 20-year policy, and when it came due, he cashed it in and bought a single loaf of bread.' The Berlin publisher Leopold Ullstein wrote that an American visitor tipped their cook one dollar. The family convened, and it was decided that a trust fund should be set up in a Berlin bank with the cook as beneficiary, the bank to administer and invest the dollar."[7]

Today we can trace the steps to hyperinflation, although some of the reasons remain unclear. Germany abandoned the gold standard of its currency in 1914 (as did the United States in 1971). The Great War was expected to be short, so it was financed by government borrowing (government's debt and deficit), not by savings and taxation. (Does this sound like the U.S. financing of the Iraq war?) In Germany, prices doubled between 1914 and 1919 and continued to double in the few years after the war. There were complaints about the high cost of living and an underground economy developed, aided by a desire to beat the tax collector. Germany's printing presses ran (supply money), and once they began to run, they were hard to stop. The price increases began to be dizzying. Menus in cafes could not be revised quickly enough. "A student at Freiburg

Freiberger Papierfabrik zu Weissenborn

A letter posted to Amsterdam on October 2, 1923, with a total cost of 3 million marks.

Roy Lingen, *German Inflation 1923* (www.world-postal-history.com, n.d.), retrieved August 17, 2006, from www.world-postal-history.com/exhibits/roy/germinfl.shtml.

University ordered a cup of coffee at a cafe. The price on the menu was 5,000 marks. He had two cups. When the bill came, it was for 14,000 marks. 'If you want to save money,' he was told, 'and you want two cups of coffee, you should order them both at the same time.'"

People quickly got rid of their money by purchasing diamonds, gold, country houses, and antiques, and as the supply of these goods dried up, minor and almost-useless items—bric-a-brac, soap, and hairpins—became attractive. Law-abiding Germany crumbled into petty thievery. "Copper pipes and brass armatures weren't safe. Gasoline was siphoned from unattended cars. When the 1,000-billion Mark note came out, few bothered to collect the change when they spent it. By November 1923, with one dollar equal to one trillion Marks, the breakdown was complete." The currency had lost all value—Germans no longer believed in their currency!

Source: Roy Lingen, *German Inflation 1923* (www.world-postal-history.com). Courtesy of Roy Lingen.

Opening Thoughts

The relationship between the world's currencies can, as Sun Tzu counsels, be powerful weapons used by nations to "entice" a relationship or to create disorder. Recently, the United States, the EU, and other developed nations have felt that China's currency has a very favourable exchange rate that benefits China's manufacturers. Americans and others feel that it is being used as a weapon to grow global market share and to build a strong balance of payments. In 2006, China reportedly held $US1 trillion in its foreign exchange (FX) reserves! As a result, China is being increasingly pressured by developed countries to adjust or revalue the yuan exchange rate further against other world currencies.

Eventually, if globalization continues, the world might have one global currency. In such a world, FX markets, FX rates, and indeed FX itself would not be required. However, until that day arrives, we are all required to travel, make payments across borders, and transfer funds globally. It is a business requirement that we stay informed and have a working knowledge of the global FX market in order to protect our organizations' and our financial interests. The opening vignette described how a nation's currency and its relationship to other global currencies can move quickly with little warning and with troubling implications. In the opening vignette, the MIGA provided "insurance" to a group lending to a Vietnam power plant to cover their interest rate-hedging instrument. We need to have an awareness of the global capital markets and the hedging instruments available to small and large business that can reduce decision makers' risks.

In 1973, the FX market was transformed significantly as nations moved from a fixed exchange rate established by the Bretton Woods agreement (1944) to a floating currency rate. Canada continues to maintain a floating currency rate today. We will examine these international monetary fixed and floating rate systems in Chapter 9, pages 261–263. In large part, the financial markets have been deregulated, thereby eliminating government control in nearly all countries. Exchange rates today are mainly established by the marketplace and competition among global financial institutions. Nations no longer find it easy to control the value of their currency due to technology and deregulation. Technology is a significant component in the success of FX markets. It enables real-time communications and transfers of large sums of money between global institutions. It has also permitted smaller investors real-time access to the FX market.

Canada has seen its dollar swing from $US1.08 to a low of US$0.63 since 1973. An understanding of the implications of this currency volatility for exporters (e.g., Western Canada's oil producers) and importers (e.g., Central Canada's manufacturers with nondomestic supply chains) is necessary. The interests of Western and Central Canada are clearly not the same. The value of the Canadian dollar can mean survival or business failure. Keep in mind, from the Sun Tzu section, the notion that all money is a matter of confidence as we examine how the FX works; the variables that impact the FX; and "insurance policies" available for businesses that exploit the benefits of, or to prevent losses from, currency swings. We will close the chapter by looking at the future of the FX.

What Is the FX Market?

In 1944, nations attending the Bretton Woods meeting attempted to stabilize international currencies, recognizing that currency speculation contributed to destabilization. They agreed to measures that would restrict the flow of money from one country to another. They agreed to try to maintain the value of their currency against the U.S. dollar, which, in turn, was to be fixed to an amount of gold. The holder of the U.S. currency could convert the U.S. paper currency to gold at the agreed fixed exchange rate. However, the dramatic increase in world trade, combined with the United States' spending on the Vietnam War and the liberal printing of "dollar bills" led to staggering amounts of capital flowing globally.[8] Like the Germans in 1914, the United States was forced to go off the gold standard in 1971.

Money has been around in one form or another since the time of pharaohs. The Babylonians were the first to use paper bills and receipts. The roots of currency traders exchanging the coins of one culture for another can be traced back to the money changers in the Middle East. By the Middle Ages, moving bags of heavy coins became unworkable. The need for another form of currency emerged. These paper bills represented transferable third-party payments of funds. This innovation made FX much easier for merchants and traders, and resulted in thriving regional economies.

Today's FX market has undergone significant transformation since 1973. Today it is known as the free-floating system. "The FX market is more than three times the size of the United States Equity and Treasury markets combined. Unlike other financial markets, the FX market has no physical location and no central exchange."[9] It is similar to the World Wide Web. It operates through an electronic network of banks, corporations, institutional investors, and individuals trading one currency for another. "The lack of a physical exchange enables the FX market to operate on a 24-hour basis, spanning from one time zone to another across the major global financial centers. . . . Over 4,600 international banks and thousands of small and large speculators participate [in the FX market]. Everyday this worldwide market exchanges more than $1.9 trillion [U.S. dollars] in dozens of different currencies. With the current growth rate, the market is projected to grow to more than $2.0 trillion per day by the year 2006."[10] Individuals and firms now have the opportunity to trade and participate in the largest, most liquid financial market in the world. A few decades ago, only major institutions enjoyed these financial advantages.

A final observation: economic textbooks note that FX rates are determined by supply and demand based on market fundamentals.[11] While this is true at the surface level, we cannot dismiss the sociopolitical factors we discussed in the opening chapters. PEST-C attributes also shape these market fundamentals, which in turn affect supply and demand on a secondary level, as does our "confidence" about the strength or weakness of a currency.

Trading Centres

Market makers are persons or firms authorized to create and maintain a market in a security. Market makers commit themselves to always being ready to deal in the range of stocks for which they are registered.[15]

An **over-the-counter (OTC) transaction** refers to a security that is not listed on an exchange, generally because it does not meet the exchange listing requirements. Broker/dealers negotiate directly with one another over computer networks and by phone, thereby creating a market for the security. The country's exchange officials monitor their activities.

In the past few years, the FX market has evolved into one transacted not only by banks but also by many other kinds of financial institutions, such as brokers and **market makers**, nonfinancial corporations, investment firms, hedge funds, and day traders. "FX is an over-the-counter (OTC) market, meaning there is no central exchange."[12] For stocks and bonds, an **over-the-counter OTC transaction** refers to "a security that is not traded on an exchange, usually due to an inability to meet listing requirements. For such securities, broker/dealers negotiate directly with one another over computer networks and by phone, and the nations' exchange officials monitor their activities. OTC stocks are usually very risky since they are the stocks that are not considered large or stable enough to trade on a major exchange. They also tend to trade infrequently, making the bid-ask spread larger. Also, research about these stocks is more difficult to obtain."[13] The FX market facilitates business "through the trading centres (in order of importance): London, New York, Tokyo, Singapore, Frankfurt, Geneva and Zurich, Paris, and Hong Kong. Market participants have various reasons for using the FX market. Asset managers, investors, and corporations such as importers and exporters utilize the FX market to diversify their portfolio holdings, hedge against their foreign- or domestic currency–denominated assets, and/or to profit from price fluctuations. They all influence the demand and supply for currencies.[14] In Chapter 9, pages 263–264, we examine a number of global capital markets in greater detail.

The Transformation of Global FX Markets

The **inter-bank market** is a network of major banks around the world. Individual banks act as brokers on behalf of customers, and trade with each other.

Derivatives can be defined as financial instruments, traded on or off an exchange, the price of which are directly dependent upon the value of one or more underlying securities, equity indices, debt instruments, commodities, other derivative instruments, or any agreed-upon pricing index or arrangement.

The genesis of global markets, commencing with the gold standard, the Bretton Woods Agreement, fixed and floating exchange rates, and the emergence of the managed float are all reviewed in Chapter 9, pages 257–263.

The FX market is undergoing rapid transformation as a result of a number of factors. Traditionally, an inter-bank market, the FX market has evolved to include other participants. Most derivative transactions related to foreign currencies occur in the **inter-bank market**, a network of major banks around the world. Individual banks act as brokers on behalf of customers, and trade with each other. The more active banks also act as market makers. These banks usually maintain dealing rooms with separate trading desks for cash, forward, and option transactions, as well as separate desks for different underlying assets. The first factor driving transformation is that asset managers, hedge funds, and commodity trading advisors are playing a much more active role in the FX markets. Second, the number of geographic markets is growing in the new large emerging economies, such as China. These rapidly emerging economies need access to the investment capital available in the FX markets. And finally, the use of **derivatives** is increasing.[16] The transformation of the FX market "provides banks with a cost-effective means of distributing their foreign exchange prices to a wide base of potential customers."[17]

Derivatives involve the trading of rights or obligations based on the underlying product but do not directly transfer property. They are used to hedge risk or to exchange a floating rate of return for a fixed rate of return. The FX market emerged in its current form in the 1980s, creating an active trading community with greater transparency and liquidity. Today, thanks to technology and the provision of electronic trading tools more small investors and businesses are joining the FX trading community. Business decision makers are using instruments such as spots, forwards, options and futures, including currency futures traded on the Chicago Mercantile Exchange as a part of their risk management planning. You and I can now trade these instruments from the convenience of our computer desktops!

The following is an extract from BCE's *Annual Report*. From the notes contained in the financial statements, you will gain the sense that FX rate instruments are widely used in Canadian businesses both large and small.

Extracts from BCE's *Annual Report* (1998)

Risk management: BCE Inc. uses cross currency swaps to hedge its foreign currency denominated long-term debt against fluctuations in foreign exchange rates. The Corporation also uses interest rate swaps to manage its exposure to interest rate fluctuations and reduce its financing costs. Bell Canada uses cross currency swaps, forward contracts and interest rate swaps to manage its foreign currency and interest rate positions associated with its debt instruments. Bell Canada generally uses these derivative contracts to reduce its financing costs and to diversify Bell Canada's access to capital markets. BCE Mobile uses a cross currency swap to hedge its only foreign currency denominated debt instrument against fluctuations in foreign exchange rates. BCI operates internationally and as such is exposed to fluctuations in foreign exchange rates. BCI does not currently use financial instruments to limit its exposure to fluctuations in foreign exchange rates on its investments or long-term debt, or to manage the risk of interest rate fluctuations on existing long-term debt.

Source: BCE, *1998 Annual Report—Notes to Consolidated Financial Statements,* retrieved August 17, 2006, from www.bce.ca/en/investors/reports/annual/bce/1998annual/financial/notes/note14.html.

Functions of the Market

The FX market performs two main functions: (1) currency convertibility and (2) insurance for government, business, and individuals. In addition, there has been an unintended function, arbitrage.

PRACTICAL ENTREPRENEURIAL FOCUS

Understanding Risk

Risk happens! It is part of life. There is always the chance that something won't work out, and this chance is called risk. Most of us are used to dealing with risk either on a positive or a negative basis. In your personal world, this is illustrated in your decision to obtain a post-secondary education. Attending this institution is essentially a case of assuming a risk; you are foregoing years of income for the chance that the increased education will pay off in more earned income over the long run. Fortunately, for most of us, this is a pretty safe investment—it usually works. There is also risk in our financial life.

Fundamentally, there are two types of risk personalities. Knowing which one you are is an important step in managing your business.

The first type we classify as the *risk taker*. This personality lives for the thrill and loves risk. This individual is comfortable in the high-risk world of options and foreign securities where the prices fluctuate hourly. Unfortunately, the risk taker is most likely to lose his investment. If you demonstrate this personality you need to be sure to re-evaluate your investment choices or obtain second opinions.

The second type we classify as the *risk avoider*. This person believes that investments will not turn out well and is most likely to say, "You can't trust anybody!" The risk avoider is most likely to miss out on opportunities; however, will likely end up with her original investment. If this classification fits your personality, then you need to consider whether you are allocating a bit too much money in bonds, money markets, or other fairly safe and liquid investments. Somewhere between the two is the right place to be for business decision makers accessing FX markets.

Adapted from "Understanding Risk" (*Money Instructor*, 2002).

REFLECTIVE THINKING QUESTION

Whatever your personality type, understand how you approach risk and craft your business investment strategy. Use the same mental model in your personal affairs. You will be compensated for the extra managed risk you undertake.

Currency Convertibility

Convertibility means that the currency can buy domestic and foreign goods and services, including foreign currencies.

"A currency's usefulness as a medium of exchange depends on its **convertibility**. Without a convertible currency, people cannot easily use money to make the decentralized exchanges that make a market economy work efficiently."[18] From time to time, governments impose currency restrictions. They do this for a number of reasons. Restrictions preserve a nation's reserve of hard currency needed to repay other nations that they are indebted to. Second, convertibility ensures that countries have sufficient hard currency to pay for imports and to finance trade deficits. Third, a government may want to protect the nation's currency from speculators. (Recall from Chapter 1, page 7, the Asian Flu, during which Thailand's private banks were forced to declare bankruptcy.) Finally, currency restrictions may prevent resident firms and individuals from investing abroad. For example, governments can impose restrictions by requiring that all financial FX transactions be conducted by the national bank. Governments can also implement an import licensing program, thereby controlling the flow of capital out of the country. They can utilize multiple FX rates by requiring high exchange rates on goods considered nonessential while setting a lower exchange rate to permit the uninterrupted flow of essential goods and service. Finally, governments can require FX import deposits be put into special accounts before import licences are issued. Importers are able to get around these FX currency constrictions by using vehicles like countertrade (Chapter 12, pages 342–344). These impediments result in different degrees of currency convertibility.

Cash convertibility is the ability to exchange a unit (say, a dollar) of bank deposits for a unit of notes and coins on demand.

Commodity convertibility is the ability to buy domestic goods and services with cash or credit.

Steve H. Hanke and Kurt Schuler[19] identify three degrees of currency convertibility. These degrees correspond to the extent that a government allows a currency to function as a medium of exchange. The most basic type of convertibility is **cash convertibility**. This is the ability to exchange a dollar of bank deposits for dollars and coins on demand. Cash convertibility is taken as a given in developed countries except when a run on the bank occurs. Unfortunately, cash convertibility does not exist in some developing countries. The second type of convertibility is **commodity convertibility**. This is the ability to buy domestic goods and services. Often it is taken for granted in developed countries but does not exist in some developing countries. Nations with commodity convertibility generally require cash or credit to buy domestic goods and services from domestic sellers. The exchange of goods and services where commodity convertibility exists is much more extensive, rapid, and efficient because commodities can be converted for cash or credit.[20]

Foreign exchange convertibility is the ability to buy foreign goods and services, including foreign currencies.

A currency with cash, commodity, and FX convertibility is said to have **full convertibility;** FX convertibility almost always implies cash and commodity convertibility.

"The third type of convertibility is **foreign exchange convertibility**. This is the ability to buy foreign goods and services, including foreign currencies. If no restrictions exist on buying foreign goods and services, including foreign currencies, at market rates of exchange a currency is said to have full foreign exchange convertibility. These developed countries have strong financial positions and large holdings of foreign exchange."[21] FX convertibility almost always implies cash and commodity convertibility, so in this text **full (FX) convertibility** will be synonymous with unrestricted FX. The currencies of most developed countries are fully convertible; unfortunately, the currencies of most developing and underdeveloped countries are only partially convertible or are inconvertible. "For example, many currencies are convertible for most current-account purchases, where residents use domestic currency to buy foreign goods and services for import, but inconvertible for many capital-account purchases, where residents use domestic currency to buy foreign financial assets such as foreign currencies and securities, and certain non-financial assets such as real estate."[22] Restrictions on capital-account transactions are called **capital controls**. Current-account convertibility is helpful for international trade, but it does not attract substantial FDI. To attract FDI, capital-account convertibility is required. Unless foreigners can repatriate some profits, they generally don't make significant FDI.

Capital controls exist when a government places restrictions on capital-account transactions, using domestic currency to purchase foreign financial assets, such as foreign currencies and securities, and certain nonfinancial assets, such as real estate.

Most of us would agree that cash and commodity convertibility are desirable. Yet economists like Hanke and Schuler[23] advise developing countries to delay full FX convertibility. Hanke and Schuler put forward three arguments to support this notion. First, the introduction of full convertibility would worsen capital flight—domestic investment would leave on a large scale. Second, immediate full convertibility would allow excessive FDI, thereby making the domestic export goods uncompetitive because FDI increases the prices of land, labour, and other nontraded goods. Prices of exported goods would then increase because they are made partly from nontraded goods. A large, sudden appreciation of the real exchange rate could make exports uncompetitive, causing a national economic depression. A third argument against immediate full convertibility is that it would create problems of moral hazard. "Chile, Argentina, and Uruguay all suffered banking crises in the 1980s after they abolished some restrictions on convertibility. Many companies and banks borrowed heavily abroad. Their liabilities were payable in foreign currency but their income was mainly in domestic currency. As real exchange rates appreciated, political pressure from export industries and economic pressure from currency speculators induced the central banks of those countries to devalue. Devaluation steeply increased the burden of debt repayment for companies and commercial banks that had borrowed in foreign currency, and bankrupted many. Their governments or central banks rescued them and assumed responsibility for repaying their debts."[24]

Insurance for Government, Business, and Individuals

Since most, if not all, of the transactions in the world involve currencies, the FX market has an incredible reach of influence into every financial facet including the equities and bond markets, private property, and manufacturing assets. Currency volatility presents risk to governments, business, and individuals. The FX market provides "insurance" to remove and/or mitigate the risk. Currency rates determined by this market play a vital role in the financing of government deficits, as well as equity ownerships in real estate holdings, and in other companies. The influence of the FX market affects purchasing power, and therefore your everyday personal and business consumption decisions. When a nation lowers the value of its currency it is called **devaluation** while raising the currency value is called **revaluation**. In 2005, China revalued its currency in response to pressure by the United States when the foreign exchange rate gap between the two currencies continued to result in huge trade deficits for the United States. (Recall the observation in the Opening Thoughts of this chapter, pages 226–227.) This is not the same as referring to a currency as being strong or weak. In 2005, the Canadian dollar was a strong currency and was referred to by many traders as a "petrodollar." Petrodollars are defined as the U.S. dollar (currently) earned from the sale of oil, or they may be simply defined as oil revenues currently denominated in U.S. dollars. A strong Canadian petrodollar has significant implications to Canada's economy at both the macro and micro levels.

Consider the example of a Canadian company like Canfor, an integrated forest products firm that insures itself against such risk. Up to 80 percent of Canfor's "product is sold in US dollars to customers located all over the world. The US dollar is called the **price of determination** because all sales of pulp and paper are denominated in US dollars."[25] Suppose Canfor enters into a contract for US$20 million worth of product. The terms of the contract provide that Canfor will receive the US$20 million payment into its U.S. dollar account in one month's time. This receivable presents significant risk. For 30 days, Canfor is exposed to rate of exchange volatility between the Canadian petrodollar and the U.S. dollar. This can be a significant risk. As a Canadian company, it will have to repatriate those U.S. dollars at some point because management has decided that FX risk is not something that they are prepared to carry. Canfor has deemed it to be peripheral to their core business. The problem has two dimensions: uncertainty and opportunity.[26]

If Canfor does not hedge the transaction in any way, it cannot know with any certainty at what rate of exchange it will be able to exchange the US$20 million for Canadian dollars after it has been paid into the company's U.S. dollar account. It could be at a better, or a worse, rate than the rate prevailing at the time of the contract. It is a gamble. What do you think the exchange rate between the two currencies will be 30 days from now? Consider today's (August 30, 2006) prevailing **spot rate** at 1.110 and the prevailing one-month-forward outright rate of 1.1091 at which Canfor could hedge. (These rates are published in the daily financial papers and are available in real time

Video 8.1

Devaluation is the lowering of the value of a country's currency by its government.

Revaluation is the raising of the value of a country's currency by its government.

In the case where all sales worldwide of a given commodity or product are denominated in U.S. dollars, the U.S. dollar is called the **price of determination**.

A **spot rate** is the FX rate at which two currencies can be exchanged in two days' time.

online.) Let's say that Canfor decides to enter into a forward contract in which it obligates itself to buy Canadian dollars and sell U.S. dollars for delivery on the same date as the delivery date of its pulp-and-paper contract (30 days into the future). The good news—the company has removed uncertainty. Management knows what the currency exchange rate will be 1.1091. The financial managers can now factor this cost into the contract price. They now know with certainty how much money they will receive in 30 days as a result of this contract. This is a double-edged sword. They have now taken on the infinite risk of opportunity loss. If the Canadian dollar weakens because of some unforeseen event like a significant drop in the price of oil that in one month's time results in a prevailing spot rate of 1.1400, then they have foregone CDN$580,000 additional profit that they could have made on the currency volatility. This is their **lost opportunity**. Why would they use this lottery ticket? The exchange rate could also increase to 1.0700 in relationship to the U.S. dollar. In this event, such a change would mean Canfor would lose about CDN$580,000 from the contract price. Such a loss might represent the entire net profit anticipated from the transaction. Business decision makers want stability and predictability in their currency dealings.

> **Lost opportunity** is a description for investments that are not earning the current available rate of return.

Currency Exchange Rate Volatility

Financial managers must understand hedging instruments, which address certainty and opportunity loss. These instruments are like insurance policies and are called derivatives or derivative products. Most financial institutions make markets for the risk management instruments involving derivative products, either as stand-alone instruments or as packages or combinations of instruments. You do not have to know the details of the derivative products, but you must know they exist and when you should seek expert advice in order to manage risk by acquiring one or more of these insurance policies. One such derivative is an FX option. A **foreign exchange option** provides a company with the right but not the obligation to buy, for example, Canadian dollars and sell U.S. dollars at a pre-set strike price. The strike price will vary day to day with the movement in the Canadian dollar/U.S. dollar exchange rate. If the Canadian dollar gets stronger, the Canadian dollar **call** becomes more valuable. If the Canadian dollar gets weaker, the Canadian dollar call becomes less valuable. Instead of entering into a forward contract to buy Canadian dollars, Canfor in our example above could purchase a Canadian dollar call with a strike price at 1.1091 for a premium from one of its financial institution counterparties.[27] Doing so reduces the certainty of the rate that the Canadian pulp and paper company, in this example, will repatriate the U.S. dollars received, but it also limits the worst-case exchange scenario by allowing it to enjoy potential opportunity gains, again conditioned by the premium paid. Figure 8.1 shows the exchange rate between the U.S. dollar and the Canadian dollar from a low of 63 cents in January 2002 to January 2005. By summer 2006, it had broken the 90-cent mark. Swings like this can cripple firms, so hedging instruments must be considered by business decision makers.

> A **foreign exchange option** on the Canadian dollar gives a company the right but not the obligation to buy, for example, Canadian dollars and sell U.S. dollars at a pre-set strike price that will vary on a day-to-day basis with the movement in the Canadian dollar/U.S. dollar exchange rate.
>
> A **call** is an agreement that gives an investor the right, but not the obligation, to buy a stock, bond, commodity, or other instrument at a specified price within a specific time period.

"Derivatives, just like any other economic mechanism, are best thought of in terms of tradeoffs. The tradeoffs here are between uncertainty and opportunity loss."[28] However, a Canadian dollar call is only one of the possible risk management solutions for Canfor to consider. There are dozens of possible hedging instruments, each having a different tradeoff between uncertainty and opportunity loss, that the pulp-and-paper company could use to manage this exposure to changes in the exchange rate. The key to hedging is to decide which of these solutions is the right fit for the firm's needs . . . remember the characteristics of risk-taking and risk-averse personalities? Hedging is not just about entering into a forward contract; "hedging is about making the best possible decision, integrating the firm's level of sophistication, systems and the preferences of their shareholders."[29] Here are some others.

FIGURE 8.1

The Canadian Dollar, Currency Exchange Rate Volatility

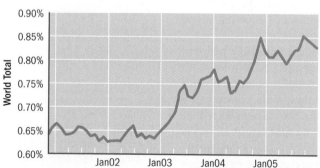

Other Instruments for Insuring against FX Risks

In addition to the instruments we have just discussed, there are other more sophisticated instruments that could be considered by business decision makers to accommodate volatility and risk in their foreign exchange dealings.

FORWARD RATE AGREEMENTS

Forward rate agreements can be used to manage (insure) short-term interest rate risk. Financial managers manage short-term interest rate exposure by adjusting maturities on commercial paper issuance or changing from one **LIBOR** reset (LIBOR interest rate adjustment) option to another on bank debt. LIBOR is the London Interbank Offered Rate (LIBOR), the interest rate charged by one international bank to another for lending money. "Borrowers lengthen maturities when rates are expected to rise and shorten them when they expect rates to drop. Sometimes, however, market movements can outstrip the financial decision maker's abilities to manage rate exposure using cash market alternatives alone. Forward Rate Agreements (FRAs) were invented to fill this gap. FRAs offer a simple way to manage short-term rate exposures without tying up the balance sheet."[30]

> **LIBOR** is the London Interbank Offered Rate, the interest rate charged by one international bank to another for lending money.

What are **forward rate agreements**? "An FRA is a tailor-made futures contract . . . to fix a future interest rate today, for example, the 6 month LIBOR rate for value 3 months from now . . . When the future date arrives, the FRA contract rate is compared to the actual market LIBOR. If market rates are higher than the contract rate, the borrower/FRA buyer receives the difference; if lower, he pays the difference. For the investor/FRA seller, the FRA flows would be reversed. Underlying borrowing or investment programs proceed normally at market rates, while the compensating payment provided by the FRA brings the hedgers' all-in cost or yield back to the base rate contracted for in the FRA."[31] Firms use FRAs to protect short-term borrowing or investment programs from market surprises. Firms that plan to borrow in the future would use FRAs to lock in a future borrowing base rate at a level lower than today's rates.

> A **forward rate agreement** is a tailor-made futures contract to fix a future interest rate today. When the future date arrives, the FRA contract rate is compared to the actual market LIBOR. If market rates are higher than the contract rate, the borrower/FRA buyer receives the difference; if lower, he pays the difference. For the investor/FRA seller, the FRA flows would be reversed. Firms use FRAs to protect short-term borrowing or investment programs from market surprises. Firms that plan to borrow in the future would use FRAs to lock in a future borrowing base rate at a level lower than today's rates.

SWAPS

Business practitioners managing interest rate risk can also consider swaps—interest rate and cross-currency swaps.

INTEREST RATE SWAPS Among the most popular of the derivative hedging instruments is the **interest rate swap**. Corporations, government entities, and financial institutions use them to manage interest rate risk. Swaps have application to a wide range of hedging needs and can be easily tailored to match a specific risk profile. Because of their simplicity and flexibility, they have become the workhorse of the risk manager's toolbox. "An interest rate swap is an agreement to exchange interest payments in a single currency for a stated time period. Note that only interest payments are exchanged, not principle. Swap terms are customized to meet the user's specific risk management objectives. Terms include starting and ending dates, settlement frequency, the notional amount on which swap payments are based, and reference rates on which swap payments are determined. Reference rates are published rates such as LIBOR [see Chapter 9, page 268] or benchmark Treasuries, or customized indexes crafted to meet the clients' needs."[32]

> An **interest rate swap** is an agreement to exchange interest payments in a single currency for a stated time period. Note that only interest payments are exchanged, not the principal.

"Treasurers use swaps to hedge against rising interest rates and to reduce borrowing costs. Among other applications, swaps give financial managers the ability to convert floating rate debt to fixed rate or from fixed rate to floating rate; lock in an attractive interest rate in advance of a future debt issue; position fixed rate liabilities in anticipation of a decline in interest rates; and arbitrage debt price differentials in the capital markets. Financial institutions, pension managers and insurers use swaps to balance asset and liability positions without leveraging up the balance sheet and to lock-in higher investment returns for a given risk level."[33] Governments also use interest rate swaps.

Since 1985, Canada's federal government has used swaps to manage liabilities in a cost-effective and flexible manner. The federal government's swap program has been cost effective with savings estimated to exceed $500 million.[34]

COMMON SWAP STRUCTURES   The most basic swap is an exchange of floating-rate interest payments for fixed-rate payments. "For example, a company that has cost-effective floating rate bank debt can use its floating rate borrowing power to create fixed rate debt. To do this, the company enters into a swap to the target maturity (e.g., five years), agreeing to exchange floating-rate payments based on LIBOR for a five year fixed rate."[35] Using swaps, the firm avoids the costs of issuing long-term debt, and gains the protection of a fixed rate, while retaining the cost advantage its bank debt enjoys.

Other typical swap applications include "fixed-for-floating swaps that allow a company to lock in liquidity through issuing long-term debt, but to pay a floating rate. The swap positions the company to gain from a decline in short-term interest rates; forward starting swaps lock in the rate today for an asset or liability to be created or sold in the future. A company that plans to issue [a] fixed rate instrument at a future date can use a forward-starting swap to hedge the future issuance rate. Forward-starting swaps allow companies to exploit favourable rates when the market offers them, not just when coming to market. Locking in the forward financing costs or investment yields allows the hedger to accurately budget cash flows and expenses related to future projects . . . Other swap structures can be created to meet different needs. This flexibility is why many companies find that interest rate swaps are an invaluable tool in managing the financial balance sheet."[36]

CROSS-CURRENCY SWAPS   A **cross-currency swap** provides a firm with the opportunity to reduce borrowing costs in both domestic and foreign markets. They are also a simple and effective solution to long-term currency hedging needs. Investors can use cross-currency swaps to manage the currency risk in foreign investment portfolios and to create synthetic assets with a specific currency risk profile. For example, a synthetic security is a Japanese investor who wants a zero coupon bond denominated in yen. Currently Japan does not have this instrument available. Therefore, the Japanese investor will create (synthesize) one from a Canadian Treasury Bill–backed zero coupon bond. A zero coupon bond is more commonly referred to a stripped bond. A stripped bond has the interest portion of the bond stripped from the instrument. Utilizing the asset swap market, the Japanese investor achieves the desired risk exposure by buying the Canadian Treasury Bill stripped bonds. In effect, the Japanese investor has exchanged a yen/Canadian dollar swap. The principal amounts of the stripped bonds will be exchanged at maturity.[37] "A cross-currency swap involves the exchange of payments denominated in one currency for payments denominated in another. Payments are based on a notional principal amount the value of which is fixed in exchange rate terms at the swap's inception. Periodic swap payments are made in the appropriate currencies based on specified reference interest rates. When the swap matures, a final payment representing the change in the value of the swap notional principal is made between the parties to the swap. Alternatively, the principal values can be re-exchanged at maturity at the original exchange rate. Because currency swaps involve exchange risk on principal, the credit risk associated with these transactions is substantially greater than with interest rate swaps."[38]

APPLYING CURRENCY SWAPS   "Corporations and financial institutions use currency swaps to manage the exchange and interest rate risks associated with foreign currency financing and investing. Currency swaps are also valuable as long-term hedges of translation risk and in many instances represent an attractive alternative to long-dated forward FX cover. Currency swaps can be used in a variety of situations. By using those companies can:

- "*Tap foreign capital markets for low-cost financing.* The ability to swap interest payments related to financing denominated in foreign currency allows domestic debt

A **cross-currency swap** involves the exchange of payments denominated in one currency for payments denominated in another. Payments are based on a notional principal amount, the value of which is fixed in exchange rate terms at the swap's inception.

issuers to tap new markets, expand the investor base, and lower borrowing costs. Foreign debt issues by top-rated companies are well received by foreign investors seeking to diversify credit risks and can be quite cost-effective compared to domestic issues. Through cross-currency swaps the debt is converted to the issuer's domestic currency, eliminating currency risk while preserving the cost advantages achieved by issuing offshore."[39]

- "*Lower financing costs for foreign subsidiaries.* Companies operating foreign subsidiaries typically prefer to finance operations in local currency to eliminate currency risk. While borrowing locally may sometimes be cost effective, the parent firm can often borrow more cheaply in its home market and base currency. Currency swaps provide the bridge to exchange-protected, least-cost financing for offshore operations."[40]

- "*Enhance buyer financing programs.* Many companies provide long-term buyer finance programs to support sales efforts. Hedging the currency and rate risk of competitively priced programs for offshore buyers is another area where currency swaps add value. Buyer financing is extended in the customer's currency of choice then swapped to the seller's local currency to eliminate exchange risk. In countries where export incentive programs are available, currency swaps allow borrowers to access incentive pricing without accepting unwanted currency and rate risk."[41]

"Cross currency swaps are an essential tool in managing cross-border business and investment activities. Their simplicity and flexibility in many different applications have made cross-currency swaps among the most frequently used derivative instruments in the corporate arena."[42]

Figure 8.2 provides the cross rates on major currencies. These are the price of one country's currency expressed in another country's currency; the rate at which one currency can be exchanged for another. You will note from the table that the Canadian dollar could have been exchanged for 1.1100 US dollars or 2.1136 British pounds on August 30, 2006. These tables are available from global capital markets sources in real-time.

Arbitrage

Since 1973, speculators like George Soros have made money using the instruments we have discussed in this chapter, as well as other instruments we have not discussed. The last and unintended function of the FX market is arbitrage. **Arbitrage** is attempting to profit by exploiting generally temporary price differences of identical or similar financial instruments, on different markets or in different forms. Occasionally, for a very few seconds, small discrepancies occur between spot price quotes in different global markets (see Figure 8.3, page 236). These discrepancies can be much less than a penny but by buying and selling identical large amounts of currency on the two global

Arbitrage (financial), as it refers to pricing differentials in financial instruments, is the attempt to profit by exploiting temporary price differences of identical or similar financial instruments, on different markets or in different forms.

	Canada dollar	U.S. dollar	British pound	Euro	Japan yen	Swiss franc
Canada dollar	–	1.1100	2.1136	1.4233	0.009481	0.9029
U.S. dollar	0.9009	–	1.9041	1.2823	0.008541	0.8134
British pound	0.4731	0.5252	–	0.6734	0.004486	0.4272
Euro	0.7026	0.7799	1.4850	–	0.006661	0.6344
Japan yen	105.4741	117.0763	222.9301	150.1213	–	95.2304
Swiss franc	1.1076	1.2294	2.3410	1.5764	0.010501	–

FIGURE 8.2
Cross Rates on Major Currencies

SOURCE: *BMO Economics: Daily FX Rates* (BMO Financial Group, August 30, 2006).

FIGURE 8.3
Currency Spot and Forward Rates

Mid-Market Rates for Large-Volume Transactions in Toronto at Noon, April 24, 2006.

U.S./Can.		$1 U.S. in Cdn.$=	$1 Cdn in U.S.$=	Country		Cdn.$ per unit	U.S. $ per unit
SPOT		1.1373	0.8793	Britain	(pound)	2.0288	1.7839
1 month	forward	1.1364	0.8800	1 m	forward	2.0278	1.7844
2 months	forward	1.1354	0.8808	2 m	forward	2.0270	1.7853
3 months	forward	1.1344	0.8815	3 m	forward	2.0263	1.7863
6 months	forward	1.1312	0.8841	6 m	forward	2.0238	1.7891
12 months	forward	1.1256	0.8884	12 m	forward	2.0195	1.7941
3 years	forward	1.1113	0.8998	Europe	(euro)	1.4076	1.2377
5 years	forward	1.0988	0.9101	1 m	forward	1.4091	1.2400
7 years	forward	1.0873	0.9197	2 m	forward	1.4107	1.2425
10 years	forward	1.0718	0.9330	3 m	forward	1.4121	1.2448
				6 m	forward	1.4159	1.2517
				12 m	forward	1.4221	1.2634
Cdn.$	High	1.1299	0.8850	Japan	(Yen)	0.009895	0.008700
in 2006:	Low	1.1794	0.8479	1 m	forward	0.009927	0.008736
	Average	1.1537	0.8668	2 m	forward	0.009961	0.008774
				3 m	forward	0.009994	0.008810
				6 m	forward	0.010092	0.008922
				12 m	forward	0.010279	0.009132

SOURCE: BMO Financial Group, *Currency Spot & Forward Rates* (BMO Financial Group 2005). Copyright Bank of Montreal 1996–2003.

Hot money refers to funds that flow into a country to exploit small differences in interest or exchange rates. Because these funds are rapidly shifted between FX markets to increase profits, hot money is highly volatile and a major factor in capital flight from developing countries. These types of transactions were largely responsible for the currency crises in Mexico and Asia during the 1990s.

markets, spectators can make money. Speculating on interest rate differentials can also be a lucrative source of revenue for speculators. However, this may not be a good thing. Because of the high-tech and globally linked trading systems, **hot money** can move electronically in real time anywhere in the world overnight for short-term currency trades. This presents potential risk for financial currencies. Recall the discussion in Chapter 1, page 7, concerning the financial crisis experienced by Thailand and other Asian nations and speculators' involvement. Can the FX market do anything to reduce this risk?

INTERNATIONAL STRATEGIC THINKING

Sometimes what starts out as a hedge ends up looking like an outright bet—and a wild one at that. Just ask analysts following Baxter International Inc., who are wondering why the Deerfield, Ill., medical-products company in 2002 opted for a hedge that locked in the dollar's movement against the euro—for four years. That is a staggeringly long term by the standards of most currency hedges, particularly in a world where global fortunes, and therefore exchange rates, can change in a matter of months or weeks. Most companies hedge out currency exposure for a period of six or 12

months. The hedge, effectively a bet that the dollar would continue to rise against the European currency, is costing Baxter and its shareholders plenty. But the company's current management "is not responsible for these problems," says Glenn Reicin, who covers the company for Morgan Stanley. Former Baxter Chairman and Chief Executive Officer Harry M. Kraemer Jr. resigned last year amid discontent about the company's financial performance and share price and was succeeded in April by current CEO Robert L. Parkinson Jr. Specifically, Baxter aimed to fix the exchange rate for

products it made in the U.S. and sold in Europe. So in 2002 it entered into a type of hedge that guaranteed every euro of goods it sold would be valued at 95 cents against the euro.

Today, [January 6, 2005] one euro fetches $1.3260 (U.S.), nearly 40% above the rate Baxter locked in. Normally, a declining dollar boosts a US firm's revenue when foreign-currency sales are translated back into the home currency. But by locking in that 95-cent rate, Baxter lost the currency kick to its earnings. "We view these hedges as more of a bet on the direction of the dollar—and one that turned out to be wrong," Morgan Stanley analysts wrote in a recent report. "We project that these hedges have significantly cost the company in potential earnings upside." Indeed, Baxter's hedging headache comes at a time when many U.S. companies have been the beneficiaries of the dollar's decline as their goods become cheaper abroad. The top 25 U.S. companies made 43% of their revenue abroad, with international sales up 15% from the previous year, according to Morgan Stanley, with most of these gains because of the dollar's move. The matter also shows how the derivatives that are the tools of many hedging programs can be a mix of blessing and curse: Used wisely, these products, which derive their value from an underlying asset, can minimize volatility and protect gains. But poorly executed or used over a long period of time, they also can amplify the very losses they are designed to minimize.

Baxter's plight goes beyond the currency hedges. Baxter also entered into another type of transaction that it refers to as net-investment hedges to protect the value of its European assets, including its European facilities and inventory, according to a Baxter spokeswoman. These hedges were in the form of so-called cross-currency swaps that fix the exchange rate between dollars and euros. The spokeswoman says these swaps originally were slated to be in place until 2009, although the company is now unwinding some of these—albeit at a cost. By the end of the company's third quarter on Sept. 30, the total market value of the losses on what the company refers to as the "net investment hedge portfolio" amounted to $956 million, according to a presentation by Chief Financial Officer John Greisch on an Oct. 21 conference call. Because the company has decided to "reduce the level of financial risk associated with these hedges," Mr. Greisch added on that call, Baxter was in the process of entering into offsetting hedges. That means, he said, that half the losses, or $478 million, will be locked in. By the end of the third quarter the company had locked in about 30% of the loss, or $296 million. Baxter planned to lock in the remainder of that $478 million in the fourth quarter just ended. The company expects the cost of entering into such offsetting hedges will amount to some $338 million in 2005 and will reduce cash flow by that amount, the spokeswoman says.

Meanwhile, the Morgan Stanley analysts calculate that the first type of hedges will have cost the company 37 cents a share over their four-year life.

The Baxter spokeswoman declined to comment on the per-share cost to the company of its hedges. In 2003, Baxter had net income of $866 million, or $1.43 a share, on sales of $8.9 billion. An irony for Baxter is that when its hedges finally lapse, its financial performance will look better compared with the previous year. "This ultimately reverses when the contracts expire and helps support our view that [earnings-per-share] growth in 2006 will be significant," Morgan Stanley analysts wrote in a December report. That leaves the remainder of the cross-currency swaps. "They will be settled as they mature or possibly sooner, depending on the level of our cash flow," the Baxter spokeswoman says. "There will be additional costs."

Source: Henny Sender, "Tracking the Numbers/Outside Audit: Baxter's Hedge in 2002 Turned into Costly Bet; Four-Year Lock of Dollar against Euro Means Loss of a Currency Kick to Profit," (*Wall Street Journal Eastern edition*, January 6, 2005). Copyright © 2006 Dow Jones & Company, Inc. All Rights Reserved.

CRITICAL THINKING QUESTION
Should businesses be gambling (hedging)? It certainly cost Baxter and its shareholders plenty betting that the dollar would continue to rise against the European currency.

How Can the FX Market Reduce Currency Speculation?

One suggestion that seems to have merit was that of James Tobin, Ph.D., a Nobel laureate economist at Yale. Tobin advocated for the implementation of a simple sales tax on currency trades across borders. The purpose of the tax is to discourage overnight or short-term currency trades, the most volatile, while leaving longer-term investments barely affected. Tobin's tax would seem to be a win-win proposition. It would slow the flow of hot money across borders, thereby potentially preventing financial currency crises. "Currency speculators trade over $1.9 trillion dollars each day across borders. The market is huge and volatile. Each trade would be taxed at 0.1 to 0.25 percent of volume (about 10 to 25 cents per hundred dollars). This would discourage short-term currency trades, about 90 percent speculative, but leave long-term productive investments intact. The currency market would thus shrink in volume, helping to restore national economic autonomy. Nations again could intervene effectively to protect their own currency from devaluation and financial crisis. Billions in revenue, estimated at $100[billion]–$300 billion per year, would be generated. Revenue could go into earmarked trust funds to fund urgent international priorities."[43] Tobin taxes can be enacted domestically by national legislatures, but they require multilateral cooperation to be effectively enforced.

JUST DOING THE RIGHT THING

France First to Support Tobin Tax

France was the first major industrialized country to support a tax on international financial transactions (in 2001). The Prime Minister said he was responding to the concerns of the anti-globalization movement, which has a strong base in France among farmers and intellectuals. The French pressure group, Attac, which has been campaigning for the Tobin tax, welcomed the move. A UK campaign group, War on Want (WoW), called for Britain to follow France's lead. The Chair of WoW noted if the Tobin tax was to be implemented, we really could change the lives of millions in the developing world by raising some serious money and calming world markets at the same time. It has the advantage of combining regulation of the international financial system with a means of raising money for development to counteract the falling aid budgets of most rich countries. Those opposing the tax claim the tax would destabilize foreign exchange markets, be difficult to implement, and would not hit the speculators it was designed to curb. In addition, many economists who believe in free capital markets claim it would be impossible to enforce and counter-productive if it prevented necessary exchange rate adjustments and capital flows to poor countries.

Source: Steve Schifferes, *France Backs Tobin Tax* (BBC News, 2001). Copyright British Broadcasting Corporation, 2006.

To date, while many see the merit in such an initiative, only a few national legislators are considering implementing it. See Just Doing the Right Thing—France First to Support Tobin Tax.

How FX Works

The first step in FX trading is to understand currency quotes. Since FX is the simultaneous purchase and sale of two currencies, the quote will always be given in pairs. Each pair has a base currency, which is the first listed currency (e.g., CDA/USA). When the quote rises, it means that the base rate has strengthened in value, since $1 could buy more francs, and vice versa. The base rate, which is normally the U.S. dollar, is set to a value of $1. There are a few major pairs in which the dollar is not the base currency, such as the Canadian dollar (CDND/USD), the British pound (GBP/USD), the euro (EUR/USD), and the Australian and New Zealand dollars (AUD/USD, NZD/USD). If the GBP/USD rises in price, then the British pound is rising in purchasing power versus the U.S. dollar.[44] Figure 8.4 shows a sampling of selected currency quotes from the financial pages that are published daily. Remember the FX rates are available in real time and will vary from the quotes you read in the paper.

Determination of FX Exchange Rates—Why Do They Go up and Down?

The two principal ways of determining the FX rate are either to fix it against another currency or to allow it to float freely in the market and find its own level. These two systems are respectively known as "fixed" rates and "floating" rates. These monetary systems (and others) are extensively covered in Chapter 9, pages 261–263. You can also

FIGURE 8.4
Selected Quotes (August 30, 2006)

Rate	Bid/Ask	High	Low
EUR/USD	1.2837/40	1.2840	1.2833
USD/JPY	117.08/12	117.19	117.04
USD/CHF	1.2273/78	1.2280	1.2270
GBP/USD	1.9045/50	1.9051	1.9033
AUD/USD	0.7626/30	0.7636	0.7625
USD/CAD	1.1083/88	1.1096	1.1077
EUR/JPY	150.30/34	150.40	150.24

SOURCE: Forex Quotes, (FOREX.com, August 30, 2006). © 2006 FOREX.com.

visit www.power.nelson.com for an overview of other exchange rate systems. There are four variables to consider in establishing FX rates. These are supply and demand, purchasing power parity, inflation and interest rates, and market psychology.

Supply and Demand

An FX exchange rate is a price like any other price. It is what you give up to acquire something else, in this case another currency. Accordingly, the FX rate establishes the price of one currency relative to another. The price can be set in various ways; the government may fix the rate or the currency could perhaps be linked to something external, like gold or backed by other currencies. (For example, as part of its revaluation, China's central bank cut the yuan's peg to the U.S. dollar and linked the value of the middle kingdom's currency to a currency basket comprising the U.S. dollar, the euro, the yen, and the South Korean won; also included are the Singapore dollar, the British pound sterling, the Malaysian ringgit, the Russian ruble, the Australian dollar, the Thai baht and the Canadian dollar.) However, the most likely method of establishing the FX rate is the marketplace—Adam Smith's invisible hand: demand and supply. Note this is the supply and demand of dollars traded on the FX market and not the amount of dollars in circulation! A high level of demand for the Canadian dollar will force up its price and shift the exchange rate. Where supply is equal to demand it is said to be at the equilibrium exchange rate, as shown in Figure 8.5.[45]

Recall that the demand for Canadian dollars comes from people abroad who are investing in Canada and need dollars, or from firms that are buying Canadian exports. Both will need dollars to pay for the goods and services. The supply comes from people in Canada who are selling dollars. This may be because they have bought goods and services from overseas (imports), or it may simply be that they are investing in another country and need that local currency; they have to sell Canadian dollars in order to obtain the other currency. The equilibrium rate is where supply is equal to demand, and this will change as supply and demand changes. Say, for example, that interest rates increase. This will tend to attract more external investment into Canada. These foreign investors will need to buy dollars and so the demands for Canadian dollars will rise. See Figure 8.6.

Note that in this figure both the exchange rate and the volume of Canadian dollars traded have increased. This will not always be the outcome as other factors may affect the exchange rate at the same time. For example, it will also be affected by whether or not the FX market expected the interest rate increase or not. However, understanding supply of and demand for the Canadian dollar provides a very useful tool for analyzing movements and explaining one of the determinants of the FX rate. In addition to supply and demand, the other determinants—interest rates, inflation, and the market physiology—also help us understand why FX rates go up and down. In order to discuss the other determinants, we need to look briefly at the law of one price and purchase power parity as both are linked to a country's FX rates.

The Law of One Price

The **law of one price** is the economic notion that in an efficient market all identical goods must have only one price because all sellers will seek the highest prevailing price, and all buyers will seek the lowest current market price. In an efficient market, the convergence on one price is instant. The price is said to be instant because, in a perfect market without impediments placed on a willing buyer and seller, they establish the market price without reference to any other party. This law is possible if competitive markets for the goods and services offered for sale are free of transportation costs and trade barriers. If these constraints are removed, the same widget should sell for the same price when the FX rates are compared in all countries. To the extent that the selling price ratio varies, so too should the currencies in question. For example, if a Dodge Caravan sells for CDN$20,000 in Canada and the current FX rate is $1.10 Canadian to US$1, then according to the law of one price, the same car in the United States should sell for US$18,000. Under NAFTA, buyers on both sides of the border can buy from either of the Dodge Caravan sellers.

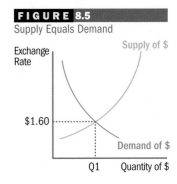

FIGURE 8.5

Supply Equals Demand

FIGURE 8.6

The Equilibrium Rate Following an Interest Rate Hike by the Bank of Canada shifts from D1 to D2

The **law of one price** is an economic law stated as "in an efficient market all identical goods must have only one price."[46]

However, when anomalies exist, for example, if the U.S. dealer sells the same car for US$16,000 with the FX rate remaining unchanged at $1.10, buyers can purchase the U.S. auto for $16,000 and sell it in Canada for a $2,000 profit. This discrepancy in the law of one price gives rise to **arbitrage opportunity**.

An **arbitrage opportunity** is the opportunity to buy an asset at a low price then immediately sell it on a different market for a higher price.

Purchasing Power Parity

The theory of purchasing power parity (PPP) also needs to be understood. Although we discussed it in Chapter 3, page 79, in this chapter we will enhance that understanding as it applies to the FX market. You will agree that if the law of one price was in effect, then we would need only one global price list for all goods and services in order to establish the PPP between nations. But, as we have noted, this is not the case because the market is not efficient; there are transportation costs and trade barriers influencing prices. PPP asserts that in equilibrium, the prevailing exchange rate between two countries will be that which equalizes the prices of traded goods in each country. There is a relationship between the prices of goods and services and FX rates. "Typically, the prices of many goods would be looked at and weighted according to their importance in the economy. Purchasing power parity exchange rates are useful for comparing living standards between countries. However, the actual exchange rates can be a misleading representation of living standards. For example, if the value of the Mexican peso falls by half compared to the dollar, the[n] [Mexico's] gross domestic product measured in dollars will also be halved. However, this doesn't necessarily mean that Mexicans are any poorer. Providing incomes and prices remain quoted in pesos, Mexicans will be no worse off—assuming that imported goods are not essential to the their quality of life."[47] Measuring different countries' income using PPP exchange rates provides a more accurate picture.

One concern with PPP is that the actual content of the PPP is often unclear. When this is the case, the statistical results are deceiving.[48] Recall the simple and humorous example of measuring PPP, the "Big Mac index," which we looked at in Chapter 3, page 80. "If a Big Mac cost US$4 in the US and £3 in Britain, the purchasing power parity exchange rate would be £3 for US$4."[49] It is this exchange rate and the shifts in the ratio that interest us. A shift in the ratio of the U.S. dollar to the pound sterling from 3:4 will indicate that the currency is either overvalued or undervalued depending upon in whose favour the ratio shifts. These relative price changes can be good precursors to FX rate shifts at a future date.

CRITICISM OF PPP

It would be wrong of us to assume that the prices of goods should be equal in all countries because people in different countries usually put different values on the same goods. "What is a luxury good in one country can be ordinary daily goods in another country. PPP disregards this."[50] For example, in Canada, a bicycle is a sports toy; in developing counties it is the main source of transportation. "The exchange rate says how much you can buy in another country with one unit of your own currency. But purchasing power parity exchange rates have nothing to do with how much you can buy because it indicates only the cost of the goods in the PPP basket, indicate the GNI per capita—disposable income."[51] See the Mini Case, page 250, to review an opinion about the value of PPP in establishing currency values. I think you will find it interesting.

Inflation and Interest Rates

The causes of inflation can be explained by looking at aggregate money supply and demand. Figure 8.7 shows how any change in either AS (aggregate supply) or AD (aggregate demand) will cause a change in the price level.

If aggregate demand increases to line AD1 or aggregate supply decreases to line AS2, the price level increases. This we call inflation. If both change simultaneously, the impact of inflation is even more significant. If the inflation is driven by an increase in demand, then it is known as demand-pull inflation; the growth in demand literally pulls up

FIGURE 8.7

Causes of Inflation through Aggregate Money Supply and Demand

prices. "However, if the inflation is caused by a change in aggregate supply, then it is usually known as cost-push inflation. In practice, the two are often linked together as increases in demand may cause labour shortages, which in turn push up wages. Firms, who have to pay the higher wages, are then forced to put their prices up to maintain their margins."[52]

It is also important to look at the role of the money supply in the economy. The quantity theory of money shows how increased growth in the money supply can cause inflation. This happens because the extra money boosts the level of demand for goods and services, and so causes demand-pull inflation. Many today are concerned with the United States' increase in their money supply. This information is available weekly for example in *The Economist*. Anticipated inflation rates also impact a nation's FX rate.

THE FISHER EFFECT

Irving Fisher first stressed the difference between nominal and real interest rates in 1930.[53] Intuitively, most of us would conclude that the interest rate includes some provision for future inflation rates. If interest rates are high then it is expected that inflation rates will be high. So then, the simply stated nominal rate of interest = the real rate of interest + inflation. This is known as the **Fisher effect**.[54] The equation tells us that, all things being equal, a rise in a country's expected inflation rate will eventually cause an equal rise in the interest rate (and vice versa). In 1930, Irving Fisher put forward the notion that the interest rate differential between two countries should be an unbiased predictor of the future change in the spot rate. "Inflation affects interest rates by driving a wedge between nominal (the interest rate unadjusted for inflation) and real interest rates. In the model of rational expectations, the nominal interest rate did all of the adjusting with inflation having no effect on the real interest rate. According to the Fisher effect, if two nations are alike in all other respects but have different inflation rates, the nation with the higher inflation should have the higher nominal interest rates."[55] If we assume that the Canadian inflation rate expected over the coming year is 4 percent while in Germany it is 12 percent, then the nominal interest rates on similar securities should be 8 percent higher in Germany than in Canada.

Consider if the real interest rate in both nations is 2 percent on one-year T-bills, then the nominal one-year T-bill rate in Canada will tend to be 6 percent while in Germany it will tend to be 14 percent. As a result, the differing inflation rates will have two results. Through PPP, the forward premium on the Canadian dollar in respect to the euro is 8 percent (the difference in expected annual inflation rates). Through the Fisher effect, the difference in nominal interest rates on similar securities is 8 percent (the difference in expected annual inflation rates) higher in Germany than in Canada. In essence, if real interest rates are the same globally, then any differential in a nation's interest rate can be attributed to the anticipated inflation. Inflation expectations and interest rates affect the FX rates.

The **Fisher effect** in simple terms is stated by the equation: nominal rate of interest = the real rate of interest + inflation. In addition, Fisher put forward the notion that the interest rate differential between two countries should be an unbiased predictor of the future change in the spot rate.

The International Fisher Effect—An Example

The nominal interest rate is the amount of interest payable translated to money terms. For example, suppose you purchase a term deposit of $100 at your bank for one year and receive interest of $10 at the end of the year. Your balance at year-end would be $110. In this case, the nominal interest rate is 10 percent per annum. The real interest rate, which measures the purchasing power of interest receipts, is calculated by adjusting the nominal rate charged to take inflation into account. If inflation in the Canadian economy has been 10 percent in the year, then the $110 in the account at the end of the year buys the same amount as the $100 did a year ago when you acquired the term deposit. The real interest rate, in this case, is zero. After the fact, the "realized" real interest rate, which has actually occurred, is

$$i_r = i_n - p$$

where p = the actual inflation rate over the year.

The expected real returns on an investment, before it is made, are

$$i_r = i_n - p^e$$

where:

i_n = nominal interest rate
i_r = real interest rate
p^e = expected or projected inflation over the year.
For more examples of the Fisher effect visit www.power.nelson.com.

Market Psychology (Belief-Confidence)

Market psychology—business and individual confidence—is the fourth and final determinant of FX rates that we will examine. People's expectations of inflation can cause inflation. This may sound odd, but consider that you and I build our expectation of inflation into our wage claim; you can see that this in itself can be a cause of inflation. If we expect inflation to be 5 percent in Canada in the near term, we reasonably expect a wage increase in excess of this. If we receive that wage increase, then that may cause further cost-push inflation as firms then face higher costs. The higher inflation may then raise people's expectations further. It is a vicious circle; expectations of higher inflation can actually cause higher inflation. The **consumer confidence index** (a monthly report that expresses how a representative sample of households measures their confidence in the country's current and future economic state) is widely used by FX markets in forecasting future inflation rates.

None of these four attributes can fully explain the FX rates. However, when viewed collectively, supply and demand, PPP, interest rates, and market psychology provide an educated sense of the direction of FX rates. If they were 100 percent accurate, we would all be rich!

The **consumer confidence index** is a monthy report that expresses how a representative sample of households measures their confidence in the country's current and future economic state. This index is widely used by FX markets in forecasting future inflation rates.

Important Global Currencies

Although the United Kingdom remains the hub for FX trading, the U.S. dollar is the preferred currency denomination. As such, it is referred to as the **vehicle currency.** Today in currency transactions, the U.S. dollar, the British pound, the euro, and the Japanese yen are the major global currencies. We will examine two of these as well as a little-known gold-backed currency, the dinar. To date it has acquired little traction but nevertheless it should be watched.

Since 1999, Europe has evolved rapidly and the euro increasingly rivals the U.S. dollar as the preferred world "vehicle" currency.

A **vehicle currency** is one that is often used as the metric to convert funds between two other currencies.

The U.S. Dollar—A Weaker but Still Dominant Dollar

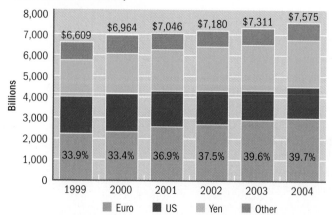

FIGURE 8.8

Euro: A Core World Currency

SOURCE: Dr. Charles Berman, *Overview of Issuance and Investment Development in the Global Local Currency Market* (OECD Headquarters, 2004). © OECD. All rights reserved.

Notwithstanding the recent decline in the value of the U.S. dollar, it continues to dominate global financial markets. It is the world's most heavily traded currency and the one preferred for issuing equities and bonds. However, there are some signs of a moving-away from the U.S. dollar. For example, the Chinese yuan's exchange rate became linked to a basket of currencies in 2005. The euro is gaining notice among the world's central bankers and now rivals the U.S. dollar's role in international finance (2004). See Figure 8.8. "In the past 30 years, the U.S. dollar has had four rounds of marked depreciation."[56] The most recent began in 2002 and continues till now (2006). During this period the U.S. dollar fell "by 28% against the euro and by 14% against a broad basket of currencies. Even so, 66% of the world's official foreign-exchange holdings were in dollars compared with 25% in euros, 4% in yen and 3% in pounds:

according to . . . the IMF."[57] The diminished status of the dollar as the world's reserve currency is attributed to America's economic and foreign policies. If America continues its large current-account deficits and persists in permitting its net foreign liabilities to rise, foreigners will have little choice but to become less willing to take the American "IOUs." Such an event will result in the dollar's depreciation, which in turn will create inflationary pressure in America, thereby further contributing to the growing unattractiveness of holding dollar reserves. The American Federal Reserve, in order to stem the hemorrhage and convince foreigners to hold the IOUs, will have little choice but to increase interest rates. This in turn will put a brake on the American economy. In 2005, the current-account deficit was over 6 percent of U.S. GNP; the highest on record. U.S. net foreign liabilities were also at an all-time high of over 22 percent of GNP. As a result, foreign central banks have commenced reducing their purchases of American Treasury-bills (IOUs). In the first seven months of 2005 foreign central banks raised their holdings of U.S. Treasury bills by only $2 billion. This is troubling as these institutions bought $295 billion in 2004 and $175 billion in promissory notes in 2003.[58] If this trend continues, and there are indications that it will, other currencies may challenge the U.S. dollar's dominance.

Figure 8.9 graphically illustrates the preference for the four major world currencies used in the acquisition and selling of financial products. Since 2004, the gap between the euro and the U.S. dollar as the preferred exchange currency is closing.

This is not a new phenomenon, the British pound experienced a reserve currency shift (meaning most developed countries and others moved away from holding British pounds in their central bank) commencing in 1914 when Britain became a net debtor. It took two decades (until World War II) for the shift to be complete. As a result, the British pound was no longer the preferred world currency for international FX and the global demand for the pound fell as the U.S. dollar assumed this role and was validated by the Bretton Woods agreement. A shift away from U.S. currency would not happen quickly today. Indeed it may involve a shift to more than one main currency reserve. There is some support for the partially gold-backed euro (15 percent gold). Although China and Japan both have an appetite to be considered an Asian global currency, currently neither is likely to achieve this status for a number of reasons. China's capital controls and financial markets are neither transparent nor liquid enough to support such consideration. The impediments in China's rule of law remove any serious consideration of an Asian currency as a global contender in the near future as the yen is not sufficiently attractive to undertake this initiative on its own.

The Euro—A Challenger?

The euro was introduced in Chapter 5, page 130. The euro had a slow start (see the video), but today it is being readily accepted at home where it has lowered interest rates and inflation, and increasingly in global capital markets. Many nations in Eastern Europe and around the Mediterranean are eager to join the European Monetary Union or peg their currency to the euro, or have already adopted the euro as their national currency. The euro

Video 8.2

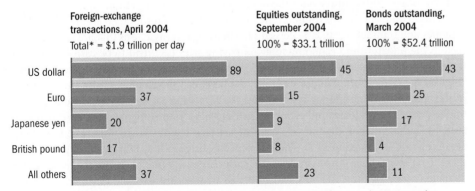

	Foreign-exchange transactions, April 2004 Total* = $1.9 trillion per day	Equities outstanding, September 2004 100% = $33.1 trillion	Bonds outstanding, March 2004 100% = $52.4 trillion
US dollar	89	45	43
Euro	37	15	25
Japanese yen	20	9	17
British pound	17	8	4
All others	37	23	11

*Figures sum to 200%, since there are two currencies in any single foreign exchange transaction.

Source: "Finance and Economics: Currency Competition; Economic Focus," *The Economist*, October 1, 2005.

FIGURE 8.9
Preferred Exchange Currency for Financial Products (percent) (2004)

VIDEO

Video 8.3

is the official currency in 31 states and territories; 10 more will join by 2008 and 8 others may join in the next six years; a further 27 nations peg their own currency to the euro. One of its attractions is that "the Governing Council of the European Central Bank (ECB), decided that gold should be included in the initial transfer of foreign reserve assets to the European Central Bank (ECB) from the national central banks participating in the euro area. The ECB agreed that 15% of this initial transfer should be in gold with the remaining 85% being transferred in foreign currency assets. This decision indicated that European central bankers continued to believe that gold strengthened the balance sheet of a central bank and enhanced public confidence in the euro as a currency. The IMF also confirmed that it saw its remaining gold holdings as giving a 'fundamental strength' to its balance sheet."[59]

However, the euro evolution is not yet complete. "The euro's share of global reserves and of invoicing in international trade remains far smaller than its share of global GDP (22 percent) or the dollar's overwhelming share on both counts (more than 60 percent). European financial markets are still fragmented along national lines."[60] Currently (2005) "Eurozone member countries' economic performances have not improved since the euro's launch, despite the decline in average interest rates. This has contributed in part to the European public's recent resistance to the proposed EU Constitution."[61]

However, the euro is a contender for recognition as a global currency. Indeed, the challenge will intensify if Europe undertakes economic reforms internally and becomes more attractive as a place to invest

The euro will challenge the U.S. dollar's dominance in three areas. The first challenge is that the euro provides investors with an alternative currency that is increasingly widely accepted, with large and growing markets to move to should there be a decline of confidence in the dollar. Indeed, increasingly there are reports many feel such a decline appears imminent because of the United States' balance of payments deficits. During earlier declines, the U.S. dollar was protected because it was "the only game in town" and at that time the available alternative currencies—the yen, pound, and deutsche mark—were not as attractive because of the size of their underlying economies and liquidity. No such limitations apply with the euro. The euro continues to gain market share as a reserve currency, in invoicing of trade, and as a vehicle for financial transactions. Competition from the euro will increase the cost of capital to the United States; in order to retain investment, the United States will have to offer more attractive interest rates and implement national foreign policy that strengthens the confidence in the United States and its dollar. The U.S. capital markets' competitive advantages will soften while demand for the euro as the denomination of transactions increases. This will be compounded by the euro's gold reserves in support of the currency—unlike the U.S. dollar, which is backed only by a promise to pay. U.S. industrial companies will experience increasing uncertainty as more products are sold with euro price tags. This is not to be interpreted as doom and gloom. But rather, as Canadian business practitioners, we must be aware of the possibility of the euro emerging as a strong contender. This will not happen overnight. But history is repeating; the U.S. dollar is undergoing exactly the process of slow decline that undercut the British pound's advantages as a reserve currency over the first half of the 20th century once the dollar emerged as a competitor.

The second challenge is found in the international underground economy. Both illegal activities and transactions that avoid taxes (such as legal transactions that are paid for with cash in the underground economy to avoid paying sales tax) tend to be cash-based. Cash used for this purpose globally creates seigniorage revenues for the issuing government. **Seigniorage** is the profit that, for example, the Bank of Canada makes from the difference in the cost of printing money (paper) and the face value of the money it puts into the marketplace. The underground economy in Eurasia is flourishing, and the euro is readily available in large denomination (€500) notes to facilitate these activities. The U.S. dollar denomination is limited to $100. The result is that the euro is rapidly increasing its market share. True, seigniorage is not a business that any nation wants to be in, but the reality is that demand is growing for €500 bills, which further weakens the demand for the U.S. dollar.

The final challenge offered by the euro is institutional. "Right now, the combined share of Eurozone votes in the IMF and World Bank exceeds that of the US (23 percent

Seigniorage, also spelled seignorage, is the net revenue derived from the issuing of currency. It represents the difference between the face value of the currency and the cost of producing and distributing it. Seigniorage is an important source of revenue for most national governments.

to 17 percent), but is fragmented across 'constituencies,' which include combinations of euro, non-euro, and even non-European countries. Should the Eurozone member-countries consolidate their representation in these institutions (and in the G-8 meetings) [as oil-producing counties did in the 1970s with the Organization of the Petroleum Exporting Countries (OPEC)], the United States would finally have a more decisive and coherent partner for international collaboration and negotiation."[62] Such a consolidation would significantly diminish the United States' influence over the World Bank and the IMF's agenda and priorities.

Established in 1960, OPEC is a cartel with a current membership of 13 oil producers. In 1973–74 and again in 1979–80, OPEC was successful in engineering enormous increases in the price of crude oil. A strong euro could result in OPEC nations and others denominating their sales in euros, or at least away from dollars toward a basket of other currencies, without any significant economic ramifications according to some economists. Over the long term, "'it would be a great mistake not to treat the threat seriously,' said Robert Mondell, a Columbia University professor whose research provided much of the theoretical foundation for the establishment of the euro."[63] Most would agree that the long-term upward trajectory of the euro's role in global finance will come largely at the expense of the U.S. dollar.

The Dinar—A Possible Lightweight?

Increasingly, nations like Iran, Venezuela, Russia, China and others concerned with the health of the greenback and the United States' foreign policy are floating the notion that oil should no longer be linked to the U.S. dollar but rather the euro or some other currency. The impact on Canada of such an eventuality, while extremely serious, should be somewhat mitigated because of Canada's petro dollar. One such initiative in 2006 gaining traction in this economic currency "war" is the gold Islamic dinar as a possible substitute for the U.S. dollar as the currency of choice for certain oil-exporting nations.

The I-dinar[64]

Islamic Gold Dinar Will Minimize Dependency on U.S. Dollar

Malaysia will start using the Islamic gold dinar starting mid-2003 in its foreign trade section with some countries replacing the U.S. dollar in a first step move toward unifying the currency used in commercial dealings between Islamic countries. The success of this idea, according to several western newspapers, may lead to minimizing the U.S. dollar hegemony as an intermediate tool in commercial dealings in the world. The idea was adopted by Malaysian Prime Minister Mahathir Mohamad who conducted bilateral talks during the year 2002 with several Islamic countries, including Bahrain, Libya, Morocco and Iran, to convince them of using the Islamic dinar as a way of payment in their commercial dealings with Malaysia. This move is considered from one side a way to recall a currency related to the history of Muslims and their monetary heritage since the time of Prophet Muhammad (peace be upon him), and from the other side, the ability to find the Islamic alternative to the dollar at a time the calls to boycott all what is labelled as American starting from goods to currency, are intensified.[65]

The idea of the Islamic gold dinar belongs to Professor Omar Ibrahim Fadillo, founder of the Morabeteen International Organization founded in 1983 in South Africa where it is widely known as well as in Europe. The organization believes that the unity of the Islamic world cannot be achieved except through the unification on the economic level. It also calls for the establishment of a united Islamic market using one currency which is the gold Islamic dinar used by the Morabeteen members, hoping it will replace the U.S. dollar. The idea of the Islamic gold dinar aims at minimizing the hegemony of the U.S. dollar and to use the gold once again as an international currency because the value of the paper currencies is in continuous fluctuation unlike the stable gold currency which preserves its value through the value of the metal itself. The system is built on the idea that the Islamic governments keep the gold in a central bank and use it in settling their commercial

A 250 dinar Iraqi note issued after the fall of Saddam Hussein

dealings instead of depending on foreign fund markets and foreign financial corporations. The first Islamic gold dinar, equivalent to 4.25 grams of 22-karat gold, was issued in 1992 on a very limited scale between the members of the Morabeteen.[66]

Several countries around the world are currently dealing directly with 100,000 Islamic gold dinars and 250,000 silver dirhams issued by the company, hoping that one day it will replace the U.S. dollar in the dealings of the 1.3 billion citizens of the Islamic countries. "Consequently, the gold dinar will be the ideal currency to facilitate and increase international trade and minimizing speculation in paper currency that led to the Asian currency crisis in 1997," Dr. Muhammad Sheriff Bashir said. The existence of a fund unity between the countries of the Muslim world will increase the amount of trade between them and will help in increasing the economic development if the conditions for the success of the gold dinar were provided, he added."[67] The dinar has not caught on in the Arab world. However, neither did the concept of the OPEC until 1973, although the concept of OPEC had been discussed for decades.

Since 2003, there have been indications that the notion of "anything but a U.S. currency" is firming up. Consider: "Qatar's central bank governor Abdullah bin Khaled al-Attiyah said [in April 2006] its central bank could hold up to 40 percent of its reserves in euros. As of mid-2005, it held more than 90 percent of reserves in dollars. Kuwait's central bank governor Sheikh Salem Abdul-Aziz al-Sabah said the bank is studying whether the euro is becoming more attractive. The United Arab Emirates central bank is also considering converting 10 percent of its reserves to euros and said it would decide next month [May 2006]. Moreover, Iran said in March [2006] it could switch its holdings out of dollars into other currencies."[68] And even more troubling for the U.S. dollar is "Iran's opening of an Oil Bourse priced in euros (and possibly ultimately in the Islamic Gold Dinar). Originally it announced it planned to open at the end of March 2006. According to the Iran Ministry of Petroleum the delayed opening is a result of 'technical glitches.' No new date has been set. While Pravda on January 21, 2006 indicated that the IOB [Iranian Oil Bourse] opened."[69]

This new oil bourse (exchange) for countries all over the world to buy and sell oil and gas in euros, if successful, will have momentous repercussions on the global FX market. The Iranian exchange will establish "a new oil 'marker' based on Iranian crude and denominated in Euros, in open rivalry to the existing West Texas, Norway Brent and UAE Dubai markers, all of which are currently calculated in U.S. dollars. If the exchange opens as planned it would reduce considerably, over time, the need for dollars by all the Eurozone and as well as much of the rest of the world Russia has already moved in this direction."[70]

Napoleon Bonaparte: War Financing

" In order to finance his invasion of Russia, in 1812 Napoleon Bonaparte set up a factory in Paris to produce a unique product to be "traded" for military supplies. The product? Counterfeit money."[71]

Forecasting Exchange Rates

We understand that it is imperative for decision makers to constantly scan their ecosystems in order to identify emerging issues at the earliest opportunity. This environmental scanning is equally important to financial managers who must "cost" the impact of currency valuation changes to their bottom line when payments are not concurrent with the transaction. We have now reviewed some of the instruments available to financial managers in the FX market to provide hedging insurance against potential losses due to currency depreciation. Can managers predict the future of currency exchange rates? There are two points of view to consider.

The Efficient Market View

The **efficient market view** accepts that the FX rates published in local financial pages are the best possible forecast of future exchange rates.

By using the **efficient market view**, you accept the FX rates published in local financial pages as being the best possible forecast of future exchange rates. This view is based on the notion that in the free FX marketplace all information that can materially affect the future currency price is widely available. Traders (buyers and sellers) of FX currency, having read these materials, establish the rates published in the financial quotes. They are willing to buy or sell the target currency at the published rate at the future fixed date. In essence, you are accepting that this view is as good as any other view.

The Inefficient Market View

Proponents of the **inefficient market view** contend that the efficient market view does not contain all of the data and/or information available. These individuals believe that some lesser-known or private information and/or data must be considered when determining the FX currency future rate. By undertaking an individual analysis to establish the future currency rate, they believe the inefficient market view's results will be more accurate.

> The **inefficient market view** contends that the efficient market view does not contain all of the data and/or information available.

Forecasting Techniques

There are two types of forecasting techniques—fundamental analysis and technical analysis—that can be adopted by proponents of the inefficient market view. A **fundamental analysis** often uses complex models containing a number of fundamental economic indicators in different combinations and permutations that are statistically analyzed in order to forecast the future exchange rate. The fundamental economic indicators used in this model include inflation, money supply, tax rates, interest rates, and government spending. The analysis may also extend to include the nation's balance of payment and any government intervention in the FX markets that may influence the future value of the currency. A **technical analysis** uses charts and past trends in the currency price(s) to predict future FX rate and currency relationships. Technical analysis also uses statistical models of charts containing past trends under known prevailing conditions. An examination of the trends will estimate the timing, directions, and magnitude of future shifts in currency rates.

> A **fundamental analysis** often uses complex models containing a number of fundamental economic indicators in different combinations and permutations that are statistically analyzed in order to forecast the future exchange rate. The fundamental economic indicators used in this model include inflation, money supply, tax rates, interest rates, and government spending.
>
> **Technical analysis** uses charts and past trends in the currency price(s) to predict future FX rate and currency relationships.

Do they work? Neither are 100 percent accurate. There are proponents of each view and forecasting technique. When one fails to meet the forecast, the shortcoming can be traced to analyst error, unforeseen events, incorrect "weighting" of variables, or a list of other reasons. However, this being said, they are the best we have available and the outcomes seem to be the same.

Management Implications

- Understanding the global FX market as part of a company's value chain or to contribute to the economic well-being of the nation is important for decision makers. The FX market presents opportunities and threats that must be exploited or mitigated as they emerge. Astute financial managers can significantly enhance their firm's bottom line by selecting the appropriate hedging instruments to mitigate risk in their global transactions. Financial managers who ignore this aspect of the business do so at their peril.
- Managers, while not able to predict with 100 percent accuracy the direction of FX rates, are able to obtain a sense of the future direction by considering the four determinants. The core problem when deciding upon a hedging policy is to strike a balance between uncertainty and the risk of opportunity loss. In determining the appropriate balance, we must consider our risk aversion, our preferences, and our shareholders. Make no mistake, setting hedging policy is a strategic decision, the outcome of which can make or break a firm.
- The opening of the Iranian bourse may be the end of the monopoly of the U.S. dollar on the global oil market and could potentially affect the dollar as the reserve currency for world trade. The longer-term result is likely to upset the international currency market, as producing countries will be able to charge their production in euros also. In parallel, European countries in particular will be able to buy oil directly in their

own currency without converting to the U.S. dollar. This creates a significant drop in demand for U.S. dollars! This double development will thus head in the same direction, i.e., a very significant reduction of the importance of the dollar as the international reserve currency, and therefore a significant and sustainable weakening of the American currency, particularly compared to the euro. Canadian business leaders must keep an eye on this possible development. Watch for the United States to prevent this from happening using all "tools" available.

- The single most important point to take away from this chapter is that financial risk management is critical to the survival of any corporation. Investors who have real money at risk must understand the exposures facing the firms in which they invest, they must know the extent of risk management undertaken by these companies and they must be able to distinguish between good risk management programs and bad ones. Without this knowledge, they may be in for some very unpleasant surprises.

CHAPTER SUMMARY

- In this chapter, we examined the global FX market. We looked at the relationship between world currencies and how this relationship can be used to influence a nation's economy. Today, individuals, businesses, and governments have little choice but to participate in the FX market in order to travel, and import and export, and for governments to fund public debt. The flow of global capital, facilitated by high-tech communications, operates 24 hours per day.

- When a nation lowers the value of its currency, it is called devaluation. When a government raises the value of its currency it is called revaluation.

- The FX market performs two functions: currency conversion, the provision of "insurance," and a third and unintended function—arbitrage. Arbitrage is defined as attempting to profit by exploiting price differences between identical or similar financial instruments on different markets or in different forms. Tobin advocated the implementation of a simple sales tax on currency trades across borders as a solution to reducing the amount of harmful speculation in the FX market.

- Not all nations' currencies are freely convertible. At times, governments, particularly in developing nations, find it necessary to impose currency restrictions on their currencies' convertibility. By doing this, they preserve the nation's reserve of hard currency needed to repay their debts to other nations. Second, it ensures that they have sufficient hard currency to pay for imports and to finance trade deficits. Third, a government may want to protect the nation's currency from speculators. And finally, restrictions may prevent resident firms and individuals from investing abroad.

- Governments can affect the convertibility of currency by requiring that all financial FX transactions be conducted by the national bank. They can implement an import licensing program, thereby controlling the flow of capital out of the country. They can put multiple FX rates in place, requiring high exchange rates on goods considered nonessential while having lower exchange rates in place to permit the uninterrupted flow of essential goods and service. Finally, governments can require FX import deposits be deposited into special accounts before import licences are issued. Importers can sometimes circumnavigate these obstacles by using countertrade.

- Impediments result in three degrees of currency convertibility: cash, commodity, and FX convertibility.

- Currencies fluctuate in their exchange rate relationship with each other. This volatility in FX rates presents threats and opportunities for financial decision makers. To reduce the risk, governments, businesses, and individuals put hedging instruments in place. Hedging instruments are similar to insurance policies against future losses resulting from FX rate fluctuations. The hedging instruments discussed in this chapter include forward and future contracts, options, and swaps.

- An FX option, for example, on the Canadian dollar, provides the right but not the obligation to buy Canadian dollars and sell U.S. dollars at a pre-set strike price. The strike price will vary on a day-to-day basis with the movement in the Canadian/U.S. dollar exchange rate.

- A forward rate agreement is a tailor-made futures contract to fix a future interest rate today. When the future date arrives, the FRA contract rate is compared to the LIBOR. If market rates are higher than the contract rate, the borrower/FRA buyer receives the difference; if lower, he pays the difference.

- An interest rate swap is an agreement to exchange interest payments in a single currency for a stated time period. Note that only interest payments are exchanged, not principle.
- A currency swap involves the exchange of payments denominated in one currency for payments denominated in another. Payments are based on a notional principal amount, the value of which is fixed in exchange rate terms at the swap's inception.
- The economic law of one price is the notion that in an efficient market all identical goods must have only one price. The reasoning is that all sellers will seek the highest prevailing price, and all buyers will seek the lowest current market price.
- The two principal ways of determining the FX rate are either to fix it against another currency or to allow it to float freely in the market and find its own level. These two systems are respectively known as "fixed" rates and "floating" rates.
- There are four determinants of the FX rates. They are supply and demand, PPP, interest rates, and market psychology.
- The PPP statistic adjusts for cost-of-living differences by replacing the normal exchange rates with rates designed to equalize the prices of a standard basket of goods and services. These are used to obtain PPP estimates of GDP per head. PPP estimates are shown on an index, taking the United States as 100 percent. There are questions as to the value of the PPP as a measure of a country's currency.

- In 1930, Irving Fisher put forward the notion, known as the international Fisher effect, that the interest rate differential between two countries should be an unbiased predictor of the future change in the spot rate.
- People's expectations of inflation can cause inflation.
- The U.S. dollar continues to dominate global financial markets. It is the world's most heavily traded currency and the preferred one for issuing equities and bonds. There are signs the FX markets are moving away from the U.S. dollar, such as the Chinese yuan's linking to a basket of currencies in 2005. The euro is gaining notice among the world's central bankers, and now rivals the U.S. dollar's role in international finance.
- Can managers predict a future currency exchange rate? There are two points of view to consider. The efficient market view states that the FX rates published in local financial pages represent the best possible forecast of future exchange rates. The second, the inefficient market view, contends that the efficient market view does not contain all of the data and/or information available and that decision makers should undertake their own analysis.

REVIEW QUESTIONS

1. What is the FX market? What are its three functions?
2. Discuss the derivative instruments that address both certainty and opportunity loss available to financial managers
3. Provide the currency spot and forward rates reported in today's newspaper.
4. What is the LIBOR?
5. Explain the Fisher effect.
6. The euro is challenging the U.S. dollar's dominance in three areas. Discuss.
7. What is seigniorage?
8. Can managers predict the future of currency exchange rates? If so, what two points of view might they adopt?

REFLECTIVE THINKING QUESTIONS

1. Having completed this chapter, reread the quotations on the first page, critically reflect on the validity of the authors' statements, and provide your opinion as to the validity of each. Evidence-based answers are preferred to rhetorical answers.
2. Speculating on interest rate differentials can be a lucrative source of revenue for speculators. However, this can be a problem; because of technology and globally linked trading systems, money can now move electronically in real time anywhere around the globe overnight or for short-term currency trades. Is it right that government initiatives interfere with this free marketplace?
3. The rapid flow of money across borders has the potential to stimulate a financial crisis. To slow the flow of "hot money," Tobin's tax could be enacted domestically by national ruling bodies. However, they require multilateral cooperation to be effectively enforced. To date, while many see the merit in such an initiative, national legislators have not implemented them. Do you support such a tax? Why has it not been implemented? Discuss.
4. To what extent can we rely on PPP as a component of determining quality of life? Discuss.
5. Do you believe that an Iranian oil bourse will result in a very significant reduction in the importance of the dollar as the international reserve currency. If so, what difference could that make to Canadian business? What steps can political and business leaders take to mitigate the damage or to exploit the opportunity?

GLOBAL E-RESEARCH

Visit www.power.nelson.com for research suggestions, questions, and a number of background discussion papers on this topic.

MINI CASE

How the U.S. Media Exaggerates America's Economic Strengths

. . . One issue that has gotten zero coverage in the press is how the media tends to exaggerate the strength of America's economy these days. And one of the major ways the media exaggerates America's economic prospects is via the widespread usage of a bizarre economic statistic called "purchasing power parity" (PPP) in its coverage of the U.S. and the global economy. PPP is a yardstick that has been used almost exclusively by the U.S. media since around 1985. Up until that time, the media simply used the current values from the world's currency markets—a much more logical and honest approach. (Interestingly enough, the mid-1980s was also a period during which other nations, including Japan and Germany, began overtaking the U.S. in per capita income levels for the first time).

Although at first glance, it might seem like PPP is an obscure topic, best left to specialized economic journals, the truth is the exact opposite. In a nutshell, the media's use of PPP misleads the American public about a number of important issues, not least of which is that it gives the public an exaggerated sense of U.S. economic clout these days. If you look at any story these days in the media that discusses issues like American GDP or U.S. income levels, the PPP figure is always used. As a result, most Americans are under the impression that per capital U.S. income levels are the highest in the world. (In reality, the U.S. is surpassed by 12 other nations in per capita income these days). PPP is basically an artificial creation of economists. It simply does not exist in the real world. Many economists believe that the U.S. dollar is unfairly valued by world currency markets. Thus, under PPP, (as an example) they assign a value of 140 yen to one dollar, Instead of the true market value of 104 yen/dollar. This would be not that big a deal were PPP relegated to obscure academic journals. . . A final major problem is that readers are completely unaware that the figures they see in the media are vastly inflating the value of the dollar. . . . The time has come for the U.S. mainstream media to stop misleading its readers about the strength of today's U.S. economy.

Source: Marc McDonald, "How the U.S. Media Exaggerates America's Economic Strengths" (BeggarsCanBeChoosers.com, March 28, 2005), retrieved August 17, 2006, from www.beggarscanbechoosers.com/2005_03_01_marcmcdonald_archive.html.

MINI CASE QUESTIONS

1. What, exactly, is PPP and how is it calculated? Is this methodology flawed as the author suggests?
2. Why does the U.S. media rely solely on PPP when it discusses issues like U.S. GDP and income levels?
3. When including PPP figures in a story or a chart, for balance, should the media also include world currency market values for the dollar?
4. Do you support the author's contention that the PPP exaggerates America's economic strength?

ENDNOTES

1. *Brainy Quote* (BrainyMedia.com, 2005), retrieved 2005, from www.brainyquote.com.
2. *Quotes* (QuoteWorld, 2006), retrieved August 17, 2006, from www.quoteworld.org.
3. *Brainy Quote.*
4. Quote Garden (The Quote Garden, 2006), retrieved August 17, 2006, from www.quotegarden.com.
5. *Quotations* (ThinkExist.com Quotations, n.d.), retrieved August 17, 2006, from http://en.thinkexist.com/quotes/top.
6. Mark McNeilly, *Sun Tzu and the Art of Business: Six Strategic Principles for Managers* (New York: Oxford University Press, 1996).
7. George J.W. Goodman, *The German Hyperinflation, 1923* (Heights Productions, 1981), retrieved August 17, 2006, from www.pbs.org/wgbh/commandingheights/shared/minitext/ess_germanhyperinflation.html.
8. Habib Neaime and Najwa Neaime, *Background of the Fx Market* (FX Trainer Financial Services, 2003), retrieved August 17, 2006, from http://www.nohypeforex.com/index2/forextrainer/.
9. *Background History* (FX Trainer Financial Services, 2004), retrieved August 17, 2006, from http://www.nohypeforex.com/index2/forextrainer/.
10. Habib Neaime and Najwa Neaime, *Background History* (FX Trainer, 2004), retrieved August 17, 2006, from http://www.nohypeforex.com/index2/forextrainer/.
11. Henry C. K. Liu, *US Dollar Hegemony Has Got to Go* (Asia Times On Line, 2002), retrieved August 17, 2006, from www.atimes.com/global-econ/DD11Dj01.html.
12. *Forex Learning Center* (FXInternationalGroup.com, 2004), retrieved August 17, 2006, from http://fxinternationalgroup.com/center.htm.
13. Investorwords.com, *Over-the-Counter* (WebFinance, 2005), retrieved August 17, 2006 from www.investorwords.com/3557/Over_the_Counter.html.

[14] *Forex Learning Center.*

[15] *Glossary* (Mondovisione), retrieved September 16, 2006, from www.exchange-handbook.co.uk/index.cfm?section=glossary&first_letter=M.

[16] Reuters Professional Products, *Foreign Exchange Markets* (Reuters, 2004). retrieved August 17, 2006, from http://about.reuters.com/productinfo/s/foreign_exchange_markets.

[17] Ibid.

[18] Steve H. Hanke and Kurt Schuler, "Currency Boards for Developing Countries: A Handbook," Institute for Contemporary Studies (San Francisco: Kurt Schuler, ICS Press, 2000). The original version of this study was published by ICS Press, San Francisco, in 1994 for the International Center for Economic Growth. It is copyrighted 1994 by the Institute for Contemporary Studies. This version, updated slightly in June 2000, is being made available electronically by permission of the Institute for Contemporary Studies.

[19] Ibid.

[20] Ibid.

[21] Ibid.

[22] Ibid.

[23] Ibid.

[24] Ibid.

[25] Chand Sooran, *What Is Hedging? Why Do Companies Hedge?* (Victory Risk Management Consulting, n.d.), retrieved August 17, 2006, from www.finpipe.com/hedge.htm.

[26] Adapted from Ibid.

[27] Ibid.

[28] Ibid.

[29] Ibid.

[30] BMO Nesbitt Burns, *Forward Rate Agreements* (BMO Nesbitt Burns, 2005), retrieved August 30, 2006, from www.bmocm.com/products/marketrisk/intrderiv/forwardrate.

[31] Ibid.

[32] BMO Nesbitt Burns, *Interest Rate Swaps* (BMO Nesbitt Burns, 2005), retrieved August 30, 2006, from www.bmocm.com/products/marketrisk/intrderiv/interestswaps.

[33] Ibid.

[34] John Kiff, Uri Ron, and Shafiq Ebrahim, *The Federal Government's Use of Interest Rate Swaps and Currency Swaps* (The Bank of Canada, 2001), retrieved 2005, from http://epe.lac-bac.gc.ca/100/201/301/bank_can_review/2001/winter/revsum.htm.

[35] BMO Nesbitt Burns, *Interest Rate Swaps.*

[36] Ibid.

[37] BMO Nesbitt Burns, *Cross Currency Swaps* (BMO Nesbitt Burns, 2005), retrieved August 30, 2006, from www.bmocm.com/products/marketrisk/intrderiv/cross.

[38] Ibid.

[39] Ibid.

[40] Ibid.

[41] Ibid.

[42] Ibid.

[43] Center for Environmental Economic Development, Tobin Tax Initiative (Center for Environmental Economic Development, 2000), retrieved August 17, 2006, from www.ceedweb.org/iirp/factsheet.htm.

[44] FXInternational, *What Is Foreign Exchange (Fx or Forex)?* (FXInternational Group.com, 2004), retrieved August 29, 2006, from www.fxinternationalgroup.com/center.htm.

[45] Institute for Learning and Research Technology, Markets—Foreign Exchange Market (Bank of Biz/ed, 2005), retrieved August 17, 2006, www.bized.ac.uk/virtual/bank/economics/markets/foreign/theories.htm.

[46] Ibid.

[47] Encyclopedia4U, *Purchasing Power Parity* (Par Web Solutions, 2005) retrieved August 17, 2006, from www.encyclopedia4u.com/p/purchasing-power-parity.html.

[48] Ibid.

[49] Ibid.

[50] Ibid.

[51] Ibid.

[52] Ibid.

[53] Irving Fisher, *The Theory of Interest: As Determined by Impatience to Spend Income and Opportunity to Invest It* (New York: The Macmillan Company, 1930).

[54] Ibid.

[55] Donald R. Byrne, *Financial Economics* (University of Detroit Mercy, 2003), retrieved August 17, 2006, from http://byrned.faculty.udmercy.edu/2003%20Volume,%20Issue%203/Fisher%20Effect.htm.

[56] "Finance and Economics Currency Competition; Economic Focus," *The Economist*, October 1, 2005.

[57] Ibid.

[58] Ibid.

[59] World Gold Council, *The New European Central Bank Decides to Hold Gold* (World Gold Council, July 7, 1998), retrieved August 30, 2006 from www.gold.org/value/reserve_asset/agreements.

[60] Posen, "The Rise of the Euro: Currency Is Emerging as Rival to the Dollar," *The Ripon Forum* (July 2005), retrieved August 30, 2006, from www.iie.com/publications/papers/paper.cfm?ResearchID=537.

[61] Ibid.

[62] Posen, "The Rise of the Euro: Currency Is Emerging as Rival to the Dollar."

[63] Robert Block, "Some Muslim Nations Advocate Dumping the Dollar for the Euro," *The Wall Street Journal*, April 15, 2003.

[64] European Institute for Interest Free Economy, *I-Dinar Working for Just Monetary System* (European Institute for Interest Free Economy, April 7, 2006), retrieved August 17, 2006, from www.ipdirect.home.pl/dinar.

[65] Malaysian Times, *Islamic Gold Dinar Will Minimize Dependency on US Dollar* (European Institute for Interest Free Economy, April 19, 2003), retrieved August 17, 2006, from www.ipdirect.home.pl/dinar/gold_dinar/malaysia/islamic_gold_dinar_will_minimize.htm.

[66] Ibid.

[67] Ibid.

[68] Natsuko Waki, "Analysis—FX Reserve Shift out of Dollars Can Be Costly" (Reuters, April 4, 2006), retrieved August 17, 2006, from http://today.reuters.com/business/newsarticle.aspx?type=tnBusinessNews&storyID=nL0418151&from=business.

[69] David J. Jonsson, "Structural Changes—Destruction of the U.S. Dollar" (*American Daily*, March 25, 2006), retrieved August 17, 2006, from www.americandaily.com/article/12589.

[70] Ibid.

[71] M. Driscoll, ed., "5087 Trivia Questions & Answers" (*Washington Post*, May 12, 2002), retrieved August 17, 2006, from http://anecdotage.com/index.php?aid=1827.

CHAPTER 9

Global International Monetary Systems and Capital Markets

"Global capital markets pose the same kinds of problems that jet planes do. They are faster, more comfortable, and they get you where you are going better. But the crashes are much more spectacular."[1]

—Larry Summers

"Capital as such is not evil; it is its wrong use that is evil. Capital in some form or other will always be needed."[2]

—Mohandas Gandhi

"The globalization of the capital market is actually part of economic globalization. This will create a change in the entire world economy, not just restricted to some fields in some countries."[3]

—Richard Grasso

"In this age of electronic money, investors are no longer seduced by a financial 'dance of a thousand veils.' Only hard and accurate information on reserves, current accounts, and monetary and fiscal conditions will keep capital from fleeing precipitously at the first sign of trouble."[4]

—Larry Summers

"The tax on capital gains directly affects investment decisions, the mobility and flow of risk capital . . . the ease or difficulty experienced by new ventures in obtaining capital, and thereby the strength and potential for growth in the economy."[5]

—John F. Kennedy

LEARNING OUTCOMES

- Understand the drivers and continuing evolution of the international monetary system since the Bretton Woods Agreement of 1944.
- Evaluate the merits of fixed and floating exchange rate systems.
- Evaluate the merits of some of the emerging issues regarding the U.S. dollar as the vehicle currency.
- Evaluate the success and the emerging patterns of the global capital market.
- Understand the functions and institutions of the global capital market.
- Evaluate the evolving role of the International Monetary Fund and its members' Special Drawing Rights.
- Demonstrate an understanding of how the global capital market contributes to the success of international business.
- Demonstrate an understanding of the considerations in selecting global debt instruments.

China's Capital Markets—Change Is Coming Fast

"Much needs to be done to make Chinese capital market more efficient and deeper," says World Bank chief Paul Wolfowitz. China's ruling Communist Party has listed bond market development as a major priority for its next five-year plan. Change is coming fast.

China's corporate bill market, launched earlier this year, is booming as cash-hungry companies seek funding alternatives, asset-backed securities have been given the go-ahead, and the private sector arm of the World Bank and the Asian Development Bank last month became the first foreign issuers of Yuan "panda" bonds in the domestic market. "Important though it was, the move represented but one step in a long process," said Paul Wolfowitz, president of the World Bank. "Much work needs to be done to make the Chinese capital

market more efficient and deeper so it can meet the needs of the businesses that fuel the economy." China must reduce the reliance on banks, which currently provide over 90 percent of the industries' financing requirements. The growing of a world-class capital market is the answer.

Currently "China's bond market is small by Asian, let alone rich-country, standards. For instance, OECD data discloses that China's total corporate bond issuance is just 1 percent of GDP compared with more than 40 percent in Malaysia. State-owned rather than private firms issued just 37 billion Yuan worth of corporate debt in China last year, compared with 135 billion Yuan in A-shares." This lack of performance is due in large part to the constricting bond quota system imposed by China's

National Development and Reform Commission. "In 2005, firms were given the go-ahead to issue such bills. Trade in short-term corporate paper is ... [speeding up] as Chinese companies tap cheaper funding costs of under 3 percent for one-year bills versus the benchmark 5.58 percent interest rate on comparable bank loans."

China also needs a reliable credit ratings system based on global best practices. Currently domestic agencies regularly dole out triple-A credentials to shaky firms. To establish the necessary credibility and global confidence needed, "stock exchange and interbank markets ... need to be linked, interest rate liberalization deepened and red tape slashed. ... The International Monetary Fund "singled out corporate reform as the vital missing ingredient: cozy ties binding state-owned firms to state-owned banks had to be cut.

"Legal framework, laws, regulation and infrastructure, ratings agencies and credit culture are not sufficient conditions for development of a thriving corporate bond market. ... A broader range of bonds would encourage the development of fixed-income institutional investors" who currently are discouraged by the limited investment choices. To establish a viable, vibrant Chinese capital market is within the government's power. But that depends on the political will.

"China Needs Thriving Bond Market" (*Daily Times*, November 2, 2005).

A SUN TZU MOMENT. . .

"Now the resources of those skilled in the use of extraordinary forces are as infinite as the heavens and earth; as inexhaustible as the flow of the great rivers."[6]

THE CRUSADES AND THE RE-EMERGENCE OF BANKING

Before the rule of Henry II, it was the practice in England, as in other feudal countries, for the king's tenants-in-chief and their retainers to owe him a period of military service, usually 40 days annually. Henry replaced this obligation with cash payments known as scutage. This tax was to be segregated to pay for a permanent professional army of mercenaries or soldiers needed for the Crusades. Indeed the modern-day term soldier comes from the solidus or king's shilling that they earned. Henry's expenditures on the Crusades had to be financed by levying heavy taxes on all movable property and all incomes. Unfortunately, while the taxing was successful and huge sums accumulated, Henry refused to spend this wealth until after the disastrous battle of Hattin in 1187. He wanted his cake and to eat it too! As a result of the lack of capital, much of the Holy Land was lost to Saladin.

Henry's successor, Richard I (the "Lion Heart") also needed money for the Third Crusade. Richard sold as many publicly owned assets as possible to raise the capital—a measure that compares to Margaret Thatcher's "privatization" policy in the 1980s, which was copied by governments around the world. Unfortunately, upon returning, he was captured in Vienna and imprisoned by Emperor Henry VI. The ransom demanded far

exceeded the average revenue of the Kingdom of England, but the loyal tenants-in-chief, their retainers, and others paid the ransom (special taxes and gifts) for his release.

However, there was a problem. At that time, payments for supplies, equipment, allies, ransoms, etc. required safe and speedy means of transferring vast resources of cash (hard coin). How could it move from country to country? The Knights of the Temple and the Hospitallers began to provide some banking services. They benchmarked against some very early initiatives developed by some Italian city-states. This led to the development of financial services including bills of exchange (not a new concept as banking had been invented in the Middle East long before of the introduction of coins; however, after the collapse of the Roman Empire, banking was abandoned and forgotten). Fortunately for us today the Crusades gave a great stimulus to its re-emergence.

Adapted from Glyn Davies, *A History of Money from Ancient Times to the Present Day*, 3rd ed. (Cardiff: University of Wales Press, 2002).

Opening Thoughts

The importance of finance in society lies in its ability to unlock human potential—but that all depends on political will. This understanding drives nations to put financial institutions and supporting technology in place to enable competitiveness in the global markets. The global capital markets democratize capital and create jobs. As business practitioners in global markets, you must be able to combine knowledge of international monetary systems with an understanding of risk in order to ensure your success. This chapter's Sun Tzu moment speaks to the importance of leaders understanding and leveraging knowledge to obtain competitive advantage. Capital market structures strengthen the ability of a nation and firms within that nation to succeed.

Global capital markets have expanded dramatically over the last decade, despite the frequency of global shocks (see Figure 9.1).

With a few exceptions, it no longer makes sense to think in terms of national financial markets. Increasingly, national capital markets are being integrated into a single global market as cross-border holdings of financial assets and cross-border flows of capital grow. In 2004, for example, "foreigners held 12 percent of US equities, 25 percent

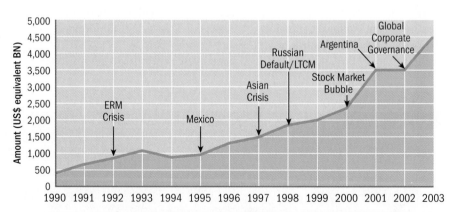

All international issues, including underwritten government bonds but excluding auctions.

SOURCE: Dr. Charles Berman, *Overview of Issuance and Investment Development in the Global Local Currency Market* (OECD Headquarters, 2004). © OECD. All rights reserved.

of US corporate bonds, and 44 percent of Treasury securities, up from 4, 1, and 20 percent, respectively, in 1975. Since 1995, cross-border capital flows have more than tripled, and they now total upwards of $4 trillion annually, including foreign purchases of equity and debt securities, foreign direct investment by corporations, and cross-border bank lending."[7] These flows create stronger integrated, evolving, interdependent links between national markets. Financial institutions that previously enjoyed significant monopoly power increasingly face stiffer competition as a result of globalization, privatization, and deregulation. Borrowers and lenders have welcomed this increased global competition and the benefits it provides. Note that the transformation of the global capital markets is driven by the exponential growth in technology, especially in communications. In the financial industry, **technopoly**[8] has democratized and enabled business and investors to make informed, real-time decisions. There is access to the global capital markets 24 hours a day.

However, there are issues. First, because of the growing global capital markets' interdependency, if one capital market were to "fail" all would be affected. A growing concern, for example, is the United States' current-account debt, which continues to exponentially bloom—to almost 80 percent of GDP in 2005. The United States requires a net capital inflow of over $2 billion every working day to finance its annual shortfall, and much of this is raised in the global capital marketplace. Additional inflationary pressures on the U.S. dollar could be brought about by the Chinese allowing the yuan to continue to appreciate against the U.S. dollar. Permitting a higher inflation level in the United States might be seen as politically expedient as a way to erode the value of its public debt and deficit. Japan and Italy, like the United States, carry extremely onerous debt burdens (with their net public debt around 80 to 100 percent of their GNP). This has not been a problem because, as we have seen, the belief in the strength of the U.S. dollar continues; therefore, the dollar continues to retain the confidence of lending countries globally like China. Will it continue?

In Chapter 8, pages 243–246, we discussed the possible potential shifts from the U.S. dollar to emerging global currencies such as the euro, the dinar, and perhaps an Asian global currency. If any one of these currencies gains traction, the economic monetary shift in the world capital markets will be significant. Canadian business decision makers must monitor these developments.

Capital markets are critical to the economic health of nations. China has insufficient domestic capital to meet its exploding domestic demands, so access to non-domestic funding is essential. From time to time however, governments place restrictions that impede the free flow of capital as illustrated by China's National Development and Reform Commission's imposing a bond quota system in the opening vignette. The current risk assessed by international credit rating agencies like Standard & Poor's is a significant part of the global capital market. These agencies respond to the legal financial framework, regulations, financial infrastructure, and the credit culture. As the Sun Tzu Moment observes, the need to access nondomestic capital is not a new phenomenon; the Knights of the Temple and Hospitallers provided international banking services required by Richard I in order to meet the ransom demands. This underscores that "the resources of those skilled in the use of extraordinary forces [banking] are infinite."[9] Recall that there are structural changes being contemplated in the global "safety nets," such as the role the IMF plays in international monetary systems.

International business decision makers must analyze today's global capital structure in terms of firm, industry, market, economic, societal, and regulatory risks. Decision makers must assess global banking trends, crisis risk of the currency and financial markets, transparency, and the cost and availability of capital for their foreign subsidiaries.

What Is Money?

Capital markets are in large part about the flow of money and derivatives, which we examined in Chapter 8, pages 228 and 232. The value of money depends on the confidence of those who use it. The U.S. dollar is accepted because of the confidence the world's

According to Neil Postman, a **technopoly** is a self-justifying, self-perpetuating system wherein technology of every kind has been cheerfully granted sovereignty over our institutions.

1963.0040.00004/Currency Museum, Bank of Canada

Card money used in New France during the 17th and early 18th century.

nations have in it. In this chapter, we will continue to discuss briefly whether that confidence is eroding and, if so, the impact on the international monetary systems and capital markets.

The Canadian dollar has value internally because it is widely accepted by Canadians and is the means by which we trade for goods and services. Regrettably, global acceptance of the Canadian dollar is declining. Historically, the value of money has been vested in certain objects, including cattle (source of the word "capital"), iron, gold, silver, diamonds, shells, and numerous other things (see New France's money card). Today, vast amounts of money are not even represented by objects—they are merely computer entries in a databank. Whether a tangible object or a computer entry, money is based on a social agreement to recognize its value, which is the very essence of the global capital market.

Card Money 1729

Authorities in New France were just as concerned as their counterparts today that it be easy for the public to use paper money. During the 17th and early 18th century, illiteracy was widespread, and each denomination of card money was a different shape to allow the uneducated to identify the value of their cards.

Source: Currency Museum Bank of Canada, *A New Issue of Card Money* (Industry Canada, n.d.), retrieved September 6, 2006, from http://collections.ic.gc.ca/bank/english/newcdmy.htm.

Money performs three principal functions. First, it is a means of exchange. Without money, we would have to exchange goods and services directly, commonly known as bartering. Money simplifies these exchanges. Second, money is a unit of measurement, allowing us to compare the value of goods and services. It is the metric for pricing goods and services and the metric of buying and selling them. Money enables us to compare costs, income, and profit over time. As a result, money is the foundation of the accounting system that enables us to plan and make economic decisions. Finally, money is a means of banking purchasing power for future use. As a reserve, money allows us to accumulate savings and to lend those savings to someone else. Money makes it much simpler for us to enter into contracts—promising to do something now for payment in the future.[10]

A nation influences its domestic economy, with two levers or tools: **fiscal policy** and **monetary policy**. Fiscal policy refers to the expenditures government makes and how it finances through taxation and borrowing to provide the necessary goods and services. Monetary policy controls the supply and availability of money in the domestic economy. In determining the amount of paper (money) to print, the national bank, such as the Bank of Canada, and its governor, David Dodge, will consider Canada's current employment rates, inflation rates, economic growth, and the balance of external payments that must be met.

Fiscal policy refers to the expenditures government makes and how it finances through taxation and borrowing to provide the necessary goods and services.

Monetary policy controls the supply and availability of money in the domestic economy.

Courtesy of the Federal Reserve Bank of San Francisco

The colour green has been associated with money since the U.S. government issued notes with green-coloured backs during the Civil War.

The Colour of Money

The colour green has been associated with money, particularly American currency, since the U.S. government issued notes with green-coloured backs during the Civil War. However, it was a Canadian—George Matthews of Montreal—who patented its use in 1857 under the name of the Canada Security Printing Tint. It was generally believed that green ink would not photograph well, so this colour was used extensively on Canadian and U.S. notes as a security measure against photographic copies.

The Invention of Banking and Coinage

Banking preceded coinage. Banking originated in Ancient Mesopotamia (Iraq) where the royal palaces and temples provided secure places for the safekeeping of grain and other commodities. The receipts provided came to be used for transfers not only to the original depositors but also to third parties. "Eventually private houses in Mesopotamia also got involved in these banking operations and laws regulating them were included in the code of Hammurabi. In Egypt too the centralization of harvests in state warehouses also led to the development of a system of banking. Written orders for the withdrawal of separate lots of grain by owners whose crops had been deposited there for safety and convenience, or which had been compulsorily deposited to the credit of the king, soon became used as a more general method of payment of debts to other persons including tax gatherers, priests and traders. Even after the introduction of coinage these Egyptian grain banks served to reduce the need for precious metals which tended to be reserved for foreign purchases, particularly in connection with military activities."[11] From these beginnings, today's international monetary systems and the global capital market have evolved. We will commence our examination with gold as the underlying value for monetary systems.

The Gold Standard

The phrase **"gold standard"** means the use of gold as the standard value for the money of a country. The relationship of gold to monetary systems has been established for millenniums. In this text we will restrict our examination to the last 100 years or so. If a country backs any of its money with gold it is said to be using the gold standard. The United States and many other Western countries adhered to the gold standard during the early 1900s. Today, gold's role in the worldwide monetary system is negligible; however,

The **gold standard** is a financial system that exists when a country backs its currency with gold and is prepared, under predetermined conditions, to exchange its currency for a fixed amount of gold.

PRACTICAL ENTREPRENEURIAL FOCUS

Canadian entrepreneurs envy the competitive advantages achieved by nations using the euro in the EU. Discussions emerge regularly as to whether Canada should dollarize (meaning adopting the U.S. dollar or the euro or some other global 'unit', as our currency). While admittedly there are many disadvantages for Canadian SMEs, there would seem to be strong support for the notion economically. Disadvantages include the loss of monetary fiscal policy; seigniorage; a perceived or actual loss of sovereignty, self-esteem, and national identity; and conveying the message to other nations that you cannot control your own affairs. (Seigniorage is discussed in Chapter 8, page 244.) Robert Mundell, a Canadian economist and a Nobel Laureate (1999) provided an interesting case in support of adopting a global currency.

"A few economists have recently recognized the merits of and need for a world currency. Whether that can be achieved or not in the near future will depend on politics as well as economics. But it is nevertheless a project that would restore a needed coherence to the international monetary system, give the International Monetary Fund a function that would help it to promote stability, and be a catalyst for international harmony. As Paul Volcker has put it, 'A global economy needs a global currency'. The benefits from a world currency would be enormous. Prices all over the world would be denominated in the same unit and would be kept equal in different parts of the world to the extent that the law of one price was allowed to work itself out. Apart from tariffs and controls, trade between countries would be as easy as it is between states of the United States. It would lead to an enormous increase in the gains from trade and real incomes of

all countries including the United States. Another dimension of the benefits from a world currency would be a great improvement in the monetary policies of perhaps two-thirds of the countries of the world. The benefits to each country from a stable currency that is also a universal currency would be enormous. If the whole world were dollarized, there would be a common inflation rate and similar interest rates, a considerable increase in trade, productivity and financial integration, all of which would produce a considerable increase in economic growth and well-being."[13]

CRITICAL THINKING QUESTION
From the perspective of Canadian business, do you agree with this Canadian-born (and educated at the University of British Columbia) Nobel Laureate's position? Should Canada take the first step and dollarize?

recently there seems to be a resurgence of interest. Britain was forced to abandon the gold standard in 1931; the United States was forced to abandon it in 1971, having first adopted it in the Bretton Words Agreement of 1944. The United States was increasingly being called upon to convert its paper to gold and found it necessary to unilaterally breach the agreement. This action in 1971 was the first time in history in which no circulating paper anywhere in the world was redeemable in gold. President Richard Nixon closed the "gold window," which resulted in today's global financial system—a system of fixed and floating currencies. The price of gold rises and falls in relation to the demand for the metal.[12] This position implies in an absolutely perfect world where money is working at the peak of efficiency, no central bank would need to hold any gold. But the world is far from perfect, and consequently there is renewed interest in linking currency to gold. Recall the possible emergence of the gold dinar and that a percentage of the euro is "somewhat" backed by gold (when first joining the EMU, a country's currency must be 15 percent back by gold; however, this percentage changes over time). To understand the current genesis of the global capital market and the importance of the gold standard following World War II, we need to once again revisit the Bretton Woods Agreement and the International Monetary Fund in so far as they affect global monetary systems and capital markets.

The Bretton Woods Agreement

During July 1944, delegates from 45 nations gathered at the United Nations Monetary and Financial Conference in Bretton Woods, New Hampshire, to discuss the postwar recovery of Europe as well as a number of monetary issues, including unstable exchange rates and protectionist trade policies. After World War I, many of the world's major economies stumbled and had unstable currency exchange rates. As a result, many nations resorted to mercantilism and restrictive trade policies. In the early 1940s, the United States and Great Britain proposed the creation of new international financial institutions that would stabilize exchange rates and increase international trade. The Bretton Woods agreement was to provide for these new international financial institutions. It also established a postwar international monetary system of convertible currencies, fixed exchange rates, and free trade. The agreement created two international institutions to facilitate these objectives, the International Monetary Fund (IMF) and the International Bank for Reconstruction and Development, which was to become the World Bank.

By the end of World War II, the United States had accumulated 80 percent of the world's gold and 40 percent of the world's production.[14] Its economic and military predominance was absolute. One goal of the Bretton Woods Agreement was to prevent currency competition and promote monetary co-operation among nations. To facilitate this goal, the IMF member countries established an exchange rate system. Exchange rates could be adjusted within a set range against the U.S. dollar or in the event of an imbalance in the balance of payments (BoP) account. This system remained until 1971. The system collapsed for a number of reasons: a large destabilizing flow of currency, e.g., significant spending on the Vietnam War; speculators betting on the value at which the fixed exchange rate would be refixed, which led to Thailand's bankruptcy, discussed in Chapter 1, page 7; and concerns that a fixed exchange rate system did not allow countries enough freedom to pursue their own monetary and fiscal policies.

Initially, Canada maintained par value with the United States dollar but within months (1946), the Canadian dollar under significant downward financial market pressure was devalued again in 1949. Troubled by what happened to the Canadian dollar's value under a fixed exchange rate system, the government decided in 1950 to allow the dollar to float. "Another 12 years would pass before Canada reinstated a fixed exchange rate. Canada's maverick years would later become a model for other countries when the fixed exchange rate system of Bretton Woods proved unworkable in the early 1970s and was replaced by a system of floating exchange rates. Many economists and bankers still periodically call for a return to fixed exchange rates."[15]

Bettmann/Corbis Canada

Lester B. Pearson, Ambassador to the United States, signing the Bretton Woods Agreement, December 28, 1945.

The International Monetary Fund (IMF)

The IMF's mission, established at Bretton Woods, was to help manage the fixed exchange rate system. The fund would make short-term loans to member countries experiencing balance of payment difficulties. Nixon's move off the gold standard and the move to flexible exchange rates in 1973 effectively ended this mission.[16] Yet today the IMF continues to operate. Should its role be expanded? Cogent arguments can be found to support both sides.

The core of the debate around the IMF is whether these loans and guarantees create a **moral hazard** problem. Countries borrowing funds from the IMF sometimes do so with the belief that if they can't meet the contractual obligations, they will not be called upon to account. The IMF bailouts, either implicitly or explicitly through their loan guarantees, lead to excessive risk taking by both borrowers and lenders, compounding the severity of the financial crisis. The Mexican peso crisis illustrates this point. In December 1994, the Clinton administration encouraged the U.S. Treasury, the U.S. Federal Reserve, and the IMF to provide Mexico with a $41 billion bailout. Many viewed this bailout as an action designed primarily to protect foreign investors (mainly American) who would have taken large losses on the Mexican loans had this funding not been put in place. The Mexican bailout spread to Asia in 1997, rolled on to the Russian devaluation and default in 1998, tore through Brazil, and, most recently, helped wreck Argentina by creating an economic imbalance between Brazil and Argentina. Globally, banks, including Canadian banks, felt secure lending to the emerging markets of Asia and South America, and were comforted by the knowledge that the IMF was standing by and therefore the risk was minimal. "Once the government steps in to protect individuals from bad outcomes, the incentive to monitor the behaviour of financial institutions declines."[17]

Those arguing against the IMF's continuing in its present condition state that increasing the power of an institution that has promoted ineffective macroeconomic adjustment programs is just wrong. The IMF's lending programs have demonstrated that they do not provide strong incentives for fundamental market reforms. Indeed there is ample evidence that the IMF interventions promote a debilitating dependence on further IMF loans. Repeated IMF bailouts encourage excessive risk taking by both lenders and borrowers, resulting in more frequent and severe financial crises. The IMF loan conditions imposed on Turkey illustrate this significant cause of tension. Turkey, long prized as NATO's best friend in the Muslim world, in 2001 found millions of Turkish citizens out of work and short on hope because of the IMF's stress on high-tax fiscal "discipline" above economic growth and political realities. Read "Turkey Tests IMF's Crisis-Handling Skills."

A better strategy would be to reduce the power of the IMF, ending its role as the global guarantor for international investors, thereby forcing global investors to increase their scrutiny of the economic policies of emerging market economies. Countries like China, Russia, and others that want access to world capital will have strong incentives to adopt political and market reforms. As a result, global capital will be used more prudently and efficiently, meaning fewer and less-severe financial problems.

A **moral hazard** is a situation in which someone will purposely engage in risky behaviour, knowing that any costs incurred will be compensated by the insurer (lender).

Turkey Tests IMF's Crisis-Handling Skills

As the financial crisis in Turkey unfolds, attention will increasingly focus on just what the International Monetary Fund (IMF) will do to shore up that economy, following its blundering on the Asian crisis in the late 1990s. So far the IMF has issued a guarded reaction to developments this week in Turkey, where the government allowed the lira to float freely on the market following a financial crisis sparked by a quarrel between the prime minister and the president. [In February 2001], the lira had lost about 36% of its value amid fears that it was in free fall. . . . The IMF's external affairs department says . . . "The goal is to discuss any changes needed to the current program necessitated by the decision by Turkey to float its currency." . . . So far, the current turmoil in Turkey appears different from the Asian crisis [see Chapter 1] and from the one that followed in Russia in 1998. This time the Turkish government is drawing support for acting decisively by adopting the new currency measures. Also, while in Russia many hedge funds responded to the first signs of trouble by borrowing more money to take even bigger positions in the country in Turkey, the response was to quietly sell off assets at the first signs of trouble [2000]. As of [September 30, 2000] major foreign creditors had $44 billion on loan to Turkey, notes the Bank for International Settlements. This contrasts with $76 billion on loan to Russia when its economy collapsed. During the Asian crisis, banks in Korea, for instance, were saddled with unhedged borrowing of up to $150 billion. In Turkey, the figure is estimated at about $10 billion. The US Treasury Secretary Paul O'Neill supported the move by Turkey to float its currency, noting that the new measure, together with "firm and determined implementation of appropriate supportive policies, can be successful in preserving the gains from the IMF program so far.

Source: *Turkey Tests IMF's Crisis-Handling Skills* by Gumisai Mutume (Third World Network, February 23, 2005).

Special Drawing Rights—A Substitute for Gold

The IMF provides its members special drawing rights (SDRs). SDRs represent a potential claim on the freely usable currencies of IMF members. These rights are neither a currency, nor a claim on the International Monetary Fund but rather an international reserve asset that exists only as accounting entries. SDRs' value are derived from a

JUST DOING THE RIGHT THING

Debt relief has become a significant vehicle of resource transfer to countries by the World Bank. However, many African countries' current debt ratios exceed the bank's sustainability level of 150 percent debt-to-exports ratio. Here is Canada's answer.

Canada Proposes 100 Per Cent Debt Relief for World's Poorest Countries

Minister of Finance Ralph Goodale today announced a debt relief proposal that will ease the burden of debt for the world's poorest countries by substantially increasing both the amount of relief available and the number of nations eligible for international debt relief assistance. He also called on other donor countries to support this Canadian initiative and provide similar debt relief for developing nations. "The Canadian proposal will provide low-income nations with the opportunity to invest in the future of their people, and

not the debt obligations of their past," said Minister Goodale. "A permanent debt relief solution may finally be within our reach." Under this initiative Canada will contribute approximately $172 million over the next five years to the International Development Association of the World Bank and the African Development Fund. This relief will be immediately open to the 15 countries that have completed the Heavily Indebted Poor Countries Initiative, a multilateral debt reduction strategy, as well as 4 other nations participating in the World Bank Poverty Reduction Support Credit program. A further 37 countries are potentially eligible for benefits. Strong governance and human rights considerations are built into this proposal, as is a link to the achievement of the Millennium Development Goals in 2015. This contribution represents 4 per cent of all debt payments to these institutions, or Canada's traditional share of global multilateral assistance. . . .

"Canada's proposal focuses on relieving the immediate burden of debt

by reducing debt-servicing obligations, and provides deeper relief than existing initiatives by effectively paying 100 per cent of debt-servicing payments coming due between now and 2015," said Minister Goodale. "Canada is also willing to explore various options to finance further debt relief through the IMF. However, if these options negatively affect the Fund's financial position or disrupt world gold markets, Canada calls upon donor countries to pay for 100 per cent debt-service relief on IMF claims directly."

Source: Department of Finance Canada, *Canada Proposes 100 Per Cent Debt Relief for World's Poorest Countries*, (February 2, 2005), retrieved August 21, 2006, from www.fin.gc.ca/news05/05-008e.html.

CRITICAL THINKING QUESTION

Are we doing enough as a developed nation? Given the corruption levels in some African nations, are we not just throwing good money after bad? Visit www.power.nelson.com to see the update on this initiative.

weighted basket of the major global currencies. Today the basket comprises the euro, the pound sterling, the Japanese yen, and the U.S. dollar. The amounts of each currency making up one SDR unit are in accordance with the relative weight of the currency in international trade and finance markets. The composition of the SDR basket and the weights attributed takes place every five years. The value is determined daily in U.S. dollars by the IMF, based on the exchange rates of the currencies in the basket. The IMF and several other international organizations also use SDRs as a unit of account. A few countries have pegged their currencies against SDRs, and from time to time SDRs have been used to denominate some private international financial instruments. SDRs were primarily created to replace gold in large international transactions. The units are referred to at times as "paper gold"— credits that nations with balance of trade surpluses can "draw" upon nations with balance of trade deficits. So-called "paper gold" is simply an accounting transaction within a ledger of accounts, thereby eliminating the problem of moving gold back and forth between nations to settle national accounts.

Monetary Systems—Fixed and Floating Rates

A debate has swirled around the advantages and disadvantages of adopting a fixed or a floating rate monetary system since 1971, and the United States' unilateral withdrawal from its undertaking to back the "greenback" with gold. The following are some considerations to assist you in formulating your opinion as to which is the most appropriate monetary system.

Fixed Rates

A **fixed exchange rate** is a system where the exchange rate has a set (fixed) value against another currency. For much of the postwar period, as we have discussed, the Canadian dollar was fixed against the U.S. dollar but floated in 1972 when a fixed rate became unsustainable. To maintain a fixed exchange rate, the government needs to have a significant level of foreign currency reserves to prevent speculators putting the currency in "play" as we saw in the Thai baht case (see Chapter 1, page 7). A fixed exchange rate required the government to intervene in the markets to maintain equilibrium between supply and demand. If, for example, referring to the model we used in Chapter 8, page 239, an increase in demand for the Canadian dollar (shown by a shift from line D1 to line D2 in Figure 9.2), would normally lead to an increase in the exchange rate. However, if the exchange rate is fixed then the government has to counter the effect of the increase in demand by increasing supply. In other words, the government sells Canadian dollars and buys other currencies for its foreign exchange reserves instead. (The government could also go "down to the basement" and print more "loonies" to increase the money supply.) This shifts the supply curve to S2, and maintains the fixed rate equilibrium.

A hybrid of the fully fixed rate is the **pegged exchange rate**. Nations adopt a pegged system when one county "ties" its currency to another. For example, China, prior to its revaluation in 2005, pegged its currency to the U.S. dollar (¥8.1: $1). Pegged systems are very popular in small economies as they tend to moderate a nation's inflation rate. An innovative control measure for pegged systems is the creation of a **currency board**, which manipulates the global capital market's supply and demand for the nation's currency so as to maintain its established pegged rate. To do this it issues (prints) new domestic currency if it can back the printing of money with foreign reserves. In essence, the domestic currency is 100 percent backed by foreign reserves holdings at all times. Currency boards are popular in emerging economies because currency backed by foreign reserves affords little opportunity for speculators to attempt to manipulate the currency. In 1997, as other Asian nations' currencies collapsed because of speculation, Hong Kong's currency board maintained the Hong Kong dollar at $15:$US1 by controlling the supply and demand for its currency on the world's markets (see Figure 9.2).

A **fixed exchange rate** is a system where the exchange rate has a set (fixed) value against another currency.

A **pegged foreign exchange system** is a hybrid of the fully fixed rate system. Nations adopt a pegged system when one country "ties" its currency to another country's currency.

A **currency board** is charged by the government with the responsibility to exchange domestic currency for foreign currency at a specified and fixed rate.

FIGURE 9.2

To Maintain the Balance in the Exchange Rate, Governments Intervene

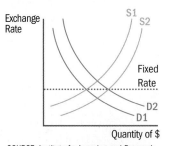

SOURCE: Institute for Learning and Research Technology, *Markets—Foreign Exchange Market* (Bank of Biz/ed, 2005).

Advantages of a Fixed Rate

There are three arguments in favour of fixed rates. First, they reduce risk in international trade. By maintaining a fixed rate, buyers and sellers of international goods can agree on a price knowing the payment will not be subject to exchange rate risks; certainty encourages investment. Second, fixed rates bring discipline into economic management. The impact of maintaining rate equilibrium is felt quickly by the domestic economy. Governments sensitive to voters have a built-in incentive not to follow inflationary policies. If they do, unemployment and balance of payment problems are certain to result as the economy becomes uncompetitive. Finally, fixed rates should eliminate destabilizing speculation. As we have discussed, speculation (the flow of hot money) can be very destabilizing for an economy. When the amount of arbitrage is small, so is speculation.[18]

Disadvantages of a Fixed Rate

There are four disadvantages to a fixed rate system. First, there is no automatic balance of payments adjustment. A floating exchange rate generally accommodates disequilibrium in the balance of payments without government interference, and without affecting the domestic economy. If there is a deficit, then the currency's exchange rate falls, making the nation competitive again. However, in a fixed system, as demand drops, people consume fewer imports (the aggregate level of demand), and the price level then falls, making the country more competitive. Second, large holdings of foreign exchange reserves are required to maintain a fixed exchange rate system to maintain the fixed rate. These reserves have an opportunity cost as they could be otherwise spent stimulating the nation's economy. Third, freedom of a national internal policy (sovereignty) is lost. The needs of the exchange rate can dominate policy, which may not be the best for the economy at that point in time. Interest rates and other policies may be set to meet the needs of the exchange rate rather than the more important macro objectives of inflation and unemployment. Finally, "fixed rates are inherently unstable. Countries within a fixed rate mechanism often follow different economic policies. The result tends to be differing rates of inflation. What this means is that some countries will have low inflation and be very competitive while others will have high inflation and not be very competitive. The uncompetitive countries will be under severe pressure continually and may, ultimately, have to devalue,"[19] as was the case with Mexico. It is unlikely that this fact will go unnoticed by foreign exchange speculators.

Floating Rates

A **floating exchange rate** is one that is allowed to find its own level according to the forces of supply and demand. The equilibrium rate is where supply is equal to demand, and this will vary as supply and demand change. The advantages for a nation adopting a floating exchange system are first, that the nation's balance of payments automatically adjust in the event of depreciation or appreciation of its currency because of exports and imports of goods and services. Second, a floating exchange rate allows governments to pursue their own internal policy objectives, such as employment levels and economic growth, without reference to external constraints. Third, floating rates permit rate changes automatically on a day-to-day basis and therefore are not subject to financial crisis as pressure mounts to devalue or revalue the nation's currency, as we have discussed in the Mexican peso illustration. Fourth, a floating rate significantly enables a country to adjust to external shocks. Finally, unlike fixed rate systems that generally require a nation to hold significant foreign exchange reserves to support its currency in the event the currency has to be defended against devaluation, as in the Asian flu illustration, floating systems adjust incrementally based on the demand and supply for the currency in the marketplace, and therefore the need for large foreign exchange holdings is less imperative.

A **floating exchange rate** is one that is allowed to find its own level according to the forces of supply and demand.

A Hybrid of the Fixed and Floating Systems

A hybrid of the fixed and floating rates system is the establishment of an exchange rate mechanism (ERM). The EU adopted such a system to enable currencies to float within a fixed band. Its purpose was to reduce exchange rate variability and achieve monetary stability in Europe in preparation for the introduction of the euro. The ERM was based on the concept of fixed currency exchange rate margins, but with exchange rates variable within those margins. See the Mini Case at the end of this chapter, pages 273–274, for an explanation and examples of the managed float and the basket of currencies exchange rate systems. In addition to fixed and floating rate systems, other systems include the pegged exchange rate, sometimes supported by a currency board, exchange rate bands, basket pegged, and others. Visit www.power.nelson.com for an overview of other exchange rate systems.

What Are Global Capital Markets?

By now, most of you will have recognized, at the macro level, the economic advantages of globalization. And if we can agree that economic growth is a good thing, then the global capital markets are an integral part of that success. Capital markets provide a venue, financial infrastructure, and the instruments necessary for borrowers and lenders to conduct business. Financial institutions routinely move trillions of dollars of assets— stocks, bonds, and other instruments—around the globe. The world market tends to move in response to common global factors. The **money market** raises, invests, and trades short-term capital using financial instruments such as treasury bills, bankers' acceptances, commercial paper, and bonds maturing in one year or less. Repurchase agreements (repos) are the most common funding instruments, and use government securities as the underlying collateral. At the centre of operating capital markets are the **market makers**. These matchmakers provide the financial infrastructure and instruments required by the parties to conduct business. The concept is not new. "The great variety of coinages originally in use in the Hellenic world meant that money changing was the earliest and most common form of Greek banking. Usually the money changers would carry out their business in or around temples and other public buildings, setting up their trapezium-shaped tables (which usually carried a series of lines and squares for assisting calculations), from which the Greek bankers—the trapezitai—derived their name, much as our name for bank comes from the Italian banca for bench or counter. The close association between banking, money changing and temples is best known to us from the episode of Christ's overturning the tables in the Temple of Jerusalem (Matthew 21:12). Money changing was not the only form of banking. One of the most important services was bottomry or lending to finance the carriage of freight by ships. Other business enterprises supported by the Greek bankers included mining and construction of public buildings."[20]

Generally, today's financial instruments are broadly classified as either debt or equity instruments. Firms take on debt or they issue equity to raise money to cover their operating expenditures. A **debt instrument** represents "an amount owed to a person or organization for funds borrowed. Debt can be represented by a loan note, bond, debenture, mortgage or other form stating repayment terms and, if applicable, interest requirements. These different forms all imply intent to pay back an amount owed by a specific date, which is set forth in the repayment terms."[22] An **equity instrument** represents "ownership interest in a corporation in the form of common stock or preferred stock."[23]

Much of the growth in global financial assets comes from a rapid expansion of corporate and government debt. The roles that major countries and regions play in capital markets are changing. "Just four areas account for more than 80 percent of the world's financial stock: the United States, the Euro zone, Japan, and the United Kingdom. . . . The Asian financial markets are relatively isolated from one another and differ in important ways. . . . China's financial market, though less than one-third the size of Japan's, is among the world's fastest growing [see the opening vignette, page 253], and the country has amassed a sizable portion of the world's bank deposits."[26]

The **money market** raises, invests, and trades short-term capital using financial instruments such as treasury bills, bankers' acceptances, commercial paper, and bonds maturing in one year or less. Repurchase agreements (repos) are the most common funding instruments, and utilize government securities as the underlying collateral.[21]

Market makers are persons or firms authorized to create and maintain a market in a security. Market makers commit themselves to always being ready to deal in the range of stocks for which they are registered.

A **debt instrument** represents "an amount owed to a person or organization for funds borrowed. Debt can be represented by a loan note, bond, debenture, mortgage, or other form stating repayment terms, and, if applicable, interest requirements. These different forms all imply intent to pay back an amount owed by a specific date, which is set forth in the repayment terms."[24]

An **equity instrument** represents ownership interest in a corporation in the form of common stock or preferred stock.[25]

Compound Global Capital Market
Annual Growth Rate

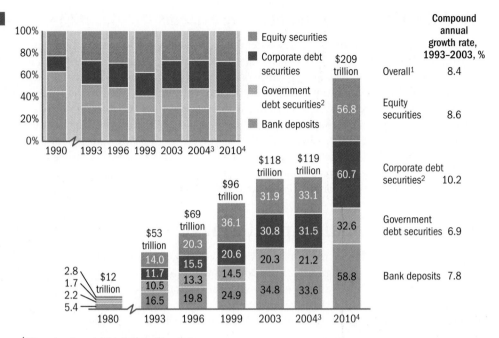

1 Figures do not sum to totals, because of rounding.

2 Includes debt issued by financial institutions and other corporations.

3 Based on latest available data: September 2004 for equities; May/June 2004 for debt; June 2004 for bank deposits.

4 Extrapolation from 2003 base with components increasing at 1993–2003 compound annual growth rates.

SOURCE: Diana Farrell, Aneta Marcheva Key, and Tim Shavers, *Mapping the Global Capital Markets: Growing Cross-Border Capital Flows* (The McKinsey Quarterly, February 8, 2005). Copyright © 1992–2006 McKinsey & Company, Inc.

The United States has $44 trillion in financial assets and accounts for 37 percent of the world's financial stock, composed primarily of private debt and equity.[27] Currently the United States remains the world's capital market centre; however, the major countries' and regions' degree of involvement in the global capital markets are shifting. Currently the United States is the world's largest financial market. "With the creation of the Euro, however, European financial markets are integrating and gaining share. Japan's financial markets are becoming less important in the global financial system, while China's are growing rapidly. Financial markets in the rest of the world—including Singapore and all of Latin America—are negligible in a global context. Latin America's financial markets are notably underdeveloped compared against those of middle-income countries in other regions: despite representing over 4 percent of global GDP, Latin America has less than 2 percent of the world's total financial assets."[28] Note that the world's capital markets are mainly transacted in U.S. dollars and that, as we will see, may be a problem. Asset price bubbles (real estate) and the issuance of excessive government debt (treasury bills) can lead to an unhealthy financial access to capital markets—and painful corrections.

The world's capital markets are huge (see Figure 9.3). McKinsey calculates "that the world's financial assets now total more than $118 trillion and will exceed $200 trillion by 2010 if current trends persist. The stock of global financial assets has grown faster than the world's GDP."[29] National financial markets are becoming deeper and more liquid. This augurs well for the world's economies, since deeper markets provide better access to capital and improve the allocation of risk. It is interesting to note **investor bias** here. Investors tend to demonstrate a propensity to purchase domestic (home) debt and equity, rather than foreign instruments. This can be attributed to their increased access regarding domestic institutions' information and generally lower transaction costs than in a non-domestic capital market. There is an investors' Muslim bias (religious bias) capital market emerging in Dubai, UAE, that could have significant consequences in the long term to the U.S. hegemony; read "High Time for a Single Gulf Cooperative Council Currency."

Investor bias refers to an investor's tendency to demonstrate a propensity to purchase domestic (home) debt and equity, rather than foreign instruments.

High Time for a Single Gulf Cooperative Council Currency

There is skepticism toward the proposed Corporation Council for the Arab (CCA) states of the Gulf single currency (2006). On the surface it seems to be a good fit; all member states have similar export-orientated economies so a single currency should be viable and not difficult to implement.

The key benefits of currency union include the elimination of transaction costs and increased trade between member states Skeptics argue that all currencies are pegged to the U.S. dollar; therefore, transaction costs are already effectively nonexistent. Further, they note that a single currency would not stimulate much new intra-Gulf Cooperation Council (GCC) trade as most of the region's trade involves exporting oil and gas to Asia and Europe. Finally, if the currency union is to be effective there will need to be a single independent central bank along with a GCC monetary authority. Indeed, what are the chances GCC leaders will actually defer to a supranational institution?

"Much of the potential success or otherwise depends on two things: a strong independent central bank and what exchange rate mechanism the region's policymakers decide to adopt post 2010. It seems that at present there is little appetite—at least publicly expressed—to move away from the dollar peg, let alone consider invoicing future oil sales in Gulf dinars. Reasons given for maintaining the status quo include the fact that the dollar is the de facto currency of international trade and that OPEC oil sales are invoiced in dollars."

But this is changing. GCC governments hold vast sums of dollar-denominated assets, such as US Treasury bonds, and a weakening of the dollar would lower the value of these assets. However, if GCC nations were to start selling some of their dollars and buying euro-denominated assets for their currency reserve prior to currency union, it would provide a good hedge against the inevitable downward decline in the dollar. Indeed if the GCC purchased oil in euros along with the Gulf dinar and other currencies, they would see their euro assets appreciate massively. In addition, a greater number of oil-importing nations holding higher levels of euros in reserve will increase this new currency's value.

"Iran's decision to open an oil and associated derivatives market in March 2006 is interesting, not least because it plans to invoice contracts in euros, not dollars. It is not likely that many energy traders will leave New York or London and set up shop in Tehran, but Iran's move does highlight a rising concern over the long-term value of the U.S. dollar. If the dollar continues to decline against the euro, more states will increase the percentage of euros they hold in their reserves because the euro will be a better store of future wealth, and major oil suppliers will prefer to sell at least some of their oil for euros or currencies other than the dollar."

Increasingly Arab and Islamic states view the proposed currency as a more "acceptable" reserve currency than that of the U.S. dollar. The notion proposed forward by U.S. officials and the petrodollar hegemony that it would be too difficult to set up a market for invoicing oil sales in any currency other than the dollar is quite frankly ridiculous.

Adapted from Emilie Rutledge, *High Time for a Single GCC Currency* (Aljazeera.Net: Opinion, October 3, 2005). Copyright Aljazeera.net 2003–2006.

Critical Thinking Questions

This article provides much to think about. Other drivers support this notion of a GCC currency; first, the U.S. federal debt. The weakening U.S. dollar has resulted in GCC European imports becoming more expensive. In 2002, for example, a Saudi riyal was worth €0.29; by 2006 it was worth only €0.21. This means that it has become 32 percent more expensive for GCC countries to import goods and services from the EU. Second a strong, independent, single GCC currency is likely to attract increased levels of FDI. Third, GCC countries will experience significantly increased seigniorage revenues. Fourth, unlike the United States, the EU does not run large trade deficits, and the European Central

Bank imposes strict limits on government deficits. There are indications during 2004–2006 that some countries, including Canada, were shifting part their currency reserves from the U.S. dollar to the euro and other currencies. If so, what does this mean for Canada, the United States, and the global economic order? What will it mean for the exchange rates for Canada, the United States, and the EU currencies?

Patterns of Global Capital Market Growth

The growth patterns of financial assets vary by regions. Corporate debt is expanding quickly and preferred in the United States, Canada, and Europe. In Canada, initial public offerings (IPOs) are a significant source of growth in equities, as are higher price-to-earnings ratios. In contrast, Europe's newly floated shares from the privatization of state-owned companies drive equities' growth. In Japan, a huge expansion of public debt has been the only source of growth for almost a decade. Only recently (2006) are there signs of financial stock equities and corporate-debt securities shifting. In China and Eastern Europe, all asset classes are rapidly growing due to FDI.

Business practitioners who seek to raise money, institutions hoping to shape the global capital market, and the policy makers who regulate them must all understand the constant evolution and shifting of the global capital markets.

Drivers of the Global Capital Market

- *For.* There are three arguments in support of the global capital market: it lowers the cost of capital, spurs investment, and encourages economic growth. Greater financial-sector competition lowers the cost of capital, thereby resulting in better risk management and improving the country's financial system efficiency. By competing in the marketplace, domestic banks will adopt new banking techniques and improve banking skills by enhancing the quality and quantity of their banking services. Such actions improve the effectiveness of using the country's savings, increasing productivity and economic growth. Domestic banks facing competition reduce their profit margins since they no longer have a monopoly; these institutions can no longer undertake inefficient projects just because the borrowers are politically connected (see the opening vignette, page 253). Capital markets encourage portfolio diversification and the better use of capital, thereby spurring investment. Open capital markets provide incentives for better government economic policy makers. For example, governments can use Public Private Partnerships (P3s) to free public funds for projects that the private sector would not undertake. Investors quickly scrutinize policy makers who initiate inflationary or anti-growth policies. Investors cast their vote by selling or buying the country's currency. (Today, this may be the case with the U.S. dollar.) A growing weakness in a nation's currency makes imports and foreign loans-payable more costly in terms of the domestic currency. Adam Smith's invisible hand will work! These variables positively affect the country's overall standard of living. "Evidence from 41 industrialized and emerging economies during the 1970's and 1980's [showed] those countries that allowed international investments [FDI] have higher levels of economic growth, productivity and capital formation."[30]
- *Against.* The Milken Institute identified a number of key drivers as emerging risks to the global capital market. They include: negative capital flows to developing and transitioning economies; reversals in global trade integration and a backlash against globalization; the absence of middle-class development in the developing world; and the absence of markets to adequately and efficiently allocate capital for entrepreneurial finance and economic growth. The trade theory of Adam Smith has equal application in the global capital market's economic operations—the supply and demand curves must be observed for early indications of "shifts." For example, shifts in capital controls can harm economic performance and reduce domestic and foreign direct investment, slowing global economic growth (see Chapter 7).

An Emerging Capital Market to Watch

Will Bahrain or Dubai be the financial centre of the Middle East? The 2004 opening of the world's newest financial centre in Dubai seems to support the vision for a single GCC currency. First, Beirut lost its banking crown to Bahrain as a result of the Arab–Israel conflict. Now Dubai is set to usurp Bahrain with the Dubai International Financial Centre (DIFC). The very presence of the IMF and World Bank meetings in Dubai in September 2003 indicated their support. The DIFC is a mega-project that will house 20,000 white-collar workers by 2010 in a purpose-built, air-conditioned complex, including the world's largest parking lot. But this is about much more than real estate. The DIFC is adopting international best practices for activities as diverse as insurance to equity trading, and is establishing its own independent, civil, and commercial law to regulate the capital market's activities. The DIFC will use English as the working language and international law, whereas Bahrain uses Arabic and Sharia courts administer the law in Bahrain. The international market makers are watching closely. ABN Amro, Credit Suisse, HSBC, and Standard Chartered Bank have relocated or established their regional headquarters in Dubai. International banks locating in the DIFC will be able to adopt a geocentric hiring practice, while Bahrain insists that local workers are hired. Islamic banking is a growing sector and, until recently, Bahrain was the major player in this banking niche. Global international banks recognize the importance of Islamic banking, which will help Dubai establish itself as part of the Islamic banking world. The real driver to establish the DIFC as the international capital market in the region will be the WTO. "Within a few years Saudi Arabia is likely to join the World Trade Organization and that should open up a massive new market for the international banks [deregulation], which are currently only allowed to own stakes in Saudi banks. Dubai, with its openness to foreign cultures, is likely to prove to be an ideal base for international banks wishing to establish a presence in the Kingdom. This is why Citigroup announced last week [2003] that it would take no further part in the management of the Saudi American Bank in which it holds a stake. The giant US bank wishes to be considered a foreign bank post-WTO. So is Dubai seizing the initiative to become an international banking sector just at the right time, while Bahrain is welded to a glorious but declining past? Some people have begun to think this might prove to be the case."[31] A further emerging issue relating to this topic is the possibility of an Euro-based oil bourse (stock exchange) in Iran that, if successful, will result in the euro gaining a significant market share as the vehicle currency in international oil trade. Such an eventuality would significantly lessen the demand for the U.S. dollar and could cause significant global economic disruption.

Global Bond Markets

Bonds are debt instruments; the lender promises to repay the principal at a predetermined rate of interest to the borrower. Bonds contain specific legal remedies in the event the lender defaults on the terms and conditions contained within any instrument. Bonds are issued by private sector firms and by governments at all levels.

There are three classifications of bonds. **Domestic bonds** raise funds within a nation and in the currency denomination of the country; there are two classifications of international bonds—foreign bonds and Eurobonds. **Foreign bonds** are issued to raise funds outside the country of origin and are denominated in the currency of the issuing entity's country. "The most important foreign bond markets are Zurich, New York, and Tokyo. In general, bonds traded in the foreign market have a nickname such as Loonie bonds in Canada, Yankee bonds in the United States, Matador bonds in Spain, Rembrandt bonds in the Netherlands, Samurai bonds in Japan, and Bulldog bonds in the United Kingdom."[32] Countries and other entities issue foreign bonds when interest rates in other jurisdictions are lower than at home. In the early part of this decade, Japan set interests rates on Samurai bonds at about 1 percent. These were attractive bond offerings for nations and entities with higher domestic interest rates seeking funding for the operation of their organizations. In 2006, Japan commenced moving interest rates up, tightening the global liquidity.

Bonds are debt instruments issued by private sector firms and by all levels of government. The lender promises to repay the principal and a predetermined rate of interest to the borrower.

Domestic bonds are issued to raise funds within a nation and in the currency denomination of the country.

Foreign bonds are issued to raise funds outside the country of origin and are denominated in the currency of the issuing entity's country.

The **Eurobond market** comprises all bonds issued and sold in a jurisdiction outside the country of the currency of denomination. Eurobonds cannot be offered in that country's capital market nor sold to the residents of the currency of denomination. Eurobonds also differ from foreign bonds, as the latter are usually sold simultaneously in the markets of several nations.

Underwriting is a contractual arrangement between investment bankers to guarantee the sale of the bond issue at a predetermined price in return for a fee, generally 5 percent of the principal.

The prefix "**euro**" is given to all bonds and currencies deposited in any country outside the country of origin.

Eurobonds have historically been the most popular of the international bonds. The **Eurobond market** comprises all bonds issued and sold in a jurisdiction outside the country of the currency of denomination. Eurobonds cannot be offered in that country's capital market nor sold to the residents of the currency of denomination. Eurobonds also differ from foreign bonds, as the latter are usually sold simultaneously in the markets of several nations. A syndicate of international banks generally underwrites the Eurobond issue. **Underwriting** is a contractual arrangement between investment bankers to guarantee the sale of the bond issue at a predetermined price in return for a fee. The fees are generally 5 percent of the principal. Those bonds not purchased by investors are purchased by members of the underwriting syndications according to the percentage set out in the underwriting agreement. It is a lucrative business.

A word about the prefix "**euro**": immediately following World War II, Communist governments and others, as a result of the Cold War, were concerned that their deposits held in American banks globally might be confiscated. This fear continues with many Muslims and others today. This situation gave rise to the need to invest funds in Europe. The London exchange historically has been the centre for the issuing of Eurobonds. As a result, the prefix "euro" is given to all bonds and currencies deposited in any country outside the country of origin; they are referred to as Eurocurrency and Eurobonds. U.S. or Canadian dollars deposited in a German bank, for example, would be referred to as Eurodollars. Japanese yen deposited in the same German bank would be referred to as Euroyen. (A Euroyen bond is denominated in Japanese yen and issued by a non-Japanese company outside of Japan. Despite what the name suggests, Euroyen bonds can be found in bond markets around the world, not just in European markets.)

The Eurobond and Eurocurrency market is attractive to borrowers because there is less regulatory interference, reduced disclosure requirements, and generally more tax advantages. Eurobonds and Eurocurrency are not regulated by any single nation. Because the denomination is in foreign currencies and sold to nondomestic holders, national governments impose less regulatory restrictions on Eurobond and Eurocurrency transactions. For example, most governments legislate that their domestic bank must maintain a percentage of their deposits with the central bank. The percentage varies, but currently in Canada the Bank Act requires 10 percent be segregated by domestic banks as a reserve and not used in the day-to-day lending by the bank. Therefore, Canadian banks can put only 90 percent of their cash deposits to work in mortgages, loans, etc. These types of regulations and constraints combined with the fewer administrative costs and disclosure requirements make euro syndicates very competitive. The result is a lower interest rate on the bonds and currency loans and higher rates on deposits and bonds for the euro transactions (see Figure 9.4). Canada's tax rates on Eurobonds held by foreigners are more attractive than the tax treatment on domestic bonds. Notwithstanding the lack of regulatory restrictions and reduced disclosure requirements, I have found only one default. In 1997, Ecuador defaulted on its Eurobonds (Brady) interest payments. It was subsequently rescheduled.[33] The Eurocurrency market is commonly quoted at the London Interbank Offer Rate (LIBOR). This is the rate of interest large international banks charge each other to borrow money. Similarly, the deposit rate offered by banks to large depositors is referred to as the **London Interbank Bid Rate** (**LIBID**). The spread (the difference between the LIBOR and the LIBID rates) is narrower than domestic offerings because of the reduced cost to the financial institution, thereby making the Eurobonds and currency attractive from both the borrower's and the depositor's perspectives (see Figure 9.4).

The United States has long dominated the world's bond market; however, globalization and other factors have introduced significant changes in the global bond mix and presented new opportunities. Bonds issued in the United States in 2003 accounted for less than half of the global bond market (see Figure 9.5). This decline is due largely to more bond issues in euro-denominated corporate debt.[34]

The **London Interbank Bid Rate** (**LIBID**) is the deposit rate offered by banks to large depositors.

FIGURE 9.4

Interest Rate Spreads, Euro versus Domestic Currency Markets

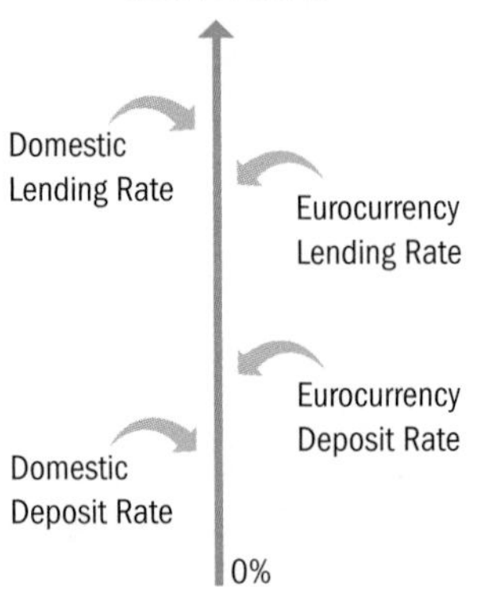

SOURCE: PIMCO Foundation, *Global Bond Market Growth Expands Opportunities* (May 2004). Copyright PIMCO Foundation, 2004.

Risks in Global Bonds

By now, most of you will recognize that one of the primary risks of investing in foreign bond markets is that returns can be significantly affected by fluctuations in currency exchange rates (see Chapter 8). Consider Canada's currency turbulence, ranging from US$0.6179 on January 21, 2002, to US$0.9099 on June 12, 2006.[35] Bonds issued at 63 cents and paid back at 90 represent a significant risk. Another potential risk is the possibility that an issuer will default and fail to pay either interest or principal. Government debt is generally rated as the least likely to default. However, non-government debt's increasing share of the global bond market is contributing to a general rise in the market's overall default risk.[36]

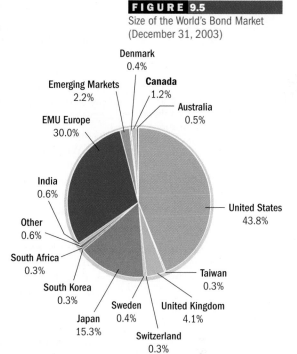

FIGURE 9.5

Size of the World's Bond Market (December 31, 2003)

SOURCE: PIMCO Foundation, *Global Bond Market Growth Expands Opportunities* (Bond Basics, May 2004). Copyright PIMCO Foundation, 2004.

Royal Bank of Canada Issues US$400 million of Subordinated Notes in the Eurobond Market

Royal Bank of Canada today announced the issuance of US$400 million of subordinated notes ("the Notes") through its European Medium Term Note Program. The Notes bear interest at a floating rate of 3-month US$ LIBOR + 0.50% payable quarterly until November 8, 2006, and at 3-month US$ LIBOR + 1.50% payable quarterly thereafter until their maturity on November 8, 2011. The issue was priced at 100.019% and is expected to close on November 8, 2001.

The bank may, at its option, and with the prior approval of the Office of the Superintendent of Financial Institutions in Canada, redeem the Notes in whole at par, on not less than 30 days' and not more than 60 days' notice to the registered holders on November 8, 2006.

The purpose of this issue is to enlarge the bank's capital base. Proceeds of the issue will be added to the bank's general funds and will be utilized for general banking purposes.

Placement into the Eurobond market allows the bank to diversify its investor base. Denominating the issue in US$ allows the bank to better align the currency composition of its capital base with that of its asset base. The Notes have not been qualified for sale in Canada pursuant to a prospectus and will not be offered or sold directly or indirectly in any province or territory of Canada. Barclays Capital and RBC Capital Markets acted as joint lead managers on the issue.

Critical Thinking Question

Reflect on the bank option to redeem the Notes in whole at par to the registered holders on November 8, 2006, in the light of the relevant currency fluctuations between 2001 and 2006. What would you do as the Royal Bank adviser?

Source: Royal Bank of Canada, *Royal Bank of Canada Issues US$400 Million of Subordinated Notes in the Eurobond Market* (News Release, October 31, 2001), retrieved August 21, 2006, from www.prnewswire.co .uk/cgi/news/release?id=76056.

Global Equity Market

"Canada, the United States and Singapore possess the most investor-friendly institutional framework that enhances stock market development. My most striking finding is that improvements in institutional efficiency, and changes in investor sentiment, appear to be the driving force behind the phenomenal expansion of global equity markets over the past two decades."[37]

The global equity market normally takes the form of shares (stocks), which represent ownership in a company. Shareholders may or may not receive dividends depending upon whether the board of directors declares a dividend for that year. This in turn is dependent on the company having retained earnings from which to pay the dividend to its shareholders.

Investors buy shares for capital appreciation and for dividends. The ability of shareholders to buy and sell their shares is determined by whether there are willing sellers and buyers in the marketplace. This is called **liquidity**. If there is a strong market demand, the market for the stock is said to be liquid. In Canada, on the Toronto Stock Exchange (TSX), stocks with a trading volume of a minimum of 100,000 shares transferred daily are termed "liquid."

With deregulation of the financial industry, the lines between the world's capital markets are becoming blurred. Canadian firms such as Bombardier, Nortel, and EnCana are listed on the Toronto Stock Exchange as well as the New York Stock Exchange. The growing number of international investors drives the multiple listing by firm; investors look globally for the best return on their investment. Specifically, there are six reasons for multilisting by international firms like Bombardier. First, deregulation of the industry and advances in communication have made global investment possible for investors of all sizes. Second, it is in the corporation's best interest that the firm's shares are made available to as many investors as possible in order to increase demand and liquidity for its stock. This in turn reduces the firm's cost of borrowing. Third, firms multilist as a prerequisite to being able to issue an initial public offering (IPO) in the host nation's capital market. They must be prepared to meet the regulatory and disclosure requirements designed to protect the domestic share purchasers, which in many cases requires the adoption of different generally accepted accounting practices (GAAP) for filings. Fourth, a domestic firm that registers in a host country's capital market will find future M&A more favourably received by the host marketplace if the issuing firm is viewed by investors as a domestic entity. The fifth advantage is that governments like to see local ownership in domestic corporations. (This has been particularly true in China.) The final advantage is that corporations frequently issue options as part of their compensation package. Options have greater perceived value when employees can view the current price of the stock and options (a derivative) on the domestic exchange and/or daily in their newspapers.

The world's capital markets are sloshing with **hot money**. The world's capital markets' volatility is increasingly affected by the movement of hot money. The collapse of

Liquidity refers to the ability to exchange shares for cash in the global equity markets. If there is a strong market demand, the market for the stock is said to be liquid.

Hot money refers to funds that flow into a country to exploit small differences in interest or exchange rates. Because these funds are rapidly shifted between FX markets to increase profits, hot money is highly volatile and a major factor in capital flight from developing countries. These types of transactions were largely responsible for the currency crises in Mexico and Asia during the 1990s.

INTERNATIONAL STRATEGIC THINKING

As business leaders you must leverage your competencies and assets, including cash. You must consider whether to park your firm's surplus cash in a certificate of deposit with your local bank at the prevailing interest rates or to consider the opportunities the global capital market offers. Maximizing the return on investment will impact your firm's bottom line in a very competitive global marketplace. If you chose the latter, then think of your firm's investment portfolio as a pie divided into three pieces. We call this asset allocation. The pie consists of three main asset classes: cash (or cash equivalents), fixed income (bonds and other debt obligations), and equities (also called stocks). Each piece of the

pie can be further subdivided into smaller pieces, known as subasset classes. For example, the fixed income allocation may be divided among subasset classes such as Eurobonds, municipal bonds, and corporate bonds in order to exploit of the different market conditions globally. This asset allocation results in another benefit—diversification. Most of you reading this text understand how rapidly markets can rise and fall. Recall the turbulence displayed in the Canadian dollar chart (Figure 8.1 on page 232). Clearly, such turbulence will have an effect on your firm's portfolio. If your firm's portfolio is concentrated in currency, a few stocks, or a single industry, your firm is vulnerable to

economic factors that can adversely impact those securities. On the other hand, a diversified portfolio that contains a wide range of investments can reduce overall portfolio risk by diluting the volatility of any particular investment; expose your firm's portfolio to growth opportunities in many different industries; take advantage of improving economic conditions; and provide a degree of protection in a falling global capital market.

CRITICAL THINKING QUESTION
What region or country would be the best capital market for a firm to "park" surplus cash for the next 12 months and why?

the Mexican peso was attributed in part to the exodus of hot money to other more attractive jurisdictions. Countries would do well to differentiate investments as either hot or **patient money**. Arbitrage uses hot money.

Management Implications

- Increasingly, managers must be aware of the locations of surplus capital. Asians have a high savings rate; Americans do not. It is anticipated that the wealthiest economies of North Asia and China will exhibit some of the same thrift characteristics that Japan exhibited a decade or so ago and will be attractive venues in which to raise capital. The return on investment will rise as the world's appetite for capital increases exponentially. Watch for initiatives that reduce risk in the various capital markets in order to attract capital.

- Canadian exchanges, while small, are among the best in the world. They are undertaking initiatives to harmonize with the global capital market. Canadian exchanges are critical to the economic health and development of Canada by providing a source of capital; nevertheless, it is necessary for market-makers to cast the net wider to achieve a lower cost of capital.

- Canadian firms and their bonds are rated highly by global investors and reporting agencies such as Standard & Poor's. The Canadian government regulators protect the Canadian capital market "brand" as a safe, stable place for investment with a solid reputation. Canadian banks are at the forefront of developing the Canadian capital markets and play a role in the global capital market. Canadian banks have attempted to make a business case with federal political leaders to permit domestic banks to consolidate in order to participate as heavyweights in the global capital market. To date they have not made their case.

- Governments and organizations are well advised to remember that the best time to issue stock and to acquire debt is when they do not need it. The low interest rates in Japan and other nations are attractive today (2005–06) but the rates are anticipated to climb later in the decade.

- The harmonization of the global capital market regarding settlement, clearing mechanisms, transparency in regulations, and legal frameworks necessary for disclosure to both domestic and foreign investors will continue.

- The increasing tension between the United States and China over currency valuations could have significant global implications if the United States insists on a higher yuan value or imposes a 27.5 percent tariff on Chinese manufactured goods. This will result in China imposing retaliatory tariffs and shifting more of its reserve foreign currency to euros and gold, which will force American interest rates up, thereby bringing downward pressure on the U.S. housing market and business borrowings. Canada's economic dependency on the United States makes this a serious issue with management implications.

Patient money is money made in FDI in factories, equipment, and land that cannot be readily withdrawn from a nation.

CHAPTER SUMMARY

- Today more than ever, nations need access to capital in order to grow their economies. Driven by deregulation and advancements in technology and telecommunications, national capital markets have integrated into one global capital market. Globally, the market is always open and has expanded exponentially during the past decade or so. This rapid growth presents some issues. First, the growing economic interdependence between nations has increased economic risk as the global economy shifts. Second, the U.S. dollar has been the lone player on the global capital stage; however, this is changing as others such as the euro increasingly capture world currency market share.

- Money and banking can be traced back to the early days of recorded history. Today's global capital market uses financial instruments such as Treasury bills, bankers' acceptance, commercial paper, and bonds maturing in one year or less. At the centre of the market are market makers, the commercial and investment bankers that play a matchmaker's role by putting global borrowers and lenders together.

- A nation influences its domestic economy with two levers or tools: fiscal policy and monetary policy. Fiscal policy refers to the expenditures government makes and how it finances through taxation and borrowing to provide necessary goods and services. Monetary policy controls the supply and availability of money in the domestic economy. In determining the amount of paper (money) to print, the national bank, such as the Bank of Canada, and its governor, David Dodge, will consider Canada's current employment rates, inflation rates, economic growth, and the balance of external payments that must be met.

- Financial instruments can be classified as either debt or equity. A debt instrument represents an amount owed for funds borrowed. The debt can be represented by a loan note, bond, debenture, mortgage, or other form that contains repayment terms and, if applicable, interest payments.

- Beware of investors' bias. Individuals tend to demonstrate a propensity to purchase domestic and equity instruments rather than foreign instruments.

- There are two bond classifications: domestic and international (foreign and euro). Domestic bonds raise funds within a nation and in the currency denomination of that country. International bonds are of two categories. Foreign bonds are issued to raise funds outside the country of origin and are denominated in the currency of the issuing entity's country. Eurobonds are issued and sold in a jurisdiction outside the country of the currency denomination, and they cannot be offered in that country's capital market nor sold to residents of the country of the currency denomination. Eurobonds are usually sold simultaneously in the markets of several nations. The prefix "euro" is given to all bonds and currencies deposited outside the countries of origin. Eurobonds and Eurocurrencies became popular because of the fear of confiscation of funds held by American banks, and their competitive advantages over the domestic lending and deposit rates.

- The world's capital markets are sloshing with hot money. Hot money describes cash that can be quickly withdrawn by investors in times of crisis or for any reason. Patient money is money invested as FDI in factories, equipment, and land and cannot be quickly withdrawn from the host nation.

- Since 1971, when the U.S. dollar abandoned the protocol established under the Bretton Woods Agreement of 1944, no world currency has been linked to a gold standard. However, the euro has provided a quasi-link to gold by restricting its euro member national banks' gold sales. There are other emerging gold-linked currency initiatives, such as the dinar, which has not been successful as a global trading currency to date.

- The IMF was established by the Bretton Woods Agreement to help manage the fixed exchange rate system by making short-term loans to member countries experiencing balance of payment difficulties. Special drawing rights by its members in accordance with a predetermined formula are a potential claim on the IMF's freely usable currency.

REVIEW QUESTIONS

1. What is money? Outline its three principal roles.
2. What are derivatives? Provide examples.
3. Explain what is meant by the gold standard.
4. What was the Bretton Woods Agreement?
5. Provide the arguments that support the IMF's actions and those that do not.
6. What are the IMF's special drawing rights?
7. Describe the fixed and floating exchange rate systems and provide the advantages and disadvantages of each.

8. A nation influences its domestic economy, with two levers. Discuss, using examples.
9. What is meant by the global capital market?
10. What are the drivers of the global capital market and are they strengthening or weakening?
11. Evaluate the successes and the emerging patterns of the global capital market.
12. What is meant by the prefix "euro" when used to describe Eurobonds and Eurocurrency?
13. Discuss the considerations SME decision makers must undertake in selecting appropriate debt instruments.

REFLECTIVE THINKING QUESTIONS

1. Having completed this chapter, reread the quotations on the first page, critically reflect on the validity of the authors' statements, and provide your opinion as to the validity of each. Evidence-based answers are preferred to rhetorical answers.
2. Evaluate the IMF's effectiveness as part of the global capital market in today's world.

3. Reflect on and describe how the global capital market contributes to the success of Canadian international business.

4. An emerging issue is the possibility of a Euro-based oil bourse (stock exchange) in Iran that, if successful, will result in the euro gaining a significant market share as the vehicle currency in international oil trade. Such an eventuality will significantly lessen the demand for the U.S. dollar and could cause significant global economic disruption. Many suggest this might be the underlying cause for the United States' rush in 2006 for United Nations sanctions relating to development of nuclear fuel. Comment.

5. Evaluate some of the emerging international monetary issues regarding the U.S. dollar as the vehicle currency. Should Canada be concerned?

6. How are the drivers of the global capital markets contributing to the evolution of this "entity"?

GLOBAL E-RESEARCH

Visit www.power.nelson.com for research suggestions, questions, and a number of background discussion papers on this topic.

MINI CASE

CHINA'S CURRENCY POLICY SHIFT

China Took an Important Step Forward in Its Move Toward a Market Economy

Norman Chan/Shutterstock

China, moving toward a market economy, announced it would increase the value of its currency, the yuan, and abandon its decade-old fixed exchange rate to the U.S. dollar in favour of a link to a basket of world currencies. This was seen by many as China's first move toward allowing the yuan (also known as the renminbi) to eventually adopt a floating currency system. The move was designed by the Chinese to ease tensions between China and the United States on a key source of trade friction—export balance of payments. The United States argued that a low-priced yuan has unfairly kept Chinese goods artificially cheap. China's critics in the United States have demanded that Beijing do more and increase the value of its currency by at least 10 percent. Congress has been threatening to impose across-the-board punitive tariffs of 27.5 percent against Chinese imports if China does not substantially raise the value of the yuan.

This small step fell short of Congress's demands. "In a statement posted on its Web site, China's central bank said it would on Friday free the Yuan to rise to 8.11 from its current 8.28 to the dollar—an increase of about 2.1 percent. The bank also said it would allow the Yuan to move within a trading range of 0.3 percent above or below the previous day's closing price, continuing its 'managed float' policy." For many, the new managed floating currency regime is seen as an interim system with the expectation that a further widening of the band will take place in the not-distant future, but this has not happened.

As a sign of China's growing regional economic influence, Malaysia followed suit and allowed its currency, the ringgit, to float within a prescribed trading band.

"For China, the move toward a more flexible currency carries potential perils. Anything that could dampen export growth is sensitive at a time when China's coastal factories are creating jobs to offset those lost by the demise of bankrupt state-owned factories. 'The Yuan appreciation will add to their difficulties and force them to lay off more workers,' said Yu Nanping, the East China Normal University economist."

China is reluctant to remove controls on the movement of money, cognizant that a surge of speculative investment into real estate followed by a hasty dash for the exits predicated Asia's last financial crisis. "China avoided the devastation in large part because of its fixed currency and strict capital controls—a policy that then drew words of gratitude from the United States."

Adapted from "China Ends Fixed-Rate Currency: Administration Hails Policy Shift" by Peter S. Goodman (*The Washington Post*, July 22, 2005). © 2000–2006 The Washington Post.

Comments

It seems from the article that China's long-term goal is to establish a floating currency. A float system will permit the yuan to rise and fall on global markets according to supply and demand. This system has been adopted by many major currencies, such as the Canadian and U.S. dollars, the euro, and the British pound.

China's adoption of a managed float might be seen as a step towards its ultimate goal of a global floating currency. The managed float will permit the Chinese currency to rise and fall but only within prescribed limits established by a basket of currencies. The basket includes China's biggest trading partners' currencies: the U.S. dollar, the yen, the Korean won, and the euro. It will also include, but weighted on a reduced scale, the currencies of other significant trade partners, including Singapore, the United Kingdom, Malaysia, Russia, Australia, Canada, and Thailand.

It is interesting to note that Singapore, before this announcement, had a very effective managed float system. Malaysia, concurrently with the Chinese initiative, adopted a managed float system using the same basket of currencies as the Chinese, thereby moving with China away from reliance solely on the U.S. dollar.

QUESTIONS

1. China's most strenuous critics in the United States have demanded that Beijing increase the value of its currency by at least 10 percent. Senators Charles E. Schumer and Lindsey O. Graham have been pressing a bill that would impose across-the-board punitive tariffs of 27.5 percent against Chinese imports if China does not substantially raise the value of the yuan. Discuss the merits of such a barrier to trade.

2. Initially, globalization was very good for developing countries. However, within two decades, developing countries, as a result of the inflow of FDI and access to the global capital market, are dramatically affecting the economic global relationship balances. Developed countries now find they have opened Pandora's Box by removing the barriers to the flow of trade. They now find themselves exposed and must constrict imports to prevent their hemorrhaging. This article illustrates how developed countries attempt to interfere with free trade by using one of the instruments available—FX rates. Do you agree?

3. Was this a good or a bad decision from China's economic perspective? From the USA economic perspective? Recall that China is the USA's "prime banker." Do you think that a 10 percent increase in the value of the yuan would make a difference in Wal-Mart's imports from China? Is the problem as simple as the United States' citizens spending too much and saving too little?

ENDNOTES

[1] *Quotations*, (ThinkExist.com Quotations, n.d.), retrieved September 6, 2006, from http://en.thinkexist.com/authors.

[2] Ibid.

[3] *Brainy Quote*, (BrainyMedia.com, n.d.), retrieved September 6, 2006, from www.brainyquote.com.

[4] Ibid.

[5] Ibid.

[6] Mark McNeilly, *Sun Tzu and the Art of Business: Six Strategic Principles for Managers* (New York: Oxford University Press, 1996).

[7] Diana Farrell, Aneta Marcheva Key, and Tim Shavers, *Mapping the Global Capital Markets: Growing Cross-Border Capital Flows* (The McKinsey Quarterly, February 8, 2005), retrieved August 21, 2006, from www.mckinseyquarterly .com/ar_g.aspx?ar=1579&L2=7&L3=10.

[8] Neil Postman, *Technopoly: The Surrender of Culture to Technology*, 1st ed. (New York: Random House Canada, 1993).

[9] McNeilly, *Sun Tzu and the Art of Business: Six Strategic Principles for Managers.*

[10] *What Is Money?* (Bank of Canada, July 2001), retrieved September 6, 2006, from www.bankofcanada.ca/en/ backgrounders/bg-m1.html.

[11] Glyn Davies, *A History of Money: From Ancient Times to the Present Day*, 3rd ed. (Cardiff: University of Wales Press, 2002).

[12] *What Is Gold and When Did It Get to Be the Standard That Backed the World's Money?* (Page Wise Inc, 2002), retrieved August 21, 2006, from http://tx.essortment.com/ goldstandards_rgvh.htm.

[13] Robert A. Mundell, *World Currency* (The Works of Robert A. Mundell, n.d.), retrieved September 6, 2006, from www.robertmundell.net/Menu/Main.asp?Type=5&Cat=09&T hemeName=World%20Currency.

[14] Sohan Sharma, Sue Tracy, and Surinder Kumar, "The Invasion of Iraq: Dollar Vs Euro: Re-Denominating Iraqi Oil in U.S. Dollars, Instead of the Euro," *Third World Traveler* (February 2004).

[15] Ibid.

[16] Robert Krol, *The Case for Open Capital Markets* (CATO Institute, March 15, 2001), retrieved August 21, 2006, from www.freetrade.org/pubs/briefs/tbp-011.pdf.

[17] Ibid.

[18] Ibid.

[19] Ibid.

[20] Roy Davies, *Origins of Money and of Banking* (History of Money from Ancient Times to the Present Day, May 25, 2005), retrieved September 6, 2006, from www.ex.ac .uk/~RDavies/arian/origins.html.

[21] Bank of Canada, *Glossary* (Bank of Canada) retrieved August 21, 2006, from www.bank-banque-canada.ca/en/ glossary/glossary.html.

[22] *Debt* (Investorwords.com, 2005), retrieved August 21, 2006, from www.investorwords.com/1313/debt.html.

[23] *Equity* (Investorwords.com, 2005), retrieved August 21, 2006, from www.investorwords.com/1726/equity.html.

[24] *Debt* (Investorwords.com, 2005).

[25] *Equity* (Investorwords.com, 2005).

[26] Farrell, Key, and Shavers, *Mapping the Global Capital Markets: Growing Cross-Border Capital Flows.*

27 Ibid.

28 Ibid.

29 Ibid.

30 Krol, *The Case for Open Capital Markets*

31 *Bahrain or Dubai to Be Financial Centre of the Middle East?*
(AME Info: Middle East Finance and Economy, September 20,
2003), retrieved August 21, 2006, from
www.ameinfo.com/28398.html.

32 Antonio de Padua Ferreira Passos, *The International Bond
Market and Brazil's Insertion as Sovereign Partner* (Fall 1996),
retrieved August 21, 2006, from www.gwu.edu/~ibi/
minerva/Fall1996/Antonio.de.Padua/Antonio.de.Padua.html.

33 Will Ollard, *The Devil Is in the Default* (Brady Bonds,
November 1999), retrieved August 21, 2006, from www.
financewise.com/public/edit/latin/latrisk2/latr2-brady.htm.

34 PIMCO Foundation, *Global Bond Market Growth Expands
Opportunities* (Bond Basics, May 2004), retrieved August 21,
2006, from www.pimco.com/LeftNav/Bond+Basics/
2004/Global+Bond+Basics.htm.

35 Author-generated data from Werner Antweiler, *Database
Retrieval System* (Pacific Exchange Rate Service, 2006), retrieved
September 7, 2006, from http://fx.sauder.ubc.ca/data.html.

36 Ibid.

37 Kai Li, *The Growth of Global Equity Markets: A Closer Look*
(Econometric Society 2004 North American Winter Meetings,
August 11, 2004), retrieved August 21, 2006, from
http://ideas.repec.org/p/ecm/nawm04/54.html.

Internal— Crafting International Strategy

I n the preceding parts of the text we critically examined selected external factors of the global business ecosystem likely to impact the firm. We drilled down into the political, economic, societal, technological, and cultural attributes (PEST-C) of potential host nations. The earlier materials have helped us understand that the growing international economic interdependence termed *globalization*, driven in part by cheap transportation and an exponential growth in technology, has resulted in a clustering of nations. Furthermore, these trade agreements are grounded in economic trade theory. We can make a case to preserve international institutions such as the International Monetary Fund, the World Bank, and the World Trade Organization to support economic globalization, albeit most would agree they need some revitalization. We concluded our examination of the external ecosystem by looking at world currencies, foreign exchange markets, international monetary systems, and the global capital markets.

Now we turn our attention to the firm itself. Internally, how does a firm prepare to go outside and play in the global village? In this part, we consider the organization's internal attributes, selected variables and processes, and their impact upon the company's international strategic plan. We will examine the generic international strategies and understand the advantages and disadvantages of modes of entry into host countries, with a specific focus on the most common mode—exporting. Once we craft our strategy and select our mode of entry, it is important to select appropriate organizational design (structure) and control systems, and, finally, we place the right bums in the right seats within our organization. Remember, business leaders fail not because of their inability to analyze the ecosystem and craft workable strategies, but because of their inability to implement "the plan." This part commences our examination of how to successfully craft and implement our international business plan.

Global Strategic Management and Modes of Entry

"The secret of business is to know something that nobody else knows."[1]

—*Aristotle Onassis (1906–1975), shipping magnate*

"If what you have done yesterday still looks big to you, you have not done much today."[2]

—*Mikhail Gorbachev, President of the USSR (1990–1991)*

"Competition is in every business; no matter how small or how large, someone is just around the corner forever trying to steal your ideas and build his success out of your imagination, struggling after that which you have toiled endless years to secure, striving to outdo you in each and every way. If such a competitor would work as hard to originate as he does to copy, he would much more quickly gain success."[3]

—*Alice Foote MacDougall (1867–1945), U.S. businesswoman*

"The essence of strategy lies in creating tomorrow's competitive advantages faster than competitors mimic the ones you possess today."[4]

—*Gary Hamel and C.K. Prahalad*

"Analysis is the critical starting point of strategic thinking."[5]

—*Kenichi Ohmae, management consultant*

LEARNING OUTCOMES

- Understand why firms go global.
- Understand the process required to craft an international business strategy and apply a number of strategic models.
- Formulate vision statements, mission statements, goals, and objectives for an international SME.
- Know how to undertake, analyze, and create value in the firm's value chain.
- Evaluate and know when to select the appropriate international strategy (multidomestic, global, transnational, or international).
- Evaluate and select the appropriate mode of entry for an international firm's market-entry strategy.
- Be able to assess the "tension" between local responsiveness and low costs as part of a firm's market-entry strategy and other problems likely to be encountered by business leaders when going international.
- Understand how to measure strategic outcomes.

Canadian Aerial Battle a Lesson for Business: WestJet Parlays Building Blocks of Competitive Advantage

Why do some firms succeed and others fail? Air Canada lies in rubble, struggling to emerge from bankruptcy this month while WestJet rules the Canadian skies. The continuing battle between Canada's titans of air travel offers lessons for small and mid-size Canadian businesses. The key to success lies, in part, in what strategists term competitive advantage.

But what is it? How do you get it? How do you keep it? Harvard Business School professor Michael Porter states that the generic building blocks of competitive advantage are superior quality, superior efficiency, superior innovation and superior customer responsiveness. If your firm develops and implements these competencies better than your competitor, your firm will succeed. Intuitively, entrepreneurs understand the importance of providing their customers with superior quality. Think about the last time you flew with Air Canada and WestJet. Although neither firm publishes the statistics on lost luggage, most of us are able to provide firsthand evidence of the quality difference between these two behemoths. In the 1970s, the Japanese exploited the same superior quality that they continue to exploit today over U.S. automobile

manufacturers. *Fortune Magazine* recently reported the decline of all U.S. car manufacturers as they lose market share to Toyota's innovative and quality product line that includes Lexus, Prius and the popular Echo. Toyota's stock market value is reportedly more than General Motors, Ford, DaimlerChrysler and Volkswagen AG combined.

Advocates such as W. Edwards Deming, the father of total quality management systems (TQMS), have been espousing the importance of TQMS to organizations for more than half a century. Increasingly, organizations are paying attention to quality and embracing standards such as the ISO 9000 series to gain competitive advantage over others within their industry. Doing more with less in a competitive global ecosystem is a necessity. Today, this underlying theme of superior efficiency is prevalent in the public, not-for-profit and private sectors.

Recently, on a trip from Victoria to Toronto, I booked my tickets electronically. The first leg of the trip was with WestJet. When I arrived at the WestJet ticket counter, they provided me with a receipt similar to one received from the grocery store. It contained my seat assignment, depar-

ture time and other relevant details. I asked the friendly attendant how much the ticket cost WestJet. She suggested it was less than a penny. On the next leg of my flight, I received the typical Air Canada boarding pass materials—the cardboard envelope, boarding passes and ticket receipts. When asked, the not-so-friendly attendant said that Air Canada would pay about 31 cents for this bundle of documentation and that computer-scannable documentation would cost more than a dollar. WestJet shows us the way to wring pennies out of the value chain to enhance the bottom line. As entrepreneurs, we must look for these opportunities to find savings.

Superior innovation and speed of implementation are strong components of a firm's competitive advantage. WestJet's early strategy of not directly attacking Air Canada, combined with a unique corporate culture of friendly service, continues to stand the firm in good stead. Supply chain innovation of the kind conceived by Michael Dell, who sold and shipped his first computers from his garage using FedEx, and innovation of the kind adopted by the 18-year-old who built Napster and threatened the very heart of the music industry are illustrative of the new mental models required by organizations. It is a matter of form and substance. The substance of the industry is necessary; the form is flexible. Consider banking. It is required, but the need for banks as the form is not. It is this type of innovative thinking that is evident in WestJet's approach to all aspects of its value chain. Superior customer relationships have also received more attention from WestJet than Air Canada. According to the 2003 Air

Travel Complaints Commissioner's Report, of all complaints filed against all domestic and foreign carriers, 53.7 per cent concerned Air Canada, while only one per cent related to WestJet. Limiting the view to Canadian airlines, 64.4 per cent of the complaints received were about Air Canada while a mere 1.3 per cent focused on WestJet. Finally, of the 1,756 complaints to the national airline ombudsman in 2002, WestJet had only 20 complaints. That's 20 complaints per 4.3 million guests—clearly customer satisfaction.

U.S. author and business strategist Gary Hamel advises us to "put competitors at a continual disadvantage." WestJet has taken this advice to heart. They have taken control and parlayed the generic building blocks of competitive advantage into continual disadvantage for their competitors. No doubt, this resonates with the near-bankrupt Air Canada and its long-suffering shareholders.

Source: "Canadian Aerial Battle a Lesson for Business" by Terrance Power (*The Business Edge*, September 16, 2004). Reproduced with permission of the author.

A SUN TZU MOMENT...

Visual Arts Library, London/Alamy

"Speed is the essence of war. Take advantage of the enemy's unpreparedness; travel by unexpected routes and strike him where he has taken no precautions."[6]

In 1939 Italian operations in North Africa, centred on Libya, required resupply from the Italian mainland. British North African operations, centred in Egypt, suffered similar but much greater supply difficulties. The British Navy convoys had to cross the entire Mediterranean Sea from depots in Gibraltar. Geographically, the Italians were well positioned. However, to protect their ships from British naval attack, the Italians left their ships clustered safely in harbour. This was the prevailing theory of a "fleet-in-being." At the time this "fleet-in-being" strategy seemed sound, the harbour at Taranto contained six battleships (although one was not battle-worthy), seven heavy and two light cruisers, and eight destroyers.

The naval Battle of Taranto took place in November 1940. This first all-aircraft naval battle in history began when the Royal Navy launched a small number of aircraft from a single aircraft carrier in the Mediterranean and attacked the Italian fleet at Taranto. It was revolutionary thinking that gave rise to naval air power.

"The first wave of 12 Fairey Swordfish torpedo bombers left the *Illustrious* just before 21:00, followed by a second wave of 9 aircraft about an hour later. The first wave approached the harbour at 22:58 and split into two groups, one attacking the ships in the outer harbour (*Mar Grande*) and a smaller group flying over the town to the inner harbour (*Mar Piccolo*). The second wave attacked from the northwest over the town about an hour later. During the attacks the battleship *Littorio* took hits from three torpedoes, while the battleships *Conte di Cavour* and *Caio Duilio* were both hit by one each, while a cruiser in the inner harbour had been damaged by bombs. The planes had dropped flares in order to see their targets at night, and although this also gave gunners on the ground better visibility, the Italians shot down only two of the Swordfish."[7]

By the end of the attack the Italian fleet suffered a mortal wound, losing half its strength in one night; the "fleet-in-being" strategy no longer existed, and the Royal Navy took uncontested control of the Mediterranean. The mental model of air-launched torpedo meant experts had previously thought that torpedo attacks against ships required deep water, at least 100 ft (30 m). Yet Taranto was only 40 ft (12 m) deep. To meet these conditions the Royal Navy innovated and used modified torpedoes dropped from a very low height. This new strategy was subsequently adopted by the Japanese at Pearl Harbour.[8]

This Sun Tzu Moment draws our attention to the importance of crafting revolutionary strategies. It is about adopting new mental models, aligning our strategies to fit the vision and mission of the organization, and implementing the strategies quickly. Here, the British Royal Navy crafted and implemented a new strategy that conventional thinking said was impossible. The Japanese ambassador in Italy wrote extensively on this event. Unfortunately, on December 7, 1941, many in the American Navy had not shifted their mental model to this new reality and believed their Navy at Pearl Harbour was safe because, like Taranto, the Hawaiian harbour was shallow.

Be a revolutionary when you craft your international business strategies; be prepared to think differently. A good book on the topic is Gary Hamel's bestseller, *Leading the Revolution*.[9]

Opening Thoughts

"Cheshire Puss," she began, rather timidly, as she did not at all know whether it would like the name: however, it only grinned a little wider. "Come, it's pleased so far," thought Alice, and she went on. "Would you tell me, please, which way I ought to go from here?" "That depends a good deal on where you want to get to," said the Cat. "I don't much care where—" said Alice. "Then it doesn't matter which way you go," said the Cat. "—so long as I get SOMEWHERE," Alice added as an explanation. "Oh, you're sure to do that," said the Cat, "if you only walk long enough."[10]

After spending considerable time examining the broad *external* global ecosystem of international business, the time has come to focus on the *internal* attributes, variables, and issues that a firm must consider to successfully compete internationally. In large part, the success of a firm's operations is dependent upon crafting and implementing a corporate strategy that exploits and leverages the firm's resources and competencies in such a fashion as to build a sustainable competitive advantage. Unlike Alice, firms must care where they are headed; it does matter! Resources are finite and cannot be squandered as Air Canada demonstrates in the opening vignette. Managers have a duty to obtain the best value from assets expended. Businesses are like rose bushes; over time suckers grow, sapping the energy from the bush. Your task as an international business manager is to be constantly vigilant; pruning off initiatives that are not aligned with, nor support the firm's vision and mission statements, in order to guide and strengthen the business's growth. In this chapter we will briefly examine the strategic planning process, the generic strategies you can evaluate, and the modes of entry a firm can consider when contemplating foreign operations.

Crafting International Strategies

Nobody needs to tell you that in the new economy, managers using conventional strategies are losing out to agile competitors who move on ideas that others overlook and who confidently act while others dither. The lessons learned from the Battle of Taranto serve as a reminder that speed and innovation at times are the only tools that firms, and in particular SMEs, have to be competitive. The fundamental problem is the old tools, training, and conceptual frameworks that worked for business-as-usual can't, and don't, work in today's turbulent environment. You must discard old business mental models and aggressively create completely new ones. The sad truth is that over the years strategic planning has been a costly, laborious, and dissatisfying experience for many who undertook the task. It needn't be.

One way these seismic shifts occur in industries is through a shift in the value perceived for the good or service in the mind of the consumer. For example, Canadians who bought insulin from Connaught Laboratories, North York, Ontario, (founded in 1914) initially were most concerned with quality, but as the product quality levels of competing firms became roughly the same, competition shifted to developing applicators that made injections easier. "Suddenly the reason people buy insulin has nothing to do with purity. . . . Similar shifts in the basis of competition occurred with the creation of the business class and frequent-flier programs by airlines. In many industries, the exploitation period for advantages is shrinking. . . . You have to keep making moves that force competitors to respond."[11] In most cases emerging opportunities are accompanied by challenges.

How do companies keep ahead of the curve in making these competitive moves? They do this by critically thinking about their strategies and the implementation. To stay ahead of the competitor, marketers must understand the target market demographics creating needs or wants in the minds of these consumers. Here is the story of two such marketers.

The Emperor's New Clothes by Hans Christian Andersen (1837)

An Emperor from the distant past loved beautiful new clothes. He spent all his money on being finely dressed. One day two swindlers [marketers] explained to the Emperor that their clothing's colours and the patterns were not only extraordinarily beautiful, but in addition, the material had the amazing property of being invisible to anyone who was incompetent or stupid. "It would be wonderful to have clothes made from that cloth," thought the emperor. "Then I would know which of my men are unfit for their positions, and I'd also be able to tell clever people from stupid ones." He hired, at an inflated price, the two swindlers [marketers] to weave their cloth for him. Their looms were set and they pretended to work late into the night. Of course there was nothing on the looms.

Regularly the emperor sent his officials to observe the weavers' progress and report back. While they saw nothing, they reported back how wonderful the material was and that he should have new clothes made from it to wear in a grand procession. The swindlers pretended to work the entire night before the procession was to take place. In the morning the Emperor donned the clothes and looked in the mirror. The emperor saw nothing but he heard "Goodness, they suit you well! What a wonderful fit!" "What a pattern! What colours! Such luxurious clothes!" Not wishing to appear incompetent or stupid, he quickly agreed. No one dared say they could see nothing.

The emperor walked beneath the beautiful canopy through the town, and all the people in the street and in their windows said, "Goodness, the emperor's new clothes are incomparable! What a beautiful train on his jacket. What a perfect fit!" No one wanted it to be noticed that he could see nothing, for then it would be said that he was unfit for his position or that he was stupid. "But he doesn't have anything on!" said a small child. Finally everyone was saying, "He doesn't have anything on!" The emperor shuddered, for he knew that they were right, but he thought, "The procession must go on!" He carried himself even more proudly, and the chamberlains walked along behind carrying the train that wasn't there.

Have you ever been tempted as a result of marketers' skills to buy a Jaguar, a Mont Blanc pen, or a Birks diamond?

Adapted from Hans Christian Andersen, *The Emperor's New Suit* (1837), retrieved August 22, 2006, from http://hca.gilead.org.il/emperor.html.

Value Creation

I tell the story a little differently to my grandson. This child's story is about value creation. I see the two swindlers not as swindlers but as skilled marketers (we need to overlook their fraudulent misrepresentation) who did their job well. They raised the value of the clothes in the mind of the emperor and all of his supporters. Your task when crafting your international strategy is to identify the values your consumers place on the attributes of your products and services and then work toward value creation either by lowering the costs or by differentiation. This chapter's Mini Case, on page 306, provides one such new mental model of successful value creation in developing countries.

In Figure 10.1 note that there are three possible selling prices. First is point "A" (actual cost). This price point represents only the fixed and variable costs (no profit). You can sell your product indefinitely at this price; indeed, for short periods this may be a good strategy to capture market share if your actual costs are lower than those of your competitors. You must find ways to achieve the lowest cost; this is the first variable that will affect the firm's profitability. One way to achieve the lowest possible cost is to undertake a value chain analysis. We will discuss this in a moment. The next price point is "S" on the figure. This represents the selling price. It consists of point "A" (the fixed and variable costs) plus a profit. The final price you need to identify is shown as the value price "V" on the figure. This is the price or value placed on your goods or services in the mind of your customers. You can influence this value. If your marketers have done as good a job in **value creation** as the marketers in our story did with the emperor, then the selling price "S" can be higher, approaching the value price. Failing that, your selling price

Value creation is undertaking activities that increase the perceived value of the goods or services provided to your customers.

FIGURE 10.1
Value Creation—Three Possible Selling Prices

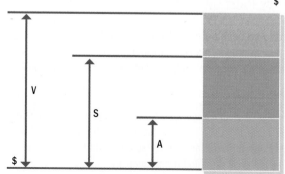

$
V = Value price
S = Selling price
A = Actual price (Fixed + Variable Costs)

V − S = Consumer value
S − A = Profit
V − A = Value added in the
       mind of the consumer

will shift downward toward the actual price and the firm's profits will be less. The selling price will seldom match the value price but can shift closer if you are able to craft a strategy that convinces your customers of the value of your "emperor's new clothes."

Value Chain Analysis

In determining value creation possibilities (cost and/or differentiation), managers should undertake a value chain analysis. This is done by viewing the firm's operations as a series of watertight, value creation activities. You will note in Figure 10.2 that there are two broad categories. The first, primary activities. range from design to after-sales customer service. The primary activities are supported by a cluster of other support activities that supply inputs to permit the primary activities to take place. In the figure we have included the company infrastructure (management, legal, administrative), human resource management, manufacture and supply chain management, and financial management activities. We will examine these activities in subsequent chapters. The figure does not include the many other support activities, such as technology development, which will not be specifically discussed. By carefully viewing each watertight activity we can attempt to identify cost savings that might be achieved, through outsourcing for example, and we can look for opportunities to differentiate our goods and services in order to accommodate the value creation opportunities identified by our customers. Your job is to "wring the pennies" out of the activities in the value chain and/or to add value to the activities to meet or create needs in the customers' minds.

A value chain analysis considers the uniqueness of customers, or small customer segments. It encourages customers to choose the product or service attributes they value most. Logistics management drives design and development, procurement, production, marketing, and service processes, all of which have to be coordinated throughout the organization to meet the different customer expectations at a profit. Logistics management will be covered in subsequent chapters.

Value chain analysis is also valuable for a competitive analysis. Using the same watertight compartments, analyze your competitors similar activities in each of the compartments. Comparatively, where are you strong? Where are you weak? How can you exploit your strengths and mitigate your weaknesses? That is your task.

The Five Tasks of Strategic Management

This is not a strategy text; nevertheless, a working knowledge of some of the basics of strategic management is needed to enhance your understanding of international business and how the materials in the text fit into business planning. Those who are competent in strategy may want to pass over this section. For those who have not taken an introductory strategy course, a quick scan of this material will be helpful in order to understand how the international strategies and modes of entry outlined later in the chapter fit into an international firm's business plan.

A firm's **strategy** can be seen as the "game plan" crafted by management to position the company in selected target markets in a sustainable fashion. How do we achieve our objectives and goals? Strategy involves considering all of the possible options and then

Strategy can be seen as the "game plan" crafted by management to position the company in selected target markets in a sustainable fashion. How do we achieve our objectives and goals? Strategy involves considering all of the possible options that could be chosen and then selecting the most appropriate option(s) having fully examined the firm's ecosystem and its internal resources and competencies to create shareholder value and ensure survival of the firm.

FIGURE 10.2

The Value Chain

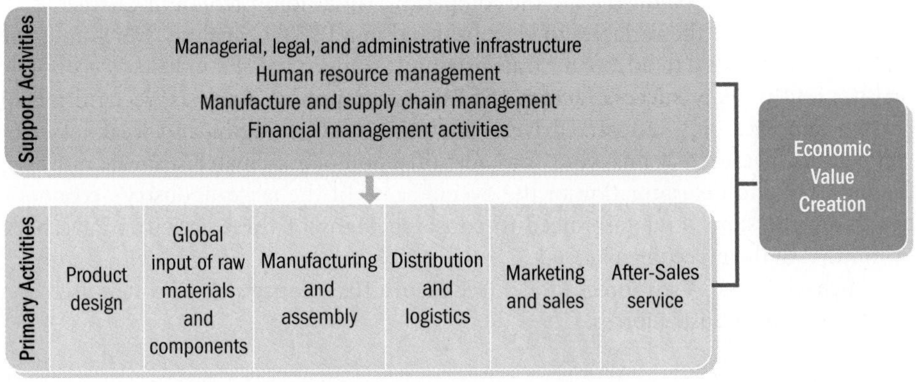

Support Activities	Managerial, legal, and administrative infrastructure Human resource management Manufacture and supply chain management Financial management activities					
Primary Activities	Product design	Global input of raw materials and components	Manufacturing and assembly	Distribution and logistics	Marketing and sales	After-Sales service

Economic Value Creation

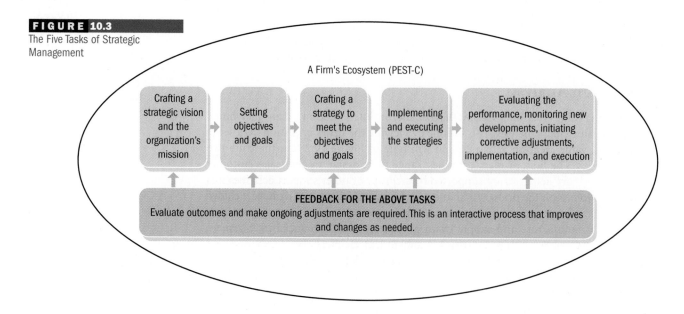

FIGURE 10.3
The Five Tasks of Strategic Management

selecting the most appropriate option(s) having fully examined the firm's ecosystem and its internal resources and competencies in order to create shareholder value and ensure survival of the firm. Unlike Alice, in international business it is important which path your firm follows. There are five interrelated managerial tasks. They are

1. Forming a strategic vision and the organization's mission
2. Setting the objectives and goals for the organization
3. Crafting strategies in support of the objectives
4. Implementing and executing the strategies
5. Evaluating the outcomes; making ongoing, iterative, corrective adjustments to the vision, mission, objectives, strategies and implementation processes.

See Figure 10.3 for an overview of the concepts of vision, mission statements, goals, objectives, strategies, action plans, competitive advantage, and distinctive competencies. Visit www.power.nelson.com for further strategic thinking concepts.

The Strategic Thinking and Analysis Process

Externally

Crafting a strategy is an analysis-driven exercise that cannot be solely based on opinions, gut feelings, and creative thinking. Managers must undertake solid analysis. Interestingly, when U.S. General Colin Powell, in the first Gulf War, was asked how much information he needed to make a decision, he replied 60 percent. While I don't recommend 60 percent, the lesson is you cannot wait for "perfect" information because the turbulence in your industry's ecosystem today requires you to be agile. If you delay too long you will miss the opportunity.

First, examine the company's external environment (see Figure 10.4) by thinking strategically about the industry and the competitive conditions present. In Chapters 2, 3, and 4 we examined the variables to be considered in a PEST-C analysis, which must be fully considered now. In addition, strategists must understand the industry's economic realities and the **key success factors (KSFs)**. A competitive analysis, recognition of current and emerging industry drivers, analysis of the strengths and weaknesses of competitors measured against your firm, identification of anticipated strategic moves in the industry, and determination of the overall sense of the target industry's economic health are the steps strategists need to consider. Many of these activities have been introduced in the preceding chapters.

Michael Porter's Five Forces Model (see Figure 10.5 on page 256) is often used as a tool to examine industry forces.

Key success factors (KSFs) can be defined as those attributes most likely to contribute to the success of a firm in the target industry. They are the attributes upon which firms must build competencies.

FIGURE 10.4
The Strategic Thinking and
Analysis Process

External strategic thinking about the industry and its ecosystem

Ask:
- Using Porter's five forces model, what are the entry barriers, strengths, and weaknesses of suppliers and buyers; how strong is the rivalry; and what are the possibility of substitutions?
- What are the current and forecasted economic conditions for the industry?
- What is driving change in the industry?
- What are the key success factors necessary to succeed in the industry?
- Is the industry an attractive investment given the other possible opportunities?

Internal strategic thinking about the firm and its competitive position

Ask:
- How well is the company's current strategy working?
- What resources does the firm have and what resources does it need to acquire or enhance skills?
- What are the firm's strengths, weaknesses, opportunities, and threats?
- How competitive are the firm's costs compared to rivals?
- What are the emerging strategic issues the firm needs to consider?
- How strong is the firm's current competitive position?

Strategic decision required by the firm to maintain its competitive position

Ask:
Does the firm need only retail changes (minor) to its existing strategy, or are wholesale changes (major) required?

Is it the right strategy?

Undertake a threefold test:
- Does it fit the company's competencies and resources?
- Will it contribute to the firm's building a sustainable competitive advantage?
- Will it enhance the firm's performance?

Internally

In this chapter and subsequent chapters, business practitioners are introduced to the questions that must be examined and answered concerning how well the company's present strategy is working: the internal resources (land, capital, labour); strengths and weaknesses; the opportunities and threats identified by a SWOT analysis; the firm's costs in relation to competitor's costs; a competitor analysis (based on the **SMART** model); the strength of competitors; and the strategic issues to be addressed by undertaking a gap analysis based on the SMART model. Prior to considering marketing products or services on a global scale, a company needs to clearly understand its internal strengths and weaknesses. This includes determining whether the company has the human resources capacity and the financial capability, systems, and maturity to implement and sustain an international marketing program.

One helpful decision-making tool is referred to as the Simple Multi-Attribute Rating Technique (SMART model). (See www.power.nelson.com.) The model is easy for business decision makers to apply and helps a firm assess the company's competitive position and its competitive strength vis-à-vis similar firms in the industry. This model will determine whether the firm's market position will remain stable or is likely to shift; the relative position of the firm in relation to other key rivals within the industry; the strengths and weaknesses of the firm's current competitive advantages or lack thereof; and the likelihood of the firm's success or failure in defending its current position in the face of shifts in the ecosystem and emerging strategies of competitors.

An effective business tool used to assess both the internal and external microenvironment of a company is a **SWOT** analysis. Using the model shown in Figure 10.6, page 286, the organization can assess and analyze its readiness to expand

SMART is an acronym for the Simple Multi-Attribute Rating Technique decision-making tool. The model is easy for business decision makers to apply and helps a firm assess the company's competitive position and its competitive strength vis-à-vis similar firms in the industry.

SWOT is an acronym for Strengths, Weaknesses, Opportunities, and Threats. A SWOT analysis is an effective business tool to assess both the internal (strengths and weaknesses) as well as the external (opportunities and threats) of the company's microenvironment.

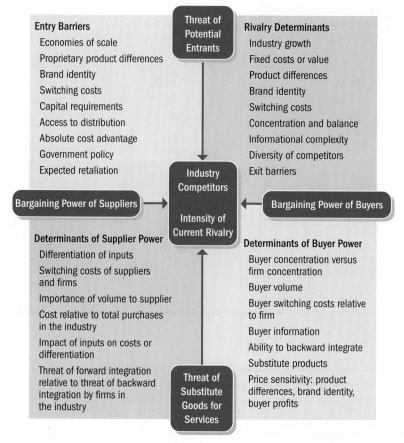

Source: Michael E. Porter, *Competitive Advantage* (New York: Free Press, 1985).

its business internationally. The SWOT includes performing a "candid" internal assessment of the company's strengths and weaknesses, and its external opportunities and threats. A company must closely examine its competitive advantages and address any deficiencies through its business planning process. A SWOT analysis is also a very effective instrument to evaluate potential international business partners and alliances to assess their overall strengths and weaknesses.

Based on the data collected and by responding to the various questions, the strategist must analyze the data and consider the firm's current situation and its available resources. Managers must determine whether the current strategy is working and, if it isn't, what other viable options are within the firm's capability and competencies. The test in determining the best strategic option is to ask a series of

Internal Organization Analysis		External Ecosystem Analysis	
↓		↓	
Controllable Factors		Uncontrollable Factors	
Relates to organizational strengths and weaknesses that the organization has the decision-making power *to change* if it chooses.		Relates to external factors over which the organization has no descision-making power. The organization can respond or not respond, but it *cannot change* the external factors.	
S	**W**	**O**	**T**
Organizational Strengths	Organizational Weaknesses	External Factors that are Opportunities	External Factors that are Threats

questions: Is the proposed option a good fit with the vision and mission statements and the firm's available resources? Will it contribute to building a sustainable competitive advantage for the firm? Will it create value for shareholders and strengthen the firm's survivability? If the answers are yes, then there is merit in adopting the strategy. Strategists must undertake hard critical thinking and analyze the data they have collected for the models and draw all of the "so what's" from their data when crafting their strategies.

When analyzing data, look beyond the surface level of a fact by asking a series of "so what's." Our competitor is opening a factory in China. So what? Well, China's labour is less expensive than ours. So what? Well, our competitor's cost base will go down. So what? They will be able to make their product for less than us. Ah-ha. This technique will help you "peel the onion" to reveal deeper meaning from the facts.

Five Generic Competitive Strategies

In 1980, Michael Porter introduced a classification scheme for five generic competitive strategies.[12] The objective of a competitive strategy is to provide management with an action plan for competing successfully in the marketplace and delivering superior value (either perceived or actual) to consumers. Porter's five strategies reduce the wide range of possible strategies to their essence. They address how a firm targets customers, and how it withstands competition and strengthens its position in the marketplace. Strategies are selected based on whether the target market is broad or narrow, and whether the firm is pursuing a competitive advantage that is driven by either low cost or product differentiation.

Porter's five generic competitive strategies, as illustrated in Figure 10.7, are (1) a low-cost leadership strategy that is crafted to attract a broad range of customers to your firm as the overall low-cost provider in the marketplace; (2) a broad differentiation strategy that provides a differentiated product that can be distinguished from rivals' products in ways that increase value in the minds of a broad range of customers; (3) a best-cost strategy that gives customers value for money by providing the lowest cost possible for goods and services that have some of the value-added attributes found in the differentiated goods and services with the aim of providing the best value for money for the goods and services offered; (4) a focused or market niche strategy that is based on low cost and provides the lowest cost possible to a very narrow customer base by providing price points lower than your competitors; (5) and finally a focused or market niche strategy based on differentiation that provides a very narrow customer base a customized product or service with attributes that differentiate it in the customers' minds better than the competition.

The Strategic Process Is Replicated Internally

The firm is now in a position to provide its corporate strategic plan. The plan is shared throughout the organization, and the decision makers at both the functional and operational levels conduct a similar process though their lenses. Figure 10.8, on page 288, indicates the responsibility for producing plans, but the process of gathering inputs is conducted at all levels; high levels of diversity and broad participation in the planning process are essential from all levels. It is only by engaging stakeholders in the strategic process that we can expect the prerequisite sense of ownership of the resulting strategy. If there is buy-in then we have the best chance for success in implementation. Strategic planning is an ongoing iterative effort that enables firms to accommodate changes in the ecosystem. In subsequent chapters we will focus on the marketing, manufacture, and supply chain management roles; the human resource management roles; and the financial management roles in strategic international business planning. We will examine selected variables and

FIGURE 10.7

Porter's Model of the Five Generic Competitive Strategies

Type of Competitive Strategy Being Pursued

	Lower Cost	Differentiation
A Broad Cross-Section of Buyers	Overall Low-Cost Leadership Strategy	Broad Differentiation Strategy
	Best-Cost Provider Strategy	
A Narrow Buyer Segment	Focused Low-Cost Strategy	Focused Differentiation Strategy

Market Target

Source: Michael E. Porter, *Competitive Strategy* (New York: Free Press, 1980).

FIGURE 10.8

Strategy Replication in a Single
Business Corporation

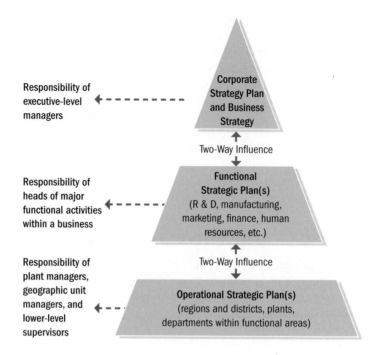

Responsibility of
executive-level ← – – – – – – –   **Corporate Strategy Plan and Business Strategy**
managers

Two-Way Influence

Responsibility of
heads of major ← – – – – – –   **Functional Strategic Plan(s)** (R & D, manufacturing, marketing, finance, human resources, etc.)
functional activities
within a business

Two-Way Influence

Responsibility of
plant managers,
geographic unit ← – –   **Operational Strategic Plan(s)** (regions and districts, plants, departments within functional areas)
managers, and
lower-level
supervisors

emerging trends that must be considered by these different functional units when crafting their supportive strategies. Remember, these strategies must align with the organization's overall vision, mission, and the corporate goals and objectives. The closer the strategies align, the greater the firm's success.

You will observe from Figure 10.8 that the corporate-level business strategy flows to the functional-level managers. Managers at this level prepare their strategic plan for their functional responsibility (human resources, finance, marketing, etc.) based on the guidance contained in the corporate strategic plan. Once complete, these functional plans are passed to the operational level within the functions where the operational strategies will be crafted. At all levels, each strategic plan must support and align horizontally and vertically throughout the corporation, ultimately supporting the corporate vision statement. This completes our brief review of strategy as it relates to international business. With this generic understanding of how to craft a strategy, we now examine the decision-making process leading to the implementation of a firm's international business strategy.

Overview of the Decision-Making Process and Implementation of International Business Strategy

Initially firms have a *reason*, a motivation, to enter foreign marketplaces. After analyzing these motivating factors and having decided that it makes good business sense to go global, we considered Porter's five generic competitive strategies and their respective advantages and disadvantages. Next, having chosen the appropriate international strategy that best fits with the organization's resources and competencies, we select one of seven modes of entry. We must consider each of these modes' advantages and disadvantages, and select the one that fits with the core competencies and resources of the firm. Then we can craft and undertake the action plans necessary to implement the corporate-, functional-, and operational-level strategies. Finally, as with any process, we must evaluate and analyze the outcomes. This ongoing feedback will guide strategic iterative adjustments in order to achieve the best performance possible (see Figure 10.9). In the next section, we will expand on this process. Remember, at the core of this process is the need for innovation and speed.

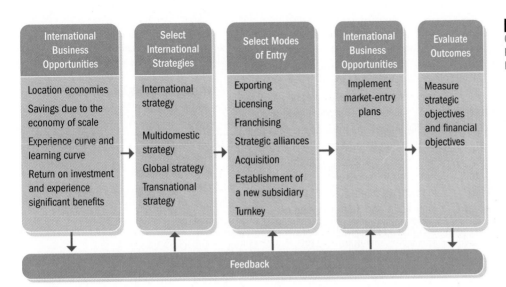

FIGURE 10.9
Overview of the Decision-Making Process and Implementation of International Strategy

JUST DOING THE RIGHT THING

Innovation Hinges on New Mental Models: Creative Thinking Pays Dividends in Business

Business leaders often talk of the need for innovation within their organizations. A large percentage of their mission statements contain the word *innovative*. But innovation doesn't just happen. It takes original thinking, a fresh view of the big picture and bold steps into the unknown to create and introduce something new. The ground must be fertile within organizations to allow innovation to take root and flourish. Studies indicate that 80 per cent of decisions are made based on past events. To be innovative, we must be aware of these old mental models as we seek new, innovative solutions to meet today's challenges. History is important, but basing future change on past results will only lead to small incremental changes, like adjusting the jib sail on a boat. In today's turbulent business ecosystem, this is a recipe for disaster.

We need new mental models. . . . (Andrew Grove, CEO, of Intel Corp) once observed there are only two types of firms: The quick and the dead. Revolutionary change is needed. In order to accomplish revolutionary

change, we must engage in fresh, unencumbered strategic thinking. We must mitigate the damage of emerging threats and exploit the opportunities presented by the instability within our business ecosystem. Proponents of the old mental models often seek their solutions in finding more people and throwing more money at the problem. The new mental model requires creative, agile and innovative thinking.

There are many high-profile examples of leaders who have adapted new mental models successfully. Examples include Dell computers, WestJet and eBay. As these corporate leaders seized new mental models and revolutionized their industries, their competitors were blindsided. The solution was not more money or more people but fresh, innovative, strategic thought. All organizations have a genetic blindness, just as land is a mystery to fish because fish are not genetically equipped to understand land. By the time the fish understands the land it is often too late. [Do you see the future coming?]

In order to create the fertile ground necessary to produce revolutionary, innovative change, Professor Gary Hamel suggests that five things must happen: *Add new voices*. Organizations must invite young people and other new voices into

the decision-making process. These fresh eyes will provide fresh insights. *Create new conversations.* Consider who has attended your strategy meetings in the past. Are they always the same people? That will lead to disaster. Organizations must break free from the scripted concentrated meetings of the past. Conversations that cross functional and geographic boundaries will lead to new thinking. The true value comes from continuing dialogues. Revolutionary change can't be crammed into one planning afternoon. Venture divisions established by organizations are useful if funded and given the authority to accelerate the innovative process within organizations. *Promote new perspectives.* Organizations can't raise the IQ of individuals, but they can change perspectives by helping them see the world in different ways. Recall the Jimmy Buffet song, "Changes in Attitudes, Changes in Latitudes." The ability to stand in a new place will help the issues to be seen in a new way. For example, business leaders should teach and academics should lead business for a time in order to provide them with powerful new perspectives. This would bring fresh new thoughts to problems when they return to their sectors. *Establish shared passions.* There must be a passion for diversity and employees must have a passion for the organization. Charles Schwab CEO David Pottruck commented, "Our employees see themselves as custodians of our customer's financial dreams." When was the last time you heard that passion expressed by your employees? *Encourage experimentation.* The route to the desired result is hidden. Often, the pursuit of efficiency and fiscal restraint drive out the very experimentation necessary to find the needed innovation. How many experiments does your organization have under way? When asked, many of my clients can't point to any innovative new

experiments within their organization. At any one time, an organization should have 20 or 30 small experiments under way. This will lead to fertile ground for revolutionary change. Do not be afraid to experiment—mistakes are a good thing.

Organizations must spend less time focusing on innovation as a "thing" and more time focusing on the things that lead to innovation. As business leaders, we need to stop talking about innovation and start adopting new mental models that permit innovative strategic thinking to take root.

Source: "Innovation Hinges on New Mental Models" by Terrance Power (*The Business Edge*, April 22, 2004). Reproduced with permission of the author.

CRITICAL THINKING QUESTIONS

Do you accept that innovation and speed are the two keys to success for Canadian business in the international marketplace?

How can you become an agent of change in your organization and contribute to the creation of "fertile ground"?

Domestic Firms Can Profit from Going Global—Four Motivating Factors

Domestic firms are motivated by four factors (opportunities) when they consider entering a foreign market. First, firms motivated by their need to enhance shareholders' value exploit global *location economies*. They do this by moving some of the firm's value chain activities to locations that offer the best value for money. Second, firms experience savings by marketing their products and services globally from a central location, achieving savings due to the *economy of scale, experience curve, and learning curve.* Third, firms *transfer part or all of their core competencies and distinctive skills to foreign subsidiaries* where indigenous competitors are at a disadvantage, achieving a greater return on investment. Finally, firms participating in the global marketplace over time experience significant benefits (including increased market size) as a result of the *foreign subsidiary developing and transferring skills, research and development, and core competencies* with the home country and other global subsidiaries.

Location Economies

You will recall from Chapter 6, pages 162–163, that comparative advantage arises from the differences in cost factors in each country. Michael Porter's determinants of national competitive advantage model defined these in part as factor endowments (advanced and basic). Firms actively seek global locations where advantages exist. However, there are further considerations beyond a preliminary cost analysis when determining whether to exploit location economies. First, transportation costs might be so exorbitant that the advantages gained by establishing a foreign subsidiary are lost because of the *high transportation cost.* Clearly there is a difference in transportation costs between silicon computer chips and a Jaguar motorcar. Second, *trade barriers*, whether direct costs or administrative, might also negate the advantage of a particular location. The third consideration, as we noted in Chapter 3, pages 67–68, is the importance of undertaking a *political risk assessment.* It might well be that on the surface the location economy cost analysis reflects a positive outcome, but the potential political instability or emerging economic risks may warrant excluding the country from consideration.

The Experience Curve, Economies of Scale, and the Learning Curve

The experience curve, economies of scale, and the learning curve contribute to the firm's bottom line. Accordingly, firms attempt to position themselves as low on the curve as possible because of the benefits they will receive. The three curve down and to the right as observed in Figure 10.10.

FIGURE 10.10

The Experience Curve, Economies of Scale and the Learning Curve

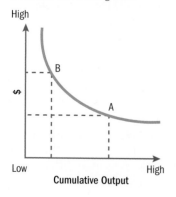

Experience Curve

You will note that the unit costs fall as the *cumulative* output increases. Studies indicate that systematic reductions in production costs will occur over the lifetime of the product due to the economies of scale and the learning curve effect.

Economies of Scale

Firms can reduce unit costs by increasing the number of units produced and spreading the fixed costs over more units, resulting in lower per unit costs. Second, increasing the number of units generally affords the opportunity to acquire larger machines and state-of-the-art technology, both of which will contribute to lowering costs. Third, workers may now specialize in their core competencies. Recall that Adam Smith's theory demonstrated that workers (nations) specializing in what they do well will produce greater efficiencies than in a small firm where workers have to undertake many production-related functions. The net effect is that firms producing a larger quantity should have, as a result of the economies of scale, a significant advantage.

Learning Curve

The learning curve reflects the notion that as workers perform a function they become more experienced and therefore it generally follows that they will become more efficient. This curve and the benefits are quite noticeable during the start-up stages; however, over time the benefits from the learning curve abate.

Increasing Return on Investment—Firms Transferring Their Core Competencies and Distinctive Skills to Foreign Subsidiaries

Both domestic and foreign firms have value chains. However, an analysis of their respective value chains may indicate gaps that can be exploited or advantages mitigated. When transferring competencies and skills to foreign subsidiaries, firms with value creation activities within their value chain generally have a competitive advantage over indigenous firms. It is important that these competitive advantages be difficult to replicate by competitors in the new location, and the value creation be recognized as being of value by the new customers. In addition, firms that lever their core competencies in foreign markets can attain cost advantages, thereby increasing their total global sales and return on investment.

Significant Benefits from Foreign Subsidiaries Transferring Skills, R&D, and Core Competencies

Today MNEs' core competencies not only reside in the home country but also are developed by all units in the firm's global operations. The transfer of skills, R&D, and production offerings move back and forth between a subsidiary and the home offices. This exchange is referred to as **global learning**. Each subsidiary learns from the others, irrespective of whether the unit is the home or a foreign subsidiary. The knowledge "grown" within the organization is leveraged. An occasional impediment to global learning is the unwillingness of certain management within the domestic firm to believe they can learn anything from their foreign subsidiaries. Firms must not adopt an ethnocentric view of knowledge but understand that the best thoughts and practices will percolate throughout the firm's global organization. Managers require the aptitude to recognize emerging innovation from whatever source in the global organization and to exploit the opportunities it will present. Global learning and innovative practices must be rewarded and the ground made fertile for everyone within the organization to feel comfortable and learning to take "root." All must be encouraged to come forward with their new ideas. Champions should be established within the firm to mentor and foster new practices.

Global learning is the transfer of skills, R&D, and production offerings that move back and forth between subsidiary offices and the home office. Each subsidiary learns from the others, irrespective of whether the unit is the home or a foreign subsidiary.

FIGURE 10.11
Four Basic Strategies

A **global strategy** focuses on increasing profitability by pursuing a low-cost strategy. Cost reductions come from the experience curve effect and location economies. Global strategists prefer to market a standardized product worldwide so they can reap the maximum benefit from economies of scale. They see the world as one global marketplace.

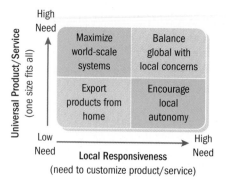

FIGURE 10.12
Need for Universal Product/Services versus Local Responsiveness Matrix

An **international strategy** is one where the home firm wishes to leverage by transferring its valuable competencies, skills, and products to foreign markets.

International Strategic Choices

In the second stage of the decision-making process and implementation of international business strategy (see Figure 10.9 on page 289), firms undertake an external and internal analysis using the strategic concepts and models we reviewed, e.g., SMART, SWOT, Porter's Five Forces, and others we have not reviewed in this text. Having completed an analysis and understanding the limits to their resources and competencies, business decision makers then craft their international strategy. There are four!

There are four basic international strategic choices for market entry. (Note these are not the modes of entry we will discuss later in the chapter). The strategic choices are international, multidomestic, global, and transnational strategies as shown in Figure 10.11. In *Managing Across Borders*, Christopher Bartlett and Sumantra Ghoshal[13] defined the four basic competitive strategies and their advantages and disadvantages. The best international strategy for your firm depends on your strategic analysis. Is there great pressure for cost reductions? How strong is the need to be locally responsive in your product or service offering? The strategy you select will be determined in large part by these two questions.

Global Strategy

A **global strategy** focuses on increasing profitability by pursuing a low-cost strategy. Cost reductions come from the experience curve effect and location economies. Global strategists prefer to market a standardized product worldwide so they can reap the maximum benefit from economies of scale. They see the world as one global marketplace. The production, marketing, and R&D functions are concentrated in a few favourable global locations. Global firms are reluctant to customize their product or service to meet the needs of the host market because of costs. Theirs is a "one size fits all" strategy. See Figure 10.12, Need for Universal Product/Services versus Local Responsiveness Matrix. They may use their cost advantage as a weapon against the competition by adopting aggressive pricing in those locations where there is strong pressure for cost reduction and demands for local responsiveness are minimal. Increasingly, conditions of minimal responsiveness and low cost prevail in many industrial goods industries and commodities. This strategy is not a good fit when demands for local responsiveness are high. Canada's firms trading in commodities like oil, lumber, copper, steel, and uranium are all examples of firms that have successfully adopted a global strategy. Over time, strategies can change. With the advent of globalization and cheap transportation, Swedish firm Ikea, producer of well-designed functional home-furnishing products, initially successfully adopted a global strategy. Its products were shipped unassembled to global host countries in order to achieve low cost by using the latest technology and supply chain methods. However, recently Ikea is being forced to accommodate local demands to tailor its furniture for host countries' consumers and is shifting some parts of its operation from a global strategy to a multinational strategy.

International Strategy

An **international strategy** is one where the home firm wishes to leverage by transferring its valuable competencies, skills, and products to foreign markets. This is possible because generally the industries in the host country do not possess these skills nor possess the competitive advantages. An international strategy works well for firms wishing to produce differentiated products in their foreign subsidiaries. Generally this strategy retains the R&D, corporate financial management, and other head office–type functions at home. While an international strategy will establish production and marketing functions in each major country, the overall control of these functions will remain with the home office. The company will undertake the minimum local customization of product offerings and experience little pressure to provide the lowest cost. Firms should not use an international strategy if the pressures for local responsiveness are high or they will soon lose their market share to those firms that are customizing product offerings to meet the needs of local conditions. By replicating manufacturing facilities in the foreign subsidiaries, the strategy has high operating costs and is therefore inappropriate in manufacturing industries where cost pressures are highly competitive. A large number of Canadian universities, for example, have successfully adopted an international strategy to leverage their competencies by providing education in developing countries. Has yours?

Multidomestic Strategy

A **multidomestic strategy** maximizes the customization of the firm's goods and services offerings. In essence, the firm is replicating the home facilities (functions), and transplanting them to the foreign subsidiary. It sees itself almost as a collection of independent subsidiaries, with foreign subsidiaries producing goods and services designed specially to meet the needs of the market each serves. A multidomestic marketing strategy specifically accommodates the different national cultures found in each host country. As a result, the firm is unable to exploit location economies, economies of scale, or the experience curve. It is also hindered from transferring and leveraging its core competencies to the foreign market. A multidomestic strategy makes the most sense where there are high pressures for local responsiveness and low pressures for cost reduction. Because of the high costs associated with replicating production facilities, the strategy does not work well where cost pressures are intense. A further weakness of a multidomestic strategy is that over time the foreign subsidiaries tend to develop into watertight decentralized organizations, with each unit seeking greater autonomy. It is a very costly model. Most will recognize KFC, Coca-Cola, Microsoft, and McDonald's as examples of multinational corporations that have successfully adopted a multidomestic strategy by adapting their products and services to meet the demands of local markets. Philips and Motorola also provide good examples of firms that have successfully followed a multidomestic strategy that has resulted in innovation from local research and development, entrepreneurial spirit, production of products that are tailored to the individual countries, and high quality due to backward integration.

> A **multidomestic strategy** maximizes the customization of the firm's goods and services offerings. In essence, the firm is replicating the home facilities (functions), and transplanting them to the foreign subsidiary. It sees itself almost as a collection of independent subsidiaries.

Transnational Strategy

A **transnational strategy** tries to capture the best of all worlds. These firms want the global scale efficiencies and the benefits derived from being locally responsive to their customers. Those adopting this strategy are trying to add value by "exploiting experience based cost economies, location economies and transferring core competencies while paying attention to the pressures for local responsiveness."[14] Many international practitioners do not accept this fourth strategy (transnational). However, Bartlett and Ghoshal suggest, and I accept, that crafting strategies for turbulent times requires firms to exploit the experience and location curves and transfer their core competencies to gain lower costs. "While holding costs down, they must pay attention to the pressures for local responsiveness. A transnational strategy makes sense when the firm faces high pressures for cost reduction and high pressures to be locally responsive. It is not an easy strategy to pursue and is very difficult to implement because of the challenge in finding the appropriate organizational structure and controls. Nevertheless, "the transnational form may be the ideal way for a firm to 'think globally' and 'act locally.' Caterpillar Inc. has tried to do both by manufacturing many identical components at a few global locations, and setting up assembly in each of its major markets where the product can be tailored to local needs."[15]

> A **transnational strategy** tries to capture the best of all worlds—the global-scale efficiencies and the benefits derived from being locally responsive to customers. Those adopting this strategy are trying to add value by "exploiting experience-based cost economies, location economies and transferring core competencies while paying attention to the pressures for local responsiveness."[16]

The advantages and disadvantages for these four international strategic choices are summarized in Figure 10.13, page 294.

Modes of Entry

Stage three in the decision-making process and implementation of international business strategy is selecting the appropriate modes of entry. (See Figure 10.9 on page 289.) We have briefly examined selected strategic management concepts that will assist us in

FIGURE 10.13
Advantages and Disadvantages of
the Four Basic Strategies

Strategy	Advantages	Disadvantages
Global	• Experience curve savings can be exploited • Location economies savings can be exploited	• Not responsive to local needs
International	• Core competencies to foreign markets are transferable	• Not responsive to local needs • Inability to exploit location economies • Failure to exploit experience curve savings
Multidomestic	• Products and marketing can be customized to meet the need for local responsiveness	• Inability to exploit location economies • Failure to exploit experience curve savings • Inability to transfer core competencies to foreign markets • Tendency to create "silos"
Transnational	• Experience curve savings can be exploited • Location economies savings can be exploited • Global learning opportunities can be exploited • Products and marketing can be customized to meet the need for local responsiveness	• Implementation difficulties because of organizational tensions—a challenge to be "all things to all people"

crafting a firm's strategic plan for entering foreign markets. Through analysis we have determined which foreign markets to enter; we have determined when to enter; and we have undertaken a risk assessment by examining the internal and external attributes discussed earlier in the text and elsewhere in this chapter. In the balance of this chapter, we examine the methods or modes available to businesses contemplating entering the global marketplace and their advantages and disadvantages.

Of the 190 or so nations available to be considered as a host country, firms generally limit their selection to a much smaller number, mainly those that are politically stable and have a free market system. Firms also require, as we discussed in Chapter 3, pages 74–75, that the host country's economic conditions be favourable. Once a firm has decided to be the first mover, the firm must turn its mind to the scale of entry. Does it wish to make a major strategic commitment? Making such a large-scale entry is likely to "poke the bear," causing the indigenous competition and their government to stir with countermeasures. Is it better advice to follow the dictum of China's former chairman, Deng Xiaoping that suggests that entering a market is like "crossing a river by feeling for each stone?" What is the appropriate balance? Answers to questions such as these will be governed by finding the best fit between the firm's core competencies and the mode of entry selected. There are seven entry modes available for consideration by firms entering a global marketplace. These can be classified primarily as *contractual* or *investment* modes.

Each mode has its own advantages and disadvantages. When we reviewed foreign direct investment (FDI) in Chapter 7, we examined several investment modes of entry—wholly owned subsidiaries, joint ventures, and greenfields. The FDI modes of entry are high in risk because they require direct investment in plant and equipment, and ongoing involvement in the foreign subsidiary's operations. They can also present significant risks due to political, economic, societal, technological, and cultural shifts. We will now examine these FDI modes and those based primarily on contractual arrangements. Primary contractual modes are generally lower in risk and require less operational control. (See Figure 10.14.)

Exporting (Contractual)

Exporting is the mode adopted by most companies entering foreign markets. Because of its popularity as an entry mode we will examine it separately and in greater detail in Chapter 12. The *advantages* of exporting include the avoidance of financial risk; the possibility of exploiting the experience curve, and the realization of location economies. Exporting *disadvantages* include that firms must be vigilant with respect to competitors who, having been exposed to the exported product, will consider replicating it in their country. Competitors able to set up production facilities leveraging the advantages of their location economies to include supplying "homemade" products to the host country will have an advantage. Adding transportation costs can make your products more expensive than those produced and sold in the host country. It is also possible that additional costs will be incurred because of trade barriers and governmental administrative impediments on imports. Finally, many firms experience difficulties with those they have engaged to conduct their marketing, sales, and service in the host country. These "independent" entities are committed only by contract and, therefore, might not have the same "passion" as the exporter does for the product and its servicing. Competitors in the host country will have a competitive advantage if this situation persists.

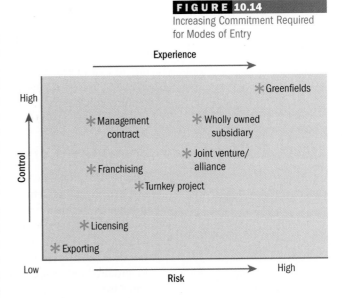

FIGURE 10.14
Increasing Commitment Required for Modes of Entry

Licensing (Contractual)

Licensing is a budget-price technique adopted by a firm (the licensor-owner of intangible property) wishing to increase its export sales by contracting with a foreign firm (the licensee-purchaser) under what is known as a **licensing agreement.** The licensor, in return for granting these rights, receives a royalty on sales. Intangible property includes copyrights, trademarks, patents, formulas, inventions, recipes, processes, designs, and other items. They are distinguished from real or tangible property, such as real estate and automobiles. The advantages of licensing include low development costs and financial risk for the licensor. Generally the licensee puts up the financial capital necessary for the development costs and undertakes the risks associated with opening and ongoing operation of the plant in the host country. Licensing is an attractive option for firms wanting to establish a global presence but not desiring to undertake significant financial risk. Often an advantage can be realized when the licensee leverages the intangible property by producing new products and services not currently provided by the licensor. For example, a number of Canadian universities license their IT online platforms to educational institutions in developing countries. It is a condition of the licensing agreement that if the developing countries' educational institutions enhance the platform then those enhancements would be available without cost to the Canadian universities. The disadvantages of licensing include the lack of tight control over the use of technology, quality of manufacturing, and marketing. By granting others the rights to build plants and sell the product, the licensor is estopped (prohibited) from exploiting location economies and lower costs from the experience curve. A further disadvantage is that licensing can become an impediment at a later date should the licensor decide to develop a different global strategy. Often young firms license their intangible assets only to find that they want to exercise control over a global strategy at a later date but find themselves hindered because of the contractual rights provided earlier to licensees. It might be, for example, contractually impossible to establish a foreign-owned subsidiary where a licence has been issued. Furthermore, the licensee's operations may not align with the licensor's eventual long-term global initiatives.

The disadvantages of licensing agreements can be reduced by the inclusion of **cross-licensing** agreements. By contractually sharing valuable know-how, both parties reduce the risk associated with licensing intangible assets. The licensee recognizes that any

Licensing is a budget-price technique adopted by a firm (the licensor-owner of intangible property) wishing to increase its export sales by contracting with a foreign firm (the licensee-purchaser) under what is known as a licensing agreement.

A **licensing agreement** is the right to use intangible property in the manufacture and sale of a firm's product under specific terms and conditions (time, venue, etc). The licensor, in return for granting these rights, receives a royalty on sales.

A **cross-licensing** agreement provides for the exchange of licensing agreements between the licensor and the licensee.

violation of the licensing contract exposes its intangible assets that have been cross-licensed to the licensor. In essence, the firms hold each other hostage. Cross-licensing reduces the probability that the parties to the agreement will lightly break the terms of the contract. Connecting the licensing agreement to a joint venture between the two parties is another method commonly practised to mitigate the disadvantages of licensing by creating a vested interest in the economic well-being of the new venture. We discussed joint ventures in Chapter 7, and will look at it again briefly here. Should we license or adopt FDI? See Figure 10.15.

Franchises (Contractual)

A franchise is another entry mode whereby the franchisor (owner) grants rights and ongoing support, including setting up the facility and continuing support with the franchisee throughout the life of the contract, in return for compensation. Franchising agreements are not standardized and vary from franchise to franchise; however, they are generally very one-sided contracts in favour of the franchisor. Franchises are generally adopted in service industries, such as restaurants, fast food, photo shops, etc. There are two forms of franchise: the product/trade name franchise and the business format franchise. **Product/trade name franchisors** have established product names, logos, and trademarks, and they sell the right to use these intangible products to another party. The contracts can be exclusive or nonexclusive depending upon the terms of the contract. **Business format franchisors**, in addition to providing intangible rights, including the product trade name, also generally provide assistance in site selection, building, staff training, products supply, advertising and marketing plans, management accounting services, systems controls, and—occasionally—financing assistance. For these initial and ongoing services the franchisor receives compensation in the form of initial franchise fees, ongoing royalty fees, training fees, management assistance fees, advertisement and promotion fees, service fees, product pricing fees, and others. Franchisees generally must buy any required equipments from the franchisor, lease the land, and contribute toward the cost of centralized bookkeeping, accounting, and data processing services. In the business format model, franchisees generally pay the total cost of establishing the facility to the franchisor, which, in turn, builds the facility with the franchisee's money and provides the franchisee with a turnkey operation.

The *advantages* of franchising include: low development costs, the low risk of entry by using other people's money, and the global consistency of quality and branding because of the contractual nature of the franchise agreement (which is also a risk). Franchising affords the opportunity for firms to expand quickly into the international marketplace, and finally, it leverages the synergy between the franchisor and the franchisee. The franchisor has the know-how and the franchisee has a better understanding of the culture of the foreign facility, has the money, and has an owner's passion for the business.

Product/trade name franchisors have established product names, logos, and trademarks, and they sell the right to use these intangible products to another party.

Business format franchisors, in addition to providing intangible rights, including the product trade name, also generally provide assistance in site selection, building, staff training, products supply, advertising and marketing plans, management accounting services, systems controls, and—occasionally—financing assistance.

FIGURE 10.15

Decision Tree: License or FDI?

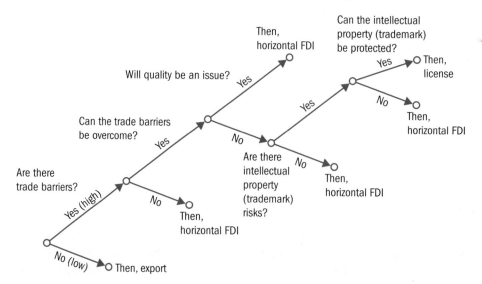

The *disadvantages* of franchising may include quality and consistency that are not at the levels contemplated by the franchise agreement. Sometimes businesses have only their brand to sell; travellers generally select accommodation and restaurants with which they are familiar. Accordingly, it is in the best interest of both the franchisor and the franchisee that quality and consistency be maintained. To mitigate the potential of this disadvantage, most franchisors establish master franchise agreements in the host country. Owners of these master franchise agreements may or may not operate their own franchises within their territory but they do receive a percentage of the compensation and "stand in the shoes" of the franchisor in the foreign country. Master franchisors can be both an advantage and a disadvantage; master franchise agreements, and franchise agreements, authorize the rights to sell the franchisor's products and services in that venue for a fixed period of time. This may impede the implementation of a different global strategy by the franchisor should it decide to adopt an investment mode of entry at a later date.

Turnkeys (Contractual)

A knowledgeable company may choose to undertake a **turnkey project** for a client. The company designs, constructs, implements processes, provides best practice guidelines and policies, and undertakes all other aspects required to complete a project and then turns the project over to the client for a fee. At that point, all that remains is to pass the client the keys to the front door and the facility is operational. In a hamburger franchise, this would mean that the fat is in the fryers and the hamburgers are on the grill ready for the first customer to come through the door: the company is open for business. In other management contracts, special know-how is sold to the client. Some are called BOTs (build-operate-transfer) in which the firm builds and operates the project, generally under a management contract for a fixed term, and then transfers the project to the client at a predetermined, agreed-upon price. Governments use this mode for some major infrastructure projects. The firm recovers its costs over a fixed period of time, generally through user fees, and then the project is transferred to the government. Highway infrastructure makes use of this model. Governments around the world are rapidly transferring the operation and financing of airports to professional airport management companies. This shift towards private operation enables governments to concentrate on maintaining regulatory control over their aviation industries, thereby ensuring the highest level of sovereignty, safety, and security. The Vancouver International Airport Authority undertakes such management contracts and turnkey projects because of the special skills its executives have acquired in growing the Vancouver International Airport into a world-class facility. Vancouver Airport Services (YVRAS), a subsidiary of Vancouver International Airport Authority (YVR), markets its expertise, operating philosophies, and leading-edge systems developed at YVR. It is one of the leading global airport operators.

Advantages of turnkey projects include the synergy between the parties. Firms with specialized core competencies can leverage their talents with clients who currently lack these competencies. Making money by selling skills in this way is particularly valuable when FDI is restricted or impeded for political or economic reasons. A disadvantage of turnkeys is that, because of the lucrative nature of the contracts, the award process can become political. The second disadvantage is that transferring these core competencies to the client firms may, in time, be growing efficient competitors.

This completes our look at the advantages and disadvantages of the *contract modes* of entry. Now we will examine three more modes that require greater risk due to the required FDI and ongoing involvement in their operation.

Joint Ventures (Investment)

A **joint venture (JV)** is the formation of a separate legal entity that is owned by two or more independent entities to achieve a common mission. The term of the joint venture can be fixed or open-ended. The partners (entities) can be public, private, or not-for-

In a **turnkey project,** a company designs, constructs, implements processes, provides best practice guidelines and policies, and undertakes all other aspects required to complete a project and then turns the project over to the client for a fee.

The **joint venture (JV)** is the formation of a separate legal entity that is owned by two or more independent entities to achieve a common mission. The term of the joint venture can be fixed or open-ended, and the partners (entities) can be public, private, or not-for-profit. Firms enter into joint ventures to gain synergy. A JV is one form of strategic alliance.

profit. Firms enter into JVs because of synergy. If the outcome of the JV is not greater than the individual parts, then the JV should not be entered. JVs work because of the fit between the partners' expertise, because of special tax considerations, to be "acceptable" to foreign government, or because of the need to access resources such as additional capital and experienced personnel. JVs are one form of a strategic alliance. **Strategic alliances** range from an informal business relationship based on a simple contract whereby the parties agree to work together toward a common goal while not losing their individuality, to a more structured JV agreement. Advantages of a JV are first that it reduces investment risk; the entities benefit by having a partner in both the host and the domestic country that are familiar with the political, economic, and cultural issues, thereby reducing the risk to the JV. The second advantage is sharing the costs of establishing the foreign venture, and funding its ongoing operations. Another advantage is that a JV may provide the opportunity for one or more of the JV entities to gain competitive advantage by moving down the efficiency curve. This can also be a disadvantage if control over the venture is lacking. The final advantage is the reduction in political risk. There is little likelihood of nationalization or political interference if firms use this mode of entry.

> **Strategic alliances** are partnership between competitors, customers, or suppliers designed to build synergy.

Disadvantages include the sharing of profits. Another disadvantage is the loss of control. How will disputes between partners be resolved? In the event the JV is terminated, who gets the R&D, the assets, the customers, etc? Another major disadvantage is related to sharing competencies and know-how between the partners. There is always a danger that one partner will lose control over the proprietary knowledge. Another disadvantage that we touched on as a possible advantage is that if the JV does not have tight control over the new entity, then the ability to exploit the experience curve may not be attained. Firms entering China in certain industries are permitted by government to hold only 49 percent of the firm. As a result, notwithstanding the significant investments, foreign firms may not have control unless the JV share distribution is widely held. Advice? Prepare a prenuptial agreement!

Here are two successful Canadian joint ventures that got it right. Canada's largest producer and exporter of home textile products, Beco Industries of Montreal, uses China as a labour supply market for its fashion bedding and comforters. Management claims, "joint ventures with Chinese manufacturers are the way to go."[17] The second is Cubex Limited, a Winnipeg manufacturer and distributor of mining equipment and municipal maintenance systems that formed a successful joint venture in India for road sweepers and sewer-cleaning equipment.[18]

Wholly Owned Subsidiaries (Investment)

> A **wholly owned subsidiary** is a mode whereby a domestic firm acquires 100 percent of a growing concern.

A **wholly owned subsidiary** is a mode whereby a domestic firm acquires a 100 percent of a growing concern. Some practitioners include greenfields in the wholly owned mode classification, but because of its distinct advantages and disadvantages it is presented in this text as a separate mode. In both cases, the plant is entirely owned and operated by a single parent company. The advantages of using a wholly owned subsidiary as a mode of entry are that managers have complete control over the facility's operations and they can access the firm's global technologies, processes, and intangible property. This control affords the opportunity to prevent competitor's benchmarking against firms adopting this mode and gaining insight into the subsidiary's operations. This mode provides control over all aspects of inputs and the products and services sold within the foreign country. By definition, the wholly owned operation means that the firm receives all profits and takes all losses from the wholly owned operation. It is a good model when strong coordination and control over global operations are required. The disadvantages of a wholly owned subsidiary are the expense: the cost of replicating plants in new locations can be high. The high-risk exposure to the firm is another disadvantage. Recall from Chapters 2, 3, and 4 that a shift in the political, economic, and societal variables can dramatically affect the success of the firm.

FIGURE 10.16
Advantages and Disadvantages
of the Seven Modes of Entry

Entry Mode	Advantages	Disadvantages
Exporting	• Location and experience curve economies can be exploited	• High transportation costs • Trade barriers • Possibility of problems with local marketing agents/representatives • Limited feedback
Turnkey Contracts	• A firm's competencies can be leveraged in countries where FDI is restricted	• Creation of efficient competitors • Lack of long-term market presence
Licensing	• Development costs and risks are low	• Location and experience curve economies cannot be exploited • A global strategy cannot be implemented
Franchising	• Development costs and risks are low	• Lack of control over quality • A global strategy cannot be implemented
Joint Ventures/ Strategic Alliances	• Access to local partner's knowledge achieves synergy and cross-cultural co-operation • Sharing of costs and risks • Politically acceptable arrangement	• Lack of control over quality • A global strategy cannot be implemented • Location and experience curve economies cannot be exploited
Wholly owned subsidiaries/ acquisitions	• Protection of technology and intellectual property • Ability to undertake a global strategy • Location and experience curve economies can be exploited	• High costs and risks
Greenfield	• All advantages of wholly owned subsidiaries and acquisitions plus the ability to build the facilities to a firm's specifications	• Higher costs and risks than wholly owned subsidiaries and acquisitions

Greenfields (Investment)

The final mode of entry is termed **greenfield,** establishing from the ground up a new operation in a foreign country. Recall that greenfields can also be defined as a wholly owned mode of entry. To design the facility to meet your needs is an advantage most of us can recognize. If you build your new home from the ground up and build in the features you require, there is no doubt that you will be happier with the end product. However, compared to buying a ready-built house, it takes longer. Therein lie the advantages and disadvantages. Indeed, on occasion, greenfields may be the only mode of entry available to a firm attempting to enter a foreign market. It may be that there are no firms (plants) available for mergers, acquisitions, or joint ventures. As a result, the only option is to build the facility from the ground up. There are advantages to greenfields as a mode of entry in that rather than acquiring an existing operation, the new foreign subsidiary will be able to introduce its corporate culture, processes, and procedures to the new workers rather than attempting to convert the culture and practices existing in an ongoing operation. Despite this, there are several disadvantages. First, it takes considerably more time to establish an operation from scratch than to take over an existing, ongoing facility. Second, there will be uncertainty about the success of a facility having no historical record of the success or failure of previous operations for guidance.

A **greenfield** mode of entry involves establishing, from the ground up, a new operation in a foreign country. It is sometimes a wholly owned subsidiary.

Finally, global competitors adopting other modes, such as mergers, acquisitions, and joint ventures, may quickly build a market presence and overshadow the greenfield operation.

Each mode has advantages and disadvantages that must be evaluated against the firm's core competencies and resources prior to selecting the appropriate mode. Figure 10.16 shows an overview of the advantages and disadvantages of the various modes of entry.

Management Problems and Risks

There are numerous problems for business leaders in stage four of the decision-making process and implementation of international business strategy (see Figure 10.9 on page 289). Next we explore a few.

Tension for Lower Costs and Local Responsiveness

There is a tension between the need for cost reductions and the need to meet the demand for local responsiveness that must be contemplated when considering the establishment of a foreign subsidiary. Managers constantly strive to find the appropriate balance between reducing costs and responding to the pressure to be locally responsive in the firm's marketplace. In Chapter 6, pages 161–162, we examined Adam Smith's supply and demand curves, so we can understand the advantage to a firm that is able to offer a standardized product in a global marketplace. Yet the consumers in the host country may want a "tailored" good or service to meet their unique needs. Therein lies the dilemma. How much customization will you undertake to grow your market share and at what cost?

Pressures for Cost Reductions

In today's competitive environment, firms must exploit every opportunity to reduce unit costs. One way to do this is to establish foreign subsidiaries in low-cost locations. Currently, the **BRIC nations** are very attractive (see the Mini Case, page 306). With global competition increasing, firms find that they are under attack and are required to lower their costs and develop new innovative products if they are to survive. This is particularly true of products and services lacking any meaningful differentiation and where price remains the significant factor as to whether the customer will buy the product. Like commodities, many industrial and consumer products are not significantly differentiated: they compete almost solely on cost. Firms operating in these industries are under intense pressure to reduce costs and find opportunities for value creation. Those that fail to reduce costs will not survive long.

Pressures for Local Responsiveness

By exploiting location economies to drive down costs, the question becomes can you produce a standardized product, or are you required to modify your product or service to meet your local customers' particular needs? Recall from the materials from Chapters 2, 3, and 4 that globally, consumer tastes, cultures, and preferences differ; infrastructure and traditional practices differ; distribution channels differ; and host governments' requirements differ. All of these factors pressure a company to be locally responsive. We noted that there are products and services that do have universal application. Theodore Levitt suggested that globalization is resulting in a convergence of tastes in the global markets. Increasingly, Coca-Cola, Levi's jeans, Much Music, and BlackBerry devices are marketed globally with very little adaptation.[19] While there is truth in Levitt's observation, also recall that a number of practitioners believe he might be overstating the proposition. Recall Huntington's position (in Chapter 2, pages 43–45) that suggested the notion that Islamic and Christian cultures are clashing because of the spread of Western liberalized democracy and its culture. Visit www.power.nelson.com for a short note on Huntington's theses.

Some industries are required to be responsive to local practices and infrastructure requirements. Although standards such as the ISO 9000 and 14000 series are emerging, there remains a need for some firms to be locally responsive. Consider, for example, electrical appliances that require different voltages, automobiles that require catalytic converters in some locales, and steering wheels placed on the opposite side of the vehicle in

The **BRIC nations** are Brazil, Russia, India, and China.

order to meet local requirements. There are differences in the global distribution channels that must be accommodated by firms as well (see Chapter 13, pages 373–374). Additionally, as a precondition of doing business, the host government may have established certain political and economic demands that must be met (see Chapter 3, pages 89–90).

The implication of this tension between universal application and tailoring for each jurisdiction results in firms finding that they may not be able to achieve the desired level of cost reduction nor provide the desired level of local responsiveness in their product and service offerings. Firms might have to settle for the best balance between the two competing strategies.

Timing Considerations

There are considerations regarding the timing to entering a market. Those first to enter the market derive what is known as **first-mover advantage**, which includes the ability to establish a strong customer base; secure the best inputs and outputs (to include best location, accounting firms, banks, and law firms); move down the experience curve, thereby enabling certain cost advantages that may not be easily replicated by those who enter the market at a later date; and increase the switching costs, which tend to grow over time. Those of you who have switched your home computer and the accompanying software between a Mac and an IBM product readily understand the difference. While the compatibility issues are diminishing today; it was a major issue only a few years ago. To be the first into the marketplace is a double-edged sword. There is a disadvantage known as **pioneering costs**, which are costs incurred by the first movers that will not have to be incurred by later entrants. Pioneer costs can be expensive if the first mover fails to establish a "beachhead" in the host country and has to close the foreign subsidiary. Late movers will have the advantage to study and benchmark against the first mover into the market. Another pioneer cost is that the first mover must create the need for the good or service in the minds of the consumers in the new market. Those who follow can piggyback on the

> Those first to enter the market attain **first-mover advantage** and gain a number of economic and strategic advantages over those that subsequently enter the market, which may include establishing a strong customer base, securing the best inputs and outputs, moving down the experience curve, and increasing switching costs.

> **Pioneering costs** are costs that are incurred by the first movers that will not have to be incurred by later entrants.

PRACTICAL ENTREPRENEURIAL FOCUS

Strategic Thinking Is at the Heart of Being an Entrepreneur

Businesses that focus on innovation and speed are the businesses that survive. Encourage employees and stakeholders to undertake strategic thinking and to adopt new mental models.

Consider these eight entrepreneurial strategic thinking concepts as you craft and implement your strategies.

1. See things from your customer's perspective. Get inside and examine the customers' perspective from inside their box.
2. Everybody plays. Business is a team sport with internal and external players. New thought must be welcome.
3. Experiment intelligently. Analysis alone will not lead to a competitive advantage. At times it is better to

undertake experimentation and refine your implementation strategy through trial and error. Learn and adapt from the mistakes.

4. Risk is part of being in business—deal with it! Accept calculated risk that could result in increased value for your firm.
5. Set priorities and exercise discipline. Establish a specific mission and goals/objectives and then aim for them. This is what Martin Luther King referred to as "keeping an eye on the prize." One of the indices of a successful entrepreneur is self-discipline. Having established the metrics for the priorities to measure your strategies, you must be disciplined to implement them.
6. Spend imagination instead of money: Strategic thinking doesn't have to be expensive. Often the most inexpensive investment, with

the greatest potential for the highest return, is the time you spend imagining and dreaming. With today's ever-increasing pace, we must push back and find time for dreaming.

7. Measure early and always: Units of measure serve as guides. They are your canary in the coal mine to forewarn you of impending problems before they become irreparable.
8. Allocate the necessary resources to achieve the strategies.

Adapted from Terrance Power, "Entrepreneurs Must Be Adaptable to Customer Needs," *The Business Edge* (July 8, 2004), retrieved September 7, 2006, from www.businessedge.ca/article.cfm/newsID/6402.cfm.

CRITICAL THINKING QUESTION

How much validity does Andrew Grove's statement have: "There are only two kinds of companies: The quick and the dead!"

first mover's efforts. Finally, it is not unusual for first movers to have to collaborate with the host government to establish regulations for the industry. The political risk can be enormous for first movers and, consequently, those who follow after the "rules" have been established realize a great benefit. This, too, is a double-edged sword. By working with government, the first mover may be able to influence government regulations to the first mover's benefit and to the detriment of those who follow. Business decision makers will have to find the appropriate balance between being the first mover and being a follower. If they select to be a follower, it is important to determine how far behind they can be before the barriers to entering the new marketplace are insurmountable.

Stage Five—Strategic Competitive Outcomes

The final stage, stage five of the decision-making process and implementation of international strategy (see Figure 10.9, page 289) is measuring strategic competitive outcomes.

Measuring Outcomes

Processes, reduced to their essence, can be graphically seen as inputs (factors, variables, etc.), entering a box (where the inputs are processed, acted upon, etc.), with outputs (products, services etc.) exiting the box. The last stage is the measuring or feedback loop (customer surveys, evaluation, and analysis resulting in adjustments to the process). It is iterative; managers must constantly undertake analysis of the international strategy process and its outputs, adjusting the model as required. There are a number of tools available for monitoring and evaluating the success of the strategies.

Until recently, businesses were structured on a well-defined, strict, military hierarchy model, similar to that used by the Chinese army 3,000 years ago. The rigid system worked well until the 1980s when it became apparent that exponential changes in our global village were taking place with such rapidity that companies, in order to survive, required real-time intelligence and the agility to shift their strategies to accommodate emerging threats and opportunities in their ecosystem. What gets measured gets managed. No longer would organizations be able to simply monitor and track key historical financial information to maintain the strategic course. To assist managers in monitoring the firm's success in achieving the objectives established, a number of tools are available.

First, a corporate dashboard that visually provides the status of a number of key metrics is popular. Dashboards are Web browser–based, and provide current measurements and goals of key performance factors in an intuitive, graphic format. The data is updated automatically through the firm's other business software, eliminating additional input errors. Most charts are plain but effectively communicate the metric and whether it is "Good," "OK," or "Needs Immediate Attention" through the use of green, yellow, and red ranges. Perhaps you have noticed this technology in action while waiting in line at your financial institution.

Another is the balanced scorecard, also based on performance indicators (perspectives), reflecting different views of the firm. These perspectives must constantly be recalibrated to accommodate your monitoring. Managers undertake a *financial perspective* that monitors traditional financial objectives established in support of the firm's strategy. This includes measures such as return on investment (ROI), revenue growth, and shareholder value. Managers can consider a *customer perspective*. A customer's perspective looks at the organization through the eyes of the customer. Use metrics to measure service levels, satisfaction ratings, and the volume of repeat business, to name a few. A **consumption chain analysis** (the process of analyzing each step of the consumption chain, from awareness through disposal) is good business practice as companies can examine opportunities to add value along the way. For example, Oral B added colour to its toothbrush bristles to show consumers when they needed to replace their toothbrushes. An *internal perspective* examines the efficiencies and effectiveness of the processes and procedures undertaken by the firm. It would, for example, establish

A **consumption chain analysis** is the process of analyzing each step of the consumption chain—from awareness to disposal—so that companies can examine opportunities to add value along the way.[20]

metrics to measure productivity, cycle time, and cost. Both the customer perspective and the internal perspective will be familiar to those who have studied operations management. Finally, the *organizational and learning perspective* views an organization largely through the eyes of the firm's "assets" (personnel). What are the firm's intellectual assets, market innovations currently being researched, and skills gaps? Has training or hiring been undertaken to mitigate these deficiencies?

These perspectives are not viewed as watertight compartments but rather as linked to each other in some fashion. The intention of the balanced scorecard is not only to assist in controlling the organization but also to communicate and leverage information in real time throughout the organization. These tools enable international businesses to enhance their competitive advantage and maximize their corporate performance in a global environment.

Implementation (Action Plans)

According to Ram Charan and Geoffrey Colvin, CEOs fail not because they have not crafted a good strategy but rather because of implementation.[21] "When CEOs fail, it is rarely because of a lack of smarts or vision. Most unsuccessful CEOs stumble because of one simple, fatal shortcoming: bad execution—not getting things done, being indecisive, and not delivering on commitments. This conclusion is based on a study of several dozen CEO failures that have been observed over the decades."[22] Ways in which many "failed" CEOs came up short were identified by Charan and Colvin.[23] One was to ensure each strategy had an *action plan* setting out the steps that need to be undertaken. An action plan describes the way members of the organization will implement the selected strategy to meet its objectives. Plans comprise a number of actions, steps, or changes that are to be brought about and generally include what actions or changes will occur; who will carry out these changes; when will they take place, and for how long; what resources (e.g., money, staff) are needed to carry out these changes; and a communications plan. Firms create action plans to demonstrate internally and externally that the organization is well managed; that no details have been overlooked; that the strategy supported by the action plan is doable; that the implementation of the strategy will be completed in the most efficient and effective manner possible; and to provide a measurement to evaluate the performance of those assigned tasks to ensure the successful implementation of the selected strategy. Strategists must apply project management processes and tools to assist them. Visit www.power.nelson.com for The Five Signs of Failure: A Self-Test for CEOs.

INTERNATIONAL STRATEGIC THINKING

Strategies for Canadian SMEs Entering the Chinese Market

The following strategies are offered for consideration by Canadian SMEs considering entering the Chinese market:

· Recognize that infrastructure and technological capacity varies greatly between regions; a strategy for one area may not be possible, practical, or profitable elsewhere.

· If the SME's value lies in its knowledge, extra precautions should be taken to protect intellectual property.

· Long-term vision, patience, and presence are extremely important. Firms must be committed to either be stationed in or visit China regularly to develop relationships and seize opportunities as they arise.

· Prepare for the financial investment and time required to develop relationships and work through the bureaucracy. The costs of doing business in China can be high for small firms, including travelling, adapting to local market needs, and translation.

· Strategies for easing the transition and reducing the risk of failure in this new marketplace could include the following:

– Form strategic alliances with larger multinationals or Chinese companies to leverage market access and networks, and to more easily build credibility.

– Enter the Mainland Chinese market through Hong Kong. Hong Kong has the unique advantage of straddling East and West: its business, political, and legal environments have strong influences from Britain; however, it has ethnic and cultural ties to China.

Threefold Test for International Business Strategy

Having now crafted your strategies, how do you test them to determine the best option for your firm? Here is a threefold test you can apply. First, there is the "fit" test. Remember, a good strategy is tailored to meet the firm's external and internal environment. The findings of your analysis must indicate that the selected strategy is a very close "fit." Second, strategies are crafted to enhance or lead to sustainable competitive advantage. The greater the strategy's contribution, the better the strategy. Third, the best strategy will enhance the company's performance. Specifically, a good strategy properly implemented will increase profitability; expand company competitive strength; and strengthen long-term market position. Test your strategy against these three metrics before implementing it.

Management Implications

- Crafting strategies in turbulent times is a complex challenge. Managers are increasingly required to adopt new mental models in order to maintain the agility and innovation required to survive in the international marketplace. Crafting and implementing strategies as contemplated only a few decades ago no longer has relevance.
- Increasingly, it is important that firms be lean. To have no waste of the firm's assets is critical to the firm's survival.
- The ability to gather data and apply it to the strategic models available to strategists is the easy part of crafting strategies. The hard part is the critical thinking about the data and assigning values and weights to the information.
- Implementation of the firm's strategy presents the greatest risk of failure. Leadership is *sine qua non* (critical). Leaders must ensure attention to detail and adherence to action plans.
- Permitting new voices to be heard and conducting meaningful discussions from all perspectives is essential to the strategic process.

CHAPTER SUMMARY

- The Sun Tzu Moment emphasizes that speed and innovation are the essence of war and that successful firms must craft revolutionary strategies. Although there are many issues to be considered, the strategist must never lose sight of creating value in the mind of the customer.
- Tools available to assist business leaders in crafting an international business strategy include the SMART analysis, value chain analysis, SWOT analysis, and applying Michael Porter's five forces model. Remember that models are just that; they serve only as tools to ensure that all factors are identified and considered by the firm's decision makers. There are other equally suitable business decision-making models. The importance of the value chain analysis as a tool to identify activities where pennies might be wrung out or value added to a firm's product or service must not be overlooked.
- The strategic process involves developing the strategic vision and mission statements, and setting goals and/or objectives. These, in turn, are supported by strategies that have one or more action plans prepared in support of each strategy. Throughout the iterative process, constant monitoring and adjustments occur.
- There are five generic competitive strategies that the firm can consider when crafting a market entry strategy. They are overall low-cost leadership with a broad customer base, broad differentiation with a broad customer base, best cost and value, focused low-cost leadership and narrow customer base, and focused differentiation with a narrow customer base. The appropriate strategy is based on cost or product differentiation, and market size being either a focused niche or a broad market.
- Once the corporate-level strategy plan is completed, it is made available to the functional and operational units within the organization. These units, in turn, craft their strategies in support of the corporate strategic plan by focusing on their resources and capabilities and the contributions they can make in support of the company's plan.

- Having selected its strategy, the firm then decides on the international strategic choices for its market entry strategy. These strategic choices are international, multidomestic, global, and transnational.
- One of the final tasks in crafting a suitable strategy is to select the appropriate mode of entry that fits with the firm's resources. Modes of entry are divided into contractual and investment modes. They include exporting, licensing, franchising, and turnkey (all contractual); and joint ventures-strategic alliances, wholly owned subsidiary and greenfield (investment) modes.
- In selecting the corporate strategy, a number of management issues must be addressed. First, there is a tension between keeping costs low by adopting a universal "one size fits all" product and the need to be responsive to the host country's customers. The more responsive a firm's strategy, the higher the costs will be because the firm is forced to operate higher on the experience and economies of scale curves.

Second, in deciding when to enter a market, timing is important. Third, business decision makers must decide what the specific advantages and disadvantages are in being a first mover rather than a follower into a new foreign market. The fourth management issue is how to promote innovation within the organization.

- Once the strategy has been crafted and implemented, monitoring must continue on an ongoing basis. One of the tools for measuring outcomes is the balanced scorecard, which can assist business decision makers in evaluating a number of metrics and ensuring that the strategic and financial objectives are being met.
- There is a threefold test that business practitioners can apply to see if they have crafted the right strategy. These are: does the strategy "fit," does the strategy enhance or lead to sustainable competitive advantage, and does the strategy enhance the company's performance?

REVIEW QUESTIONS

1. Using a diagram, explain the three possible selling prices for goods and services.
2. What is a value chain analysis, and why is it important to business decision makers?
3. What are the five tasks of strategic management?
4. Briefly explain Porter's five forces model using a Canadian industry as an example.
5. Describe the five generic international business competitive strategies.
6. Discuss the four factors that explain why firms go global.
7. Describe the four basic international strategic choices for market entry strategy.
8. Discuss the advantages and disadvantages of the seven entry modes available for consideration by firms entering a global marketplace. Provide examples of Canadian firms using each mode.
9. Discuss problems business leaders encounter in stage four, implementation of market-entry plans, of the decision process and Implementation of international business strategy.
10. What is a balanced scorecard?
11. Why do CEOs fail?
12. What are the three tests to measure the success of an international business strategy?

REFLECTIVE THINKING QUESTIONS

1. Having completed the chapter, reread the quotes on the first page and critically reflect on the validity of the authors' statements and provide your opinion. Evidence-based answers are preferred to rhetorical answers.
2. "Would you tell me, please, which way I ought to go from here?" "That depends a good deal on where you want to get to," said the Cat. "I don't much care where—" said Alice. "Then it doesn't matter which way you go," said the Cat. "—so long as I get SOMEWHERE," Alice added as an explanation. "Oh, you're sure to do that," said the Cat, "if you only walk long enough." Comment on the accuracy of the Cheshire Puss's counsel to Alice.[24]
3. Examine any one of the strategic choices adopted by a Canadian SME.
4. Undertake a value chain analysis for a Canadian SME.
5. Do you agree with Bartlett and Ghoshal and the text author that a transnational strategy is sustainable?

GLOBAL E-RESEARCH

Visit www.power.nelson.com for research suggestions, questions, and a number of background discussion papers on this topic.

MINI CASE

5.4 Billion New Customers?

The challenges of succeeding in emerging markets are forcing the Western powers to come up with bold new strategies. They're under pressure to innovate like crazy, pioneer new ways of doing business, and outmanoeuvre their feisty new competitors. "The pattern in the past was to sell the same stuff to the same kind of customers. But that won't work, and it has to change," says C.K. Prahalad. . . . "What's required is a fundamental rethinking of how to design products and make money."

Consider, a young woman itinerant photographer entrepreneur in Andhra Pradesh province in southern India. She visits farming communities carrying a small backpack crammed with a digital camera, printer, and solar battery charger. This is part of a Hewlett-Packard Co. (HPQ) new marketing strategy. She has doubled her family income by charging the equivalent of 70 cents apiece for photos of newborns, weddings, and other proud moments of her village's life. HPQ, instead of selling the gear outright, rents the equipment for $9 a month.

She has become a star in the two-room house with a dirt floor that she and her stonecutter husband, Krishnamurthy, share with his parents and brother. What are Neelamma's dreams? "I want to buy a television and a ceiling fan. And I want to build a small photo studio in my home," she says. One young woman's life and aspirations have been changed by the arrival of technology.

Cultural Customization. New marketing and product innovations designed for the developing world emerge daily. How about a cell phone for the world's 1.3 billion Muslims? A small Dubai-based Ilkone Mobile Telecommunication firm is selling a phone that not only comes loaded with the Koran but also alerts people at prayer times. Yes it also has a compass, and points toward Mecca. To accommodate cultural differences like the "Muslim phone," companies are conducting in-depth studies of people's needs. "Intel, for instance, has a team of 10 ethnographers traveling the world to find out how to redesign existing products or come up with new ones that fit different cultures or demographic groups." One interesting finding was that many Chinese families were reluctant to buy PCs, even if they could afford them. Parents were concerned that their children would listen to pop music or surf the Web, distracting them from schoolwork. "Intel turned that insight into a product." . . . It now sells the China Home Learning PC. "It comes with four education applications and a physical lock and key that allow parents to prevent their kids from goofing off when they should be studying."

Often emerging markets will have demanding specifications. They need to be simple to use and capable of operating in harsh environments. India's TVS Electronics Ltd., sells "a new kind of all-in-one business machine called Sprint designed especially for India's 1.2 million small shopkeepers. It's part cash register and part computer and designed to tolerate heat, dust, and power outages. The cost is just $180 for the smallest model." Pricing is often the make-or-break factor in developing countries. In rural South Africa the average person makes less than $1 a day. HP recognized that few South Africans could afford to buy their own personal computers. They developed the 441 PC that permits four users for each computer. The machine is set up in a school or library and connects to four keyboards and four screens, so multiple people can get on the Net or send e-mail at the same time.

Patience is the most important attribute for firms trying to get established in emerging markets. IBM has been in Brazil for 87 years. Hewlett-Packard has spent three years establishing the pilot programs we have discussed in India and South Africa. Canadian SMEs must look past the traditional developed nations marketing base of 1 billion customers and adopt new mental models and strategies to access the untouched 5.4 billon potential new consumers.

Adapted from Steve Hamm, Manjeet Kripalani, Bruce Einhorn, and Andy Reinhardt, *Tech's Future* (McGraw-Hill, September 27, 2004).

CRITICAL THINKING QUESTIONS

1. Consider five billion customers making less than $2 a day. Can we do business with these folks? We need a new mental model. In his book *The Fortune at the Bottom of the Pyramid*,[25] C.K. Pralahad offers us a way. He states in the Mini Case, "What's required is a fundamental rethinking of how to design products and make money." Identify and discuss how a number of products that might be marketed in a non-North American size and fashion to customers in developing and underdeveloped countries.

2. Think about the observation in the Mini Case for "cultural customization" when doing business in the BRIC countries. I believe that you have to go back to the technology of the 1980s to find what can be marketed today in the BRIC countries. Why? Do you agree?

3. Remember the words of Andrew Grove, CEO, Intel Corp.: "There are only two types of firms—the quick and the dead." Can you think of behemoths that are stumbling because they fail to adopt new strategic mental models?

ENDNOTES

1 *Brainy Quote* (BrainyMedia.com, 2005), retrieved August 22, 2006, www.brainyquote.com.

2 *Quotations* (ThinkExist.com Quotations), retrieved August 22, 2006, from http://en.thinkexist.com/quotes/top/.

3 Alice Foote MacDougall, *The Autobiography of a Business Woman* (Columbia University Press, 1928), retrieved August 22, 2006, http://education.yahoo.com/reference/quotations/quote/46792.

4 Gary Hamel and C. K. Prahalad, "Strategic Intent," *Harvard Business Review*, no. 69, May–June (1989).

5 Kenichi Ohmae, *The Mind of the Strategist: The Art of Japanese Business* (New York: McGraw-Hill, 1982).

6 Mark McNeilly, *Sun Tzu and the Art of Business: Six Strategic Principles for Managers* (New York: Oxford University Press, 1996).

7 Thomas P. Lowry, John W.G. Wellham, *The Attack on Taranto: Blueprint for Pearl Harbor*, (Mechanicsburg, PA: Stackpole Books, 2000).

8 Ibid.

9 Gary Hamel, *Leading the Revolution*, (Boston, MA: HBS Press, October 2002).

10 Rev. Charles Lutwidge Dodgson (Lewis Carroll), *Alice's Adventures in Wonderland* (1862), retrieved August 22, 2006, available from www.cs.indiana.edu/metastuff/wonder/wonder.txt.gz.

11 Rita Gunther McGrath and Ian MacMillan, *The Entrepreneurial Mindset* (Boston, MA: HBS Press, 2000).

12 Michael E. Porter, *Competitive Strategy* (New York: Free Press, 1980).

13 C.A. Bartlett and S. Ghoshal, *Managing across Borders: The Transnational Solution* (Boston, MA: HSB Press, 1989).

14 Ibid.

15 Patrick E. Mears and Carol M. Sánchez, "Going Global: How Do Law Firms Do It and What Does It Change?" *Business Law Today*, (March/April 2001), retrieved September 7, 2006, from www.abanet.org/buslaw/blt/bltmar01mearssanchez.html.

16 Ibid.

17 International Trade Canada, *In Sync with China* (DFAIT, January 13, 2005), retrieved August 23, 2006, from www.dfait-maeci.gc.ca/tna-nac/stories112-en.asp#beco.

18 International Trade Canada, *Cleaning India's Streets* (DFAIT, February 3, 2004), retrieved August 23, 2006, from www.dfait-maeci.gc.ca/tna-nac/stories87-en.asp#cube.

19 Theodore Levitt, "The Globalization of Markets," *Harvard Business Review* (May–June 1983).

20 Ibid.

21 Ram Charan and Geoffrey Colvin, *Why CEOs Fail* (CNN, June 21, 1999), retrieved August 23, 2006, from www.pycco.com/why_ceos_fail.pdf.

22 Ibid.

23 Ibid.

24 Rev. Charles Lutwidge Dodgson (Lewis Carroll), *Alice's Adventures in Wonderland*.

25 C.K. Prahalad, *The Fortune at the Bottom of the Pyramid* (Pearson Education, 2005).

Global Organizational Structures and Control Systems

"The secret of all victory lies in the organization of the non-obvious."[1]

—*Marcus Aurelius, Roman soldier*

"Most human organizations that fall short of their goals do so not because of stupidity or faulty doctrines, but because of internal decay and rigidification. They grow stiff in the joints. They get in a rut. They go to seed."[2]

—*James A. Garfield, 20th President of the United States*

"No institution can possibly survive if it needs geniuses or supermen to manage it. It must be organized in such a way as to be able to get along under a leadership composed of average human beings."[3]

—*Peter F. Drucker, writer, management consultant, and university professor*

"A mountain of evidence shows that 85 to 90 percent of errors originate in the organization's structure, system or process. Yet all too many executives look for who rather than what went wrong."[4]

—*Jim Clemmer, organizational improvement expert*

"Every company has two organizational structures: The formal one is written on the charts; the other is the everyday relationship of the men and women in the organization."[5]

—*Harold S. Geneen, former chairman,* International Telephone and Telegraph

LEARNING OUTCOMES

- Assess the impact of globalization on the transformation of today's firms' organizational structures.
- Understand how the elements or parts of a firm can affect each other according to the organizational structural relationship they form.
- Recognize that old, rigid hierarchies are out, and flat, speedy, virtual organizations are in.
- Understand the two core classification models: mechanistic and organic.
- Evaluate the merits of functional, divisional, matrix, hybrid, virtual, and network organizational structures.
- Understand a control system's two main objectives: output and behaviour.
- Understand the three main components of organizational structure: horizontal complexity, vertical complexity, and their integrated controlling mechanisms.
- Evaluate the merits of cross-functional control integration mechanisms: hierarchy, direct contact, liaison roles, task groups, integrating role, integrating department, and matrix structure.

Will a New Organizational Structure Save Sony?

TOSHIYUKI AIZAWA/Reuters/Landow

"Sony has lost credibility as a premium consumer brand. Left behind by the latest technological advances and unable to justify its prices against cheaper rivals, its profits are in reverse. Now for the first time the Japanese company has put an 'outsider'—Sir Howard Stringer—at the controls, in the hope that the Welshman can raise its game." Stringer has a reputation as a deal-maker and cost cutter. "Stringer will be the first '*gaijin*' (foreigner) to run the company as chairman and chief executive officer. . . . The Welshman will cut further swathes of jobs and bureaucracy from Sony's bloated corporate structure, and try to recapture the essence of Sony's one-time status as the world's leading electronics brand."

Sony was the world's undisputed leader in entertainment electronics; however, today its share of its core markets is hemorrhaging. The Sony Walkman, launched in 1979, was the industry's gold standard for portable music. But it ceased to be a revolutionary; it lost the "fire in the belly." Apple's iPod has taken the pole position in the portable music industry. In televisions, again, Sony had set the pace, but it failed to scan the ecosystem. Asian manufacturers like Samsung, Sony's Korean archrival, are selling flat-screen TVs at a significantly lower price and were the earlier adapters of flat-screen technology, plasma, and liquid crystal display screens. Sony has only recently attempted to catch up by investing in new semi-conductor technology. As of 2006, the company had not achieved any breakthroughs.

Sony's worldwide problems are akin to those experienced by Marks & Spencer in the mid-1990s. That long- and well-established British clothing store, like Sony, failed to notice new market trends, as it basked in the light of its earlier success. "Sony has become 'complacent.' Having successful products such as the PlayStation and powerful music and film studio interests has led its management to pay scant attention to other areas such as consumer electronics. . . . The appointment of Stringer is a reaction to how quickly you fall foul if you take your eye off the ball. Sony has not taken opportunities and made investments in key technologies; there was a certain amount of arrogance in its operation and this has led to complacency."

Sony's focus was on film and music production, mobile phones, and wanting to create synergy through convergence of content, hardware, and communications. However, the company has not attained the success to date necessary to make a difference. There wasn't a consumer out there saying: "Can you put all these things together for me?" Unlike Intel's team of 10 ethnographers travelling the world to find out how to redesign existing products (or come up with new ones that fit different cultures or demographic groups as we discussed in Chapter 9's Mini Case, on pages 273–274), Sony was disconnected from its target market.

Structure follows strategy. "The structure of the company has also worked against making the convergence vision a reality . . . With staff bonuses related to sales in their own product areas, there has been little impetus to think in a joined-up way." Clearly Sony's "silo" mentality created by its current organizational design needs revisiting. Taking over as CEO, Stringer recognized this and stated, "Sony has an unparalleled legacy of boldness, innovation and leadership around the world. We look forward to joining our twin pillars of engineering and technology with our commanding presence in entertainment and content creation to deliver the most advanced devices and forms of entertainment to the consumer."

So, a new CEO, vision, mission, and strategy—will it work?

A SUN TZU MOMENT. . .

"Now the army's disposition of force (hsing) is like water. Water's configuration (hsing) avoids heights and races downward. The army's disposition of force (hsing) avoids the substantial and strikes the vacuous. Water configures (hsing) its flow in accord with the terrain; the army controls its victory in accord with the enemy. Thus the army does not maintain any constant strategic configuration of power (shih), water has no constant shape (hsing). One who is able to change and transform in accord with the enemy and wrest victory is termed spiritual. Thus [none of] the five phases constantly dominates; the four seasons do not have constant positions; the sun shines for longer and short periods; and the moon wanes and waxes."

Source: Ralph D. Sawyer, *The Art of War: New Translation* (Barnes and Noble, 1994).

CANADIAN NAVY TEAMS UP WITH U.S. CARRIER BATTLE GROUPS

One of the best examples of the effectiveness of Canadian and American defence co-operation is the integration of Canadian Navy frigates into United States Carrier Battle Groups. Since the end of the Gulf War in 1991, Canada has contributed to the Persian Gulf (Arabian Gulf) Multinational Interdiction Force enforcing UN sanctions against Iraq. In 1998, HMCS *Ottawa* integrated into a U.S. Carrier Battle Group as part of this force.

This was the first time since the Korean War that another country had this level of interoperability with the U.S. Navy.

. . . Since that first deployment, the Canadian Navy integrated into several United States Navy Carrier Battle Groups during sanction enforcement operations and multinational exercises. HMCS *Charlottetown* is the first frigate from Maritime Forces Atlantic to be integrated into a United States Navy Carrier Battle Group. . . . 'We're ready,' said HMCS *Charlottetown*'s Commanding Officer, Commander Ron Lloyd. 'A great deal of work has been done to ensure that we are capable of fully integrating into the technically complex environment of an American aircraft carrier battle group. We're probably one of the few non–U.S. ships in the world that are ready now to do so.' HMCS *Winnipeg*, also deploying as part of a United States Navy Carrier Battle Group, leaves for the Persian Gulf (Arabian Gulf) in March 2001 and will join the Multinational Interdiction Force as part of a U.S. Surface Task Force. The Canadian Navy is the only foreign navy to successfully operate as part of U.S. Carrier Battle Groups. This success is due to the extensive training that the American and Canadian navies conduct together. Furthermore, the Halifax-class frigate is a welcome addition to any coalition naval force because of the ship's highly skilled crew and its modern communications, sensors, and weapons systems. At 442 feet in length and only 4,750 tonnes, it is considered by Canada's allies as the most capable ship of its size in the world.

Source: National Defence, *Canadian Navy Teams up with U.S. Carrier Battle Groups* (National Defence (Canada), 2005-06-07). Copyright Public Works & Government Canada.

Opening Thoughts

This chapter is about Sun Tzu's observation that business, like water, configures its flow (hsing) in accord with the terrain. Having crafted a strategy for the Persian Gulf (Arabian Gulf) Multinational Interdiction Force to enforce UN sanctions against Iraq, naval units were collected to form a "'structure" called a Carrier Battle Group. Of the number of structures available, the decision makers chose this model. Why? By the end of this chapter you will know.

I joined the army at a very young age and learned some powerful lessons. The smallest unit in the infantry is called a section (some might suggest it is the individual soldier, but bear with me). In those days, it comprised 11 soldiers in two functional subunits; one made up of riflemen (9) and the other a Bren machine gun team (2). At times, in order to carry out missions, the section would move across terrain. As it did, the section adopted, like water, different structures (formations). For example, when approaching a defile, (a narrow path) the section would form single file; upon emerging from the defile into open ground, like water the section would adopt an arrowhead (wedge-like) formation. If moving into an assault position, the rifle subunit would adopt a straight-line-abreast structure while covering fire was provided from a flank by the machine gun team. Each structure had its advantages, disadvantages, and control mechanisms. Business is no different. As you move your firm through the environmental terrain, you must be constantly adjusting your organizational structure to align with your firm's changing strategy, goals, mission, vision, and ecosystem. The firm must flow like water and conform to its ecosystem. Clearly, from the opening vignette, we can see that

Sony's management failed to react to its shifting turbulent ecosystem, bloated corporate structure, and isolated corporate silos, and suffered as iPod and Samsung tore off chunks of its market share.

An organization's elements, such as its people, resources, aspirations, market trends, levels of competence, reward systems, departmental mandates, and so on, affect each other according to the relationship they form. Interestingly, most small business organizational structures are rarely designed in support of the firm's strategy but tend to evolve over time. This is not a good thing; structure should follow strategy! Adopting an organization's structure to support the crafted strategy, as outlined in Chapter 10, is often one of the key determining factors in whether an organization is successful in the global market. Canadian SMEs must consider structure in the business planning process.

Strategic choice and organizational design are extremely complex, but there is an underlying logic based on the concept of fit. Keep this in mind as you select the appropriate structure for your firm.

A reflective thought—Once I saw an unusual pumpkin at the Saanich village weekend farmers' market. One farmer had grown a small pumpkin in a four-cornered Mason jar. With time, the jar had to be broken and the pumpkin removed. The pumpkin that was confined was shaped exactly like its small incarceration space—the small Mason jar. The other pumpkins were allowed to grow without constraints and were five times bigger. Organizational structures and systems have the same effect on a firm's human resources. The firm's structure and control systems can either limit or liberate the teams' performance potential.

A caveat—Any structural change is likely to meet resistance from those holding power in the current structure.

Globalization's Impact on Organizational Structure

When considering the type of structure you will put in place, be aware of the impact globalization has had and will continue to have on the firm's organizational structure. What impact does globalization have on an organization's structure?

First, organizations have been affected by the exponential growth in technology. In fact, during the past 30 years, transportation, communication, and information technologies have dramatically transformed the business environment. At the time of Canada's Confederation (1867), it took months to get a message from Halifax to Japan. Today, you can communicate instantly using a variety of technologies like the free voice over Internet protocol (VoIP). Cheap transportation has made it possible for firms to transport products to and from any major city on the planet in about 20 hours. Accordingly, the firm's structure has to reflect the reality that firms have global customers, and may have to maintain offices or subsidiaries around the world.

Second, globalization has produced rapid growth of truly global firms, both large and small. These global firms exploit national differences in customers' needs and production capabilities (e.g., location economies, worker expertise, costs, government aid; see Chapter 10). In addition, the markets in many countries, including Canada, have become largely saturated for many products. For example, firms wishing to increase sales of televisions in Canada will have to convince Canadian users to have multiple televisions, or make the televisions obsolete more quickly over time, or convince Canadians to have more children because, at this point, almost every Canadian who could possibly afford a TV has one. As a result, new global emerging markets are where firms can position themselves on the growth portion of the product lifecycle rather than being positioned in saturated markets located on the mature or declining portion of the product life curve (see Chapter 10's Mini Case, page 306, and C.K. Prahalad's observations on the challenges of succeeding in emerging markets).

Third, globalization has also contributed to a demographic shift in the workplace that will have to be accommodated when selecting the firm's structure. Organizations will need new coordinating mechanisms to accommodate different kinds of people in the workplace. For example, as more women have entered the workforce, organizations have had to deal with a whole range of issues, including sexual harassment and pregnancy. The response to increased diversity has, in many cases, been increased organizational flexibility. Visit www.power.nelson for a discussion paper on the impact of globalization on woman.

Some organizations allow different workers to have very different work and payment schedules, such as "fast tracks" and "mommy tracks," full-time and part-time. Many organizations (and workers) have found it convenient to treat some workers as independent consultants rather than employees. In certain occupations, advances in communication and information technologies have enabled "telecommuting," working at home via computer. (See the Mini Case, pages 330–331.) New mental models will require new organizational structures.

Today's business environment is turbulent; change is so quick that organizational response time is at a premium. Organizations that can develop new technologies faster, or can adapt to changes in the market faster, will survive the competition. This means different organizational structures must be adopted to meet this sometimes-chaotic environment. To minimize response time, organizations have been flattening, downsizing, and encouraging networking. Flat organizational structures make decisions more quickly because each person is closer to the ultimate decision makers. Smaller Canadian SMEs are faster because there are simply fewer different things going on—fewer competing goals, fewer people to coordinate, etc. This, in turn, requires further structural consideration. Organizations that flatten tend to simultaneously encourage horizontal communication among workers. Rather than work through the **hierarchy**, it is often faster for workers that need to coordinate with each other to simply communicate directly.[6] Yes, this can lead to chaos, and many managers and supervisors feel threatened by this model; however, flat organizations tend to be highly networked.

> A **hierarchy** is a system of ranking and organizing things.

Networked organizations establish relationships with other organizations and are particularly important in industries with complex products where technologies and customer needs change rapidly, such as in high-tech industries. Close ties among a network of companies enable them to work with each other in ways that are faster than arms-length contracts would permit, and yet retain the flexibility of being able to drop the relationship if needed. To cease operations of "in-house" activity is more complex when staff reductions, plant facilities, etc. have to be made redundant. The "network" concept is not new to Japanese firms; it is called **keiretsu**. The major keiretsu firms in Japan are Mitsubishi, Mitsui, Sumitomo Group, Fuyo Group, Nissan Group, Itochu, and Hankyu-Toho Group. Visit www.power.nelson.com for a brief overview of keiretsu-like non-Japanese firms that have adopted this model.

> **Keiretsu** companies are the Japanese companies formed from the dismantling of the *zaibatsu* (pre–World War II "partnering" business groupings) that reconnected through share purchases to form horizontally integrated alliances across many industries. Where possible, these firms supply one another, making the alliances also vertically integrated to some extent.

Increasingly, organizations are outsourcing functions that used to be done in-house. This is another reality that will affect a firm's organizational structural design. To avoid losing time and effort managing contracts with suppliers, organizations have learned to develop very close ties or partnerships with their suppliers, so that social mechanisms of coordination replace legal mechanisms, which are slow and costly. In many industries, such as the garment industry in Italy, strong relationships have developed between manufacturers and suppliers (and other manufacturers), so that considerable work is done without a contract or even without working out a firm price.

We examined international, multidomestic, global, and transnational strategies in Chapter 10, pages 292–293. It is in the context of these globalization realities that we must examine our current organizational design and consider the traditional as well as new organizational structural models emerging in order to select the best fit for the organization's needs today and tomorrow.

Organizational Structure

Appropriate organizational design (structure) is valued as one of the four key criteria for business successes in the twenty-first century.[7] The other three criteria for business success are a customer- and quality-driven organization with a flatter management hierarchy; having a sense of vision; and an organization's capacity to add significant value to products and services. "Senior executives give high priority to the issue of organizational design because it represents the process of determining the best overall macro structure for the organization and its subcomponents. It also characterizes such structural elements as span of control (the range of employees who report to a managerial position) and departmentalization."[8] We have established that firms' organizational design must align with the *internal* capabilities and conditions of the firm and the *external* ecosystem, and must *support* the firm's corporate strategies within the global realities.[9] So if strategy can be viewed as responding to the firm's ecosystem and the organizational design flows from strategy, then it follows that there is a relationship between the firm's organizational design and its environment.

Organizational structure exists to perform two essential functions within the organization. The first function is *control*. Organizations must design their structures to permit the firm's assets, competencies, and labour to be grouped and positioned so that the best possible competitive advantage can be achieved by their application. Second, the organizational design provides coordination of all activities within the firm in an *efficient and effective* manner so as to ensure the firm meets its objectives in support of its vision.

When designing the structure for the organization it helps to think of and to view the firm as a living, evolving entity: a system comprising parts and elements. **Systems** can be the entire organization, or its departments, groups, processes, etc. Each organization has numerous subsystems, as well. Each subsystem has its own supporting goals/objectives. Common examples of subsystems are departments, programs, projects, teams, people, and processes to produce products or services, etc. Firms' organizational charts, job descriptions, marketing materials, etc. provide us with a sense of what the organization is about. The organizational system is controlled and maintained by policies and procedures, budgets, information management systems, quality management systems, performance review systems, etc. By way of analogy, consider viewing the firm as a human body. Once the brain crafts the vision, mission, and goals to be accomplished by the body, it is necessary to develop the appropriate structure (bulking up, weight loss, exercise). By analogy then, a skeleton is also required for our corporate body. Does the firm need the skeleton (structure) of a sumo wrestler (bureaucratic, hierarchical) or the skeleton of a 100-metre sprinter (organic, flat, and fast-moving)? Once the bone structure has been decided upon, the controlling mechanisms that align with the needs of the structure must be selected and put into place. This can be viewed as the nervous system of the corporate body. How will the firm communicate messages and exercise control quickly throughout the structure—from the firm's directing minds at its headquarters (brain) to the employees (fingertips) on the front line? To complete the analogy, we will see in Chapter 15 that human resources are then added as the blood of the firm. Get the right bums in the right seats!

Others view organizations as people management systems having three main components—*horizontal complexity*, *vertical complexity* and *integrated controlling mechanisms*. **Horizontal complexity** of the structure refers to the degree of clustering of the firm's units on the basis of function, the type of business the units conduct, or the geographic area they service. **Vertical complexity** is the degree of **authority** retained by the top decision makers; is it **centralized** or **decentralized**, with decision-making authority delegated to decision makers higher or lower in the organization? Finally, we examine the firm's **integrated controlling mechanisms**. How does the firm communicate and coordinate the firm's activities of its units and subunits internally and externally? Are the integrated controlling mechanisms informal or formal?

The possible structural models range from simple hierarchies based on military-type, traditional lines to the more recent complex networks incorporating computer systems and telecommunications. When correct, organizational structures can foster cost-effectiveness and employee commitment.

Organizational structures can be classified in a number of types. The first business model was a functional structure; however, during the past half-century, new models have been adopted. The major new models are divisional, matrix, hybrid, virtual, and network

Systems are an organized collection of parts or elements that are highly integrated in order to accomplish an overall goal.

Horizontal complexity refers to the number of units and subunits across an organization.

Vertical complexity is where (location) decisions are made.

Authority is the formally granted influence of a position to make decisions, pursue goals, and get resources to pursue the goals; authority in a managerial role may exist only to the extent that subordinates agree to grant this authority or follow the orders from that position.

Centralized or centralization refers to the extent to which decision-making functions are concentrated in the organization.

Decentralized or decentralization refers to the extent to which decision-making functions are dispersed in the organization, either in terms of integration with other functions or geographically.

A firm's **integrated controlling mechanisms** describe the extent to which rules, policies, and procedures control the organization.

organizational structures, and emerged in response to globalization and technology. We'll now examine each of these models, and their advantages and disadvantages. As a business leader, you'll need to be familiar with each to know if and when to adopt each in support of your strategy. In a global market the considerations are complex and require careful critical thinking.

Two Core Organizational Structural Classifications

Development of global competition and multinational corporations coupled with, and in part fuelled by, the fast pace of technological change has made the external environment both more complex and more unpredictable for business. Out of competitive necessity, firms have abandoned the traditional functional design in favour of better organizational structure. Today, organizations, both SMEs and MNEs, respond to external ecosystem variables by identifying with one of two core classifications of models—mechanistic (bureaucratic) or organic (project and team based facilitated by technology). It might be helpful for you to think of mechanistic as a machine's organizational structure versus organic organizational structures, which can be considered biological, living organisms. The continuum shown in Figure 11.1 displays the organizational design structures based on this thought.

In an ecosystem "where the amount of change is relatively low, firms tend to [continue to] use a **mechanistic model** characterized by rigidity, bureaucracy, and a strict hierarchy."[10] A mechanistic structure is characterized by high complexity and formalization, centralized decision making, rigid relationships, fixed duties, downward communication, and little participation in decision making. At this end of a continuum we refer to the structure as functional. It is the traditional model.

At the opposite end of the continuum we find the organic models. "In dynamic, unstable environments, firms tend to apply an **organic model**, which is characterized by openness, responsiveness, and lack of hierarchy."[11] The organic structural model is characterized by low complexity and formalization, decentralized decision making, adaptable duties, flexible relationships, and horizontal and upward communication. The modern marketplace has resulted in more companies adopting the organic models. Here we will find the network and virtual organizational structures. There are a number of models between these two extremes that we also need to examine.

In 1988, Peter Drucker correctly predicted the shift from the command-and-control functional organizational structure to the organization of departments and divisions (divisional-matrix-hybrids), and to the information-based organization (network-virtual). In his view, the new organizations would be "composed largely of specialists who direct and discipline their own performance through organized feedback from colleagues, customers and headquarters."[12] Drucker observed that "to remain competitive—maybe even to survive" businesses would have to convert themselves into organizations of knowledgeable specialists. This has, over the past two decades, become the case for most Canadian firms.

Organizational Structures—Design Concepts

Organizations are subject to a variety of constantly changing internal and external influences, such as adopting and implementing new strategies and conducting business in turbulent environmental conditions. Clearly, access to the global marketplace, increasing global competition, and the emergence of a knowledge-based economy characterized by a high level of communications and the growth of information

The **mechanistic model** is characterized by rigidity, bureaucracy, and a strict hierarchy. The structure is characterized by high complexity and formalization, centralized decision making, rigid relationships, fixed duties, downward communication, and little participation in decision making.

The **organic model**, which is characterized by openness, responsiveness, and lack of hierarchy, tends to be applied in dynamic, unstable environments. The structure is characterized by low complexity and formalization, decentralized decision making, adaptable duties, flexible relationships, and horizontal and upward communication.

FIGURE 11.1

Mechanistic to Organic Continuum

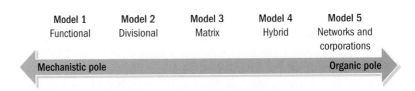

Model 1	Model 2	Model 3	Model 4	Model 5
Functional	Divisional	Matrix	Hybrid	Networks and corporations

Mechanistic pole → Organic pole

technologies all mandate the need for firms to be prepared to change rapidly. Canadian SMEs and others find their market stability is threatened by short product life cycles, shorter design product cycles, constantly emerging new technology, and frequent entry by unexpected global foreign competitors into "their" markets. To respond, firms must adopt better organizational designs and continuously review their organizational structure for "currency" against emerging turbulence in their ecosystem. Be prepared to experiment. When evaluating new possibilities, be aware of the tension between achieving organizational design efficiency and fostering a learning organization. Establishing the correct relationship between these two positions is at the heart of the analysis.

Vertical structures must be fully evaluated against horizontal structures. *Vertical structures* are designed for efficiency through specialized tasks; strict bureaucratic hierarchy with many rules, policies, and procedures controlling activities; vertical reporting (the go-through-channels syndrome); few teams, with staff remaining in their functional "box"; and centralized decision making. *Horizontal structures*, on the other hand, are designed for learning. Tasks are shared; workers are empowered; everyone works in a relaxed environment that is largely controlled by the corporate culture with few rules, policies, and processes formally set out; horizontal, face-to-face communication is permitted, thereby gaining speed and building relationships; a large number of specific activities are team-based; and decision making is decentralized. Establishing the appropriate balance between vertical and horizontal structures is critical when designing the organizational structure that is the right fit for your firm. Reflect for a moment on Figure 11.2.

Organizational Structure—Functional (Vertical Organization)

When firms have a historical dependence on specialization, it results in an organizational design based on *functions* such as marketing, purchasing, operations, advertising, and finance. This results in a vertically structured organization. From the 1950s through the 1980s, this vertical organizational structural design prevailed due in large part to the relative stability of the firms' ecosystems. Even today, many new SMEs adopt this model, designing their organizational structure by dividing the enterprise into relatively simple parts defined by major activities such as production, marketing, and personnel. As they achieve success and become complex, many adopt one of the new organizational structures. Figure 11.3, page 316, shows a generic functional design model. In this model the organization is grouped by task (each group does something different).

Functional Structure—Advantages

This model responds best to price and quality performance pressures. Economies of scale are realized by centralized functional activity, which is most effective with only one or a few products. The greater degree of specialization and reinforcement of expertise are realized from grouping people with other functional experts. Functional organizations

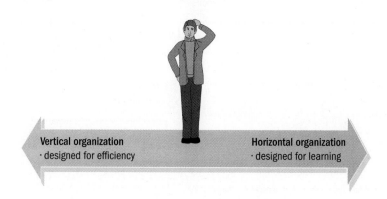

Vertical organization
· designed for efficiency

Horizontal organization
· designed for learning

FIGURE 11.2
The Relationship of Organizational Design to Efficiency versus Learning Outcomes

FIGURE 11.3
Functional Model—Generic

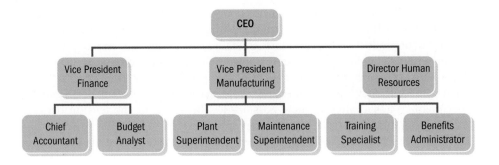

have the advantage of being simple to understand with clear lines of command, and specified tasks and responsibilities. Staff can develop in-depth knowledge and skills in a particular business area, such as production or marketing, and follow well-defined career paths. A functional structure promotes task specialization and expertise development. This model contains no redundancy of functions across groups. It enables the organization to accomplish functional goals.

Functional Structure—Disadvantages

There are major disadvantages to functional structures. Managers have to control interdepartmental conflict that often degenerates into "them" and "us" tribal warfare. Silos emerge. Coherence, good communication, and good horizontal coordination are particularly hard to achieve between virtually independent functions, contributing to less innovation. For example, in Figure 11.3, how does the training specialist talk to the plant superintendent? This model makes it difficult to identify who is responsible for failures; who in the figure is responsible for poor sales? The functional model involves a restricted view of organizational goals.

Functional models are slow to respond to environmental changes. Figure 11.4 shows a Canadian example of a functional structure, Amecan (Canada) Inc. Amecan is an exporter in Mississauga, Ontario, with "associates" around the world. Study Figure 11.4 for a moment and reflect upon the advantages and disadvantages of Amecan's functional model. What do you notice?

FIGURE 11.4
Organizational Chart of Amecan (Canada) Inc.

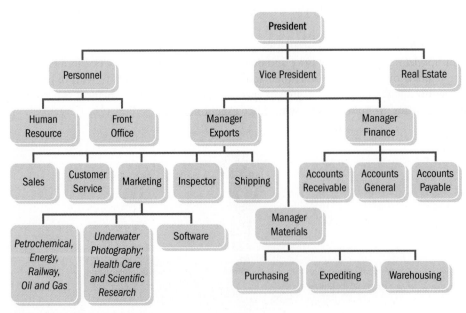

SOURCE: Adapted from *Organization Chart* (Amecan Canada Inc, 2002).

Horizontal Organizations

In the early 1990s, a new form of organizational structure began to emerge in response to complex, rapidly changing, and highly competitive global environments. This new type of structure is based largely on *processes* rather than on functions. The group of consultants at McKinsey & Co. named this new structure the **horizontal organization**. In a functional hierarchy of a vertically built company, individual jobs and information flow are geared toward control. The cross-functional teams of the horizontal company do not require the same level of formal managerial control because their work is aligned with customers' needs, and "controlled" by a judgment of the final result. If the teams are arranged to complete their projects in parallel (from start to finish), thus minimizing subdivision of the processes, the hierarchy becomes flattened. Horizontal structural models include divisional, matrix, hybrid, virtual, and network organizational models.

The **horizontal organization** consists of autonomous, cross-functional work teams designed around critical processes.

Horizontal Structure—Advantages

Advantages of the horizontal structure include flexibility and rapid response to changes in customer needs. The model directs the attention of everyone toward the production and delivery of value to the customer. Because each employee has a broader view of the organizational goals, the model promotes a focus on teamwork and collaboration, and creates a common commitment to meeting objectives. This model also improves the quality of life for employees by offering them the opportunity to share responsibility, make decisions, and be accountable for outcomes.[13]

Horizontal Structure—Disadvantages

One disadvantage of the horizontal model is that determining core processes to organize around is difficult and time-consuming; additionally, this model requires changes in culture, job design, management philosophy, and information and reward systems. Traditional managers may balk when they have to give up power and authority. The model requires significant training of employees to work effectively in a horizontal team environment, and can limit in-depth skill development. As we move along the continuum from the functional model at the mechanistic pole toward the organic pole (see Figure 11.1, page 314), the first model we encounter is the divisional organizational structure.

Organizational Structure—Divisional

A divisional organizational structure forms groups by product, customer, location, topic, etc. Each group performs the same tasks; each for a different topic, customer, product, or location. This structure responds best to time and service performance pressures; works best in large organizations with several products; and provides a greater degree of coordination achieved by grouping all those working on a single product or project together. Coordination is achieved through a single common goal. Sometimes divisional structures are called multidivisional or "M-form" organizations. See Figure 11.5.

As the ecosystem places demands or performance pressure on an organization, the organization then responds by altering its structure, thus moving from functional to divisional or to other models further along the continuum. Remember, quality and cost performance pressures push the structure toward the mechanistic (functional) end of the continuum, while time and service pressures push the structure toward the organic end of the continuum. Divisional structures should be used only when the following three conditions exist. First there are *multiple performance pressures*. If the firm is faced with time, quality, and service issues *and* can pass on the costs, then it should adopt a divisional structure. If quality and cost are important, but time is not, then it

FIGURE 11.5

Generic Divisional Model for Product, Geographic, Process, and Customer Departmentalization

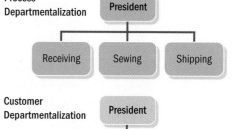

should adopt a functional structure. Second, there are benefits from *economies of scale.* If the company is big enough that it can provide all the expertise needed in the separate divisions, and fully utilize these people, then it should adopt a divisional structure. However, if the company is more toward the conglomerate end of the diversification continuum (rather than the concentric end) it probably will not benefit from economies of scale except for broad-based administrative services. A company is overstaffed if it has surplus or underutilized experts. Finally, divisional structures should be used where there are *high information processing needs.* This will be particularly true when there is a relatively large amount of new product development.

Divisional Structure—Advantages

Because coordination within product lines is easier, a divisional structure enables managers to identify with accuracy what is responsible for the success or failure of the firm's activities. Because product responsibility and contact points are clear, this structure provides greater service expertise related to single customer needs, thereby leading to client satisfaction. It involves high coordination across functions; by grouping into self-contained units, this structure is able to react to ecosystem changes quickly, making larger firms able to compete against SMEs. Divisional structures are more adaptable to changes in ecosystem (e.g., can shut down an international division when a product is no longer selling), and are therefore well suited for fast change in an unstable ecosystem. They can readily adapt to differences in products, regions, or clients.

Divisions encourage team spirit and identification with a product or region. Competition across divisions can serve as a motivator but is a double-edged sword as we will see in the discussion of disadvantages. Managers develop broad skills in order to control all of the basic functions within the unit. This structure decentralizes decision making.

Divisional Structure—Disadvantages

Since each division is likely to have all major functions represented, there is a risk of duplicating activities and providing a redundancy of functions between head office and the divisions (e.g., marketing, R&D), thereby making this model more costly. Conflict and competition for resources and power between staff in successful and unsuccessful divisions may emerge. The divisional function may play a coordinating role, a complex task of reconciling decisions taken at the corporate and business unit levels. By adopting a divisional structure, the economies of scale achieved in functional departments will be eliminated. There is poor coordination, integration, and standardization across product lines. Finally, staff may fail to develop in-depth competencies and technical specialization in their functional areas.

Figure 11.6 shows the divisional (geographic) structure for Apple Computer.

Organizational Structure—Matrix

Today's large global organizations have multiple matrix structures with overlapping business, country, and function areas; however, only a few SMEs will have the resources to adopt this model. The matrix structure theoretically balances power between the functional manager and the project manager, both of whom have budgets and influence over personnel decisions. The matrix structure is designed to force a conflict between the functional manager's desire for quality and the project manager's push for time and service. The matrix structure also exploits economies of scale by encouraging the fluid deployment and redeployment of expertise to projects as needed. Those readers who saw *Mission Impossible* will understand the concept of pulling together experts required for a specific task. Once the task is completed they revert back to their functional areas, awaiting the call to participate in the next task.

Matrix structures are difficult to manage and require leadership and conflict resolution styles different from traditional functional structures. In a matrix, administrative functions

FIGURE 11.6
Geographic Structure for Apple Computer

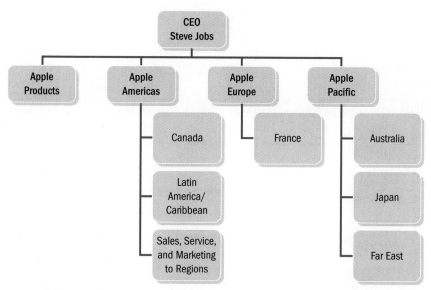

SOURCE: Adapted from H. Baker, III, "Fundamentals of Organization Structure" in *Essentials of Organization Theory and Design*, 2nd ed. Copyright 1999 H. Eugene Baker III.

are generally the responsibility of the functional managers who supervise employees assigned to projects for a fixed period of time; the project managers generally provide the day-to-day operational direction. Companies can, of course, divide the operation and administrative tasking in other configurations but this is one common method.

Matrix structures can be regarded as an early form of network structure; like the network structures we will examine further in a moment, matrix structures focus on project teams, bringing skilled individuals together from different parts of the organization. However, network structures make individuals responsible both to their line manager and the project manager. Before the advent of network technology, many matrix organizations were dogged by duplication and confusion sometimes referred to as the "matrix muddle." The matrix structure is best used by medium-sized organizations with multiple products.

Matrix Structure—Advantages

Matrix structures provide benefits from economies of scale. If a firm is large enough to provide all the expertise required to meet the needs of the product managers (see Figure 11.7, page 320) and if they can be fully utilized, then a matrix structure should be considered. It should also be considered if there are high information processing needs, and a relatively large amount of new product development. The matrix structure uses resources more efficiently than many other structures. The product teams increase technical quality and product integrity simultaneously because of the increased sense of ownership. Other advantages of the matrix structure are its suitability for complex decision making and frequent changes in an unstable environment; achieving the coordination necessary to meet dual demands from customers; flexible sharing of resources across products; and providing opportunities for both functional and product skill development.[14]

Matrix Structure—Disadvantages

Matrix structures require lots of communication and coordination (e.g., between functional and divisional management), and they expose participants to dual authority, which can be frustrating and confusing. Have you ever worked for two or more bosses at the same time? (See the Practical Entrepreneurship Focus box, page 321) Those participating in this model need good interpersonal skills and extensive training. The matrix structure is time-consuming and involves frequent meetings and conflict resolution sessions. Matrix

FIGURE 11.7
Matrix Organization

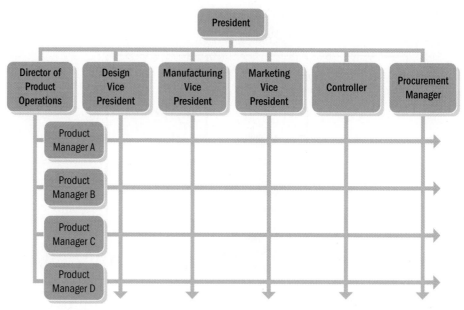

Adapted from H. Baker, III, "Fundamentals of Organization Structure" in *Essentials of Organization Theory and Design*, 2nd ed. Copyright 1999 H. Eugene Baker III.

structures fail because participants don't understand the model and fail to adopt collegial rather than vertical-type relationships.[15] The project leaders must continue to provide significant effort to maintain the appropriate level of control over those assigned to the project from functional areas within the firm. See the Practical Entrepreneurial Focus box. Figure 11.8 shows Worldwide Steel Company, which uses a matrix structure.

Hybrid Organization

Hybrids combine the functional and divisional organizational structures. A hybrid model is functional at one level and divisional at another level simultaneously, and is built on cross-functional project teams. It may even include, from time to time, some additional

FIGURE 11.8
Matrix Structure for Worldwide Steel Company

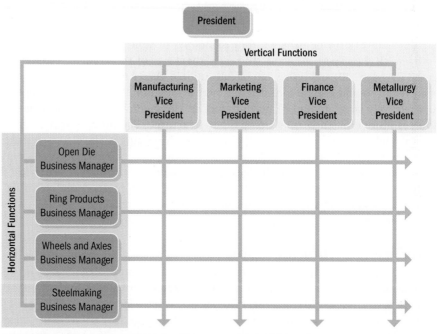

SOURCE: Robert Duncan, "What Is the Right Organization Structure? Decision Tree Analysis Provides the Answer," *Organizational Dynamics* (Winter, 1979).

PRACTICAL ENTREPRENEURIAL FOCUS

Office Democracies: How Many Bosses Can One Person Have?

When Eric Knudsen worked at a software company, he started out with just one boss. But when he was picked to help lead a new product and set of services, his bosses suddenly multiplied and divided. There was a sales director and a marketing director from one group, and a marketing director and a business-operations manager from another group. "Those four people were always in some way trying to direct me," he says. "It gets even weirder," he adds, as a vice president also wanted to direct his efforts. "What I actually did in my job and what I was being told to do had no relation to one another," he says. "It was difficult to know who was holding the purse strings, who to support and who to ignore." He was surprised he made it through the process, but he ultimately quit because of burnout.

Large staffs certainly can be difficult to manage as you reach the edge of the span of control for the position, but managing a number of bosses can be extremely challenging as Knudsen points out. The proliferation of managers can take place because of "empire builders (whoever has the biggest team wins), glory seekers (anything touched can be taken credit for) and ubiquitous leaders-in-training (potential and potentate are close enough)."

But there are problems. "Such flattening of an organization, as it's often called, means by definition that the bottom is a lot closer to the top, which doesn't always suit the bottom very well. Dick Nicholson used to work for a packaging manufacturer that employed a matrix design. "Everyone who could fog a mirror thought he was my boss," he says. "It was especially true of the bean counter and HR types." Did it simplify the organization? "It didn't in my experience," he says. "Everybody just became a boss."

It was President Kennedy's call to the moon that shifted organizations from the military model (functional), with clear chains of command. The moon race was a complex undertaking that required new mental models about organizational design that could provide multiple centres of control. However they found that to "confine *matrix design* within the walls of a normal corporation and 'all hell breaks loose.' . . . Factional rivalries, personal frictions and other political degradations conspire to make it backfire. 'Inside companies it fails more often than it succeeds.'"

Source: Adapted from Jared Sandberg, "Office Democracies: How Many Bosses Can One Person Have?" (*The Wall Street Journal*, November 22, 2005).

At times it can seem like a kind of managerial free-for-all. One of the latest trends in organizational design is a network form of governance that we will refer to in a moment—teams of leaderless groups that are self-directed. Yes the network model can have creative benefits, but it can also create a Lord-of-the-Flies scenario, with self-appointed leaders run amok. Keep these observations in mind as you review and consider adopting matrix organizational designs.

---

organizational structure that we will discuss below when we examine new organizational trends. The objective of the hybrid structure is to increase the efficiency of the decision-making process. The design of the structure (see Figure 11.9) enables individuals to rapidly carry out tasks through communication that cuts across organizations within the scope of their responsibility. The person responsible for a proposal can freely select members according to the project's characteristics within a prescribed range. Ford Customer Service Division is an example of a hybrid structure (see Figure 11.10, page 322).

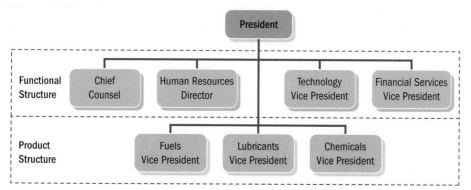

FIGURE 11.9
Hybrid Organization—Generic

Adapted from H. Baker, III, "Fundamentals of Organization Structure" in *Essentials of Organization Theory and Design*, 2nd ed. Copyright 1999 H. Eugene Baker III.

FIGURE 11.10
Ford Customer Service Division

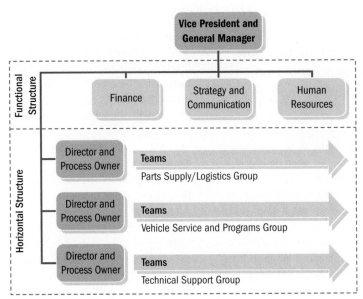

Adapted from H. Baker, III, "Fundamentals of Organization Structure" in *Essentials of Organization Theory and Design*, 2nd ed. Copyright 1999 H. Eugene Baker III.

Hybrid Structure—Advantages

Functional support at the top for product groups can eliminate the redundancy problem of divisional design and increase the expertise available. This structure can use functional groupings where the firm needs the advantages of functional grouping, and divisional groupings where it needs the advantages gained by using a divisional grouping.

Hybrid Structure—Disadvantages

Difficulties in coordination can occur across levels because of different modes of operating. Power struggles can develop because of the nonauthority of functional groups at headquarters over the product groups below.

The Virtual Corporation Organization

A wonderful playing field leveller for SMEs is the organizational structure of the virtual corporation! This use of the term *virtual* comes from the computer industry, where virtual memory is used to make a computer act as if it has more storage capacity than it really does. Similarly, the virtual corporation appears to be a single firm with vast capacities, when in reality it is a collection of many smaller firms or individuals who work together to achieve a specific goal. The virtual corporation represents a *temporary network* of independent companies or workers who come together quickly to exploit fast-changing opportunities. Within a virtual corporation, companies can share costs, skills, and access to global markets, with each contributing to the common goal what it is best at. Today, the virtual corporation has become an important form of business organization structure, particularly in the services sector.

Some of the key attributes of the virtual corporation are:

- Technology—using information networks, entrepreneurs within companies connect and work together from start to finish
- Opportunism—bringing companies together to meet a specific market opportunity; once the opportunity has been exploited, the network will disband
- Trust—making companies far more reliant on one another because the fate of each partner is dependent upon the others
- Excellence—making it possible to achieve a "best of everything" organization; since each partner contributes its key capabilities, every function and process can be world class. There are no borders as a result of a high degree of cooperation between competitors, suppliers, and customers.

Virtual Structure—Advantages

SMEs adopt a virtual organizational structure in order to capture the synergies available from networking with other small firms in the supply chain both upstream and down. These small firms tend to be the early adopters of emerging technology. Because of their small size they can exploit new technology advances that permit them to come together quickly to exploit fast-changing opportunities. Within a virtual corporation, companies can share costs, skills, and access to global markets; each contributing to the common goal by contributing their specific core competencies to the tasks.

Virtual Structure—Disadvantages

There are a number of downsides to the virtual structure such as the possibility that a member-company may lose control of the functions it cedes to its partners, who will not perform adequately to the task; proprietary information or technology may be lost; and management faces the not inconsiderable challenge of learning how to build trust with outsiders and manage beyond the firm's own walls.

Network Structure

The **network organizational structure** can be internal or extended to include key external contacts (see the discussion on hybrid organizations, pages 320–322). Internal network structures provide an informal method of communications within the firm. A network structure is built on personal relationships developed over time; the more extensive the personal network, the better. This structure is in addition to the firm's organizational structure and is to be seen as an enhancement. A network structure can assist in the coordination of activities between the participants in the network. But there can be difficulties similar to those experienced in the matrix structure discussed in the Practical Entrepreneurial Focus box on page 321. Technology has been a great help to this organizational structure; the creation of intranets and virtual teams undertaking projects online are increasing the relationship networks of firms. Recall that the Japanese keiretsu are linked networks where one core firm may own a part of another. German companies similarly promote networks but do not have a German word to describe them.

Networks can be expanded to include key external participants. This represents a disaggregating of organizations by use of independent contractors, joint ventures, etc. In this case, the internal lines of communication and control are aligned horizontally. At the same time the organization is aligned with external organizations at the value-adding level. (See Figure 11.11) MNEs are adopting network structures in response to complex opposing forces of global integration and local responsiveness. From the perspective of MNEs, the network avoids the problem of duplication of effort, inefficiency, and resistance to ideas developed elsewhere by giving subsidiaries the latitude, encouragement, and tools necessary to pursue local business development within the framework of the global strategy. Headquarters considers each unit as a source of ideas, skills, capabilities, and knowledge that can be utilized for the benefit of the entire organization. This de-emphasis of the hierarchical levels by network structures permits a bird's-eye view of the organization and the key stakeholders. The role of the manager in a network structure is transformed from expert to coordinator.[16] A network hybrid structure that permits outside inputs into the firm's network structure is called a project-oriented organizational structure.

> A **network organizational structure** can be internal or extended to include key external contacts. Internal network structures provide an informal method of communications within the firm. A network structure is built on personal relationships developed over time; the more extensive the personal network, the better.

Project-Oriented Organization Structures

A project-oriented organization is designed to execute a specific strategy. Its mandate is to efficiently and effectively balance and resolve business strategy issues.

In Figure 11.12, note that a project-oriented organization functions without regard to a hierarchy when executing new business strategies. Upon completion of the project, the staff assigned revert to their normal positions within the organizational structure.

FIGURE 11.11

Simple Network Model

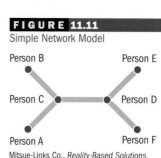

Mitsue-Links Co., *Reality-Based Solutions*, (Tokyo: Mitsue-Links, Co., 2006).

FIGURE 11.12

Conceptual Diagram of a Project-Oriented Organization

Mitsue-Links Co., *Reality-Based Solutions*, (Tokyo: Mitsue-Links, Co., 2006).

INTERNATIONAL STRATEGIC THINKING

There is no "right" organizational structure model, nor are you constrained to stay within the "box" of the generic models discussed in this chapter. Firms experiment daily, each seeking competitive advantage while remaining cognizant of the concepts and relationships of organizational design that we have examined. Figure 11.13 shows a new (2005) organizational structure that combines functional, project, and matrix-oriented structures.

Mitsue-Links attempts to capture the best of the hierarchical, project, and matrix-oriented organizational structures. The firm believes the three organizational structures are respectively preservation-, strategy-, and efficiency-oriented, allowing them to "play to their strengths."

FIGURE 11.13

Mitsue-Links Co.–Rotary Organization (Continually Shifting Strategic Centre)

SOURCE: Mitsue-Links Co., *Reality-Based Solutions* (Tokyo: Mitsue-Links Co., 2006).

"Furthermore, rather than having all three function equally, we continually shift our strategic center according to market fluctuations. This enables us to choose which organizational structure to prioritize according to whether we should preserve the organization, make an effort to promote a strategy, or try to promote efficiency. Mitsue-Links developed this unique organizational structure system, which it refers to as a 'rotary organization.'"[17] Another name for organizational design is a rotary formation.

Network—Advantages

The network structure allows organizations more flexibility, which increases competitiveness. The network structure doesn't require as many resources as it obtains some of its inputs (e.g., employees, office space, equipment, etc.) from independent contractors, joint ventures, and others.

Network—Disadvantages

This structure may result in difficulty controlling quality. The need for contract management skills increase because of the need to coordinate and communicate effectively with everyone involved.

Global Trends in Organizational Design

The management of international business used to be a neat discipline with comforting rules and knowable best practices. But globalization and the arrival of the information economy have rapidly demolished all the old mental models. Today the management of global Canadian SMEs must innovate and speed information through horizontal, globe-spanning networks, a daunting challenge. Old, rigid hierarchies found in Canadian MNEs are out, and flat, speedy, virtual organizations are in. These new flat, agile organizational structures enable SMEs to more readily enter the global marketplace. Increasingly, teamwork is a must and compensation schemes have to be redesigned to reward team players. Canadian business leaders must think beyond just the firm's organizational chart: the structure must accommodate workflows. If people don't teamwork across structural boundaries, the organization will revert into silos of self-sufficient generalists. The structure implementation process must permit fluid cross-boundary workflows as an integral part of the design.

Today, strategists have to custom-design their organizations' structure to accommodate their ecosystem, their industry, their own corporate legacy, and key global customers. Indeed, they may have to revamp more than once to get it right, as we read in the opening vignette, page 309. Air Canada, Alberta's Eurogas Corporation, Canadian Pacific Limited, and Precision Drilling Corporation are examples of Canadian firms that have been through several organizational reincarnations in the past decade to boost global

JUST DOING THE RIGHT THING

Don't Rush to Discard the Corporate Memory—The Old Folks

The corporate memory is a very important "soft" asset that cannot be lost when adopting new organizational design structures.

All organizations contain a corporate body of knowledge, some of it obvious and some not so obvious. In large measure, it is acquired over time by the firm's long-time staff. The loss of this knowledge could significantly affect the firm's future corporate performance. For example, the firm's organizational culture or "how we do things around here" is an intangible form of knowledge. If this knowledge is lost it could damage intellectual property, the corporate "memory," and the firm's identity. To prevent this, the full corporate body of knowledge needs to be understood in context before embarking on organizational design change.

Firms must identify where they are at risk if they adopt a new organizational structure. They will need to examine the new structure from the perspective of all stakeholders. "Talent and knowledge mapping are obvious steps, but a skills inventory can easily miss the less obvious: 'How we make things happen'; 'What's the best way to do x'; and other parts of the company culture, including the 'genesis of products' (the processes that are gone through to develop new products and services)."[18] Remember the firm's corporate memory (old folks) is an organizational asset that must be protected before, during, and after organization design change. Think before you downsize!

competitiveness. In restructuring your firm's organization, remember to provide for the "soft" skills in your structural design, and anticipate challenges in implementing the new models. See Just Doing the Right Thing.

Controlling Strategies

Having crafted the organization's strategy and designed the supporting organizational structure, it is now necessary to put in place the firm's "nervous system"—the control mechanism that will provide the means to verify how well activities are being conducted and to permit remedial action to ensure the organization's goals/objectives are met. Controls are designed to reduce uncertainty, increase predictability, and ensure that the behaviour of the organization is aligned with the firm's corporate values and objectives, notwithstanding idiosyncratic factors, distance between units, and diversity of the firm's human resources. In attempting to establish the approach to control measures, it is important to note that we are seeking a balance between the need for headquarters to ensure that activities are conducted in the best interest of the firm, while at the same time ensuring the rules, regulations, and policies that have been implemented do not stifle innovation.

Organizational Control—Design

When designing control systems, first clarify the objective of the control measure. There are two main objectives: output controls and behaviour controls. **Output controls** are formalized control systems that serve as benchmarks for managers to evaluate past and future performance. They include balance sheets, sales and production data, and personnel performance reviews. Today this information is available in most cases in real time. Canadian firms must be aware of the technological advances in this software area and adopt where there is value for money. In Chapter 10, pages 302–303, we discussed a number of tools, including the balanced scorecard, consumption chain analysis, and corporate dashboards, available to assist in monitoring and providing early warning of possible control measure concerns.

Behavioural control measures attempt to influence employees' actions by training individuals to share corporate beliefs and values. In Chapter 15, we examine in some detail the importance of corporate culture as a behavioural control measure; therefore, it will not be examined in great depth in this chapter.

When designing control systems, management must consider the cost of the establishing and maintaining the system versus the potential benefit. It is important to remember that a control system requires investment in a management structure and system

Output controls are formalized control systems that include the firm's balance sheets, sales data, production data, product line growth, and personnel performance reviews. The establishment of output controls involves management control by establishing goals or objectives that act as the criteria in the decision-making process.

Behavioural control measures attempt to influence employees' actions by training individuals to share the corporate beliefs and values.

design. The impact goes beyond administrative components. Controls that are misguided or too time-consuming undermine the implementation process. The implementation of controls requires great sensitivity to behavioural dimensions and the environment. The control measures must be an appropriate and reflective of actual performance; individuals should be judged only on factors over which they have some degree of control.

Organizational Control—Generic Types of Control Mechanisms

Firms' control systems require a base of power and a control mechanism. There are four generic types of control mechanisms: centralized decision making; formalized guides to the decision-making process; exercised output control; and cloning. Using **centralization**, managers achieve control over decision making by either making all decisions themselves or by requiring the decision makers to have all decisions approved before implementation. **Formalization** of controls takes place when a firm provides rules, procedures, guidelines, and policies that guide the decision-making process. The establishment of *output controls* involves management control by establishing goals or objectives that act as the criteria in the decision-making process (see the margin definition on page 325). Recall in Chapter 10 that we covered goals and objectives as control measures at some length. Finally **cloning** is achieved by establishing a set of shared values and expectations that act to guide the decision-making process. With this behavioural control mechanism, a strong base of power is not necessary. Cloning is the basis of organizational culture. Many argue that organizational culture and organizational structure are functional alternatives, that is, they both function to achieve control. When culture is strong, strong controlling structures are unnecessary.

Cross-Functional Control Integration Mechanisms

The need for coordination increases directly as the firm shifts its structure from mechanistic to organic. That is to say that control measures become increasing important as the firm decentralizes its decision-making authority. Because mechanistic structures retain tight control, few resources and relatively little effort need to be directed toward coordination of the firm's activities. As firms move further from this end of the continuum toward the organic pole, managers must undertake more coordination efforts, make constant adjustments, provide enhanced communication, and resolve conflicts. As a result, more resources are necessary to facilitate communication and conflict resolution in an integrative (win-win) manner. The requirements of cross-functional control integration mechanisms are greatest during the development and product introduction (early) stages of a product's life cycle. Accordingly, firms with multiple products and short life cycles have the greatest need for cross-functional control integration mechanisms. Cross-functional control integration mechanisms can be arranged in order of increased cost, as well as increased effectiveness.

The **hierarchy control mechanism** achieves cross-functional control integration through communication between senior functional managers. Conflict among functional units is resolved through the mutual supervisors negotiating. This mechanism, while requiring the least resources, creates time delays. In addition, where multiple products exist, the firm's general manager, who focuses on operational issues of all products, will be required to participate in controlling his own relationship between functional units from time to time. Hence the hierarchy control mechanism requires the fewest additional resources but is the weakest mechanism when increased complexity (amount of reciprocal interdependence) exists. The cross-functional control integration mechanisms can be viewed as a hierarchy ranging from simple to complex. See Figure 11.14.

Direct Contact

When the chain of command gets overburdened from using the hierarchy cross-functional control mechanism model, individuals begin communicating directly with their counterparts

Centralization of decision making permits managers to achieve control over decision making by either making all decisions themselves or by requiring the decision makers to have all decisions approved before implementation.

Formalization of control takes place when a firm provides rules, procedures, guidelines, and policies that act to guide the decision-making process.

Cloning is achieved by establishing a set of shared values and expectations that act to guide the decision-making process. With this behavioural control mechanism, a strong base of power is not necessary.

The **hierarchy control mechanism** achieves cross-functional control integration through communication between senior functional managers; conflict is resolved through negotiation. This mechanism requires the fewest resources but creates time delays, and is the weakest mechanism for complex organizations.

in other functional departments, thereby providing another integrative control mechanism—direct contact. Recall that in the functional and divisional organization there is no communication channel established to enable this activity. Communication in these models went up, across and then down. In this model, employees are encouraged to initiate direct contact with subunits throughout all functional and divisional areas. Communication with, and the involvement of, the appropriate functional units is left to the discretion and initiative of individuals. Direct contact has a propensity to speed up decision making. When conflict occurs between these individuals, their relative power tends to determine the outcome. An integrative (win-win) decision is not encouraged. Whether this control measure is effective depends in large part on the individuals and managers engaging in and supporting direct contact. This control mechanism leads to a tradeoff of performance pressures, rather than development of an innovative way to meet multiple performance pressures.

FIGURE 11.14
Cross-Functional Control Integration Mechanisms

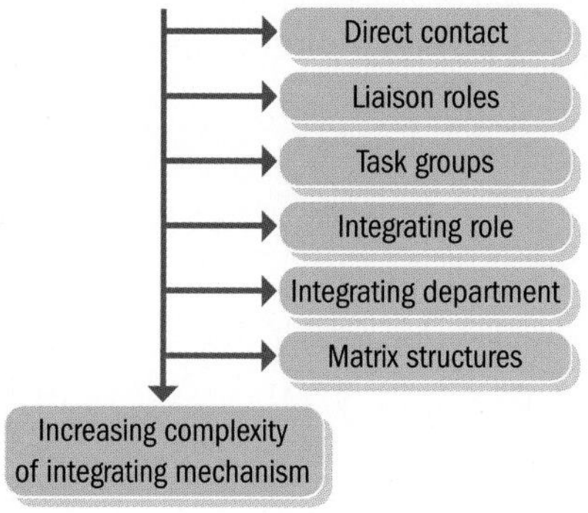

Liaison Role

This control mechanism requires a facilitator, expediter, or project manager–type person who is appointed to smooth conflicts and encourage communication among those working on a single project or product. There is no formal base of power; individuals appointed to this position must rely on building identification with the project (referent power). Often they tend to get work done through reciprocity (exchange of favours). Lack of formal power often puts this type of project manager at a disadvantage; when faced with competing demands from a project manager and functional manager, the employee generally attempts to satisfy the functional manager. The liaison positions are assigned. There is some degree of recognition and "standing" within the units, and there are recognized tasks. The increased recognized interaction between the same people assigned to the liaison role and the subunits generally result in a "bonding" relationship. This can be a positive control measure and outcome.

Task Groups

This cross-functional control integration mechanism provides for a project manager to have specifically assigned individuals from the various functional units to work on a specific activity or project. The task group will either be permanent or for a fixed term. Generally, committees and teams are very effective when more than three subunits are required to undertake an activity. The team meets regularly and motivation is achieved through identification with the team. The ongoing, regular meetings facilitate increased communication. The success of this mechanism is directly dependent upon the project leader's conflict mediation and facilitation skills. The project leader must focus on both team goals as well as accommodating the functional members' interests in order to be effective. Team members who are well led will often develop a sense of "ownership" of the project. As a result, all team members tend to devote more time and energy toward "their" project than they would without this sense of ownership. Team leaders must ensure team members know their efforts are making a measurable difference in the results of the project. This is further enhanced when positive project outcomes can be directly attributed to their competencies and to their contribution. However, a team member's motivation can be marred when the time and effort spent on the project is seen by her functional manager as being accomplished at the expense of the functional unit's performance.

Integrating Role

This mechanism is similar to the cross-functional task group control integration mechanism in that the project leader's titles may be the same (project manager, expediter, etc.). However, this individual can allocate resources in support of the task. The ability to allocate resources in turn provides the project leader with increased power (in all other cross-functional control integration mechanisms resources are distributed among functional departments). Resources are divided between functional managers and project managers for the duration of the task.

Integrating Department

The integrating department cross-functional control integration mechanism is a task group with a budget.

Matrix Structure

The final cross-functional control integration mechanism is a matrix, the most complex control mechanism. Recall the advantages and disadvantages of a matrix organizational design discussed earlier. In a matrix there is a theoretical balance of power between the functional manager and the project manager, who both have budgets and influence over personnel decisions. The matrix is designed to force a conflict between the functional manager's desire for quality, and the project manager's push for time and service. The matrix also exploits the economies of scale necessary to hold down costs by encouraging the fluid deployment and redeployment of expertise to projects as needed. Matrix structures are difficult to manage and require different leadership and conflict resolution styles than traditional functional structures.

Management Implications

- The 1990s brought a decade of managerial innovation and organizational experimentation that will bring new forms of organizational systems and managerial approaches into the 21st century. Today, modern organizations identify the organization of tomorrow characterized by a high level of flexibility, a lack of hierarchy, and a strong focus on communications. Current trends indicate that companies of the future will become organizations with fluid boundaries, where even large companies may be networked to smaller ones that constantly interchange with one another. This development has worked in the favour of Canadian SMEs by levelling the international market playing field.
- Canada's global customers become empowered and stronger because of globalization and technology. Canadian SMEs must shift from a product management mentality to a customer service management mentality. Organizational structures must be designed for this fact. Global service organizations are the wave of the future for Canada. Canadian multinationals will continue to have business units with global mandates, global account managers (apart from the business units), and small, powerless country managers.
- The culture of a company is probably more important than the lines on an organizational chart. Rather than a structure that is rigid, organizational charts should be drawn in pencil. In today's fast-paced, turbulent ecosystems, firms must be prepared to make adjustments to the organizational design as often as necessary to get the job done and maintain the cultural values developed over time.
- Global realities shaping organizational structures include worldwide expansion of scientific knowledge; exponential growth in the number of global competitors; increasingly fragmented markets and shifting customer preferences; and diverse and transforming process technology that leads to increased flexibility. Technology has never been more important, yet it has never been harder to gain a competitive edge using technology alone. Managers must link technical capabilities with their global customer requirements and then design the organizational structure to best meet those needs. Canadian SMEs must be aware of and adopt the technological advances and link them to the firm's strategic intent. Canadian SMEs must take a world-view of technical competence. Speed is probably the major advantage of SMEs and is essential in a very competitive global marketplace. The firm's organizational structure must align with and support this advantage. Firms must also understand the principles of operations management and the science of production in order to design the best-fitting organizational structure.
- Globalization places high value on the ability to adapt and be open to other peoples' values and traditions. That challenge requires a different mental model; it's not only

a bridge that is needed but also the ability to stand on new terrain. Companies can use cultural differences to spark new ideas, make the organization more effective, and generate new ways of thinking about their organizational design structure.

- Remember the firm's corporate memory (old folks) is an organizational asset that must be protected before, during, and after organizational design change. Think before you downsize.

CHAPTER SUMMARY

- Business, like water, configures its flow (hsing) in accord with the terrain. It is helpful to think of a firm as being constructed of elements, such as people, resources, aspirations, market trends, levels of competence, reward systems, departmental mandates, and so on, that affect each other according to the structural relationship they form.

- An organization's structure is often one of the key determining factors in whether an organization is successful at being global. The firm's structure and control systems either limit or liberate the project teams' performance potential.

- Globalization and the information economy have rapidly demolished old precepts. The management of global companies, which must innovate simultaneously and speed information through horizontal, globe-spanning networks, has become a daunting challenge. Old, rigid hierarchies are out, and flat, speedy, virtual organizations are in. Teamwork is crucial, and compensation schemes have to be redesigned to reward team players.

- Organizations will need new coordinating mechanisms to accommodate different kinds of people in the workplace.

- Today's business environment is turbulent. Change is so quick that organizational response time is at a premium. Those organizations that can develop new technologies faster, or can adapt to changes in the market faster, that will survive the competition. This means different structures must be adopted to meet the sometimes-chaotic environment.

- Appropriate organizational design is valued as one of the four key criteria for business success in the 21st century. The other three criteria for business success are a customer- and quality-driven organization with a flat management hierarchy; a sense of vision; and the capacity to add significant value to products and services.

- Organizational structure exists to perform two essential functions within the organization. The first function is control. Organizations must design their structures to permit the firm's assets, competencies, and labour to be grouped and positioned so that the best possible competitive advantage can be achieved. Second, the design provides coordination of all activities within the firm in an efficient and effective manner to ensure the firm meets its objectives.

- Today, organizations can be viewed as people management systems having three main components: horizontal complexity, vertical complexity, and integrated controlling mechanisms.

- The appropriate balance between vertical and horizontal structures must be kept in mind as you design the organizational structure that has the right "fit" for your firm.

- Vertical structures are designed for efficiency. They provide for specialized tasks; have a strict bureaucratic hierarchy with many rules, policies, and procedures controlling activities; employ vertical reporting (the go-through-channels syndrome); have few teams as staff must remain in their functional "box"; and maintain centralized decision making. These features must be fully evaluated against the tradeoffs available when adopting a horizontal structure.

- Horizontal structures are designed for learning. Tasks are shared; workers are empowered; everyone works in a relaxed environment that is largely controlled by the corporate culture, with few rules, policies, and processes formally set out; horizontal face-to-face communication is permitted, thereby gaining speed and building relationships; a large number of specific activities are team-based; and decision making is decentralized.

- When designing control systems, first determine the object of the control measure. There are two main objectives: output controls and behavioural controls. Firms' control systems require a base of power and a control mechanism. There are four generic types of control mechanisms to meet the objectives of establishing control mechanisms.

- Today, organizations respond to external environmental factors by identifying with one of two core classifications of models: mechanistic (characterized by rigidity, bureaucracy, and a strict hierarchy) and organic (project- and team-based facilitated by technology and characterized by openness, responsiveness, and lack of hierarchy). The structural models range from simple hierarchies based on military-type traditional lines to the more recent complex networks having computer systems and telecommunications at their centre. There are functional, divisional, matrix, hybrid, virtual, and network organizational structures. The newer models have emerged in response to globalization and technology.

REVIEW QUESTIONS

1. How has globalization changed firms' organizational structures?
2. Organizational structure exists to perform two essential functions within the organization. What are they? Discuss.
3. Today, organizations can be viewed as people management systems having three main components. What are they? Discuss.
4. Discuss the two core classifications of organizational structural models.
5. What is meant by the "tension between vertical and horizontal organizational structures"?

6. Select any three organizational structures and discuss their advantages and disadvantages. Provide a Canadian firm as an example of each.
7. Explain why, when designing control systems, management should first determine the object of the control measure.
8. What are the four generic types of control mechanisms?
9. The need for coordination increases directly as the firm shifts its structure from mechanistic to organic. Discuss the different cross-functional control integration mechanisms available to managers.

REFLECTIVE THINKING QUESTIONS

1. Having completed this chapter, reread the quotations on the first page, critically reflect on the validity of the authors' statements, and provide your opinion as to the validity of each. Evidence-based answers are preferred to rhetorical answers.
2. New forms of organizational structure have emerged, such as the virtual corporation. Do you think these structures are adequate to meet the constantly changing world into which we are moving? Can they meet the needs of organizations in varying situations, in different economies, in disparate countries, and with different cultures?

3. Many argue that organizational culture and organizational structure are functional alternatives, that is, they both function to achieve control. When culture is strong, strong structures are unnecessary. What do you think?
4. Professor Julian Birkenshaw of the London Business School observed, "Country managers have gone from being king of the company to administrative coordinators and local ambassadors. They are nominally responsible to get things done, but they have no power."[19] Do you agree that country managers have gone from being king of the company to administrative coordinators and local ambassadors? Support your position.

GLOBAL E-RESEARCH

Visit www.power.nelson.com for research suggestions, questions, and a number of background discussion papers on this topic.

MINI CASE

Users Grow Virtual Call Centres

Office Depot is in the process of shutting down nearly all its internally operated call centres and shifting the load to outsourcers—in particular, outsourcers who use home-based agents. The office supply retailer has been exploring the "virtual call centre" model for more than three years, and today relies on about 1,400 remote agents employed by its outsourcing partners. Virtual call centres are gaining popularity because of fierce competition in the industry. The traditional, in-house call centre or using an offshore outsourcer is increasingly becoming yesterday's news. While outsourcing

work-at-home agents doesn't have the same cost-savings potential as offshore outsourcing, it does resolve many of the cultural challenges presented by using offshore providers.

For five years, Jet Blue has run its reservations department using 900 home-based reservation agents working in the Salt Lake City area. Staff turnover is significantly less with home-based agents. "Turnover rates at JetBlue are exceptionally low at 4% annually. Agents enjoy the flexibility of working from home, and it shows in their performance, he said. 'When agents are happy, revenue is going to go up.'" Before moving to a virtual organizational design model, Office Depot historically had a 60% annual turnover of its call centre agents. When they adopted the virtual model, they immediately experienced a 50 percent cut in attrition rates and attendance was also is up. For Office Depot it has proven to be a good alternative to completely going offshore.

What is driving the adoption of this virtual organizational design?

First, dissatisfaction with offshore outsourcing. "There's a problem with quality in some of the offshore call centers. . . . Using U.S.–based agents working from home gives companies access to a broader, more educated workforce that is suited to up-sell customers and handle more complex questions. . . . The desire for more skilled, flexible workers drives many companies to use outsourced services. . . . With a virtual workforce, you're not confined to a 25-mile radius around a brick-and-mortar building that you built. You can go find those skilled workers regardless of where they reside." These issues faced by large U.S. firms have presented Canadian call centres a wonderful opportunity. Second is a growth in broadband services. Third is management-related. Work-at-home initiatives require different organizational design and management skills than in traditional call centres. There must, for example, be greater reliance on control and coordination using software applications such

as workforce automation software that facilitates tasks such as planning, scheduling, and activity management. An Office Depot spokesperson observed, "The biggest hurdle is making sure that employees feel they are part of the company. . . . The virtual call center is not necessarily applicable to every single industry . . . It depends on the types of calls a company gets and whether those calls require advanced skills or geographic affinity."

Adapted from Ann Bednarz, "Users Grow Virtual Call Centers," *Network World* (January 31, 2005), retrieved September 8, 2006, from http://www .networkworld.com/news/2005/013105virtualcall.html.

QUESTIONS

1. Do you think they are onto something? Are virtual call centres, as adopted by JetBlue Airways and others as truly a viable, innovative, new organizational design model or a passing fad?

2. Reflect on the challenges faced by corporations in the Mini Case when using offshore call centres and comment on their relevancy today. Are they strengthening? Diminishing? What will be the impact on the "flourishing" Canadian call centre industry?

ENDNOTES

1 *Brainy Quote* (BrainyMedia.com, 2005), retrieved August 23, 2006, from www.brainyquote.com.

2 Ibid.

3 Ibid.

4 Jim Clemmer, *Measurement Traps* (Kitchener, ON: The CLEMMER Group), retrieved August 22, 2006, from www.clemmer.net/excerpts/measurement_ traps.shtml.

5 *Brainy Quote.*

6 Richard L. Daft, *Organization Theory and Design*, 6th ed. (Cincinnati, OH: South-Western College Publishing, 1998).

7 "The Next Paradigm?" *Chief Executive* (June 1992), retrieved September 8, 2006.

8 Alexander Nikolenko and Brian H. Kleiner, "Global Trends in Organizational Design" (*Work Study*, Vol. 45 1996), retrieved August 23, 2006, from www.emeraldinsight.com/10.1108/00438029610150966.

9 Ibid.

10 J.M. Higgins, *The Management Challenge*, 2nd ed., (New York: Macmillan College Publishing Co., 1994).

11 Ibid.

12 Peter Drucker, "The Coming of the New Organisation," *Harvard Business Review*, (January–February 1988).

13 Frank Ostroff, *The Horizontal Organization: What the Organization of the Future Looks Like and How It Delivers Value to Customers* (New York: Oxford University Press, 1999).

14 Adapted from H. Baker, III, "Fundamentals of Organization Structure" in *Essentials of Organization Theory and Design*, 2nd ed. Retrieved September 8, 2006, from www.unf.edu/ ~gbaker/Man4201/Chapt003a.PDF.

15 Robert Duncan, "What Is the Right Organization Structure? Decision Tree Analysis Provides the Answer," *Organizational Dynamics* (Winter, 1979).

16 Sonia M. Goltz, *Organizational Structure* (Michigan Tech's School of Business and Economics, 2005), retrieved August 23, 2006, from www.sbea.mtu.edu/smgoltz/ba3700/ OrgStructure.html.

17 Mitsue-Links Co., *Reality-Based Solutions* (Company Overview: Corporate Structure, 2006), retrieved August 23, 2006, available from www.mitsue.co.jp/english/company/ chart.html.

18 Martyn Smith, "Safeguarding Knowledge During Change" (*Knowledge Management Review*, May/June 2005).

19 Julian Birkenshaw, "Custom-Designing the Global Corporation: Pointers from Some of Management's Masters," *BusinessWeek* (August 28, 2000), retrieved September 21, 2006, from www.businessweek.com/2000/00_35/b3696036.htm.

Export, Import, and Countertrade Practices

"The idea that Canada and China still have a special relationship has passed. We had a head start in the 1970s . . . but the rest of the world has caught up, and today, Canada has to compete for the attention of the Chinese government."[1]

—Yuen Pau Woo, chief economist of the Asia Pacific Foundation of Canada

"No nation was ever ruined by trade."[2]

—Benjamin Franklin

"Trade is the best cure for prejudice."[3]

—Baron de Montesquieu, (1689–1755), French lawyer and political philosopher

"My father's generation knew that they were playing by different rules from the West. When it came to trade, they pretended they didn't understand the rules. That's why they won."[4]

—Hideo Morita, executive at Sony Music Entertainment, Japan

"Americans should never underestimate the constant pressure on Canada which the mere presence of the United States has produced. We're different people from you and we're different people because of you."[5]

—Pierre Elliott Trudeau, Prime Minister of Canada,
1968–1979, 1980–1984

LEARNING OUTCOMES

- Understand why Canada must continue to be a world leader in exports.
- Evaluate the merits and reasons for exporting, importing, and countertrade practices.
- Understand the pitfalls for SMEs when crafting export strategy.
- Formulate opinions regarding Canada's need to diversify its international trade markets.
- Contrast two fundamental forms of export strategies, indirect and direct.
- Identify and evaluate the merits of the different kinds of export intermediaries.
- Evaluate existing Canadian international trading patterns and formulate an opinion as to whether today's trade patterns still align with Canada's best economic interest.
- Understand countertrade arrangements for selected developing and underdeveloped countries.
- Develop an awareness of Canada's trade supports for SME importers and exporters.

Solar-Powered Marine Lights Carmanah Technologies Inc., Victoria, British Columbia

Carmanah's Model 701 solar-powered LED marine light installed on a navigational buoy in Singapore.

"Countries around the world are brighter and safer thanks to products manufactured by Carmanah Technologies Inc. The Victoria-based company designs and produces solar-powered LED (light-emitting diode) lights for marking channels, waterways, moored vessels and docks, as well as highlighting hazards and high-caution areas on roads, highways and railways."[6] It commenced business in 1996 and had sales of $38.7 million for the year ending 31 December 2005.[7] Ninety-two percent of the sales are derived from exports.[8] "About 85 percent of Carmanah's production is exported to port and roadway authorities, marinas and rail yards, as well as other commercial and private users. The company also serves the needs of the Canadian and United States coast guards and the United Kingdom's Trinity House."[9]

"With 12 major ports, 150 minor ports and 12,000 kilometres of coastline and navigable inland waterways, India represents a large market for marine navigation products. During the Canada Trade Mission to the region in 2002, Carmanah signed a contract for the sale of 22 of its Model 701 marine lights to the Port of Kandla, the connecting hub for one million square kilometres of north-western India. 'Buyers there recognize that our short-range marine navigation lights are the best in the world,' says Carmanah CEO Art Aylesworth, 'and the Model 701 has the lowest cost of acquisition, installation and operation in its class.' Like all Carmanah lights, the 701 has a self-contained power source and requires no battery/bulb replacement or other maintenance during its lifespan."[10]

A SUN TZU MOMENT. . .

"Those who do not use local guides are unable to obtain the advantages of ground."[11]

According to Greek mythology, after nine years of unsuccessfully attempting to bring the City of Troy to its knees around 1150 BC, the Greeks abandoned the battlefield and left a Trojan horse, which the citizens of Troy believed to be tribute, outside the gates of Troy. The Greeks deceived Troy's king into believing that they had abandoned the fight and returned to Greece. Some citizens of Troy brought the Trojan horse inside the city walls. Later that night, by stealth from within the wooden Trojan horse, a small band of Greek soldiers emerged and opened Troy's gates—and the rest is history.

In this chapter, we will examine some of the local guides (assistance) that are available to Canadian SMEs when considering entering the gates of host countries. It is important that Canadian SME managers know themselves and their business. When entering the global marketplace, they must also know the "enemy"—the competition. We have read that partnerships, alliances, and joint ventures are good business FDI modes of entry that provide SMEs with the services of local guides in host countries. In this chapter, we will examine the local guides and supports available to exporting and importing Canadian SMEs.

Opening Thoughts

Why Export, Import, and Countertrade?

Exports are the cornerstone of Canada's economic well-being. One in three jobs directly relies on international trade. It is estimated that for every $1 billion invested in Canada, 45,000 new jobs are created.[12] Daily world exports and imports add up to several billion dollars. Canada can't afford not to participate.

Many trade and other barriers prevent SMEs from looking outside Canada for expansion opportunities. Barriers such as the relative value of the Canadian dollar versus other currencies can have a major impact on exporters. Many countries continue to have "buy-at-home" policies and provide preferential treatment for indigenous companies. The customs process can be complex, and delivery and transportation in a foreign country add to the challenges of an international undertaking. Cultural differences and language barriers also add challenges for Canadian businesses. Finally, there are many regulatory mechanisms, such as taxation, health and safety regulations, environmental policies, and regulating competition, which must be understood and provided for by exporting and importing SMEs. Fortunately, for the most part these trade barriers are falling.

Notwithstanding these barriers, firms like British Columbia's Carmanah Technology Inc. export for three reasons. First, the company increases revenues through expanding total sales when the domestic market has become mature. It exploits the advantages to be gained by spreading the fixed cost of production over more units (economies of scale), as well as possibly obtaining experience curve benefits. Generally, the more goods or services it can sell, the lower the unit costs will be. As a result, Carmanah achieves greater efficiencies and so is able to provide its goods or services to more customers at lower costs. Reducing the unit costs can also serve as a barrier to imitators entering the market that find themselves unable to sell for these low unit costs. Second, exporting provides the company with the opportunity to diversify its sales base. As a result, it will be in a better position to withstand regional economic recessions. Also, exporting companies' revenues from diversified sales can be an advantage when used to pay international creditors. Finally, firms like Carmanah use exporting as a low-cost, low-risk strategy (mode) to enter a foreign market, thereby acquiring international trade expertise that may in time lead to more sophisticated, integrated market-entry strategies (see Chapter 10, pages 292–293, and Figure 10.13).

By now, most of you will agree that globalization of business is a reality. In Chapter 10, we examined several international management strategies, and their advantages and disadvantages, and we reviewed in some detail possible market entry modes available to decision makers. Exporting is the most common market entry strategy for SMEs wishing to participate in global trade as it is a conservative way to test the waters. Carmanah's success is a good example of a small firm succeeding in the global market by initially using an export strategy.

One factor driving increased Canadian exports is the reality that the Canadian domestic market is likely to grow at a slower rate than the world economy.[13] SMEs must consider these faster-growing global markets. There are 2.6 million small businesses and self-employed people in Canada who could participate; SMEs are a key engine of growth in the Canadian economy, accounting for some 60 percent of private sector employment and 43 percent of private sector output.[14]

There are additional export drivers. Increasingly, SMEs are attempting to participate in the global marketplace driven by global competition, cheap efficient transportation, falling trade barriers, and the need for global cost competitiveness. Trade opportunities are growing: "exports of Canadian goods and services increased 5.2 per cent to $516.4 billion in 2005, surpassing the previous record reached in 2000 ($489.0 billion) (see Figure 12.1). As with exports, imports also rose, increasing 5.8 per cent to $463.1 billion."[15] See Figure 12.2.

However, Canada's trade performance with the United States appears to be declining. This can, in part, possibly be attributed to Canada–U.S. trade relations. In 2005, the U.S. market was the destination for 71.5 percent of Canadian exports and the source of

55.8 percent of Canadian imports.[16] Some factors resulting in the decline of Canadian exports to the United States from an all-time high of 85.8 percent in 2004 include U.S. cuts in spending due to the war in Iraq; the ban of Canadian beef because of bovine spongiform encephalopathy (BSE); severe acute respiratory syndrome (SARS), which precipitated a marked decline in commercial and travel services; the decline in forest products caused by an increase in B.C. forest fires; U.S. tariffs imposed on softwood lumber;[17] and increased trade with other nations. As a result, Canada experienced a decline in labour rates. This, combined with an overall decrease in spending, resulted in slightly lower imports than previous years. Remember that trade is not just about exporting and importing goods; services account for about 67 percent of total economic activity in Canada. Canada's recorded services exports exceeded $62 billion in 2004,[18] "about one dollar of every eight dollars earned from Canadian exports."[19]

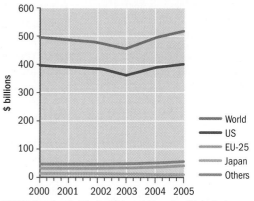

FIGURE 12.1

Exports of Goods and Services by Major Areas, 2000–05

SOURCE: Department of Foreign Affairs and International Trade, *Trade Update 2006* (Seventh Annual Report on Canada's State of Trade, July 5, 2006). Copyright Public Works & Government Services Canada.

Export–Import

In order to participate in **exporting** and/or **importing**, traders must learn, among other things, financial flows, the export and import processes, and Internet technologies. Unfortunately, many new SME managers fear the unknown and therefore do not proactively explore new global markets. Exporting presents minimal risk and lower investment than other available market entry strategies. When SMEs adopt an exporting strategy, much of the operational control and most of the marketing control is passed to others in the distribution channel. SMEs should rely on intermediaries, who know the export/import best practices of the selected host countries' distribution and marketing functions, thereby reducing the discomfort level for novice global trading Canadian SMEs. In the early days, many small firms welcomed the opportunity to divest themselves of these responsibilities. However, with the advancement of user-friendly technology and growing sophistication in the conduct of international business SME managers increasingly consider participating in this export activity. Exporting is a good strategy for small or novice international entrepreneurs to consider. However, when adopting an export market entry strategy, ensure that the strategy fits with the company's future overall global plans.

Exporting is selling goods and services to locations outside the home country.

Importing is buying goods and services abroad and bringing them into the home country.

The questions an *exporting* entrepreneur must consider include: What does the firm gain from exporting? Does the firm have sufficient resources (human, financial, production) and is exporting it the most efficient use of these resources? Is exporting consistent with the company's overall mission and other goals? Are the risks identified in a PEST-C analysis managed? The questions an *importing* entrepreneur must consider include: Are the management risks identified, such as currency fluctuations, political stability, and other variables, acceptable? Will the quality of the import meet the SME's standards? Are there any corporate social responsibility considerations (see Chapter 17, pages 472–478)? Keep these questions in mind as you read this chapter.

SMEs have two advantages in a global marketplace. First, the emergence of virtual corporations levering technology has dramatically levelled the exporting marketplace's playing field with MNEs. Second, SMEs' business models tend to be more organic and sensitive to market shifts than the larger bureaucratic organizations. Speed and innovation are powerful attributes for any organization (see Chapter 11).

Can exporting be maintained over the long term? Many SMEs will enter the export market timidly exporting by chance rather than as a result of a well-thought-out strategy, and can be termed "dabblers." For some reason, possibly an inquiry from a trade show, a potential foreign customer contacts the SME to enquire whether the firm exports. The journey begins. Sporadically, marginal exporting takes place. The results

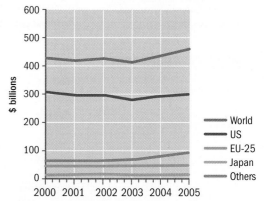

FIGURE 12.2

Imports of Goods and Services by Major Areas, 2000–05

SOURCE: Department of Foreign Affairs and International Trade, *Trade Update 2006* (Seventh Annual Report on Canada's State of Trade, July 5, 2006). Copyright Public Works & Government Services Canada.

A **strategic inflection point** occurs when the ecosystem of an industry or firm experiences a seismic shift that is so dramatic it requires the organization to radically revise its strategy—a wholesale, rather than a retail change.

are favourable and before long the exporting initiative is having an impact on the SME's bottom line. The export demand continues to increase. At this point, many entrepreneurs reach a **strategic inflection point**. At this juncture, the SME is required to either increase its foreign commitment (risk investment) or risk abandoning the market to others. Indeed, it may be that the company has little choice but to adopt a more committed strategy if there is a significant likelihood that other offshore entrepreneurs, having noted the success of the domestic SME, decide to move quickly to replicate and take away the SME's foreign market share. Exporting is a wonderful way to commence the journey of becoming an international trader.

Export Strategy—Caveats

Exporting SMEs would be well advised to observe these four caveats when crafting their strategy. First, the initial entry should be on a small scale to minimize risk. Second, offer a minimum number of product lines until a foothold has been established. Third, hire and involve locals within your organization at the earliest opportunity. And fourth, consider the degree of difficulty in cutting through red tape when crafting the firm's export strategy. (See Chapter 7.)

A look at the World Bank's *Doing Business: Benchmarking Business Regulations*,[20] enables an interesting comparison between Canada and other popular FDI destinations. As shown in Figure 12.3, the World Bank collected information as it relates to the number of procedures required to set up a business in countries around the world as well as the time and costs involved—a very important consideration for SME intending to enter one of these identified markets.

Forms of Export—Two Levels of Involvement

There are two fundamental levels of involvement to consider when crafting an export strategy. They are low-level involvement (indirect exporting) and high-level involvement (direct exporting). We will also examine a third level, intra-corporate transfers, that is seldom considered by SMEs. Both direct and indirect exporters and importers will frequently contract the services of trade intermediaries (local guides) to do business in the host country because they can provide assistance in expediting and identifying important details, such as transportation, financing, and documentation, required by the SME. Intermediaries are also valuable to assist in developing the firm's strategic, business, and marketing plans in support of market entry. Direct and indirect trade intermediaries help by providing knowledge of the foreign market's competitive conditions, a network of potential foreign buyers, an evaluation of risk assessment of the SME's foreign buyers, the sales staff and infrastructure to effectively and efficiently represent your firm to your foreign customers, and the physical delivery of the product to foreign buyers.

In addition to these intermediaries, there are numerous other intermediaries offering more specialized services. **Manufacturers' agents** solicit domestic orders on behalf of foreign manufacturers. They are generally remunerated on a commission basis. **Manufacturers' export agents** perform the role of the foreign sales department for

Manufacturers' agents solicit domestic orders on behalf of foreign manufacturers.

Manufacturers' export agents perform the role of the foreign sales department for the domestic manufacturers by selling the domestic firms' goods in the foreign target market.

FIGURE 12.3
Doing Business: Benchmarking Business Regulations, 2006

Country	Number of Procedures	Time (days)	Cost (USD)
Brazil	17	152	341
Canada	**2**	**3**	**278**
China	13	35	162
India	11	35	531
Mexico	8	27	1035
Russia	7	28	121
South Africa	9	35	341

World Bank, *Starting a Business* (Doing Business: Benchmarking Business Regulations, 2006). © 2006 The World Bank Group. All Rights Reserved.

domestic manufacturers by selling the domestic firms' goods in the foreign target market. **Export and import brokers** facilitate matchmaking between international buyers and sellers offering standardized commodities such as wheat, coffee, and rice. **Freight forwarders** specialize in the actual transportation of goods, the facilitation of customs documentation, and logistics and transportation services. There are many other smaller specialists supporting exporters and importers within Canada. For more specifics of these intermediaries visit www.power.nelson.com.

Indirect—Low-Level Involvement

Indirect exporting is an attractive, low-level involvement for companies with few export resources, or for those concerned about the intricacies of taking their products offshore. The indirect intermediaries include agents, export management companies (EMC), and export trading companies.

- **Agents** can represent one or more principals and are usually compensated through commissions based on sales. Accordingly, agents are a budget-priced way for novice exporting entrepreneurs to be represented in host markets. Agents have a fiduciary duty to their principal. However, there are risks. In practice, agents tend to be more attentive to and represent the exporters that offer the larger commissions. The potential for conflict of interest is always present when agents represent more than one principal. The exporter retains ownership (title) of the goods until the product is sold to the buyer in the host country. This presents a significant risk because the agent may have possession of the exported goods and receipts from time to time and will need to be closely monitored.

- **Export management companies (EMCs)** hold themselves out to have experience in international business and specifically in a particular geographic area. The important distinction between an agent and an EMC is that in most cases EMCs, as distributors, purchase the products from the domestic firms; they take title and take on all the trading risk. EMCs sell in their own name and as a result have an opportunity for greater profit or loss than acting as an agent. The major risk for SMEs when dealing with distributors is undercapitalization of the smaller EMCs, which may result in these organizations ceasing operation with little notice. Recall that you will pass title of your products to this intermediary and it may not have enough money to pay for them. A second disadvantage of adopting this model is that you will be less likely to gain an understanding of the complexities of the international market and will be slow at developing in-house international business expertise. Sometimes the EMC agrees to act as an agent. In this case, EMCs are generally remunerated on a commission basis, and title remains with the exporting firm under an agency agreement. Ensure that if your EMC is acting as an agent, it is able to adequately represent you and has not undertaken too many agency accounts.

- The third and final low-level intermediary is an international **export trading company (ETC)**. These companies provide a vast range of additional services than those supplied by the EMC. The EMC is restricted solely to export and related activities while the export trading company (ETC) services may included importing; exporting; countertrading services; developing and expanding distribution channels; providing storage facilities; as well as financing trading, investment projects, and, occasionally, manufacturing. In some countries, ETCs can be viewed as a collective or network because of their wide range of supporting services. In Japan, ETCs are called sogo shosha (general trading companies). The sogo shosha might be a small family network or large conglomerate such as Kanematsu Corp.; Marubeni Corp.; Mitsubishi Corp.; Mitsui & Co., Ltd.; Nichimen Corp.; Nissho Iwai Corp.; Sumitomo Corp.; and Tomen Corp. The ETC collective is also in evidence in South Korea where it is called a chaebol. Visit www.power.nelson.com for specifics of the world's five largest sogo shosha.

Export and import brokers facilitate matchmaking between international buyers and sellers offering standardized commodities such as wheat, coffee, and rice.

Freight forwarders specialize in the actual transportation of goods, the facilitation of customs documentation, and logistics and transportation services.

Indirect exporting is a strategy whereby an exporter contracts with an intermediary located in the home country to sell its product or service to a designated foreign market.

Agents are individual organizations that "stand in the shoes" of the principal (the exporter). They are generally remunerated on a set commission based on sales and, although they often have possession of the goods and receipts, title remains with the exporter until the product is sold. Agents have a fiduciary duty to their principal; however, conflict of interest is a potential risk.

Export management companies (EMCs), self-proclaimed experts in international business in a specific geographic area, provide their services either on a commission basis (as an agent) or as a distributor. As a distributor, the most common role, the EMC takes title to the goods and takes on all of the trading risks and opportunities. The EMC is restricted solely to exports and related activities.

Export trading company (ETC) services may include importing; exporting; countertrading services; developing and expanding distribution channels; providing storage facilities; and financing trade, investment projects, and occasionally manufacturing. In some countries, ETCs can be viewed as a collective or network.

The close working relationships between Asian firms within the ETC aid collaboration on all activities from financing and manufacturing to distribution. These influential collectives, explained in part by cultural considerations, have powered the Asian ETCs to dominant positions in global markets. Large North American companies have recently tried to replicate similar relationships. To date, they have not had the same measure of success.

Direct—High-Level Involvement

Direct exporting is full involvement by the exporting company in selling its product directly to buyers *within* the target market. Exporting companies do not use intermediaries; rather they rely upon sales representatives and/or distributors. **Sales representatives** can be either a corporation or individual engaged to use best efforts to represent the exporter's product in the target market. Sales representatives are compensated similarly to employees. Generally, sales representatives' compensation includes a fixed salary plus commissions. They are not agents, and title to the product remains with the exporting company. **Distributors** take ownership of the product and accept all risks relating to the product's subsequent sale. Distributors use their own channels of distribution to sell to retailers, wholesalers, or end-users. Be aware that the direct exporter loses control of the final selling price of the product in the target market. If this price is inconsistent with the exporting firm's international pricing strategy, it can represent a significant impediment to the exporter's planned growth in market share.

Intra-Corporate Transfers—A Third Level of Involvement

A third level of export involvement exists. However, SMEs will not generally use **intra-corporate transfers**; they are used by MNCs. Gildan Activewear Inc., a Canadian company headquartered in Montreal, PQ, provides a good example. Gildan knits its T-shirt fabrics in its Ville Saint Laurent, Quebec, factory. The fabric is shipped to the cutting facility in Malone, New York, and recorded as an export from Canada and an import by the U.S. subsidiary. The cut fabric is exported from the United States and imported by the Honduras subsidiary where garment assembly takes place in one of Gildan's three Honduras facilities. The garments are exported from Honduras and imported by Canada where they are dyed and finished in Quebec. Finally, 85 percent of the finished garments are then exported to the United States for sale.[21] Keep this exporting model in mind when you examine nations' balance of payments. The United States has a number of firms like Gildan and, as a result, its BoP numbers may be misleading.

Direct exporting is full involvement by the exporting company in selling its product directly to buyers within the target market, supported by sales representatives or distributors.

Sales representatives can be either a corporation or an individual engaged to use best efforts to represent the exporter's product in the target market. Similar to an employee, they do not hold title to the goods and are generally paid a small base salary supplemented by commission.

Distributors take ownership of the product and accept all risks relating to the product's subsequent sale. They use their own channels of distribution to sell to retailers, wholesalers, or end-users.

Intra-corporate transfers are the sale of goods and services to a related corporate entity.

INTERNATIONAL STRATEGIC THINKING

When beginning an offshore initiative, rely upon the services of an export management company to assist in identifying threats and opportunities meeting administrative rules and regulations. Given that there are 193 countries in the world,[22] it is best to initially focus on only one or two countries to move up the learning curve before entering additional markets. Keep the entry scale small in order to minimize risk. Be aware of the additional commitment of resources (human, financial, production) required by the exporting venture.

Build trust. We have discussed the importance of establishing a relationship of trust when dealing offshore. Be prepared to spend time at this activity.

The opening Sun Tzu Moment advises us to use local guides in foreign countries. Build a relationship with these local guides. Constantly scan your ecosystem for export opportunities. Be proactive rather than reactive. Craft strategies to include well-thought-out action plans to implement your export initiative. Be aware of strategic inflection points. Remember, if you are successful, competitors will want to replicate your success. The competition will come not only from the domestic market but also from foreign markets.

Why import? Companies import to obtain less expensive goods or services, or because the goods or services are not available in the domestic market. Outsourcing is frequently in the news and will be examined in Chapter 14.

Export–Import Financing

The paramount concern for both importers and exporters is the question of trust. Will the parties live up to their agreement? Exporters fear that once the goods are shipped they will not receive payment; importers, faced with the mirror image of the question, ask, if they pay up-front for the goods, will they be delivered? Over time, protocols and procedures have been put in place to enable trade.

Methods of Payment

It is important that international business practitioners become familiar with the fundamentals of import and export payment. There are a number of methods; here are two.

Advance Payments

Advance payments occur when the terms of the contract require the importer to pay for the goods in advance of receipt. Clearly, this is the most favourable method of payment for exporters while being the least favourable for importers. Payments can be made through a number of methods including credit cards and wire transfers.

An **advance payment** occurs when the terms of the contract require that the importer pay for the goods in advance of receipt.

Documentary Collections

Documentary collections provide for payment against receipt of acceptable documentation using a third party as an intermediary. In almost all cases, the intermediaries are banks, although occasionally international law firms use their trust accounts to perform this function. Here is a typical collection process.

Documentary collection provides for payment against receipt of acceptable documentation, using a third party as intermediary.

COLLECTION PROCESS

There are nine steps required to complete the collection process. We will use China as the importer and Canada as the exporter in this example.

Step 1. The Canadian exporter and the Chinese importer negotiate the terms of a contract using legal and accounting advice as necessary.

Step 2. A draft (bill of exchange) is prepared by the Canadian exporter and his bank, in this example, the Royal Bank of Canada. (An alternative is for the Chinese importer to use a bank that is acceptable to the Canadian exporter's bank to prepare the bill of exchange.) Once the bill of exchange is complete and contains the specific terms required by all parties, the draft is given by the Royal Bank of Canada to the Canadian exporter. A draft is somewhat similar to a cheque. When presented, it orders the importer to pay the agreed-upon specific sum at the agreed-upon specific time. There are two types of drafts: a sight draft and a time draft. It is a condition of the contract that is open at the outset for negotiation between the parties. A **sight draft** requires payment at the time the goods are delivered to the importer. For an importer, a **time draft** provides valuable time to sell the goods and use the proceeds to pay the time draft when it comes due. For the exporter, providing the importer this concession, increases the likelihood that the exporter will experience greater sales. The downside, of course, is that the importer has the use of the exporter's money for the time set out in the time draft. In effect, the exporter has become the importer's bank. A time draft is a negotiable instrument that can be pledged or sold to other financial institutions. It may be that the Canadian exporter, although having initially agreed to a time draft, unexpectedly requires these funds prior to the due date. In this case, the Canadian exporter can obtain cash by **factoring**.

A **sight draft** requires payment at the time the goods are delivered to the importer.

A **time draft** is a negotiable instrument that extends the payment date by mutual agreement between the parties to some time after the importer has received the goods. The most commonly negotiated times are 30, 60, or 90 days.

Factoring allows the holder of a time draft to obtain cash by assigning or selling the instrument at a discount to a third party.

Step 3. The exporter then delivers the merchandise for shipment to the Chinese importer. The shipping company, upon receipt of the goods from the exporter, will issue a packing list clearly identifying items shipped and a document called a **bill of lading** to the exporter. Dependent on whether the goods are being transported by air, land, or sea, the title of the bill of lading is called an airway bill of lading, ocean bill of lading, or inland bill of lading. It is sometimes referred to simply as a waybill. The bill of lading represents title (ownership), a receipt, and a contract for transporting the goods.

A **bill of lading** represents three things. It is a contract containing all of the terms and conditions of shipping between the exporter and the shipper, it represents title to goods shipped, and it is a receipt for the goods.

Step 4. The exporter, now in possession of a packing list of the items shipped and the bill of lading, takes these documents confirming "the goods are on the way" to the Royal Bank of Canada (the exporter's bank).

Step 5. The Royal Bank forwards these documents to the importer's bank. In this example, we will use the Bank of China (Hong Kong). The two banks have established contact regarding this transaction at an earlier date, and generally the trust issue is significantly reduced.

Step 6. The Chinese importer arranges with the Bank of China (Hong Kong) to have the required funding on deposit at the bank. The Chinese bank is responsible to ensure that contract funds are available in accordance with the terms of the draft. In most cases, the source of funding will be discussed at the very early stages of the process by the importer and his bank.

Step 7. The importer's bank, satisfied that the funding arrangements are in place to make payment, passes the bill of lading to the Chinese importer. Recall that the bill of lading represents title (ownership) of the goods. The transportation company will release the goods only to the holder of the bill of lading (title).

Step 8. In the case of a sight draft, at the same moment as the bill of lading is passed to the importer, the importer's bank sends the payment for the goods to the Canadian exporter's bank in accordance with terms of the draft. In the case of a time draft, this step will not take place until the agreed-upon time has passed. The importer's bank remains responsible to ensure the time draft is paid when due. (Recall step 6, in which the importer's bank will have taken steps to ensure payment by the importer.)

Step 9. The Royal Bank advises the Canadian exporter that the funds are available and the transaction is concluded.

Letters of Credit

There are occasions when the exporter needs to confirm that funding will be available to pay for the goods upon delivery. One method is for the importer's bank to issue a document called a letter of credit. The exporting SME will formally request a letter of credit when the importer's creditworthiness is in question or unknown; when the exporting SME needs evidence that the invoice for the goods will be paid in order for the exporter to raise capital to produce the goods; or when required by market regulations.

A **letter of credit** is a document issued by a bank following due diligence guaranteeing payment available in the event the importer defaults.

The importer's bank carries out its due diligence regarding the financial health of the importer and makes whatever arrangements are necessary with the importer (pledging of security) for it to agree to issue the document. By issuing the **letter of credit**, the importer's bank has become the guarantor that the goods will be paid for in the event that the importer defaults. The importer's bank will charge a small fee for issuing the letter, generally less than 5 percent of the face value of the letter of credit. The fee is determined by the creditworthiness of the importer and the negotiating power it has with its bank.

An **irrevocable letter of credit** permits the importer's bank to modify the terms only with the approval of both the exporter and the importer.

Exporting SMEs must be aware that there are three forms of letters of credit. An **irrevocable letter of credit** permits the importer's bank to modify the terms only with the approval of both the exporter and the importer. The second is called a **revocable letter of credit** that can be modified at any time without consultation with the exporter or the importer. This is a very dangerous and tenuous letter of credit. The final is a **confirmed letter of credit** guaranteeing payment by both the exporter's bank and the importer's bank.

A **revocable letter of credit** can be modified at any time without consultation with the exporter or the importer; this is a very dangerous and tenuous letter of credit.

A **confirmed letter of credit** guarantees payment by both the exporter's bank and the importer's bank.

Open Accounts

This form of payment is used only for the exporter's most trusted customers. It is no different from the credit arrangements that the SME uses domestically. The exporter will ship the goods and send an invoice requesting payment. The importer will pay the invoice in its normal course of business after it has received the goods. Generally, payment terms will have been established, e.g., 30 days. An open account is used with greater frequency between importers and exporters in Canada and the United States. Both nations' laws are similar, and credit information, banking references, collection processes, and reciprocal agreements facilitate this form of payment. This is not a recommended form of payment for SMEs to adopt when initially establishing accounts in most other nations. However, with the passage of time and the development of relationship and trust between the parties, other methods of payment can evolve into an **open account**.

Pitfalls for Exporters and Importers

Canadian SMEs must be aware of the following importing and exporting pitfalls.

- Floating currencies are not stable (see Chapter 8). Accordingly, attention must be paid to mitigating this risk.
- Generally accepted accounting principles vary from nation to nation (see Chapter 16, pages 446–447). Make sure you have the appropriate accounting advice in place.
- The rule of law in some nations will be significantly different in substance, form, and enforceability. Make sure you are cognizant of the legal and accounting risks as part of your market entry strategy.
- Statistical reliability varies greatly from nation to nation. Do not expect to rely on some foreign governments' statistics to the same extent you would with those provided by the Canadian government. Conduct due diligence, undertake a market analysis, and undertake a PEST-C analysis (see Chapters 2–4).
- Be prepared to customize your product to meet the needs of foreign customers.
- Take time to understand the distribution channels available in the target market.
- Be very cognizant of cultural nuances when preparing your public relations and promotional campaign materials.
- Understand the impediments to obtaining financing both domestically and within the foreign country related to your market entry strategy. This includes repatriating profits.
- Do not underestimate the resources needed to support the strategy. This includes the time you will need to cultivate new foreign accounts, which can be considerable.
- Finally, be prepared for administrative paperwork.

With an **open account,** payment is received after delivering the goods to the purchaser. It is understood that the invoice will be paid in accordance with the terms of the open account agreement.

PRACTICAL ENTREPRENEURIAL FOCUS

Practical Importing Tips

Canada's Export and Import Controls Bureau (EICB) is responsible for authorizing the import and export of goods restricted by quotas and/or tariffs. The Bureau also ensures the personal security of Canadians and citizens of other countries by restricting trade of dangerous goods and other materials. Today, as a result of a variety of trade agreements and regionalization, just about any good may be imported into Canada, provided the importer complies with the law. Regulations pose certain questions such as: "Is the article prohibited entry into Canada? A narrow range of goods are listed as prohibited under Annex VII of the Customs Tariff, e.g., hate literature and pornography."[23] Is it banned from import because of international sanctions? Is the item permitted entry only under the Export and Import Permits

Act? The Act controls "imports of textiles and clothing, steel, wheat, barley and their products, supply-managed farm products (dairy, chicken, eggs, and turkey), firearms and suchlike, and a few miscellaneous items. These are all found on the Import Control List."[24] Is the imported item subject to some other federally imposed condition? For example, goods for retail sale have to comply with labelling laws to include those specific regulations required by the province of Quebec. Those contemplating bringing automobiles in from California, for example, will find they have to meet emission control standards different from the original equipment; food and agricultural products have to pass the necessary health and sanitary checks. Certain articles can be subject to some privately certified standards. For example, the Canadian Standards Association International

must certify all electrical appliances and equipment before they can be sold in Canada. Indeed, it is just not federal law and regulations that must be followed. The importing of liquor, wine, and beer requires prior authorization from the appropriate provincial liquor commission to clear Customs. Unfortunately, just about all goods imported into Canada are subject to customs duties and the Goods and Services Tax. The tax is collected by Canada Revenue Agency (CRA) at the time of importation, and levied on the landed value of the goods. CRA also collects antidumping and countervailing duties on a few goods that have been found to be sold under unfair conditions. Canadian SMEs should consider using freight forwarders or custom brokers to facilitate moving goods through this maze. For more practical importing tips visit, www.power.nelson.com.

Countertrade

Countertrade is the exchange of goods or services for either all or part of the purchase price.

You will recall from Chapter 8 that there are occasions when countries do not have sufficient foreign exchange to pay for imports or the importing nation restricts the convertibility of its currency. During the 1980s, China implemented currency convertibility restrictions to grow its foreign currency reserves. Nigeria has an absolute ban under the penalty of death for expatriating American dollars and other currencies, so international traders have to find creative ways to conduct international trade without currency. I am sure many of you have exchanged your services (bartered), or know somebody who has obtained goods and services from others. Some nations do the same thing. **Countertrade** is an innovative way to finance trade; it is a creative marketing tool that should not be overlooked!

However, there are restrictions on governments countertrading. Only NAFTA and WTO members that are not signatories to the plurilateral WTO Agreement on Government Procurement (GPA) can use countertrade. This agreement has made countertrade arrangements "illegal" for those subject to the agreement. Consequently, current examples are well hidden. However, countries that are not members of WTO or NAFTA still use countertrade. Signatories to the agreement are Canada, the European Community (including its 25 member states: Austria, Belgium, Cyprus, Czech Republic, Denmark, Estonia, Finland, France, Germany, Greece, Hungary, Ireland, Italy, Latvia, Lithuania, Luxembourg, Malta, Netherlands, Poland, Portugal, Slovak Republic, Slovenia, Spain, Sweden, United Kingdom), Hong Kong China, Iceland, Israel, Japan, Korea, Liechtenstein, the Netherlands (including Aruba), Norway, Singapore, Switzerland, and the United States. Currently others are negotiating their participation in the GPA.

Here are a number of practical examples. "Australia is the only major industrialized country that is not a signatory to the GPA. As such, Australia is not bound by the GPA's rules on open and non-discriminatory policies in government procurement. At both the Commonwealth and State/Territory level, requirements for offsets and similar GPA-inconsistent arrangements are systemic. Domestic supplier price preferences are common at the State/Territory level. Under the Australian and New Zealand Government Procurement Agreement, New Zealand suppliers are afforded domestic supplier [preferential] treatment. . . . In January 2002, the Kuwaiti government transformed its offset program into the major vehicle for inducing foreign investment in Kuwait. The new requirements imposed an offset obligation on civilian contracts with the Kuwaiti Government of 10 million Kuwaiti Dinar (approximately $30 million euros) or more and on defence contracts of KD 1 million (approximately $3 million euros) or more. The obligation will amount to 35 percent of the contract value, which must be invested in an approved offset business venture. Kuwait is also not a signatory to the WTO Agreement on Government Procurement. . . . India has an unpublished policy that favours countertrade. Private companies are encouraged to use countertrade. Global tenders usually include a clause stating that, all other factors being equal, preference will be given to companies willing to agree to countertrade. The exact nature of offsetting exports is unspecified as is the export destination. The Indian government does try, nonetheless, to eliminate the use of re-exports in countertrade."[25]

Tips for Countertraders

- The success of countertrade will be measured by the ability of the parties to market the product or service countertraded.
- Do not quote a price until the countertrade terms are clear.
- An important rule in selecting which products will be countertraded is to identify high-value, low-volume products; products that will not take up much warehouse space; and lightweight items that are high in value.
- Evaluate and mitigate the risks. Recall the financial instruments available in the section on hedging in Chapter 8, pages 232–235.

Five Forms of Countertrade

There are five forms of countertrade. These are barter, counterpurchase, offset, switch trading, and compensation or buy back.

Barter

Barter is simple in concept but difficult in practice. How do you take a container of sulphur from a firm in Vancouver and exchange (barter) it with a Chinese firm in order to be paid with a container load of bicycles? Clearly SMEs are at a disadvantage because of their size and lack of a global network to convert the bicycles into currency in some other country. Risk is another significant consideration in this form of countertrade. The exchange of goods and services must be concurrent because of the lack of trust between the trading partners. In the case of bicycles bartered for sulphur, it did happen. The Canadian company shipped sulphur in exchange for Raleigh bicycles. Having accepted the bicycles as payment for the sulphur in China, the Canadian company was able to sell them in Singapore for a tidy profit. Why Singapore? In Singapore, a bicycle is a form of daily transportation, not the recreational toy that it tends to be in Canada.

> **Barter** is the direct exchange of goods or services between parties without the use of currencies.

Counterpurchase

Counterpurchase is a more common buying agreement. A **counterpurchase agreement** requires that, as a condition of sale, the firm selling the goods or services to a nation is required to spend a portion of the receipts purchasing specific goods or services stipulated as a condition of contract by the purchasing nation. For example, in the Canadian–Mexican Agreement on Industrial and Energy Cooperation signed in 1980, Ottawa said it would buy Mexican crude oil if Mexico considered buying a CANDU reactor. (Read the box Just Doing the Right Thing on pages 351–352.)

> A **counterpurchase agreement** requires that, as a condition of sale, the firm selling the goods or services to a nation is required to spend a portion of the receipts purchasing specific goods or services stipulated as a condition of contract by the purchasing nation.

Offset

An offset requires the seller to acquire unspecified goods from the purchasing nation in order to offset a hard-currency sale. Note the difference from a counterpurchase: the **offset agreement** does not specify the type of product that must be purchased, just the amount that must be spent. This provides the company greater flexibility in spending the purchase price hard currency. For example, "The United Arab Emirates (UAE) does not require that a portion of any government tender be subcontracted to local firms, but it grants a 10 percent price preference for local firms in government procurement. The UAE requires a company to be registered to be invited to receive government tender documents. To be registered, a company must have 51 percent UAE-ownership. However, these rules do not apply on major projects or defence contracts where there is no local company able to provide the goods or services required. Established in 1990, the UAE's offset program requires defence contractors that are awarded contracts valued at more than $10 million to establish joint venture projects that yield profits equivalent to 60 percent of the contract value within a specified period (usually seven years). There are also reports, as well as anecdotal evidence, indicating that defence contractors can sometimes satisfy their offset obligations through an up-front, lump-sum payment directly to the UAE Offsets Group. The projects must be commercially viable joint ventures with local business partners, and are designed to further the UAE objective of diversifying its economy away from oil. To date, more than 40 projects have been launched, including, *inter alia*, a hospital, an imaging and geological information facility, a leasing company, a cooling system manufacturing company, an aquiculture enterprise, Berlitz Abu Dhabi, and a firefighting equipment production facility. Two of the largest offset ventures are an international gas pipeline project (Dolphin) and the Oasis International leasing company—a British Aerospace offsets venture. The UAE is not a signatory to the WTO Agreement on Government Procurement."[26]

> An **offset agreement** requires the seller to acquire unspecified goods from the purchasing nation in order to offset a hard-currency sale. Unlike a counterpurchase agreement, the goods or services to be purchased and the amount to be spent are not specified.

Switch Trading

Sometimes companies, having completed the transaction with the host nation, have no interest in purchasing the products or services they agreed to as a condition of the initial contract. In this case, the firm can sell its obligation to purchase, for a fee, to some other company who does intend to purchase products or services within the host country, thereby fulfilling the contractual obligation of the initial company by **switch trading**. Brokers make a business out of acquiring these obligations for resale.

In **switch trading,** one company sells for a fee (payable to the purchaser) its obligation to make a purchase in the host nation.

Compensation or Buy Back

Compensation or buy back is an innovative countertrade method. The exporter who sells equipment to a host country must purchase products assembled with that equipment as a condition of the sale.

Countertrade Contracts

There are three main contracts generally used in countertrade. They are the standard sales contract, the standard purchase contract, and the protocol agreement. The sales and the purchase contracts are the most common contracts used by exporting companies. The protocol agreement ties the two pieces of the contract together and defines the terms of the countertrade transaction. Protocol agreements include such items as an overall statement as to the intent of the parties, commencement and end dates, obligations of the parties, value (price) of the contract, terms of payment, choice of goods, details regarding completion timing, terms of commitment, liquidated damages if the countertrade is not completed, any marketing limitations or restrictions regarding sale of the products sold, and the ability to assign the protocol agreement.

Canada's Most Likely Trading Partners

Canada's GNP is 1.1 trillion PPP (est. 2005).[27] So with whom should we trade? Most SMEs immediately think of the United States. It is a good choice: minimal risk; close proximity; similar culture; long-standing good trading relationship; shared language, and on the list goes. However, consider that in 2003, Canada's six major import and export countries included the United States, Japan, the United Kingdom (EU), China, Mexico, and Germany (EU) (see Figure 12.4). However, many Canadians increasingly feel that Canada has sleepwalked into a dangerous reliance on trade with the United States and that diversification is needed quickly. The emergence of new markets in the global economy presents the best opportunities for Canadian exporters and investors to reduce this dependency. Today (2005) Canada and the Export Development Corporation have identified BRIC nations (Brazil, Russia, India, and China) as the key

FIGURE 12.4
Canada's Top 10 Export and Import Markets by Country, 2005

Country	% Share of Total Exports	Country	% Share of Total Imports
United States	71.5	United States	55.8
Japan	2.1	China	7.8
United Kingdom	1.9	Mexico	3.8
China	1.6	Japan	3.8
Mexico	0.7	United Kingdom	2.7
Germany	0.7	Germany	2.7
South Korea	0.6	Norway	1.6
France	0.6	South Korea	1.4
Belgium	0.5	France	1.3
Netherlands	0.5	Italy	1.2
Total of Top 10	**80.7**	**Total of Top 10**	**82.1**

SOURCE: Author generated from data at Industry Canada, *Trade Data Online* (Government of Canada, March 14 2006).

emerging markets. The federal government is proactively encouraging SMEs to explore trade and investment with these countries as they have gained considerable purchasing and financial power. These nations have undertaken substantial economic reforms to open their economies. Let us examine some of these likely trading partners for Canadian SMEs more closely.

> Export Development Canada (EDC) and other organizations produce free country-based risk assessments that SMEs should review prior to entering foreign markets. EDC's analysis is divided into six sections: political foundations, current political environment, governance and sustainability, economic policies, investment environment, and state disparities. Visit www.power.nelson.com for a link and further discussion on this valuable service regarding doing business in India and other countries.
>
> Another good country intelligence source is *The World Factbook* (see www.cia.gov/cia/publications/factbook). *The Economist* also has excellent intelligence reports (Country Briefings); however, the full reports are available to SMEs only for a fee; see www.economist.com/countries.

Video 12.1

"The US has the highest level of output in the world, with GDP valued at US$12.5 trn [trillion] in 2005. . . . Inflationary pressures have been kept in check by both structural and cyclical factors."[28] Although the recession of 2001 did shrink the trade deficit marginally, the trade gap has widened significantly again, reaching a record high of US$723.6 billion in 2005; US external debt [was estimated at] $8.837 trillion."[29] In 2004, the top five destinations for U.S. exports were "Canada 23%, Mexico 13.6%, Japan 6.7%, UK 4.4%, China 4.3%."[30] The United States is the principal destination for Canadian exports.

The powerful trade relationship between Canada and the United States has been a win-win partnership; both countries have done well over the centuries and have seen their trade grow exponentially since the adoption of the Free Trade Act in 1989 and in subsequent years under the provisions of NAFTA (1994). Figure 12.5 shows the regional distribution of Canada's trade with the United States in 2003. Unfortunately, increasingly protectionist measures are being implemented on both sides of the border. Nevertheless, it is a comfortable relationship for business. The political, economic, technical, societal, and cultural attributes of the two countries are very closely aligned. The proximity and the advanced transportation infrastructure have also driven SME trade initiatives. However, as we have discussed, many in Canada feel that we must diversify our trade through agreements with BRIC nations and others.

Canadian SME Business in the European Union

The EU's 2005 GNP is estimated at 12.4 trillion PPP[31] and in 2004 accounted for 6.0 percent and 10.2 percent of Canada's merchandise exports and imports, respectively. "The top 10 exporting sectors accounted for some two-thirds of all merchandise exports

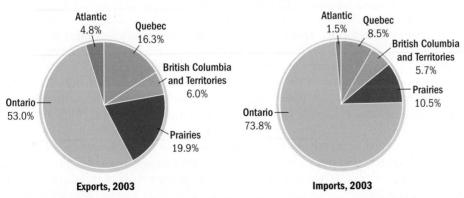

Exports, 2003   Imports, 2003

FIGURE 12.5

Canada's Regional Distribution of U.S. Merchandise Trade 2003

SOURCE: Department of Foreign Affairs and International Trade, *Fifth Annual Report on Canada's State of Trade* (Trade Update, March 2004). Copyright Public Works and Government Services Canada.

to the EU. Precious stones/metals and jewellery, mostly in the form of diamonds, were Canada's top exports to the EU, at $3.3 billion, or 15.0 per cent of all merchandise exports to the region. Several other high value added sectors, such as mechanical machinery and equipment, precision instruments, aircraft, and automotive products, were also amongst the largest exports to this region."[32]

Canadian SME Business in India

India's 2005 GNP is estimated at 3.7 trillion PPP.[33] "Over the past decade, Canada has approached the Indian market in different ways. In the 1990s, as India's government commenced its drive towards economic liberalization, Canada opened its eyes to the commercial potential of this market and was strategizing on ways Canadians could take part. However, this enthusiasm was quickly transformed into disenchantment when, in May 1998, India carried out five nuclear tests which consequently raised tensions between India and Pakistan. At this point, Canada (like many other western countries) disengaged from India politically and commercially. It was not until 2003 that Canada started to seriously re-engage. In October 2003, [then] Prime Minister Jean Chrétien made a visit to India highlighting these re-engagement efforts. Today, [December 2004] Export Development Canada (EDC) and the Canadian Government identify India along with Brazil, China and Russia as being the key strategic emerging markets. . . . However, it is also important to be cognizant of India's political landscape given its influence on the business environment."[34]

The EDC risk assessment on India reveals that "post-independence India suffered significant violence as a result of ethnic and religious divides as well as economic and societal impurities. India's history is tainted with sporadic acts of communal violence in the form of Sikh extremism, Hindu-Muslim violence, independence movements, anti-poverty rebellion and caste-based agitation. In spite of this discord, India has been able to maintain a democracy and has built a deep network of institutions allowing most of the interest groups within this diverse country to be represented in the political sphere. Today, India can boast being the world's largest democracy."[35] India is increasingly playing a larger international role in global politics.

India's economic policy direction shifted dramatically in the mid-1990s from a closed centralized state-dominated economy to an open somewhat decentralized mixed economy. As a result of the recent economic liberalization, it is increasingly attracting FDI (see Chapter 7). "The main impediments for business in India include the cultural and institutional remnants of India's post-independence economic model of self-sufficiency, pervasive corruption, policy unpredictability and the lack of investment in the country's infrastructure. There is hope for improvement in some areas however corruption and policy unpredictability are likely here to stay for the foreseeable future. Despite these challenges, India's IT sector showcases the possibility to prosper in the current investment environment."[36]

India is not homogenous. The diverse country has its population scattered across 28 states and 7 territories, all of which hold some decision-making powers. With the recent economic reforms, state-level governments have been given more and more discretion with regards to approving and licensing investments in their territory. Many states have been very successful in cultivating a dynamic private sector.[37]

The catalyst for much of the bilateral trade between Canada and India has been Canada's large and dynamic Indo-Canadian community. It is an international trade competitive advantage! Canada boasts over 1 million Indo-Canadians. With a rapidly expanding middle class, India has the largest emerging consumer market in the world. At the time of writing, India was the 12th largest economy in the world and the 4th largest in terms of purchasing power, yet it is only our 18th largest export market. India is Canada's largest trading partner in South Asia. Record trade was valued at over $2.8 billion for 2005.[38]

Canadian SME Business in China

China's estimated 2005 GNP is 8.2 trillion PPP.[39] China's political landscape has changed dramatically over the last century, moving from the traditional Dynasty model through civil war to a closed Communist model, to an increasingly open political model allowing individual entrepreneurial development and actively pursuing international trade linkages. We should understand, however, that our ethnocentric view of democracy is not necessarily the Chinese view of democracy. The Chinese model may well be as unique as their Communist model, which adopted Lenin's communist ideology of Russia but personalized it with the thoughts of Mao Zedong.

"With a population officially just over 1.3 billion and an estimated growth rate of about 0.6%, China is very concerned about its population growth and has attempted with mixed results to implement a strict birth limitation policy. . . . The government's goal is to stabilize the population in the first half of the 21st century, and current projections are that the population will peak at around 1.6 billion by 2050."[40] The Canada–China relationship is cooperative and includes trade, human rights dialogue, defence relations, legal cooperation, and cultural and academic exchanges. Unfortunately, Canada has not exploited the favoured position we had as the home of Norman Bethune and the early recognition of the Communist government by Prime Minister Trudeau. In 2005, former Prime Minister Martin still referred to China as an emerging market. Of course, this perception antagonized Chinese leadership and is not supported by the global trade evidence. "Canada ranks as the 13th-largest direct investor in China. Canada's direct investment stock in China increased from $6 million in 1990 to $647 million in 2004."[41] Despite the small growth in FDI, Canada recognizes the need to build its trade relationship with the Middle Kingdom. "China received [only] about 1.8 percent of Canadian FDI in the region and about 0.1 percent of total Canadian FDI abroad."[42]

Furthermore, the meeting of Canada's former Prime Minster Martin with the Dalai Lama (2004) and subsequent awarding of Canadian citizenship (2006); Ottawa's refusal to deport alleged smuggling kingpin Lai Changxing (2004); and other similar acts continue to impede the expansion of our trade relationship. China has become the manufacturing centre of the world and Canada is one of the few Western nations that does not have an agreement protecting foreign investors.[43] "'Canadian businesses in China are left unprotected and vulnerable,' said Jack Tang, a Vancouver entrepreneur who lost a $6-million investment in China when his dairy herd was slaughtered by local officials."[44]

"China exports to the USA (21.1%), Hong Kong (17.0%), Japan (12.4%) and South Korea (4.7%)."[45] Canada ranks 10th representing 1.3% of China's exports.[46] "China imports from Japan (16.8%), Taiwan (11.6%), South Korea (11.1%) and the USA (8.0%)."[47] Canada ranks 17th at 1.1% of China's imports.[48] "China has become the fourth largest market for Canadian exports behind the United States, Japan and the United Kingdom. In total, Chinese imports from Canada have more than tripled since 1998, rising at an average annual rate of 21%. Nevertheless, in 2004, China's total imports of Canadian goods, worth US $7 billion, accounted for only 1.3% of China's total imports. To put that into perspective, China imported more than US $94 billion from Japan in 2004."[49] For details on Canada's trade with China, see Figures 12.6 and 12.7. For an illustration of the trade gap between the two countries, see Figure 12.8.

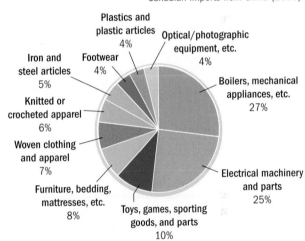

FIGURE 12.6
Canadian Imports from China (2005)

SOURCE: Author generated from data at Industry Canada, *Trade Data Online* (Government of Canada, March 14, 2006).

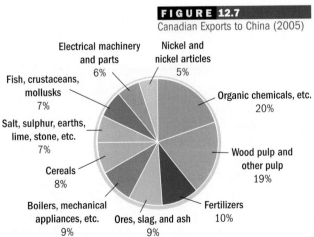

FIGURE 12.7
Canadian Exports to China (2005)

SOURCE: Author generated from data at Industry Canada, *Trade Data Online* (Government of Canada, March 14, 2006).

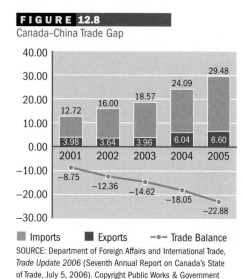

FIGURE 12.8
Canada-China Trade Gap

Imports   Exports   Trade Balance

SOURCE: Department of Foreign Affairs and International Trade, *Trade Update 2006* (Seventh Annual Report on Canada's State of Trade, July 5, 2006). Copyright Public Works & Government Services Canada.

In its January 2006 *World Outlook* report, the Conference Board of Canada said it expects the global economy to slow from 3.0 percent in 2005 to 2.8 percent in 2006. "Weaker economic activity in the United States and China will be offset to a certain extent by higher growth in Japan and in parts of Europe. . . . China's rapidly expanding middle class has created a growing demand for some of the technologically advanced goods produced in countries like Japan and South Korea."[50]

Canadian SME Business in Brazil

Brazil's 2005 GNP was estimated to be $1.7 trillion PPP.[51] "Tight fiscal and monetary policies resulted in a growth rate of 0.5% in 2003. Economic recovery became apparent by the fourth quarter and was consolidated in 2004, when the Brazilian economy grew by 4.9%, the highest growth rate in ten years. In 2005, for the first time in three decades, Brazil experienced an external and fiscal equilibrium and low inflation."[52] "Brazil is officially designated as a priority market for Canada and is Canada's most important trading partner in South America. Two-way trade reached $4.2 billion in 2005. Canadian merchandise exports to Brazil expanded to almost $953 million in 2004, an increase of 7% over the previous year. Major exports included fertilizers, paper products, mechanical machinery, mineral fuels, electrical equipment and minerals. Canadian merchandise imports from Brazil totalled $3.1 billion in 2005. Major imports included industrial goods such as iron and steel, manufactured goods, such as automobiles and mechanical machinery, agricultural goods (raw sugar, prepared fruit and vegetable products), as well as wood, footwear and precious stones."[53] Canada's trade deficit was just over CDN$2 billion.[54] For an illustration of Canada's trade with Brazil, see Figure 12.9.

Canadian SME Business in Mexico

Mexico's 2005 GNP was estimated to be 1.1 trillion PPP.[55] As a result of NAFTA, Mexico is a trading partner with Canada and the United States. Canadian SMEs should explore the possibly of trade with this North American nation. Once strongly nationalist and interventionist, the leaders of Partido Revolucionario Institucional (PRI) governments in the 1990s embraced free market policies and economic liberalization. Following the victory in July 2000 of Vicente Fox Quesada, the presidential candidate of the center-right party, the Partido Acción Nacional (PAN) commenced changes to the political system. It is unclear whether these changes will root or if the country will revert to the political philosophy of the previous government. The 2006 federal election ended with uncertainty. Mexico's Federal Electoral Institute subsequently declared pro-corporate conservative Felipe Calderon of the ruling conservative National Action Party elected.

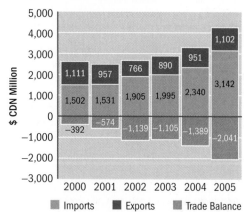

FIGURE 12.9
Canada's Trade with Brazil

$ CDN Million

Imports   Exports   Trade Balance

SOURCE: Author generated from data at Industry Canada, *Trade Data Online* (Government of Canada, March 14, 2006).

The tension between the two major parties remains. This outcome could make a significant difference to Canadian firms doing business there. In 2005, exports totalled US$213.7 billion and imports US$223.7 billion, producing a trade deficit of US$10 billion. The current-account deficit was just under US$9 billion, less than 1 percent of GDP. The leading markets for Mexico in 2004 were the United States (87.6 percent), Canada (1.8 percent), and Spain (1.1 percent). Mexico imports from the United States (55.1 percent), China (7.1 percent), and Japan (5.3 percent).[56]

Canada's International Trade Supports

Not surprisingly, as a more socialist nation than the United States, Canada has greater trade supports for entrepreneurs. Industry Canada reports that as of June 2003, there were approximately 2.2 million SMEs in Canada that employed close to 6.6 million people.[57] Small businesses are defined as companies with fewer than 100 people employed, and medium businesses employ fewer than 500 people. Parka maker Metro Sportswear Ltd. is an example of a Canadian company doing business globally and highlights the growing contribution that SMEs have made to the Canadian economy recently.[58] The family-owned outerwear company now has clients across the globe in places such as Western Europe, Japan, Russia, and the United States. Metro Sportswear had a sales increase of more than 60 percent in 2003, totalling more than $10 million.[59]

Overall, there are many resources available to Canadian businesses attempting to enter the global marketplace. These include federal, provincial, and private organizations that are able to offer business information and support. However, many of the government resources overlap; as a result, finding the support best suited to your particular needs might take some time. Also, some resources require purchasing membership; are tailored to goods, not services; or do not provide one-to-one service. As well, some organizations are tailored only to international relations with specific countries. Obtain the federal government's *Your Guide to Government of Canada Services and Support for Small Business* for inclusion in your export/import reference readings. It contains useful information on federal government programs and services available to small businesses, including detailed information regarding key support and information services, and exporting.

Export Development Canada has established a Forum for International Trade Training (FITT). Its courses provide practical international trade training programs and services specifically designed for Canadian SMEs in or contemplating international business.

Export Support Services in Canada

Exporting services that SMEs are most likely to consider include the following:

- Canada Export Centre (CEC) supports increasing international sales and visibility for Canadian businesses. Located in Vancouver, it provides companies with the opportunity to showcase their goods and services year-round to some 200 annual inbound trade missions to British Columbia, and the 8.3 million international travellers who visit Vancouver every year.
- The Canadian Commercial Corporation (CCC) serves as an export-contracting agency for Canada as it works to bring buyers and exporters together. In addition, it acts as a prime contractor and procurement agency for buyers interested in Canadian products and services. The CCC works with businesses during all stages of the contract and partnership process. The CCC also provides government-backed guarantees to foreign businesses. CCC charges a fee for its services.
- The National Research Council of Canada is a federal government organization whose mandate is to promote and support research and development.
- Industry Canada's website provides information on topics such as international investment opportunities, trade and investment statistics, trade and investment policy, investment promotion, and internal trade. The website also provides tools for creating market reports, finding business partners and sales leads, and compiling trade information. Strategis guides and weekly e-mail updates are available. The Industry Canada website does not provide detailed country-specific information.
- Statistics Canada (StatsCan) provides international trade information such as Canadian and international merchandising trade figures. StatsCan has compiled detailed information on Canadian imports, exports, and trade balances of goods. It can also provide information on market shares, foreign and domestic market trends, Canada's trading status, transportation implications, and price and volume of traded goods.
- Canadian International Development Agency (CIDA) supports Canadian businesses planning sustainable business activities in developing countries in order to reduce poverty and to contribute to a more secure, equitable, and prosperous world. CIDA helps Canadian firms reduce their risks by sharing the costs of doing business in developing countries, in countries promoting the participation of women, and in those stressing a clean environment.

- Export Development Canada (EDC) provides financing to access export markets. It also provide financing for foreign buyers of Canadian capital goods and/or services in over 200 markets. EDC provides financing to Canadian companies through equity investments, preshipment financing, note purchases, Canadian FDI, direct loans, lines of credit, contract bonding, corporate loan syndication, and special leasing plans.
- Team Canada Inc. provides a network of 20 federal agencies and departments to offer comprehensive information on developing an export plan; identifying a market; export financing; and industry sector resources. Team Canada is headed by the prime minister, the minister for International Trade, provincial premiers, and territorial government leaders. Team Canada's efforts are to support and help develop international trade partnerships for Canadian businesses. It emphasizes small to medium-sized businesses and women- and aboriginal-owned businesses. To facilitate the exporting partnership process, Team Canada organizes international missions of less than a dozen to several hundred business people to countries where business in foreign markets is possible.
- Trade Team BC is a federally and provincially funded network comprising 25 export-service organizations. Trade Team BC serves as a link to these organizations and a resource for promoting industry events. A number of provinces have similar organizations.
- New Exporters to Border States (NEBS) program is a two-day hands-on seminar held by the Ontario government, where new exporters visit Buffalo or Detroit to understand the exporting process. Ontario Exports Inc. assists Ontario companies wishing to learn about exporting. The program includes presentations on identifying market opportunities, export pricing, legal considerations, export finance and insurance, and customs protocols.
- The Agriculture Financial Services Corporation helps Alberta manufacturers export goods anywhere outside the province.
- The Virtual Trade Commissioner website provides market information, business opportunities, online service delivery, and information to trade commissioners abroad.
- The Canadian Trade and Commissioner Service in Canada is a service for small to large Canadian businesses that have researched and selected a target market and that are committed to doing business in the global marketplace. A trade commissioner will provide up-to-date information on the chosen country, furnish specific advice for successfully entering the market, discuss barriers and upcoming marketing and trade events, and suggest next steps. The Canadian Trade and Commissioner Service in Canada can also provide dedicated businesses with key contact information, help organize a visit to the country they want to do business in, provide a face-to-face briefing, troubleshoot services, and provide referrals to third-party services. The organization will not provide services to businesses just starting out.
- The Canadian Trade and Commissioner Service Abroad provides similar service to the in-Canada service; however, it is located in 140 cities worldwide. Trade commissioners in these cities can help develop the businesses' export potential and provide key contact information. In addition, they can provide advice and intelligence and market reports. The Canadian Trade Commissioner Services are not available in all countries.
- Canada Business Service Centres are provincial business services that are a cooperative arrangement between, federal, provincial, territorial, and private-sector organizations. Operating in partnership with the Canadian government, Provincial Business Service Centres offer small to medium-sized businesses business information and support. They also provide direct assistance to trade-related information. Canada Business Service Centres consider themselves the first stop to export and import information, and are a direct information source to Team Canada Inc. Most Business Service Centres are open to the public during regular business hours. They provide access to a trade library, Internet access, export-related seminars, workshops, one-on-one coaching, and other learning resources. Although Business Service Centres provide great information for businesses starting out in international trade, they do not provide country-specific information or detailed trade consulting.

- International Trade Canada (ITCan) is a federal agency providing information and services for Canadians involved in or looking to become involved in exporting. ITCan provides links to information sources and direct assistance through 12 offices located in various Canadian provinces. ITCan also has under its mandate the role of providing other export, import, and investor resources, such as Team Canada Inc., Canadian Trade Commissioner Service in Canada, Canadian Trade Commissioner Service Abroad, and the Export and Import Controls Bureau. It also administers the Program for Export Market Development (PEMD), which can provide medium- to large-sized businesses with funding for doing business in the international marketplace, as well as other programs and services. In addition, the agency provides information on Canada's trade and economic policy, develops policy, and works to support investment into Canada.

Comprehensive business information and a broad range of supports (financing, research and development, banks, associations, and public and private agencies at all levels of government) have been collected and can be viewed at www.power.nelson.com. They provide an extremely valuable resource to Canadian SMEs considering entry into the international markets. Visit this section of the text website in order to be familiar with the wide range of assistance available to Canadian SMEs.

Impacts of International Trade on Canada and International Business

Canada has experienced many changes since becoming a major player in international trade. Economic activity has risen, which allows for increases in political and commercial relations with other countries. In addition, overall national revenues have increased and more jobs have been created, which has resulted in an overall higher quality of life for many Canadians. International trade has also allowed more choice, and access to more innovations and advancements as trade barriers fall. On a business level, a worldwide marketplace has opened the door to increased business globally. Overall, demand for many goods and services have increased, creating the need for higher national output. Business relations have also improved as countries work together to create mutual benefits.

JUST DOING THE RIGHT THING

Let's Not Help India Build More Nuclear Weapons

U.S. President George Bush has struck a deal with India that directly violates the nuclear Non-Proliferation Treaty, or NPT, as well as several major U.S. laws, setting off criticism in the U.S. and around the world. Yet Canada has not taken part in that criticism. [Canada sells atomic reactors and their supplies through Atomic Energy of Canada Limited, using the trade name CANDU.] Instead, the nation that helped India build its first nuclear weapon may now help it build dozens more.

The Bush deal would directly encourage and assist India's nuclear bomb program, in contradiction to Article 1 of the NPT, which prohibits any signatory nation from helping another nation develop nuclear weapons. . . . Still other countries, including France, Russia and Canada, are tempted by the profit in nuclear sales to the world's second-most-populous nation. Nuclear industries in these countries are salivating at potentially billions of dollars in trade and hoping the construction of dozens of new reactors in India and China could restart their long-stalled industry. So-called "realists" in foreign policy establishments dismiss proliferation concerns, focusing instead on the need to forge strong ties with India. Neo-conservatives are eager to forge a grand alliance against China. . . .

Canada will play a key role in determining whether this deal lives or dies. It has a special responsibility in this matter—more than any Indian scientist, this country can be called the true mother of the Indian nuclear bomb. In 1955, Canada agreed to build a 40MW research reactor for India, known as the CIRUS (Canada-India-Reactor-United-States).

India promised that both the reactor and related fission materials would only be used for peaceful purposes. . . .

Many of its nuclear reactors, both operational and planned, are based on CANDU technology and designs. All were supposed to be exclusively for peaceful use. But in 1974, India cheated on its commitments. It took fuel rods from the CIRUS reactor, extracted the plutonium and detonated its first nuclear test. India called it a "peaceful" nuclear explosion, but the country now admits it was a test of a weapon design. In response, Canada ceased all nuclear co-operation with India. Now, following the U.S. lead, Canada has begun to revive that co-operation. In September, then–foreign affairs minister Pierre Pettigrew met with his Indian counterpart, Natwar Singh. . . . They agreed to develop a broad bilateral co-operation framework, possibly by mid-2006. Canada agreed to open the supply of nuclear technology to any Indian civilian nuclear facility. . . .

Full-scope safeguards mean that a country agrees all its nuclear facilities will be open to thorough inspection by the International Atomic Energy Agency. These inspectors will make sure no nuclear fuel is diverted to weapons purposes. But the Bush-India deal exempts fully one-third of India's reactors from any inspections. . . . If the deal stands, India will use foreign fuel for its power reactors, freeing up Indian uranium for military reactors. India will be able to double or triple the weapons it can make annually. The consequences could be severe. Regionally, it could ignite a new nuclear arms race. Pakistan will not stand idly by, nor will China. Globally, the deal cripples the main diplomatic and legal barrier to the spread of nuclear weapons. The United States is now trying to restrain the Iranian program by relying on the very treaty it has just weakened with the India deal. . . .

Pakistani officials have already asked for a similar deal. Israel is surely waiting in the wings. Other nations may decide they can break the rules, too, to grant special deals to their friends. . . . Canadian officials can help. But they must now decide if they want to. A bit of reflection on their past history with India wouldn't hurt."

Source: Joseph Cirincione, "Let's Not Help India Build More Nuclear Weapons," *The Globe and Mail*, March 11, 2006. Copyright © 2006 Bell Globemedia Publishing Inc. All Rights Reserved.

REFLECTIVE QUESTIONS

Atomic Energy Canada (AECL) and the Canadian government seem to be driven by "bottom line" considerations rather than considering violating human rights, encouraging corruption, and aiding potential proliferation of nuclear weapons. Is this a fair statement? How important is it that Canadian SMEs consider issues other than the bottom line when considering importing or exporting goods and services?

Management Implications

- Several billion dollars worth of goods and services enter and leave Canada daily. It is likely that some aspect of any domestic firm's operation relates directly or indirectly to exports or imports. Do you purchase raw materials from foreign suppliers? In today's global business climate, there are few firms that operate in a purely domestic environment. This reality must be recognized by Canadian business leaders.

- How does the import and export market affect you? Are you competing against low-cost goods from countries with lower wage levels? Are your operating costs or profit margins influenced by the rise and fall of the Canadian dollar in relation to U.S. currency or the powerful euro and British pound sterling? Perhaps you are a domestic firm looking to enter foreign markets to capitalize on some of the faster-growing economies around the world.

- Entering the export market, or establishing import relationships, adds a layer of challenge and risk for domestic firms. Who are your foreign buyers or suppliers, and how will you establish trade? What is the method of payment, and is it required before or after delivery of the goods? What are the shipping logistics, and what is the time to market? What are the risks and guarantees on product quality and reliability of delivery?

- You may also have to deal with cultural differences, as well as legal and governmental challenges, in distributing or purchasing goods abroad. New entrants to the export market may find indirect exporting helps to facilitate greater ease of entry. While indirect intermediaries, such as export/import brokers, freight forwarders, export management companies (EMCs) and export trading companies (ETCs) will cut into your profit margins, their knowledge of your target foreign market may increase your likelihood of success. Services such as facilitation of customs documentation and establishing distribution channels are invaluable to exporters. Even if you choose a direct export strategy, you may benefit from the engagement of local sales representatives or distributors in your target foreign markets. Follow Sun Tzu's counsel—seek local guides.

- The Canadian government offers a wide range of support to domestic SMEs looking to enter or expand their export operations. Remember to visit www.power.nelson.com for a comprehensive listing of and contact information for a wide range of supports for Canadian SMEs considering importing and exporting.
- Despite all the governmental and industry services and support for foreign trade, the export/import market is accompanied by risk. Yet, in this new era of globalization, with risks come opportunities—opportunities that are likely found beyond Canada's borders where bigger and faster growing markets offer goods, services, and the demand for "Made in Canada."

CHAPTER SUMMARY

- Canada is a trading nation, and our standard of living is dependent on our ability to trade. The United States is Canada's primary trading partner, accounting for 85.8 percent of exports in 2004, and 68.9 percent of our imports. By 2005, the U.S. market declined to 71.5 percent of Canadian exports and the source of 55.8 percent of Canadian imports.[60] Some factors resulting in the decline of Canadian exports to the United States from an all-time high of 85.8 percent include U.S. cuts in spending due to the war in Iraq; the ban of Canadian beef because of bovine spongiform encephalopathy (BSE); severe acute respiratory syndrome (SARS), which precipitated a marked decline in commercial and travel services; the decline in forest products caused by an increase in B.C. forest fires; and U.S. tariffs imposed on softwood lumber,[61] in addition to increase trade with other nations.
- The Canadian government supports exports via a number of programs and initiatives, including trade commissioners, trade missions, and online services for researching and developing contacts in foreign markets. Canada's six major import and export countries include the United States, Japan, China, United Kingdom, Mexico, and Germany. Recently the desire to trade with the BRIC countries and other developing countries has increased significantly.
- Exporting means selling goods or services to locations outside the home country. Exports enable Canadian firms to expand sales through international trade and support increased profit margins by spreading fixed costs of production over more units. Canadian firms seek export opportunities due to efficient transportation; falling trade barriers; low-cost, high-speed communications; higher-growth economies offshore; and the influx of foreign firms competing for market share in this country.

- Importing is buying goods or services abroad and bringing them into the home country. Firms import to obtain less expensive goods or services, or because the goods or services are not available in the domestic market. Goods imported into Canada are subject to compliance with conditions imposed by the federal and, sometimes, provincial governments. Federally imposed conditions on imports include labelling laws for retail goods, various health and safety standards, regulations and checks for agricultural products, electrical appliances and equipment, and certain other goods. Most products imported into Canada are subject to customs duties and GST, both of which are collected by Canada Revenue Agency (CRA) at the time of importation.
- Nations export for three reasons. First, exporting increases revenues through expanding total sales when the domestic market has become mature. Second, it provides the opportunity for exporters to diversify their sales base. And finally, it is a low-cost, low risk strategy (mode) to enter a foreign market, thereby resulting in the acquisition of international trade expertise that may in time lead to more sophisticated integrated market entry strategies.
- It is important that Canadian exporting and importing SMEs avail themselves of local guides and the supports available.
- SMEs have two advantages in a global marketplace. First, the emergence of virtual corporations harnessing technology has dramatically levelled the exporting marketplace playing field and enabled SMEs to participate on a more equal footing with large multinational firms. Second, SME business models tend to be more organic and sensitive to market shifts than the larger bureaucratic organizations. Speed and innovation are powerful attributes for any organization.

- There are two fundamental forms of export: indirect strategies and direct strategies. There is a third low-level intermediary used by MNEs, an international export trading company, which isn't used often by SMEs. Indirect export is a low-level involvement strategy in which the exporter contracts with an intermediary to sell its products or services in target foreign markets. Indirect intermediaries include agents, export management companies (EMCs), and export trading companies (ETCs). Agents can represent one or more foreign firms. They may be manufacturers' agents who solicit orders in the foreign markets, manufacturers' export agents, who serve as a foreign sales department, or export/import brokers facilitating matches between buyers and sellers internationally. Freight forwarders facilitate customs documentation, transportation services, and logistics, and, sometimes, transportation. EMCs provide their services either on a commission basis (agent) or as a distributor taking title to the goods and distributing them in target markets. ETCs provide the same services as EMCs and more, dealing with import, export, and countertrade services, distribution channels, storage facilities, trade financing, and investments. Direct exporting is full involvement by the exporting company in selling its product directly to buyers within the target market, without the support of intermediaries. Direct exporters may hire local sales representatives (corporations or individuals) and/or distributors. Distributors take ownership of the product, and use their own sales channels. A third export strategy, sometimes used by MNCs, is intra-corporate transfers. Intra-corporate transfers are the sale of goods and services to a related corporate entity.

- International business practitioners must become familiar with the fundamentals of import and export payments, including advance payments, documentary collection, letters of credit, open accounts, and, occasionally, countertrade.

- Countertrade is the exchange of goods or services instead of currency for all or part of the purchase price of a product or service. Typically large firms engage in countertrade when nations restrict convertibility of currency or expatriation of currency to the seller's country. Nations lacking sufficient foreign exchange to pay for imports may require countertrade.

- There are five forms of countertrade: barter, counterpurchase, offset, switch trading, and compensation or buy back. Barter is the direct exchange of goods and services between parties without the use of currencies. A counterpurchase is an agreement in which the firm selling the goods or services to a nation is required to spend a portion of the contracted funds on buying goods or services as specified by the nation. Offset trading requires the purchaser to acquire unspecified goods from the nation in order to offset the hard-currency sale. Switch trading occurs when one company sells for a fee (payable to the purchaser) its obligation to another company to make a purchase in the host nation. Compensation or buy back is a countertrade method requiring the exporter that sells equipment to a host country to purchase products produced with that equipment from the host country as a condition of the sale.

REVIEW QUESTIONS

1. Provide three reasons Canadian SMEs export.
2. Explain the two advantages SMEs have over MNEs in the global marketplace.
3. What are the four caveats exporting SMEs would be well advised to observe when crafting their export strategy? Discuss.
4. Discuss the two fundamental levels of involvement to be considered by entrepreneurs when crafting an export strategy.
5. Briefly outline import and export financing options. Provide examples of companies using these options.
6. Explain the exporting collection process.
7. What are the two types of financing drafts?
8. What does a bill of lading represent?
9. What is countertrade? Briefly outline its five forms.
10. Outline any three Canadian trade supports appropriate for a venture of your choosing.

REFLECTIVE THINKING QUESTIONS

1. Having completed this chapter, reread the quotations on the first page, critically reflect on the validity of the authors' statements, and provide your opinion as to the validity of each. Evidence-based answers are preferred to rhetorical answers.
2. How does Sun Tzu's observation; "Those who do not use local guides are unable to obtain the advantages of ground" provide sage counsel to Canadian SMEs when crafting their export strategy?
3. SMEs that export will face daily challenges. Comment with examples on potential challenges involving human

rights, bribes, and other cultural and ethical tensions. It is imperative that you undertake critical reflection about these issues when you develop your marketing plans. Let's not help India build more nuclear weapons stores.

4. Canada's merchandise exports to the United States are now 8.8 percent lower than their peak of $359.3 billion in 2000. Provide your critical thinking as to what pre-

cipitated this decline in U.S.–Canada trade and is it likely to continue?

5. Can you make a case for the Canadian government's wide range of supports to domestic SMEs looking to enter or expand their export operations? If so, how do you accommodate the economic trade theories we discussed earlier?

GLOBAL E-RESEARCH

Visit www.power.nelson.com for research suggestions, questions, and a number of background discussion papers on this topic.

MINI CASE

Top-Notch Canadian Animation—Bardel Entertainment, Vancouver, British Columbia

Bardel Entertainment is an international award-winning animation production services firm. "Among its high-profile clients are Warner Brothers, Disney, DreamWorks SKG, Fox, Nelvana, Turner Broadcasting System and Electronic Arts. The studio is about to launch *Dragons—Fire & Ice*, its first proprietary animated movie using computer-generated imagery (CGI). Based on the mega-successful line of toys from Montreal's Mega Bloks Inc. (Canada's Exporter of the Year in 2003), the 72-minute medieval fantasy will debut on TELETOON on September 11, 2004 and will be released internationally on DVD for Christmas. Another television production, *Silverwing*, soared to the top ten in Denmark in December, 2003, while multi-award winning *The Christmas Orange* has been sold in eight countries."

Running a production company in Canada, particularly in Vancouver, has its advantages, according to Cathy Schoch, Bardel's Vice President, Development and Productions. "We

are very competitive, even with the strong dollar," she says. "Canadians are sought after as international co-production partners, thanks to our government subsidies and excellent tax credit programs. These co-productions are a mainstay of the Canadian film industry and have kept us prominent on the world stage." To date, Bardel has worked on 11 animated feature films, 3 home videos, 35 television series and specials, 15 interactive media projects as well as numerous websites and commercials.

"When Canada Celebrates Film" (*Why Trade Matters*, September 14, 2004), Department of Foreign Affairs and International Trade, 2005. Copyright Public Works and Government Services.

CRITICAL THINKING QUESTIONS

1. How successful would this exporting firm be without government subsidies and tax credits?

2. As a taxpayer, do you support these types of federal and provincial expenditures?

3. What do you think would happen if Ontario decreased its movie tax credits significantly?

ENDNOTES

1 Yuen Pau Woo, "PM Shifts Tactics to Woo China," *The Globe and Mail*, January 20, 2005.

2 *Quotations* (ThinkExist.com Quotations), retrieved August 23, 2006, from http://en.thinkexist.com/quotes/top.

3 *Quotes about Trade* (zQuotes, 2006), retrieved August 23, 2006, from www.zaadz.com/quotes/topics/trade.

4 Ibid.

5 *Great Canadian Quotes* (Canada—The Best Country, 2002), retrieved August 23, 2006, from www.thebestcountry .ca/info5.htm.

6 International Trade Canada, *Trade and the Canadian Economy: New and Emerging Markets—Canadian Companies in India*, (Why Trade Matters, February 19, 2004), retrieved August 23, 2006, from www.dfait-maeci.gc.ca/tna-nac/stories87-en.asp.

7 Carmanah Technologies Corporation, *Annual Report 2005*. (Carmanah Technologies, 2005), retrieved August 23, 2006, from www.carmanah.com/documents/financials/annual_ report_2005.pdf.

8 Carmanah Technologies Corporation, *Interim Financial Statements for Nine Months ended September 30, 2004 and 2003* (Carmanah Technologies Corporation, 2004), retrieved September 20, 2006, from www.carmanah.com/documents/ financials/q3sep04.pdf.

9 International Trade Canada, *New and Emerging Markets— Canadian Companies in India*.

10 Ibid.

11 Mark McNeilly, *Sun Tzu and the Art of Business: Six Strategic Principles for Managers* (New York: Oxford University Press, 1996).

12 Canadian Manufacturers and Exporters Portal (International Trade and Development, 2004), retrieved August 24, 2006, from www.cme-mec.ca/national/template_na.asp?p=3.

13 Government of Canada, *Canadian Economy Online* (2004), retrieved August 24, 2006, from http://canadianeconomy .gc.ca/english/economy/index.cfm.

14 Industry Canada, *Minister's Message* (Business Support and Financing, SME Guide, April 4, 2001), retrieved

August 24, 2006, from http://strategis.ic.gc.ca/SSG/me00005e.html.

[15] Department of Foreign Affairs and International Trade, *Trade Update 2006* (Seventh Annual Report on Canada's State of Trade, July 5, 2006), retrieved August 24, 2006, from www.international.gc.ca/eet/trade/sot_2006/sot-2006-en.asp#aiv13.

[16] Ibid. Author calculated from data.

[17] Statistics Canada, "Canadian International Merchandise Trade" (*The Daily*, August 13, 2004), retrieved August 24, 2006, from www.statcan.ca/Daily/English/040813/d040813a.htm.

[18] Department of Foreign Affairs and International Trade, *Trade Update April 2005* (Sixth Annual Report on Canada's State of Trade, 2005), retrieved September 12, 2006, from www.international.gc.ca/eet/trade/sot_2005/sot_2005-en.asp.

[19] Ibid.

[20] World Bank, *Starting a Business* (Doing Business: Benchmarking Business Regulations, 2006), retrieved August 24, 2006, from www.doingbusiness.org/ExploreTopics/StartingBusiness.

[21] "Section Five: Corporate Profiles" (*A Needle in a Haystack: Tracing Canadian Garment Connections in Mexico and Central America*, 2000), retrieved August 24, 2006, from www.maquilasolidarity.org/resources/garment/haystack.htm.

[22] Matt Rosenberg, "The Number of Countries in the World" (*The New York Times*, February 8, 2006), retrieved August 24, 2006, from http://geography.about.com/cs/countries/a/numbercountries.htm.

[23] Export and Import Control Bureau, *Importing into Canada* (How to Obtain a Permit, February 26, 2003), retrieved August 24, 2006, from www.dfait-maeci.gc.ca/eicb/general/impcan-en.asp.

[24] Ibid.

[25] Robert B. Zoellick, "National Trade Estimate Report on Foreign Trade Barriers (NTE)," *Foreign Trade Barriers* (The Office of the United States Trade Representative, 2004).

[26] Ibid.

[27] Central Intelligence Agency, *Canada*, retrieved August 24, 2006, from www.cia.gov/cia/publications/factbook/geos/ca.html.

[28] *The Economist*, "Factsheet" (Country Briefings, 2006), retrieved August 24, 2006, from www.economist.com/countries.

[29] Central Intelligence Agency, *United States* (CIA, May 2, 2006), retrieved August 24, 2006, from www.cia.gov/cia/publications/factbook/index.html.

[30] Ibid.

[31] Central Intelligence Agency, *European Union* (CIA, May 2, 2006), retrieved August 24, 2006, from www.cia.gov/cia/publications/factbook/geos/ee.html.

[32] Department of Foreign Affairs and International Trade, *Sixth Annual Report on Canada's State of Trade*.

[33] Central Intelligence Agency, *India* (CIA, January 10, 2005), retrieved August 24, 2006, from https://www.cia.gov/cia/publications/factbook/geos/in.html#Econ.

[34] Dominique Bergevin, *A Perspective into India's Political Masala* (EDC Political Report, December 1, 2004), retrieved September 13, 2006, from www.edc.ca/english/docs/12_04_india_report_e.pdf.

[35] Ibid.

[36] Ibid.

[37] Ibid.

[38] Industry Canada, *Trade Data Online* (Government of Canada, March 14, 2006), retrieved August 24, 2006, from http://strategis.ic.gc.ca/sc_mrki/tdst/engdoc/tr_homep.html.

[39] Central Intelligence Agency, *China* (CIA, May 2, 2006), retrieved August 24, 2006, from https://www.cia.gov/cia/publications/factbook/geos/ch.html.

[40] U.S. Department of State, *Background Note: China* (Bureau of East Asian and Pacific Affairs, April 2006), retrieved August 24, 2006, from www.state.gov/r/pa/ei/bgn/18902.htm.

[41] Canadian Department of Foreign Affairs & International Trade, *People's Republic of China Fact Sheet* (Asia Pacific, 2004), retrieved August 24, 2006, from www.dfait-maeci.gc.ca/asia/main/china/factsheet-en.asp.

[42] Ibid.

[43] Yuen Pau Woo, "PM Shifts Tactics to Woo China," *The Globe and Mail*, January 20, 2005.

[44] Ibid.

[45] Industry Canada, *People's Republic of China: Economic Overview* (Country/Region Information: Asia, August 29, 2005), retrieved August 24, 2006, from http://strategis.ic.gc.ca/epic/internet/inibi-iai.nsf/en/bi18683e.html.

[46] Ibid.

[47] Ibid.

[48] Ibid.

[49] Statistics Canada, "Study: Canadian Exporters and a Booming China" (*The Daily*, March 14, 2006), retrieved August 24, 2006, from www.statcan.ca/Daily/English/060314/d060314b.htm.

[50] Kip Beckman, *World Outlook Winter 2006: Global Economic Trends and Prospects* (The Conference Board of Canada, January 2006), retrieved September 13, 2006, from www.conferenceboard.ca/boardwiseii/temp/BoardWise2JLBAOFCDAMLBGOGNMPNKANOA2006913164858/158-06%20WOWinter2006%20for%20web.pdf.

[51] Central Intelligence Agency, *Brazil* (CIA, May 2, 2006), retrieved September 20, 2006, from https://www.cia.gov/cia/publications/factbook/geos/br.html.

[52] World Bank, *Brazil Country Brief* (Brazil, July 2006), retrieved November 9, 2006, from http://wbln0018.worldbank.org/LAC/lacinfoclient.nsf/b4fbc1f98ac19293852567360066f32e/d98123e25863079085256d7b00684606/$FILE/Brazil_Eng.pdf.

[53] Canadian Department of Foreign Affairs & International Trade, *Opening Doors to Central and South America* (Opening Doors to the World, April 18, 2005), retrieved August 24, 2006, www.dfait-maeci.gc.ca/tna-nac/2005/6_05-en.asp.

[54] Author generated from Industry Canada, *Trade Data Online*.

[55] Central Intelligence Agency, *Mexico* (CIA, May 2, 2006), retrieved September 20, 2006, from https://www.cia.gov/cia/publications/factbook/geos/mx.html.

[56] Ibid.

[57] Industry Canada, *Key Small Business Financing Statistics—August 2005* (DFAIT, August 19, 2005), retrieved September 20, 2006, from http://strategis.ic.gc.ca/epic/internet/insme_fdi-prf_pme.nsf/en/h_01642e.html.

[58] Erin Pooley, "Small Business Poised for Strong Growth" (*The Globe and Mail*, September 5, 2004), retrieved August 24, 2006, from www.theglobeandmail.com/series/business/sb2/globe/06232004c.html.

[59] Ibid.

[60] Department of Foreign Affairs and International Trade, *Trade Update 2006* (Seventh Annual Report on Canada's State of Trade, July 5, 2006), retrieved August 24, 2006, from www.international.gc.ca/eet/trade/sot_2006/sot-2006-en.asp#aiv13.

[61] Statistics Canada, "Canadian International Merchandise Trade."

PART 6

Internal– Value Chain Activities

Continuing our journey along the road toward our international "pot of gold," in these final five chapters you will adopt the roles of specific functional decision makers responsible for crafting and implementing international business strategies, and leading the firm's functional units in support of the overarching corporate strategy discussed in Chapter 10. You will examine selected value chain activities (functions) in an international setting. These primary and supporting activities are marketing, manufacturing and supply chain management, human resources management and labour relations, and global accounting. We conclude with a chapter on ethics and corporate social responsibility—notions that are pervasive considerations to be taken into account by all managers within the firm no matter what their functional area. There are, of course, other watertight compartment activities in a firm's value chain that might also have been examined. However, we have restricted our review to these major functional activities. Consider now the specific challenges faced by international business through the lenses of marketers, accountants, operations managers, project managers, and human resource managers. Each decision maker stands on different terrain and sees many things in the ecosystem differently. The opportunities and threats observed must be provided for in the functional unit's business plan to seamlessly align with and support the firm's corporate strategic plan.

CHAPTER 13

Global Marketing and Research and Development

"The elements of success in this business do not differ from the elements of success in any other. Competition is keen and bitter. Advertising is as large an element as in any other business, and since the usual avenues of successful exploitation are closed to the profession, the adage that the best advertisement is a pleased customer is doubly true for this business."[1]

—*Madeleine Blair, prostitute and madam*

"All our factories and facilities could burn down tomorrow but you'd hardly touch the value of the company; all that actually lies in the goodwill of our brand franchise and the collective knowledge in the company."[2]

—*Roberto Goizueta, late CEO of Coca-Cola*

"Failure to take into account business risks, market differences from the West, and underestimating local competition are among the biggest mistakes global consumer market companies continue to make when looking to expand or start up in China."[3]

—*KPMG*

"Business has only two functions—marketing and innovation."[4]

—*Peter F. Drucker, management consultant*

"It is neither the strongest species that survive, nor the most intelligent, but those that are best prepared for change."[5]

—*Commonly attributed to Charles Darwin*

LEARNING OUTCOMES

- Evaluate the increased complexity of the political, economic, societal, technological, and cultural attributes that affect SMEs' global marketing strategies.
- Understand from a marketing perspective how to accommodate tradition-based and modern-based cultures.
- Evaluate the merits of adopting a new mental marketing model of market convergence.
- Understand how adopting new marketing technology can enhance a firm's competitive advantages.
- Formulate a new mental model about the opportunity to market to global consumers in the emerging markets.
- Evaluate the increased complexity that the global environment presents to an SME's marketing mix (4Ps).
- Evaluate four cost concepts that are important in international pricing decisions.
- Understand the ability to commercialize research and development (R&D) as a critical determinant of Canada's capacity to innovate.
- Be able to evaluate the strengths and weaknesses of potential global locations for Canadian SME R&D.
- Understand and be able to accommodate additional considerations when SMEs market services rather than goods in a global environment.

Snack Maker Seeks Fat Rewards from Slimming Bars

Hannah Sutter was so frustrated with the lack of available healthy snack foods that she gave up a partnership in a law firm and started to make her own. "I went into the kitchen armed with some scientific journals but I had no other skills," . . . [she] came up with her first recipe for a snack bar from her Edinburgh kitchen in early 2004. Six months later, it was on sale.

In (2005), her firm "Go Lower" sells between 150,000 and 200,000 bars a month. Her marketing niche is "seeds and nut [snack bars] that are low in carbohydrates, contain no added sugars, and no sweetening ingredients. . . . Ms Sutter argues that the food industry does not care about consumers, and is more concerned with profit than what they put in their products. 'The person behind Go Lower is a real consumer,' she says. 'I am the guardian of the low sugar message.'"

Source: Jenny Wiggins, "Snack Maker Seeks Fat Rewards from Slimming Bars," *The Financial Times*, August 30, 2005, retrieved August 25, 2006, from http://us.ft .com/ftgateway/superpage.ft?news_id= fto083020051827267830.

A SUN TZU MOMENT . . .

Visual Arts Library, London/Alamy

"In war, numbers alone confer no advantage. Do not advance relying on sheer military power."[6]

THE BATTLE OF THE ATLANTIC

"The Battle of the Atlantic was waged in order to keep allied shipping lanes open. Around the beginning of July 1940, German U-Boats were attacking merchant ships sailing across the Atlantic in their deadly 'Wolf Pack' formation. The largest problem the allies had was that all their coastal patrol aircraft were not designed to fly across the ocean, which made the merchant ships vulnerable in the mid-Atlantic. This gave the 26 German submarines virtual impunity over the high seas. In 1941, around 2.9 million tonnes of allied cargo [primarily shipped from Halifax and other eastern ports] destined for England was sent to the ocean floor. In 1942, around 6 million tonnes was sunk. The solution to this problem came from a coastal patrol ship known as a corvette. These ships were small; the first class ships only being 59 metres in length and the second class or Castle class were 77 metres in length. Designed like whaling ships, they were simple and inexpensive ships to build. Their primary design function was to patrol the Canadian coast. However their versatility made them excellent escorts for the vulnerable merchant ships. Corvettes were armed with anti-submarine torpedoes, anti-aircraft guns, depth charges to fend off attacks from German U-boats lurking all around them, and one 4-inch deck gun. Also, the Corvettes were equipped with listening devices to detect them. The HMCS *Lewis* was our first naval loss. It was sunk September 19, 1941.

Throughout all of the Battle of the Atlantic, Hitler rarely used his surface ships, relying almost entirely on U-Boats. The German U-Boat attacks peaked with the destruction of 27 merchant vessels. The Battle of the Atlantic never really ended until the end of the war; however, as the war dragged on and German resources ran low, the threat of a U-boat attack decreased. In all, 217 merchant vessels were destroyed from the deadly Wolf Pack attacks. With the Canadian Corvettes, the seas were secure enough for troops and supplies to be ferried across the Atlantic."[7] As a matter of interest, immediately following World War II, the Canadian Navy was the third largest in the world.

Opening Thoughts

Arvind Rangaswamy's quote sets the stage perfectly for the materials in this marketing chapter when he urges us to adopt a new mental model, "The future is all about convergence: Dot.coms + not.coms, TV + computer, first world + third world, marketing + finance, and so on. At the end of this future is the centaur—the hybrid consumer who is tech savvy + uniquely human."[8] How we think about global marketing requires the adoption of new mental models like those of Hannah Sutter identifying a new niche for her seed and nut bar, or Canada's corvettes meeting the emerging threats of Hitler's U-boats. Although neither large nor strong by harnessing new technology, speed, and agility, Canada's corvettes made a difference. Canadian SMEs can do the same.

Technology has been a major catalyst to encourage change in how we view our customers. Increasingly, electronic networks enable customers to access a wealth of information about products and services that heretofore was not readily available. In thinking about our international global marketing strategies we must be aware that the power has shifted in large measure to our customers. The traditional Henry Ford "push" strategy and the more recent "pull" marketing strategies need to be revisited and adapted. Today, our customers are centaurs, half techie and half traditional. As a result, the new mental model of convergence marketing is washing over us. The use of technology combined with the realities of cheap transportation and communication devices enable centaurs to purchase and sell goods and services to a vast array of international suppliers and buyers. You are competing in the global marketplace whether you like it or not.

Increasingly, Canadian businesses are exploring international markets to stimulate growth and grow revenue. If they don't, they will not last long because international sellers offering similar goods and services will enter their domestic markets and sell to their Canadian customers. It would be a mistake, as Sun Tzu counsels, to try to match the foreign challengers strength for strength. Guard against this Western cultural phenomenon of wanting to go toe to toe with opponents. Think smarter; do not simply match the competition. Traditionally Canadian SMEs market to North American and Western European customers with little risk. However, this myopic view limits their potential customer base. From Chapter 10's Mini Case, "5.4 Billion New Customers?" (page 306), recall that 80 percent of the world lives on $2 a day or less. If we believe the statistics, we would seldom trade with anyone not in North America and Western Europe. This would be wrong, as statistics don't always reflect reality. Other global customers have cash or are ready to barter. It will take a new mental model to meet the needs of these people. Like water, we must flow around the obstacles swiftly. While these new customers may not be able to buy the large, economic, super-sized products sold in North America, they will buy large numbers of smaller-sized, packaged products. Yes, there is business risk in these new, overlooked, emerging market economies. But these markets represent approximately 80 percent of the global population and about 20 percent of the world's economy. These emerging markets offer lucrative business potential that can no longer be overlooked by Canadian SMEs.

The international business environment is complex. New questions need to be answered. Are the political, economic, societal, technical, and cultural variables significantly different in the international setting? Can we assume the global market will accept goods and services with universal attributes? Will firms be required to modify the product or service to reflect the tastes and cultural preferences of the host marketplace? What changes are needed in the firm's communication, distribution, and marketing strategies to meet the international market's needs? Are the considerations different for the marketing of services as opposed to the marketing of goods? Are there advantages to sourcing abroad? Which R&D strategy should be adopted in an international setting? These are just a few of the questions we will examine in this chapter. Be prepared to think differently!

The Global Market's Ecosystem (PEST-C)

In Chapter 2, pages 43–45, we examined Huntington's warning of the impending clash of civilizations. Much of what he had to say in 1996 has come to pass. Globalization and global marketing of Western liberalized democracy and their goods and services are both good and bad. Many young Iraqi Muslims and other Asians enjoy listening to American music and watching American movies, for example. However, such actions are very threatening to others in the traditional non-Western cultures. The uproar over Disney's entry into France is proof that not only poor and developing nations can feel threatened by what is perceived as the imposition of a different culture. Canadian marketers must be sensitive to and accommodate these concerns.

Theodore Levitt observed in 1980 that "a powerful force drives the world towards a converging commonality, and that force is technology."[9] It has proletarianized communications, transport, and travel. The result is a new commercial reality—the emergence of global markets for standardized consumer products on a previously unimagined scale of magnitude. Gone are the accustomed differences in national and regional preferences. The globalization of markets is now commonplace. So if the multinational commercial world is nearing its end, so must be the multinational corporation. The multinational corporation operates in a number of countries and adjusts its products and practices to each at high relative costs. The global corporation operates with resolute consistency at low relative cost. These global corporations function as if the entire world were a single entity; they sell the same thing in the same way everywhere. Commercially, the success of McDonald's from the shops on the Champs Élysées to Ginza,[10] of Coca-Cola in Bahrain and Pepsi-Cola in Moscow, and of rock music, Greek salad, Hollywood movies, Revlon cosmetics, Sony television, and Levi jeans everywhere confirm this thought. Ancient differences in national tastes or modes of doing business disappear. The commonality of preference leads inescapably to the standardization of products, manufacturing, and the institutions of trade and commerce."[11] Thomas L. Friedman[12] put forward the "Golden Arches Theory of Conflict Prevention." Friedman notes that no two countries both having a McDonald's outlet have ever gone to war against each other. Venezuela's 80 McDonald's outlets must be a comforting thought for populist President Hugo Chavez!

A universal approach to marketing, and to the manufacture of goods and services where one size fits all, will hold great appeal for global firms wishing to capture efficiencies derived from moving down the production possibility frontier (PPF) curve and producing goods at a lower cost per unit because of the economies of scale and the efficiency curve (see Chapter 6, pages 161–162). However, during the past two decades it has become clear to most that Levitt has overstated the position. To a greater or lesser degree, today global marketing must accommodate many of the "local" issues that emerge from a PEST-C (political, economic, societal, technological, and cultural) analysis.

International Variables—PEST-C

International markets, particularly emerging markets, offer lucrative business opportunities. However, these opportunities are accompanied by unique hazards. To protect your business and reduce your vulnerability, you must be aware of the issues both present and emerging from a number of international variables. Accordingly, our discussion in this chapter will briefly refresh your thoughts from the earlier materials and add a few new observations as to how these variables relate to global marketing.

Specifically, Canadian SMEs must be watching for *political risks* "arising from government; lack of transparency and consistency in regulatory, business and accounting practices, which create uncertainty; *economic risks* arising from volatility in economic growth rates, investment values and exchange rates; *legal risks* occurring from differences in banking and insolvency laws, as well as underdeveloped or unreliable regulatory frameworks; *communications risks* and other *cultural issues* due to entering overseas environments; *infrastructure risks* that impede business development and investment opportunities; corruption and fraud risks such as bribery, and other under-the-table dealings; [and finally, SMEs must be watching for] *security and terrorism risks* that are seen as threats against certain foreign individuals in politically volatile countries."[13] Let's examine these risks more closely.

Political and Legal Factors

It is important that Canadian SMEs and others are aware of the host country's business laws and regulations that may affect their marketing operations. Canada has important legislation in place to protect our indigenous firms; it ratified the Organisation for Economic Co-operation and Development's Convention that established standards for dealing with bribery of foreign government officials, and in 1999 passed the Corruption of Foreign Public Officials Act (CFPOA). The act makes it illegal for Canadian companies or individuals to make a "corrupt" payment to a foreign official in order to obtain or direct business. The act also covers "facilitation payments" used to speed up or secure any official documentation, ranging from permits and licences to visas or other documents needed to conduct business. The act does seem to permit some discretion as to how the definition of payments is interpreted. Each case will be determined on the facts and circumstances surrounding the payments as to whether the firm or individual has come into conflict with the legislation, but those who are found guilty will face sanctions. Unlike the United States' Foreign Corrupt Practices Act (FCPA), Canada's act is viewed by many as the most rigorous of all the global anticorruption legislations. There have been only a small number of CFPOA enforcement actions. Canadian SMEs doing business directly or indirectly in the United States and conducting business in other foreign jurisdictions must be aware of this legislation and seek professional assistance when an issue arises. Interestingly, Canadian firms and individuals have been sanctioned under the U.S. legislation. The penalties include, "criminal and civil enforcement actions, large fines, and suspension or debarment from federal procurement contracting."[14]

Video 13.1

There are many legal constraints likely to be encountered by Canadian SMEs in the global marketplace. Most countries will have laws and regulations relating to workplace safety, consumer protection, environmental standards, food and drug standards, advertising restrictions, piracy and counterfeit goods laws, and many others that will require the attention of business leaders. (See Video 13.1.)

A growing and complex area of law—jurisdiction—is emerging because of the success of globalization. Web messages and e-business occur everywhere in the world, and sometimes the transactions give rise to prosecution. In one jurisdiction the activity may be perfectly acceptable while in another it is not. Generally the issues in these cases arise from moral issues, such as gambling or the distribution of pornography. The blurring of the international boundary means the origin of the service provider or the business often is not clear. Canadian SMEs must exercise great care to determine just where they're doing business and that they are obeying the laws of the host jurisdictions. Like the tax havens discussed in Chapter 16, pages 457–459, some jurisdictions attract and protect businesses of a morally questionable nature. To date, there are no global legal standards.

Another legal area of concern to business is whether the different venues have reciprocal agreements with Canada to enforce judgments obtained in host countries. If there are no international agreements, it may be prudent for firms to add disclaimers such as "void where prohibited by law" or "available only to residents of Canada" to warranties provided on goods sold over the Internet. These political and legal variables are important considerations to a firm's marketing success.

Economic Factors

Purchasing power parity varies widely throughout the global marketplace. Developed countries' products often have many attributes that are neither required by nor affordable for foreign consumers in developing and poor nations. Accordingly, marketing decision makers must think carefully about the appropriateness of the goods they are intending to offer in the host countries. Often stripped-down versions of current product lines, packaged in budget-sized units, will be required. For example, Microsoft offers a Windows XP Starter Edition for sale in India, Russia, Indonesia, Malaysia, and Thailand that is less expensive than the Canadian product offering.[15] "For international markets, either small or large package sizes could be preferred, depending upon the market. Snack food consumers in Latin America, for example, are relatively price-sensitive. In Mexico, this cost-sensitivity is satisfied with small package sizes whereas consumers in Argentina prefer to improve their cost-per-volume by purchasing larger packages. "Package sizes in Canada vary widely. The popularity of snacks for children results in small package sizes while the growth of club stores supports large package sizes."[16]

Technology Factors

The advances in technology from a global marketing perspective are presenting opportunities as well as significant challenges for Canadian SMEs participating in the global marketplace. Clearly, e-commerce has levelled the playing field for small Canadian firms wishing to access the global market. The growth in e-business sales volume has been dramatic. In Canada, the value of online sales (private and public) in 2004 was $28.3 billion;

business-to-consumer (B2C) sales in 2004 was $6.6 billion; business-to-business (B2B) sales in 2004 was $19.8 billion; firms (connected to the Internet) using high-speed Internet access in 2004 was 72 percent; and the percentage of firms connected to the Internet using low-speed Internet access in 2004 was 18.[17] See Figure 13.1 for a comparison of similar indicators across eight OECD countries.

Technology has enabled marketers to identify smaller, more discrete, market segments in the marketplace and can communicate very accurate and relevant information efficiently to these smaller segments. Advertising choices only a few decades ago were limited to radio, television, and print ads. Today there is a mind-boggling array of alternatives available to deliver the firm's message; therefore, firms must understand their market segmentation and select media most likely to attract the attention of those potential customers. Technology also has an impact on service delivery—both good and bad. The banking industry, while improving efficiency by engaging automated banking machines, interactive voice-response telephone systems, and call management software, has also significantly hampered their customer relationships. As a result, customer loyalty has been diminished. Technology can assist in providing better service; however, firms cannot lose sight of the importance of building customer loyalty. A troubling advance in technology is the ability to monitor customers' activities, one of the biggest issues faced in the next decade. The question of how businesses use the customer information collected through technology must be balanced against their customers' right to privacy (see Chapter 14, pages 393–394).

With e-commerce, it is now possible to conduct business globally without ever leaving the home office. Internet technology has made every connected computer an international market where we can obtain information, place orders, and receive goods from anywhere on the globe. Our clients and competitors can be anywhere in the world. Marketing techniques are growing as quickly as the Internet enables electronic marketing. The transformation from the push–pull marketing approach to convergence marketing is possible only because of technology. Electronic marketing is integral in every aspect of marketing. Firms will incorporate electronic media, e-mail, CD-ROMs, the Internet, and rapidly growing infomercials into their marketing strategies. "The marketplace in the 21st century will be exposed to every new marketing technique that will be producing volume sales for thousands of outlets and corporations any time in today's marketplace."[18]

Visit www.power.nelson.com for a number of charts and the latest statistics on Canadian firms' adoption of technology to conduct e-business.

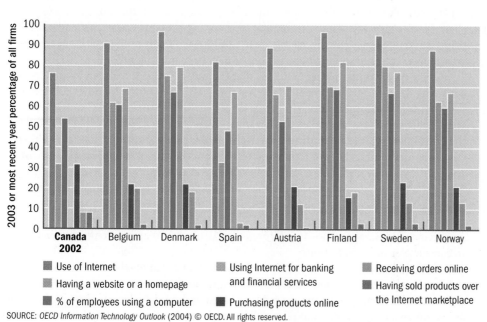

FIGURE 13.1

High Business Connectivity but Low e-Commerce Adoption

Legend:
- Use of Internet
- Having a website or a homepage
- % of employees using a computer
- Using Internet for banking and financial services
- Purchasing products online
- Receiving orders online
- Having sold products over the Internet marketplace

THE SEVEN TECHNOLOGICAL e-BUSINESS MARKETING RULES TO FOLLOW

1. Identify your location on the home page of your website. Remember that the website reaches a global audience; include your full telephone number, including the country code, area code, and business phone number.
2. While graphics and photographs add sizzle to the site, ensure that the page takes less than 10 seconds to load.
3. The exponential growth in new Web technology, while exciting and interesting, may be a "bridge too far" for your customer. Advising your customers that your site is best viewed with the newest browser and that they must download the new version may be a barrier that prevents further exploration of your site.
4. Make navigation intuitive. Don't make your customers work to find the information they need. Include plenty of links on each page.
5. Ensure that the information on your Web page is current, and provide an online map of how to get to your facility.
6. On the home page of your website, invite and provide a way for visitors to subscribe to your membership, mailing list, or database. This will enable you to e-mail newsletters, website updates, or notices of coming events to your subscribers.
7. Don't ask for too much information. You want your customer to feel comfortable about signing up to your e-mail list database. If you need demographic information, this can be collected at a future date with a "feature" offering that will interest your customers after trust in the site has been built.

Societal and Cultural Factors

Video 13.2

Societal and cross-cultural problems provide more challenges and opportunities for marketers, particularly as the Eastern bloc and Asian countries enter the global marketplace (see Video 13.2).

SMEs must consider what societal and cultural factors will affect their marketing strategies. Should they undertake international initiatives or remain focused only on their domestic market? Should their products be standardized or be adapted to meet the societal and cultural needs of the international market? How important are the societal and cultural dimensions of marketing research? How will SMEs provide for the societal and cultural aspects of the marketing mix (products, price, promotion, and distribution)? What must be done to address the societal and cultural aspects of service marketing? What are the societal and cultural implications of the aftermarket? How much societal and cultural marketing education and professional training will be needed for the firm's expatriates, family members, and suppliers to succeed in the host country? (See Chapter 15, pages 425–426.) An international setting presents many challenges for the firm's marketing managers. In the text we have addressed many of these challenges as they arose; however, some specific observations related to marketing follow.

Cross-cultural marketing is the strategic process of marketing among consumers whose culture differs from that of the marketer's own culture at least in one of the fundamental cultural aspects, such as language, religion, social norms and values, education, and living style.[20]

Guoqin refers to the special situation or character of China.

Cross-cultural marketing demands that Canadian SMEs develop an awareness and sensitivity for cultural differences. Marketers must respect the rights of other cultures and nondomestic consumers in various marketplaces. If Canadian firms want to be the winners in cross-cultural marketing, they must create the marketing mix that provides for the consumers' values, including their right to their own culture. "Take the Chinese culture as an example. For western marketers to be successful, it is important for them to respect the Chinese and their government's claim for **guoqin**."[19]

Marketing in a host country presents the potential for cultural misunderstandings due to lack of effective communication or being unaware of unwritten rules. Know as much as possible about your potential business partners and the country. Develop sensitivity and tolerance. Hire an interpreter, particularly if there's potential language risk in contracts or in conversation.

In Chapter 2, pages 37–38, and Figure 2.1, page 39, we examined culture. To add to that understanding, marketers and others find it helpful to characterize a society's culture as a continuum between two extremes: tradition-based and modern-based. This classification can be subdivided along two interrelated dimensions: economic and cultural. The culture of tradition-based societies is incorporated in its market system. "It might not be easy for marketers from Western countries, defined as modern-based culture, to understand the market system in developing countries, which are categorized as tradition-based cultures. This uneasiness could also happen within modern-based cultural societies. For instance, . . . many U.S. marketers are hard pressed to understand the French government's actions restricting retail store size, especially after the success of efficient supermarkets."[21] Many believe the French government's efforts to protect local mom-and-pop retailers may be cultural in nature. If so, it comes at a significant economic cost.

Canadian marketers must understand a host country's marketing culture before attempting to match the marketing mix with consumer preferences, purchasing behaviour, and product-use patterns in a potential market. This is not to say marketers should focus only on cultural differences when crafting their foreign marketing programs; they must also identify cultural similarities and provide for them in the marketing mix (see Chapter 14, pages 394–395). This cultural analysis is a very important part of getting the right marketing mix strategy.

Here is an example of marketers getting it right: during the early 1980s after the fall of the Bamboo curtain, many foreign TV set manufacturers, primarily Japanese and Europeans, conducted significant marketing studies of the Chinese TV market. They concluded that the low GDP per capita in China would result in very poor sales. What most of the studies (except the Japanese) missed was the cultural reality that in China, people hand down savings from generation to generation, and they did not use banks. A further cultural revelation was that although China had domestic budget-priced colour TV set makers, they preferred imported products. The Japanese marketers dominated the imported TV set market in China till the late 1990s (recall the Sony case in the opening vignette of Chapter 11, page 309) because they understood the cultural nuances.

Global Market Management

Marketing managers, like their counterparts in other functional areas of a firm, are similarly tasked with the responsibility of evaluating their contribution to the firm's value chain in order to find ways to both "wring pennies out of the activities" they are responsible for and add value to their activities that will contribute to a higher value in the mind of their consumers. In undertaking this task, the same generic domestic strategic considerations need to be undertaken except they are far more complex because of the international ecosystem. In this section we will look at selected management activities that are more challenging than those faced in the domestic marketplace. Specifically, we will look at some of the international factors and considerations impacting the 4Ps of marketing (product, price, placement, and promotion); specifically marketing strategy, product attributes, branding, market segmentation, distribution strategy, communication, push-pull-convergence marketing, global advertising, strategic pricing, and distribution channels.

Marketing managers must understand the roles of their salespeople as marketers. They must collaborate and support them. "The detailed data that these professionals are good at generating can be a treasure trove."[22] Marketing managers must work with other supply chain functional managers to adjust the firm's supply chain activities to quickly accommodate international customer preferences. "For example, information from sales and marketing indicating that customers are beginning to prefer a certain version of a product—in a particular shape or size, say—helps the supply chain manager to move rapidly,"[23] ascertain the cost implications of that trend and find sources for the needed materials.

It is important that the firm's global marketing communications structure provides for the flow of information up and down the chain quickly in order to respond to emerging international marketing threats and opportunities. For example, the firm's supply chain manager knows if a certain shape or size of product has implications beyond cost. If salespeople recognize that "consumers prefer a particular size yogurt [it] might influence package design, which in turn could affect shipment sizes and hence the way product is transported to market. It becomes the supply chain manager's job to inform marketers, early in the game, about the logistical challenges that certain product configurations pose and to suggest possible alternatives. In order for this to work, the various departments in the firm must make the latest information available to one another"[24] and work towards solutions collaboratively. The firm's marketing teams are an integral and important part of this process. Although they are the best information intelligence gatherers, many firms overlook the value of debriefing these individuals. Effective communication and knowing the business culture will not ensure marketing success; you must effectively monitor your business.

A caveat—in emerging markets, widely dispersed marketing operations with decentralized management, local staff, and poor internal reporting systems can present significant risk. It is essential to monitor the firm's global marketing efforts in an emerging market. If you do not, then your firm will be prone to corruption, fraud, or theft. So hire the right people, encourage quality control, and train and raise the managers' awareness of these challenges.

Today, marketing managers must no longer adopt the paradigm of simply selling product in the traditional sense. The new mental model requires marketing strategies crafted in such a way that products and services are offered that satisfy customers' needs and fulfill their expectations and allow them to participate in the process. Firms must permit and welcome participation (marketing convergence) in the process by their customers. As developing countries grow stronger with their competitive advantages of low labour costs and other location economies, SMEs will be required to focus on adding sustainable value to their products. Canada's ability to compete with price on manufactured goods where labour costs represent a significant portion of the cost is quickly shrinking. For Canadian businesses to be sustainable we must offer value instead of simply supplying product. A Bic pen is a Bic pen; the cost will be largely the determining selling factor. In contrast, the manufacture and sale of a Mont Blanc pen, with its unique attributes and value in the mind of the consumer, reveals the new way for Canadian SMEs to maintain market share.

INTERNATIONAL STRATEGIC THINKING

Canadian SMEs Must Fully Consider Market Segmentation

Market segmentation defines and enables targeting of specific markets. It is the process of dividing a market into a distinct group of buyers that has common attributes. Segmentation enables firms to develop different products or marketing mixes to focus marketing resources on these niches. To succeed in today's marketplace, Canadian SMEs must find attributes to differentiate themselves and thereby obtain a marketing edge over their competitors.

"Markets can be segmented or targeted using a variety of societal and other factors. The bases for segmenting consumer markets include: demographic bases (age, family size, life cycle, occupation); geographic bases (states, regions, countries); behaviour bases (product knowledge, usage, attitudes, responses); and psychographic bases (lifestyle, values, personality). A business must analyze the needs and wants of different market segments before determining its own niche. To be effective in market segmentation, keep the following things in mind: segments or target markets should be accessible to the business; each segmented group must be large enough to provide a solid customer base; and each segmented group requires a separate marketing plan. Large companies segment their markets by conducting extensive market research projects. This research is often too expensive for small businesses to invest in, but there are alternative ways for to a small business to segment their markets."[25]

Canadian SMEs must gain knowledge and information on how to segment their markets. To do this they can use secondary data sources and undertake qualitative research. External secondary data is available from many of the Canadian supports we examined in Chapter 12, pages 349–351. They can also learn by watching key competitors' marketing efforts and adapting them as necessary, talking to key buyers, and conducting needs analysis with potential customers. When SMEs first recognize significant, measurable differences in their market, they must quickly consider market segmentation. It will facilitate easier marketing, indicate new niche markets, and enhance the efficient expenditure of scarce marketing resources.

Four Basic Standardization Choices

When a firm enters a global market, a fundamental marketing decision is the degree of standardization needed for the firm's product. There are four basic standardization choices. The firm may choose to sell the domestic product unchanged; adapt the domestic product for specific new markets, countries, or regions; design new products for foreign markets; or incorporate all the adaptations into one product and introduce it globally. These will be discussed in more detail in Chapter 14 but we'll examine them briefly from a marketing viewpoint.

The degree of adaptation will range from trivial, such as translating the user's manual to substantial changes that might include manufacturing a "stripped-down," more economical version of the product for the host country. Author Virginia Yorio has suggested that three bundles of characteristics[26] will influence the marketing manager's decisions as to whether the product must be adapted. The *first* bundle of characteristics is defined as regional, country, or local. This bundle will include an analysis of government regulations, non-tariff barriers, customer characteristics, customer expectations and preferences, purchasing patterns, the economic status of potential users, the country's stage of economic development, competitive offerings, and the climate and geography of the country. The *second* bundle (product characteristics) include the product constituents, brand, packaging, physical form or appearance (e.g., size, style, colour), functions, attributes, features, methods of operation or usage, durability, quality, ease of installation, maintenance, after-sales services, and country of origin. The *third* bundle relates to company considerations. This bundle includes the expected degree of profitability, market opportunities (e.g., market potential, product–market fit), cost of adapting policies (e.g., commonality, consistency), organization, resources, and the need to be viewed as a corporate socially responsible organization. Many of these factors have been touched upon in this and other chapters of the text.

The potential for a product or service to be standardized can be measured by applying models such as Figure 13.2. To illustrate the extent to which a product can be marketed globally without modification, examine Figure 13.3, page 368, and the factors that would be considered if marketing beer or disposable gel pens. In this example we have taken some elements of standardization and assigned weights (high, average, and low). By reflectively thinking about each of these elements (and others) we can apply

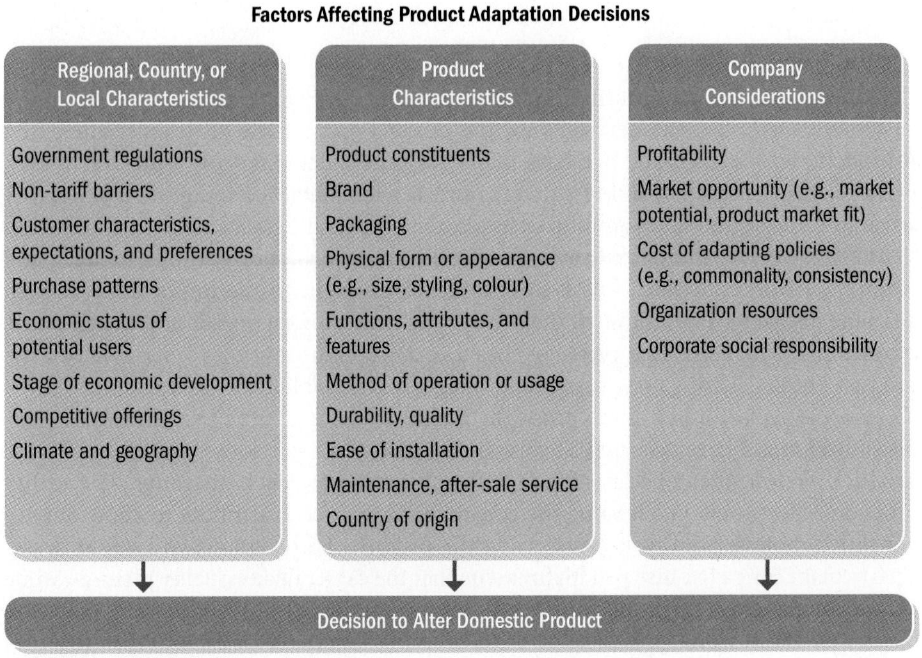

Factors Affecting Product Adaptation Decisions

Regional, Country, or Local Characteristics	Product Characteristics	Company Considerations
Government regulations	Product constituents	Profitability
Non-tariff barriers	Brand	Market opportunity (e.g., market potential, product market fit)
Customer characteristics, expectations, and preferences	Packaging	Cost of adapting policies (e.g., commonality, consistency)
Purchase patterns	Physical form or appearance (e.g., size, styling, colour)	Organization resources
Economic status of potential users	Functions, attributes, and features	Corporate social responsibility
Stage of economic development	Method of operation or usage	
Competitive offerings	Durability, quality	
Climate and geography	Ease of installation	
	Maintenance, after-sale service	
	Country of origin	

Decision to Alter Domestic Product

FIGURE 13.2
Factors Influencing Product Standardization–Adaptation

SOURCE: Adapted from Virginia M. Yorio, *Adapting Products for Export* (New York: Conference Board, 1983).

FIGURE 13.3

Standardization Profile of Sleeman's Grolsch Premium Beer and a Disposable Gel Pen

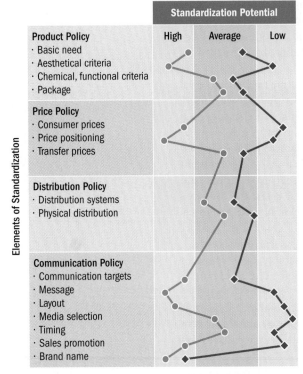

- -●- Standardization profile of a special drink (Sleeman's Beer)
- -◆- Standardization profile of a special disposable gel pen

Adapted from Virginia M. Yorio, *Adapting Products for Export* (New York: Conference Board, 1983).

Yorio's characteristics influencing product standardization, as applicable, to obtain a graphic sense of the standardization potential for our product or service. We will examine a number of these factors and elements in this chapter.

Strategic Considerations for the Product, Price, Placement, and Promotion (4Ps) of International Goods

Marketing managers will craft their product, price, placement, and promotion strategies considering the same factors they would consider in the domestic market except, once again, the analysis will be more complex. Product strategies will be concerned with the product's variety, quality, design, features, brand name, packaging, sizes, services, warranties, and return processes. Pricing strategies will be concerned with the list price, discounts, allowances, payment methods, and credit terms. Placement strategy will be concerned with the channels of distribution, website, product locations, transportation, and logistics. Promotional strategy will consider advertising, personal selling, website, publicity, and public relations. We have examined a number of these topics in other sections of the text; however, we will consider a number of interesting adjustments to the 4Ps required by the international ecosystem.

Product Considerations

We have to determine which products we will export and what product improvements or modifications will be required to meet the host country's PEST-C marketplace variables. The packaging standards and shipping requirements will also have to be examined. It is often a good strategy to provide a sample of your product to potential clients to ensure it meets the host country's requirements.

Product Attributes

Customers purchasing internationally will adopt the same concept as domestic customers. *First* the customer will view the product as a bundle of product attributes. A product, service, or brand can have many attributes, including cost, value for money, prestige, taste, usability, liking (affect), and a wide range of image or personality attributes. To use one very common example, the car brand class includes attributes such as prestige, cost, reliability, exclusivity, availability, type (e.g., sporty, family, luxury), and country of origin. *Second*, a consumer attaches a weight to the importance of each attribute insofar as a specific attribute contributes to meeting her needs and wants. *Third*, a consumer, when selecting products, has a certain predisposition to her belief in the product's brand. This is known as brand image. It is possible that the consumer's belief about a particular brand differs from the reality of the product's true attributes. This disconnect might have occurred because of the customer's previous experience with the product. *Fourth*, the consumer has a utility function for each attribute. The utility function reflects how much value the consumer expects each attribute to contribute to her satisfaction derived from purchasing the product. For example, you might prefer a particular camera because you highly value that the camera takes quality pictures, while at the same time you might place little utility value on the size of the camera. To you, size doesn't matter. It is the highest value of these utility functions for each of the attributes in combination that helps the consumer decide which product best meets her needs.

When considering the utility function of their product, marketers often find it helpful to undertake an analysis called attribute mapping. Attribute mapping looks at the bundle of product characteristics and, using a model similar to the one shown in Figure 13.3, weights the customers' perception of the desirability of each feature. Attributes could range from "nonnegotiable" (features expected by the customers) through "differentiators" (features that positively differentiate your product from the competition) and "exciters" (features customers find positively delightful) to "tolerable" (features not really liked, but not hated either) and "enragers" (features customers absolutely hate or fear). By undertaking this analysis, international marketing managers are better able to understand the utility value of the product attributes.

Global marketing managers must provide for these four concepts whether the locations of their customers are domestic or foreign. Remember, the products and services must be fully considered nation to nation and sometimes even differentiated within nations. Marketing to Canadians in Quebec is clearly different from marketing to Canadians in British Columbia.

Branding

A strong brand may be the firm's most valuable asset. Recall this chapter's opening quote by Roberto Goizueta, late CEO of Coca-Cola, regarding the importance he places on branding. A recognizable name that provides a favourable image has become even more important in a global setting. Those of you who have travelled will recognize the validity of this observation. I suspect many of you selected McDonald's, Holiday Inn, Perrier water, and other recognizable brands because of your comfort level in knowing exactly what you are acquiring in host countries. It is important that firms revisit their brands to ensure they are suitable in the global market. A failure to do so may result in an unintended offence to your prospective customers. (See Cultural Sensitivity Communications Faux Pas on page 376.)

Consumers usually evaluate global brands through five different lenses.

1. *Perceived Quality.* In the 1950s and 1960s, North American consumers thought little of Japanese imported products. By the 1970s and 1980s, that perception had changed. Today, we all want Japanese cameras, televisions, and cars. Why? The perceived quality of Japanese products in the minds of consumers has soared. People expect Japanese companies to produce higher quality electronic and automobile products.
2. *Global Status.* The idea that global brands confer an elite status on the buyer is the second lens. Jaguar cars, Mont Blanc fountain pens, Swiss Rolex watches, and Cuban cigars are all "better" because they are recognized as high-quality, foreign goods.
3. *Country-of-Origin Quality.* A "food chain" of production means that higher-quality goods are created in Canada, the United States, Europe, and Japan. Canada's clean, clear water is especially attractive globally because it comes from Canada. However, as our supply chain inputs increasingly come from outsourcing, this lens can become clouded. The product may have the Canadian label but the reality is that most of the product was made by workers in developing nations.
4. *Citizenship.* While abroad, Canadians take great pride in wearing the maple leaf insignia to identify themselves as Canadians and not Americans. Indeed, there are reports that many Americans wear the maple leaf for the same reason. In a similar example, Arab nations will buy little from Israeli firms.
5. *Social Cachet.* A global firm's products or services may be either admired or derided for their perceived power as social forces. Increasingly the spread of Western liberalized democracy is becoming an issue for China and many Muslim countries. Recall Levitt's and Huntington's earlier observations and the linkages to American value icons—Coca-Cola, Marlboro, Nike, Pepsi, and McDonald's. Canadian SMEs need to accommodate and exploit these views as they consider branding issues and contemplate taking their products international. Recall the preference for Canadian education and textbooks (see Chapter 2, pages 35–36).

Price

Selecting the right price point for goods and services will be critical to success in the international marketplace. In selecting the pricing strategy, marketing managers will be guided by the corporate strategy (see Chapter 10, see pages 292–293, and Figure 10.13). If the company has decided to adopt a low-cost strategy, then marketing managers will select a low-cost price point.

A **world price strategy** involves selling the firm's products at the same price everywhere in the world.

Initially you might be inclined to adopt a **world-price strategy**, meaning selling the product at the same price everywhere in the world. To permit adoption of this strategy, there are four challenges to overcome. First, location economies result in different production costs from nation to nation. These costs will influence the price of the product from nation to nation. Second, producing all goods at a few plants means incurring the same costs of production. However, with only a few facilities, transportation and distribution channel costs are likely to vary greatly. So once again it will be difficult to establish a universal price. Third, purchasing power parity varies widely between international customers. Accordingly, their ability to acquire goods will depend on the buying power of the host country's currency. As a result, setting one worldwide price will be difficult. Fourth, currency fluctuation will result in different unit costs.

Before we look at specific strategies the economic concept of price elasticity of demand will be helpful in determining pricing strategy.

Price Elasticity of Demand

Price elasticity of demand is a measurement of how the marketplace will respond to changes in price.

Demand is **inelastic** when a large change in price produces only a small change in demand.

Demand is **elastic** when a small change in price produces a large change in demand.

When establishing the price point for a good or service it's important to understand the concept of **price elasticity of demand**. If we change the price, what happens to the demand? We say that the demand is **inelastic** when a large change in price produces only a small change in demand. The demand is **elastic** when a small change in price produces a large change in demand (see Figure 13.4). Both the customer's purchasing power parity and the competitiveness of the industry influence the demand elasticity for a good or service in a country.

Clearly, customers with little purchasing power will be very price-conscious; an upward shift in the price will result in price elasticity of demand for the good. This is shown in Figure 13.4B where the price moves up from P1 to P2 resulting in a dramatic drop in sales from Q1 to Q2. The greater the competition in the marketplace, the greater the bargaining power of the consumer. In the absence of high switching costs, consumers will choose to obtain a similar product at a lower price. This is shown in Figure 13.4A where the price moves up from P1 to P2 resulting in a much smaller drop in sales from Q1 to Q2. We say there is an inelastic demand for the good. Accordingly, a firm charging a higher price will not achieve a corresponding increase in the ratio of price to sales.

Controlling International Costs

The profit equation in an international setting is no different from the profit equation domestically. Profit equals total revenue minus total cost. It is important that marketing managers understand and fully calculate all the costs when making marketing decisions

FIGURE 13.4

Price Elasticity of Demand

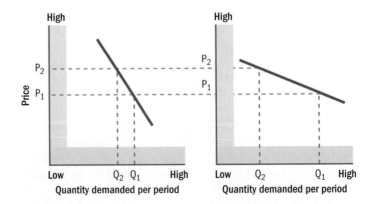

and in particular when making pricing decisions. The five cost concepts important in international pricing decisions are total cost, fixed costs, variable costs, unit variable costs, and marginal costs. See Figure 13.5.

Break-Even Point

International marketing managers must understand at what point there is little reason to continue to sell their goods because the incremental cost of production exceeds the incremental revenue. To ascertain this point, managers undertake a **marginal analysis**, which is central to the concept of maximizing profit in an international environment. As long as the revenue received from the sale of an additional product (marginal revenue) is greater than the additional cost of production and selling that product (marginal cost), the firm should continue to expend its resources to expand output. In undertaking a marginal analysis marketing managers often use a **break-even analysis**. It identifies the point where total revenue and total costs are equal and beyond which profit will occur. (See Figure 13.6, page 372.)

Global Pricing Strategies

There are three primary global pricing strategies to be considered. They are predatory pricing, multipoint pricing, and experience curve pricing. Marketing managers must be aware that at times setting prices in the international market cannot be done unilaterally. Foreign governments will be watching closely to ascertain whether nondomestic firms entering their market are dumping or undertaking other questionable practices to obtain domestic market share. Recall that a nation's political and legal factors will influence global marketing.

PREDATORY PRICING

As the name suggests, firms use **predatory pricing** as a competitive weapon to force weaker competitors, generally in the host country, out of their national market. Once they have achieved this goal, then they are at liberty to increase prices, which in turn result in higher profits because of the elasticity of demand. Predatory pricing is of major concern to developing and poor nations when, as a result of globalization and deregulation, developed nations' firms with their efficiencies and resources enter their market. In response, developing countries undertake certain political and legal remedies that we will discuss in a moment.

MULTIPOINT PRICING

When two or more international firms compete against each other in two or more national marketplaces often one will adopt a **multipoint pricing strategy**. This strategy is sometimes referred to as "poking the bear." If one firm aggressively prices its product in

A **marginal analysis** is central to the concept of maximizing profit in an international environment. As long as the revenue received from the sale of an additional product (marginal revenue) is greater than the additional cost of production and selling that product (marginal cost), the firm should continue to expend its resources to expand output.

A **break-even analysis** identifies the point where total revenue and total costs are equal and beyond which profit will occur.

Predatory pricing is the use of price as a competitive weapon to force weaker competitors, generally in the host country, out of the market.

Multipoint pricing arises when the firm's pricing strategy in one shared market may have an impact on a competitor's pricing strategy in another shared market.

- Total cost (TC) is the sum of all the expenses incurred by a firm in producing and marketing the product. Adding all fixed and variable costs equals total cost.

$$TC = FC + VC$$

- Fixed costs (FC) are the firm's costs that do not vary depending on production or sales levels. These include expenses such as building rent, executive and administrative salaries, property taxes, interest expenses, and insurance.
- Variable costs (VC) are the firm's expenses, such as direct labour, materials, sales commissions, and overhead that fluctuate depending on the number of product units that are produced and sold. While the total variable cost changes with increased production, the total fixed costs stay the same.
- Unit variable cost (UVC) is the variable cost expressed on a per unit basis. Variable costs are directly linked to production; therefore, every increase in production results in an increase in variable costs that can be calculated to be a defined per unit dollar amount.
- Marginal cost (MC), also called incremental cost, is the cost associated with producing and marketing one additional unit.

FIGURE 13.5
Five Cost Concepts

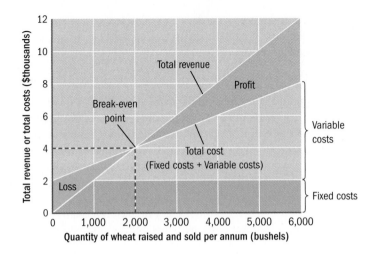

one country to the detriment of the competitor in that country, then the injured competitor may reciprocate in another country where the injured competitor has a marketplace advantage over the offender. Marketing managers must be aware that increasing or decreasing the prices for their good in one country may well have a ripple effect and provoke a response from competitors in another venue.

EXPERIENCE CURVE PRICING

The third pricing strategy we will look at has, in part, been previously discussed. This price-point strategy is determined by the firm's experience curve. Recognizing that the price per unit drops as the quantity is increased, firms will move quickly, even if it means taking a short-term loss to move down the production possibility frontier (PPF) curve and capture efficiencies to enable the firm to produce goods at a significantly lower price than others in the market or others contemplating entering the market. This marketing strategy provides a strong barrier to entry for those who might follow. If successful, this strategy will generally drive many competitors out of the market and may result in a monopoly. Governments may intervene if this strategy is too successful.

Political and Legal Variables

As we have noted, political and legal variables (factors) may affect a firm's ability to pursue either predatory pricing or experience curve pricing strategies. Specifically, if governments become concerned about the impact on indigenous firms because of the potential for the emergence of oligarchy or monopoly situations to develop, then they will become involved. Generally this involvement will take the form of the anti-**dumping** regulations and competition regulations. In the ongoing anti-dumping lumber dispute between the United States and Canada, the United States argue that Canadian lumber is "dumped" on the U.S. market at lower than the cost of production. Canada, like most nations, has put regulations in place to promote competition and to restrict monopolies in key industries. Canada's movie cinema industry provides a good example. Canada's Competition Bureau found that given the degree of concentration in the industry and the barriers to entry into the market, it was essential that Cineplex sell off 35 theatres to ensure that a merger did not result in a substantial prevention or lessening of competition.[27] Government can control prices or mark-ups; pass anti-trust legislation; impose import duties; pass tax laws; and implement transfer-pricing controls (see Chapter 16, pages 454–455).

Dumping is defined as selling goods at less than the cost of production.

Placement

Marketing placement is concerned with the distribution of a firm's goods and services. This involves managing distribution channels and developing market segmentation.

Distribution Channels

Distribution channels are the essential links either direct (owned and managed by the firm) or indirect (third parties, e.g., agents, distributors, wholesalers) that connect the firm with its customers; they are part of the firm's value chain. Selecting distribution channels is another of the major marketing mix decisions that once made will be difficult to change. Accordingly, it is important that all variables be fully considered prior to entering into distribution channel arrangements. Often the firm will have to relinquish some control over the marketing of its products. It is important that distribution channels be properly imbedded and staffed in order to seamlessly integrate the activity into the firm's value chain. In designing the distribution channel, marketing managers will consider whether the market is concentrated or fragmented and the length and width of the channel. Some channels will be direct and others can be "sourced" to independent distribution channel managers.

CONCENTRATED OR FRAGMENTED

Retail systems are said to be concentrated or fragmented. They are **concentrated** when a few retailers supply most of the market. Conversely, where there are many retailers with no particular market leader, the retail market is referred to as **fragmented**. There is evidence to support the notion that developed countries generally have a concentrated retail system. This has come about in part because of the economies of scale, size of firms, transportation infrastructure, and communications. However, some developed countries, such as Japan, because of historical and cultural considerations, have maintained traditional distribution channels. Fragmented marketplaces are more likely to be found in developing countries where these variables just mentioned are not as advanced. Accordingly, a great number of firms and individuals are needed in the distribution channels to move product from manufacturers to consumers who may well be 2,000 miles in the outback. Research conducted "in a minority region in China (a tradition-based culture) indicates that culture influences consumer behaviour regarding product distribution. It is noted that the cultural orientation of the ethnic group of consumers has helped to establish and maintain, through vendor loyalty, plenty of small retailers supported by inefficient, multi-tiered distribution networks. It makes the Chinese state-owned retail businesses far from . . . profitable let alone the foreign commercial institutions. Similarly, . . . cultural overtones in marketing operations are derived, to some extent, from consumer preferences. . . . They suggest that 'the cultural characteristics of a target market will be responsive to certain culturally bound channel structures, such as local stores, or bazaars. . . .' "[28]

LENGTH

We use the term **channel length** to describe the number of intermediaries between a manufacturer and the final consumer. If the manufacturer sells directly to the consumer, we say the channel is very short. The founder of Dell Inc., Michael Dell, shortened his firm's distribution channel in order to obtain sustainable competitive advantage over Big Blue (IBM) because IBM was unable to readily replicate a shorter distribution channel, thereby mitigating Dell's competitive advantage. Fragmented retail systems, for the reasons just stated, will tend to have longer channel lengths than Canadian firms in Canada. With 45 percent of business being conducted online, channel lengths have shortened. Manufacturers using this technology sell directly to the ultimate consumer using only a delivery service as an intermediary.

WIDTH

The width of existing national distribution channels can present challenges for foreign firms. A **narrow distribution channel** exists when there are few options available to move product from the manufacturer to the consumer or when it is difficult for outsiders to access the channel. This situation can come about for historical, cultural, and sometimes political reasons. It results in distribution channels with invisible barriers that are difficult for foreign manufacturers to breach. Japan provides an example of cultural relationships and norms that do not permit easy access to nonindigenous firms. Fortunately,

Distribution channels are the essential links either direct (owned and managed by the firm) or indirect (third parties, e.g., agents, distributors, wholesalers) that connect the firm with its customers.

The market is said to be **concentrated** when a few retailers supply most of the market.

Where there are many retailers and no particular market leader, the retail market is referred to as **fragmented**.

Channel length describes the number of intermediaries between a manufacturer and the final consumer.

A **narrow distribution channel** exists when there are few options available to move product from the manufacturer to the consumer or when it is difficult for outsiders to access the channel.

A **wide distribution channel** occurs when there are many options to move the goods from the manufacturer to the ultimate consumer and barriers to entering the channel are few.

globalization is breaking down these traditional barriers and the global distribution channels' playing fields are becoming more level. A **wide distribution channel** occurs when there are many options to move the goods from the manufacturer to the ultimate consumer and barriers to entry of the nature we just discussed are few.

FACTORS TO CONSIDER WHEN DESIGNING A NEW DISTRIBUTION CHANNEL

Marketing managers should consider a number of factors when establishing a new distribution channel:

- *Customers.* What are the demographic and psychographic characteristics of the firm's customers? You will need to know their needs, and why and how they will use your product when determining the distribution channel.
- *Culture.* What is the distribution culture of the market? Are firms entering host countries required to adopt existing distribution structures and channels? Indeed, some countries have legislation requiring, for example, that only firms that are 100 percent host-country-owned firms provide distribution activities. Other countries prohibit the use of independent dealers as was the case in China with Avon and Amway.
- *Competitors.* Do all competitors use the same channels?
- *Company Objectives.* Does the firm's management strategy conflict with the channel design being considered? Often the marketing division of the firm will get out in front of the administrative side of the firm. As a result, the supply and service support activities "lines" are stretched.
- *Nature of the Product.* The nature of the good will affect the design of the channel. Is the product specialized, expensive, bulky, perishable, or does it require after-sales services? If so, it is likely that the channel will be relatively short.
- *Capital Cost.* Is the initial capital available to establish the contemplated distribution channel? The stronger the firm's finances the more likely the firm will own and control the activity.
- *Ongoing Cost.* What are the ongoing costs to maintain the channel?
- *Coverage.* How well will the firm be represented, and over what geographical area?
- *Control.* Does the strategy or product require the firm to exercise strong control? Generally, the longer the channel the more difficult it is for marketing managers to control pricing, promotion, and venue.
- *Ongoing Support.* Foreign distributors generally want regular product upgrades, new lines, and support for the product.
- *Communication.* Two-way communication flowing in a timely fashion is necessary for all parties in the supply chain.
- *E-Commerce.* Offering goods and services over the Web has grown significantly and has enabled shorter distribution channels. This is a 24-hour service that requires marketing managers to understand the regulatory rules and possess customs handling expertise for each jurisdiction in which they conduct business. Many of the previous challenges with respect to response delivery capabilities have been overcome by outsourcing services or by building international distribution with air express carriers that offer full-service packaging, enable access to their own Internet infrastructure 24 hours a day, and provide customs clearance and e-mail shipment notification. Notwithstanding English being perceived as the lingua franca of the Web, studies indicate that customers are three times more likely to purchase products offered for sale in their own language.[29] Accordingly, firms competing in a global marketplace may consider having their website offerings in several languages. Once again, firms are cautioned to be aware of governments' growing governance role in e-commerce.

Market Segmentation

Markets consist of customers with similar needs and others whose needs are not so similar. Customers differ in the benefits they want; the price they are able or willing to pay; media they view (e.g., television, newspapers, radio stations); the quantities they purchase; and the place and time they purchase the product. The challenge for marketers is to design and deliver relevant products and services efficiently and effectively to their customers. To do this they need to sell using a "rifle approach" rather than an expensive "shot gun" approach that has little focus and wastes the firm's valuable resource. They need to achieve value for money by segmenting the market. **Segmentation** involves subdividing markets, channels, or customers into groups with different needs, and delivering tailored products or services that meet these needs as precisely as possible. While marketing segmentation has in the past been widely thought of as an art, not a science, today's technology and pervasive electronic databases are shifting this view. There are two segmentation variables: needs and profilers.

The basic criterion for segmenting a market is to do it along the lines of customers' needs. To find the needs of customers it will be necessary to undertake market research, both secondary and primary.

Profilers are the descriptive, measurable customer characteristics (such as location, age, nationality, gender, and income). The four most common profilers used in customer segmentation are geographic (region of the country, urban or rural); demographic (age, sex, family size, income, occupation, education, religion, race, and nationality); psychographic (social class, lifestyle type, personality type); and behavioural (product usage—e.g., light, medium, heavy users; brand loyalty—none, medium, high; and the type of user—e.g., with meals, special occasions). See the International Strategic Thinking box on page 366.

> **Segmentation** involves subdividing markets, channels, or customers into groups with different needs, and delivering tailored products or services that meet these needs as precisely as possible.

Promotion

A major challenge for marketing managers is promotion and its relationship to the other elements of the marketing mix. The tools for communicating marketing messages are referred to as a promotional mix. The promotional mix includes advertising, personal selling, sales promotion, publicity, and public relations. Each has a distinct role. The goal of these activities is to raise awareness, educate, and promote the offering in the broadest sense in order to sell the product or service in the host marketplace. It is important to underscore that promotional activities are not solely focused on the firm's customers but are also designed to raise the awareness of all those involved and those who might be able to influence the success of the firm. This at times could include educating governments, NGOs, and others. The questions raised by the international marketing managers are the same questions raised with other functional managers within the firm's value chain, such as production. For example, can the same message be used in all countries or will a modified or different message be required?

Global Advertising

Advertising approaches can be viewed on a continuum with the tailored approach at one end, a hybrid approach in the centre, and the universal approach, where one size fits all, at the other end.

THE TAILORED APPROACH

Sometimes the societal-cultural differences found in various host marketplaces can be so significant that each venue must be seen as a watertight compartment. Tailored approaches are designed to meet a specific customer view, often within a specific region. Even in Canada, there are significant difference in regions: consider a Quebec customer vis-à-vis a Newfoundland customer. Would you promote products differently? Indeed, would the respective provincial legislation mandate that you do? See the Evidence Box for a number of wonderful examples. I specifically liked the Gerber baby food clip with the picture of the baby on the label; clearly a case requiring that advertising adopt a tailored approach.

THE HYBRID APPROACH

The hybrid approach, as the name suggests, blends two or more cultures in the marketing promotional activities. Increasingly in Canada, diversity advertising showing visible minorities using the products demonstrates the success of this approach. Recently I watched a television advertisement in California, which has a very large Hispanic population. The Subway sandwich commercial featured Chinese actors emphasizing the taste of the product. While the company's pitch to the general market is as a healthy alternative to fast food, Hispanic customers are more concerned about taste. This advertisement focused on a Hispanic message without a word of Spanish or any Hispanic faces. Not a very good advertising approach.

THE UNIVERSAL APPROACH

Market leaders that target global segments usually adopt the universal advertising approach. Generally, things like industrial machinery can be advertised using the universal approach. This approach can be very efficient when used with the appropriate product (e.g., advertising commodities like crystal-clear Canadian water).

Cultural Sensitivity Communications Faux Pas

Here are few examples of how even a small lack of cultural sensitivity can quickly defeat a firm's marketing effort. In making these observations, we of course understand that we're dealing with individuals and the national stereotypes that we refer to will not always apply. Enjoy!

"Crayola has changed color names over time due to the civil rights movement and other social pressures. In 1962, Binney & Smith replaced flesh with peach, in recognition of the wide variety of skin tones. More recently, in 1999, they changed Indian red to chestnut. The color was not named after Native Americans, it was actually named for a special pigment that came from India. But school children often assumed the incorrect origin of the name."

"Volkswagen named the sedan version of Golf the Jetta. However, the letter 'J' doesn't exist in the Italian alphabet, so Jetta is pronounced 'Ietta,' which means Misfortune."

"A few years back Reed Business News relaunched itself with the branding: 'If it's news to you, it's news to us.' It was replaced after a couple of days."

"According to TravelBiz.com.au in April, 2003 the Hong Kong Tourist Board tried to either pull their ads or have their slogan changed. But it was too late to change the campaign that was on billboards throughout Hong Kong and in British versions of *Cosmopolitan* and *Condé Nast Traveller*. The slogan that was running *'Hong Kong: It will take your breath away'* unfortunately coincided with the SARS epidemic that resulted in numerous deaths. Shortness of breath is one of the main symptoms of SARS."

"When American Airlines wanted to advertise its new leather first class seats in the Mexican market, it translated its 'Fly In Leather' campaign literally, which meant 'Fly Naked' ('vuela en cuero') in Spanish!"

"Clairol introduced the 'Mist Stick,' a curling iron, into Germany only to find out that 'mist' is slang for manure. Not too many people had use for the 'manure stick.'"

"Coors put its slogan, 'Turn it loose' into Spanish, where it was read as 'Suffer from diarrhea.'"

Urban legend has it that "when Gerber started selling baby food in Africa, they used the same packaging as in the US, with the beautiful Caucasian baby on the label. Later they learned that in Africa, companies routinely put pictures on the label of what's inside, since most people can't read."

"In Chinese, the Kentucky Fried Chicken slogan 'finger-lickin' good' came out as 'eat your fingers off.'"

It is important to remember Sun Tzu's advice to employ local guides when designing your marketing materials for foreign lands!

Adapted from Tex Texin, *Translations That (Allegedly) Embarrassed Their Marketing Departments* (Marketing Translation Mistakes, March 5, 2006).

Communication Strategy

Communication strategy involves choosing suitable communication objectives, and identifying brand awareness and brand attitude strategies that are in harmony with marketplace consumer behaviours.

Another component of the marketing mix is the firm's communication strategy. **Communication strategy** involves choosing suitable communication objectives, and identifying brand awareness and brand attitude strategies that are in harmony with marketplace consumer behaviours. How should a firm inform target customers about products and services? Will it adopt a push, pull, or convergence marketing strategy? To what extent can communications adopt a global "one size fits all" strategy for advertising? Are there any cultural impediments that must be accommodated? Is there a need for separate languages in the communications strategy? Are there different dialects? Different geography may require a distinctive advertising theme. Countries with lower literacy rates will require user labels that are very simple and possibly shown in a pictorial fashion. What difference does colour make? Will religion affect communications? Are there special legal requirements for advertising products, such as cigarettes and pharmaceuticals, that must be observed? Is there media available? What is the trademark law? Are there taxes on advertising? These are just a few of the factors that must be considered in crafting the firm's communication plan. We will examine some below; others have been introduced elsewhere in the text. The Just Doing the Right Thing box shows a new communication plan with a new mental model.

Push-Pull-Convergence Marketing

To sell your product you must effectively promote and advertise it. The two traditional promotion strategies are push and pull. Within the last few years, a third model has emerged, driven by technology and cheap transportation: convergence marketing.

Push Strategy

The **push strategy** maximizes the use of all available channels of distribution, including the firm's sales force and trade promotion activities, to create consumer demand for a product. A push strategy centres on personal selling rather than mass media advertising. It tends to focus on the next member down the distribution channel rather than on the end consumer. In essence, the manufacturer pushes the offering down the value chain to the customer. This traditional approach may be dangerous to your international marketing efforts: pushing your services and capabilities at your clients could, because of culture and other factors, result in them being turned off. A push strategy tries to sell directly to the consumer (e.g.,

> A **push strategy** centres on personal selling rather than mass media advertising. It tends to focus on the next member down the distribution channel rather than on the end consumer. In essence, the manufacturer pushes the offering down the value chain to the customer.

JUST DOING THE RIGHT THING

Is Wal-Mart Just Doing the Right Thing?

Twice since November 2005, Wal-Mart has made significant announcements about how it buys seafood. Wal-Mart is changing how it buys shrimp, and how it buys the wild-caught fish that it sells in grocery stores across North America. . . . [Wal-Mart is the #1 retailer in Mexico, Canada, and the United States.] Two things are striking about the seafood buying news from Wal-Mart. First, if Wal-Mart takes its own rules seriously, the new standards could have a dramatic impact on fish, the environment, and on competitors. Wal-Mart has taken the uncharacteristic step of turning to third parties to provide both the environmental standards and the certification that suppliers are meeting those standards. In the case of the shrimp it buys from shrimp

farms—shrimp is a third of all seafood Wal-Mart sells—the company is working with the Global Aquaculture Alliance and the Aquaculture Certification Council. The standards for shrimp farms include the protection of indigenous mangrove and seagrass beds, and effluent standards regulating the discharge of pollution from the shrimp farms.

Wal-Mart's wild-caught fish will only come from certified sustainable waters. The Marine Stewardship Council monitors and certifies that selected waters are managed in a healthy and sustainable fashion so that the natural stocks of fish will replenish themselves. . . . Why is this initiative of interest? Because Wal-Mart's sales of shrimp and fish are so large they can significantly impact the good practice standards of global shrimp farms. Wal-Mart's initiative will influence other firms who will have little choice but to follow the

leviathan's lead. "Environmental and sustainability standards aren't about 'always low prices, always'—they are about making sure that the price of seafood in the display case at a Wal-Mart . . . actually includes the real costs of the seafood, including things like the 'cost' of preventing pollution." Clearly this time Wal-Mart is just doing the right thing!

Adapted from Charles Fishman, *The Wal-Mart Blog: Day Two* (FC Now: The Fast Company Weblog, March 7, 2006).

CRITICAL THINKING QUESTIONS

Should we be cynical about this marketing communication? Is Wal-Mart wrapping itself in green? Has Wal-Mart adopted a new marketing mental model that competitors will have to follow? Do you think you could make a business case for your firm to follow Wal-Mart's lead?

selling insurance or holidays directly), bypassing other distribution channels. With this type of strategy, consumer promotions and advertising are the most likely promotional tools. However, none of us want to be receiving hundreds of telemarketing pitches every day! A second shortcoming for international markets is that production and distribution are based on often-erroneous forecasts resulting in, for example, over- or undersupply of the product. A good example of push selling is mobile phones; major handset manufacturers such as Nokia promote their products via retailers like Shaw in Canada. Nokia offers subsidies on the handsets to encourage retailers like Shaw to sell higher volumes.

Pull Strategy

A **pull strategy** requires the customer to demand that the product be available in the marketplace. It is generally accomplished with a major commitment to advertising and promotion, thereby creating a demand the retailers (channels) cannot ignore.

A **pull strategy** requires that customers demand that the product be available in the marketplace. It is generally accompanied by a major commitment to advertising and promotion, thereby creating a demand the retailers (channels) cannot ignore. Those of you old enough to recall the original Cabbage Patch Kids will remember that parents actually fought each other in the stores to purchase them for Christmas when they were first introduced. Clearly a great example of a pull strategy, as parents demanded that the retail toy stores order them. Today, of course, it is no longer dolls that adopt very successful international pull strategies but technology like the Microsoft X-box 360 game system.

Convergence Marketing

Convergence marketing occurs when customers collaborate with their suppliers to tailor a product or service that better meets the needs of the customer.

Wal-Mart's Efficient Consumer Response (ECR) initiatives emphasize information sharing and collaboration between grocers and their suppliers, also known as convergence marketing. **Convergence marketing** occurs when customers work (collaborate) with their suppliers to tailor a product or service to better meet the needs of the customer. Convergence marketing is widely available on the Web to purchase automobiles, furniture, clothes, and other products. Customers are given the electronic tools to design and tailor the products they wish to buy. Convergence marketing is not pushed at them, nor is it pulled down the value chain; rather, it is a hybrid between these two traditional strategies that permits the customer to research the product offering and make an informed decision. In this example, "retailers work with suppliers to select the optimal mix of products to display on store shelves. To replenish store shelves, retailers inform suppliers as soon as goods leave a store, which helps suppliers to better manage store inventory. New products are jointly developed by manufacturers and retailers to improve the chances of product success."[30] Technology is the driver.

Strengthening Marketing Relationships

In closing this section, a word about the "army of one." Customers want to feel special. They want to be treated as individuals. They want a one-to-one relationship. As a result of globalization and technological advances, this is increasingly possible. Canadian SMEs must build strong one-to-one international customer relationships. Marketing experts suggest "in trying to appeal to a more powerful customer base, your company might pursue a strategy of relationship marketing."[31] Today, firms develop and emphasize customer satisfaction metrics, create consistency in customer interfaces, build better products through Total Quality Management, and enhance personalized service. Customer Relationship Management (CRM) software provides the data and functionality needed for one-to-one marketing and the prerequisite consistent interface. "By putting the 'custom' back in customers, these companies can target their customers better and can deliver persuasive information and promotions more efficiently."[32] However, be careful in how you use this "army of one" mental model. When used correctly, firms can create a close positive relationship with customers; however, if used poorly, the customer will see it as an invasive and somewhat questionable ethical marketing tactic.

New CRM software will enable you to grow large databases to identify segments; nevertheless, by using that information to target aggressive e-mail, phone, or Internet promotions, with or without customer permission, your impertinence and aggressive cross-selling can make customers feel you have exploited the relationship. "No wonder 55% of CRMs have not succeeded. If your CRM is a push system, it is not going to work well in this world of customer power. You need to fulfill the dream of CRM by building a long-run trust, but even this may not be enough. Advocacy is an effective new strategy and you should consider it. Your company might choose to embrace advocacy by becoming a faithful representative of your customers' interests. Under this approach, you provide customers and prospects with open, honest, and complete information. You give them advice so that they can find the best products, even if those products are not your company's products. . . . Of course, if you embrace honesty, you will need to have very good, if not the best, products. . . . Advocacy is not a way for your company to speak *at* customers. Rather, . . . It is a partnership between you and your customers for everyone's mutual benefit. You are building trust and levering that trust to build your brand. You advocate for their interest, and they advocate for you by buying your products and helping you design better products. Most importantly, they tell other customers about your firm and products."[33]

Research and Development

The ability to commercialize research and development (R&D) is a critical determinant of a country's capacity to innovate. R&D is also a key contributor to the competitiveness of Canadian firms. High-growth Canadian SMEs are more likely to invest in R&D for products, services, and process activities. While one-quarter of Canadian SMEs stated that they invested in R&D in 2000, this number increased to 34 percent among high-growth SMEs.[34] However, no matter the size, R&D activities are a key part of firms' business investment strategies. Even in the smallest firms, one in five makes an investment in R&D. In our open world economy, R&D and innovation will be essential for maintaining the competitiveness of Canada's economy.

More R&D and innovation translates into productivity gains and enterprises better equipped to face international competition. Innovation and productivity go hand in hand. Innovation helps to improve production processes, produce at better cost, and reinforce management processes, resulting in more productive, more profitable enterprises better equipped to sustain competition. Measurements of productivity include labour productivity, capital productivity or total productivity of production factors, but the most frequently used unit of measurement is value added per hour worked, or labour productivity.

If Canadian firms are to remain competitive in the international marketplace, they must increase innovation, adopt new technology, and adopt new mental models. "In the face of an increasingly complex international business environment, a management culture is needed . . . based on an open, decentralized corporate leadership style, continuing development of new competencies, establishment of internal and external networks, and ongoing use of innovation derived from research and development in all its forms."[35]

Unfortunately, Canada lags far behind the United States and the average of G7 countries with respect to gross domestic expenditure on R&D.[36] Canada's backwardness with respect to the G7 countries is primarily attributable to its R&D funding structure. In 2004, the private sector accounted for only 47.1 percent of gross expenditures in R&D (GERD) in Canada, compared with 61.9 percent for the OECD nations, despite the existence in Canada of R&D tax incentives among the most generous of any industrialized country.[37] Notwithstanding the generous R&D tax support, Canada must provide increased funding for both the direct and indirect costs of research, the renewal and expansion of research infrastructure, and the expansion of programs for graduate studies. If Canada is to excel as a knowledge-based nation, Canadian researchers must be given the tools to push the frontier of knowledge, thereby positioning Canada to succeed in the international marketplace.

"New, much more demanding business processes are a necessity for SMEs, such as integration of logistics chains, just-in-time production and delivery, prime contractors' ever-growing requirements in terms of quality and ongoing cost reduction, much shorter product development cycles and a substantial reduction in products' useful lives."[38] To accomplish this, Canadian SMEs will have to undertake more R&D. Canadian MNEs have understood the need to adopt new, higher-performance business practices; unfortunately this reality seems much less obvious to Canadian SMEs: "Traditionally isolated most of the time, SMEs now have to learn to operate in networks (of suppliers, competitors, clients and specialists) and to conduct strategic, technological and commercial watch activities."[39]

As mentioned earlier, innovation ensures the sustained productivity growth that is essential to maintaining enterprises' competitiveness. For example, "new information and communications technology (NICT) can be used to do business differently and is a powerful strategic lever accessible to SMEs to enhance their productivity and competitiveness. Electronic business goes far beyond mere e-commerce to encompass all the SMEs' business and management processes including work organization, production, inventory management and relations with suppliers and clients. NICTs also help reinforce the . . . [ecosystem scanning capabilities] that are essential for maintaining [their] competitiveness."[40] Canadian SMEs must undertake R&D on new information communications technology and harness its power to enhance their competitive performance in the global marketplace.

"Government R&D expenditures are an integral part of a comprehensive innovation support strategy. . . . Public support for innovation and research is not restricted to direct government spending. Over the past few decades, Canada has developed an R&D and innovation tax incentive system (including R&D tax credits) that is among the most generous in the industrialized world, striding ahead of the United States, France, Japan and Sweden in this regard, according to the experts. Within Canada, Quebec is the province that offers the most attractive tax treatment for R&D both for large corporations and for SMEs. In comparison, Ontario ranks eighth for large corporations and sixth for SMEs."[41]

"Canada's performance in innovation is slightly declining. Canada's gross domestic expenditure on research and development (GERD) as a percentage of GDP has decreased from 2.05% in 2001 to 1.89% in 2004. In terms of other measures of innovation, such as Canada's world share in triadic patent families and science and engineering article outputs, Canada is behind the U.S. and other G-7 countries."[42] The numbers presented here vary slightly from those provided by the OECD shown in Figure 13.7. However, the message is the same: Canada does not spend enough on R&D!

"The weak support for R&D from Canada's private sector is, nonetheless, somewhat offset by a more intense effort from the university community, which performs 30% of R&D in Canada compared with 13.9% for the U.S. and 17.1% for the OECD."[43] Specifically, Canada's top 50 research universities posted over $5 billion in sponsored research income for fiscal 2004.[44] Canada's top R&D firms in 2005 were Nortel Networks Corporation, Bell Canada, Magna International Inc., Pratt & Whitney Canada Corp and ATI Technologies Inc.[45] Visit www.power.nelson.com for an in-depth overview of Canada's top 20 R&D firms.

FIGURE 13.7

Gross Domestic Expenditures on R&D (GERD) as a Percentage of Gross Domestic Product for Selected OECD Countries

Country	1998	1999	2000	2001	2002	2003	2004
Canada	**1.76**	**1.80**	**1.92**	**2.09**	**2.03**	**1.97**	**1.96**
France	2.17	2.18	2.18	2.23	2.26	2.19	–
Germany	2.31	2.44	2.49	2.51	2.53	2.55	–
Italy	1.07	1.04	1.07	1.11	1.16	–	–
Japan	2.95	2.96	2.99	3.07	3.12	3.15	–
Sweden[1]	–	3.65	–	4.27	–	–	–
U.K.	1.80	1.87	1.86	1.87	1.90	1.89	–
U.S.A[2]	2.60	2.65	2.72	2.73	2.66	2.60	–

[1]Underestimated or based on underestimated data.

[2]Excludes most or all capital expenditures

SOURCE: Main Science and Technology Indicators, No. 1, DSTI, OECD, 2005. Copyright OECD. All rights reserved.

R&D Global Considerations

Canadian firms that successfully develop and market new products as a result of R&D are well positioned to earn above-average returns. First, after deciding whether to undertake research, how to obtain development funding, and the source of funding (government or private sector), firms must also consider the best location to conduct their research and development. The Canadian government fiscally supports research in the university sector. Global firms will research funding availability when selecting R&D locations. Firms will also consider, and be influenced by, consumers' demands and expectations of the product or service, and consumers with disposable income to purchase the new innovative outputs. Recall Michael Porter's determinants of national competitive advantage model in Chapter 6, pages 167–169. The selection of R&D locations will be influenced in a positive way if the competition is fierce.

A second consideration is to ensure that R&D is not undertaken in "silos" but rather as a seamlessly integrated activity that includes input from all functional managers within the supply chain, specifically production and marketing. Remember, the firm's marketing team is on the front line and collects new market intelligence daily. This includes observations of customers' satisfaction with the current product and identifies possible new product offerings or modifications they would like to see on existing products. The marketing team can provide fertile ground for the R&D staff to examine when looking for ways to innovate. By taking an integrated approach that includes all managers within the supply chain, specifically marketing, production, and R&D, the firm can be sure that new product development innovations will be undertaken in direct response to the firm's customers' needs; that the new products or services offered will be manufactured and designed most efficiently; that the firm's research and development initiatives are focused, thereby keeping development costs under control; and the firm's innovative new products and services will be supplied in a speedy and timely basis. A caveat: decision makers should be prepared to accept that only a small percentage of R&D initiatives will make a return on investment. But when they do, the rewards may be extraordinary.

Third, the firm might consider establishing a cross-functional team for R&D and/or selection/approval teams. Headed by a strong "champion," the team would consist of decision makers representing all activities in the firm's value chain. While technology permits for video conferencing and team meetings conducted at a distance, it is important that the team bond. Therefore, firms should consider face-to-face meetings occasionally. The cross-functional team must establish policies and processes to evaluate new initiatives. The evaluation must be open, transparent, and swift in accepting or rejecting new R&D proposals. The policies and procedures must be well communicated to all in the firm. The process approval must be easy to carry out, transparent, and designed to encourage input from all team members.

Fourth, the entire R&D process must be proactive and free of bureaucratic barriers. Finally, the firm's culture must encourage innovation. Employees can be encouraged by bonuses and incentives for submitting new thoughts.

Marketing of Services

We need to spend a few moments looking specifically at the nuances of marketing services—a major component of Canada's GNP. While there are many similarities between marketing tangible products and marketing services, some key differences will require attention when marketing in an international environment. Although it is difficult to find a product that does not have some service component (see Figure 13.8, page 382), to the extent that the firm provides mostly services, the more important the following observations become.

The special nature of service comes about because of the characteristics that distinguish it from a tangible product. These characteristics create special marketing challenges for international Canadian SMEs. The first characteristic is the notion that a service is intangible. It cannot be tasted, felt, seen, heard, or smelled. As a consequence, when advertising your service, it is important that you emphasize the benefit to be derived rather than the service itself. This can be accomplished in a number of ways—first, by visualization. For example, you can communicate travel services by showing customers on a beach with their laptop, or you might communicate through association with a tangible object, person, or place. For example, the Australian airline communicates the warm and friendly image of Australia by using a koala bear. Physical representation can also be used to communicate. Examples displaying the positive images of service representatives demonstrate trustworthiness, dependency, and cleanliness when marketing seniors' housing. The physical documentation you provide with your service, such as warranties, demonstrates a commitment of service quality to the customer—the muffler is guaranteed for life.

The second characteristic is that services are inseparable. The service is created, dispensed, and consumed simultaneously. Customers' opinions about the service are based on the firm's consumption chain—the points of contact with the firm from one end of the purchasing process to the after-service follow-up. The face-to-face interaction customers have with your firm's personnel will form their impressions of the company. It is important that the firm's international personnel think of themselves not just as producers of product and marketers but also as "creators of service."

The third characteristic is that service is diverse in character, meaning that it is generally difficult for global service providers to standardize their service. Each "unit of service" varies from employee to employee, from customer to customer, and from country to country. Recently, technology has assisted by bringing innovative, and sometimes not so innovative, service products to assist in quality control of the services provided. For example, voice messaging systems and bank machines for dispensing money assist firms in quality control. Remember, service is perishable and the demands for it fluctuate. Consultants, who sell their time, quickly recognize this reality. Their time cannot be stored. Demand for their services increases and decreases often beyond the control of the consultant service provider, thereby making it difficult to instantly accommodate the fluctuating demand with the same service provider.

Four Rs of Service Marketing

Just as there are the 4Ps of marketing; there are 4Rs of international service marketing. In marketing services, we still pay attention to the 4Ps but they are insufficient to ensure customers' satisfaction. It is also important for a firm's service providers to provide for relationship, retention, referrals, and recovery. Service providers must build relationships; theirs must be more than a contractual contact. Take an interest in the customers' well-being and family. It will pay great dividends. For example, retailers of Saturn automobiles hold picnics and barbecues for Saturn owners. In Mexico, often the family is more important than business considerations. As we have discussed, technology-enabled customer databases promote these relationships. Firms that build relationships are profitable as customer loyalty is critical to success of the service firm.

You want to forge an emotional connection with your customers. The importance of satisfied customers is reflected when you retain their business and they refer your firm's services to their friends and associates. In Asian cultures, this aspect takes on even greater significance (see Chapter 2, page 43).

FIGURE 13.8

Degree of Service

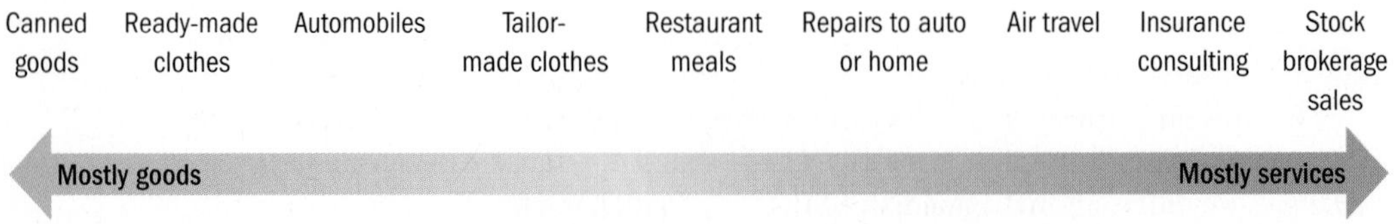

Canned goods	Ready-made clothes	Automobiles	Tailor-made clothes	Restaurant meals	Repairs to auto or home	Air travel	Insurance consulting	Stock brokerage sales

← Mostly goods   Mostly services →

Word-of-mouth referrals produce large volumes of new business. Conversely, a dissatisfied customer speaking negatively about the service she received can do great injury.

Recovery is the last characteristic. When something goes wrong with a service, marketers must recover the customer's satisfaction. You cannot afford to do nothing. The service quality that customers perceive is generally very difficult to measure. However, service quality that does not meet customer expectations can result in lost sales and failure to attract new customers. It is therefore important that the firm's global service manager introduce programs that lead to service quality and measure customer satisfaction. Remember, good service is what the customer says it is!

Customers consider five service factors as being critical. These are the primary service—the nature of the service itself; the secondary support services—the quality of the service required to ensure the primary service performs to expectations; technology service interface—the technical aspects of the process by which the service is delivered; the human dimension—the interaction with people who deliver the service; and the customer's perception of the service—how the customer feels during his interaction with the company and its employees—his feelings or impression. Management can influence these five factors.

Management Implications

- Marketing globally can be risky business if you don't divest yourself of your ethnocentric thinking. Consider your new market's language, work schedules, tastes, lifestyle choices, and cultural associations. We have yet to see the full impact of the open, global marketplace. Today, all raw materials and technology are available everywhere in the world. The only differences between countries and markets will be skill levels, education, and the level of empowerment of the workplace.

- Marketing leadership is important not only in vision and strategy setting, but also execution. Risks are company specific, and small companies face different risks and opportunities from big companies. Bridging scale and scope, local and global, is important. The importance of value chain integration cannot be overlooked, nor can international marketers' needs for local expertise. There is no single frame of mind or simple solution for any market. You must tailor your solution to your circumstances. Many risks Canadian SMEs face are driven by the bigger problem of political and economic instability, which also creates opportunities.

- Two trends will place even more pressure on Canadian SMEs' performance in the future. First, the revolution in international trade (global commerce) has entered a new phase called "integrative trade," which captures all of the elements firms use to achieve the lowest possible cost and maximize return on their products. Despite its membership in the G7, Canada is not among the seven leading economies of the world in terms of GDP. Its place in global economic rankings has been slipping.

PRACTICAL ENTREPRENEURIAL FOCUS

Guidelines to Minimize Cross-Cultural Mistakes

Adopt these guidelines to minimize possible cross-cultural marketing mistakes: "Be sensitive to do's and taboos. Develop cultural empathy. Recognize, understand, and respect another's culture and difference. Be culturally neutral and realize that different is not necessarily better or worse. Never assume transferability of a concept from one culture to another." For instance, if local businesspeople in developing countries tell you that they do not like Canadians, they may not mean that they do not want to buy Canadian goods. It simply means they are expected to say certain things in public, but that they may operate differently in private. And "get cultural [advisors] involved in the decision makings. Cultural [advisors] could be local businesspeople or very well trained anthropologists."

Adapted from Robert Guang Tian, "Cross-Cultural Issues in the 21st Century Marketing," *The Journal of Modern Business*, May 24, 2006.

Canada should seek to build a G20 of developed and emerging economic powers that reflects these new geopolitical circumstances. Second, the rise of the BRIC nations is a strong, and perhaps irresistible, force shaping the global economy. Canada should pursue new marketing opportunities overseas, particularly in emerging markets, while continuing to nurture our primary relationship with the United States.

- Managers must be prepared to challenge existing mental models. General Motors knows that national advertising is ineffective but spends billions on national advertising anyway because that is the way the company has always done it. There is hard evidence to look at advertising from the bottom up and to adopt a convergence-marketing model.
- Internet shopping is the number-two shopping destination—second only to discount department stores. Consumers cited convenience as the key factor.[46]
- Beware of "survival bias." We have a tendency to draw inferences from instances of success. For each instance of success, remember that there are thousands of other managers who have tried to do the same thing and failed. Conduct your due diligence prior to implementing your market entry strategy.
- R&D experimentation is critical: form hypotheses and test them. Success stories arise from the process. We learn from mistakes; they must be permitted.

CHAPTER SUMMARY

- The future is all about convergence: Dot.coms + not.coms, TV + computer, first world + third world, marketing + finance, and so on. At the end of this future is the centaur—the hybrid consumer who is tech savvy + uniquely human. We require new mental models.
- Technology has been a major catalyst to encourage change in how we view our customers. Increasingly, electronic networks enable customers to access a wealth of information about products and services that wasn't previously readily available. In thinking about our international marketing strategies we must be aware that the power has shifted in large measure to customers.
- Typically, emerging markets, including the BRIC countries and other countries in Eastern Europe, Asia, Africa, and South America, offer lucrative business potential and cannot be overlooked by Canadian SMEs. These countries represent approximately 80 percent of the global population and about 20 percent of the world's economies.
- The environment of international business is far more complex than the business environment faced by firms operating only in local venues; political, economic, societal, technical, and cultural marketing variables are generally significantly different in an international setting. International markets, particularly emerging markets, offer lucrative business opportunities. However, these opportunities

are accompanied by unique hazards. To protect your business and reduce your vulnerability, you must be aware of the issues, both present and emerging, from a number of international variables—PEST-C.

- Cross-cultural marketing demands that Canadian SMEs develop an awareness and sensitivity for cultural differences. Cross-cultural marketing is defined as the strategic process of marketing among consumers whose culture differs from that of the marketer's own culture in at least one of the fundamental cultural aspects (language, religion, social norms and values, education, and living style).
- Marketing managers have responsibility for evaluating their contribution to the firm's international value chain in order to find ways to "wring pennies out of the activities" and find ways to add value that will contribute to a higher product value in the mind of their firm's consumers.
- Three bundles of characteristics will influence the marketing manager's decisions as to whether the product must be adapted to the host country. The first is defined as regional, country, or local. The second bundle (product characteristics) includes the product constituents, brand, packaging, physical form or appearance (e.g., size, style, colour), functions, attributes, features, methods of operation or usage, durability, quality, ease of installation, maintenance, after-sales services, and country of origin. The third bundle is company considerations.

- The 4Ps are more complex in an international setting. Product strategies will be concerned with product variety, quality, design, features, brand name, packaging, sizes, services, warranties, and return processes. Pricing strategies will address the list price, discounts, allowances, and payment and credit terms. Placement strategy will be concerned with the channels of distribution, website, locations, transportation, and logistics. Promotional strategy will consider advertising, personal selling, website, publicity, and public relations. We have examined a number of these topics in other sections of the text; however, we reviewed a number of interesting adjustments to the 4Ps made necessary by the international ecosystem.

- The degree of goods and services adaptation will range from trivial, such as translating the user's manual, to substantial changes that might include manufacturing a "stripped-down" more economical version of the product for the host country.

- Customers want to feel special and to be treated as individuals. They want a one-to-one relationship. As a result of globalization and technological advances, this is becoming increasingly possible. Canadian SMEs must build strong one-to-one customer relationships.

- The ability to commercialize research and development (R&D) is a critical determinant of a country's capacity to innovate. R&D is also a key contributor to the competitiveness of Canadian firms; to ensure their future growth, Canadian SMEs will have to raise their innovation levels, increase their use of new technology, and agree to take a fresh look at their traditional ways of doing things. In the face of an increasingly complex international business environment, a new mental model of management culture is needed.

- In considering the best location to conduct R&D, firms will consider influences of demanding consumers, customers' disposable income, and the fierceness of competition.

- Service marketing requires special consideration because of the characteristics that distinguish it from a tangible product. These characteristics create special marketing challenges for Canadian SMEs.

REVIEW QUESTIONS

1. Provide some observations on the PEST-C variables as they relate to global marketing.
2. Research indicates that a society's culture can be characterized as a continuum between two extremes; tradition-based and modern-based. Explain what this means.
3. Sales professionals can be a treasure trove. What does this observation mean?
4. Virginia Yorio has suggested that there are three bundles of characteristics that will influence the marketing manager's decisions as to whether a product must be adapted. Outline them.
5. Marketing managers will craft their product, price, placement, and promotion strategies considering the same factors as they would for the domestic market except their analysis will be more complex. Explain some of these international marketplace complexities.
6. Using a model, explain the concept of price elasticity of demand.

7. The four cost concepts important in international pricing decisions are total cost, fixed costs, variable costs, and marginal costs. Explain each.
8. What are the global pricing strategies to be considered when setting international prices?
9. The challenge for marketers is to design and deliver relevant products and services efficiently and effectively to their customers. How do we do this?
10. What activities does the promotional mix include?
11. Explain push, pull, and convergence marketing strategies using examples.
12. Customers want to feel special and to be treated as individuals. How can this be accomplished?
13. How important is R&D to Canada?
14. What makes a location attractive for R&D?
15. Describe the characteristics that distinguish a service from a product.
16. What are the 4Rs of service marketing?

REFLECTIVE THINKING QUESTIONS

1. Having completed this chapter, reread the quotations on the first page, critically reflect on the validity of the authors' statements, and provide your opinion as to the validity of each. Evidence-based answers are preferred to rhetorical answers.
2. How we think about global marketing requires the adoption of a new mental model. Comment on the validity of this observation.

3. A troubling advance in technology is the ability to monitor customers' activities. It will be one of the biggest issues faced in the next decade. The question of how businesses use the customer information collected through technology will be balanced against the customers' right to privacy. Provide your thoughts.
4. Globalization and global marketing of Western liberalized democracy and its goods and services are both good and bad. Do you agree or disagree? Provide your reasons.

5. "Canada's performance in innovation is slightly declining. Canada's gross domestic expenditure on research and development (GERD) as a percentage of GDP has decreased from 2.05% in 2001 to 1.89% in 2004."[47] Should this be a concern?

GLOBAL E-RESEARCH

Visit www.power.nelson.com for research suggestions, questions, and a number of background discussion papers on this topic.

MINI CASE

Here are some interesting extracts from a wonderful and thought-provoking book. Although published over two decades ago, the material is still very relevant.

"In 1981 Joel Garreau, a writer for the *Washington Post,* wrote the book: *The Nine Nations of North America* (Houghton Mifflin, Boston). In that book Garreau writes: 'Forget the pious wisdom you've been handed about North America. Forget the borders dividing the United States, Canada, and Mexico, those pale barriers so thoroughly porous to money, immigrants, and ideas. Forget the bilge you were taught in sixth-grade geography about East and West, North and South, faint echoes of glorious pasts that never really existed save in sanitized textbooks. Forget the maze of state and provincial boundaries, those historical accidents and surveyors' mistakes. The reason no one except the trivia expert can name all fifty of the United States is that they hardly matter. Forget the political almanacs full of useless data on local elections rendered meaningless by strangely carved districts and precincts. Consider, instead, the way North America really works. It is Nine Nations. Each with its capital and distinctive web of power and influence. . . . These nations look different, feel different, and sound different from each other, and few of their boundaries match the political lines drawn on current

maps. . . . Most importantly, each nation has a distinctive prism through which it views the world.'"

Well, we won't completely forget the boundaries found on current maps, but we should turn our minds to the Nine Nations as defined by Garreau. Reflect on Garreau's view of North America as an aid to understanding marketing in North America.

Adapted from Joel Garreau, *Nine Nations of North America* (Houghton Miffin, 1981), as quoted by Mark L. Healy, *North America: Nine Nations* (World Regional Geography, Fall 2006).

QUESTIONS

1. As a marketer, can you find some support for the notion that we should view North America as "Nine Nations"?
2. If there is validity to the notion, how can you use this information in crafting North American marketing strategies?

Source: Joel Garreau, *Nine Nations of North America* (Houghton Mifflin, 1981), as quoted by Mark L. Healy, *North America: Nine Nations* (World Regional Geography, Fall 2006), retrieved September 16, 2006, from www.harpercollege.edu/~mhealy/g101ilec/namer/nac/nacnine/na9intro/nacninfr.htm.

ENDNOTES

[1] *Madeleine: An Autobiography,* Book 1 Chapter V (New York and London: Harper & Brothers Publishers, 1919), retrieved September 14, 2006, from http://digital.library.upenn.edu/women/madeleine/madeleine/madeleine.html.

[2] Roberto Goizueta, *BizWriter* (May 19, 2005), retrieved September 25, 2006, from http://bizwriter.wordpress.com/2005/05/19/marketing-quotes.

3 KPMG, *Companies Underestimate Challenges of Doing Business in China: KPMG Survey* (Media release, KPMG in Canada, 2004), retrieved August 25, 2006, from www.kpmg.ca/en/news/pr20040608.html.

4 Peter F. Drucker, *The Practice of Management* (New York: Harper Collins, 1954).

5 *Quote Garden* (2006), retrieved August 25, 2006, from www.quotegarden.com.

6 Leonard Arianto (Tan), *Sun Tzu's Art of War* (1996), retrieved August 25, 2006, from www.geocities.com/Athens/4884.

7 James McAllister, *The Battle of the Atlantic* (Phil's WWII Pages, May 15, 1998), retrieved August 25, 2006, from www.secondworldwar.co.uk/canada.html.

8 Yoram Wind, Vijay Mahajan, and Robert E. Gunther, *Convergence Marketing: Strategies for Reaching the New Hybrid Consumer* (Upper Saddle River, NJ: Prentice Hall, 2002).

9 Theodore Levitt, "The Globalization of Markets," *Harvard Business Review*, May–June 1983.

10 Ginza is the most exclusive and expensive shopping area in Japan. It is also known for having the most expensive real estate on earth.

11 Levitt, "The Globalization of Markets."

12 Thomas L. Friedman, *The World Is Flat*, 1st ed. (New York: Farrar, Straus and Giroux, 2005).

13 Ibid.

14 Canada Deloitte & Touche LLP, *Doing Business in Emerging Markets: Emerging Markets Can Be Lucrative. But How Can You Protect Your Company from Potential Risk?* (Deloitte Canada, 2004), retrieved August 25, 2006, from www.deloitte.com/dtt/article/0,1002,cid%253D83923,00.html.

15 "India's Windows XP Starter Delayed" (*Software Technology News*, March 17, 2005) retrieved September 13, 2006, from www.techweb.com/wire/software/159901570.

16 Agriculture and Agri-Food Canada, *The Canadian Snack Food Industry* (Food Processing, June 2, 2004), retrieved August 25, 2006, from www.agr.gc.ca/misb/fb-ba/index_e.php?s1=proc-trans&s2=prof&page=snack-grignot.

17 *OECD Information Technology Outlook* (2004), retrieved August 25, 2006, from www.oecd.org/dataoecd/20/47/33951035.pdf.

18 Robert Guang Tian, "Cross-Cultural Issues in the 21st Century Marketing," *The Journal of Modern Business*, May 24, 2006.

19 Tian, *Cross-Cultural Issues in the 21st Century Marketing*.

20 Ibid.

21 Ibid.

22 Kevin O'Marah, "Supply Chain-Driven Innovation," *Working Knowledge for Business Leaders*, December 12, 2005, retrieved September 13, 2006, from http://hbswk.hbs.edu/archive/5139.html.

23 Ibid.

24 Ibid.

25 Laura Lake, "Market Segmentation for the Small Business," *Marketing*, 2006, retrieved August 25, 2006, from http://marketing.about.com/cs/sbmarketing/a/smbizmrktseg_p.htm.

26 Virginia M.Yorio, *Adapting Products for Export* (New York: Conference Board, 1983).

27 Tim Weil, *Competition Bureau Screens Cinema Merger: Cineplex Must Sell Off 35 Theatres* (Government of Canada, Competition Bureau, July 26, 2005), retrieved

August 25, 2006, from www.competitionbureau.gc.ca/internet/index.cfm?itemID=1866&lg=e.

28 Tian, *Cross-Cultural Issues in the 21st Century Marketing*

29 Hope Katz Gibbs, "Taking Global Local," *Global Business Online*, December 12, 1999, as cited by Philip J. Rosson, "The Internet and SME Exporting: Canadian Success Stories" (*Internet Exporting*, September 2000), retrieved September 13, 2006, from http://cibs.management.dal.ca/a013-papers/DP-179.pdf#search=%22Gibbs%20%22Taking%20Global%20Local%22%22.

30 Stephen Martinez and Hayden Stewart, "From Supply Push to Demand Pull: Agribusiness Strategies for Today's Consumers" (*Amber Waves*, November 2003), retrieved September 13, 2006, from www.strategicagreview.com/e_article000196616.cfm?x=[[IMN.LID]],[[IMN.USER_ID.

31 Glen L. Urban, *Don't Just Relate—Advocate! Now Is the Time to Advocate for Your Customers* (Philadelphia: Wharton School Publishing, 2005).

32 Ibid.

33 Ibid.

34 Patrick Huot and Christine Carrington, "High Growth SMEs" (*Small Business Financing Profiles*, May 2006), retrieved September 16, 2006, from www.sme-fdi.gc.ca/epic/internet/insme_fdi-prf_pme.nsf/en/h_01540e.html.

35 Ibid.

36 Organisation for Economic Co-operation and Development, *Main Science and Technology Indicators (MSTI: 2006/1 edition)*, retrieved August 25, 2006, from www.oecd.org/dataoecd/49/45/24236156.pdf.

37 Ibid.

38 "Canada Economic Development for Quebec Regions, Chapter 3: Innovation" (*The Economy of Quebec and Its Regions—Analysis of Trends 2003*), retrieved September 13, 2006, from www.dec-ced.gc.ca/Complements/Publications/ADT2003/en/3.html.

39 Ibid.

40 Ibid.

41 Ibid.

42 *Canada's Performance 2005: The Government of Canada's Contribution*, (November 23, 2005), retrieved August 25, 2006, from www.tbs-sct.gc.ca/report/govrev/05/cp-rc12_e.asp.

43 "Canada Economic Development for Quebec Regions, Chapter 3: Innovation."

44 "Research Income Hits $5 Billion for the First Time" (*Canada's Top 50 Research Universities List 2005 Analysis, 2005*), retrieved September 16, 2006, from www.researchinfosource.com/media/2005-top50-article.pdf.

45 "Top 100 Spending Recovers" (Canada's Top 100 Corporate R&D Spenders List 2005 Analysis, 2005), retrieved September 16, 2006, from www.researchinfosource.com/2005-analysis.pdf.

46 "Grocery Gateway Acquisition Accelerates Longo's E-Business Strategy" (*Deloitte Canada RSS Feeds*), retrieved September 16, 2006, from www.deloitte.com/dtt/case_study/0,1005,sid%253D3630%2526cid%253D71204,00.htm.

47 Treasury Board of Canada Secretariat, *Appendix A: Performance Highlights* (Treasury Board of Canada Secretariat, November 23, 2005), retrieved August 25, 2006, from www.tbs-sct.gc.ca/report/govrev/05/cp-rc12_e.asp.

Global Manufacturing and the Supply Chain

"It must be considered that there is nothing more difficult to carry out, nor more doubtful of success, nor more dangerous to handle than to initiate a new order of things."[1]

—Niccolò Machiavelli

"There is at least one point in the history of any company when you have to change dramatically to rise to the next performance level. Miss the moment and you start to decline."[2]

—Andrew Grove, Chairman, Intel

"Kaizen is like a hotbed that nurtures small and ongoing changes, while innovation is like magma that appears in abrupt eruptions from time to time."[3]

—Masaaki Imai, Japanese change and quality management guru

"The bitterness of poor quality remains long after low pricing is forgotten."[4]

—Leon M. Cautillo, management consultant

"Quality is not an act. It is a habit."[5]

—Aristotle

LEARNING OUTCOMES

- Understand the importance of adopting new paradigms for global manufacturing and supply chain management.
- Understand how political boundaries and other variables influence manufacturing and supply chain management.
- Evaluate the advances in manufacturing and supply chain management technology and determine their value to Canadian SMEs.
- Understand the importance of supply chain management to a firm's sustainable competitive advantage.
- Evaluate the advantages and disadvantages of the different modes of transportation.
- Evaluate security initiatives since 9/11 insofar as they affect manufacturing and supply chain management within Canadian firms.
- Evaluate new mental models regarding production factors, including capacity allocation planning, concentrated-decentralized facilities, and standardization versus customization of products.
- Understand the need for the organization to implement quality practices.
- Understand the significant transformation from the old models, and evaluate the five new supply chain models.
- Understand where and when to source components.

Japanese Model Near Triumph in Auto Making

HARUYOSHI YAMAGUCHI/Bloomberg News/Landov

Fifteen years ago, James Womack and two collaborators at the Massachusetts Institute of Technology wrote a book that revolutionized our understanding of the global auto industry. Japanese automakers were not gaining ground based on sneaky government aid or the inbred productivity of Japanese workers ... Instead, Toyota, the dominant producer, had simply developed a better system, one it dubbed lean manufacturing. ... [which] demanded constant improvement in the manufacturing process, a departure from the typical manufacturing focus of meeting financial goals. Manufacturing defects, for example, weren't simply repaired at the end of the assembly line; instead, their causes were hunted down immediately and corrected.

Lean manufacturing was revolutionary. Companies cut costs yet they were also able to boost quality. Toyota didn't rest on this competitive advantage. American competitors have now adopted lean manufacturing, but the delay has cost them significantly. General Motors has lost half its market share over the past three decades, which means economies of scale have turned into diseconomies of shrinkage. "By next year [2006], Womack predicts, Toyota will pass GM as the world's largest car company. After all, he cracks: 'It's not hard to pass a guy who's going in reverse.' As this watershed approaches, it's not by accident more and more of Toyota's magazine ads now show happy North American employees working in its U.S. and Canadian plants. 'Toyota's biggest management problem now is avoiding blame for the collapse of GM.' "

Adapted from Jay Bryan, "Japanese Model near Triumph in Auto Making," Victoria Times Colonist December 2, 2005. © CanWest Interactive, a division of CanWest MediaWorks Publications Inc. All rights reserved.

A SUN TZU MOMENT...

Visual Arts Library, London/Alamy

"If we go forth and the enemy can also advance, it is termed 'accessible.' In an accessible configuration, first occupy the heights and yang (side), and improve the routes for transportation of provisions. Then when we engage in battle, it will be advantageous."[5]

1939–45—WORLD WAR II TRANSFORMED THE CANADIAN ECONOMY

"More than 40,000 Canadians sacrificed their lives during World War II, which began with Hitler's invasion of Poland on September 1, 1939. Just two days after the invasion, Britain, France, Australia, and New Zealand declared war on Germany, and Canada followed almost immediately on September 10, 1939.

By the time the war ended in Europe on May 8, 1945, it would have profound and long lasting effects on the economic and social lives of Canadians. During the war, agriculture became increasingly mechanized, manufacturing showed unprecedented growth, exports jumped, government spending increased substantially, unemployment virtually disappeared, and more than 1 million women who were previously engaged in home-making moved into the workforce.

The economy not only recovered from the Great Depression, which had preceded the war, but also gained the momentum that would lead to rapid postwar prosperity."

The war created an unprecedented demand for military and civilian goods manufacturing. Canada was Britain's principal supplier of war materials until the United States entered the war.

To meet the demand, in 1940 the Canadian government created the Department of Munitions and Supply, headed by C.D. Howe. "Under Howe's direction, the government created 28 Crown corporations for large-scale production of manufactured goods. Production expanded rapidly: by 1942, Canada was producing more than 4,000 aircraft a year, and exports to the United Kingdom were [skyrocketing]. . . . From 1939 to 1941, the number of employees in Canada's manufacturing sector increased by 50%."

By 1945, Canada had a highly skilled labour force and firms, which contributed to sustained economic growth. When the men returned home and took up positions in the workplace, many women returned to their traditional role as homemakers. Marriages that had been postponed now took place and the baby boom followed.

"Canada and the United States were the only two major industrialized countries whose infrastructures were substantially expanded during the war rather than devastated. By the end of the war, the United States emerged as the most powerful economy in the world, which also helped the Canadian economy in terms of its exports and growth. The two countries undertook major building projects such as the St. Lawrence Seaway. The supreme sacrifice of [Canada's military], the increased co-operation with the United States, a greater role for government in the economy, the emergence of Crown corporations, the large-scale participation of women in the labour force, and prosperity were the main legacies of World War II."

Source: Government of Canada, *1939–1945—World War II Transformed the Canadian Economy* (Key Economic Events, 2005), retrieved August 25, 2006, from http://canadianeconomy.gc.ca/english/economy/1939ww2.html.

Opening Thoughts

World War II, by necessity, forced Canada to adopt Sun Tzu's advice to "occupy the heights and yang (side), and improve the routes for transportation of provisions." As a result, when Canada engaged in the global economic battle both during the war years and those that followed, it benefited. Canadian businesses continue to seek the heights and the yang. Since the early 1990s, Canadian firms readily adopted global manufacturing and supply chain management's new paradigms; however, the contribution of industry and manufacturing to Canada's GNI has fallen in 2005 to only 29.1 percent,[7] while our service industries' contribution has increased to 68.7 percent.[8] Agriculture (which includes forestry, fishing, and hunting[9]) makes up the difference at 2.2 percent of Canada's GNI.[10] Keep this in mind as we review manufacturing and supply chain material. Supply chains comprise activities linked together in a series of customer–supplier relationships that eventually result in the delivery of finished products to the customer.

Many of the concepts discussed have equal application for service-based firms in the international environment. Firms in the global marketplace must adopt new paradigms or they risk following General Motor's lead.

In this chapter, we examine new concepts through the lenses of global manufacturing and supply chain managers charged with "wringing pennies out of the value chain" or adding value to their product or service. These leaders must ask what contribution their team can make to the firm's bottom line. To answer this, they have to understand the factors that will affect their success. How will the firm gain access to inputs? How will it transport the inputs? Does the firm's global capacity meet the needs of the firm? Are there advantages to be gained from outsourcing? Where should the firm locate its service centres to ensure customer satisfaction? Should the production activities be centralized or decentralized? Is it more profitable to standardize or modify products and services in order to satisfy the needs of international customers? If so, what global standards, such as quality, should the firm adopt? What new emerging technology would enhance its competitive position in the global marketplace? These are a few of the complex questions global manufacturing and supply chain managers must answer correctly. They must be prepared to adopt new mental models that build on the foundation models of lean manufacturing systems rather than continuing the traditional functional silos approach of the 1980s and 1990s.

In considering how to gain access to manufacturing inputs, business leaders are encouraged to think of business as being like water; business will flow around obstacles and seek the most attractive venues to source inputs. The factors (obstacles) to be analyzed and accommodated when crafting market entry strategies are once again the PEST-C factors and others such as geography. Let us briefly examine some additional PEST-C considerations to those we have discussed in earlier chapters through the lenses of the manufacturing and supply chain managers. As well, we will examine a number of logistical challenges, including transportation, security, and several critical emerging production issues.

James Lipton observed, "Since opportunity and danger are inseparable, it is impossible to make a significant step forward without encountering danger; and, obversely, the scent of danger should alert us to the fact that we may be headed in the right direction."[11] These new paradigms we are about to consider are all about change and therefore, not for the faint of heart.

Political, Economic, and Cultural Considerations

Video 14.1

Although we reviewed materials regarding the political impact on international business in Chapter 2, our thoughts here specifically relate to global manufacturing and supply chain management. Political boundaries introduce considerations that influence how business will be conducted in different venues and on the activities required to move goods globally. Examples of relevant political issues include law, which may require the use of local supplies for manufacturing in a particular country; labour relations; environmental regulations; and export/import laws. The decision maker must consider all. Dell provides a worthwhile political example. Prior to China's joining the WTO in 2002, Dell decided not to build a plant in China because China's government leaders indicated that they would maintain control over Dell's operations.[12]

In the short term, a shift in political conditions may affect delivery and production schedules; in the longer term, a shift may undermine Canadian SMEs' business plans if they were based on assured supply and predictable cost assumptions. Oil provides an example of this kind of uncertainty. Hurricane Katrina's North American impact resulted in the world market prices for oil briefly hitting US$70/barrel. The ripple effect throughout the globally interrelated economies was quickly felt. Canadian airlines' strategy to secure oil prompted the firm to enter into hedging instrument agreements to assure stable prices (see Chapter 8, pages 232–235). Regional conflict provides another example. A critical material, coltan (columbite-tantalite, a black tar-like mineral), is found in the Democratic Republic of Congo. The mineral is used to produce tantalum used in capacitors in a vast array of small electronic devices, especially mobile phones, pagers, and laptop computers. Supply chains like Nortel were disrupted because of civil strife in the Congo.

A second dimension to geopolitical sourcing concerns is the need for government-to-government agreements as part of sourcing decisions. For instance, weapons systems are often developed by international consortia and require not only agreements among the many companies involved but also negotiated agreements among the countries in which those companies reside. For example in Canada, Colt (Canada) and the American parent firm Colt acquired Diemaco, a Canadian logistics and defence firm. The Diemaco business operates as Colt Canada Corporation. It is a wholly owned subsidiary of Colt. "Colt Canada, based in Kitchener, Ontario . . . is a defence contractor that supplies small arms to military and law enforcement agencies. Since 1976, Diemaco has served as Canada's Small Arms Center for Excellence. . . . Weapons manufactured by Colt Canada supply military troops of NATO countries as well as Canadian Forces and the Royal Canadian Mounted Police."[13] In cases like these, the transaction costs of establishing business relationships can be extremely high. One reason the expense may be justifiable is the need to sell globally. Governments may also see these agreements as instruments of foreign policy. The North American Missile Defense Shield proposal contemplated such government-to-government agreements that will be underscored with foreign policy issues. This proposal was designed to support the Bush administration's foreign policy requiring closer integration and control of Canada's airspace in the American "War on Terror" planning.

Developing and underdeveloped countries' legal systems often do not adequately support the security needs of many Canadian SMEs. For example, some countries' legal systems do not enable firms to apply for patents or protect previously developed intellectual property. For instance, it has been noted that despite China's membership in the WTO, "manufacturing executives say China still does not offer the kinds of protection for know-how, patents and other sorts of intellectual property that are common in the U.S., Canada, and Europe."[14]

Another legal security concern of a different nature is whether there is a strong naval presence in the host country. Why? Protection against piracy is a global problem. "In 2003 there were 445 global attacks. Indonesia continues to have the world's most treacherous waters with 121 attacks. Bangladesh followed with 58 attacks and Nigeria with 39. Malaysia and Singapore's better-policed waterways had 35 reported incidents. Piracy attacks tend to cluster near some of the Third World's busiest ports. "A January International Maritime Bureau report noted that attacks on tankers in 2003 grew by up to 22 percent. 'That these ships carrying dangerous cargoes may fall temporarily under the control of unauthorized and unqualified individuals is a matter of concern, for both environmental and safety reasons.' "[15] Security certificates are required under recent legislation to comply with the International Ship and Port Facility Security Code and to facilitate entry to ISPS Code–compliant port facilities in Canada and abroad. Canadian ships attacked to date include the *Scotia Pearl, Baltic Heritage, Sol de Medinoche, Nanuk*, and the *Northern Magic*.[16] While commercial ships are obligated to report piracy incidents, concerns about insurance rate penalties have resulted in few private owners reporting incidents and have received little Canadian press coverage.

Once again we build upon our earlier discussion regarding the impact of economic variables on the firm's ecosystem. Of specific interest to those involved in all manufacturing and supply chain management will be issues relating to the GNP per capita (see Chapter 3), current labour costs (see Chapter 15), the foreign-exchange market (see Chapter 8), and specifically the currencies in question. Certainly, most of us have experienced firsthand the impact, both good and bad, of a strong Canadian dollar (US$0.91 in May 2006).

Technology

Advances in technology have been a boon to international business. The growing sophistication of manufacturing and supply chain management software, Global Radio Frequency Identification (RFID), Electronic Data Interchange (EDI) and voice over Internet protocol (VoIP) technology are paying big dividends for early adopters. Consider Dell's reliance on these advances and the use of software programs and other IT processes that have made very efficient information transfers possible. This efficiency has resulted in Dell's keeping an efficient and effective balance between supplier deliveries and customer orders. Dell's global supply chain model continues to grow its efficiencies using new technology. In the mid-1990s, the most important component of Dell's IT was its Information to Run the Business (IRB) system. The IRB system resulted in the optimization of production, quality, and distribution both globally and locally.[17] Dell continues to update its IT capabilities; in 2001 the company deployed its TradeMatrix Supply Chain tools to gain a "cost-effective, flexible solution . . . to sustain a global, 24 × 7 manufacturing operation."[18] Some generic technologies being widely adopted by public and private sectors are explained below.

Radio Frequency Identification

Radio frequency identification (**RFID**) systems often include bar codes or tags, optical character readers, and sometimes advanced biotechnologies such as retinal and fingerprint scans. They are different from the traditional UPC bar code systems we see in the shopping malls; RFID is designed to enable readers to capture data on tags and

Radio frequency identification (**RFID**) tags are portable databases that enable the access of information that has been updated in real-time through reader/writers at any point along the supply chain. They are a noncontact, non-line-of-sight method to automatically gather, inspect, and distribute detailed information.[19]

transmit the information to a computer system without human intervention. Currently the tag's chip capacity can contain as much as 2 kilobytes of data. This data can include product specifications, manufacturing and shipment dates, and destination and sales information. The RFID reader continuously emits radio waves and receives signals back from the tag that in turn is sent in real time to a computer system. RFID applications are "used for such functions as security [and] access control, toll collection, animal tracking, and automobile immobilization, as well as stocking Wal-Mart, Metro AG, Target, and Tesco shelves, and for 'other uses' by the U.S. Department of Defense."[20] Wal-Mart was an early adopter of RFID technology. This technology significantly reduced its out-of-stocks, allowed supply chain visibility in real or "near-real" time, and reduced costs and labour. The benefit for Wal-Mart is clear: "higher costs and poor inventory control in the supply chain do not help anyone, especially the largest retailer. With Wal-Mart selling over $245 billion worth of goods in fiscal year 2003, a 1% improvement in the out-of-stock issue could generate nearly $2.5 billion in very profitable sales."[21]

What is the incentive for Wal-Mart suppliers? The primary benefit is the additional sales revenue suppliers generate by early notice of out-of-stock levels. Another benefit is lower operating costs through labour reduction and improved business process efficiencies. Wal-Mart also encourages its suppliers to use RFID to look for a return on investment within their own operations, e.g., there is less shrinkage if articles are clamshelled and RFID tagged.

"However, people are increasingly worried about the loss of privacy in widespread RFID usage, given the ability to easily track RFID-tagged products. And such fears, if not addressed, could hobble the RFID industry."[22] We have every right to be very concerned. RFID will make products and therefore the people wearing and carrying them trackable from non-line-of-sight positions. "The infelicitously-titled IBM [patent] filing 'Identification and Tracking of Persons Using RFID-Tagged Items,' and a Phillips Electronics 2003 patent application advocates placing RFID tags in shoes so they can be detected by RFID scanners embedded in floors."[23] All of us must be vigilant when this technology is marketed under the name of efficiency. For example, cell phone manufacturers offer tracking devices as a "safety feature" for parents to follow the movements of their children. Should we be concerned about this trend?

JUST DOING THE RIGHT THING

Shaving Shoppers to Be Saved from Surveillance?

Big Brother technology trained on razor buyers—hairy men beware.

Derek Capitaine

"Consumer group Caspian is challenging Gillette over its trial of RFID technology on packs of Mach3 razors, now in place in supermarkets in the UK and the US. Caspian—Consumers Against Supermarket Privacy Invasion and Numbering—has taken issue with the company's 'smart shelf' system and are demanding an explanation. The Gillette tracking system senses when a product is removed from the shelf and takes a photograph of the shopper, which is then compared to another snap taken when the razors reach the checkout. One such system was found to be in operation in a Massachusetts Wal-Mart supermarket, but it was removed shortly after Caspian queried its presence in the shop."

Retailers, with some merit, claim radio tracking technology is essential to maintain stock levels and avoid shrinkage. Opponents to RFID, like the civil liberties groups, also with some justification, express concerns this technology could be put to a more sinister use. Interestingly, the U.S. defence department is said to be keen to develop the technology. Fortunately, with threats come opportunities. New RFID deactivating devices are emerging to resolve the major threat to personal privacy. These will prevent tracking after the product leaves the store.

Adapted from Jo Best, "Shaving Shoppers to Be Saved from Surveillance?" *Law & Policy*, July 21, 2003. Reproduced with permission of Jo Best.

According to some estimates, the worldwide market for RFID technology was $1.49 billion in 2004. The demand for RFID systems is increasing exponentially. Some estimates are that the industry will be worth $6.1 billion in 2006 and as much as $26.9 billion in 2015.[24] New applications are announced almost daily.

As the manufacturing centre for the globe, China is an early adopter. RFID is used in many sectors in Shanghai, "such as the management of driver's licenses for cabbies, police ticketing, local customs offices, pet license regulation and tickets for the Master's tennis tournament. Hualian Supermarket, one of city's major food chains, is in negotiation with Cisco Systems to adopt RFID networks in its outlets. In the second quarter (2005), China's RFID market size reached 228 million Yuan (US$28.2 million), 38 percent coming from second-generation identity cards, according to Analysis International."[25]

Whose data is it? Putting the ethics and corporate governance issues aside for a moment, an interesting question arises from RFID technology—whose data is it? Clearly the manufacturer owns the product initially; therefore, we can conclude that data about that product belongs to the manufacturer. But when distributors purchase the product from the manufacturer and then retailers purchase the product from the distributors; and finally the consumer buys it from the retailer—who owns the data? Imagine the manufacturer's response to the idea that the consumer and those in between own the entire data lifecycle of any product they buy. It provides much to think about; possibly a class action lawsuit?

Electronic Data Interchange

Electronic data interchange (EDI) is the electronic exchange of business information (data) between companies using networks or the Internet to enhance efficiencies in the buying, selling, and trading of information.

Since the mid-1990s **electronic data interchange (EDI)** has become increasingly important as an easy mechanism for companies to buy, sell, trade, and communicate information. EDI is the electronic exchange of business information (data) between companies using networks or the Internet to enhance efficiencies in the buying, selling, and trading of information. It has been described as the backbone of electronic commerce and generally is combined with e-mail and VoIP into a single communications system for original equipment manufacturers (OEMs) and their suppliers. Wal-Mart once again leads the way in harnessing the power of EDI with its global suppliers.

Voice over Internet Protocol

Voice over Internet protocol (VoIP) is a technology that allows telephone calls through a broadband Internet connection in lieu of a regular (or analog) phone line.

Voice over Internet protocol (VoIP) is quickly becoming another technical innovation that can be readily adopted by Canadian SMEs. VoIP enables analog audio signals, like the kind you hear when you talk on the phone, to be turned into digital data that can be transmitted over the Internet. Some services using VoIP may allow you to call only other people using the same service, but others may allow you to call anyone who has a telephone number—including local, long distance, mobile, and international numbers. Through a standard Internet connection, VoIP permits firms to make telephone calls anywhere in the world free of long distance charges. The software is currently available to businesses. Canadian SMEs must change the way they think about long distance phone calls. Rather than absorbing huge monthly phone bills, SMEs could access a VoIP provider such as Skype, Vonage, or other broadband telephone service for a fraction of the cost or free.

Culture

Video 14.2

We have spent considerable time exploring culture and identifying the dangers of adopting an ethnocentric view of the world. The concepts and lessons learned have application when thinking about the firm's global manufacturing strategy and its supply chain management. The relationship with a firm's stakeholders in an international setting has great bearing on a firm's competitiveness. Unless we're selling commodities like coal and sulphur, to be successful it will be imperative that we understand the host country's culture. Recall that the British continue to insist on driving on the "wrong" side of the road! As a result, when manufacturing automobiles, cultural values, such as driving on the "wrong" side of the road, must be accommodated. The cultural factors are referred to frequently throughout the text and therefore will not be further examined here; nevertheless, they must be fully considered though the lens of the manufacturing and supply chain managers.

International Transportation Issues

As discussed, in Chapter 6, pages 167–169, Michael Porter's diamond established the determinants of national competitive advantage and the role government can play in making these determinants either attractive or unattractive to firms seeking to source their inputs globally. Porter's theory forms part of how we explain the new economic trade theory. Supply chain management involves transportation across borders. By enhancing the transportation infrastructure (recall Porter referred to this as an advanced factor endowment), governments can make the ground "fertile" for national competitive advantage by encouraging private sector investment; they can implement safety regulations and tax incentives; and they can formulate policies to promote business efficacy—e.g., transportation policies including customs requirements, documentation of export and import regulation compliance, and advance notification of shipment content to attract global manufacturing and participation in international firms' supply chains. The data management burden resulting from these requirements can be very high, particularly since 9/11 and increased security vigilance. There is increasing concern within Canadian international businesses that these impediments to the free flow of goods and services add significant additional costs and lower gross national product. As international sourcing increases, so does the need for overseas transportation. Nations must develop a seamless inter-modal (sea, air, rail, and ground) transportation system for the movement of goods. Each transition between transportation modes increases cost, time, and the possibility of loss or damage. Canadian businesses must constantly monitor their environment and avail themselves of these and other government initiatives. SMEs must be aware, for example, that an insurance provider for the international cargo container industry estimates that "as many as 5% of container movements in the world develop problems during transit."[26] Managers must understand how and when the goods will be received, and the transportation cost, which can represent between 10 and 30 percent of the final cost of goods.[27] The transportation component of a firm's supply chain management can be divided into infrastructure, modes, and choice of the best fit.

Infrastructure

In developed countries, transportation systems generally present few challenges for international firms. Developed countries have established inter-modal systems that will deliver goods efficiently. This is not the case with developing and underdeveloped countries, however, so special attention will be required in the movement of goods in these venues. Some of these countries might have an excellent inbound and outbound transportation system, but the movement of goods from the docks and airports in the country may be poor.

Sea

Surrounded by three oceans, Canada has a competitive advantage for accessing inter-modal movements. Canadian firms regularly use combinations of land, sea, and airfreight modes to move goods and services. As of 2005, Canada had 169 Canadian registered ships and 112 registered offshore.[28] There are three types of ocean shipping: liner, bulk, and tramp and charter service. Liner service offers regular shuttle accommodation on established routes; bulk services are contracted services for individual voyages or for prolonged periods of time; tramp and charter service are available for irregular routes and are scheduled on demand. Supply chain managers and others must not only be familiar with these three services, but also understand the type of cargo the vessels providing the service can carry. Most common are the conventional (break bulk) cargo vessels, container ships, and "roll on–roll off" vessels.

Conventional cargo vessels are good for irregular and awkward goods, e.g., livestock, barges, and other ships, and goods on pallets that for whatever reason can not easily be containerized. Most container ships carry standardized containers that facilitate loading and unloading of cargo for integration into inter-modal transportation systems. Containerization has greatly improved the speed and efficiency of the carriage of goods by sea during the past three decades.

Roll on–roll off vessels are seagoing ferries. Trucks and automobiles roll up the ramp to load, and roll off at their destination.

Air

Airfreight is available to most countries. The total volume of airfreight in relation to total global shipping volumes remains quite small. However, when measured by value, 40 percent of the world's manufactured exports use this mode. High-value items referred to as high density (weight to volume) tend to be moved by airfreight.

Modes of Shipment Selection

In selecting the appropriate mode, managers must consider the needs of the firm and its customers. Specifically they must consider transit time, predictability, cost, and noneconomic factors.

Transit Time

The transit time to move goods by air or by ocean can be significantly different: from 40 days for goods transported by ocean service to only 24 hours if the goods are delivered by airfreight. Business decision makers will note that although the initial cost may be higher for airfreight, there are some advantages. First, this mode may eliminate the need for overseas storage facilities because inventories can be significantly reduced by adopting the just-in-time (JIT) resupply system. Second, the firm's funds will be freed up and can be put to work sooner rather than waiting for the extended delivery time when sent by sea (40 days). Third, airfreight may meet the "emergency" needs of customers. Fourth, for perishable goods, airfreight may be the only mode available that will enable participation in offshore markets. Fruits, vegetables, and flowers all use airfreight successfully.

It is important that supply chain managers seek out and improve the weakest link in their airfreight supply chain. Levi Strauss has embarked on a manufacturing process that permits the customer to have her body computer-scanned at one of Levi's specialized locations. Her specific measurements are then instantly transferred electronically to a manufacturing facility. The manufacturing managers have the jeans made to measure within a few hours but Levi Strauss can exploit this new technology only if the transportation mode (airfreight) activity in the supply chain takes very little time to deliver the goods. A systems approach must be applied throughout all of the firm's activities.

Predictability

Generally, air travel tends to be more predictable than ocean freight. Technology has made significant strides in helping managers determine predictability in terms of both air and ocean shipping. Using technology, shippers and customers are now able to track goods at any point during shipment. This ability can be a significant competitive advantage to manufacturers. For example, the ability for a firm to divert shipments to meet customers' changing demands is often cited. The RFID microchip, as we have read, is very much part of this transformation of business and society.

Cost and Noneconomic Factors

Shipping by air may have significantly higher costs and need to be justified. The density of the goods will be a determining factor. Bulky goods, such as automobiles, are generally too expensive to ship by air while very compact goods, like computer chips, are suitable for air transportation. High-priced items with low density are good candidates for airfreight transportation. We all understand that the shipment of diamonds by airfreight makes more sense than shipping coal by air! Supply chain managers must be prepared to mix and match the different modes available in order to achieve the most efficient and effective outcome. Strategically, the choice between airfreight and ocean freight can be influenced if the firm is attempting to obtain a foothold with the buyer by providing prompt and efficient service. In this case, the additional cost of air may be justifiably absorbed as part of the firm's aggressive marketing expansion strategy.

Security

Since 9/11, security has become a significant cost factor (measured in both time and money) in the movement of goods and services. Firms' decision makers must constantly monitor the transportation infrastructure and be prepared to move those parts of the supply chain affected by deterioration in a nation's transportation systems. Security obstacles are being addressed both globally and regionally.

First, the Asia-Pacific Economic Cooperation (APEC) is developing a Framework for the Security and Facilitation of Global Trade, which is based on the World Customs Organization (WCO) Framework of Standards to Secure and Facilitate Global Trade. The goal of both initiatives is to "create an environment for the secure and efficient movement of goods, services, and people across the borders."[29] It is anticipated that the APEC Framework will result in "international standards for securing and facilitating the global supply chain within the APEC region."[30]

Second, the United States has implemented a new program that will significantly affect Canadian businesses. It is called Customs-Trade Partnership Against Terrorism (C-TPAT), a worldwide supply chain security initiative. It has been designed to reduce the threat of terrorism while facilitating secure, legitimate commerce for employers, suppliers, and clients involved in the global supply chain industry. C-TPAT offers Canadian SMEs and others the opportunity to be a certified partner working directly with the U.S. Customs and Border Protection (CBP) to strengthen border security while ensuring the integrity of international supply chain practices. As certified partners, Canadian firms have the assurance that their extended supply chain provider has met, and will maintain, rigorous supply chain security standards. In return for participating, the partnering firm will receive priority processing to help in minimizing border delays. The goal of the C-TPAT initiative is to identify low-risk, trusted import leaders from businesses, border brokers, and others who have implemented solid supply chain security procedures.

A third initiative is the Free and Secure Trade (FAST) program. It is a "joint Canada–U.S. initiative involving the Canada Border Services Agency, and the United States Bureau of Customs and Border Protection (CBP). FAST supports moving pre-approved eligible goods across the border quickly and verifying trade compliance away from the border. It is a commercial process offered to pre-approved importers, carriers, and registered drivers. Shipments for approved companies, transported by approved carriers using registered drivers, will be cleared into either country with greater speed and certainty, and at a reduced cost of compliance. In Canada, FAST builds on the Customs Self-Assessment (CSA) program and its principles of pre-approval and self-assessment, as well as increased security measures under the Partners in Protection (PIP) program. FAST participants must meet the requirements of Canada's PIP program or the United States Customs Trade Partnership Against Terrorism (C-TPAT) program. As part of these programs, companies must adopt and implement security procedures to be compatible with guidelines set by both the CBSA and CBP."[31] (FAST allows U.S./Canada partnering importers expedited release for qualifying commercial shipments. C-TPAT is a voluntary government–business initiative to build cooperative relationships that strengthen and improve overall international supply chain and border security.)

All of these initiatives come at a cost! My request to government, on behalf of Canadian SMEs, is as modest as that of Diogenes to Alexander: "Get out of my light."[32] Do you agree? Are these security measures really needed for Canada to participate in the global marketplace, or have we overreacted to the War on Terror? Visit www.power.nelson.com for an op ed article on counterterrorism security.

Production Issues

There are several key production issues in addition to the ecosystem factors (PEST-C), transportation, and security considerations that must be provided for by firms undertaking global manufacturing and supply chain management. International manufacturing and supply chain managers must adopt new supply chain paradigms and new mental models regarding production factors including capacity allocation planning, concentrated-decentralized facilities, and standardization versus customization of products. Old paradigms provided the minimum requirements for business systems, such as financial management, inventory control, order management, and production scheduling. Competitive pressures over the past decade have forced OEMs to adopt new paradigms, in which suppliers must become lean and mean. Today, firms adopt and fine-tune new methodologies, such as JIT manufacturing, EDI, VoIP, order release management, ERP systems, and quality ratings, such as the ISO 9000 and the Six Sigma Programs. These new methodologies and software must be integrated within a systems approach to become part of the firm's DNA. They must be viewed in the macro sense, so the interface and linkages between OEMs and suppliers are understood, nurtured, and well established.

A Systems Approach

International logistics can be defined as the design and management of a system that controls the flow, both forward and reverse, of materials, service, and information in, through, and out of the firm encompassing the firm's entire range of import and export movements. Today, firms take a **management systems** (holistic) approach rather than viewing these activities as separate silos. The systems approach includes the incorporation of and interaction with outside organizations and individuals. Consider Canada's Magna International, a diversified automobile supplier with 224 production and 60 engineering and R&D centres in 22 countries located on 4 continents. Certainly, contractual arrangements are at the core of the interaction between Magna and its suppliers, but the parties to the contract agreed to build on a commonality of purpose so that all win. To achieve this end, all parties in Magna's supply chain view performance, quality, and timing as being the essence of their arrangement. To achieve this vision, Magna, and other companies like Magna, adopt JIT delivery in order to lower the cost of inventory. They adopt EDI to improve efficiency of the order processing. They undertake early supplier involvement (ESI) for better planning of goods development and movement. They develop efficient customer response systems (ECR) using RFID and other methods to track sales activities on the retail level, and they implement quality programs to eliminate waste and achieve efficiencies.

In viewing the international logistics as a system, firms concentrate on their core competencies and rely upon partners for inputs grounded on those companies' core competencies. See Figure 14.1.

International logistics can be defined as the design and management of a system that controls the flow, both forward and reverse, of materials, service, and information in, through, and out of the firm. It encompasses the firm's entire range of import and export movements.

A **management system** refers to the organization's structure for managing its processes and activities that will transform inputs into a product or service.

FIGURE 14.1

iPod: Using Everyone Else's Technology

Just-in-time Inventory (JIT)

Just-in-time (JIT) is a management philosophy that actively promotes the elimination of manufacturing waste by producing the right part in the right place at the right time. Unnecessarily moving, loading, unloading, and storing products, for example, adds cost without adding value. JIT will "improve profits and return on investment by reducing inventory levels (increasing the inventory turnover rate), improving product quality, reducing production and delivery lead times, and reducing other costs (such as those associated with machine setup and equipment breakdown)."[33]

Virtually every company has taken steps to reduce costs associated with holding inventory. "The challenge in making appropriate inventory decisions is to clearly understand all the costs associated with holding inventory."[34] A typical manufacturing firm must seek to "wring the pennies out" of warehouse inventory, banking fees, pre-assembly, and scrap. Warehousing inventory commits a firm to pay for such things as fixtures, equipment, maintenance, building depreciation (or rent), and operating costs such as light and heat. Whether you use a credit line from the bank, or pay out of cash flow, you pay for more than just the cost of materials. There is insurance on the inventory, and sometimes inventory taxes, and you run the risk of material becoming obsolete, damaged, or requiring additional preparation as a consequence of exposure to the elements. Some of the expenses incurred to process the materials before they are ready for production can be provided more cost-effectively through sourcing. This eliminates, for example, the need for some material processing equipment, simplifies handling, and frees up personnel for other tasks. When materials end up in the scrap bin, it is at a significant cost. Selling to a scrap dealer realizes only a small fraction of the original purchase price. Mistakes made in the manufacturing process cutting material can significantly affect a firm's bottom line. Buying pre-cut and assembled material shifts that risk to suppliers. "Warehousing inventory requires people to receive, store and sometimes move it; people to operate fork lifts and pre-processing equipment; people to collect scrap; and clerical personnel to plan, track and monitor the inventory."[35] When asked where its warehouses are located, Wal-Mart is sometimes quoted as saying its warehouse inventory is in the back of a 5-ton truck on highway so-and-so and it will be at the loading dock at 3:00 PM today.

Flexible Manufacturing—Lean Production

Flexible manufacturing "integrates combinations of various types of capital equipment, and is a system that is capable of processing a number of different work-pieces simultaneously and automatically, with the machines in the system carrying out the system's operation in any sequence."[36] Recall that JIT is in large part a philosophy of waste elimination while **lean production** is an assembly-line manufacturing methodology that pursues waste elimination (see the opening vignette, page 389). The goal of lean production is described as getting "the right things to the right place at the right time, the first time, while minimizing waste and being open to change."[38] The ten rules of lean production are eliminate waste; minimize inventory; maximize flow; pull production from customer demand; meet customer requirements; do it right the first time; empower workers; design for rapid changeover; partner with suppliers; and create a culture of continuous improvement.[39]

Engineer Taiichi Ohno, a founding father of the principles of lean production, discovered that in addition to eliminating waste, his enterprise resource planning led to improved product flow and better quality.[41] **Enterprise resource planning (ERP)** systems are the central nervous system of the organization. ERP attempts to integrate all departments and functions across a company onto a single computer system that can serve all those different departments' particular needs. ERP leverages knowledge and provides real-time information to decision makers. "Dell Computers and Boeing Aircraft have embraced the philosophy of lean production [and ERP] with great success."[42]

Just-in-time (JIT) is a management philosophy that strives to eliminate sources of manufacturing waste by producing the right part in the right place at the right time.

Flexible manufacturing "integrates combinations of various types of capital equipment, and is a system that is capable of processing a number of different work-pieces simultaneously and automatically, with the machines in the system carrying out the system's operation in any sequence."[37]

Lean production is an assembly-line manufacturing methodology. The goal of lean production is described as getting "the right things to the right place at the right time, the first time, while minimizing waste and being open to change."[40]

Enterprise resource planning (ERP) attempts to integrate all departments and functions across a company onto a single computer system that can serve all those different departments' particular needs by leveraging knowledge and providing real-time information to decision makers.

Total Quality Management

"Total quality management (**TQM**) is both a philosophy and a set of guiding principles that represent the foundation of a continuously improving organization."[43]

Total quality management (TQM) has become a major operations management success factor in the manufacturing and supply chain management. "Total Quality Management is both a philosophy and a set of guiding principles that represent the foundation of a continuously improving organization. TQM is the application of quantitative methods and human resources to improve the materials and services supplied to an organization and all the processes within an organization, and the degree to which needs of customers are met, now and in future. TQM integrates fundamental management techniques, existing improving efforts, and technical tools under a disciplined approach focused on continuous improvement."[44]

There is a relationship between quality and cost. Figure 14.2 shows that by improving the quality of a firm's product, the unit cost will be reduced. These cost savings will come about because time is not wasted in manufacturing poor quality product that cannot be sold. The savings in time permits the firm to produce more units that will result in a reduction in the unit price. We have discussed the benefits of economies of scale in earlier chapters. The second reduction in costs is derived from a reduction in defective scrap and rework materials. Finally there are savings achieved from a reduced number of product warranty claims. To achieve these cost savings, manufacturers implement TQM and quality assurance programs. TQM has become a major production issue in operations management and specifically in manufacturing and supply chain management. As Henry Ford observed, "Quality means doing it right when no one is looking."[45]

Although TQM has been introduced and practised by a number of firms in North America prior to the 1990s, it was only during the 1990s that TQM became inculcated in North American firms' manufacturing and value chains. The practice of TQM can be traced back to the works of W. Edward Deming, Joseph M. Juran, and Philip Crosby. "In 1950, W. Edwards Deming . . . conducted a series of lectures on statistical methods to Japanese engineers and on the quality responsibility to the CEOs of the largest organisations in Japan. The foundation of the Japanese quality miracle and resurgence as an economic power is credited to Dr. Deming. Dr. Deming, the best known of the early pioneers or quality gurus, is recognised for popularising quality control in Japan."[46] TQM is grounded on the thoughts of these three quality gurus' efforts to promote quality. More recently, a number of not-for-profit organizations have commenced encouraging firms to focus on quality.

Canadians are encouraged to pursue quality by the Canada Awards for Business Excellence. This joint industry–government program evolved into the Canada Awards for Excellence in the 1990s, which is similar to the American Society of Quality Control's Baldrige Award. The Canadian program "recognises quality in education, government, and healthcare as well as entrepreneurship, innovation, manufacturing quality, and quality service. All sectors in the Canadian economy compete on a common set of criteria, built on the quality principles and practices."[47] There are similar programs worldwide, such as the Australian Business Excellence Awards and the European Quality Foundation

FIGURE 14.2
How Quality Lowers Costs

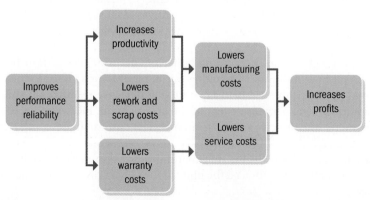

SOURCE: David A. Garvin, "What Does Product Quality Really Mean?" *Sloan Management Review* (Vol. 26, No. 1 Fall 1984).

Excellence Awards. New Zealand, South Africa, and Japan all offer recognition with a similar process.

International Organization for Standardization

Of course, standards contribute to quality. In an international environment with many of the manufacturing inputs being sourced globally, it is an absolute necessity that global standards be adopted. The EU's International Organization for Standardization champions the current leading initiative. One such organization in Canada concerned with standards is The National Quality Institute.

The European's International Organization for Standardization has established the ISO 9000 and ISO 14000 families, which are among ISO's most widely known standards. ISO first published its quality standards in 1987, revised them in 1994, and then republished an updated version in 2000. These new standards, which reflect the needs of service industries and also incorporate a process approach to quality management, are referred to as the ISO 9000:2000 standards. By 2005, the ISO 9000 and ISO 14000 standards had been implemented by more than 760,900 organizations in 154 countries.[48] The ISO 9000 family of standards, primarily concerned with quality management, has become an international reference for quality management in business-to-business dealings, and the ISO 14000 family of standards is well on the way to achieving similar success in enabling organizations to meet their environmental challenges.

The ISO 9000 certification standards specifically support global manufacturers. This set of standards has been well received within Europe, Asia, and is taking root in North

PRACTICAL ENTREPRENEURIAL FOCUS

Deming's 14 Points

1. Create constancy of purpose toward improvement of product and service, with the aim to become competitive and to stay in business, and to provide jobs.
2. Adopt the new philosophy. We are in a new economic age. Western management must awaken to the challenge, must learn their responsibilities, and take on leadership for change.
3. Cease dependence on inspection to achieve quality. Eliminate the need for inspection on a mass basis by building quality into the product in the first place.
4. End the practice of awarding business on the basis of price tag. Instead, minimize total cost. Move toward a single supplier for any one item, on a long-term relationship of loyalty and trust.
5. Improve constantly and forever the system of production and service, to improve quality and productivity, and thus constantly decrease costs.

6. Institute training on the job.
7. Institute leadership. The aim of supervision should be to help people and machines and gadgets to do a better job. Supervision of management is in need of overhaul as well as supervision of production workers.
8. Drive out fear, so that everyone may work effectively for the company.
9. Break down barriers between departments. People in research, design, sales, and production must work as a team, to foresee problems of production and in use that may be encountered with the product or service.
10. Eliminate slogans, exhortations, and targets for the work force asking for zero defects and new levels of productivity. Such exhortations only create adversarial relationships, as the bulk of the causes of low quality and low productivity belong to the system and thus lie beyond the power of the work force.

11. Eliminate work standards (quotas) on the factory floor. Substitute leadership. Eliminate management by objective. Eliminate management by numbers, numerical goals. Substitute leadership.
12. Remove barriers that rob the hourly worker of his right to joy of workmanship. The responsibility of supervisors must be changed from sheer numbers to quality. Remove barriers that rob people in management and in engineering of their right to joy of workmanship. This means abolishment of the annual merit rating and of management by objective.
13. Institute a vigorous program of education and self-improvement.
14. Put everybody in the company to work to accomplish the transformation. The transformation is everybody's job.

Source: Jim Clauson, *Deming's 14 Points* (Deming Electronic Network Website, October 5, 1997). The W. Edwards Deming Institute®, All Rights Reserved & Copyright © 2000.

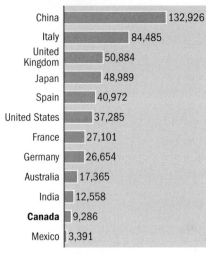

FIGURE 14.3

Top Ten Countries for ISO 9001:2000 Certificates (2004)

China	132,926
Italy	84,485
United Kingdom	50,884
Japan	48,989
Spain	40,972
United States	37,285
France	27,101
Germany	26,654
Australia	17,365
India	12,558
Canada	9,286
Mexico	3,391

SOURCE: Adapted from ACNielsen, *The ISO Survey—2004* (ISO Central Secretariat, 2004).

A **Six Sigma program** focuses on the control of a process to the point of ± six sigma (standard deviations) from a centre line or, put another way, a failure rate of 3.4 parts per million or 99.9997 items.

America (see Figures 14.3 and 14.4). Many manufacturing companies, particularly Japanese software firms, require their suppliers to be ISO-certified as a condition for being awarded a contract. ISO certification provides great comfort to manufacturers; knowing that their suppliers follow strict quality processes in the manufacture of the inputs that will contribute to the overall quality of the manufactured product.

Interested in becoming ISO registered? Visit www.power.nelson.com for the links to undertake this registration.

Six Sigma Systematic Quality Program

A number of large multinational firms implement a **Six Sigma program**, which focuses on the control of a process to the point of ± six sigma (standard deviations) from a centre line or, put another way, a failure rate of 3.4 or fewer parts per million or 99.9997 items. Using statistical analysis, the Six Sigma quality assurance system aims to prevent defects by establishing a tolerance range; measuring key internal processes critical to quality; determining why the defects occurred; and identifying improvement activities. As a result, organization-wide statistical training is a key emphasis of the Six Sigma quality measurement and improvement program originally developed in the mid-1980s by Motorola. The Six Sigma process is shown in Figure 14.5.

Since being adopted by Motorola, Six Sigma has spread to many other manufacturing companies, such as GE Aircraft Engines. A.E. Petsche Company, a supplier of high-performance wire, cable, and related interconnect products, implemented a sophisticated supply program in 2001 with Bombardier. As a result of Bombardier's Six Sigma initiative launched in 1997 and this supply arrangement, Bombardier will eliminate virtually all of its in-house wire and cable inventory. Recognizing the value of the program, the public sector is also adopting Six Sigma programs. In 2000, Fort Wayne, Indiana, became the first city to implement the program in a city government. A Six Sigma systematic quality program provides businesses with the tools to improve the capability of their business processes.

Capacity Allocation Planning

Firms must anticipate the capacity they will require in the future. The analysis will include forecasts as to whether demand is increasing or decreasing for their product or service. General Motors undertook such a study and determined it needs less global capacity. Accordingly, the company has announced it will be discharging 30,000 employees by 2008. Similarly, CIBC, as a result of its dismal financial returns in 2005, terminated the employment of 900 employees and 15 percent of management.

Capacity planning is extremely important both for manufacturing and the service industry. If a firm decides that additional capacity is required, then facility location planning must be undertaken. Decision makers will look for location economy factors, such as low wages, access to the customer to reduce transportation costs and enhance customer satisfaction, and supply issues, including the modes of transportation available to move goods within the firm's supply chain. As we have seen, sometimes the location is determined by political and economic risks. With pragmatic globalization decision making, firms must have a clear understanding of these attributes when they establish or close their facilities. There are ramifications to assess in both eventualities. Japanese automobile companies, sensing the growing tension expressed by Americans as domestic producers like GM hemorrhage, have moved quickly to establish a solid and positive corporate presence in the United States and Canada. Similarly, the perception of an emerging "fortress" Europe has attracted American automobile manufacturers and others to establish a presence in Europe.

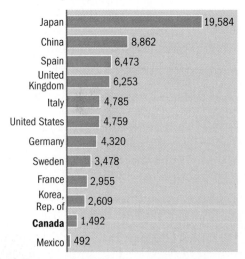

FIGURE 14.4

Top Ten Countries for ISO 14001 Certificates (2004)

Japan	19,584
China	8,862
Spain	6,473
United Kingdom	6,253
Italy	4,785
United States	4,759
Germany	4,320
Sweden	3,478
France	2,955
Korea, Rep. of	2,609
Canada	1,492
Mexico	492

SOURCES: *ISO 9000 and ISO 14000—in Brief* (International Organization for Standardization, August 22, 2006).

These firms concluded that it was better to locate within the EU in order to be eligible for residential tax and other concessions, and to provide protection from future trade barriers that might be imposed on non-resident firms.

Structure Follows Strategy

The next production issue was introduced in Chapter 10, where we observed that many practitioners advocate that structure follows strategy. A firm's organizational structure will be crafted in such a way as to permit the different functions' and units' activities within the firm to best support the firm's vision and mission statements, and the corporate goals. Organizational structure must enable command and control of the organization effectively and efficiently. In Chapter 11, pages 312–324, we examined a number of organizational structures and their advantages and disadvantages. In this chapter we will look at the advantages and disadvantages of centralizing the firm's activities versus decentralizing. We will also briefly discuss again the tension faced by manufacturing decision makers regarding whether to standardize or customize their product. It should be noted that today some advocates, like Tom Peters, suggest strategy also follows structure.[49]

Centralized versus Decentralized

In trying to achieve the goal of "wringing the pennies," Canadian SMEs will consider the locations of their customers and the sourcing opportunities available in the global marketplace. In order to realize sustainable competitive advantage, a firm must understand how to best integrate its manufacturing and supply chain activities in a complex network of international vendors, suppliers, other third parties, and customers. The nature of the product is a production issue, and we have discussed the "weight to value" consideration earlier. If we were producing automobiles (high weight–high value) then we would want to give favourable consideration to manufacturing facilities close to the marketplace. However, if we are producing RIM's high value–low weight BlackBerry devices, we are likely to place less importance on the proximity of our customer.

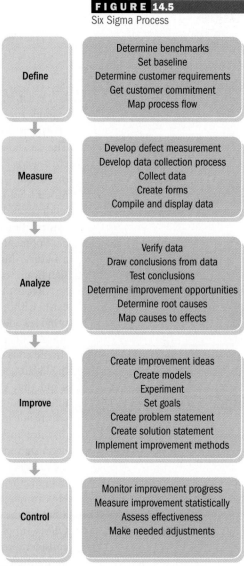

FIGURE 14.5
Six Sigma Process

Define
Determine benchmarks
Set baseline
Determine customer requirements
Get customer commitment
Map process flow

Measure
Develop defect measurement
Develop data collection process
Collect data
Create forms
Compile and display data

Analyze
Verify data
Draw conclusions from data
Test conclusions
Determine improvement opportunities
Determine root causes
Map causes to effects

Improve
Create improvement ideas
Create models
Experiment
Set goals
Create problem statement
Create solution statement
Implement improvement methods

Control
Monitor improvement progress
Measure improvement statistically
Assess effectiveness
Make needed adjustments

SOURCE: "Six Sigma in Engineering," *Six Sigma Tutorial* (2004).

INTERNATIONAL STRATEGIC THINKING

Process Excellence: Battling Inefficiencies at Canada Post

In 2003, Canada Post implemented a Six Sigma program, and, by the end of 2005, the benefits topped $10 million. "According to Louis O'Brien, vice president of business transformation and sourcing management, 'It's an unequalled savings and performance engine that ultimately delivers measurable value to the customer,' he said of Six Sigma. 'By the end of 2004, we had invested $3 million in the program, and realized hard savings of $4 million.' 'The whole initiative is built on employee engagement,' said Jean Shaw, advisor for process leadership development. 'A project can only be successful and sustainable when employees are involved in, commit to and take ownership of the solution.' Shaw has seen various projects in which postal clerks, sorters, and other frontline employees were successfully engaged, thus becoming a formal part of the change process."[50] Merely embracing process excellence no longer ensures Canada Post's economic viability in a globalized world. Lean and Six Sigma methodologies will become the essential underpinnings of a new strategic management culture for firms wishing to succeed. Many companies have pursued Lean and Six Sigma as separate improvement methodologies with separate improvement organizations and separate improvement objectives. A combined approach like that taken by Canada Post to "Lean/Six Sigma" helps firms achieve both Lean speed and efficiency and Six Sigma quality through a single improvement organization initiative.

FIGURE 14.6

Centralization versus Decentralization—Degrees of Delegation

Highly delegated and decentralized organization

No delegation and highly centralized organization

We'll open the discussion as to whether to centralize or decentralize a firm's manufacturing facilities with an observation: it will be unlikely for a firm to universally adopt an organizational structure that provides only for a centralized or decentralized structure. The decision must be tailored to the individual variables present in the host countries' ecosystems. Generally there will be a balance between the two structures. If you do adopt a one-size-fits-all model, then the outcome might be similar to that experienced by General Motors. Saturn used to promote its plastic side panels in commercials that showed them fending off dents from trashcans and bicycles. "Some had argued that they were integral to Saturn's brand identity, but there was no room for them in GM's complex global product development system."[51] So the soft side panels had to go. In times of stress, there seems to be a natural human instinct toward centralization. But centralization can impose some significant restrictions on adaptability and speed—and in today's world, that can be ruinous.

Recall that centralization and decentralization referred to the degree of delegation that exists within the firm. Visualize a continuum; Figure 14.6 shows that a centralized firm provides only a few activities and authority delegated to subordinates. A decentralized firm adopts the opposite organizational structure. When deciding which structure managers should consider, there are questions. What size is the organization? If the firm is large, then the likelihood is greater that the decentralized structure would provide the best fit. Bear in mind that delegation of activities and authority permits increased workload to be undertaken by senior management. On the other hand, decentralization and delegation will result in increased costs. Where are the firm's customers located? The greater the distance both in time and space, the greater the case that can be made for a decentralized organization. Unless the firm is selling commodities, management needs to be close to the customers. Magna International has adopted a decentralized structure for its manufacturing divisions because it makes the firm more responsive to customers' needs. How homogeneous is the firm's product portfolio? The more heterogeneous or diversified a firm is, the greater the case for the firm to adopt a decentralized structure. Where are the OEMs' suppliers located? We have noted that transportation costs and time are important considerations when selecting venues for the firm's subsidiaries. The greater the distance inputs are required to move through the supply chain, the greater the case for the firm to adopt a decentralized structure. How responsive must the firm be to its stakeholders? If time is of the essence in providing answers to stakeholders, the greater the case for a decentralized structure. How innovative and creative must the organization be? Decentralized structures that empower workers throughout the organization provide a greater likelihood, albeit at a cost, that the firm will undertake innovative initiatives.

Supply Chain Management

Supply chain management (SCM) can be defined as the management of the entire value chain, from the initial supplier of inputs to the manufacturer right through to the retailer, the final customer, and the after-service activities.

Supply chain management (SCM) can be defined as the management of the entire value chain, from the initial supplier of inputs to the manufacturer right through to the retailer, the final customer, and the after-service activities. SCM has three primary goals: reduce inventory, increase the transaction speed by using real-time IT technology, and increase sales by adding value and meeting the needs of the customer more efficiently. There are a number of other SCM definitions but these form the core. Firms constantly seek to improve the SCM efficiency by re-evaluating two key types of transactions: first, the actual physical flows of material that move "forward" from suppliers to customers and, second, the dataflow moving "backward" from customers to suppliers (the data takes the form of orders placed and payments made for materials, services, parts, supplies, and customer feedback). Critical to these re-evaluations is the firm's IT infrastructure. If state of the art, it enables real-time information to flow throughout the firm's supply chain, providing the firm with a significant competitive advantage. See the Mini Case, pages 413–414.

Early in the 20th century, manufacturing industries were very concerned about the performance of their supply chains. One of the most common organizational strategies was vertical integration, in which the entire supply chain was brought within the firm's ownership structure. Henry Ford, for example, built a vertically integrated company in the 1920s and 1930s; his firm owned not only automobile parts production and assembly, but also the downstream car dealerships, and the upstream steel mills, iron ore mines, and rubber plantations.[52]

"The advantages of vertical integration in centralizing decision making and maintaining coordination across the supply chain were sufficient to make it the organizational strategy of choice"[53] until the later few decades of that century. Increasingly the disadvantages became apparent: "firms often found themselves running operations in which they had little expertise, such as Ford's rubber plantations. These non-core businesses were likely to have inferior technology and thus higher costs than more focused competitors. Vertical integration often raised antitrust concerns, especially if the industries in which the firm operated were highly concentrated."[54] Increasingly firms with the traditional vertically integrated and centralized structure were faced with rapid technological change, increasing global competition, and accelerating quality improvement expectations. Their agility in the marketplace was weighed down by the rigidity of their corporate organizational design.

To meet this challenge, they concentrated on leveraging core competencies. If it was something they did well or was critical to the firm's core well-being, they retained it. If not, they spun it off and outsourced. "The necessity of developing core competencies, along with the arrival of low-cost computing and communication via the Internet catalyzed the beginnings of vertical disintegration."[55] A firm focusing its resources in its own areas of expertise leads to great advantages. This mental model of concentrating on core competencies fostered new forms of organizational design that leverage modern information and production technologies (see Chapter 11). "A critical need for ensuring success in these organizations is the creation of inter-firm information systems, embodied in ERP software or SCI systems. These systems look at the entire supply chain as a virtual enterprise that may include a global network of suppliers, factories, warehouses, distribution centers, retailers, and service centers. The virtual enterprise acquires raw materials, transforms them into products, markets and delivers products to customers, and services products over their lifetime."[56]

Supply chains must operate in a coordinated, holistic manner to optimize performance. In today's turbulent marketplace supply chain management systems must coordinate plans and schedules across all supply chain functions. "The efficiency of the production system is ultimately determined by the agility with which the supply chain is managed at the tactical and operational levels to enable timely dissemination of information, accurate coordination of decisions, and management of actions among people."[57] Today, software assists firms in their supply chain management, including programs such as Enterprise Resource Planning (ERP), Customer Resource Management (CRM), and Product Lifecycle Management (PLM). These programs are both supplier-side and customer-side applications. A graphic overview of today's typical international supply chain can be seen in Figure 14.7, page 406.

Drivers of Internationalizing Supply Chains

The four factors that drive the globalization of a firm's supply chain are access to complementary assets, cost savings, marketing necessity, and trade regulations and other constraints.

Complementary Assets

Firms find that if certain resources (e.g., raw materials) are located in a particular country, then they are strongly motivated to perform other supply chain activities (e.g., manufacture products) in that country, dependent, of course, on other variables,

FIGURE 14.7
Today's Typical International
Supply Chain

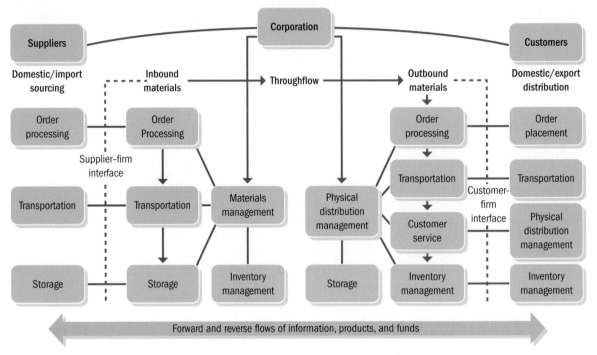

SOURCE: Michael R. Czinkota, Illka A. Ronkainen, and Michael H. Moffett, *International Business*, 7th ed. (Mason, OH: Thomson South-Western, 2005).

such as the cost of labour not being prohibitive. As an alternative example, a firm might consider moving its R&D supply chain activities to a host country to ensure that employees working on manufacturing and R&D are located in the same geographic vicinity. This would permit exploitation of the synergy produced by having the two units interacting with each other.

Cost Savings

The most common reason for outsourcing is the cost of inputs. In many cases, decreased production costs outweigh any added cost due to elaborate and possibly unpredictable logistics (e.g., transportation). In general, the greater the contribution of labour to product cost, the greater the appeal of countries with location economies, such as low wage rates. Prime examples of developed and developing countries adopting this global perspective for their supply chain are evident in the apparel, textiles, and electronics industries. Recall David Ricardo's law of comparative advantage in Chapter 6, pages 167–169, and Figure 6.3, page 162, that proved it is more efficient for countries to specialize in a few products rather than produce many goods at a high opportunity cost. Today firms understand the cost savings they can achieve by moving certain job functions and process facilities to the most cost-effective location. As a result, outsourcing will increase.

When McKinsey and Company surveyed "7,300 senior executives from companies around the world [they] found that roughly 4 out of 5 of the executives said outsourcing was good for the global economy."[58] The approval ratio "was virtually the same in Europe, Asia and the United States."[59] They were also asked how outsourcing affected their business. "In Europe, 70 percent of executives said outsourcing was good for business. So did 86 percent of Chinese executives and 97 percent of those in India. Yet in the United States, headquarters to many of the most aggressive and successful globalizing companies, the fraction of executives that said outsourcing was either very positive or somewhat positive for their company dropped to 58 percent"[60]—clearly a growing political hostility against outsourcing.

The paramount issues these managers face are where they should locate their subsidiaries in order to access location economies; what role the subsidiaries should play both short term and long term in the firm's global strategy; and which activities conducted by the firm should remain internal and which, including management, should be outsourced. Location economies are at the top of the list of variables to be considered.

Marketing Necessity

Another reason for outsourcing is that it is a marketing necessity; the sales and marketing advantages accrue because of a firm's presence and contribution to the local economy. Marketing necessity is likely to be important for industries characterized by low volumes and high product prices that require global sales for business success. Aerospace and the sale of regional jets are a good example of such an industry— Canada's Bombardier and Brazil's Embraer currently compete for favour in China and as a result find it a necessity to establish a presence in, and collaborate with, Chinese aerospace firms.

Trade Regulations and Other Constraints

The final driver of internationalizing supply chains is local trade restrictions and other constraints encountered by international firms. These constraints will increase the risk and the cost of doing business. The frequency of encountering these constraints will increase in proportion to the number of host markets the domestic firm has decided to enter. Host countries' political complexities, the degree to which the rule of law has been adopted, the state of transportation infrastructure, business culture, currency, data and communication standards, and new geopolitical concerns arising in part because of the War on Terror are some of the complexities that will contribute to a firm's supply chain costs and risks. In addition, international firms will be required to maintain and coordinate multiple supply chain systems to accommodate the uniqueness of each host country within which they operate.

Today's Conceptual Models

There has been significant transformation in the supply chain models over the past few decades. Today's conceptual supply chain models can be viewed on a continuum (see Figure 14.8) that is characterized by the degree of control over the OEM. At one end of the continuum is the single corporation that manages and operates facilities at every step of the supply chain. It is a traditional, vertically integrated firm. At the other end of the continuum is the virtual corporation. Virtual corporations (see Chapter 11, pages 322–323) have no function in the supply chain other than product design, sales, and marketing functions. Each of these five models is briefly described below.

The **vertically integrated firm** manages all supply chain activities from sourcing of materials to delivery and after-service. These firms manufacture almost all of the components required for the product in-house. They may outsource small amounts of noncritical inputs. The next step along the continuum is defined as **decentralized manufacturing** led by the OEM model. The OEM at these firms undertakes the final assembly of the goods by outsourcing most of the supply chain activities to independent suppliers. The advantage of this model is that the firm and its suppliers may increase cost

The **vertically integrated** firm manages all supply chain activities from sourcing of materials to delivery and after-service.

Decentralized manufacturing is the final assembly of goods by outsourcing most of the supply chain activities to independent suppliers.

FIGURE 14.8

Decreasing-Control Supply Chain Models

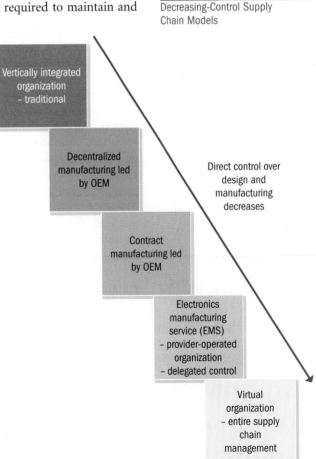

Vertically integrated organization – traditional

Decentralized manufacturing led by OEM

Contract manufacturing led by OEM

Electronics manufacturing service (EMS) – provider-operated organization – delegated control

Virtual organization – entire supply chain management

Direct control over design and manufacturing decreases

savings and quality advantages as a result of each of the suppliers focusing on its own core competencies. Unlike the vertically integrated firm, these organizations must establish good information flow between the firm and its suppliers to ensure that adequate inventory, quality, and other variables are attended. To keep control, the OEM might provide component design, process engineering, and facility tooling to its suppliers. Today, most automobile manufacturers have adopted this supply chain model.

Firms using the **contract-manufacturing** model contract out all production to suppliers, including the final assembly of the product.

In the middle of the continuum are firms adopting a **contract-manufacturing** model led by the OEM. These firms contract out all production to suppliers, including the final assembly of the product. Contract manufacturing firms adopt this model to permit them to focus solely on product design, sales, and marketing. These activities are considered to be the core competencies of these firms. The advantage of this model is that by outsourcing, the firm can be more flexible as it no longer has responsibility for labour or production management. If the product does not meet the specifications, the firm can cancel the contract and find another supplier. The disadvantage of this model is giving up control of the quality and performance of the finished product exposes the firm to considerable risk. The information flow between the firm and its suppliers is critical.

Firms adopting the **electronics manufacturing service (EMS)** model delegate control of not just the manufacturing but also the design and engineering supply chain activities.

The next model is the **electronics manufacturing service (EMS)**. This model provides for the firm to delegate control of not just the manufacturing but also the design and engineering supply chain activities. Often the firm will contract with the supplier to manage the entire process. The OEM brand name will be on the final product and it is responsible for marketing and selling the product. But the EMS provider controls most of the supply chain activities. In this model almost the entire risk has shifted to the EMS firm. However, quality defects and supply disruptions will negatively affect the OEM.

At the other end of the continuum is the virtual corporation supply chain. This model provides for a service provider that controls and manages the entire supply chain. That firm, in essence, stands in the shoes of the OEM. The OEM contracts for the service, and has its brand placed on the product, but has no control or input into the manufacturing process. Its role can best be defined as that of a spectator. Firms adopting the virtual corporation model are entirely disconnected and contribute only sales and marketing to the supply chain activities.

When considering these five models, supply chain managers examine the tradeoff between the process control and the advantages of distributing responsibility for supply chain activities to others. At the core of their decision is, as we have seen, the question, "will the model permit wringing pennies out of the value chain and/or add value to the product in the mind of the consumer?" In determining which model to select, the decision makers will consider three factors. First, what is the product? The supply chain manager must consider the size of the components; transportation costs; whether products are large, small, customized, or specialized; and whether time is of the essence. All contribute to the supply chain manager's model selection. Second, what are the target markets? The geographic and societal characteristics of the marketplace affect the suitability of the supply chain model. For example, it might be necessary to manufacture goods in another country in order to expedite delivery. Third, the state of the firm's IT infrastructure will limit or enable certain models. Clearly, the virtual corporation is grounded in communications and technology.

Supply Chain Innovators

Here are three companies that have led the way in innovative supply chain management. Observe the way they have led the revolution within their industries by focusing on internal optimization, external relationships, and inventory management.

On-Demand Supply Chain—The IBM Transformation

International Business Machines (IBM) has transformed and improved its supply chain efficiency. In the early 1990s, IBM started consolidating its organizational structure and was left little choice but to adopt advances in technology after company data processing costs reached three times the industry average.[61] Specifically, IBM deployed extensive middleware to reduce repetition in data entry and ease access to the company's vast information resources. "The company has leveraged the use of many third-party solutions, such as SAP for Enterprise Resource Planning (ERP), Siebel for Customer Relationship Management (CRM), i2 for Supply Chain Management (SCM), and Ariba for procurement. However, IBM believes that its value chain ideology has allowed a symbiotic relationship to form with many of its suppliers. This value network is defined by an IBM white paper as 'a group of trading partners, focused on core competencies and connected via web-enabled technology, collaborating to provide total solutions to customers.'"[62]

A New Mental Model—The Li & Fung Virtual Enterprise

Can you imagine being an entrepreneur establishing a firm that permits you to work at home in your pyjamas? Can you imagine a firm that harnesses technology to maintain a comprehensive database; that identifies the "best" global supply chain activities and services to meet its client's needs? Li & Fung Virtual Enterprise is doing just that. This firm receives orders, selects suppliers, and arranges for the delivery of materials on behalf of clients. It has perfected the virtual corporation. Clients include Wal-Mart, JC Penney, Kohl's, and Meijer. Amazingly, Li & Fung's achieves success without ever coming into possession of any part of the product; the firm relies totally on selling its expertise in managing supply chains of firms that prior to introducing this service undertook SCM activities in-house. Today they find great saving in using the services of this firm. It has successfully exploited "new technology as a primary means of maintaining competitive advantage. Using Internet capabilities, Li & Fung developed and maintains a **customer relationship management (CRM)** system that provides the critical fast and seamless information flow. Through dedicated Internet sites, Li & Fung's customers have access to their past orders and billing, can track current orders, and place new orders. They can also see other clients' orders."[63] Indeed if a client likes what another client has ordered, it can "piggyback" on the initial order, thereby lowering costs because of economies of scale. "Li & Fung has excelled at finding extremely low-cost labour and raw or processed materials and then identifying the most efficient manufacturers."[64] Figure 14.9 displays the complex nature of Li & Fung's business model. Li & Fung is the nexus between the developing countries offering low-cost, labour-intensive manufacturing and the consumers in the developed nations. Truly innovative, harnessing emerging technology—a new mental model!

> **Customer relationship management (CRM)** entails managing all aspects of interaction a company has with its customers.

Build-to-Order Supply Chain—The Dell Model

In 1994, Dell was struggling to keep afloat in the fiercely competitive PC market, but one decision set Dell on a winning path. Dell's management team adopted a new mental model concerning supply chain operations. Dell changed to a build-to-order procedure,

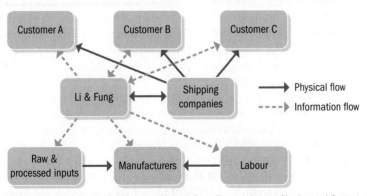

> **FIGURE 14.9**
> The Complex Nature of Li & Fung's Business Model

SOURCE: Adapted from William J. White, Alan C. O'Connor, and Brent R. Rowe, *Economic Impact of Inadequate Infrastructure for Supply Chain Integration* (Research Triangle Park, NC: RTI International, 2004).

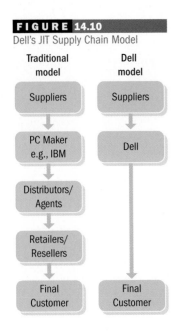

FIGURE 14.10

Dell's JIT Supply Chain Model

eliminated inventory costs, and became not only a pioneer of just-in-time delivery, but also the number one computer systems company in 2001.

Supplier and customer relationships are the key to the success of the Dell model. By partnering with stable companies interested in consistently high-quantity supplies and targeting large IT–based customers interested in routine PC upgrades, Dell was able to successfully implement its very successful business model. Dell empowers PC buyers to use convergence marketing to design computers to their personal specifications. Dell's new mental model included selling directly to customers, thereby eliminating numerous distribution channels while the primary competitors, Apple, IBM, and Compaq, continued to use the traditional distributors, retailers, and resellers (see Figure 14.10).

To Source or Not to Source?

Another production and supply chain issue we have earlier briefly discussed is whether to source components for the firm's products. It is clear that the Apple executive's decision to source the components for the iPod shows the power of getting it right! The success of the iPod is contributing significantly to Apple's comeback in the industry. One of the advantages to a firm vertically integrating is that it may result in a lower cost per unit, provided it is an activity in which the firm has a sustainable competitive advantage. If, on the other hand, it is not a core competency and can be provided externally at a lower cost, then the firm should probably consider outsourcing. At times, special manufacturing machinery and/or facilities will be required because of the uniqueness of the product or its components; for example, perhaps a new die and tap to create an engineer-specified thread pattern for a structural screw or a metric factory required to build something to imperial measure. The cost for the firm to acquire this new machinery might be prohibitive so outsourcing to a third party that may well have other clients needing the same unique engineering features could be considered. Unfortunately, the decision to outsource is a double-edged sword. To make it in-house provides the firm with security of supply and ensures control over the inputs although they may be more expensive than if the firm outsourced. However, sourcing from third parties may expose the firm to considerable risk. For example, the supplier may cease production, increase costs unilaterally, sell the component to others or experience labour strife. From the suppliers' perspective, once the significant capital investment required to produce the specialized components is considered, it may view the opportunity to supply as a substantial risk. For example, the OEM may decide it no longer requires the component, thereby leaving the supplier with useless machinery and facilities, or encouraged by its strong bargaining position, OEMs may wish to renegotiate the terms of the contact. By not outsourcing, proprietary risk is managed; the production of certain components will be core competencies for the firm. To outsource core competencies allows the core competency within the firm to atrophy, not a strategically sound decision. What then prevents others replicating the product? The final advantage is scheduling. Firms controlling their own manufacturing process and availability of inputs are unlikely to miss target dates. Dependency on external sources increases the risk of supply interruption. The advantages of acquiring components from external sources include flexibility in the choice of suppliers and cost. Acquiring inputs from a variety of suppliers encourages marketplace competition to ensure supply of the firm's inputs at the lowest possible price.

A wonderful example of sourcing to obtain sustainable competitive advantage is inside Apple's iPod. Figure 14.1 on page 398 reveals that others substantially make the iPod! Contributing to this innovative marvel are "Toshiba, Sony, Portal Player, Samsung, Texas Instruments, Wolfson Microelectronics, Cypress Semiconductor, Synaptics and others—a veritable who's who in the high tech hardware industry. These suppliers keep their technology ahead of the performance and cost curves, and Apple benefits. Apple integrates these discrete components (through software intelligence) and packages them in the clean white-and-chrome 'bathtub.'"[65]

Management Implications

- The exponential advances in technology have affected positively manufacturing and supply chain management practices for Canadian SMEs. Today new mental models are required in order to participate in this new marketplace. A continuous value chain analysis must be undertaken by managers in order to identify at the earliest opportunity shifts that may affect the firm's value chain activities. In the competitive global market, all firms must leverage their resources to remain competitive. Managers must "wring the pennies out" or add value to each functional area's activity. When crafting the right strategy to accommodate the variables within their unique ecosystem, managers must take a systems view of the firm's activities and not, as many have done in the past, examine only their discrete functional areas.

- Savings accrue through the lean manufacturing approach. Achieving savings from quality must be a part of the firm's DNA. Successful implementation of TQM requires the organization to be committed to quality and to believe in continuous improvement. TQM is a new way of thinking about organizations. Its primary goal is to meet the end-users' requirements—a quality product or service. TQM–managed organizations must be learning organizations. They must advocate teamwork and thrive in a high-trust culture environment. At times these goals may require new vision and leadership within the firm.

CHAPTER SUMMARY

- During the past two decades, Canadian, firms have dramatically adopted global manufacturing and supply chain management's new paradigms. These new paradigms require leaders prepared to adopt new mental models. These new models build on a foundation of lean manufacturing systems.
- Adoption of new supply chain paradigms regarding production factors, such as capacity allocation planning, concentrated-decentralized facilities, and standardization, versus customization of products will be essential.
- Political boundaries introduce considerations that influence how business will be conducted in different venues and on the activities needed to move goods globally. Relevant issues include laws requiring the use of local supplies for manufacturing in a particular country, labour relations, environmental regulations, and export/import laws. A second dimension of geopolitical sourcing is the need for government-to-government agreements as part of sourcing decisions.
- The advances in technology have been a boon to international business. The growing sophistications of manufacturing and supply chain management software, global radio frequency identification, and electronic data interchange and other technology are paying big dividends for early adopters.
- Supply chain management involves transportation across borders. Transportation infrastructure is one of many supply chain factors that must be analyzed. Government has a role in making the ground fertile by supporting advanced factor endowments that will attract global manufacturing and enable domestic firms to participate in international firms' supply chains.
- Since 9/11, security has become a significant cost factor for the movement of goods and services for Canadian business when measured in both time and money.
- Today firms take a systems approach rather than viewing activities as separate silos. The systems approach includes the incorporation and interaction with outside organizations and individuals. To achieve this, firms adopt JIT delivery to lower the cost of inventory, adopt the electronic data interchange to make the order processing more efficient, undertake early supplier involvement for better planning of goods development and movement, develop efficient customer response systems using RFID and other methods to track sales activities on the retail side, and implement quality programs to eliminate waste and achieve efficiencies.
- In viewing international logistics as a system, firms must increasingly concentrate on their core competencies to remain competitive and rely upon partners for the provision of other supply chain inputs.
- Lean manufacturing is the continuous pursuit of waste elimination. Enterprise resource plan

systems are the central nervous system of the organization. ERP attempts to integrate all departments and functions across a company onto a single computer system that can serve all those different departments' particular needs. It leverages knowledge and provides real-time information to decision makers.

- There is a relationship between quality and cost. To achieve these cost savings, manufacturing firms implement TQM programs and quality assurance programs. Total quality management has become a major factor in operations management, particularly in the conduct of manufacturing and supply chain management.

- TQM is both a philosophy and a set of guiding principles that represent the foundation of a continuously improving organization. TQM is the application of quantitative methods and human resources to improve the materials and services supplied to an organization and all the processes within an organization, and the degree to which needs of customers are met, now and in future. TQM integrates fundamental management practices with the firm's improvement efforts, and applies technical tools to undertake a disciplined approach focused on continuous improvement.

- When undertaking facility location planning, decision makers will look for location economies that provide low wages, access to the customer to reduce transportation costs and enhance customer satisfaction, and supply-suitable solutions to issues such as the modes of transportation to support the locations under consideration. Think of business as being like water!

- Many practitioners suggest that structure follows strategy. A firm's organizational structure will be crafted in such a way as to permit the functions' and units' activities to best support the firm's vision and mission statements, and the corporate goals.

Organizational structure must enable command and control of the organization effectively and efficiently.

- The terms *centralization* and *decentralization* refer to the degree of delegation that exists within the firm.

- Supply chain management can be defined as the management of the entire value chain, from the initial supplier of inputs to the manufacturer, right through to the retailer, the final customer, and the after-service activities. SCM's three primary goals are to reduce inventory, increase transaction speed by using real-time IT technology, and increase sales by adding value and meeting the needs of the customer more efficiently.

- The four factors driving the globalization of a firm's supply chain are access to complementary assets, cost savings, marketing necessity, and trade regulations and other constraints.

- Global supply chain managers must be aware of the increased system heterogeneity, increased political complexity, decreased legal security, transportation modality changes, greater delivery times and higher volumes, and new geopolitical concerns.

- There has been significant transformation in supply chain models characterized by OEMs' degree of control. At one end of the continuum is the single corporation that manages and operates facilities at every step of the supply chain. It is a traditional, vertically integrated firm. At the other end of the continuum is the virtual corporation. Virtual corporations have no function in the supply chain other than product design, sales, and marketing functions.

- Decision makers will consider cost per unit, special manufacturing machinery and facilities required, the capital investment required, and the importance of scheduling when deciding whether to source components for the firm's products. The advantages of acquiring components from external sources are flexibility in the choice of suppliers and input cost.

REVIEW QUESTIONS

1. Briefly outline some emerging PEST-C issues specific to global manufacturing and supply chains that Canadian firms might face when contemplating entry into foreign markets.

2. Explain how global radio frequency identification (RFID), ta interchange (EDI), and voice over Internet P) technology can enhance business.

rtation component of the firm's supply ement can be divided into an examination re, availability of modes, and the choice Discuss.

4. There are three types of ocean shipping. Discuss.

5. In selecting the appropriate transportation mode, managers must consider the needs of the firm and its customers. What four factors might they consider?

6. Currently, security obstacles to free trade are being addressed both globally and regionally. Discuss three recent initiatives in which Canada is playing a role.

7. What are ISO 9000 and the Six Sigma programs? Why is it important that Canadian firms register in these programs?

8. What are JIT inventory, flexible manufacturing, enterprise resource planning, and TQM?

9. Why is capacity planning extremely important for both Canadian manufacturing and service industries?

10. Centralization and decentralization refer to the degree of delegation that exists within the firm. What six questions will management consider in determining the appropriate degree of delegation for the firm?

11. What is supply chain management?

12. What four factors drive globalization of a firm's supply chain?

13. What are five advantages for firms that vertically integrate?

REFLECTIVE THINKING QUESTIONS

1. Having completed this chapter, reread the quotations on the first page, critically reflect on the validity of the authors' statements, and provide your opinion as to the validity of each. Evidence-based answers are preferred to rhetorical answers.

2. The new economic order has witnessed an economic power shift to China, primarily because of its low-cost labour and valuation of its currency. The government has served notice that it considers the automobile industry, a "pillar" industry in China's economic global strategic plan. Is Canada as focused? Do you think Canada undertakes sufficient long-term strategic planning to enable Canadian manufacturing SMEs to participate in the new global economic order?

3. Canada is expending scarce resources participating in initiatives such as the Customs Self-Assessment program, Partners in Protection, and the U.S. Customs

Trade Partnership Against Terrorism programs. Are these security measures really needed for Canada to participate in the global marketplace or have we over-reacted to the War on Terror?

4. The outsource suppliers for iPod keep their technology ahead of the performance and cost curves, and Apple benefits. What prevents you from replicating iPod's success and entering into similar supply arrangements? Do you think iPod's comparative advantage is sustainable?

5. The North American Missile Defense shield proposal contemplated a government-to-government agreement. Do you view such an initiative with trade and economic benefits as an instrument of foreign policy? If so, who benefits and who loses?

6. Ethics and corporate governance issues aside for a moment, an interesting question arises from RFID technology—whose data is it? Discuss.

GLOBAL E-RESEARCH

Visit www.power.nelson.com for research suggestions, questions, and a number of background discussion papers on this topic.

MINI CASE

Kirin Brewery Company Accurately Forecasts—and Meets—Demand

Inventory control is one of the key business goals for any manufacturer. Accordingly, effective supply chain management (SCM) must be a priority. Firms that fail to control their inventory will experience lost sales or incur unnecessary costs because of excess inventory.

A Japanese firm, Kirin Brewery, markets approximately 700 products, including domestic and imported beer, whisky, liqueur, shouchu, and wine. In 2003, Kirin completely rebuilt its supply/demand planning system using technology and supporting software to correct significant inventory issues. Almost immediately the company improved the accuracy of its demand forecast and succeeded in automating a very complicated procurement processes.

"The spirits and wine business is largely dependent on imported products. We trade with thirty-four suppliers in fourteen countries. The business requires an extremely long lead-time from placing an order to import clearance proce-

dures. Some products can be obtained only by making a reservation more than one year in advance. The lead-time also depends on the area, season, and order lot, as well as the tonnage capacity of trucks, which is restricted by law in some nations. These complex factors and conditions are stored in the master database. All decision-making processes, including the timing and volume of placing orders, are automated. In the past, these processes were dependent on individual staff knowledge and experience and carried out with spreadsheets. We succeeded in dramatically improving efficiency for such processes, says Katsutoshi Ishii, of Kirin's Logistics Division."

The new SCM system has two major strengths. First, the procurement operation, including order planning and future stock simulation, that in the past was processed by the individual staff largely from memory is now systemized and automated. Second, the new efficient demand forecast and shipment plan are based on the most appropriate analytical model. The models were specially designed by arranging dozens of analytical methods, including methods based on past data, methods reflecting the latest performance, and methods for seasonality. Simulations with different variables and patterns chosen for product characteristics take place daily. One popular feature was the alarm function in the new SCM software that notifies the user of deviations from the forecast in the actual figures—a great dashboard tool!

Source: *Always Enough, Never Too Much: Kirin Brewery Company, Limited Accurately Forecasts—and Meets—Demand* (Customer Success, 2006).

QUESTIONS

1. How important do you think it is to have all members of the firm buy into a concept like Kirin's new SCM system? Will the old guard be comfortable with the existing SCM system or will they feel threatened? If so, how would you sell a new SCM system similar to Kirin's?

2. The case states "effective supply chain management (SCM) must be a priority." Do you agree or disagree?

3. How would you make a business case to your board of directors that the money and effort required for a SCM program will enhance a firm's bottom line over the long term? What specific points might you put forward to bolster your business case?

ENDNOTES

1. Niccolò Machiavelli, *The Prince and the Discourses* (Page 21, Chapter VI) (The Modern Library, Random House Inc., 1950), retrieved August 25, 2006, from www.design.caltech.edu/erik/Misc/Machiavelli.html.

2. Andrew S. Grove, *Strengthen Your Management Team* (Steps to Growth Capital, July 12, 2005), retrieved August 25, 2006, from http://strategis.ic.gc.ca/sc_mangb/stepstogrowth/engdoc/step4/ssg-4-6.php.

3. Masaaki Imai, *Famous Quotes on Change and Organizations* (12 Manage, Rigor and Relevance, April 9, 2006), retrieved August 25, 2006, from www.12manage.com/quotes_co.html.

4. *Leon M. Cautillo Quotes* (Historic Quotes and Proverbs Archive, 2003), retrieved August 25, 2006, from www.worldofquotes.com/author/Leon-M.-Cautillo/1/index.html.

5. *Aristotle Quotes*, (ThinkExist.com Quotations), retrieved November 16, 2006, from http://www3.thinkexist.com/quotation/quality_is_not_an_act_it_is_a_habit/147153.html.

6. Leonard Arianto (Tan), *Sun Tzu's Art of War* (1996), retrieved August 25, 2006, from www.geocities.com/Athens/4884.

7. "Canada" (*The World Fact Book*, September 7, 2006), retrieved September 18, 2006, from www.cia.gov/cia/publications/factbook/geos/ca.html.

8. Ibid.

9. *The State of Food and Agriculture 2005* (Rome, Italy: Food and Agriculture Organization of the United Nations, 2005), retrieved September 18, 2006, from ftp://ftp.fao.org/docrep/fao/008/a0050e/a0050e_full.pdf.

10. "Canada."

11. Bill Ginnodo and Celia Ginnodo, *Our Favorite Quality Quotes* (Arlington Heights, IL: Pride Publications, 1996).

12. Scott Frahm, "China and the World Trade Organization," (*Supply Chain Management*, February 3, 2004), retrieved August 25, 2006, from http://scm.ncsu.edu/public/facts/facs040203.html.

13. Carlton Chen, "Colt Defense Completes Diemaco Acquisition" (*Colt Defense News*, May 20, 2005), retrieved September 17, 2006, from www.colt.com/mil/news.asp.

14. J. S. McClenahen, "Waking up to a New World" (*Industry Week*, June 1, 2003), retrieved September 18, 2006, from www.industryweek.com/ReadArticle.aspx?ArticleID=1260.

15. Andrea R. Mihailescu, "Piracy Still Lurks the High Seas," *The Washington Times*, July 16, 2004.

16. Klaus Hympendahl, "Registration of Pirate Attacks since 1996" (*Yacht Piracy*, 2005), retrieved August 25, 2006, from www.yachtpiracy.org/en/list_of_attacked_yachts.htm.

17. Jason Dedrick, Kenneth Kraemer, and Sandra Yamashiro, *Refining and Extending the Business Model with Information Technology: Dell Computer Corporation* (Center for Research on Information Technology and Organizations at the University of California at Irvine, May 19, 1999), retrieved September 27, 2006, from www.indiana.edu/~tisj/readers/full-text/16-1%20kraemer.pdf.

18. William J. White, Alan C. O'Connor, and Brent R. Rowe, *Economic Impact of Inadequate Infrastructure for Supply Chain Integration* (Planning Report 04-2, May–June 2004), retrieved August 25, 2006, from www.nist.gov/director/prog-ofc/report04-2.pdf.

19. David Sims, *Omron Sets Sights on U.S. RFID Market* (Technology Marketing Corporation, November 29, 2005), retrieved August 25, 2006, from http://news.tmcnet.com/news/2005/nov/1215576.htm.

20. Ibid.

21. Michael J. Liard, *RFID in the Supply Chain: The Wal-Mart Factor* (Venture Development Corporation, November 11, 2003), retrieved November 11, 2006, from http://www.mhmonline.com/nID/1213/MHM/viewStory.asp.

22. Sims, *Omron Sets Sights on U.S. RFID Market.*

23. Ibid.

24. *Growth of RFID* (RFID Lowdown, November 3, 2005), retrieved September 17, 2006, from www.rfidlowdown.com/standards/index.html.

25. Zhu Shenshen, "Wave of the Future: IDs by Radio," *Shanghai Daily*, November 28, 2005.

26. D. Machalaba and A.Pasztor, "Thinking Inside the Box: Shipping Containers Get Smart" (*Wall Street Journal*, January 15, 2004), retrieved August 25, 2006, from www.skybitz.com/newsroom/pdf/WSJ1.15.04.pdf.

27. Robert T. Hise, "The Implications of Time-Based Competition on International Logistics Strategy, (*Business Horizons*, Vol. 38, Iss. 5, 1995).

28. "Canada."

29. "APEC Backs Security Initiatives, Completion of WTO Trade Round" (*Washington File*, November 16, 2005), retrieved August 25, 2006, from http://usinfo.state.gov/usinfo/Archive/2005/Nov/16-65384.html.

30 Ibid.

31 *The Free and Secure Trade (FAST) Program* (Importers, February 21, 2006), retrieved August 25, 2006, from www.cbsa-asfc.gc.ca/import/fast/menu-e.html.

32 Terry Ballad, *A Day with Diogenes, Section 3*, retrieved September 18, 2006, from http://faculty.quinnipiac.edu/libraries/tballard/diogenes.htm.

33 *Just-in-Time (JIT) Inventory* (Services Solutions, 2004), retrieved August 25, 2006, from www.tubularsteel.com/solutions_sol004.asp.

34 Ibid.

35 Ibid.

36 "Flexible Manufacturing System" (*Lean Glossary*, 2004), retrieved August 25, 2006, from www.leanadvisors.com/Lean/glossary/definition.cfm/Word/Flexible%20Manufacturing%20System.cfm.

37 Ibid.

38 "Acronyms and Term Definitions: L" (*CIO Resources: Glossaries*, 2000), retrieved September 18, 2006, from http://searchcio.techtarget.com/gDefinition/0,294236,sid19_gci810519_alpL,00.html.

39 Ibid.

40 Ibid.

41 Ibid.

42 Ibid.

43 Dr. Bernardo F. Adiviso, *TQM: Concepts, Evolution, and Prospects* (Seameo Voctech, 1998), retrieved August 25, 2006, from www.voctech.org.bn/virtual_lib/tqmconcepts.htm.

44 Ibid.

45 *Brainy Quote* (BrainyMedia.com, 2005), retrieved August 25, 2006, from www.brainyquote.com.

46 Dr. Bernardo F. Adiviso, *TQM: Concepts, Evolution, and Prospects.*

47 Larry Taylor, "A Comparison of the Criteria and Strategies of Different Awards," *The Innovation Journal*, Vol. 5, Iss. 1, 2000, retrieved November 17, 2006, from http://www.innovation.cc/awards/baldrige-taylor.htm.

48 *ISO 9000 and ISO 14000—in Brief* (International Organization for Standardization, August 22, 2006), retrieved September 18, 2006, from www.iso.org/iso/en/iso9000-14000/understand/inbrief.html.

49 Tom Peters, *Liberation Management: Necessary Disorganization for the Nanosecond Nineties*, 1st ed. (New York: Ballantine Books, 1994).

50 E. Lisa Moses, *Process Excellence: Battling Inefficiencies at Canada Post* (Six Sigma, 2005), retrieved September 18, 2006, from www.isixsigma.com/library/content/c051114a.asp.

51 David Foster, *General Motors and Organization Design* (ChicagoBoyz, May 3, 2005), retrieved August 25, 2006, from www.chicagoboyz.net/archives/003111.html.

52 White, O'Connor, and Rowe, *Economic Impact of Inadequate Infrastructure for Supply Chain Integration.*

53 Ibid.

54 Ibid.

55 Ibid.

56 Ibid.

57 Ibid.

58 Eduardo Porter, "Outsourcing Is Becoming a Harder Sell in the U.S" (*The New York Times*, March 6, 2004), retrieved August 26, 2006, from http://classwork.busadm.mu.edu/Economics%20Newspaper%20Articles/International%20Economics/2004/2004%2003%2006%20Outsourcing%20is%20becoming%20a%20harder%20sell%20in%20the%20US.PDF.

59 Ibid.

60 Ibid.

61 White, O'Connor, and Rowe, *Economic Impact of Inadequate Infrastructure for Supply Chain Integration.*

62 Ibid.

63 Ibid.

64 Ibid.

65 James Conley, "Trademarks, Not Patents: The Real Competitive Advantage of the Apple iPod" (*Current Articles*, 2005), retrieved August 25, 2006, from www.core77.com/reactor/12.05_ipod_trademark.asp.

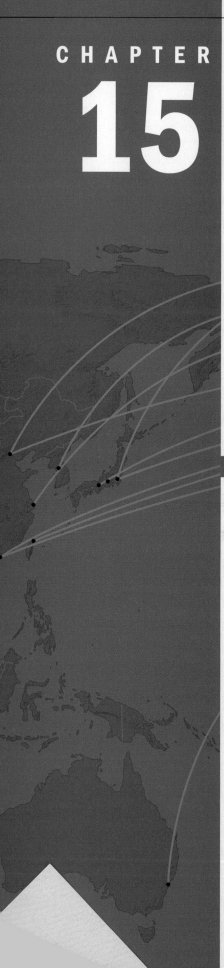

Global Human Resources and Labour Management

"It's almost worse than sending a Westerner, to send someone who has the Chinese language but not the Chinese values."[1]

—Kay Kutt, VP, Paragon Decision Resources

"The best executive is the one who has sense enough to pick good men to do what he wants done, and self-restraint enough to keep from meddling with them while they do it."[2]

—Theodore Roosevelt, 26th President of the United States

"When people go to work, they shouldn't have to leave their hearts at home."[3]

—Betty Bender, former president, American School Food Service Association

"So much of what we call management consists of making it difficult for people to work."[4]

—Peter Drucker, business theorist

"Globalization has changed us into a company that searches the world, not just to sell or to source, but to find intellectual capital—the world's best talents and greatest ideas."[5]

—Jack Welch, former CEO, General Electric

LEARNING OUTCOMES

- Recognize how Canada's cultural diversity can be exploited to gain competitive advantage in a firm's international human resource management.
- Understand the strategic importance of human resource management to an organization's sustainability in a global environment.
- Examine the five major human resource management processes.
- Identify the impediments restricting an employee's willingness to undertake foreign assignments.
- Understand why expatriate managers experience a high failure rate when undertaking foreign assignments.
- Evaluate ethnocentric, polycentric, and geocentric staffing policies.
- Evaluate the success predictors to assist in evaluation of suitable expatriates for foreign assignments.
- Compare employee compensation and benefits packages.
- Understand the importance of having a repatriation plan for expatriates.
- Examine new labour directions and emerging labour issues in a global setting.
- Examine some of the regional and cultural barriers to female expatriate managers in the global workplace.
- Understand the importance of developing a global mindset.
- Evaluate emerging global threats in human resource management.

Cultural Diversity a Jewel Yet to Be Discovered

Don Mason/Corbis Canada

"Cultural diversity is making an increasingly important contribution to the economic well-being of Western Canada. It is a jewel yet to be discovered and exploited by most of . . . [Canada's] small and mid-sized businesses (SMEs). . . . In B.C. [for example], the significant increase in the immigrant population is no secret to those living in Greater Vancouver. During the past two decades, more than 1 million immigrants, primarily from Asia, have moved [t]here. Statistics show that in 2001, immigrants represented 26.1 percent of the total provincial population.[6] Most of these immigrants—nearly three in four—live in the Vancouver metropolitan area where they represent more than 37 percent of the population.[7] This cultural diversity provides an open window to the world. In terms of trade, B.C. exported goods and services valued at $47.9 billion while importing $43.7 billion in 2005.[8] In December 2005, the United Nations Conference on Trade and Development reported that China remains the most attractive FDI destination in the world in 2005 for the fourth consecutive year. India rose from third to second to bump the United States down to third.[9] This evidence of strong economic growth and improved investment environment in Asia is driving the need for realignment by . . . [Canadian] SMEs."[10]

". . . SMEs must immediately shift their business strategies to exploit the new business opportunities emerging in Asia, and place less reliance for growth on the U.S. market."[11] SMEs sell to, and increasingly employ, immigrants. Canadian firms will have to "work with governments to raise the skill level of workers and ensure a more successful integration of immigrants into the Canadian economy. I suspect that by luck, rather than design, . . . [many provinces] find themselves uniquely positioned in a global, multicultural environment. We have new Canadians who know the culture, and have for example the contacts and the entrepreneurial skill to enable . . . [Canada] to do well in a hot Asian market. Provincial governments . . . must recognize and support the our diversity competitive advantage and reflectively think about how we can best support and leverage our cultural diversity. It is an overlooked jewel that needs to be polished."[12]

A SUN TZU MOMENT. . .

Visual Arts Library, London/Alamy

"One whose upper and lower ranks have the same desires will be victorious."[13]

Some of the greatest human resource management (HRM) challenges Canada has faced were the transition of hundreds of thousands of men and women from peacetime jobs to wartime positions. At the commencement of the war with Germany in 1939, the RCAF had only 4,000 personnel and 195 mostly obsolete aircraft. By the end of the war, 131,000 pilots, navigators, and other air crew graduated from Canada's air training programs. Of this number some 70,000 were Canadians, and most of them served overseas. Eventually 47 RCAF squadrons served overseas, and a large number of RCAF personnel served in British units. Altogether, nearly a quarter of a million Canadians, including over 17,000 members of the Women's Division, served in the RCAF at home or abroad during World War II. Canada's air force had become the fourth largest among the Allied powers.[14]

The shifts experienced in military culture—hiring, staffing, controlling, and managing—were Herculean. Today globalization presents similar, significant, human resource challenges.

Opening Thoughts

Globalization is decreasing the barriers to trade between nations. Modern technological developments have opened the door to this phenomenon through the minimization of barriers, cheap transportation, and increased speed of communication. "Like many other industrialized nations, Canada is going through a second wave of globalization. In the first wave, the largest companies set up offices and plants outside their home countries. During the current second wave, small and medium-sized companies are expanding outside their home countries and becoming international. The second wave of globalization is sometimes a consequence of the first one. In the automotive business, for example, the fact that car manufacturers want to use the same parts for their cars and trucks regardless of location has driven auto parts suppliers [both large and small] to establish offices and plants abroad."[15] Canada's Magna Corporation, a global supplier of technologically advanced automotive systems with subsidiaries in North and South America, Europe, and Asia, is one of the most diversified automotive suppliers in the world. Magna has had little choice but to accompany its automobile clients or lose them.

Consequently, monoculture is being replaced by a pluralistic society, and the concept of the global village is becoming a reality, as discussed in the opening vignette. For organizations that want to compete and prosper in this diverse and complex global environment, an international understanding of a broad range of variables, including acquiring cross-cultural sensitivity and adaptation, becomes the key to survival. Effectively managing employees in a global environment demands skilled human resource (HR) managers with global competencies. Skills in deployment, transfer of knowledge, and development and retention of talent, are just a few. These skill sets are not new to HR managers, but they have become more complex and critical to the overall success of an organization. HR managers must adjust their traditional mental models and adapt to their changing environment based on a PEST-C analysis (see Chapter 2) to ensure the organization's sustainability. Moreover, to achieve global integration, aligning the firm's international business and HRM functions has never been more critical.

The HRM process includes recruitment and selection, training and development, performance management, compensation and benefits, and labour relations. These five steps (the HRM process) are iterative, and collectively they contribute to an organization's effectiveness. When a domestic firm enters the global marketplace, these HRM activities become more complex as knowledge of the host country's labour markets, culture, legal systems, and economic systems must be acquired (see Chapters 2 to 4). There will be differences in the compensation practices from country to country. The choice a company makes in considering its HR requirements will depend on the stability and structure of the foreign country; its local customs, language, and culture; the availability of a qualified talent pool that will ensure the organization can meet its strategic objectives; and, of course, the cost to deploy any or all of these options. Bear in mind the four competitive strategies firms can consider: multidomestic, global, transnational, and international, and the advantages and disadvantages of each (see Chapter 10, pages 292–293, and Figure 10.13). International human resource management (IHRM) is a major organizational function to support these international strategies and the firm's organizational design.

A generation ago, employees would have more willingly undertaken overseas deployments; however, today workers are less likely to react to a company's bidding. Many factors constrict an employee's willingness to accept a foreign posting; dual-income families are almost *de rigueur* in contemporary Canadian society and many families are neither willing nor able to afford to lose the economic opportunities associated with the second income, career goals, and prospects of an accompanying spouse. Disruption to the entire family unit may be increasingly unpalatable, especially in situations where children may have unique needs (academic and/or medical). In this "sandwich generation," many families have elderly and ailing parents as well as children, which affects their willingness to relocate. Other constrictions are "career blockage, culture shock, lack of cross-cultural training, overemphasis on technical qualifications, and a tendency to use foreign assignments as a way to get rid of problem employees."[16]

The opening vignette, on page 417, notes that Canada, while not immune to international HRM (IHRM) issues resulting from globalization, is well positioned when compared to many other countries. Canada's cultural mosaic presents a clear advantage related to diversity training, cultural awareness, and the associated risks of failure in managing and staffing foreign subsidiaries. But do we exploit this advantage? Strategic IHRM today is an academic discipline, profession, and critical management issue as organizations globalize their operations. HR managers must have a seat at the highest decision-making level of the table in an international firm. Figure 15.1 shows the IHRM process and will be our guide for much of this chapter.

Recruitment and Selection—Staffing

The first task for IHRM in a strategic context is recruitment and selection—staffing. Once your firm has crafted its international strategy, it is important that the appropriate corporate structural design and HRM plan be developed to support the firm's international vision, mission, and corporate strategy. The closer the HRM plan aligns (fits) with the corporate strategy, the greater the enhancement of shareholder value. Remember once again that most practitioners suggest that structure follows strategy (see Chapter 10). Increasingly Canadian businesses, including small and medium-sized ones, are becoming aware of the importance and the sustainable competitive advantage to be gained by finding the right people to manage their organizations overseas. As global competition increases, businesses in Canada are confronted with HR challenges such as attracting and retaining talented employees, especially in light of the shortage of skilled workers. Labour shortages in Canada exist primarily due to the rapid growth of the economy, significant aging in our demographics, the attractiveness of emerging markets (Asia), and the dynamic nature of private enterprises.[17] This reality imposes a host of challenges on organizations as they contend with recruiting, training, compensation, workforce planning, labour legislation, immigration laws, and the corresponding requirement to undertake strategic HR planning to achieve and support organizational alignment.

The tension that managers experience when staffing key management positions in the global marketplace is similar to the experiences of marketing managers, as discussed in Chapter 13, pages 365–366. Managers must find the appropriate balance between the desire to have a one-size-fits-all HRM, thereby achieving cost reductions, and the demand to differentiate (through local responsiveness) the firm's HR products, services, and processes to accommodate the realities of the host countries. It will take hard critical thinking to achieve the appropriate balance between these two positions.

Depending on the orientation of the organization, staffing can be accomplished in a variety of ways. As part of IHRM strategic planning, managers must consider whether to adopt an ethnocentric, polycentric, or geocentric staffing policy (see Figure 15.2, page 420). It is critical that firms get the wrong people off the bus, get the right people on the bus and then get the right bums in the right seats.[18] You will agree that getting the right bums in the right seats was at the top of the list of things to do in the Sun Tzu Moment, in terms of both the transition of hundreds of thousands of men and women from peacetime jobs to wartime positions and the alignment with the same vision—victory!

Ethnocentric Staffing

Ethnocentric staffing describes an HR policy that requires that key management positions in the foreign subsidiary be filled by domestic nationals. This staffing policy is generally used to support an international competitive strategy. Firms adopt an ethnocentric staffing policy because, first, they believe there is an insufficient pool of talent in the host country with the appropriate skill set to fill senior positions. Second, firms consider it important for their corporate well-being that the corporate culture migrates to the host country. Finally, firms believe that their core competencies can best

FIGURE 15.1

The Human Resource Management Process

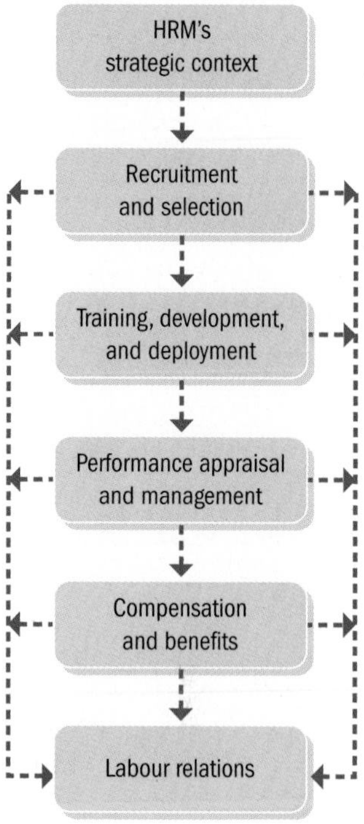

Ethnocentric staffing describes an HR policy where domestic nationals fill key management positions in the foreign subsidiary.

Staffing Philosophy	Global Strategy	Pros	Cons
Ethnocentric • Key overseas assignments staffed by home country managers	International	• Puts qualified managers in place • Creates global culture • Transfer of core competencies • High comfort level by head office management • Develops international management competencies in domestic staff	• Local resentment of foreign management • Cultural myopia • Immigration barriers • Costly
Polycentric • Key overseas assignments staffed by new indigenous managers	Multidomestic	• Alleviates cultural myopia • Inexpensive to implement • Corporate culture at risk	• Limits career mobility • Isolates HQ from overseas subs—creates silos
Geocentric • Best qualified from any nation to fill key host country positions	Global and Transnational	• Uses HR efficiency • Builds strong global culture and informal management network • Grows an international management pool	• Costly • Immigration barriers

be transferred to the foreign subsidiaries by filling the senior positions in the host country from their domestic talent pool. While this policy had merit a few decades ago, it is on the wane because the new reality is that many of the developing countries have grown an educated workforce; there could be detrimental optics to consider in terms of the educated (host) country's workforce being troubled by foreign managers taking senior positions; and, finally, an inherent cultural myopia may lead to organizational homogeneity and cultural short-sightedness—a problem that can be an exacerbated tension if the company is trying to integrate itself in local culture. If, for example, a Canadian firm were to establish a facility in Beijing that was completely staffed by Canadians, there is the likelihood of a lack of cultural sensitivity in interfacing with Chinese suppliers, customers, and others. Diversity is a good thing.

Polycentric Staffing

Polycentric staffing describes an HR policy whereby key management positions are filled by indigenous managers within the host country. By undertaking such a staffing policy, the cultural myopic danger presented in an ethnocentric staffing policy is removed. However, polycentric staffing is a double-edged sword in that it presents a potential for a gap between the home and host countries' operations. Polycentric staffing is generally used in support of a multidomestic strategy. Its advantages include a reduction in cultural myopia and reduced costs filling key positions with locals rather than transferring and retaining personnel for these positions from outside the country. The disadvantages are that a polycentric staffing policy prevents domestic managers from acquiring cross-cultural skills and international management experience. Without international exposure, firms will not develop the domestic talent base into one that is competent to operate in an international environment. The second disadvantage is the likelihood that the domestic company and the foreign subsidiary will converge into "watertight compartments." Management in both entities may have little in common and will not likely share the same corporate culture over time without some degree of interface.

Polycentric staffing describes an HR policy whereby indigenous managers within the host country fill key management positions.

Geocentric Staffing

Geocentric staffing describes an HR policy that requires hiring the best-trained personnel for the host management position from anywhere in the world regardless of nationality. This policy provides organizations with people who possess a strong diversified global culture and an international informal business network. Geocentric staffing is used in support of a firm adopting a global or transnational strategy. Unfortunately, from time to time, nations place barriers to impede the flow of labour across borders by implementing nonfriendly immigration policies. This may hamper the adoption of a geocentric staffing policy. The advantage of geocentric staffing is that the best people fill key management positions, and the firm is strengthened by the depth and diversity of its key management team. The disadvantages are the occasional barriers presented by the host country's immigration policy that constrict the use of geocentric staffing, and the cost associated with recruiting and transferring key management personnel to the host country.

The assessment of individual suitability must be augmented by an organizational commitment to issues such as cross-cultural training, knowledgeable IHRM managers who view IHRM as a distinct competency within the HR profession, integrated career planning, attention to repatriation goals and needs, a compensation package that ensures expatriates do not lose financially but yet is still cost-effective from the firm's position, proper orientation, and performance management and mentoring.

> **Geocentric staffing** describes an HR policy that requires hiring the best-trained personnel for the host management position from anywhere in the world regardless of nationality.

Staffing—Success Predictors

Those charged with the HR responsibility to select suitable expats for foreign assignments need to evaluate the following success predictors in their candidates. In addition to the required technical skills and job know-how, successful expatriates should possess the following attributes that typically fall into the soft-skills domain.

Candidates' Internal Orientation

Expats must be extroverts and possess a strong sense of self-esteem, self-confidence, and a very robust feeling of well-being. Candidates must be willing and interested in experiencing new food, music, sports, and outside interests. They must have superior technical competencies. They must also have **emotional stability**, which is the intrapersonal ability to adapt and cope with stress in professional and personal spheres of one's life.

> **Emotional stability** is the intrapersonal ability to adapt and cope with stress in professional and personal spheres of one's life.

Candidates' External Orientation

Expats must be eager to interact with host nationals and develop relationships. They must be team players, demonstrated by developing reciprocal social alliances and building social capital in the organization.

Perceptual Aptitude

Expats must understand, appreciate, and adjust to the host country's culture. This will require a certain degree of cross-cultural sensitivity, openness, and intellect. Expats must also acquire a broad background knowledge of the host nation's history and culture, leave their ethnocentric view at home, and adopt a pragmatic view of the world.

Staffing—Failure and Posting Costs

Staffing—When Expatriates Fail

Historically, and particularly in North America, expatriates have been the most favoured staffing choice because of the amount of technical skill and corporate knowledge they bring to the subsidiary. **Expatriate managers**, defined as managers assigned to a foreign subsidiary in a country other than their national origin, experience a significant failure rate. They generally undertake two- to three-year assignments abroad, and then return to their home country upon completion of the assignment. Failure can be attributed to

> **Expatriate managers** are defined as managers assigned to a foreign subsidiary in a country other than their national origin.

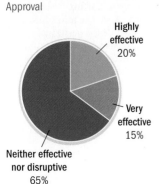

FIGURE 15.3

Overseas Effectiveness: Peer/Client Approval

Highly effective 20%

Very effective 15%

Neither effective nor disruptive 65%

SOURCE: David Mitrovica, "Expatriate Recruitment and Effectiveness" (*CSEG Recorder*, February 2001). Copyright © Canadian Society of Exploration Geophysicists.

a wide range of factors, including less desire to move associated with organizational loyalty, family lifestyle and issues (spouse's career), children's education, and parental elder care issues; career blockage; lack of cross-cultural training for the expatriates (expats) and family; culture shock; too much reliance on technical qualifications for the position; and firms frequent use of foreign assignments as a way to get rid of problem employees. In order of importance, Canadian expats fail primarily because the spouse cannot adjust culturally; the manager cannot adjust culturally; other family adjustment problems occur; the manager lacks personal and emotional maturity; or the manager is unable to cope with responsibilities offshore. Contrast this to high failure rates by Japanese expats who fail because of their inability to cope with the broader responsibilities offshore; the lack of ability to adjust culturally; the manager's lack of personal and emotional maturity; the lack of technical competence; and, lastly, the spouse's inability to adjust culturally. If you wonder why this anomaly exists, recall Hofstede's five dimensions model (see Chapter 2, pages 56–59, including Figures 2.6 to 2.12). Successful expatriate experiences require a holistic screening approach that considers technical as well as interpersonal skills, emotional intelligence, family circumstances, and forward-thinking plans for repatriation. You may want to rent the movie *Gung Ho* starring Michael Keaton (1986), a wonderful example of cross-cultural sensitivity training.

Only about 20 percent of expatriates are considered by their peers and clients to be highly effective. (See Figure 15.3.) Effectiveness is defined in terms of an expat's experience, ability to adapt, and communication skills.

The consequence of failure is not only a cost consideration but also a practical consideration insofar as disruption to the business, loss of time, and the potential damaged relationships—both professional and personal. The cost of sending a manager abroad is in the order of three to five times the expat's salary, and these are direct costs. Real costs are higher if we include costs of selection and replacement, training, preparation, moving, lost revenue, lost reputation, lost opportunity, and lost future value. Family matters not only heavily influence the success or failure of expatriates once deployed, but also factor into the decision whether an assignment will be accepted at the outset. A complete examination of the family in its lifecycle and any extenuating circumstances must be undertaken. It is critical to determine candidates' (and family) suitability from the start, not as an afterthought once the expatriation selection, training, and development are underway. Repatriation also requires careful consideration. It must be planned in advance of the deployment in order to mitigate culture shock, and to ensure career planning and goals are consistent with the subsequent assignment for the manager. Imagine for a moment you are the director of HR for your firm. If you select the wrong candidate for the foreign subsidiary, it can cost the firm $500,000 or more. How many mistakes can the SME's bottom line afford? It is, therefore, important to understand why an expatriate experience failed and strategically plan to mitigate these factors in the future.

We have said much about the impact of culture on an employee, the employee's family, and the manner in which the employee conducts herself in business in this chapter and in the earlier materials. Worth a brief examination are the subtleties that can occur in situations between NAFTA partners (see Figure 15.4). NAFTA has worked well for Canada since 1994. The trade exchanged between the trading partners is large. Interestingly, there is a tendency to consider Canadians and Americans as fairly homogenous yet much anecdotal evidence suggests this is not necessarily the case. The differing traits range from values and beliefs to customs and mannerisms. Even after a decade of interaction, SME business leaders still fall short of the cultural sensitivity required in this most important regional grouping. It is easy to see how cultures may be misunderstood if cues are misread and individual biases exist. A failure to demonstrate cultural sensitivity in the workplace can hurt your business. When considering staffing foreign subsidies, you would be well advised to create such tables to assist in understanding where the cultural gaps exist. Hofstede's model and others will assist in this regard (see Chapter 2, pages 56–59). Have a look at these labour cultural differences. Do any surprise you? Reflect for a few minutes and ask yourself what difference these cultural attributes would have on your staffing plans. There is much here to reflect upon.

FIGURE 15.4
A Comparison of the NAFTA's
Labour Cultural Differences

Aspect	Mexico	Canada/USA
Family	• Family is the first priority. • Children are celebrated and sheltered. • Wife fulfills domestic role. • Mobility is limited.	• Family is usually second to work. • Children are often minimally parented; are independent. • Mobility quite common.
Religion	• Long Roman Catholic tradition. • Fatalistic outlook. "As God wills."	• Mixed religions. • "Master of own life" outlook.
Education	• Memorization. • Emphasis on theoretical. • Rigid, broad curriculum.	• Analytical approach. • Emphasis on the practical. • Narrow, in-depth specialization.
Nationalism	• Very nationalistic. • Proud of long history and traditions. • Reluctant to settle outside Mexico.	• (U.S.) Very patriotic. • Proud of "American way of life."
Personal Sensitivity	• Difficulty separating work and personal relationships. • Sensitive to differences of opinion. • Fear loss of face, especially publicly. • Shuns confrontation.	• Separates work from emotions/ personal relationships. • Sensitivity seen as weakness. • Tough business front. • Has difficulty with subtlety.
Etiquette	• "Old world" formality. • Etiquette and manners seen as measure of breeding.	• Formality often sacrificed for efficiency. • "Let's get to the point" approach.
Personal Appearance	• Dress and grooming are status symbols.	• Appearance is secondary to performance.
Status	• Title and position more important than money in eyes of society.	• Money is main status measure and is reward for achievement.
Aesthetics	• Aesthetic side of life is important even at work.	• No time for "useless frills."
Ethics	• Truth is tempered by need for diplomacy. • Truth is a relative concept.	• Direct yes/no answers given and expected. • Truth seems absolute.

SOURCE: Eva Kras, *Comparing Cultural Differences: Mexico with Canada & the United States* (Mexico Connect, 1996). © Mexico Connect 1996–2006.

Staffing—Women in the Global Workplace

Globalization has made a significant impact on women in general and women in the workplace specifically. (Visit www.power.nelson.com for more discussion on this topic.) Before moving to the second step in the HRM process, it is important to our understanding of HRM that we spend a few moments discussing women employed in the global workplace.

When international firms send personnel from their home country to manage operations overseas, they must consider the receptivity of staff in the host country to foreign managers. Receptivity to women in management varies from country to country. Paul Wolfowitz, neo-con and president of the World Bank Group remarked, "Jobs are a priority for every country, and especially the poorest countries. Doing more to improve regulation and help entrepreneurs is key to creating more jobs—and more growth. It is also a key to fighting poverty. Women, who make up three quarters of the workforce in some developing economies, will be big beneficiaries. So will young people looking for their first job. The past year's diverse range of successful reformers—from Serbia to Rwanda—is showing the way forward. We can all learn from their experience."[19] There is a perception in developed countries that women "take care" while men "take charge,"[20] a point not unnoticed by relationship counsellor John Gray in his bestseller, *Men Are from*

Mars, Women Are from Venus: A Practical Guide for Improving Communication and Getting What You Want in Your Relationships.[21] "Women hold 50.3% of all management and professional positions yet only 7.9% of the top Fortune 500 earners and 1.4% of Fortune 500 CEOs are women."[22] In Canada, the situation is not much better. "Women hold 14.4 percent of corporate officer positions in Canada (770/5347 corporate officers), a less than one-half percent increase since 2002, according to the *2004 Catalyst Census of Women Corporate Officers and Top Earners of Canada.* . . . Among the 2004 Catalyst Census key findings: Women hold 14.4 percent of corporate officer positions in the FP500, up from 14.0 percent in [2002]; 61.4 percent of FP500 companies have at least one woman corporate officer, down from 62.4 percent in 2002; 95 FP500 companies have 25 percent or more women corporate officers, up from 87 companies in 2002; women hold 9.4 percent of line officer positions, up from 9.0 percent in 2002; women hold 7.1 percent of the highest corporate officer titles, up from 6.7 percent in 2002; and women hold 14.8 percent of positions in the 'Executive Pipeline,' up from 12.5 percent in 2002."[23]

The unseen barrier to women's corporate mobility is referred to as the glass ceiling, the height of which changes in different cultures. "The term 'glass ceiling' was coined in a 1986 *Wall Street Journal* report on corporate women by Hymowitz and Schellhardt."[24] The **glass ceiling** refers to the notion that barriers impede or prevent a discrete population from obtaining senior positions and/or higher salary levels in organizations. The glass ceiling is not restricted to women; it can also refer to barriers to advancement experienced by racial and ethnic minorities and some men.[25] In this chapter, the term *glass ceiling* will refer to women in business with a focus on advancement to senior positions. "The term **glass elevator** at times refers to the rapid promotion of men over women, especially into management, in female-dominated fields like nursing.[26] Similarly, you may hear the term **glass cliff** used to describe a situation where someone, particularly a woman, has been promoted into a risky, difficult job where the chances of failure are high.[27]

Glass Ceilings You Might Encounter

As organizations begin adapting their strategies to ensure inclusive practices, firms will need to adjust their focus and adapt to their changing environment to ensure they remain competitive in the marketplace.

JAPAN

Although there are examples in Japan of female executives appointed to major corporations, such as Sanyo Electric Co., Japan continues to maintain a glass ceiling to female executives. However, the situation is improving: "Matsushita Electric Industrial Co. says it boosted the number of female managers by 170% last year; . . . Nissan in February [2005] said that by 2007 it wants to triple the number of female managers to 120—5% of the company's work force compared with the Japanese average of just 2.8%."[30]

GERMANY

Women managers are still underrepresented in executive positions in Germany. In 2004, "women accounted for 47% of all persons in dependent employment, but for only 33% of all executives."[31]

UNITED STATES

A 2004 study of U.S. firms that "broke" the glass ceiling demonstrates that they have prospered financially. "Of 353 Fortune 500 companies, those with the highest representation of women on their top management teams had better financial performance than did the group with the lowest women's representation: the Return on Equity (ROE) was 35% higher and the Total Return to Shareholders (TRS) was 34% higher. . . . Women are perceived to be disadvantaged, compared with men, regarding international mobility, balancing work and personal responsibilities, and building business relationships outside the United States."[32]

The **glass ceiling** refers to the notion that barriers impede or prevent a discrete population from obtaining senior positions and or higher salary levels in organizations.

The **glass elevator** refers to the rapid promotion of men over women, especially into management, in female-dominated fields like nursing.[28]

The term **glass cliff** describes a situation where someone, particularly a woman, has been promoted into a risky, difficult job where the chances of failure are high.[29]

Training, Development, and Deployment of Expats

As we noted in the Sun Tzu moment, page 417, getting the right people in the right positions is one of the first steps to a sustainable enterprise. The second step in the HRM process, including activities such as succession planning and leadership identification and development, is essential in building an organization. In order to meet strategic goals, organizations often weave staff development into their succession planning strategy. For most corporations conducting global business, expatriates have been a key element of their employment strategy. Notwithstanding the skill and educational levels in host countries are increasing, it seems the demand for expats will not fall. According to PricewaterhouseCoopers, "despite reports of reductions due to an overall global economic slowdown, an overwhelming majority of companies continue to expect growth in the number of international assignments."[33] This need, however, may not be met as the expatriation refusal rates are also increasing.[34] According to the National Association of Corporate Directors, "forty-five per cent of companies worth over 500 million US dollars still did not have a clear succession plan."[35] It is imperative that HR strategic plans include a succession scheme for expats and lever the value brought back to the firm as a result of out-of-country assignments. Those who admit to not having a succession plan rationalize that the scope of the multinational organization is so large that collecting information about employees is difficult; and that the cultural biases in the process often cause talented people to be overlooked.

IHRM requires a comprehensive repatriation plan for expatriates. Although a large amount of time is spent sourcing, interviewing, and testing competency for an international assignment, many organizations do not consider the re-entry of expatriates, and fail to have a policy in place or follow best practices guidelines. Concerns surrounding cultural reintegration, diminished position and status, and loss of social network are often overlooked. The impact of this practice, or lack thereof, is cited as one of the reasons expatriate refusal rates are rising. Although some organizations have begun looking at a more holistic approach to expatriates, by utilizing tools such as the Hofstede classification system, career advancement, and guaranteed placements, many international assignments continue to be unattractive because of the failure to provide adequately for re-entry into the domestic organization.

The transferring of knowledge must also be considered in this second step of the HRM process. The purpose of knowledge transfer is to build and retain intellectual capital across business units and national boundaries, ultimately creating best-fit practices where applicable. **Knowledge transfer** is the process of "systematically organized exchange of information and skills between entities. Westerners often find themselves grappling with transferring knowledge in transitional economies, such as between . . . [multinationals] and their subsidiaries."[36] The notion of knowledge transfer is not new; however, it has become the corporate flavour of the day. Disseminating best practices and knowledge organizationally through standardized processes, cross-functional teaming, or expatriates has become the standard. Whether dissemination is occurring through expatriates or business systems, this centre-out approach does not necessarily create the structure for locations to provide or receive information concurrently. Moreover, when dissemination is completed in these ways, there is little regard to cultural dissimilarity. Recall from Chapter 11 that the firm's organizational design must provide for the knowledge transfer between the functional units. This transfer can be accomplished, for example, through mentorship, on-the-job training, and classroom-type training.

Two key issues emerge from these current methods. First, there is a gap in transferring knowledge from one geographic region to another, and second, most technical classroom training is taught without considering learning styles or diversity. The impact of losing knowledge or intellectual capital, and/or sharing information in

Knowledge transfer is the process of a "systematically organized exchange of information and skills between entities."[37]

a manner that may not be used in other countries, is unknown in dollars or cents but may mean the difference between corporate lagging or leading in the chosen industry. Consequently, the standardized approach is beginning to give way to a barrier-free and culturally sensitive method. Academic and organizational studies, as well as failed experiences, illustrate the need to recognize the challenges and possible benefits that traditional culture and values can create. The transfer of culture and knowledge can take many forms including planned management training programs, parent-subsidiary relationships, and joint ventures. Thus, a culturally based approach is replacing a standardized approach when managing employees both remotely and when bringing them to headquarters. According to global HR practitioners, "Multinational companies do not and cannot submerge the individuality of different cultures. That is, strong as a corporate culture may be, the template for behaviours isn't from the company, but from the national culture."[38] In order to truly transfer knowledge and corporate culture, individual culture must be understood, respected, and accepted by the HR decision makers and their counterparts throughout the organization.

Additionally, knowledge transfer has been a current focus not only for speed and efficiency when managing employees but also for the amount of knowledge managers can disseminate and employees can utilize. Literature illustrates that in "2006 there [are] more 55–64 year olds than 16–24 year olds, for the first time since records began. By 2006 45–59 year olds [were] the largest age group in the workforce. By 2010 only 17% of the workforce will be aged between 18 and 24, while almost 40% will be over 45 years of age. . . . This will mean a revolution in HR policies and practices. Working up to the age of 70 and beyond seems likely to become the norm."[39] Not everyone agrees however. According to Peter Cappelli, "people keep talking about the 'coming labour shortfall.' Well, they were talking about the 'coming shortfall' 10 years ago, and they're still talking about it today, but we haven't seen it. Demographics don't drive labour markets. Demographic changes are gradual and predictable, and the economy and the labour force have enough time to adjust to them."[40] Whether or not the HR community believes in an impending labour shortage, the certainty of a changing workforce due to demographics is a reality. Organizations must transfer knowledge effectively in order to retain their intellectual capital for years to come.

Performance Management

Performance management is the third step in the HRM process. Generally focusing on competencies and results, it is used to enhance other HRM processes, such as career development, performance improvement, employee involvement, and reward determinations. "Performance management in its fullest sense is based on the belief that everything that people do at work at any level contributes to achieving the overall purpose of the organization."[41] Unfortunately for individuals on expatriate assignments, current practice may not enable organizations to see their true value or contribution. Due to short assignment postings, employees often take one year before their learning curve plateaus and then they begin to worry about their next assignment, which may reduce productivity. The second year on assignment, the organization and employee begin to see the rewards of the assignment, but often it is the third year before a true reflection of the job can be completed and continual improvement trends can be seen.

In response, approaches to performance management (specifically evaluations) are placing a stronger focus on calibration and metrics beyond results. Although previously an evaluation often focused on the "what," trends show evaluations now focus on the "what" and the "how." This change in thinking centres on managing employees effectively so that they are learning the skills to manage, work, or lead in a diverse environment through leadership competency, communication, and understanding. Indeed, an often-asked question is who undertakes the expat's evaluation—the host- or the home-office manager? "Another performance management approach that has become more popular over the last five years is multi-rater or 360-degree feedback evaluation. It includes an assessment instrument that collects ratings on behavioural items from multiple observers and a feedback process that summarizes the input from different raters and helps the ratee interpret and act upon the feedback. . . . Raters typically include direct reports, peers, and upper management"[42] as well as a self-assessment. "Multi-rater . . . feedback was used by 90% of Fortune 500 companies in 2003."[43] It is generally believed to be a highly effective performance evaluation tool, yet there are many who doubt its benefits. "Candid performance feedback from peers, direct reports, and supervisors is generally difficult to obtain because sharing such feedback (particularly if it is not positive) can be risky. . . . [The] reliability and validity of the assessment instrument take on special importance when assessment results support personnel decisions such as awarding promotions or bonuses. . . . The manner in which feedback is provided is also important. . . . Implementation of a multi-rater assessment and feedback process is a major undertaking for most organizations, and open communication among those involved is key to success."[44] When this method is utilized in the wrong environment, the results can be detrimental.

Strategic and personal goal alignment has become a key success factor in managing a remote workforce. It is often difficult for employees to see the link between the firm's overall strategy and their everyday tasks. Ensuring goal congruence, for example, between the firm's ethics and corporate social responsibility values and the individual's ethical and corporate social responsibility values results in a much stronger and productive global workforce. Individuals will identify and support goals they personally champion and believe in. Finally, technology plays a vital role in managing and developing employees globally. Performance management systems can be as simple as a paper form filed in the expat's employee file, or the adoption of sophisticated software systems that link individuals to their business units throughout the global organization. Managers conducting performance reviews and succession planning at all levels must have access to current information to make a timely fact-based decision. One caveat—a performance management system is only as good as the information provided.

Compensation and Benefits

The administration of compensation and benefits is the fourth step in the HRM process. As discussed, expatriate assignments are extremely expensive for an organization. With remuneration packages generally costing between $150,000 and $500,000, HR managers must link the employee's base salary with assignment premiums, cost differential allowances, and other expenses.[45] Although most employee benefit issues can be dealt with effortlessly, health coverage can create challenges as well as expenses. Thus, movement toward an all-inclusive global compensation system has become the norm. Although most companies have moved to practices such as banding host-country pay, or national pay scales, most have missed the point of a total rewards package. (Banding compensation systems enable more flexible salary administration and enhanced career growth opportunities for employees. The traditional system of pay grades and job classes are being replaced with broad salary ranges, or bands, encompassing specific occupational areas.) Providing equitable remuneration, benefits, and support for expatriates requires looking at the package as a whole, rather than the sum of its parts. Unfortunately, language and employee assistance programs, cultural sensitivity training, and spousal outplacement are not always available to relocating employees and their families. These activities should be provided and the costs included in the expats' total compensation package. In fact, according to the Global Relocation Trends Survey, only 60 percent of organizations in 2005 offered any form of cross-cultural training before assignments and, of that, only 26 percent stated the training was mandatory.[46] The cost of not providing this type of total compensation includes a high expatriate failure rate (20 to 50 percent for Canadian firms),[47] as most failed assignments are due to inabilities to integrate in the culture, spousal dissatisfaction, and family concerns.[48]

In determining the appropriate level of expatriate compensation, a common approach is referred to as the *balance sheet approach* (BSA). It has been adopted by a majority of Canadian companies. The BSA is based on a comparison of the purchasing power of the countries being considered. The intent is to provide a level of payment that will maintain the same standard of living for the expats that they enjoyed at home plus provide an addition inducement to undertake the assignment. If the transfer is from a developed country like Canada to a less-developed country, the setting of appropriate compensation is even more difficult. The *base salary* for each venue is normally in the same band range as a similar position in the home country. It is paid in either the home country's currency or the foreign subsidiary's currency. The decision as to what currency—domestic, host, or a global vehicle currency (euro or the U.S. dollar)—is negotiated between the expat and her firm. In addition to the base salary, the expatriate generally receives, as an inducement to accept the foreign subsidiary posting, a *foreign transfer premium*. This premium compensates the expat for the country differences experienced as a result of the transfer. For example, expats might be in a start-up situation living out of a trailer in a remote area; in this case, greater compensation would be expected than transferring between a firm's subsidiaries in developed countries. This premium is generally based on the base salary and ranges between 10 and 30 percent. In addition to the base salary and foreign transfer premium allowances, a hardship allowance, based on the degree of hardship the expat is likely to experience because of the lack of amenities and other factors (health, school, and climate), may be included. In addition, a housing allowance may be provided to maintain the same quality housing in the host country as the expat had in the home country.

According to the 2006 cost of living survey by Mercer Human Resource Consulting, Moscow and Seoul rank first and second as the world's most expensive cities, respectively.[49] The United States had six cities in the world's 50 most expensive: New York (10th), Los Angeles (29th), San Francisco (34th), Chicago (38th), Miami (39th), and White Plains (43rd).[50] China had four: Hong Kong (4th), Beijing (14th), Shanghai (20th), and Shenzhen (40th).[51] Toronto was the only Canadian city to rank among the world's 50 most expensive cities at 47th.

A cost-of-living allowance may also be provided to offset other cost anomalies so that expats can maintain their domestic standard of living. This would include assistance in private school costs for dependants. Anomalies in the methods of taxation between the home and the host countries must also be provided. Finally, it is important that the benefits received by expatriates, such as medical, pension, and savings, are aligned with the home country's benefits.

Overview of Unions and Labour Relations

The fifth and final step in the HRM iterative process is the need to fully appreciate the complexities of unions and their transformation in the international marketplace. Management decision makers must acquire a global mindset in order to understand unions and workers. There have been significant declines in union membership in the United States. Fifty years ago, one-third of the American workforce held union jobs. Jump forward to 2005 and that number has dropped to only 13 percent.[52] This is a serious situation for unions, as it means significantly decreased revenues, and a declining membership base, which translates into less influence. Andy Stern, president of Service Employees International, asserts that unions are responsible for creating the middle class, with good wages and health care. However, Stern is seeing a decline in wages resulting in a decreased quality of life for those people.[53] The need for Canadian business to do more with less results in Canadian workers working longer hours for marginal wage increases, which directly affects their ability to maintain a balance between work and home. Increasingly, there is resistance to this need for increased productivity such as "Germany's big unions remain[ing] opposed to breaking the 35-hour-week barrier"[54] to move to a 40-hour workweek. Today it is a reality of globalization that, in order to compete with the global low-cost nations, developed countries come under increased pressure to also lower costs and benefits or face the possibility their jobs will move. Canada is no exception (see Video 15.1).

VIDEO

Video 15.1

One of the most significant effects of globalization on unions is outsourcing. The benefits to the consumer at the surface level of outsourcing or offshoring have already been established in this text; people want cheaper and better goods and services. Exploiting location economies to obtain lower labour costs that provide cheaper goods to the consumer and enhance the firm's bottom line is very much a part of what firms do in a global environment.

Today, firms understand the cost savings they can achieve by moving certain job functions and process facilities to the most cost-effective location. As a result, outsourcing will increase.

Unions are attempting to respond to this changing business environment precipitated by the success of outsourcing. Increasingly, they are looking for ways to increase their membership both locally and globally. Unions establish fair wages, fair labour practices, and a full range of other benefits. In fact, "big spikes in union membership have always coincided with efforts to accord certain disenfranchised groups the full rights and benefits of American citizenship."[55] For example, after World War II, the labour movement looked to organize the large wave of second-generation immigrants so they too could enjoy the full benefits of working in a white Anglo Saxon Protestant (WASP)–dominated workforce.

Are Unions Necessary in Canada?

Are unions really necessary in Canada today? No longer are workers denied minimum wages, children are not being forced into slave labour, and men are not working unreasonably long and gruelling shifts in dangerous mineshafts. This issue can be argued from both sides.

Yes, Unions Are Necessary in Canada

The union movement must continue to evolve and gain strength in Canada, so that its message can be carried to underdeveloped countries where reform is so desperately needed. Developed countries, their firms, and the labour movement have a responsibility to these developing countries to implement standards that are equivalent to North American standards. For example, unions can advocate that workers in developing countries be given the same workplace standards as developed countries' workers as provided by Workers Compensation Board standards. One could argue that this is "required" social responsibility as part of managing their triple bottom line. We will be examining this notion in some detail in Chapter 17. In balancing their duties, large corporations must consider their stakeholders and shareholders, remembering that "public demand for responsible corporate behaviour has now reached a critical mass, and firms that ignore it do so of their own peril."[56] To simply ignore social responsibility, and continue outsourcing to the country with the cheapest labour, could have dire bottom-line consequences (see Chapter 17).

No, Unions Are Not Necessary in Canada

Conversely, one could argue that unions are no longer necessary in Canada. However, were a decertification movement to begin in Canada, it is doubtful that it would have any effect on slowing outsourcing. To keep the unions out of their workplaces, employers would have to continue to be as competitive with wages and benefits as they were when their employees were unionized. And if, in fact, workers did decertify in an effort to slow the outsourcing job loss, it would mean that employers would have to decrease wages and benefits to be more competitive with these underdeveloped countries. This could be a very slippery slope back to the poor working conditions that existed when unions first began.

Threats to Unions by Canadian International Firms

First, a firm can divert product and resource flows to facilities in different countries to reduce the risk of union action. Large corporations may only have a very small portion of their total operations in one country and hence the exposure to union activism is minimal in the global environment. For this reason, large global corporations tend to be less responsive to the demands of labour. International firms forced to close facilities in a particular country as a result of labour action may still consider importing and selling products obtained from other global facilities with surpluses. Accordingly, the strike may have minimal impact as consumers will still purchase goods in the location of the unit subject to union action. The firm would, of course, face transportation and possible additional tariff costs that may have been the underlying reason for establishing facilities in the host country initially. Work stoppages might be damaging to the international company if it was, for example, in the process of raising financing to enhance the facility undergoing strike action. Work stoppages would also be damaging if these particular facilities were producing component parts for other facilities outside the jurisdiction. Consequently a strike can have far-reaching effects (see Video 15.2).

Video 15.2

Second, often companies when faced with union action will threaten to move production to another country in order to extract location labour economies. For example, if one company owns facilities in several countries and Canadian workers demand and get substantial wage increases that raise the price of the Canadian product, then there will be a clear incentive for the Canadian firm to consider moving all of its operations to a lower-cost location. If the Canadian company does not switch locations and continues to provide higher product prices, then competitors will likely exploit the opportunity to build their Canadian market share using their inherent offshore location economies and export the products to the Canadian marketplace. The Canadian firm will not survive long.

Third, the size and complexity of some Canadian MNEs operating in the global environment have made it increasingly more difficult for unions to influence the firm's decision makers. Often these decision makers are located in the home-country headquarters while negotiating unions are located on the front line with the workers in the foreign jurisdictions. Although unions regularly examine the financial statements in order to understand the firm's ability to meet its demands, the complexity of the data (see Chapter 16) makes the task very difficult. For example, the firm's statements might use transfer pricing in order to give the appearance that the subsidiary does not have the financial strength to meet labour's demands. The situation may be alleviated to some extent with the advent of the International Accounting Standards discussed in Chapter 16, pages 450–452.

Fourth, local host governments are hesitant to provide rights to unions as they fear this will discourage the much-needed FDI. So as Canadian corporations strive to achieve the lowest costs, and are encouraged by foreign governments attempting to attract FDI, it is unlikely that host governments will intercede on a union's behalf and thereby make their country unattractive to these global firms' FDI. It will require the electorate demanding political action of the nature that seems to be emerging in the United States, and to a significantly lesser extent in Canada, regarding outsourcing to change this outcome.

Labour's Response

To meet the growing threat of globalization, unions are trying new approaches to re-establish their strength. First, information sharing is increasingly taking place between unions. This intelligence gathering and collaboration is necessary in order to validate a company's claim, for example, that it can't afford to meet minimum health and safety standards. Information sharing is also needed to understand a country's labour environment. Second, unions are increasingly joining international confederations that have memberships spanning single or multiple industries. These confederations provide the support base for local negotiators. Assistance to foreign bargaining units is increasing when unions recognize it is to their advantage to support their "brothers and sisters" in other countries. However, there are problems; in order to protect their members, some

INTERNATIONAL STRATEGIC THINKING

As you read this article, think reflectively about the battle between the consumers and labour. Look at the manufacturing labels on your clothes. How many are made in Canada? The tension between consumers wanting low-cost products comes at the cost of national job losses. When it is your money you are spending, how do you vote? Whom will you hire?

Press 1 for Delhi, 2 for Dallas: Latest Wrinkle in Jobs Fight: Letting Customers Choose Where Their Work Is Done

Customers using online lender E-Loan Inc. now have a choice about who will process their application: They can let the company make use of workers in India. Or they can request to have their loan processed domestically by U.S. workers—and wait as many as two days longer. With the movement of U.S. jobs overseas becoming a hot political issue, companies are trying to find new ways to avoid the backlash. E-Loan's move is the latest wrinkle: disclosing that they have workers overseas, and letting customers themselves decide whether to opt for the advantages they offer. . . . Since the company started offering the option four weeks ago, roughly 86% of its customers for home equity loans have chosen the India route. To offer the faster service, E-Loan contracts with a unit of Wipro Ltd., a big Indian outsourcing company that is growing so rapidly it is expanding its work force by 3,000 each quarter. . . "This is really a massive struggle between consumers and labour," says Mr. Larsen, whose company did $6 billion in loans last year.

. . . As concern mounts, legislation has been proposed in Congress and in dozens of state capitals to crimp such moves abroad. Among the proposed techniques: barring government purchasing that involves work sent abroad; imposing tax penalties on companies that send work offshore; and requiring companies to disclose such moves. . . . Many economists argue that offshore outsourcing both helps economic development overseas and lowers prices domestically, which frees up capital to invest in new jobs in the U.S. and increases consumers' purchasing power. . . . Wipro, which does the work for E-Loan, has been watching the furor from India. "We're very concerned about the angst that is there," says Sangita Singh, Wipro's chief marketing officer. "Our heart reaches out to the people getting affected with all the job losses."

unions remain reluctant to adopt the new mental model of global union confederations, still seeing each other as competitors. For example, the Canadian and the U.S. automobile industry workers are competitors. General Motors, if treated harshly in Canada, might move its operations to its facilities in the United States, which would be seen as a very positive move by the American automobile unions. Accordingly, it is unlikely that the Canadian union will fight vigorously to protect American union auto jobs if there is a likelihood of those jobs migrating to Ontario. A number of jurisdictions, including Japan and Germany, have legislated that union membership have representation on the MNE's board of directors. On balance, this has a very positive effect. Notwithstanding the patriotic view, these international initiatives are slowly emerging. Third, occasionally simultaneous negotiations and strikes emerge in several countries. Simultaneous actions are not the norm, as cooperation across borders remains difficult because the memberships' objectives are not aligned. However, with regionalization, there are movements to support this labour initiative of cooperation across borders.

International Labour Movements

Canada's unions are joining with other influential groups in an attempt to stop the trend of outsourcing that is driving many of their members into the unemployment pool, and thus reducing the union's revenue base. They are trying to accomplish this with proposed measures that include barring government purchasing that involves work sent abroad, imposing tax penalties on companies that send work offshore, and requiring companies to disclose such moves.[57]

Increasingly, there are calls for unions to consolidate and focus all of their money, time, and energy on organizing.[58] Many of these unions have been very focused in the past on negotiating good contracts for members and have thus neglected to recruit new members.

The result is that "in the past three years, the 'official' net loss in U.S. jobs was 1 million. But this includes a loss of 3 million well-paid, often union, jobs in manufacturing while 2 million jobs were gained, if the official figures are accurate, mainly in the low-paid, non-union service sector."[59] This trend cannot continue if unions are to remain a thriving and driving force. However, the recruitment issue is difficult to resolve, because as Canadian manufacturing jobs disappear, unions must sign up members in industries such as the service sector where there has never been a strong union presence. Furthermore, they must convince their current members to allow them to shift resources normally available to service them to recruiting.

"Global unions must develop global organizing strategies. Local and national unions are best placed to recruit members," according to Union Network International (UNI).[60] Global unions can assist by using their global presence, bringing pressure to global companies to recognize their employees' right to join a union everywhere. A global union can use its power to assist the global company undergoing difficult negotiations at the national government level. A global union with a large membership presence in the country is able to use moral suasion to motivate the nation's decision makers to move the negotiations along. Using global organizing campaigns, global unions can pull together strong unions to help weaker unions. At times there is synergy when a global union brings all of its international members together to spur new workers in a new host country to organize. Increasingly, global unions are undertaking membership drives in small and medium enterprises, with freelancers, and in new areas such as call centres.[61]

One recent example of global labour unions pressuring global corporate giants for certification is UNI's campaign to unionize Wal-Mart worldwide. UNI includes 900 unions in 140 countries and they are aggressively seeking to make union members global players.[62] UNI says that "unions are adapting to a borderless world."[63] This initiative is in response to Wal-Mart being accused by unions of driving down wages for its 1.6 million employees. In their bid to organize Wal-Mart employees, the unions accuse the employer of "paying poverty wages, shipping jobs to countries where sweatshops are prevalent, and in the US, shifting enormous healthcare costs onto taxpayers."[64] The unions believe that Wal-Mart is creating the "new global economic model to be followed by many other firms."[65] Visit www.power.nelson.com for a paper on the topics of transformational change in Canadian unions resulting from globalization.

What Does the Future Hold for Unions?

In a globalized, interconnected world, unions must move away from the one-size-fits-all union model built in the 1930s. Unions must adopt a new mental model that addresses the changes occurring in the economic environment. The new model will organize "around major industries, taking over benefits like healthcare, pensions and training, and having companies contribute a predictable amount into a pool."[66] This model could appeal to those who don't participate in or support traditional collective bargaining, but are looking for assurances around job security and a comfortable retirement. The key to this new model will be recognizing that different groups of workers have disparate needs. Nurses may look for support in achieving adequate staffing levels and fair hours of work, while those more transient, educated workers who change jobs regularly may be looking for assurances in receiving benefits. Also under consideration are the many benefits to be recognized from creating a retirement plan for employees that isn't tied to any one employer, making moving from job to job that much easier in a changing economy.

Another initiative underway to change the face of how the union operates is an effort to close the digital divide for members and nonmembers alike. Unions recognize the power that emerging technology brings to enhance communications to disseminate the union message. The more people unions are able to reach regularly, the more efficiently they can spread their message and recruit new members. Another alternative that has been proposed is to offer workers affiliate membership to unions, which offer all the benefits of unionization provided under labour law and regulations except for collective bargaining and grievance protections.[67] This may have a broader appeal to those who in the past have typically not been interested in joining the union movement. Would you agree?

The Global Mindset

To conclude this chapter on global HRM, we examine the need for all international managers to develop a global mindset. International managers must nurture and grow the mental and behavioural characteristics set out in Figure 15.5. In addition, managers need to look at growing issues precipitated by globalization; for example, the increasing mobility of workers. The quantity and quality of available labour is affected by various factors, such as new immigrants and unemployment rates. According to Citizenship and Immigration Canada's most recent Census results, in 2001 "5.4 million people, or 18.4% of the total population, were born outside the country. This was the highest proportion since 1931."[68] About 1.8 million foreigners have arrived in Canada between 1991 and May 2001.[69] Roughly

FIGURE 15.5

Characteristics of Leaders with a Global Mindset

Mental Characteristics		**Behavioural Characteristics**	
Characteristic	*Importance to Global Leadership*	*Characteristic*	*Importance to Global Leadership*
Optimism	• Optimism is a base for motivation: one feels motivated only for what one thinks is possible. • Maintain a positive and proactive "can-do" attitude under complex circumstances. • Learn from mistakes. • Courage.	Social Skills	• Effectiveness in leading change and being a change catalyst. • Capacity to motivate and align people to one vision. • Conflict management. • Manage first impressions, and multicultural communicative competence.
Self-Regulation	• Control or redirect disruptive impulses and moods; suspend judgment to think before acting. • Capacity for emotional stability and adaptive capacity. • Know when to make a decision and when to gather more information.	Networking Skills	• Build partnerships and alliances. • Relationships and linking capabilities and activities globally.
Social Judgment Skills	• Perspective-taking capacity. • Extend the context beyond a particular problem or situation. • Observe and accurately profile the culture of others. • Acknowledge that any solution is implemented and applied in distinctly social contexts.	Knowledge	• Technical knowledge needed to perform certain tasks, that is, to fill the job description. • Understand the global nature of one's business and be able to analyze current trends/market conditions.
Empathy	• Level of empathy has a strong influence on such skills as ability to cope with people and situations, emotionally connect with people from various backgrounds, listening skills and ability to understand different viewpoints, and understanding people.	Experience	• Internationally experienced managers who are responsive to global opportunities and threats are also viewed as a source of competitive advantage.
Motivation to Work in an International Environment	• Commitment, personal drive, goal orientation, perseverance and dedication.		
Cognitive Skills	• Ability for complex thinking can help a global leader interpret situations using past experience as guide, not a set of instructions. • Handle complexity and all its contradictions.		

SOURCE: Tiina Jokinen, "Global Leadership Competencies: A Review and Discussion," *Journal of European Industrial Training* (Vol. 29, No. 3, April 2005). © Emerald Group Publishing Limited.

160,000 foreign-born people become Canadian citizens each year with approximately 85 percent of immigrants eventually becoming Canadian citizens.[70] "Of the 1.8 million immigrants who arrived between 1991 and 2001, 58% came from Asia, including the Middle East; 20% from Europe; 11% from the Caribbean, Central and South America; 8% from Africa; and 3% from the United States."[71]

Similarly, our major trading partner reports, "according to US Census Bureau Data, there were 34.2 million foreign-born people in the US in 2004, a rise of 2.3 percent compared with 2003. About 6.1 million foreigners have arrived in the US after 2000. 13.1 million foreign-born people had become US citizens, while 21.1 million have not naturalized. The population of foreign-born Hispanic people is increasing, with an estimated 53 percent of immigrants now coming from Latin America. 25 percent of foreign-born immigrants are from Asia, 14 percent from Europe, and 8 percent from other regions."[72] The United States has only a slightly higher number of immigrant workers than Japan. "Japan in 2003 hosted under two million foreigners making up about 1.5 per cent of the population."[73] In Germany, "according to Government figures . . . 768,000 migrants came to Germany in 2003"[74]—the lowest figure for the first time in many years. "Germany plans to keep its current [2006] ban on foreign workers from new European Union states entering its labour market till 2009. . . . By extending the restrictions to the free movement of labour from the 8 new EU states, Germany wants to defer tension to its labour market. The German rate of unemployment currently stands at 12%."[75] To manage diversity in the workplace requires a global mindset. Today's leaders require certain mental behavioural characteristics to succeed in a global marketplace.

The global mindset will include understanding temporary migrant workers. We have seen that globalization has been very successful, with the flow of capital across borders. Although there are impediments, the flow of goods and services has also made significant strides. The missing link in globalization and a corporate mindset is attention to the flow of workers across borders. Economists calculate that if rich companies would permit 3 percent of their labour force to comprise migrant workers for a limited period this would translate for the developing world into $200 billion of extra revenue per year.[76] A United Nations 2005 report supported these economists' findings. The UN report examined the historical experience of the Germans under their "*Gastarbeiter* program that invited Turks, Yugoslavians and others to fill the temporary factory jobs resulting from the post–World War II"[77] economic boom. A similar program in the United States from 1942 to 1964 called the *bracero* program that involved recruiting Mexican field hands also failed.[78] At the core of the failures was a self-evident fact that temporary workers remain in the host country. Developed countries do not want the additional responsibility of providing social safety nets for migrant workers. The temporary workers' home countries also want the workers to return, as the longer the worker stayed outside the country, the more the flow of foreign currency from their paycheque home diminished. Both host and home countries want short stays of young workers. Those arguing against migrant worker programs suggest that as long as cheap labour exists, innovation and new technology will not be forthcoming. In Germany, observers commented, "Japan is getting robots while Germany gets the Turks."[79]

So what is the answer? Suggestions include visa pools: "In South Korea, temporary workers contribute to a special account that is refunded to them if they leave on time and forfeited if they linger. The British government is thinking of asking some migrants to post a bond, like a defendant on bail, which they will lose if they choose not to return."[80] The issue of temporary migrants needs to catch up with the market forces of globalization and find democratic solutions. This issue will not wait long for resolution; consider France experiencing 11 days of riots in 300 towns and cities in 2005. Unrest broke out in areas with large African and Arab communities after the deaths of two youths who were accidentally electrocuted at an electricity substation in the run-down Paris suburb of Clichy-sous-Bois. Locals said the police were chasing them, but the police deny this. More than 2,000 cars were torched and the police arrested thousands of people. "The leader of France's far-right National Front (FN), Jean-Marie Le Pen, described the situation as nearing 'the brink of civil war.'"[81] Earlier the French government passed a law banning Islamic headscarves; many feel it contributed to the current problems affecting French Muslims.

This type of tension could be experienced globally. German industrial workers are now unemployed in greater numbers than at any time since the Great Depression. "New rules in Germany effective from January 1, [2005] will make entering and staying in Germany easier for skilled migrants, while keeping tight restrictions on unskilled immigration."[82] German wages are not set competitively. Instead, they are set "consensually," reflecting the relative bargaining power of industry-wide unions and employer federations. Germany's politicians are loath to break apart these "social partners." German corporations also labour under the weight of mandatory contributions to the public insurance systems that pay for the sick, the retired, and the unemployed. Germany's legions of jobless, in particular, place a double burden on the state: both what they take out of the state coffers in unemployment benefits and what they do not contribute to the payroll taxes that fund Germany's pension system.[83]

Emerging Trends

As countries begin to regionalize and organizations grow internationally, the concept of ethnocentric and polycentric approaches to managing and staffing subsidiaries has transformed. Instead, organizations are applying geocentric strategies in order to integrate employees on an inclusive basis.[84] Consequently, adapting current strategies to future needs creates a paradigm shift in business. Deployment, knowledge transfer, and development are all key ingredients to this new way of managing employees. With historical roots in traditional expatriate assignments, the cost and failure level has forced organizations to rethink their strategy. "The challenge of global deployment is getting the needed skills from one part of the organization to another [effectively] and inexpensively."[85]

Three emerging global HRM trends seemed to be at the forefront: aspatial careers, rotational assignments, and managing employees remotely.

The newest emerging trend is that of aspatial careers. "**Aspatial careerists** have borderless careers, typically working in multiple countries over the course of their work lives. The chief difference between the aspatial career and the expatriate assignment is that

"**Aspatial careerists** have borderless careers, typically working in multiple countries over the course of their work lives. The chief difference between the aspatial career and the expatriate assignment is that these careers exist in an environment where authority and expertise are no longer thought to reside exclusively at the parent company."[89]

JUST DOING THE RIGHT THING

What about those countries that have no labour movement? What can we do? Who speaks for them? Consider this story.

Unions Assail WTO for Ignoring Worker Rights

"Critics of economic globalization, including unions and scores of non-governmental organizations (NGOs), have long argued that, in the absence of enforceable global standards for environmental protection, human rights, and other workplace standards, multinational corporations will tend to invest in countries with less regulation in these areas in order to reduce costs. The result is the so-called 'race to the bottom' as countries compete for these multinationals' foreign direct investment by . . . repressing labour unions

[Mexico], failing to enforce environmental laws [China], or offering far-reaching tax breaks or other incentives to foreign investors" (see Chapter 7 of this text). "Because MNCs' supply chain management is a 'global assembly line' in which different parts of a final product may be produced, manufactured, and assembled in different countries, NGOs and unions insist that the WTO should play a key role in enforcing international standards." There are no "effective" multilateral trade rules currently in place to support these standards and so the negative downward spiral of lower standards continues.

Consider for example the Mexican "free zones" or "maquilas" whose "workers are made to take amphetamines to get them to work harder and faster, where violence and abuse are a daily reality for

thousands upon thousands of workers, and where attempts to form unions and bargain collectively for a fair deal are often met with reprisals, sackings and even death threats. . . . Similarly, China's economic zones, where independent unions are actively repressed, have drawn tens of billions of dollars in investment in recent years due to a relatively well-educated workforce that toils for as little as US$1.20 a day." China's success as the dominant FDI global player in part "not only has come at the expense of assembly industries in the rest of Asia, but is also responsible for the closings of maquilas as far away as the Caribbean Basin and Mexico."

Adapted from Jim Lobe, *Unions Assail WTO for Ignoring Worker Rights* (Common Dreams News Center, September 8, 2003). © Copyright 1997–2006 Common Dreams.

these careers exist in an environment where authority and expertise are no longer thought to reside exclusively at the parent company."[86] This form of career can take multiple forms; first an individual can reside in a permanent geographic home base and travel extensively (thereby allowing his family to acquire a sense of permanency), or an individual can live or work overseas and relocate frequently.[87] This latter form may appeal to younger "unattached" workers who are interested in rapidly acquiring international business experience. Although this does not necessarily overcome all of the cost concerns of the traditional expatriate model, it does allow the retention of employees with dual-career families that might have otherwise left the organization for another with a more flexible career learning model. Moreover, employees willing to work in an aspatial framework become invaluable to an organization as they often become spatially neutral and have an "in-depth understanding of global organizations because they have managed across cultures and know how culture affects work."[88] This emerging trend is not yet fully realized, yet the underlying logic is sound; employees who have a global perspective and network are required at the executive level of an organization.

The second emerging trend is focused around **rotational awareness building assignments**. "The primary purpose of [rotational] awareness building assignments is to develop [cultural] sensitivity in high-potential employees."[90] These assignments generally last less than one year and allow employees to frequently commute. Again, the cost is not necessarily less than an expatriate assignment, but such assignments may be more appealing to those whose families are unable or unwilling to relocate.

Aspatial careerists and rotational assignments benefit the corporation in two ways: cultural awareness and practice deployment. Organizations are beginning to recognize the advantages of integrating a culturally disparate workforce, and the entire organization is regarded as an interdependent system operating from different locations. Relationships

> "The primary purpose of **rotational awareness** *building assignments* is to develop [cultural] sensitivity in high-potential employees."[91] These assignments generally last less than one year and allow employees to commute.

PRACTICAL ENTREPRENEURIAL FOCUS

Managing Employees in Global Organizations of the Future

Adopt these strategies for managing employees and leading change.

- *A Persistent Sense of Urgency.* An increased sense of urgency will help organizations change. Create a state in which complacency is virtually absent; a state in which people are always looking for both problems and opportunities, and in which the norm is "do it now."
- *Teamwork at the Top.* "In a fast-moving world, teamwork is enormously helpful." In an environment of change, even the brightest and most talented individuals will not have "enough time or expertise to absorb rapidly shifting competitor, customer, market, and technological information. They will not have enough time to communicate all the important decisions to hun-

dreds or thousands of others" scattered in different parts of the world. More hands make light work, even at the top!

- *Create and Communicate Vision.* Successful global organizations will be incubators of leadership. Develop leaders with vision, communication skills, and the skills to empower people. New organizations will be flatter and leaner structures with less control and increased risk taking. They will have an organizational culture where succession planning and knowledge transfer are the norms.
- *Broad-Based Empowerment.* "Without sufficient empowerment, critical information about quality sits unused in workers' minds and energy to implement change lies dormant." Lead more and manage less.
- *Delegate for Excellent Short-Term Performance.* Delegate responsibilities. You will be in a superior posi-

tion to manoeuvre an organization than micro-managers who do not believe in delegation. Trust subordinates, be patient, train them, and share responsibility.

- *No Unnecessary Interdependence.* Coordinate all subunits. "Interdependencies left over from earlier eras that add no value . . . [will have no place]. . . . Fewer structural cobwebs and less procedural dust will make surfaces slicker and faster." Continuously scan your organizational design and remove any barriers to ensure a dynamic, adaptive work environment.
- *An Adaptive Corporate Culture.* Adopt an adaptive corporate culture that supports competent leadership and management, encourages teamwork, and demands minimum layers, bureaucracy, and interdependencies.

Adapted from John P. Kotter, *Leading Change* (Boston, MA: Harvard Business School Press, 1996), Chapter 11.

between headquarters and the subsidiaries are collaborative, and communication is respected from both directions and at all levels. Aspatial careers and rotational assignments still face many of the pitfalls experienced by expatriates. Lack of cultural understanding or training and global pay practices continue to be a concern for organizations that lack the foresight or planning to include their entire human resources flow into their strategy.

The next emerging trend is a **virtual or remote workforce**. Although it has been prevalent through circumstance, the concept is truly just in its infancy of being explored and assessed. A virtual or remote workforce utilizes technology in order to complete work from geographically dispersed locations. Often, the Internet, intranet, e-mail, video conferencing, and Web tools are utilized. For positions that service remote areas or do not require teammates or bricks and mortar to complete required tasks, organizations are allowing employees to work from home or in subsidiary offices instead of relocating. As the nature of work changes, this emerging trend becomes a vital attraction and retention tool. Canadian HR managers, and their firm's other functional managers, must be constantly scanning the ecosystem for emerging issues and implement proactive responses.

A **virtual or remote workforce** utilizes technology in order to complete work from geographically dispersed locations.

Management Implications

- During the past several decades we have witnessed a transformation in the management of employees. We have travelled far from the day of the personnel manager who also served as the first-aid officer and an organizer of Christmas parties to a complex position that requires increasing competencies and skills in order to contribute to the sustainability of a global firm operating in a turbulent environment.
- These skills and competencies are required by not only MNEs but all businesses undertaking global ventures, no matter their size. The HR manager must be given an equal position at the corporate decision-making table. Staffing, recruitment and selection, training, development, and compensation require much critical thinking contributing to strategic planning in order to maintain a firm's sustainable competitive advantage(s).
- With the shift in demographics to a more diversified workforce in Canada, and the stalled population growth forecast to remain at about 32 million citizens out to 2050, businesses will find the labour market increasingly more competitive. Diversity must be made a Canadian competitive advantage, with employees seen as assets rather than liabilities. This new mental model requires management to invest in people through training and development and not think of them as a liability requiring a paycheque on the 1st and 15th of each month.

CHAPTER SUMMARY

- One of Canada's national core competencies is our diversity. Recent Canadian immigrants provide a wonderful opportunity for businesses both large and small to establish trade and business connections in other nations.
- The challenges for HRM and organizational labour relations have become significantly more complex as a result of globalization. Recruitment and selection, training and development, performance appraisals, compensation and benefits, and labour relations all contribute to the firm's organizational effectiveness. They require HR managers with new skills and competencies.

- Unions and labour relations are also experiencing significant transformation. Union members' numbers have been dropping. Multinational firms' ability to move because of their size and complexity, the ease of outsourcing, and the general support of government are all factors contributing to troubling times for unions. Unions have responded by sharing information, assisting foreign bargaining units, and simultaneous labour actions. Until recently, unions were more comfortable with a national approach to organization, but recently there are initiatives to create international labour movements to preserve their bargaining positions with MNEs.

- Firms have three staffing policies available to them: ethnocentric staffing, which requires key management positions in foreign subsidies to be filled with domestic nationals; polycentric staffing, which requires key management positions to be filled by indigenous managers within the host country; and geocentric staffing, which requires hiring of the best-trained personnel for the host management positions from anywhere in the world regardless of nationality. Today, global firms are shifting from an ethnocentric and polycentric to a geocentric staffing policy.
- Expat managers assigned to a foreign subsidiary other than their national origin, experience high failure rates. North American expat failure rates are higher than those of some other cultures; North American expats are only 20 percent effective in filling their off-shore appointments. This can be explained in part by the cultural dimensions of the expats' nationality. Expats require certain internal and external aptitudes to reduce the chances of failure.

- Costs for filling foreign subsidiaries with expatriates include additional funding for tax allowances, repatriation expenses, relocation expenses, foreign service premiums, home leave, salaries, housing, living expenses, schooling, and other costs in addition to those normally experienced by domestic managers.
- A particular area of interest to HR managers will be the employment of women in the global workplace. Female expats will have to be thoroughly briefed and understand the host country's glass ceiling and other cultural impediments to their success.
- It is important that a repatriation plan be in place for returning expats.
- There are emerging trends that must be considered by management when staffing and managing subsidiaries. These trends are the aspatial careers, rotational assignments, and managing employees remotely.
- It is important that management and employees filling offshore positions have mental and behavioural characteristics of a global mindset.

REVIEW QUESTIONS

1. What are the five major HRM activities? Briefly discuss.
2. What are today's impediments to finding employees willing to accept a foreign posting?
3. Using examples, describe what is meant by ethnocentric, polycentric, and geocentric staffing policies.
4. Why do some expatriates fail?
5. Outline the success predictors that assist in evaluating the suitability of an employee for foreign assignments.
6. Discuss what is meant by the "glass ceiling."
7. What is knowledge transfer and why is it important in HRM?
8. Explain multi-rater (360-degree) feedback.
9. Using a diagram, explain the balance sheet approach to evaluating employees' compensation packages.
10. Are unions necessary? Explain.
11. What are the threats to Canadian unions? How has labour both nationally and internationally responded to these threats?
12. What is meant by a "global mindset," and why is it important from a HR perspective?
13. Are temporary migrant workers in Canada a good thing or a bad thing?
14. Discuss some of the emerging threats in IHRM.

REFLECTIVE THINKING QUESTIONS

1. Having completed this chapter, reread the quotations on the first page, critically reflect on the validity of the authors' statements, and provide your opinion as to the validity of each. Evidence-based answers are preferred to rhetorical answers.
2. "Organizations are beginning to embrace the connection between global culture and the bottom line; a positive and accepting culture can have a positive impact on financial results, while a negative culture can interfere with performance. The need for cultural learning, diversity, and acceptance will create a new market for diversity and cultural awareness training, and a new way of thinking within organizations. This thinking will create trust, and therefore enhance relationships and knowledge-transfer efficiency, increasing the opportunity for a competitive advantage." Prove or disprove the validity of this notion.
3. The cost of sending a manager abroad is in the order of three to five times the expatriate's salary, and these are direct costs. How many $500,000 mistakes can you make before your decision-making ability is questioned? Discuss.
4. According to Cappelli, "people keep talking about the 'coming labour shortfall.' Well, they were talking about the 'coming shortfall' 10 years ago, and they're still talking about it today, but we haven't seen it. Demographics don't drive labour markets. Demographic changes are gradual and predictable, and the economy and the labour force have enough time to adjust to them."[92] Discuss the validity of Cappelli's

observation. Will Canada's future demographics be an issue for Canadian business?

5. As countries compete for foreign investment by repressing labour unions, failing to enforce environmental laws, or offering far-reaching tax breaks or other incentives to foreign investors, governments find it more difficult to afford essential social and health services. Does this "race to the bottom" concern you? Why or why not?

6. Theodore William Schultz, Nobel Prize Winner (1979), said, "The mere thought of investment in human beings is offensive to some among us. Our values and beliefs inhibit us from looking upon human beings as capital goods, except in slavery, and this we abhor. . . . To treat human beings as wealth that can be augmented by investment runs counter to deeply held values."[93] Should we see our employees as assets or liabilities? Discuss.

GLOBAL E-RESEARCH

Visit www.power.nelson.com for research suggestions, questions, and a number of background discussion papers on this topic.

MINI CASE

A Province for Sale—A Union Perspective

As B.C. assets shift into foreign hands, some unions suggest that the move comes at a big cost—the ability to chart B.C.'s economic future. In 1979, Canadian Pacific expressed its interest in purchasing British Columbia's largest lumber company, MacMillan Bloedel (McBlo). Premier Bill Bennett was widely quoted as saying, "B.C. is not for sale." Today, large portions of the BC economy are shifting into foreign hands. In June 1999, giant forestry company Weyerhaeuser (Washington) acquired McBlo for $2.45 billion. "A month later, Louisiana Pacific (Portland, Oregon) bought Evans Forest Products for $133 million. As a result, over the years, of the three top forestry companies operating in British Columbia in 2005—Weyerhaeuser, Canfor, and Abitibi—only one, Canfor, is based in British Columbia. . . . The current government encourages sales of Crown corporation assets."

The ripple effect goes beyond the boardrooms. American firm Kinder Morgan acquired a controlling interest in Terasen, B.C.'s seventh-largest corporation in 2004, with assets of nearly $5 billion and about 2,000 employees. Many fear that when corporations like Terasen become global, the regional culture and their concern for British Columbia's well-being inevitably changes. In August 2005, the Industrial Wood and Allied Workers of Canada (IWA Canada) voted to merge with the United Steelworkers of America. Gary Kobayashi, a union member from Vancouver Island, was in favour. He said, "To me it made a lot of sense to be locked into an international union when we're dealing with an international company. Weyerhaeuser is a typically ugly American corporation. They want to weaken unions, contract out as much as possible, all the typical union-busting tactics. We've got an international campaign going against Weyerhaeuser. We wouldn't have been able to do something like that as a national union." However, four B.C. union

locals viewed the matter differently. "In the Prince George local, the opposition to the merger was particularly fierce: 90 percent of the 6,000 members voted no. . . . We didn't buy into the story that big was always better. If you do your research, if you know the business that you're bargaining with, then you can do a good job for the membership. There's going to be competing interests in the United Steelworkers. . . . According to a Statistics Canada Report, in 2002, 14.5 percent of B.C.'s corporations were controlled by foreign owners. The U.S. had the biggest share of the pie—5.6 percent."

"A Province for Sale?" by Claudia Cornwall (January 14, 2005), copyright thetyee.ca © 2003–2006.

QUESTIONS

1. Gary Kobayashi of IWA local 2171 on Vancouver Island commented that "To me it made a lot of sense to be locked into an international union when we're dealing with an international company. Weyerhaeuser is a typically ugly American corporation. They want to weaken unions, contract out as much as possible, all the typical union-busting tactics. We've got an international campaign going against Weyerhaeuser. We wouldn't have been able to do something like that as a national union."[94] Is this a trend? Do you feel a loss of Canadian sovereignty? Discuss.

2. "Many fear that when corporations like Terasen become global, the regional culture and their concern for BC's well being inevitably changes."[95] How valid is this statement?

3. According to a Statistics Canada report, in 2002, foreign owners controlled 14.5 per cent of B.C.'s corporations. The United States had "the biggest share of the pie—5.6 per cent."[96] Should this observation concern unions? Should it concern Canadian HR managers of unionized firms?

ENDNOTES

1 Kay Kutt, "Leaders of the Right Stuff in Big Demand," *Financial Times*, June 7, 2000.

2 *Quote Garden* (A Harvest of Quotes for Word Lovers, 2006), retrieved August 26, 2006, from www.quotegarden.com.

3 *Brainy Quote* (BrainyMedia.com, 2005), retrieved August 26, 2006, from www.brainyquote.com/.

4 *Quotes* (QuoteWorld, 2006), retrieved August 26, 2006, from www.quoteworld.org/.

5 *Brainy Quote.*

6 Terrance Power, "Cultural Diversity Could Be Business Boost: Immigrant Population Plays Key Role in Western Economy,"*Business Edge*, Vol. 4, No. 38, October 28, 2004, retrieved August 26, 2006, from www.businessedge.ca/article.cfm/newsID/7291.cfm.

7 "Special Feature: B.C. Immigrant Population," *BC Stats Immigration Highlights*, Issue 03-1, retrieved September 21, 2006, from www.bcstats.gov.bc.ca/pubs/immig/imm031sf.pdf.

8 *Provincial Pocket Facts* (Canada's Merchandise Trade, May 2006), retrieved September 24, 2006, from www.dfait-maeci.gc.ca/eet/pdf/prov_pfacts_2005_Aug%202006-en.pdf.

9 *Prospects for Foreign Direct Investment and the Strategies of Transnational Corporations, 2005–2008* (United Nations Conference on Trade and Development, December 1, 2005), retrieved September 24, 2006, from www.unctad.org/en/docs/iteiit20057_en.pdf.

10 Power, "Cultural Diversity."

11 Ibid.

12 Ibid.

13 Ralph D. Sawyer, *The Art of War: New Translation* (Barnes and Noble, 1994).

14 Hugh A. Halliday, "Canada's Air Force in War and Peace," *Military History*, May 6, 2005, retrieved August 26, 2006, from www.civilization.ca/cwm/disp/dis006_e.html.

15 Lionel Laroche, *Relocating Abroad: A High Stakes Venture* (ITAP International, 1999), retrieved August 26, 2006, from www.itapintl.com/relocatingabroad.htm.

16 Sonja Treven, "Human Resource Management in International Organizations," *Management*, Vol. 6, No. 178, 2001.

17 William Parrett, "Deloitte CEO William Parrett Identifies Key Human Resource Challenges for Multinational Corporations in China," *Fortune*, May 17, 2005, retrieved August 26, 2006, from www.deloitte.com/dtt/press_release/0,1014,ssid%253D46669%2526cid%253D83011,00.html.

18 Jim Collins, *Do You Have the Right People on the Bus?* (First Who, Then What, 2002), retrieved September 18, 2006, from www.jimcollins.com/lab/firstWho/p2.html.

19 World Bank Group, *CIS Economies Pick up the Pace of Reform* (Doing Business in 2006, September 12, 2005), retrieved September 18, 2006, from http://web.worldbank.org/WBSITE/EXTERNAL/NEWS/0,,contentMDK:20643534~menuPK:34466~pagePK:34370~piPK:34424~theSitePK:4607,00.html.

20 Susan Nierenberg and Caroline Marvin, "Women 'Take Care,' Men 'Take Charge': Stereotyping of U.S. Business Leaders Exposed" (*Catalyst*, 2004), retrieved August 26, 2006, from www.catalystwomen.org/files/fact/Stereotype%20factsheet.pdf.

21 John Gray, *Men Are from Mars, Women Are from Venus: A Practical Guide for Improving Communication and Getting What You Want in Your Relationships* (New York: Harper Collins, 1992).

22 Nierenberg and Marvin, "Women 'Take Care.'"

23 Claire M. Tallarico and Susan Black, "Latest Count of Top Women in Canadian Business Shows Little Progress since Last Catalyst Census" (*Catalyst*, April 27, 2005), retrieved August 26, 2006, from www.catalystwomen.org/pressroom/press_releases/4-27-05%202004%20COTE%20News.pdf.

24 Nancy R. Lockwood, *The Glass Ceiling: Domestic and International Perspectives* (Society for Human Resource Management, June 2004), retrieved September 20, 2006, from www.shrm.org/research/quarterly/0402glass_essay.asp.

25 Ibid.

26 "Glass Ceiling" (*Dictionary by Laborlaw Talk*), retrieved September 20, 2006, from http://dictionary.laborlawtalk.com/glass%20ceiling.

27 Ibid.

28 Ibid.

29 Ibid.

30 Hiroko Tashiro and Ian Rowley, "Japan: The Glass Ceiling Stays Put," *Business Week*, May 2, 2005, retrieved August 26, 2006, from www.businessweek.com/magazine/content/05_18/b3931066.htm.

31 *Few Women in Executive Positions* (Press Release, Federal Statistical Office Germany, March 22, 2005), retrieved August 26, 2006, from www.destatis.de/presse/englisch/pm2005/p1370024.htm.

32 Lockwood, *The Glass Ceiling: Domestic and International Perspectives.*

33 Human Resource Services, *International Assignments: Global Policy and Practice—Key Trends 2005* (PricewaterhouseCoopers International, 2005), retrieved August 26, 2006, from www.pwc.com/uk/eng/ins-sol/publ/pwc_assignments-keytrends2005.pdf.

34 Michael Harvey, Cheri Speir, and Milorad M. Novicevic, "Strategic Human Resource Staffing of Global Subsidiaries," *Research and Practice in Human Resources Management*, Vol. 9, No. 2, 2001, retrieved November 17, 2006, from http://rphrm.curtin.edu.au/2001/issue2/strategic.html.

35 Jana Ritter, *Succession Planning: A Tool for Success* (The Galt Global Review, April 15, 2005), retrieved August 26, 2006, from www.galtglobalreview.com/business/succession.html.

36 Ruth C. May, Sheila M. Puffer, and Daniel J. McCarthy, "Transferring Management Knowledge to Russia: A Culturally Based Approach," *Academy of Management Executive*, Vol. 19, no. 2, May 2005.

37 Ibid.

38 Andre Laurent, "The Cross-Cultural Puzzle of Human Resource Management," *Human Resource Management*, Spring, 1986.

39 Shaun Tyson, "Synchronise Your Strategies," *Human Resources*, November 2004.

40 Penn State University, *What Labor Shortage? Debunking a Popular Myth* (Research at Penn, August 27, 2003), retrieved August 26, 2006, from www.upenn.edu/researchatpenn/article.php?708&bus.

41 Michael Armstrong, *Strategic Human Resources Management* (London: Kogan Page, 2000).

42 Dr. Beverly Dugan and Dr. Deirdre Knapp, "Multi-Rater Assessment and Feedback" (*Research Profiles*, 2000), retrieved August 26, 2006, from www.humrro.org/corpsite/html/research/multiraterfeedback.htm.

43 Terri Linman, *360-Degree Feedback: Weighing the Pros and Cons* (2004), retrieved August 26, 2006, from http://edweb.sdsu.edu/people/ARossett/pie/Interventions/360_1.htm.

44 Dugan and Knapp, *Multi-Rater Assessment and Feedback.*

45 Jodie Carter, "Globe Trotters," *Training,* Vol. 42, Iss. 24, August 2005.

46 Ibid.

47 Keith Head, *Elements of Multinational Strategy* (Overheads from Lecture, March 2006), retrieved September 20, 2006, from http://strategy.sauder.ubc.ca/head/book/chapter13.ppt.

48 Mary A Schumacher, *Global Employment Trends* (1999), retrieved September 20, 2006, from www.schumachergroup.net/PDF/Global%20Employment%20Trends.pdf#search=%22Schumacher%20Global%20Employment%20Trends%22.

49 *Cost of Living Survey 2006–Worldwide Rankings* (Mercer Human Resource Consulting, March, 2006), retrieved September 20, 2006, from www.mercerhr.com/attachment.dyn?idContent=1231390&filePath=/attachments/English/Mercer_Cost_of_living_2006_summary_table.pdf.

50 Ibid.

51 Ibid.

52 Luke Burbank, *Outsourcing, Globalization Eroding Unions* (NPR Radio, Morning Edition, November 12, 2004), retrieved September 20, 2006, from www.npr.org/templates/story/story.php?storyId=4166839.

53 Ibid.

54 "Business in Germany and France: Europe's Workplace Revolution," *The Economist,* July 29, 2004, retrieved August 26, 2006, from www.economist.com/business/displayStory.cfm?story_id=2967451.

55 Shari Caudron et al., "80 People, Events & Trends That Shaped HR," *Workforce,* Vol.81, Iss. 1, January 2002.

56 Terrance Power, *The Triple Bottom Line: Something Old, Something New, Something Borrowed, Something Blue, . . . Or . . . What You Can't Measure Doesn't Get Done* (Royal Roads University, 2004).

57 Caudron, "80 People, Events & Trends That Shaped HR.

58 Burbank, *Outsourcing, Globalization Eroding Unions.*

59 Jeff Mackler, "Split in the AFL-CIO?" *Socialist Action,* January 2005, retrieved September 24, 2006, from www.socialistaction.org/jan05_10.htm.

60 *Our Global Union* (UNI Global Union, July 4, 2005), retrieved August 26, 2006, from www.union-network.org/uniflashes.nsf/By+Date/832E3AA27FC18A17C1256FDC00392D26?OpenDocument.

61 Ibid.

62 *About Us: UNI's Strategic Objectives* (UNI Global Union, 2002), retrieved August 26, 2006, from www.union-network.org/ UNIsite/About_Us/Presentation_of_UNI/10points-en.html.

63 *In Globalization Twist, Unions Target Wal-Mart Worldwide* (AFP, August 21, 2005), retrieved August 26, 2006, from www.organicconsumers.org/BTC/unionize082405.cfm.

64 Ibid.

65 Ibid.

66 Ibid.

67 Gary Fields, "Reinventing the Union; Faced with Factory-Job Loss, Outsourcing, Services Growth, Labor Seeks New Strategies," *Wall Street Journal,* July 27, 2005, retrieved September 20, 2006, from http://online.wsj.com/public/article/SB112243080451697041-MS8mHyS2ZgDFlZfshzLaFxCO3aY_20060727.html?mod=blogs.

68 *Foreign-Born Population, 2001* (Natural Resources Canada, October 17, 2005), retrieved August 26, 2006, from http:// atlas.gc.ca/site/english/maps/peopleandsociety/immigration/imfb_01/1.

69 Ibid.

70 *Serving Canada and the World* (Citizenship and Immigration Canada, November 1, 2003), retrieved August 26, 2006, from www.cic.gc.ca/english/department/brochure/service.html.

71 *Foreign-Born Population, 2001.*

72 *Immigrants Making up Bigger Share of US Population* (Workpermit.com, February 24, 2005), retrieved August 26, 2006, from www.workpermit.com/news/2005_02_24/us/immigrants_big_share_of_us_population.htm.

73 Niels Planel, *Japan Takes a Hard Look at Immigration* (DAWN, April 2, 2005), retrieved August 26, 2006, from www.dawn.com/2005/04/02/int16.htm.

74 *German Immigration at Lowest Level for Many Years* (Workpermit.com, January 19, 2005), retrieved August 26, 2006, from www.workpermit.com/news/2005_01_19/germany/german_immigration_drops_to_long_term_low.htm.

75 *Germany Holds Off Immigrant Workers from the East* (Workpermit.com, March 22, 2006), retrieved August 26, 2006, from www.workpermit.com/news/2006_03_22/europe/germany_holds_off_immigrants.htm.

76 "Be My Guest: The Economic Case for Temporary Migration Is Compelling; the Historical Record Less So," *The Economist,* October 6, 2005, retrieved August 26, 2006, from www.economist.com/finance/displayStory.cfm?story_id=4488614.

77 Ibid.

78 Ibid.

79 Ibid.

80 Ibid.

81 Ibid.

82 *German Immigration Law Targets Skilled Workers* (Workpermit.com, January 13, 2005), retrieved August 26, 2006, from www.workpermit.com/news/2005_01_13/germany/german_immigration_law_targets_skilled_workers.htm.

83 Thomas Mayer, *Germany Is Fading* (Focus Europe, February 9, 2004), retrieved August 26, 2006, from www.cesifo-group.de/pls/portal/docs/PAGE/IFOCONTENT/NEUESEITEN/ME-MEDIENECHO/ME-DOKUMENTE/IFO_PRESS_ECHO_INTERNATIONAL_2004/DB_RESEARCH09-02-04.PDF.

84 Treven, "Human Resource Management in International Organizations."

85 Karen Roberts, Ellen Ernst Kossek, and Cynthia Ozeki, "Managing the Global Workforce: Challenges and Strategies," *Academy of Management Executive,* Vol. 12, No. 4, November 1998, p. 100.

86 Ibid.

87 Ibid.

88 Ibid.

89 Ibid.

90 Ibid.

91 Ibid.

92 Penn State, *What Labor Shortage? Debunking a Popular Myth.*

93 *Brainy Quote.*

94 Claudia Cornwall, *A Province for Sale?* (The Tyee News, January 14, 2005), retrieved August 26, 2006, from www.thetyee.ca/News/current/AProvinceforSale.htm.

95 Ibid.

96 Ibid.

Global Accounting in International Business

"In the game of business . . . [accountants] aspired to be players, or at least umpires, but were relegated to the humble office of scorekeepers. Their revenge for this ignominy was to keep the score in such a way that neither the players nor the umpires could ascertain the state of the game."[1]

—*R.G.A. Boland, former director of the UCT Graduate School of Business*

"Money for which no receipt has been taken is not to be included in the accounts."[2]

—*Hammurabi (ca. 2000 BC)*

"When there is an income tax, the just man will pay more and the unjust less on the same amount of income."[3]

—*Plato*

"The world that is fast emerging from the clash of new values and technologies, new geopolitical relationships, new life-styles and modes of communication, demands wholly new ideas and analogies, classifications and concepts."[4]

—*Alvin Toffler, American writer and futurist*

"We have the most crude accounting tools. It's tragic because our accounts and our national arithmetic doesn't tell us the things that we need to know."[5]

—*Susan George, British actress*

LEARNING OUTCOMES

- Evaluate the merits of the International Financial Reporting Standards (IFRS) harmonization initiative from a Canadian perspective.
- Demonstrate a knowledge and understanding of the five divergent forces that cause international accounting systems' differences.
- Understand what to finance, how to finance it, and how to conduct ongoing management of the firm's financial affairs.
- Understand the financial advantages and disadvantages of providing inter-company loans.
- Know when and how to make dividend payments between the subsidiary and the parent firm.
- Know how to make provision for royalty payments where applicable.
- Be able to arrange transfer and payment of management and service fees.
- Understand the importance of the ongoing management of short-term investments worldwide.
- Understand the collection and transfer of funds relating to accounts receivable.
- Enable transfer pricing while observing and staying within the law and regulations.
- Understand the duty to pay all the legal taxes owed to all jurisdictions within which the firm operates yet seek ways to reduce and avoid taxes to the maximum extent permitted by law.
- Understand how to exploit the opportunities presented by tax competition between nations.
- Understand how to avail the firm of the services provided by tax havens.

Bean-Counting Goes Global: International Accounting Standards Are Finally Becoming International

The new year is a time to break old habits and form new, better ones. For European companies, this ritual takes on a heightened level of seriousness in 2005. Starting on January 1st, the 7,000 quoted companies in Europe will be required by law to ditch the mishmash of national accounting rules used in the past for International Financial Reporting Standards (IFRS). The idea is that such "convergence" will boost the efficiency of Europe's markets. Investors will make better decisions because comparing firms across borders will be simpler; companies will save time and money by reporting under one accounting standard (with the exception of derivatives) rather than a multiplicity of them. The new rules emphasize market values and economic substance rather than smooth earnings, as the old ones did. For

example, they require companies to record pension deficits at their current (ever-fluctuating) value rather than letting firms hide these shortfalls off the balance sheet and "smooth" their impact on profits little by little over many years. Inevitably, rules like this will mean more volatility and, for many investors, more confusion—at least at first. All the more so because, although most firms have been hard at work for months training staff and installing the systems needed for the new accounting framework, some smaller outfits are unprepared. Moreover, applying the new accounting framework will involve subjective judgments by company accountants and auditors. These interpretations will no doubt vary in the early stages, leading to more inconsistency in financial reporting during the first few years.

Europe is not alone in facing these challenges. In total, almost 100 countries on six continents will be using international standards by 2005, either directly or through national accounting rules aligned to them. Even some American companies—which are governed by American rules and not international ones—will feel the sting, including American subsidiaries of European firms or those with big, foreign investors that require international accounting. The ultimate goal is a single set of accounting rules worldwide. Since 2002 American and international standard-setters have slowly but steadily worked to narrow the gap between American rules and IFRS. Next on the agenda is Japan. Stay tuned.

Source: Joanne Ramos, *Bean-Counting Goes Global* (The World in 2005). © The Economist Newspaper Limited 2006. All rights reserved.

A SUN TZU MOMENT. . .

"The State is impoverished by the Army when it transports provisions far off. When provisions are transported far off, the hundred surnames [aristocracy; today we would say all citizens] are impoverished."[6]

HITLER'S SILENT PARTNERS— SWISS BANKS

Revelations about Swiss banks and their business dealings with Nazi Germany during World War II occurred at the Nuremberg trials. "It was common knowledge that the German occupiers had looted the national banks of the occupied; that jewellery was seized from concentration camp and death camp victims, and the gold fillings of the dead yanked out of their mouths; that all this looted gold was resmelted and sent to the Reichsbank; and finally, that the Swiss Bank for International Settlements bought this gold, paying for it in convertible Swiss francs which Germany used to import materials for its war

effort."[7] It is fair to conclude that Swiss banks were guilty of fencing stolen goods and money-laundering worth about $600,000,000 in wartime dollars for Hitler's regime. It seems, at the time, the Swiss conscience was untroubled. "The issue of laundering stolen Nazi gold was part of a general stream of revelations about Swiss money-laundering for organized crime, drug lords, and dictators. Swiss foot-dragging over the numbered bank accounts of Holocaust victims, when heirs came to claim what was rightfully theirs, was long known. . . . What was not known until recently was that from the 1950s to the 1970s, Swiss banks had pirated the unclaimed dormant accounts of East European Holocaust victims to compensate Swiss nationals for property nationalized by Communist regimes."[8] The Swiss government and its banking establishment, relying in part on the country's banking law, provided enormous barriers to those who sought truth, justice, and transparency into ethically challenged monetary transactions. Switzerland continues to be a tax haven today.

Opening Thoughts

Our old friend Sun Tzu provides sage advice as he warns us that nations are weakened if their citizens take their wealth and transport it to other nations' banks. The practice of organizations and individuals moving their wealth in order to obtain location economic advantage is not a new concept. The opening vignette reports on the actions of some Germans and Swiss banking institutions during World War II in order to fence stolen goods and launder money. Today, similar tax havens offering location economies continue to be used for the same purposes and attract capital to the detriment of Canada and other nations.

This chapter concludes our internal focus on the firm's value chain and the contribution of some of the secondary support activities to the sustainability of the organization. Financial managers, like other functional managers, must take every opportunity to "wring the pennies out" or add value to the firm's value chain. They do this in three ways. They can make the appropriate investment decisions that fit the specific needs of the organization; they can use the global capital markets to finance the firm's financial requirements; and they can prudently manage the firm's capital in order to obtain the best financial outcomes. The complexity in making decisions about *what* to finance, *how* to finance it, and how to conduct *ongoing management* of the firm's financial affairs in a sometimes turbulent international environment once again involves scanning for PEST-C factors. This will occur through the lens of the firm's financial decision makers just as the other functional-level managers scanned through their lenses in order to achieve a sustainable competitive advantage.

In this chapter we will briefly examine global accounting and the accounting standards of Canada and many of its trading partners. We do this because, as business leaders, we must be familiar with the generally accepted accounting principles (GAAP) of the nations with which we trade in order to view the entire global accounting picture of the firm. We will examine underlying rationale to explain a nation's idiosyncratic GAAP. We will also examine some additional aspects of corporate governance as they relate to the appropriate use of tax havens and transfer pricing. Finally, we will conclude the chapter with a review of selected initiatives to harmonize global accounting practices as reported in the opening vignette. One caveat: This chapter is not intended to be the definitive statement on global accounting practices but rather is designed for those in a nonaccounting stream who wish to develop an awareness of a number of emerging international accounting issues that will affect Canadian business.

A well-known and respected American jurist, Judge Learned Hand, is often quoted as stating: "Anyone may arrange his affairs so that his taxes shall be as low as possible; he is not bound to choose that pattern which best pays the Treasury; there is not even a patriotic duty to increase one's taxes . . . nobody owes any public duty to pay more than the law demands. Taxes are an enforceable extraction and not a voluntary contribution."[9] This is equally good law in Canada. In this chapter, you will form your own opinion as to Judge Hand's dictum and the ethics of such a position in light of tax havens and how his thoughts seem at odds with the thoughts of Sun Tzu.

What to Finance

The first complexity in making financial decisions is *what* to finance. Financial decision makers, in determining what to finance, will generally start with the firm's capital budget for the project. The challenges are compounded when a firm undertakes nondomestic ventures, which produce their own budgeting information and specifically their own cash flows. The firm will have to translate the cash flow of the foreign subsidiary in order to determine what impact it will make to the cash flow of the home office. Cash flows will differ between the parent and the subsidiary for a number of reasons. Chief among these is that the repatriation of capital could be restricted or may be blocked by the host country; the taxes in the host nation may significantly affect any residual capital left for repatriation; or the host country may require that a profit or a percentage thereof be invested within the country rather than repatriated to the parent company (see Chapter 12, pages 342–344). This interference in the free flow of the firm's capital from its subsidiaries must be costed by the parent in determining whether to finance the venture once established. Will the firm be able to get its profits out? Financial decision makers must calculate the net present value of funding that would have been received had it not been for these impediments and adjust their capital budgets accordingly. The good news is that with globalization and deregulation, the number of impediments of this nature is declining.

Further factors requiring analysis when determining whether to finance a particular venture arise from evaluating the political and economic risks that are likely to affect the success of the venture. We have examined these variables at some length in Chapters 2–4. Today political and economic risks shift quickly, and require ongoing monitoring by the firm's financial decision makers. Canadian mining companies, such as Toronto-based Crystallex International Corporation, a gold producer with operations and exploration properties in Venezuela, face these risks daily. In determining whether to proceed, the capital budget must provide, among other things, a suitable return on investment (ROI) for the additional political and economic risk exposure. These costs must be included when determining the capital budget and whether the venture should be financed.

How to Finance

The second complexity in making financial decisions is *how* to finance. In host countries, operational risk is an old problem with a crucial new significance. The transformation of the accounting services industry in the past few years is fundamentally changing the landscape. Globalization, reliance on technology, and a more stringent regulatory environment mean that the opportunities and consequences of operational risk have proliferated. The firm's financial decision makers, like other functional managers, are required to globally source the lowest cost of capital as part of the firm's value chain. Firms of all sizes often access the global capital markets to seek external financing for operations and projects. In Chapter 8, pages 243–245, we discussed a number of financial instruments, such as Eurocurrency and Eurobonds, that can aid the firm in achieving significant capital cost savings. At times, accessing funds from the global capital markets within the host nation can be a good strategic move. For example, a Canadian firm may reduce its operational risk by raising debt or equity funding through capital markets within China. It would seem less likely that a Canadian firm would be nationalized by China if its capital base represented a large domestic financial exposure for Chinese citizens should the venture close its doors. However, it can happen; during 2005, the tension between China and Japan included veiled threats of nationalization to Japanese businesses operating in China.

At times, host countries may have restrictions on the financing of projects with local debt and equity financing instruments. Conversely, a nation may have regulations requiring FDI capital be sourced outside of the host country. We discussed in Chapter 7, page 202, how governments might adjust tax acts and regulations in order to attract capital. These adjustments may include low-cost interest, subsidies, and other tax initiatives designed to lower the cost of capital and to make the host country more attractive than the competitors—"a beauty contest." Financial decision makers, as part of analyzing the operational risk, will also consider PEST-C factors though the lenses of financial managers. We have discussed this process in earlier chapters and will not repeat it here, but it remains a very important component of the required analysis and critical thought. When crafting their financial business strategy, business leaders must consider these factors and many others, such as whether the host country's currency is anticipated to depreciate or appreciate on the foreign exchange market (see Chapter 8, pages 246–247).

Ongoing Management of the Firm's Financial Affairs

The third and final complexity in making financial decisions, we will examine is how to conduct *ongoing management* of the firm's financial affairs in a sometimes-turbulent international environment. Globalization, global foreign exchange markets, and new technology have provided SMEs with more profit-making opportunities when managing the firm's financial affairs. However, these opportunities also present operational risks. Business managers recognize that proactively managing the firm's financial affairs offers a real business benefit. In a competitive marketplace, firms have little choice but to participate in these opportunities and manage the attendant risk. Financial managers can no longer simply park their surplus capital in the corner bank as a low-interest-bearing term deposit until required. Access to the global capital markets requires financial managers to manage the firm's global cash resources in the most efficient way possible. Recall that the role of the financial manager in the firm's value chain is "to wring the pennies out" and/or create additional value for the product or service in the mind of the consumer. The challenge for financial managers is to achieve the appropriate balance to meet the firm's need for sufficient liquid capital while investing the balance of its surplus nonrequired cash in the global capital markets to achieve the maximum rate of return on the cash reserves. In addition, many firms find that pooling the entire firm's surplus capital in a *consolidated account* affords efficiency. This efficiency is in part derived from economies of scale by not permitting every subsidiary to maintain its own surplus capital investment initiatives. Further savings can be achieved by maintaining a consolidated account for the firm to enable lower **transaction costs**. We discussed these opportunities in Chapters 8 and 9. Today, financial managers must avail themselves of the investment opportunities, invest these consolidated funds in the global capital markets, and exploit foreign exchange fluctuations. Increasingly the global capital markets are competing for firms' capital market business, and reducing transaction costs. Readers may be familiar with online trading and have watched competition drive down the cost of buying and selling stocks. A firm's financial manager must identify similar savings as part of her ongoing management of the firm's financial affairs.

Transaction costs are the costs paid to the market makers by buyers and sellers to acquire or sell debt and equity instruments.

International Generally Accepted Accounting Principles (GAAP)

A critical element in any market is its accounting system. A nation's accounting system provides an accounting language, information required by investors, creditors, and regulators regarding a company's affairs. Accounting is often referred to as the language of business. Developed nations and most developing nations have each over time crafted their own unique set of **Generally Accepted Accounting Principles (GAAP)**. Business leaders reading the financial statements of a firm with its head office in Halifax can take comfort that the same definitions and protocols are being applied by accountants in all provinces—the language is the same. Unfortunately, specific protocols and accounting definitions vary from nation to nation, resulting in most nations having their own distinctive set of GAAP. This presents a significant difficulty and cost for Canadian international businesses. Let us examine the historic, political, and economic drivers that have resulted in establishing a global set of differing accounting languages.

Generally accepted accounting principles (GAAP) are a set of accounting rules used to standardize the reporting of financial statements throughout a country.

The accounting process in Canada provides accounting information of the firm's financial position mainly through the production of profit and loss statements, balance sheets, budgets, investment analysis, and tax analysis. This information is used by investors to determine whether they will invest in the firm; by creditors as part of their risk due diligence in determining whether to extend credit to the firm; and by government in order to collect taxes owed. Today, accounting information is increasingly being produced in real time and has become a major control function of an organization. In turbulent markets, financial statements that are 3, 6, or 12 months old serve little purpose. Today, accounting information must be real time, leveraged, and accessible by all who need the information as part of the firm's decision-making process. The importance of accounting to the successful operation of a firm in a global environment has risen exponentially.

Transparent and accurate information is also the foundation of a nation's economy, the markets' well-being, and the maintenance of regulatory efficiency. With globalization has come the recognition that all trading nations need to have a clear, comprehensive, and consistent accounting language that is universally accepted. While most nations see the absolute necessity of a global accounting language, a number of nations have been reluctant to harmonize their GAAP with others; nevertheless, as we read in the opening vignette, page 443, a global accounting language is taking hold.

History—Accounting around the World

"The history of accounting is as old as civilization, among the most important professions in economic and cultural development, and fascinating. That's right, fascinating! Accountants invented writing, developed money and banking, innovated the double entry bookkeeping system that fuelled the Italian Renaissance, were needed by Industrial Revolution inventors and entrepreneurs for survival, helped develop the capital markets necessary for big business [and] so essential for capitalism, turned it into a profession that brought credibility to complex business practices that sparked the economic boom of the 20th century, and are central to the information revolution that is now transforming the global economy."[10] Today, accounting has harnessed the latest technology and is among the most critical professions. Interestingly there are no household names among the accounting innovators; in fact, virtually no names survive before the Italian Renaissance. The Crash of 1929 and the subsequent Great Depression brought to the surface problems with capital markets, business practices, and deficiencies in accounting practices. In response, the Roosevelt administration introduced numerous business regulations.

Therefore, it will come as no surprise that accounting practices are shaped in large part by the past and present environment of a nation. PEST-C factors shape a nation's accounting system, which is crafted to meet the needs of the nation's unique marketplace. The drivers shaping any nation's accounting system include the nation's view of inflation, the prevailing culture of the nation, the level of economic and technical development, the political and economic history of the nation and its relationship with other countries, and the legal system, including the accounting system's relationship with business and its role in the global capital markets. To read about the world's first accounting system using tokens in the ancient city of Jericho in what is now Israel, visit www.power.nelson.com.

A Nation's View of Inflation

The first driver shaping a nation's accounting system is its view on inflation. Most developed and developing countries adopt the view of inflation that it is not to be accounted for in their accounting records. This view of inflation is called the **historic cost principal**. Countries like Japan, Canada, Germany, and the United States make no provision for currency shifts in books of account. The expenditure is the cost recorded in the firm's financial records. You can readily appreciate the distortions that appear by adopting the historic cost principal. For example, by adopting this method a plant purchased 10 years ago would be shown on a firm's books as the cost paid at that time. We all recognize that the value of the plant (land values) in most venues has appreciated significantly since the date of purchase 10 years ago, yet nowhere in

The **historic cost principal** takes the view that inflation is not to be accounted for in a nation's accounting records. Assets are valued according to their net book value; net book value equals historical cost less accumulated depreciation, where depreciation is calculated on a straight-line basis using historical cost.

Current cost approach is an attempt to reflect the true value of asset transactions. Assets are valued at their current or inflation-adjusted cost, and depreciation is based on these costs, usually on a straight-line basis.

the firm's financial records is provision made for this increase in equity to be reflected in the worth of the firm. During the 1980s, most developing countries including Canada experienced significant inflation accompanied by extremely high interest rates. It was not uncommon for Canadian mortgage rates to be over 18 percent and Canadian chartered banks to charge 21 to 22 percent interest on their loans. The value of assets appreciated quickly. What value to the firm's decision makers, investors, or lenders are the firms' statements in such a turbulent environment? In response to the historically high inflation rate, Great Britain adopted a **current cost approach** to accounting in an attempt to reflect the true value of asset transactions. With the return to what might be described as inflation rate normalcy, the current cost approach is no longer used.

The Role of Culture

The second driver shaping a nation's accounting system is the impact of its culture. The "Uncertainty Avoidance Index (UAI) focuses on the level of tolerance for uncertainty and ambiguity within the society—i.e. unstructured situations. A high uncertainty avoidance ranking indicates the country has a low tolerance for uncertainty and ambiguity. This creates a rule-oriented society that institutes laws, rules, regulations, and controls in order to reduce the amount of uncertainty. A low uncertainty avoidance ranking indicates the country has less concern about ambiguity and uncertainty and has more tolerance for a variety of opinions. This is reflected in a society that is less rule-oriented, more readily accepts change, and takes more and greater risks."[11] Hofstede's lowest uncertainty score is awarded to Singapore with 8; the highest to Greece with a score of 112. Hofstede's scores Canada at 48, Australia 51 and Brazil at 76. Accordingly, Canada's accounting system will be characterized by low uncertainty avoidance. Low uncertainty avoidance cultures generally have a strong independent accounting profession. Joining Canada with similar cultures are Singapore, Britain, the United States, and Sweden. Nations like Argentina, Brazil, Japan, Mexico, and Greece place significantly higher on Hofstede's uncertainty avoidance dimension and, as a result, have a less independent accounting profession.

The Level of Economic and Technical Development

The third driver shaping a nation's accounting system is the level of development and the technical resources and infrastructure available to the nation. Porter calls them advanced factor endowments (see Chapter 6, page 169). Developed nations are able to avail themselves of the latest technology combined with real-time access to the global capital markets, investors, lenders, and regulators—and have more sophisticated accounting systems. Regretfully, underdeveloped countries and many developing countries lacking these resources use only very rudimentary accounting practices. This gap provides significant advantage to firms fortunate enough to be in a developed country and impedes FDI into these less technically advanced nations. We also note that the best-trained accounting practitioners gravitate to developed nations (i.e., cause a brain drain) while those lacking these high-tech skills remain in the poor nations. The higher the skill sets and more advanced the nation's technology, the more developed the nation's accounting system.

Shaping a Nation's Accounting System—Political and Economic History, and Relationships with Other Countries

The fourth driver shaping a nation's accounting system is its political and economic history. Former colonies like Canada, the United States, Australia, and many African nations have their accounting genesis grounded in the political and economic linkages with two European nations, either Britain or France. Three accounting clusters can be readily identified: the British-Canadian-American-Dutch; the European-Japanese; and the South American. These clusters are rooted in the political/legal, economic, societal, technological, and cultural variables we have examined earlier in this text.

Global capital markets increasingly require foreign firms to adopt their regulations, which, when combined with growing regionalization, result in nations promoting convergence of global accounting standards. Driven by economics, NAFTA, Mercosur, the EU, and ASEAN regions are developing some commonalities in their accounting systems. For example, "the UK has a long history of wide share ownership, with not only multinationals but also medium-sized domestic companies obtaining listings on the London market. The requirements of shareholders and the desire of companies to demonstrate continuously upward profit trends have, as a result, influenced significantly, the development of UK accounting practice. In the past, German industry was dominated by the '**Mittelstand**'—private companies (many of which are effectively family businesses), whose capital has traditionally been provided by the banking sector. Consequently, the major developments in German accounting have been driven by the needs of the creditors (the so called "Gläubigerschutzprinzip") rather than those of the shareholders. Indeed, it is possible to argue that whilst profitability (the profit and loss account) is most important to the general user of UK financial statements, financial security (the balance sheet) has traditionally been of greatest significance to the German user (generally banks). There is, however, a clear trend in Germany towards wider share ownership and the attractiveness of the legal form of public company is coming to bear."[13]

> **Mittelstand** refers to private German companies, many of which are effectively family businesses, whose capital has traditionally been provided by the banking sector.[12]

In China, accounting in the past has focused not on the needs of investors and bankers, but rather on how many units of production would be produced because the state needed to know. The source of capital, whether government, lending institutions, or investors, significantly influences a country's accounting system. In this chapter we will discuss the move by most nations away from these historical roots towards the adoption of a global accounting business language.

Legal System

The final driver shaping a nation's accounting system is its legal system. For example, UK, Canadian, and American accounting practices "have developed separately from tax law and reconciliations between tax accounts and statutory accounts are often complex, whereas German accounting has been significantly affected by tax rules."[14] The important German principles of "Massgeblichkeit," which links the commercial financial statements and tax laws (they must be consistent) and "umgekehrte Massgeblichkeit," which reverses the financial reporting rules are chosen, interpreted, or shaped with the tax effect in mind. This results in many tax incentives available to business only if the commercial financial statements follow the same accounting treatment. There are no precise Canadian equivalents for these two principles. Germany's recent legislation has minimized the differences between tax and financial accounts; however, significant differences still remain, particularly in the detailed methods of computing profits. "These differences are partly attributable to . . . business traditions within the two countries and the different historical development of the legal systems. The heavily codified law in Germany, with its comprehensive legal provisions, contrasts sharply with the common law . . . [stare decisis—case law precedent] in the United Kingdom [and Canada]. As a result, accounting in Germany has been basically governed by detailed legal regulations."[15] Similarly, the Japanese accounting principles are established by statutes.

These five drivers and the resulting classification of national systems have been captured by C.W. Nobes, which is included for historical reference in Figure 16.1, on page 450. The reality of today means the redrawing of lines to provide convergence from Nobes's view to a universal globally harmonized set of international accounting standards.

Nobes Classification of National
Accounting Systems

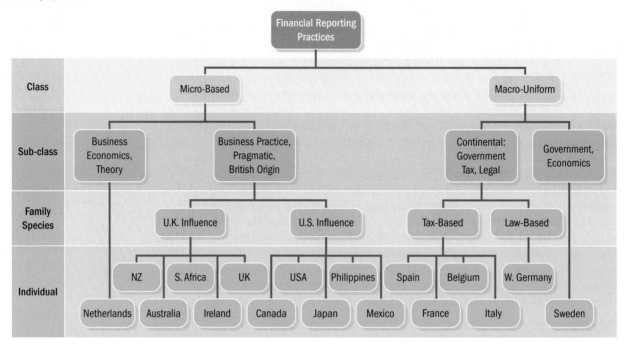

Global Accounting Harmonization

A global real-time integrated accounting system for most developed countries is a near reality. "Despite remarkable efforts of international harmonization for more than 25 years, accounting regulation is still the domain of national legislators or delegated standard setters."[16] Fortunately, this situation is shifting toward a global authority establishing a universally accepted set of accounting standards. Global financial markets demand international consistency in accounting and auditing standards and approaches. Several countries have either adopted international financial reporting standards (IFRS) or are basing their local standards on IFRS. Leading the way is the EU. "Multiple, country-based accounting standards in Europe make it very difficult to compare results of companies registered in different countries."[17] This has served as a catalyst to the creation of the International Accounting Standards (IAS) Board. "The International Accounting Standards Committee is an independent organization, established in 1973, through an agreement made by professional accounting bodies from Australia, Canada, France, Germany, Japan, Mexico, the Netherlands, the UK, Ireland and [the] USA. At present 140 accounting bodies are members of the IASC, representing 101 countries and 2 million accountants."[18] The European Union requires all companies listed on a stock exchange in a EU country to comply with IAS as of January 1, 2005. "Unlike Directives, EU Regulations have the force of law without requiring transposition into national legislation. Member States have the option of extending the requirements of this Regulation to unlisted companies and to the production of individual accounts."[19]

The EU's influence with its trading partners is now resulting in the IAS going global. Hong Kong, Korea, Singapore, Australia, Canada, and Russia, have announced either their support for, or adoption of the IAS. The IAS are adopted as national standards or widely used in the Middle East; Eastern Europe; Russia; Pakistan, Bangladesh, India; much of Africa, the West Indies, and China; Italy, Germany, the Netherlands, France, Turkey, and parts of South America. The EU's adoption of IAS will provide investors with reliable and widely accepted international financial statements, and lower European issuers' cost of capital. It will also enable the European Union to encourage others, including the United States, to adopt the IAS to ensure the full international comparability that the investing community requires. IAS is an older set of standards stating how particular types of transactions and other events should be reflected in financial statements. In the past, the Board of the International Accounting Standards Committee (IASC) issued the International Accounting Standards (IAS). Since 2001, the new set of standards has been known as the international financial reporting standards (IFRS) and has been issued by the International Accounting Standards Board (IASB).

"The Russian Finance Ministry announced plans to force Russian enterprises to use international financial accounting standards by 2010."[20] However, it seems the Russian initiative might be delayed. Press reports suggest that "A bureaucratic foul-up has caused the government to fall behind the business community in the drive to adopt international accounting standards. Although Russia's top companies already do their books under international standards, the delay could put a brake on other businesses following suit."[21] The United States is also moving, with reservations, toward adopting the global standard. The United States contends that, because European capital markets are organized in a different way from capital markets in the United States or Asia, European investors need different information. The Association for Investment Management and Research does not accept this position. It states, "Investors in every capital market need the same information on which to base their investment decisions and to make fair and reliable comparisons of performance, regardless of specific market structures or practices. They require this information to be provided according to the highest quality reporting and disclosure standards. . . . Australia has become one of the first countries to balk at the implementation of the international accounting rules."[22] Having accepted the international standards in 2001, Australian accounting professionals say the London-based International Financial Reporting Interpretations Committee (IFRIC), the little-known rule-making arm of the IASB is taking too long to make needed rule-clarifying decisions. Still, in other countries, such as Australia, accounting professional leaders want to interpret the global standards their own way. They say they want the drive-through version instead of the long wait at the restaurant.

Competing Standards

The two competing global accounting standards (models) are regulated by the American Financial Accounting Standards Board (AFASB) and the International Accounting Standards Board, based in London. In the private sector, the American Financial Accounting Standards Board has been the designated organization since 1973. It is responsible for establishing the financial accounting and reporting standards that govern financial report preparation, and is officially recognized by the Securities and Exchange Commission and the American Institute of Certified Public Accountants. Standards are essential to the credibility, transparency, and comparison of financial information that interested parties rely upon. For more information about the FASB, visit www.power. nelson.com. Firms wishing to access the U.S. capital markets and to be listed must adopt these standards.

The other emerging model is the International Accounting Standards Board (IASB), based in London. It replaced the IASC when it began operations in 2001. Funded by contributions from the international private and public sectors, the IASB collaborates with national accounting boards to achieve a set of global accounting standards that will result in general purpose financial statements that are both transparent and comparable. For more information about the IASB, visit www.power.nelson.com.

Driven by globalization and the needs of business, these competitors (models) are expected to converge into one set of global accounting standards.

The Canadian Position

Canada initially commenced aligning its GAAP with American GAAP but in 2005 stopped this accounting convergence in favour of the IAS. The IAS, now recognized by most stock exchanges worldwide, require businesses to adopt their processes, practices, and systems to bring about uniformity in financial reporting on a global basis.

The January 2006 statement by the Canadian Institute of Chartered Accountants' Accounting Standards Board (AcSB) announced it will move toward the global convergence of accounting standards. The best way to achieve the objective of a single set of globally accepted, high-quality accounting standards is to converge Canadian GAAP with International Financial Reporting Standards (IFRS) over a transitional period, expected to be five years.[23] The AcSB stated that by 2011 "Canadian GAAP will cease to exist as a separate, distinct basis of financial reporting for public companies."[24] It is important that business leaders be made aware of this pending shift in Canada's GAAP. Canadian managers must follow this initiative closely and commence planning today to realign their current practices with these new accounting standards. Currently the plan envisions 2010 as the last year that publicly accountable enterprises will report under current Canadian GAAP. The following year (2011) will be the first year of reporting under a complete set of IFRS-based Canadian standards. Since some current Canadian standards are already IFRS-based, and others will become IFRS-based before 2011, the changeover to IFRS-based Canadian standards should be gradual,

The AcSB currently accepts U.S. GAAP as an appropriate alternative when regulators and other competent authorities choose to permit its use. For private businesses, the AcSB states that GAAP applies only to entities that have significant nonresident users of their financial statements. For those entities, the AcSB will determine the most appropriate model for meeting the entities' needs. For example, "for not-for-profit organizations, the AcSB will continue to apply the applicable elements of GAAP for profit-oriented enterprises and develop other standards dealing with the special circumstances found in the not-for-profit sector."[25] The decision to propose the convergence of Canadian standards for public companies with IFRS is another crucial step toward achieving a global financial market and the consequent removal of artificial barriers to investment in new businesses and hence new jobs. However, Canada's position is rather unique because of our high dependency on U.S. capital markets and therefore Canada continues to be required to meet the SEC standards while shifting towards the IFRS. Truly Canadian! (See the Mini Case, pages 463–464.)

Financial Managers Must Consider Accessing the Global Capital Markets

Canadian SMEs and other international firms have little choice but to access the services of the global capital markets in order to utilize the firm's cash resources in the most efficient way. This will require the firm's financial decision makers to prudently handle the firm's internal funds flow; and the use of funds positioning and **intra-subsidiary netting**. To achieve these three outcomes, financial managers must

> **Intra-subsidiary netting** occurs when a firm's internal divisions sell to each other using the head office clearing accounts so that their sales and their internal debits and credits are quickly electronically entered into the firms accounts (netted out) to include currency conversion where necessary.

- Consider the financial advantages and disadvantages of providing inter-company loans
- Make dividend payments between the subsidiary and the parent firm
- Make provision for royalty payments where applicable
- Arrange transfer and payment of management and service fees
- Undertake the ongoing management of short-term investments
- Understand the collection and transfer of funds relating to accounts receivable
- Enable transfer pricing while observing the law and regulations
- Pay the taxes owed to all jurisdictions within which the firm operates while seeking ways to reduce and avoid taxes to the maximum extent permitted by law
- Exploit the opportunities presented by tax competition between nations
- Avail the firm of the services provided by tax havens where appropriate

The tax treatment of these various activities may be different and thus it is not usually advisable to lump them all together into a bundle. The separation of these various payments is called *unbundling*. I think you'll agree that today's financial managers' level of job sophistication has significantly increased with globalization. We explore these activities below.

Inter-Company Loans

Loans from the parent company may carry an interest charge above the cost of debt capital. This additional interest is a method firms can use to transfer profits to the parent. Conversely, a subsidiary may loan money to the parent when it is located in a venue where the prevailing interest rate is below the parent company's rate. Lastly, leading or lagging transaction payments between the parent and the subsidiary can temporarily influence the profit statements for one entity at the expense of the other. For example, if the subsidiary buys supplies from the parent and pays for them in advance, this in effect is a loan from the subsidiary to the parent. If the subsidiary sells supplies to the parent and the parent permits the payments to be delayed (lagged) then this also serves as a loan from the subsidiary to the parent. These are corporate governance issues (see Chapter 17, pages 482–488). At times a country's regulations may prohibit loans from a subsidiary to a parent company but allow the transfer of funds to financial intermediaries (such as large international banks). In this situation, financial decision makers may want to consider **fronting a loan** to transfer capital from the subsidiary to the parent. The interest on the parent company's loan is partially offset by the interest received on the subsidiary's deposit.

Fronting a loan occurs when the subsidiary deposits funds, generally in a large international bank, which are held by the bank as collateral for a loan the bank, in turn, provides to the parent company.

Dividend Payments

The Canadian Income Tax Act does not fully define a dividend. Canada's tax department contends ". . . it must be given its generally accepted meaning. Accordingly, any distribution by a corporation of its income or capital gains made pro rata among its shareholders may properly be described as a dividend unless the corporation can show that it is another type of payment. The fact that a distribution of this kind may not be called a dividend does not affect the nature of the distribution."[26] A subsidiary may declare dividends payable in any amount from retained earnings; however, dividends cannot exceed retained earnings. For example, "The dividends paid by Dell were paid through a patent royalty company called Dell Research Ltd. It had accumulated $91.7 [million] in retained profits, none of which is subject to tax under current Irish legislation."[27] Canada has tax legislations that permit the flow of dividends tax-free between subsidiaries and the parent. Dividends payable to the parent company are one of the most common methods of transferring funds. In undertaking this transfer method, financial managers will have to calculate factors such as the tax regulations in the jurisdiction of interest and the currency conversion costs, and understand that the same dividend must be paid out not only to the parent company but also to all holders of the stock to which the dividend declared refers (pro rata). This means that any distribution of funds to the parent will also be distributed to shareholders within the host country. What are the tax implications for all of the firm's shareholders? Is it still an attractive option after these calculations? Because the subsidiary can declare dividends at any time, they should be declared when they will be of the most benefit to the parent company; for example, immediately before or immediately after the company's year-end.

Royalty Payments, Management Fees, and Service Fees

Financial managers must consider and exploit the various jurisdictions' tax treatments for each of the transfer funds methods. Some locations may block or restrict payment of dividends. In such situations, financial managers will often use some combination of royalty fees, management fees, and service fees as a method of transferring funds from the subsidiary to the parent. Indeed, some jurisdictions provide certain tax advantages in favour of royalty payments, management, and service fees over dividends. Financial managers will have to examine the host country's tax rates to determine its relationship to the home country's tax rate. Generally royalty payments and management and service fees are fully deductible as an expense by the subsidiary as a result of making payment of these funds to the parent. Royalty payments and interest payments to nonresidents within Canada and most other jurisdictions are subject to a withholding tax.

Nations like Ireland and others participate in a global tax "beauty contest." To enhance its attractiveness, Ireland has passed legislation making royalty payment treatment very appealing for some. Consider the Irish patent exemption on patented inventions, which are a large source of revenue to the pharmaceutical industry. "Irish tax legislation provides an exemption from tax for income derived from 'qualifying patents' when received by a person resident in Ireland and not resident in any other country. A 'qualifying patent' is defined as a patent in relation to which the research, planning, processing, experimenting, testing, devising, designing, developing or similar activity leading to the invention, the subject of the patent, was carried out in Ireland."[28]

Taxation relief derived from patented inventions goes further than to exempt the income from patent royalties from tax. It also provides that certain distributions by companies made out of certain patent's income that has been disregarded for corporation tax purposes can also be disregarded for the purposes of income tax on the part of a shareholder. This has had significant implications for investors in pharmaceutical companies considering carrying out R&D in Ireland. The tax initiative works: "Ireland's annual corporate tax revenue is about €5.3 billion ($6.3 billion). *The Wall Street Journal* said in its report that a Microsoft Dublin-based company that is used for routing patent . . . [and] royalty income from overseas operations, paid the Irish Revenue [Service] $300 million in taxes last year [2004]."[29]

Managing Short-Term Investments

Positioning funds within the international business is one of the financial managers' main tasks. They must consider the possible locations and currencies they will hold. In Chapter 8, page 232, we discussed the volatility of the foreign exchange currency market, and most would agree that the firm's surplus capital should be held within a consolidated fund. Financial decision makers charged with the management of a consolidated fund must have a high level of financial and global capital market sophistication. Financial managers' goals are to achieve the best after-tax, risk-adjusted returns on the firm's financial assets while balancing this strategy against the needs for financial liquidity by the subsidiaries. In essence, then, financial decision makers must answer the question, what mix of assets should the firm hold, and in which affiliate should the assets be positioned? The parent company must undertake daily intra-subsidiary netting. This takes place in an internal clearing centre to "net out" the inter-affiliate capital flows to the greatest extent possible by offsetting internal debits and credits rather than issuing cheques and other payment instruments, which is a value-added benefit that cannot be ignored.

Accounts Receivable

Advances in technology have greatly aided international firms' cash flow payments from their accounts receivable. The delays in receiving capital today can seldom be justified. Electronic fund transfers and the interdependency between world banks permit almost instant transfer of funds between branches in different countries. This ability means international firms' accounts can be credited or debited in moments. International business decision makers must work with their banking institutions to ensure they have a network of corresponding banks in the venues in which the business is operating. Accounts receivable must not be delayed by banking bureaucracy, which is an unnecessary cost.

Transfer Pricing

Transfer prices are those prices charged between parents and subsidiaries, and between two subsidiaries for goods and services provided by one to the other.

Transfer prices are those prices charged between parents and subsidiaries and between two subsidiaries for goods and services provided by one to the other. The pricing of goods and services may serve to transfer profits from the subsidiary to the parent. The use of transfer pricing for this purpose generally results in reduced taxes. But this could be a problem! In determining the appropriate transfer price for the goods and services, financial managers will attempt to achieve their goal of reducing the firms' taxes, but this must be accomplished having full regard for the applicable tax law for the host and domestic countries involved. Accordingly, they will set the transfer prices to the firms' best interest. In many cases, income tax acts may well be the critical consideration in establishing transfer prices. Parent firms in high-tax jurisdictions, such as Canada, are often tempted to establish transfer prices charged by their subsidiaries as high as possible in order to reduce the Canadian tax owed. Similarly, import taxes can be an onerous burden and, in some jurisdictions, may offer a reason to establish a low transfer price. In these situations a Canadian firm might reduce its foreign tax burden by charging its subsidiaries substantially below-arm's-length prices for the same goods and services sold to other subsidiaries within other jurisdictions in order to reduce the tax payable as a result of the tariff. Financial managers might charge a premium, with some justification, if the subsidiaries are located in venues where there is political uncertainty or currency devaluation potential. Such situations would make the subsidiary a risky place to store retained earnings; therefore, financial managers could make a case for the higher transfer pricing than the global rate for its goods and services. As we have seen for royalty payments and management and service fees, transfer pricing is a more flexible way to move funds among subsidiaries than dividends. Generally, host countries do not interfere with the transfer of royalty payments but might interfere with the flow of dividends. Many jurisdictions have legislation with significant sanctions if the transfer prices are determined to be a form of tax evasion rather than tax avoidance. This line is often blurred. Financial managers must have the best global accounting advice when establishing transfer prices. Consider an Ernst & Young's 2005 survey of 476 companies in 22 countries. It found that "almost two-thirds had been the subject of transfer pricing probes over the last three years, with 40% of the respondents reporting that reviews had led to a readjustment by the authorities of the amount of tax owed."[30]

Taxation

The American Declaration of Independence put it succinctly when it said of King George III that: "He has erected a multitude of new offices, and sent hither swarms of officers to harass our people and eat out their substance."[31] In Canada "between 1975 and 1999, over 117,000 new federal and provincial regulations were enacted, an average of 4,700 every year. Over this twenty-four year period, federal and provincial governments have published over 505,000 pages of regulations contained in volumes that measure 10 stories when stacked."[32] The Canadian Income Tax Act and its regulations are contained in 2,707 very complex pages. When taxation levels become less onerous, nations will economically break free.

Have a look at Figure 16.2, page 456, and check the number of days you will have to work in order pay the taxes levied by Canadian governments at all levels. Does it makes you reflect on Rousseau's observation that "Man is born free yet everywhere he is in chains"[33]?

Only government has the power to tax, so with globalization, countries often enter into reciprocal tax treaties in order to prevent double taxation on their citizens' worldwide income. Canada and the United States have such a reciprocal tax agreement. Generally, nations follow one of two basic approaches to international taxation: the **residential approach** or a source or **territorial approach**. Canada and most other countries have adopted a balance between the two approaches. In Canada, we tax both foreign and domestic entities. We apply the residential approach to taxing residents, including corporations, and a territorial approach to income earned by nonresidents within our territorial jurisdiction. Many different combinations are adopted globally; in Germany, for example, the territorial approach is applied to dividends that have been paid to domestic firms by their foreign subsidiaries under the assumption that the dividends have been taxed abroad and are therefore exempt from further taxation in Germany.

Taxes are generally classified as being either **direct taxes** or **indirect taxes**. In the EU, the primary revenue source is a value-added tax (VAT). VAT is applied to the value added to a product during the production process. Corporate tax rates in Canada range

Video 16.1

The **residential approach** to international taxation determines the tax owing regardless of where the income is earned. For example, a Canadian resident company would pay Canadian tax on all world income to the Canadian government.

The **territorial approach** to international taxation taxes entities within its territorial jurisdiction regardless of the country of residence. This is a source-based taxation approach; therefore, a Canadian company with operations in, for example, Canada, Australia, and South Africa, would pay taxes on the income earned in each country (territory) to that country's government. To provide tax equity, many countries have reciprocal tax agreements that permit taking into account the "territorial" taxes paid in determining the amount owed the domestic government. Canada has many of these reciprocal tax agreements in place.

Direct taxes are calculated on the actual income of a firm or an individual.

Indirect taxes include sales tax, goods and services tax, provincial sales tax, health tax, death tax, severance tax, tariffs, and value-added taxes that are applied to the purchase price, material costs, quantities of natural resources, and commodities.

FIGURE 16.2
Tax Freedom Day Tables

	1981	1985	2000[re]	2004[re]	2005[re]	2006[pe]
Newfoundland	18 May	9 May	20 May	6 June	19 June	17 June
Prince Edward Island	6 May	7 June	21 May	5 June	14 June	11 June
Nova Scotia	11 May	17 May	4 June	12 June	20 June	18 June
New Brunswick	6 May	2 June	5 June	8 June	15 June	12 June
Quebec	7 June	17 June	13 June	3 July	30 June	27 June
Ontario	29 May	26 May	13 June	20 June	19 June	16 June
Manitoba	17 May	5 May	12 June	21 June	24 June	20 June
Saskatchewan	24 May	17 May	13 June	30 June	3 July	26 June
Alberta	30 May	22 May	5 June	21 June	18 June	6 June
British Columbia	9 June	16 June	13 June	25 June	22 June	16 June
Canada	30 May	6 June	12 June	25 June	24 June	19 June

[re] revised estimate

[pe] preliminary estimate

Based on total taxes as a percentage of cash income for families with two or more individuals.

SOURCE: *Tax Freedom Day Tables—2006* (The Fraser Institute's Canadian Tax Simulator, 2006).

between 36 percent and 40 percent while in Saudi Arabia there are no corporate taxes. Financial decision makers must undertake a financial tax analysis of different jurisdictions when considering transferring the firm's funds, which can yield significant benefits for a firm when determining where and when to transfer funds. I am reminded of billionaire hotel owner Leona Helmsley at her trial for tax evasion in 1989. She stated, "Only the little people pay taxes." There is at times a very fine line between **tax avoidance** and **tax evasion** that financial managers will be hard pressed to discern. Once again, business practitioners are advised to obtain professional counsel regarding the blurred line between tax avoidance and evasion in relation to their specific facts. Recall the words of Judge Learned Hand, that "anyone may arrange his affairs so that his taxes shall be as low as possible; he is not bound to choose that pattern which best pays the Treasury" in the Opening Thoughts, page 444.

Tax avoidance means seeking to pay the least amount of tax as possible as provided for by law (e.g., the Canada Income Tax Act). Tax avoidance is not to be confused with tax evasion.

Tax evasion is the illegal practice of intentionally evading taxes. Common examples include underreporting income or hiding assets from the tax authorities.

Tax Competition

Ireland offers one of the most beneficial corporate tax environments in the world, with a corporation tax rate of 12.5 percent applied to all corporate trading profits. The tax position of companies carrying out approved activities prior to July 31, 1998 will remain unchanged at 10 percent until 2010.[34] Is Canada doing enough to compete? Can we?

Tax competition is in a sense a "beauty contest" where nations attempt to persuade investors to established offshore operations in their country.

Where did the idea of tax competition come from? In a global economy, nations compete to persuade investors to establish offshore operations in their country. This "beauty contest" is commonly referred to as a **tax competition**. Nations participate by lowering taxes paid on profits, providing tax holidays, accelerating income tax allowances permitted for capital asset expenditures, providing subsidies, reducing all kinds of regulations, refraining from reciprocal agreements with other nations requiring the participation in a withholding tax scheme and sharing of tax information, and other forms of tax inducements.

Tax competition plays a significant role in directing worldwide investment flow, and the IMF, World Bank, and a number of regions like the European Union encourage it. From the perspective of a developed country like Canada blessed with resources, there seems little reason not to participate in the tax competition to compete globally. Unfortunately, from the perspective of underdeveloped countries, tax competition has been harmful. Poor countries are unable to raise the tax revenue they need to improve their lot. Three specific tax strategies come to mind. First, tax competition results in nations lowering their corporate tax rates to attract foreign investment. The result of this strategy is that less tax needed to undertake quality-of-life initiatives is collected by these nations. Consider: "the Irish tax exemption on patent income could well fund over 5% of the Irish Government's planned total spending (current and capital) of €48.5 billion, in 2006."[35] Second, globalization has deprived developing countries of import taxes. In order to participate in the global economy, developing nations are required to reduce their barriers to trade. In some cases, this strategy results in these nations losing up to one-third of their tax revenue. "According to the International Monetary Fund (IMF), in low-income countries, for every US$1 lost in trade taxes, only 30 US cents has been recovered in sales and consumption taxes."[36] The final strategy is to become a tax haven. For almost 40 percent of the world's developing and some underdeveloped nations, this is a way to achieve location economies and to compete against the competitive advantages of developed countries. Multinational companies, wealthy individuals, criminals, corrupt leaders, and terrorists all avail themselves of the benefits of tax havens. Tax havens affect the tax revenues of all nations, rich and poor alike.

Tax Havens

A **tax haven** can be defined as a country that provides a no-tax or low-tax environment. These countries impose little or no tax on the profits from transactions carried on or routed through that country, especially income from dividends and interest. Tax havens control their public expenditures and acquire the funding they need from licensing fees and other revenue streams. To illustrate, we will examine Bermuda as a tax haven and how it funds its government's needs later in the chapter. In addition, many also provide banking secrecy. This concept was developed in Europe at the time of the French Revolution (for the benefit of the French aristocracy) but became enshrined in Swiss law in the 1930s. In the Sun Tzu moment, page 443, we noted how the Swiss recognized and quickly exploited the competitive advantage that a tax haven status could provide a small, land-locked state in a hostile European environment. Canadians also use these venues in support of their best interest. A Canadian MP stated: "there is no greater example of that than the New Brunswick multi-billionaire, Mr. K.C. Irving, who left a will a few years ago for his sons, turning over all of the assets of his very successful business to the children on the condition that they could not live in Canada. In other words, they had to go to a tax haven offshore, the Cayman Islands or perhaps the Bahamas, where they would pay no taxes."[37]

> A **tax haven** can be defined as a country that provides a no-tax or low-tax environment.

"Today, of the 72 tax havens [the number is falling due to the influence of OECD countries] almost half are British territories, dependencies or Commonwealth members. Britain alone loses some US $170 billion a year in avoided taxes."[38] "Almost every part of the world now has access to havens. Europeans can use the old-established havens like Jersey and Liechtenstein or the newer ones, like Cyprus and Malta; the Asian Pacific uses the Pacific Islands and Singapore; India and southern Africa have the Seychelles and Mauritius; and North America has the Caribbean Islands and Central America."[39] A conservative estimate indicates that at least $1 trillion of Canada's wealth is held offshore. This, according to America's statistics, "does not include the laundered profits of businesses that operate through offshore tax havens to avoid tax. Nor does it include the financial assets of those whose wealth amounts to less than US$1 million. The total sum of money currently held offshore is not known."[40] Tax havens are respected and widely used. Indeed, "45 of the world's top 50 banks have subsidiary or branch operations in Cayman"[41] including most of Canada's major banks. In 2003, the Caymans received $415 billion in deposits.[42] For a comparison of tax havens, see Figure 16.3, page 458.

Is using these tax havens considered a legal tax and estate planning strategy, or is it tax evasion? Are there ethical considerations? Read these reports and form your own opinion on the merits of tax havens.

"An example of [possible] corporate evasion is Rupert Murdoch's News Corporation. 'In March 1999, the *Economist* reported, that in the four years to 30 June of the previous year, News Corporation and its subsidiaries paid an effective tax rate of only around 6 per cent. This compared with 31 per cent paid by Disney.' . . . [At that time] the 'basic corporate tax rates in Australia, America and Britain, the three main countries in which News Corporation operated were 36%, 35%, and 30% respectively'. The article points to

FIGURE 16.3
The Rise of Tax Havens, 1999
and 2002 Compared (profits are
in millions of U.S. dollars)

		1999				2002	
Rank	Country	Before-Tax Profits	Effective Tax Rate	Rank	Country	Before-Tax Profits	Effective Tax Rate
1	United Kingdom	$29,368	30%	1	Ireland	$36.835	8%
2	**Canada**	**21,244**	**22**	2	Bermuda	25,212	2
3	Netherlands	19,390	10	3	Netherlands	20,802	9
4	Ireland	13,355	8	4	United Kingdom	19,717	31
5	Switzerland	11,699	6	**5**	**Canada**	**19,626**	**26**
6	Germany	11,636	27	6	Luxembourg	18,405	1
7	Japan	9,010	45	7	Switzerland	14,105	4
8	Bermuda	8,529	3	8	Japan	11,526	39
9	Mexico	7,049	34	9	Mexico	7,659	37
10	Cayman Islands	5,635	3	10	Singapore	7,533	11
14	Singapore	4,370	12	13	Germany	5,371	27
16	Luxembourg	4,032	2	21	Cayman Islands	2,809	5

Notes: Effective tax rates include only foreign taxes. Data for 2002 are preliminary. Eight countries were in top 10 both years. Last 2 rows show 1999 rank of the other two 2002 top 10 countries and the 2002 rank of the two other 1999 top 10 countries.

SOURCE: *U.S. Multinationals Profit from Tax Havens* (Finfacts Ireland, November 21, 2005).

the difficulties of finding out the specifics of News Corporations' tax affairs because of the company's complex corporate structure. 'In its latest accounts, the group lists roughly 800 subsidiaries, including some 60 incorporated in such tax havens as the Cayman Islands, Bermuda, the Netherlands Antilles and the British Virgin Islands, where the secrecy laws are as attractive as the climate.' The article continues, 'This . . . elaborate tax planning has bizarre consequences. The most profitable of News Corporation's British operations in the 1990s was not the Sunday Times, or its successful satellite television business, BSkyB. It was News Publishers, a company incorporated in Bermuda. News Publishers has, in the seven years to June 30th 1996, made around £1.6 billion in net profit. This is a remarkable feat for a company that seems not to have employees, nor any obvious source of income from outside Mr Murdoch's companies.'"[43] Canada's business leaders also adopt tax havens as a sound business strategy.

How well do tax havens like Bermuda work as a tax strategy? In 2004, the U.S. journal *Tax Notes* said: "In low-tax Ireland, for instance, profits of subsidiaries of US multinationals have doubled in four years, from $13.4 billion to $26.8 billion. Profits from operations of U.S. multinationals in no-tax Bermuda have tripled, from $8.5 billion

JUST DOING THE RIGHT THING

The CSL Albatross

No matter how hard Paul Martin tries to get the CSL issue off his back, the more it seems to stick to him like glue. Canada Steamship Lines is sailor Paul's albatross and won't disappear overnight once he's Prime Minister. . . . A recent column by Chantal Hebert, the *Toronto Star*'s national affairs columnist, has her hearing people talking and arguing about CSL and its influence on Martin. These people are focusing on CSL as

a character indicator. These people are saying that CSL is flying flags of convenience that hurt Canadian workers. They're saying CSL, by using the Bermuda tax haven, is cheating the Canadian government out of needed tax revenues. These Canadians are not impressed with the argument that these are standard business practices. Martin's attempts to dodge the CSL issue in the hopes that it will go away don't seem to be working. . . . The Bermuda tax haven of Martin's company

raises the charge that Martin as finance minister did nothing to plug tax loopholes because he didn't want to hurt CSL financially. That's probably an absurd charge, but it's a charge that goes to Martin's character and credibility. . . . If nothing happens, CSL will continue to hang around Martin's neck like an albatross.

Source: Larry Zolf, *The CSL Albatross* (CBC News Analysis and Viewpoint, November 27, 2003). Copyright © CBC 2006.

to $25.2 billion. Not surprisingly, those two tax havens rank as the number one and number two locations in terms of profitability for U.S. corporations operating abroad—surpassing long-time leading investment partners like the United Kingdom and Canada."

Those advocating closing tax havens argue recipients of IMF funding and other funding agencies see millions of dollars siphoned off to these tax havens annually.

Political figures who use tax havens include "Haiti's 'Baby Doc' Duvalier, Zaire's President Mobutu, Sani Abacha, the former president of Nigeria, and Raul Salinas, the brother of the former Mexican president. Mr Abacha, during his period as president, had a standing order to transfer $15m (£8.4m at current [September 2004] exchange rates) a day of stolen funds to his Swiss bank account. . . . In 1999, the *Economist* estimated that African leaders had $20bn in Swiss bank accounts alone, twice the amount that sub-Saharan Africa spends on servicing debts. Among the latest countries offering such services is Somalia, which Mr Christensen describes as 'an example of what can happen when the cancer is not cut out.' He believes that the main function of the financial markets in Somalia will be money laundering."[44]

Does tax avoidance breed unethical habits? The Enron investigation in 2001 disclosed 881 offshore subsidiaries. Of these, 692 were incorporated in the Cayman Islands. The Enron partners included a large list of banks that paid to settle allegations that they had helped Enron engage in misleading transactions. Canada's "Canadian Imperial Bank of Commerce has paid the SEC $80 million to settle Enron-related charges. . . . The $80 million fine includes $37.5 million of ill-gotten gains, a $37.5 million fine, and $5 million in interest. The SEC also sued three current or former CIBC executives."[45]

Another argument against them is that tax havens hurt the majority. " 'The implications of tax avoidance on development are manifold. . . . While transnational corporations endeavour to hold on to cash by shoring it up in tax havens, millions are lost that could have been used in the fight against poverty. Every time we investigate corruption in the oil industry, we find that looted public money has been laundered through offshore tax havens,' said Gavin Hayman of Global Witness, the international resource watchdog group. Billions of dollars pass from public to private hands this way with no comeback. The collateral damage to the illicit international system and to international development is truly enormous and the only people who benefit are those who have something bad to hide. Tax havens are the seedy backstreet bars of the financial world, where corporations and multi-millionaires huddle in shadowy corners to pursue their business out of sight of respectable citizens."[46] Oxfam reports, that "as a conservative estimate, tax havens have contributed to revenue losses of developing countries of at least US$50 billion a year. To put this figure in context, it is roughly equivalent to annual aid flows to developing countries."[47]

So should we support the OECD initiative to close down tax havens? Are developed countries' motives grounded in the best interests of all or in their inability to compete with the tax havens' location economies (a banking competitive advantage)? Developed countries cannot do away with taxation and some might say they are using the OECD to level the playing field and remove very agile competitors. What do you think? We have examined many reasons for closing tax havens. Here are some arguments in favour of tax havens.

Those of the right-wing persuasion can make a strong case for tax havens. They find favour in the inherently secretive nature of low- or no-tax venue and the moral case espoused by organizations like the Fraser Institute and others (see the International Strategic Thinking box, page 460) concerned about tax efficiency, restraints on government power, the preservation of capital, and the freedom to enjoy that capital. Interestingly, "just one per cent of the world's population who hold more than 57 per cent of total global wealth use these havens to escape taxation."[48]

Corporate Governance

The discussion of international global accounting is not complete until financial managers make themselves aware of the corporate governance requirements in Canada and other jurisdictions. These requirements must also be fully considered when firms think about using tax havens (see Chapter 17, pages 482–488).

INTERNATIONAL STRATEGIC THINKING

The Moral Case for Tax Havens

"Bermuda has a terrible reputation with foreign government elites. The . . . problem is that Bermudians do not pay income tax on their earnings, capital gains taxes, or corporate taxes on profits. OECD countries see this as a great menace to the financial well-being of Western civilization on the grounds that tax havens siphon off their legitimate tax revenues. OECD countries claim tax haven depositors are dodging their legitimate tax obligations and as a result unfairly compelling their citizens to pay higher taxes. OECD countries also contend tax havens facilitate money laundering, linked to drug trafficking, and are the banks of terrorists.

There is a huge morally important point at stake. Government taking is usually justified by the fact that it performs good works and provides endless benefits to its citizens. The state is somehow more important than the individual [Plato], and we should willingly stump up our share because of all the benefits showered on us by benevolent rulers. Others . . . argue that the individual takes precedence over government [Aristotle] and there are inalienable rights to privacy, life, liberty, and property and that the compulsory sequestration of the individual's property through taxation makes the rights of man dependent on the goodwill of the state."

Bear in mind that government's role a century ago tended to be restricted to "maintaining an army against foreign aggression, a police force to protect law-abiding citizens against robbers and thieves, and a limited number of social activities such as public health and education. In most countries, less than 10 percent of incomes were taken in taxation." Today our bloated governments have "a desire to redistribute incomes from the rich to the poor, and the recognition that governments by spending huge amounts on social programs could effectively bribe voters with their own money to vote high spending politicians into office. Elections became in the words of H.L. Mencken 'advance auctions of stolen goods.' . . . Once the government bite on individual incomes reaches 30 percent or thereabouts a silent tax revolt takes place [Canada's underground economy]. People either stop working, . . . they cheat on their tax returns, or they shift assets, [like KC Irving], and their commercial activities, [like Paul Martin], abroad to countries where the tax regime is less hostile to earnings and the preservation of capital. . . . The most important activity of the misnamed tax havens is to avoid governmental unproductive spending and to allow entrepreneurs freely to invest and produce the goods and services needed for the world to prosper. . . . Can there be a more moral case for tax havens than tax efficiency, restraints on government power to grab the income of its citizens,

the preservation of capital to increase prosperity, and freedom to enjoy private property? I think not."

Adapted from Robert Stewart, *The Moral Case for Tax Havens* (LewRockwell.com, October 30, 2002).

REFLECTIVE THINKING QUESTION

These extracts from Bob Stewart, former CEO of the Royal/Dutch Shell Group of Companies in Bermuda, present a strong case for tax havens and for those holding similar views to Aristotle, Adam Smith, and others, by supporting free trade and the role of the invisible guiding hand in the economy. Unfortunately for them, the OECD countries are making headway in constricting the competitive advantages of "tax havens." Some might see the OECD countries' initiative as "sour grapes" because they are unable to compete with Bermuda and other tax havens' location economies in a global setting. Accordingly, OECD nations must find a way to place barriers to this form of "trade." Some of you, as business practitioners, will have to face this challenge as baby boomers inheriting your parents' wealth. Will you keep your inheritance in Canada or will you seek alternative locations such as Bermuda? See the Bentley College Ethical Test, Chapter 17, page 482, and recall Sun Tzu's observation about taking wealth out of the nation. There are no easy answers.

Management Implications

- In a global economy, transnational financing is a requirement. Canadian firms entering the international marketplace must avail themselves of the most attractive capital market to buy and sell debt and equity instruments to support the firm's activities. As a consequence, financial managers require a greater knowledge of global accounting than in the past. Today, most firms prepare financial statements according to the set of GAAP for each nation within which it operates. These statements must be translated and/or consolidated into the parent accounting language (GAAP). This is a very expensive and time-consuming exercise.
- The activity of consolidating financial statements has stimulated a growing interest in eliminating major differences between national and international standards. With the

PRACTICAL ENTREPRENEURIAL FOCUS

How to Choose the Right Offshore Jurisdiction

Having read the arguments for and against exploiting the advantages to be gained both personally and for your firm, you now wish to set up an offshore account, here are some initial thoughts as to the best venue. Remember, tax havens are for tax avoidance, not tax evasion. Their purpose is to provide access to specific benefits or incentives (mostly tax concessions) and for asset protection. Which tax haven is best? Consider the following.[49]

- *Your Profile*. What is your intended business? Will your prospective customers be concerned that your firm is registered in a particular offshore territory or will they care? Bear in mind Paul Martin's experience. Have your prospective market countries imposed any restrictions against transfers of funds to the particular offshore jurisdiction?
- *Political and Economic Stability*. The most important consideration is to select a venue that provides both political and economic stability.
- *Legislation*. Is the tax haven's legislation modern, flexible, and well proven?
- *Reduced Corporations Law Administrative Requirements*. Many offshore jurisdictions have reduced their corporations law administrative requirements. This includes "minimal or optional statutory filing obligations, availability of bearer shares, non-disclosure of beneficial ownership, minimum number of directors, minimum information on public file, ability to hold directors meetings anywhere in the world, lack of requirement to file audited records, flexibility in regards the amount and paying-up of the authorized capital, and similar."[50]
- *Infrastructure*. The infrastructure of an offshore jurisdiction is important. What is the state of its telecommunications and transportation systems?
- *Cost*. How much are the registration fees and flat rate taxes? What is the incorporation fee? What are the continuing domiciliary and ongoing management fees? What are the audit and other statutory compliance requirements? It has been my experience that you can open an account for a few thousand dollars using, for example, the CIBC in the Cayman Islands. Visit www.power.nelson.com for information on how to set up an offshore account for your firm.

EU's initiative, drawing on the best of U.S. GAAP and other national standards, the world's capital markets are creating a set of global accounting standards that investors can trust. Canada has adopted the EU's International Financial Reporting Standards (IFRS). Canadian managers must follow this initiative closely and commence planning today to realign their current practices with these new accounting standards. Currently the plan envisions 2010 as the last year that publicly accountable enterprises will report under current Canadian GAAP. The following year (2011) will be the first year of reporting under a complete set of IFRS-based Canadian standards. Since some current Canadian standards are already IFRS-based, and others will become IFRS-based before 2011, the changeover to IFRS-based Canadian standards should be gradual.

- Canadian SMEs must now understand that global, integrated, real-time accounting systems are a near reality. Firms must be early adopters and embrace this financial enhancing software technology.
- Increasingly, Canadian firms are setting up shops and manufacturing hubs in foreign countries. As a result, the impact of transfer pricing assumes significance. Managers must be careful not to use transfer pricing as an instrument to escape tax liability, either by overpricing or underinvoicing goods. Transfer pricing is a dominant issue for international firms. The imposition of documentation requirements, a focus on transfer pricing audits, and transfer pricing risk management have become daily tasks for international managers. Managers consider the economies of tax havens; their competition will.
- A final thought: we need to adopt new mental models in how we think about our business vocabulary and reports. Consider for example the word we have used in this global accounting chapter with some frequency "budget." The very word conjures up performance measurement, control, and rewards. Not very inspiring! In the *Harvard Business Review*, Robert Howell suggests we "get rid of the word 'budget.' From now on we will use 'profit plan' or 'value-creating plan.'" What do you think?

CHAPTER SUMMARY

- A global, integrated, real-time accounting system for most developed countries is a near reality. The globalization of markets has increased the demand for internationally comparable, high-quality accounting information, giving rise to the creation of universal GAAP. Several countries have either adopted IFRS (international financial reporting standards) or are basing their local standards on IFRS. The EU is leading the way. On January 1, 2005, the 7,000 quoted companies in Europe were required by law to use the IFRS. The IASC is an independent organization, established in 1973, through an agreement made by professional accounting bodies from Australia, Canada, France, Germany, Japan, Mexico, the Netherlands, the United Kingdom, Ireland, and the United States. At present 140 accounting bodies are members of the IASC, representing 101 countries and 2 million accountants. Canada agreed in 2005 to adopt the IAS.

- Firms driven by global competition must seek location economies. The firm's financial managers, like other functional managers, must "wring the pennies out" or add value to the firm's value chain. To do this, they must consider the complexity in making decisions about *what* to finance, *how* to finance it, and how to conduct *ongoing management* of the firm's financial affairs in a sometimes-turbulent international environment. This requires the same level of PEST-C scanning undertaken by the firm's other functional managers in order to maintain a sustainable competitive advantage.

- Notwithstanding the fact that we are moving toward one universal standard of accounting rules, the drivers shaping any nation's accounting system include the nation's view of inflation; the prevailing culture; the level of economic and technical development; the political and economic history of the nation, and its relationship with other countries; the legal system; and finally its relationship with business and its role in the global capital markets.

- Canadian SMEs and other international firms have little choice but to access the services of the global capital markets in order to utilize the firm's cash resources in the most efficient way possible. This requires prudent handling of the firm's internal funds' flow, use of funds positioning, and intra-subsidiary netting.

- Intra-subsidiary netting involves having internal divisions within a firm sell to each other and use the head office clearing accounts in order to have their sales and their internal debits and credits quickly electronically entered into the firms accounts (netted out), including currency conversion where necessary.

- Financial managers must consider the financial advantages and disadvantages of providing intercompany loans; when and how to make dividend payments between the subsidiary and the parent firm; how to make provision for royalty payments where applicable; and how to arrange transfer and payment of service fees. They must undertake the ongoing management of short-term investments worldwide; understand the collection and transfer of funds relating to accounts receivable; enable transfer pricing while observing and staying inside the law and regulations; pay all the legal taxes owed to all jurisdictions within which the firm operates yet seek ways to reduce and avoid taxes to the maximum extent permitted by law; exploit the opportunities presented by tax competition between nations; and avail the firm of the services provided by tax havens where appropriate. The tax treatment of the various activities may be different and thus it is not usually advisable to lump them all together into a bundle. The separation of these various payments is called unbundling.

REVIEW QUESTIONS

1. Financial managers, like other functional managers, must take every opportunity to "wring the pennies out" or add value to the firm's value chain. In what three ways do they make investment decisions?

2. Discuss the five drivers shaping a nation's accounting system.

3. Discuss the two competing global accounting standards.

4. Explain Canada's current status regarding the global convergence of accounting standards.

5. What is meant by the terms: intra-subsidiary netting, unbundling, fronting a loan, transfer pricing, tax avoidance, tax evasion, and tax haven?

6. Financial managers require prudent handling of the firm's internal funds flow, use of funds positioning, and intra-subsidiary netting. Briefly outline the financial manager's concerns when undertaking these tasks.

7. Taxes are generally classified as being either direct or indirect. Explain.

8. Make a case for and against tax havens.

REFLECTIVE THINKING QUESTIONS

1. Having completed this chapter, reread the quotations on the first page, critically reflect on the validity of the authors' statements, and provide your opinion as to the validity of each. Evidence-based answers are preferred to rhetorical answers.

2. Larry Zolf reports: "These people are saying that CSL is flying flags of convenience that hurt Canadian workers. They're saying CSL, by using the Bermuda tax haven, is cheating the Canadian government out of needed tax revenues. These Canadians are not impressed with the argument that these are standard business practices."[51] What do you think? What would you do if your parents died and left you $500,000? Would you consider moving it offshore?

3. "In Canada between 1975 and 1999, over 117,000 new federal and provincial regulations were enacted, an average of 4,700 every year. Over this twenty-four year period, federal and provincial governments have published over 505,000 pages of regulations contained in volumes that measure 10 stories when stacked."[52] The Canadian Income Tax Act and its regulations are contained in 2,707 very complex pages. When taxation levels become less onerous, Canada will economically break free. Do you agree or disagree? Are you a proponent of Plato's or Aristotle's political economic theory?

GLOBAL E-RESEARCH

Visit www.power.nelson.com for research suggestions, questions, and a number of background discussion papers on this topic.

MINI CASE

When people think of a foreign tax shelter, they imagine an idyllic Caribbean island where anyone can squirrel away dollars, far from the prying eyes of the taxman. It's not that simple.

Clody Kinkade's company, Offshore Inc. (not real names), wanted to establish a tax shelter in Barbados, but quickly learned that setting up a legal tax shelter is not a simple matter of going to a tropical paradise and registering a company. Offshore spent six months getting the job done, and it took Kinkade, the comptroller, another six months to make the enhancements and improvements needed to get transfer pricing contracts in order and to ensure the company was in compliance with national and international legislation and regulations. Offshore's lawyers and accountants spent much of that time reviewing and improving the proposed Barbados limited liability corporation (LLC) by ensuring that Offshore was not violating any rules and creating a structure that would be relatively stable in the event of changing tax rules. . . . The company decided to move all of its intellectual property to an LLC incorporated in the state of Wyoming, because of less onerous corporate tax laws, and to make the LLC resident in Barbados, because of its low tax rate—*2.5% versus approximately 40% in Canada.* . . . Kinkade says [his advisors are] "by the book and don't allow any gray areas." If Kinkade didn't care whether the tax shelter was legal, he could have created it much more quickly. Offshore could have established a shell company in Barbados and reported a portion of its income in the island. It could have then claimed that the new company was not a Canadian entity and therefore not subject to Canadian tax. However, that would have been tax avoidance, which was not what Offshore wanted when it created the offshore tax shelter.

. . . Offshore's LLC has been up and running nine years, and Kinkade says the initial outlay in effort was worth it: "I would recommend a tax shelter because the tax savings are enormous." He estimates his organization—which has US$35 million in revenue—saves about US$2 million annually in taxes because of the shelter. "We avoid taxes in Canada that can be between 40% to 45% and additional US taxes, versus Barbados at 2.5%." . . . Senior members of Offshore's staff attend key meetings in Barbados annually to discuss budgets, operational risks, forecasted product sales and to provide updates to the LLC. Since the shelter was implemented in 1995, the Canada Revenue Agency (CRA) has not questioned it. However, Kinkade says a few years ago the U.S. Internal Revenue Service did. "It ultimately gave the blessing that it was proper and not tax evasion," he says. If his organization had not established the entity in Barbados, Kinkade believes the only other option for the company to minimize taxes would have been to purchase organizations with losses and then apply the losses to his company's gains. But its policy is to make acquisitions with products that are first or second in the market and therefore enhance its revenue. Kinkade feels this option was less strategic than the offshore structure it has in place now. "It takes a lot of time to invest in the structure," he says. "But it's a small price to pay for the savings."

Christian Girouard, spokesperson for CRA, says it is important to remember that Canadians are taxed on income earned anywhere in the world as if it was all earned in Canada. While tax shelters are not illegal, he says, Canadians and Canadian entities have to report all their income. Problems occur when they don't. In 2003, international auditors reviewed 1,782 individual and corporate cases involving international treaties and re-assessed $900 million in taxes. Of the 1,782 audited cases, Girouard says, 1,004 were large international corporations that represented $761 million in re-assessed taxes. Generally, offshore tax shelters are created by large corporations, so if they get audited, all their holdings, including the offshore ones, are audited. However, the CRA has no numbers on how many firms that have been audited actually have offshore holdings. . . . The CRA . . . [prevents] tax avoidance, Girouard says. On the multilateral front, the CRA teams with organizations such as the Organization for Economic and Co-operative Development and the Pacific Association of Tax Administrators to develop strategies and projects to limit the occurrence of tax avoidance on an international level. The CRA also has a bilateral approach where it shares information about organizations with countries—including those considered tax havens. On the domestic front, Girouard says, the CRA deals with abusers by conducting ongoing audits and assessing risk. For instance, if certain transactions are considered to be based on the motivation for establishing a tax haven instead of a legitimate business reason, the transaction will be examined with greater scrutiny.

. . . . Cameron McIntosh, president of Calgary's Overseas Tax Consultants, suggests offshore shelters to clients, especially to his high-income clients, primarily for asset protection, not to avoid taxes. One of the advantages of using offshore shelters for asset protection is that creditors cannot attack money held offshore through nondisclosure arrangements. McIntosh recommends these shelters for those in highly litigious positions such as doctors and lawyers. He says most clients do not understand the costs associated with offshore shelters, such as maintaining the structure and legal expenses. And you need to have significant amounts of money to justify the cost of creating and maintaining one. "A lot of people have a false impression and think you should put $200,000 offshore," says McIntosh. "You need about $1 million." According to McIntosh, currently the most popular places for an offshore shelter are the Bahamas, Belize, the Channel Islands and the Isle of Man. Other choices include the Cayman Islands, Barbados, and Turks and Caicos. McIntosh's personal favorite is the Bahamas, because its laws are

entrenched in that type of business. Many laws are modeled after the British system, which has more stability and credibility.

Canadians who do invest in the Bahamas should be aware that the Bahamas (as well as other tax havens) have entered into Mutual Legal Assistance Treaties with Canada. "The treaty with Canada provides for mutual legal assistance in all matters relating to the investigation, prosecution and suppression of offences," Warren says. This means the Bahamas will take witness testimony; locate and identify persons, objects and sites; execute requests for searches and seizures; service documents and provide documents and records. . . . "There is no shortage of quality islands that are bona fide," says [David Wentzell, partner at McMillan Binch LLP]. "I would do a comprehensive due diligence to scope out what it is." Once you've completed your due diligence with your advisers, you're well on your way to deciding if a tax shelter is for you.

. . . Offshore tax shelters won't work for everyone yet can have tremendous benefits. The issue is finding a structure that is legal and has these benefits.

Source: Sharda Prashad, "Offshore Havens?" (*CAmagazine*, March 2005). Reprinted with permission of Sharda Prashad.

QUESTIONS

1. "We avoid taxes in Canada that can be between 40% to 45% and additional U.S. taxes, versus Barbados at 2.5%." How can Canada compete against venues offering firms a 2.5 percent corporate tax rate?
2. Provide a business case to your management team to avail themselves of tax havens in support of implementing transfer pricing favourable to your firm.
3. "Offshore tax shelters won't work for everyone yet can have tremendous benefits. The issue is finding a structure that is legal and has these benefits." Is it enough for a firm to just meet the test to keep it legal?

Keep this thought in mind as we now turn to Chapter 17 and consider the appropriate standards for firms faced with the dilemma set out in question 1—social responsibility versus social obligation and ethics.

ENDNOTES

1 R.G.A. Boland, *Accounting Quotes* (Financial Times, June 14, 2003), retrieved August 27, 2006, from www.users.globalnet .co.uk/~rxv/orgmgt/accounting.htm.

2 "Accounting Quotes," (MBAMap.com, 2006), retrieved November 16, 2006, from http://www.MBAMap.com/ mba-essentials/business-quotes/accounting-quotes.htm.

3 "Income Tax Quotes," (New York: About Inc., 2006), retrieved November 16, 2006, from http://quotations.about .com/od/moretypes/a/taxquotes2.htm.

4 Alvin Toffler, *The Third Wave* (Bantam Books, 1980), retrieved August 27, 2006, from www.webcom.com/intvoice/ editor26.html.

5 *Brainy Quote* (BrainyMedia.com, 2005), retrieved August 27, 2006, from www.brainyquote.com/.

6 Mark McNeilly, *Sun Tzu and the Art of Business: Six Strategic Principles for Managers* (New York: Oxford University Press, 1996).

7 "Hitler's Silent Partners: Swiss Banks, Nazi Gold, and the Pursuit of Justice," *University of Toronto Quarterly*, Vol. 68,

No 1, Winter 1998/99, retrieved September 23, 2006, from www.utpjournals.com/product/utq/681/hitler136.html.

[8] Ibid.

[9] Robert Stewart, *The Moral Case for Tax Havens* (LewRockwell.com, October 30, 2002), retrieved August 27, 2006, from www.lewrockwell.com/orig2/stewart2.html.

[10] Dr. Gary Giroux, "Accounting History Page," retrieved September 23, 2006, from http://acct.tamu.edu/giroux/history.html.

[11] Geert Hofstede, *Cultural Dimensions* (1967–2003), retrieved August 27, 2006, from www.geert-hofstede.com.

[12] Adrian Campton, Sasha Dorofeyev, Susanne Kolb, and Wolfram Meyer-Hollatz, *European Comparison: UK and Germany, The Main Differences Between UK and German Accounting Practice* (Deloitte & Touche, 2001), retrieved August 27, 2006, from www.iasplus.com/dttpubs/uk_ger.pdf.

[13] Ibid.

[14] Ibid.

[15] Ibid.

[16] Günther Gebhardt, "The Evolution of Global Standards of Accounting," Center for Financial Studies, (CFS Working Paper No. 2000/05 December 1999).

[17] *Governance and Compliance* (Oracle, n.d.), retrieved August 27, 2006, from www.oracle.com/solutions/corporate_governance/ias.html.

[18] International Accounting Standards Committee, *International Accounting Standards Explained* (John Wiley & Sons Ltd, October 23, 2000).

[19] *IASB Chairman Welcomes the EU's Decision to Adopt International Accounting Standards* (International Accounting Standards Board Press Release, June 7, 2002), retrieved August 27, 2006, from www.iasplus.com/pressrel/2002pr08.pdf.

[20] "Russia to Adopt International Financial Accounting Standards by 2010," *SANS AuditBits*, Vol. II, Iss. 3, July 16, 2004.

[21] Mikhail Balyasny, "Accounting Reform Loses Steam," *The Moscow Times,* July 5, 2004.

[22] Bolkestein, "AIMR Supports Full Adoption by Europe of International Accounting Standards."

[23] *Canada's Accounting Standards Board Ratifies Its Strategic Plan: Approves Convergence with International Reporting Standards* (The Canadian Institute of Chartered Accountants Press Release, January 10, 2006), retrieved November 13, 2006, from http://www.cica.ca/index.cfm/ci_id/29532/la_id/1.htm.

[24] Ibid.

[25] Ibid.

[26] *IT67R3 Taxable Dividends from Corporations Resident in Canada* (Canada Revenue Agency Forms and Publications, May 15, 1992), retrieved August 27, 2006, from www.cra-arc.gc.ca/E/pub/tp/it67r3/it67r3-e.html.

[27] *US Multinationals Overseas Profits: Ireland's Patent Income Tax-Exemption May Fund over 5% of Irish Government Annual Spending in 2006* (Finfacts Ireland, November 21, 2005), retrieved August 27, 2006, from www.finfacts.com/irelandbusinessnews/publish/printer_10003995.shtml.

[28] Ibid.

[29] Ibid.

[30] Jason Gorringe, *Transfer Pricing Becomes Key Tax Issue for Authorities and Multinationals* (TAX-NEWS.COM, November 17, 2005), retrieved August 27, 2006, from www.tax-news.com/asp/story/story_open.asp? storyname=21793.

[31] *The Unanimous Declaration of the Thirteen United States of America* (The Declaration of Independence 1776, July 4, 1995), retrieved August 27, 2006, from www.ushistory.org/declaration/document.

[32] Laura Jones and Stephen Graf, "Canada's Regulatory Burden: How Many Regulations? At What Cost?" (*Fraser Forum*, August 2001), retrieved August 27, 2006, from www.fraserinstitute.ca/shared/readmore.asp?sNav=pb&id=150.

[33] Jean Jacques Rousseau, *The Social Contract* (1762), retrieved August 27, 2006, from www.mdx.ac.uk/www/study/xrou.htm.

[34] *US Multinationals Overseas Profits: Ireland's Patent Income Tax-Exemption May Fund over 5% of Irish Government Annual Spending in 2006.*

[35] *US Multinationals Overseas Profits: Ireland's Patent Income Tax-Exemption May Fund over 5% of Irish Government Annual Spending in 2006.*

[36] Anup Shah, *Evasion of Tax and Other Responsibilities,* (GlobalIssues.org, 2005), retrieved November 16, 2006, from http://www.globalissues.org/TradeRelated/Corporations/Evasion.asp.

[37] Dick Proctor, *36th Parliament, 1st Session* (HANSARD, Iss. 079, 1140, March 24, 1998), retrieved August 27, 2006, from www.parl.gc.ca/36/1/parlbus/chambus/house/debates/079_1998-03-24/han079_1140-e.htm.

[38] Shah, *Evasion of Tax and Other Responsibilities.*

[39] Duncan Campbell, "Havens That Have Become a Tax on the World's Poor," *The Guardian*, September 21, 2004, retrieved August 27, 2006, from. www.guardian.co.uk/international/story/0,3604,1309079,00.html.

[40] Shah, *Evasion of Tax and Other Responsibilities.*

[41] Ibid.

[42] Ibid.

[43] Shah, *Evasion of Tax and Other Responsibilities.*

[44] Campbell, *Havens That Have Become a Tax on the World's Poor.*

[45] Peter Behr, "Canadian Bank to Pay $80 Million in Enron Investigation," *The Washington Post*, December 23, 2003.

[46] Campbell, *Havens That Have Become a Tax on the World's Poor*

[47] *Tax Havens: Releasing the Hidden Billions for Poverty Eradication* (Oxfam International, June 2000), retrieved August 27, 2006, from www.oxfam.org.uk/what_we_do/issues/debt_aid/tax_havens.htm.

[48] Stewart, *The Moral Case for Tax Havens.*

[49] *How to Choose the Right Offshore Jurisdiction?* (Fidelity Corporate Services, n.d.), retrieved August 27, 2006, from www.offshoregibraltar.com/index.php?page=1_4_2.

[50] Ibid.

[51] Larry Zolf, *The CSL Albatross* (CBC News Analysis and Viewpoint, November 27, 2003), retrieved August 27, 2006, from www.cbc.ca/news/viewpoint/vp_zolf/20031127.html.

[52] Jones and Graf, Canada's Regulatory Burden: How Many Regulations? At What Cost?

CHAPTER 17

Global Ethics and Corporate Social Responsibility

"The truth is, we can't afford not to become involved in social problems. It has got to be a cost of doing business—and it will be costly—so that your community will be worth doing business in and living in."[1]

—*Elisha Gray II, former head of Whirlpool Corporation*

"Almost half the world's population lives on less than two dollars a day and yet even this statistic fails to capture the humiliation, powerlessness and brutal hardship that is the daily lot of the world's poor."[2]

—*Kofi Annan, UN Secretary-General*

"The shortest and surest way to live with honour in the world is to be in reality what we would appear to be; all human virtues increase and strengthen themselves by the practice and experience of them."[3]

—*Socrates*

"When money speaks, the truth keeps silent."[4]

—*Russian proverb*

"The role of leadership today is to encourage the embrace of a global ethic. An ethic that abhors the present imbalance in the basic human condition—an imbalance in access to health care, to a nutritious diet, to shelter, to education. An ethic that extends to all men, to all space, and through all time. An ethic that is based on confidence in one's fellow man."[5]

—*Pierre Elliott Trudeau, Prime Minister of Canada, 1968–1979, 1980–1984*

LEARNING OUTCOMES

- Understand what corporate social responsibility (CSR) is, its drivers, and the arguments for and against it.
- Understand the importance of having a strong, accepted, corporate culture and the four impacts culture will have on a firm's sustainability.
- Understand the five dimensions that influence corporate culture.
- Understand how corporate culture can influence a firm's view of corporate social responsibly and ethical behaviour.
- Evaluate the importance of ethics in the day-to-day operation of an organization and be able to apply the Bentley College Center for Business Ethics Test.
- Be aware of what is driving the increased attention to corporate governance.
- Evaluate Canada's new corporate governance regulations.
- Form an opinion as to the major dilemma facing business practitioners—the tension between adopting a social responsibility strategy and a social obligation strategy.
- Understand the importance of making a business case in support of corporate social responsibility initiatives.

- Formulate an opinion as to whether we have passed the age of the triple bottom line.
- Identify the four flashpoints where most offences have occurred in corporate governance.
- Discuss corporate governance in selected international settings.

Corporate Ethical Crises Eroding Public Trust: Shareholders Left Holding Bag in CIBC Fiasco

Courtesy of Anita Wolfe, photograph by Carolyn Davey

Bad things happen to good people when nobody is minding the store. Post-Enron media reports on the absence of corporate governance appear daily on the financial pages.... because our eyes tend to glaze over when discussions of corporate governance take place, transgressors are able to ... go unchallenged.

There is an ethical crisis in corporate Canada that is eroding the public trust and breaking down organizational cultures. The perpetrators play their roles without regard to the human suffering, unemployment and losses sustained by investors, including widows and orphans. Yes, widows and orphans whose funds have been invested in institutions with the expectation that they have made a safe investment in a blue-chip bank that will pay dividends needed to pay for their food and monthly mortgages. The strength of the Canadian economy

is in large part the strength of our equity market. The actions of CIBC and others that diminish the strength of Canada's equity market and therefore the Canadian economy must be condemned. "Organizations are becoming and must become more transparent in the wake of recent regulatory initiatives," notes Anita Wolfe, president of Environment for Change, a Victoria-based environmental consulting group. Unfortunately, even increased transparency is not enough to prevent the frivolous erosion of shareholders' wealth. Consider that one of the most chilling observations arises from a brief examination of the remuneration paid by shareholders to those charged with corporate governance of the CIBC. The outgoing CEO John Hunkin, on whose watch the CIBC corporate governance transgression was perpetrated, received about CDN$52 million in stock and other securities as his retirement package. In addition, while under this fiduciary duty, he pocketed nearly $15 million in salary and bonuses since his appointment as CEO in 1999. At a time when the average bank teller was expected to live on part-time hours and a wage of about $10 to $15 per hour, the CIBC chief received compensation more than 100 times the salary of the tellers.

Ask the question: Have employees and shareholders received value for money? Wolfe said: "Firms must have leadership with integrity. It is about serving the organization. As a consultant when I work with boards, it is critical to identify at the outset their collective accountability. It is imperative that the responsibilities of the

board and senior executive be clearly established." New regulations assist in establishing accountability. In July 2002, Senator Paul Sarbanes and Representative Michael Oxley introduced the Sarbanes-Oxley Act in the United States. The act's objective was to protect investors through improving accuracy and reliability in corporate disclosures; punish corporate fraud and corruption; ... ensure justice for wrong-doers; and ... protect the interests of workers and shareholders. It was well received by investors.... Two years later, in March 2004, Canadian regulators followed suit by adopting three sets of corporate governance rules similar to the Sarbanes-Oxley.... These new rules for corporate governance present new challenges for business.

... "In this environment, consumers and businesses buy the same thing—a company's reputation," said Don Colegrave, manager of ... a credit union. "The reputation of the brand, achieved in part as a result of sound corporate governance among other things, is the firm's value proposition," he said. Businesses must make positive contributions to society through their core business activities, their social investment and philanthropy programs, and their engagement in public policy. Greed cannot be the determinant. Firms that ignore corporate social responsibility should not be permitted to do business in Canada.

Source: Terrance Power, "Corporate Ethical Crises Eroding Public Trust: Shareholders Left Holding Bag in CIBC Fiasco," *The Business Edge*, August 18, 2005.

A SUN TZU MOMENT . . .

"He whose ranks are united in purpose will be victorious."[6]

An organization must build a corporate culture that will support its strategies and it subsequent implementation. The culture will provide a productive work climate and an organizational esprit de corps so that all members of the team do what has to be done to meet the performance goals and objectives of the firm. Nowhere is this observation more evident than the Royal Newfoundland Regiment's participation in the Battle of Beaumont-Hamel.

"On July 1, 1916, British forces began the bloodiest day of their history. The objective of the day was to smash through the German lines located in the Somme region of France behind the artillery barrage they believed had smashed all of the enemy's defences. The Newfoundland regiment (as part of the British army pre-1949) was assigned the section of the line at Beaumont-Hamel. . . . Soon after the attack began it was clear that the German machine guns were not silenced and the barbed wire had not been destroyed. The bravery of the Newfoundlanders was as undeniable: their chances for success practically non-existent."

"The Newfoundlanders were situated in 'St. John's Road,' a support trench, 200 meters behind the British forward line and out of sight of the enemy. Because the communication trenches were congested with dead and wounded and under shell fire, the Battalion Commander, Lieutenant Colonel Hadow, decided to move immediately into attack formation and advance across the surface. . . .The Newfoundlanders were now on their own—supported only by limited mortar and machine gun fire."

"The Newfoundlanders started their advance at 9:15 a.m., moving in their pre-rehearsed formation with A and B Companies leading in lines of platoons in file or single file at forty pace intervals and twenty five paces between sections, followed at one hundred yards distance by C and D Companies in similar formation. As they breasted the skyline behind the British first line, they were effectively the only troops moving on the battlefield and were subjected to the full wrath of the enemy's 119th (Reserve) Infantry Regiment manning the positions ahead and the German artillery. A great many fell before they even crossed the British line. . . .With exemplary courage, the survivors picked up their assault formations as best they could and 'with chins tucked down as if walking into a blizzard' continued towards the German line about 400 meters further on."

"By 9:45 a.m. the advance had failed. Within fifteen to twenty minutes of leaving St. John's Road trench approximately 85% of those who had started forward were dead, dying or wounded. Isolated survivors continued to engage the Germans from No Man's Land and about forty men, taken under command of a Captain G.E. Malcolm of 1st KOSB, attempted to continue the attack but were finally stopped just short of the enemy line. Of this Captain Malcolm, who was wounded, later reported, 'I should like to congratulate the Newfoundland Regiment on their extreme steadiness under trying conditions.'"

The Newfoundland Regiment lost 700 out of 800 men on that day. I want you to reflect for a moment and ask, what makes a person stand by side another in the face of such risk? The answer lies in the power of a corporate culture; in this case, the regimental system. The feeling of a brotherhood overcomes personal interests. The esprit de corps of the regiment prevails against all. The same lesson applies in all organizations. You must develop a strong corporate culture to support your international strategies if you are to succeed.

Adapted from SchoolNet Digital Collections, *The Beaumont Hamel (Newfoundland) Memorial* (Industry Canada), http://collections.ic.gc.ca/courage/landforcesmemorials.html.

Opening Thoughts

The Canadian Centre for Philanthropy conducted a survey of 27 business schools across Canada in 2003. Two-thirds of the deans interviewed ranked the importance of teaching corporate responsibility as high.[7] The profile of the issue continues to increase, primarily as a result of recent high-profile corporate scandals in Canada and the United States. The foremost business schools in North America are in favour of an integrated approach to incorporating the elements of corporate responsibility in their programs rather than segregated delivery. Clearly, corporate responsibility is an idea whose time has come. Accordingly, we provide in this chapter a conceptual overview of corporate social responsibility, and we include in our discussion corporate culture, ethics, and corporate governance in Canada.

In 2000, Peter Drucker observed, "The truth is, there's no such thing as a 'tax decision' or a 'marketing decision'; there are only business decisions." Drucker offers a poignant observation. We, as business practitioners require a more holistic long-term view when crafting our strategies rather than the traditional myopic view that considers only short-term profits, which is behind many of the business corporate governance failures of the nature described in the opening vignette, page 467.

Businesses looking to leverage their core competencies must be governed in such a way that more than just the financial bottom line guides business decisions. How do we introduce this governance to our firms? We start by growing a strong corporate culture, one closely aligned with the values of all stakeholders. But there is a problem. A corporation is a legal entity with all the rights and responsibilities of humans. But it doesn't have a soul or a mind. Just as humans have "social contract" with the state; corporations need a "social contract" that promotes and supports corporate social responsibility, ethics, and corporate governance in alignment with the expectations of all stakeholders and society. The theory of a social contract was advocated by Jacques Rousseau in 1762 and others, and is the basis for the relationship between individuals and the state. All citizens consent to be governed by the state and the state in turn agrees to protect individuals' natural rights. This consent is what gives legitimacy to the government.

Government's laws, regulations, and policies require corporations to meet these societal expectations; however, a corporation's managers, the "directing minds" unfortunately require more than these written measures. The organization needs a soul. In some firms, this is found in the entity's corporate culture. We will discuss attributes of the corporate soul in this chapter.

Another major component of a firm's culture is its attitude towards corporate social responsibility. "The **corporate social responsibility (CSR)** movement has been gathering momentum for the past ten years. This growth has raised questions—how to define the concept, how to measure it, and how to make good on its promises. The Dow Jones Sustainability Index created a commonly accepted definition of CSR as: 'a business approach that creates long-term shareholder value by embracing opportunities and managing risks deriving from economic, environmental and social developments.' This definition encompasses a broad range of corporate values and concerns, including reputation, transparency, social impact, ethical sourcing, profitability and civil society— the list goes on. As a result of the interdependent nature of CSR, integration of its values remains a challenge for many organizations."[9] We will include in our examination of CSR a look at the **triple bottom line** as one popular cluster of values to be measured when crafting international business strategies. "One of the fundamental opportunities for the CSR movement is how to effectively align consumer and employee values with corporate strategy to generate long-term [sustainable] benefits—a better understanding of precisely with whom, what, when, where, how, and why an enterprise makes a profit or surplus. CSR requires more holistic strategic thinking and a wider stakeholder perspective."[10] Consider using the balanced scorecard to assist in monitoring a firm's CSR initiatives (see Chapter 10, page 302).

Another attribute of a firm's corporate culture is ethics. We talk freely about ethics, but what are they? Are yours the same as mine? Ethical conduct is not a guaranteed recipe for profits or sustainability; however, the lack of ethical conduct, particularly in the light of social scrutiny, is a recipe for failure. The ethical dilemma becomes more difficult when we are anchored in the beliefs of Canadian society, yet seek competitive advantage by exploiting ethical and moral variances in foreign countries. The tension between the bottom line and just doing the right thing seems never far from the international business decision maker's mind. Some Canadian manufacturers, when adopting business strategies for their subsidiaries in third-world countries, hide behind the "corporate veil." They feel they have passed the ethical and moral "tests" by simply complying with the host-country's regulations and governance standards. Yes, legally they have met the standard. But is just meeting a developing or underdeveloped host country standards right? We know better. Emerging trends in global corporate responsibility standards promise to raise the bar of corporate due diligence and ethical conduct. Ethically challenged corporations gaining a competitive advantage by utilizing cheap uneducated labour in foreign countries are coming under increased public scrutiny. And these firms don't like the light. But it is a double-edged sword; if they don't seek these location economies, their international competitors will. How long will the firm survive? Therein lies the question; this chapter doesn't provide specific answers; readers must determine their own ethical beliefs.

A commonly accepted definition of **corporate social responsibility (CSR)** is a business approach that creates long-term shareholder value by embracing opportunities and managing risks deriving from economic, environmental and social developments.[8]

Elkington defines the **triple bottom line** as "the simultaneous pursuit of economic prosperity, environmental quality, and social equity."[11]

"**Corporate governance** is a system of checks and balances between the board, management, and investors that contribute to the efficient functioning of the corporation, resulting in long-term value."[12]

Corporate governance is the last attribute we will examine as part of a firm's corporate culture. Corporate governance is a system of checks and balances between the board, management, and investors that contribute to the efficient functioning of the corporation, resulting in long-term value. "All corporate governance systems throughout the world are the product of a series of legal, regulatory, and best practice elements. Each country's regulatory and corporate law system will shape the specifics of its corporate governance."[13] Corporate governance can never be far from the business decision maker's mind when crafting international strategies.

Practitioners must establish a strong corporate culture that fosters ethical behaviour; positions the firm to be viewed as a socially responsible, global corporate citizen; and provides corporate governance not only for its Canadian operations, but also for its global operations. Firms must not simply wrap themselves in "green"; they must observe not only the letter of the law, but also the spirit of the law as part of their corporate culture. Dizzy Gillespie purportedly said of music, "If you can't feel it, you can't play it!" You and your firm's employees must feel the corporate culture. You must build and grow these attributes if you want success.

The "Players"

A **corporation** is a creature of statute and comes into existence when the corporate registrar receives properly documented articles of incorporation, which contain specific information about the corporation, accompanied by the requisite fee, and certifies that the application for incorporation is registered.

- *Corporation.* A **corporation** is a creature of statute and comes into existence when the corporate registrar receives properly documented articles of incorporation, which contain specific information about the corporation, accompanied by the requisite fee, and certifies that the application for incorporation is registered. From the moment of inception, the fundamental impetus of corporate governance provides structure and drives the conduct of corporate directors and officers as well as the evolution of corporations.
- *Directors.* Common shareholders at annual general meetings elect directors. Corporate legislation provides directors with the power to manage and supervise the management of the business and the affairs of the corporation. Although directors are given the ultimate authority to run the corporation, corporate legislation authorizes directors to delegate most, but not all, of their power to committees of directors, and officers. Directors are agents for the corporation under common law and by legislation. The directors have a duty to the corporation not to be negligent. They must exercise care, due diligence, and skill. Directors can rely on management, committees, and experts to assist in their due diligence. Directors also owe a fiduciary duty, well established in common law—to act honestly and in good faith, in the best interests of the corporation, overriding any self-interest. Recent case law has expanded this fiduciary duty and now suggests that in exercising their powers, directors must also have regard to the interests of shareholders and creditors. Directors are required to disclose a potential or actual conflict of interest, including any material interest in contracts. Disclosure must be in writing and delivered to the board at the earliest opportunity. Recent amendments to the Canada Business Corporations Act allow shareholders to examine such disclosure. Today almost all firms listed on the Toronto Stock Exchange have a corporate governance committee. Canadian corporate governance rules and regulations following Sarbanes-Oxley encourage the composition of these committees to comprise a majority of members who are "outside" directors.
- *Business Executive/Senior Management.* The CEO is responsible for the operation of the firm and reports to the board of directors. Generally the CEO may appoint other managers including a president. The corporate executive generally refers to the chairman of the board, CEO, president, CFO, executive directors, and sometimes "insiders" (officers of a corporation who have access to private information about the corporation's operations).
- *Shareholders.* Shareholders are the owners of the corporation and, with few exceptions, have limited liability for the debts of the business. As a corporation is

a legal entity, the debts and assets of the business belong to the corporation. Shareholders do not operate the business; they elect the board of directors. The corporate executive and the firm's directors are the *directing minds* of the organization.

Corporate Culture

Corporate culture is a system of shared values and beliefs that influence the behaviour of the organization's members. Most readers will be familiar with the friendly and at times humorous corporate culture pervasive in Canada's airline WestJet. Clearly, this firm's corporate culture makes a significant contribution to its success. A firm's culture consists of values such as being helpful and supportive toward employees and customers.

Five dimensions influence corporate culture. First, *values* form the foundation of the organizational culture. These values are an expression of the firm's philosophy and guide members in their day-to-day relationships. Commitments to quality or a desire to please stakeholders illustrate the values that are important to the firm. Second, *relative diversity* is one measure of the strength of a firm's corporate culture. A strong corporate culture assumes some degree of homogeneous composition. The youthful innovative energies found in the workforce of software startup firms support this notion. Establishing the right balance of deviation that will be tolerated within the firm must be established. For a firm to be innovative there must be dialogue and differences expressed at all levels without fear; however, once the dialogue has been completed and a decision arrived at the members of the organization must move on to the next issue as one. *Resource allocation and rewards* are the third dimension. How a firm allocates its money and other resources directly affects the firm's culture. What the firm supports and measures will get done. For example, if the customer service department is fully staffed and funded, then members of the firm will conclude that customer service is important to the company. The fourth dimension is the firm's *attitude toward change*. Today, managers who lack energy when operating in a turbulent environment send the message that they are unwilling to consider innovation and change. Firms operating in a global environment must possess a corporate culture that accepts change as part of the normal course of business. CEO Herb Kelleher of Southwest Airlines commented, "We tell our people all the time, you have to be ready for change. In fact, sometimes only in change there is security."[14] Today, firms must have speed and innovation to succeed. The attitude of Kelleher's firm toward change offers a good role model for Canadian business. Finally, *the strength of the culture*, like the strong culture of the brave Royal Newfoundland Regiment in the opening Sun Tzu Moment, page 468, is an important dimension. It provides an excellent example of the outcomes that can be expected from organizations with a strong culture. The stronger a firm's corporate culture the fewer policies and procedures required.

It is important to note the difference between policies and rules and regulations. A **policy** implies there is discretion given to the decision maker while a rule and regulation imply no discretion and must be followed. Remember policies, regulations, and even sometimes rules, do not replace judgment. An ethical leader provides a way for stakeholders to "push back." There must be a way for dissenters to express their views for consideration by the organization's business leaders. Many leaders speak of having a learning culture, and others may say they have a working corporate culture, but the true test is how people are given a place to articulate their concerns. All members of an organization contribute toward the development, adoption, acceptance, and ongoing support for the firm's corporate culture. You must nurture and feel the corporate culture and its values and beliefs. They must become part of you and your firm's DNA. Socrates posed the question, "How do we live?" I pose the question, "How should we live as individuals and as businesses?" The answer lies in part in reflectively thinking about your values and beliefs and how closely they are aligned with your organization's culture.

Corporate culture is a system of shared values and beliefs that actively influence the behaviour of the organization's members.

A **policy** implies there is discretion given to the decision maker; a rule and regulation imply no discretion and must be followed.

A strong corporate culture will have five significant impacts on an organization:

1. The firm's productivity, quality, and morale can be positively affected by corporate culture inculcated by its members and stakeholders. A firm that promotes the dignity of its workers and recognizes them as assets will have a higher morale, and its workers will have greater job satisfaction.

2. Corporate cultures that favour high productivity, quality, and morale will in turn strengthen the firm's competitive advantage. Consistency in valuing a strong corporate culture will, over time, result in a greater competitive advantage.

3. Mergers and acquisitions are successful only if the corporate cultures of the merged firms are compatible. (The trail of failed mergers and acquisitions, reported to be in excess of 70 percent, are well documented in the financial pages. Visit www.power.nelson.com for more statistics of interest regarding mergers and acquisitions.) The chances of failure are compounded when international firms merge country cultures and corporate cultures. Business practitioners must carefully evaluate the risk involved in bringing together two or more corporate cultures.

4. Culture has an impact on the corporate leadership. CEOs often regard the growth of a strong corporate culture to be one of their primary functions. To do this, the CEO and senior management lead by example and demonstrate the desired attitudes and behaviour. Their behaviour must be consistent with the values they wish to inculcate in the organization. As leaders, senior management can also assist in establishing corporate culture by implementing a well-thought-out reward system that will reinforce the corporate culture. For example, they might implement awards for innovative activity. Recall that what gets measured gets done. The firm's leaders, wishing to promote a strong corporate culture, must ensure that the HR management team's new hires personally demonstrate the values that are important to the organization. The closer the alignment between the individual's values and the organization's values, the greater the job satisfaction and, as a result, the better the firm's competitive advantage.

5. Senior management must provide training and development programs that foster the firm's corporate culture.

Culture is the inner voice of the individuals and the firm; it is always there for guidance. It must be nurtured and supported both internally and externally.

Corporate Social Responsibility (CSR)

"Only after the last tree has been cut down, Only after the last river has been poisoned, Only after the last fish has been caught, Only then will you find that money cannot be eaten."[15]—Cree Indian proverb

What Is CSR?

It's the future of business. We are made aware of the importance of CSR daily, without even noticing it; most customers choose products with a good reputation. Most investors buy shares in firms with values similar to their own. Firms whose brands become tarnished, quickly lose investor support. (See Hollinger's Code of Ethics on page 481.)

Why CSR? The Rewards Are Enormous

In a world where brand value and reputation are increasingly seen as a company's most valuable assets, CSR can build the loyalty and trust that ensure a bright sustainable future. A key part of CSR is the notion of sustainability. A 1987 paper prepared for the World Commission on Environment and Development, expressed in the language of business, defined **sustainable development** as follows: "we should live off the earth's interest, not its capital."[16] Not a bad thought! "The next big thing in brands is corporate social responsibility. . . . It will be clever to say there is nothing different about our product or price, but we do behave well."[18] Recall Don Colegrave's observation in the opening vignette, page 467, "In this environment, consumers and businesses buy the same thing—

Sustainable development has been defined as living "off the earth's interest, not its capital."[17]

a company's reputation."[19] The reputation of the brand, achieved in part as a result of sound corporate governance among other things, is the firm's value proposition. So provide CSR training for employees, and you will gain loyalty and commitment in return.

In our complex global society, corporations are becoming increasingly visible, and are judged not only on their results but also on their behaviour. This transformation can be an opportunity; by integrating CSR into your business as a core value and as part of your corporate culture, you are making a significant contribution to a better society and, just as importantly, you will be recognized for doing so. "Corporate social responsibility is about integrating the issues of the workplace, human rights, the community, and the marketplace into core business strategies."[20] Benefits derived will include improved financial performance, reduced operating costs, enhanced brand value and reputation, long-term sustainability, long-term return on investments, better risk and crisis management, increased worker commitment, good relations with governments and communities, a licence to operate and increased productivity.[21] Truly value for money!

What Drives CSR?

Bob Willard, a sustainability consultant and author provides 10 major market forces that compel firms to adopt CSR values as part of their corporate culture. Willard divides these 10 major forces into mega-issues and stakeholders. "The Five Mega-Issues [are]: Climate change/pollution, health, globalization backlash, the energy crunch, [and] the erosion of trust. Five Demanding Stakeholders [are]: 'Green' consumers, activist shareholders, civil society [and] NGOs, governments and regulators, [and] the financial sector."[22]

KPMG's *International Survey of Corporate (Social) Responsibility Reporting 2005* surveyed more than 1,600 companies worldwide and listed the "top ten motivators driving corporations to engage in CSR for competitive reasons. . . . [They] are: economic considerations, ethical considerations, innovation and learning, employee motivation, risk management or risk reduction, access to capital or increased shareholder value, reputation or brand, market position or share, strengthened supplier relationships, [and] cost savings."[23] It is clear from the CSR drivers described by Willard and KPMG that there is strong evidence that organizations can benefit by adopting CSR.

What Is the Triple Bottom Line?

In their decision making, socially responsible firms consider values other than simply the bottom line. A cluster of values popular in the 1990s are referred to as the TBL. Although proponents ascribe to a number of definitions, the definition I have adopted was put forward by John Elkington. Elkington has been described as a dean of the corporate-responsibility movement for over three decades. He provides this definition, "Sustainable development involves the simultaneous pursuit of economic prosperity, environmental quality, and social equity. Companies aiming for sustainability need to perform not against a single, financial bottom line but against a triple bottom line."[24] Most corporate social responsibility practitioners agree with Elkington's definition; however, others like Schwartz and Carol hold a different view and put forth a three-dimensional model for consideration in 2003. Their framework is a view of a triple bottom line from an ethicist's perspective, and encourages firms to consider the ethical, economic, and legal attributes.

My institution, Royal Roads University in Victoria, British Columbia, was previously a Canadian military university. The campus has many artifacts from the military era. One is an iron statute— "Three Iron Men" stating the military "triple bottom line" attributes as— "Truth, Valour and Duty." My point is that firms today must move past the triple bottom line values espoused by Elkington, Schwartz and Carol, Royal Roads Military College, and others to develop their own.

The concept of looking at more than just the bottom line is not a new concept; companies have adjusted their guiding principles over time. For example, when asked how his firm adhered to these fundamental principles, Norm Lockington, Vice-President—Technology, of Dofasco, a manufacturer of flat rolling steel (among other products), responded, "first, they adopted an open door policy, and second, they live by the Golden Rule"[25] [meaning do unto others as you would have them do unto you]. Dofasco has a long history of doing the right thing; since the 1930s, the company has demonstrated social responsibility: "Dofasco didn't refer to the term as triple bottom-line nor sustainability, but they have found that CSR is just good business."[26] Lockington illustrated the value of CSR by pointing to Dofasco's success when it created mini-mills in Ghent, Kentucky and Hamilton, Ontario. The company found that building mini-mills rather than larger facilities reduced energy consumption by almost 20 percent; reduced greenhouse gas emissions by 22 percent; and ensured that all material used in and scrap metal created by these operations were 100 percent recycled to steel manufacturing.[27] The benefits of this initiative flowed to Dofasco's bottom line. Dofasco observes that it has also benefited from harnessing the energy of volunteers and holding town hall meetings in affected communities to acquire input from all stakeholders have proven to be valuable, championing a number of green initiatives such as the mini-mills over the years.

Figure 17.1 reflects how business and society have evolved through paradigms ranging from corporate social responsibility in the 1960s, to today's broader perspective of corporate citizenship. Today's paradigm is transforming into something beyond the triple bottom line. Today we must consider other values in addition to the traditional triple-bottom-line values when crafting our business strategies.

Arguments for and against CSR

Arguments supporting corporate social responsibility include public expectations, long-run profits, ethical obligations, public image, bettering the environment, discouraging further government regulation, balancing responsibility and power, stockholder interests, possession of resources, and the superiority of prevention over cure.

Arguments against social responsibility consist of violation of profit maximization, dilution of purpose, costs, lack of skills, lack of accountability, and lack of broad public support. Some see the triple bottom line as an antishareholder theory.

So What Is the Correct View of CSR?

When making strategic decisions we cannot "zoom in and out" of the CSR values as if they were a change of clothes to be donned when the situation dictates. Rather, because of the growing transparency within organizations, companies must now find holistic solutions.

FIGURE 17.1

Transformation in Competing Corporate Responsibility Paradigms in Business—1960s to Present

	Corporate Social Responsibility	Business Ethics	Stakeholder Management	Sustainability	Corporate Citizenship
Time Frame	1960s	1970s	1980s	1990s	2000s
Grounded in	Social impact	Morality	Inclusion of nonshareholders	Global environment	Philanthropy/ community
Overarching Concept	Do good	Avoid harm	Balance interest (Stakeholder analysis)	Ensure future-life of the interest	Contribute to society Golden rule
Evidenced by	CSR managers Social investments Social audits Reputation management	Establishing: Ethics officers Ethics programs and ethics audits Ethical investment Risk management	Corporate governance Officers Corporate consistency Legislation	Triple bottom line Balanced scorecard Sustainability reports Social investment	Past the triple bottom line (Shifting to values past the TBL) Community officers Citizen reports Strategic philanthropy Corporate governance adoption Ethical codes adoption

No longer should firms hire based solely on economic or societal considerations. Today, they must consider the total individual or outsourcing firm. Corporations must now deal in a collaborative way with all stakeholders, including suppliers, employees, and customers. Firms must frame how we do business and trade with each other in such a way that we all move forward together (a win-win outcome). So what does this mean for business?

Unfortunately, it seems increasingly apparent that there exists a growing divergence between what society wants and what individuals want. For example, society wants fuel-efficient and highly sustainable automobiles that produce lower pollution levels. Collectively, we all would support that position! Yet when given a chance to support those values, what do we do? We often buy fuel-guzzling autos and SUVs. Yet we share "the Commons"[28] in this global village. We must quickly recognize this reality. Those readers who saw Al Gore's film, *An Inconvenient Truth*, will understand his concern for the climate crisis. It is time for wholesale change. Issues such as the Kyoto Accord, automobile pollution, and the hydrogen economy, all need champions. Those who don't have the same sense of urgency and are satisfied with doing no more than meeting their *social obligation*, it seems to me, do not have a sustainable mental model. They claim it is not for the private sector but for the community/ government to implement green initiatives of this nature. Is it sufficient for a firm to *only meet* its social obligation on issues like this, or is it obligated as a citizen to improve the world?

Social Responsibility versus Social Obligation

One of the major dilemmas business practitioners face daily is the tension between being socially responsible and just meeting the firm's social obligation. This tension is prevalent when firms have to make choices in the international marketplace. **Social obligation** describes the notion that a firm has no responsibility beyond economic obligation to the owners and stockholders as may be prescribed by law or contract. Maximizing shareholder value (profits) has been the paramount goal of business and, indeed, without profits nothing else is possible. Firms adopting this standard as their level of commitment to CSR will pursue social goals so long as they match the firms' economic goals. These firms will not pursue social goals just because they are the right things to do. Supporters of this traditional view include Milton Friedman, who referred to "social responsibility in business as a 'fundamentally subversive doctrine' in which there is one and only one social responsibility of business—to use its resources and engage in activities designed to increase its profits so long as it stays within the rules of the game, which is to say, engages in open and free competition without deception or fraud."[29]

Many firms now do more. These socially responsible firms attempt to find the appropriate balance between the minimum standard (social obligation) and a standard past the minimum (social responsiveness). Social responsibility requires business leaders to determine what is right or wrong, and thus seek fundamental truths, even if they turn out to be "inconvenient truths." When determining the right course of action, business leaders will be guided by the firm's corporate culture, and the importance it places on corporate social responsibility, social norms, and ethics. CSR practices must align with good corporate governance that will result in benefits to the organization, its employees, the community, the economy, and the environment.

Social obligation describes the notion that a firm has no responsibility beyond economic obligation to the owners and stockholders, as may be prescribed by law or contract.

Five Stages of Corporate Social Responsibility

Simon Zadek, CEO of the U.K.–based institute AccountAbility, contends that "Organizations learn in unique ways, but they inevitably pass through five stages of corporate responsibility, from defensive ('It's not our fault') to compliance ('We'll do only what we have to') to managerial ('It's the business') to strategic ('It gives us a competitive edge') and, finally, to civil ('We need to make sure everybody does it')."[30] Zadek argues that companies need to stay abreast of society's evolving ideas about corporate roles and responsibilities, further supporting my contention that we are entering a period of corporate responsibility that is "past the triple bottom line" of the last decade.

Firms transforming themselves through Kadek's five stages will be challenged. Roger Martin outlines the struggles executives face in trying to reposition their organizations as better corporate citizens. "If they undertake costly initiatives and their rivals don't, they risk eroding their company's competitive advantage. If they invite government oversight, they may be hampered by costly regulations. If they adopt wages and working conditions comparable to North American manufacturers, they may drive jobs to countries with less stringent standards."[31] CSR will not be an easy ride! How do you convince the many skeptics?

How Do You Sell CSR to Decision Makers?

I believe the only way to sell CSR to decision makers is to present a business case. Provide evidence, not rhetoric, to business decision makers. You will find that until it costs money or resources, most people will claim to be social responsibility advocates. Therefore, prove the CSR initiative will drive down costs, increase revenues, and increase shareholders' value. Indeed, a few companies will voluntarily take socially responsible action, despite the costs involved. To persuade companies to adopt social responsibility, Bob Willard suggests framing its "sale" as a business case and enlisting the support of other advocates.[32] Demonstrate that the firm will attract the best talent. Procter & Gamble, for example, attracts long-term, loyal employees because the best employees prefer to work for a socially responsible firm. Research has proven the business case for CSR with a long list of potential benefits including "better anticipation and management of an ever-expanding spectrum of risk, . . . improved reputation management, . . . enhanced ability to recruit, develop and retain staff . . . improved competitiveness and market positioning, . . . enhanced operational efficiencies and cost savings, . . . improved ability to attract and build effective and efficient supply chain relationships, . . . enhanced ability to address change, . . . more robust 'social licence' to operate in the community, . . . access to capital, . . . [and] improved relations with regulators."[33] CSR firms know they don't have to spend a lot of time "policing" contracts (see the discussion on Wal-Mart below). Levi Strauss has been very effective in establishing foreign subsidiaries because the host nations know of Strauss's reputation for treating its employees fairly. Ben and Jerry's and The Body Shop are able to charge a premium price for their products because of strong brand recognition as environmental leaders. Finally, a good CSR reputation results in easier financing. For a long time, Rubbermaid has been seen as a desirable long-term investment because of its CSR reputation.

But, the road can be difficult. "Leading global businesses like Wal-Mart struggle to find the appropriate metrics but are not always successful. Following Kathie Lee Gifford's negative publicity in 1997, Wal-Mart implemented stringent CSR accounting standards and put in place a self-policing supplier audit system. To implement the system, the firm hired PricewaterhouseCoopers and Cal Safety Compliance Organizations to inspect and audit Wal-Mart's overseas suppliers. Unfortunately, even the professional auditors had difficulty figuring out what was going on. *BusinessWeek* reported the actions of a Wal-Mart offshore supplier who crowded workers in dormitories, and charged $15 per month for food and lodging, even though workers made only about $22 per month in wages. The employer took personal ID cards so workers were kept virtual prisoners. The workers were allowed only 60 minutes per day for all the day's meals, and were fined for each instance they spent too much time in the bathroom. During the protest, one worker reported that he had only had $6 after three months work at 90 hours per week.[34] The offending offshore firm had put up a phony factory to meet Wal-Mart's audit inspection requests and avoid compliance. The question is, how much effort and due diligence is required by firms like Wal-Mart to avoid being brought into the critical light of public opinion?

Where Is CSR Now?

Social norms in North America are advanced in comparison with those of emerging countries. One factor for this disparity is the relative wealth of North America. With fundamental needs like food, clothing, clean water, shelter, and safety in abundance, as Maslow's Hierarchy of Needs[35] predicts, North Americans have turned to elevating societal and business values.

Global headlines reveal a heightened awareness of corporate governance and corporate social responsibility emerging worldwide. The *Financial Times* reported in 2005: "In response to what is now a growing pressure on energy corporations worldwide to consider the plight of those living close to their projects, BP [British Petroleum] is undertaking an ambitious social experiment [in the remote province of Papua, Indonesia], one with the potential to reshape the way resource projects are undertaken around the world."[36] From the United Kingdom, *Insurance Day* stated in 2005, "Large insurers will note with interest the UK government's announcement of plans to promote corporate social responsibility (CSR) around the world."[37] BusinessWorld, in 2005: "In the Philippines alone social investment of the local business sector from 2003 to 2004, reached P2.7 billion. The Philippine Business for Social Progress (PBSP) is promoting a framework designed to help managers develop and implement strategic, effective, and sustainable corporate citizenship."[38] The *East African* (a Kenya news publication) stated in 2005: "While the world's mind was focused on Asia at the start of the year, the international and business spotlight must now illuminate Africa once again—and businesses in Africa must show themselves worthy of this spotlight. The growing movement towards corporate social responsibility (CSR) reflects the feeling that business has an obligation to give something back."[39] *The Los Angeles Times*, in 2004: "As increasing numbers of Western manufacturers shift production to China and other developing countries, leading toy maker Mattel's experience underscores how difficult it is to guarantee humane working conditions and still make the ever-cheaper goods that consumers demand. It also raises the question of how much responsibility a single company should bear when it operates in parts of the world where poverty is omnipresent and the exploitation of workers is rampant."[40] It is clear that businesses that take environmental and social issues seriously will be best placed to gain access to capital in the future. (See Video 17.1.)

Video 17.1

INTERNATIONAL STRATEGIC THINKING

The Crisis of Globalization Stimulates Corporate Social Responsibility

Three trends related to globalization are stimulating the rise of CSR: the rising protest movement against economic globalization, the War on Terror, and recent corporate scandals.[41]

The antiglobalization movements have become global in scope. Using the Internet and other new technology, a broad range of environmental, labour, and social activists daily challenge globalization and the World Trade Organization. These activists exchange heated dialogue with corporations for their lack of corporate social responsibility. This debate primarily centres around environmental and human rights issues including "biodiversity, child labour, climate change, endocrine disruptors, genetically modified foods,

globalization, green politics, the growth of megacities, ozone depletion, recycling, renewable resources, socially responsible investing, sustainable forestry, and urban air quality"[42] to name but a few. The antiglobalization activists contend that these issues provide ample evidence as to why corporations cannot be trusted to oversee the emerging new global order. The view among activists is that "international capitalism is nothing more than a byword for oppression, exploitation, and injustice by rapacious multinationals."[43] Many cite the actions of the United States in the War on Terror in Iraq as an economically driven foreign policy. They argue that companies will stop at nothing to maximize profits even if it means degrading the environment, abusing workers, exploiting developing markets, and committing a host of other sins such as the recent corporate scandals.[44] (See Hollinger's Code of Ethics

on page 481.) Unfortunately, there is evidence to support this position.

To meet these charges, corporations increasingly adopt CSR initiatives as vehicles to reassure the public that corporate globalization is a good thing. Often they do this by partnering with NGOs to enhance the message. Guy Boucher, vice-president, Environment, Domtar Inc. commented that "we don't own the forest, we borrowed it!"[45] What a wonderful mental model! Domtar's CSR mental model, sensitive to forest sustainability, has achieved lower inventories, and the increased use of technology in its supply chain management has in turn driven out the waste from this organization. These new efficiencies have enhanced Domtar's bottom line.[46] Firms are beginning to understand that there is a positive correlation between social responsibility and profitability, which will result in the firms doing the right things.

What Does CSR Mean for You?

It is important that your personal values align with your firm's values. Increasingly, HR managers are placing significant weight on new hires' culture, values and ethics, and their alignment with the firm's culture, values, and ethics. For example, Jennifer Hooper, DuPont Canada's Director of Corporate Safety, Health & Environment, commented that when hiring employees, DuPont attempts to identify characteristics such as integrity and team-based skills. She considers questions like: Do the applicant's values align with the corporation's values? Does the applicant demonstrate a high energy level and experience coupled with the need to be pushing the frontier within his disciplines? When pushed, she commented that these attributes were 98 percent of the selection criteria and experience was only 2 percent.[47]

What Is Ethics?

Ethics is the moral obligation to separate right from wrong. "Whereas compliance means choosing right versus wrong, ethics is about right versus right. And whereas law is obedience to the enforceable, ethics is obedience to the unenforceable."[48]

Ethics is the moral obligation to separate right from wrong. Acts can be legal or illegal, and while illegal acts should not be difficult to resolve due to the obvious misdemeanour, legal acts can sometimes present ethical challenges for business practitioners. For example, when Prime Minister Martin was confronted about taking five flights on private sector corporate jets, Martin responded that while he was a little uncomfortable with his decision it was within the current ethical guidelines. Clearly his mental model sees meeting the social obligation requirements as sufficient; he has no responsibility past

---

JUST DOING THE RIGHT THING

Is Downloading Music Stealing? Napster Tests Our Notion of Right and Wrong

Most people will gladly and emphatically tell you that they don't steal. What they don't tell you is that their definition of what constitutes stealing may differ significantly from yours. I bring this up because many people, mostly recording industry executives and performers, will tell you that they consider downloading copyrighted music from the Internet to be stealing, while a significant majority of Internet users who were surveyed feel otherwise.

[Consider], "in the first scenario, imagine that your car—with its warranty newly expired—develops a problem with an onboard computer. Installing a new one, your only option, will cost you $1,000. But you need the car, so you agree. When the car is finished the service person says, 'Well, you're lucky. The car is still under warranty, so this won't cost you anything.' The question is whether you, knowing the warranty had actually expired, own up to the fact and fork over the

$1,000. Most people—about 99 percent—say they wouldn't. Now imagine that you're at the same dealership, and, while you're there, an armoured car comes to pick up a load of cash. When you leave the dealership, you notice a bundle of money lying on the ground where the armoured car was parked. It's a neatly packaged pile of bills, totalling $1,000, with a label that says 'Property of General Motors.' The question now is whether you stuff the money in your pocket or take it back into the dealership and turn it in. Again, most people—about 99 percent—would return the money.

What I want to know is what is so different about these two cases that we come up with completely opposite answers? Although many people have tried various explanations, I haven't heard any that settle the question adequately for me. Some of the explanations lean heavily on the fact that the price of the computer doesn't represent the actual value—although the same thing could be said about the money, which is, after all, only pieces of paper. Others bring up the fact that the armoured car driver

could get in trouble when the shortage comes to light. They ignore the fact that the service person could get in trouble if the mistake about the warranty were discovered. Some people, after thinking about it, change their minds about the first scenario while very few change their minds about the second. . . . We have significant differences about whether a particular act is stealing, despite the fact that we all think stealing, as a concept, is ethically wrong.

We find the same sort of ethical problem when we confront the situation with Napster or any other use of copyrighted material on the Internet—or even in something as low-tech as photocopying and distributing protected material, which many people don't consider stealing. Yet these same people wouldn't for a moment consider going into a store and taking a CD or a book without paying for it. There are no easy answers.

Source: Carlton Vogt, "Is Downloading Music Stealing? Napster Tests Our Notion of Right and Wrong" (*Ethics Matter*, 2001), www.infoworld.com/articles/op/xml/01/04/13/010413opethics.html.

that! "Compliance and ethics are two different concepts, says Dr. Rushworth Kidder, president of the Institute for Global Ethics. Whereas compliance means choosing right versus wrong, ethics is about right versus right. And whereas law is obedience to the enforceable, ethics is obedience to the unenforceable."[49]

Ethics is important in society; without standards of behaviour as a civil society, life would be, as Thomas Hobbes (1588–1679) observed in the *Leviathan*, "solitary, poor, nasty, brutish and short."[50] We have also seen that when businesses behave unethically, they can avoid outside restrictions, as attempted by Conrad Black. However, some ethical standards have been made law in Canada; however, as we will see it is only a small step. The new rules regarding corporate governance in Canada have been implemented as a direct result of high-profile media cases reporting on the absence of ethics in Canadian and U.S. MNEs. In response, the United States passed the Sarbanes-Oxley Act (as noted in the Opening Vignette). The U.S. act included governance reforms promulgated by the SEC and the U.S. stock exchanges. The Canadian initiatives are reviewed in this chapter.

Ethics in the Workplace

An Aspen Institute survey reports, "ethical conduct in the workplace has become increasingly important to students at leading business schools; however, learners are concerned that their study programs might teach questionable values that may later contribute to mismanagement and corporate fraud."[51] The Aspen Institute study finds that 73.9 percent of respondents consider meeting customers' needs to be a top priority of a company, while 70.6 percent of those polled believe that maximizing shareholder value is the second most important priority.[52] Clearly in addition to economic and legal obligations, ethical obligations should be explicitly acknowledged and lived up to by companies if sustainability is to be assured.

In Canadian society, we rely upon business to create jobs, provide incomes, assemble resources, and produce, sell, and service most of the goods and services we need or want. Accordingly, the standards that businesses employ in these activities are of the utmost importance. Some standards are recognized as important enough to the community to be written into law. Other standards are set by the competitive forces in the market system. Many believe that in the long term, Adam Smith's invisible hand will ensure that the standards the marketplace wants will be supplied. However, in the short term the situation is troubling, with gaps between legal and market-driven standards. In the latter case, there is much room for business discretion, at least in the short run, in deciding which ethical standards a firm will adopt in its dealings with its stakeholders (customers, employees, owners and investors, suppliers and host communities). Firms' stakeholders are taking an increased interest in and responding to the firm's ethical standards. (See Video 17.2.)

Video 17.2

As entrepreneurs, while we have an understanding of ethics and corporate social responsibility, we have to be aware that ethics can cost. "Just doing the right thing" can be expensive! Many members of my generation were influenced by organizations such as Cubs, Brownies, Boy Scouts, and Girl Guides. Regretfully, in my opinion, these organizations no longer contribute to our individual ethical growth to the extent they once did. Our youths' moral compasses are predominantly established by the time they leave their teenage years, so what has replaced these organizations in moulding today's youth?

When asked what value the market places on ethics, executives typically respond that the marketplace is quick to punish any firm caught engaging in an egregiously unethical activity. But are firms that introduce a first-class ethics program rewarded to the same degree? Clearly some firms, such as Johnson & Johnson, are rewarded. The company's long history of ethical behaviour was evidenced when it didn't shrink; indeed it also came forward to offer refunds, which was a proactive response in the face of the Tylenol scandal.

Ethics is a dynamic and individual concept strongly influenced by societal governances, laws, regulations, and codes of conduct. Technological advances, allowing broad access to information and real-time communications, require businesses to re-evaluate moral and ethical policies. These technological advances provide data and information about customers that have traditionally not been available, but would be tempting to use to enhance the firm's bottom line—notwithstanding using this information transgresses the privacy rights of individuals. For example, in 2006, Hewlett-Packard Co.'s chief ethics officer appointed an outside investigator to investigate two HP board members he suspected of leaking information to the press. He specifically directed the investigator to obtain the personal telephone records of the HP board members. Rapidly changing corporate governance regulations, media coverage, and growing market transparency are exposing unethical behaviour and directors and owners to sanctions for unethical conduct. Martha Stewart's conviction for insider trading and Mark Hill's resignation from WestJet following allegations of inappropriately obtaining sensitive Air Canada data are two such cases. The allegations were eventually proven against WestJet in a high-profile Canadian "corporate espionage" case. WestJet admitted culpability, apologized to Air Canada, and agreed to pay settlement costs of $15.5 million.[53] How did shareholders react to WestJet's bad behaviour? Ethical conduct is not a guaranteed recipe for profits or sustainability; however, the lack of ethical conduct, particularly in the light of social scrutiny, is a recipe for failure.

Ethical Codes of Conduct

Professional bodies in Canada and other jurisdictions have adopted codes of ethics (conduct) for many years. Increasingly, corporations are following their lead and publishing an organization's code of ethics. A corporate code of ethics (conduct) defines the anticipated ethical standards for all members of the organization. There is wide variation in these codes of ethics. For the most part, corporate codes of ethics are completely voluntary. Their implementation and enforcement depends in very large part on the firm's management. These codes are generally crafted by the board of directors, CEO, top management, legal departments and, occasionally, outside consultants and representatives. *Compliance codes of ethics* provide direct statements giving guidance and prohibit certain kinds of conduct; *corporate credos* are broad general statements for corporations ethics; and *management's philosophical ethical statements* provide guidance on the organization's way of doing business.

Although an ethical code of conduct is no guarantee that a business or its stakeholders will act ethically, it does provide a reference for acceptable ethical conduct (see Hollinger's Code of Ethics on page 481).

Most large corporations now have a code in place as part of their corporate values. Petro-Canada's code states that "Petro-Canada strives to maintain the highest standards of corporate governance, with a focus on a strong and diligent Board of Directors and transparency for shareholders. The Company has solid governance and disclosure practices, a commitment to continuously improve those practices, and an ethical corporate culture. Our Code of Business Conduct is required reading for all employees, who must acknowledge their awareness and understanding of the Code every two years. The Board of Directors is responsible for the oversight of the management of the Company's business and affairs. The Board has the statutory authority and obligation to protect and enhance the value of the Company, in the interest of all shareholders. Members of the Board of Directors, along with management and employees, believe that good corporate governance contributes to the creation of shareholder value."[54] But do ethical codes of conduct work?

Ethical Codes—Do They Work?

Formal guidelines governing executive and employee conduct are very much in vogue these days. But firms must do more than draft and publish their ethical codes. The Evidence Box shows Hollinger's Code of Ethics.

Did Anybody Even Read This? Hollinger's Code of Ethics

Hollinger International Inc.'s eloquent Code of Business Conduct and Ethics, introduced in early 2003 and "designed to deter wrongdoing," offers a compelling case study. Sifting through recent legal complaints, corporate disclosures and court rulings, it's difficult to find a single provision within this fledgling code that has not been allegedly trampled or disregarded . . .

HONEST AND ETHICAL CONDUCT: Black has described himself as "an honest man." Delaware Chancery Court Judge Leo Strine disagreed. He said Black lied to his fellow directors and was "evasive and unreliable" as a witness. "His explanations of key events and of his own motivations do not have the ring of truth."

CONFLICTS OF INTEREST: Despite the code's straightforward language, Hollinger's 2002 annual report told investors that related-party transactions were common, and that Black's interests might conflict with their own. Moreover, the code expressly prohibits executives from making off with Hollinger's property and opportunities. Strine found that Black attempted exactly that by negotiating his secret deal with Britain's Barclay brothers, and that he'd used "confidential company information for his own purposes."

DISCLOSURE: The code stipulates that Hollinger's public disclosures must be accurate and timely. According to the SEC and Hollinger's own special committee, they were neither. For example, the SEC alleges that Hollinger improperly transferred millions to Black and other insiders, and made "false statements" and withheld material information to conceal these transfers.

LEGAL COMPLIANCE: The code specifically discourages insider trading and bribery. Mercifully, no such allegations have surfaced. General compliance with laws and regulations is another matter. The SEC claims Hollinger International violated federal securities laws. Black also faces numerous allegations of nonconformist behaviour, the most serious being purported contraventions of the Racketeer Influenced and Corrupt Organizations Act.

INTERNAL REPORTING: The code includes a whistle-blowing mechanism. It doesn't appear to have worked. Most alleged misdeeds at Hollinger were discovered by the special committee—which formed in response to complaints from investors, not employees. What's more, the mechanism is supposed to protect complainants from retaliation, but seems to have proven of little use to special committee members. Black threatened them with dismissal and lawsuits in order to derail their investigation, according to U.S. District Court Judge Blanche Manning in Illinois.

ACCOUNTABILITY: With many court actions still unresolved, it remains to be seen who will be held accountable for alleged wrongdoing at Hollinger, or how, or for what. But tellingly, the code appears to be a non-issue. Perhaps British barrister Lord Edward Thurlow was right when, two centuries ago, he said: "Corporations have neither bodies to be punished, nor souls to be condemned; they therefore do as they like."

Source: Matthew McClearn, "Did Anybody Even Read This?" *Canadian Business*, May 24–June 6, 2004. Reprinted with permission of Matthew McClearn.

Conrad Black says all deals and fees were approved.

John Gress/Reuters/Corbis Canada

While it may be said that morals and ethics govern human interactions and laws and regulations govern business conduct, the corporate veil is coming off. As Frank Maguire, founding senior executive at Federal Express stated in an interview: "Business is people. We are in the people business, no matter what our product. People do business with people they like. It is passion, not process, that forms the soul of a company. A passionate workforce inspired by its leaders has a direct positive effect on productivity and earnings."[55] In order to foster an ethical workplace and resolve ethical dilemmas, business leaders must go beyond measured guidelines, policies, and procedures, and nurture fundamental ethical conduct.

The ethical dilemma begins with individual concepts of right and wrong and extends to a dichotomy of considering what is right for stakeholders in conjunction with what is right for maintaining a competitive business advantage. This can be challenging. The dilemma exists internally and externally and may require the development of new policies or revisiting existing policies to mandate an equitable solution, whether in business, research, employee relations, or society in general.

The ethical dilemma is compounded when firms go global. Businesses anchored in the beliefs of Canadian society may increasingly seek competitive advantage by exploiting ethical and moral divisions in other societies. The concept of right and wrong in one society may directly conflict with that concept in another society. Do ethics have a universal application? As decision makers, most of the time, you will be on your own when you answer a question such as this. To assist your decision-making process, I encourage you to memorize the following ethics test.

Ethics Test—Center for Business Ethics at Bentley College

I recommend taking this six-question test when you face an ethical question. If you are at ease with your answers, then you probably don't have an ethical problem. The Center for Business Ethics at Bentley College suggests decision makers who face ethical questions ask themselves:

1. Is it right?
2. Is it fair?
3. Who could get hurt?
4. Would you be comfortable if the details of your decision were reported on the front page of the paper?
5. Would you tell your child to do it?
6. How does it "smell"?[56]

Video 17.3

Do you think Prime Minister Paul Martin would have made the same decision had he applied this test prior to accepting corporate jet rides? What about physicians who accepted perks from drug companies? Interestingly, doctors have ceased taking gifts from pharmaceutical representatives and firms (see Video 17.3). Did the ethical shift come about because the practice was brought to light?

Corporate Governance

"What is corporate governance? When asked, many respond, 'I know it's important. And it has a lot to do with accountability, communications and decision-making. But it's hard to describe. . . . Discussions on governance have generally been with regard to regulatory and compliance rules imposed on Canadian publicly traded or larger companies. However, corporate governance is starting to be viewed as a tool for growth and sustainability for all companies, large and small. What is corporate governance? In the literature on corporate governance, there is disagreement about the boundaries of corporate governance. Depending on their perspective, different authors define corporate governance in different ways. Corporate governance can be defined . . . from very broad to demonstrably specific. . . . Corporate governance is defined narrowly as the relationship of a company to its shareholders or, more broadly, as its relationship to society. . . . J Wolfensohn, president of the World Bank in 1999 was quoted as saying, 'Corporate governance is about promoting corporate fairness, transparency and accountability.' In its narrowest sense, corporate governance can be viewed as a set of arrangements internal to the corporation that define the relationship between the owners and managers of the corporation. An example is the definition by Monks and Minow . . . corporate governance 'is the relationship among various participants in determining the direction and performance of corporations. The primary participants are (1) the shareholders, (2) the management, and (3) the board of directors.' The World Bank defines corporate governance from two different perspectives. From the standpoint of a corporation, the emphasis is put on the relations between the owners, management board, and other stakeholders (the employees, customers, suppliers, investors and communities). Major significance in corporate governance is given to the board of directors and its ability to attain long-term, sustained value by balancing these interests.

From a public policy perspective, corporate governance refers to providing for the survival, growth and development of the company, and at the same time its accountability in the exercise of power and control over companies. The role of public policy is to discipline companies and, at the same time, to stimulate them to minimize differences between private and social interests. The OECD's (1999) original definition is: 'Corporate governance is the system by which business corporations are directed and controlled. The corporate governance structure specifies the distribution of rights and responsibilities among different participants in the corporation, such as the board, managers, shareholders and other stakeholders, and spells out the rules and procedures for making decisions on corporate affairs. By doing this, it also provides the structure through which the company objectives are set, and the means of attaining those objectives and monitoring performance.' . . . The OECD [2001] also offers a broader definition: 'corporate governance refers to the private and public institutions, including laws, regulations and accepted business practices, which together govern the relationship in a market economy, between corporate managers and entrepreneurs ('corporate insiders') on one hand, and those who invest resources in corporations, on the other.' "[57]

"And yet another perspective in defining corporate governance is called 'path dependence.' Central to the idea of path dependence is that initial historical conditions matter in determining the corporate governance structures that are prevalent today. A national system of corporate governance evolves in order to exploit the advantages of the corporate form of organization while mitigating concomitant agency costs in a manner consistent with a country's history and legal, political, and social traditions. Therefore, a nation's system of corporate governance can be seen as an institutional matrix that structures the relations among owners, boards, and top managers, and determines the goals pursued by the corporation. The nature of this institutional matrix is one of the principal determinants of the economic vitality of a society. . . . In order to understand the problem of corporate governance, it is most important to stress that it is, first of all, dependent on the political system of any country and the country's historical and cultural characteristics."[58] I prefer and will use this definition: "**Corporate governance** is a system of checks and balances between the board, management, and investors that contribute to the efficient functioning of the corporation, producing long-term value. All corporate governance systems throughout the world are the product of a series of legal, regulatory, and best practice elements. Each country's regulatory and corporate law system will shape the specifics of its corporate governance."[59] Corporate governance reflects the company's values found in its corporate culture, and its attitude toward corporate social responsibility and ethics. It is this mechanism that attempts to ensure that the interests of business executives and senior management are aligned with the interests of shareholders.

> **Corporate governance** is a system of checks and balances between the board, management, and investors that contribute to the efficient functioning of the corporation, producing long-term value. All corporate governance systems throughout the world are the product of a series of legal, regulatory, and best practice elements.

Why Now?

The exposure of corporate wrongdoing at all levels and across many industries in North America spurred investors, concerned citizens, and activist groups like those discussed earlier to protest corporate conduct. Between 1992 and 2001, Enron (initially incorporated in 1985), one of the largest and most successful corporations in America, was built on political connections, fraudulent business practices, and aggressive unethical accounting methods. In 2000, Enron had reached $880 billion in sales; however, in August 2001, Enron's unethical business practices were uncovered. Enron had concealed debt through aggressive accounting methods, lied about and artificially inflated profits, and committed fraud by using the company's own stock to bet against its own future value. Canada has had its share of offenders, such as Hollinger International, which is 78 percent owned by Conrad Black's private company, Ravelston Corporation.[60] Other countries are facing similar corporate responsibility challenges. "Two thirds of the American people believe that corporate executives are dishonest."[61]

It is not just a North American problem. "Calisto Tanzi, the founder and former chairman of Parmalat, the collapsed Italian dairy giant dubbed 'Europe's Enron' after a

€14 billion (£9.5bn) black hole was found in its accounts, is facing charges in Milan."[62] This case has called corporate governance standards into question across Europe. The company admitted that a €3.95 billion (£2.7 billion) account that Bonlat, a Cayman Islands-based subsidiary, claimed to hold with Bank of America, did not exist. Parmalat later filed for bankruptcy protection.[63]

The common thread in all these cases was that managers and directors did not always subordinate their self-interest to the interest of the owners (shareholders) and other stakeholders. The danger is exacerbated when managers and directors are not subject to the review of independent auditors, lawyers, analysts, and other gatekeepers. Something needed to be done to ensure scrutiny and transparency. Enter the regulatory bodies.

How Have Regulators Responded to the Public Pressure to Do Something?

In 2002, U.S. President Bush signed into law the Sarbanes-Oxley Act. The act tightened federal controls over the accounting industry and imposed tough new criminal penalties for fraud. President Bush proclaimed, "The era of low standards and false profits is over."[64] The first phase of the Ontario Securities Commission's (OSC's) response to similar dwindling investor confidence, and stakeholder concerns was passing three made-in-Canada investor confidence rules. They parallel much of what was contained in the Sarbanes-Oxley Act. The rules, backed by 12 of 13 provinces and territories, require CEOs and CFOs to personally certify that financial reports are free of errors; that effective internal controls are in place; and that the firm's financial positions are fairly stated.[65] The second phase, post-Enron, approved issuance of new disclosure and governance requirements in March 2004. This phase includes filing board-approved, CEO- and CFO-certified-error-free reports fairly representing financial conditions and transactions for the three most recent years. These reports include off-balance-sheet arrangements, conformance with GAAP and GAAS, and any changes in preparing financial statements. Reporting issuers must have a three-member financially literate independent audit committee to which external auditors provide full disclosure directly.[66] In addition to the pressure from high-profile cases, demand is also coming from global sources. Heightened awareness of global corporate governance standards and a broad suspicion of Western business practices by developing and underdeveloped countries, is also driving a need for greater transparency and more stringent government-regulated reporting standards. This broad suspicion of Western business practices because of cases like Enron and Black et al. is making it more difficult for Canadian and other business ventures to enter and compete in foreign markets. Yes, the new corporate governance rules help; but there is a problem. In 2004, there were more than 2.3 million businesses operating in Canada.[67] Fewer than half of all businesses are "employer businesses," employing more than one person.[68] "Approximately 59% of all business establishments in Canada are located in Ontario and Quebec. Virtually all the rest are divided up between the western provinces (around 35%) and the Atlantic provinces (around 6%). The Northwest Territories, the Yukon and Nunavut only represent 0.3% of Canada's businesses. . . . Of the 1,046,345 employer businesses, slightly less than 3000 or about 0.3% have more than 500 employees. The vast majority of Canadian businesses (98%) have fewer than 100 employees; nearly 75% have fewer than 10; and 58% had 1 to 4 employees. . . . About one-quarter of all business[es] . . . produce goods, while the remainder provides services. Small firms, with fewer than 100 employees, make up 97% of goods-producing employer businesses and 98% of all service-producing employer businesses. . . . Using an alternative definition of small businesses in the service-producing sector (defined as small businesses with fewer than 50 employees), small firms account for 95% of all service-producing employer firms."[69] "Currently, [January, 2003] there are 1,300 companies listed on the TSX, only about 172 of which are inter-listed in the US. Forty-four percent of TSX listed companies have market capitalizations of less than $50 million. . . . Another 2,500 companies are listed on the TSX Venture Exchange, with five of these also listed on NASDAQ."[70]

These statistics are critical because the legislated intent of the Sarbanes-Oxley Act and the OSC regulations in Canada are aimed at less than 0.16 percent of Canadian businesses. Therefore, 98.04 percent—mainly Canadian SMEs—are not subject to these corporate governance regulations. It is hoped that these corporate governance practices adopted by 0.16 percent of Canadian businesses will cascade down to all Canadian businesses. What do you think?

Corporate Governance: Four Common Flash Points

First, corporate governance at its core is concerned with aligning strategic decisions with corporate culture so that the firm's attitude toward CSR is observed, and that high ethical standards are met. The tension is found between the conflicting interests of the firm's owners (shareholders) and its business executives and senior management. Business executives and senior management may occasionally undertake termed **managerial opportunism** and, as we have seen, they occasionally get caught. *Fraudulent actions* are the first flashpoint.

> **Managerial opportunism** is defined as managers putting self-interest before the interest of the firm's shareholders.

Second, *executive compensation* is often a flash point between the owners of the company and its board of directors. The board of directors is responsible for an effective and acceptable executive compensation system for the firm. However, compensation should be structured such that it encourages managerial decisions that reflect the shareholders' best interests. According to *Benefits Canada*, "many boards in Canada are becoming more assertive in linking executive compensation to company financial performance. Those that paid bonuses to their CEOs typically outperformed those that did not pay bonuses. Of the 214 companies surveyed, 176 paid bonuses in 2003. Those companies generated a median total return to shareholders of 30.6%, compared to 6% returned by the 39 companies that did not pay bonuses."[71] Companies are increasingly tying executive compensation to financial performance goals. However, this can be a problem too, in that all decisions are made only in terms of the bottom line and short-term financial results. Therefore, patience and wise counsel aren't necessarily rewarded.

Compensation disclosure, whether voluntary or regulated, appears to be improving. "In 2003, 80% of TSX-listed companies provided some insights in their reports on executive compensation to inform shareholders about incentives for executives."[72] "The salaries of Canadian executives have been relatively modest—at least compared to their U.S. counterparts. The median base salary of a Canadian CEO was up 6% to $600,000 in 2002 from a year earlier. That compares to more than US$750,000 for American executives. At the core of shareholder anger has been overly generous option plans designed to align the interest of management with investors. Unfortunately, in most cases that didn't happen. Warren Buffett called option plans "a royalty on the passage of time, which allowed even mediocre executives to get rich on the back of a bullish stock market. At worst, they tempted managers to engage in risky behaviour or even cook their books to force their stock up long enough for them to cash in options."[73] Nortel's shareholders are still paying for the earlier mistake of granting options to align the interests of management and shareholders.

The third contentious issue is the *composition of the board of directors*. What will be the number of insiders, related outsiders, and outsiders? The challenge for boards is to create long-term incentive plans and performance criteria that are justifiable and transparent. The committee that makes such decisions needs to comprise independent directors who are able to fully grasp the implications of their decisions. "The compensation committee is one of the toughest committees to be on . . . Do directors really understand the business? You rely on them to have a good grasp on the business. If they don't, it doesn't matter how independent they are."[74]

The fourth area of conflict is the *ownership concentration*. Are large numbers of shares owned by a small cluster of shareholders? Does a block in effect control the company at the expense of the minor shareholders? Magna Corporation and Bombardier do this effectively using different classes of shares. Firms at times issue class A and class B shares, each with different rights. This can be a bad thing in that the share conditions might enable the interests of the few (class A) shareholders to exploit the majority of the shareholders (class B) in that class B might not have the same weight of voting rights, notwithstanding collectively the share capitalization is significantly more than that of the class A shareholders. A diffused ownership (broadly held) results in weak monitoring and control of managerial decisions by the shareholders. Recently, however, shareholder activism led by institutional investors, and joined by the small shareholders, has resulted in "clustering" and voting in a block to balance the directors' and business executives' managerial decisions.

Shareholder Activism

"Shareholder activism is a way that shareholders can claim their power as company owners to influence a corporation's behaviour. It consists of both dialogue and formal shareholder proposals, also known as shareholder resolutions. . . . Historically, the shareholder activism process is an attempt by investors to get information out of a firm and points of view into a firm that otherwise would not be there."[75] Shareholder activism has intensified because of the lack of corporate governance and the loss of investor's share value. Many fund managers are demanding a greater role in the operations of firms. "Through shareholder activity, investors are demanding greater transparency, democracy, and responsibility in corporate [Canada and] America."[76] Shareholder activists use efforts like "shareholder dialogue" to effect change by prompting discussion or negotiation on an issue, and "shareholder proposals" to recommend or request that boards take a particular action relevant to company policy.[77] Blog sites have proven to be a very effective tool for promoting discussion. "In 1997, the Social Investment Forum reported that three-quarters of a trillion dollars were controlled by investors who play an active role in shareholder advocacy. That same year, the shareholder activists successfully fought proposed SEC rules that would have severely limited the ability of shareholders to introduce social resolutions."[78] Figure 17.2 shows Canada's most respected corporations as ranked by CEOs.

Global Corporate Governance Agencies

Standardizing global corporate governance promises to raise the level of corporate integrity and ethical conduct for corporations conducting business in a global arena. Even in countries such as China and Russia, we find evidence of corporate governance emerging. For example, PetroChina, in order to be publicly listed on the New York Stock and Hong Kong Stock Exchanges, was required to adopt the Sarbanes-Oxley corporate governance standards. Following are some agencies engaged in improving corporate governance worldwide.

The Canadian Coalition for Good Governance

The Canadian Coalition for Good Governance represents "Canadian institutional shareholders through the promotion of best corporate governance practices . . . aligns the interests of boards and management with those of the shareholder . . . [to ensure] that all public corporations have highly qualified boards of directors who understand that they are accountable only to the shareholders in the carrying out of their fiduciary duties."[79] Included on the text website at www.power.nelson.com is a *Corporate Governance Self Appraisal Guidelines Review* prepared by the Canadian Coalition for Good Governance. Readers can learn much from reviewing this document.

European Corporate Governance Institute (ECGI)

The European Corporate Governance Institute (ECGI) is an international, scientific, nonprofit association that undertakes, commissions, and disseminates research on corporate governance. The ECGI provides a forum for debate and dialogue between academics, legislators, and practitioners. It promotes best practices by focusing on major corporate governance issues. (See www.ecgi.org.)

World Council for Corporate Governance

The World Council for Corporate Governance is an independent, not-for-profit international network. The council was established to help improve the quality of corporate governance practices worldwide. It promotes greater transparency, integrity, probity, accountability and responsibility. (See www.wcfcg.net.)

Asian Corporate Governance Association

The Asian Corporate Governance Association (ACGA), founded in 1999, believes that corporate governance is fundamental to the long-term development of Asian economies and capital markets. Like the other associations, ACGA is an independent, nonprofit membership organization. They are dedicated to working with investors, companies, and regulators in the implementation of effective corporate governance practices throughout Asia. (See www.acga-asia.org.)

FIGURE 17.2

The Top 25 Most Respected Canadian Corporations as Ranked by Canadian CEOs

Ranking			Company	Sector	CEO
2005	*2004*	*2003*			
1	1	1	RBC Financial Group	Financial Services	Gordon M. Nixon
2	2	6	Research In Motion Limited	Electronics	Jim Balsillio/Michael Lazaridis
3	12	8	EnCana Corporation	Energy	Randall K. Eresman
4	3	2	WestJet Airlines Ltd.	Transportation	Clive J. Beddoe
5	5	7	Scotiabank	Financial Services	Richard E. Waugh
6	6	15	Manulife Financial Group	Financial Services	Dominic D'Alessandro
7	11	18	TD Bank Financial Group	Financial Services	W. Edmund Clark
8	4	3	BCE Inc.	Communications	Michael J. Sabia
9	7	9	BMO Financial Group	Financial Services	Tony Comper
10	9	4	Loblaw Companies Limited	Retail	John. A. Lederer
11	22	16	Dofasco Inc.	Industrial Products	Donald A. Pether
12	26	27	Toyota Canada Inc.	Automotive	Ken Tomikawa
13	8	36	Power Corporation of Canada	Financial Services	André Desmarais/ Paul Desmarais, Jr.
14	21	20	Microsoft Canada Inc.	Software	Phil Sorgen
15	23	10	Magna International Inc.	Automotive Manufacturing	Donald Walker/Siegfried Wolf
16	28	23	Enbridge Inc.	Energy	Patrick D. Daniel
17	37	40	Rogers Communications Inc.	Communications	Edward S. Rogers
18	10	13	Canadian Imperial Bank of Commerce	Financial Services	Gerald T. McCaughey
18	24	17	Wal-Mart Canada Corp.	Retail	Mario Pilozzi
19	17	22	IBM Canada Ltd.	Electronics	Dan Fortin
20	22	31	TELUS Corporation	Communications	Darren Entwistle
21	19	28	Imperial Oil Limited	Energy	Tim J. Hearn
22	40	19	General Electric Canada	Industrial Products	Elyse Allan
23	18	14	Four Seasons Hotels Inc.	Hospitality	Isadore Sharp
24	15	25	Petro-Canada	Energy	Ron A. Brenneman
25	20	11	Canadian Tire Corporation Limited	Retail	Wayne C. Sales
25	25	30	Dell Canada Inc.	Electronics	Gregory Davis

SOURCE: *The Top 25 Most Respected Canadian Corporations Honour Roll* (KPMG, January 30, 2005).

PRACTICAL ENTREPRENEURIAL FOCUS

Designing Corporate Governance Education for Your Board

In Canada and elsewhere, corporate governance means more education for board directors. This heightened interest is driven by an increase in the number of lawsuits, stock exchange and government regulations, the desire to stay out of the light of increased media coverage, increasing corporate transparency that enables shareholder awareness and activism, and a wish to demonstrate good governance to stakeholders. Here are eight suggestions to assist business leaders in crafting corporate governance education for Canadian SMEs.

1. Appoint a project champion from the firm's executive-level management.
2. Be prepared to tailor the program to meet the current needs of the firm.
3. Educate individual committees separately. This will permit focus and the ability to use relevant external experts such as lawyers and accountants to speak to their special areas of expertise.
4. Make learning convenient and enjoyable. Often this is best accomplished by contracting the services of external facilitators.
5. Use plain language. Fit the content to the audience.
6. Provide in advance an aide de memoir and other reading materials. Remember to keep the materials short and on point.
7. Corporate governance is an ongoing iterative process. The materials must be customized and part of a multiyear director's education plan.
8. Develop a corporate governance best practices manual for current and subsequently appointed board members. It may provide good evidence in the case of a director's malfeasance. (misconduct or wrongdoing).

Management Implications

- Emerging troubling issues and international organizations for corporate governance call for increased vigilance and transparency in decision making, accountability for conduct, and safeguarding the interests of stakeholders and investors.
- Directors are no longer "window dressing"; today they are part of the firm's corporate governance and an essential component of the company's valuation and risk assessment processes. Directors must ask themselves whether the board is managed effectively. What processes need to be to put in place to enable awareness at the earliest opportunity of any "red flag" issues in the company's operations? What is the appropriate balance between the directors' duty to properly monitor the firm and relying on senior management and external experts such as the firm's accountants, lawyers, and consultants?
- Consider how corporate governance processes can enhance the firm's viability and public confidence in the capital markets. How will instituting corporate governance best practices reduce corporate risk? These are questions board members must consider in filling their fiduciary responsibility of oversight. No longer can they simply be "ventriloquist's dummies" and draw their director's fees. In the future, corporate governance will increasingly align business activates in one country with business activities in another country. Directors will be held accountable to higher standards of conduct globally.
- Global responses to the increasing presence of North American businesses are one factor driving the mandate for increased corporate social responsibility and corporate governance. Corporations view globalization in terms of economic opportunities associated with developing markets in emerging countries, thereby making CSR and corporate governance global issues. Business leaders must increasingly inculcate these values in order to reassure the public that corporate globalization is viable.
- Standardizing global corporate governance, promises to raise the level of corporate integrity, and ethical conduct for corporations conducting business in a global arena are all timely initiatives. The new global imperative for Canadian businesses venturing offshore is to build confidence to ensure sustainability and competitive advantage in the global marketplace. To be the 14th least corrupt nation in the world is just not good enough. Business practitioners must make CSR part of their DNA, observe ethical values, and support corporate governance to ensure the sustainability of their firms and the economic well-being of the nation.

CHAPTER SUMMARY

- Bad things happen to good people when nobody is minding the store. During the past decade, the transgressions of those directing Canadian and other corporations have raised corporate social responsibility, ethics, and corporate governance profiles. As a result, learning institutions, government, regulatory bodies, and businesses are spending resources and providing education to reduce the risk of committing further acts that violate the law or moral code. Business practitioners can undertake a number of actions to correct these shortcomings.

- Establish a culture that will provide the firm with an internal voice that will direct the corporation to do the right thing. Corporate culture is a system of shared values and beliefs that actively influence the behaviour of the organization's members. There are five dimensions that influence corporate culture. The dimensions include the values themselves that form the foundation of the organization's culture; the relative diversity within the organization; the allocation of the firm's resources and rewards to identify the importance placed on the task by the firm; the attitude of the firm to change; and the strength of the culture's inculcation within the organization.

- A strong corporate culture has four significant impacts on the organization. These include the impact on the firms' productivity, quality, and morale; the impact on the firm's competitive advantage in the marketplace; the impact on the firm's success in undertaking mergers and acquisitions; and the impact on corporate leadership.

- The notion of firms doing the right thing has been present in Canada for a considerable period of time. The more recent notion of triple bottom line values has been widely adopted by firms aiming to consider more than just the financial bottom line in their decision making. There are, however, a number of other values I have termed as "past the triple bottom line" that can equally be measured by firms undertaking CSR.

- The arguments for CSR include meeting public expectations, long-term profits, ethical obligations, public image, bettering the environment, discouraging further government regulations, balancing responsibility and power, stockholder interest, possession of resources, and the superiority of prevention over cure.

- Arguments against CSR include violation of the profit maximization goal, dilution of purpose, cost, lack of skills, lack of accountability, and lack of broad public support. Indeed, some see CSR as an anti-shareholder theory.

- A major dilemma facing business practitioners is the tension between social responsibility and social obligation. Social obligation is the notion that a firm has no responsibility past meeting its economic obligations to its owners and stockholders as may be prescribed by law or contracts. Social responsibility requires firms do more than just meet this minimum test. To convince decision makers to undertake corporate social responsibility, make a business case.

- Ethics is a moral obligation to separate right from wrong. When faced with ethical dilemmas, it is helpful to reinforce your moral compass by considering the Bentley College Center for Business Ethics six-question test on page 482. Increasingly, firms are establishing an ethical code. All employees must participate in ethical practices and adopt the organization's code of ethics. The code is of little value if only posted on the website or on the wall behind the reception desk.

- Corporate governance is a system of checks and balances between the board, management, and investors that contributes to the efficient functioning of the corporation, producing long-term value. Recent corporate failures have driven renewed interest by government and policy makers in strengthening corporate governance.

- There are four flashpoints where most offences occur. The first is managerial opportunism where managers put their self-interest ahead of the firm's best interest. Second is executive compensation, including salaries, bonuses, options, and golden parachutes that draw the ire of the firm's owners, the shareholders. Third is the composition of the board. What is the appropriate balance between the number of insiders, related outsiders, and outsiders? The final flashpoint is the question of ownership concentration.

- There are emerging new initiatives to standardize global corporate governance.

REVIEW QUESTIONS

1. What is CSR?
2. Why should firms undertake corporate social responsibility?
3. What are the drivers of corporate social responsibility?
4. Present the arguments for and against corporate social responsibility.
5. Differentiate between social obligation and social responsibility.
6. What is ethics? Apply the Bentley College Center of Business Ethics Test, page 482, to an ethical dilemma you have recently confronted. Would the outcome remain unchanged had you used the test before facing the dilemma?
7. Define corporate governance and discuss why it has taken on such importance in business today.
8. Describe the four most common flashpoints in a firm's corporate governance.
9. What is shareholder activism? Provide a recent example.

REFLECTIVE THINKING QUESTIONS

1. Having completed this chapter, reread the quotations on the first page, critically reflect on the validity of the authors' statements, and provide your opinion as to the validity of each. Evidence-based answers are preferred to rhetorical answers.
2. Roger Martin explores the struggles executives face in trying to reposition their organizations as better corporate citizens. "If they undertake costly initiatives and their rivals don't, they risk eroding their company's competitive advantage. If they invite government oversight, they may be hampered by costly regulations. And if they adopt wages and working conditions comparable to North American manufacturers, they may drive jobs to countries with less stringent standards."[80] Is this a valid argument to exclude countries like the United States that produce 25 percent of the global emissions from participating in the Kyoto accord? Is it a valid argument for a Canadian firm not to adopt CSR practices? Discuss at both the national and corporate level.
3. The ethical dilemma is compounded when firms go global. Businesses anchored in the beliefs of Canadian society increasingly seek competitive advantage by exploiting ethical and moral divisions in other societies. They will be challenged by these opportunities as they try to maintain ethical business conduct because the concept of right and wrong for individuals in one society may directly conflict with the concept of right and wrong for individuals in another society. For example, the views of China regarding copyright law or those of India regarding bribes. Can ethics have a universal application? Discuss.
4. "Paul Haggis, the new CEO of the Ontario Municipal Employees Retirement Board, also has little time for dual-share structures. 'How do you have it that someone who has 5 or 7 per cent of the equity controls management?' he asks. 'To me that's not fair.' Such opposition from powerful shareholders can create plenty of extra headaches for the person or group trying to hold onto their special shares."[81] Reflecting on the materials in this chapter, do you support Bombardier's dual-share structure? Discuss.
5. In 2000, Peter Drucker observed, "the truth is, there's no such thing as a 'tax decision' or a 'marketing decision'—there are only business decisions." Do you agree? Discuss.
6. Two centuries ago British barrister Lord Edward Thurlow said: "Corporations have neither bodies to be punished, nor souls to be condemned; they therefore do as they like." Do you agree? If so, what are the implications if we adopt Thurlow's view?

GLOBAL E-RESEARCH

Visit www.power.nelson.com for research suggestions, questions, and a number of background discussion papers on this topic.

MINI CASE

Excuse Me—Is that Dr. or Mr. Craft?

As head of a foundation that funds arts programs in a southern city, Connie helped initiate a program to bring artists-in-residence into the middle schools. Her seven-member committee had received numerous applications, including one from Hamilton Craft, perhaps the best-known painter in the region. His national reputation and amiable personality made him a natural for Connie's program—and he had let it be known around the city that he was applying. Reviewing the applications, Connie had little doubt he would be selected. On the resume submitted with his application, Craft had listed a Ph.D. in art history, received from an east-coast university in the late 1960s. So Connie's assistant, doing routine background checks on the artists, was astonished to discover that the university had no record of such a degree.

Craft had indeed enrolled in a doctoral program, but had never completed it. He did not hold a Ph.D. His resume plainly misstated the facts. Connie told the committee, and then confronted Craft. Cordial as ever, he explained that just as he was completing the work for his doctorate, he had been drafted into the army. What he had meant to write on the resume, he explained, was, "Course work completed for Ph.D."—a phrase often used in resumes to indicate that the candidate never completed the writing of the dissertation. But somehow that phrase got shortened simply to "Ph.D."

Then, turning surprisingly tough, Craft warned her that if the committee refused him on this technicality—an issue that surely had little bearing on his ability to work with a classroom of middle-schoolers—he would sue them for mishandling his application and potentially defaming his character. . . . Sobered, the committee assessed its options. Some, arguing from the ends-based perspective of the greatest good for the greatest number, felt the whole matter should be quietly overlooked. The city's entire arts community knew he was planning to join this program. His stature would greatly enhance the new program. To refuse him would amount to a public reprimand—and perhaps produce such fallout that the entire artists-in-residence program would be jeopardized. Wouldn't it be the greatest good for a great number of kids to study with one of the nation's best? Be realistic, they said. Think of the horrendous consequences of rejecting him, as opposed to the negligible problems of accepting him.

Others, taking a more rule-based approach, insisted that the infraction was no small issue. How could they hold up as a role model for their children a man who sought to deceive others? No matter how good the art, that kind of dishonesty was unacceptable. The committee, they felt, had no choice but to stand by the principle they would like everyone in the world to obey: no cheating, no fraud, no deception. Besides, what if some enterprising newspaper reporter discovered that the resume was false—and the committee, knowing that fact, had appointed him anyway? Wouldn't that jeopardize the program? Still others argued for a care-based approach. They should do to Craft as they would like others to do to them if they were in his position. If I were guilty of stretching the truth a bit in private, they argued, should I be subjected to a public reprimand that could seriously compromise my reputation? On the other hand, if I were deliberately trying to deceive others, wouldn't it be best if someone had the courage to stop me? Chairing the committee, Connie watched it deadlock in a three-to-three vote. It fell to her to break the tie.

Source: Institute for Global Ethics, *Excuse Me—Is That Dr. or Mr. Craft?* (Dilemma: Right vs. Right, n.d.), retrieved August 28, 2006, from www.globalethics.org/ resources/dilemmas/excuse_me.htm.

QUESTIONS

1. What should she do? Remember the Bentley College Center for Business Ethics test, page 482.
2. Apply the Bentley College Center for Business Ethics test. From Craft's perspective, is the outcome different?

This dilemma is without a real-life resolution. I encourage you to think for yourself about how you might resolve the questions raised since the nature of each dilemma is highly individualistic.

ENDNOTES

1 *Quotes from the Ethics File* (Institute for Global Ethics, June 9, 2005), retrieved August 28, 2006, from www.globalethics .org/newsline/members/quotes.tmpl.

2 Kofi Annan, "Poverty Facts and Stats" (*Trade-related Issues: Causes of Poverty*, July 20, 1998), retrieved August 28, 2006, from www.globalissues.org/TradeRelated/Facts.asp.

3 *The Quotations Page*, (QuotationsPage.com, 2005), retrieved November 17, 2006, from http://www.quotationspage.com/ quote/29492.html.

4 *The Frictionary*, September 11, 2005, retrieved November 17, 2006, from http://frictionary.blogspot.com/2005_09_01_ frictionary_archive.html.

5 Ivan L. Head and Pierre Trudeau, *The Canadian Way: Shaping Canada's Foreign Policy 1968–1984* (Toronto: McClelland & Stewart, 1995).

6 Leonard Arianto (Tan), *Sun Tzu's Art of War* (1996), retrieved August 28, 2006, from www.geocities.com/Athens/4884.

7 Norm Lockington, "Dofasco Panel Discussion" (paper presented at the Schulich School of Business conference, Schulich School of Business, November 2–3, 2003).

8 David Crawford and Todd Scaletta, "The Balanced Scorecard and Corporate Social Responsibility: Aligning Values for Profit," *CMA Management*, October 2005, retrieved September 22, 2006, from www.managementmag.com/ index.cfm/ci_id/2391/la_id/1.

9 Ibid.

10 Ibid.

11 John Elkington, *Cannibals with Forks: The Triple Bottom Line of the 21st Century* (Oxford, England: Capstone Publishing Limited, 1998).

12 Carolyn Kay Brancato and Christian A. Plath, *Corporate Governance Handbook 2005: Developments in Best Practices, Compliance, and Legal Standards* (The Conference Board Special Report SR-05-02, June 2005), retrieved August 28, 2006, from www.conferenceboard.ca/documents.asp?rnext=1299.

13 Ibid.

14 Arthur A. Thompson Jr. and A.J. Strickland III, *Strategic Management: Concepts and Cases*, 13th ed. (Boston: McGraw Hill, 2003).

15 *Quotations* (ThinkExist Famous Quotes, 1999), retrieved August 28, 2006, from http://en.thinkexist.com/quotes/top/.

16 United Nations Department of Economic and Social Affairs, *Report of the World Commission on Environment and Development* (United Nations General Assembly, December 11, 1987), retrieved August 28, 2006, from www.un.org/documents/ga/res/42/ares42-187.htm.

17 Ibid.

18 "Brands: Who's Wearing the Trousers?" *The Economist*, September 6, 2001, retrieved August 28, 2006, from www.economist.com/displaystory.cfm?story_id=770992.

19 Terrance Power, "Corporate Ethical Crises Eroding Public Trust: Shareholders Left Holding Bag in CIBC Fiasco," *The Business Edge*, August 18, 2005, retrieved August 28, 2006, from www.businessedge.ca/article.cfm/newsID/10274.cfm.

20 Yale School of Management, "Corporate Social Responsibility: Description of the Field," retrieved November 13, 2006, from http://www.som.yale.edu/careerinfo/roadmaps/socialresponsibility.asp.

21 *Corporate Social Responsibility* (Business Leaders Forum, April 1–2, 2004), retrieved August 28, 2006, from www.blf.cz/csr/en/csr.php.

22 Crawford and Scaletta, "The Balanced Scorecard and Corporate Social Responsibility: Aligning Values for Profit."

23 Ibid.

24 Elkington, *Cannibals with Forks*.

25 Lockington, "Dofasco Panel Discussion."

26 Ibid.

27 "At Home in the World," *Dofasco 2002 Annual Report*, 2002, retrieved September 22, 2006, from http://media.corporate-ir.net/media_files/irol/97/97859/reports/DFS_2002AR_eng.pdf.

28 Garrett Hardin, "The Tragedy of the Commons," *Science Magazine*, Vol. 162, no. 3859, 1968.

29 Milton Friedman, "The Social Responsibility of Business Is to Increase Its Profits," *The New York Times Magazine*, September 13, 1970.

30 Simon Zadek, "The Path to Corporate Responsibility," *Harvard Business Review*, Vol. 82, no. 12, December 2004.

31 Roger L. Martin, "The Virtue Matrix: Calculating the Return on Corporate Responsibility," *Harvard Business Review*, Vol. 80, no. 3, March 2002.

32 Bob Willard, *The Sustainability Advantage: Seven Business Case Benefits of a Triple Bottom Line* (Gabriola Island, B.C: New Society Publishers, May 2002).

33 *Corporate Social Responsibility,* (Industry Canada, January 31, 2006), retrieved September 22, 2006, from http://strategis.ic.gc.ca/epic/internet/incsr-rse.nsf/en/rs00129e.html.

34 Dexter Roberts and Aaron Bernstein, "Inside a Chinese Sweatshop: A Life of Fines and Beating" *BusinessWeek* (October 2, 2000), retrieved August 28, 2006, from www.businessweek.com/archives/2000/b3701119.arc.htm?campaign_id=search.

35 Abraham Harold Maslow, *Motivation and Personality*, 3rd ed. (London: HarperCollins Publishers, 1987)

36 Shawn Donnan, "Energy Special: The Houses That Gas Built," *Financial Times*, March 26 2005, retrieved August 28, 2006, from www.christusrex.org/www1/news/ft-3-26-05b.html.

37 "UK Will Promote Social Responsibility Globally" (*Insurance Day*, March 23, 2005), retrieved August 28, 2006, from www.insuranceday.com/insday/homepage.jsp.

38 "Framing Corporate Responsibility," *Business World*, February 14, 2005.

39 James Laing, "Private Sector Can Help Africa Emerge from Poverty," *The East African*, February 7, 2005.

40 Abigail Goldman, "Sweat, Fear and Resignation Amid All the Toys," *Los Angeles Times*, November 26, 2004, retrieved August 28, 2006, from www.globalexchange.org/campaigns/sweatshops/3060.html.

41 Sheldon Rampton, "Corporate Social Responsibility and the Crisis of Globalization," *PR Watch*, Vol. 9, No. 3, Third Quarter, 2002, retrieved August 28, 2006, from www.prwatch.org/prwissues/2002Q3/csr.html.

42 Ibid.

43 Ibid.

44 Ibid.

45 Guy Boucher, "Panel Discussion" (paper presented at the Conference, Schulich School of Business, November 2–3, 2003).

46 Ibid.

47 Jennifer Hooper, "Dofasco Panel Discussion" (paper presented at the Schulich School of Business conference, Schulich School of Business, November 2–3, 2003).

48 Sally Praskey, "Canadian Grocer: Putting Ethics into Technology," *EthicScan Canada*, Fall 2003, retrieved August 28, 2006, from www.ethicscan.ca/aboutus/media/canadian_grocer.html.

49 Ibid.

50 Thomas Hobbes, Chapter XIII of the Natural Condition of Mankind as Concerning Their Felicity and Misery (*The Leviathan*, 1997), retrieved September 22, 2006, from http://oregonstate.edu/instruct/phl302/texts/hobbes/leviathan-c.html#THESECONDPART.

51 Lynnley Browning, "Ethics Lacking in Business School Curriculum, Students Say in Survey," *The New York Times*, May 20, 2003.

52 Ibid.

53 Chris Sorensen, "WestJet Apologizes to Air Canada for Snooping," *Financial Post*, May 30, 2006, retrieved September 22, 2006, from www.canada.com/nationalpost/financialpost/story.html?id=6ca8461a-fb61-4bcc-be49-002f092c337f&k=61096.

54 *Corporate Governance* (Petro-Canada, June 10, 2006), retrieved August 28, 2006, from www.petro-canada.ca/eng/investor/9250.htm.

55 Frank Maguire, *Executive Interview* (August 8, 2004), retrieved August 28, 2006, from www.ameinfo.com/news/Detailed/43675.html.

56 Center for Business Ethics, (Bentley College), retrieved August 28, 2006, from www.bentley.edu/cbe.

57 Nagendra V Chowdary, *Corporate Governance in Emerging Markets*-Vol. II (The ICFAI University Press, 2005), retrieved August 28, 2006, from www.icfaipress.org/books/Corporate%20Governance%20in%20Emerging%20Markets%20_%20Vol_2.asp.

58 Ibid.

59 Brancato and Plath, *Corporate Governance Handbook 2005: Developments in Best Practices, Compliance, and Legal Standards.*

60 CBC News, *Hollinger Delays Financial Filing; 'Inaccuracies' Uncovered* (CBC, December 4, 2003), retrieved August 28, 2006, from www.cbc.ca/stories/2003/11/14/hollinger141103.

61 Scott Green, *Managers Guide to the Sarbanes-Oxley Act* (Hoboken, NJ: John Wiley and Sons, 2004).

62 Rhys Blakely and Agencies in Milan, "Parmalat Founder Stands Trial," *Times Online*, September 28, 2005, retrieved September 22, 2006, from www.timesonline.co.uk/article/ 0,,13509-1801800,00.html.

63 Ibid.

64 *President Bush Signs Corporate Corruption Bill*, (The White House: Corporate Responsibility, July 30, 2002), retrieved September 22, 2006, from www.whitehouse.gov/news/ releases/2002/07/20020730.html.

65 Ontario Securities Commission, *OSC Issues Investor Confidence Rules* (Ontario Securities Commission, June 27, 2003), retrieved August 28, 2006, from www.osc.gov.on .ca/Media/NewsReleases/ 2003/nr_20030627_osc- investor-rules.jsp.

66 Ibid.

67 "Key Small Business Statistics—January 2005" (*Small Business Research and Policy*, June 20, 2005), retrieved August 28, 2006, from http://strategis.ic.gc.ca/epic/internet/insbrp-rppe .nsf/en/rd00999e.html.

68 Ibid.

69 Ibid.

70 *Financial Reporting News* (PricewaterhouseCoopers, January 27, 2003), retrieved August 28, 2006, from www.pwc.com/ extweb/pwcpublications.nsf/DocID/85256A6F0064847885256 D47006ED618.

71 Kate McCaffery, "What Is a CEO Worth?" (*Benefits Canada*, March 24, 2005), retrieved August 28, 2006, from www.benefitscanada.com/news/article.jsp?content=20050328_ 093920_5308.

72 Ibid.

73 John Gray, "Having Their Cake," *Canadian Business Magazine*, March 2004, retrieved August 28, 2006, from www.canadianbusiness.com/article.jsp?content=20040315_ 58952_58952.

74 McCaffery, "What Is a CEO Worth?"

75 "Shareholder Activity as a Tool for Corporate Transparency & Democracy" (*Confronting Companies Using Shareholder Power: A Handbook on Socially-Oriented Shareholder Activism*, 2005), retrieved August 28, 2006, from www.foe.org/international/ shareholder/toolsfordemocracy.html.

76 Ibid.

77 Ibid.

78 Ibid.

79 Canadian Coalition for Good Governance, "Mandate and Mission" (*The Voice of the Shareholder*, June 2006), retrieved August 28, 2006, from www.ccgg.ca/mission-and-mandate.

80 Martin, "The Virtue Matrix: Calculating the Return on Corporate Responsibility."

81 Elizabeth Church, "Special Share Classes Hard to Give Up," *The Globe and Mail*, (September 25, 2003), retrieved August 28, 2006, from www.theglobeandmail.com/series/ boardgames2k3/news/ten.html.

Glossary

The traditional **4Ps of marketing** are product, price, place, and promotion. (p. 111)

Administrative trade policies are bureaucratic rules and regulations that are specifically designed to impede free trade. (p. 178)

An **ad valorem tariff** is a percentage based on the value of the goods imported. For example, imported garlic bulbs from China are taxed at 10 percent of the declared value of the garlic bulbs. (p. 171)

Advanced factor conditions are enhancements made to improve the competitive advantage of the nation's industry. (p. 168)

An **advance payment** occurs when the terms of the contract require that the importer pay for the goods in advance of receipt. (pp. 168, 339)

Agents are individual organizations that "stand in the shoes" of the principal (the exporter). They are generally remunerated on a set commission based on sales and, although they often have possession of the goods and receipts, title remains with the exporter until the product is sold. Agents have a fiduciary duty to their principal; however, conflict of interest is a potential risk. (p. 337)

Arbitrage (financial), as it refers to pricing differentials in financial instruments, is the attempt to profit by exploiting temporary price differences of identical or similar financial instruments, on different markets or in different forms. (pp. 130, 235)

Arbitrage (goods), as it refers to pricing differentials in sourcing goods, is the artificial trade of goods between countries solely for the purpose of exploiting any price differential caused by shifting exchange rates. (p. 130)

An **arbitrage opportunity** is the opportunity to buy an asset at a low price then immediately sell it on a different market for a higher price. (p. 240)

Aspatial careerists have borderless careers, typically working in multiple countries over the course of their work lives. The chief difference between the aspatial career and the expatriate assignment is that these careers exist in an environment where authority and expertise are no longer thought to reside exclusively at the parent company. (p. 435)

Authority is the formally granted influence of a position to make decisions, pursue goals, and get resources to pursue the goals; authority in a managerial role may exist only to the extent that subordinates agree to grant this authority or follow the orders from that position. (p. 313)

Barter is the direct exchange of goods or services between parties without the use of currencies. (p. 343)

The **basic factor conditions** are those found naturally and without enhancements within a nation, such as a large labour force, natural resources, surface features, and geography. (p. 168)

Behavioural control measures attempt to influence employees' actions by training individuals to share the corporate beliefs and values. (p. 325)

A **bill of lading** represents three things. It is a contract containing all of the terms and conditions of shipping between the exporter and the shipper, it represents title to goods shipped, and it is a receipt for the goods. (p. 339)

Bonds are debt instruments issued by private sector firms and by all levels of government. The lender promises to repay the principal and a predetermined rate of interest to the borrower. (p. 267)

A country's balance of payment (**BoP**) account tracks both payments to and receipts from other nations. (p. 195)

Brain drain is the emigration by the brightest and best of a nation's workplace talent to foreign countries. (p. 49)

A **break-even analysis** identifies the point where total revenue and total costs are equal and beyond which profit will occur. (p. 371)

The **BRIC nations** are Brazil, Russia, India, and China. (p. 300)

Buddhism was founded by a Hindu Prince, Gautama, in India, 2,600 years ago. Buddhist teachings provided an alternative to Hinduism. There are currently approximately 378 million Buddhists established mostly in Asian nations, such as China, Korea, Tibet, Japan, Thailand, and Vietnam. (p. 42)

Business format franchisors, in addition to providing intangible rights, including the product trade name, also generally provide assistance in site selection, building, staff training, products supply, advertising and marketing plans, management accounting services, systems controls, and—occasionally—financing assistance. (p. 296)

A **business model** is how a company sustains itself by generating revenue. It is a summary of how a company plans to serve its customers involving both strategy and implementation. (p. 101)

Reduced to its essence, the **business paradigm** is quite simple. A firm produces a good or service and sells it to customers with the expectation that the revenue from those sales will exceed the cost of operation, resulting in a profit. (p. 101)

A **call** is an agreement that gives an investor the right, but not the obligation, to buy a stock, bond, commodity, or other instrument at a specified price within a specific time period. (p. 232)

Canon law contributes concepts to family and estate law. Law merchant provided legal concepts relating to commercial law and guilds (unions). (p. 83)

Canada's **capital account** records the sale and purchase of Canadian assets. For example, when Husky Oil was sold to a Hong Kong company in 1983, the transaction was included as a credit on Canada's capital account. This is because the capital (the money used to make the purchase) flowed into Canada as FDI. (p. 195)

Capital controls exist when a government places restrictions on capital-account transactions, using domestic currency to purchase foreign financial assets, such as foreign currencies and securities, and certain nonfinancial assets, such as real estate. (p. 230)

Capitalism is grounded in the thoughts of Aristotle, Adam Smith, David Ricardo, John Stuart Mills, and others who supported the notion that all the major factors of production are to be privately owned rather than under the control of the state. (p. 66)

Cash convertibility is the ability to exchange a unit (say, a dollar) of bank deposits for a unit of notes and coins on demand. (p. 230)

The **caste system** stratifies the entire society into four groups, called varnas, each with an assigned class of work. These are the Brahmins—priests; the Kshatryas (politicians and landowners)—warriors; the Vaishyas (merchants)—traders; and the Shudras—labourers. Those not included in one of these basic four varnas are assigned to a fifth group referred to as the "outcasts—untouchables." (p. 41)

Centralization of decision making permits managers to achieve control over decision making by either making all decisions themselves or requiring the decision makers to have all decisions approved before implementation. (p. 326)

Centralized or centralization refers to the extent to which decision-making functions are concentrated in the organization. (p. 313)

Chaebol is the economic and political dominance of giant family-controlled business conglomerates. (p. 72)

Channel length describes the number of intermediaries between a manufacturer and the final consumer. (p. 373)

A **chose in action** means a right to sue and applies to intangible rights, such as a claim for debt. Bonds, shares, and negotiable instruments are examples of choses in action. (p. 85)

Christianity boasts some 300 denominations, with the majority belonging to the Roman Catholic, Protestant, and Eastern Orthodox churches. It is by far the largest of the world's religions and is adopted to some degree by about 30 percent of the world. Most Christians live in Europe and the Americas, with an increasingly strong presence in Africa. Its fundamentals can be found in the teachings of Jesus of Nazareth over 2,000 years ago. (p. 39)

Civil law is found at the other end of the continuum of civilian laws. This legal system is based on a "code." Examples include the Criminal Code of Canada and Quebec's civil code, which is based on the 19th-century Napoleonic Code of France. (p. 83)

A **class system** is defined as social status determined by the family into which a person is born and subsequent socioeconomic achievements. (p. 47)

Cloning is achieved by establishing a set of shared values and expectations that act to guide the decision-making process. With this behavioural control mechanism, a strong base of power is not necessary. (p. 326)

Grounded in the thoughts of Karl Marx, a **command economy**, also known as a centrally planned economy, is one where the factors of production are owned by the government, and government planning agencies specify the production goals and the prices for the country. (p. 76)

Commodity convertibility is the ability to buy domestic goods and services with cash or credit. (p. 230)

Common law developed from customs and traditions, and borrowed heavily on Roman civil law, canon or church law, and law merchant. (p. 83)

Communication strategy involves choosing suitable communication objectives, and identifying brand awareness and brand attitude strategies that are in harmony with marketplace consumer behaviours. (p. 376)

Communism advocates social change that will result in a classless society and requires state ownership of all major factors of production. (p. 66)

A **compound tariff** is a combination of both a specific and an ad valorem tax being levied. Canada is one of the few countries with this tariff classification. (p. 171)

The market is said to be **concentrated** when a few retailers supply most of the market. (p. 373)

A **confirmed letter of credit** guarantees payment by both the exporter's bank and the importer's bank. (p. 340)

Confucianism was founded over 2,500 years ago by a politician and philosopher, K'ung-Fu-tzu (pronounced Confucius in English). With over 225 million followers in China and partial acceptance by countries such as Japan, South Korea, and other nations with a large ethnic Chinese population, the teachings of Confucianism are growing as the economic stature of these countries develops. Loyalty to one superior is highly prized. But not just loyalty up; loyalty down is equally expected. This reciprocal relationship (guanxi) is central to Confucianism. (p. 43)

A **conservative ideology** in Canada generally means reducing governments' control or ownership of the basic factors of production and placing these factors in the hands of the private sector to operate at a profit. In other countries, conservatism means maintaining the status quo or returning to a previous state. In Russia and China for example, those wishing to return to the previous command economies are referred to as *conservatives*. (p. 67)

The **consumer confidence index** is a monthly report that expresses how a representative sample of households measures their confidence in the country's current and future economic state. This index is widely used by FX markets in forecasting future inflation rates. (p. 242)

A **consumption chain analysis** is the process of analyzing each step of the consumption chain—from awareness to disposal—so that companies can examine opportunities to add value along the way. (p. 302)

Firms using the **contract-manufacturing** model contract out all production to suppliers, including the final assembly of the product. (p. 408)

Convergence marketing occurs when customers collaborate with their suppliers to tailor a product or service that better meets the needs of the customer. (p. 378)

Convertibility means that the currency can buy domestic and foreign goods and services, including foreign currencies. (p. 230)

Copyrights provide exclusive legal right to authors, composers, playwrights, recording artists, movie firms, and publishers for ownership of their work. (p. 88)

Corporate culture is a system of shared values and beliefs that actively influence the behaviour of the organization's members. (p. 471)

Corporate governance is a system of checks and balances between the board, management, and investors that contribute to the efficient functioning of the corporation, producing long-term value. All corporate governance systems throughout the world are the product of a series of legal, regulatory, and best practice elements. (pp. 470, 483)

A commonly accepted definition of **corporate social responsibility (CSR)** is a business approach that creates long-term shareholder value by embracing opportunities and managing risks deriving from economic, environmental and social developments. (p. 469)

A **corporation** is a creature of statute and comes into existence when the corporate registrar receives properly documented articles of incorporation, which contain specific information about the corporation, accompanied by the requisite fee, and certifies that the application for incorporation is registered. (p. 470)

Corruption is a lack of integrity or honesty (especially susceptibility to bribery) or use of a position of trust for dishonest gain. For example, political corruption is the misuse of public office for private gain. (p. 215)

Corruption perception scores relate to the perceptions of the degree of corruption as seen by business people, academics, and risk analysts, and range between 0 (highly clean) and 10 (highly corrupt). This includes police corruption, business corruption, political corruption, etc. (p. 215)

A **counterpurchase agreement** requires that, as a condition of sale, the firm selling goods or services to a nation must use an agreed portion of the receipts to purchase specific goods or services as stipulated by the purchasing nation. (p. 343)

Countertrade is the exchange of goods or services for either all or part of the purchase price. (p. 342)

A **coup d'état** (literally a "blow against the state") is a seizure of political power by a small number of people. Such a coup may usher in a revolution, but usually it does not. (p. 73)

Cross-cultural literacy is an understanding and an awareness of cultural differences between countries (and their citizens) and how these differences can affect the conduct and success of our business. (p. 37)

Cross-cultural marketing is the strategic process of marketing among consumers whose culture differs from that of the marketer's own culture at least in one of the fundamental cultural aspects, such as language, religion, social norms and values, education, and living style. (p. 364)

A **cross-currency swap** involves the exchange of payments denominated in one currency for payments denominated in another. Payments are based on a notional principal amount, the value of which is fixed in exchange rate terms at the swap's inception. (p. 234)

A **cross-licensing** agreement provides for the exchange of licensing agreements between the licensor and the licensee. (p. 295)

Cultural proxies are the conduits by which ideas, beliefs, and values are transmitted. One way to measure the globalization of culture is to chart the movement of popular media (a proxy), which have more impact on our thinking than some of the other, more frequently cited symbols of cultural globalization such as the proliferation of Starbucks coffee shops around the world. (p. 49)

Culture is an agreed-upon set of values, beliefs, and norms by a definable segment of people. (p. 37)

A **currency board** is charged by the government with the responsibility to exchange domestic currency for foreign currency at a specified and fixed rate. (p. 261)

A **current account deficit** exists when a country imports more goods and services than it exports. (p. 195)

The **current-account section** of the BoP account reflects credits and debits of all transactions involving the export (credit) and import (debit) of goods and services, income receipts from abroad, and income payments for foreign assets inside the country. (p. 195)

A **current account surplus** exists when a nation exports more goods and services than it imports. (p. 195)

Current cost approach is an attempt to reflect the true value of asset transactions. Assets are valued at their current or inflation-adjusted cost, and depreciation is based on these costs, usually on a straight-line basis. (p. 448)

Customer relationship management (CRM) entails managing all aspects of interaction a company has with its customers. (p. 409)

A **debt instrument** represents an amount owed to a person or organization for funds borrowed. Debt can be represented by a loan note, bond, debenture, mortgage, or other form stating repayment terms, and, if applicable, interest requirements. These different forms all imply intent to pay back an amount owed by a specific date, which is set forth in the repayment terms. (p. 263)

Decentralized or decentralization refers to the extent to which decision-making functions are dispersed in the organization, either in terms of integration with other functions or geographically. (p. 313)

Decentralized manufacturing is the final assembly of goods by outsourcing most of the supply chain activities to independent suppliers. (p. 407)

Derivatives can be defined as financial instruments, traded on or off an exchange, the price of which are directly dependent upon the value of one or more underlying securities, equity indices, debt instruments, commodities, other derivative instruments, or any agreed-upon pricing index or arrangement. (p. 228)

Devaluation is the lowering of a country's currency by its government. (p. 231)

Developing countries and less developed countries are used interchangeably in this text. The terms describe a country whose per capita income is low by world standards but does not meet the UN criteria for least developed nation status in at least two of the three categories. It does not necessarily connote that the country's income is rising. (p. 197)

Direct exporting is full involvement by the exporting company in selling its product directly to buyers within the target market, supported by sales representatives or distributors. (p. 338)

Direct taxes are calculated on the actual income of a firm or an individual. (p. 455)

Distribution channels are the essential links either direct (owned and managed by the firm) or indirect (third parties, e.g., agents, distributors, wholesalers) that connect the firm with its customers. (p. 373)

Distributors take ownership of the product and accept all risks relating to the product's subsequent sale. They use their own channels of distribution to sell to retailers, wholesalers, or end-users. (p. 338)

Documentary collection provides for payment against receipt of acceptable documentation, using a third party as intermediary. (p. 339)

Domestic bonds are issued to raise funds within a nation and in the currency denomination of the country. (p. 267)

Dumping is defined as the selling of goods in a host market below the cost of production. This definition has been expanded by those affected who argue that dumping also takes place when goods are sold in the host market below the fair market value. (pp. 178, 372)

E-commerce can be defined as the buying, selling, and distribution of goods and services over the Internet. (p. 101)

Economic systems determine the process surrounding and controlling the factors of production: land, capital, and labour. There are three broad classifications that can be placed on a continuum, with the command economy at one extreme, the market economy at the other, and the mixed economy somewhere between. (p. 75)

An **ecosystem** is a living community of interacting organisms and their physical environment. (p. 36)

The **efficient market view** accepts that the FX rates published in local financial pages are the best possible forecast of future exchange rates. (p. 246)

Demand is **elastic** when a small change in price produces a large change in demand. (p. 370)

Electronic data interchange (EDI) is the electronic exchange of business information (data) between companies using networks or the Internet to enhance efficiencies in the buying, selling, and trading of information. (p. 394)

Firms adopting the **electronics manufacturing service (EMS)** model delegate control of not just the manufacturing but also the design and engineering supply chain activities. (p. 408)

Emotional stability is the intrapersonal ability to adapt and cope with stress in professional and personal spheres of one's life. (p. 421)

Enterprise resource planning (ERP) attempts to integrate all departments and functions across a company onto a single computer system that can serve all those different departments' particular needs by leveraging knowledge and providing real-time information to decision makers. (p. 399)

Environment is the physical surroundings and conditions. (p. 36)

An **equity instrument** represents ownership interest in a corporation in the form of common stock or preferred stock. (p. 263)

Ethical values are grounded in religion and can be defined as the moral "ought to-do's" that sustain a civilized society. (p. 38)

Ethics is the moral obligation to separate right from wrong. Whereas compliance means choosing right versus wrong, ethics is about right versus right. And whereas law is obedience to the enforceable, ethics is obedience to the unenforceable. (p. 478)

Ethnocentric staffing describes an HR policy where domestic nationals fill key management positions in the foreign subsidiary. (p. 419)

Ethnocentric view is holding a belief or demonstrating a behaviour that one's own ethnic group or culture is superior to others. At times the view is so extreme that the ethnic group will exhibit contempt for or disregard other cultures. (p. 50)

The prefix "**euro**" is given to all bonds and currencies deposited in any country outside the country of origin. (p. 268)

The **Eurobond market** comprises all bonds issued and sold in a jurisdiction outside the country of the currency of denomination. Eurobonds cannot be offered in that country's capital market nor sold to the residents of the currency of denomination. Eurobonds also differ from foreign bonds, as the latter are usually sold simultaneously in the markets of several nations. (p. 268)

Expatriate managers are defined as managers assigned to a foreign subsidiary in a country other than their national origin. (p. 421)

Export and import brokers facilitate matchmaking between international buyers and sellers offering standardized commodities such as wheat, coffee, and rice. (p. 337)

Exporting is selling goods and services to locations outside the home country. (p. 335)

Export management companies (EMCs), self-proclaimed experts in international business in a specific geographic area, provide their services either on a commission basis (as an agent) or as a distributor. As a distributor, the most common role, the EMC takes title to the goods and takes on all of the trading risks and opportunities. The EMC is restricted solely to exports and related activities. (p. 337)

Export Processing Zones (EPZs) are formal industrial zones with special incentives to attract foreign investment. (p. 22)

Export Trading Company (ETC) services may include importing; exporting; countertrading services; developing and expanding distribution channels; providing storage facilities; and financing trade, investment projects, and occasionally manufacturing. In some countries, ETCs can be viewed as a collective or network. (p. 337)

The **extended family** typically includes three or more generations, such as grandparents, aunts, uncles, and cousins, in addition to the nuclear family. (p. 46)

Extranet refers to an intranet that is partially accessible to authorized outsiders. Whereas an intranet resides behind a firewall and is accessible only to people who are members of the same organization or are authorized, an extranet provides various levels of accessibility to outsiders. Outsiders will be issued a username and password. Your identity determines which "levels" of the extranet you can access. Extranets increasingly are becoming a tool for business partners to exchange information in real time. (p. 10)

Face is a multi-faceted term, and its meaning is inextricably linked with culture and other terms such as honour and its opposite, humiliation. Saving face or giving face has different levels of importance, depending on the culture or society with which one is dealing. Perhaps the most familiar term to many is "saving face," which we understand simply to mean not being disrespectful to others in public, or taking preventive actions so that we will not appear to lose face in the eyes of others. (p. 43)

Factoring allows the holder of a time draft to obtain cash by assigning or selling the instrument at a discount to a third party. (p. 339)

The **FDI stock** is the accumulated total of all of a nation's FDI. (p. 193)

A country's **fertility rate** is the rate at which the population replaces itself. (p. 48)

Those first to enter the market attain **first-mover advantage** and gain a number of economic and strategic advantages over those that subsequently enter the market, which may include establishing a strong customer base, securing the best inputs and outputs, moving down the experience curve, and increasing switching costs. (pp. 167, 301)

Fiscal policy refers to the expenditures government makes and how it finances through taxation and borrowing to provide the necessary goods and services. (p. 256)

The **Fisher effect** in simple terms is stated by the equation: nominal rate of interest = the real rate of interest + inflation. In addition, Fisher put forward the notion that the interest rate differential between two countries should be an unbiased predictor of the future change in the spot rate. (p. 241)

A **fixed exchange rate** is a system where the exchange rate has a set (fixed) value against another currency. (p. 261)

Flexible manufacturing integrates combinations of various types of capital equipment, and is a system that is capable of processing a number of different work-pieces simultaneously and automatically, with the machines in the system carrying out the system's operation in any sequence. (p. 399)

A **floating exchange rate** is one that is allowed to find its own level according to the forces of supply and demand. (p. 262)

The **flow of FDI** is that amount of FDI flowing in and out of a country over a fixed period of time. (p. 193)

Folkways are norms grounded in acceptable social behaviour such as good table manners, dressing appropriately for dinner, or standing when a lady enters the room. Transgressions seldom bring formal sanctions but those observing may well form a lower opinion of those who fail to observe the social niceties. (p. 38)

Foreign bonds are issued to raise funds outside the country of origin and are denominated in the currency of the issuing entity's country. (p. 267)

Foreign direct investment can be defined as significant investment made by external individuals, firms, and governments (investors) in local facilities to produce or market goods or services. Significant investment will be deemed to have taken place whenever a 10 percent or greater equity interest in the target investment has been obtained by the external entity. (p. 193)

Foreign exchange convertibility is the ability to buy foreign goods and services, including foreign currencies. (p. 230)

A **foreign exchange option** on the Canadian dollar gives a company the right but not the obligation to buy, for example, Canadian dollars and sell U.S. dollars at a pre-set strike price that will vary on a day-to-day basis with the movement in the Canadian dollar/U.S. dollar exchange rate. (p. 232)

Foreign portfolio investment (FPI) can be defined as investments undertaken by individuals, firms, and governments that represent less than 10 percent equity interest in the target investment. (p. 193)

Formalization of control takes place when a firm provides rules, procedures, guidelines, and policies that act to guide the decision-making process. (p. 326)

A **forward rate agreement** is a tailor-made futures contract to fix a future interest rate today. When the future date arrives, the FRA contract rate is compared to the actual market LIBOR. If market rates are higher than the contract rate, the borrower/FRA buyer receives the difference; if lower, he pays the difference. For the investor/FRA seller, the FRA flows would be reversed. Firms use FRAs to protect short-term borrowing or investment programs from market surprises. Firms that plan to borrow in the future would use FRAs to lock in a future borrowing base rate at a level lower than today's rates. (p. 233)

Where there are many retailers and no particular market leader, the retail market is referred to as **fragmented**. (p. 373)

Those who accept the **free market view** adopt the position that nations must not interfere with FDI, but open up their country and permit the free flow of FDI. (p. 198)

Free trade exists when governments make no attempt to interfere with businesses buying or selling products or services directly or indirectly in the global marketplace. (p. 171)

Freight forwarders specialize in the actual transportation of goods, the facilitation of customs documentation, and logistics and transportation services. (p. 337)

Fronting a loan occurs when the subsidiary deposits funds, generally in a large international bank, which are held by the bank as collateral for a loan the bank, in turn, provides to the parent company. (p. 453)

A currency with cash, commodity, and FX convertibility is said to have **full convertibility**; FX convertibility almost always implies cash and commodity convertibility. (p. 230)

A **fundamental analysis** often uses complex models containing a number of fundamental economic indicators in different combinations and permutations that are statistically analyzed in order to forecast the future exchange rate. The fundamental economic indicators used in this model include inflation, money supply, tax rates, interest rates, and government spending. (p. 247)

Generally accepted accounting principles (GAAP) are a set of accounting rules used to standardize the reporting of financial statements throughout a country. (p. 446)

Geocentric staffing describes an HR policy that requires hiring the best-trained personnel for the host management position from anywhere in the world regardless of nationality. (p. 421)

The **glass ceiling** refers to the notion that barriers impede or prevent a discrete population from obtaining senior positions and or higher salary levels in organizations. (p. 424)

The term **glass cliff** describes a situation where someone, particularly a woman, has been promoted into a risky, difficult job where the chances of failure are high. (p. 424)

The **glass elevator** refers to the rapid promotion of men over women, especially into management, in female-dominated fields like nursing. (p. 424)

Globalism is the ideology that advocates the liquidation of nations; it is the opposite of nationalism. Globalism describes the reality of being interconnected, while globalization is the speed at which these connections increase or decrease. (p. 6)

Globalization is the increasing economic and political interdependence between nations in scope and intensity. Globalism describes the reality of being interconnected, while globalization is the speed at which these connections increase or decrease.

It is not a fad or a passing trend, but rather a system that has quickly replaced the Cold War system after the fall of the Berlin Wall in 1989. (p. 6)

The **globalization of markets** is the convergence or union of all countries' markets into one global marketplace. (p. 11)

Global learning is the transfer of skills, R&D, and production offerings that move back and forth between subsidiary offices and the home office. Each subsidiary learns from the others, irrespective of whether the unit is the home or a foreign subsidiary. (p. 291)

A **global strategy** focuses on increasing profitability by pursuing a low-cost strategy. Cost reductions come from the experience curve effect and location economies. Global strategists prefer to market a standardized product worldwide so they can reap the maximum benefit from economies of scale. They see the world as one global marketplace. (p. 292)

The **gold standard** is a financial system that exists when a country backs its currency with gold and is prepared, under predetermined conditions, to exchange its currency for a fixed amount of gold. (p. 257)

A **greenfield** mode of entry involves establishing, from the ground up, a new operation in a foreign country. It is sometimes a wholly owned subsidiary. (p. 299)

Gross domestic product (GDP) represents the total of the goods and services produced domestically within a 12-month period (normally the calendar year) to include income received from abroad. (p. 78)

Gross fixed capital formation, as defined by the European System of Accounts (ESA), consists of "resident producers' acquisitions, less disposals, of fixed assets during a given period plus certain additions to the value of non-produced assets realised by the productive activity of producer or institutional units." (p. 205)

Gross national income (GNI) includes income received from other countries set off against similar payments made to other countries. (p. 78)

Guoqin refers to the special situation or character of China. (p. 364)

The **Heckscher-Ohlin theory** states that when resources (factors of production both basic and advanced) are abundant in one nation, while at the same time scarce in other competing nations, then the nation with the abundance will have an international competitive advantage in those specific resources and the goods or services that require those resources. This theory is focused on the advantage of producing and exporting goods and services using factors of production that are most abundant and therefore cheaper compared to international competitors. (p. 164)

A **hierarchy** is a system of ranking and organizing things. (p. 312)

The **hierarchy control mechanism** achieves cross-functional control integration through communication between senior functional managers; conflict is resolved through negotiation. This mechanism requires the fewest resources but creates time delays, and is the weakest mechanism for complex organizations. (p. 326)

Hinduism is seen by many as a way of life rather than a formal religion. It has no founder nor recognized central authority or spiritual leader. It is practised by more than 870 million of India's population (1.1 billion). (p. 41)

The **historic cost principal** takes the view that inflation is not to be accounted for in a nation's accounting records. Assets are valued according to their net book value; net book value equals historical cost less accumulated depreciation, where depreciation is calculated on a straight-line basis using historical cost. (p. 447)

Horizontal complexity refers to the number of units and subunits across an organization. (p. 313)

The **horizontal organization** consists of autonomous, cross-functional work teams designed around critical processes. (p. 317)

Hot money refers to funds that flow into a country to exploit small differences in interest or exchange rates. Because these funds are rapidly shifted between FX markets to increase profits, hot money is highly volatile and a major factor in capital flight from developing countries. These types of transactions were largely responsible for the currency crises in Mexico and Asia during the 1990s. (pp. 236, 270)

Importing is buying goods and services abroad and bringing them into the home country. (p. 335)

An **import quota** is a government restriction on the quantity of a product that will be admitted into the host country. (p. 175)

Indirect exporting is a strategy whereby an exporter contracts with an intermediary located in the home country to sell its product or service to a designated foreign market. (p. 337)

Indirect taxes include sales tax, goods and services tax, provincial sales tax, health tax, death tax, severance tax, tariffs, and value-added taxes that are applied to the purchase price, material costs, quantities of natural resources, and commodities. (p. 455)

The **inefficient market view** contends that the efficient market view does not contain all of the data and/or information available. (p. 247)

Demand is **inelastic** when a large change in price produces only a small change in demand. (p. 370)

A firm's **integrated controlling mechanisms** describe the extent to which rules, policies, and procedures control the organization. (p. 313)

Intellectual property is intangible personal property that includes copyright, patents, trademarks, industrial design, confidential information, and trade secrets. (p. 85)

The **inter-bank market** is a network of major banks around the world. Individual banks act as brokers on behalf of customers, and trade with each other. (p. 228)

An **interest rate swap** is an agreement to exchange interest payments in a single currency for a stated time period. Note that only interest payments are exchanged, not the principal. (p. 233)

The **international dollar** is a hypothetical unit of currency that has the same purchasing power that the U.S. dollar has in the United States at a given point in time. It is used to make comparisons both between countries and over time. (p. 79)

International logistics can be defined as the design and management of a system that controls the flow, both forward and reverse, of materials, service, and information in, through, and out of the firm. It encompasses the firm's entire range of import and export movements. (p. 398)

International product-trade-life-cycle theory is similar to the marketing product-life-cycle model. Countries begin by exporting their product; then they undertake foreign direct investment and establish international facilities. Later, they enter the final stage and become an importer of the product. This cycle will occur because others will have entered the global market and taken market share by exploiting their own respective low-cost-factor endowments. (p. 165)

An **international strategy** is one where the home firm wishes to leverage by transferring its valuable competencies, skills, and products to foreign markets. (p. 292)

Internet connectivity can be defined as the existence, availability, and affordability of the communication infrastructure. (p. 108)

Intra-corporate transfers are the sale of goods and services to a related corporate entity. (p. 338)

An **intranet** is a network based on an Internet protocol belonging to an organization. An intranet is used to share information among an organization's members, employees, and others with authorization. Intranet websites are similar to other websites, but a firewall blocks unauthorized access. Because they are much less expensive to build and manage than private networks based on proprietary protocols, secure intranets are now the fastest growing segment of the Internet. (p. 10)

Intra-subsidiary netting occurs when a firm's internal divisions sell to each other using the head office clearing accounts so that their sales and their internal debits and credits are quickly electronically entered into the firms accounts (netted out) to include currency conversion where necessary. (p. 452)

Intra-trade is international trade among countries that belong to the same group (for example, a regional or trade grouping). (p. 128)

Investor bias refers to an investor's tendency to demonstrate a propensity to purchase domestic (home) debt and equity, rather than foreign instruments. (p. 264)

Adam Smith put forth that the **"invisible hand"** is the notion that an individual who "intends only his own gain," is, as it were, "led by an invisible hand . . . [and] will promote . . . the public interest." Smith did not assert that this was invariably true, but he contributed to a dominant tendency of thought that assumes decisions reached individually will be the best decisions for an entire society. (p. 69)

An **irrevocable letter of credit** permits the importer's bank to modify the terms only with the approval of both the exporter and the importer. (p. 340)

Islam is the world's second largest religion (1.3 billion) founded in 622 (the first year of the Islamic calendar) by the Prophet Muhammad and followed by the majority in more than 35 countries. Islam is the youngest of the three monotheistic world religions. An adherent to Islam is a Muslim, an Arab term for "one who surrenders oneself to God." (p. 40)

The **joint venture (JV)** is the formation of a separate legal entity that is owned by two or more independent entities to achieve a common mission. The term of the joint venture can be fixed or open-ended, and the partners (entities) can be public, private, or not-for-profit. Firms enter into joint ventures to gain synergy. A JV is one form of strategic alliance. (p. 297)

Judaism is one of the three monotheistic world religions and dates back to the 6th century B.C.E. Its religious and ethical beliefs are contained within a sacred text—the Hebrew Bible, particularly in the Torah (the five books of Moses) and the Talmud (the laws and commandments). Judaism's central authority is not vested in any person or group but rather in its writings and traditions. At the core of the religious belief is that the people of Israel are God's chosen people and every member of the faith strives to live within God's law. (p. 42)

Just-in-time (JIT) is a management philosophy that strives to eliminate sources of manufacturing waste by producing the right part in the right place at the right time. (p. 399)

Keiretsu companies are the Japanese companies formed from the dismantling of the *zaibatsu* (pre–World War II "partnering" business groupings) that reconnected through share purchases to form horizontally integrated alliances across many industries. Where possible, these firms supply one another, making the alliances also vertically integrated to some extent. (p. 312)

Key success factors (KSFs) can be defined as those attributes most likely to contribute to the success of a firm in the target industry. They are the attributes upon which firms must build competencies. (p. 284)

Knowledge transfer is the process of a systematically organized exchange of information and skills between entities. (p. 425)

Kosher describes food that meets the standards of Kashrut. Kashrut is the body of Jewish law dealing with what foods Jews can and cannot eat, and how those foods must be prepared and eaten. The word *kosher* can also be used, and often is used, to describe ritual objects that are made in accordance with Jewish law and are fit for ritual use. Contrary to popular misconception, rabbis or other religious officials do not "bless" food to make it kosher. (p. 42)

Laissez-faire is short for "*laissez faire, laissez aller, laissez passer*," a French phrase meaning "let do, let go, let pass." The term was first used in France by the 18th-century enlightened thinkers as an injunction against government interference with trade. Today it is a synonym for strict free market economics, according to its own economic laws as stated by Adam Smith and others, and is generally understood to be a doctrine opposing economic interventionism by the state beyond what many believe to be the core roles of government—maintaining peace and preserving property rights. (pp. 11, 76)

Law can be described as the body of rules that are enforced by nations' courts or by delegate government agencies such as provincial workers' compensation boards. (p. 82)

The **law of one price** is an economic law stated as "in an efficient market all identical goods must have only one price." (p. 239)

Lean production is an assembly-line manufacturing methodology. The goal of lean production is described as getting the right things to the right place at the right time, the first time, while minimizing waste and being open to change. (p. 399)

A **letter of credit** is a document issued by a bank following due diligence guaranteeing payment available in the event the importer defaults. (p. 340)

Liberal ideology today means increasing governments' control or ownership of the basic factors of production on a not-for-profit basis. (p. 67)

Libertarians advocate that individuals' liberty is to be preferred over the power of the state. (p. 67)

LIBOR is the London Interbank Offered Rate, the interest rate charged by one international bank to another for lending money. (p. 233)

Licensing is a budget-price technique adopted by a firm (the licensor-owner of intangible property) wishing to increase its export sales by contracting with a foreign firm (the licensee-purchaser) under what is known as a licensing agreement. (p. 295)

A **licensing agreement** is the right to use intangible property in the manufacture and sale of a firm's product under specific terms and conditions (time, venue, etc.). The licensor, in return for granting these rights, receives a royalty on sales. (p. 295)

Liquidity refers to the ability to exchange shares for cash in the global equity markets. If there is a strong market demand, the market for the stock is said to be liquid. (p. 270)

Local-content requirements are implemented by nations by specifying that some portion of the product must be produced domestically. (p. 176)

Location economies can be defined as those locations that offer the lowest cost factors of production—land, labour, and capital—in the broadest sense. (p. 201)

The **London Interbank Bid Rate (LIBID)** is the deposit rate offered by banks to large depositers. (p. 269)

Lost opportunity is a description for investments that are not earning the current available rate of return. (p. 232)

A **management system** refers to the organization's structure for managing its processes and activities that will transform inputs into a product or service. (p. 398)

Managerial opportunism is defined as managers putting self-interest before the interest of the firm's shareholders. (p. 485)

Manufacturers' agents solicit domestic orders on behalf of foreign manufacturers. (p. 336)

Manufacturers' export agents perform the role of the foreign sales department for the domestic manufacturers by selling the domestic firms' goods in the foreign target market. (p. 336)

A **marginal analysis** is central to the concept of maximizing profit in an international environment. As long as the revenue received from the sale of an additional product (marginal revenue) is greater than the additional cost of production and selling that product (marginal cost), the firm should continue to expend its resources to expand output. (p. 371)

A **market economy**, located at the opposite end of the continuum, provides for all of the factors of production to be privately owned. (p. 76)

Market makers are persons or firms authorized to create and maintain a market in a security. Market makers commit themselves to always being ready to deal in the range of stocks for which they are registered. (pp. 228, 263)

The **mechanistic model** is characterized by rigidity, bureaucracy, and a strict hierarchy. The structure is characterized by high complexity and formalization, centralized decision making, rigid relationships, fixed duties, downward communication, and little participation in decision making. (p. 314)

Mental models are the decision-making frameworks that are applied when presented with a situation that requires us to make a decision. Neuroscience studies indicate that over 80 percent of the time we make our decisions within the context and framework of mental models we have acquired over time. (p. 50)

Nations that adopt **mercantilism** strive for total economic independence from all other countries by embracing protectionist and isolationist policies. This trade theory supports the notion that it is in the nation's best interest to sell as much of its exports as possible while restricting the value of its imports from its trading partners. (p. 159)

Mittelstand refers to private German companies, many of which are effectively family businesses, whose capital has traditionally been provided by the banking sector. (p. 449)

A **mixed economy** reflects some of the attributes of market and command economies. It is an economy whereby some production is done by the private sector and some by the state. The degree to which the private sector or the state control "commanding heights" determines where on the continuum the nation should be placed. The reality is all nations can be classified as mixed economies! (p. 77)

Monetary policy controls the supply and availability of money in the domestic economy. (p. 256)

The **money market** raises, invests, and trades short-term capital using financial instruments such as treasury bills, bankers' acceptances, commercial paper, and bonds maturing in one year or less. Repurchase agreements (repos) are the most common funding instruments, and utilize government securities as the underlying collateral. (p. 263)

A **moral hazard** is a situation in which someone will purposely engage in risky behaviour, knowing that any costs incurred will be compensated by the insurer (lender). (pp. 148, 259)

Mores (major repercussions) are norms that have great impact on the functioning of society. They are the customs and conventions that are strongly held by a definable culture. Transgression of mores can bring sanctions. (p. 38)

A **multidomestic strategy** maximizes the customization of the firm's goods and services offerings. In essence, the firm is replicating the home facilities (functions), and transplanting them to the foreign subsidiary. It sees itself almost as a collection of independent subsidiaries. (p. 293)

Multipoint pricing arises when the firm's pricing strategy in one shared market may have an impact on a competitor's pricing strategy in another shared market. (p. 371)

Nanotechnology aims to create new materials from nano-sized resources. The Greek prefix *nano* means one-billionth, which in nanotechnology relates to measurement. One nanometre equals one-billionth of a metre, where 75,000 nanometres measure the thickness of a human hair, and 1,000,000 nanometres is the width of a dime. (p. 109)

A **narrow distribution channel** indicates there are few options available to move product from the manufacturer to the consumer or that it is difficult for outsiders to access the channel. (p. 373)

Neo-conservative, or neocon, refers to the political movement, ideology, and public policy goals of "new conservatives" in the United States. Proponents are mainly characterized by critics as having relatively interventionist and hawkish views on foreign policy of the nature conducted in Afghanistan and Iraq by the Bush administration. Neocons, as conservatives, generally lack support for restricting the size of government and they tolerate more social spending, compared to other American conservatives such as traditional or paleoconservatives. (p. 147)

A **network organizational structure** can be internal or extended to include key external contacts. Internal network structures provide an informal method of communications within the firm. A network structure is built on personal relationships developed over time; the more extensive the personal network, the better. (p. 323)

The **new trade theory** states three premises: firms can gain an advantage through specialization and by exploiting economies of scale; companies that are first into the marketplace will gain a number of advantages as well as the ability to put in place barriers to entry by competitors; and, on occasion, governments can play a very important role in assisting home companies to succeed internationally. (p. 167)

A **non-governmental organization (NGO)** is an organization that is privately funded, generally by donations from the public and is independent from the public sector and governments and their policies. (p. 23)

Norms are generally specific social rules and guidelines that prescribe the acceptable behaviour of a member of a definable society. (p. 37)

A **nuclear** family typically includes parents and their children. (p. 46)

An **offset agreement** requires the seller to acquire unspecified goods from the purchasing nation in order to offset a hard-currency sale. Unlike a counterpurchase agreement, the goods or services to be purchased and the amount to be spent are not specified. (p. 343)

Offshoring involves giving jobs to foreigners in developing countries instead of keeping those jobs at home. (p. 179)

With an **open account**, payment is received after delivering the goods to the purchaser. It is understood that the invoice will be paid in accordance with the terms of the open account agreement. (p. 341)

The **organic model**, which is characterized by openness, responsiveness, and lack of hierarchy, tends to be applied in dynamic, unstable environments. The structure is characterized by low complexity and formalization, decentralized decision making, adaptable duties, flexible relationships, and horizontal and upward communication. (p. 314)

Output controls are formalized control systems that include the firm's balance sheets, sales data, production data, product line growth, and personnel performance reviews. The establishment of output controls involves management control by establishing goals or objectives that act as the criteria in the decision-making process. (p. 325)

An **over-the-counter (OTC) transaction** refers to a security that is not listed on an exchange, generally because it does not meet the exchange listing requirements. Broker/dealers negotiate directly with one another over computer networks and by phone, thereby creating a market for the security. The country's exchange officials monitor their activities. (p. 228)

A **patent** is a grant to an inventor who has produced a new product that provides for exclusive rights for a fixed period of time over the manufacture, use, or sale of the inventor's invention. (p. 88)

Patient money is money made in FDI in factories, equipment, and land that cannot be readily withdrawn from a nation. (p. 271)

A **pegged foreign exchange system** is a hybrid of the fully fixed rate system. Nations adopt a pegged system when one country "ties" its currency to another country's currency. (p. 261)

Personal property includes ownership of all things other than real property, including chattels; intangible rights, such as bonds, shares, and negotiable instruments; and intellectual property. (p. 85)

PEST-C is a common acronym for political (law), economic, societal, technological, and cultural (attributes that must be thoroughly understood and analyzed in order to succeed in the international marketplace). (p. 96)

Pioneering costs are costs that are incurred by the first movers that will not have to be incurred by later entrants. (p. 301)

A **policy** implies there is discretion given to the decision maker; a rule and regulation imply no discretion and must be followed. (p. 471)

Political systems describe the structures, processes, and control mechanisms that support and sustain a nation's political ideologies. They can be differentiated along the political philosophies of collectivism versus individualism and democracy versus totalitarianism regimes. (p. 69)

Political union is found at one extreme of a continuum or at the top of the stairs. There is political union when the regional groups centralize their political apparatus to coordinate all governance aspects generally associated with those found in a nation's state. (p. 126)

Polycentric staffing describes an HR policy whereby indigenous managers within the host country fill key management positions. (p. 420)

Porter's theory of competitive advantage of nations holds that four kinds of determinants affect the ability of domestic firms to utilize the nation's resources to gain international competitive advantage. The four specific country attributes are factor endowments; demand conditions; related and supporting industries; and the firm's strategy, structure, and rivalry. (p. 167)

The **pragmatic nationalism view** utilizes a cost-benefit analysis to determine whether to accept FDI. If the benefits outweigh the costs to the host country then FDI should be encouraged; if not, it should be rejected. (p. 198)

Predatory pricing is the use of price as a competitive weapon to force weaker competitors, generally in the host country, out of the market. (p. 371)

Price elasticity of demand is a measurement of how the marketplace will respond to changes in price. (p. 370)

In the case where all sales worldwide of a given commodity or product are denominated in U.S. dollars, the U.S. dollar is called the **price of determination**. (p. 231)

Product/trade name franchisors have established product names, logos, and trademarks, and they sell the right to use these intangible products to another party. (p. 296)

The **production possibility frontier (PPF)** is a curve or line depicting all maximum output possibilities of two or more goods given a set of inputs (resources, labour, capital, technology etc.). The PPF assumes that all inputs are used efficiently. (p. 161)

The **Protestant work ethic** is a widely known tenet. Its focus on hard work, wealth creation (for the glory of God), frugality, and the accumulation of capital for investment was high on the list of cultural values of Protestants. (p. 39)

A **pull strategy** requires the customer to demand that the product be available in the marketplace. It is generally accomplished with a major commitment to advertising and promotion, thereby creating a demand the retailers (channels) cannot ignore. (p. 378)

The **purchasing power parity (PPP)** metric allows us to compare the purchase price for a fixed basket of goods in every country. The basket includes basic items found in common daily use, such as apples, soap, toothpaste, and so on, thereby capturing the difference in the cost of living from country to country. PPP allows us to make more accurate comparisons of standards of living across countries. (pp. 22, 79)

A **pure democracy** is a political system where all citizens participate freely and actively in the decision making required by the political process. (p. 70)

A **push strategy** centres on personal selling rather than mass media advertising. It tends to focus on the next member down the distribution channel rather than on the end consumer. In essence, the manufacturer pushes the offering down the value chain to the customer. (p. 377)

Supporters of the **radical view** of FDI, grounded in the thoughts of Plato and shaped by Karl Marx, hold an economic rationale for rejecting or nationalizing developed countries' FDI because they fear that FDI will spread Western liberalized democracy and imperialism that will suffocate and exploit lesser developed and underdeveloped nations that accept FDI. (p. 198)

Radio frequency identification (RFID) tags are portable databases that enable the access of information that has been updated in real-time through reader/writers at any point along the supply chain. They are a noncontact, non-line-of-sight method to automatically gather, inspect, and distribute detailed information. (p. 392)

The term *realism* comes from the German compound word *realpolitik*, from the words *real*—meaning *realistic, practical,* or *actual*—and *politik*—meaning *politics*. **Realpolitik** is crafting a nation's foreign policy based on a pragmatic political analysis rather than ideals or ethics. (p. 71)

Real property are land and items considered fixed or attached to the land. (p. 85)

Regionalism is the regional integration of nations by entering trade agreements. It can be traced back to early trading times when geographic proximity was an important factor in nurturing favourable trade arrangements. Often these trade agreements expand over time to other interdependencies between the trade "partners." (p. 124)

Regionalization for our purposes refers to clusters of trading nations. (p. 124)

One major purpose of **regional trading blocs** is to reduce, and ultimately remove, all tariff and non-tariff barriers that impede the free flow of goods and services between the participating members. (p. 124)

Religion is a system of shared beliefs and rituals concerned with the role of the sacred. (p. 38)

A **representative democracy** is a political system that permits citizens to delegate decision-making authority to representatives for an established period. At the expiry of the period, the representatives are accountable to the citizens (electorate) for their actions. Through voting processes, the existing representatives are affirmed for a further established period if it is the wish of the electorate; if not, new representatives are selected. (p. 70)

The **residential approach** to international taxation determines the tax owing regardless of where the income is earned. For example, a Canadian resident company would pay Canadian tax on all world income to the Canadian government. (p. 505)

Revaluation is the raising of a country's currency by its government. (p. 231)

A **revocable letter of credit** can be modified at any time without consultation with the exporter or the importer; this is a very dangerous and tenous letter of credit. (p. 340)

Roman law provides much of the property law we rely upon today. (p. 83)

The primary purpose of **rotational awareness building assignments** is to develop cultural sensitivity in high-potential employees. These assignments generally last less than one year and allow employees to commute. (p. 436)

Round tripping occurs when an investment is made abroad for tax reasons and ends up back in the home country. (p. 203)

Rule of law states that everyone is subject to the law; no one, no matter how important or powerful, is above the law. (p. 71)

Rules of origin are the "laws, regulations and administrative procedures that determine the origin of a good. Rules of origin may be designed to determine the eligibility of a good for preferential access under the terms of a free trade agreement, or they may be designed to determine a good's country of origin for various [other] purposes. . . . These rules can vary from country to country and from purpose to purpose." (p. 134)

Sales representatives can be either a corporation or an individual engaged to use best efforts to represent the exporter's product in the target market. Similar to an employee, they do hold title to the goods and are generally paid a small base salary supplemented by commission. (p. 338)

Segmentation involves subdividing markets, channels, or customers into groups with different needs, and delivering tailored products or services that meet these needs as precisely as possible. (p. 375)

Seigniorage, also spelled seignorage, is the net revenue derived from the issuing of currency. It represents the difference between the face value of the currency and the cost of producing and distributing it. Seigniorage is an important source of revenue for most national governments. (p. 244)

Selling short is an action taken by an investor to speculate on the pending decline of the future value of an asset with the expectation they will be able to profit from the subsequent decline in the value of the asset. (p. 7)

Shintoism, derived from the Chinese words *shin tao* ("the way of the Gods"), is the indigenous religion of Japan. Started about 500 B.C.E, arising from legends and without a founder or sacred text, over 4 million Japanese have accepted this native religion. (p. 42)

A **sight draft** requires payment at the time the goods are delivered to the importer. (p. 339)

A **Six Sigma program** focuses on the control of a process to the point of ± six sigma (standard deviations) from a centre line or, put another way, a failure rate of 3.4 parts per million or 99.9997 items. (p. 402)

SMART is an acronym for the Simple Multi-Attribute Rating Technique decision-making tool. The model is easy for business decision makers to apply and helps a firm assess the company's competitive position and its competitive strength vis-à-vis similar firms in the industry. (p. 285)

Socialism is the notion that governments own or control the basic factors of production and that they should do so on a not-for-profit basis. (p. 67)

Social mobility is the ease with which members of a society can move up or down the "ladder" of social status. (p. 47)

Social obligation describes the notion that a firm has no responsibility beyond economic obligation to the owners and stockholders, as may be prescribed by law or contract. (p. 475)

Sovereignty is government free from external controls; in other words, a government that is the supreme authority within a territory. (p. 24)

A **specific tariff** is a fixed charge levied for each unit of a good imported. For example, a tax of 50¢ for each bushel of California tomatoes being imported into Canada would be a specific tariff. (p. 171)

A **split-run magazine** is a Canadian edition of a magazine published originally in another country that has basically the same content as the original but replaces more than 5 percent of its original advertisements with ads targeted to Canadians. (p. 54)

The **spot rate** is the FX rate at which two currencies can be exchanged in two days' time. (p. 231)

Stare decisis is the process of following the precedent of other courts. A lower court within the same jurisdiction must follow precedent established by a higher court and all courts are bound by the Supreme Court of Canada's rulings. (p. 83)

Strategic alliances are partnerships between competitors, customers, or suppliers designed to build synergy. (p. 298)

A **strategic inflection point** occurs when the ecosystem of an industry or firm experiences a seismic shift that is so dramatic it requires the organization to radically revise its strategy—a wholesale, rather than a retail change. (p. 336)

Strategy can be seen as the "game plan" crafted by management to position the company in selected target markets in a sustainable fashion. How do we achieve our objectives and goals? Strategy involves considering all of the possible options that could be chosen and then selecting the most appropriate option(s) having fully examined the firm's ecosystem and its internal resources and competencies to create shareholder value and ensure survival of the firm. (p. 283)

A **subsidy** is the gratuitous direct or indirect payment of monies by a government to a domestic firm. (p. 173)

Supply chain management (SCM) can be defined as the management of the entire value chain, from the initial supplier of inputs to the manufacturer right through to the retailer, the final customer, and the after-service activities. (p. 404)

Sustainable development has been defined as living "off the earth's interest, not its capital." (p. 472)

A **sweatshop** is a place of employment in a host country that offends our cultural senses of laws governing minimum wage and overtime, child labour, industrial homework, occupational safety and health, workers' compensation, or industry registration. (p. 20)

In **switch trading**, one company sells for a fee (payable to the purchaser) its obligation to make a purchase in the host nation. (p. 344)

SWOT is an acronym for Strengths, Weaknesses, Opportunities, and Threats. A SWOT analysis is an effective business tool to assess both the internal (strengths and weaknesses) as well as the external (opportunities and threats) of the company's microenvironment. (p. 285)

Systems are an organized collection of parts or elements that are highly integrated in order to accomplish an overall goal. (p. 313)

Systems biology is the study of biological systems as a whole rather than a collection of the individual components. It is a holistic approach to analyzing the entire system including all types of biological information (DNA and its genes and proteins) to reveal how biological systems work. (p. 110)

A **tariff** is a tax levied on imports. In most countries, tariffs fall into two categories. Canada has three: specific, ad valorem, and compound. (p. 171)

Tax avoidance means seeking to pay the least amount of tax as possible as provided for by law (e.g., the Canada Income Tax Act). Tax avoidance is not to be confused with tax evasion. (p. 456)

Tax competition is in a sense a "beauty contest" where nations attempt to persuade investors to established offshore operations in their country. (p. 456)

Tax evasion is the illegal practice of intentionally evading taxes. Common examples include underreporting income or hiding assets from the tax authorities. (p. 456)

A **tax haven** can be defined as a country that provides a no-tax or low-tax environment. (p. 457)

Technical analysis uses charts and past trends in the currency price(s) to predict future FX rate and currency relationships. (p. 247)

A **technology park** is a property-based development that has a high-quality physical environment in a park-like setting; is located adjacent to or at a reasonable distance from a research institute or university; and emphasizes activities promoting growth of research, technology, and knowledge-based enterprise. (p. 104)

According to Neil Postman, a **technopoly** is a self-justifying, self-perpetuating system wherein technology of every kind has been cheerfully granted sovereignty over our institutions. (p. 255)

The **territorial approach** to international taxation taxes entities within its territorial jurisdiction regardless of the country of residence. This is a source-based taxation approach; therefore, a Canadian company with operations in, for example, Canada, Australia, and South Africa, would pay taxes on the income earned in each country (territory) to that country's government. To provide tax equity, many countries have reciprocal tax agreements that permit taking into account the "territorial" taxes paid in determining the amount owed the domestic government. Canada has many of these reciprocal tax agreements in place. (p. 455)

A **theocracy** is a system in which political power rests with the clergy. (p. 73)

Theocratic is derived from "two Greek words meaning 'rule by the deity,' and is the name given to political regimes that claim to represent the Divine on earth both directly and immediately." (p. 73)

Theocratic law is based on religious teachings. The most prominent theocratic laws are Islamic, Hindu, and Jewish law. While Hindu and Jewish law tend to be more cultural and spiritual forces now, Islamic law continues to be very much in evidence in Islamic countries today. (p. 84)

The **theory of absolute advantage** holds that a country should export only those goods and services for which it is more productive than other countries and should import only those goods and services from countries that are more productive than it is. (p. 161)

The **theory of comparative advantage** was published by English economist David Ricardo who, building on Adam Smith's theory, proved that even though a nation was less efficient than other nations, it could still profit by exporting goods if it held an advantage in the production of the exported goods compared to other nations. (p. 162)

A **time draft** is a negotiable instrument that extends the payment date by mutual agreement between the parties to some time after the importer has received the goods. The most commonly negotiated times are 30, 60, or 90 days. (p. 339)

Total quality management (TQM) is both a philosophy and a set of guiding principles that represent the foundation of a continuously improving organization. (p. 400)

Totalitarianism is a political system is adopted by citizens who support a government in which one person or political party exercises absolute control over all aspects of human life. It is imposed authority. (p. 72)

Trademarks are the names and designs normally registered by producers of goods and services in order to differentiate their products. (p. 88)

A **trade deficit** is the condition where the value of the trade imports exceeds the value of the nation's exports. (p. 159)

A **trade surplus** occurs when the value of the nation's exports exceeds the value of the nation's imports. This is the goal of mercantilism. (p. 159)

Transaction costs are the costs paid to the market makers by buyers and sellers to acquire or sell debt and equity instruments. (p. 446)

Transfer prices are those prices charged between parents and subsidiaries and between two subsidiaries for goods and services provided by one to the other. (p. 454)

A **transnational strategy** tries to capture the best of all worlds—the global-scale efficiencies and the benefits derived from being locally responsive to customers. Those adopting this strategy are trying to add value by "exploiting experience-based cost economies, location economies and transferring core competencies while paying attention to the pressures for local responsiveness." (p. 293)

Triads refer to the world's three major global regional clusters or trading blocs. These supranational, regional blocs are also the world's most powerful economies: the United States, the European Union, and, in combination, China and India. (p. 127)

Tribal ethnocentric-based political systems are established by a specific "tribe" and ruled by a dictator or small oligarchy from that tribe. (p. 74)

Elkington defines the **triple bottom line** as "the simultaneous pursuit of economic prosperity, environmental quality, and social equity." (p. 469)

The WTO adopted an intellectual property agreement commonly referred to as **TRIPS** (trade-related aspects of intellectual property rights). It is an attempt to set global rules for trade and investment in ideas and creativity. (p. 149)

In a **turnkey project**, a company designs, constructs, implements processes, provides best practice guidelines and policies, and undertakes all other aspects required to complete a project and then turns the project over to the client for a fee. (p. 297)

Types of FDI include mergers and joint ventures (the combining of two or more firms into generally a new entity), subsidiaries acquisitions (the 100 percent takeover of another firm), and greenfields (establishing from the ground up a new operation in a foreign country). (p. 193)

Underwriting is a contractual arrangement between investment bankers to guarantee the sale of the bond issue at a predetermined price in return for a fee, generally 5 percent of the principal. (p. 268)

Undeveloped countries and least developed countries are used interchangeably in this text. The terms describe countries with no more than 10 percent of their GNP resulting from manufacturing. Since 1971, the United Nations has denominated Least Developed Countries (LDCs), a category of low-income states that are deemed structurally disadvantaged in their development process, and facing more than other countries the risk of failing to come out of poverty. The three measurement criteria are low income, weak human assets, and economic vulnerability. (p. 197)

A **value chain** is defined as viewing and identifying all of the firm's functions, activities, and processes as "watertight compartments" that contribute to the design, production, marketing, delivery, and after-sales servicing of a good or a service. (p. 201)

Value creation is undertaking activities that increase the perceived value of the goods or services provided to your customers. (p. 282)

Values and beliefs are abstract ideas relating to the concept of what is good and what is bad. (p. 37)

A **vehicle currency** is one that is often used as the metric to convert funds between two other currencies. (p. 242)

Vertical complexity is where (location) decisions are made. (p. 313)

Vertical integration is the extension of a firm's activities into adjacent stages of production. It can mean taking control of the inputs (backward) or control over the outputs (forward). Firms undertake FDI in industries abroad that provide inputs into that firm's domestic industries, or provide FDI to foreign industries that sell and distribute the goods of the domestic firm. (p. 200)

The **vertically integrated** firm manages all supply chain activities from sourcing of materials to delivery and after-service. (p. 407)

A **virtual or remote workforce** utilizes technology in order to complete work from geographically dispersed locations. (p. 437)

Voice over Internet protocol (VoIP) is a technology that allows telephone calls through a broadband Internet connection in lieu of a regular (or analog) phone line. (p. 394)

A **voluntary export restriction (VER)** is a quota that has been self-imposed by the exporting country. On many occasions, VERs are put in place at the request of the importing country's government. (p. 175)

A **wholly owned subsidiary** is a mode whereby a domestic firm acquires 100 percent of a growing concern. (p. 298)

A **wide distribution channel** occurs when there are many options to move the goods from the manufacturer to the ultimate consumer and barriers to entering the channel are few. (p. 374)

A **world price strategy** involves selling the firm's products at the same price everywhere in the world. (p. 370)

Index